# Sexuality and Obscenity
# Supreme Court Decisions

## Edited by Robert Dittmer

"The Court, in this decision, holds same-sex couples may exercise the
fundamental right to marry in all States. It follows that the Court also must hold and it
now does hold that there is no lawful basis for a State to refuse to recognize a lawful
same-sex marriage performed in another State on the ground of its same-sex character."
-Obergefell v. Hodges (June 26, 2015)

Note on the text: most italics and bold has been removed.

Acknowledgements

Websites (in no particular order):

www.law.cornell.edu
supreme.justia.com
caselaw.findlaw.com
public.resource.org
scholar.google.com
en.wikipedia.org

"In this Nation, every writer, actor, or producer, no matter what medium of expression he may use, should be freed from the censor."
-Justice Douglas' concurrence in Superior Films, Inc. v. Dept. of Education of Ohio, Division of Film Censorship, Hissong, Superintendent (January 18, 1954)

"If a board of censors can tell the American people what it is in their best interests to see or to read or to hear (cf. Public Utilities Comm'n v. Pollak, 343 U.S. 451 ), then thought is regimented, authority substituted for liberty, and the great purpose of the First Amendment to keep uncontrolled the freedom of expression defeated."
-Justice Douglas' concurrence in Gelling v. Texas (June 2, 1952)

**Table of Contents**

## Contents

## National Broadcasting Co., Inc. v. US (May 10, 1943)

MR. JUSTICE FRANKFURTER delivered the opinion of the Court.

In view of our dependence upon regulated private enterprise in discharging the far-reaching role which radio plays in our society, a somewhat detailed exposition of the history of the present controversy and the issues which it raises is appropriate.

These suits were brought on October 30, 1941, to enjoin the enforcement of the Chain Broadcasting Regulations promulgated by the Federal Communications Commission on May 2, 1941, and amended on October 11, 1941. We held last Term in Columbia Broadcasting System v. United States, 316 U. S. 407, and National Broadcasting Co. v. United States, 316 U. S. 447, that the suits could be maintained under § 402(a) of the Communications Act of 1934, 48 Stat. 1093, 47 U.S.C. § 402(a) (incorporating by reference the Urgent Deficiencies Act of October 22, 1913, 38 Stat. 219, 28 U.S.C. § 47), and that the decrees of the District Court dismissing the suits for want of jurisdiction should therefore be reversed. On remand, the District Court granted the Government's motions for summary judgment and dismissed the suits on the merits. 47 F.Supp. 940. The cases are now here on appeal. 28 U.S.C. § 47. Since they raise substantially the same issues and were argued together, we shall deal with both cases in a single opinion.

On March 18, 1938, the Commission undertook a comprehensive investigation to determine whether special regulations applicable to radio stations engaged in chain broadcasting [1] were required in the "public interest, convenience, or necessity." The Commission's order directed that inquiry be made, inter alia, in the following specific matters: the number of stations licensed to or affiliated with networks, and the amount of station time used or controlled by networks; the contractual rights and obligations of stations under their agreements with networks; the scope of network agreements containing exclusive affiliation provisions and restricting the network from affiliating with other stations in the same area; the rights and obligations of stations with respect to network advertisers; the nature of the program service rendered by stations licensed to networks; the policies of networks with respect to character of programs, diversification, and accommodation to the particular requirements of the areas served by the affiliated stations; the extent to which affiliated stations exercise control over programs, advertising contracts, and related matters; the nature and extent of network program duplication by stations serving the same area; the extent to which particular networks have exclusive coverage in some areas; the competitive practices of stations engaged in chain broadcasting; the effect of chain broadcasting upon stations not licensed to or affiliated with networks; practices or agreements in restraint of trade, or in furtherance of monopoly, in connection with chain broadcasting; and the scope of concentration of control over stations, locally, regionally, or nationally, through contracts, common ownership, or other means.

On April 6, 1938, a committee of three Commissioners was designated to hold hearings and make recommendations to the full Commission. This committee held public hearings for 73 days over a period of six months, from November 14, 1938, to May 19, 1939. Order No. 37, announcing the investigation and specifying the particular matters which would be explored at the hearings, was published in the Federal Register, 3 Fed.Reg. 637, and copies were sent to every station licensee and network organization. Notices of the hearings were also sent to these parties. Station licensees, national and regional networks, and transcription and recording companies were invited to appear and give evidence. Other persons who sought to appear were afforded an opportunity to testify. 96 witnesses were heard by the committee, 45 of whom were called by the national networks. The evidence covers 27 volumes, including over 8,000 pages of transcript and more than 700 exhibits. The testimony of the witnesses called by the national networks fills more than 6,000 pages, the equivalent of 46 hearing days.

The committee submitted a report to the Commission on June 12, 1940, stating its findings and recommendations. Thereafter, briefs on behalf of the networks and other interested parties were filed before the full Commission, and on November 28, 1940, the Commission issued proposed regulations which the parties were requested to consider in the oral arguments held on December 2 and 3, 1940. These proposed regulations dealt with the same matters as those covered by the regulations eventually adopted by the Commission. On January 2, 1941, each of the national networks filed a supplementary brief discussing at length the questions raised by the committee report and the proposed regulations.

On May 2, 1941, the Commission issued its Report on Chain Broadcasting, setting forth its findings and conclusions upon the matters explored in the investigation, together with an order adopting the Regulations here assailed. Two of the seven members of the Commission dissented from this action. The effective date of the Regulations was deferred for 90 days with respect to existing contracts and arrangements of network-operated stations, and subsequently the effective date was thrice again postponed. On August 14, 1941, the Mutual Broadcasting Company petitioned the Commission to amend two of the Regulations. In considering this petition, the Commission invited interested parties to submit their views. Briefs were filed on behalf of all of the national networks, and oral argument was had before the Commission on September 12, 1941. And on October 11, 1941, the Commission (again with two members dissenting) issued a Supplemental Report, together with an order amending three Regulations. Simultaneously, the effective date of the Regulations was postponed until November 15, 1941, and provision was made for further postponements from time to time if necessary to permit the orderly adjustment of existing arrangements. Since October 30, 1941, when the present suits were filed, the enforcement of the Regulations has been stayed either voluntarily by the Commission or by order of court.

Such is the history of the Chain Broadcasting Regulations. We turn now to the Regulations themselves, illumined by the practices in the radio industry disclosed by the Commission's investigation. The Regulations, which the Commission characterized in its Report as "the expression of the general policy we will follow in exercising our licensing power," are addressed in terms to station licensees and applicants for station licenses. They provide, in general, that no licenses shall be granted to stations or applicants having specified relationships with networks. Each Regulation is directed at a particular practice found by the Commission to be detrimental to the "public interest," and we shall consider them seriatim. In doing so, however, we do not overlook the admonition of the Commission that the Regulations as well as the network practices at which they are aimed are interrelated:

"In considering above the network practices which necessitate the regulations we are adopting, we have taken each practice singly, and have shown that, even in isolation, each warrants the regulation addressed to it. But the various practices we have considered do not operate in isolation; they form a compact bundle or pattern, and the effect of their joint impact upon licensees necessitates the regulations even more urgently than the effect of each taken singly."

(Report, p. 75.)

The Commission found that, at the end of 1938, there were 660 commercial stations in the United States, and that 341 of these were affiliated with national networks. 135 stations were affiliated exclusively with the National Broadcasting Company, Inc., known in the industry as NBC, which operated two national networks, the "Red" and the "Blue." NBC was also the licensee of 10 stations, including 7 which operated on so-called clear channels with the maximum power available, 50 kilowatts; in addition, NBC operated 5 other stations, 4 of which had power of 50 kilowatts, under management contracts with their licensees. 102 stations were affiliated exclusively with the Columbia Broadcasting System, Inc., which was also the licensee of 8 stations, 7 of which were clear-channel stations operating with power of 50 kilowatts. 74 stations were under exclusive affiliation with the Mutual Broadcasting System, Inc. In addition, 25 stations were affiliated with both NBC and Mutual, and 5 with both CBS and Mutual. These figures, the Commission noted, did not accurately reflect the relative prominence of the three companies, since the stations affiliated with Mutual were, generally speaking, less desirable in frequency, power, and coverage. It pointed out that the stations affiliated with the national networks utilized more than 97% of the total night-time broadcasting power of all the stations in the country. NBC and CBS together controlled more than 85% of the total night-time wattage, and the broadcast business of the three national network companies amounted to almost half of the total business of all stations in the United States.

The Commission recognized that network broadcasting had played and was continuing to play an important part in the development of radio. "The growth and development of chain broadcasting," it stated,

"found its impetus in the desire to give widespread coverage to programs which otherwise would not be heard beyond the reception area of a single station. Chain broadcasting makes possible a wider reception for expensive entertainment and cultural programs, and also for programs of national or regional significance which would otherwise have coverage only in the locality of origin. Furthermore, the access to greatly enlarged audiences made possible by chain broadcasting has been a strong incentive to advertisers to finance the production of expensive programs. . . . But the fact that the chain broadcasting method brings benefits and advantages to both the listening public and to broadcast station licensees does not mean that the prevailing practices and policies of the networks and their outlets are sound in all respects, or that they should not be altered. The Commission's duty under the Communications Act of 1934 is not only to see that the public receives the advantages and benefits of chain broadcasting, but also, so far as its powers enable it, to see that practices which adversely affect the ability of licensees to operate in the public interest are eliminated."

(Report, p. 4.)

The Commission found that eight network abuses were amenable to correction within the powers granted it by Congress:

Regulation 3.101 -- Exclusive affiliation of station. The Commission found that the network affiliation agreements of NBC and CBS customarily contained a provision which prevented the station from broadcasting the programs of any other network. The effect of this provision was to hinder the growth of new networks, to deprive the listening public in many areas of service to which they were entitled, and to prevent station licensees from exercising their statutory duty of determining which programs would best serve the needs of their community. The Commission observed that, in areas where all the stations were under exclusive contract to either NBC or CBS, the public was deprived of the opportunity to hear programs presented by Mutual. To take a case cited in the Report: in the fall of 1939, Mutual obtained the exclusive right to broadcast the World Series baseball games. It offered this program of outstanding national interest to stations throughout the country, including NBC and CBS affiliates in communities having no other stations. CBS and NBC immediately invoked the "exclusive affiliation" clauses of their agreements with these stations, and, as a result, thousands of persons in many sections of the country were unable to hear the broadcasts of the games.

"Restraints having this effect," the Commission observed,

"are to be condemned as contrary to the public interest irrespective of whether it be assumed that Mutual programs are of equal, superior, or inferior quality. The important consideration is that station licensees are denied freedom to choose the programs which they believe best suited to their needs; in this manner, the duty of a station licensee to operate in the public interest is defeated. . . . Our conclusion is that the disadvantages resulting from these exclusive arrangements far outweigh any advantages. A licensee station does not operate in the public interest when it enters into exclusive arrangements which prevent it from giving the public the best service of which it is capable, and which, by closing the door of opportunity in the network field, adversely affect the program structure of the entire industry."

(Report, pp. 52, 57.) Accordingly, the Commission adopted Regulation 3.101, providing as follows:

"No license shall be granted to a standard broadcast station having any contract, arrangement, or understanding, express or implied, with a network organization under which the station is prevented or hindered from, or penalized for, broadcasting the programs of any other network organization."

Regulation 3.102 -- Territorial exclusivity. The Commission found another type of "exclusivity" provision in network affiliation agreements whereby the network bound itself not to sell programs to any other station in the same area. The effect of this provision, designed to protect the affiliate from the competition of other stations serving the same territory, was to deprive the listening public of many programs that might otherwise be available. If an affiliated station rejected a network program, the "territorial exclusivity" clause of its affiliation agreement prevented the network from offering the program to other stations in the area. For example, Mutual presented a popular program, known as "The American Forum of the Air," in which prominent persons discussed topics of general interest. None of the Mutual stations in the Buffalo area decided to carry the program, and a Buffalo station not affiliated with Mutual attempted to obtain the program for its listeners. These efforts failed, however, on account of the "territorial exclusivity" provision in Mutual's agreements with its outlets. The result was that this program was not available to the people of Buffalo.

The Commission concluded that

"It is not in the public interest for the listening audience in an area to be deprived of network programs not carried by one station where other stations in that area are ready and willing to broadcast the programs. It is as much against the public interest for a network affiliate to enter into a contractual arrangement which prevents another station from carrying a network program as it would be for it to drown out that program by electrical interference."

(Report, p. 59.)

Recognizing that the "territorial exclusivity" clause was unobjectionable insofar as it sought to prevent duplication of programs in the same area, the Commission limited itself to the situations in which the clause impaired the ability of the licensee to broadcast available programs. Regulation 3.102, promulgated to remedy this particular evil, provides as follows:

"No license shall be granted to a standard broadcast station having any contract, arrangement, or understanding, express or implied, with a network organization which prevents or hinders another station serving substantially the same area from broadcasting the network's programs not taken by the former station, or which prevents or hinders another station serving a substantially different area from broadcasting any program of the network organization. This regulation shall not be construed to prohibit any contract, arrangement, or understanding between a station and a network organization pursuant to which the station is granted the first call in its primary service area upon the programs of the network organization."

Regulation 3.103 -- Term of affiliation. The standard NBC and CBS affiliation contracts bound the station for a period of five years, with the network having the exclusive right to terminate the contracts upon one year's notice. The Commission, relying upon § 307(d) of the Communications Act of 1934, under which no license to operate a broadcast station can be granted for a longer term than three years, found the five-year affiliation term to be contrary to the policy of the Act:

"Regardless of any changes that may occur in the economic, political, or social life of the Nation or of the community in which the station is located, CBS and NBC affiliates are bound by contract to continue broadcasting the network programs of only one network for 5 years. The licensee is so bound even though the policy and caliber of programs of the network may deteriorate greatly. The future necessities of the station and of the community are not considered. The station licensee is unable to follow his conception of the public interest until the end of the 5-year contract."

(Report, p. 61.) The Commission concluded that, under contracts binding the affiliates for five years, "stations become parties to arrangements which deprive the public of the improved service it might otherwise derive from competition in the network field; and that a station is not operating in the public interest when it so limits its freedom of action." (Report, p. 62.) Accordingly, the Commission adopted Regulation 3.103:

"No license shall be granted to a standard broadcast station having any contract, arrangement, or understanding, express or implied, with a network organization which provides, by original term, provisions for renewal, or otherwise for the affiliation of the station with the network organization for a period longer than two years: [2] Provided, That a contract, arrangement, or understanding for a period up to two years, may be entered into within 120 days prior to the commencement of such period."

Regulation 3.104 -- Option time. The Commission found that network affiliation contracts usually contained so-called network optional time clauses. Under these provisions, the network could, upon 28 days' notice, call upon its affiliates to carry a commercial program during any of the hours specified in the agreement as "network optional time." For CBS affiliates, "network optional time" meant the entire broadcast day. For 29 outlets of NBC on the Pacific Coast, it also covered the entire broadcast day; for substantially all of the other NBC affiliates, it included 8 1/2 hours on weekdays and 8 hours on Sundays. Mutual's contracts with about half of its affiliates contained such a provision, giving the network optional time for 3 or 4 hours on weekdays and 6 hours on Sundays.

In the Commission's judgment, these optional time provisions, in addition to imposing serious obstacles in the path of new networks, hindered stations in developing a local program service. The exercise by the networks of their options over the station's time tended to prevent regular scheduling of local programs at desirable hours. The Commission found that

"shifting a local commercial program may seriously interfere with the efforts of a [local] sponsor to build up a regular listening audience at a definite hour, and the long-term advertising contract becomes a highly dubious project. This hampers the efforts of the station to develop local commercial programs, and affects adversely its ability to give the public good program service. . . . A station licensee must retain sufficient freedom of action to supply the program and advertising needs of the local community. Local program service is a vital part of community life. A station should be ready, able, and willing to serve the needs of the local community by broadcasting such outstanding local events as community concerts, civic meetings, local sports events, and other programs of local consumer and social interest. We conclude that national network time options have restricted the freedom of station licensees and hampered their efforts to broadcast local commercial programs, the programs of other national networks, and national spot transcriptions. We believe that these considerations far outweigh any supposed advantages from 'stability' of network operations under time options. We find that the optioning of time by licensee stations has operated against the public interest."

(Report, pp. 63, 65.)

The Commission undertook to preserve the advantages of option time, as a device for "stabilizing" the industry without unduly impairing the ability of local stations to develop local program service. Regulation 3.104 called for the modification of the option-time provision in three respects: the minimum notice period for exercise of the option could not be less than 56 days; the number of hours which could be optioned was limited; and specific restrictions were placed upon exercise of the option to the disadvantage of other networks. The text of the Regulation follows:

"No license shall be granted to a standard broadcast station which options for network programs any time subject to call on less than 56 days' notice, or more time than a total of three hours within each of four segments of the broadcast day, as herein described. The broadcast day is divided into 4 segments, as follows: 8:00 a.m. to 1:00 p.m.; 1:00 p.m. to 6:00 p.m.; 6:00 p.m. to 11:00 p.m.; 11:00 p.m. to 8:00 a.m. Such options may not be exclusive as against other network organizations, and may not prevent or hinder the station from optioning or selling any or all of the time covered by the option, or other time, to other network organizations."

Regulation 3.105 -- Right to reject programs. The Commission found that most network affiliation contracts contained a clause defining the right of the station to reject network commercial programs. The NBC contracts provided simply that the station "may reject a network program the broadcasting of which would not be in the public interest, convenience, and necessity." NBC required a licensee who rejected a program to "be able to support his contention that what he has done has been more in the public interest than had he carried on the network program." Similarly, the CBS contracts provided that if the station had

"reasonable objection to any sponsored program or the product advertised thereon as not being in the public interest, the station may, on 3 weeks' prior notice thereof to Columbia, refuse to broadcast such program, unless, during such notice period, such reasonable objection of the station shall be satisfied."

While seeming in the abstract to be fair, these provisions, according to the

Commission's finding, did not sufficiently protect the "public interest." As a practical matter, the licensee could not determine in advance whether the broadcasting of any particular network program would or would not be in the public interest.

"It is obvious that from such skeletal information [as the networks submitted to the stations prior to the broadcast], the station cannot determine in advance whether the program is in the public interest, nor can it ascertain whether or not parts of the program are in one way or another offensive. In practice, if not in theory, stations affiliated with networks have delegated to the networks a large part of their programming functions. In many instances, moreover, the network further delegates the actual production of programs to advertising agencies. These agencies are far more than mere brokers or intermediaries between the network and the advertiser. To an ever-increasing extent, these agencies actually exercise the function of program production. Thus, it is frequently neither the station nor the network, but rather the advertising agency, which determines what broadcast programs shall contain. Under such circumstances, it is especially important that individual stations, if they are to operate in the public interest, should have the practical opportunity, as well as the contractual right, to reject network programs. . . ."

"It is the station, not the network, which is licensed to serve the public interest. The licensee has the duty of determining what programs shall be broadcast over his station's facilities, and cannot lawfully delegate this duty or transfer the control of his station directly to the network or indirectly to an advertising agency. He cannot lawfully bind himself to accept programs in every case where he cannot sustain the burden of proof that he has a better program. The licensee is obliged to reserve to himself the final decision as to what programs will best serve the public interest. We conclude that a licensee is not fulfilling his obligations to operate in the public interest, and is not operating in accordance with the express requirements of the Communications Act, if he agrees to accept programs on any basis other than his own reasonable decision that the programs are satisfactory."

(Report, pp. 39, 66.)

The Commission undertook in Regulation 3.105 to formulate the obligations of licensees with respect to supervision over programs:

"No license shall be granted to a standard broadcast station having any contract, arrangement, or understanding, express or implied, with a network organization which (a), with respect to programs offered pursuant to an affiliation contract, prevents or hinders the station from rejecting or refusing network programs which the station reasonably believes to be unsatisfactory or unsuitable; or which (b), with respect to network programs so offered or already contracted for, prevents the station from rejecting or refusing any program which, in its opinion, is contrary to the public interest, or from substituting a program of outstanding local or national importance."

Regulation 3.106 -- Network ownership of stations. The Commission found that NBC, in addition to its network operations, was the licensee of 10 stations, 2 each in New

York, Chicago, Washington, and San Francisco, 1 in Denver, and 1 in Cleveland. CBS was the licensee of 8 stations, 1 in each of these cities: New York, Chicago, Washington, Boston, Minneapolis, St. Louis, Charlotte, and Los Angeles. These 18 stations owned by NBC and CBS, the Commission observed, were among the most powerful and desirable in the country, and were permanently inaccessible to competing networks.

"Competition among networks for these facilities is nonexistent, as they are completely removed from the network-station market. It gives the network complete control over its policies. This 'bottling-up' of the best facilities has undoubtedly had a discouraging effect upon the creation and growth of new networks. Furthermore, common ownership of network and station places the network in a position where its interest as the owner of certain stations may conflict with its interest as a network organization serving affiliated stations. In dealings with advertisers, the network represents its own stations in a proprietary capacity and the affiliated stations in something akin to an agency capacity. The danger is present that the network organization will give preference to its own stations at the expense of its affiliates."

(Report, p. 67.)

The Commission stated that, if the question had arisen as an original matter, it might well have concluded that the public interest required severance of the business of station ownership from that of network operation. But since substantial business interests have been formed on the basis of the Commission's continued tolerance of the situation, it was found inadvisable to take such a drastic step. The Commission concluded, however, that "the licensing of two stations in the same area to a single network organization is basically unsound and contrary to the public interest," and that it was also against the "public interest" for network organizations to own stations in areas where the available facilities were so few or of such unequal coverage that competition would thereby be substantially restricted. Recognizing that these considerations called for flexibility in their application to particular situations, the Commission provided that

"networks will be given full opportunity, on proper application for new facilities or renewal of existing licenses, to call to our attention any reasons why the principle should be modified or held inapplicable."

(Report, p. 68.)

Regulation 3.106 reads as follows:

"No license shall be granted to a network organization, or to any person directly or indirectly controlled by or under common control with a network organization, for more than one standard broadcast station where one of the stations covers substantially the service area of the other station, or for any standard broadcast station in any locality where the existing standard broadcast stations are so few or of such unequal desirability (in terms of coverage, power, frequency, or other related matters) that competition would be substantially restrained by such licensing."

Regulation 3.107 -- Dual network operation. This regulation provides that:

"No license shall be issued to a standard broadcast station affiliated with a network organization which maintains more than one network: Provided, That this regulation shall not be applicable if such networks are not operated simultaneously, or if there is no substantial overlap in the territory served by the group of stations comprising each such network."

In its Supplemental Report of October 11, 1941, the Commission announced the indefinite suspension of this regulation. There is no occasion here to consider the validity of Regulation 3.107, since there is no immediate threat of its enforcement by the Commission.

Regulation 3.108 -- Control by networks of station rates. The Commission found that NBC's affiliation contracts contained a provision empowering the network to reduce the station's network rate, and thereby to reduce the compensation received by the station, if the station set a lower rate for non-network national advertising than the rate established by the contract for the network programs. Under this provision, the station could not sell time to a national advertiser for less than it would cost the advertiser if he bought the time from NBC. In the words of NBC's vice-president,

"This means simply that a national advertiser should pay the same price for the station whether the buys it through one source or another source. It means that we do not believe that our stations should go into competition with ourselves."

(Report, p. 73.)

The Commission concluded that

"it is against the public interest for a station licensee to enter into a contract with a network which has the effect of decreasing its ability to compete for national business. We believe that the public interest will best be served and listeners supplied with the best programs if stations bargain freely with national advertisers."

(Report, p. 75.) Accordingly, the Commission adopted Regulation 3.108, which provides as follows:

"No license shall be granted to a standard broadcast station having any contract, arrangement, or understanding, express or implied, with a network organization under which the station is prevented or hindered from, or penalized for, fixing or altering its rates for the sale of broadcast time for other than the network's programs."

The appellants attack the validity of these Regulations along many fronts. They contend that the Commission went beyond the regulatory powers conferred upon it by the Communications Act of 1934; that, even if the Commission were authorized by the Act to deal with the matters comprehended by the Regulations, its action is nevertheless invalid because the Commission misconceived the scope of the Act, particularly § 313 which deals with the application of the antitrust laws to the radio industry; that the Regulations are arbitrary and capricious; that, if the Communications Act of 1934 were construed to authorize the promulgation of the Regulations, it would be an unconstitutional delegation of legislative power; and that, in any event, the Regulations abridge the appellants' right of free speech in violation of the First Amendment. We are thus called upon to determine whether Congress has authorized the Commission to exercise the power asserted by the Chain Broadcasting Regulations, and if it has, whether the Constitution forbids the exercise of such authority.

Federal regulation of radio [3] begins with the Wireless Ship Act of June 24, 1910, 36 Stat. 629, which forbade any steamer carrying or licensed to carry fifty or more persons to leave any American port unless equipped with efficient apparatus for radio communication, in charge of a skilled operator. The enforcement of this legislation was entrusted to the Secretary of Commerce and Labor, who was in charge of the administration of the marine navigation laws. But it was not until 1912, when the United States ratified the first international radio treaty, 37 Stat. 1565, that the need for general regulation of radio communication became urgent. In order to fulfill our obligations under the treaty, Congress enacted the Radio-Communications Act of August 13, 1912, 37 Stat. 302. This statute forbade the operation of radio apparatus without a license from the Secretary of Commerce and Labor; it also allocated certain frequencies for the use of the Government, and imposed restrictions upon the character of wave emissions, the transmission of distress signals, and the like.

The enforcement of the Radio Act of 1912 presented no serious problems prior to the World War. Questions of interference arose only rarely because there were more than enough frequencies for all the stations then in existence. The war accelerated the development of the art, however, and, in 1921, the first standard broadcast stations were established. They grew rapidly in number, and, by 1923, there were several hundred such stations throughout the country. The Act of 1912 had not set aside any particular frequencies for the use of private broadcast stations; consequently, the Secretary of Commerce selected two frequencies, 750 and 833 kilocycles, and licensed all stations to operate upon one or the other of these channels. The number of stations increased so rapidly, however, and the situation became so chaotic, that the Secretary, upon the recommendation of the National Radio Conferences which met in Washington in 1923 and 1924, established a policy of assigning specified frequencies to particular stations. The entire radio spectrum was divided into numerous bands, each allocated to a particular kind of service. The frequencies ranging from 550 to 1500 kilocycles (96 channels in all, since the channels were separated from each other by 10 kilocycles) were assigned to the standard broadcast stations. But the problems created by the enormously rapid development of radio were far from solved. The increase in the number of channels was not enough to take care of the constantly growing number of stations. Since there were more stations than available frequencies, the Secretary of Commerce attempted to find room for everybody by limiting the power and hours of operation of stations in order that several stations might use the same channel. The number of stations multiplied so rapidly, however, that by November, 1925, there were almost 600 stations in the country, and there were 175 applications for new stations. Every channel in the standard broadcast band was, by that time, already occupied by at least one station, and many by several. The new stations could be accommodated only by extending the standard broadcast band, at the expense of the other types of services, or by imposing still greater limitations upon time and power. The National Radio Conference which met in November, 1925, opposed both of these methods, and called upon Congress to remedy the situation through legislation.

The Secretary of Commerce was powerless to deal with the situation. It had been held that he could not deny a license to an otherwise legally qualified applicant on the ground that the proposed station would interfere with existing private or Government stations. Hoover v. Intercity Radio Co., 52 App.D.C. 339, 286 F. 1003. And, on April 16, 1926, an Illinois district court held that the Secretary had no power to impose restrictions as to frequency, power, and hours of operation, and that a station's use of a frequency not assigned to it was not a violation of the Radio Act of 1912. United States v. Zenith Radio Corp., 12 F.2d 614. This was followed on July 8, 1926, by an opinion of Acting Attorney General Donovan that the Secretary of Commerce had no power, under the Radio Act of 1912, to regulate the power, frequency or hours of operation of stations. 35 Op.Atty.Gen. 126. The next day, the Secretary of Commerce issued a statement abandoning all his efforts to regulate radio and urging that the stations undertake self-regulation.

But the plea of the Secretary went unheeded. From, July, 1926, to February 23, 1927, when Congress enacted the Radio Act of 1927, 44 Stat. 1162, almost 200 new stations went on the air. These new stations used any frequencies they desired, regardless of the interference thereby caused to others. Existing stations changed to other frequencies and increased their power and hours of operation at will. The result was confusion and chaos. With everybody on the air, nobody could be heard. The situation became so intolerable that the President in his message of December 7, 1926, appealed to Congress to enact a comprehensive radio law:

"Due to the decisions of the courts, the authority of the Department [of Commerce] under the law of 1912 has broken down; many more stations have been operating than can be accommodated within the limited number of wave lengths available; further stations are in course of construction; many stations have departed from the scheme of allocations set down by the Department, and the whole service of this most important public function has drifted into such chaos as seems likely, if not remedied, to destroy its great value. I most urgently recommend that this legislation should be speedily enacted."

(H.Doc.483, 69th Cong., 2d Sess., p. 10.)

The plight into which radio fell prior to 1927 was attributable to certain basic facts about radio as a means of communication -- its facilities are limited; they are not available to all who may wish to use them; the radio spectrum simply is not large enough to accommodate everybody. There is a fixed natural limitation upon the number of stations that can operate without interfering with one another. [4] Regulation of radio was therefore as vital to its development as traffic control was to the development of the automobile. In enacting the Radio Act of 1927, the first comprehensive scheme of control over radio communication, Congress acted upon the knowledge that if the potentialities of radio were not to be wasted, regulation was essential.

The Radio Act of 1927 created the Federal Radio Commission, composed of five members, and endowed the Commission with wide licensing and regulatory powers. We do not pause here to enumerate the scope of the Radio Act of 1927 and of the authority entrusted to the Radio Commission, for the basic provisions of that Act are incorporated in the Communications Act of 1934, 48 Stat. 1064, 47 U.S.C. § 151 et seq., the legislation immediately before us. As we noted in Federal Communications Comm'n v. Pottsville Broadcasting Co., 309 U. S. 134,

"In its essentials, the Communications Act of 1934 (so far as its provisions relating to radio are concerned) derives from the Federal Radio Act of 1927. . . . By this Act, Congress, in order to protect the national interest involved in the new and far-reaching science of broadcasting, formulated a unified and comprehensive regulatory system for the industry. The common factors in the administration of the various statutes by which Congress had supervised the different modes of communication led to the creation, in the Act of 1934, of the Communications Commission. But the objectives of the legislation have remained substantially unaltered since 1927."

Section 1 of the Communications Act states its

"purpose of regulating interstate and foreign commerce in communication by wire and radio so as to make available, so far as possible, to all the people of the United States a rapid, efficient, Nationwide, and world-wide wire and radio communication service with adequate facilities at reasonable charges."

Section 301 particularizes this general purpose with respect to radio:

"It is the purpose of this Act, among other things, to maintain the control of the United States over all the channels of interstate and foreign radio transmission; and to provide for the use of such channels, but not the ownership thereof, by persons for limited periods of time, under licenses granted by Federal authority, and no such license shall be construed to create any right, beyond the terms, conditions, and periods of the license."

To that end, a Commission composed of seven members was created, with broad licensing and regulatory powers.

Section 303 provides:

"Except as otherwise provided in this Act, the Commission from time to time, as public convenience, interest, or necessity requires, shall --"

"(a) Classify radio stations; "

"(b) Prescribe the nature of the service to be rendered by each class of licensed stations and each station within any class;"

"* * * *"

"(f) Make such regulations not inconsistent with law as it may deem necessary to prevent interference between stations and to carry out the provisions of this Act . . .;"

"(g) Study new uses for radio, provide for experimental uses of frequencies, and generally encourage the larger and more effective use of radio in the public interest;"

"* * * *"

"(i) Have authority to make special regulations applicable to radio stations engaged in chain broadcasting;"

"* * * *"

"(r) Make such rules and regulations and prescribe such restrictions and conditions, not inconsistent with law, as may be necessary to carry out the provisions of this Act. . . ."

The criterion governing the exercise of the Commission's licensing power is the "public interest, convenience, or necessity." §§ 307(a)(d), 309(a), 310, 312. In addition, § 307(b) directs the Commission that,

"In considering applications for licenses, and modifications and renewals thereof, when and insofar as there is demand for the same, the Commission shall make such distribution of licenses, frequencies, hours of operation, and of power among the several States and communities as to provide a fair, efficient, and equitable distribution of radio service to each of the same."

The Act itself establishes that the Commission's powers are not limited to the engineering and technical aspects of regulation of radio communication. Yet we are asked to regard the Commission as a kind of traffic officer, policing the wave lengths to prevent stations from interfering with each other. But the Act does not restrict the Commission merely to supervision of the traffic. It puts upon the Commission the burden of determining the composition of that traffic. The facilities of radio are not large enough to accommodate all who wish to use them. Methods must be devised for choosing from among the many who apply. And since Congress itself could not do this, it committed the task to the Commission.

The Commission was, however, not left at large in performing this duty. The touchstone provided by Congress was the "public interest, convenience, or necessity," a criterion which "is as concrete as the complicated factors for judgment in such a field of delegated authority permit." Federal Communications Comm'n v. Pottsville Broadcasting Co., 309 U. S. 134, 309 U. S. 138.

"This criterion is not to be interpreted as setting up a standard so indefinite as to confer an unlimited power. Compare New York Central Securities Corp. v. United States, 287 U. S. 12, 287 U. S. 24. The requirement is to be interpreted by its context, by the nature of radio transmission and reception, by the scope, character, and quality of services. . . ."

Federal Radio Comm'n v. Nelson Bros. Bond & Mortgage Co., 289 U. S. 266, 289 U. S. 285.

The "public interest" to be served under the Communications Act is thus the interest of the listening public in "the larger and more effective use of radio." § 303(g). The facilities of radio are limited, and therefore precious; they cannot be left to wasteful use without detriment to the public interest.

"An important element of public interest and convenience affecting the issue of a license is the ability of the licensee to render the best practicable service to the community reached by his broadcasts."

Federal Communications Comm'n v. Sanders Bros. Radio Station, 309 U. S. 470, 309 U. S. 475. The Commission's licensing function cannot be discharged, therefore, merely by finding that there are no technological objections to the granting of a license. If the criterion of "public interest" were limited to such matters, how could the Commission choose between two applicants for the same facilities, each of whom is financially and technically qualified to operate a station? Since the very inception of federal regulation by radio, comparative considerations as to the services to be rendered have governed the application of the standard of "public interest, convenience, or necessity." See Federal Communications Comm'n v. Pottsville Broadcasting Co., 309 U. S. 134, 309 U. S. 138 n. 2.

The avowed aim of the Communications Act of 1934 was to secure the maximum benefits of radio to all the people of the United States. To that end, Congress endowed the Communications Commission with comprehensive powers to promote and realize the vast potentialities of radio. Section 303(g) provides that the Commission shall "generally encourage the larger and more effective use of radio in the public interest"; subsection (i) gives the Commission specific "authority to make special regulations applicable to radio stations engaged in chain broadcasting"; and subsection (r) empowers it to adopt

"such rules and regulations and prescribe such restrictions and conditions, not inconsistent with law, as may be necessary to carry out the provisions of this Act."

These provisions, individually and in the aggregate, preclude the notion that the Commission is empowered to deal only with technical and engineering impediments to the "larger and more effective use of radio in the public interest." We cannot find in the Act any such restriction of the Commission's authority. Suppose, for example, that a community can, because of physical limitations, be assigned only two stations. That community might be deprived of effective service in any one of several ways. More powerful stations in nearby cities might blanket out the signals of the local stations so that they could not be heard at all. The stations might interfere with each other, so that neither could be clearly heard. One station might dominate the other with the power of its signal. But the community could be deprived of good radio service in ways less crude. One man, financially and technically qualified, might apply for and obtain the licenses of both stations and present a single service over the two stations, thus wasting a frequency otherwise available to the area. The language of the Act does not withdraw such a situation from the licensing and regulatory powers of the Commission, and there is no evidence that Congress did not mean its broad language to carry the authority it expresses.

In essence, the Chain Broadcasting Regulations represent a particularization of the Commission's conception of the "public interest" sought to be safeguarded by Congress in enacting the Communications Act of 1934. The basic consideration of policy underlying the Regulations is succinctly stated in its Report:

"With the number of radio channels limited by natural factors, the public interest demands that those who are entrusted with the available channels shall make the fullest and most effective use of them. If a licensee enters into a contract with a network organization which limits his ability to make the best use of the radio facility assigned him, he is not serving the public interest. . . . The net effect [of the practices disclosed by the investigation] has been that broadcasting service has been maintained at a level below that possible under a system of free competition. Having so found, we would be remiss in our statutory duty of encouraging 'the larger and more effective use of radio in the public interest' if we were to grant licenses to persons who persist in these practices."

(Report, pp. 81, 82.)

We would be asserting our personal views regarding the effective utilization of radio were we to deny that the Commission was entitled to find that the large public aims of the Communications Act of 1934 comprehend the considerations which moved the Commission in promulgating the Chain Broadcasting Regulations. True enough, the Act does not explicitly say that the Commission shall have power to deal with network practices found inimical to the public interest. But Congress was acting in a field of regulation which was both new and dynamic.

"Congress moved under the spur of a widespread fear that, in the absence of governmental control, the public interest might be subordinated to monopolistic domination in the broadcasting field."

Federal Communications Comm'n v. Pottsville Broadcasting Co., 309 U. S. 134, 309 U. S. 137. In the context of the developing problems to which it was directed, the Act gave the Commission not niggardly, but expansive, powers. It was given a comprehensive mandate to "encourage the larger and more effective use of radio in the public interest," if need be, by making "special regulations applicable to radio stations engaged in chain broadcasting." § 303(g)(i).

Generalities unrelated to the living problems of radio communication of course cannot justify exercises of power by the Commission. Equally so, generalities empty of all concrete considerations of the actual bearing of regulations promulgated by the Commission to the subject matter entrusted to it, cannot strike down exercises of power by the Commission. While Congress did not give the Commission unfettered discretion to regulate all phases of the radio industry, it did not frustrate the purposes for which the Communications Act of 1934 was brought into being by attempting an itemized catalogue of the specific manifestations of the general problems for the solution of which it was establishing a regulatory agency. That would have stereotyped the powers of the Commission to specific details in regulating a field of enterprise the dominant characteristic of which was the rapid pace of its unfolding. And so Congress did what experience had taught it in similar attempts at regulation, even in fields where the subject matter of regulation was far less fluid and dynamic than radio. The essence of that experience was to define broad areas for regulation and to establish standards for judgment adequately related in their application to the problems to be solved.

For the cramping construction of the Act pressed upon us, support cannot be found in its legislative history. The principal argument is that § 303(i), empowering the

Commission "to make special regulations applicable to radio stations engaged in chain broadcasting," intended to restrict the scope of the Commission's powers to the technical and engineering aspects of chain broadcasting. This provision comes from § 4(h) of the Radio Act of 1927. It was introduced into the legislation as a Senate committee amendment to the House bill (H.R. 9971, 69th Cong., 1st Sess.). This amendment originally read as follows:

"(C) The commission, from time to time, as public convenience, interest, or necessity requires, shall --"

"* * * *"

"(j) When stations are connected by wire for chain broadcasting, determine the power each station shall use and the wavelengths to be used during the time stations are so connected and so operated, and make all other regulations necessary in the interest of equitable radio service to the listeners in the communities or areas affected by chain broadcasting."

The report of the Senate Committee on Interstate Commerce, which submitted this amendment, stated that, under the bill, the Commission was given "complete authority . . . to control chain broadcasting." Sen.Rep.No.772, 69th Cong., 1st Sess., p. 3. The bill as thus amended was passed by the Senate and then sent to conference. The bill that emerged from the conference committee, and which became the Radio Act of 1927, phrased the amendment in the general terms now contained in § 303(i) of the 1934 Act: the Commission was authorized "to make special regulations applicable to radio stations engaged in chain broadcasting." The conference reports do not give any explanation of this particular change in phrasing, but they do state that the jurisdiction conferred upon the Commission by the conference bill was substantially identical with that conferred by the bill passed by the Senate. See Sen.Doc.No.200, 69th Cong., 2d Sess., p. 17; H.Rep.1886, 69th Cong., 2d Sess., p. 17. We agree with the District Court that, in view of this legislative history, § 303(i) cannot be construed as no broader than the first clause of the Senate amendment, which limited the Commission's authority to the technical and engineering phases of chain broadcasting. There is no basis for assuming that the conference intended to preserve the first clause, which was of limited scope, and abandon the second clause, which was of general scope, by agreeing upon a provision which was broader and more comprehensive than those it supplanted. [5]

A totally different source of attack upon the Regulations if found in § 311 of the Act, which authorizes the Commission to withhold licenses from persons convicted of having violated the antitrust laws. Two contentions are made -- first, that this provision puts considerations relating to competition outside the Commission's concern before an applicant has been convicted of monopoly or other restraints of trade, and second, that, in any event, the Commission misconceived the scope of its powers under § 311 in issuing the Regulations. Both of these contentions are unfounded. Section 311 derives from § 13 of the Radio Act of 1927, which expressly commanded, rather than merely authorized, the Commission to refuse a license to any person judicially found guilty of having violated the antitrust laws. The change in the 1934 Act was made, in the words of Senator Dill, the manager of the legislation in the Senate, because "it seemed fair to the committee to do that." 78 Cong.Rec. 8825. The Commission was thus permitted to exercise its judgment as to whether violation of the antitrust laws disqualified an applicant from operating a station in the "public interest." We agree with the District Court that

"The necessary implication from this [amendment in 1934] was that the Commission might infer from the fact that the applicant had in the past tried to monopolize radio, or had engaged in unfair methods of competition, that the disposition so manifested would continue and that if it did it would make him an unfit licensee."

47 F.Supp. 940, 944.

That the Commission may refuse to grant a license to persons adjudged guilty in a court of law of conduct in violation of the antitrust laws certainly does not render irrelevant consideration by the Commission of the effect of such conduct upon the "public interest, convenience, or necessity." A licensee charged with practices in contravention of this standard cannot continue to hold his license merely because his conduct is also in violation of the antitrust laws and he has not yet been proceeded against and convicted. By clarifying in § 311 the scope of the Commission's authority in dealing with persons convicted of violating the antitrust laws, Congress can hardly be deemed to have limited the concept of "public interest" so as to exclude all considerations relating to monopoly and unreasonable restraints upon commerce. Nothing in the provisions or history of the Act lends support to the inference that the Commission was denied the power to refuse a license to a station not operating in the "public interest," merely because its misconduct happened to be an unconvicted violation of the antitrust laws.

Alternatively, it is urged that the Regulations constitute an ultra vires attempt by the Commission to enforce the antitrust laws, and that the enforcement of the antitrust laws is the province not of the Commission, but of the Attorney General and the courts. This contention misconceives the basis of the Commission's action. The Commission's Report indicates plainly enough that the Commission was not attempting to administer the antitrust laws:

"The prohibitions of the Sherman Act apply to broadcasting. This Commission, although not charged with the duty of enforcing that law, should administer its regulatory powers with respect to broadcasting in the light of the purposes which the Sherman Act was designed to achieve. . . . While many of the network practices raise serious questions under the antitrust laws, our jurisdiction does not depend on a showing that they do, in fact, constitute a violation of the antitrust laws. It is not our function to apply the antitrust laws as such. It is our duty, however, to refuse licenses or renewals to any person who engages or proposes to engage in practices which will prevent either himself or other licensees or both from making the fullest use of radio facilities. This is the standard of public interest, convenience, or necessity which we must apply to all applications for licenses and renewals. . . . We do not predicate our jurisdiction to issue the regulations on the ground that the network practices violate the antitrust laws. We are issuing these regulations because we have found that the network practices prevent the maximum utilization of radio facilities in the public interest."

(Report, pp. 46, 83, 83n. 3.)

We conclude, therefore, that the Communications Act of 1934 authorized the Commission to promulgate regulations designed to correct the abuses disclosed by its investigation of chain broadcasting. There remains for consideration the claim that the Commission's exercise of such authority was unlawful.

The Regulations are assailed as "arbitrary and capricious." If this contention means that the Regulations are unwise, that they are not likely to succeed in accomplishing what the Commission intended, we can say only that the appellants have selected the wrong forum for such a plea. What was said in Board of Trade v. United States, 314 U. S. 534, 314 U. S. 548, is relevant here:

"We certainly have neither technical competence nor legal authority to pronounce upon the wisdom of the course taken by the Commission."

Our duty is at an end when we find that the action of the Commission was based upon findings supported by evidence, and was made pursuant to authority granted by Congress. It is not for us to say that the "public interest" will be furthered or retarded by the Chain Broadcasting Regulations. The responsibility belongs to the Congress for the grant of valid legislative authority, and to the Commission for its exercise.

It would be sheer dogmatism to say that the Commission made out no case for its allowable discretion in formulating these Regulations. Its long investigation disclosed the existences of practices which it regarded as contrary to the "public interest." The Commission knew that the wisdom of any action it took would have to be tested by experience:

"We are under no illusion that the regulations we are adopting will solve all questions of public interest with respect to the network system of program distribution. . . . The problems in the network field are interdependent, and the steps now taken may perhaps operate as a partial solution of problems not directly dealt with at this time. Such problems may be examined again at some future time after the regulations here adopted have been given a fair trial."

(Report, p. 88.) The problems with which the Commission attempted to deal could not be solved at once and for all time by rigid rules-of-thumb. The Commission therefore did not bind itself inflexibly to the licensing policies expressed in the Regulations. In each case that comes before it, the Commission must still exercise an ultimate judgment whether the grant of a license would serve the "public interest, convenience, or necessity." If time and changing circumstances reveal that the "public interest" is not served by application of the Regulations, it must be assumed that the Commission will act in accordance with its statutory obligations.

Since there is no basis for any claim that the Commission failed to observe procedural safeguards required by law, we reach the contention that the Regulations should be denied enforcement on constitutional grounds. Here, as in New York Central

Securities Corp. v. United States, 287 U. S. 12, 287 U. S. 24, 25, the claim is made that the standard of "public interest" governing the exercise of the powers delegated to the Commission by Congress is so vague and indefinite that, if it be construed as comprehensively as the words alone permit, the delegation of legislative authority is unconstitutional. But, as we held in that case,

"It is a mistaken assumption that this is a mere general reference to public welfare without any standard to guide determinations. The purpose of the Act, the requirements it imposes, and the context of the provision in question show the contrary."

Id. See Federal Radio Comm'n v. Nelson Bros. Bond & Mortgage Co., 289 U. S. 266, 289 U. S. 285; Federal Communications Comm'n v. Pottsville Broadcasting Co., 309 U. S. 134, 309 U. S. 137-138. Compare Panama Refining Co. v. Ryan, 293 U. S. 388, 293 U. S. 428. Intermountain Rate Cases, 234 U. S. 476, 234 U. S. 486-489; United States v. Lowden, 308 U. S. 225.

We come, finally, to an appeal to the First Amendment. The Regulations, even if valid in all other respects, must fall because they abridge, say the appellants, their right of free speech. If that be so, it would follow that every person whose application for a license to operate a station is denied by the Commission is thereby denied his constitutional right of free speech. Freedom of utterance is abridged to many who wish to use the limited facilities of radio. Unlike other modes of expression, radio inherently is not available to all. That is its unique characteristic, and that is why, unlike other modes of expression, it is subject to governmental regulation. Because it cannot be used by all, some who wish to use it must be denied. But Congress did not authorize the Commission to choose among applicants upon the basis of their political, economic or social views, or upon any other capricious basis. If it did, or if the Commission, by these Regulations, proposed a choice among applicants upon some such basis, the issue before us would be wholly different. The question here is simply whether the Commission, by announcing that it will refuse licenses to persons who engage in specified network practices (a basis for choice which we hold is comprehended within the statutory criterion of "public interest"), is thereby denying such persons the constitutional right of free speech. The right of free speech does not include, however, the right to use the facilities of radio without a license. The licensing system established by Congress in the Communications Act of 1934 was a proper exercise of its power over commerce. The standard it provided for the licensing of stations was the "public interest, convenience, or necessity." Denial of a station license on that ground, if valid under the Act, is not a denial of free speech.

A procedural point calls for just a word. The District Court, by granting the Government's motion for summary judgment, disposed of the case upon the pleadings and upon the record made before the Commission. The court below correctly held that its inquiry was limited to review of the evidence before the Commission. Trial de novo of the matters heard by the Commission and dealt with in its Report would have been improper. See Tagg Bros. v. United States, 280 U. S. 420; Acker v. United States, 298 U. S. 426.

Affirmed.

Notes

[1] Chain broadcasting is defined in § 3(p) of the Communications Act of 1934 as the "simultaneous broadcasting of an identical program by two or more connected stations." In actual practice, programs are transmitted by wire, usually leased telephone lines, from their point of origination to each station in the network for simultaneous broadcast over the air.

[2] Station licenses issued by the Commission normally last two years. Section 3.34 of the Commission's Rules and Regulations governing Standard and High-Frequency Broadcast Stations, as amended October 14, 1941.

[3] The history of federal regulation of radio communication is summarized in Herring and Gross, Telecommunications (1936) 239-86; Administrative Procedure in Government Agencies, Monograph of the Attorney General's Committee on Administrative Procedure, Sen.Doc. No. 186, 76th Cong., 3d Sess., Part 3, dealing with the Federal Communications Commission, pp. 82-84; 1 Socolow, Law of Radio Broadcasting (1939) 38-61; Donovan, Origin and Development of Radio Law (1930).

[4] See Morecroft, Principles of Radio Communication (3d ed. 1933) 355-402; Terman, Radio Engineering (2d ed. 1937) 593-645.

[5] In the course of the Senate debates on the conference report upon the bill that became the Radio Act of 1927, Senator Dill, who was in charge of the bill, said:

"While the commission would have the power under the general terms of the bill, the bill specifically sets out as one of the special powers of the commission the right to make specific regulations for governing chain broadcasting. As to creating a monopoly of radio in this country, let me say that this bill absolutely protects the public, so far as it can protect them, by giving the commission full power to refuse a license to anyone who it believes will not serve the public interest, convenience, or necessity. It specifically provides that any corporation guilty of monopoly shall not only not receive a license, but that its license may be revoked; and if, after a corporation has received its license for a period of three years, it is then discovered and found to be guilty of monopoly, its license will be revoked. . . . In addition to that, the bill contains a provision that no license may be transferred from one owner to another without the written consent of the commission, and the commission, of course, having the power to protect against a monopoly, must give such protection. I wish to state further that the only way by which monopolies in the radio business can secure control of radio here, even for a limited period of time, will be by the commission's becoming servile to them. Power must be lodged somewhere, and I myself am unwilling to assume in advance that the commission proposed to be created will be servile to the desires and demands of great corporations of this country."

68 Cong.Rec. 2881.

## Chatwin v. United States (January 2, 1946)

MR. JUSTICE MURPHY delivered the opinion of the Court.

The Federal Kidnapping Act [1] punishes any one who knowingly transports or aids in transporting in interstate or foreign commerce

"any person who shall have been unlawfully seized, confined, inveigled, decoyed, kidnapped, abducted, or carried away by any means whatsoever and held for ransom or reward or otherwise, except, in the case of a minor, by a parent thereof."

The sole issue confronting us in these cases is whether the stipulated facts support the convictions of the three petitioners under this Act, the indictment having charged that they unlawfully inveigled, decoyed, and carried away a minor child of the age of 15, held her for a stated period, and transported her from Utah to Arizona with knowledge that she had been so inveigled and held. We are not called upon to determine or characterize the morality of their actions. Nor are we concerned here with their liability under any other statute, federal or state.

Petitioners are members of the Fundamentalist cult of the Mormon faith, a cult that sanctions plural or "celestial" marriages. In August, 1940, petitioner Chatwin, who was then a 68-year old widower, employed one Dorothy Wyler as a housekeeper in his home in Santaquin, Utah. This girl was nearly 15 years old at this time, although the stipulation indicates that she had only a mental age of 7. [2] Her employment by Chatwin was approved by her parents. While residing at Chatwin's home, the girl was continually taught by Chatwin and one Lulu Cook, who also resided there, that plural marriage was essential to her salvation. Chatwin also told her that it was her grandmother's desire that he should take her in celestial marriage, and that such a marriage was in conformity with the true principles of the original Mormon Church. As a result of these teachings, the girl was converted to the principle of celestial marriage and entered into a cult marriage with Chatwin on December 19, 1940. Thereafter she became pregnant, which fact was discovered by her parents on July 24, 1941. The parents then informed the juvenile authorities of the Utah of the situation, and they took the girl into custody as a delinquent on August 4, 1941, making her a ward of the juvenile court.

On August 10, 1941, the girl accompanied a juvenile probation officer to a motion picture show at Provo, Utah. The officer left the girl at the show and returned later to all for her. The girl asked to be allowed to stay on for a short time, and the officer consented. Thereafter, and prior to the second return of the officer, the girl "left the picture show and went out onto the street in Provo." There she met two married daughters of Chatwin who gave her sufficient money to go from Provo to Salt Lake City. Shortly after arriving there, she was taken to the home of petitioners Zitting and Christensen. They, together with Chatwin, convinced her that she should abide, as they put it, "by the law of God, rather than the law of man," and that she was perfectly justified in running away from the juvenile court in order to live with Chatwin. They further convinced her that she should go with them to Mexico to be married legally to Chatwin and then remain in hiding until she had reached her majority under Utah law. Thereafter, on October 6, 1941, the three petitioners transported the girl in Zitting's automobile from Salt Lake City of Juarez,

Mexico, where she went through a civil marriage ceremony with Chatwin on October 14. She was then brought back to Utah, and thence to Short Creek, Arizona. There she lived in hiding with Chatwin under assumed names until discovered by federal authorities over two years later, December 9, 1943. While in Short Creek, she gave birth to two children by Chatwin. The transportation of the girl from Provo to Salt Lake City, thence to Juarez, Mexico, and finally to Short Creek was without the consent and against the wishes of her parents and without authority from the juvenile court officials. [3]

Having waived jury trials, the three petitioners were found guilty as charged and were given jail sentences. United States v. Cleveland, 56 F.Supp. 890. The court below affirmed the convictions. 146 F.2d 730. We granted certiorari, 324 U.S. 835, because of our doubts as to the correctness of the judgment that the petitioners were guilty under the Federal Kidnapping Act on the basis of the foregoing facts.

The Act, by its own terms, contemplates that the kidnapped victim shall have been (1) "unlawfully seized, confined, inveigled, decoyed, kidnapped, abducted, or carried away by any means whatsoever" and (2) "held for ransom or reward or otherwise." The Government contends that both elements appear from the stipulated facts in this case. The petitioners, it is argued, unlawfully "inveigled" or "decoyed" the girl away from the custody of her parents and the juvenile court authorities, the girl being "incapable of understanding the full significance of petitioners' importunities" because of her tender years and extremely low mentality. It is claimed, moreover, that the girl was "held" during the two-month period from August 10 to October 6, 1941, prior to the legal marriage, for the purpose of enabling Chatwin to cohabit with her, and that this purpose, being of "benefit to the transgressor," is within the statutory term "or otherwise" as defined in Gooch v. United States, 297 U. S. 124, 297 U. S. 128.

We are unable to approve the Government's contention. The agreed statement that the girl "left the picture show and went out onto the street in Provo" without any apparent motivating actions by the petitioners casts serious doubts on the claim that they "inveigled" or "decoyed" her away from the custody of the juvenile court authorities. But we do not pause to pursue this matter, for it is obvious that there has been a complete lack of competent proof that the girl was "held for ransom or reward or otherwise" as that term is used in the Federal Kidnapping Act.

The act of holding a kidnapped person for a proscribed purpose necessarily implies an unlawful physical or mental restraint for an appreciable period against the person's will and with a willful intent so to confine the victim. If the victim is of such an age or mental state as to be incapable of having a recognizable will, the confinement then must be against the will of the parents or legal guardian of the victim. In this instance, however, the stipulated facts fail to reveal the presence of any of these essential elements.

(1) There is no proof that Chatwin or any of the other petitioners imposed at any time an unlawful physical or mental restraint upon the movements of the girl. Nothing indicates that she was deprived of her liberty, compelled to remain where she did not wish to remain, or compelled to go where she did not wish to go. For aught that appears

from the stipulation, she was perfectly free to leave the petitioners when and if she so desired. In other words, the Government has failed to prove an act of unlawful restraint.

(2) There is no proof that Chatwin or any of the other petitioners willfully intended, through force, fear, or deception, to confine the girl against her desires. While bona fide religious beliefs cannot absolve one from liability under the Federal Kidnapping Act, petitioners' beliefs are not shown to necessitate unlawful restraints of celestial wives against their wills. Nor does the fact that Chatwin intended to cohabit with the girl and to live with her as husband and wife serve as a substitute for an intent to restrain her movements contrary to her wishes, as required by the Act.

(3) Finally, there is no competent or substantial proof that the girl was of such an age or mentality as necessarily to preclude her from understanding the doctrine of celestial marriage and from exercising her own free will, thereby making the will of her parents or the juvenile court authorities the important factor. At the time of the alleged inveiglement in August, 1941, she was 15 years and 8 months of age, and the alleged holding occurred thereafter. There is no legal warrant for concluding that such an age is ipso facto proof of mental incapacity in view of the general rule that incapacity is to be presumed only where a child is under the age of 14. 9 Wigmore on Evidence (3d ed.) § 2514. [4] Nor is there any statutory warrant in this instance for holding that the consent of a child of this age is immaterial. Cf. In re Morrissey, 137 U. S. 157; United States v. Williams, 302 U. S. 46; State v. Rhoades, 29 Wash. 61, 69 P. 389. In Utah, parenthetically, any alleged victim over the age of 12 is considered sufficiently competent so that his consent may be used by an alleged kidnapper in defense to a charge under the state kidnapping statute. Utah Code Ann. (1943) 103-33-2. And a person over the age of 14 in Utah is stated to be capable of committing a crime, the presumption of incapacity applying only to those younger. § 103-1-40. Sadleir v. Young, 97 Utah 291, 85 P.2d 810; State v. Terrell, 55 Utah, 314, 186 P. 108.

Great stress is placed by the Government, however, upon the admitted fact that the girl possessed a mental age of 7 in 1940, one year before the alleged inveiglement and holding. It is unnecessary here to determine the validity, the reliability, or the proper use of mental tests, particularly in relation to criminal trials. It suffices to note that the method of testing the girl's mental age is not revealed, and that there is a complete absence of proof in the record as to the proper weight and significance to be attached to this particular mental age. Nothing appears save a bare mathematical approximation unrestricted in terms to the narrow legal issue in this case. Under such circumstances, a stipulated mental age of 7 cannot be said necessarily to preclude one from understanding and judging the principles of celestial marriage and from acting in accordance with one's beliefs in the matter. The serious crime of kidnapping should turn on something more substantial than such an unexplained mathematical approximation of the victim's mental age. There must be competent proof beyond a reasonable doubt of a victim's mental incapacity in relation to the very acts in question before criminal liability can be sanctioned in a case of this nature. [5]

The stipulated facts of this case reveal a situation quite different from the general problem to which the framers of the Federal Kidnapping Act addressed themselves. This statute was drawn in 1932 against a background of organized violence. 75 Cong.Rec. 13282-13304. Kidnapping by that time had become an epidemic in the United States. Ruthless criminal bands utilized every known legal and scientific means to achieve their aims and to protect themselves.

Victims were selected from among the wealthy with great care and study. Details of the seizures and detentions were fully and meticulously worked out in advance. Ransom was the usual motive.

"Law enforcement authorities, lacking coordination, with no uniform system of intercommunication and restricted in authority to activities in their own jurisdiction, found themselves laughed at by criminals bound by no such inhibitions or restrictions. . . . The procedure was simple -- a man would be kidnapped in one State and whisked into another, and still another, his captors knowing full well that the police in the jurisdiction where the crime was committed had no authority as far as the confinement and concealment was concerned."

Fisher and McGuire, "Kidnapping and the So-called Lindbergh Law," 12 New York U.L.Q.Rev. 646, 653. See also Hearing before the House Committee on the Judiciary (72d Cong., 1st Sess.) on H.R. 5657, Serial 4; Finley, "The Lindbergh Law," 28 Georgetown L.J. 908.

It was to assist the states in stamping out this growing and sinister menace of kidnapping that the Federal Kidnapping Act was designed. Its proponents recognized that, where victims were transported across state lines, only the federal government had the power to disregard such barriers in pursuing the captors. H.Rep. No. 1493 (72d Cong., 1st Sess.); S.Rep. No. 765 (72d Cong., 1st Sess.). Given added impetus by the emotion which gripped the nation due to the famous Lindbergh kidnapping case, the federal statute was speedily adopted. See 75 Cong.Rec. 5075-5076, 13282-13304. Comprehensive language was used to cover every possible variety of kidnapping followed by interstate transportation. Armed with this legislative mandate, federal officials have achieved a high and effective control of this type of crime.

But the broadness of the statutory language does not permit us to tear the words out of their context, using the magic of lexigraphy to apply them to unattractive or immoral situations lacking the involuntariness of seizure and detention which is the very essence of the crime of kidnapping. Thus, if this essential element is missing, the act of participating in illicit relations or contributing to the delinquency of a minor or entering into a celestial marriage, followed by interstate transportation, does not constitute a crime under the Federal Kidnapping Act. No unusual or notorious situation relating to the inability of state authorities to capture and punish participants in such activities evidenced itself at the time this Act was created; no authoritative spokesman indicated that the Act was to be used to assist the states in these matters, however unlawful and obnoxious the character of these activities might otherwise be. Nor is there any indication that Congress desired or contemplated that the punishment of death or long imprisonment, as authorized by the Act, might be applied to those guilty of immoralities lacking the characteristics of true kidnappings. In short, the purpose of the Act was to outlaw interstate kidnappings, rather than general transgressions of morality involving the crossing of state lines. And the broad language of the statute must be interpreted and applied with that plain fact in mind. See United States v. American Trucking Associations, 310 U. S. 534, 310 U. S. 543-544.

Were we to sanction a careless concept of the crime of kidnapping or were we to disregard the background and setting of the Act, the boundaries of potential liability would be lost in infinity. A loose construction of the statutory language conceivably could lead to the punishment of anyone who induced another to leave his surroundings and do some innocent or illegal act of benefit to the former, state lines subsequently being traversed. The absurdity of such a result, with its attendant likelihood of unfair punishment and blackmail, is sufficient by itself to foreclose that construction.

The judgment of the court below affirming the convictions of the petitioners must therefore be

Reversed.

Notes

[1] 47 Stat. 326; 48 Stat. 781, 18 U.S.C. § 408a.

[2] At the time of her employment by Chatwin, the girl's physical age was 14 years and 8 months; her mental age was 7 years and 2 months; her intelligence quotient was 67. At the time of the stipulation in March, 1944, she was a "high grade moron" with a mental age of 9 years and 8 months and an intelligence quotient of 64.

[3] In Chatwin v. Terry, 153 P.2d 941, the Utah Supreme Court held that the juvenile court had authority to hold the girl in custody until she reached the age of 21, despite her legal marriage to Chatwin.

[4] See Commonwealth v. Nickerson, 5 Allen 518, 87 Mass. 518 (child of 9 held incompetent to assent to forcible transfer of custody); State v. Farrar, 41 N.H. 53 (child of 4 held incapable of consenting to forcible seizure and abduction); Herring v. Boyle, 1 C.M. & R. 377 (child of 10 could not recover for false imprisonment without proof that he knew of alleged restraint upon him); In re Lloyd, 3 Man. & Gr. 547 (child between 11 and 12 held competent to decide whether to live with father or mother).

[5] See State v. Kelsie, 93 Vt. 450, 108 A. 391; State v. Schilling, 95 N.J.L. 145, 112 A. 400; People v. Oxnam, 170 Cal. 211, 149 P. 165; State v. Schafer, 156 Wash. 240, 286 P. 833; Commonwealth v. Stewart, 255 Mass. 9, 151 N.E. 74, 44 A.L.R. 579; Commonwealth v. Trippi, 268 Mass. 227, 167 N.E. 354; Woodbridge, "Physical and Mental Infancy in the Criminal Law," 87 U. of Pa.L.Rev. 426.

**Hannegan v. Esquire, Inc. (February 4, 1946)**

Mr. Justice DOUGLAS delivered the opinion of the Court.

Congress has made obscene material nonmailable, 35 Stat. 1129, 18 U.S.C. 334, 18 U.S.C.A. § 334, and has applied criminal sanctions for the enforcement of that policy. It has divided mailable matter into four classes, periodical publications constituting the second-class. 1 § 7 of the Classification Act of 1879, 20 Stat. 358, 43 Stat. 1067, 39 U.S.C. 221, 39 U.S.C.A. § 221. And it has specified four conditions upon which a publication shall be admitted to the second-class. § 14 of the Classification Act of 1879, 20 Stat. 358, 48 Stat. 928, 39 U.S.C. 226, 39 U.S.C.A. § 226. The Fourth condition, which is the only one relevant here, 2 provides:

'Except as otherwise provided by law, the conditions upon which a publication shall be admitted to the second class are as follows * * * Fourth. It must be originated and published for the dissemination of information of a public character, or devoted to literature, the sciences, arts, or some special industry, and having a legitimate list of subscribers. Nothing herein contained shall be so construed as to admit to the second class rate regular publications designed primarily for advertising purposes, or for free circulation, or for circulation at nominal rates.'

Respondent is the publisher of Esquire Magazine, a monthly periodical which was granted a second-class permit in 1933. In 1943, pursuant to the Act of March 3, 1901, 31 Stat. 1107, 39 U.S.C. 232, 39 U.S.C.A. § 232, a citation was issued to respondent by the then Postmaster General (for whom the present Postmaster General has now been substituted as petitioner) to show cause why that permit should not be suspended or revoked. 3 A hearing was held before a board designated by the then Postmaster General. 4 The board recommended that the permit not be revoked. Petitioner's predecessor took a different view. He did not find that Esquire Magazine contained obscene material and therefore was nonmailable. He revoked its second-class permit because he found that it did not comply with the Fourth condition. The gist of his holding is contained in the following excerpt from his opinion:

'The plain language of this statute does not assume that a publication must in fact be 'obscene' within the intendment of the postal obscenity statutes before it can be found not to be 'originated and published for the dissemination of information of a public character, or devoted to literature, the sciences, arts, or some special industry.'

'Writings and pictures may be indecent, vulgar, and risque and still not be obscene in a technical sense. Such writings and pictures may be in that obscure and treacherous borderland zone where the average person hesitates to find them technically obscene, but still may see ample proof that they are morally improper and not for the public welfare and the public good. When such writings or pictures occur in isolated instances their dangerous tendencies and malignant qualities may be considered of lesser importance.

'When, however, they become a dominant and systematic feature they most certainly cannot be said to be for the public good, and a publication which uses them in that manner is not making the 'special contribution to the public welfare' which Congress intended by the Fourth condition.

'A publication to enjoy these unique mail privileges and special preferences is bound to do more than refrain from disseminating material which is obscene or bordering on the obscene. It is under a positive duty to contribute to the public good and the public welfare.'

Respondent thereupon sued in the District Court for the District of Columbia to enjoin the revocation order. The parties stipulated at a pre-trial conference that the suit would not be defended on the ground that Esquire Magazine was obscene or was for any other reason nonmailable. 5 The District Court denied the injunction and dismissed the complaint. 55 F.Supp. 1015. The Court of Appeals reversed. 151 F.2d 49. The case is here on a petition for a writ of certiorari which we granted because of the importance of the problem in the administration of the postal laws.

The issues of Esquire Magazine under attack are those for January to November inclusive of 1943. The material complained of embraces in bulk only a small percentage of those issues. 6 Regular features of the magazine (called 'The Magazine for Men') include articles on topics of current interest, short stories, sports articles or stories, short articles by men prominent in various fields of activities, articles about men prominent in the news, a book review department headed by the late William Lyon Phelps, a theatrical department headed by George Jean Nathan, a department on the lively arts by Gilbert Seldes, a department devoted to men's clothing, and pictorial features, including war action paintings, color photographs of dogs and water colors or etchings of game birds and reproductions of famous paintings, prints and drawings. There was very little in these features which was challenged. But petitioner's predecessor found that the objectionable items, though a small percentage of the total bulk, were regular recurrent features which gave the magazine its dominant tone or characteristic. These include jokes, cartoons, pictures, articles, and poems. They were said to reflect the smoking-room type of humor, featuring, in the main, sex. Some witnesses found the challenged items highly objectionable, calling them salacious and indecent. Others thought they were only racy and risque. Some condemned them as being merely in poor taste. Other witnesses could find no objection to them.

An examination of the items makes plain, we think, that the controversy is not whether the magazine publishes 'information of a public character' or is devoted to 'literature' or to the 'arts.' It is whether the contents are 'good' or 'bad.' To uphold the order of revocation would, therefore, grant the Postmaster General a power of censorship. Such a power is so abhorrent to our traditions that a purpose to grant it should not be easily inferred.

The second-class privilege is a form of subsidy. 7 From the beginning Congress has allowed special rates to certain classes of publications. The Act of February 20, 1792, 1 Stat. 232, 238, granted newspapers a more favorable rate. These were extended to magazines and pamphlets by the Act of May 8, 1794, 1 Stat. 354, 362. Prior to the Classification Act of 1879, periodicals were put into the second-class, 8 which by the Act of March 3, 1863, 12 Stat. 701, 705, included 'all mailable matter exclusively in print, and regularly issued at stated periods, without addition by writing, mark, or sign.' That Act plainly adopted a strictly objective test and left no discretion to the postal authorities to withhold the second-class privilege from a mailable newspaper or periodical because it failed to meet some standard of worth or value or propriety. There is nothing in the language or history of the Classification Act of 1879 which suggests that Congress in that law made any basic change in its treatment of second-class mail, let alone such an abrupt and radical change as would be entailed by the inauguration of even a limited form of censorship.

The postal laws make a clear-cut division between mailable and nonmailable material. The four classes of mailable matter are generally described by objective standards which refer in part to their contents, but not to the quality of their contents. 9 The more particular descriptions of the first, 10 third, 11 and fourth 12 classes follow the same pattern, as do the first three conditions specified for second-class matter. 13 If, therefore, the Fourth condition is read in the context of the postal laws of which it is an integral part, it, too, must be taken to supply standards which relate to the format of the publication and to the nature of its contents, but not to their quality, worth, or value. In that view, 'literature' or the 'arts' mean no more than productions which convey ideas by words, pictures, or drawings.

If the Fourth condition is read in that way, it is plain that Congress made no radical or basic change in the type of regulation which it adopted for second-class mail in 1879. The inauguration of even a limited type of censorship would have been such a startling change as to have left some traces in the legislative history. But we find none. Congressman Money, a member of the Postal Committee who defended the bill on the floor of the House, stated that it was 'nothing but a simplification of the postal code. There are no new powers granted to the Department by this bill, none whatever.' 8 Cong.Rec. 2134. The bill contained registration provisions which were opposed on the ground that they might be the inception of a censorship of the press. Id., p. 2137. These were deleted. Id., pp. 2137, 2138. It is difficult to imagine that the Congress, having deleted them for fear of censorship, gave the Postmaster General by the Fourth condition discretion to deny periodicals the second-class rate, if in his view they did not contribute to the public good. Congressman Money indeed referred to 'the daily newspapers, with their load of gossip and scandal and every-day topics that are floating through the press' as being entitled without question to the second-class privilege. Id., p. 2135. To the charge that the bill imposed a censorship, he pointed out that it only withheld the privileged rate from publications 'made up simply of advertising concerns not intended for public education'; and added:

'We know the reason for which papers are allowed to go at a low rate of postage, amounting almost to the franking privilege, is because they are the most efficient educators of our people. It is because they go into general circulation and are intended for the dissemination of useful knowledge such as will promote the prosperity and the best interests of the people all over the country. Then all this vast mass of matter is excluded from that low rate of postage. I say, instead of being a censorship upon the press, it is for the protection of the legitimate journals of the country.' Id., 2135.

The policy of Congress has been clear. It has been to encourage the distribution of periodicals which disseminated 'information of a public character' or which were devoted to 'literature, the sciences, arts, or some special industry,' because it was thought that those publications as a class contributed to the public good. 14 The standards prescribed in the Fourth condition have been criticized, but not on the ground that they provide for censorship. 15 As stated by the Postal Commission of 1911, H.Doc. 559, 62nd Cong., 2d Sess., p. 142: 'The original object in placing on second-class matter a rate far below that on any other class of mail was to encourage the dissemination of news and of current literature of educational value. This object has been only in part attained. The low rate has helped to stimulate an enormous mass of periodicals, many of which are of little utility for the cause of popular education. Others are of excellent quality, but the experience of the post office has shown the impossibility of making a satisfactory test based upon literary or educational values. To attempt to do so would be to set up a censorship of the press. Of necessity the words of the statute—'devoted to literature, the sciences, arts, or some special industry'—must have a broad interpretation.'

We may assume that Congress has a broad power of classification and need not open second-class mail to publications of all types. The categories of publications entitled to that classification have indeed varied through the years. 16 And the Court held in Ex parte Jackson, 96 U.S. 727, 24 L.Ed. 877, that Congress could constitutionally make it a crime to send fraudulent or obscene material through the mails. But grave constitutional questions are immediately raised once it is said that the use of the mails is a privilege which may be extended or withheld on any grounds whatsoever. See the dissents of Mr. Justice Brandeis and Mr. Justice Holmes in United States ex rel. Milwaukee Social Democrat Publishing Co. v. Burleson, 255 U.S. 407, 421—423, 430—432, 437, 438, 41 S.Ct. 352, 357, 358, 360, 361, 363, 65 L.Ed. 704. Under that view the second-class rate could be granted on condition that certain economic or political ideas not be disseminated. The provisions of the Fourth condition would have to be far more explicit for us to assume that Congress made such a radical departure from our traditions 17 and undertook to clothe the Postmaster General with the power to supervise the tastes of the reading public of the country. 18

It is plain, as we have said, that the favorable second-class rates were granted periodicals meeting the requirements of the Fourth condition, so that the public good might be served through a dissemination of the class of periodicals described. But that is a far cry from assuming that Congress had any idea that each applicant for the second-class rate must convince the Postmaster General that his publication positively contributes to the public good or public welfare. Under our system of government there is an accommodation for the widest varieties of tastes and ideas. 19 What is good literature, what has educational value, what is refined public information, what is good art, varies with individuals as it does from one generation to another. There doubtless would be a contrariety of views 20 concerning Cervantes' Don Quixote, Shakespeare's Venus & Adonis, or Zola's Nana. But a requirement that literature or art conform to some norm prescribed by an official smacks of an ideology foreign to our system. The basic values implicit in the requirements of the Fourth condition can be served only by uncensored distribution of literature. From the multitude of competing offerings the public will pick and choose. What seems to one to be trash may have for others fleeting or even enduring values. But to withdraw the second-class rate from this publication today because its contents seemed to one official not good for the public wou d sanction withdrawal of the second-class rate tomorrow from another periodical whose social or economic views seemed harmful to another official. The validity of the obscenity laws is recognition that the mails may not be used to satisfy all tastes, no matter how perverted. But Congress has left the Postmaster General with no power to prescribed standards for the literature or the art which a mailable periodical disseminates.

This is not to say that there is nothing left to the Postmaster General under the Fourth condition. It is his duty to 'execute all laws relative to the Postal Service.' Rev.Stat. § 396, 5 U.S.C. 369, 5 U.S.C.A. § 369. For example, questions will arise as they did in Houghton v. Payne, 194 U.S. 88, 24 S.Ct. 590, 48 L.Ed. 888; Bates & Guild Co. v. Payne, 194 U.S. 106, 24 S.Ct. 595, 48 L.Ed. 894, and Smith v. Hitchcock, 226 U.S. 53, 33 S.Ct. 6, 57 L.Ed. 119, whether the publication which seeks the favorable second-class rate is a periodical as defined in the Fourth condition or a book or other type of publication. And it may appear that the information contained in a periodical may not be of a 'public character.' But the power to determine whether a periodical (which is mailable) contains information of a public character, literature or art does not include the further power to determine whether the contents meet some standard of the public good or welfare.

Affirmed.

Notes

1 'mailable matter of the second class shall embrace all newspapers and other periodical publications which are issued at stated intervals, and as frequently as four times a year and are within the conditions named in sections twelve and fourteen.' § 10 of the Classification Act of 1879, 20 Stat. 358, 39 U.S.C. 224, 39 U.S.C.A. § 224. For other periodical publications which are included in second-class matter, see 37 Stat. 550, 39 U.S.C. 229, 39 U.S.C.A. § 229; 31 Stat. 660, 39 U.S.C. 230, 39 U.S.C.A. § 230.

2 The first three conditions are:

'First. It must regularly be issued at stated intervals, as frequently as four times a year, and bear a date of issue, and be numbered consecutively. Second. It must be issued from a known office of publication. Third. It must be formed of printed paper sheets, without board, cloth, leather, or other substantial binding, such as distinguish printed books for preservation from periodical publications: Provided, That publications produced by the stencil, mimeograph, or hectograph process or in imitation of typewriting shall not be regarded as printed within the meaning of this clause.'

3 Sec. 1 of that Act provides:

'When any publication has been accorded second-class mail privileges, the same shall not be suspended or annulled until a hearing shall have been granted to the parties interested.'

4 See 7 Fed.Reg. 3001.

5 It was not contended that Esquire Magazine does not comply with the first three conditions of 39 U.S.C. 226, 39 U.S.C.A. § 226, set forth in note 2, supra.

6 Items taking up a part or all of 86 pages out of a total of 1972 pages.

7 It was found to be worth $500,000 a year to Esquire Magazine. 'A newspaper editor fears being put out of business by the administrative denial of the second-class mailing privilege much more than the prospect of prison subject to a jury trial.' Chafee, Freedom of Speech (1920), p. 199.

8 Rates on periodicals, designed primarily for advertising purposes or for free circulation, were increased by the Act of July 12, 1876, 19 Stat. 78, 82.

9 Sec. 7 of the Classification Act of 1879, as amended, 39 U.S.C. 221, 39 U.S.C.A. § 221, provides:

'Mailable matter shall be divided into four classes:

'First, written matter;

'Second, periodical publications;

'Third, miscellaneous printed matter and other mailable matter not in the first, second, or fourth classes;

'Fourth, merchandise and other mailable matter weighing not less than eight ounces and not in any other class.'

10 First class. 'Mailable matter of the first class shall embrace letters, postal cards, and all matters wholly or partly in writing * * *.' 39 U.S.C. 222, 39 U.S.C.A. § 222.

11 Third class. 'Mail matter of the third class shall include books, circulars, and other matter wholly in print (except newspapers and other periodicals entered as second-class matter), proof sheets, corrected proof sheets, and manuscript copy accompanying same, merchandise (including farm and factory products) and all other mailable matter not included in the first or second class, or in the fourth class * * *.' 39 U.S.C. 235, 39 U.S.C.A. § 235.

12 Fourth class. 'Mail matter of the fourth class shall weigh in excess of eight ounces, and shall include books, circulars, and other matter wholly in print (except newspapers and other periodicals entered as second-class matter), proof sheets, corrected proof sheets and manuscript copy accompanying same, merchandise (including farm and factory products), and all other mailable matter not included in the first or second class, or in the third class as defined in section 235 of this title, not exceeding eleven pounds in weight, nor greater in size than seventy-two inches in length and girth combined, nor in form or kind likely to injure the person of any postal employee or damage the mail equipment or other mail matter and not of a character perishable within a period

reasonably required for transportation and delivery.' 39 U.S.C. 240, 39 U.S.C.A. § 240.

13 See note 2, supra.

14 See Lewis Publishing Co. v. Morgan, 229 U.S. 288, 301, 33 S.Ct. 867, 870, 57 L.Ed. 1190; Annual Report of Postmaster General (1892), p. 71.

15 See Report of the Postal Commission of 1906, H.Doc, 608, 59th Cong., 2d Sess., pp. xxxvi—xxxvii:

'But in what way can it be said that a requirement that a certain printed matter should be 'devoted to literature' serves to mark it off from anything else that can be put into print. There is practically no form of expression of the human mind that can not be brought within the scope of 'public information,' 'literature, the sciences, art, or some special industry.' It would have been just as effective and just as reasonable for the statute to have said, 'devoted to the interests of humanity,' or ' devoted to the development of civilization,' or 'devoted to human intellectual activity.'

'The prime defect in the statute is, then, that it defines not by qualities but by purposes, and the purpose described is so broad as to include everything and exclude nothing.

'With the exception of a few instances where the publication has been excluded because the information was deemed not to be public, no periodical has ever been classified by the application of tests of this kind. Any attempt to apply them generally would simply end in a press censorship.'

16 As we have seen, the Fourth condition bars admission to second-class privileges of publications 'designed primarily for advertising purposes, or for free circulation, or for circulation at nominal rates.' Publications of state departments of agriculture were not granted the special rate until the Act of June 6, 1900, 31 Stat. 660, 39 U.S.C. 230, 39 U.S.C.A. § 230. And that was not done for publications of benevolent and fraternal societies, of institutions of learning, trade unions, strictly professional, literary, historical and scientific societies until the Act of August 24, 1912, 37 Stat. 550, 39 U.S.C. 229, 39 U.S.C.A. § 229.

17 See Deutsch, Freedom of the Press and of the Mails, 36 Mich.L.Rev. 703, 715—727.

18 When Congress has been concerned with the content of matter passing through the mails, it has enacted criminal statutes making, for example, obscene material (35 Stat. 1129, 18 U.S.C. 334, 18 U.S.C.A. § 334), fraudulent material (35 Stat. 1130, 18 U.S.C. 338, 18 U.S.C.A. § 338), and seditious literature (40 Stat. 230, 18 U.S.C. 344, 18 U.S.C.A. § 344), nonmailable in any class. And it has granted the Postmaster General power to refuse to deliver mail for any person whom he finds to be using the mails in conducting lotteries or fraudulent schemes. Rev.Stat. § 3929, 39 U.S.C. 259, 39 U.S.C.A. § 259.

But that power has been zealously watched and strictly confined. See, for example, S.Rep. 118, 24th Cong., 1st Sess., reporting adversely on the recommendation of President Jackson that a law be passed prohibiting the use of the mails for the transmission of publications intended to instigate the slaves to insurrection. It was said, p. 3:

'But to understand more fully the extent of the control which the right of prohibiting circulation through the mail would give to the Government over the press, it must be borne in mind, that the power of Congress over the Post Office and the mail is an exclusive power. It must also be remembered that Congress, in the exercise of this power, may declare any road or navigable water to be a post road; and that, by the act of 1825, it is provided 'that no stage, or other vehicle which regularly performs trips on a post road, or on a road parallel to it, shall carry letters.' The same provision extends to packets, boats, or other vessels, on navigable waters. Like provision may be extended to newspapers and pamphlets; which, if it be admitted that Congress has the right to discriminate in reference to their character, what papers shall or what shall not be transmitted by the mail, would subject the freedom of the press, on all subjects, political, moral, and religious, completely to its will and pleasure. It would, in fact, in some respects, more effectually control the freedom of the press than any sedition law, however severe its penalties. The mandate of the Government alone would be sufficient to close the door against circulation through the mail, and thus, at its sole will and pleasure, might intercept all communications between the press and the people * * *.'

19 'The foolish judgments of Lord Eldon about one hundred years ago, proscribing the works of Byron and Southey, and the finding by the jury under a charge by Lord Denman that the publication of Shelley's 'Queen Mab' was an indictable offense are a warning to all who have to determine the limits of the field within which authors may exercise themselves.' United States v. One Book Entitled Ulysses, 2 Cir., 72 F.2d 705, 708.

20 In the present case petitioner's predecessor said in his report:

'when the polls of public opinion submitted by the publication are examined, it is found that these pictures were characterized as obscene or indecent by 19 to 22% of the persons interviewed, and that 20 to 26% of the persons polled would object to having them in their homes.'


## Winters v. New York (March 29, 1948)

MR. JUSTICE REED delivered the opinion of the Court.

Appellant is a New York City bookdealer, convicted, on information, [1] of a misdemeanor for having in his possession with intent to sell certain magazines charged to violate subsection 2 of § 1141 of the New York Penal Law, Consol.Laws, c. 40. It reads as follows:

"§ 1141. Obscene prints and articles"

"1. A person . . . who,"

"2. Prints, utters, publishes, sells, lends, gives away, distributes or shows, or has in his possession with intent to sell, lend, give away, distribute or show, or otherwise offers for sale, loan, gift or distribution, any book, pamphlet, magazine, newspaper or other printed paper devoted to the publication, and principally made up of criminal news, police reports, or accounts of criminal deeds, or pictures, or stories of deeds of bloodshed, lust or crime; . . ."

"* * * *"

"Is guilty of a misdemeanor, . . . "

Upon appeal from the Court of Special Sessions, the trial court, the conviction was upheld by the Appellate Division of the New York Supreme Court, 268 App.Div. 30, 48 N.Y.S.2d 230, whose judgment was later upheld by the New York Court of Appeals. 294 N.Y. 545, 63 N.E.2d 98.

The validity of the statute was drawn in question in the state courts as repugnant to the Fourteenth Amendment to the Constitution of the United States in that it denied the accused the right of freedom of speech and press, protected against state interference by the Fourteenth Amendment. Gitlow v. New York, 268 U. S. 652, 268 U. S. 666; Pennekamp v. Florida, 328 U. S. 331, 328 U. S. 335. The principle of a free press covers distribution as well as publication. Lovell v. City of Griffin, 303 U. S. 444, 303 U. S. 452. As the validity of the section was upheld in a final judgment by the highest court of the state against this constitutional challenge, this Court has jurisdiction under Judicial Code, § 237(a). This appeal was argued at the October 1945 Term of this Court and set down for reargument before a full bench at the October 1946 Term. It was then reargued and again set down for further reargument at the present term.

The appellant contends that the subsection violates the right of free speech and press because it is vague and indefinite. It is settled that a statute so vague and indefinite, in form and as interpreted, as to permit within the scope of its language the punishment of incidents fairly within the protection of the guarantee of free speech is void on its face as contrary to the Fourteenth Amendment. Stromberg v. California, 283 U. S. 359, 283 U. S. 369; Herndon v. Lowry, 301 U. S. 242, 301 U. S. 258. A failure of a statute limiting freedom of expression to give fair notice of what acts will be punished and such a statute's inclusion of prohibitions against expressions, protected by the principles of the First Amendment violates an accused's rights under procedural due process and freedom of speech or press. Where the alleged vagueness of a state statute had been cured by an opinion of the state court, confining a statute, Rem. & Bal.Code, § 2564, punishing the circulation of publications "having a tendency to encourage or incite the commission of any crime" to "encouraging an actual breach of law," this Court affirmed a conviction under the stated limitation of meaning. The accused publication was read as advocating the commission of the crime of indecent exposure. Fox v. Washington, 236 U. S. 273, 236 U. S. 277.

We recognize the importance of the exercise of a state's police power to minimize all incentives to crime, particularly in the field of sanguinary or salacious publications with their stimulation of juvenile delinquency. Although we are dealing with an aspect of a free press in its relation to public morals, the principles of unrestricted distribution of publications admonish us of the particular importance of a maintenance of standards of certainty in the field of criminal prosecution for violation of statutory prohibitions against distribution. We do not accede to appellee's suggestion that the constitutional protection for a free press applies only to the exposition of ideas. The line between the informing and the entertaining is too elusive for the protection of that basic right. Everyone is familiar with instances of propaganda through fiction. What is one man's amusement teaches another's doctrine. Though we can see nothing of any possible value to society in these magazines, they are as much entitled to the protection of free speech as the best of literature. Cf. Hannegan v. Esquire, 327 U. S. 146, 327 U. S. 153, 327 U. S. 158. They are equally subject to control if they are lewd, indecent, obscene or profane. Ex parte Jackson, 96 U. S. 727, 96 U. S. 736; Chaplinsky v. New Hampshire, 315 U. S. 568.

The section of the Penal Law, § 1141(2), under which the information was filed is a part of the "indecency" article of that law. It comes under the caption "Obscene prints and articles." Other sections make punishable various acts of indecency. For example, § 1141(1), a section not here in issue but under the same caption, punishes the distribution of obscene, lewd, lascivious, filthy, indecent or disgusting magazines. [2] Section 1141(2) originally was aimed at the protection of minors from the distribution of publications devoted principally to criminal news and stories of bloodshed, lust or crime. [3] It was later broadened to include all the population and other phases of production and possession.

Although many other states have similar statutes, they, like the early statutes restricting paupers from changing residence, have lain dormant for decades. Edwards v. California, 314 U. S. 160, 314 U. S. 176. Only two other state courts, whose reports are printed, appear to have construed language in their laws similar to that here involved. In Strohm v. Illinois, 160 Ill. 582, 43 N.E. 622, a statute to suppress exhibiting to any minor child publications of this character was considered. The conviction was upheld. The case, however, apparently did not involve any problem of free speech or press or denial of due process for uncertainty under the Fourteenth Amendment.

In State v. McKee, 73 Conn. 18, 46 A. 409, the court considered a conviction under a statute which made criminal the sale of magazines

"devoted to the publication or principally made up of criminal news, police reports, or pictures, and stories of deeds of bloodshed, lust, or crime."

The gist of the offense was thought to be a

"selection of immoralities so treated as to excite attention and interest sufficient to command circulation for a paper devoted mainly to the collection of such matters."

Page 27. It was said, a propos of the state's constitutional provision as to free speech, that the act did not violate any constitutional provision relating to the freedom of the press. It was held, p. 31, that the principal evil at which the statute was directed was "the circulation of this massed immorality." As the charge stated that the offense might be committed

"whenever the objectionable matter is a leading feature of the paper, or special attention is devoted to the publication of the prohibited items,"

the court felt that it failed to state the full meaning of the statute and reversed. As in the Strohm case, denial of due process for uncertainty was not raised.

On its face, the subsection here involved violates the rule of the Stromberg and Herndon cases, supra, that statutes which include prohibitions of acts fairly within the protection of a free press are void. It covers detective stories, treatises on crime, reports of battle carnage, et cetera. In recognition of this obvious defect, the New York Court of Appeals limited the scope by construction. Its only interpretation of the meaning of the pertinent subsection is that given in this case. After pointing out that New York statutes against indecent or obscene publications have generally been construed to refer to sexual impurity, it interpreted the section here in question to forbid these publications as "indecent or obscene" in a different manner. The Court held that collections of criminal deeds of bloodshed or lust

"can be so massed as to become vehicles for inciting violent and depraved crimes against the person, and, in that case, such publications are indecent or obscene in an admissible sense, . . ."

294 N.Y. at 550. "This idea," its opinion goes on to say, "was the principal reason for the enactment of the statute." The Court left open the question of whether "the statute extends to accounts of criminal deeds not characterized by bloodshed or lust" because the magazines in question "are nothing but stories and pictures of criminal deeds of bloodshed and lust." As the statute in terms extended to other crimes, it may be supposed that the reservation was on account of doubts as to the validity of so wide a prohibition. The court declared:

"In short, we have here before us accumulations of details of heinous wrongdoing which plainly carried an appeal to that portion of the public who (as many recent records remind us) are disposed to take to vice for its own sake."

Further, the Court of Appeals, 294 N.Y. at 549, limited the statute so as not to "outlaw all commentaries on crime from detective tales to scientific treatises" on the ground that the legislature did not intend such literalness of construction. It thought that the magazines the possession of which caused the filing of the information were indecent in the sense just explained. The Court had no occasion to and did not weigh the character of the magazine exhibits by the more frequently used scales of § 1141(1), printed in note 2 It did not interpret § 1141(2) to punish distribution of indecent or obscene publications, in the usual sense, but that the present magazines were indecent and obscene because they "massed" stories of bloodshed and lust to incite crimes. Thus, interpreting § 1141(2) to include the expanded concept of indecency and obscenity stated in its opinion, the Court of Appeals met appellant's contention of invalidity from indefiniteness and uncertainty of the subsection by saying, 294 N.Y. at 551,

"In the nature of things, there can be no more precise test of written indecency or obscenity than the continuing and changeable experience of the community as to what types of books are likely to bring about the corruption of public morals or other analogous injury to the public order. Consequently, a question as to whether a particular publication is indecent or obscene in that sense is a question of the times which must be determined as matter of fact, unless the appearances are thought to be necessarily harmless from the standpoint of public order or morality."

The opinion went on to explain that publication of any crime magazine would be no more hazardous under this interpretation than any question of degree and concluded, p. 552,

"So, when reasonable men may fairly classify a publication as necessarily or naturally indecent or obscene, a mistaken view by the publisher as to its character or tendency is immaterial."

The Court of Appeals, by this authoritative interpretation, made the subsection applicable to publications that, besides meeting the other particulars of the statute, so massed their collection of pictures and stories of bloodshed and of lust "as to become vehicles for inciting violent and depraved crimes against the person." Thus, the statute forbids the massing of stories of bloodshed and lust in such a way as to incite to crime against the person. This construction fixes the meaning of the statute for this case. The interpretation by the Court of Appeals puts these words in the statute as definitely as if it had been so amended by the legislature. Hebert v. Louisiana, 272 U. S. 312, 272 U. S. 317; Skiriotes v. Florida, 313 U. S. 69, 313 U. S. 79. We assume that the defendant, at the time he acted, was chargeable with knowledge of the scope of subsequent interpretation. Compare Lanzetta v. New Jersey, 306 U. S. 451. As lewdness in publications is punishable under § 1141(1) and the usual run of stories of bloodshed, such as detective stories, are excluded, it is the massing as an incitation to crime that becomes the important element.

Acts of gross and open indecency or obscenity, injurious to public morals, are indictable at common law as violative of the public policy that requires from the offender retribution for acts that flaunt accepted standards of conduct. 1 Bishop, Criminal Law, 9th Ed., § 500; Wharton, Criminal Law, 12th Ed., § 16. When a legislative body concludes that the mores of the community call for an extension of the impermissible limits, an enactment aimed at the evil is plainly within its power, if it does not transgress the boundaries fixed by the Constitution for freedom of expression. The standards of certainty in statutes punishing for offenses is higher than in those depending primarily upon civil sanction for enforcement. The crime "must be defined with appropriate definiteness." Pierce v. United States, 314 U. S. 306, 314 U. S. 311; Cantwell v. Connecticut, 310 U. S. 296. There must be ascertainable standards of guilt. Men of common intelligence cannot be required to guess at the meaning of the enactment. [4] The vagueness may be from uncertainty in regard to persons within the scope of the act, Lanzetta v. New Jersey, 306 U. S. 451, or in regard to the applicable tests to ascertain guilt. [5]

Other states than New York have been confronted with similar problems involving statutory vagueness in connection with free speech. In State v. Diamond, 27 N.Mex. 477, 202 P. 988, a statute punishing "any act of any kind whatsoever which has for its purpose or aim the destruction of organized government, federal, state or municipal, or to do or cause to be done any act which is antagonistic to or in opposition to such organized government, or incite or attempt to incite revolution or opposition to such organized government"

was construed. The court said, p. 479:

"Under its terms, no distinction is made between the man who advocates a change in the form of our government by constitutional means, or advocates the abandonment of organized government by peaceful methods, and the man who advocates the overthrow of our government by armed revolution, or other form of force and violence."

Later in the opinion, the statute was held void for uncertainty, p. 485:

"Where the statute uses words of no determinative meaning, or the language is so general and indefinite as to embrace not only acts commonly recognized as reprehensible, but also others which it is unreasonable to presume were intended to be made criminal, it will be declared void for uncertainty."

Again in State v. Klapprott, 127 N.J.L. 395, 22 A.2d 877, a statute was held invalid on an attack against its constitutionality under state and federal constitutional provisions that protect an individual's freedom of expression. The statute read as follows, p. 396:

"Any person who shall, in the presence of two or more persons, in any language, make or utter any speech, statement or declaration, which in any way incites, counsels, promotes, or advocates hatred, abuse, violence or hostility against any group or groups of persons residing or being in this state by reason of race, color, religion or manner of worship, shall be guilty of a misdemeanor."

The court said, pp. 401-402:

"It is our view that the statute, supra, by punitive sanction, tends to restrict what one may say lest, by one's utterances, there be incited or advocated hatred, hostility or violence against a group 'by reason of race, color, religion or manner of worship.' But additionally and looking now to strict statutory construction, is the statute definite, clear and precise so as to be free from the constitutional infirmity of the vague and indefinite? That the terms 'hatred,' 'abuse,' 'hostility,' are abstract and indefinite admits of no contradiction. When do they arise? Is it to be left to a jury to conclude beyond reasonable doubt when the emotion of hatred or hostility is aroused in the mind of the listener as a result of what a speaker has said? Nothing in our criminal law can be invoked to justify so wide a discretion. The Criminal Code must be definite and informative, so that there may be no doubt in the mind of the citizenry that the interdicted act or conduct is illicit."

This Court goes far to uphold state statutes that deal with offenses, difficult to define, when they are not entwined with limitations on free expression. [6] We have the same attitude toward federal statutes. [7] Only a definite conviction by a majority of this Court that the conviction violates the Fourteenth Amendment justifies reversal of the court primarily charged with responsibility to protect persons from conviction under a vague state statute.

The impossibility of defining the precise line between permissible uncertainty in statutes caused by describing crimes by words well understood through long use in the criminal law -- obscene, lewd, lascivious, filthy, indecent or disgusting -- and the unconstitutional vagueness that leaves a person uncertain as to the kind of prohibited conduct -- massing stories to incite crime -- has resulted in three arguments of this case in this Court. The legislative bodies in draftsmanship obviously have the same difficulty as do the judicial in interpretation. Nevertheless, despite the difficulties, courts must do their best to determine whether or not the vagueness is of such a character "that men of common intelligence must necessarily guess at its meaning." Connally v. General Constr. Co., 269 U. S. 385, 269 U. S. 391. The entire text of the statute or the subjects dealt with may furnish an adequate standard. [8] The present case as to a vague statute abridging free speech involves the circulation of only vulgar magazines. The next may call for decision as to free expression of political views in the light of a statute intended to punish subversive activities.

The subsection of the New York Penal Law, as now interpreted by the Court of Appeals, prohibits distribution of a magazine principally made up of criminal news or stories of deeds of bloodshed, or lust, so massed as to become vehicles for inciting violent and depraved crimes against the person. But even considering the gloss put upon the literal meaning by the Court of Appeals' restriction of the statute to collections of stories

"so massed as to become vehicles for inciting violent and depraved crimes against the person . . . not necessarily . . . sexual passion,"

we find the specification of publications, prohibited from distribution, too uncertain and indefinite to justify the conviction of this petitioner. Even though all detective tales and treatises on criminology are not forbidden, and though publications made up of criminal deeds not characterized by bloodshed or lust are omitted from the interpretation of the Court of Appeals, we think fair use of collections of pictures and stories would be interdicted because of the utter impossibility of the actor or the trier to know where this new standard of guilt would draw the line between the allowable and the forbidden publications. No intent or purpose is required -- no indecency or obscenity in any sense heretofore known to the law. "So massed as to incite to crime" can become meaningful only by concrete instances. This one example is not enough. The clause proposes to punish the printing and circulation of publications that courts or juries may think influence generally persons to commit crime of violence against the person. No conspiracy to commit a crime is required. See Musser v. Utah, 333 U. S. 95. It is not an effective notice of new crime. The clause has no technical or common law meaning. Nor can light as to the meaning be gained from the section as a whole or the Article of the Penal Law under which it appears. As said in the Cohen Grocery Co. case, supra, p. 255 U. S. 89:

"It leaves open, therefore, the widest conceivable inquiry, the scope of which no one can foresee and the result of which no one can foreshadow or adequately guard against."

The statute as construed by the Court of Appeals does not limit punishment to the indecent and obscene, as formerly understood. When stories of deeds of bloodshed, such as many in the accused magazines, are massed so as to incite to violent crimes, the statute is violated. It does not seem to us that an honest distributor of publications could know when he might be held to have ignored such a prohibition. Collections of tales of war horrors, otherwise unexceptionable, might well be found to be "massed" so as to become "vehicles for inciting violent and depraved crimes." Where a statute is so vague as to make criminal an innocent act, a conviction under it cannot be sustained. Herndon v. Lowry, 301 U. S. 242, 301 U. S. 259.

To say that a state may not punish by such a vague statute carries no implication that it may not punish circulation of objectionable printed matter, assuming that it is not protected by the principles of the First Amendment, by the use of apt words to describe the prohibited publications. Section 1141, subsection 1, quoted in note 2 is an example. Neither the states nor Congress are prevented by the requirement of specificity from carrying out their duty of eliminating evils to which, in their judgment, such publications give rise.

Reversed.

Notes

[1] The counts of the information upon which appellant was convicted charged, as the state court opinions show, violation of subsection 2 of § 1141. An example follows:

"Fourth Count"

"And I, the District Attorney aforesaid, by this information, further accuse the said defendant of the Crime of Unlawfully Possessing Obscene Prints, committed as follows:"

"The said defendant, on the day and in the year aforesaid, at the city and in the county aforesaid, with intent to sell, lend, give away and show, unlawfully did offer for sale and distribution, and have in his possession with intent to sell, lend, give away and show, a certain obscene, lewd, lascivious, filthy, indecent and disgusting magazine entitled 'Headquarters Detective, True Cases from the Police Blotter, June 1940,' the same being devoted to the publication and principally made up of criminal news, police reports, and accounts of criminal deeds, and pictures and stories of deeds of bloodshed, lust and crime."

[2] "§ 1141. . . . 1. A person who sells, lends, gives away, distributes or shows, or offers to sell, lend, give away, distribute, or show, or has in his possession with intent to sell, lend, distribute or give away, or to show, or advertises in any manner, or who otherwise offers for loan, gift, sale or distribution, any obscene, lewd, lascivious, filthy, indecent or disgusting book, magazine, pamphlet, newspaper, story paper, writing, paper, picture, drawing, photograph, figure or image, or any written or printed matter of an indecent character; . . ."

"* * * *"

"Is guilty of a misdemeanor. . . ."

[3] Ch. 380, New York Laws 1884; ch. 692, New York Laws 1887; ch. 925, New York Laws 1941.

[4] Connally v. General Const. Co., 269 U. S. 385, 269 U. S. 391, 269 U. S. 392:

"But it will be enough for present purposes to say generally that the decisions of the court, upholding statutes as sufficiently certain, rested upon the conclusion that they employed words or phrases having a technical or other special meaning, well enough known to enable those within their reach to correctly apply them, . . . or a well settled common law meaning, notwithstanding an element of degree in the definition as to which estimates might differ, . . . or, as broadly stated by Mr. Chief Justice White in United States v. Cohen Grocery Co., 255 U. S. 81, 255 U. S. 92,"

"that, for reasons found to result either from the text of the statutes involved or the subjects with which they dealt, a standard of some sort was afforded."

[5] United States v. Cohen Grocery Co., 255 U. S. 81, 255 U. S. 89-93; Champlin Refining Co. v. Corporation Commission, 286 U. S. 210, 286 U. S. 242; Smith v. Cahoon, 283 U. S. 553, 283 U. S. 564.

[6] Omaechevarria v. Idaho, 246 U. S. 343; Waters-Pierce Oil Co. v. Texas, 212 U. S. 86.

[7] United States v. Petrillo, 332 U. S. 1; Gorin v. United States, 312 U. S. 19.

[8] Hygrade Provision Co. v. Sherman, 266 U. S. 497, 266 U. S. 501; Mutual Film Corp. v. Ohio Industrial Commission, 236 U. S. 230, 236 U. S. 245-246; Screws v. United States, 325 U. S. 91, 325 U. S. 94-100.

## US v. Alpers (February 6, 1950)

Mr. Justice MINTON delivered the opinion of the Court.

The question in this case is whether the shipment of obscene phonograph records in interstate commerce is prohibited by § 245 of the Criminal Code, which makes illegal the interstate shipment of any 'obscene * * * book, pamphlet, picture, motionpicture film, paper, letter, writing, print, or other matter of indecent character.' Respondent was charged by an information in three counts with knowingly depositing with an express company for carriage in interstate commerce packages 'containing certain matter of an indecent character, to-wit: phonograph records impressed with recordings of obscene, lewd, lascivious and filthy language and obscene, lewd, lascivious and filthy stories.' Respondent, having waived jury trial, was found guilty by the District Court on two counts and was assessed a fine on each. The Court of Appeals reversed, 9 Cir., 175 F.2d 137. We granted certiorari to examine the applicability of § 245 of the Criminal Code to the facts of this case. 338 U.S. 813, 70 S.Ct. 75.

The pertinent provisions of the statute are as follows: 'Whoever shall * * * knowingly deposit or cause to be deposited with any express company or other common carrier (for carriage in interstate commerce) any obscene, lewd, or lascivious, or any filthy book, pamphlet, picture, motion-picture film, paper, letter, writing, print, or other matter of indecent character * * * shall be fined not more than $5,000 or imprisoned not more than five years, or both.' 41 Stat. 1060, 18 U.S.C. 396, now 18 U.S.C. 1462, 18 U.S.C.A. § 1462.

It is conceded that the phonograph records were obscene and indecent. The only question is whether they come within the prohibition of the statute.

We are aware that this is a criminal statute and must be strictly construed. This means that no offense may be created except by the words of Congress used in their usual and ordinary sense. There are no constructive offenses. United States v. Resnick, 299 U.S. 207, 210, 57 S.Ct. 126, 127, 81 L.Ed. 127. The most important thing to be determined is the intent of Congress. The language of the statute may not be distorted under the guise of construction, or so limited by construction as to defeat the manifest intent of Congress. United States v. Raynor, 302 U.S. 540, 552, 58 S.Ct. 353, 358, 82 L.Ed. 413. 1

In interpreting the statute as applied to this case the Court of Appeals invoked the rule of ejusdem generis. Since the words 'book, pamphlet, picture, motion-picture film, paper, letter, writing, print' appearing in the statute refer to objects comprehensible by sight only, the court construed the general words 'other matter of indecent character' to be limited to matter of the same genus. The Court of Appeals held phonograph records without the statute, so interpreted, since phonograph records are comprehended by the sense of hearing.

When properly applied, the rule of ejusdem generis is a useful canon of construction. But it is to be resorted to not to obscure and defeat the intent and purpose of Congress, but to elucidate its words and effectuate its intent. It cannot be employed to render general words meaningless. Mason v. United States, 260 U.S. 545, 554, 43 S.Ct. 200, 202, 67 L.Ed. 396. What is or is not a proper case for application of the rule was discussed in Gooch v. United States, 297 U.S. 124, 56 S.Ct. 395, 396, 80 L.Ed. 522. In that case a bandit and a companion had kidnaped two police officers for the purpose of avoiding arrest and had transported them across a state line. The defendant was convicted of kidnaping under a federal statute which made it an offense to transport across state lines any person who had been kidnaped 'and held for ransom or reward or otherwise.' The police officers had been held not for ransom or reward but for protection, and it was contended that the words 'or otherwise' did not cover the defendant's conduct, since under the rule of ejusdem generis, the general phrase was limited in meaning to some kind of monetary reward. This Court rejected such limiting application of the rule, saying: 'The rule of ejusdem generis, while firmly established, is only an instrumentality for ascertaining the correct meaning of words when there is uncertainty. Ordinarily, it limits general terms which follow specific ones to matters similar to those specified; but it may not be used to defeat the obvious purpose of legislation. And, while penal statutes are narrowly construed, this does not require rejection of that sense of the words which best harmonizes with the context and the end in view.' 297 U.S. at page 128, 56 S.Ct. at page 397.

We think that to apply the rule of ejusdem generis to the present case would be 'to defeat the obvious purpose of legislation.' The obvious purpose of the legislation under consideration was to prevent the channels of interstate commerce from being used to disseminate any matter that, in its essential nature, communicates obscene, lewd, lascivious or filthy ideas. The statute is more fully set out in the margin. 2 It will be noted that Congress legislated with respect to a number of evils in addition to those proscribed by the portion of the statute under which respondent was charged. Statutes are construed in their entire context. This is a comprehensive statute, which should not be constricted by a mechanical rule of construction.

We find nothing in the statute or its history to indicate that Congress intended to limit the applicable portion of the statute to such indecent matter as is comprehended through the sense of sight. True, this statute was amended in 1920 to include 'motion-picture film.' We are not persuaded that Congress, by adding motion-picture film to the specific provisions of the statute, evidenced an intent that obscene matter not specifically added was without the prohibition of the statute; nor do we think that Congress intended that only visual obscene matter was within the prohibition of the statute. The First World War gave considerable impetus to the making and distribution of motion-picture films. And in 1920 the public was considerably alarmed at the indecency of many of the films. 3 It thus appears that with respect to this amendment, Congress was preoccupied with making doubly sure that motion-picture film was within the Act, and was concerned with nothing more or less. 4

Upon this record we could not hold, nor do we wish to be understood to hold, that the applicable portion of the statute is all-inclusive. As we have pointed out, the same statute contains other provisions relating to objects intended for an indecent or immoral use. But the portion of the statute here in issue does proscribe the dissemination of matter which, in its essential nature, communicates obscene ideas. We are clear therefore that obscene phonograph records are within the meaning of the Act. The judgment of the Court of Appeals is reversed, and the judgment of the District Court is affirmed.

Reversed.

Notes

1. See Horack, The Disintegration of Statutory Construction, 24 Ind.L.J. 335, 343—344 (1949).

2. 'Whoever shall bring or cause to be brought into the United States, or any place subject to the jurisdiction thereof, from any foreign country, or shall therein knowingly deposit or cause to be deposited with any express company or other common carrier (for carriage in interstate or foreign commerce) any obscene, lewd, or lascivious, or any filthy book, pamphlet, picture, motion-picture film, paper, letter, writing, print, or other matter of indecent character, or any drug, medicine, article, or thing designed, adapted, or intended for preventing conception, or producing abortion, or for any indecent or immoral use; or any written or printed card, letter, circular, book, pamphlet,

advertisement, or notice of any kind giving information, directly or indirectly, where, how, or of whom, or by what means any of the hereinbefore mentioned articles, matters, or things may be obtained or made; or whoever shall knowingly take or cause to be taken from such express company or other common carrier any matter or thing the depositing of which for carriage is herein made unlawful, shall be fined not more than $5,000 or imprisoned not more than five years, or both.' 18 U.S.C. 396, now 18 U.S.C. 1462, 18 U.S.C.A. § 1462.

    3. See The Motion Picture Industry, 254 Annals of the American Academy of Political and Social Science, pp. 7—9, 140, 155, 157 (1947).

    4. H.R.Rep.No.580, 66th Cong., 2d Sess. (1920); S.Rep.No.528, 66th Cong., 2d Sess. (1920); 59 Cong.Rec. 2178—2179, 7162, 7297, 8280, 8334 (1920).

## Joseph Burstyn, Inc. v. Wilson (May 26, 1952) [Notes omitted]

    MR. JUSTICE CLARK delivered the opinion of the Court.

    The issue here is the constitutionality, under the First and Fourteenth Amendments, of a New York statute which permits the banning of motion picture films on the ground that they are "sacrilegious." That statute makes it unlawful

    "to exhibit, or to sell, lease or lend for exhibition at any place of amusement for pay or in connection with any business in the state of New York, any motion picture film or reel [with specified exceptions not relevant here], unless there is at the time in full force and effect a valid license or permit therefor of the education department. . . . [1]"

    The statute further provides:

    "The director of the [motion picture] division [of the education department] or, when authorized by the regents, the officers of a local office or bureau shall cause to be promptly examined every motion picture film submitted to them as herein required, and unless such film or a part thereof is obscene, indecent, immoral, inhuman, sacrilegious, or is of such a character that its exhibition would tend to corrupt morals or incite to crime, shall issue a license therefor. If such director or, when so authorized, such officer shall not license any film submitted, he shall furnish to the applicant therefor a written report of the reasons for his refusal and a description of each rejected part of a film not rejected in toto. [2]"

    Appellant is a corporation engaged in the business of distributing motion pictures. It owns the exclusive rights to distribute throughout the United States a film produced in Italy entitled "The Miracle." On November 30, 1950, after having examined the picture, the motion picture division of the New York education department, acting under the statute quoted above, issued to appellant a license authorizing exhibition of "The Miracle," with English subtitles, as one part of a trilogy called "Ways of Love." [3] Thereafter, for a period of approximately eight weeks, "Ways of Love" was exhibited publicly in a motion picture theater in New York City under an agreement between appellant and the owner of the theater whereby appellant received a stated percentage of the admission price.

During this period, the New York State Board of Regents, which by statute is made the head of the education department, [4] received "hundreds of letters, telegrams, post cards, affidavits and other communications" both protesting against and defending the public exhibition of "The Miracle." [5] The Chancellor of the Board of Regents requested three members of the Board to view the picture and to make a report to the entire Board. After viewing the film, this committee reported to the Board that, in its opinion, there was basis for the claim that the picture was "sacrilegious." Thereafter, on January 19, 1951, the Regents directed appellant to show cause, at a hearing to be held on January 30, why its license to show "The Miracle" should not be rescinded on that ground. Appellant appeared at this hearing, which was conducted by the same three-member committee of the Regents which had previously viewed the picture, and challenged the jurisdiction of the committee and of the Regents to proceed with the case. With the consent of the committee, various interested persons and organizations submitted to it briefs and exhibits bearing upon the merits of the picture and upon the constitutional and statutory questions involved. On February 16, 1951, the Regents, after viewing "The Miracle," determined that it was "sacrilegious," and for that reason ordered the Commissioner of Education to rescind appellant's license to exhibit the picture. The Commissioner did so.

Appellant brought the present action in the New York courts to review the determination of the Regents. [6] Among the claims advanced by appellant were (1) that the statute violates the Fourteenth Amendment as a prior restraint upon freedom of speech and of the press; (2) that it is invalid under the same Amendment as a violation of the guaranty of separate church and state and as a prohibition of the free exercise of religion; and, (3) that the term "sacrilegious" is so vague and indefinite as to offend due process. The Appellate Division rejected all of appellant's contentions and upheld the Regents' determination. 278 App.Div. 253, 104 N.Y.S.2d 740. On appeal the New York Court of Appeals, two judges dissenting, affirmed the order of the Appellate Division. 303 N.Y. 242, 101 N.E.2d 665. The case is here on appeal. 28 U.S.C. § 1257(2).

As we view the case, we need consider only appellant's contention that the New York statute is an unconstitutional abridgment of free speech and a free press. In Mutual Film Corp. v. Industrial Comm'n, 236 U. S. 230 (1915), a distributor of motion pictures sought to enjoin the enforcement of an Ohio statute which required the prior approval of a board of censors before any motion picture could be publicly exhibited in the state, and which directed the board to approve only such films as it adjudged to be "of a moral, educational or amusing and harmless character." The statute was assailed in part as an unconstitutional abridgment of the freedom of the press guaranteed by the First and Fourteenth Amendments. The District Court rejected this contention, stating that the first eight Amendments were not a restriction on state action. 215 F. 138, 141 (D.C.N.D. Ohio 1914). On appeal to this Court, plaintiff in its brief abandoned this claim and contended merely that the statute in question violated the freedom of speech and publication guaranteed by the Constitution of Ohio. In affirming the decree of the District Court denying injunctive relief, this Court stated:

"It cannot be put out of view that the exhibition of moving pictures is a business pure and simple, originated and conducted for profit, like other spectacles, not to be regarded, nor intended to be regarded by the Ohio constitution, we think, as part of the press of the country or as organs of public opinion. [7]"

In a series of decisions beginning with Gitlow v. New York, 268 U. S. 652 (1925), this Court held that the liberty of speech and of the press which the First Amendment guarantees against abridgment by the federal government is within the liberty safeguarded by the Due Process Clause of the Fourteenth Amendment from invasion by state action. [8] That principle has been followed and reaffirmed to the present day. Since this series of decisions came after the Mutual decision, the present case is the first to present squarely to us the question whether motion pictures are within the ambit of protection which the First Amendment, through the Fourteenth, secures to any form of "speech" or "the press." [9]

It cannot be doubted that motion pictures are a significant medium for the communication of ideas. They may affect public attitudes and behavior in a variety of ways, ranging from direct espousal of a political or social doctrine to the subtle shaping of thought which characterizes all artistic expression. [10] The importance of motion pictures as an organ of public opinion is not lessened by the fact that they are designed to entertain as well as to inform. As was said in Winters v. New York, 333 U. S. 507, 333 U. S. 510 (1948):

"The line between the informing and the entertaining is too elusive for the protection of that basic right [a free press]. Everyone is familiar with instances of propaganda through fiction. What is one man's amusement, teaches another's doctrine."

It is urged that motion pictures do not fall within the First Amendment's aegis because their production, distribution, and exhibition is a large-scale business conducted for private profit. We cannot agree. That books, newspapers, and magazines are published and sold for profit does not prevent them from being a form of expression whose liberty is safeguarded by the First Amendment. [11]

We fail to see why operation for profit should have any different effect in the case of motion pictures.

It is further urged that motion pictures possess a greater capacity for evil, particularly among the youth of a community, than other modes of expression. Even if one were to accept this hypothesis, it does not follow that motion pictures should be disqualified from First Amendment protection. If there be capacity for evil it may be relevant in determining the permissible scope of community control, but it does not authorize substantially unbridled censorship such as we have here.

For the foregoing reasons, we conclude that expression by means of motion pictures is included within the free speech and free press guaranty of the First and Fourteenth Amendments. To the extent that language in the opinion in Mutual Film

Corp. v. Industrial Comm'n, supra, is out of harmony with the views here set forth, we no longer adhere to it. [12]

To hold that liberty of expression by means of motion pictures is guaranteed by the First and Fourteenth Amendments, however, is not the end of our problem. It does not follow that the Constitution requires absolute freedom to exhibit every motion picture of every kind at all times and all places. That much is evident from the series of decisions of this Court with respect to other media of communication of ideas. [13] Nor does it follow that motion pictures are necessarily subject to the precise rules governing any other particular method of expression. Each method tends to present its own peculiar problems. But the basic principles of freedom of speech and the press, like the First Amendment's command, do not vary. Those principles, as they have frequently been enunciated by this Court, make freedom of expression the rule. There is no justification in this case for making an exception to that rule.

The statute involved here does not seek to punish, as a past offense, speech or writing falling within the permissible scope of subsequent punishment. On the contrary, New York requires that permission to communicate ideas be obtained in advance from state officials who judge the content of the words and pictures sought to be communicated. This Court recognized many years ago that such a previous restraint is a form of infringement upon freedom of expression to be especially condemned. Near v. Minnesota ex rel. Olson, 283 U. S. 697 (1931). The Court there recounted the history which indicates that a major purpose of the First Amendment guaranty of a free press was to prevent prior restraints upon publication, although it was carefully pointed out that the liberty of the press is not limited to that protection. [14] It was further stated that "the protection even as to previous restraint is not absolutely unlimited. But the limitation has been recognized only in exceptional cases." Id. at 283 U. S. 716. In the light of the First Amendment's history and of the Near decision, the State has a heavy burden to demonstrate that the limitation challenged here presents such an exceptional case.

New York's highest court says there is "nothing mysterious" about the statutory provision applied in this case:

"It is simply this: that no religion, as that word is understood by the ordinary, reasonable person, shall be treated with contempt, mockery, scorn and ridicule. . . . [15]"

This is far from the kind of narrow exception to freedom of expression which a state may carve out to satisfy the adverse demands of other interests of society. [16] In seeking to apply the broad and all-inclusive definition of "sacrilegious" given by the New York courts, the censor is set adrift upon a boundless sea amid a myriad of conflicting currents of religious views, with no charts but those provided by the most vocal and powerful orthodoxies. New York cannot vest such unlimited restraining control over motion pictures in a censor. Cf. Kunz v. New York, 340 U. S. 290 (1951). [17] Under such a standard the most careful and tolerant censor would find it virtually impossible to avoid favoring one religion over another, and he would be subject to an inevitable tendency to ban the expression of unpopular sentiments sacred to a religious minority. Application of the "sacrilegious" test, in these or other respects, might raise substantial questions under the First Amendment's guaranty of separate church and state with freedom of worship for all. [18] However, from the standpoint of freedom of speech and the press, it is enough to point out that the state has no legitimate interest in protecting any or all religions from views distasteful to them which is sufficient to justify prior restraints upon the expression of those views. It is not the business of government in our nation to suppress real or imagined attacks upon a particular religious doctrine, whether they appear in publications, speeches, or motion pictures. [19]

Since the term "sacrilegious" is the sole standard under attack here, it is not necessary for us to decide, for example, whether a state may censor motion pictures under a clearly drawn statute designed and applied to prevent the showing of obscene films. That is a very different question from the one now before us. [20] We hold only that, under the First and Fourteenth Amendments, a state may not ban a film on the basis of a censor's conclusion that it is "sacrilegious."

Reversed.

## Butler v. Michigan (February 25, 1957)

MR. JUSTICE FRANKFURTER delivered the opinion of the Court.

This appeal from a judgment of conviction entered by the Recorder's Court of the City of Detroit, Michigan, challenges the constitutionality of the following provision, § 343, of the Michigan Penal Code:

"Any person who shall import, print, publish, sell, possess with the intent to sell, design, prepare, loan, give away, distribute or offer for sale, any book, magazine, newspaper, writing, pamphlet, ballad, printed paper, print, picture, drawing, photograph, publication or other thing, including any recordings, containing obscene, immoral, lewd or lascivious language, or obscene, immoral, lewd or lascivious prints, pictures, figures or descriptions, tending to incite minors to violent or depraved or immoral acts, manifestly tending to the corruption of the morals of youth, or shall introduce into any family, school or place of education or shall buy, procure, receive or have in his possession, any such book, pamphlet, magazine, newspaper, writing, ballad, printed paper, print, picture, drawing, photograph, publication or other thing, either for the purpose of sale, exhibition, loan or circulation, or with intent to introduce the same into any family, school or place of education, shall be guilty of a misdemeanor."

Appellant was charged with its violation for selling to a police officer what the trial judge characterized as

"a book containing obscene, immoral, lewd, lascivious language, or descriptions, tending to incite minors to violent or depraved or immoral acts, manifestly tending to the corruption of the morals of youth."

Appellant moved to dismiss the proceeding on the claim that application of § 343 unduly restricted freedom of speech as protected by the Due Process Clause of the

Fourteenth Amendment in that the statute (1) prohibited distribution of a book to the general public on the basis of the undesirable influence it may have upon youth; (2) damned a book and proscribed its sale merely because of some isolated passages that appeared objectionable when divorced from the book as a whole; and (3) failed to provide a sufficiently definite standard of guilt. After hearing the evidence, the trial judge denied the motion, and, in an oral opinion, held that

". . . the defendant is guilty because he sold a book in the City of Detroit containing this language [the passages deemed offensive], and also because the Court feels that, even viewing the book as a whole, it [the objectionable language] was not necessary to the proper development of the theme of the book, nor of the conflict expressed therein."

Appellant was fined $100.

Pressing his federal claims, appellant applied for leave to appeal to the Supreme Court of Michigan. Although the State consented to the granting of the application

"because the issues involved in this case are of great public interest, and because it appears that further clarification of the language of . . . [the statute] is necessary,"

leave to appeal was denied. In view of this denial, the appeal is here from the Recorder's Court of Detroit. We noted probable jurisdiction. 350 U.S. 963.

Appellant's argument here took a wide sweep. We need not follow him. Thus, it is unnecessary to dissect the remarks of the trial judge in order to determine whether he construed § 343 to ban the distribution of books merely because certain of their passages, when viewed in isolation, were deemed objectionable. Likewise, we are free to put aside the claim that the Michigan law falls within the doctrine whereby a New York obscenity statute was found invalid in Winters v. New York, 333 U. S. 507.

It is clear on the record that appellant was convicted because Michigan, by § 343, made it an offense for him to make available for the general reading public (and he in fact sold to a police officer) a book that the trial judge found to have a potentially deleterious influence upon youth. The State insists that, by thus quarantining the general reading public against books not too rugged for grown men and women in order to shield juvenile innocence, it is exercising its power to promote the general welfare. Surely, this is to burn the house to roast the pig. Indeed, the Solicitor General of Michigan has, with characteristic candor, advised the Court that Michigan has a statute specifically designed to protect its children against obscene matter "tending to the corruption of the morals of youth." * But the appellant was not convicted for violating this statute.

We have before us legislation not reasonably restricted to the evil with which it is said to deal. The incidence of this enactment is to reduce the adult population of Michigan to reading only what is fit for children. It thereby arbitrarily curtails one of those liberties of the individual, now enshrined in the Due Process Clause of the Fourteenth Amendment, that history has attested as the indispensable conditions for the maintenance and progress of a free society. We are constrained to reverse this conviction.

Reversed.

## Kingsley Books, Inc. v. Brown (June 24, 1957)

MR. JUSTICE FRANKFURTER delivered the opinion of the Court.

This is a proceeding under § 22-a of the New York Code of Criminal Procedure (L.1941, c. 925), as amended in 1954 (L.1954, c. 702). This section supplements the existing conventional criminal provision dealing with pornography by authorizing the chief executive, or legal officer, of a municipality to invoke a "limited injunctive remedy," under closely defined procedural safeguards, against the sale and distribution of written and printed matter found after due trial to be obscene, and to obtain an order for the seizure, in default of surrender, of the condemned publications. [1]

A complaint dated September 10, 1954, charged appellants with displaying for sale paper-covered obscene booklets, fourteen of which were annexed, under the general title of "Nights of Horror." The complaint prayed that appellants be enjoined from further distribution of the booklets, that they be required to surrender to the sheriff for destruction all copies in their possession, and, upon failure to do so, that the sheriff be commanded to seize and destroy those copies. The same day, the appellants were ordered to show cause within four days why they should not be enjoined pendente lite from distributing the booklets. Appellants consented to the granting of an injunction pendente lite, and did not bring the matter to issue promptly, as was their right under subdivision 2 of the challenged section, which provides that the persons sought to be enjoined

"shall be entitled to a trial of the issues within one day after joinder of issue, and a decision shall be rendered by the court within two days of the conclusion of the trial."

After the case came to trial, the judge, sitting in equity, found that the booklets annexed to the complaint and introduced in evidence were clearly obscene -- were "dirt for dirt's sake"; he enjoined their further distribution and ordered their destruction. He refused to enjoin "the sale and distribution of later issues" on the ground that "to rule against at volume not offered in evidence would . . . impose an unreasonable prior restraint upon freedom of the press." 208 Misc. 150, 167, 142 N.Y.S.2d 735, 750.

Not challenging the construction of the statute or the finding of obscenity, appellants took a direct appeal to the New York Court of Appeals, a proceeding in which the constitutionality of the statute was the sole question open to them. That court (one judge not sitting) found no constitutional infirmity: three judges supported the unanimous conclusion by detailed discussion, the other three deemed a brief disposition justified by "ample authority." 1 N.Y.2d 177, 189, 151 N.Y.S.2d 639, 134 N.E.2d 461, 468. A claim under the Due Process Clause of the Fourteenth Amendment made throughout the state litigation brought the case here on appeal. 352 U.S. 962.

Neither in the New York Court of Appeals nor here did appellants assail the legislation insofar as it outlaws obscenity. The claim they make lies within a very narrow compass. Their attack is upon the power of New York to employ the remedial scheme of § 22-a. Authorization of an injunction pendente lite, as part of this scheme, during the period within which the issue of obscenity must be promptly tried and adjudicated in an adversary proceeding for which "[a]dequate notice, judicial hearing, [and] fair determination" are assured, 208 Misc. 150, 164, 142 N.Y.S.2d 735, 747, is a safeguard against frustration of the public interest in effectuating judicial condemnation of obscene matter. It is a brake on the temptation to exploit a filthy business offered by the limited hazards of piecemeal prosecutions, sale by sale, of a publication already condemned as obscene. New York enacted this procedure on the basis of study by a joint legislative committee. Resort to this injunctive remedy, it is claimed, is beyond the constitutional power of New York in that it amounts to a prior censorship of literary product, and, as such, is violative of that "freedom of thought and speech" which has been "withdrawn by the Fourteenth Amendment from encroachment by the states." Palko v. Connecticut, 302 U. S. 319, 302 U. S. 326-327. Reliance is particularly placed upon Near v. Minnesota, 283 U. S. 697.

In an unbroken series of cases extending over a long stretch of this Court's history, it has been accepted as a postulate that "the primary requirements of decency may be enforced against obscene publications." Id. at 283 U. S. 716. And so, our starting point is that New York can constitutionally convict appellants of keeping for sale the booklets incontestably found to be obscene. Alberts v. California, post, p. 354 U. S. 476. The immediate problem, then, is whether New York can adopt as an auxiliary means of dealing with such obscene merchandising the procedure of § 22-a.

We need not linger over the suggestion that something can be drawn out of the Due Process Clause of the Fourteenth Amendment that restricts New York to the criminal process in seeking to protect its people against the dissemination of pornography. It is not for this Court thus to limit the State in resorting to various weapons in the armory of the law. Whether proscribed conduct is to be visited by a criminal prosecution or by a qui tam action, or by an injunction, or by some or all of these remedies in combination, is a matter within the legislature's range of choice. See Tigner v. Texas, 310 U. S. 141, 310 U. S. 148. If New York chooses to subject persons who disseminate obscene "literature" to criminal prosecution and also to deal with such books as deodands of old, or both, with due regard, of course, to appropriate opportunities for the trial of the underlying issue, it is not for us to gainsay its selection of remedies. Just as Near v. Minnesota, supra, one of the landmark opinions in shaping the constitutional protection of freedom of speech and of the press, left no doubts that "Liberty of speech, and of the press, is also not an absolute right," 283 U.S. at 283 U. S. 708, it likewise made clear that "the protection even as to previous restraint is not absolutely unlimited." Id. at 283 U. S. 716. To be sure, the limitation is the exception; it is to be closely confined so as to preclude what may fairly be deemed licensing or censorship.

The judicial angle of vision in testing the validity of a statute like § 22-a is "the operation and effect of the statute in substance." Id. at 283 U. S. 713. The phrase "prior restraint" is not a self-wielding sword. Nor can it serve as a talismanic test. The duty of closer analysis and critical judgment in applying the thought behind the phrase has thus been authoritatively put by one who brings weighty learning to his support of constitutionally protected liberties: "What is needed," writes Professor Paul A. Freund,

"is a pragmatic assessment of its operation in the particular circumstances. The generalization that prior restraint is particularly obnoxious in civil liberties cases must yield to more particularistic analysis."

The Supreme Court and Civil Liberties, 4 Vand.L.Rev. 533, 539.

Wherein does § 22-a differ in its effective operation from the type of statute upheld in Alberts? Section 311 of California's Penal Code provides that "Every person who wilfully and lewdly . . . keeps for sale . . . any obscene . . . book . . . is guilty of a misdemeanor. . . ." Section 1141 of New York's Penal Law is similar. One would be bold to assert that the in terrorem effect of such statutes less restrains booksellers in the period before the law strikes than does § 22-a. Instead of requiring the bookseller to dread that the offer for sale of a book may, without prior warning, subject him to a criminal prosecution with the hazard of imprisonment, the civil procedure assures him that such consequences cannot follow unless he ignores a court order specifically directed to him for a prompt and carefully circumscribed determination of the issue of obscenity. Until then, he may keep the book for sale and sell it on his own judgment, rather than steer "nervously among the treacherous shoals." Warburg, Onward And Upward With The Arts, The New Yorker, April 20, 1957, pp. 98, 101, in connection with R. v. Martin Secker Warburg, Ltd., [1954] 2 All Eng. 683 (C.C.C.).

Criminal enforcement and the proceeding under § 22-a interfere with a book's solicitation of the public precisely at the same stage. In each situation, the law moves after publication; the book need not in either case have yet passed into the hands of the public. The Alberts record does not show that the matter there found to be obscene had reached the public at the time that the criminal charge of keeping such matter for sale was lodged, while here, as a matter of fact, copies of the booklets whose distribution was enjoined had been on sale for several weeks when process was served. In each case, the bookseller is put on notice by the complaint that sale of the publication charged with obscenity in the period before trial may subject him to penal consequences. In the one case, he may suffer fine and imprisonment for violation of the criminal statute; in the other, for disobedience of the temporary injunction. The bookseller may, of course, stand his ground and confidently believe that in any judicial proceeding the book could not be condemned as obscene, but both modes of procedure provide an effective deterrent against distribution prior to adjudication of the book's content -- the threat of subsequent penalization. [2]

The method devised by New York in § 22-a for determining whether a publication is obscene does not differ in essential procedural safeguards from that provided under many state statutes making the distribution of obscene publications a misdemeanor. For example, while the New York criminal provision brings the State's criminal procedure into operation, a defendant is not thereby entitled to a jury trial. In each case, a judge is the conventional trier of fact; in each, a jury may, as a matter of discretion, be summoned. Compare N.Y.City Criminal Courts Act, § 31, Sub. 1(c) and Sub. 4, with N.Y.Civil Practice

Act, § 430. (Appellants, as a matter of fact, did not request a jury trial, they did not attack the statute in the courts below for failure to require a jury, and they did not bring that issue to this Court.) Of course, the Due Process Clause does not subject the States to the necessity of having trial by jury in misdemeanor prosecutions.

Nor are the consequences of a judicial condemnation for obscenity under § 22-a more restrictive of freedom of expression than the result of conviction for a misdemeanor. In Alberts, the defendant was fined $500, sentenced to sixty days in prison, and put on probation for two years on condition that he not violate the obscenity statute. Not only was he completely separated from society for two months, but he was also seriously restrained from trafficking in all obscene publications for a considerable time. Appellants, on the other hand, were enjoined from displaying for sale or distributing only the particular booklets theretofore published and adjudged to be obscene. Thus, the restraint upon appellants as merchants in obscenity was narrower than that imposed on Alberts.

Section 22-a's provision for the seizure and destruction of the instruments of ascertained wrongdoing expresses resort to a legal remedy sanctioned by the long history of Anglo-American law. See Holmes, The Common Law 24-26; Van Oster v. Kansas, 272 U. S. 465; Goldsmith-Grant Co. v. United States, 254 U. S. 505, 254 U. S. 510-511; Lawton v. Steele, 152 U. S. 133, and see United States v. Urbuteit, 335 U. S. 355, dealing with misbranded articles under § 304(a) of the Food, Drug, and Cosmetic Act, 52 Stat. 1044. It is worth noting that, although the Alberts record does not reveal whether the publications found to be obscene were destroyed, provision is made for that by §§ 313 and 314 of the California Penal Code. Similarly, § 1144 of New York's Penal Law provides for destruction of obscene matter following conviction for its dissemination.

It only remains to say that the difference between Near v. Minnesota, supra, and this case is glaring in fact. The two cases are no less glaringly different when judged by the appropriate criteria of constitutional law. Minnesota empowered its courts to enjoin the dissemination of future issues of a publication because its past issues had been found offensive. In the language of Mr. Chief Justice Hughes, "This is of the essence of censorship." 283 U.S. at 283 U. S. 713. As such, it was found unconstitutional. This was enough to condemn the statute wholly apart from the fact that the proceeding in Near involved not obscenity, but matters deemed to be derogatory to a public officer. Unlike Near, § 22-a is concerned solely with obscenity, and, as authoritatively construed, it studiously withholds restraint upon matters not already published and not yet found to be offensive.

The judgment is

Affirmed.

Notes

[1] "§ 22-a. Obscene prints and articles; jurisdiction. The supreme court has jurisdiction to enjoin the sale or distribution of obscene prints and articles, as hereinafter

specified:"

"1. The chief executive officer of any city, town or village or the corporation counsel, or if there be none, the chief legal officer of any city, town, or village, in which a person, firm or corporation sells or distributes or is about to sell or distribute or has in his possession with intent to sell or distribute or is about to acquire possession with intent to sell or distribute any book, magazine, pamphlet, comic book, story paper, writing, paper, picture, drawing, photograph, figure, image or any written or printed matter of an indecent character, which is obscene, lewd, lascivious, filthy, indecent or disgusting, or which contains an article or instrument of indecent or immoral use or purports to be for indecent or immoral use or purpose; or in any other respect defined in section eleven hundred forty-one of the penal law, may maintain an action for an injunction against such person, firm or corporation in the supreme court to prevent the sale or further sale or the distribution or further distribution or the acquisition or possession of any book, magazine, pamphlet, comic book, story paper, writing, paper, picture, drawing, photograph, figure or image or any written or printed matter of an indecent character, herein described or described in section eleven hundred forty-one of the penal law."

"2. The person, firm or corporation sought to be enjoined shall be entitled to a trial of the issues within one day after joinder of issue and a decision shall be rendered by the court within two days of the conclusion of the trial."

"3. In the event that a final order or judgment of injunction be entered in favor of such officer of the city, town or village and against the person, firm or corporation sought to be enjoined, such final order of judgment shall contain a provision directing the person, firm or corporation to surrender to the sheriff of the county in which the action was brought any of the matter described in paragraph one hereof and such sheriff shall be directed to seize and destroy the same."

"4. In any action brought as herein provided, such officer of the city, town or village shall not be required to file any undertaking before the issuance of an injunction order provided for in paragraph two hereof, shall not be liable for costs and shall not be liable for damages sustained by reason of the injunction order in cases where judgment is rendered in favor of the person, firm or corporation sought to be enjoined."

"5. Every person, firm or corporation who sells, distributes, or acquires possession with intent to sell or distribute any of the matter described in paragraph one hereof, after the service upon him of a summons and complaint in an action brought by such officer of any city, town or village pursuant to this section is chargeable with knowledge of the contents thereof."

[2] This comparison of remedies takes note of the fact that we do not have before us a case where, although the issue of obscenity is ultimately decided in favor of the bookseller, the State nevertheless attempts to punish him for disobedience of the interim injunction. For all we know, New York may impliedly condition the temporary injunction, so as not to subject the bookseller to a charge of contempt if he prevails on the issue of obscenity.

## Roth v. US (June 24, 1957)

MR. JUSTICE BRENNAN delivered the opinion of the Court.

The constitutionality of a criminal obscenity statute is the question in each of these cases. In Roth, the primary constitutional question is whether the federal obscenity statute [n1] violates the provision of the First Amendment that "Congress shall make no law . . . abridging the freedom of speech, or of the press. . . ." In Alberts, the primary constitutional question is whether the obscenity provisions of the California Penal Code [n2] invade the freedoms of speech and press as they may be incorporated in the liberty protected from state action by the Due Process Clause of the Fourteenth Amendment.

Other constitutional questions are: whether these statutes violate due process, [n3] because too vague to support conviction for crime; whether power to punish speech and press offensive to decency and morality is in the States alone, so that the federal obscenity statute violates the Ninth and Tenth Amendments (raised in Roth), and whether Congress, by enacting the federal obscenity statute, under the power delegated by Art. I, § 8, cl. 7, to establish post offices and post roads, preempted the regulation of the subject matter (raised in Alberts).

Roth conducted a business in New York in the publication and sale of books, photographs and magazines. He used circulars and advertising matter to solicit sales. He was convicted by a jury in the District Court for the Southern District of New York upon 4 counts of a 26-count indictment charging him with mailing obscene circulars and advertising, and an obscene book, in violation of the federal obscenity statute. His conviction was affirmed by the Court of Appeals for the Second Circuit. [n4] We granted certiorari. [n5]

Alberts conducted a mail-order business from Los Angeles. He was convicted by the Judge of the Municipal Court of the Beverly Hills Judicial District (having waived a jury trial) under a misdemeanor complaint which charged him with lewdly keeping for sale obscene and indecent books, and with writing, composing and publishing an obscene advertisement of them, in violation of the California Penal Code. The conviction was affirmed by the Appellate Department of the Superior Court of the State of California in and for the County of Los Angeles. [n6] We noted probable jurisdiction. [n7]

The dispositive question is whether obscenity is utterance within the area of protected speech and press. [n8] Although this is the first time the question has been squarely presented to this Court, either under the First Amendment or under the Fourteenth Amendment, expressions found in numerous opinions indicate that this Court has always assumed that obscenity is not protected by the freedoms of speech and press. Ex parte Jackson, 96 U.S. 727, 736-737; United States v. Chase, 135 U.S. 255, 261; Robertson v. Baldwin, 165 U.S. 275, 281; Public Clearing House v. Coyne, 194 U.S. 497, 508; Hoke v. United States, 227 U.S. 308, 322; Near v. Minnesota, 283 U.S. 697, 716; Chaplinsky v. New Hampshire, 315 U.S. 568, 571-572; Hannegan v. Esquire, Inc., 327 U.S.

146, 158; Winters v. New York, 333 U.S. 507, 510; Beauharnais v. Illinois, 343 U.S. 250, 266. [n9]

The guaranties of freedom of expression [n10] in effect in 10 of the 14 States which by 1792 had ratified the Constitution, gave no absolute protection for every utterance. Thirteen of the 14 States provided for the prosecution of libel, [n11] and all of those States made either blasphemy or profanity, or both, statutory crimes. [n12] As early as 1712, Massachusetts made it criminal to publish "any filthy, obscene, or profane song, pamphlet, libel or mock sermon" in imitation or mimicking of religious services. Acts and Laws of the Province of Mass. Bay, c. CV, § 8 (1712), Mass.Bay Colony Charters & Laws 399 (1814). Thus, profanity and obscenity were related offenses.

In light of this history, it is apparent that the unconditional phrasing of the First Amendment was not intended to protect every utterance. This phrasing did not prevent this Court from concluding that libelous utterances are not within the area of constitutionally protected speech. Beauharnais v. Illinois, 343 U.S. 250, 266. At the time of the adoption of the First Amendment, obscenity law was not as fully developed as libel law, but there is sufficiently contemporaneous evidence to show that obscenity, too, was outside the protection intended for speech and press. [n13]

The protection given speech and press was fashioned to assure unfettered interchange of ideas for the bringing about of political and social changes desired by the people. This objective was made explicit as early as 1774 in a letter of the Continental Congress to the inhabitants of Quebec:

The last right we shall mention regards the freedom of the press. The importance of this consists, besides the advancement of truth, science, morality, and arts in general, in its diffusion of liberal sentiments on the administration of Government, its ready communication of thoughts between subjects, and its consequential promotion of union among them, whereby oppressive officers are shamed or intimidated into more honourable and just modes of conducting affairs.

1 Journals of the Continental Congress 108 (1774).

All ideas having even the slightest redeeming social importance -- unorthodox ideas, controversial ideas, even ideas hateful to the prevailing climate of opinion -- have the full protection of the guaranties, unless excludable because they encroach upon the limited area of more important interests. [n14] But implicit in the history of the First Amendment is the rejection of obscenity as utterly without redeeming social importance. This rejection for that reason is mirrored in the universal judgment that obscenity should be restrained, reflected in the international agreement of over 50 nations, [n15] in the obscenity laws of all of the 48 States, [n16] and in the 20 obscenity laws enacted by the Congress from 1842 to 1956. [n17] This is the same judgment expressed by this Court in Chaplinsky v. New Hampshire, 315 U.S. 568, 571-572:

... There are certain well defined and narrowly limited classes of speech, the prevention and punishment of which have never been thought to raise any Constitutional problem. These include the lewd and obscene. ... It has been well observed that such utterances are no essential part of any exposition of ideas, and are of such slight social value as a step to truth that any benefit that may be derived from them is clearly outweighed by the social interest in order and morality. . . .

(Emphasis added.) We hold that obscenity is not within the area of constitutionally protected speech or press.

It is strenuously urged that these obscenity statutes offend the constitutional guaranties because they punish incitation to impure sexual thoughts, not shown to be related to any overt antisocial conduct which is or may be incited in the persons stimulated to such thoughts. In Roth, the trial Judge instructed the jury:

The words "obscene, lewd and lascivious" as used in the law, signify that form of immorality which has relation to sexual impurity and has a tendency to excite lustful thoughts.

(Emphasis added.) In Alberts, the trial judge applied the test laid down in People v. Wepplo, 78 Cal.App.2d Supp. 959, 178 P.2d 853, namely, whether the material has "a substantial tendency to deprave or corrupt its readers by inciting lascivious thoughts or arousing lustful desires." (Emphasis added.) It is insisted that the constitutional guaranties are violated because convictions may be had without proof either that obscene material will perceptibly create a clear and present danger of anti-social conduct, [n18] or will probably induce its recipients to such conduct. [n19] But, in light of our holding that obscenity is not protected speech, the complete answer to this argument is in the holding of this Court in Beauharnais v. Illinois, supra, at 266:

Libelous utterances not being within the area of constitutionally protected speech, it is unnecessary, either for us or for the State courts, to consider the issues behind the phrase "clear and present danger." Certainly no one would contend that obscene speech, for example, may be punished only upon a showing of such circumstances. Libel, as we have seen, is in the same class.

However, sex and obscenity are not synonymous. Obscene material is material which deals with sex in a manner appealing to prurient interest. [n20] The portrayal of sex, e.g., in art, literature and scientific works, [n21] is not itself sufficient reason to deny material the constitutional protection of freedom of speech and press. Sex, a great and mysterious motive force in human life, has indisputably been a subject of absorbing interest to mankind through the ages; it is one of the vital problems of human interest and public concern. As to all such problems, this Court said in Thornhill v. Alabama, 310 U.S. 88, 101-102:

The freedom of speech and of the press guaranteed by the Constitution embraces at the least the liberty to discuss publicly and truthfully all matters of public concern without previous restraint or fear of subsequent punishment. The exigencies of the colonial period and the efforts to secure freedom from oppressive administration developed a broadened conception of these liberties as adequate to supply the public need for information and education with respect to the significant issues of the times. . . . Freedom of discussion, if it would fulfill its historic function in this nation, must embrace all issues about which information is needed or appropriate to enable the members of society to cope with the exigencies of their period.

(Emphasis added.)

The fundamental freedoms of speech and press have contributed greatly to the development and wellbeing of our free society and are indispensable to its continued growth. [n22] Ceaseless vigilance is the watchword to prevent their erosion by Congress or by the States. The door barring federal and state intrusion into this area cannot be left ajar; it must be kept tightly closed, and opened only the slightest crack necessary to prevent encroachment upon more important interests. [n23] It is therefore vital that the standards for judging obscenity safeguard the protection of freedom of speech and press for material which does not treat sex in a manner appealing to prurient interest.

The early leading standard of obscenity allowed material to be judged merely by the effect of an isolated excerpt upon particularly susceptible persons. Regina v. Hicklin, [1868] L.R. 3 Q.B. 360. [n24] Some American courts adopted this standard, [n25] but later decisions have rejected it and substituted this test: whether, to the average person, applying contemporary community standards, the dominant theme of the material, taken as a whole, appeals to prurient interest. [n26] The Hicklin test, judging obscenity by the effect of isolated passages upon the most susceptible persons, might well encompass material legitimately treating with sex, and so it must be rejected as unconstitutionally restrictive of the freedoms of speech and press. On the other hand, the substituted standard provides safeguards adequate to withstand the charge of constitutional infirmity.

Both trial courts below sufficiently followed the proper standard. Both courts used the proper definition of obscenity. In addition, in the Alberts case, in ruling on a motion to dismiss, the trial judge indicated that, as the trier of facts, he was judging each item as a whole as it would affect the normal person, [n27] and, in Roth, the trial judge instructed the jury as follows:

. . . The test is not whether it would arouse sexual desires or sexual impure thoughts in those comprising a particular segment of the community, the young, the immature or the highly prudish or would leave another segment, the scientific or highly educated or the so-called worldly wise and sophisticated indifferent and unmoved. . . .

\* \* \* \*

The test in each case is the effect of the book, picture or publication considered as a whole not upon any particular class, but upon all those whom it is likely to reach. In other words, you determine its impact upon the average person in the community. The books, pictures and circulars must be judged as a whole, in their entire context, and you are not to consider detached or separate portions in reaching a conclusion. You judge the circulars, pictures and publications which have been put in evidence by present-day standards of the community. You may ask yourselves does it offend the common conscience of the community by present-day standards.

\* \* \* \*

In this case, ladies and gentlemen of the jury, you and you alone are the exclusive judges of what the common conscience of the community is, and, in determining that conscience, you are to consider the community as a whole, young and old, educated and uneducated, the religious and the irreligious -- men, women and children.

It is argued that the statutes do not provide reasonably ascertainable standards of guilt, and therefore violates the constitutional requirements of due process. Winters v. New York, 333 U.S. 507. The federal obscenity statute makes punishable the mailing of material that is "obscene, lewd, lascivious, or filthy . . . or other publication of an indecent character." [n28] The California statute makes punishable, inter alia, the keeping for sale or advertising material that is "obscene or indecent." The thrust of the argument is that these words are not sufficiently precise, because they do not mean the same thing to all people, all the time, everywhere.

Many decisions have recognized that these terms of obscenity statutes are not precise. [n29] This Court, however, has consistently held that lack of precision is not itself offensive to the requirements of due process. ". . . [T]he Constitution does not require impossible standards"; all that is required is that the language "conveys sufficiently definite warning as to the proscribed conduct when measured by common understanding and practices. . . ." United States v. Petrillo, 332 U.S. 1, 7-8. These words, applied according to the proper standard for judging obscenity, already discussed, give adequate warning of the conduct proscribed, and mark

. . . boundaries sufficiently distinct for judges and juries fairly to administer the law. . . . That there may be marginal cases in which it is difficult to determine the side of the line on which a particular fact situation falls is no sufficient reason to hold the language too ambiguous to define a criminal offense. . . .

Id. at 7. See also United States v. Harriss, 347 U.S. 612, 624, n. 15; Boyce Motor Lines, Inc. v. United States, 342 U.S. 337, 340; United States v. Ragen, 314 U.S. 513, 523-524; United States v. Wurzbach, 280 U.S. 396; Hygrade Provision Co. v. Sherman, 266 U.S. 497; Fox v. Washington, 236 U.S. 273; Nash v. United States, 229 U.S. 373. [n30]

In summary, then, we hold that these statutes, applied according to the proper standard for judging obscenity, do not offend constitutional safeguards against convictions based upon protected material, or fail to give men in acting adequate notice of what is prohibited.

Roth's argument that the federal obscenity statute unconstitutionally encroaches upon the powers reserved by the Ninth and Tenth Amendments to the States and to the people to punish speech and press where offensive to decency and morality is hinged upon his contention that obscenity is expression not excepted from the sweep of the provision of the First Amendment that "Congress shall make no law . . . abridging the freedom of speech, or of the press. . . ." (Emphasis added.) That argument falls in light of our holding that obscenity is not expression protected by the First Amendment. [n31] We therefore hold that the federal obscenity statute punishing the use of the mails for obscene material is a proper exercise of the postal power delegated to Congress by Art. I,

§ 8, cl. 7. [n32] In United Public Workers v. Mitchell, 330 U.S. 75, 95-96, this Court said:

. . . The powers granted by the Constitution to the Federal Government are subtracted from the totality of sovereignty originally in the states and the people. Therefore, when objection is made that the exercise of a federal power infringes upon rights reserved by the Ninth and Tenth Amendments, the inquiry must be directed toward the granted power under which the action of the Union was taken. If granted power is found, necessarily the objection of invasion of those rights, reserved by the Ninth and Tenth Amendments, must fail. . . .

Alberts argues that, because his was a mail-order business, the California statute is repugnant to Art. I, § 8, cl. 7, under which the Congress allegedly preempted the regulatory field by enacting the federal obscenity statute punishing the mailing or advertising by mail of obscene material. The federal statute deals only with actual mailing; it does not eliminate the power of the state to punish "keeping for sale" or "advertising" obscene material. The state statute in no way imposes a burden or interferes with the federal postal functions.

. . . The decided cases which indicate the limits of state regulatory power in relation to the federal mail service involve situations where state regulation involved a direct, physical interference with federal activities under the postal power or some direct, immediate burden on the performance of the postal functions. . . .

Railway Mail Assn. v. Corsi, 326 U.S. 88, 96.

The judgments are

Affirmed.


Notes

1. The federal obscenity statute provided, in pertinent part:

Every obscene, lewd, lascivious, or filthy book, pamphlet, picture, paper, letter, writing, print, or other publication of an indecent character, and --

\* \* \* \*

Every written or printed card, letter, circular, book, pamphlet, advertisement, or notice of any kind giving information, directly or indirectly, where, or how, or from whom, or by what means any of such mentioned matters, articles, or things may be obtained or made, . . . whether sealed or unsealed . . .

\* \* \* \*

Is declared to be nonmailable matter and shall not be conveyed in the mails or delivered from any post office or by any letter carrier.

Whoever knowingly deposits for mailing or delivery, anything declared by this section to be nonmailable, or knowingly takes the same from the mails for the purpose of circulating or disposing thereof, or of aiding in the circulation or disposition thereof, shall be fined not more than $5,000 or imprisoned not more than five years, or both.

18 U.S.C. § 1461.

The 1955 amendment of this statute, 69 Stat. 13, is not applicable to this case.

2. The California Penal Code provides, in pertinent part:

Every person who willfully and lewdly, either:

\* \* \* \*

3. Writes, composes, stereotypes, prints, publishes, sells, distributes, keeps for sale, or exhibits any obscene or indecent writing, paper, or book; or designs, copies, draws, engraves, paints, or otherwise prepares any obscene or indecent picture or print; or molds, cuts, casts, or otherwise makes any obscene or indecent figure; or,

4. Writes, composes, or publishes any notice or advertisement of any such writing, paper, book, picture, print or figure; . . .

\* \* \* \*

6. . . . is guilty of a misdemeanor. . . .

West's Cal.Penal Code Ann., 1955, § 311.

3. In Roth, reliance is placed on the Due Process Clause of the Fifth Amendment, and, in Alberts, reliance is placed upon the Due Process Clause of the Fourteenth Amendment.

4. 237 F.2d 796.

5. 352 U.S. 964. Petitioner's application for bail was granted by MR. JUSTICE HARLAN in his capacity as Circuit Justice for the Second Circuit. 1 L.Ed.2d 34, 77 Sup.Ct. 17.

6. 138 Cal.App.2d Supp. 909, 292 P.2d 90. This is the highest state appellate court available to the appellant. Cal.Const., Art. VI, § 5; see Edwards v. California, 314 U.S. 160.

7. 352 U.S. 962.

8. No issue is presented in either case concerning the obscenity of the material involved.

9. See also the following cases in which convictions under obscenity statutes have been reviewed: Grimm v. United States, 156 U.S. 604; Rosen v. United States, 161 U.S. 29; Swearingen v. United States, 161 U.S. 446; Andrews v. United States, 162 U.S. 420; Price v. United States, 165 U.S. 311; Dunlop v. United States, 165 U.S. 486; Bartell v. United States, 227 U.S. 427; United States v. Limehouse, 285 U.S. 424.

10. Del.Const., 1792, Art. I, § 5; Ga.Const., 1777, Art. LXI; Md.Const., 1776, Declaration of Rights, § 38; Mass.Const., 1780, Declaration of Rights, Art. XVI; N.H.Const., 1784, Art. I, § XXII; N.C. Const., 1776, Declaration of Rights, Art. XV; Pa.Const., 1776, Declaration of Rights, Art. XII; S.C.Const., 1778, Art. XLIII; Vt.Const., 1777, Declaration of Rights, Art. XIV; Va. Bill of Rights, 776, § 12.

11. Act to Secure the Freedom of the Press (1804), 1 Conn.Pub.Stat.Laws 355 (1808); Del.Const., 1792, Art. I, § 5; Ga.Penal Code, Eighth Div., §VIII (1817), Digest of the Laws of Ga. 364 (Prince 1822); Act of 1803, c. 54, II Md.Public General Laws 1096 (Poe 1888); Commonwealth v. Kneeland, 37 Mass. 206, 232 (1838); Act for the Punishment of Certain Crimes Not Capital (1791), N.H.Laws 1792, 253; Act Respecting Libels (1799), N.J.Rev.Laws 411 (1800); People v. Croswell, 3 Johns. (N.Y.) 337 (1804);

Act of 1803, c. 632, 2 Laws of N.C. 999 (1821); Pa.Const., 1790, Art. IX, § 7; R.I.Code of Laws (1647), Proceedings of the First General Assembly and Code of Laws 44-45 (1647); R.I.Const., 1842, Art. I, § 20; Act of 1804, 1 Laws of Vt. 366 (Tolman 1808); Commonwealth v. Morris, 1 Brock. & Hol. (Va.) 176 (1811).

12. Act for the Punishment of Divers Capital and Other Felonies, Acts and Laws of Conn. 66, 67 (1784); Act Against Drunkenness, Blasphemy, §§ 4, 5 (1737), 1 Laws of Del. 173, 174 (1797); Act to Regulate Taverns (1786), Digest of the Laws of Ga. 512, 513 (Prince 1822); Act of 1723, c. 16, § 1, Digest of the Laws of Md. 92 (Herty 1799); General Laws and Liberties of Mass. Bay, c. XVIII, § 3 (1646), Mass. Bay Colony Charters & Laws 58 (1814); Act of 1782, c. 8, Rev.Stat. of Mass. 741, § 15 (1836); Act of 1798, c. 33, §§ 1, 3, Rev.Stat. of Mass. 741, § 16 (1836); Act for the Punishment of Certain Crimes Not Capital (1791), N.H.Laws 1792, 252, 256; Act for the Punishment of Profane Cursing and Swearing (1791), N.H.Laws 1792, 258; Act for Suppressing Vice and Immorality, §§ VIII, IX (1798), N.J.Rev.Laws 329, 331 (1800); Act for Suppressing Immorality, § IV (1788), 2 Laws of N.Y. 257, 258 (Jones & Varick 1777-1789); People v. Ruggles, 8 Johns. (N.Y.) 290 (1811); Act . . . for the More Effectual Suppression of Vice and Immorality, § III (1741), 1 N.C.Laws 52 (Martin Rev. 1715-1790); Act to Prevent the Grievous Sins of Cursing and Swearing (1700), II Statutes at Large of Pa. 49 (1700-1712); Act for the Prevention of Vice and Immorality, § II (1794), 3 Laws of Pa. 177, 178 (1791-1802); Act to Reform the Penal Laws, §§ 33, 34 (1798), R.I.Laws 1798, 584, 595; Act for the More Effectual Suppressing of Blasphemy and Prophaneness (1703), Laws of S.C. 4 (Grimke 1790); Act, for the Punishment of Certain Capital, and Other High Crimes and Misdemeanors, § 20 (1797), 1 Laws of Vt. 332, 339 (Tolman 1808); Act for the Punishment of Certain Inferior Crimes and Misdemeanors, § 20 (1797), 1 Laws of Vt. 352, 361 (Tolman 1808); Act for the Effectual Suppression of Vice, § 1 (1792), Acts of General Assembly of Va. 286 (1794).

13. Act Concerning Crimes and Punishments, § 69 (1821), Stat.Laws of Conn. 109 (1824); Knowles v. State, 3 Day (Conn.) 103 (1808); Rev.Stat. of 1835, c. 130, § 10, Rev.Stat. of Mass. 740 (1836); Commonwealth v. Holmes, 17 Mass. 335 (1821); Rev.Stat. of 1842, c. 113, § 2, Rev.Stat. of N.H. 221 (1843); Act for Suppressing Vice and Immorality, § XII (1798), N.J.Rev.Laws 329, 331 (1800); Commonwealth v. Sharpless, 2 S. & R. (Pa.) 91 (1815).

14. E.g., United States v. Harriss, 347 U.S. 612; Breard v. Alexandria, 341 U.S. 622; Teamsters Union v. Hanke, 339 U.S. 470; Kovacs v. Cooper, 336 U.S. 77; Prince v. Massachusetts, 321 U.S. 158; Labor Board v. Virginia Elec. & Power Co., 314 U.S. 469; Cox v. New Hampshire, 312 U.S. 569; Schenck v. United States, 249 U.S. 47.

15. Agreement for the Suppression of the Circulation of Obscene Publications, 37 Stat. 1511; Treaties in Force 209 (U.S. Dept. State, October 31, 1956).

16. Hearings before Subcommittee to Investigate Juvenile Delinquency of the Senate Committee on the Judiciary, pursuant to S.Res. 62, 84th Cong., 1st Sess. 49-52 (May 24, 1955).

Although New Mexico has no general obscenity statute, it does have a statute giving to municipalities the power "to prohibit the sale or exhibiting of obscene or immoral publications, prints, pictures, or illustrations." N.M.Stat.Ann., 1953, §§ 14-21-3, 14-21-12.

17. 5 Stat. 548, 566; 11 Stat. 168; 13 Stat. 504, 507; 17 Stat. 302; 17 Stat. 598; 19 Stat. 90; 25 Stat. 187, 188; 25 Stat. 496; 26 Stat. 567, 614-615; 29 Stat. 512; 33 Stat. 705; 35 Stat. 1129, 1138; 41 Stat. 1060; 46 Stat. 688; 48 Stat. 1091, 1100; 62 Stat. 768; 64 Stat. 194; 64 Stat. 451; 69 Stat. 183; 70 Stat. 699.

18. Schenck v. United States, 249 U.S. 47"] 249 U.S. 47. This approach is typified by the opinion of Judge Bok (written prior to this Court's opinion in 249 U.S. 47. This approach is typified by the opinion of Judge Bok (written prior to this Court's opinion in Dennis v. United States, 341 U.S. 494) in Commonwealth v. Gordon, 66 Pa. D. & C. 101, aff'd sub nom. Commonwealth v. Feigenbaum, 166 Pa.Super. 120, 70 A.2d 389.

19. Dennis v. United States, 341 U.S. 494. This approach is typified by the concurring opinion of Judge Frank in the Roth case, 237 F.2d at 801. See also Lockhart & McClure, Literature, The Law of Obscenity, and the Constitution, 38 Minn.L.Rev. 295 (1954).

20. I.e., material having a tendency to excite lustful thoughts. Webster's New International Dictionary (Unabridged,2d ed., 1949) defines prurient, in pertinent part, as follows:

. . . Itching; longing; uneasy with desire or longing; of persons, having itching, morbid, or lascivious longings; of desire, curiosity, or propensity, lewd. . . .

Pruriency is defined, in pertinent part, as follows:

. . . Quality of being prurient; lascivious desire or thought. . . .

See also Mutual Film Corp. v. Industrial Comm'n, 236 U.S. 230, 242, where this Court said as to motion pictures:

. . . They take their attraction from the general interest, eager and wholesome it may be, in their subjects, but a prurient interest may be excited and appealed to. . . .

(Emphasis added.)

We perceive no significant difference between the meaning of obscenity developed in the case law and the definition of the A.L.I., Model Penal Code, § 207.10(2) (Tent.Draft No. 6, 1957), viz.:

. . . A thing is obscene if, considered as a whole, its predominant appeal is to prurient interest, i.e., a shameful or morbid interest in nudity, sex, or excretion, and if it goes substantially beyond customary limits of candor in description or representation of such matters. . . .

See Comment, id. at 10, and the discussion at page 29 et seq.

21. See, e.g., United States v. Dennett, 39 F.2d 564.

22. Madison's Report on the Virginia Resolutions, 4 Elliot's Debates 571.

23. See note 14, supra.

24. But see the instructions given to the jury by Mr. Justice Stable in Regina v. Martin Secker Warburg, [1954] 2 All Eng. 683 (C.C.C.).

25. United States v. Kennerley, 209 F. 119; MacFadden v. United States, 165 F. 51; United States v. Bennett, 24 Fed.Cas. 1093; United States v. Clarke, 38 F. 500; Commonwealth v. Buckley, 200 Mass. 346, 86 N.E. 910.

26. E.g., Walker v. Popence, 80 U.S.App.D.C. 129, 149 F.2d 511; Parmelee v. United States, 72 App.D.C. 203, 113 F.2d 729; United States v. Levine, 83 F.2d 156; United States v. Dennett, 39 F.2d 564; Khan v. Feist, Inc., 70 F.Supp. 450, aff'd, 165 F.2d 188; United States v. One Book Called "Ulysses," 5 F.Supp. 182, aff'd, 72 F.2d 705; American Civil Liberties Union v. Chicago, 3 Ill.2d 334, 121 N.E.2d 585; Commonwealth v. Isenstadt, 318 Mass. 543, 62 N.E.2d 840; Missouri v. Becker, 364 Mo. 1079, 272 S.W.2d 283; Adams Theatre Co. v. Keenan, 12 N.J. 267, 96 A.2d 519; Bantam Books, Inc. v. Melko, 25 N.J.Super. 292, 96 A.2d 47; Commonwealth v. Gordon, 66 Pa. D. & C. 101, aff'd sub nom. Commonwealth v. Feigenbaum, 166 Pa.Super. 120, 70 A.2d 389; cf. Roth v. Goldman, 172 F.2d 788, 794-795 (concurrence).

27. In Alberts, the contention that the trial judge did not read the materials in their entirety is not before us because not fairly comprised within the questions presented. U.S.Sup.Ct.Rules, 15(1)(c)(1).

28. This Court, as early as 1896, said of the federal obscenity statute:
. . . Every one who uses the mails of the United States for carrying papers or publications must take notice of what, in this enlightened age, is meant by decency, purity, and chastity in social life, and what must be deemed obscene, lewd, and lascivious.
Rosen v. United States, 161 U.S. 29, 42.

29. E.g., Roth v. Goldman, 172 F.2d 788, 789; Parmelee v. United States, 72 App.D.C. 203, 204, 113 F.2d 729, 730; United States v. 4200 Copies International Journal, 134 F.Supp. 490, 493; United States v. One Unbound Volume, 128 F.Supp. 280, 281.

30. It is argued that, because juries may reach different conclusions as to the same material, the statutes must be held to be insufficiently precise to satisfy due process requirements. But it is common experience that different juries may reach different results under any criminal statute. That is one of the consequences we accept under our jury system. Cf. Dunlop v. United States, 165 U.S. 486, 499-500.

31. For the same reason, we reject, in this case, the argument that there is greater latitude for state action under the word "liberty" under the Fourteenth Amendment than is allowed to Congress by the language of the First Amendment.

32. In Public Clearing House v. Coyne, 194 U.S. 497, 506-508, this Court said:
The constitutional principles underlying the administration of the Post Office Department were discussed in the opinion of the court in Ex parte Jackson, 96 U.S. 727, in which we held that the power vested in Congress to establish post offices and post roads embraced the regulation of the entire postal system of the country; that Congress might designate what might be carried in the mails and what excluded. . . . It may . . . refuse to include in its mails such printed matter or merchandise as may seem objectionable to it upon the ground of public policy. . . . For more than thirty years, not

only has the transmission of obscene matter been prohibited, but it has been made a crime, punishable by fine or imprisonment, for a person to deposit such matter in the mails. The constitutionality of this law we believe has never been attacked. . . .

## Smith v. California (December 14, 1959)

MR. JUSTICE BRENNAN delivered the opinion of the Court.

Appellant, the proprietor of a bookstore, was convicted in a California Municipal Court under a Los Angeles City ordinance which makes it unlawful

"for any person to have in his possession any obscene or indecent writing, [or] book . . . in any place of business where . . . books . . . are sold or kept for sale. [1]"

The offense was defined by the Municipal Court, and by the Appellate Department of the Superior Court, [2] which affirmed the Municipal Court judgment imposing a jail sentence on appellant, as consisting solely of the possession, in the appellant's bookstore, of a certain book found upon judicial investigation to be obscene. The definition included no element of scienter -- knowledge by appellant of the contents of the book -- and thus the ordinance was construed as imposing a "strict" or "absolute" criminal liability. [3] The appellant made timely objection below that, if the ordinance were so construed it would be in conflict with the Constitution of the United States. This contention, together with other contentions based on the Constitution, [4] was rejected, and the case comes here on appeal. 28 U.S.C. § 1257(2); 358 U.S. 926.

Almost 30 years ago, Chief Justice Hughes declared for this Court:

"It is no longer open to doubt that the liberty of the press and of speech is within the liberty safeguarded by the due process clause of the Fourteenth Amendment from invasion by state action. It was found impossible to conclude that this essential personal liberty of the citizen was left unprotected by the general guaranty of fundamental rights of person and property. . . ."

Near v. Minnesota, 283 U. S. 697, 283 U. S. 707. It is too familiar for citation that such has been the doctrine of this Court, in respect of these freedoms, ever since. And it also requires no elaboration that the free publication and dissemination of books and other forms of the printed word furnish very familiar applications of these constitutionally protected freedoms. It is, of course, no matter that the dissemination takes place under commercial auspices. See Joseph Burstyn, Inc., v. Wilson, 343 U. S. 495; Grosjean v. American Press Co., 297 U. S. 233. Certainly a retail bookseller plays a most significant role in the process of the distribution of books.

California here imposed a strict or absolute criminal responsibility on appellant not to have obscene books in his shop. "The existence of a mens rea is the rule of, rather than the exception to, the principles of Anglo-American criminal jurisprudence." Dennis v. United States, 341 U. S. 494, 341 U. S. 500. [5] Still, it is doubtless competent for the States to create strict criminal liabilities by defining criminal offenses without any element of scienter -- though even where no freedom of expression question is involved, there is precedent in this Court that this power is not without limitations. See Lambert v. California, 355 U. S. 225. But the question here is as to the validity of this ordinance's elimination of the scienter requirement -- an elimination which may tend to work a substantial restriction on the freedom of speech and of the press. Our decisions furnish examples of legal devices and doctrines in most applications consistent with the Constitution, which cannot be applied in settings where they have the collateral effect of inhibiting the freedom of expression, by making the individual the more reluctant to exercise it. The States generally may regulate the allocation of the burden of proof in their courts, and it is a common procedural device to impose on a taxpayer the burden of proving his entitlement to exemptions from taxation, but where we conceived that this device was being applied in a manner tending to cause even a self-imposed restriction of free expression, we struck down its application. Speiser v. Randall, 357 U. S. 513. See Near v. Minnesota, supra, at 283 U. S. 712-713. It has been stated here that the usual doctrines as to the separability of constitutional and unconstitutional applications of statutes may not apply where their effect is to leave standing a statute patently capable of many unconstitutional applications, threatening those who validly exercise their rights of free expression with the expense and inconvenience of criminal prosecution. Thornhill v. Alabama, 310 U. S. 88, 310 U. S. 97-98. Cf. Staub v. City of Baxley, 355 U. S. 313. [6] And this Court has intimated that stricter standards of permissible statutory vagueness may be applied to a statute having a potentially inhibiting effect on speech; a man may the less be required to act at his peril here, because the free dissemination of ideas may be the loser. Winters v. New York, 333 U. S. 507, 333 U. S. 509-510, 333 U. S. 517-518. Very much to the point here, where the question is the elimination of the mental element in an offense, is this Court's holding in Wieman v. Updegraff, 344 U. S. 183. There an oath as to past freedom from membership in subversive organizations, exacted by a State as a qualification for public employment, was held to violate the Constitution in that it made no distinction between members who had, and those who had not, known of the organization's character. The Court said of the elimination of scienter in this context: "To thus inhibit individual freedom of movement is to stifle the flow of democratic expression and controversy at one of its chief sources." Id. at 344 U. S. 191.

These principles guide us to our decision here. We have held that obscene speech and writings are not protected by the constitutional guarantees of freedom of speech and the press. Roth v. United States, 354 U. S. 476. [7] The ordinance here in question, to be sure, only imposes criminal sanctions on a bookseller if, in fact, there is to be found in his shop an obscene book. But our holding in Roth does not recognize any state power to restrict the dissemination of books which are not obscene; and we think this ordinance's strict liability feature would tend seriously to have that effect by penalizing booksellers even though they had not the slightest notice of the character of the books they sold. The appellee and the court below analogize this strict liability penal ordinance to familiar forms of penal statutes which dispense with any element of knowledge on the part of the person charged, food and drug legislation being a principal example. We find the analogy instructive in our examination of the question before us. The usual rationale for such statutes is that the public interest in the purity of its food is so great as to warrant the imposition of the highest standard of care on distributors -- in fact, an absolute standard which will not hear the distributor's plea as to the amount of care he has used. Cf. United States v. Balint, 258 U. S. 250, 258 U. S. 252-253, 258 U. S. 254. His ignorance of the character of the food is irrelevant. There is no specific constitutional inhibition against making the distributors of good the strictest censors of their merchandise, but the constitutional guarantees of the freedom of speech and of the press stand in the way of imposing a similar requirement on the bookseller. By dispensing with any requirement of knowledge of the contents of the book on the part of the seller, the ordinance tends to impose a severe limitation on the public's access to constitutionally protected matter. For if the bookseller is criminally liable without knowledge of the contents, and the ordinance fulfills its purpose, [8] he will tend to restrict the books he sells to those he has inspected; and thus the State will have imposed a restriction upon the distribution of constitutionally protected, as well as obscene literature. It has been well observed of a statute construed as dispensing with any requirement of scienter that:

"Every bookseller would be placed under an obligation to make himself aware of the contents of every book in his shop. It would be altogether unreasonable to demand so near an approach to omniscience. [9]"

The King v. Ewart, 25 N.Z.L.R. 709, 729 (C.A.). And the bookseller's burden would become the public's burden, for, by restricting him, the public's access to reading matter would be restricted. If the contents of bookshops and periodical stands were restricted to material of which their proprietors had made an inspection, they might be depleted indeed. The bookseller's limitation in the amount of reading material with which he could familiarize himself, and his timidity in the face of his absolute criminal liability, thus would tend to restrict the public's access to forms of the printed word which the State could not constitutionally suppress directly. The bookseller's self-censorship, compelled by the State, would be a censorship affecting the whole public, hardly less virulent for being privately administered. Through it, the distribution of all books, both obscene and not obscene, would be impeded.

It is argued that unless the scienter requirement is dispensed with, regulation of the distribution of obscene material will be ineffective, as booksellers will falsely disclaim knowledge of their books' contents or falsely deny reason to suspect their obscenity. We might observe that it has been some time now since the law viewed itself as impotent to explore the actual state of a man's mind. See Pound, The Role of the Will in Law, 68 Harv.L.Rev. 1. Cf. American Communications Assn. v. Douds, 339 U. S. 382, 339 U. S. 411. Eyewitness testimony of a bookseller's perusal of a book hardly need be a necessary element in proving his awareness of its contents. The circumstances may warrant the inference that he was aware of what a book contained, despite his denial.

We need not and most definitely do not pass today on what sort of mental element is requisite to a constitutionally permissible prosecution of a bookseller for carrying an obscene book in stock; whether honest mistake as to whether its contents in fact constituted obscenity need be an excuse; whether there might be circumstances under which the State constitutionally might require that a bookseller investigate further, or might put on him the burden of explaining why he did not, and what such circumstances might be. Doubtless any form of criminal obscenity statute applicable to a bookseller will induce some tendency to self-censorship and have some inhibitory effect on the dissemination of material not obscene, but we consider today only one which goes to the extent of eliminating all mental elements from the crime.

We have said:

"The fundamental freedoms of speech and press have contributed greatly to the development and wellbeing of our free society, and are indispensable to its continued growth. Ceaseless vigilance is the watchword to prevent their erosion by Congress or by the States. The door barring federal and state intrusion into this area cannot be left ajar; it must be kept tightly closed, and opened only the slightest crack necessary to prevent encroachment upon more important interests."

Roth v. United States, supra, at 354 U. S. 488. [10] This ordinance opens that door too far. The existence of the State's power to prevent the distribution of obscene matter does not mean that there can be no constitutional barrier to any form of practical exercise of that power. Cf. Dean Milk Co. v. City of Madison, 340 U. S. 349. It is plain to us that the ordinance in question, though aimed at obscene matter, has such a tendency to inhibit constitutionally protected expression that it cannot stand under the Constitution.

Reversed.

Notes

[1] The ordinance is § 41.01.1 of the Municipal Code of the City of Los Angeles. It provides:

"INDECENT WRITINGS, ETC. -- POSSESSION PROHIBITED"

"It shall be unlawful for any person to have in his possession any obscene or indecent writing, book, pamphlet, picture, photograph, drawing, figure, motion picture film, phonograph recording, wire recording or transcription of any kind in any of the following places:"

"1. In any school, school-grounds, public park or playground or in any public place, grounds, street or way within 300 yards of any school, park or playground;"

"2. In any place of business where ice-cream, soft drinks, candy, food, school supplies, magazines, books, pamphlets, papers, pictures or postcards are sold or kept for sale;"

"3. In any toilet or restroom open or the public;"

"4. In any poolroom or billiard parlor, or in any place where alcoholic liquor is sold or offered for sale to the public;"

"5. In any place where phonograph records, photographs, motion pictures, or transcriptions of any kind are made, used, maintained, sold or exhibited."

[2] In this sort of proceeding, "the highest court of a State in which a decision could be had." 28 U.S.C. § 1257. Cal.Const. art. VI, §§ 4, 4b, 5. See Edwards v. People of State of California, 314 U. S. 160, 314 U. S. 171.

[3] See Hall, General Principles of Criminal Law, p. 280. The Appellate Department's opinion is at 161 Cal.App.2d Supp. 860, 327 P.2d 636. The ordinance's elimination of scienter was, in fact, a reason assigned by that court for upholding it as permissible supplementary municipal legislation against the contention that the field was occupied by California Penal Code, § 311, a statewide obscenity statute which requires scienter.

[4] These other contentions, which are made again here, are that evidence of a nature constitutionally required to be allowed to be given for the defense as to the obscene character of a book was not permitted to be introduced; that a constitutionally impermissible standard of obscenity was applied by the trier of the facts, and that the book was not, in fact, obscene. In the light of our determination as to the constitutional permissibility of a strict liability law under the circumstances presented by this case, we need not pass on these questions. For the purposes of discussion, we shall assume without deciding that the book was correctly adjudged below to be obscene.

[5] See also Williams, Criminal Law -- The General Part, p. 238 et seq.

[6] See Note, 61 Harv.L.Rev. 1208.

[7] In the Roth opinion, there was also decided Alberts v. California, which dealt with the power of the States in this area.

[8] The effectiveness of absolute criminal liability laws in promoting caution has been subjected to criticism. See Hall, General Principles of Criminal Law, pp. 300-301. See generally Williams, Criminal Law -- The General Part, pp. 267-274; Sayre, Public Welfare Offenses, 33 Col.L.Rev. 55; Mueller, On Common Law Mens Rea, 42 Minn.L.Rev. 1043; Morissette v. United States, 342 U. S. 246.

[9] Common law prosecutions for the dissemination of obscene matter strictly adhered to the requirement of scienter. See the discussion in Attorney-General v. Simpson, 93 Irish L.T. 33, 37-38 (Dist.Ct.). Cf. Obscene Publications Act, 1959, 7 & 8 Eliz. 2, c. 66, § 2(5); American Law Institute Model Penal Code § 207.10(7) (Tentative Draft No. 6, May 1957), and Comments, pp. 49-51.

The general California obscenity statute, Penal Code, § 311, requires scienter, see note 3 and was, of course, sustained by us in Roth v. United States, supra. See note 7.

[10] We emphasized in Roth, at p. 354 U. S. 484, that there is a "limited area" where such other interests prevail, and we listed representative decisions in note 14 at that page

**Times Film Corp. v. City of Chicago (January 23, 1961)**

MR. JUSTICE CLARK delivered the opinion of the Court.

Petitioner challenges on constitutional grounds the validity on its face of that portion of § 155-4 [1] of the Municipal Code of the City of Chicago which requires submission of all motion pictures for examination prior to their public exhibition. Petitioner is a New York corporation owning the exclusive right to publicly exhibit in Chicago the film known as "Don Juan." It applied for a permit, as Chicago's ordinance required, and tendered the license fee, but refused to submit the film for examination. The appropriate city official refused to issue the permit, and his order was made final on appeal to the Mayor. The sole ground for denial was petitioner's refusal to submit the film for examination as required. Petitioner then brought this suit seeking injunctive relief ordering the issuance of the permit without submission of the film and restraining the city officials from interfering with the exhibition of the picture. Its sole ground is that the provision of the ordinance requiring submission of the film constitutes, on its face, a prior restraint within the prohibition of the First and Fourteenth Amendments. The District Court dismissed the complaint on the grounds, inter alia, that neither a substantial federal question nor even a justiciable controversy was presented. 180 F.Supp. 843. The Court of Appeals affirmed, finding that the case presented merely an abstract question of law, since neither the film nor evidence of its content was submitted. 272 F.2d 90. The precise question at issue here never having been specifically decided by this Court, we granted certiorari, 362 U.S. 917 (1960).

We are satisfied that a justiciable controversy exists. The section of Chicago's ordinance in controversy specifically provides that a permit for the public exhibition of a motion picture must be obtained; that such

"permit shall be granted only after the motion picture film for which said permit is requested has been produced at the office of the commissioner of police for examination;"

that the commissioner shall refuse the permit if the picture does not meet certain standards; [2] and that, in the event of such refusal, the applicant may appeal to the mayor for a de novo hearing, and his action shall be final. Violation of the ordinance carries certain punishments. The petitioner complied with the requirements of the ordinance, save for the production of the film for examination. The claim is that this concrete and specific statutory requirement, the production of the film at the office of the commissioner for examination, is invalid as a previous restraint on freedom of speech. In Joseph Burstyn, Inc. v. Wilson, 343 U. S. 495, 343 U. S. 502 (1952), we held that motion pictures are included "within the free speech and free press guaranty of the First and Fourteenth Amendments." Admittedly, the challenged section of the ordinance imposes a previous restraint, and the broad justiciable issue is therefore present as to whether the ambit of constitutional protection includes complete and absolute freedom to exhibit, at least once, any and every kind of motion picture. It is that question alone which we decide. We have concluded that § 155-4 of Chicago's ordinance requiring the submission of films prior to their public exhibition is not, on the grounds set forth, void on its face.

Petitioner's narrow attack upon the ordinance does not require that any consideration be given to the validity of the standards set out therein. They are not challenged, and are not before us. Prior motion picture censorship cases which reached this Court involved questions of standards. [3] The films had all been submitted to the authorities, and permits for their exhibition were refused because of their content. Obviously, whether a particular statute is "clearly drawn," or "vague," or "indefinite," or whether a clear standard is in fact met by a film are different questions involving other constitutional challenges to be tested by considerations not here involved.

Moreover, there is not a word in the record as to the nature and content of "Don Juan." We are left entirely in the dark in this regard, as were the city officials and the other reviewing courts. Petitioner claims that the nature of the film is irrelevant, and that even if this film contains the basest type of pornography, or incitement to riot, or forceful overthrow of orderly government, it may nonetheless be shown without prior submission for examination. The challenge here is to the censor's basic authority; it does not go to any statutory standards employed by the censor or procedural requirements as to the submission of the film.

In this perspective, we consider the prior decisions of this Court touching on the problem. Beginning over a third of a century ago, in Gitlow v. New York, 268 U. S. 652 (1925), they have consistently reserved for future decision possible situations in which the claimed First Amendment privilege might have to give way to the necessities of the public welfare. It has never been held that liberty of speech is absolute. Nor has it been suggested that all previous restraints on speech are invalid. On the contrary, in Near v. Minnesota, 283 U. S. 697, 283 U. S. 715-716 (1931), Chief Justice Hughes, in discussing the classic legal statements concerning the immunity of the press from censorship, observed that the principle forbidding previous restraint

"is stated too broadly, if every such restraint is deemed to be prohibited. . . . [T]he protection even as to previous restraint is not absolutely unlimited. But the limitation has been recognized only in exceptional cases."

These included, the Chief Justice found, utterances creating "a hindrance" to the Government's war effort, and "actual obstruction to its recruiting service or the publication of the sailing dates of transports or the number and location of troops." In addition, the Court said that "the primary requirements of decency may be enforced against obscene publications" and the

"security of the community life may be protected against incitements to acts of violence and the overthrow by force of orderly government."

Some years later, a unanimous Court, speaking through Mr. Justice Murphy, in Chaplinsky v. New Hampshire, 315 U. S. 568, 315 U. S. 571-572 (1942), held that there were

"certain well defined and narrowly limited classes of speech, the prevention and punishment of which have never been thought to raise any Constitutional problem. These include the lewd and obscene, the profane, the libelous, and the insulting or 'fighting' words -- those which, by their very utterance, inflict injury or tend to incite an immediate breach of the peace."

Thereafter, as we have mentioned, in Joseph Burstyn, Inc. v. Wilson, supra, we found motion pictures to be within the guarantees of the First and Fourteenth Amendments, but we added that this was

"not the end of our problem. It does not follow that the Constitution requires absolute freedom to exhibit every motion picture of every kind at all times and all places."

At p. 343 U. S. 502. Five years later, in Roth v. United States, 354 U. S. 476, 354 U. S. 483 (1957), we held that "in light of . . . history, it is apparent that the unconditional phrasing of the First Amendment was not intended to protect every utterance." Even those in dissent there found that

"Freedom of expression can be suppressed if, and to the extent that, it is so closely brigaded with illegal action as to be an inseparable part of it."

Id. at 354 U. S. 514. And, during the same Term, in Kingsley Books, Inc. v. Brown, 354 U. S. 436, 354 U. S. 441 (1957), after characterizing Near v. Minnesota, supra, as "one of the landmark opinions" in its area, we took notice that Near

"left no doubts that 'Liberty of speech, and of the press, is also not an absolute right . . . the protection even as to previous restraint is not absolutely unlimited.' . . . The judicial angle of vision,"

we said there,

"in testing the validity of a statute like § 22-a [New York's injunctive remedy against certain forms of obscenity] is 'the operation and effect of the statute in substance.'"

And as if to emphasize the point involved here, we added that "The phrase prior restraint' is not a self-wielding sword. Nor can it serve as a talismanic test." Even as recently as our last Term, we again observed the principle, albeit in an allied area, that the State possesses some measure of power "to prevent the distribution of obscene matter." Smith v. California, 361 U. S. 147, 361 U. S. 155 (1959).

Petitioner would have us hold that the public exhibition of motion pictures must be allowed under any circumstances. The State's sole remedy, it says, is the invocation of criminal process under the Illinois pornography statute, Ill.Rev.Stat. (1959), c. 38, § 470, and then only after a transgression. But this position, as we have seen, is founded upon the claim of absolute privilege against prior restraint under the First Amendment -- a claim without sanction in our cases. To illustrate its fallacy, we need only point to one of the "exceptional cases" which Chief Justice Hughes enumerated in Near v. Minnesota, supra, namely, "the primary requirements of decency [that] may be enforced against obscene publications." Moreover, we later held specifically "that obscenity is not within the area of constitutionally protected speech or press." Roth v. United States, 354 U. S. 476, 354 U. S. 485 (1957). Chicago emphasizes here its duty to protect its people against the dangers of obscenity in the public exhibition of motion pictures. To this argument petitioner's only answer is that, regardless of the capacity for, or extent of, such an evil, previous restraint cannot be justified. With this we cannot agree. We recognized in

Burstyn, supra, that "capacity for evil . . . may be relevant in determining the permissible scope of community control," 343 U.S. at 343 U. S. 502, and that motion pictures were not "necessarily subject to the precise rules governing any other particular method of expression. Each method," we said, "tends to present its own peculiar problems." At p. 343 U. S. 503. Certainly petitioner's broadside attack does not warrant, nor could it justify on the record here, our saying that -- aside from any consideration of the other "exceptional cases" mentioned in our decisions -- the State is stripped of all constitutional power to prevent, in the most effective fashion, the utterance of this class of speech. It is not for this Court to limit the State in its selection of the remedy it deems most effective to cope with such a problem, absent, of course, a showing of unreasonable strictures on individual liberty resulting from its application in particular circumstances. Kingsley Books, Inc. v. Brown, supra, at 354 U. S. 441. We, of course, are not holding that city officials may be granted the power to prevent the showing of any motion picture they deem unworthy of a license. Joseph Burstyn, Inc. v. Wilson, supra, at 343 U. S. 504-505.

As to what may be decided when a concrete case involving a specific standard provided by this ordinance is presented, we intimate no opinion. The petitioner has not challenged all -- or, for that matter, any -- of the ordinance's standards. Naturally we could not say that every one of the standards, including those which Illinois' highest court has found sufficient, is so vague on its face that the entire ordinance is void. At this time, we say no more than this -- that we are dealing only with motion pictures, and, even as to them, only in the context of the broadside attack presented on this record.

Affirmed.

Notes

[1] The portion of the section here under attack is as follows:

"Such permit shall be granted only after the motion picture film for which said permit is requested has been produced at the office of the commissioner of police for examination or censorship. . . "

[2] That portion of § 155-4 of the Code providing standards is as follows:

"If a picture or series of pictures, for the showing or exhibition of which an application for a permit is made, is immoral or obscene, or portrays, depravity, criminality, or lack of virtue of a class of citizens of any race, color, creed, or religion and exposes them to contempt, derision, or obloquy, or tends to produce a breach of the peace or riots, or purports to represent any hanging, lynching, or burning of a human being, it shall be the duty of the commissioner of police to refuse such permit; otherwise it shall be his duty to grant such permit."

"In case the commissioner of police shall refuse to grant a permit as hereinbefore provided, the applicant for the same may appeal to the mayor. Such appeal shall be presented in the same manner as the original application to the commissioner of police. The action of the mayor on any application for a permit shall be final."

It should be noted that the Supreme Court of Illinois, in an opinion by Schaefer,

C.J., has already considered and rejected an argument against the same Chicago ordinance, similar to the claim advanced here by petitioner. The same court also sustained certain of the standards set out above. American Civil Liberties Union v. City of Chicago, 3 Ill.2d 334, 121 N.E.2d 585 (1954).

[3] Joseph Burstyn, Inc. v. Wilson, supra ("sacrilegious"); Gelling v. State of Texas, 343 U. S. 960 (1952) ("prejudicial to the best interests of the people of said City"); Commercial Pictures Corp. v. Regents, 346 U. S. 587 (1954) ("immoral"); Superior Films, Inc. v. Department of Education, 346 U. S. 587 (1954) ("harmful"); Kingsley International Pictures Corp. v. Regents, 360 U. S. 684 (1959) ("sexual immorality").

**Marcus v. Search Warrant of Property at . . . (June 19, 1961) [Notes omitted]**

MR. JUSTICE BRENNAN delivered the opinion of the Court.

This appeal presents the question whether due process under the Fourteenth Amendment was denied the appellants by the application in this case of Missouri's procedures authorizing the search for and seizure of allegedly obscene publications preliminarily to their destruction by burning or otherwise if found by a court to be obscene. The procedures are statutory, but are supplemented by a rule of the Missouri Supreme Court. [1] The warrant for search for and seizure of obscene material issues on a sworn complaint filed with a judge or magistrate. [2]

If the complainant states "positively and not upon information or belief," or states "evidential facts from which such judge or magistrate determines the existence of probable cause" to believe that obscene material "is being held or kept in any place or in any building,"

"such judge or magistrate shall issue a search warrant directed to any peace officer commanding him to search the place therein described and to seize and bring before such judge or magistrate the personal property therein described. [3]"

The owner of the property is not afforded a hearing before the warrant issues; the proceeding is ex parte. However, the judge or magistrate issuing the warrant must fix a date, not less than five nor more than 20 days after the seizure, for a hearing to determine whether the seized material is obscene. [4] The owner of the material may appear at such hearing and defend against the charge. [5] No time limit is provided within which the judge must announce his decision. If the judge finds that the material is obscene, he is required to order it to be publicly destroyed, by burning or otherwise; if he finds that it is not obscene, he shall order its return to its owner. [6]

The Missouri Supreme Court sustained the validity of the procedures as applied in this case. 334 S.W.2d 119. The appellants brought this appeal here under 28 U.S.C. § 1257(2). We postponed consideration of the question of our jurisdiction to the hearing of the case on the merits. 364 U.S. 811. We hold that the appeal is properly here, see Dahnke-Walker Milling Co. v. Bondurant, 257 U. S. 282, and turn to the merits.

Appellant, Kansas City News Distributors, managed by appellant, Homer Smay, is a wholesale distributor of magazines, newspapers and books in the Kansas City area. The other appellants operate five retail newsstands in Kansas City. In October 1957, Police Lieutenant Coughlin of the Kansas City Police Department Vice Squad was conducting an investigation into the distribution of allegedly obscene magazines. On October 8, 1957, he visited Distributors' place of business and showed Smay a list of magazines. Smay admitted that his company distributed all but one of the magazines on the list. The following day, October 9, Lieutenant Coughlin visited the five newsstands and purchased one magazine at each. [7] On October 10, the officer signed and filed six sworn complaints in the Circuit Court of Jackson County, stating in each complaint that "of his own knowledge" the appellant named therein, at its stated place of business, "kept for the purpose of [sale] . . . obscene . . . publications. . . ." No copy of any magazine on Lieutenant Coughlin's list, or purchased by him at the newsstands, was filed with the complaint or shown to the circuit judge. The circuit judge issued six search warrants authorizing, as to the premises of the appellant named in each,

"any peace officer in the State of Missouri . . . [to] search the said premises . . . within 10 days after the issuance of this warrant by day or night, and . . . seize . . . [obscene materials] and take same into your possession. . . ."

All of the warrants were executed on October 10, but by different law enforcement officers. Lieutenant Coughlin, with two other Kansas City police officers and an officer of the Jackson County Sheriff's Patrol, executed the warrant against Distributors. Distributors' stock of magazines runs "into hundreds of thousands . . . [p]robably closer to a million copies." The officers examined the publications in the stock on the main floor of the establishment, not confining themselves to Lieutenant Coughlin's original list. They seized all magazines which, "[i]n our judgment," were obscene; when an officer thought "a magazine . . . ought to be picked up," he seized all copies of it. After three hours, the examination was completed, the the magazines seized were "hauled away in a truck, and put on the 15th floor of the courthouse." A substantially similar procedure was followed at each of the five newsstands. Approximately 11,000 copies of 280 publications, principally magazines but also some books and photographs, were seized at the six places. [8]

The circuit judge fixed October 17 for the hearing, which was later continued to October 23. Timely motions were made by the appellants to quash the search warrants and to suppress as evidence the property seized, and for the immediate return of the property. The motions were rested on a number of grounds, but we are concerned only with the challenge to the application of the procedures in the context of the protections for free speech and press assured against state abridgement by the Fourteenth Amendment. [9] Unconstitutionality in violation of the Fourteenth Amendment was asserted because the procedures as applied (1) allowed a seizure by police officers

"without notice or any hearing afforded to the movants prior to seizure for the purpose of determining whether or not these . . . publications are obscene . . . ,"

and (2) because they

"allowed police officers and deputy sheriffs to decide and make a judicial determination after the warrant was issued as to which . . . magazines were . . . obscene . . . and were subject to seizure, impairing movants' freedom of speech and publication."

The circuit judge reserved rulings on the motions, and heard testimony of the police officers concerning the events surrounding the issuance and execution of the several warrants. On December 12, 1957, the circuit judge filed an unreported opinion in which he overruled the several motions and found that 100 of the 280 seized items were obscene. A judgment thereupon issued directing that the 100 items, and all copies thereof,

"shall be retained by the Sheriff of Jackson County . . . as necessary evidence for the purpose of possible criminal prosecution or prosecutions, and, when such necessity no longer exists, said Sheriff . . . shall publicly destroy the same by burning within thirty days thereafter;"

it ordered further that the 180 items not found to be obscene, and all copies thereof, "shall be returned forthwith by the Sheriff . . . to the rightful owner or owners. . . ."

I

The use by government of the power of search and seizure as an adjunct to a system for the suppression of objectionable publications is not new. Historically, the struggle for freedom of speech and press in England was bound up with the issue of the scope of the search and seizure power. See generally Siebert, Freedom of the Press in England, 1476-1776; Hanson, Government and the Press, 1695-1763. It was a principal instrument for the enforcement of the Tudor licensing system. The Stationers' Company was incorporated in 1557 to help implement that system, and was empowered

"to make search whenever it shall please them in any place, shop, house, chamber, or building or any printer, binder or bookseller whatever within our kingdom of England or the dominions of the same of or for any books or things printed, or to be printed, and to seize, take hold, burn, or turn to the proper use of the aforesaid community, all and several those books and things which are or shall be printed contrary to the form of any statute, act, or proclamation, made or to be made. . . . [10]"

An order of counsel confirmed and expanded the Company's power in 1566, [11] and the Star Chamber reaffirmed it in 1586 by a decree

"That it shall be lawful for the wardens of the said Company for the time being or any two of the said Company thereto deputed by the said wardens, to make search in all workhouses, shops, warehouses of printers, booksellers, bookbinders, or where they shall have reasonable cause of suspicion, and all books [etc.] . . . contrary to . . . these present ordinances to stay and take to her Majesty's use. . . . [12]"

Books thus seized were taken to Stationers' Hall where they were inspected by ecclesiastical officers, who decided whether they should be burnt. These powers were exercised under the Tudor censorship to suppress both Catholic and Puritan dissenting literature. [13]

Each succeeding regime during turbulent Seventeenth Century England used the search and seizure power to suppress publications. James I commissioned the ecclesiastical judges comprising the Court of High Commission

"to enquire and search for . . . all heretical, schismatical and seditious books, libels, and writings, and all other books, pamphlets and portraitures offensive to the state or set forth without sufficient and lawful authority in that behalf, . . . and the same books [etc.] and their printing presses themselves likewise to seize and so to order and dispose of them . . . as they may not after serve or be employed for any such unlawful use. . . . [14]"

The Star Chamber decree of 1637, reenacting the requirement that all books be licensed, continued the broad powers of the Stationers' Company to enforce the licensing laws. [15] During the political overturn of the 1640's, Parliament on several occasions asserted the necessity of a broad search and seizure power to control printing. Thus, an order of 1648 gave power to the searchers

"to search in any house or place where there is just cause of suspicion that Presses are kept and employed in the printing of Scandalous and lying Pamphlets, . . . [and] to seize such scandalous and lying pamphlets as they find upon search. . . . [16]"

The Restoration brought a new licensing act in 1662. Under its authority, "messengers of the press" operated under the secretaries of state, who issued executive warrants for the seizure of persons and papers. These warrants, while sometimes specific in content, often gave the most general discretionary authority. For example, a warrant to Roger L'Estrange, the Surveyor of the Press, empowered him to "seize all seditious books and libels and to apprehend the authors, contrivers, printers, publishers, and dispersers of them," and to

"search any house, shop, printing room, chamber, warehouse, etc. for seditious, scandalous or unlicensed pictures, books, or papers, to bring away or deface the same, and the letter press, taking away all the copies. . . . [17]"

Another warrant gave L'Estrange power to

"search for & seize authors, contrivers, printers, . . . publishers, dispensers, & concealers of treasonable, schismaticall, seditious or unlicensed books, libells, pamphlets, or papers . . . together with all copys exemplaryes of such Books, libells, pamphlets or paper as aforesaid. [18]"

Although increasingly attacked, the licensing system was continued in effect for a time even after the Revolution of 1688, and executive warrants continued to issue for the search for and seizure of offending books. The Stationers' Company was also ordered

"to make often and diligent searches in all such places you or any of you shall know or have any probable reason to suspect, and to seize all unlicensed, scandalous books and pamphlets. . . . [19]"

And even when the device of prosecution for seditious libel replaced licensing as the principal governmental control of the press, [20] it too was enforced with the aid of general warrants -- authorizing either the arrest of all persons connected with the publication of a particular libel and the search of their premises or the seizure of all the papers of a named person alleged to be connected with the publication of a libel. [21]

Enforcement through general warrants was finally judicially condemned in England. This was the consequence of the struggle of the 1760's between the Crown and the opposition press led by John Wilkes, author and editor of the North Briton. From this struggle came the great case of Entick v. Carrington, 19 How.St.Tr. 1029, which this Court has called "one of the landmarks of English liberty." Boyd v. United States, 116 U. S. 616, 116 U. S. 626. A warrant based on a charge of seditious libel issued for the arrest of Entick, writer for an opposition paper, and for the seizure of all his papers. The officers executing the warrant ransacked Entick's home for four hours and carted away great quantities of books and papers. Lord Camden declared the general warrant for the seizure of papers contrary to the common law, despite its long history. Camden said:

"This power so assumed by the secretary of state is an execution upon all the party's papers, in the first instance. His house is rifled; his most valuable secrets are taken out of his possession, before the paper for which he is charged is found to be criminal by any competent jurisdiction, and before he is convicted either of writing, publishing, or being concerned in the paper."

At 1064. Camden expressly dismissed the contention that such a warrant could be justified on the grounds that it was

"necessary for the ends of government to lodge such a power with a state officer; and . . . better to prevent the publication before than to punish the offender afterwards."

At 1073. In Wilkes v. Wood, 19 How.St.Tr. 1153, Camden also condemned the general warrants employed against John Wilkes for his publication of issue No. 45 of the North Briton. He declared that these warrants, calling for the arrest of unnamed persons connected with the alleged libel and seizure of their papers, amounted to a

"discretionary power given to messengers to search wherever their suspicions may chance to fall. If such a power is truly invested in a secretary of state, and he can delegate this power, it certainly may affect the person and property of every man in this kingdom, and is totally subversive of the liberty of the subject."

Id., 1167. [22]

This history was, of course, part of the intellectual matrix within which our own constitutional fabric was shaped. The Bill of Rights was fashioned against the background of knowledge that unrestricted power of search and seizure could also be an instrument for stifling liberty of expression. For the serious hazard of suppression of innocent expression inhered in the discretion confided in the officers authorized to exercise the power.

II

The question here is whether the use by Missouri in this case of the search and seizure power to suppress obscene publications involved abuses inimical to protected expression. We held in Roth v. United States, 354 U. S. 476, 354 U. S. 485, [23] that "obscenity is not within the area of constitutionally protected speech or press." But, in

Roth itself, we expressly recognized the complexity of the test of obscenity fashioned in that case and the vital necessity in its application of safeguards to prevent denial of "the protection of freedom of speech and press for material which does not treat sex in a manner appealing to prurient interest." Id., p. 354 U. S. 488. We have since held that a State's power to suppress obscenity is limited by the constitutional protections for free expression. In Smith v. California, 361 U. S. 147, 361 U. S. 155, we said,

"The existence of the State's power to prevent the distribution of obscene matter does not mean that there can be no constitutional barrier to any form of practical exercise of that power,"

inasmuch as "our holding in Roth does not recognize any state power to restrict the dissemination of books which are not obscene." Id., p. 361 U. S. 152. We therefore held that a State may not impose absolute criminal liability on a bookseller for the possession of obscene material even if it may dispense with the element of scienter in dealing with such evils as impure food and drugs. We remarked the distinction between the cases:

"There is no specific constitutional inhibition against making the distributors of food the strictest censors of their merchandise, but the constitutional guarantees of the freedom of speech and of the press stand in the way of imposing a similar requirement on the bookseller."

Id. at 361 U. S. 152-153. The Missouri Supreme Court's assimilation of obscene literature to gambling paraphernalia or other contraband for purposes of search and seizure does not, therefore, answer the appellants' constitutional claim, but merely restates the issue whether obscenity may be treated in the same way. The authority to the police officers under the warrants issued in this case, broadly to seize "obscene . . . publications," poses problems not raised by the warrants to seize "gambling implements" and "all intoxicating liquors" involved in the cases cited by the Missouri Supreme Court. 334 S.W.2d at page 125. For the use of these warrants implicates questions whether the procedures leading to their issuance and surrounding their execution were adequate to avoid suppression of constitutionally protected publications.

". . . [T]he line between speech unconditionally guaranteed and speech which may legitimately be regulated, suppressed, or punished is finely drawn. . . . The separation of legitimate from illegitimate speech calls for . . . sensitive tools. . . ."

Speiser v. Randall, 357 U. S. 513, 357 U. S. 525. [24] It follows that, under the Fourteenth Amendment, a State is not free to adopt whatever procedures it pleases for dealing with obscenity as here involved, without regard to the possible consequences for constitutionally protected speech.

We believe that Missouri's procedures, as applied in this case, lacked the safeguards which due process demands to assure nonobscene material the constitutional protection to which it is entitled. Putting to one side the fact that no opportunity was afforded the appellants to elicit and contest the reasons for the officer's belief, or otherwise to argue against the propriety of the seizure to the issuing judge, still the warrants issued on the strength of the conclusory assertions of a single police officer, without any scrutiny by the judge of any materials considered by the complainant to be obscene. The warrants gave the broadest discretion to the executing officers; they merely repeated the language of the statute and the complaints, specified no publications, and left to the individual judgment of each of the many police officers involved the selection of such magazines as in his view constituted "obscene . . . publications." So far as appears from the record, none of the officers except Lieutenant Coughlin had previously examined any of the publications which were subsequently seized. It is plain that, in many instances, if not in all, each officer actually made ad hoc decisions on the spot and, gauged by the number of publications seized and the time spent in executing the warrants, each decision was made with little opportunity for reflection and deliberation. As to publications seized because they appeared on the Lieutenant's list, we know nothing of the basis for the original judgment that they were obscene. It is no reflection on the good faith or judgment of the officers to conclude that the task they were assigned was simply an impossible one to perform with any realistic expectation that the obscene might be accurately separated from the constitutionally protected. They were provided with no guide to the exercise of informed discretion, because there was no step in the procedure before seizure designed to focus searchingly on the question of obscenity. See generally 1 Chafee, Government and Mass Communications, pp. 200-218. In consequence, there were suppressed and withheld from the market for over two months 180 publications not found obscene. [25] The fact that only one-third of the publications seized were finally condemned strengthens the conclusion that discretion to seize allegedly obscene materials cannot be confided to law enforcement officials without greater safeguards than were here operative. Procedures which sweep so broadly and with so little discrimination are obviously deficient in techniques required by the Due Process Clause of the Fourteenth Amendment to prevent erosion of the constitutional guarantees. [26]

III

The reliance of the Missouri Supreme Court upon Kingsley Books, Inc., v. Brown, 354 U. S. 436, is misplaced. The differences in the procedures under the New York statute upheld in that case and the Missouri procedures as applied here are marked. They amount to the distinction between "a "limited injunctive remedy," under closely defined procedural safeguards, against the sale and distribution of written and printed matter found after due trial to be obscene," Kingsley Books, supra, at 354 U. S. 437, and a scheme which, in operation, inhibited the circulation of publications indiscriminately because of the absence of any such safeguards. First, the New York injunctive proceeding was initiated by a complaint filed with the court which charged that a particular named obscene publication had been displayed, and to which were annexed copies of the publication alleged to be obscene. [27] The court, in restraining distribution pending final judicial determination of the claim, thus had the allegedly obscene material before it, and could exercise an independent check on the judgment of the prosecuting authority at a point before any restraint took place. Second, the restraints in Kingsley Books, both temporary and permanent, ran only against the named publication; no catchall restraint against the distribution of all "obscene" material was imposed on the defendants there, comparable to the warrants here which authorized a mass seizure and the removal of a broad range of items from circulation. [28] Third, Kingsley Books does not support the proposition that the State may impose the extensive restraints imposed here on the distribution of these publications prior to an adversary proceeding on the issue of obscenity, irrespective of whether or not the material is legally obscene. This Court expressly noted there that the State was not attempting to punish the distributors for disobedience of any interim order entered before hearing. The Court pointed out that New York might well construe its own law as not imposing any punishment for violation of an interim order were the book found not obscene after due trial. 354 U.S. at 354 U. S. 443, note 2. But there is no doubt that an effective restraint -- indeed, the most effective restraint possible -- was imposed prior to hearing on the circulation of the publications in this case, because all copies on which the police could lay their hands were physically removed from the newsstands and from the premises of the wholesale distributor. An opportunity comparable to that which the distributor in Kingsley Books might have had to circulate the publication despite the interim restraint and then raise the claim of nonobscenity by way of defense to a prosecution for doing so was never afforded these appellants because the copies they possessed were taken away. Their ability to circulate their publications was left to the chance of securing other copies, themselves subject to mass seizure under other such warrants. The public's opportunity to obtain the publications was thus determined by the distributor's readiness and ability to outwit the police by obtaining and selling other copies before they, in turn, could be seized. In addition to its unseemliness, we do not believe that this kind of enforced competition affords a reasonable likelihood that nonobscene publications, entitled to constitutional protection, will reach the public. A distributor may have every reason to believe that a publication is constitutionally protected and will be so held after judicial hearing, but his belief is unavailing as against the contrary judgment of the police officer who seizes it from him. [29] Finally, a subdivision of the New York statute in Kingsley Books required that a judicial decision on the merits of obscenity be made within two days of trial, which, in turn, was required to be within one day of the joinder of issue on the request for an injunction. [30] In contrast, the Missouri statutory scheme drawn in question here has no limitation on the time within which decision must be made -- only a provision for rapid trial of the issue of obscenity. And, in fact,over two months elapsed between seizure and decision. [31] In these circumstances, the restraint on the circulation of publications was far more thoroughgoing and drastic than any restraint upheld by this Court in Kingsley Books.

Mass seizure in the fashion of this case was thus effected without any safeguards to protect legitimate expression. The judgment of the Missouri Supreme Court sustaining the condemnation of the 100 publications therefore cannot be sustained. We have no occasion to reach the question of the correctness of the finding that the publications are obscene. Nor is it necessary for us to decide in this case whether Missouri lacks all power under its statutory scheme to seize and condemn obscene material. Since a violation of the Fourteenth Amendment infected the proceedings, in order to vindicate appellants' constitutional rights, the judgment is reversed, and the cause is remanded for further proceedings not inconsistent with this opinion.

It is so ordered.

## Manual Enterprises, Inc. v. Day (June 25, 1962) [Notes omitted]

MR. JUSTICE HARLAN announced the judgment of the Court and an opinion in which MR. JUSTICE STEWART joins.

This case draws in question a ruling of the Post Office Department, sustained both by the District Court and the Court of Appeals, 110 U.S.App.D.C. 78, 289 F.2d 455, barring from the mails a shipment of petitioners' magazines. That ruling was based on alternative determinations that the magazines (1) were themselves "obscene," and (2) gave information as to where obscene matter could be obtained, thus rendering them nonmailable under two separate provisions of 18 U.S.C. § 1461, known as the Comstock Act. [1] Certiorari was granted (368 U.S. 809) to consider the claim that this ruling was inconsistent with the proper interpretation and application of § 1461, and with principles established in two of this Court's prior decisions. Roth v. United States, 354 U. S. 476; Smith v. California, 361 U. S. 147. [2]

Petitioners are three corporations respectively engaged in publishing magazines titled MANual, Trim, and Grecian Guild Pictorial. They have offices at the same address in Washington, D.C., and a common president, one Herman L. Womack. The magazines consist largely of photographs of nude, or near-nude, male models, and give the names of each model and the photographer, together with the address of the latter. They also contain a number of advertisements by independent photographers offering nudist photographs for sale.

On March 25, 1960, six parcels containing an aggregate of 405 copies of the three magazines, destined from Alexandria, Virginia, to Chicago, Illinois, were detained by the Alexandria postmaster, pending a ruling by his superiors at Washington as to whether the magazines were "nonmailable." After an evidentiary hearing before the Judicial Officer of the Post Office Department, there ensued the administrative and court decisions now under review.

I

On the issue of obscenity, as distinguished from unlawful advertising, the case comes to us with the following administrative findings, which are supported by substantial evidence and which we, and indeed the parties, for the most part, themselves, accept: (1) the magazines are not, as asserted by petitioners, physical culture or "body-building" publications, but are composed primarily, if not exclusively, for homosexuals, and have no literary, scientific or other merit; [3] (2) they would appeal to the "prurient interest" of such sexual deviates, but would not have any interest for sexually normal individuals; and (3) the magazines are read almost entirely by homosexuals, and possibly a few adolescent males; the ordinary male adult would not normally buy them.

On these premises, the question whether these magazines are "obscene," as it was decided below and argued before us, was thought to depend solely on a determination as to the relevant "audience" in terms of which their "prurient interest" appeal should be judged. This view of the obscenity issue evidently stemmed from the belief that, in Roth v. United States, 354 U. S. 476, 354 U. S. 489, this Court established the following single test for determining whether challenged material is obscene:

"whether to the average person, applying contemporary community standards, the dominant theme of the material taken as a whole appeals to prurient interest."

(Footnote omitted.) On this basis, the Court of Appeals, rejecting the petitioners' contention that the "prurient interest" appeal of the magazines should be judged in terms of their likely impact on the "average person," even though not a likely recipient of the magazines, held that the administrative finding respecting their impact on the "average homosexual" sufficed to establish the Government's case as to their obscenity.

We do not reach the question thus thought below to be dispositive on this aspect of the case. For we find lacking in these magazines an element which, no less than "prurient interest," is essential to a valid determination of obscenity under § 1461, and to which neither the Post Office Department nor the Court of Appeals addressed itself at all: these magazines cannot be deemed so offensive on their face as to affront current community standards of decency -- a quality that we shall hereafter refer to as "patent offensiveness" or "indecency." Lacking that quality, the magazines cannot be deemed legally "obscene," and we need not consider the question of the proper "audience" by which their "prurient interest" appeal should be judged.

The words of § 1461, "obscene, lewd, lascivious, indecent, filthy or vile," connote something that is portrayed in a manner so offensive as to make it unacceptable under current community mores. While, in common usage, the words have different shades of meaning, [4] the statute since its inception has always been taken as aimed at obnoxiously debasing portrayals of sex. [5] Although the statute condemns such material irrespective of the effect it may have upon those into whose hands it falls, the early case of United States v. Bennett, 24 Fed.Cas. p. 1093, No. 14571, put a limiting gloss upon the statutory language: the statute reaches only indecent material which, as now expressed in Roth v. United States, supra, at 354 U. S. 489, "taken as a whole appeals to prurient interest." This "effect" element, originally cast in somewhat different language from that of Roth (see 354 U.S. at 354 U. S. 487, 354 U. S. 489), was taken into federal obscenity law from the leading English case of Regina v. Hicklin, [1868] L.R. 3 Q.B. 360, of which a distinguished Australian judge has given the following illuminating analysis:

"As soon as one reflects that the word 'obscene,' as an ordinary English word, has nothing to do with corrupting or depraving susceptible people, and that it is used to describe things which are offensive to current standards of decency, and not things which may induce to sinful thoughts, it becomes plain, I think, that Cockburn, C.J., in . . . R. v. Hicklin . . . was not propounding a logical definition of the word 'obscene,' but was merely explaining that particular characteristic which was necessary to bring an obscene publication within the law relating to obscene libel. [6] The tendency to deprave is not the characteristic which makes a publication obscene, but is the characteristic which makes an obscene publication criminal. It is at once an essential element in the crime and the justification for the intervention of the common law. But it is not the whole and sole test of what constitutes an obscene libel. There is no obscene libel unless what is published is both offensive according to current standards of decency and calculated or likely to have the effect described in R. v. Hicklin. . . . [7]"

Regina v. Close, [1948] Vict.L.R. 445, 463, Judgment of Fullagar, J. (Emphasis in original.)

The thoughtful studies of the American Law Institute reflect the same two-fold concept of obscenity. Its earlier draft of a Model Penal Code contains the following definition of "obscene":

"A thing is obscene if, considered as a whole, its predominant appeal is to prurient interest . . . and if it goes substantially beyond customary limits of candor in description or representation of such matters."

A.L.I., Model Penal Code, Tent. Draft No. 6 (1957), § 207.10(2). (Emphasis added.) The same organization's currently proposed definition reads:

"Material is obscene if, considered as a whole, its predominant appeal is to prurient interest . . . and if, in addition, it goes substantially beyond customary limits of candor in describing or representing such matters."

A.L.I., Model Penal Code, Proposed Official Draft (May 4, 1962), § 251.4(1). (Emphasis added.) [8]

Obscenity under the federal statute thus requires proof of two distinct elements: (1) patent offensiveness; and (2) "prurient interest" appeal. Both must conjoin before challenged material can be found "obscene" under § 1461. In most obscenity cases, to be sure, the two elements tend to coalesce, for that which is patently offensive will also usually carry the requisite "prurient interest" appeal. It is only in the unusual instance where, as here, the "prurient interest" appeal of the material is found limited to a particular class of persons that occasion arises for a truly independent inquiry into the question whether or not the material is patently offensive.

The Court of Appeals was mistaken in considering that Roth made "prurient interest" appeal the sole test of obscenity. [9] Reading that case as dispensing with the requisite of patently offensive portrayal would be not only inconsistent with § 1461 and its common law background, but out of keeping with Roth's evident purpose to tighten obscenity standards. The Court there both rejected the "isolated excerpt" and "particularly susceptible persons" tests of the Hicklin case, 354 U.S. at 354 U. S. 488-489, and was at pains to point out that not all portrayals of sex could be reached by obscenity laws, but only those treating that subject "in a manner appealing to prurient interest."

354 U.S. at 354 U. S. 487. That, of course, was but a compendious way of embracing in the obscenity standard both the concept of patent offensiveness, manifested by the terms of § 1461 itself, and the element of the likely corruptive effect of the challenged material, brought into federal law via Regina v. Hicklin.

To consider that the "obscenity" exception in "the area of constitutionally protected speech or press," Roth at 354 U. S. 485, does not require any determination as to the patent offensiveness vel non of the material itself might well put the American public in jeopardy of being denied access to many worthwhile works in literature, science, or art. For one would not have to travel far even among the acknowledged masterpieces in any of these fields to find works whose "dominant theme" might, not beyond reason, be claimed to appeal to the "prurient interest" of the reader or observer. We decline to attribute to Congress any such quixotic and deadening purpose as would bar from the mails all material, not patently offensive, which stimulates impure desires relating to sex. Indeed, such a construction of § 1461 would doubtless encounter constitutional barriers. Roth at 354 U. S. 487-489. Consequently we consider the power exercised by Congress in enacting § 1461 as no more embracing than the interdiction of "obscenity" as it had theretofore been understood. It is only material whose indecency is self-demonstrating and which, from the standpoint of its effect, may be said predominantly to appeal to the prurient interest that Congress has chosen to bar from the mails by the force of § 1461.

We come then to what we consider the dispositive question on this phase of the case. Are these magazines offensive on their face? Whether this question be deemed one of fact or of mixed fact and law, see Lockhart and McClure, Censorship of Obscenity: The Developing Constitutional Standards, 45 Minn.L.Rev. 5, 114-115 (1960), we see no need of remanding the case for initial consideration by the Post Office Department or the Court of Appeals of this missing factor in their determinations. That issue, involving factual matters entangled in a constitutional claim, see Grove Press, Inc. v. Christenberry, 276 F.2d 433, 436, is ultimately one for this Court. The relevant materials being before us, we determine the issue for ourselves.

There must first be decided the relevant "community" in terms of whose standards of decency the issue must be judged. We think that the proper test under this federal statute, reaching as it does to all parts of the United States whose population reflects many different ethnic and cultural backgrounds, is a national standard of decency. We need not decide whether Congress could constitutionally prescribe a lesser geographical framework for judging this issue [10] which would not have the intolerable consequence of denying some sections of the country access to material, there deemed acceptable, which in others might be considered offensive to prevailing community standards of decency. Cf. Butler v. Michigan, 352 U. S. 380.

As regards the standard for judging the element of "indecency," the Roth case gives little guidance beyond indicating that the standard is a constitutional one which, as with "prurient interest," requires taking the challenged material "as a whole." Roth at 354 U. S. 489. Being ultimately concerned only with the question whether the First and

Fourteenth Amendments protect material that is admittedly obscene, [11] the Court there had no occasion to explore the application of a particular obscenity standard. At least one important state court and some authoritative commentators have considered Roth and subsequent cases [12] to indicate that only "hard core" pornography can constitutionally be reached under this or similar state obscenity statutes. See, People v. Richmond County News, Inc., 9 N.Y.2d 578, 216 N.Y.S.2d 369, 175 N.E.2d 681; Lockhart and McClure, supra, at 58-60. Whether "hard core" pornography, or something less, be the proper test, we need go no further in the present case than to hold that the magazines in question, taken as a whole, cannot, under any permissible constitutional standard, be deemed to be beyond the pale of contemporary notions of rudimentary decency.

We cannot accept in full the Government's description of these magazines which, contrary to Roth (354 U.S. at 354 U. S. 488-489), tends to emphasize and in some respects overdraw certain features in several of the photographs at the expense of what the magazines, fairly taken as a whole, depict. [13] Our own independent examination of the magazines leads us to conclude that the most that can be said of them is that they are dismally unpleasant, uncouth, and tawdry. But this is not enough to make them "obscene." Divorced from their "prurient interest" appeal to the unfortunate persons whose patronage they were aimed at capturing (a separate issue), these portrayals of the male nude cannot fairly be regarded as more objectionable than many portrayals of the female nude that society tolerates. Of course, not every portrayal of male or female nudity is obscene. See Parmelee v. United States, 72 App.D.C. 203, 206-208, 113 F.2d 729, 732-734; Sunshine Book Co. v. Summerfield, 355 U. S. 372; Mounce v. United States, 355 U. S. 180. Were we to hold that these magazines, although they do not transcend the prevailing bounds of decency, may be denied access to the mails by such undifferentiated legislation as that before us, we would be ignoring the admonition that

"the door . . . into this area [the First Amendment] cannot be left ajar; it must be kept tightly closed, and opened only the slightest crack necessary to prevent encroachment upon more important interests."

(Footnote omitted.). Roth at 354 U. S. 488. [14]

We conclude that the administrative ruling respecting nonmailability is improvident insofar as it depends on a determination that these magazines are obscene.

II

There remains the question of the advertising. It is not contended that the petitioners held themselves out as purveyors of obscene material, or that the advertisements, as distinguished from the other contents of the magazines, were obscene on their own account. The advertisements were all by independent third-party photographers. And neither with respect to the advertisements nor the magazines themselves do we understand the Government to suggest that the "advertising" provisions of § 1461 are violated if the mailed material merely "gives the leer that promises the customer some obscene pictures." United States v. Hornick, 229 F.2d 120, 121. Such an approach to the statute could not withstand the underlying precepts of Roth.

See Poss v. Christenberry, 179 F.Supp. 411, 415; cf. United States v. Schillaci, 166 F.Supp. 303, 306. The claim on this branch of the case rests, then, on the fact that some of the third-party advertisers were found in possession of what undoubtedly may be regarded as "hard core" photographs, [15] and that postal officials, although not obtaining the names of the advertisers from the lists in petitioners' magazines, received somewhat less offensive material through the mails from certain studios which were advertising in petitioners' magazines.

A question of law must first be dealt with. Should the "obscene advertising" proscription of § 1461 be construed as not requiring proof that the publisher knew that at least some of his advertisers were offering to sell obscene material? In other words, although the criminal provisions of § 1461 do require scienter ( note 1 supra), can the Post Office Department, in civil proceedings under that section, escape with a lesser burden of proof? We are constrained to a negative answer. First, Congress has required scienter in respect of one indicted for mailing material proscribed by the statute. In the constitutional climate in which this statute finds itself, we should hesitate to attribute to Congress a purpose to render a publisher civilly responsible for the innocuous advertisements of the materials of others in the absence of any showing that he knew that the character of such materials was offensive. And with no express grant of authority to the Post Office Department to keep obscene matter from the mails (see note 2 supra), we should be slow to accept the suggestion that an element of proof expressly required in a criminal proceeding may be omitted in an altogether parallel civil proceeding. Second, this Court's ground of decision in Smith v. California, 361 U. S. 147, indicates that a substantial constitutional question would arise were we to construe § 1461 as not requiring proof of scienter in civil proceedings. For the power of the Post Office to bar a magazine from the mails, if exercised without proof of the publisher's knowledge of the character of the advertisements included in the magazine, would as effectively "impose a severe limitation on the public's access to constitutionally protected matter," 361 U.S. at 361 U. S. 153, as would a state obscenity statute which makes criminal the possession of obscene material without proof of scienter. Since publishers cannot practicably be expected to investigate each of their advertisers, and since the economic consequences of an order barring even a single issue of a periodical from the mails might entail heavy financial sacrifice, a magazine publisher might refrain from accepting advertisements from those whose own materials could conceivably be deemed objectionable by the Post Office Department. This would deprive such materials, which might otherwise be entitled to constitutional protection, of a legitimate and recognized avenue of access to the public. To be sure, the Court found it unnecessary in Smith to delineate the scope of scienter which would satisfy the Fourteenth Amendment. Yet it may safely be said that a federal statute which, as we construe it, required the presence of that element is not satisfied, as the Government suggests it might be, merely by showing that a defendant did not make a "good faith effort" to ascertain the character of his advertiser's materials.

On these premises, we turn to the record in this case. Although postal officials had informed petitioners' president, Womack, that their Department was prosecuting several of his advertisers for sending obscene matter through the mails, there is no evidence that any of this material was shown to him. He thus was afforded no opportunity to judge for himself as to its alleged obscenity. Contrariwise, one of the government witnesses at the administrative hearing admitted that the petitioners had deleted the advertisements of several photographic studios after being informed by the Post Office that the proprietors had been convicted of mailing obscene material. [16]

The record reveals that none of the postal officials who received allegedly obscene matter from some of the advertisers obtained their names from petitioners' magazines; this material was received as a result of independent test checks. Nor, on the record before us, can petitioners be linked with the material seized by the police. Note 15 supra. The only such asserted connection -- that "hard core" matter was seized at the studio of one of petitioners' advertisers -- falls short of an adequate showing that petitioners knew that the advertiser was offering for sale obscene matter. Womack's own conviction for sending obscene material through the mails, Womack v. United States, 111 U.S.App.D.C. 8, 294 F.2d 204, is remote from proof of like conduct on the part of the advertisers. At that time, he was acting as president of another studio; the vendee of the material, while an advertiser in petitioners' magazines, had closed his own studio before the present issues were published. Finally, the general testimony by one postal inspector to the effect that, in his experience, advertisers of this character, after first leading their customers on with borderline material, usually followed up with "hard core" matter, can hardly be deemed of probative significance on the issue at hand.

At best, the Government's proof showed no more than that petitioners were chargeable with knowledge that these advertisers were offering photographs of the same character, and with the same purposes, as those reflected in their own magazines. This is not enough to satisfy the Government's burden of proof on this score. [17]

In conclusion, nothing in this opinion of course remotely implies approval of the type of magazines published by these petitioners, still less of the sordid motives which prompted their publication. All we decide is that, on this record, these particular magazines are not subject to repression under § 1461.

Reversed.


## Bantam Books, Inc. v. Sullivan (February 18, 1963)

MR. JUSTICE BRENNAN delivered the opinion of the Court.

The Rhode Island Legislature created the "Rhode Island Commission to Encourage Morality in Youth," whose members and Executive Secretary are the appellees herein, and gave the Commission, inter alia,

"... the duty ... to educate the public concerning any book, picture, pamphlet, ballad, printed paper or other thing containing obscene, indecent or impure language, or manifestly tending to the corruption of the youth as defined in sections 13, 47, 48 and 49 of chapter 610 of the general laws, as amended, and to investigate and recommend the prosecution of all violations of said sections. . . . [1]"

The appellants brought this action in the Superior Court of Rhode Island (1) to declare the law creating the Commission in violation of the First and Fourteenth Amendments, and (2) to declare unconstitutional and enjoin the acts and practices of the appellees thereunder. The Superior Court declined to declare the law creating the Commission unconstitutional on its face, but granted the appellants an injunction against the acts and practices of the appellees in performance of their duties. The Supreme Court of Rhode Island affirmed the Superior Court with respect to appellants first prayer, but reversed the grant of injunctive relief. ___ R.I. ___, 176 A.2d 393 (1961). [2] Appellants brought this appeal, and we noted probable jurisdiction, 370 U.S. 933. [3]

Appellants are four New York publishers of paperback books which have for sometime been widely distributed in Rhode Island. Max Silverstein & Sons is the exclusive wholesale distributor of appellants publications throughout most of the State. The Commission's practice has been to notify a distributor on official Commission stationery that certain designated books or magazines distributed by him had been reviewed by the Commission and had been declared by a majority of its members to be objectionable for sale, distribution or display to youths under 18 years of age. Silverstein had received at least 35 such notices at the time this suit was brought. Among the paperback books listed by the Commission as "objectionable" were one published by appellant Dell Publishing Co., Inc., and another published by appellant Bantam Books, Inc. [4]

The typical notice to Silverstein either solicited or thanked Silverstein, in advance, for his "cooperation" with the Commission, usually reminding Silverstein of the Commission's duty to recommend to the Attorney General prosecution of purveyors of obscenity. [5] Copies of the lists of "objectionable" publications were circulated to local police departments, and Silverstein was so informed in the notices.

Silverstein's reaction on receipt of a notice was to take steps to stop further circulation of copies of the listed publications. He would not fill pending orders for such publications, and would refuse new orders. He instructed his field men to visit his retailers and to pick up all unsold copies, and would then promptly return them to the publishers. A local police officer usually visited Silverstein shortly after Silverstein's receipt of a notice to learn what action he had taken. Silverstein was usually able to inform the officer that a specified number of the total of copies received from a publisher had been returned. According to the testimony, Silverstein acted as he did on receipt of the notice "rather than face the possibility of some sort of a court action against ourselves, as well as the people that we supply." His "cooperation" was given to avoid becoming involved in a "court proceeding" with a "duly authorized organization."

The Superior Court made fact findings and the following two, supported by the evidence and not rejected by the Supreme Court of Rhode Island, are particularly relevant:

"8. The effect of the said notices (those received by Silverstein, including the two listing publications of appellants) were [sic] clearly to intimidate the various book and magazine wholesale distributors and retailers and to cause them, by reason of such intimidation and threat of prosecution, (a) to refuse to take new orders for the proscribed publications, (b) to cease selling any of the copies on hand, (c) to withdraw from retailers all unsold copies, and (d) to return all unsold copies to the publishers."

"9. The activities of the Respondents (appellees here) have resulted in the suppression of the sale and circulation of the books listed in said notices. . . ."

In addition to these findings, it should be noted that the Attorney General of Rhode Island conceded on oral argument in this Court that the books listed in the notices included several that were not obscene within this Court's definition of the term.

Appellants argue that the Commission's activities under Resolution 73, as amended, amount to a scheme of governmental censorship devoid of the constitutionally required safeguards for state regulation of obscenity, and thus abridge First Amendment liberties, protected by the Fourteenth Amendment from infringement by the States. We agree that the activities of the Commission are unconstitutional, and therefore reverse the Rhode Island court's judgment and remand the case for further proceedings not inconsistent with this opinion. [6]

We held in Alberts v. California, decided with Roth v. United States, 354 U. S. 476, 354 U. S. 485, that "obscenity is not within the area of constitutionally protected speech or press," and may therefore be regulated by the States. But this principle cannot be stated without an important qualification:

". . . [I]n Roth itself, we expressly recognized the complexity of the test of obscenity fashioned in that case and the vital necessity in its application of safeguards to prevent denial of 'the protection of freedom of speech and press for material which does not treat sex in a manner appealing to prurient interest.' [354 U.S. at 354 U. S. 488]. . . . It follows that, under the Fourteenth Amendment, a State is not free to adopt whatever procedures it pleases for dealing with obscenity . . . without regard to the possible consequences for constitutionally protected speech."

Marcus v. Search Warrant, 367 U. S. 717, 367 U. S. 730-731.

Thus, the Fourteenth Amendment requires that regulation by the States of obscenity conform to procedures that will ensure against the curtailment of constitutionally protected expression, which is often separated from obscenity only by a dim and uncertain line. It is characteristic of the freedoms of expression in general that they are vulnerable to gravely damaging, yet barely visible, encroachments. Our insistence that regulations of obscenity scrupulously embody the most rigorous procedural safeguards, Smith v. California, 361 U. S. 147; Marcus v. Search Warrant, supra, is therefore but a special instance of the larger principle that the freedoms of expression must be ringed about with adequate bulwarks. See, e.g., Thornhill v. Alabama, 310, U.S. 88; Winters v. New York, 333 U. S. 507; NAACP v. Button, 371 U. S. 415.

"[T]he line between speech unconditionally guaranteed and speech which may legitimately be regulated . . . is finely drawn. . . . The separation of legitimate from illegitimate speech calls for . . . sensitive tools. . . ."

    Speiser v. Randall, 357 U. S. 513, 357 U. S. 525.

    But, is it contended, these salutary principles have no application to the activities of the Rhode Island Commission, because it does not regulate or suppress obscenity, but simply exhorts booksellers and advises them of their legal rights. This contention, premised on the Commission's want of power to apply formal legal sanctions, is untenable. It is true that appellants books have not been seized or banned by the State, and that no one has been prosecuted for their possession or sale. But though the Commission is limited to informal sanctions -- the threat of invoking legal sanctions and other means of coercion, persuasion, and intimidation -- the record amply demonstrates that the Commission deliberately set about to achieve the suppression of publications deemed "objectionable," and succeeded in its aim. [7] We are not the first court to look through forms to the substance and recognize that informal censorship may sufficiently inhibit the circulation of publications to warrant injunctive relief. [8]

    It is not as if this were not regulation by the State of Rhode Island. The acts and practices of the members and Executive Secretary of the Commission disclosed on this record were performed under color of state law, and so constituted acts of the State within the meaning of the Fourteenth Amendment. Ex parte Young, 209 U. S. 123. Cf. Terry v. Adams, 345 U. S. 461. These acts and practices directly and designedly stopped the circulation of publications in many parts of Rhode Island. It is true, as noted by the Supreme Court of Rhode Island, that Silverstein was "free" to ignore the Commission's notices, in the sense that his refusal to "cooperate" would have violated no law. But it was found as a fact -- and the finding, being amply supported by the record, binds us -- that Silverstein's compliance with the Commission's directives was not voluntary. People do not lightly disregard public officers' thinly veiled threats to institute criminal proceedings against them if they do not come around, and Silverstein's reaction, according to uncontroverted testimony, was no exception to this general rule. The Commission's notices, phrased virtually as orders, reasonably understood to be such by the distributor, invariably followed up by police visitations, in fact stopped the circulation of the listed publications ex proprio vigore. It would be naive to credit the State's assertion that these blacklists are in the nature of mere legal advice when they plainly serve as instruments of regulation independent of the laws against obscenity. [9] Cf. Joint Anti-Fascist Refugee Committee v. McGrath, 341 U. S. 123.

    Herein lies the vice of the system. The Commission's operation is a form of effective state regulation superimposed upon the State's criminal regulation of obscenity and making such regulation largely unnecessary. In thus obviating the need to employ criminal sanctions, the State has at the same time eliminated the safeguards of the criminal process. Criminal sanctions may be applied only after a determination of obscenity has been made in a criminal trial hedged about with the procedural safeguards of the criminal process. The Commission's practice is in striking contrast, in that it provides no safeguards whatever against the suppression of nonobscene, and therefore constitutionally protected, matter. It is a form of regulation that creates hazards to protected freedoms markedly greater than those that attend reliance upon the criminal law.

What Rhode Island has done, in fact, has been to subject the distribution of publications to a system of prior administrative restraints, since the Commission is not a judicial body and its decisions to list particular publications as objectionable do not follow judicial determinations that such publications may lawfully be banned. Any system of prior restraints of expression comes to this Court bearing a heavy presumption against its constitutional validity. See Near v. Minnesota, 283 U. S. 697; Lovell v. City of Griffin, 303 U. S. 444, 303 U. S. 451; Schneider v. New Jersey, 308 U. S. 147, 308 U. S. 164; Cantwell v. Connecticut, 310 U. S. 296, 310 U. S. 306; Niemotko v. Maryland, 340 U. S. 268, 340 U. S. 273; Kunz v. New York, 340 U. S. 290, 340 U. S. 293; Staub v. City of Baxley, 355 U. S. 313, 355 U. S. 321. We have tolerated such a system only where it operated under judicial superintendence and assured an almost immediate judicial determination of the validity of the restraint. [10] Kingsley Books, Inc. v. Brown, 354 U. S. 436. The system at bar includes no such saving features. On the contrary, its capacity for suppression of constitutionally protected publications is far in excess of that of the typical licensing scheme held constitutionally invalid by this Court. There is no provision whatever for judicial superintendence before notices issue or even for judicial review of the Commission's determinations of objectionableness. The publisher or distributor is not even entitled to notice and hearing before his publications are listed by the Commission as objectionable. Moreover, the Commission's statutory mandate is vague and uninformative, and the Commission has done nothing to make it more precise. Publications are listed as "objectionable," without further elucidation. The distributor is left to speculate whether the Commission considers this publication obscene or simply harmful to juvenile morality. For the Commission's domain is the whole of youthful morals. Finally, we not that although the Commission's supposed concern is limited to youthful readers, the "cooperation" it seeks from distributors invariably entails the complete suppression of the listed publications; adult readers are equally deprived of the opportunity to purchase the publications in the State. Cf. Butler v. Michigan, 352 U. S. 380.

The procedures of the Commission are radically deficient. They fall far short of the constitutional requirements of governmental regulation of obscenity. We hold that the system of informal censorship disclosed by this record violates the Fourteenth Amendment.

In holding that the activities disclosed on this record are constitutionally proscribed, we do not mean to suggest that private consultation between law enforcement officers and distributors prior to the institution of a judicial proceeding can never be constitutionally permissible. We do not hold that law enforcement officers must renounce all informal contacts with persons suspected of violating valid laws prohibiting obscenity.

Where such consultation is genuinely undertaken with the purpose of aiding the distributor to comply with such laws and avoid prosecution under them, it need not retard the full enjoyment of First Amendment freedoms. But that is not this case. The appellees are not law enforcement officers; they do not pretend that they are qualified to give or that they attempt to give distributors only fair legal advice. Their conduct as disclosed by this record shows plainly that they went for beyond advising the distributors of their legal rights and liabilities. Their operation was in fact a scheme of state censorship effectuated by extra-legal sanctions; they acted as an agency not to advise but to suppress.

Reversed and remanded.

Notes

[1] Resolution No. 73 H 1000, R.I.Acts and Resolves, January Session 1956, 1102-1103. The resolution created a "commission to encourage morality in youth," to be composed of nine members appointed by the Governor of the State. The members were to serve for staggered, five-year terms. They were to receive no compensation, but their expenses, as well as the expenses incurred in the operation of the Commission generally, were to be defrayed out of annual appropriations. The original mandate of the Commission was superseded in part by Resolution No. 95 S. 444 R.I.Acts and Resolves, January Session 1959, 880, which reads as follows:

"It shall be the duty of said commission to educate the public concerning any book, picture, pamphlet, ballad, printed paper or other thing containing obscene, indecent or impure language, as defined in chapter 11-31 of the general laws, entitled 'Obscene and objectionable publications and shows,' and to investigate and recommend the prosecution of all violations of said sections, and it shall be the further duty of said commission to combat juvenile delinquency and encourage morality in youth by (a) investigating situations which may cause, be responsible for or give rise to undesirable behavior of juveniles, (b) educate the public as to these causes and (c) recommend legislation, prosecution and/or treatment which would ameliorate or eliminate said causes."

The Commission's activities are not limited to the circulation of lists of objectionable publications. For example, the annual report of the Commission issued in January 1960, recites in part:

"In September, 1959, because of the many complaints from outraged parents at the type of films being shown at the Rhode Island Drive-Ins and also the lack of teen-age supervision while parked, this Commission initiated and completed a survey on the Drive-In Theatres in the State. High points of the survey note that there are II (2) Drive-in theatres in Rhode Island which operate through summer months and remain open until November and then for week-ends during the winter, providing car heaters."

"* * * *"

"Acting on its power to investigate causes of delinquency, the Commission has met with several state officials for a discussion of juvenile drinking, the myriad and complex causes of delinquency, and legal aspects of the Commission's operations. It also held a special meeting with Rhode Island police and legal officials in September, 1959, for a discussion on the extent of delinquency in Rhode Island and the possible formation of statewide organization to combat it."

[2] The action was brought pursuant to Title 9, c. 30, Gen.Laws R.I., 1956 ed., as amended (Uniform Declaratory Judgments Act).

[3] Our appellate jurisdiction is properly invoked, since the state court judgment sought to be reviewed upheld a state statute against the contention that, on its face and applied, the statute violated the Federal Constitution. 28 U.S.C. § 1257(2). Dahnke-Walker Milling Co. v. Bondurant, 257 U. S. 282.

[4] Peyton Place, by Grace Metalious, published (in paperback edition) by appellant Dell Publishing Co., Inc.; The Bramble Bush, by Charles Mergendahl, published (in paperback edition) by appellant Bantam Books, Inc. Most of the other 106 publications which, as of January, 1960, had been listed as objectionable by the Commission were issues of such magazines as "Playboy," "Rogue," "Frolic," and so forth. The Attorney General of Rhode Island described some of the 106 publications as "horror" comics which he said were not obscene as this Court has defined the term.

[5] The first notice received by Silverstein reads, in part, as follows:

"This agency was established by legislative order in 1956 with the immediate charge to prevent the sale, distribution or display of indecent and obscene publications to youths and [sic] eighteen years of age."

"The Commissions (sic) have reviewed the following publications, and by majority vote have declared they are completely objectionable for sale, distribution or display for youths under eighteen years of age."

"The Chiefs of Police have been given the names of the aforementioned magazines with the order that they are not to be sold, distributed or displayed to youths and [sic] eighteen years of age."

"The Attorney General will act for us in case of noncompliance."

"The Commissioners trust that you will cooperate with this agency in their work. . . ."

"Another list will follow shortly."

"Thanking you for your anticipated cooperation, I am,"

"Sincerely yours"

"Albert J. McAloon"

"Executive Secretary"

Another notice received by Silverstein reads in part:

"This list should be used as a guide in judging other similar publications not named."

"Your cooperation in removing the listed and other objectionable publications from your newstands [sic] will be appreciated. Cooperative action will eliminate the necessity of our recommending prosecution to the Attorney General's department."

An undated "News Letter" sent to Silverstein by the Commission reads in part:

"The lists (of objectionable publications) have been sent to distributors and police departments. To the present, cooperation has been gratifying."

[6] Appellants standing has not been, nor could it be, successfully questioned. The appellants have in fact suffered a palpable injury as a result of the acts alleged to violate federal law, and at the same time their injury has been a legal injury. See Joint Anti-Fascist Refugee Committee v. McGrath, 341 U. S. 123, 341 U. S. 151-152 (concurring opinion). The finding that the Commission's notices impaired sales of the listed publications, which include two books published by appellants, establishes that appellants suffered injury. It was a legal injury, although more needs be said to demonstrate this. The Commission's notices were circulated only to distributors and not, so far as appears, to publishers. The Commission purports only to regulate distribution; it has made no claim to having jurisdiction of out-of-state publishers. However, if this were a private action, it would present a claim, plainly justiciable, of unlawful interference in advantageous business relations. American Mercury, Inc., v. Chase, 13 F.2d 224 (D.C.D.Mass.1926). Cf. 1 Harper and James, Torts (1956), §§ 6.11-6.12. See also Pocket Books, Inc. v. Walsh, 204 F.Supp. 297 (D.C.D.Conn.1962). It makes no difference, so far as appellants' standing is concerned, that the allegedly unlawful interference here is the product of state action. See Pierce v. Society of Sisters, 268 U. S. 510; Truax v. Raich, 239 U. S. 33; Terrace v. Thompson, 263 U. S. 197, 263 U. S. 214-216; Columbia Broadcasting System v. United States, 316 U. S. 407, 316 U. S. 422-423. Furthermore, appellants are not in the position of mere proxies arguing another's constitutional rights. The constitutional guarantee of freedom of the press embraces the circulation of books, as well as their publication, Lovell v. City of Griffin, 303 U. S. 444, 303 U. S. 452, and the direct and obviously intended result of the Commission's activities was to curtail the circulation in Rhode Island of books published by appellants. Finally, pragmatic considerations argue strongly for the standing of publishers in cases such as the present one. The distributor who is prevented from selling a few titles is not likely to sustain sufficient economic injury to induce him to seek judicial vindication of his rights. The publisher has the greater economic stake, because suppression of a particular book prevents him from recouping his investment in publishing it. Unless he is permitted to sue, infringements of freedom of the press may too often go unremedied. Cf. NAACP v. State of Alabama ex rel. Patterson, 357 U. S. 449, 357 U. S. 459.

[7] For discussions of the problem of "informal censorship," see Lockhart and McClure, Censorship of Obscenity: The Developing Constitutional Standards, 45 Minn.L.Rev. 5, 6-9 and n. 7-22 (1960); Note, Extra-legal Censorship of Literature, 33 N.Y.U.L.Rev. 989 (1958); Note, Entertainment: Public Pressures and the Law, 71 Harv.L.Rev. 326, 344-347 (1957); Note, Regulation of Comic Books, 68 Harv.L.Rev. 489, 494-499 (1955); Comment, Censorship of Obscene Literature by Informal Governmental Action, 22 Univ. of Chi.L.Rev. 216 (1954); Lockhart and McClure, Literature, the Law of

Obscenity, and the Constitution, 38 Minn.L.Rev. 295, 309-316 (1954).

[8] Threats of prosecution or of license revocation, or listings or notifications of supposedly obscene or objectionable publications or motion pictures, on the part of chiefs of police or prosecutors, have been enjoined in a number of cases. See Kingsley International Pictures Corp. v. Blanc, 396 Pa. 448, 153 A.2d 243 (1959); Bunis v. Conway, 17 A.D.2d 207, 234 N.Y.S.2d 435 (1962) (dictum); Sunshine Book Co. v. McCaffrey, 4 A.D.2d 643, 168 N.Y.S.2d 268 (1957); Random House, Inc., v. Detroit, No. 555684 Chancery, Cir.Ct., Wayne County, Mich., March 29, 1957; HMH Publishing Co. v. Garrett, 151 F.Supp. 903 (D.C.N.D.Ind.1957); New American Library of World Literature v. Allen, 114 F.Supp. 823 (D.C.N.D.Ohio 1953); Bantam Books, Inc. v. Melko, 25 N.J.Super. 292, 96 A.2d 47 (Chancery 1953), modified on other grounds, 14 N.J. 524, 103 A.2d 256 (1954); Dearborn Publishing Co. v. Fitzgerald, 271 F. 479 (D.C.N.D.Ohio 1921); Epoch Producing Corp. v. Davis, 19 Ohio N.P. (N.S.) 465 (C.P.1917). Cf. In re Louisiana News Co., 187 F.Supp. 241 (D.C.E.D.La.1960); Roper v. Winner, 244 S.W.2d 355, 357 (Tex.Civ.App.1951); American Mercury, Inc. v. Chase, 13 F.2d 224 (D.C.D.Mass.1926). Relief has been denied in the following cases: Pocket Books, Inc. v. Walsh, 204 F.Supp. 297 (D.C.D.Conn.1962); Dell Publishing Co. v. Beggans, 110 N.J.Eq. 72, 158 A. 765 (Chancery 1932). See also Magtab Publishing Corp. v. Howard, 169 F.Supp. 65 (D.C.W.D.La.1959). None of the foregoing cases presents the precise factual situation at bar, and we intimate no view one way or the other as to their correctness.

[9] We note that the Commission itself appears to have understood its function as the proscribing of objectionable publications, and not merely the giving of legal advice to distributors. See the first notice received by Silverstein, quoted in note 5 supra. The minutes of one of the Commission's meetings read in part:

". . . Father Flannery [a member of the Commission] noted that he had been called about magazines proscribed by the Commission remaining on sale after lists had been scent [sic] to distributors and police, to which Mr. McAloon suggested that it could be that the same magazines were seen, but that it probably was not the same edition proscribed by the Commission."

"Father Flannery questioned the statewide compliance by the police, or anyone else, to get the proscribed magazines off the stands. Mr. McAloon showed the Commissioners the questionnaires sent to the chiefs of police from this office and returned to us."

The minutes of another meeting read in part:

". . . Mr. Sullivan [member of the Commission] suggested calling the Cranston Chief of Police to inquire the reason Peyton Place was still being sold, distributed and displayed since the Police departments had been advised of the Commission's vote."

Of course, it is immaterial whether, in carrying on the function of censor, the Commission may have been exceeding its statutory authority. Its acts would still constitute state action. Ex parte Young, 209 U. S. 123. The issue of statutory authority was not raised or argued in this litigation.

Our holding that the scheme of informal censorship here constitutes state action is in no way inconsistent with Standard Computing Scale Co. v. Farrell, 249 U. S. 571. In that case, it was held that a bulletin of specifications issued by the State Superintendent of Weights and Measures could not be deemed state action for Fourteenth Amendment purposes because the bulletin was purely advisory; the decision turned on the fact that the bulletin was not coercive in purport.

[10] Nothing in the Court's opinion in Times Film Corp. v. Chicago, 365 U. S. 43, is inconsistent with the Court's traditional attitude of disfavor toward prior restraints of expression. The only question tendered to the Court in that case was whether a prior restraint was necessarily unconstitutional under all circumstances. In declining to hold prior restraints unconstitutional per se, the Court did not uphold the constitutionality of any specific such restraint. Furthermore, the holding was expressly confined to motion pictures.

## Jacobellis v. Ohio (June 22, 1964)

MR. JUSTICE BRENNAN announced the judgment of the Court and delivered an opinion in which MR. JUSTICE GOLDBERG joins.

Appellant, Nico Jacobellis, manager of a motion picture theater in Cleveland Heights, Ohio, was convicted on two counts of possessing and exhibiting an obscene film in violation of Ohio Revised Code (1963 Supp.), § 2905.34. [1] He was fined $500 on the first count and $2,000 on the second, and was sentenced to the workhouse if the fines were not paid. His conviction, by a court of three judges upon waiver of trial by jury, was affirmed by an intermediate appellate court, 115 Ohio App. 226, 175 N.E.2d 123, and by the Supreme Court of Ohio, 173 Ohio St. 22, 179 N.E.2d 777. We noted probable jurisdiction of the appeal, 371 U.S. 808, and subsequently restored the case to the calendar for reargument, 373 U.S. 901. The dispositive question is whether the state courts properly found that the motion picture involved, a French film called "Les Amants" ("The Lovers"), was obscene, and hence not entitled to the protection for free expression that is guaranteed by the First and Fourteenth Amendments. We conclude that the film is not obscene, and that the judgment must accordingly be reversed.

Motion pictures are within the ambit of the constitutional guarantees of freedom of speech and of the press. Joseph Burstyn, Inc. v. Wilson, 343 U. S. 495. But, in Roth v. United States and Alberts v. California, 354 U. S. 476, we held that obscenity is not subject to those guarantees. Application of an obscenity law to suppress a motion picture thus requires ascertainment of the "dim and uncertain line" that often separates obscenity from constitutionally protected expression. Bantam Books, Inc. v. Sullivan, 372 U. S. 58, 372 U. S. 66; see Speiser v. Randall, 357 U. S. 513, 357 U. S. 525. [2] It has been suggested that this is a task in which our Court need not involve itself. We are told that the determination whether a particular motion picture, book, or other work of expression is obscene can be treated as a purely factual judgment on which a jury's verdict is all but conclusive, or that, in any event, the decision can be left essentially to state and lower federal courts, with this Court exercising only a limited review such as that needed to determine whether the ruling below is supported by "sufficient evidence." The suggestion is appealing, since it would lift from our shoulders a difficult, recurring, and unpleasant task. But we cannot accept it. Such an abnegation of judicial supervision in this field would be inconsistent with our duty to uphold the constitutional guarantees. Since it is only "obscenity" that is excluded from the constitutional protection, the question whether a particular work is obscene necessarily implicates an issue of constitutional law. See Roth v. United States, supra, 354 U.S. at 354 U. S. 497-498 (separate opinion). Such an issue, we think, must ultimately be decided by this Court. Our duty admits of no "substitute for facing up to the tough individual problems of constitutional judgment involved in every obscenity case." Id., at 354 U. S. 498; see Manual Enterprises, Inc. v. Day, 370 U. S. 478, 370 U. S. 488 (opinion of Harlan, J.). [3]

In other areas involving constitutional rights under the Due Process Clause, the Court has consistently recognized its duty to apply the applicable rules of law upon the basis of an independent review of the facts of each case. E.g., Watts v. Indiana, 338 U. S. 49, 338 U. S. 51; Norris v. Alabama, 294 U. S. 587, 294 U. S. 590. [4] And this has been particularly true where rights have been asserted under the First Amendment guarantees of free expression. Thus in Pennekamp v. Florida, 328 U. S. 331, 328 U. S. 335, the Court stated:

"The Constitution has imposed upon this Court final authority to determine the meaning and application of whose words of that instrument which require interpretation to resolve judicial issues. With that responsibility, we are compelled to examine for ourselves the statements in issue and the circumstances under which they were made to see whether or not they . . . are of a character which the principles of the First Amendment, as adopted by the Due Process Clause of the Fourteenth Amendment, protect. [5]"

We cannot understand why the Court's duty should be any different in the present case, where Jacobellis has been subjected to a criminal conviction for disseminating a work of expression, and is challenging that conviction as a deprivation of rights guaranteed by the First and Fourteenth Amendments. Nor can we understand why the Court's performance of its constitutional and judicial function in this sort of case should be denigrated by such epithets as "censor" or "super-censor." In judging alleged obscenity, the Court is no more "censoring" expression than it has in other cases "censored" criticism of judges and public officials, advocacy of governmental overthrow, or speech alleged to constitute a breach of the peace. Use of an opprobrious label can neither obscure nor impugn the Court's performance of its obligation to test challenged judgments against the guarantees of the First and Fourteenth Amendments, and, in doing so, to delineate the scope of constitutionally protected speech. Hence, we reaffirm the principle that, in "obscenity" cases, as in all others involving rights derived from the First Amendment guarantees of free expression, this Court cannot avoid making an independent constitutional judgment on the facts of the case as to whether the material involved is constitutionally protected. [6]

The question of the proper standard for making this determination has been the subject of much discussion and controversy since our decision in Roth seven years ago. Recognizing that the test for obscenity enunciated there --

"whether, to the average person, applying contemporary community standards, the dominant theme of the material, taken as a whole, appeals to prurient interest,"

354 U.S. at 354 U. S. 489 -- is not perfect, we think any substitute would raise equally difficult problems, and we therefore adhere to that standard. We would reiterate, however, our recognition in Roth that obscenity is excluded from the constitutional protection only because it is "utterly without redeeming social importance," and that

"[t]he portrayal of sex, e.g., in art, literature and scientific works, is not itself sufficient reason to deny material the constitutional protection of freedom of speech and press."

Id., 354 U.S. at 354 U. S. 484, 354 U. S. 487. It follows that material dealing with sex in a manner that advocates ideas, Kingsley Int'l Pictures Corp. v. Regents, 360 U. S. 684, or that has literary or scientific or artistic value or any other form of social importance, may not be branded as obscenity and denied the constitutional protection. [7] Nor may the constitutional status of the material be made to turn on a "weighing" of its social importance against its prurient appeal, for a work cannot be proscribed unless it is "utterly" without social importance. See Zeitlin v. Arnebergh, 59 Cal.2d 901, 920, 31 Cal.Rptr. 800, 813, 383 P.2d 152, 165 (1963). It should also be recognized that the Roth standard requires, in the first instance, a finding that the material "goes substantially beyond customary limits of candor in description or representation of such matters." This was a requirement of the Model Penal Code test that we approved in Roth, 354 U.S. at 354 U. S. 487, n. 20, and it is explicitly reaffirmed in the more recent Proposed Official Draft of the Code. [8] In the absence of such a deviation from society's standards of decency, we do not see how any official inquiry into the allegedly prurient appeal of a work of expression can be squared with the guarantees of the First and Fourteenth Amendments. See Manual Enterprises, Inc. v. Day, 370 U. S. 478, 370 U. S. 482-488 (opinion of Harlan, J.).

It has been suggested that the "contemporary community standards" aspect of the Roth test implies a determination of the constitutional question of obscenity in each case by the standards of the particular local community from which the case arises. This is an incorrect reading of Roth. The concept of "contemporary community standards" was first expressed by Judge Learned Hand in United States v. Kennerley, 209 F. 119, 121 (D.C.S.D.N.Y.1913), where he said:

"Yet, if the time is not yet when men think innocent all that which is honestly germane to a pure subject, however little it may mince its words, still I scarcely think that they would forbid all which might corrupt the most corruptible, or that society is prepared to accept for its own limitations those which may perhaps be necessary to the weakest of its memberships. If there be no abstract definition, such as I have suggested, should not the word 'obscene' be allowed to indicate the present critical point in the compromise between candor and shame at which the community may have arrived here and now? . . . To put thought in leash to the average conscience of the time is perhaps tolerable, but to fetter it by the necessities of the lowest and least capable seems a fatal policy."

"Nor is it an objection, I think, that such an interpretation gives to the words of the statute a varying meaning from time to time. Such words as these do not embalm the precise morals of an age or place; while they presuppose that some things will always be shocking to the public taste, the vague subject matter is left to the gradual development of general notions about what is decent. . . ."

(Italics added.) It seems clear that in this passage Judge Hand was referring not to state and local "communities," but rather to "the community" in the sense of "society at large; . . . the public, or people in general." [9] Thus, he recognized that, under his standard, the concept of obscenity would have "a varying meaning from time to time" -- not from county to county, or town to town.

We do not see how any "local" definition of the "community" could properly be employed in delineating the area of expression that is protected by the Federal Constitution. MR. JUSTICE HARLAN pointed out in Manual Enterprises, Inc. v. Day, supra, 370 U.S. at 370 U. S. 488, that a standard based on a particular local community would have

"the intolerable consequence of denying some sections of the country access to material, there deemed acceptable, which in others might be considered offensive to prevailing community standards of decency. Cf. Butler v. Michigan, 352 U. S. 380."

It is true that Manual Enterprises dealt with the federal statute banning obscenity from the mails. But the mails are not the only means by which works of expression cross local community lines in this country. It can hardly be assumed that all the patrons of a particular library, bookstand, or motion picture theater are residents of the smallest local "community" that can be drawn around that establishment. Furthermore, to sustain the suppression of a particular book or film in one locality would deter its dissemination in other localities where it might be held not obscene, since sellers and exhibitors would be reluctant to risk criminal conviction in testing the variation between the two places. It would be a hardy person who would sell a book or exhibit a film anywhere in the land after this Court had sustained the judgment of one "community" holding it to be outside the constitutional protection. The result would thus be "to restrict the public's access to forms of the printed word which the State could not constitutionally suppress directly." Smith v. California, 361 U. S. 147, 361 U. S. 154.

It is true that local communities throughout the land are, in fact, diverse, and that, in cases such as this one, the Court is confronted with the task of reconciling the rights of such communities with the rights of individuals. Communities vary, however, in many respects other than their toleration of alleged obscenity, and such variances have never been considered to require or justify a varying standard for application of the Federal Constitution. The Court has regularly been compelled, in reviewing criminal convictions challenged under the Due Process Clause of the Fourteenth Amendment, to reconcile the conflicting rights of the local community which brought the prosecution and of the individual defendant. Such a task is admittedly difficult and delicate, but it is inherent in the Court's duty of determining whether a particular conviction worked a deprivation of rights guaranteed by the Federal Constitution. The Court has not shrunk from discharging that duty in other areas, and we see no reason why it should do so here. The Court has explicitly refused to tolerate a result whereby "the constitutional limits of free expression in the Nation would vary with state lines," Pennekamp v. Florida, supra, 328 U.S. at 328 U. S. 335, we see even less justification for allowing such limits to vary with town or county lines. We thus reaffirm the position taken in Roth to the effect that the constitutional status of an allegedly obscene work must be determined on the basis of a national standard. [10] It is, after all, a national Constitution we are expounding.

We recognize the legitimate and indeed éxigent interest of States and localities throughout the Nation in preventing the dissemination of material deemed harmful to children. But that interest does not justify a total suppression of such material, the effect of which would be to "reduce the adult population . . . to reading only what is fit for children." Butler v. Michigan, 352 U. S. 380, 352 U. S. 383. State and local authorities might well consider whether their objectives in this area would be better served by laws aimed specifically at preventing distribution of objectionable material to children, rather than at totally prohibiting its dissemination. [11] Since the present conviction is based upon exhibition of the film to the public at large, and not upon its exhibition to children, the judgment must be reviewed under the strict standard applicable in determining the scope of the expression that is protected by the Constitution.

We have applied that standard to the motion picture in question. "The Lovers" involves a woman bored with her life and marriage who abandons her husband and family for a young archaeologist with whom she has suddenly fallen in love. There is an explicit love scene in the last reel of the film, and the State's objections are based almost entirely upon that scene. The film was favorably reviewed in a number of national publications, although disparaged in others, and was rated by at least two critics of national stature among the best films of the year in which it was produced. It was shown in approximately 100 of the larger cities in the United States, including Columbus and Toledo, Ohio. We have viewed the film, in the light of the record made in the trial court, and we conclude that it is not obscene within the standards enunciated in Roth v. United States and Alberts v. California, which we reaffirm here.

Reversed.

Notes
[1] "Selling, exhibiting, and possessing obscene literature or drugs for criminal purposes."

"No person shall knowingly sell, lend, give away, exhibit, or offer to sell, lend, give away, or exhibit, or publish or offer to publish or have in his possession or under his control an obscene, lewd, or lascivious book, magazine, pamphlet, paper, writing, advertisement, circular, print, picture, photograph, motion picture film, or book, pamphlet, paper, magazine not wholly obscene but containing lewd or lascivious articles, advertisements, photographs, or drawing, representation, figure, image, cast, instrument, or article of an indecent or immoral nature, or a drug, medicine, article, or thing intended for the prevention of conception or for causing an abortion, or advertise any of them for sale, or write, print, or cause to be written or printed a card, book, pamphlet, advertisement, or notice giving information when, where, how, of whom, or by what means any of such articles or things can be purchased or obtained, or manufacture, draw, print, or make such articles or things, or sell, give away, or show to a minor, a book, pamphlet, magazine, newspaper, story paper, or other paper devoted to the publication, or principally made up, of criminal news, police reports, or accounts of criminal deeds, or pictures and stories of immoral deeds, lust, or crime, or exhibit upon a street or highway or in a place which may be within the view of a minor, any of such books, papers, magazines, or pictures."

"Whoever violates this section shall be fined not less than two hundred nor more than two thousand dollars or imprisoned not less than one nor more than seven years, or both."

[2] It is too late in the day to argue that the location of the line is different, and the task of ascertaining it easier, when a state, rather than a federal, obscenity law is involved. The view that the constitutional guarantees of free expression do not apply as fully to the States as they do to the Federal Government was rejected in Roth-Alberts, supra, where the Court's single opinion applied the same standards to both a state and a federal conviction. Cf. Ker v. California, 374 U. S. 23, 374 U. S. 33; Malloy v. Hogan, 378 U. S. 1, 378 U. S. 10-11.

[3] See Kingsley Int'l Pictures Corp. v. Regents, 360 U. S. 684, 360 U. S. 708 (separate opinion):

"It is sometimes said that this Court should shun considering the particularities of individual cases in this difficult field, lest the Court become a final 'board of censorship.' But I cannot understand why it should be thought that the process of constitutional judgment in this realm somehow stands apart from that involved in other fields, particularly those presenting questions of due process. . . ."

See also Lockhart and McClure, Censorship of Obscenity: The Developing Constitutional Standards, 45 Minn.L.Rev. 5, 116 (1960):

"This obligation -- to reach an independent judgment in applying constitutional standards and criteria to constitutional issues that may be cast by lower courts 'in the form of determinations of fact' -- appears fully applicable to findings of obscenity by juries, trial courts, and administrative agencies. The Supreme Court is subject to that obligation, as is every court before which the constitutional issue is raised."

And see id. at 119:

"It may be true . . . that judges 'possess no special expertise' qualifying them 'to supervise the private morals of the Nation' or to decide 'what movies are good or bad for local communities.' But they do have a far keener understanding of the importance of free expression than do most government administrators or jurors, and they have had considerable experience in making value judgments of the type required by the constitutional standards for obscenity. If freedom is to be preserved, neither government censorship experts nor juries can be left to make the final effective decisions restraining free expression. Their decisions must be subject to effective, independent review, and we know of no group better qualified for that review than the appellate judges of this country under the guidance of the Supreme Court."

[4] See also Fiske v. Kansas, 274 U. S. 380, 274 U. S. 385-386; Haynes v. Washington, 373 U. S. 503, 373 U. S. 515-516; Chambers v. Florida, 309 U. S. 227, 309 U. S. 229; Hooven & Allison Co. v. Evatt, 324 U. S. 652, 324 U. S. 659; Lisenba v. California, 314 U. S. 219, 314 U. S. 237-238; Ashcraft v. Tennessee, 322 U. S. 143, 322 U. S. 147-148; Napue v. Illinois, 360 U. S. 264, 360 U. S. 271.

[5] See also Niemotko v. Maryland, 340 U. S. 268, 340 U. S. 271; Craig v. Harney, 331 U. S. 367, 331 U. S. 373-374; Bridges v. California, 314 U. S. 252, 314 U. S. 271; Edwards v. South Carolina, 372 U. S. 229, 372 U. S. 235; New York Times Co. v. Sullivan, 376 U. S. 254, 376 U. S. 285.

[6] This is precisely what the Court did in Times Film Corp. v. City of Chicago, 355 U. S. 35; One, Inc. v. Olesen, 355 U. S. 371; and Sunshine Book Co. v. Summerfield, 355 U. S. 372. The obligation has been recognized by state courts as well. See, e.g., State v. Hudson County News Co., 41 N.J. 247, 256-257, 196 A.2d 225, 230 (1963); Zeitlin v. Arnebergh, 59 Cal.2d 901, 909-911, 31 Cal.Rptr. 800, 805-806, 383 P.2d 152, 157-158 (1963); People v. Richmond County News, Inc., 9 N.Y.2d 578, 580-581, 216 N.Y.S.2d 369, 370, 175 N.E.2d 681, 681-682 (1961). See also American Law Institute, Model Penal Code, Proposed Official Draft (May 4, 1962), § 251.4(4).

Nor do we think our duty of constitutional adjudication in this area can properly be relaxed by reliance on a "sufficient evidence" standard of review. Even in judicial review of administrative agency determinations, questions of "constitutional fact" have been held to require de novo review. Ng Fung Ho v. White, 259 U. S. 276, 259 U. S. 284-285; Crowell v. Benson, 285 U. S. 22, 285 U. S. 54-65.

[7] See, e.g., Attorney General v. Book Named "Tropic of Cancer," 345 Mass. 11, 184 N.E.2d 328 (Mass.1962); Zeitlin v. Arnebergh, 59 Cal.2d 901, 31 Cal.Rptr. 800, 383 P.2d 152 (1963).

[8] American Law Institute, Model Penal Code, Proposed Official Draft (May 4, 1962), § 251.4(1):

"Material is obscene if, considered as a whole, its predominant appeal is to prurient interest . . ., and if, in addition, it goes substantially beyond customary limits of candor in describing or representing such matters."

(Italics added.)

[9] Webster's New International Dictionary (2d ed. 1949) at 542.

[10] See State v. Hudson County News Co., 41 N.J. 247, 266, 196 A.2d 225, 235 (1963). Lockhart and McClure, note 3 supra, 45 Minn.L.Rev. at 108-112; American Law Institute, Model Penal Code, Tentative Draft No. 6 (May 6, 1957) at 45; Proposed Official Draft (May 4, 1962), § 251.4(4)(d).

[11] See State v. Settle, 90 R.I. 195, 156 A.2d 921 (1959).

## A Quantity of Books v. Kansas (June 22, 1964)

MR. JUSTICE BRENNAN announced the judgment of the Court and delivered an opinion in which THE CHIEF JUSTICE, MR. JUSTICE WHITE, and MR. JUSTICE GOLDBERG join.

Under a Kansas statute authorizing the seizure of allegedly obscene books before an adversary determination of their obscenity and, after that determination, their destruction by burning or otherwise, [1] the Attorney General of Kansas obtained an order from the District Court of Geary County directing the sheriff of the county to seize and impound, pending hearing, copies of certain paperback novels at the place of business of P-K News Service, Junction City, Kansas. After hearing, the court entered a second order directing the sheriff to destroy the 1,715 copies of 31 novels which had been seized. The Kansas Supreme Court held that the procedures met constitutional requirements, and affirmed the District Court's order. 191 Kan. 13, 379 P.2d 254. Probable jurisdiction was noted, 375 U.S. 919. We conclude that the procedures followed in issuing the warrant for the seizure of the books, and authorizing their impounding pending hearing, were constitutionally insufficient because they did not adequately safeguard against the suppression of nonobscene books. For this reason, we think the judgment must be reversed. Therefore, we do not reach, and intimate no view upon, the appellants' contention that the Kansas courts erred in holding that the novels are obscene.

Section 4 of the Kansas statute requires the filing of a verified information stating only that, "upon information and belief . . ., there is [an] . . . obscene book . . . located within his county." The State Attorney General went further, however, and filed an information identifying by title 59 novels, and stating that "each of said books [has] been published as This is an original Nightstand Book.'" He also filed with the information copies of seven novels published under that caption, six of which were named by title in the information; particular passages in the seven novels were marked with penciled notations or slips of paper. Although also not expressly required by the statute, the district judge, on application of the Attorney General, conducted a 45-minute ex parte inquiry during which he "scrutinized" the seven books; at the conclusion of this examination, he stated for the record that they "appear to be obscene literature as defined" under the Kansas statute "and give this Court reasonable grounds to believe that any paper-backed publication carrying the following: 'This is an original Night Stand book' would fall w thin the same category. . . ."

He issued a warrant which authorized the sheriff to seize only the particular novels identified by title in the information. When the warrant was executed on the date it was issued, only 31 of the titles were found on P-K's premises. All copies of such titles, however, 1,715 books in all, were seized and impounded. At the hearing held 10 days later pursuant to a notice included in the warrant, P-K made a motion to quash the information and the warrant on the ground, among others, that the procedure preceding the seizure was constitutionally deficient. The claim was that, by failing first to afford P-K a hearing on the question whether the books were obscene, the procedure "operates as a prior restraint on the circulation and dissemination of books," in violation of the constitutional restrictions against abridgment of freedom of speech and press. The motion was denied, and, following a final hearing held about seven weeks after the seizure (the hearing date was continued on motion of P-K), the court held that all 31 novels were obscene and ordered the sheriff to stand ready to destroy the 1,715 copies on further order.

The steps taken beyond the express requirements of the statute were thought by the Attorney General to be necessary under our decision in Marcus v. Search Warrant, 367 U. S. 717, decided a few weeks before the information was filed. Marcus involved a proceeding under a strikingly similar Missouri search and seizure statute and implementing rule of court. See 367 U. S. 719 at notes 2 3 In Marcus, the warrant gave the police virtually unlimited authority to seize any publications which they considered to be obscene, and was issued on a verified complaint lacking any specific description of the publications to be seized, and without prior submission of any publications whatever to the judge issuing the warrant.

We reversed a judgment directing the destruction of the copies of 100 publications held to be obscene, holding that, even assuming that they were obscene, the procedures leading to their condemnation were constitutionally deficient for lack of safeguards to prevent suppression of nonobscene publications protected by the Constitution.

It is our view that, since the warrant here authorized the sheriff to seize all copies of the specified titles, and since P-K was not afforded a hearing on the question of the obscenity even of the seven novels before the warrant issued, the procedure was likewise constitutionally deficient. [2] This is the teaching of Kingsley Books, Inc. v. Brown, 354 U. S. 436. See Marcus at pp. 367 U. S. 734-738. The New York injunctive procedure there sustained does not afford ex parte relief, but postpones all injunctive relief until "both sides have had an opportunity to be heard." Tenney v. Liberty News Distributors, 13 A.D.2d 770, 215 N.Y.S.2d 663, 664. In Marcus, we explicitly said that Kingsley Books

"does not support the proposition that the State may impose the extensive restraints imposed here on the distribution of these publications prior to an adversary proceeding on the issue of obscenity, irrespective of whether or not the material is legally obscene."

367 U.S. at 367 U. S. 735-736. A seizure of all copies of the named titles is indeed more repressive than an injunction preventing further sale of the books. State regulation of obscenity must

"conform to procedures that will ensure against the curtailment of constitutionally protected expression, which is often separated from obscenity only by a dim and uncertain line."

Bantam Books, Inc. v. Sullivan, 372 U. S. 58, 372 U. S. 66; the Constitution requires a procedure "designed to focus searchingly on the question of obscenity," Marcus, p. 367 U. S. 732. We therefore conclude that in not first affording P-K an adversary hearing, the procedure leading to the seizure order was constitutionally deficient. What we said of the Missouri procedure, id. at 367 U. S. 736-737, also fits the Kansas procedure employed to remove these books from circulation:

". . . there is no doubt that an effective restraint -- indeed, the most effective restraint possible -- was imposed prior to hearing on the circulation of the publications in this case, because all copies on which the [sheriff] could lay [his] hands were physically removed . . . from the premises of the wholesale distributor. An opportunity . . . to circulate the [books] . . . and then raise the claim of nonobscenity by way of defense to a prosecution for doing so was never afforded these appellants, because the copies they possessed were taken away. Their ability to circulate their publications was left to the chance of securing other copies, themselves subject to mass seizure under other such warrants. The public's opportunity to obtain the publications was thus determined by the distributor's readiness and ability to outwit the police by obtaining and selling other copies before they, in turn, could be seized. In addition to its unseemliness, we do not believe that this kind of enforced competition affords a reasonable likelihood that nonobscene publications, entitled to constitutional protection, will reach the public. A distributor may have every reason to believe that a publication is constitutionally protected and will be so held after judicial hearing, but his belief is unavailing as against the contrary [ex parte] judgment [pursuant to which the sheriff] . . . seizes it from him."

It is no answer to say that obscene books are contraband, and that, consequently, the standards governing searches and seizures of allegedly obscene books should not differ from those applied with respect to narcotics, gambling paraphernalia and other contraband. We rejected that proposition in Marcus. We said, 367 U.S. at 367 U. S. 730-731:

"The Missouri Supreme Court's assimilation of obscene literature to gambling paraphernalia or other contraband for purposes of search and seizure does not, therefore, answer the appellants' constitutional claim, but merely restates the issue whether obscenity may be treated in the same way. The authority to the police officers under the warrants issued in this case broadly to seize 'obscene . . . publications' poses problems not raised by the warrants to seize 'gambling implements' and 'all intoxicating liquors' involved in the cases cited by the Missouri Supreme Court. 334 S.W.2d at 125. For the use of these warrants implicates questions whether the procedures leading to their issuance and surrounding their execution were adequate to avoid suppression of constitutionally protected publications."

" . . . [T]he line between speech unconditionally guaranteed and speech which may legitimately be regulated, suppressed, or punished is finely drawn. . . . The separation of legitimate from illegitimate speech calls for . . . sensitive tools. . . ."

"Speiser v. Randall, 357 U. S. 513, 357 U. S. 525. It follows that, under the Fourteenth Amendment, a State is not free to adopt whatever procedures it pleases for dealing with obscenity as here involved without regard to the possible consequences for constitutionally protected speech."

See also Smith v. California, 361 U. S. 147, 361 U. S. 152-153.

Nor is the order under review saved because, after all 1,715 copies were seized and removed from circulation, P-K News Service was afforded a full hearing on the question of the obscenity of the novels. For if seizure of books precedes an adversary determination of their obscenity, there is danger of abridgment of the right of the public in a free society to unobstructed circulation of onobscene books. Bantam Books v. Sullivan, supra; Roth v. United States, 354 U. S. 476; Marcus v. Search Warrant, supra; Smith v. California, supra. Here, as in Marcus, "[s]ince a violation of the Fourteenth Amendment infected the proceedings, in order to vindicate appellants' constitutional rights," 367 U.S. at 367 U. S. 738, the judgment resting on a finding of obscenity must be reversed.

Reversed.

Notes

[1] The statute is Kan.Gen.Stat. § 21-1102 et seq. (Supp.1961). Section 1 of Kan.Laws 1961, c. 186 (§ 21-1102), constitutes the selling or distribution of obscene materials (obscenity is defined in § 1(b)) a criminal misdemeanor punishable by fine or imprisonment or both. Section 4 (§ 21-1102c) provides for the search and seizure procedure here involved:

"Whenever any district, county, common pleas, or city court judge or justice of the peace shall receive an information or complaint, signed and verified upon information and belief by the county attorney or the attorney general, stating there is any prohibited lewd, lascivious or obscene book, magazine, newspaper, writing, pamphlet, ballad, printed paper, print, picture, motion pictures, drawing, photograph, publication or other thing, as set out in section 1[21-1102](a) of this act, located within his county, it shall be the duty of such judge to forthwith issue his search warrant directed to the sheriff or any other duly constituted peace officer to seize and bring before said judge or justice such a prohibited item or items. Any peace officer seizing such item or items as hereinbefore described shall leave a copy of such warrant with any manager, servant, employee or other person appearing or acting in the capacity of exercising any control over the premises where such item or items are found or, if no person is there found, such warrant may be posted by said peace officer in a conspicuous place upon the premises where found and said warrant shall serve as notice to all interested persons of a hearing to be had at a time not less than ten (10) days after such seizure. At such hearing, the judge or justice issuing the warrant shall determine whether or not the item or items so seized and brought before him pursuant to said warrant were kept upon the premises where found in violation of any of the provisions of this act. If he shall so find, he shall order such item or items to be destroyed by the sheriff or any duly constituted peace officer by burning or otherwise, at such time as such judge shall order, and satisfactory return thereof made to him: Provided, however, such item or items shall not be destroyed so long as they may be needed as evidence in any criminal prosecution."

[2] P-K News Service also asserts that its constitutional right against unreasonable searches and seizures was violated. The result here makes it unnecessary to pass upon this contention.

## Freedman v. Maryland (March 1, 1965)

MR. JUSTICE BRENNAN delivered the opinion of the Court.

Appellant sought to challenge the constitutionality of the Maryland motion picture censorship statute, Md.Ann.Code, 1957, Art. 66A, and exhibited the film "Revenge at Daybreak" at his Baltimore theatre without first submitting the picture to the State Board of Censors as required by § 2 thereof. [1] The State concedes that the picture does not violate the statutory standards [2] and would have received a license if properly submitted, but the appellant was convicted of a § 2 violation despite his contention that the statute in its entirety unconstitutionally impaired freedom of expression. The Court of Appeals of Maryland affirmed, 233 Md. 498, 197 A.2d 232, and we noted probable jurisdiction, 377 U.S. 987. We reverse.

I

In Times Film Corp. v. City of Chicago, 365 U. S. 43, we considered and upheld a requirement of submission of motion pictures in advance of exhibition. The Court of Appeals held, on the authority of that decision, that

"the Maryland censorship law must be held to be not void on its face as violative of the freedoms protected against State action by the First and Fourteenth Amendments."

233 Md. at 505, 197 A.2d at 235. This reliance on Times Film was misplaced. The only question tendered for decision in that case was "whether a prior restraint was necessarily unconstitutional under all circumstances." Bantam Books, Inc. v. Sullivan, 372 U. S. 58, 372 U. S. 70, n. 10 (emphasis in original). The exhibitor's argument that the requirement of submission without more amounted to a constitutionally prohibited prior restraint was interpreted by the Court in Times Film as a contention that the

"constitutional protection includes complete and absolute freedom to exhibit, at least once, any and every kind of motion picture . . . even if this film contains the basest

type of pornography, or incitement to riot, or forceful overthrow of orderly government. .
. .'"

365 U.S. at 365 U. S. 46, 47. The Court held that, on this "narrow" question, id. at
365 U. S. 46, the argument stated the principle against prior restraints too broadly; citing
a number of our decisions, the Court quoted the statement from Near v. State of
Minnesota, 283 U. S. 697, that "[t]he protection even as to previous restraint is not
absolutely unlimited." In rejecting the proffered proposition in Times Film, the Court
emphasized, however, that "[i]t is that question alone which we decide," 365 U.S. at 365
U. S. 46, and it would therefore be inaccurate to say that Times Film upheld the specific
features of the Chicago censorship ordinance.

Unlike the petitioner in Times Film, appellant does not argue that § 2 is
unconstitutional simply because it may prevent even the first showing of a film whose
exhibiting may legitimately be the subject of an obscenity prosecution. He presents a
question quite distinct from that passed on in Times Film; accepting the rule in Times
Film, he argues that § 2 constitutes an invalid prior restraint because, in the context of the
remainder of the statute, it presents a danger of unduly suppressing protected expression.
He focuses particularly on the procedure for an initial decision by the censorship board,
which, without any judicial participation, effectively bars exhibition of any disapproved
film unless and until the exhibitor undertakes a time-consuming appeal to the Maryland
courts and succeeds in having the Board's decision reversed. Under the statute, the
exhibitor is required to submit the film to the Board for examination, but no time limit is
imposed for completion of Board action, § 17. If the film is disapproved, or any
elimination ordered, § 19 provides that

"The person submitting such film or view for examination will receive immediate
notice of such elimination or disapproval, and if appealed from, such film or view will be
promptly reexamined, in the presence of such person, by two or more members of the
Board, and the same finally approved or disapproved promptly after such reexamination,
with the right of appeal from the decision of the Board to the Baltimore City Court of
Baltimore City. There shall be a further right of appeal from the decision of the Baltimore
City Court to the Court of Appeals of Maryland, subject generally to the time and manner
provided for taking appeal to the Court of Appeals."

Thus, there is no statutory provision for judicial participation in the procedure
which bars a film, nor even assurance of prompt judicial review. Risk of delay is built into
the Maryland procedure, as is borne out by experience; in the only reported case
indicating the length of time required to complete an appeal, the initial judicial
determination has taken four months, and final vindication of the film on appellate
review six months. United Artists Corp. v. Maryland State Board of Censors, 210 Md. 586,
124 A.2d 292.

In the light of the difference between the issues presented here and in Times
Film, the Court of Appeals erred in saying that, since appellant's refusal to submit the film
to the Board was a violation only of § 2,

"he has restricted himself to an attack on that section alone, and lacks standing to challenge any of the other provisions (or alleged shortcomings) of the statute."

233 Md. at 505, 197 A.2d at 236. Appellant has not challenged the submission requirement in a vacuum, but in a concrete statutory context. His contention is that § 2 effects an invalid prior restraint because the structure of the other provisions of the statute contributes to the infirmity of § 2; he does not assert that the other provisions are independently invalid.

In the area of freedom of expression, it is well established that one has standing to challenge a statute on the ground that it delegates overly broad licensing discretion to an administrative office, whether or not his conduct could be proscribed by a properly drawn statute, and whether or not he applied for a license.

"One who might have had a license for the asking may . . . call into question the whole scheme of licensing when he is prosecuted for failure to procure it."

Thornhill v. State of Alabama, 310 U. S. 88, 310 U. S. 97; see Staub v. City of Baxley, 355 U. S. 313, 355 U. S. 319; Saia v. New York, 334 U. S. 558; Thomas v. Collins, 323 U. S. 516; Hague v. CIO, 307 U. S. 496; Lovell v. City of Griffin, 303 U. S. 444, 303 U. S. 452-453. Standing is recognized in such cases because of the

". . . danger of tolerating, in the area of First Amendment freedoms, the existence of a penal statute susceptible of sweeping and improper application."

NAACP v. Button, 371 U. S. 145, 371 U. S. 433; see also Amsterdam, Note, The Void for Vagueness Doctrine in the Supreme Court, 109 U.Pa.L.Rev. 67, 75- 76, 80-81, 96-104 (1960). Although we have no occasion to decide whether the vice of overbroadness infects the Maryland statute, [3] we think that appellant's assertion of a similar danger in the Maryland apparatus of censorship -- one always fraught with danger and viewed with suspicion -- gives him standing to make that challenge. In substance, his argument is that, because the apparatus operates in a statutory context in which judicial review may be too little and too late, the Maryland statute lacks sufficient safeguards for confining the censor's action to judicially determined constitutional limits, and therefore contains the same vice as a statute delegating excessive administrative discretion.

II

Although the Court has said that motion pictures are not "necessarily subject to the precise rules governing any other particular method of expression," Joseph Burstyn, Inc. v. Wilson, 343 U. S. 495, 343 U. S. 503, it is as true here as of other forms of expression that "[a]ny system of prior restraints of expression comes to this Court bearing a heavy presumption against its constitutional validity." Bantam Books, Inc. v. Sullivan, supra, at 372 U. S. 70.

". . . [U]nder the Fourteenth Amendment, a State is not free to adopt whatever procedures it pleases for dealing with obscenity . . . without regard to the possible consequences for constitutionally protected speech."

Marcus v. Search Warrant, 367 U. S. 717, 367 U. S. 731. The administration of a censorship system for motion pictures presents peculiar dangers to constitutionally protected speech. Unlike a prosecution for obscenity, a censorship proceeding puts the initial burden on the exhibitor or distributor. Because the censor's business is to censor, there inheres the danger that he may well be less responsive than a court-part of an independent branch of government -- to the constitutionally protected interests in free expression. [4] And if it is made unduly onerous, by reason of delay or otherwise, to seek judicial review, the censor's determination may, in practice, be final.

Applying the settled rule of our cases, we hold that a noncriminal process which requires the prior submission of a film to a censor avoids constitutional infirmity only if it takes place under procedural safeguards designed to obviate the dangers of a censorship system. First, the burden of proving that the film is unprotected expression must rest on the censor. As we said in Speiser v. Randall, 357 U. S. 513, 357 U. S. 526,

"Where the transcendent value of speech is involved, due process certainly requires . . . that the State bear the burden of persuasion to show that the appellants engaged in criminal speech."

Second, while the State may require advance submission of all films, in order to proceed effectively to bar all showings of unprotected films, the requirement cannot be administered in a manner which would lend an effect of finality to the censor's determination whether a film constitutes protected expression. The teaching of our cases is that, because only a judicial determination in an adversary proceeding ensures the necessary sensitivity to freedom of expression, only a procedure requiring a judicial determination suffices to impose a valid final restraint. See Bantam Books, Inc. v. Sullivan, supra; A Quantity of Books v. State of Kansas, 378 U. S. 205; Marcus v. Search Warrant, supra; Manual Enterprises, Inc. v. Day, 370 U. S. 478, 370 U. S. 518-519. To this end, the exhibitor must be assured, by statute or authoritative judicial construction that the censor will, within a specified brief period, either issue a license or go to court to restrain showing the film. Any restraint imposed in advance of a final judicial determination on the merits must similarly be limited to preservation of the status quo for the shortest fixed period compatible with sound judicial resolution. Moreover, we are well aware that, even after expiration of a temporary restraint, an administrative refusal to license, signifying the censor's view that the film is unprotected, may have a discouraging effect on the exhibitor. See Bantam Books, Inc. v. Sullivan, supra. Therefore, the procedure must also assure a prompt final judicial decision, to minimize the deterrent effect of an interim and possibly erroneous denial of a license.

Without these safeguards, it may prove too burdensome to seek review of the censor's determination. Particularly in the case of motion pictures, it may take very little to deter exhibition in a given locality. The exhibitor's stake in any one picture may be insufficient to warrant a protracted and onerous course of litigation. The distributor, on the other hand, may be equally unwilling to accept the burdens and delays of litigation in a particular area when, without such difficulties, he can freely exhibit his film in most of the rest of the country; for we are told that only four States and a handful of municipalities have active censorship laws. [5]

It is readily apparent that the Maryland procedural scheme does not satisfy these criteria. First, once the censor disapproves the film, the exhibitor must assume the burden of instituting judicial proceedings and of persuading the courts that the film is protected expression. Second, once the Board has acted against a film, exhibition is prohibited pending judicial review, however protracted. Under the statute, appellant could have been convicted if he had shown the film after unsuccessfully seeking a license, even though no court had ever ruled on the obscenity of the film. Third, it is abundantly clear that the Maryland statute provides no assurance of prompt judicial determination. We hold, therefore, that appellant's conviction must be reversed. The Maryland scheme fails to provide adequate safeguards against undue inhibition of protected expression, and this renders the § 2 requirement of prior submission of films to the Board an invalid previous restraint.

III

How or whether Maryland is to incorporate the required procedural safeguards in the statutory scheme is, of course, for the State to decide. But a model is not lacking: In Kingsley Books, Inc. v. Brown, 354 U. S. 436, we upheld a New York injunctive procedure designed to prevent the sale of obscene books. That procedure postpones any restraint against sale until a judicial determination of obscenity following notice and an adversary hearing. The statute provides for a hearing one day after joinder of issue; the judge must hand down his decision within two days after termination of the hearing. The New York procedure operates without prior submission to a censor, but the chilling effect of a censorship order, even one which requires judicial action for its enforcement, suggests all the more reason for expeditious determination of the question whether a particular film is constitutionally protected.

The requirement of prior submission to a censor sustained in Times Film is consistent with our recognition that films differ from other forms of expression. Similarly, we think that the nature of the motion picture industry may suggest different time limits for a judicial determination. It is common knowledge that films are scheduled well before actual exhibition, and the requirement of advance submission in § 2 recognizes this. One possible scheme would be to allow the exhibitor or distributor to submit his film early enough to ensure an orderly final disposition of the case before the scheduled exhibition date -- far enough in advance so that the exhibitor could safely advertise the opening on a normal basis. Failing such a scheme or sufficiently early submission under such a scheme, the statute would have to require adjudication considerably more prompt than has been the case under the Maryland statute. Otherwise, litigation might be unduly expensive and protracted, or the victorious exhibitor might find the most propitious opportunity for exhibition past. We do not mean to lay down rigid time limits or procedures, but to suggest considerations in drafting legislation to accord with local exhibition practices, and in doing so to avoid the potentially chilling effect of the Maryland statute on protected expression.

Reversed.

Notes

[1] Md.Ann.Code, 1957, Art. 66A, § 2:

"It shall be unlawful to sell, lease, lend, exhibit or use any motion picture film or view in the State of Maryland unless the said film or view has been submitted by the exchange, owner or lessee of the film or view and duly approved and licensed by the Maryland State Board of Censors, hereinafter in this article called the Board."

[2] Md.Ann.Code, 1957, Art. 66A, § 6:

"(a) Board to examine, approve or disapprove films. -- The Board shall examine or supervise the examination of all films or views to be exhibited or used in the State of Maryland and shall approve and license such films or views which are moral and proper, and shall disapprove such as are obscene, or such as tend, in the judgment of the Board, to debase or corrupt morals or incite to crimes. All films exclusively portraying current events or pictorial news of the day, commonly called news reels, may be exhibited without examination and no license or fees shall be required therefor."

"(b) What films considered obscene. -- For the purposes of this article, a motion picture film or view shall be considered to be obscene if, when considered as a whole, its calculated purpose or dominant effect is substantially to arouse sexual desires, and if the probability of this effect is so great as to outweigh whatever other merits the film may possess."

"(c) What films tend to debase or corrupt morals. -- For the purposes of this article, a motion picture film or view shall be considered to be of such a character that its exhibition would tend to debase or corrupt morals if its dominant purpose or effect is erotic or pornographic; or if it portrays acts of sexual immorality, lust or lewdness; or if it expressly or impliedly presents such acts as desirable, acceptable or proper patterns of behavior."

"(d) What films tend to incite to crime. -- For the purposes of this article, a motion picture film or view shall be considered of such a character that its exhibition would tend to incite to crime if the theme or the manner of its presentation presents the commission of criminal acts or contempt for law as constituting profitable, desirable, acceptable, respectable or commonly accepted behavior, or if it advocates or teaches the use of, or the methods of use of, narcotics or habit-forming drugs."

[3] Appellant also challenges the constitutionality of § 6, establishing standards, as invalid for vagueness under the Due Process Clause; § 11, imposing fees for the inspection and licensing of a film, as constituting an invalid tax upon the exercise of freedom of speech; and § 23, allowing exemptions to various classes of exhibitors, as denying him the equal protection of the laws. In view of our result, we express no views upon these claims.

[4] See Emerson, The Doctrine of Prior Restraint, 20 Law & Contemp.Prob. 648, 656-659 (1955). This is well illustrated by the fact that the Maryland Court of Appeals has reversed the Board's disapproval in every reported case. United Artists Corp. v. Maryland

State Board of Censors, supra; Maryland State Board of Censors v. Times Film Corp., 212 Md. 454, 129 A.2d 833; Fanfare Films, Inc. v. Motion Picture Censor Board, 234 Md. 10, 197 A.2d 839.

[5] An appendix to the brief amici curiae of the American Civil Liberties Union and its Maryland Branch lists New York, Virginia and Kansas as the three States having statutes similar to the Maryland statute, and the cities of Chicago, Detroit, Fort Worth and Providence as having similar ordinances. Twenty-eight of the remaining 39 municipal ordinances and codes are listed as "inactive."

## A Book Named "John Cleland's Memoirs of a Woman of Pleasure" v. AG of Massachusetts (March 21, 1966) [Appendix omitted]

MR. JUSTICE BRENNAN announced the judgment of the Court and delivered an opinion in which THE CHIEF JUSTICE and MR. JUSTICE FORTAS join.

This is an obscenity case in which Memoirs of a Woman of Pleasure (commonly known as Fanny Hill), written by John Cleland in about 1750, was adjudged obscene in a proceeding that put on trial the book itself, and not its publisher or distributor. The proceeding was a civil equity suit brought by the Attorney General of Massachusetts, pursuant to General Laws of Massachusetts, Chapter 272, §§ 28C-28H, to have the book declared obscene. [1] Section 28C requires that the petition commencing the suit be "directed against [the] book by name" and that an order to show cause "why said book should not be judicially determined to be obscene" be published in a daily newspaper and sent by registered mail "to all persons interested ill the publication." Publication of the order in this case occurred in a Boston daily newspaper, and a copy of the order was sent by registered mail to G. P. Putnam's Sons, alleged to be the publisher and copyright holder of the book.

As authorized by § 28D, G. P. Putnam's Sons intervened in the proceedings in behalf of the book, but it did not claim the right provided by that section to have the issue of obscenity tried by a jury. At the hearing before a justice of the Superior Court, which was conducted, under § 28F, "in accordance with the usual course of proceedings in equity," the court received the book in evidence and also, as allowed by the section, heard the testimony of experts [2] and accepted other evidence, such as book reviews, in order to assess the literary, cultural, or educational character of the book. This constituted the entire evidence, as neither side availed itself of the opportunity provided by the section to introduce evidence "as to the manner and form of its publication, advertisement, and distribution." [3] The trial justice entered a final decree, which adjudged Memoirs obscene and declared that the book

"is not entitled to the protection of the First and Fourteenth Amendments to the Constitution of the United States against action by the Attorney General or other law enforcement officer pursuant to the provisions of . . . 28B, or otherwise. [4]"

The Massachusetts Supreme Judicial Court affirmed the decree. 349 Mass. 69,

206 N.E.2d 403 (1965). We noted probable jurisdiction. 382 U. S. 900. We reverse. [5]

I

The term "obscene" appearing in the Massachusetts statute has been interpreted by the Supreme Judicial Court to be as expansive as the Constitution permits: the "statute covers all material that is obscene in the constitutional sense." Attorney General v. The Book Named "Tropic of Cancer," 345 Mass. 11, 13, 184 N.E.2d 328, 330 (1962). Indeed, the final decree before us equates the finding that Memoirs is obscene within the meaning of the statute with the declaration that the book is not entitled to the protection of the First Amendment. [6] Thus, the sole question before the state courts was whether Memoirs satisfies the test of obscenity established in Roth v. United States, 354 U. S. 476.

We defined obscenity in Roth in the following terms:

"[W]hether to the average person, applying contemporary community standards, the dominant theme of the material taken as a whole appeals to prurient interest."

354 U.S. at 354 U. S. 489. Under this definition, as elaborated in subsequent cases, three elements must coalesce: it must be established that (a) the dominant theme of the material taken as a whole appeals to a prurient interest in sex; (b) the material is patently offensive because it affronts contemporary community standards relating to the description or representation of sexual matters, and (c) the material is utterly without redeeming social value.

The Supreme Judicial Court purported to apply the Roth definition of obscenity and held all three criteria satisfied. We need not consider the claim that the court erred in concluding that Memoirs satisfied the prurient appeal and patent offensiveness criteria; for reversal is required because the court misinterpreted the social value criterion. The court applied the criterion in this passage:

"It remains to consider whether the book can be said to be 'utterly without social importance.' We are mindful that there was expert testimony, much of which was strained, to the effect that Memoirs is a structural novel with literary merit; that the book displays a skill in characterization and a gift for comedy; that it plays a part in the history of the development of the English novel, and that it contains a moral, namely, that sex with love is superior to sex in a brothel. But the fact that the testimony may indicate this book has some minimal literary value does not mean it is of any social importance. We do not interpret the 'social importance' test as requiring that a book which appeals to prurient interest and is patently offensive must be unqualifiedly worthless before it can be deemed obscene."

349 Mass. at 73, 206 N.E.2d at 406. The Supreme Judicial Court erred in holding that a book need not be "unqualifiedly worthless before it can be deemed obscene. " A book cannot be proscribed unless it is found to be utterly without redeeming social value. This is so even though the book is found to possess the requisite prurient appeal and to be patently offensive. Each of the three federal constitutional criteria is to be applied independently; the social value of the book can neither be weighed against nor canceled by its prurient appeal or patent offensiveness. [7] Hence, even on the view of the court

below that Memoirs possessed only a modicum of social value, its judgment must be reversed as being founded on an erroneous interpretation of a federal constitutional standard.

II

It does not necessarily follow from this reversal that a determination that Memoirs is obscene in the constitutional sense would be improper under all circumstances. On the premise, which we have no occasion to assess, that Memoirs has the requisite prurient appeal and is patently offensive, but has only a minimum of social value, the circumstances of production, sale, and publicity are relevant in determining whether or not the publication or distribution of the book is constitutionally protected. Evidence that the book was commercially exploited for the sake of prurient appeal, to the exclusion of all other values, might justify the conclusion that the book was utterly without redeeming social importance. It is not that, in such a setting the social value test is relaxed so as to dispense with the requirement that a book be utterly devoid of social value, but rather that, as we elaborate in Ginzburg v. United States, post, pp. 383 U. S. 470-473, where the purveyor's sole emphasis is on the sexually provocative aspects of his publications, a court could accept his evaluation at its face value. In this proceeding, however, the courts were asked to judge the obscenity of Memoirs in the abstract, and the declaration of obscenity was neither aided nor limited by a specific set of circumstances of production, sale, and publicity. [8]

All possible uses of the book must therefore be considered, and the mere risk that the book might be exploited by panderers because it so pervasively treats sexual matters cannot alter the fact -- given the view of the Massachusetts court attributing to Memoirs a modicum of literary and historical value -- that the book will have redeeming social importance in the hands of those who publish or distribute it on the basis of that value.

Reversed.

MR. JUSTICE BLACK and MR. JUSTICE STEWART concur in the reversal for the reasons stated in their respective dissenting opinions in Ginzburg v. United States, post, p. 383 U. S. 476 and p. 383 U. S. 497 and Mishkin v. New York, post, p. 383 U. S. 515 and p. 383 U. S. 518.

Notes

[1] The text of the statute appears in the Appendix.

[2] In dissenting from the Supreme Judicial Court's disposition in this case, 349 Mass. 69, 775, 206 N.E.2d 403, 406-407 (1965), Justice Whittemore summarized this testimony:

"In the view of one or another or all of the following viz., the chairman of the English department at Williams College, a professor of English at Harvard College, an associate professor of English literature at Boston University, an associate professor of English at Massachusetts Institute of Technology, and an assistant professor of English and American literature at Brandeis University, the book is a minor 'work of art' having 'literary merit' and 'historical value' and containing a good deal of 'deliberate, calculated comedy.' It is a piece of 'social history of interest to anyone who is interested in fiction as a way of understanding society in the past.'[1] A saving grace is that, although many scenes, if translated"

" 1. One of the witnesses testified in part as follows: "Cleland is part of what I should call this cultural battle that is going on in the 18th century, a battle between a restricted Puritan, moralistic ethic that attempts to suppress freedom of the spirit, freedom of the flesh, and this element is competing with a freer attitude towards life, a more generous attitude towards life, a more wholesome attitude towards life, and this very attitude that is manifested in Fielding's great novel Tom Jones' is also evident in Cleland's novel. . . . [Richardson's] `Pamela' is the story of a young country girl; [his] `Clarissa' is the story of a woman trapped in a house of prostitution. Obviously, then Cleland takes both these themes, the country girl, her initiation into life and into experience, and the story of a woman in a house of prostitution, and what he simply does is to take the situation and reverse the moral standards. Richardson believed that chastity was the most important thing in the world; Cleland and Fielding obviously did not, and thought there were more important significant moral values.""

"into the present day language of 'the realistic, naturalistic novel, could be quite offensive' these scenes are not described in such language. The book contains no dirty words and its language 'functions . . . to create a distance, even when the sexual experiences are portrayed.' The response, therefore, is a literary response. The descriptions of depravity are not obscene because 'they are subordinate to an interest which is primarily literary;' Fanny's reaction to the scenes of depravity was 'anger,' 'disgust, horror, [and] indignation.' The book 'belongs to the history of English literature, rather than the history of smut.'"

" 2. In the opinion of the other academic witness, the headmaster of a private school, whose field is English literature, the book is without literary merit and is obscene, impure, hard core pornography, and is patently offensive."

[3] The record in this case is thus significantly different from the records in Ginzburg v. United States, post, p. 383 U. S. 463, and Mishkin v. New York, post, p. 383 U. S. 502. See pp 383 U. S. 420-421, infra.

[4] Section 28B makes it a criminal offense, inter alia, to import, print, publish, sell, loan, distribute, buy, procure, receive, or possess for the purpose of sale, loan, or distribution, "a book, knowing it to be obscene." Section 28H provides that, in any prosecution under § 2813, the decree obtained in a proceeding against the book "shall be admissible in evidence," and further that,

"[i]f prior to the said offence a final decree had been entered against the book, the defendant, if the book be obscene . . . shall be conclusively presumed to have known said book to he obscene. . . ."

Thus a declaration of obscenity such as that obtained in this proceeding is likely to result in the total suppression of the book in the Commonwealth.

The constitutionality of § 28H has not been challenged in this appeal.

[5] Although the final decree provides no coercive relief, but only a declaration of the hook's obscenity, our adjudication of the merits of the issue tendered, viz., whether the state courts erred in declaring the book obscene, is not premature. There is no uncertainty as to the content of the material challenged, and the Attorney General's petition commencing this suit states that the book "is being imported, sold, loaned, or distributed in the Commonwealth." The declaration of obscenity is likely to have a serious inhibitory effect on the distribution of the book, and this probable impact is to no small measure derived from possible collateral uses of the declaration in subsequent prosecutions under the Massachusetts criminal obscenity statute. See n 4, supra.

[6] We infer from the opinions below that the other adjectives describing the proscribed books in §§ 28C-28H, "indecent" and "impure," have either been read out of the statute or deemed synonymous with "obscene."

[7] "[M]aterial dealing with sex in a manner that advocates ideas, . . . or that has literary or scientific or artistic value or any other form of social importance, may not be branded as obscenity and denied the constitutional protection. Nor may the constitutional status of the material be made to turn on a 'weighing' of its social importance against its prurient appeal, for a work cannot be proscribed unless it is 'utterly' without social importance. See Zeitlin v. Arnebergh, 59 Cal.2d 901, 920, 383 P.2d 152, 165, 31 Cal.Rptr. 800, 813 (1963)."

Jacobellis v. Ohio, 378 U. S. 184, 378 U. S. 191 (opinion of BRENNAN, J.). Followed in, e.g., People v. Bruce, 31 Ill.2d 459, 461, 202 N.E.2d 497, 498 (1964); Trans-Lux Distributing Corp. v. Maryland Bd. of Censors, 240 Md. 98, 104-105, 213 A.2d 235, 238-239 (1965).

[8] In his dissenting opinion, 349 Mass. at 76-78, 206 N.E.2d at 408-409, Justice Cutter stated that, although in his view the book was not "obscene" within the meaning of Roth, "it could reasonably be found that distribution of the book to persons under the age of eighteen would be a violation of G. L. c. 272, § 28, as tending to corrupt the morals of youth." (Section 28 makes it a crime to sell to "a person under the age of eighteen years a book . . . which is obscene . . . or manifestly tends to corrupt the morals of youth.") He concluded that the court should

"limit the relief granted to a declaration that distribution of this book to persons under the age of eighteen may be found to constitute a violation of [G. L.] c. 272, § 28, if that section is reasonably applied. . . ."

However, the decree was not so limited and we intimate no view concerning the constitutionality of such a limited declaration regarding Memoirs. Cf. Jacobellis v. Ohio, 378 U.S. at 378 U. S. 195.

## Ginzburg v. US (March 21, 1966) [Notes omitted]

MR. JUSTICE BRENNAN delivered the opinion of the Court.

A judge sitting without a jury in the District Court for the Eastern District of Pennsylvania [1] convicted petitioner Ginzburg and three corporations controlled by him upon all 28 counts of an indictment charging violation of the federal obscenity statute, 18 U.S.C. § 1461 (1964 ed.). [2] 224 F.Supp. 129. Each count alleged that a resident of the Eastern District received mailed matter, either one of three publications challenged as obscene, or advertising telling how and where the publications might be obtained. The Court of Appeals for the Third Circuit affirmed, 338 F.2d 12. We granted certiorari, 380 U.S. 961. We affirm. Since petitioners do not argue that the trial judge misconceived or failed to apply the standards we first enunciated in Roth v. United States, 354 U. S. 476, [3] the only serious question is whether those standards were correctly applied. [4]

In the cases in which this Court has decided obscenity questions since Roth, it has regarded the materials as sufficient in themselves for the determination of the question. In the present case, however, the prosecution charged the offense in the context of the circumstances of production, sale, and publicity, and assumed that, standing alone, the publications themselves might not be obscene. We agree that the question of obscenity may include consideration of the setting in which the publications were presented as an aid to determining the question of obscenity, and assume without deciding that the prosecution could not have succeeded otherwise. As in Mishkin v. New York, post, p. 383 U. S. 502, and as did the courts below, 224 F.Supp., at 134, 338 F.2d at 14-15, we view the publications against a background of commercial exploitation of erotica solely for the sake of their prurient appeal. [5] The record in that regard amply supports the decision of the trial judge that the mailing of all three publications offended the statute. [6]

The three publications were EROS, a hard-cover magazine of expensive format; Liaison, a bi-weekly newsletter, and The Housewife's Handbook on Selective Promiscuity (hereinafter the Handbook), a short book. The issue of EROS specified in the indictment, Vol. 1, No. 4, contains 15 articles and photo-essays on the subject of love, sex, and sexual relations. The specified issue of Liaison, Vol. 1, No. 1, contains a prefatory "Letter from the Editors" announcing its dedication to "keeping sex an art and preventing it from becoming a science." The remainder of the issue consists of digests of two articles concerning sex and sexual relations which had earlier appeared in professional journals and a report of an interview with a psychotherapist who favors the broadest license in sexual relationships. As the trial judge noted,

"[w]hile the treatment is largely superficial, it is presented entirely without restraint of any kind. According to defendants' own expert, it is entirely without literary merit."

224 F.Supp. at 134. The Handbook purports to be a sexual autobiography detailing with complete candor the author's sexual experiences from age 3 to age 36. The text includes, and prefatory and concluding sections of the book elaborate, her views on such subjects as sex education of children, laws regulating private consensual adult sexual practices, and the equality of women in sexual relationships. It was claimed at trial that

women would find the book valuable, for example, as a marriage manual or as an aid to the sex education of their children.

Besides testimony as to the merit of the material, there was abundant evidence to show that each of the accused publications was originated or sold as stock in trade of the sordid business of pandering -- "the business of purveying textual or graphic matter openly advertised to appeal to the erotic interest of their customers." [7] EROS early sought mailing privileges from the postmasters of Intercourse and Blue Ball, Pennsylvania. The trial court found the obvious, that these hamlets were chosen only for the value their names would have in furthering petitioners' efforts to sell their publications on the basis of salacious appeal; [8] the facilities of the post offices were inadequate to handle the anticipated volume of mail, and the privileges were denied. Mailing privileges were then obtained from the postmaster of Middlesex, New Jersey. EROS and Liaison thereafter mailed several million circulars soliciting subscriptions from that post office; over 5,500 copies of the Handbook were mailed.

The "leer of the sensualist" also permeates the advertising for the three publications. The circulars sent for EROS and Liaison stressed the sexual candor of the respective publications, and openly boasted that the publishers would take full advantage of what they regarded as an unrestricted license allowed by law in the expression of sex and sexual matters. [9] The advertising for the Handbook, apparently mailed from New York, consisted almost entirely of a reproduction of the introduction of the book, written by one Dr. Albert Ellis. Although he alludes to the book's informational value and its putative therapeutic usefulness, his remarks are preoccupied with the book's sexual imagery. The solicitation was indiscriminate, not limited to those, such as physicians or psychiatrists, who might independently discern the book's therapeutic worth. [10] Inserted in each advertisement was a slip labeled "GUARANTEE" and reading,

"Documentary Books, Inc. unconditionally guarantees full refund of the price of THE HOUSEWIFE'S HANDBOOK ON SELECTIVE PROMISCUITY if the book fails to reach you because of U.S. Post Office censorship interference."

Similar slips appeared in the advertising for EROS and Liaison; they highlighted the gloss petitioners put on the publications, eliminating any doubt what the purchaser was being asked to buy. [11]

This evidence, in our view, was relevant in determining the ultimate question of obscenity, and, in the context of this record, serves to resolve all ambiguity and doubt. The deliberate representation of petitioners' publications as erotically arousing, for example, stimulated the reader to accept them as prurient; he looks for titillation, not for saving intellectual content. Similarly, such representation would tend to force public confrontation with the potentially offensive aspects of the work; the brazenness of such an appeal heightens the offensiveness of the publications to those who are offended by such material. And the circumstances of presentation and dissemination of material are equally relevant to determining whether social importance claimed for material in the courtroom was, in the circumstances, pretense or reality -- whether it was the basis upon which it was traded in the marketplace or a spurious claim for litigation purposes. Where the purveyor's sole emphasis is on the sexually provocative aspects of his publications, that fact may be decisive in the determination of obscenity. Certainly in a prosecution which, as here, does not necessarily imply suppression of the materials involved, the fact that they originate or are used as a subject of pandering is relevant to the application of the Roth test.

A proposition argued as to EROS, for example, is that the trial judge improperly found the magazine to be obscene as a whole, since he concluded that only four of the 15 articles predominantly appealed to prurient interest and substantially exceeded community standards of candor, while the other articles were admittedly nonoffensive. But the trial judge found that

"[t]he deliberate and studied arrangement of EROS is editorialized for the purpose of appealing predominantly to prurient interest and to insulate through the inclusion of nonoffensive material."

224 F.Supp. at 131. However erroneous such a conclusion might be if unsupported by the evidence of pandering, the record here supports it. EROS was created, represented and sold solely as a claimed instrument of the sexual stimulation it would bring. Like the other publications, its pervasive treatment of sex and sexual matters rendered it available to exploitation by those who would make a business of pandering to "the widespread weakness for titillation by pornography." [12] Petitioners' own expert agreed, correctly we think, that " [i]f the object [of a work] is material gain for the creator through an appeal to the sexual curiosity and appetite," the work is pornographic. In other words, by animating sensual detail to give the publication a salacious cast, petitioners reinforced what is conceded by the Government to be an otherwise debatable conclusion.

A similar analysis applies to the judgment regarding the Handbook. The bulk of the proofs directed to social importance concerned this publication. Before selling publication rights to petitioners, its author had printed it privately; she sent circulars to persons whose names appeared on membership lists of medical and psychiatric associations, asserting its value as an adjunct to therapy. Over 12,000 sales resulted from this solicitation, and a number of witnesses testified that they found the work useful in their professional practice. The Government does not seriously contest the claim that the book has worth in such a controlled, or even neutral, environment. Petitioners, however, did not sell the book to such a limited audience, or focus their claims for it on it supposed therapeutic or educational value; rather, they deliberately emphasized the sexually provocative aspects of the work in order to catch the salaciously disposed. They proclaimed its obscenity, and we cannot conclude that the court below erred in taking their own evaluation at its face value and declaring the book as a whole obscene despite the other evidence. [13]

The decision in United States v. Rebhuhn, 109 F.2d 512, is persuasive authority for our conclusion. [14] That was a prosecution under the predecessor to § 1461, brought in the context of pandering of publications assumed useful to scholars and members of learned professions. The books involved were written by authors proved in many instances to have been men of scientific standing, as anthropologists or psychiatrists. The Court of Appeals for the Second Circuit therefore assumed that many of the books were entitled to the protection of the First Amendment, and "could lawfully have passed through the mails, if directed to those who would be likely to use them for the purposes for which they were written. . . ." 109 F.2d at 514. But the evidence, as here, was that the defendants had not disseminated them for their "proper use, but . . . woefully misused them, and it was that misuse which constituted the gravamen of the crime." Id. at 515. Speaking for the Court in affirming the conviction, Judge Learned Hand said:

". . . [T]he works themselves had a place, though a limited one, in anthropology and in psychotherapy. They might also have been lawfully sold to laymen who wished seriously to study the sexual practices of savage or barbarous peoples, or sexual aberrations; in other words, most of them were not obscene per se. In several decisions, we have held that the statute does not in all circumstances forbid the dissemination of such publications. . . . However, in the case at bar, the prosecution succeeded . . . when it showed that the defendants had indiscriminately flooded the mails with advertisements, plainly designed merely to catch the prurient, though under the guise of distributing works of scientific or literary merit. We do not mean that the distributor of such works is charged with a duty to insure that they shall reach only proper hands, nor need we say what care he must use, for these defendants exceeded any possible limit; the circulars were no more than appeals to the salaciously disposed, and no [factfinder] could have failed to pierce the fragile screen, set up to cover that purpose."

109 F.2d at 514-515.

We perceive no threat to First Amendment guarantees in thus holding that, in close cases, evidence of pandering may be probative with respect to the nature of the material in question, and thus satisfy the Roth test. [15] No weight is ascribed to the fact that petitioners have profited from the sale of publications which we have assumed, but do not hold, cannot themselves be adjudged obscene in the abstract; to sanction consideration of this fact might indeed induce self-censorship, and offend the frequently stated principle that commercial activity, in itself, is no justification for narrowing the protection of expression secured by the First Amendment. [16] Rather, the fact that each of these publications was created or exploited entirely on the basis of its appeal to prurient interests [17] strengthens the conclusion that the transactions here were sales of illicit merchandise, not sales of constitutionally protected matter. [18] A conviction for mailing obscene publications, but explained in part by the presence of this element, does not necessarily suppress the materials in question, nor chill their proper distribution for a proper use. Nor should it inhibit the enterprise of others seeking, through serious endeavor, to advance human knowledge or understanding in science, literature, or art. All that will have been determined is that questionable publications are obscene in a context which brands them as obscene as that term is defined in Roth -- a use inconsistent with any claim to the shelter of the First Amendment. [19]

"The nature of the materials is, of course, relevant as an attribute of the defendant's conduct, but the materials are thus placed in context from which they draw color and character. A wholly different result might be reached in a different setting."

Roth v. United States, 354 U.S. at 354 U. S. 495 (WARREN, C.J., concurring).

It is important to stress that this analysis simply elaborates the test by which the obscenity vel non of the material must be judged. Where an exploitation of interests in titillation by pornography is shown with respect to material lending itself to such exploitation through pervasive treatment or description of sexual matters, such evidence may support the determination that the material is obscene even though, in other contexts, the material would escape such condemnation.

Petitioners raise several procedural objections, principally directed to the findings which accompanied the trial court's memorandum opinion, Fed.Rules Crim.Proc. 23. Even on the assumption that petitioners' objections are well taken, we perceive no error affecting their substantial rights.

Affirmed.

## Mishkin v. New York (March 21, 1966) [Notes and appendix omitted]

MR. JUSTICE BRENNAN delivered the opinion of the Court.

This case, like Ginzburg v. United States, 383 U. S. 463, also decided today, involves convictions under a criminal obscenity statute. A panel of three judges of the Court of Special Sessions of the City of New York found appellant guilty of violating § 1141 of the New York Penal Law [1] by hiring others to prepare obscene books, publishing obscene books, and possessing obscene books with intent to sell them. [2] 26 Misc.2d 152, 207 N.Y.S.2d 390 (1960). He was sentenced to prison terms aggregating three years and ordered to pay $12,000 in fines for these crimes. [3] The Appellate Division, First Department, affirmed those convictions. 17 A.D.2d 243, 234 N.Y.S.2d 342 (1962). The Court of Appeals affirmed without opinion. 15 N.Y.2d 671, 255 N.Y.S.2d 881, 204 N.E.2d 209 (1964), remittitur amended, 15 N.Y.2d 724, 256 N.Y.S.2d 936, 205 N.E.2d 201 (1965). We noted probable jurisdiction. 380 U.S. 960. We affirm.

Appellant was not prosecuted for anything he said or believed, but for what he did, for his dominant role in several enterprises engaged in producing and selling allegedly obscene books. Fifty books are involved in this case. They portray sexuality in many guises. Some depict relatively normal heterosexual relations, but more depict such deviations as sadomasochism, fetishism, and homosexuality. Many have covers with drawings of scantly clad women being whipped, beaten, tortured, or abused. Many, if not most, are photo-offsets of typewritten books written and illustrated by authors and artists according to detailed instructions given by the appellant. Typical of appellant's instructions was that related by one author who testified that appellant insisted that the books be "full of sex scenes and lesbian scenes. . . . [T]he sex had to be very strong, it had to be rough, it had to be clearly spelled out. . . . I had to write sex very bluntly, make the sex scenes very strong. . . . [T]he sex scenes had to be unusual sex scenes between men and women, and women and women, and men and men. . . . [H]e wanted scenes in which women were making love with women. . . . [H]e wanted sex scenes . . . in which there were lesbian scenes. He didn't call it lesbian, but he described women making love to women and men . . . making love to men, and there were spankings and scenes -- sex in an abnormal and irregular fashion."

Another author testified that appellant instructed him "to deal very graphically with . . . the darkening of the flesh under flagellation. . . ." Artists testified in similar vein as to appellant's instructions regarding illustrations and covers for the books.

All the books are cheaply prepared paper-bound "pulps" with imprinted sales prices that are several thousand percent above costs. All but three were printed by a photo-offset printer who was paid 40� or 15� per copy, depending on whether it was a "thick" or "thin" book. The printer was instructed by appellant not to use appellant's name as publisher, but to print some fictitious name on each book, to "make up any name and address." Appellant stored books on the printer's premises and paid part of the printer's rent for the storage space. The printer filled orders for the books, at appellant's direction, delivering them to appellant's retail store, Publishers' Outlet, and, on occasion, shipping books to other places. Appellant paid the authors, artists, and printer cash for their services, usually at his bookstore.

I

Appellant attacks § 1141 as invalid on its face, contending that it exceeds First Amendment limitations by proscribing publications that are merely sadistic or masochistic, that the terms "sadistic" and "masochistic" are impermissibly vague, and that the term "obscene" is also impermissibly vague. We need not decide the merits of the first two contentions, for the New York courts held in this case that the terms "sadistic" and "masochistic," as well as the other adjectives used in § 1141 to describe proscribed books, are "synonymous with obscene.'" 26 Misc.2d at 154, 207 N.Y.S.2d at 393. The contention that the term "obscene" is also impermissibly vague fails under our holding in Roth v. United States, 354 U. S. 476, 354 U. S. 491-492. Indeed, the definition of "obscene" adopted by the New York courts in interpreting § 1141 delimits a narrower class of conduct than that delimited under the Roth definition, People v. Richmond County News, Inc., 9 N.Y.2d 578, 586-587, 216 N.Y.S.2d 369, 175 N.E.2d 681, 685-686 (1961), [4] and thus § 1141, like the statutes in Roth, provides reasonably ascertainable standards of guilt. [5]

Appellant also objects that § 1141 is invalid as applied, first, because the books he was convicted of publishing, hiring others to prepare, and possessing for sale are not obscene, and second, because the proof of scienter is inadequate.

1. The Nature of the Material. -- The First Amendment prohibits criminal prosecution for the publication and dissemination of allegedly obscene books that do not

satisfy the Roth definition of obscenity. States are free to adopt other definitions of obscenity only to the extent that those adopted stay within the bounds set by the constitutional criteria of the Roth definition, which restrict the regulation of the publication and sale of the books to that traditionally and universally tolerated in our society.

The New York courts have interpreted obscenity in § 1141 to cover only so-called "hard-core pornography," see People v. Richmond County News, Inc., 9 N.Y.2d 578, 586-587, 216 N.Y.S.2d 369, 175 N.E.2d 681, 685-686 (1961), quoted in note 4 supra. Since that definition of obscenity is more stringent than the Roth definition, the judgment that the constitutional criteria are satisfied is implicit in the application of § 1141 below. Indeed, appellant's sole contention regarding the nature of the material is that some of the books involved in this prosecution, [6] those depicting various deviant sexual practices, such as flagellation, fetishism, and lesbianism, do not satisfy the prurient appeal requirement because they do not appeal to a prurient interest of the "average person" in sex, that, "instead of stimulating the erotic, they disgust and sicken." We reject this argument as being founded on an unrealistic interpretation of the prurient appeal requirement.

Where the material is designed for and primarily disseminated to a clearly defined deviant sexual group, rather than the public at large, the prurient appeal requirement of the Roth test is satisfied if the dominant theme of the material taken as a whole appeals to the prurient interest in sex of the members of that group. The reference to the "average" or "normal" person in Roth, 354 U.S. at 354 U. S. 489-490, does not foreclose this holding. [7] In regard to the prurient appeal requirement, the concept of the "average" or "normal" person was employed in Roth to serve the essentially negative purpose of expressing our rejection of that aspect of the Hicklin test, Regina v. Hicklin, [1868] L.R. 3 Q.B. 360, that made the impact on the most susceptible person determinative. We adjust the prurient appeal requirement to social realities by permitting the appeal of this type of material to be assessed in terms of the sexual interests of its intended and probable recipient group; and since our holding requires that the recipient group be defined with more specificity than in terms of sexually immature persons, [8] it also avoids the inadequacy of the most susceptible person facet of the Hicklin test.

No substantial claim is made that the books depicting sexually deviant practices are devoid of prurient appeal to sexually deviant groups. The evidence fully establishes that these books were specifically conceived and marketed for such groups. Appellant instructed his authors and artists to prepare the books expressly to induce their purchase by persons who would probably be sexually stimulated by them. It was for this reason that appellant

"wanted an emphasis on beatings and fetishism and clothing -- irregular clothing, and that sort of thing, and again sex scenes between women; always, sex scenes had to be very strong."

And to be certain that authors fulfilled his purpose, appellant furnished them with such source materials as Caprio, Variations in Sexual Behavior, and Krafft-Ebing,

Psychopathia Sexualis. Not only was there proof of the books' prurient appeal, compare United States v. Klaw, 350 F.2d 155 (C.A.2d Cir. 1965), but the proof was compelling; in addition appellant's own evaluation of his material confirms such a finding. See Ginzburg v. United States, 383 U. S. 463.

2. Scienter. -- In People v. Finkelstein, 9 N.Y.2d 342, 344-345, 214 N.Y.S.2d 363, 364, 174 N.E.2d 470, 471 (1961), the New York Court of Appeals authoritatively interpreted § 1141 to require the "vital element of scienter," and it defined the required mental element in these terms:

"A reading of the statute [§ 1141] as a whole clearly indicates that only those who are in some manner aware of the character of the material they attempt to distribute should be punished. It is not innocent, but calculated purveyance of filth which is exorcised. . . . [9]"

(Emphasis added.) Appellant's challenge to the validity of § 1141 founded on Smith v. California, 361 U. S. 147, is thus foreclosed, [10] and this construction of § 1141 makes it unnecessary for us to define today "what sort of mental element is requisite to a constitutionally permissible prosecution." Id. at 361 U. S. 154. The Constitution requires proof of scienter to avoid the hazard of self-censorship of constitutionally protected material and to compensate for the ambiguities inherent in the definition of obscenity. The New York definition of the scienter required by § 1141 amply serves those ends, and therefore fully meets the demands of the Constitution. [11] Cf. Roth v. United States, 354 U.S. at 354 U. S. 495-496 (Warren, C.J., concurring).

Appellant's principal argument is that there was insufficient proof of scienter. This argument is without merit. The evidence of scienter in this record consists, in part, of appellant's instructions to his artists and writers; his efforts to disguise his role in the enterprise that published and sold the books; the transparency of the character of the material in question, highlighted by the titles, covers, and illustrations; the massive number of obscene books appellant published, hired others to prepare, and possessed for sale; the repetitive quality of the sequences and formats of the books; and the exorbitant prices marked on the books. This evidence amply shows that appellant was "aware of the character of the material," and that his activity was "not innocent, but calculated purveyance of filth."

II

Appellant claims that all but one of the books were improperly admitted in evidence because they were fruits of illegal searches and seizures. This claim is not capable, in itself, of being brought here by appeal, but only by a petition for a writ of certiorari under 28 U.S.C. § 1257(3) (1964 ed.) as specifically setting up a federal constitutional right. [12] Nevertheless, since appellant challenged the constitutionality of § 1141 in this prosecution, and the New York courts sustained the statute, the case is properly here on appeal, and our unrestricted notation of probable jurisdiction justified appellant's briefing of the search and seizure issue. Flournoy v. Weiner, 321 U. S. 253, 321 U. S. 263; Prudential Ins. Co. v. Cheek, 259 U. S. 530, 259 U. S. 547. The nonappealable issue is treated, however, as if contained in a petition for a writ of certiorari, see 28 U.S.C. § 2103 (1964 ed.), and the unrestricted notation of probable jurisdiction of the appeal is to be understood as a grant of the writ on that issue. The issue thus remains within our certiorari jurisdiction, and we may, for good reason, even at this stage, decline to decide the merits of the issue, much as we would dismiss a writ of certiorari as improvidently granted. We think that this is a case for such an exercise of our discretion.

The far-reaching and important questions tendered by this claim are not presented by the record with sufficient clarity to require or justify their decision. Appellant's standing to assert the claim in regard to all the seizures is not entirely clear; there is no finding on the extent or nature of his interest in two book stores, the Main Stem Book Shop and Midget Book Shop, in which some of the books were seized. The State seeks to justify the basement storeroom seizure, in part, on the basis of the consent of the printer-accomplice; but there were no findings as to the authority of the printer over the access to the storeroom, or as to the voluntariness of his alleged consent. It is also maintained that the seizure in the storeroom was made on the authority of a search warrant; yet neither the affidavit upon which the warrant issued nor the warrant itself is in the record. Finally, while the search and seizure issue has a First Amendment aspect because of the alleged massive quality of the seizures, see A Quantity of Books v. Kansas, 378 U. S. 205, 378 U. S. 206 (opinion of BRENNAN, J.); Marcus v. Search Warrant, 367 U. S. 717, the record in this regard is inadequate. There is neither evidence nor findings as to how many of the total available copies of the books in the various bookstores were seized, and it is impossible to determine whether the books seized in the basement storeroom were on the threshold of dissemination. Indeed, this First Amendment aspect apparently was not presented or considered by the state courts, nor was it raised in appellant's jurisdictional statement; it appeared for the first time in his brief on the merits.

In light of these circumstances, which were not fully apprehended at the time we took the case, we decline to reach the merits of the search and seizure claim; insofar as notation of probable jurisdiction may be regarded as a grant of the certiorari writ on the search and seizure issue, that writ is dismissed as improvidently granted.

"Examination of a case on the merits . . . may bring into 'proper focus' a consideration which . . . later indicates that the grant was improvident."

The Monrosa v. Carbon Black Export, Inc., 359 U. S. 180, 359 U. S. 184.

Affirmed.

## Redrup v. New York (May 8, 1967)

PER CURIAM.

These three cases arise from a recurring conflict -- the conflict between asserted state power to suppress the distribution of books and magazines through criminal or civil proceedings and the guarantees of the First and Fourteenth Amendments of the United

States Constitution.

### I

In No. 3, Redrup v. New York, the petitioner was a clerk at a New York City news stand. A plainclothes patrolman approached the news stand, saw two paperback books on a rack -- Lust Pool, and Shame Agent -- and asked for them by name. The petitioner handed him the books and collected the price of $1.65. As a result of this transaction, the petitioner was charged in the New York City Criminal Court with violating a state criminal law. [1] He was convicted, and the conviction was affirmed on appeal.

In No. 16, Austin v. Kentucky, the petitioner owned and operated a retail bookstore and news stand in Paducah, Kentucky. A woman resident of Paducah purchased two magazines from a salesgirl in the petitioner's store, after asking for them by name -- High Heels, and Spree. As a result of this transaction, the petitioner stands convicted in the Kentucky courts for violating a criminal law of that State. [2]

In No. 50, Gent v. Arkansas, the prosecuting attorney of the Eleventh Judicial District of Arkansas brought a civil proceeding under a state statute [3] to have certain issues of various magazines declared obscene, to enjoin their distribution, and to obtain a judgment ordering their surrender and destruction. The magazines proceeded against were: Gent, Swank, Bachelor, Modern Man, Cavalcade, Gentleman, Ace, and Sir. The County Chancery Court entered the requested judgment after a trial with an advisory jury, and the Supreme Court of Arkansas affirmed, with minor modifications. [4]

In none of the cases was there a claim that the statute in question reflected a specific and limited state concern for juveniles. See Prince v. Massachusetts, 321 U. S. 158; cf. Butler v. Michigan, 352 U. S. 380. In none was there any suggestion of an assault upon individual privacy by publication in a manner so obtrusive as to make it impossible for an unwilling individual to avoid exposure to it. Cf. Breard v. Alexandria, 341 U. S. 622; Public Utilities Comm'n v. Pollak, 343 U. S. 451. And in none was there evidence of the sort of "pandering" which the Court found significant in Ginzburg v. United States, 383 U. S. 463.

### II

The Court originally limited review in these cases to certain particularized questions, upon the hypothesis that the material involved in each case was of a character described as "obscene in the constitutional sense" in Memoirs v. Massachusetts, 383 U. S. 413, 383 U. S. 418. [5] But we have concluded that the hypothesis upon which the Court originally proceeded was invalid, and, accordingly, that the cases can and should be decided upon a common and controlling fundamental constitutional basis, without prejudice to the questions upon which review was originally granted. We have concluded, in short, that the distribution of the publications in each of these cases is protected by the First and Fourteenth Amendments from governmental suppression, whether criminal or civil, in personam or in rem. [6]

Two members of the Court have consistently adhered to the view that a State is utterly without power to suppress, control, or punish the distribution of any writings or pictures upon the ground of their "obscenity." [7] A third has held to the opinion that a State's power in this area is narrowly limited to a distinct and clearly identifiable class of material. [8] Others have subscribed to a not dissimilar standard, holding that a State may not constitutionally inhibit the distribution of literary material as obscene unless

"(a) the dominant theme of the material, taken as a whole appeals to a prurient interest in sex; (b) the material is patently offensive because it affronts contemporary community standards relating to the description or representation of sexual matters, and (c) the material is utterly without redeeming social value,"

emphasizing that the "three elements must coalesce," and that no such material can "be proscribed unless it is found to be utterly without redeeming social value." Memoirs v. Massachusetts, 383 U. S. 413, 383 U. S. 418-419. Another Justice has not viewed the "social value" element as an independent factor in the judgment of obscenity. Id. at 383 U. S. 460-462 (dissenting opinion).

Whichever of these constitutional views is brought to bear upon the cases before us, it is clear that the judgments cannot stand. Accordingly, the judgment in each case is reversed

It is so ordered.

Notes

[1] N.Y. Pen .Law § 1141 (1).

[2] Ky.Rev.Stat. § 436.100. The Kentucky Court of Appeals denied plenary review of the petitioners conviction, the Chief Justice dissenting. 386 S. w.2d 270.

[3] Ark.Stat.Ann. §§ 41-2713 to 41-2728.

[4] 239 Ark. 474, 393 S.W.2d 219.

[5] Redrup v. New York, 384 U.S. 916; Austin v. Kentucky. 384 U.S. 916; Gent v. Arkansas, 384 U.S. 937.

[6] In each of the cases before us, the contention that the publications involved were basically protected by the First and Fourteenth Amendments was timely but unsuccessfully asserted in the state proceedings. In each of these cases, this contention was properly and explicitly presented for review here.

[7] See Ginzburg v. United States, 383 U. S. 463, 383 U. S. 476, 482 (dissenting opinions); Jacobellis v. Ohio, 378 U. S. 184, 378 U. S. 196 (concurring opinion); Roth v. United States, 354 U. S. 476, 354 U. S. 508 (dissenting opinion).

[8] See Ginzburg v. United States, 383 U. S. 463, 383 U. S. 499, and n. 3 (dissenting opinion). See also Magrath, The Obscenity Cases: Grapes of Roth, 1966 Supreme Court Review 7, 69-77.

**Albert Smith v. Walter Seibly (WA Supreme Ct, Dept. One) (August 31, 1967)**

SHORETT, J.[†]

This litigation results from a vasectomy operation performed upon the person of

Albert G. Smith, the appellant, by the respondent, Walter W. Seibly, a practicing physician at Clarkston. At the time of the operation the appellant was 18 years old, married and the father of a child. He was gainfully employed, supported his family and maintained a home for himself, his wife and child. He was afflicted with a progressive muscular disease, myasthenia gravis, which is chronic and incurable and would possibly affect his future earning capacity and ability to support his family. Under these circumstances he and his wife decided to limit their family by having appellant sterilized.

The family doctor refused to perform the operation because of appellant's youth and the doctor's knowledge of the instability of the marriage. Whereupon, appellant and his wife sought another doctor and on March 9, 1961, visited the respondent's offices requesting that respondent perform the vasectomy. The appellant represented that the sterilization was desired because of his affliction with myasthenia gravis. Respondent illustrated the operation with a diagram and explained that it would result in permanent sterilization. There is a dispute as to whether the appellant represented that he was of legal age. The respondent read aloud and presented the following statement to appellant and his wife:

TO WHOM IT MAY CONCERN: We, the undersigned, hereby consent to the sterilization operation to be performed on the husband, having been told that the operation is a permanent thing, that there is no chance for a reestablishment of a viable sperm in the semen.

The doctor then told appellant and his wife to go home, think about the operation and if they still wished it performed, sign the paper and return to his office.

Twelve days later appellant returned, presented the consent signed by himself and his wife, and the operation was performed.

After appellant reached his majority, he brought this action alleging that the respondent was negligent in performing the vasectomy upon an infant of 18 years, was negligent in failing to explain to appellant the permanent consequences of the surgery, and that such surgery was performed without valid permission. The appellant asked damages in the amount of $52,000. The respondent's answer denied the allegations of negligence and liability and alleged that the appellant was barred from recovery because he had signed a consent to the operation.

Although the complaint contained allegations based on a theory of negligence, all parties agree that the trial court properly submitted the case to the jury on an assault theory. One of the instructions read: "... The vasectomy is an assault and battery if surgery was performed without valid consent." Appellant's theory was that a minor could not give valid consent to such surgery. The respondent's view, adopted by the trial court, was that under some conditions a minor may be emancipated for the purpose of giving consent to surgery. The jury returned a verdict for respondent and judgment having been entered thereon, this appeal followed.

[1] Error is assigned to the exclusion of testimony by a Richland psychiatrist on the standard of medical care required for the performance of a vasectomy in the

Clarkston area. After the court had sustained an objection to this testimony, the appellant made no offer of proof. We therefore have no way of knowing what testimony would have been presented and we cannot speculate on its content, for the rule in this jurisdiction is:

[I]t is the duty of a party to make clear to the trial court what it is that he offers in proof, and the reason why he deems the offer admissible over the objections of his opponent, so that the court may make an informed ruling. If the party fails to so aid the trial court, then the appellate court will not make assumptions in favor of the rejected offer. (Citing cases.) Tomlinson v. Bean, 26 Wn.2d 354, 361, 173 P.2d 972 (1964).

An offer of proof is necessary to save the point on appeal. Cameron v. Boone, 62 Wn.2d 420, 383 P.2d 277 (1963); Dakin v. Dakin, 62 Wn.2d 687, 384 P.2d 639 (1963); Blood v. Allied Stores Corp., 62 Wn.2d 187, 381 P.2d 742 (1963).

[2] The next error assigned by appellant relates to the trial court's allowance of cross-examination of the plaintiff concerning his failure to make support payments for his child in accordance with the requirements of a divorce decree. Sometime after the vasectomy was performed appellant and his wife were divorced and appellant had not supported the child in accordance with the requirements of the decree of divorce. Ordinarily, testimony upon the failure to support would be completely irrelevant to the issue presented in this case. However, appellant had presented medical testimony relating to his concern for his child, his great desire to have children of his own, and the psychological damage caused by the vasectomy. Thus, in his effort to prove damages, the appellant injected into the case the topic of his interest and concern with children. This gave the trial court a wide latitude in permitting cross-examination. In State v. Robinson, 61 Wn.2d 107, 109, 377 P.2d 248 (1962), we said:

The scope of cross-examination is peculiarly within the province of the trial judge. We will not disturb his determination of its boundaries unless there is a manifest abuse of discretion. [Citing cases.] Since defendant introduced the issue, he cannot be heard to complain of the limited cross-examination permitted by the trial court. State v. King, 58 Wn. (2d) 77, 78, 360 P. (2d) 757 (1961).

See also State v. Eichman, 69 Wn.2d 327, 418 P.2d 418 (1966); State v. Oldham, 56 Wn.2d 696, 355 P.2d 9 (1960); Miller v. Edwards, 25 Wn.2d 635, 171 P.2d 821 (1946).

Appellant next contends that error was committed in giving instructions Nos. 13, 14, 15 and 16[1] and in refusing to give appellant's requested instructions Nos. 7 and 8[2].

The exceptions taken to the trial court's action on these instructions were all on one ground, namely, that appellant, being a minor, could not give consent to the operation, that his consent was void, and that parental consent was necessary to insulate respondent from liability. It has long been recognized in this state that for certain purposes, emancipation of minors may occur even in the absence of a statute. In re Hollopeter, 52 Wash. 41, 100 Pac. 159 (1909); State v. McPherson, 72 Wash. 371, 130 Pac. 481 (1913); Morgan v. Cunningham, 109 Wash. 105, 186 Pac. 309 (1919).

Respondent contends that appellant was emancipated for the purpose of giving consent to the operation, or, at least that a jury question was presented on this issue. In

American Prods. Co. v. Villwock, 7 Wn.2d 246, 267-68, 109 P.2d 570, 132 A.L.R. 1010 (1941), this court quoted from 1 Schouler, Domestic Relations (6th ed.) 897, § 807 as follows:

"`Emancipation' of a child is the relinquishment by the parent of control and authority over the child, conferring on him the right to his earnings and terminating the parent's legal duty to support the child. It may be express, as by voluntary agreement of parent and child, or implied from such acts and conduct as import consent; it may be conditional or absolute, complete or partial...."

To the same effect see DeLay v. DeLay, 54 Wn.2d 63, 337 P.2d 1057 (1959). The subject "What amounts to implied emancipation of a minor child" is annotated in 165 A.L.R. 723, 745, where it is stated:

[I]t is settled by the weight of authority that the marriage of a minor with parent's consent (according to some cases) or even without the parent's consent (according to other cases) works an emancipation, for the reason that the marriage gives rise to a new relation inconsistent with the subjection to the control and care of the parent. In such case the emancipated child is the head of a new family and as such is subject to obligations and duties to his wife and children which require him to be the master of himself, his time, his labor, earnings, and conduct.

We limit this discussion of the instructions to the exception taken by appellant. See Horwath v. Washington Water Power Co., 68 Wn.2d 835, 416 P.2d 92 (1966); Burlingham-Meeker Co. v. Thomas, 58 Wn.2d 79, 360 P.2d 1033 (1961); Klise v. Seattle, 52 Wn.2d 412, 325 P.2d 888 (1958).

[3] Tested by the exception taken, the instructions given were not erroneous. A married minor, 18 years of age, who has successfully completed high school and is the head of his own family, who earns his own living and maintains his own home, is emancipated for the purpose of giving a valid consent to surgery if a full disclosure of the ramifications, implications and probable consequences of the surgery has been made by the doctor in terms which are fully comprehensible to the minor. Thus, age, intelligence, maturity, training, experience, economic independence or lack thereof, general conduct as an adult and freedom from the control of parents are all factors to be considered in such a case.

Appellant was married, independent of parental control and financial support and it was for the jury to decide if he was sufficiently intelligent, educated and knowledgeable to make a legally binding decision. As we stated in Grannum v. Berard, 70 Wn.2d 304, 307, 422 P.2d 812 (1967): "The mental capacity necessary to consent to a surgical operation is a question of fact to be determined from the circumstances of each individual case."

The jury was correctly instructed as to the factors to be weighed in determining appellant's capacity to consent to the operation.

The judgment is affirmed.

FINLEY, C.J., HILL, WEAVER, and ROSELLINI, JJ., concur.

Notes

[1] "You are instructed that a minor who is capable of understanding or appreciating the consequences of surgery is legally capable of giving the consent that a physician is required to obtain from his patient before performing surgery." (Instruction No. 13.)

"In considering a minor's capability of understanding or appreciating the consequences, you may consider the minor's age, intelligence, maturity, training and experience, marital status, control or the absence thereof by his parents, whether he was dependent or self-supporting and whether his general conduct was that of an adult or that of a child." (Instruction No. 14.)

"You are instructed that a release or consent made by an infant is voidable and subject to disaffirment, unless because the infant misrepresented his majority, or engaged in business as an adult, the other person has good reason to believe the infant was capable of giving his consent." (Instruction No. 15.)

"You are instructed that a minor is bound by his consent to submit to surgery unless he disaffirms such consent within a reasonable time after he attains his majority." (Instruction No. 16.)

[2] "You are instructed that under the law of the State of Washington, a male less than 21 years old is an infant.

"You are further instructed that no operation may be performed by a surgeon upon an infant unless consent is first obtained of the natural guardian or parents of the infant, unless the operation is for the benefit of the infant and is done with the purpose of saving his life or limb.

"Therefore, if you find from the evidence in this case that the defendant Walter Seibly performed a surgical operation upon the plaintiff at a time when the plaintiff was less than 21 years old, and if you further find that at the time of said operation the defendant Walter Seibly had not obtained the consent of the parents of the plaintiff, then you should completely disregard any evidence of a release having been signed by the plaintiff.

"This is the law, even though you should find that the plaintiff was married at the time the operation was performed." (Proposed instruction No. 7.)

"You are instructed that in this case the Court has determined as a matter of law that the operation performed by the defendant Seibly on the plaintiff was an unauthorized operation.

"You are therefore directed to return a verdict in favor of the plaintiff and against the defendants Seibly, and fix damages in accordance with the instructions the Court has given you concerning damages." (Proposed instruction No. 8.)

**Ginsberg v. New York (April 22, 1968) [Appendix omitted]**

MR. JUSTICE BRENNAN delivered the opinion of the Court.

This case presents the question of the constitutionality on its face of a New York criminal obscenity statute which prohibits the sale to minors under 17 years of age of material defined to be obscene on the basis of its appeal to them, whether or not it would be obscene to adults.

Appellant and his wife operate "Sam's Stationery and Luncheonette" in Bellmore, Long Island. They have a lunch counter, and, among other things, also sell magazines, including some so-called "girlie" magazines. Appellant was prosecuted under two informations, each in two counts, which charged that he personally sold a 16-year-old boy two "girlie" magazines on each of two dates in October, 1965, in violation of § 484-h of the New York Penal Law. He was tried before a judge without a jury in Nassau County District Court and was found guilty on both counts. [1] The judge found (1) that the magazines contained pictures which depicted female "nudity" in a manner defined in subsection 1(b), that is

"the showing of . . . female . . . buttocks with less than a full opaque covering, or the showing of the female breast with less than a fully opaque covering of any portion thereof below the top of the nipple . . .,"

and (2) that the pictures were "harmful to minors" in that they had, within the meaning of subsection 1(f),

"that quality of . . . representation . . . of nudity . . . [which] . . . (i) predominantly appeals to the prurient, shameful or morbid interest of minors, and (ii) is patently offensive to prevailing standards in the adult community as a whole with respect to what is suitable material for minors, and (iii) is utterly without redeeming social importance for minors."

He held that both sales to the 16-year-old boy therefore constituted the violation under § 484-h of "knowingly to sell . . . to a minor" under 17 of "(a) any picture . . . which depicts nudity . . . and which is harmful to minors," and "(b) any . . . magazine . . . which contains . . . [such pictures] . . . and which, taken as a whole, is harmful to minors." The conviction was affirmed without opinion by the Appellate Term, Second Department, of the Supreme Court. Appellant was denied leave to appeal to the New York Court of Appeals, and then appealed to this Court. We noted probable jurisdiction. 388 U.S. 904. We affirm. [2]

I

The "girlie" picture magazines involved in the sales here are not obscene for adults, Redrup v. New York, 386 U. S. 767. [3] But § 484-h does not bar the appellant from stocking the magazines and selling them to persons 17 years of age or older, and therefore the conviction is not invalid under our decision in Butler v. Michigan, 352 U. S. 380.

Obscenity is not within the area of protected speech or press. Roth v. United States, 354 U. S. 476, 354 U. S. 485. The three-pronged test of subsection 1(f) for judging the obscenity of material sold to minors under 17 is a variable from the formulation for determining obscenity under Roth stated in the plurality opinion in Memoirs v. Massachusetts, 383 U. S. 413, 383 U. S. 418. Appellant's primary attack upon § 484-h is leveled at the power of the State to adapt this Memoirs formulation to define the material's obscenity on the basis of its appeal to minors, and thus exclude material so defined from the area of protected expression. He makes no argument that the magazines are not "harmful to minors" within the definition in subsection 1(f). Thus, "[n]o issue is presented . . . concerning the obscenity of the material involved." Roth, supra, at 354 U. S. 481, n. 8.

The New York Court of Appeals "upheld the Legislature's power to employ variable concepts of obscenity" [4] in a case in which the same challenge to state power to enact such a law was also addressed to § 484-h. Bookcase, Inc. v. Broderick, 18 N.Y.2d 71, 218 N.E.2d 668, appeal dismissed for want of a properly presented federal question, sub nom. Bookcase, Inc. v. Leary, 385 U. S. 12. In sustaining state power to enact the law, the Court of Appeals said, Bookcase, Inc. v. Broderick, at 75, 218 N.E.2d at 671:

"[M]aterial which is protected for distribution to adults is not necessarily constitutionally protected from restriction upon its dissemination to children. In other words, the concept of obscenity or of unprotected matter may vary according to the group to whom the questionable material is directed or from whom it is quarantined. Because of the State's exigent interest in preventing distribution to children of objectionable material, it can exercise its power to protect the health, safety, welfare and morals of its community by barring the distribution to children of books recognized to be suitable for adults."

Appellant's attack is not that New York was without power to draw the line at age 17. Rather, his contention is the broad proposition that the scope of the constitutional freedom of expression secured to a citizen to read or see material concerned with sex cannot be made to depend upon whether the citizen is an adult or a minor. He accordingly insists that the denial to minors under 17 of access to material condemned by § 484-h, insofar as that material is not obscene for persons 17 years of age or older, constitutes an unconstitutional deprivation of protected liberty.

We have no occasion in this case to consider the impact of the guarantees of freedom of expression upon the totality of the relationship of the minor and the State, cf. In re Gault, 387 U. S. 1, 387 U. S. 13. It is enough for the purposes of this case that we inquire whether it was constitutionally impermissible for New York, insofar as § 484-h does so, to accord minors under 17 a more restricted right than that assured to adults to judge and determine for themselves what sex material they may read or see. We conclude that we cannot say that the statute invades the area of freedom of expression constitutionally secured to minors. [5]

Appellant argues that there is an invasion of protected rights under § 484-h constitutionally indistinguishable from the invasions under the Nebraska statute forbidding children to study German, which was struck down in Meyer v. Nebraska, 262 U. S. 390; the Oregon statute interfering with children's attendance at private and parochial schools, which was struck down in Pierce v. Society of Sisters, 268 U. S. 510, and the statute compelling children, against their religious scruples, to give the flag salute, which was struck down in West Virginia State Board of Education v. Barnette, 319 U. S. 624. We reject that argument. We do not regard New York's regulation in defining obscenity on he basis of its appeal to minors under 17 as involving an invasion of such minors' constitutionally protected freedoms. Rather, § 484-h simply adjusts the definition of obscenity "to social realities by permitting the appeal of this type of material to be assessed in terms of the sexual interests . . ." of such minors. Mishkin v. New York, 383 U. S. 502, 383 U. S. 509; Bookcase, Inc. v. Broderick, supra, at 75, 218 N.E.2d at 671. That the State has power to make that adjustment seems clear, for we have recognized that, even where there is an invasion of protected freedoms, "the power of the state to control the conduct of children reaches beyond the scope of its authority over adults. . . ." Prince v. Massachusetts, 321 U. S. 158, 321 U. S. 170. [6] In Prince, we sustained the conviction of the guardian of a nine-year-old girl, both members of the sect of Jehovah's Witnesses, for violating the Massachusetts Child Labor Law by permitting the girl to sell the sect's religious tracts on the streets of Boston.

The wellbeing of its children is, of course, a subject within the State's constitutional power to regulate, and, in our view, two interests justify the limitations in § 484-h upon the availability of sex material to minors under 17, at least if it was rational for the legislature to find that the minors' exposure to such material might be harmful. First of all, constitutional interpretation has consistently recognized that the parents' claim to authority in their own household to direct the rearing of their children is basic in the structure of our society.

"It is cardinal with us that the custody, care and nurture of the child reside first in the parents, whose primary function and freedom include preparation for obligations the state can neither supply nor hinder."

Prince v. Massachusetts, supra, at 321 U. S. 166. The legislature could properly conclude that parents and others, teachers for example, who have this primary responsibility for children's wellbeing are entitled to the support of laws designed to aid discharge of that responsibility. Indeed, subsection 1(f)(ii) of § 484-h expressly recognizes the parental role in assessing sex-related material harmful to minors according "to prevailing standards in the adult community as a whole with respect to what is suitable material for minors." Moreover, the prohibition against sales to minors does not bar parents who so desire from purchasing the magazines for their children. [7]

The State also has an independent interest in the wellbeing of its youth. The New York Court of Appeals squarely bottomed its decision on that interest in Bookcase, Inc. v. Broderick, supra, at 75, 218 N.E.2d at 671. Judge Fuld, now Chief Judge Fuld, also emphasized its significance in the earlier case of People v. Khan, 15 N.Y.2d 311, 206 N.E.2d 333, which had struck down the first version of § 484-h on grounds of vagueness. In his concurring opinion, id. at 312, 206 N.E.2d at 334, he said:

"While the supervision of children's reading may best be left to their parents, the knowledge that parental control or guidance cannot always be provided and society's transcendent interest in protecting the welfare of children justify reasonable regulation of the sale of material to them. It is, therefore, altogether fitting and proper for a state to include in a statute designed to regulate the sale of pornography to children special standards, broader than those embodied in legislation aimed at controlling dissemination of such material to adults."

In Prince v. Massachusetts, supra, at 321 U. S. 165, this Court, too, recognized that the State has an interest "to protect the welfare of children" and to see that they are "safeguarded from abuses" which might prevent their "growth into free and independent well developed men and citizens." The only question remaining, therefore, is whether the New York Legislature might rationally conclude, as it has, that exposure to the materials proscribed by § 484-h constitutes such an "abuse."

Section 484-e of the law states a legislative finding that the material condemned by § 484-h is "a basic factor in impairing the ethical and moral development of our youth and a clear and present danger to the people of the state." It is very doubtful that this finding expresses an accepted scientific fact. [8] But obscenity is not protected expression, and may be suppressed without a showing of the circumstances which lie behind the phrase "clear and present danger" in its application to protected speech. Roth v. United States, supra, at 486-487. [9] To sustain state power to exclude material defined as obscenity by § 484-h requires only that we be able to say that it was not irrational for the legislature to find that exposure to material condemned by the statute is harmful to minors. In Meyer v. Nebraska, supra, at 262 U. S. 400, we were able to say that children's knowledge of the German language "cannot reasonably be regarded as harmful." That cannot be said by us of minors' reading and seeing sex material. To be sure, there is no lack of "studies" which purport to demonstrate that obscenity is or is not "a basic factor in impairing the ethical and moral development of . . . youth and a clear and present danger to the people of the state." But the growing consensus of commentators is that,

"while these studies all agree that a causal link has not been demonstrated, they are equally agreed that a causal link has not been disproved, either. [10]"

We do not demand of legislatures "scientifically certain criteria of legislation." Noble State Bank v. Haskell, 219 U. S. 104, 219 U. S. 110. We therefore cannot say that § 484-h, in defining the obscenity of material on the basis of its appeal to minors under 17, has no rational relation to the objective of safeguarding such minors from harm.

II

Appellant challenges subsections (f) and (g) of § 484-h as, in any event, void for vagueness. The attack on subsection (f) is that the definition of obscenity "harmful to minors" is so vague that an honest distributor of publications cannot know when he might be held to have violated § 484-h. But the New York Court of Appeals construed this definition to be

"virtually identical to the Supreme Court's most recent statement of the elements of obscenity. [Memoirs v. Massachusetts, 383 U. S. 413, 383 U. S. 418],"

Bookcase, Inc. v. Broderick, supra, at 76, 218 N.E.2d at 672. The definition therefore gives "men in acting adequate notice of what is prohibited," and does not offend the requirements of due process. Roth v. United States, supra, at 354 U. S. 492; see also Winters v. New York, 333 U. S. 507, 333 U. S. 520.

As is required by Smith v. California, 361 U. S. 147, § 484-h prohibits only those sales made "knowingly." The challenge to the scienter requirement of subsection (g) centers on the definition of "knowingly" insofar as it includes "reason to know" or

"a belief or ground for belief which warrants further inspection or inquiry of both: (i) the character and content of any material described herein which is reasonably susceptible of examination by the defendant, and (ii) the age of the minor, provided however, that an honest mistake shall constitute an excuse from liability hereunder if the defendant made a reasonable bona fide attempt to ascertain the true age of such minor."

As to (i), § 484-h was passed after the New York Court of Appeals decided People v. Finkelstein, 9 N.Y.2d 342, 174 N.E.2d 470, which read the requirement of scienter into New York's general obscenity statute, § 1141 of the Penal Law. The constitutional requirement of scienter, in the sense of knowledge of the contents of material, rests on the necessity

"to avoid the hazard of self-censorship of constitutionally protected material and to compensate for the ambiguities inherent in the definition of obscenity,"

Mishkin v. New York, supra, at 383 U. S. 511. The Court of Appeals in Finkelstein interpreted § 1141 to require "the vital element of scienter" and defined that requirement in these terms:

"A reading of the statute [§ 1141] as a whole clearly indicates that only those who are in some manner aware of the character of the material they attempt to distribute should be punished. It is not innocent but calculated purveyance of filth which is exorcised. . . ."

9 N.Y.2d at 344-345, 174 N.E.2d at 471. (Emphasis supplied.) In Mishkin v. New York, supra, at 383 U. S. 510-511, we held that a challenge to the validity of § 1141 founded on Smith v. California, supra, was foreclosed in light of this construction. When § 484-h was before the New York Legislature, its attention was directed to People v. Finkelstein as defining the nature of scienter required to sustain the statute. 1965 N.Y.S.Leg.Ann. 54-56. We may therefore infer that the reference in provision (i) to knowledge of "the character and content of any material described herein" incorporates the gloss given the term "character" in People v. Finkelstein. In that circumstance, Mishkin requires rejection of appellant's challenge to provision (i) and makes it unnecessary for us to define further today "what sort of mental element is requisite to a constitutionally permissible prosecution," Smith v. California, supra, at 361 U. S. 154.

Appellant also attacks provision (ii) as impermissibly vague. This attack however is leveled only at the proviso according the defendant a defense of "honest mistake" as to the age of the minor. Appellant argues that "the statute does not tell the bookseller what effort he must make before he can be excused." The argument is wholly without merit.

The proviso states expressly that the defendant must be acquitted on the ground of "honest mistake" if the defendant proves that he made "a reasonable bona fide attempt to ascertain the true age of such minor." Cf. 1967 Penal Law § 235.22(2), n 1, supra.

Affirmed.

Notes

[1] Appellant makes no attack upon § 484-h as applied. We therefore have no occasion to consider the sufficiency of the evidence, or such issues as burden of proof, whether expert evidence is either required or permissible, or any other questions which might be pertinent to the application of the statute. Appellant does argue that, because the trial judge included a finding that two of the magazines "contained verbal descriptions and narrative accounts of sexual excitement and sexual conduct," an offense not charged in the informations, the conviction must be set aside under Cole v. Arkansas, 333 U. S. 196. But this case was tried, and the appellant was found guilty, only on the charges of selling magazines containing pictures depicting female nudity. It is therefore not a case where defendant was tried and convicted of a violation of one offense when he was charged with a distinctly and substantially different offense.

The full text of § 484-h is attached as Appendix A. It was enacted in L. 1965, c. 327, to replace an earlier version held invalid by the New York Court of Appeals in People v. Kahan, 15 N.Y.2d 311, 206 N.E.2d 333, and People v. Bookcase, Inc., 14 N.Y.2d 409, 201 N.E.2d 14. Section 484-h, in turn, was replaced by L.1967, c. 791, now §§ 235.20-235.22 of the Penal Law. The major changes under the 1967 law added a provision that the one charged with a violation "is presumed to [sell] with knowledge of the character and content of the material sold . . .," and the provision that

"it is an affirmative defense that: (a) The defendant had reasonable cause to believe that the minor involved was seventeen years old or more, and (b) Such minor exhibited to the defendant a draft card, driver's license, birth certificate or other official or apparently official document purporting to establish that such minor was seventeen years old or more."

Neither addition is involved in this case. We intimate no view whatever upon the constitutional validity of the presumption. See in general Smith v. California, 361 U. S. 147; Speiser v. Randall, 357 U. S. 513; 41 N.Y.U.L.Rev. 791 (1966); 30 Albany L.Rev. 133 (1966).

The 1967 law also repealed outright § 484-i, which had been enacted one week after § 484-h. L.1965, c. 327. It forbade sales to minors under the age of 18. The New York Court of Appeals sustained its validity against a challenge that it was void for vagueness. People v. Tannenbaum, 18 N.Y.2d 268, 220 N.E.2d 783. For an analysis of § 484-i and a comparison with § 484-h, see 33 Brooklyn L.Rev. 329 (1967).

[2] The case is not moot. The appellant might have been sentenced to one year's imprisonment, or a $500 fine or both. N.Y.Penal Law § 1937. The trial judge, however, exercised authority under N.Y.Penal Law § 2188, and, on May 17, 1966, suspended

sentence on all counts. Under § 47a of the New York Code of Criminal Procedure, the judge could thereafter recall appellant and impose sentence only within one year, or before May 17, 1967. The judge did not do so. Although St. Pierre v. United States, 319 U. S. 41, held that a criminal case had become moot when the petitioner finished serving his sentence before direct review in this Court, St. Pierre also recognized that the case would not have been moot had

"petitioner shown that, under either state or federal law, further penalties or disabilities can be imposed on him as result of the judgment which has now been satisfied."

Id. at 319 U. S. 43. The State of New York concedes in its brief in this Court addressed to mootness "that certain disabilities do flow from the conviction." The brief states that among these is "the possibility of ineligibility for licensing under state and municipal license laws regulating various lawful occupations. . . ." Since the argument, the parties advised the Court that, although this is the first time appellant has been convicted of any crime, this conviction might result in the revocation of the license required by municipal law as a prerequisite to engaging in the luncheonette business he carries on in Bellmore, New York. Bellmore is an "unincorporated village" within the Town of Hempstead, Long Island, 1967 N.Y.S.Leg.Man. 1154. The town has a licensing ordinance which provides that the "Commissioner of Buildings . . . may suspend or revoke any license issued, in his discretion, for . . .(e) conviction of any crime." LL 21, Town of Hempstead, eff. December 1, 1966, § 8.1(e). In these circumstances, the case is not moot, since the conviction may entail collateral consequences sufficient to bring the case within the St. Pierre exception. See Fiswick v. United States, 329 U. S. 211, 329 U. S. 220-222. We were not able to reach that conclusion in Tannenbaum v. New York, 388 U. S. 439, or Jacobs v. New York, 388 U. S. 431, in which the appeals were dismissed as moot. In Tannenbaum, there was no contention that the convictions under the now repealed § 484-i entailed any collateral consequences. In Jacobs, the appeal was dismissed on motion of the State which alleged, inter alia, that New York law did not impose "any further penalty upon conviction of the misdemeanor here in issue." Appellant did not there show, or contend, that his license might be revoked for "conviction of any crime"; he asserted only that the conviction might be the basis of a suspension under a provision of the Administrative Code of the City of New York requiring the Department of Licenses to assure that motion picture theatres are not conducted in a manner offensive to "public morals."

[3] One of the magazines was an issue of the magazine "Sir." We held in Gent v. Arkansas, decided with Redrup v. New York, 386 U. S. 767, 386 U. S. 769, that an Arkansas statute which did not reflect a specific and limited state concern for juveniles was unconstitutional insofar as it was applied to suppress distribution of another issue of that magazine. Other cases which turned on findings of nonobscenity of this type of magazine include: Central Magazine Sales, Ltd. v. United States, 389 U. S. 50; Conner v. City of Hammond, 389 U. S. 48; Potomac News Co. v. United States, 389 U. S. 47; Mazes

v. Ohio, 388 U. S. 453; A Quantity of Books v. Kansas, 388 U. S. 452; Books, Inc. v. United States, 388 U. S. 449; Aday v. United States, 388 U. S. 447; Avansino v. New York, 388 U. S. 446; Shepherd v. New York, 388 U. S. 444; Friedman v. New York, 388 U. S. 441; Keney v. New York, 388 U. S. 440; see also Rosenbloom v. Virginia, 388 U. S. 450; Sunshine Book Co. v. Summerfield, 355 U. S. 372

[4] People v. Tannenbaum, 18 N.Y.2d 268, 270, 220 N.E.2d 783, 785, dismissed as moot, 388 U. S. 439. The concept of variable obscenity is developed in Lockhart & McClure, Censorship of Obscenity: The Developing Constitutional Standards, 45 Minn.L.Rev. 5 (1960). At 85, the authors state:

"Variable obscenity . . . furnishes a useful analytical tool for dealing with the problem of denying adolescents access to material aimed at a primary audience of sexually mature adults. For variable obscenity focuses attention upon the makeup of primary and peripheral audiences in varying circumstances, and provides a reasonably satisfactory means for delineating the obscene in each circumstance."

[5] Suggestions that legislatures might give attention to laws dealing specifically with safeguarding children against pornographic material have been made by many judges and commentators. See, e.g., Jacobellis v. Ohio, 378 U. S. 184, 378 U. S. 195 (opinion of JUSTICES BRENNAN and Goldberg); id. at 378 U. S. 201 (dissenting opinion of THE CHIEF JUSTICE); Ginzburg v. United States, 383 U. S. 463, 383 U. S. 498, n. 1 (dissenting opinion of MR. JUSTICE STEWART); Interstate Circuit, Inc. v. City of Dallas, 366 F.2d 590, 593; In re Louisiana News Co., 187 F.Supp. 241, 247; United States v. Levine, 83 F.2d 156; United States v. Dennett, 39 F.2d 564; R. Kuh, Foolish Figleaves? 258-260 (1967); Emerson, Toward a General Theory of the First Amendment, 72 Yale L.J. 877, 939 (1963); Gerber, A Suggested Solution to the Riddle of Obscenity, 112 U.Pa.L.Rev. 834, 848 (1964); Henkin, Morals and the Constitution: The Sin of Obscenity, 63 Col.L.Rev. 391, 413, n. 68 (1963); Kalven, The Metaphysics of the Law of Obscenity, 1960 Sup.Ct.Rev. 1, 7; Magrath, The Obscenity Cases: Grapes of Roth, 1966 Sup.Ct.Rev. 7, 75.

The obscenity laws of 35 other States include provisions referring to minors. The laws are listed in Appendix B to this opinion. None is a precise counterpart of New York's § 48-h, and we imply no view whatever on questions of their constitutionality.

[6] Many commentators, including many committed to the proposition that "[n]o general restriction on expression in terms of obscenity' can . . . be reconciled with the first amendment," recognize that "the power of the state to control the conduct of children reaches beyond the scope of its authority over adults," and accordingly acknowledge a supervening state interest in the regulation of literature sold to children, Emerson, Toward a General Theory of the First Amendment, 72 Yale L.J. 877, 938, 939 (1963):

"Different factors come into play, also, where the interest at stake is the effect of erotic expression upon children. The world of children is not strictly part of the adult realm of free expression. The factor of immaturity, and perhaps other considerations, impose different rules. Without attempting here to formulate the principles relevant to freedom of expression for children, it suffices to say that regulations of communication addressed to them need not conform to the requirements of the first amendment in the same way as those applicable to adults."

See also Gerber, supra, at 848; Kalven, supra, at 7; Magrath, supra, at 75. Prince v. Massachusetts is urged to be constitutional authority for such regulation. See, e.g., Kuh, supra, at 258-260; Comment, Exclusion of Children from Violent Movies, 67 Col.L.Rev. 1149, 1159-1160 (1967); Note, Constitutional Problems in Obscenity Legislation Protecting Children, 54 Geo.L.J. 1379 (1966).

[7] One commentator who argues that obscenity legislation might be constitutionally defective as an imposition of a single standard of public morality would give effect to the parental role and accept laws relating only to minors. Henkin, Morals and the Constitution: The Sin of Obscenity, 63 Col.L.Rev. 391, 413, n. 68 (1963):

"One must consider also how much difference it makes if laws are designed to protect only the morals of a child. While many of the constitutional arguments against morals legislation apply equally to legislation protecting the morals of children, one can well distinguish laws which do not impose a morality on children, but which support the right of parents to deal with the morals of their children as they see fit."

See also Elias, Sex Publications and Moral Corruption: The Supreme Court Dilemma, 9 Wm. & Mary L.Rev. 302, 320-321 (1967).

[8] Compare Memoirs v. Massachusetts, 383 U.S. at 383 U. S. 424 (opinion of DOUGLAS, J.) with id. at 383 U. S. 441 (opinion of Clark, J.). See Kuh, supra, cc. 18-19; Gaylin, Book Review, 77 Yale L.J. 579, 591-595 (1968); Magrath, supra, at 52.

[9] Our conclusion in Roth, at 354 U. S. 486-487, that the clear and present danger test was irrelevant to the determination of obscenity made it unnecessary in that case to consider the debate among the authorities whether exposure to pornography caused antisocial consequences. See also Mishkin v. New York, supra; Ginzburg v. United States, supra; Memoirs v. Massachusetts, supra.

[10] Magrath, supra, at 52. See, e.g., id. at 49-56; Dibble, Obscenity: State Quarantine to Protect Children, 39 So.Cal.L.Rev. 345 (1966); Wall, Obscenity and Youth: The Problem and a Possible Solution, Crim.L.Bull., Vol. 1, No. 8, pp. 28, 30 (1965); Note, 55 Cal.L.Rev. 926, 934 (1967); Comment, 34 Ford.L.Rev. 692, 694 (1966). See also J. Paul & M. Schwartz, Federal Censorship: Obscenity in the Mail, 191-192; Blakey, Book Review, 41 Notre Dame Law. 1055, 1060, n. 46 (1966); Green, Obscenity, Censorship, and Juvenile Delinquency, 14 U. Toronto L.Rev. 229, 249 (1962); Lockhart & McClure, Literature, The Law of Obscenity, and the Constitution, 38 Minn.L.Rev. 295, 373-385 (1954); Note, 52 Ky.L.J. 429, 447 (1964). But despite the vigor of the ongoing controversy whether obscene material will perceptibly create a danger of antisocial conduct, or will probably induce its recipients to such conduct, a medical practitioner recently suggested that the possibility of harmful effects to youth cannot be dismissed as frivolous. Dr. Gaylin of the Columbia University Psychoanalytic Clinic, reporting on the views of some psychiatrists in 77 Yale L.J. at 592-593, said:

"It is in the period of growth [of youth] when these patterns of behavior are laid down, when environmental stimuli of all sorts must be integrated into a workable sense of self, when sensuality is being defined and fears elaborated, when pleasure confronts security and impulse encounters control -- it is in this period, undramatically and with time, that legalized pornography may conceivably be damaging."

Dr. Gaylin emphasizes that a child might not be as well prepared as an adult to make an intelligent choice as to the material he chooses to read:

"[P]sychiatrists . . . made a distinction between the reading of pornography, as unlikely to be per se harmful, and the permitting of the reading of pornography, which was conceived as potentially destructive. The child is protected in his reading of pornography by the knowledge that it is pornographic, i.e., disapproved. It is outside of parental standards, and not a part of his identification processes. To openly permit implies parental approval, and even suggests seductive encouragement. If this is so of parental approval, it is equally so of societal approval -- another potent influence on the developing ego."

Id. at 94.

### Interstate Circuit, Inc. v. City of Dallas (April 22, 1968) [Notes and appendix omitted]

MR. JUSTICE MARSHALL delivered the opinion of the Court.

Appellants are an exhibitor and the distributor of a motion picture named "Viva Maria," which, pursuant to a city ordinance, the Motion Picture Classification Board of the appellee City of Dallas classified as "not suitable for young persons." A county court upheld the Board's determination and enjoined exhibition of the film without acceptance by appellants of the requirements imposed by the restricted classification. The Texas Court of Civil Appeals affirmed, [1] and we noted probable jurisdiction, 387 U.S. 903, to consider the First and Fourteenth Amendment issues raised by appellants with respect to appellee's classification ordinance.

That ordinance, adopted in 1965, may be summarized as follows. [2] It establishes a Motion Picture Classification Board, composed of nine appointed members, all of whom serve without pay. The Board classifies films as "suitable for young persons" or as "not suitable for young persons," young persons being defined as children who have not reached their 16th birthday. An exhibitor must be specially licensed to show "not suitable" films.

The ordinance requires the exhibitor, before any initial showing of a film, to file with the Board a proposed classification of the film together with a summary of its plot and similar information. The proposed classification is approved if the Board affirmatively agrees with it, or takes no action upon it within five days of its filing.

If a majority of the Board is dissatisfied with the proposed classification, the exhibitor is required to project the film before at least five members of the Board at the earliest practicable time. At the showing, the exhibitor may also present testimony or other support for his proposed classification. Within two days, the Board must issue its classification order. Should the exhibitor disagree, he must file within two days [3] a notice of nonacceptance. The Board is then required to go to court within three days to seek a temporary injunction, and a hearing is required to be set on that application within five days thereafter; if the exhibitor agrees to waive notice and requests a hearing on the merits of a permanent injunction, the Board is required to waive its application for a temporary injunction and join in the exhibitor's request. If an injunction does not issue within 10 days of the exhibitor's notice of nonacceptance, the Board's classification order is suspended. [4] The ordinance does not define the scope of judicial review of the Board's determination, but the Court of Civil Appeals held that de novo review in the trial court was required. [5] If an injunction issues and the exhibitor seeks appellate review, or if an injunction is refused and the Board appeals, the Board must waive all statutory notices and times, and join a request of the exhibitor to advance the case on the appellate court's docket, i.e., do everything it can to assure a speedy determination.

The ordinance is enforced primarily by a misdemeanor penalty: an exhibitor is subject to a fine of up to $200 if he exhibits a film that is classified "not suitable for young persons" without advertisements clearly stating its classification or without the classification being clearly posted, exhibits on the same program a suitable and a not suitable film, knowingly admits a youth under age 16 to view the film without his guardian or spouse accompanying him, [6] makes any false or willfully misleading statement in submitting a film for classification, or exhibits a not suitable film without having a valid license therefor.

The same penalty is applicable to a youth who obtains admission to a not suitable film by falsely giving his age as 16 years or over, and to any person who sells or gives to a youth under 16 a ticket to a not suitable film, or makes any false statements to enable such a youth to gain admission. [7]

Other means of enforcement, as against the exhibitor, are provided. Repeated violations of the ordinance, or persistent failure

"to use reasonable diligence to determine whether those seeking admittance to the exhibition of a film classified 'not suitable for young persons' are below the age of sixteen,"

may be the basis for revocation of a license to show not suitable films. [8] Such a persistent failure, or exhibition of a not suitable film by an exhibitor with three convictions under the ordinance, inter alia, are defined as "public nuisances," which the Board may seek to restrain by a suit for injunctive relief.

The substantive standards governing classification are as follows:

"'Not suitable for young persons' means: "

"(1) Describing or portraying brutality, criminal violence or depravity in such a manner as to be, in the judgment of the Board, likely to incite or encourage crime or delinquency on the part of young persons; or"

"(2) Describing or portraying nudity beyond the customary limits of candor in the community, or sexual promiscuity or extramarital or abnormal sexual relations in such a manner as to be, in the judgment of the Board, likely to incite or encourage delinquency or sexual promiscuity on the part of young persons or to appeal to their prurient interest."

"A film shall be considered 'likely to incite or encourage' crime delinquency or sexual promiscuity on the part of young persons, if, in the judgment of the Board, there is a substantial probability that it will create the impression on young persons that such conduct is profitable, desirable, acceptable, respectable, praiseworthy or commonly accepted.

A film shall be considered as appealing to 'prurient interest' of young persons if in the judgment of the Board, its calculated or dominant effect on young persons is substantially to arouse sexual desire. In determining whether a film is 'not suitable for young persons,' the Board shall consider the film as a whole, rather than isolated portions, and shall determine whether its harmful effects outweigh artistic or educational values such film may have for young persons."

Appellants attack those standards as unconstitutionally vague. We agree. Motion pictures are, of course, protected by the First Amendment, Joseph Burstyn, Inc. v. Wilson, 343 U. S. 495 (1952), and thus we start with the premise that "[p]recision of regulation must be the touchstone," NAACP v. Button, 371 U. S. 415, 371 U. S. 438 (1963). And while it is true that this Court refused to strike down, against a broad and generalized attack, a prior restraint requirement that motion pictures be submitted to censors in advance of exhibition, Times Film Corp. v. City of Chicago, 365 U. S. 43 (1961), there has been no retreat in this area from rigorous insistence upon procedural safeguards and judicial superintendence of the censor's action. See Freedman v. Maryland, 380 U. S. 51 (1965). [9]

In Winters v. New York, 333 U. S. 507 (1948), this Court struck down as vague and indefinite a statutory standard interpreted by the state court to be "criminal news or stories of deeds of bloodshed or lust, so massed as to become vehicles for inciting violent and depraved crimes. . . ." Id. at 333 U. S. 518. In Joseph Burstyn, Inc. v. Wilson, supra, the Court dealt with a film licensing standard of "sacrilegious," which was found to have such an all-inclusive definition as to result in "substantially unbridled censorship." 343 U.S. at 343 U. S. 502. Following Burstyn, the Court held the following film licensing standards to be unconstitutionally vague: "of such character as to be prejudicial to the best interests of the people of said City," Gelling v. Texas, 343 U. S. 960 (1952); "moral, educational or amusing and harmless," Superior Films, Inc. v. Department of Education, 346 U. S. 587 (1954); "immoral," and "tend to corrupt morals," Commercial Pictures Corp. v. Regents, 346 U. S. 57 (1954); "approve such films . . . [as] are moral and proper; . . . disapprove such as are cruel, obscene, indecent or immoral, or such as tend to debase or corrupt morals," Holmby Productions, Inc. v. Vaughn, 350 U.S. 870 (1955). [10] See also Kingsley Int'l Pictures Corp. v. Regents, 360 U. S. 684, 360 U. S. 699-702 (Clark, J., concurring in result).

The vice of vagueness is particularly pronounced where expression is sought to be subjected to licensing. It may be unlikely that what Dallas does in respect to the licensing of motion pictures would have a significant effect upon film makers in Hollywood or Europe. But what Dallas may constitutionally do, so may other cities and States. Indeed, we are told that this ordinance is being used as a model for legislation in other localities. Thus, one who wishes to convey his ideas through that medium, which, of course, includes one who is interested not so much in expression as in making money, must consider whether what he proposes to film, and how he proposes to film it, is within the terms of classification schemes such as this. If he is unable to determine what the ordinance means, he runs the risk of being foreclosed, in practical effect, from a significant portion of the movie-going public. Rather than run that risk, he might choose nothing but the innocuous, perhaps save for the so-called "adult" picture. Moreover, a local exhibitor who cannot afford to risk losing the youthful audience when a film may be of marginal interest to adults -- perhaps a "Viva Maria" -- may contract to show only the totally inane. The vast wasteland that some have described in reference to another medium might be a verdant paradise in comparison. The First Amendment interests here are, therefore, broader than merely those of the film maker, distributor, and exhibitor, and certainly broader than those of youths under 16.

Of course, as the Court said in Joseph Burstyn, Inc. v. Wilson, 343 U.S. at 343 U. S. 502,

"[i]t does not follow that the Constitution requires absolute freedom to exhibit every motion picture of every kind at all times and all places."

What does follow, at the least, as the cases above illustrate, is that the restrictions imposed cannot be so vague as to set "the censor . . . adrift upon a boundless sea . . .," id. at 343 U. S. 504. In short, as Justice Frankfurter said, "legislation must not be so vague, the language so loose, as to leave to those who have to apply it too wide a discretion . . .," Kingsley Int'l Pictures Corp. v. Regents, 360 U.S. at 360 U. S. 694 (concurring in result), one reason being that

"where licensing is rested, in the first instance, in an administrative agency, the available judicial review is, in effect, rendered inoperative [by vagueness],"

Joseph Burstyn, Inc. v. Wilson, supra, at 343 U. S. 532 (concurring opinion). Thus, to the extent that vague standards do not sufficiently guide the censor, the problem is not cured merely by affording de novo judicial review. Vague standards, unless narrowed by interpretation, encourage erratic administration whether the censor be administrative or judicial;

"individual impressions become the yardstick of action, and result in regulation in accordance with the beliefs of the individual censor, rather than regulation by law,"

Kingsley Int'l Pictures Corp. v. Regents, supra, at 360 U. S. 701 (Clark, J., concurring in result). [11]

The dangers inherent in vagueness are strikingly illustrated in these cases. Five members of the Board viewed "Viva Maria." Eight members voted to classify it as "not suitable for young persons," the ninth member not voting. The Board gave no reasons for its determination. [12] Appellee alleged in its petition for an injunction that the classification was warranted because the film portrayed

"sexual promiscuity in such a manner as to be in the judgment of the Board likely to incite or encourage delinquency or sexual promiscuity on the part of young persons or to appeal to their prurient interests."

Two Board members, a clergyman and a lawyer, testified at the hearing. Each adverted to several scenes in the film which, in their opinion, portrayed male-female relationships in a way contrary to "acceptable and approved behavior." Each acknowledged, in reference to scenes in which clergymen were involved in violence, most of which was farcical, that "sacrilege" might have entered into the Board's determination. And both conceded that the asserted portrayal of "sexual promiscuity" was implicit, rather than explicit, i.e., that it was a product of inference by, and imagination of, the viewer.

So far as "judicial superintendence" [13] and de novo review are concerned, the trial judge, after viewing the film and hearing argument, stated merely:

"Oh, I realize you gentlemen might be right. There are two or three features in this picture that look to me would be unsuitable to young people. . . . So I enjoin the exhibitor . . . from exhibiting it. [14]"

Nor did the Court of Civil Appeals provide much enlightenment or a narrowing definition of the ordinance. United Artists argued that the obscenity standards similar to those set forth in Roth v. United States, 354 U. S. 476 (1957), and other decisions of this Court ought to be controlling. [15] The majority of the Court of Civil Appeals held, alternatively, (1) that such cases were not applicable because the legislation involved in them resulted in suppression of the offending expression, rather than its classification; (2) that, if obscenity standards were applicable, then "Viva Maria" was obscene as to adults (a patently untenable conclusion), and therefore entitled to no constitutional protection, and (3) that, if obscenity standards were modified as to children, the film was obscene as to them, a conclusion which was not in terms given as a narrowing interpretation of any specific provision of the ordinance. 402 S.W.2d 770, 775-776. In regard to the last alternative holding, we must conclude that the court in effect ruled that the "portrayal . . . of sexual promiscuity as acceptable," id. at 775, is, in itself, obscene as to children. [16] The court also held that the standards of the ordinance were "sufficiently definite." Ibid.

Thus, we are left merely with the film and directed to the words of the ordinance. The term "sexual promiscuity" is not there defined, [17] and was not interpreted in the state courts. It could extend, depending upon one's moral judgment, from the obvious to any sexual contacts outside a marital relationship. The determinative manner of the "describing or portraying" of the subjects covered by the ordinance (see supra at 390 U. S. 681), including "sexual promiscuity," is defined as

"such a manner as to be, in the judgment of the Board, likely to incite or encourage delinquency or sexual promiscuity on the part of young persons."

A film is so

"'likely to incite or encourage' crime delinquency or sexual promiscuity on the part of young persons, if, in the judgment of the Board, there is a substantial probability that it will create the impression on young persons that such conduct is profitable, desirable, acceptable, respectable, praiseworthy or commonly accepted."

It might be excessive literalism to insist, as do appellants, that, because those last six adjectives are stated in the disjunctive, they represent separate and alternative subtle determinations the Board is to make, any of which results in a not suitable classification. Nonetheless,

"[w]hat may be to one viewer the glorification of an idea as being 'desirable, acceptable or proper' may to the notions of another be entirely devoid of such a teaching. The only limits on the censor's discretion is his understanding of what is included within the term 'desirable, acceptable or proper.' This is nothing less than a roving commission. . . ."

Kingsley Int'l Pictures Corp. v. Regents, 360 U.S. at 360 U. S. 701 (Clark, J., concurring in result). [18]

Vagueness and the attendant evils we have earlier described, see supra at 390 U. S. 683-685, are not rendered less objectionable because the regulation of expression is one of classification, rather than direct suppression. Cf. 372 U. S. S. 689� Books, Inc. v. Sullivan,@ 372 U. S. 58 (1963). [19] Nor is it an answer to an argument that a particular regulation of expression is vague to say that it was adopted for the salutary purpose of protecting children. The permissible extent of vagueness is not directly proportional to, or a function of, the extent of the power to regulate or control expression with respect to children. As Chief Judge Fuld has said:

"It is . . . essential that legislation aimed at protecting children from allegedly harmful expression -- no less than legislation enacted with respect to adults -- be clearly drawn and that the standards adopted be reasonably precise so that those who are governed by the law and those that administer it will understand its meaning and application."

People v. Kahn, 15 N.Y.2d 311, 313, 206 N.E.2d 333, 335 (1965) (concurring opinion). [20]

The vices -- the lack of guidance to those who seek to adjust their conduct and to those who seek to administer the law, as well as the possible practical curtailing of the effectiveness of judicial review -- are the same.

It is not our province to draft legislation. Suffice it to say that we have recognized that some believe "motion pictures possess a greater capacity for evil, particularly among the youth of a community, than other modes of expression," Joseph Burstyn, Inc. v. Wilson, supra, at 343 U. S. 502, and we have indicated more generally that, because of its strong and abiding interest in youth, a State may regulate the dissemination to juveniles of, and their access to, material objectionable as to them, but which a State clearly could not regulate as to adults. Ginsberg v. New York, ante, p. 390 U. S. 629. [21] Here, we conclude only that "the absence of narrowly drawn, reasonable and definite standards for the officials to follow," Niemotko v. Maryland, 340 U. S. 268, 340 U. S. 271 (1951), is fatal. [22]

The judgment of the Texas Court of Civil Appeals is reversed, and the cases are remanded for further proceedings not inconsistent with this opinion.

It is so ordered.

## Tinker v. Des Moines Independent Community School District (February 24, 1969)

MR. JUSTICE FORTAS delivered the opinion of the Court.

Petitioner John F. Tinker, 15 years old, and petitioner Christopher Eckhardt, 16 years old, attended high schools in Des Moines, Iowa. Petitioner Mary Beth Tinker, John's sister, was a 13-year-old student in junior high school.

In December, 1965, a group of adults and students in Des Moines held a meeting at the Eckhardt home. The group determined to publicize their objections to the hostilities in Vietnam and their support for a truce by wearing black armbands during the holiday season and by fasting on December 16 and New Year's Eve. Petitioners and their parents had previously engaged in similar activities, and they decided to participate in the program.

The principals of the Des Moines schools became aware of the plan to wear armbands. On December 14, 1965, they met and adopted a policy that any student wearing an armband to school would be asked to remove it, and, if he refused, he would be suspended until he returned without the armband. Petitioners were aware of the regulation that the school authorities adopted.

On December 16, Mary Beth and Christopher wore black armbands to their schools. John Tinker wore his armband the next day. They were all sent home and suspended from school until they would come back without their armbands. They did not return to school until after the planned period for wearing armbands had expired -- that is, until after New Year's Day.

This complaint was filed in the United States District Court by petitioners, through their fathers, under § 1983 of Title 42 of the United States Code. It prayed for an injunction restraining the respondent school officials and the respondent members of the board of directors of the school district from disciplining the petitioners, and it sought nominal damages. After an evidentiary hearing, the District Court dismissed the complaint. It upheld the constitutionality of the school authorities' action on the ground that it was reasonable in order to prevent disturbance of school discipline. 258 F.Supp. 971 (1966). The court referred to, but expressly declined to follow, the Fifth Circuit's holding in a similar case that the wearing of symbols like the armbands cannot be prohibited unless it "materially and substantially interfere[s] with the requirements of appropriate discipline in the operation of the school." Burnside v. Byars, 363 F.2d 744,

749 (1966). [n1]

On appeal, the Court of Appeals for the Eighth Circuit considered the case en banc. The court was equally divided, and the District Court's decision was accordingly affirmed without opinion. 383 F.2d 988 (1967). We granted certiorari. 390 U.S. 942 (1968).

I

The District Court recognized that the wearing of an armband for the purpose of expressing certain views is the type of symbolic act that is within the Free Speech Clause of the First Amendment. See West Virginia v. Barnette, 319 U.S. 624 (1943); Stromberg v. California, 283 U.S. 359 (1931). Cf. Thornhill v. Alabama, 310 U.S. 88 (1940); Edwards v. South Carolina, 372 U.S. 229 (1963); Brown v. Louisiana, 383 U.S. 131 (1966). As we shall discuss, the wearing of armbands in the circumstances of this case was entirely divorced from actually or potentially disruptive conduct by those participating in it. It was closely akin to "pure speech" which, we have repeatedly held, is entitled to comprehensive protection under the First Amendment. Cf. Cox v. Louisiana, 379 U.S. 536, 555 (1965); Adderley v. Florida, 385 U.S. 39 (1966).

First Amendment rights, applied in light of the special characteristics of the school environment, are available to teachers and students. It can hardly be argued that either students or teachers shed their constitutional rights to freedom of speech or expression at the schoolhouse gate. This has been the unmistakable holding of this Court for almost 50 years. In Meyer v. Nebraska, 262 U.S. 390 (1923), and Bartels v. Iowa, 262 U.S. 404 (1923), this Court, in opinions by Mr. Justice McReynolds, held that the Due Process Clause of the Fourteenth Amendment prevents States from forbidding the teaching of a foreign language to young students. Statutes to this effect, the Court held, unconstitutionally interfere with the liberty of teacher, student, and parent. [n2] See also Pierce v. Society of Sisters, 268 U.S. 510 (1925); West Virginia v. Barnette, 319 U.S. 624 (1943); McCollum v. Board of Education, 333 U.S. 203 (1948); Wieman v. Updegraff, 344 U.S. 183, 195 (1952) (concurring opinion); Sweezy v. New Hampshire, 354 U.S. 234 (1957); Shelton v. Tucker, 364 U.S. 479, 487 (1960); Engel v. Vitale, 370 U.S. 421 (1962); Keyishian v. Board of Regents, 385 U.S. 589, 603 (1967); Epperson v. Arkansas, ante, p. 97 (1968).

In West Virginia v. Barnette, supra, this Court held that, under the First Amendment, the student in public school may not be compelled to salute the flag. Speaking through Mr. Justice Jackson, the Court said:

The Fourteenth Amendment, as now applied to the States, protects the citizen against the State itself and all of its creatures -- Boards of Education not excepted. These have, of course, important, delicate, and highly discretionary functions, but none that they may not perform within the limits of the Bill of Rights. That they are educating the young for citizenship is reason for scrupulous protection of Constitutional freedoms of the individual, if we are not to strangle the free mind at its source and teach youth to discount important principles of our government as mere platitudes.

319 U.S. at 637. On the other hand, the Court has repeatedly emphasized the need for affirming the comprehensive authority of the States and of school officials, consistent with fundamental constitutional safeguards, to prescribe and control conduct in the schools. See Epperson v. Arkansas, supra, at 104; Meyer v. Nebraska, supra, at 402. Our problem lies in the area where students in the exercise of First Amendment rights collide with the rules of the school authorities.

II

The problem posed by the present case does not relate to regulation of the length of skirts or the type of clothing, to hair style, or deportment. Cf. Ferrell v. Dallas Independent School District, 392 F.2d 697 (1968); Pugsley v. Sellmeyer, 158 Ark. 247, 250 S.W. 538 (1923). It does not concern aggressive, disruptive action or even group demonstrations. Our problem involves direct, primary First Amendment rights akin to "pure speech."

The school officials banned and sought to punish petitioners for a silent, passive expression of opinion, unaccompanied by any disorder or disturbance on the part of petitioners. There is here no evidence whatever of petitioners' interference, actual or nascent, with the schools' work or of collision with the rights of other students to be secure and to be let alone. Accordingly, this case does not concern speech or action that intrudes upon the work of the schools or the rights of other students.

Only a few of the 18,000 students in the school system wore the black armbands. Only five students were suspended for wearing them. There is no indication that the work of the schools or any class was disrupted. Outside the classrooms, a few students made hostile remarks to the children wearing armbands, but there were no threats or acts of violence on school premises.

The District Court concluded that the action of the school authorities was reasonable because it was based upon their fear of a disturbance from the wearing of the armbands. But, in our system, undifferentiated fear or apprehension of disturbance is not enough to overcome the right to freedom of expression. Any departure from absolute regimentation may cause trouble. Any variation from the majority's opinion may inspire fear. Any word spoken, in class, in the lunchroom, or on the campus, that deviates from the views of another person may start an argument or cause a disturbance. But our Constitution says we must take this risk, Terminiello v. Chicago, 337 U.S. 1 (1949); and our history says that it is this sort of hazardous freedom -- this kind of openness -- that is the basis of our national strength and of the independence and vigor of Americans who grow up and live in this relatively permissive, often disputatious, society.

In order for the State in the person of school officials to justify prohibition of a particular expression of opinion, it must be able to show that its action was caused by something more than a mere desire to avoid the discomfort and unpleasantness that always accompany an unpopular viewpoint. Certainly where there is no finding and no showing that engaging in the forbidden conduct would "materially and substantially interfere with the requirements of appropriate discipline in the operation of the school," the prohibition cannot be sustained. Burnside v. Byars, supra at 749.

In the present case, the District Court made no such finding, and our independent examination of the record fails to yield evidence that the school authorities had reason to anticipate that the wearing of the armbands would substantially interfere with the work of the school or impinge upon the rights of other students. Even an official memorandum prepared after the suspension that listed the reasons for the ban on wearing the armbands made no reference to the anticipation of such disruption. [n3]

On the contrary, the action of the school authorities appears to have been based upon an urgent wish to avoid the controversy which might result from the expression, even by the silent symbol of armbands, of opposition to this Nation's part in the conflagration in Vietnam. [n4] It is revealing, in this respect, that the meeting at which the school principals decided to issue the contested regulation was called in response to a student's statement to the journalism teacher in one of the schools that he wanted to write an article on Vietnam and have it published in the school paper. (The student was dissuaded. [n5] )

It is also relevant that the school authorities did not purport to prohibit the wearing of all symbols of political or controversial significance. The record shows that students in some of the schools wore buttons relating to national political campaigns, and some even wore the Iron Cross, traditionally a symbol of Nazism. The order prohibiting the wearing of armbands did not extend to these. Instead, a particular symbol -- black armbands worn to exhibit opposition to this Nation's involvement in Vietnam -- was singled out for prohibition. Clearly, the prohibition of expression of one particular opinion, at least without evidence that it is necessary to avoid material and substantial interference with schoolwork or discipline, is not constitutionally permissible.

In our system, state-operated schools may not be enclaves of totalitarianism. School officials do not possess absolute authority over their students. Students in school, as well as out of school, are "persons" under our Constitution. They are possessed of fundamental rights which the State must respect, just as they themselves must respect their obligations to the State. In our system, students may not be regarded as closed-circuit recipients of only that which the State chooses to communicate. They may not be confined to the expression of those sentiments that are officially approved. In the absence of a specific showing of constitutionally valid reasons to regulate their speech, students are entitled to freedom of expression of their views. As Judge Gewin, speaking for the Fifth Circuit, said, school officials cannot suppress "expressions of feelings with which they do not wish to contend." Burnside v. Byars, supra, at 749.

In Meyer v. Nebraska, supra, at 402, Mr. Justice McReynolds expressed this Nation's repudiation of the principle that a State might so conduct its schools as to "foster a homogeneous people." He said:

In order to submerge the individual and develop ideal citizens, Sparta assembled the males at seven into barracks and intrusted their subsequent education and training to official guardians. Although such measures have been deliberately approved by men of great genius, their ideas touching the relation between individual and State were wholly different from those upon which our institutions rest; and it hardly will be affirmed that any legislature could impose such restrictions upon the people of a State without doing violence to both letter and spirit of the Constitution.

This principle has been repeated by this Court on numerous occasions during the intervening years. In Keyishian v. Board of Regents, 385 U.S. 589, 603, MR. JUSTICE BRENNAN, speaking for the Court, said:

"The vigilant protection of constitutional freedoms is nowhere more vital than in the community of American schools." Shelton v. Tucker, [ 364 U.S. 479,] at 487. The classroom is peculiarly the "marketplace of ideas." The Nation's future depends upon leaders trained through wide exposure to that robust exchange of ideas which discovers truth "out of a multitude of tongues, [rather] than through any kind of authoritative selection."

The principle of these cases is not confined to the supervised and ordained discussion which takes place in the classroom. The principal use to which the schools are dedicated is to accommodate students during prescribed hours for the purpose of certain types of activities. Among those activities is personal intercommunication among the students. [n6] This is not only an inevitable part of the process of attending school; it is also an important part of the educational process. A student's rights, therefore, do not embrace merely the classroom hours. When he is in the cafeteria, or on the playing field, or on the campus during the authorized hours, he may express his opinions, even on controversial subjects like the conflict in Vietnam, if he does so without "materially and substantially interfer[ing] with the requirements of appropriate discipline in the operation of the school" and without colliding with the rights of others. Burnside v. Byars, supra, at 749. But conduct by the student, in class or out of it, which for any reason -- whether it stems from time, place, or type of behavior -- materially disrupts classwork or involves substantial disorder or invasion of the rights of others is, of course, not immunized by the constitutional guarantee of freedom of speech. Cf. Blackwell v. Issaquena County Board of Education., 363 F.2d 740 (C.A. 5th Cir.1966).

Under our Constitution, free speech is not a right that is given only to be so circumscribed that it exists in principle, but not in fact. Freedom of expression would not truly exist if the right could be exercised only in an area that a benevolent government has provided as a safe haven for crackpots. The Constitution says that Congress (and the States) may not abridge the right to free speech. This provision means what it says. We properly read it to permit reasonable regulation of speech-connected activities in carefully restricted circumstances. But we do not confine the permissible exercise of First Amendment rights to a telephone booth or the four corners of a pamphlet, or to supervised and ordained discussion in a school classroom.

If a regulation were adopted by school officials forbidding discussion of the Vietnam conflict, or the expression by any student of opposition to it anywhere on school property except as part of a prescribed classroom exercise, it would be obvious that the regulation would violate the constitutional rights of students, at least if it could not be justified by a showing that the students' activities would materially and substantially disrupt the work and discipline of the school. Cf. Hammond v. South Carolina State College, 272 F.Supp. 947 (D.C.S.C.1967) (orderly protest meeting on state college campus); Dickey v. Alabama State Board of Education, 273 F.Supp. 613 (D.C.M.D. Ala. 967) (expulsion of student editor of college newspaper). In the circumstances of the present case, the prohibition of the silent, passive "witness of the armbands," as one of the children called it, is no less offensive to the Constitution's guarantees.

As we have discussed, the record does not demonstrate any facts which might reasonably have led school authorities to forecast substantial disruption of or material interference with school activities, and no disturbances or disorders on the school premises in fact occurred. These petitioners merely went about their ordained rounds in school. Their deviation consisted only in wearing on their sleeve a band of black cloth, not more than two inches wide. They wore it to exhibit their disapproval of the Vietnam hostilities and their advocacy of a truce, to make their views known, and, by their example, to influence others to adopt them. They neither interrupted school activities nor sought to intrude in the school affairs or the lives of others. They caused discussion outside of the classrooms, but no interference with work and no disorder. In the circumstances, our Constitution does not permit officials of the State to deny their form of expression.

We express no opinion as to the form of relief which should be granted, this being a matter for the lower courts to determine. We reverse and remand for further proceedings consistent with this opinion.

Reversed and remanded.

Notes

1. In Burnside, the Fifth Circuit ordered that high school authorities be enjoined from enforcing a regulation forbidding students to wear "freedom buttons." It is instructive that, in Blackwell v. Issaquena County Board of Education, 363 F.2d 749 (1966), the same panel on the same day reached the opposite result on different facts. It declined to enjoin enforcement of such a regulation in another high school where the students wearing freedom buttons harassed students who did not wear them, and created much disturbance.

2. Hamilton v. Regents of Univ. of Cal., 293 U.S. 245 (1934), is sometimes cited for the broad proposition that the State may attach conditions to attendance at a state university that require individuals to violate their religious convictions. The case involved dismissal of members of a religious denomination from a land grant college for refusal to participate in military training. Narrowly viewed, the case turns upon the Court's conclusion that merely requiring a student to participate in school training in military "science" could not conflict with his constitutionally protected freedom of conscience. The decision cannot be taken as establishing that the State may impose and enforce any

conditions that it chooses upon attendance at public institutions of learning, however violative they may be of fundamental constitutional guarantees. See, e.g., West Virginia v. Barnette, 319 U.S. 624 (1943); Dixon v. Alabama State Board of Education, 294 F.2d 150 (C.A. 5th Cir.1961); Knight v. State Board of Education, 200 F.Supp. 174 (D.C. M.D. Tenn.1961); Dickey v. Alabama State Board of Education, 273 F.Supp. 613 (D.C. M.D. Ala.1967). See also Note, Unconstitutional Conditions, 73 Harv.L.Rev. 1595 (1960); Note, Academic Freedom, 81 Harv.L.Rev. 1045 (1968).

3. The only suggestions of fear of disorder in the report are these:

A former student of one of our high schools was killed in Viet Nam. Some of his friends are still in school, and it was felt that, if any kind of a demonstration existed, it might evolve into something which would be difficult to control.

Students at one of the high schools were heard to say they would wear armbands of other colors if the black bands prevailed.

Moreover, the testimony of school authorities at trial indicates that it was not fear of disruption that motivated the regulation prohibiting the armbands; the regulation was directed against "the principle of the demonstration" itself. School authorities simply felt that "the schools are no place for demonstrations," and if the students didn't like the way our elected officials were handling things, it should be handled with the ballot box, and not in the halls of our public schools.

4. The District Court found that the school authorities, in prohibiting black armbands, were influenced by the fact that

[t]he Viet Nam war and the involvement of the United States therein has been the subject of a major controversy for some time. When the armband regulation involved herein was promulgated, debate over the Viet Nam war had become vehement in many localities. A protest march against the war had been recently held in Washington, D.C. A wave of draft card burning incidents protesting the war had swept the country. At that time, two highly publicized draft card burning cases were pending in this Court. Both individuals supporting the war and those opposing it were quite vocal in expressing their views.

258 F.Supp. at 92-973.

5. After the principals' meeting, the director of secondary education and the principal of the high school informed the student that the principals were opposed to publication of his article. They reported that

we felt that it was a very friendly conversation, although we did not feel that we had convinced the student that our decision was a just one.

6. In Hammond v. South Carolina State College, 272 F.Supp. 947 (D.C. S.C.1967), District Judge Hemphill had before him a case involving a meeting on campus of 300 students to express their views on school practices. He pointed out that a school is not like a hospital or a jail enclosure. Cf. Cox v. Louisiana, 379 U.S. 536 (1965); Adderley v. Florida, 385 U.S. 39 (1966). It is a public place, and its dedication to specific uses does not imply that the constitutional rights of persons entitled to be there are to be gauged as

if the premises were purely private property. Cf. Edwards v. South Carolina, 372 U.S. 229 (1963); Brown v. Louisiana, 383 U.S. 131 (1966).

## Stanley v. Georgia (April 7, 1969)

MR. JUSTICE MARSHALL delivered the opinion of the Court.

An investigation of appellant's alleged bookmaking activities led to the issuance of a search warrant for appellant's home. Under authority of this warrant, federal and state agents secured entrance. They found very little evidence of bookmaking activity, but, while looking through a desk drawer in an upstairs bedroom, one of the federal agents, accompanied by a state officer, found three reels of eight-millimeter film. Using a projector and screen found in an upstairs living room, they viewed the films. The state officer concluded that they were obscene and seized them. Since a further examination of the bedroom indicated that appellant occupied it, he was charged with possession of obscene matter and placed under arrest. He was later indicted for "knowingly hav[ing] possession of . . . obscene matter" in violation of Georgia law. [n1] Appellant was tried before a jury and convicted. The Supreme Court of Georgia affirmed. Stanley v. State, 224 Ga. 259, 161 S.E.2d 309 (1968). We noted probable jurisdiction of an appeal brought under 28 U.S.C. § 1257(2). 393 U.S. 819 (1968).

Appellant raises several challenges to the validity of his conviction. [n2] We find it necessary to consider only one. Appellant argues here, and argued below, that the Georgia obscenity statute, insofar as it punishes mere private possession of obscene matter, violates the First Amendment, as made applicable to the States by the Fourteenth Amendment. For reasons set forth below, we agree that the mere private possession of obscene matter cannot constitutionally be made a crime.

The court below saw no valid constitutional objection to the Georgia statute, even though it extends further than the typical statute forbidding commercial sales of obscene material. It held that

[i]t is not essential to an indictment charging one with possession of obscene matter that it be alleged that such possession was "with intent to sell, expose or circulate the same."

Stanley v. State, supra, at 261, 161 S.E.2d at 311. The State and appellant both agree that the question here before us is whether "a statute imposing criminal sanctions upon the mere [knowing] possession of obscene matter" is constitutional. In this context, Georgia concedes that the present case appears to be one of "first impression . . . on this exact point," [n3] but contends that, since "obscenity is not within the area of constitutionally protected speech or press," Roth v. United States, 354 U.S. 476, 485 (1957), the States are free, subject to the limits of other provisions of the Constitution, see, e.g., Ginsberg v. New York, 390 U.S. 629, 637-645 (1968), to deal with it any way deemed necessary, just as they may deal with possession of other things thought to be detrimental to the welfare of their citizens. If the State can protect the body of a citizen, may it not, argues Georgia, protect his mind?

It is true that Roth does declare, seemingly without qualification, that obscenity is not protected by the First Amendment. That statement has been repeated in various forms in subsequent cases. See, e.g., Smith v. California, 361 U.S. 147, 152 (1959); Jacobellis v. Ohio, 378 U.S. 184, 186-187 (1964) (opinion of BRENNAN, J.); Ginsberg v. New York, supra, at 635. However, neither Roth nor any subsequent decision of this Court dealt with the precise problem involved in the present case. Roth was convicted of mailing obscene circulars and advertising, and an obscene book, in violation of a federal obscenity statute. [n4] The defendant in a companion case, Alberts v. California, 354 U.S. 476 (1957), was convicted of "lewdly keeping for sale obscene and indecent books, and [of] writing, composing and publishing an obscene advertisement of them. . . ." Id. at 481. None of the statements cited by the Court in Roth for the proposition that "this Court has always assumed that obscenity is not protected by the freedoms of speech and press" were made in the context of a statute punishing mere private possession of obscene material; the cases cited deal for the most part with use of the mails to distribute objectionable material or with some form of public distribution or dissemination. [n5] Moreover, none of this Court's decisions subsequent to Roth involved prosecution for private possession of obscene materials. Those cases dealt with the power of the State and Federal Governments to prohibit or regulate certain public actions taken or intended to be taken with respect to obscene matter. [n6] Indeed, with one exception, we have been unable to discover any case in which the issue in the present case has been fully considered. [n7]

In this context, we do not believe that this case can be decided simply by citing Roth. Roth and its progeny certainly do mean that the First and Fourteenth Amendments recognize a valid governmental interest in dealing with the problem of obscenity. But the assertion of that interest cannot, in every context, be insulated from all constitutional protections. Neither Roth nor any other decision of this Court reaches that far. As the Court said in Roth itself,

[c]easeless vigilance is the watchword to prevent . . . erosion [of First Amendment rights] by Congress or by the States. The door barring federal and state intrusion into this area cannot be left ajar; it must be kept tightly closed and opened only the slightest crack necessary to prevent encroachment upon more important interests.

354 U.S. at 488. Roth and the cases following it discerned such an "important interest" in the regulation of commercial distribution of obscene material. That holding cannot foreclose an examination of the constitutional implications of a statute forbidding mere private possession of such material.

It is now well established that the Constitution protects the right to receive information and ideas. "This freedom [of speech and press] . . . necessarily protects the right to receive. . . ." Martin v. City of Struthers, 319 U.S. 141, 143 (1943); see Griswold v. Connecticut, 381 U.S. 479, 482 (1965); Lamont v. Postmaster General, 381 U.S. 301, 307-308 (1965) (BRENNAN, J., concurring); cf. Pierce v. Society of Sisters, 268 U.S. 510 (1925). This right to receive information and ideas, regardless of their social worth, see

Winters v. New York, 333 U.S. 507, 510 (1948), is fundamental to our free society. Moreover, in the context of this case -- a prosecution for mere possession of printed or filmed matter in the privacy of a person's own home -- that right takes on an added dimension. For also fundamental is the right to be free, except in very limited circumstances, from unwanted governmental intrusions into one's privacy.

The makers of our Constitution undertook to secure conditions favorable to the pursuit of happiness. They recognized the significance of man's spiritual nature, of his feelings and of his intellect. They knew that only a part of the pain, pleasure and satisfactions of life are to be found in material things. They sought to protect Americans in their beliefs, their thoughts, their emotions and their sensations. They conferred, as against the Government, the right to be let alone -- the most comprehensive of rights and the right most valued by civilized man.

Olmstead v. United States, 277 U.S. 438, 478 (1928) (Brandeis, J., dissenting). See Griswold v. Connecticut, supra; cf. NAACP v. Alabama, 357 U.S. 449, 462 (1958).

These are the rights that appellant is asserting in the case before us. He is asserting the right to read or observe what he pleases -- the right to satisfy his intellectual and emotional needs in the privacy of his own home. He is asserting the right to be free from state inquiry into the contents of his library. Georgia contends that appellant does not have these rights, that there are certain types of materials that the individual may not read or even possess. Georgia justifies this assertion by arguing that the films in the present case are obscene. But we think that mere categorization of these films as "obscene" is insufficient justification for such a drastic invasion of personal liberties guaranteed by the First and Fourteenth Amendments. Whatever may be the justifications for other statutes regulating obscenity, we do not think they reach into the privacy of one's own home. If the First Amendment means anything, it means that a State has no business telling a man, sitting alone in his own house, what books he may read or what films he may watch. Our whole constitutional heritage rebels at the thought of giving government the power to control men's minds.

And yet, in the face of these traditional notions of individual liberty, Georgia asserts the right to protect the individual's mind from the effects of obscenity. We are not certain that this argument amounts to anything more than the assertion that the State has the right to control the moral content of a person's thoughts. [n8] To some, this may be a noble purpose, but it is wholly inconsistent with the philosophy of the First Amendment. As the Court said in Kingsley International Pictures Corp. v. Regents, 360 U.S. 684, 688-689 (1959),

[t]his argument misconceives what it is that the Constitution protects. Its guarantee is not confined to the expression of ideas that are conventional or shared by a majority. . . . And, in the realm of ideas, it protects expression which is eloquent no less than that which is unconvincing.

Cf. Joseph Burstyn, Inc. v. Wilson, 343 U.S. 495 (1952). Nor is it relevant that obscene materials in general, or the particular films before the Court, are arguably devoid of any ideological content. The line between the transmission of ideas and mere entertainment is much too elusive for this Court to draw, if indeed such a line can be drawn at all. See Winters v. New York, supra, at 510. Whatever the power of the state to control public dissemination of ideas inimical to the public morality, it cannot constitutionally premise legislation on the desirability of controlling a person's private thoughts.

Perhaps recognizing this, Georgia asserts that exposure to obscene materials may lead to deviant sexual behavior or crimes of sexual violence. There appears to be little empirical basis for that assertion. [n9] But, more important, if the State is only concerned about printed or filmed materials inducing antisocial conduct, we believe that, in the context of private consumption of ideas and information we should adhere to the view that "[a]mong free men, the deterrents ordinarily to be applied to prevent crime are education and punishment for violations of the law. . . ." Whitney v. California, 274 U.S. 357, 378 (1927) (Brandeis, J., concurring). See Emerson, Toward a General Theory of the First Amendment, 72 Yale L.J. 877, 938 (1963). Given the present state of knowledge, the State may no more prohibit mere possession of obscene matter on the ground that it may lead to antisocial conduct than it may prohibit possession of chemistry books on the ground that they may lead to the manufacture of homemade spirits.

It is true that, in Roth, this Court rejected the necessity of proving that exposure to obscene material would create a clear and present danger of antisocial conduct or would probably induce its recipients to such conduct. 354 U.S. at 486-487. But that case dealt with public distribution of obscene materials and such distribution is subject to different objections. For example, there is always the danger that obscene material might fall into the hands of children, see Ginsberg v. New York, supra, or that it might intrude upon the sensibilities or privacy of the general public. [n10] See Redrup v. New York, 386 U.S. 767, 769 (1967). No such dangers are present in this case.

Finally, we are faced with the argument that prohibition of possession of obscene materials is a necessary incident to statutory schemes prohibiting distribution. That argument is based on alleged difficulties of proving an intent to distribute or in producing evidence of actual distribution. We are not convinced that such difficulties exist, but even if they did we do not think that they would justify infringement of the individual's right to read or observe what he pleases. Because that right is so fundamental to our scheme of individual liberty, its restriction may not be justified by the need to ease the administration of otherwise valid criminal laws. See Smith v. California, 361 U.S. 147 (1959).

We hold that the First and Fourteenth Amendments prohibit making mere private possession of obscene material a crime. [n11] Roth and the cases following that decision are not impaired by today's holding. As we have said, the States retain broad power to regulate obscenity; that power simply does not extend to mere possession by the individual in the privacy of his own home. Accordingly, the judgment of the court below is reversed and the case is remanded for proceedings not inconsistent with this opinion.

It is so ordered.

Notes

1. Any person who shall knowingly bring or cause to be brought into this State for sale or exhibition, or who shall knowingly sell or offer to sell, or who shall knowingly lend or give away or offer to lend or give away, or who shall knowingly have possession of, or who shall knowingly exhibit or transmit to another, any obscene matter, or who shall knowingly advertise for sale by any form of notice, printed, written, or verbal, any obscene matter, or who shall knowingly manufacture, draw, duplicate or print any obscene matter with intent to sell, expose or circulate the same, shall, if such person has knowledge or reasonably should know of the obscene nature of such matter, be guilty of a felony, and, upon conviction thereof, shall be punished by confinement in the penitentiary for not less than one year nor more than five years: Provided, however, in the event the jury so recommends, such person may be punished as for a misdemeanor. As used herein, a matter is obscene if, considered as a whole, applying contemporary community standards, its predominant appeal is to prurient interest, i.e., a shameful or morbid interest in nudity, sex or excretion.

Ga.Code Ann. § 26-6301 (Supp. 1968).

2. Appellant does not argue that the films are not obscene. For the purpose of this opinion, we assume that they are obscene under any of the tests advanced by members of this Court. See Redrup v. New York, 386 U.S. 767 (1967).

3. The issue was before the Court in Mapp v. Ohio, 367 U.S. 643 (1961), but that case was decided on other grounds. MR. JUSTICE STEWART, although disagreeing with the majority opinion in Mapp, would have reversed the judgment in that case on the ground that the Ohio statute proscribing mere possession of obscene material was "not 'consistent with the rights of free thought and expression assured against state action by the Fourteenth Amendment.'" Id. at 672.

4. 18 U.S.C. § 1461.

5. Ex parte Jackson, 96 U.S. 727, 736-737 (1878) (use of the mails); United States v. Chase, 135 U.S. 255, 261 (1890) (use of the mails); Robertson v. Baldwin, 165 U.S. 275, 281 (1897) (publication); Public Clearing House v. Coyne, 194 U.S. 497, 508 (1904) (use of the mails); Hoke v. United States, 227 U.S. 308, 322 (1913) (use of interstate facilities); Near v. Minnesota, 283 U.S. 697, 716 (1931) (publication); Chaplinsky v. New Hampshire, 315 U.S. 568, 571-572 (1942) (utterances); Hannegan v. Esquire, Inc., 327 U.S. 146, 158 (1046) (use of the mails); Winters v. New York, 333 U.S. 507, 510 (1948) (possession with intent to sell); Beauharnais v. Illinois, 343 U.S. 250, 266 (1952) (libel).

6. Many of the cases involved prosecutions for sale or distribution of obscene materials or possession with intent to sell or distribute. See Redrup v. New York, 386 U.S. 767 (1967); Mishkin v. New York, 383 U.S. 502 (1966); Ginzburg v. United States, 383 U.S. 463 (1966); Jacobellis v. Ohio, 378 U.S. 184 (1964); Smith v. California, 361 U.S. 147 (1959). Our most recent decision involved a prosecution for sale of obscene material to

children. Ginsberg v. New York, 390 U.S. 629 (1968); cf. Interstate Circuit, Inc. v. City of Dallas, 390 U.S. 676 (1968). Other cases involved federal or state statutory procedures for preventing the distribution or mailing of obscene material, or procedures for pre-distribution approval. See Freedman v. Maryland, 380 U.S. 51 (1965); Bantam Books, Inc. v. Sullivan, 372 U.S. 58 (1963); Manual Enterprises, Inc. v. Day, 370 U.S. 478 (1962). Still another case dealt with an attempt to seize obscene material "kept for the purpose of being sold, published, exhibited . . . or otherwise distributed or circulated. . . ." Marcus v. Search Warrant, 367 U.S. 717, 719 (1961); see also A Quantity of Books v. Kansas, 378 U.S. 205 (1964). Memoirs v. Massachusetts, 383 U.S. 413 (1966), was a proceeding in equity against a. book. However, possession of a book determined to be obscene in such a proceeding was made criminal only when "for the purpose of sale, loan or distribution." Id. at 422.

7. The Supreme Court of Ohio considered the issue in State v. Mapp, 170 Ohio St. 427, 166 N.E.2d 387 (1960). Four of the seven judges of that court felt that criminal prosecution for mere private possession of obscene materials was prohibited by the Constitution. However, Ohio law required the concurrence of "all but one of the judges" to declare a state law unconstitutional. The view of the "dissenting" judges was expressed by Judge Herbert:

I cannot agree that mere private possession of . . . [obscene] literature by an adult should constitute a crime. The right of the individual to read, to believe or disbelieve, and to think without governmental supervision is one of our basic liberties, but to dictate to the mature adult what books he may have in his own private library seems to the writer to be a clear infringement of his constitutional rights as an individual.

170 Ohio St., at 437, 166 N.E.2d at 393.

Shortly thereafter, the Supreme Court of Ohio interpreted the Ohio statute to require proof of "possession and control for the purpose of circulation or exhibition." State v. Jacobellis, 173 Ohio St. 22, 27-28, 179 N.E.2d 777, 781 (1962), rev'd on other grounds, 378 U.S. 184 (1964). The interpretation was designed to avoid the constitutional problem posed by the "dissenters" in Mapp. See State v. Ross, 12 Ohio St.2d 37, 231 N.E.2d 299 (1967).

Other cases dealing with nonpublic distribution of obscene material or with legitimate uses of obscene material have expressed similar reluctance to make such activity criminal, albeit largely on statutory grounds. In United States v. Chase, 135 U.S. 255 (1890), the Court held that federal law did not make criminal the mailing of a private sealed obscene letter on the ground that the law's purpose was to purge the mails of obscene matter "as far as was consistent with the rights reserved to the people, and with a due regard to the security of private correspondence. . . ." 135 U.S. at 261. The law was later amended to include letters and was sustained in that form. Andrews v. United States, 162 U.S. 420 (1896). In United States v. 31 Photographs, 156 F.Supp. 350 (D.C.S.D.N.Y.1957), the court denied an attempt by the Government to confiscate certain materials sought to be imported into the United States by the Institute for Sex Research,

Inc., at Indiana University. The court found, applying the Roth formulation, that the materials would not appeal to the "prurient interest" of those seeking to import and utilize the materials. Thus, the statute permitting seizure of "obscene" materials was not applicable. The court found it unnecessary to reach the constitutional questions presented by the claimant, but did note its belief that

the statement . . . [in Roth] concerning the rejection of obscenity must be interpreted in the light of the widespread distribution of the material in Roth.

156 F.Supp. at 360, n. 40. See also Redmond v. United States, 384 U.S. 264 (1966), where this Court granted the Solicitor General's motion to vacate and remand with instructions to dismiss an information charging a violation of a federal obscenity statute in a case where a husband and wife mailed undeveloped films of each other posing in the nude to an out-of-state firm for developing. But see Ackerman v. United States, 293 F.2d 449 (C.A. 9th Cir.1961).

8. Communities believe, and act on the belief, that obscenity is immoral, is wrong for the individual, and has no place in a decent society. They believe, too, that adults as well as children are corruptible in morals and character, and that obscenity is a source of corruption that should be eliminated. Obscenity is not suppressed primarily for the protection of others. Much of it is suppressed for the purity of the community and for the salvation and welfare of the "consumer." Obscenity, at bottom, is not crime. Obscenity is sin.

Henkin, Morals and the Constitution: The Sin of Obscenity. 63 Col.L.Rev. 391, 395 (1963).

9. See, e.g., Cairns, Paul, & Wishner, Sex Censorship: The Assumptions of Anti-Obscenity Laws and the Empirical Evidence, 46 Minn.L.Rev. 1009 (1962); see also M. Jahoda, The Impact of Literature: A Psychological Discussion of Some Assumptions in the Censorship Debate (1954), summarized in the concurring opinion of Judge Frank in United States v. Roth, 237 F.2d 796, 814-816 (C.A.2d Cir.1956).

10. The Model Penal Code provisions dealing with obscene materials are limited to cases of commercial dissemination. Model Penal Code § 251.4 (Prop. Official Draft 1962); see also Model Penal Code § 207.10 and comment 4 (Tent.Draft No. 6, 1957); H. Packer, The Limits of the Criminal Sanction 316-328 (1968); Schwartz, Morals Offenses and the Model Penal Code, 63 Col.L.Rev. 669 (1963).

11. What we have said in no way infringes upon the power of the State or Federal Government to make possession of other items, such as narcotics, firearms, or stolen goods, a crime. Our holding in the present case turns upon the Georgia statute's infringement of fundamental liberties protected by the First and Fourteenth Amendments. No First Amendment rights are involved in most statutes making mere possession criminal.

Nor do we mean to express any opinion on statutes making criminal possession of other types of printed, filmed, or recorded materials. See, e.g., 18 U.S.C. § 793(d), which makes criminal the otherwise lawful possession of materials which "the possessor has reason to believe could be used to the injury of the United States or to the advantage of any foreign nation. . . ." In such cases, compelling reasons may exist for overriding the right of the individual to possess those materials.

## Rowan v. US Post Office Dept. (May 4, 1970)

MR. CHIEF JUSTICE BURGER delivered the opinion of the Court.

Appellants challenge the constitutionality of Title III of the Postal Revenue and Federal Salary Act of 1967, 81 Stat. 645, 39 U.S.C. § 4009 (1964 ed., Supp. IV), under which a person may require that a mailer remove his name from its mailing lists and stop all future mailings to the householder. The appellants are publishers, distributors, owners, and operators of mail order houses, mailing list brokers, and owners and operators of mail service organizations whose business activities are affected by the challenged statute.

A brief description of the statutory framework will facilitate our analysis of the questions raised in this appeal. Section 4009 is entitled "Prohibition of pandering advertisements in the mails." It provides a procedure whereby any householder may insulate himself from advertisements that offer for sale "matter which the addressee in his sole discretion believes to be erotically arousing or sexually provocative." 39 U.S.C. § 4009(a) (1964 ed., Supp. IV). [n1]

Subsection (b) mandates the Postmaster General, upon receipt of a notice from the addressee specifying that he has received advertisements found by him to be within the statutory category, to issue on the addressee's request an order directing the sender and his agents or assigns to refrain from further mailings to the named addressee. Additionally, subsection (c) requires the Postmaster General to order the affected sender to delete the name of the designated addressee from all mailing lists owned or controlled by the sender and prohibits the sale, rental, exchange, or other transactions involving mailing lists bearing the name of the designated addressee.

If the Postmaster General has reason to believe that an order issued under this section has been violated, subsection (d) authorizes him to notify the sender by registered or certified mail of his belief and the reasons therefor, and grant him an opportunity to respond and have a hearing on whether a violation has occurred.

If the Postmaster General thereafter determines that the order has been or is being violated, he is authorized to request the Attorney General to seek an order from a United States District Court directing compliance with the prohibitory order. Subsection (e) grants to the district court jurisdiction to issue a compliance order upon application of the Attorney General.

Appellants initiated an action in the United States District Court for the Central District of California upon a complaint and petition for declaratory relief on the ground that 39 U.S.C. § 4009 (1964 ed., Supp. IV) is unconstitutional. They alleged that they had received numerous prohibitory orders pursuant to the provisions of the statute.

Appellants contended that the section violates their rights of free speech and due process guaranteed by the First and Fifth Amendments to the United States Constitution. Additionally, appellants argued that the section is unconstitutionally vague, without standards, and ambiguous.

A three-judge court was convened pursuant to 28 U.S.C. § 2284 and it determined that the section was constitutional when interpreted to prohibit advertisements similar to those initially mailed to the addressee. [n2] 300 F.Supp. 1036.

The District Court construed subsections (b) and (c) to prohibit "advertisements similar" to those initially mailed to the addressee. Future mailings, in the view of the District Court, "are to be measured by the objectionable material of such first mailing." 300 F.Supp. at 1041. In our view, Congress did not intend so restrictive a scope to those provisions.

I. BACKGROUND AND CONGRESSIONAL OBJECTIVES

Section 4009 was a response to public and congressional concern with use of mail facilities to distribute unsolicited advertisements that recipients found to be offensive because of their lewd and salacious character. Such mail was found to be pressed upon minors, as well as adults, who did not seek and did not want it. Use of mailing lists of youth organizations was part of the mode of doing business. At the congressional hearings, it developed that complaints to the Postmaster General had increased from 50,000 to 250,000 annually. The legislative history, including testimony of child psychology specialists and psychiatrists before the House Committee on the Post Office and the Civil Service, reflected concern over the impact of the materials on the development of children. A declared objective of Congress was to protect minors and the privacy of homes from such material and to place the judgment of what constitutes an offensive invasion of those interests in the hands of the addressee.

To accomplish these objectives, Congress provided in subsection (a) that the mailer is subject to an order "to refrain from further mailings of such materials to designated addressees." Subsection (b) states that the Postmaster General shall direct the sender to refrain from "further mailings to the named addressees." Subsection (c), in describing the Postmaster's order, states that it shall "expressly prohibit the sender. . . from making any further mailings to the designated addressees. . . ." Subsection (c) also requires the sender to delete the addressee's name "from all mailing lists," and prohibits the sale, transfer, and exchange of lists bearing the addressee's name.

There are three plausible constructions of the statute with respect to the scope of the prohibitory order. The order could prohibit all future mailings to the addressees, all future mailings of advertising material to the addressees, or all future mailings of similar materials.

The seeming internal statutory inconsistency is undoubtedly a residue of the language of the section as it was initially proposed. The section as originally reported by the House Committee prohibited "further mailings of such pandering advertisements," § 4009(a), "further mailings of such matter," § 4009(b), and "any further mailings of pandering advertisements," § 4009(c). H.R.Rep. No. 722, 90th Cong., 1st Sess., 125 (1967). The section required the Postmaster General to make a determination whether the particular piece of mail came within the proscribed class of pandering advertisements, "as that term is used in the Ginzburg case." Id. at 69.

The section was subsequently amended by the House of Representatives to eliminate from the Post Office any censorship function. Congressman Waldie, who proposed the amendment, envisioned a minimal role for the Post Office. The amendment was intended to remove "the right of the Government to involve itself in any determination of the content and nature of these objectionable materials. . . ." 113 Cong.Rec. 28660 (1967). The only determination left for the Postmaster General is whether or not the mailer has removed the addressee's name from the mailing list. Statements by the proponents of the legislation in both the House and Senate manifested an intent to prohibit all further mailings from the sender. In describing the effect of his proposed amendment, Congressman Waldie stated:

So I have said in my amendment that, if you receive literature in your household that you consider objectionable . . ., you can inform the Postmaster General to have your name stricken from that mailer's mailing list.

113 Cong.Rec. 28660. The Senate Committee Report on the bill contained similar language:

If a person receives an advertisement which . . . he . . . believes to be erotically arousing . . . he may notify the Postmaster General of his determination. The Postmaster General is then required to issue an order to the sender directing him to refrain from sending any further mailings of any kind to such person.

S.Rep. No. 801, 90th Cong., 1st Sess., 38. Senator Monroney, a major proponent of the legislation in the Senate, described the bill as follows:

With respect to the test contained in the bill, if the addressee declared it to be erotically arousing or sexually provocative, the Postmaster General would have to notify the sender to send no more mail to that address. . . .

113 Cong.Rec. 34231 (1967). [n3]

The legislative history of subsection (a) thus supports an interpretation that prohibits all future mailings independent of any objective test. This reading is consistent with the provisions of related subsections in the section. Subsection (c) provides that the Postmaster General

shall also direct the sender and his agents or assigns to delete immediately the names of the designated addressees from all mailing lists owned or controlled by the sender or his agents or assigns and, further, shall prohibit the sender and his agents or assigns from the sale, rental, exchange, or other transaction involving mailing lists bearing the names of the designated addressees.

39 U.S.C. § 4009(c) (1964 ed., Supp. IV).

It would be anomalous to read the statute to affect only similar material or advertisements, and yet require the Postmaster General to order the sender to remove the addressee's name from all mailing lists in his actual or constructive possession. The section was intended to allow the addressee complete and unfettered discretion in electing whether or not he desired to receive further material from a particular sender. See n. 6, infra. The impact of this aspect of the statute is on the mailer, not the mail. The interpretation of the statute that most completely effectuates that intent is one that prohibits any further mailings. Limiting the prohibitory order to similar materials or advertisements is open to at least two criticisms: (a) it would expose the householder to further burdens of scrutinizing the mail for objectionable material and possible harassment, and (b) it would interpose the Postmaster General between the sender and the addressee and, at the least, create the appearance, if not the substance, of governmental censorship. [n4] It is difficult to see how the Postmaster General could decide whether the materials were "similar" or possessing touting or pandering characteristics without an evaluation suspiciously like censorship. Additionally, such an interpretation would be incompatible with the unequivocal language in subsection (c).

## II. FIRST AMENDMENT CONTENTIONS

The essence of appellants' argument is that the statute violates their constitutional right to communicate. One sentence in appellants' brief perhaps characterizes their entire position:

The freedom to communicate orally and by the written word and, indeed, in every manner whatsoever, is imperative to a free and sane society.

Brief for Appellants 15. Without doubt, the public postal system is an indispensable adjunct of every civilized society, and communication is imperative to a healthy social order. But the right of every person "to be let alone" must be placed in the scales with the right of others to communicate.

In today's complex society, we are inescapably captive audiences for many purposes, but a sufficient measure of individual autonomy must survive to permit every householder to exercise control over unwanted mail. To make the householder the exclusive and final judge of what will cross his threshold undoubtedly has the effect of impeding the flow of ideas, information, and arguments that, ideally, he should receive and consider. Today's merchandising methods, the plethora of mass mailings subsidized by low postal rates, and the growth of the sale of large mailing lists as an industry, in itself, have changed the mailman from a carrier of primarily private communications, as he was in a more leisurely day, and have made him an adjunct of the mass mailer who sends unsolicited and often unwanted mail into every home. It places no strain on the doctrine of judicial notice to observe that, whether measured by pieces or pounds, Everyman's mail today is made up overwhelmingly of material he did not seek from persons he does not know. And, all too often, it is matter he finds offensive.

In Martin v. Struthers, 319 U.S. 141 (1943), MR. JUSTICE BLACK, for the Court, while supporting the "[f]reedom to distribute information to every citizen," id. at 146, acknowledged a limitation in terms of leaving "with the homeowner himself" the power to decide "whether distributors of literature may lawfully call at a home." Id. at 148.

Weighing the highly important right to communicate, but without trying to determine where it fits into constitutional imperatives, against the very basic right to be free from sights, sounds, and tangible matter we do not want, it seems to us that a mailer's right to communicate must stop at the mailbox of an unreceptive addressee.

The Court has traditionally respected the right of a householder to bar, by order or notice, solicitors, hawkers, and peddlers from his property. See Martin v. Struthers, supra; cf. Hall v. Commonwealth, 188 Va. 72, 49 S.E.2d 369, appeal dismissed, 335 U.S. 875 (1948). In this case, the mailer's right to communicate is circumscribed only by an affirmative act of the addressee giving notice that he wishes no further mailings from that mailer.

To hold less would tend to license a form of trespass, and would make hardly more sense than to say that a radio or television viewer may not twist the dial to cut off an offensive or boring communication, and thus bar its entering his home. Nothing in the Constitution compels us to listen to or view any unwanted communication, whatever its merit; we see no basis for according the printed word or pictures a different or more preferred status because they are sent by mail. The ancient concept that "a man's home is his castle" into which "not even the king may enter" has lost none of its vitality, and none of the recognized exceptions includes any right to communicate offensively with another. See Camara v. Municipal Court, 387 U.S. 523 (1967).

Both the absoluteness of the citizen's right under § 4009 and its finality are essential; what may not be provocative to one person may well be to another. In operative effect, the power of the householder under the statute is unlimited; he may prohibit the mailing of a dry goods catalog because he objects to the contents -- or indeed the text of the language touting the merchandise. Congress provided this sweeping power not only to protect privacy, but to avoid possible constitutional questions that might arise from vesting the power to make any discretionary evaluation of the material in a governmental official.

In effect, Congress has erected a wall -- or, more accurately, permits a citizen to erect a wall -- that no advertiser may penetrate without his acquiescence. The continuing operative effect of a mailing ban, once imposed, presents no constitutional obstacles; the citizen cannot be put to the burden of determining on repeated occasions whether the offending mailer has altered its material so as to make it acceptable. Nor should the householder have to risk that offensive material come into the hands of his children before it can be stopped.

We therefore categorically reject the argument that a vendor has a right, under the Constitution or otherwise, to send unwanted material into the home of another. If this prohibition operates to impede the flow of even valid ideas, the answer is that no one has a right to press even "good" ideas on an unwilling recipient. That we are often "captives" outside the sanctuary of the home and subject to objectionable speech and other sound does not mean we must be captives everywhere. See Public Utilities Comm'n v. Pollak, 343 U.S. 451 (1952). The asserted right of a mailer, we repeat, stops at the outer boundary of every person's domain.

The statutory scheme at issue accords to the sender an "opportunity to be heard upon such notice and proceedings as are adequate to safeguard the right for which the constitutional protection is invoked." Anderson Nat. Bank v. Luckett, 321 U.S. 233, 246 (1944). It thus comports with the Due Process Clause of the Fifth Amendment. The statutory scheme accomplishes this by providing that the Postmaster General shall issue a prohibitory order to the sender on the request of the complaining addressee. Only if the sender violates the terms of the order is the Postmaster General authorized to serve a complaint on the sender, who is then allowed 15 days to respond. The sender can then secure an administrative hearing. [n5] The sender may question whether the initial material mailed to the addressee was an advertisement and whether he sent any subsequent mailings. If the Postmaster General thereafter determines that the prohibitory order has been violated, he is authorized to request the Attorney General to make application in a United States District Court for a compliance order; [n6] a second hearing is required if an order is to be entered.

The only administrative action not preceded by a full hearing is the initial issuance of the prohibitory order. Since the sender risks no immediate sanction by failing to comply with that order -- it is only a predicate for later steps -- it cannot be said that this aspect of the procedure denies due process. It is sufficient that all available defenses, such as proof that no mail was sent, may be presented to a competent tribunal before a contempt finding can be made. See Nickey v. Mississippi, 292 U.S. 393, 396 (1934).

The appellants also contend that the requirement that the sender remove the addressee's name from all mailing lists in his possession violates the Fifth Amendment because it constitutes a taking without due process of law. The appellants are not prohibited from using, selling, or exchanging their mailing lists; they are simply required to delete the names of the complaining addressees from the lists and cease all mailings to those persons.

Appellants next contend that compliance with the statute is confiscatory because the costs attending removal of the names are prohibitive. We agree with the conclusion of the District Court that the

burden does not amount to a violation of due process guaranteed by the Fifth Amendment of the Constitution. Particularly when, in the context presently before this Court, it is being applied to commercial enterprises.

300 F.Supp. at 1041. See California State Auto Ins. Bureau v. Malone, 341 U.S. 105 (1951).

There is no merit to the appellants' allegations that the statute is unconstitutionally vague. A statute is fatally vague only when it exposes a potential actor to some risk or detriment without giving him fair warning of the nature of the proscribed conduct. United States v. Cardiff, 344 U.S. 174, 176 (1952). Here, the appellants know precisely what they must do on receipt of a prohibitory order. The complainants' names must be removed from the sender's mailing lists, and he must refrain from future mailings to the named addressees. The sender is exposed to a contempt sanction only if he continues to mail to a particular addressee after administrative and judicial proceedings. Appellants run no substantial risk of miscalculation.

For the reasons stated, the judgment appealed from is affirmed.

It is so ordered.

Notes

1. Subsection (g) provides that, upon the addressee's request, the order shall include the names of the addressee's minor children who reside with him and who have not attained their nineteenth birthday.

2. Judge Hufstedler, concurring specially but without dissent, would require the District Court, prior to issuing a compliance order, to determine de novo whether the sender is a person who has mailed or has caused to be mailed any pandering advertisements.

3. Senator Hruska spoke similarly:

Title III would allow the recipient of obscene mail to return it to the Postmaster General with a request that the Postmaster General notify the sender to stop mailings to the addressee. . . .

113 Cong.Rec. 34232 (1967).

4. Subsection (d) vests the Postmaster General with the duty to determine whether the sender has violated the order. This determination was intended to be primarily a ministerial one involving an adjudication whether the initial material was an advertisement and whether the sender mailed materials to the addressee more than 30 days after the receipt of the prohibitory order. An interpretation which requires the Postmaster General to determine whether the subsequent material was pandering and/or similar would tend to place him "astride the flow of mail. . . ." Lamont v. Postmaster General, 381 U.S. 301, 306 (1965).

5. Although subsection (h) specifically excludes the pre-complaint hearing from the provisions of the Administrative Procedure Act, 5 U.S.C. § 554 et seq. (1964 ed., Supp. IV), the Post Office Department has promulgated regulations setting forth procedures governing the departmental administrative hearings. 39 CFR pt. 916.

6. The function of the district court is similar to that of the Postmaster General. It is to determine whether the initial mailing included advertising material and whether there was a mailing by the sender to the addressee more than 30 days after receipt of the order. We reject the suggestions that the section should be read to require the district judge to make a determination of the addressee's good faith, or to conduct an independent adjudication of the pandering nature of the material. The statute was intended to entrust unreviewable discretion to the addressee to determine whether or not the advertisement was "erotically arousing or sexually provocative."

[T]he sole determination as to whether the literature you receive is objectionable or not is within your discretion, and you are not second-guessed on that discretion.

113 Cong.Rec. 28660 (1967) (remarks of Congressman Waldie).

## Blount v. Rizzi (January 14, 1971)

MR. JUSTICE BRENNAN delivered the opinion of the Court.

No. 55 (hereafter Mail Box) draws into question the constitutionality of 39 U.S.C. § 4006 (now 39 U.S.C. § 3006, Postal Reorganization Act,** 84 Stat. 747), under which the Postmaster General, following administrative hearings, may halt use of the mails and of postal money orders for commerce in allegedly obscene materials. No. 58 (hereafter Book Bin) also draws into question the constitutionality of § 4006, and, in addition, the constitutionality of 39 U.S.C. § 4007 (now 39 U.S.C. § 3007), 84 Stat. 748, under which the Postmaster General may obtain a court order permitting him to detain the defendant's incoming mail pending the outcome of § 4006 proceedings against him.

39 U.S.C. § 4006 provides in pertinent part:

"Upon evidence satisfactory to the Postmaster General that a person is obtaining or attempting to obtain remittances of money or property of any kind through the mail for an obscene . . . matter . . . or is depositing or causing to be deposited in the United States mail information as to where, how, or from whom the same may be obtained, the Postmaster General may --"

"(1) direct postmasters at the office at which registered letters or other letters or mail arrive, addressed to such a person or to his representative, to return the registered letters or other letters or mail to the sender marked 'Unlawful'; and"

"(2) forbid the payment by a postmaster to such a person or his representative of any money order or postal note drawn to the order of either and provide for the return to the remitters of the sums named in the money orders or postal notes."

Proceedings under § 4006 are conducted according to departmental regulations. A proceeding is begun by the General Counsel of the Post Office Department by written complaint and notice of hearing. 39 CFR §§ 952.5, 952.7, 952.8. The Judicial Officer of the Department holds a trial-type hearing at which a full record is transcribed. He renders an opinion which includes findings of fact and a statement of reasons. 39 CFR §§ 952.9952.25. The decision is to "be rendered with all due speed," 39 CFR § 952.24(a), and there is an administrative appeal. 39 CFR § 952.25. No § 4006 order may issue against the defendant until completion of the administrative proceeding. If, however, the Postmaster General wishes to detain the defendant's incoming mail before the termination of the § 4006 proceedings, he may apply to the United States District Court for the district in which the defendant resides, under 39 U.S.C. § 4007, which in pertinent part provides: [1]

"In preparation for or during the pendency of proceedings under [§ 4006] of this title, the United States district court in the district in which the defendant receives his mail shall, upon application therefor by the Postmaster General and upon a showing of probable cause to believe the statute is being violated, enter a temporary restraining order and preliminary injunction pursuant to rule 65 of the Federal Rules of Civil Procedure directing the detention of the defendant's incoming mail by the postmaster pending the conclusion of the statutory proceedings and any appeal therefrom. The district court may provide in the order that the detained mail be open to examination by the defendant and such mail be delivered as is clearly not connected with the alleged unlawful activity. An action taken by a court hereunder does not affect or determine any fact at issue in the statutory proceedings. [2] "

In Mail Box, the Postmaster General began administrative proceedings under § 4006 on November 1, 1968. The administrative hearing was concluded December 5, 1968. The Judicial Officer filed his decision December 31, 1968, finding that the specified magazines were obscene, and therefore entered a § 4006 order -- 61 days after the complaint was filed. Mail Box filed a complaint in the United States District Court for the Central District of California seeking a declaratory judgment that § 4006 was unconstitutional and an injunction against enforcement of the administrative order. A three-judge court was convened, and held that 39 U.S.C. § 4006 "is unconstitutional on its face, because it fails to meet the requirements of Freedman v. Maryland (1965) 380 U. S. 51. . . ." 305 F.Supp. 634, 635 (1969). The court therefore vacated the administrative order, directed the delivery "forthwith" of all mail addressed to Mail Box, and enjoined any proceedings to enforce § 4006.

In Book Bin, the Postmaster General applied to the District Court for the Northern District of Georgia for a § 4007 order pending the completion of § 4006 proceedings against Book Bin. [3] Book Bin counterclaimed, asserting that both §§ 4006 and 4007 were unconstitutional and that their enforcement should be enjoined. A three-judge court was convened, and held both sections unconstitutional. It agreed with the three-judge court in Mail Box that the procedures of § 4006 were fatally deficient under Freedman v. Maryland, 380 U. S. 51 (1965), and also held that the finding under § 4007 merely of "probable cause" to believe material was obscene was not a constitutionally sufficient standard to support a temporary mail detention order. 306 F.Supp. 1023 (1969).

We noted probable jurisdiction of the Government's appeals. 397 U.S. 959, 960 (1970). We affirm the judgment in each case.

Our discussion appropriately begins with Mr. Justice Holmes' frequently quoted admonition that

"The United States may give up the Post Office when it sees fit, but, while it carries it on, the use of the mails is almost as much a part of free speech as the right to use our tongues. . . ."

Milwaukee Social Democratic Pub. Co. v. Burleson, 255 U. S. 407, 255 U. S. 437 (1921) (dissenting opinion); see also Lamont v. Postmaster General, 381 U. S. 301 (1965). Since § 4006, on its face, and § 4007, as applied, are procedures designed to deny use of the mails to commercial distributors of obscene literature, those procedures violate the First Amendment unless they include built-in safeguards against curtailment of constitutionally protected expression, for Government

"is not free to adopt whatever procedures it pleases for dealing with obscenity . . . without regard to the possible consequences for constitutionally protected speech."

Marcus v. Search Warrant, 367 U. S. 717, 367 U. S. 731 (1961). Rather, the First Amendment requires that procedures be incorporated that

"ensure against the curtailment of constitutionally protected expression, which is often separated from obscenity only by a dim and uncertain line. . . . Our insistence that regulations of obscenity scrupulously embody the most rigorous procedural safeguards . . . is . . . but a special instance of the larger principle that the freedoms of expression must be ringed about with adequate bulwarks. . . ."

Bantam Books, Inc. v. Sullivan, 372 U. S. 58, 372 U. S. 66 (1963). Since we have recognized that

"the line between speech unconditionally guaranteed and speech which may legitimately be regulated . . . is finely drawn, . . . [t]he separation of legitimate from illegitimate speech calls for . . . sensitive tools. . . ."

Speiser v. Randall, 357 U. S. 513, 357 U. S. 525 (1958).

The procedure established by § 4006 and the implementing regulations omit those "sensitive tools" essential to satisfy the requirements of the First Amendment. The three-judge courts correctly held in these cases that our decision in Freedman v. Maryland, 380 U. S. 51 (1965) compels this conclusion. We there considered the constitutionality of a motion picture censorship procedure administered by a State Board of Censors. We held that, to avoid constitutional infirmity, a scheme of administrative censorship must: place the burdens of initiating judicial review and of proving that the material is unprotected expression on the censor; require "prompt judicial review" -- a final judicial determination on the merits within a specified, brief period -- to prevent the administrative decision of the censor from achieving an effect of finality; and limit to preservation of the status quo for the shortest, fixed period compatible with sound judicial resolution, any restraint imposed in advance of the final judicial determination. 380 U.S. at 380 U. S. 58-60.

These safeguards are lacking in the administrative censorship scheme created by §§ 4006, 4007, and the regulations. [4]

The scheme has no statutory provision requiring governmentally initiated judicial participation in the procedure which bars the magazines from the mails, or even any provision assuring prompt judicial review. The scheme does differ from the Maryland scheme involved in Freedman in that, under the Maryland scheme, the motion picture could not be exhibited pending conclusion of the administrative hearing, whereas, under § 4006, the order to return mail or to refuse to pay money orders is not imposed until there has been an administrative determination that the magazines are obscene. This, however, does not redress the fatal flaw of the procedure in failing to require that the Postmaster General seek to obtain a prompt judicial determination of the obscenity of the material; rather, once the administrative proceedings disapprove the magazines the distributor "must assume the burden of instituting judicial proceedings and of persuading the courts that the . . . [magazines are] protected expression." 380 U.S. at 380 U. S. 59-60. The First Amendment demands that the Government must assume this burden.

"The teaching of our cases is that, because only a judicial determination in an adversary proceeding ensures the necessary sensitivity to freedom of expression, only a procedure requiring a judicial determination suffices to impose a valid final restraint."

380 U.S. at 380 U. S. 58. [5]

Moreover, once a § 4006 administrative order has been entered against the distributor, there being no provision for judicial review, the Postmaster may stamp as "Unlawful" and immediately return to the sender orders for purchase of the magazines addressed to the distributor, and prohibit the payment of postal money orders to him. Such a scheme

"presents peculiar dangers to constitutionally protected speech. . . . Because the censor's business is to censor, there inheres the danger that he may well be less responsive than a court -- part of an independent branch of government -- to the constitutionally protected interests in free expression. And if it is made unduly onerous, by reason of delay or otherwise, to seek judicial review, the censor's determination may in practice be final."

380 U.S. at 380 U. S. 57-58. [6] Appellants suggest that we avoid the constitutional question raised by the failure of § 4006 to provide that the Government seek a prompt judicial determination by construing that section to deny the administrative order any effect whatever, if judicial review is sought by the distributor, until the completion of that review. Apart from the fact that this suggestion neither requires that the appellants initiate judicial proceedings, nor provides for a prompt judicial determination, it is for Congress, not this Court, to rewrite the statute.

The authority of the Postmaster General under § 4007 to apply to a district court for an order directing the detention of the distributor's incoming mail pending the conclusion of the § 4006 administrative proceedings and any appeal therefrom plainly does not remedy the defects in § 4006. That section does not provide a prompt proceeding for a judicial adjudication of the challenged obscenity of the magazine. [7] First, it is entirely discretionary with the Attorney General whether to institute a § 4007 action and, therefore, the section does not satisfy the requirement that the appellants assume the burden of seeking a judicial determination of the alleged obscenity of the magazines. Second, the district court is required to grant the relief sought by the Postmaster General upon a showing merely of "probable cause" to believe § 4006 is being violated. We agree with the three-judge court in Book Bin that to satisfy the demand of the First Amendment,

"it is vital that prompt judicial review on the issue of obscenity -- rather than merely probable cause -- be assured on the Government's initiative before the severe restrictions in §§ 4006, 4007, are invoked."

306 F.Supp. at 1028. Indeed, the statute expressly provides that "An action taken

by a court hereunder does not affect or determine any fact at issue in the statutory proceedings." [8]

Moreover, § 4007 does not, in any event, itself meet the requisites of the First Amendment. Any order issued by the district court remains in effect "pending the conclusion of the statutory proceedings and any appeal therefrom." [9] Thus, the statute not only fails to provide that the district court should make a final judicial determination of the question of obscenity, expressly giving that authority to the Judicial Officer, but it fails to provide that

"[a]ny restraint imposed in advance of a final judicial determination on the merits must . . . be limited to preservation of the status quo for the shortest fixed period compatible with sound judicial resolution."

380 U.S. at 380 U. S. 59.

The appellees here not only were not afforded "prompt judicial review," but they

"can only get full judicial review on the question of obscenity -- by which the Postmaster would be actually bound -- after lengthy administrative proceedings, and then only by [their] own initiative. During the interim, the prolonged threat of an adverse administrat[ive] decision in § 4006 or the reality of a sweeping § 4007 order, will have a severe restriction on the exercise of [appellees'] First Amendment rights -- all without a final judicial determination of obscenity."

306 F.Supp. at 1028.

The judgments of the three-judge courts in Nos. 55 and 58 are

Affirmed.

** The codification of the Act will appear in the 1970 edition of the United States Code. This opinion treats the old Code sections as current.

Notes

[1] Section 4006 was enacted in 1950. 64 Stat. 451. In 1956, the Postmaster General sought and obtained the power himself to enter an order, pending administrative proceedings under § 4006, that all mail addressed to the defendant in the § 4006 proceeding be impounded. The order was to expire at the end of 20 days unless the Postmaster General sought in a federal district court, an order continuing the impounding. 70 Stat. 699. In 1959, extensive hearings were held in the House on the Post Office's request that the 20-day period be extended to 45 days, and that the standard of necessity be changed to "public interest." Hearings on Obscene Matter Sent Through the Mail before the Subcommittee on Postal Operations of the House Committee on Post Office and Civil Service, 86th Cong., 1st Sess., pt.s. 1, 2, and 3 (1959); Hearings on Detention of Mail for Temporary Periods before the House Committee on Post Office and Civil Service, 86th Cong., 1st Sess. (1959). Instead, Congress enacted § 4007, which stripped the Postmaster General of his power to issue an interim order for any period and directed him to seek such an order in a federal district court. One Senate Report expressed misgivings when the Postmaster General had originally sought the impounding

power:

"The committee recognizes that, even in its present form, the bill gives the Postmaster General extraordinary and summary powers to impose a substantial penalty by impounding a person's mail for up to 20 days in advance of any hearing or any review by the courts. Such power is directly contrary to the letter and spirit of normal due process, as exemplified by the Administrative Procedure Act, which requires a hearing before any penalty may be imposed. The Post Office Department has made its case for this legislation on the grounds that a temporary and summary procedure is required to deal with fly-by-night operators using the mails to defraud or to peddle pornography, who may go out of business -- or change the name of their business or their business address -- before normal legal procedures can be brought into operation. The Post Office Department has not recommended, nor does this committee approve, the use of the temporary impounding procedure under this bill as a substitute for the normal practice of an advance hearing or the bringing of an indictment for violation of the criminal code in all cases involving legitimate and well established business operations. The committee would not approve the use of the extraordinary summary procedure under the bill against legitimate publishers of newspapers, magazines, or books in cases in which a Postmaster General might take objection to an article, an issue, or a volume."

S.Rep. No. 2234, 84th Cong., 2d Sess., 2-3 (1956).

[2] Section 4007 also authorizes the Postmaster General to apply for an impounding order during the pendency of proceedings under 39 U.S.C. § 4005 (1964 ed., Supp. V), now § 3005. Section 4005, as amended (82 Stat. 1153), permits the return to the sender of any mail sent to the perpetrator of what the Postmaster General finds to be a scheme for obtaining money by means of false representations. That section has been upheld against First Amendment attack. Donaldson v. Read Magazine, 333 U. S. 178 (1948). The Government does not argue in its brief that Donaldson compels the conclusion that § 4006 also is constitutional, but only that "Section 4006, like the fraud statute upheld in Donaldson, . . . meets all necessary constitutional standards." Brief for Appellants 20. On oral argument, the Government suggested that an affirmance in this case might jeopardize the validity of § 4005 and the continued vitality of Donaldson. But no argument was offered to support the suggestion.

[3] The order was sought with respect to a single issue of one magazine.

[4] We therefore have no occasion to consider the argument of appellees that Stanley v. Georgia, 394 U. S. 557 (1969), presupposes that an individual has a constitutional right to obtain possession of the challenged materials by delivery through the mail.

[5] In 1962, three Justices of the Court stated:

"[We have] . . . no doubt that Congress could constitutionally authorize a noncriminal process in the nature of a judicial proceeding under closely defined procedural safeguards. But the suggestion that Congress may constitutionally authorize any process other than a fully judicial one immediately raises the gravest doubts."

Manual Enterprises v. Day, 370 U. S. 478, 370 U. S. 518-519 (1962) (opinion of BRENNAN, J.).

[6] The Judicial Officer is appointed by the Postmaster General to "perform such quasi-judicial duties as the Postmaster General may designate." 39 U.S.C. § 308a. He functions as hearing examiner in many proceedings in addition to those under § 4006. The appellants argue that the Judicial Officer enjoys "many of the insulations that judges enjoy." What the Constitution requires, however, is that a noncriminal censoring process require governmentally initiated full judicial participation. Clearly, § 4006 does not so provide.

[7] The Court said in Freedman v. Maryland that the procedure considered in Kingsley Books, Inc. v. Brown, 354 U. S. 436 (1957), provides "a model . . . [of an] . . . injunctive procedure designed to prevent the sale of obscene books." 380 U.S. at 380 U. S. 60.

[8] This provision was added at the request of Postmaster General Summerfield, who desired it expressly to forestall judicial review pending completion of the administrative proceeding.

"This would guarantee that counsel for a mailer will not be able to raise successfully a bar to all further administrative proceedings in a case in which the Government failed to prevail on its motion for a preliminary injunction."

Letter from Arthur E. Summerfield, Postmaster General, to Senator Olin D. Johnston, Chairman, Senate Committee on Post Office and Civil Service, U.S.Code Cong. & Admin. News, 86th Cong., 2d Sess., 3249 (1960). In 1959, Postmaster General Summerfield had testified:

"In spite of the frustrations and the legal complications, and even the court decisions [which the Postmaster General had described as handing down 'the very broad definition of obscenity'], I feel a responsibility to the public to attempt to prevent the use of the mails for indecent material, and to seek indictments and prosecutions for such offenses, even though it may be argued that it falls in the category of material concerning which there have been previous rulings favorable to the promoters."

Hearing on Obscene Matter Sent Through the Mail before the Subcommittee on Postal Operations of the House Committee on Post Office and Civil Service, 86th Cong., 1st Sess., pt. 1, p. 6 (1959).

[9] Appellants point out that orders under §§ 4006 and 4007 generally allow the addressee to open his mail at the post office and receive any first class mail demonstrated clearly not to be connected with the allegedly unlawful use. This provision is provided in light of 39 U.S.C. § 4057, which provides that

"[o]nly an employee opening dead mail by authority of the Postmaster General, or a person holding a search warrant authorized by law may open any letter or parcel of the first class which is in the custody of the Department."

See also 39 CFR § 117.1. But query whether such provision of the order requires an "official act," viz., examining the mail, which constitutes an unconstitutional limitation on the addressee's First Amendment rights. Lamont v. Postmaster General, 381 U. S. 301 (1965).

## US v. Reidel (May 3, 1971)

MR. JUSTICE WHITE delivered the opinion of the Court.

Section 1461 of Title 18, U.S.C. prohibits the knowing use of the mails for the delivery of obscene matter. [1] The issue presented by the jurisdictional statement in this case is whether § 1461 is constitutional as applied to the distribution of obscene materials to willing recipients who state that they are adults. The District Court held that it was not. [2] We disagree and reverse the judgment.

I

On April 15, 1970, the appellee, Norman Reidel, was indicted on three counts, each count charging him with having mailed a single copy of an illustrated booklet entitled The True Facts About Imported Pornography. One of the copies had been mailed to a postal inspector stipulated to be over the age of 21, who had responded to a newspaper advertisement. [3] The other two copies had been seized during a search of appellee's business premises; both of them had been deposited in the mail by Reidel, but had been returned to him in their original mailing envelopes bearing the mark "undelivered." As to these two booklets, the Government conceded that it had no evidence as to the identity or age of the addressees or as to their willingness to receive the booklets. Nor does the record indicate why the booklets were returned undelivered.

Reidel moved in the District Court before trial to dismiss the indictment, contending, among other things, that § 1461 was unconstitutional. Assuming for the purpose of the motion that the booklets were obscene, the trial judge granted the motion to dismiss on the ground that Reidel had made a constitutionally protected delivery, and hence that § 1461 was unconstitutional as applied to him. The Government's direct appeal is here under 18 U.S.C. § 3731.

II

In Roth v. United States, 354 U. S. 476 (1957), Roth was convicted under § 1461 for mailing obscene circulars and advertising. [4] The Court affirmed the conviction, holding that "obscenity is not within the area of constitutionally protected speech or press," id., tit. 485, and that § 1461,

"applied according to the proper standard for judging obscenity, do[es] not offend constitutional safeguards against convictions based upon protected material, or fail to give men in acting adequate notice of what is prohibited."

Id. at 354 U. S. 492. Roth has not been overruled. It remains the law in this Court and governs this case. Reidel, like Roth, was charged with using the mails for the distribution of obscene material. His conviction, if it occurs and the materials are found in fact, to be obscene, would be no more vulnerable than was Roth's.

Stanley v. Georgia, 394 U. S. 557 (1969), compels no different result. There, pornographic films were found in Stanley's home and he was convicted under Georgia statutes for possessing obscene material. This Court reversed the conviction, holding that the mere private possession of obscene matter cannot constitutionally be made a crime. But it neither overruled nor disturbed the holding in Roth. Indeed, in the Court's view, the constitutionality of proscribing private possession of obscenity was a matter of first impression in this Court, a question neither involved nor decided in Roth. The Court made its point expressly:

"Roth and the cases following that decision are not impaired by today's holding. As we have said, the States retain broad power to regulate obscenity; that power simply does not extend to mere possession by the individual in the privacy of his own home."

Id. at 394 U. S. 568. Nothing in Stanley questioned the validity of Roth insofar as the distribution of obscene material was concerned. Clearly the Court had no thought of questioning the validity of § 1461 as applied to those who, like Reidel, are routinely disseminating obscenity through the mails and who have no claim, and could make none, about unwanted governmental intrusions into the privacy of their home. The Court considered this sufficiently clear to warrant summary affirmance of the judgment of the United States District Court for the Northern District of Georgia rejecting claims that under Stanley v. Georgia, Georgia's obscenity statute could not be applied to book sellers. Gable v. Jenkins, 397 U. S. 592 (1970).

The District Court ignored both Roth and the express limitations on the reach of the Stanley decision. Relying on the statement in Stanley that "the Constitution protects the right to receive information and ideas . . . regardless of their social worth," 394 U.S. at 394 U. S. 564, the trial judge reasoned that "if a person has the right to receive and possess this material, then someone must have the right to deliver it to him." He concluded that § 1461 could not be validly applied

"where obscene material is not directed at children, or it is not directed at an unwilling public, where the material such as in this case is solicited by adults. . . ."

The District Court gave Stanley too wide a sweep. To extrapolate from Stanley's right to have and peruse obscene material in the privacy of his own home a First Amendment right in Reidel to sell it to him would effectively scuttle Roth, the precise result that the Stanley opinion abjured. Whatever the scope of the "right to receive" referred to in Stanley, it is not so broad as to immunize the dealings in obscenity in which Reidel engaged here -- dealings that Roth held unprotected by the First Amendment.

The right Stanley asserted was "the right to read or observe what he pleases -- the right to satisfy his intellectual and emotional needs in the privacy of his own home."

394 U.S. at 394 U. S. 565. The Court's response was that

"a State has no business telling a man, sitting alone in his own house, what books he may read or what films he may watch. Our whole constitutional heritage rebels at the thought of giving government the power to control men's minds."

Ibid. The focus of this language was on freedom of mind and thought and on the privacy of one's home. It does not require that we fashion or recognize a constitutional right in people like Reidel to distribute or sell obscene materials. The personal constitutional rights of those like Stanley to possess and read obscenity in their homes and their freedom of mind and thought do not depend on whether the materials are obscene or whether obscenity is constitutionally protected. Their rights to have and view that material in private are independently saved by the Constitution.

Reidel is in a wholly different position. He has no complaints about governmental violations of his private thoughts or fantasies, but stands squarely on a claimed First Amendment right to do business in obscenity and use the mails in the process. But Roth has squarely placed obscenity and its distribution outside the reach of the First Amendment, and they remain there today. Stanley did not overrule Roth, and we decline to do so now.

### III

A postscript is appropriate. Roth and like cases have interpreted the First Amendment not to insulate obscenity from statutory regulation. But the Amendment itself neither proscribes dealings in obscenity nor directs or suggests legislative oversight in this area. The relevant constitutional issues have arisen in the courts only because lawmakers having the exclusive legislative power have consistently insisted on making the distribution of obscenity a crime or otherwise regulating such materials, and because the laws they pass are challenged as unconstitutional invasions of free speech and press.

It is urged that there is developing sentiment that adults should have complete freedom to produce, deal in, possess, and consume whatever communicative materials may appeal to them, and that the law's involvement with obscenity should be limited to those situations where children are involved or where it is necessary to prevent imposition on unwilling recipients of whatever age. The concepts involved are said to be so elusive, and the laws so inherently unenforceable without extravagant expenditures of time and effort by enforcement officers and the courts, that basic reassessment is not only wise, but essential. This may prove to be the desirable and eventual legislative course. But if it is, the task of restructuring the obscenity laws lies with those who pass, repeal, and amend statutes and ordinances. Roth and like cases pose no obstacle to such developments.

The judgment of the District Court is reversed.

So ordered.

[For dissenting opinion of MR. JUSTICE BLACK, see post, p. 402 U. S. 379.]

### Notes

[1] The statute in pertinent part provides:

"Every obscene, lewd, lascivious, indecent, filthy or vile article, matter, thing, device, or substance; and --"

"* * * *"

"Every written or printed card, letter, circular, book, pamphlet, advertisement, or notice of any kind giving information, directly or indirectly, where, or how, or from whom, or by what means any of such mentioned matters, articles, or things may be obtained or made, or where or by whom any act or operation of any kind for the procuring or producing of abortion will be done or performed, or how or by what means conception may be prevented or abortion produced, whether sealed or unsealed. . . ."

"* * * *"

"Is declared to be nonmailable matter and shall not be conveyed in the mails or delivered from any post office or by any letter carrier."

"Whoever knowingly uses the mails for the mailing, carriage in the mails, or delivery of anything declared by this section to be nonmailable, or knowingly causes to be delivered by mail according to the direction thereon, or at the place at which it is directed to be delivered by the person to whom it is addressed, or knowingly takes any such thing from the mails for the purpose of circulating or disposing thereof, or of aiding in the circulation or disposition thereof, shall be fined not more than $5,000 or imprisoned not more than five years, or both, for the first such offense, and shall be fined not more than $10,000 or imprisoned not more than ten years, or both, for each such offense thereafter."

[2] The trial judge did not issue a written opinion, but ruled orally from the bench.

[3] The advertisement was as follows:

"IMPORTED PORNOGRAPHY -- learn the true facts before sending money abroad. Send $1.00 for our fully illustrated booklet. You must be 21 years of age and so state. Normax Press, P. O. Box 989, Fontana, California, 92335."

[4] Roth v. United States was heard and decided with Alberts v. California, in which the Court upheld the obscenity provisions of the California Penal Code.

## US v. 37 Photographs (Luros, Claimant) (May 3, 1971)

MR. JUSTICE WHITE announced the judgment of the Court and an opinion in which THE CHIEF JUSTICE, MR. JUSTICE BRENNAN, and MR. JUSTICE BLACKMUN join. *

When Milton Luros returned to the United States from Europe on October 24, 1969, he brought with him in his luggage the 37 photographs here involved. United States customs agents, acting pursuant to § 305 of the Tariff Act of 1930, as amended, 46 Stat. 688, 19 U.S.C. § 1305(a), [1] seized the photographs as obscene. They referred the matter to the United States Attorney, who, on November 6, instituted proceedings in the United States District Court for forfeiture of the material. Luros, as claimant, answered, denying the photographs were obscene and setting up a counterclaim alleging the unconstitutionality of § 1305(a) on its face and as applied to him. He demanded that a three-judge court be convened to issue an injunction prayed for in the counterclaim. The parties stipulated a time for hearing the three-judge court motion. A formal order convening the court was entered on November 20. The parties then stipulated a briefing schedule expiring on December 16. The court ordered a hearing for January 9, 1970, also suggesting the parties stipulate facts, which they did. The stipulation revealed, among other things, that some or all of the 37 photographs were intended to be incorporated in a hard cover edition of The Kama Sutra of Vatsyayana, a widely distributed book candidly describing a large number of sexual positions. Hearing was held as scheduled on January 9, and on January 27 the three-judge court filed its judgment and opinion declaring § 1305(a) unconstitutional and enjoining its enforcement against the 37 photographs, which were ordered returned to Luros. 309 F.Supp. 36 (CD Cal.1970). The judgment of invalidity rested on two grounds: first, that the section failed to comply with the procedural requirements of Freedman v. Maryland, 380 U. S. 51 (1965), and second, that, under Stanley v. Georgia, 394 U. S. 557 (1969), § 1305(a) could not validly be applied to the seized material. We shall deal with each of these grounds separately.

I

In Freedman v. Maryland, supra, we struck down a state scheme for administrative licensing of motion pictures, holding

"that, because only a judicial determination in an adversary proceeding ensures the necessary sensitivity to freedom of expression, only a procedure requiring a judicial determination suffices to impose a valid final restraint."

380 U.S. at 380 U. S. 58. To insure that a judicial determination occurs promptly so that administrative delay does not, in itself, become a form of censorship, we further held, (1) there must be assurance,"by statute or authoritative judicial construction, that the censor will, within a specified brief period, either issue a license or go to court to restrain showing the film;" (2) "[a]ny restraint imposed in advance of a final judicial determination on the merits must similarly be limited to preservation of the status quo for the shortest fixed period compatible with sound judicial resolution"; and (3) "the procedure must also assure a prompt final judicial decision" to minimize the impact of possibly erroneous administrative action. Id. at 380 U. S. 58-59.

Subsequently, we invalidated Chicago's motion picture censorship ordinance because it permitted an unduly long administrative procedure before the invocation of judicial action, and also because the ordinance, although requiring prompt resort to the courts after administrative decision and an early hearing, did not assure "a prompt judicial decision of the question of the alleged obscenity of the film." Teitel Film Corp. v. Cusack, 390 U. S. 139, 390 U. S. 141 (1968). So, too, in Blount v. Rizzi, 400 U. S. 410 (1971), we held unconstitutional certain provisions of the postal laws designed to control use of the mails for commerce in obscene materials. Under those laws, an administrative order restricting use of the mails could become effective without judicial approval, the burden of obtaining prompt judicial review was placed upon the user of the mails, rather than the Government, and the interim judicial order, which the Government was permitted, though not required, to obtain.pending completion of administrative action was not limited to preserving the status quo for the shortest fixed period compatible with sound judicial administration.

As enacted by Congress, § 1305(a) does not contain explicit time limits of the sort required by Freedman, Teitel, and Blount. [2] These cases do not, however, require that we pass upon the constitutionality of § 1305(a), for it is possible to construe the section to bring it in harmony with constitutional requirements.

It is true that we noted in Blount that "it is for Congress, not this Court, to rewrite the statute," 400 U.S. at 400 U. S. 419, and that we similarly refused to rewrite Maryland's statute and Chicago's ordinance in Freedman and Teitel. On the other hand, we must remember that,

"[w]hen the validity of an act of the Congress is drawn in question, and . . . a serious doubt of constitutionality is raised, it is a cardinal principle that this Court will first ascertain whether a construction of the statute is fairly possible by which the question may be avoided."

Crowell v. Benson, 285 U. S. 22, 285 U. S. 62 (1932). Accord, e.g., Haynes v. United States, 390 U. S. 85, 390 U. S. 92 (1968) (dictum); Schneider v. Smith, 390 U. S. 17, 390 U. S. 27 (1968); United States v. Rumely, 345 U. S. 41, 345 U. S. 45 (1953); Ashwander v. Tennessee Valley Authority, 297 U. S. 288, 297 U. S. 348 (1936) (Brandeis, J., concurring). This cardinal principle did not govern Freedman, Teitel, and Blount only because the statutes there involved could not be construed so as to avoid all constitutional difficulties.

The obstacle in Freedman and Teitel was that the statutes were enacted pursuant to state, rather than federal, authority; while Freedman recognized that a statute failing to specify time limits could be saved by judicial construction, it held that such construction had to be "authoritative," 380 U.S. at 380 U. S. 59, and we lack jurisdiction authoritatively to construe state legislation. Cf. General Trading Co. v. State Tax Comm'n, 322 U. S. 335, 322 U. S. 337 (1944). In Blount, we were dealing with a federal statute, and thus had power to give it an authoritative construction; salvation of that statute, however, would have required its complete rewriting in a manner inconsistent with the expressed intentions of some of its authors. For the statute at issue in Blount not only failed to specify time limits within which judicial proceedings must be instituted and completed; it also failed to give any authorization at all to the administrative agency, upon a determination that material was obscene, to seek judicial review. To have saved the statute, we would thus have been required to give such authorization and to create mechanisms for carrying it into effect, and we would have had to do this in the face of legislative history indicating that the Postmaster General, when he had testified before Congress, had expressly sought to forestall judicial review pending completion of administrative proceedings. See 400 U.S. at 400 U. S. 420 n. 8.

No such obstacles confront us in construing § 1305(a). In fact, the reading into the section of the time limits required by Freedman is fully consistent with its legislative purpose. When the statute, which in its present form dates back to 1930, was first presented to the Senate, concern immediately arose that it did not provide for determinations of obscenity to be made by courts, rather than administrative officers, and that it did not require that judicial rulings be obtained promptly. In language strikingly parallel to that of the Court in Freedman, Senator Walsh protested against the "attempt to enact a law that would vest an administrative officer with power to take books and confiscate them and destroy them, because, in his judgment, they were obscene or indecent," and urged that the law "oblige him to go into court and file his information there . . . and have it determined in the usual way, the same as every other crime is determined." 72 Cong.Rec. 5419. Senator Wheeler likewise could not "conceive how any man" could "possibly object" to an amendment to the proposed legislation that required a customs officer, if he concluded material was obscene, to "tur[n] it over to the district attorney, and the district attorney prosecutes the man, and he has the right of trial by jury in that case." 71 Cong.Rec. 4466. Other Senators similarly indicated their aversion to censorship "by customs clerks and bureaucratic officials," id. at 4437 (remarks of Sen. Dill), preferring that determinations of obscenity should be left to courts and juries. See, e.g., id. at 4433-4439, 4448, 4452-4459; 72 Cong.Rec. 5417-542, 5492, 5497. Senators also expressed the concern later expressed in Freedman that judicial proceedings be commenced and concluded promptly. Speaking in favor of another amendment, Senator Pittman noted that a customs officer seizing obscene matter "should immediately report to the nearest United States district attorney having authority under the law to proceed to confiscate. . . ." Id. at 5420 (emphasis added). Commenting on an early draft of another amendment that was ultimately adopted, Senator Swanson noted that officers would be required to go to court "immediately." Id. at 5422. Then he added:

"The minute there is a suspicion on the part of a revenue or customs officer that a certain book is improper to be admitted into this country, he presents the matter to the district court, and there will be a prompt determination of the matter by a decision of that court."

Id. at 5424 (emphasis added).

Before it finally emerged from Congress, § 1305(a) was amended in response to objections of the sort voiced above: it thus reflects the same policy considerations that induced this Court to hold in Freedman that censors must resort to the courts "within a specified brief period" and that such resort must be followed by "a prompt final judicial decision. . . ." 380 U.S. at 380 U. S. 59. Congress' sole omission was its failure to specify exact time limits within which resort to the courts must be had and judicial proceedings be completed. No one during the congressional debates ever suggested inclusion of such limits, perhaps because experience had not yet demonstrated a need for them. Since 1930, however, the need has become clear. Our researches have disclosed cases sanctioning delays of as long as 40 days and even six months between seizure of obscene goods and commencement of judicial proceedings. See United States v. 77 Cartons of Magazines, 300 F.Supp. 851 (ND Cal.1969); United States v. One Carton Positive Motion Picture Film Entitled "491," 247 F.Supp. 450 (SDNY 1965), rev'd on other grounds, 367 F.2d 889 (CA2 1966). Similarly, we have found cases in which completion of judicial proceedings has taken as long as three, four, and even seven months. See United States v.

Ten Erotic Paintings, 311 F.Supp. 884 (Md.1970); United States v. 6 MM Color Motion Picture Film Entitled "Lanuae of Love," 311 F.Supp. 108 (SDNY 1970); United States v. One Carton Positive Motion Picture Film Entitled "491," supra. We conclude that to sanction such delays would be clearly inconsistent with the concern for promptness that was so frequently articulated during the course of the Senate's debates, and that fidelity to Congress' purpose dictates that we read explicit time limits into the section. The only alternative would be to hold § 1305(a) unconstitutional in its entirety, but Congress has explicitly directed that the section not be invalidated in its entirety merely because its application to some persons be adjudged unlawful. See 19 U.S.C. § 1652. Nor does the construction of § 1305(a) to include specific time limits require us to decide issues of policy appropriately left to the Congress or raise other questions upon which Congress possesses special legislative expertise, for Congress has already set its course in favor of promptness and we possess as much expertise as Congress in determining the sole remaining question -- that of the speed with which prosecutorial and judicial institutions can, as a practical matter, be expected to function in adjudicating § 1305(a) matters. We accordingly see no reason for declining to specify the time limits which must be incorporated into § 1305(a) -- a specification that is fully consistent with congressional purpose and that will obviate the constitutional objections raised by claimant. Indeed, we conclude that the legislative history of the section and the policy of giving legislation a saving construction in order to avoid decision of constitutional questions require that we undertake this task of statutory construction.

We begin by examining cases in the lower federal courts in which proceedings have been brought under § 1305(a). That examination indicates that, in many of the cases that have come to our attention, the Government, in fact, instituted forfeiture proceedings within 14 days of the date of seizure of the allegedly obscene goods, see United States v. Reliable Sales Co., 376 F.2d 803 (CA4 1967); United States v. 1,000 Copies of a Magazine Entitled "Solis," 254 F.Supp. 595 (Md.1966); United States v. 6 Cartons Containing 19,500 Copies of a Magazine Entitled "Hellenic Sun," 253 F.Supp. 498 (Md.1966), aff'd, 373 F.2d 635 (CA4 1967); United States v. 92 Copies of a Magazine Entitled "Exclusive," 253 F.Supp. 485 (Md.1966); and judicial proceedings were completed within 60 days of their commencement. See United States v. Reliable Sales Co., supra; United States v. 1,000 Copies of a Magazine Entitled "Solis," supra; United States v. 66 Cartons Containing 19,500 Copies of a Magazine Entitled "Hellenic Sun," supra; United States v. 92 Copies of a Magazine Entitled "Exclusive," supra; United States v. 127,29 Copies of Magazines, More or Less, 295 F.Supp. 1186 (Md.1968). Given this record, it seems clear that no undue hardship will be imposed upon the Government and the lower federal courts by requiring that forfeiture proceedings be commenced within 14 days and completed within 60 days of their commencement; nor does a delay of as much as 74 days seem undue for importers engaged in the lengthy process of bringing goods into this country from abroad. Accordingly, we construe § 1305(a) to require intervals of no more than 14 days from seizure of the goods to the institution of judicial proceedings for their forfeiture, and no longer than 60 days from the filing of the action to final decision in the district court. No seizure or forfeiture will be invalidated for delay, however, where the claimant is responsible for extending either administrative action or judicial determination beyond the allowable time limits or where administrative or judicial proceedings are postponed pending the consideration of constitutional issues appropriate only for a three-judge court.

Of course, we do not now decide that these are the only constitutionally permissible time limits. We note, furthermore, that constitutionally permissible limits may vary in different contexts; in other contexts, such as a claim by a state censor that a movie is obscene, the Constitution may impose different requirements with respect to the time between the making of the claim and the institution of judicial proceedings or between their commencement and completion than in the context of a claim of obscenity made by customs officials at the border. We decide none of these questions today. We do nothing in this case but construe § 1305(a) in its present form, fully cognizant that Congress may reenact it in a new form specifying new time limits, upon whose constitutionality we may then be required to pass.

So construed, § 1305(a) may constitutionally be applied to the case before us. Seizure in the present case took place on October 24 and forfeiture proceedings were instituted on November 6 -- a mere 13 days after seizure. Moreover, decision on the obscenity of Luros' materials might well have been forthcoming within 60 days had claimant not challenged the validity of the statute and caused a three-judge court to be convened. We hold that proceedings of such brevity fully meet the constitutional standards set out in Freedman, Teitel, and Blount. Section 1305(a) accordingly may be applied to the 37 photographs, providing that, on remand, the obscenity issue is resolved in the District Court within 60 days, excluding any delays caused by Luros.

II

We next consider Luros' second claim, which is based upon Stanley v. Georgia, supra. On the authority of Stanley, Luros urged the trial court to construe the First Amendment as forbidding any restraints on obscenity except where necessary to protect children or where it intruded itself upon the sensitivity or privacy of an unwilling adult. Without rejecting this position, the trial court read Stanley as protecting, at the very least, the right to read obscene material in the privacy of one's own home, and to receive it for that purpose. It therefore held that § 1305(a), which bars the importation of obscenity for private use as well as for commercial distribution, is overbroad, and hence unconstitutional. [3]

The trial court erred in reading Stanley as immunizing from seizure obscene materials possessed at a port of entry for the purpose of importation for private use. In United States v. Reidel, ante, p. 402 U. S. 351, we have today held that Congress may constitutionally prevent the mails from being used for distributing pornography. In this case, neither Luros nor his putative buyers have rights that are infringed by the exclusion of obscenity from incoming foreign commerce. By the same token, obscene materials may be removed from the channels of commerce when discovered in the luggage of a returning foreign traveler even though intended solely for his private use. That the private user under Stanley may not be prosecuted for possession of obscenity in his home does not mean that he is entitled to import it from abroad free from the power of Congress to exclude noxious articles from commerce. Stanley's emphasis was on the freedom of thought and mind in the privacy of the home. But a port of entry is not a traveler's home. His right to be let alone neither prevents the search of his luggage nor the seizure of unprotected, but illegal, materials when his possession of them is discovered during such a search. Customs officers characteristically inspect luggage, and their power to do so is not questioned in this case; it is an old practice, and is intimately associated with excluding illegal articles from the country. Whatever the scope of the right to receive obscenity adumbrated in Stanley, that right, as we said in Reidel, does not extend to one who is seeking, as was Luros here, to distribute obscene materials to the public, nor does it extend to one seeking to import obscene materials from abroad, whether for private use or public distribution. As we held in Roth v. United States, 354 U. S. 476 (1957), and reiterated today in Reidel, supra, obscenity is not within the scope of First Amendment protection. Hence, Congress may declare it contraband and prohibit its importation, as it has elected in § 1305(a) to do.

The judgment of the District Court is reversed, and the case is remanded for further proceedings consistent with this opinion.

It is so ordered.

[For dissenting opinion of MR. JUSTICE MARSHALL, see ante, p. 402 U. S. 360.]

* MR. JUSTICE HARLAN and MR. JUSTICE STEWART also join Part I of the opinion.

Notes

[1] 119 U.S.C. § 1305(a) provides in pertinent part:

"All persons are prohibited from importing into the United States from any foreign country . . . any obscene book, pamphlet, paper, writing, advertisement, circular, print, picture, drawing, or other representation, figure, or image on or of paper or other material, or any cast, instrument, or other article which is obscene or immoral. . . . No such articles whether imported separately or contained in packages with other goods entitled to entry, shall be admitted to entry; and all such articles and, unless it appears to the satisfaction of the collector that the obscene or other prohibited articles contained in the package were inclosed therein without the knowledge or consent of the importer, owner, agent, or consignee, the entire contents of the package in which such articles are contained, shall be subject to seizure and forfeiture as hereinafter provided. . . . Provided, further, That the Secretary of the Treasury may, in his discretion, admit the so-called classics or books of recognized and established literary or scientific merit, but may, in his discretion, admit such classics or books only when imported for noncommercial purposes."

"Upon the appearance of any such book or matter at any customs office, the same shall be seized and held by the collector to await the judgment of the district court as hereinafter provided; and no protest shall be taken to the United States Customs Court from the decision of the collector. Upon the seizure of such book or matter the collector shall transmit information thereof to the district attorney of the district in which is situated the office at which such seizure has taken place, who shall institute proceedings in the district court for the forfeiture, confiscation, and destruction of the book or matter seized. Upon the adjudication that such book or matter thus seized is of the character the entry of which is by this section prohibited, it shall be ordered destroyed and shall be destroyed. Upon adjudication that such book or matter thus seized is not of the character the entry of which is by this section prohibited, it shall not be excluded from entry under the provisions of this section."

"In any such proceeding any party in interest may upon demand have the facts at issue determined by a jury and any party may have an appeal or the right of review as in the case of ordinary actions or suits."

[2] The United States urges that we find time limits in 19 U.S.C. §§ 1602 and 1604. Section 1602 provides that customs agents who seize goods must "report every such seizure immediately" to the collector of the district, while § 1604 provides that, once a case has been turned over to a United States Attorney, it shall be his duty "immediately to inquire into the facts" and "forthwith to cause the proper proceedings to be commenced and prosecuted, without delay," if he concludes judicial proceedings are appropriate. We need not decide, however, whether §§ 1602 and 1604 can properly be applied to cure the invalidity of § 1305(a), for even if they were applicable, they would not provide adequate time limits and would not cure its invalidity. The two sections contain no specific time limits, nor do they require the collector to act promptly in referring a matter to the United States Attorney for prosecution. Another flaw is that § 1604 requires that, if the United States Attorney declines to prosecute, he must report the facts to the Secretary of the Treasury for his direction, but the Secretary is under no duty to act with speed. The final flaw is that neither section requires the District Court in which a case is commenced to come promptly to a final decision.

[3] The District Court's opinion is not entirely clear. The court may have reasoned that Luros had a right to import the 37 photographs in question for planned distribution to the general public, but our decision today in United States v. Reidel, ante, p. 402 U. S. 351, makes it clear that such reasoning would have been in error. On the other hand, the District Court may have reasoned that, while Luros had no right to import the photographs for distribution, a person would have a right under Stanley to import them for his own private use, and that § 1305(a) was therefore void as overbroad because it prohibits both sorts of importation. If this was the court's reasoning, the proper approach, however, was not to invalidate the section in its entirety, but to construe it narrowly and hold it valid in its application to Luros. This was made clear in Dombrowski

v. Pfister, 380 U. S. 479, 380 U. S. 491-492 (1965), where the Court noted that, once the overbreadth of a statute has been sufficiently dealt with, it may be applied to prior conduct foreseeably within its valid sweep.

## Cohen v. California (June 7, 1971)

MR. JUSTICE HARLAN delivered the opinion of the Court.

This case may seem at first blush too inconsequential to find its way into our books, but the issue it presents is of no small constitutional significance.

Appellant Paul Robert Cohen was convicted in the Los Angeles Municipal Court of violating that part of California Penal Code § 415 which prohibits "maliciously and willfully disturb[ing] the peace or quiet of any neighborhood or person . . . by . . . offensive conduct. . . ." [n1] He was given 30 days' imprisonment. The facts upon which his conviction rests are detailed in the opinion of the Court of Appeal of California, Second Appellate District, as follows:

On April 26, 1968, the defendant was observed in the Los Angeles County Courthouse in the corridor outside of division 20 of the municipal court wearing a jacket bearing the words "Fuck the Draft" which were plainly visible. There were women and children present in the corridor. The defendant was arrested. The defendant testified that he wore the jacket knowing that the words were on the jacket as a means of informing the public of the depth of his feelings against the Vietnam War and the draft.

The defendant did not engage in, nor threaten to engage in, nor did anyone as the result of his conduct in fact commit or threaten to commit any act of violence. The defendant did not make any loud or unusual noise, nor was there any evidence that he uttered any sound prior to his arrest.

1 Cal.App.3d 94, 97-98, 81 Cal.Rptr. 503, 505 (1969).

In affirming the conviction, the Court of Appeal held that "offensive conduct" means "behavior which has a tendency to provoke others to acts of violence or to in turn disturb the peace," and that the State had proved this element because, on the facts of this case,

[i]t was certainly reasonably foreseeable that such conduct might cause others to rise up to commit a violent act against the person of the defendant or attempt to forcibly remove his jacket.

1 Cal.App.3d at 99-100, 81 Cal.Rptr. at 506. The California Supreme Court declined review by a divided vote. [n2] We brought the case here, postponing the consideration of the question of our jurisdiction over this appeal to a hearing of the case on the merits. 399 U.S. 904. We now reverse.

The question of our jurisdiction need not detain us long. Throughout the proceedings below, Cohen consistently claimed that, as construed to apply to the facts of this case, the statute infringed his rights to freedom of expression guaranteed by the First and Fourteenth Amendments of the Federal Constitution. That contention has been rejected by the highest California state court in which review could be had. Accordingly, we are fully satisfied that Cohen has properly invoked our jurisdiction by this appeal. 28 U.S.C. § 1257(2); Dahnke-Walker Milling Co. v. Bondurant, 257 U.S. 282 (1921).

I

In order to lay hands on the precise issue which this case involves, it is useful first to canvass various matters which this record does not present.

The conviction quite clearly rests upon the asserted offensiveness of the words Cohen used to convey his message to the public. The only "conduct" which the State sought to punish is the fact of communication. Thus, we deal here with a conviction resting solely upon "speech," cf. Stromberg v. California, 283 U.S. 359"] 283 U.S. 359 (1931), not upon any separately identifiable conduct which allegedly was intended by Cohen to be perceived by others as expressive of particular views but which, on its face, does not necessarily convey any message, and hence arguably could be regulated without effectively repressing Cohen's ability to express himself. Cf. United States v. O'Brien, 391 U.S. 367 (1968). Further, the State certainly lacks power to punish Cohen for the underlying content of the message the inscription conveyed. At least so long as there is no showing of an intent to incite disobedience to or disruption of the draft, Cohen could not, consistently with the First and Fourteenth Amendments, be punished for asserting the evident position on the inutility or immorality of the draft his jacket reflected. 283 U.S. 359 (1931), not upon any separately identifiable conduct which allegedly was intended by Cohen to be perceived by others as expressive of particular views but which, on its face, does not necessarily convey any message, and hence arguably could be regulated without effectively repressing Cohen's ability to express himself. Cf. United States v. O'Brien, 391 U.S. 367 (1968). Further, the State certainly lacks power to punish Cohen for the underlying content of the message the inscription conveyed. At least so long as there is no showing of an intent to incite disobedience to or disruption of the draft, Cohen could not, consistently with the First and Fourteenth Amendments, be punished for asserting the evident position on the inutility or immorality of the draft his jacket reflected. Yates v. United States, 354 U.S. 298 (1957).

Appellant's conviction, then, rests squarely upon his exercise of the "freedom of speech" protected from arbitrary governmental interference by the Constitution, and can be justified, if at all, only as a valid regulation of the manner in which he exercised that freedom, not as a permissible prohibition on the substantive message it conveys. This does not end the inquiry, of course, for the First and Fourteenth Amendments have never been thought to give absolute protection to every individual to speak whenever or wherever he pleases, or to use any form of address in any circumstances that he chooses. In this vein, too, however, we think it important to note that several issues typically associated with such problems are not presented here.

In the first place, Cohen was tried under a statute applicable throughout the entire State. Any attempt to support this conviction on the ground that the statute seeks to preserve an appropriately decorous atmosphere in the courthouse where Cohen was arrested must fail in the absence of any language in the statute that would have put appellant on notice that certain kinds of otherwise permissible speech or conduct would nevertheless, under California law, not be tolerated in certain places. See Edwards v. South Carolina, 372 U.S. 229, 236-237, and n. 11 (1963). Cf. Adderley v. Florida, 385 U.S. 39 (1966). No fair reading of the phrase "offensive conduct" can be said sufficiently to inform the ordinary person that distinctions between certain locations are thereby created. [n3]

In the second place, as it comes to us, this case cannot be said to fall within those relatively few categories of instances where prior decisions have established the power of government to deal more comprehensively with certain forms of individual expression simply upon a showing that such a form was employed. This is not, for example, an obscenity case. Whatever else may be necessary to give rise to the States' broader power to prohibit obscene expression, such expression must be, in some significant way, erotic. Roth v. United States, 354 U.S. 476 (1957). It cannot plausibly be maintained that this vulgar allusion to the Selective Service System would conjure up such psychic stimulation in anyone likely to be confronted with Cohen's crudely defaced jacket.

This Court has also held that the States are free to ban the simple use, without a demonstration of additional justifying circumstances, of so-called "fighting words," those personally abusive epithets which, when addressed to the ordinary citizen, are, as a matter of common knowledge, inherently likely to provoke violent reaction. Chaplinsky v. New Hampshire, 315 U.S. 568 (1942). While the four-letter word displayed by Cohen in relation to the draft is not uncommonly employed in a personally provocative fashion, in this instance it was clearly not "directed to the person of the hearer." Cantwell v. Connecticut, 310 U.S. 296, 309 (1940). No individual actually or likely to be present could reasonably have regarded the words on appellant's jacket as a direct personal insult. Nor do we have here an instance of the exercise of the State's police power to prevent a speaker from intentionally provoking a given group to hostile reaction. Cf. Feiner v. New York, 340 U.S. 315 (1951); Termniello v. Chicago, 337 U.S. 1 (1949). There is, as noted above, no showing that anyone who saw Cohen was, in fact, violently aroused, or that appellant intended such a result.

Finally, in arguments before this Court, much has been made of the claim that Cohen's distasteful mode of expression was thrust upon unwilling or unsuspecting viewers, and that the State might therefore legitimately act as it did in order to protect the sensitive from otherwise unavoidable exposure to appellant's crude form of protest. Of course, the mere presumed presence of unwitting listeners or viewers does not serve automatically to justify curtailing all speech capable of giving offense. See, e.g., Organization for a Better Austin v. Keefe, 402 U.S. 415 (1971). While this Court has recognized that government may properly act in many situations to prohibit intrusion into the privacy of the home of unwelcome views and ideas which cannot be totally banned from the public dialogue, e.g., Rowan v. Post Office Dept., 397 U.S. 728 (1970), we have at the same time consistently stressed that "we are often 'captives' outside the sanctuary of the home and subject to objectionable speech." Id. at 738. The ability of government, consonant with the Constitution, to shut off discourse solely to protect others from hearing it is, in other words, dependent upon a showing that substantial privacy interests are being invaded in an essentially intolerable manner. Any broader view of this authority would effectively empower a majority to silence dissidents simply as a matter of personal predilections.

In this regard, persons confronted with Cohen's jacket were in a quite different posture than, say, those subjected to the raucous emissions of sound trucks blaring outside their residences. Those in the Los Angeles courthouse could effectively avoid further bombardment of their sensibilities simply by averting their eyes. And, while it may be that one has a more substantial claim to a recognizable privacy interest when walking through a courthouse corridor than, for example, strolling through Central Park, surely it is nothing like the interest in being free from unwanted expression in the confines of one's own home. Cf. Keefe, supra. Given the subtlety and complexity of the factors involved, if Cohen's "speech" was otherwise entitled to constitutional protection, we do not think the fact that some unwilling "listeners" in a public building may have been briefly exposed to it can serve to justify this breach of the peace conviction where, as here, there was no evidence that persons powerless to avoid appellant's conduct did in fact, object to it, and where that portion of the statute upon which Cohen's conviction rests evinces no concern, either on its face or as construed by the California courts, with the special plight of the captive auditor, but, instead, indiscriminately sweeps within its prohibitions all "offensive conduct" that disturbs "any neighborhood or person." Cf. Edwards v. South Carolina, supra. [n4]

II

Against this background, the issue flushed by this case stands out in bold relief. It is whether California can excise, as "offensive conduct," one particular scurrilous epithet from the public discourse, either upon the theory of the court below that its use is inherently likely to cause violent reaction or upon a more general assertion that the States, acting as guardians of public morality, may properly remove this offensive word from the public vocabulary.

The rationale of the California court is plainly untenable. At most, it reflects an "undifferentiated fear or apprehension of disturbance [which] is not enough to overcome the right to freedom of expression." Tinker v. Des Moines Indep. Community School Dist., 393 U.S. 503"] 393 U.S. 503, 508 (1969). We have been shown no evidence that substantial numbers of citizens are standing ready to strike out physically at whoever may assault their sensibilities with execrations like that uttered by Cohen. There may be some persons about with such lawless and violent proclivities, but that is an insufficient base upon which to erect, consistently with constitutional values, a governmental power to force persons who wish to ventilate their dissident views into avoiding particular forms of expression. The argument amounts to little more than the self-defeating proposition that, to avoid physical censorship of one who has not sought to provoke such a response by a hypothetical coterie of the violent and lawless, the States may more appropriately effectuate that censorship themselves. Cf. Ashton v. Kentucky, 384 U.S. 195, 200 (1966); 393 U.S. 503, 508 (1969). We have been shown no evidence that substantial numbers of citizens are standing ready to strike out physically at whoever may assault their sensibilities with execrations like that uttered by Cohen. There may be some persons about with such lawless and violent proclivities, but that is an insufficient base upon which to erect, consistently with constitutional values, a governmental power to force persons who wish to ventilate their dissident views into avoiding particular forms of expression. The argument amounts to little more than the self-defeating proposition that, to avoid physical censorship of one who has not sought to provoke such a response by a hypothetical coterie of the violent and lawless, the States may more appropriately effectuate that censorship themselves. Cf. Ashton v. Kentucky, 384 U.S. 195, 200 (1966); Cox v. Louisiana, 379 U.S. 536, 550-551 (1965).

Admittedly, it is not so obvious that the First and Fourteenth Amendments must be taken to disable the States from punishing public utterance of this unseemly expletive in order to maintain what they regard as a suitable level of discourse within the body politic. [n5] We think, however, that examination and reflection will reveal the shortcomings of a contrary viewpoint.

At the outset, we cannot overemphasize that, in our judgment, most situations where the State has a justifiable interest in regulating speech will fall within one or more of the various established exceptions, discussed above but not applicable here, to the usual rule that governmental bodies may not prescribe the form or content of individual expression. Equally important to our conclusion is the constitutional backdrop against which our decision must be made. The constitutional right of free expression is powerful medicine in a society as diverse and populous a ours. It is designed and intended to remove governmental restraints from the arena of public discussion, putting the decision as to what views shall be voiced largely into the hands of each of us, in the hope that use of such freedom will ultimately produce a more capable citizenry and more perfect polity and in the belief that no other approach would comport with the premise of individual dignity and choice upon which our political system rests. See Whitney v. California, 274 U.S. 357, 375-377 (1927) (Brandeis, J., concurring).

To many, the immediate consequence of this freedom may often appear to be only verbal tumult, discord, and even offensive utterance. These are, however, within established limits, in truth necessary side effects of the broader enduring values which the process of open debate permits us to achieve. That the air may at times seem filled with verbal cacophony is, in this sense not a sign of weakness but of strength. We cannot lose sight of the fact that, in what otherwise might seem a trifling and annoying instance of individual distasteful abuse of a privilege, these fundamental societal values are truly implicated. That is why "[w]holly neutral futilities . . . come under the protection of free speech as fully as do Keats' poems or Donne's sermons," Winters v. New York, 333 U.S. 507, 528 (1948) (Frankfurter, J., dissenting), and why, "so long as the means are peaceful, the communication need not meet standards of acceptability," Organization for a Better Austin v. Keefe, 402 U.S. 415, 419 (1971).

Against this perception of the constitutional policies involved, we discern certain more particularized considerations that peculiarly call for reversal of this conviction. First, the principle contended for by the State seems inherently boundless. How is one to distinguish this from any other offensive word? Surely the State has no right to cleanse public debate to the point where it is grammatically palatable to the most squeamish among us. Yet no readily ascertainable general principle exists for stopping short of that result were we to affirm the judgment below. For, while the particular four-letter word being litigated here is perhaps more distasteful than most others of its genre, it is nevertheless often true that one man's vulgarity is another's lyric. Indeed, we think it is largely because governmental officials cannot make principled distinctions in this area that the Constitution leaves matters of taste and style so largely to the individual.

Additionally, we cannot overlook the fact, because it is well illustrated by the episode involved here, that much linguistic expression serves a dual communicative function: it conveys not only ideas capable of relatively precise, detached explication, but otherwise inexpressible emotions as well. In fact, words are often chosen as much for their emotive as their cognitive force. We cannot sanction the view that the Constitution, while solicitous of the cognitive content of individual speech, has little or no regard for that emotive function which, practically speaking, may often be the more important element of the overall message sought to be communicated. Indeed, as Mr. Justice Frankfurter has said,

[o]ne of the prerogatives of American citizenship is the right to criticize public men and measures -- and that means not only informed and responsible criticism, but the freedom to speak foolishly and without moderation.

Baumgartner v. United States, 322 U.S. 665, 673-674 (1944).

Finally, and in the same vein, we cannot indulge the facile assumption that one can forbid particular words without also running a substantial risk of suppressing ideas in the process. Indeed, governments might soon seize upon the censorship of particular words as a convenient guise for banning the expression of unpopular views. We have been able, as noted above, to discern little social benefit that might result from running the risk of opening the door to such grave results.

It is, in sum, our judgment that, absent a more particularized and compelling reason for its actions, the State may not, consistently with the First and Fourteenth Amendments, make the simple public display here involved of this single four-letter expletive a criminal offense. Because that is the only arguably sustainable rationale for the conviction here at issue, the judgment below must be

Reversed.

Notes

1. The statute provides in full:

Every person who maliciously and willfully disturbs the peace or quiet of any neighborhood or person, by loud or unusual noise, or by tumultuous or offensive conduct, or threatening, traducing, quarreling, challenging to fight, or fighting, or who, on the public streets of any unincorporated town, or upon the public highways in such unincorporated town, run any horse race, either for a wager or for amusement, or fire any gun or pistol in such unincorporated town, or use any vulgar, profane, or indecent language within the presence or hearing of women or children, in a loud and boisterous manner, is guilty of a misdemeanor, and upon conviction by any Court of competent jurisdiction shall be punished by fine not exceeding two hundred dollars, or by imprisonment in the County Jail for not more than ninety days, or by both fine and imprisonment, or either, at the discretion of the Court.

2. The suggestion has been made that, in light of the supervening opinion of the California Supreme Court in In re Bushman, 1 Cal.3d 767, 463 P.2d 727 (1970), it is "not at all certain that the California Court of Appeal's construction of § 415 is now the authoritative California construction." Post at 27 (BLACKMUN, J., dissenting). In the course of the Bushman opinion, Chief Justice Traynor stated:

[One] may . . . be guilty of disturbing the peace through "offensive" conduct [within the meaning of § 415] if, by his actions, he willfully and maliciously incites others to violence or engages in conduct likely to incite others to violence. (People v. Cohen (1969) 1 Cal.App.3d 94, 101, [81 Cal.Rptr. 503].)

1 Cal.3d at 773, 463 P.2d at 730.

We perceive no difference of substance between the Bushman construction and that of the Court of Appeal, particularly in light of the Bushman court's approving citation of Cohen.

3. It is illuminating to note what transpired when Cohen entered a courtroom in the building. He removed his jacket and stood with it folded over his arm. Meanwhile, a policeman sent the presiding judge a note suggesting that Cohen be held in contempt of court. The judge declined to do so, and Cohen was arrested by the officer only after he emerged from the courtroom. App. 119.

4. In fact, other portions of the same statute do make some such distinctions. For example, the statute also prohibits disturbing "the peace or quiet . . . by loud or unusual noise" and using "vulgar, profane, or indecent language within the presence or hearing of women or children, in a loud and boisterous manner." See n. 1, supra. This second-quoted provision in particular serves to put the actor on much fairer notice as to what is prohibited. It also buttresses our view that the "offensive conduct" portion, as construed and applied in this case, cannot legitimately be justified in this Court as designed or intended to make fine distinctions between differently situated recipients.

5. The amicus urges, with some force, that this issue is not properly before us, since the statute, as construed, punishes only conduct that might cause others to react violently. However, because the opinion below appears to erect a virtually irrebuttable presumption that use of this word will produce such results, the statute, as thus

construed, appears to impose, in effect, a flat ban on the public utterance of this word. With the case in this posture, it does not seem inappropriate to inquire whether any other rationale might properly support this result. While we think it clear, for the reasons expressed above, that no statute which merely proscribes "offensive conduct" and has been construed as broadly as this one was below can subsequently be justified in this Court as discriminating between conduct that occurs in different places or that offends only certain persons, it is not so unreasonable to seek to justify its full broad sweep on an alternate rationale such as this. Because it is not so patently clear that acceptance of the justification presently under consideration would render the statute overbroad or unconstitutionally vague, and be cause the answer to appellee's argument seems quite clear, we do not pass on the contention that this claim is not presented on this record.

## Rabe v. Washington (March 20, 1972)

PER CURIAM.
Petitioner was the manager of the Park Y Drive-In Theatre in Richland, Washington, where the motion picture Carmen Baby was shown. The motion picture is a loose adaptation of Bizet's opera Carmen, containing sexually frank scenes, but no instances of sexual consummation are explicitly portrayed. After viewing the film from outside the theater fence on two successive evenings, a police officer obtained a warrant and arrested petitioner for violating Washington's obscenity statute. Wash.Rev.Code § 9.68.010. Petitioner was later convicted and, on appeal, the Supreme Court of Washington affirmed. 79 Wash.2d 254, 484 P.2d 917 (1971). We granted certiorari. 404 U.S. 909. We reverse petitioner's conviction.
The statute under which petitioner was convicted, Wash.Rev.Code § 9.68.010, made criminal the knowing display of "obscene" motion pictures:
"Every person who -- "
"(1) Having knowledge of the contents thereof shall exhibit, sell, distribute, display for sale or distribution, or having knowledge of the contents thereof shall have in his possession with the intent to sell or distribute any book, magazine, pamphlet, comic book, newspaper, writing, photograph, motion picture film, phonograph record, tape or wire recording, picture, drawing, figure, image, or any object or thing which is obscene; or"
"(2) Having knowledge of the contents thereof shall cause to be performed or exhibited, or shall engage in the performance or exhibition of any show, act, play, dance or motion picture which is obscene;"
"Shall be guilty of a gross misdemeanor."
In affirming petitioner's conviction, however, the Supreme Court of Washington did not hold that Carmen Baby was obscene under the test laid down by this Court's prior decisions. E.g., Roth v. United States, 354 U. S. 476; Memoirs v. Massachusetts, 383 U. S. 413. Uncertain

"whether the movie was offensive to the standards relating to sexual matters in that area and whether the movie advocated ideas or was of artistic or literary value,"

the court concluded that, if it

"were to apply the strict rules of Roth, the film 'Carmen Baby' probably would pass the definitional obscenity test if the viewing audience consisted only of consenting adults."

79 Wash.2d at 263, 484 P.2d at 922. Respondent read the opinion of the Supreme Court of Washington more narrowly, but nonetheless implied that, because the film had "redeeming social value," it was not, by itself, "obscene" under the Roth standard. The Supreme Court of Washington nonetheless upheld the conviction, reasoning that in "the context of its exhibition," Carmen Baby was obscene. Ibid.

To avoid the constitutional vice of vagueness, it is necessary, at a minimum, that a statute give fair notice that certain conduct is proscribed. The statute under which petitioner was prosecuted, however, made no mention that the "context" or location of the exhibition was an element of the offense somehow modifying the word "obscene." Petitioner's conviction was thus affirmed under a statute with a meaning quite different from the one he was charged with violating.

"It is as much a violation of due process to send an accused to prison following conviction of a charge on which he was never tried as it would be to convict him upon a charge that was never made."

Cole v. Arkansas, 333 U. S. 196, 333 U. S. 201. Petitioner's conviction cannot, therefore, be allowed to stand. Gregory v. City of Chicago, 394 U. S. 111; Garner v. Louisiana, 368 U. S. 157; Cole v. Arkansas, supra.

Under the interpretation given § 9.68.010 by the Supreme Court of Washington, petitioner is criminally punished for showing Carmen Baby in a drive-in, but he may exhibit it to adults in an indoor theater with impunity. The statute, so construed, is impermissibly vague as applied to petitioner because of its failure to give him fair notice that criminal liability is dependent upon the place where the film is shown.

What we said last Term in Cohen v. California, 403 U. S. 15, 403 U. S. 19, answers respondent's contention that the peculiar interest in prohibiting out-door displays of sexually frank motion pictures justifies the application of this statute to petitioner:

"Any attempt to support this conviction on the ground that the statute seeks to preserve an appropriately decorous atmosphere in the courthouse where Cohen was arrested must fail in the absence of any language in the statute that would have put appellant on notice that certain kinds of otherwise permissible speech or conduct would nevertheless, under California law, not be tolerated in certain places. . . . No fair reading of the phrase 'offensive conduct' can be said sufficiently to inform the ordinary person that distinctions between certain locations are thereby created."

We need not decide the broad constitutional questions tendered to us by the parties. We hold simply that a State may not criminally punish the exhibition at a drive-in theater of a motion picture where the statute used to support the conviction has not given fair notice that the location of the exhibition was a vital element of the offense.

The judgment of the Supreme Court of Washington is

Reversed.

## Kois v. Wisconsin (June 26, 1972)

PER CURIAM.

Petitioner was convicted in the state trial court of violating a Wisconsin statute prohibiting the dissemination of "lewd, obscene or indecent written matter, picture, sound recording, or film." Wis.Stat. § 944.21(1)(a) (1969). He was sentenced to consecutive one-year terms in the Green Bay Reformatory and fined $1,000 on each of two counts. The Supreme Court of Wisconsin upheld his conviction against the contention that he had been deprived of freedom of the press in violation of the Fourteenth Amendment. 51 Wis.2d 668, 188 N.W.2d 467. Petitioner was the publisher of an underground newspaper called Kaleidoscope. In an issue published in May, 1968, that newspaper carried a story entitled "The One Hundred Thousand Dollar Photos" on an interior page. The story itself was an account of the arrest of one of Kaleidoscope's photographers on a charge of possession of obscene material. Two relatively small pictures, showing a nude man and nude woman embracing in a sitting position, accompanied the article and were described in the article as "similar" to those seized from the photographer. The article said that the photographer, while waiting in the district attorney's office, had heard that bail might be set at $100,000. The article went on to say that bail had, in fact, been set originally at $100, then raised to $250, and that, later, the photographer had been released on his own recognizance. The article purported to detail police tactics that were described as an effort to "harass" Kaleidoscope and its staff. Roth v. United States, 354 U. S. 476 (1957), held that obscenity was not protected under the First or Fourteenth Amendments. Material may be considered obscene when,

"to the average person, applying contemporary community standards, the dominant theme of the material, taken as a whole, appeals to the prurient interest."

354 U.S. at 354 U. S. 489. In enunciating this test, the Court in Roth quoted from Thornhill v. Alabama, 310 U. S. 88, 310 U. S. 101-102:

"The freedom of speech and of the press guaranteed by the Constitution embraces at the least the liberty to discuss publicly and truthfully all matters of public concern without previous restraint or fear of subsequent punishment. The exigencies of the colonial period and the efforts to secure freedom from oppressive administration developed a broadened conception of these liberties as adequate to supply the public need for information and education with respect to the significant issues of the times. . . ."

(Emphasis supplied.)

We do not think it can fairly be said, either considering the article as it appears or the record before the state court, that the article was a mere vehicle for the publication of the pictures. A quotation from Voltaire in the flyleaf of a book will not constitutionally redeem an otherwise obscene publication, but if these pictures were indeed similar to the one seized -- and we do not understand the State to contend differently -- they are relevant to the theme of the article. We find it unnecessary to consider whether the State could constitutionally prohibit the dissemination of the pictures by themselves, because, in the context in which they appeared in the newspaper, they were rationally related to an article that itself was clearly entitled to the protection of the Fourteenth Amendment. Thornhill v. Alabama, supra. The motion for leave to proceed in forma pauperis and the petition for writ of certiorari are granted. The conviction on count one must therefore be reversed.

In its August, 1968, issue, Kaleidoscope published a two-page spread consisting of 11 poems, one of which was entitled "Sex Poem." The second count of petitioner's conviction was for the dissemination of the newspaper containing this poem. The poem is an undisguisedly frank, play-by-play account of the author's recollection of sexual intercourse. But, as the Roth Court emphasized,

"sex and obscenity are not synonymous. . . . The portrayal of sex, e.g., in art, literature and scientific works, is not itself sufficient reason to deny material the constitutional protection of freedom of speech and press."

354 U.S. at 354 U. S. 487. A reviewing court must, of necessity, look at the context of the material, as well as its content.

In this case, considering the poem's content and its placement amid a selection of poems in the interior of a newspaper, we believe that it bears some of the earmarks of an attempt at serious art. While such earmarks are not inevitably a guarantee against a finding of obscenity, and while, in this case, many would conclude that the author's reach exceeded his grasp, this element must be considered in assessing whether or not the "dominant" theme of the material appeals to. prurient interest. While "contemporary community standards," Roth v. United States, 354 U.S. at 354 U. S. 489, must leave room for some latitude of judgment, and while there is an undeniably subjective element in the test as a whole, the "dominance" of the theme is a question of constitutional fact. Giving due weight and respect to the conclusions of the trial court and to the Supreme Court of Wisconsin, we do not believe that it can be said that the dominant theme of this poem appeals to prurient interest. The judgment on the second count, therefore, must also be reversed.

Reversed.

## Miller v. California (June 21, 1973) [Notes omitted]

MR. CHIEF JUSTICE BURGER delivered the opinion of the Court.

This is one of a group of "obscenity-pornography" cases being reviewed by the Court in a reexamination of standards enunciated in earlier cases involving what Mr. Justice Harlan called "the intractable obscenity problem." Interstate Circuit, Inc. v. Dallas, 390 U. S. 676, 390 U. S. 704 (1968) (concurring and dissenting).

Appellant conducted a mass mailing campaign to advertise the sale of illustrated books, euphemistically called "adult" material. After a jury trial, he was convicted of violating California Penal Code § 311.2(a), a misdemeanor, by knowingly distributing obscene matter, [1] and the Appellate Department, Superior Court of California, County of Orange, summarily affirmed the judgment without opinion. Appellant's conviction was specifically based on his conduct in causing five unsolicited advertising brochures to be sent through the mail in an envelope addressed to a restaurant in Newport Beach, California. The envelope was opened by the manager of the restaurant and his mother. They had not requested the brochures; they complained to the police.

The brochures advertise four books entitled "Intercourse," "Man-Woman," "Sex Orgies Illustrated," and "An Illustrated History of Pornography," and a film entitled "Marital Intercourse." While the brochures contain some descriptive printed material, primarily they consist of pictures and drawings very explicitly depicting men and women in groups of two or more engaging in a variety of sexual activities, with genitals often prominently displayed.

I

This case involves the application of a State's criminal obscenity statute to a situation in which sexually explicit materials have been thrust by aggressive sales action upon unwilling recipients who had in no way indicated any desire to receive such materials. This Court has recognized that the States have a legitimate interest in prohibiting dissemination or exhibition of obscene material [2] when the mode of dissemination carries with it a significant danger of offending the sensibilities of unwilling recipients or of exposure to juveniles. Stanley v. Georgia, 394 U. S. 557, 394 U. S. 567 (1969); Ginsberg v. New York, 390 U. S. 629, 390 U. S. 637-643 (1968); Interstate Circuit, Inc. v. Dallas, supra, at 390 U. S. 690; Redrup v. New York, 386 U. S. 767, 386 U. S. 769 (1967); Jacobellis v. Ohio, 378 U. S. 184, 378 U. S. 195 (1964). See Rabe v. Washington, 405 U. S. 313, 405 U. S. 317 (1972) (BURGER, C.J., concurring); United States v. Reidel, 402 U. S. 351, 402 U. S. 360-362 (1971) (opinion of MARSHALL, J.); Joseph Burstyn, Inc. v. Wilson, 343 U. S. 495, 343 U. S. 502 (1952); Breard v. Alexandria, 341 U. S. 622, 341 U. S. 644 645 (1951); Kovacs v. Cooper, 336 U. S. 77, 336 U. S. 88-89 (1949); Prince v. Massachusetts, 321 U. S. 158, 321 U. S. 169-170 (1944). Cf. Butler v. Michigan, 352 U. S. 380, 352 U. S. 382-383 (1957); Public Utilities Comm'n v. Pollak, 343 U. S. 451, 343 U. S. 464-465 (1952) It is in this context that we are called on to define the standards which must be used to identify obscene material that a State may regulate without infringing on the First Amendment as applicable to the States through the Fourteenth Amendment.

The dissent of MR. JUSTICE BRENNAN reviews the background of the obscenity problem, but since the Court now undertakes to formulate standards more concrete than those in the past, it is useful for us to focus on two of the landmark cases in the somewhat tortured history of the Court's obscenity decisions. In Roth v. United States, 354 U. S. 476 (1957), the Court sustained a conviction under a federal statute punishing the mailing of "obscene, lewd, lascivious or filthy . . ." materials. The key to that holding was the Court's rejection of the claim that obscene materials were protected by the First Amendment. Five Justices joined in the opinion stating:

"All ideas having even the slightest redeeming social importance -- unorthodox ideas, controversial ideas, even ideas hateful to the prevailing climate of opinion -- have the full protection of the [First Amendment] guaranties, unless excludable because they encroach upon the limited area of more important interests. But implicit in the history of the First Amendment is the rejection of obscenity as utterly without redeeming social importance. . . . This is the same judgment expressed by this Court in Chaplinsky v. New Hampshire, 315 U. S. 568, 315 U. S. 571-572: "

". . . There are certain well defined and narrowly limited classes of speech, the prevention and punishment of which have never been thought to raise any Constitutional problem. These include the lewd and obscene. . . . It has been well observed that such utterances are no essential part of any exposition of ideas, and are of such slight social value as a step to truth that any benefit that may be derived from them is clearly outweighed by the social interest in order and morality. . . ."

[Emphasis by Court in Roth opinion.]

"We hold that obscenity is not within the area of constitutionally protected speech or press."

354 U.S. at 354 U. S. 48 85 (footnotes omitted).

Nine years later, in Memoirs v. Massachusetts, 383 U. S. 413 (1966), the Court veered sharply away from the Roth concept and, with only three Justices in the plurality opinion, articulated a new test of obscenity. The plurality held that, under the Roth definition,

"as elaborated in subsequent cases, three elements must coalesce: it must be established that (a) the dominant theme of the material, taken as a whole, appeals to a prurient interest in sex; (b) the material is patently offensive because it affronts contemporary community standards relating to the description or representation of sexual matters; and (c) the material is utterly without redeeming social value."

Id. at 383 U. S. 418. The sharpness of the break with Roth, represented by the third element of the Memoirs test and emphasized by MR. JUSTICE WHITE's dissent, id. at 383 U. S. 460-462, was further underscored when the Memoirs plurality went on to state:

"The Supreme Judicial Court erred in holding that a book need not be 'unqualifiedly worthless before it can be deemed obscene.' A book cannot be proscribed unless it is found to be utterly without redeeming social value."

Id. at 383 U. S. 419 (emphasis in original).

While Roth presumed "obscenity" to be "utterly without redeeming social importance," Memoirs required that to prove obscenity it must be affirmatively established that the material is "utterly without redeeming social value." Thus, even as they repeated the words of Roth, the Memoirs plurality produced a drastically altered test that called on the prosecution to prove a negative, i.e., that the material was "utterly without redeeming social value" -- a burden virtually impossible to discharge under our criminal standards of proof. Such considerations caused Mr. Justice Harlan to wonder if the "utterly without redeeming social value" test had any meaning at all. See Memoirs v. Massachusetts, id. at 383 U. S. 459 (Harlan, J., dissenting). See also id. at 383 U. S. 461 (WHITE, J., dissenting); United States v. Groner, 479 F.2d 577, 579581 (CA5 1973).

Apart from the initial formulation in the Roth case, no majority of the Court has at any given time been able to agree on a standard to determine what constitutes obscene, pornographic material subject to regulation under the States' police power. See, e.g., Redrup v. New York, 386 U.S. at 386 U. S. 770-771. We have seen "a variety of views among the members of the Court unmatched in any other course of constitutional adjudication." Interstate Circuit, Inc. v. Dallas, 390 U.S. at 390 U. S. 704-705 (Harlan, J., concurring and dissenting) (footnote omitted). [3] This is not remarkable, for in the area of freedom of speech and press the courts must always remain sensitive to any infringement on genuinely serious literary, artistic, political, or scientific expression. This is an area in which there are few eternal verities.

The case we now review was tried on the theory that the California Penal Code § 311 approximately incorporates the three-stage Memoirs test, supra. But now the Memoirs test has been abandoned as unworkable by its author, [4] and no Member of the Court today supports the Memoirs formulation.

II

This much has been categorically settled by the Court, that obscene material is unprotected by the First Amendment. Kois v. Wisconsin, 408 U. S. 229 (1972); United States v. Reidel, 402 U.S. at 402 U. S. 354; Roth v. United States, supra, at 354 U. S. 485. [5] "The First and Fourteenth Amendments have never been treated as absolutes [omitted]." Breard v. Alexandria, 341 U.S. at 341 U. S. 642, and cases cited. See Times Film Corp. v. Chicago, 365 U. S. 43, 365 U. S. 47-50 (1961); Joseph Burstyn, Inc. v. Wilson, 343 U.S. at 343 U. S. 502. We acknowledge, however, the inherent dangers of undertaking to regulate any form of expression. State statutes designed to regulate obscene materials must be carefully limited. See Interstate Circuit, Inc. v. Dallas, supra, at 390 U. S. 682-685. As a result, we now confine the permissible scope of such regulation to works which depict or describe sexual conduct. That conduct must be specifically defined by the applicable state law, as written or authoritatively construed. [6] A state offense must also be limited to works which, taken as a whole, appeal to the prurient interest in sex, which portray sexual conduct in a patently offensive way, and which, taken as a whole, do not have serious literary, artistic, political, or scientific value.

The basic guidelines for the trier of fact must be: (a) whether "the average person, applying contemporary community standards" would find that the work, taken as a whole, appeals to the prurient interest, Kois v. Wisconsin, supra, at 408 U. S. 230, quoting Roth v. United States, supra, at 354 U. S. 489; (b) whether the work depicts or describes, in a patently offensive way, sexual conduct specifically defined by the applicable state law; and (c) whether the work, taken as a whole, lacks serious literary, artistic, political, or scientific value. We do not adopt as a constitutional standard the "utterly without redeeming social value" test of Memoirs v. Massachusetts, 383 U.S. at 383 U. S. 419; that concept has never commanded the adherence of more than three Justices at one time. [7] See supra at 413 U. S. 21. If a state law that regulates obscene material is thus limited, as written or construed, the First Amendment values applicable to the States through the Fourteenth Amendment are adequately protected by the ultimate power of appellate courts to conduct an independent review of constitutional claims when necessary. See Kois v. Wisconsin, supra, at 408 U. S. 232; Memoirs v. Massachusetts, supra, at 383 U. S. 459-460 (Harlan, J., dissenting); Jacobellis v. Ohio, 378 U.S. at 204 (Harlan, J., dissenting); New York Times Co. v. Sullivan, 376 U. S. 254, 376 U. S. 284-285 (1964); Roth v. United States, supra, at 354 U. S. 497-498 (Harlan, J., concurring and dissenting).

We emphasize that it is not our function to propose regulatory schemes for the States. That must await their concrete legislative efforts. It is possible, however, to give a few plain examples of what a state statute could define for regulation under part (b) of the standard announced in this opinion, supra:

(a) Patently offensive representations or descriptions of ultimate sexual acts, normal or perverted, actual or simulated.

(b) Patently offensive representations or descriptions of masturbation, excretory functions, and lewd exhibition of the genitals.

Sex and nudity may not be exploited without limit by films or pictures exhibited or sold in places of public accommodation any more than live sex and nudity can be exhibited or sold without limit in such public places. [8] At a minimum, prurient, patently offensive depiction or description of sexual conduct must have serious literary, artistic, political, or scientific value to merit First Amendment protection. See Kois v. Wisconsin, supra, at 408 U. S. 230-232; Roth v. United States, supra, at 354 U. S. 487; Thornhill v. Alabama, 310 U. S. 88, 310 U. S. 101-102 (1940). For example, medical books for the education of physicians and related personnel necessarily use graphic illustrations and descriptions of human anatomy. In resolving the inevitably sensitive questions of fact and law, we must continue to rely on the jury system, accompanied by the safeguards that judges, rules of evidence, presumption of innocence, and other protective features provide, as we do with rape, murder, and a host of other offenses against society and its individual members. [9]

MR. JUSTICE BRENNAN, author of the opinions of the Court, or the plurality opinions, in Roth v. United States, supra; Jacobellis v. Ohio, supra; Ginzburg v. United States, 383 U. S. 463 (1966), Mishkin v. New York, 383 U. S. 502 (1966), and Memoirs v. Massachusetts, supra, has abandoned his former position and now maintains that no formulation of this Court, the Congress, or the States can adequately distinguish obscene material unprotected by the First Amendment from protected expression, Paris Adult Theatre I v. Slaton, post, p. 413 U. S. 73 (BRENNAN, J., dissenting). Paradoxically, MR.

JUSTICE BRENNAN indicates that suppression of unprotected obscene material is permissible to avoid exposure to unconsenting adults, as in this case, and to juveniles, although he gives no indication of how the division between protected and nonprotected materials may be drawn with greater precision for these purposes than for regulation of commercial exposure to consenting adults only. Nor does he indicate where in the Constitution he finds the authority to distinguish between a willing "adult" one month past the state law age of majority and a willing "juvenile" one month younger.

Under the holdings announced today, no one will be subject to prosecution for the sale or exposure of obscene materials unless these materials depict or describe patently offensive "hard core" sexual conduct specifically defined by the regulating state law, as written or construed. We are satisfied that these specific prerequisites will provide fair notice to a dealer in such materials that his public and commercial activities may bring prosecution. See Roth v. United States, supra, at 354 U. S. 491-492. Cf. Ginsberg v. New York, 390 U.S. at 390 U. S. 643. [10] If the inability to define regulated materials with ultimate, god-like precision altogether removes the power of the States or the Congress to regulate, then "hard core" pornography may be exposed without limit to the juvenile, the passerby, and the consenting adult alike, as, indeed, MR. JUSTICE DOUGLAS contends. As to MR. JUSTICE DOUGLAS' position, see United States v. Thirty-seven Photographs, 402 U. S. 363, 402 U. S. 379-380 (1971) (Black, J., joined by DOUGLAS, J., dissenting); Ginzburg v. United States, supra, at 383 U. S. 476, 383 U. S. 491-492 (Black, J., and DOUGLAS, J., dissenting); Jacobellis v. Ohio, supra, at 378 U. S. 196 (Black, J., joined by DOUGLAS, J., concurring); Roth, supra, at 354 U. S. 508-514 (DOUGLAS, J., dissenting). In this belief, however, MR. JUSTICE DOUGLAS now stands alone.

MR. JUSTICE BRENNAN also emphasizes "institutional stress" in justification of his change of view. Noting that "[t]he number of obscenity cases on our docket gives ample testimony to the burden that has been placed upon this Court," he quite rightly remarks that the examination of contested materials "is hardly a source of edification to the members of this Court." Paris Adult Theatre I v. Slaton, post, at 413 U. S. 92, 413 U. S. 93. He also notes, and we agree, that "uncertainty of the standards creates a continuing source of tension between state and federal courts. . . ."

"The problem is . . . that one cannot say with certainty that material is obscene until at least five members of this Court, applying inevitably obscure standards, have pronounced it so."

Id. at 413 U. S. 93, 413 U. S. 92.

It is certainly true that the absence, since Roth, of a single majority view of this Court as to proper standards for testing obscenity has placed a strain on both state and federal courts. But today, for the first time since Roth was decided in 1957, a majority of this Court has agreed on concrete guidelines to isolate "hard core" pornography from expression protected by the First Amendment. Now we may abandon the casual practice of Redrup v. New York, 386 U. S. 767 (1967), and attempt to provide positive guidance to federal and state courts alike.

This may not be an easy road, free from difficulty. But no amount of "fatigue" should lead us to adopt a convenient "institutional" rationale -- an absolutist, "anything goes" view of the First Amendment -- because it will lighten our burdens. [11] "Such an abnegation of judicial supervision in this field would be inconsistent with our duty to uphold the constitutional guarantees." Jacobellis v. Ohio, supra, at 378 U. S. 187-188 (opinion of BRENNAN, J.). Nor should we remedy "tension between state and federal courts" by arbitrarily depriving the States of a power reserved to them under the Constitution, a power which they have enjoyed and exercised continuously from before the adoption of the First Amendment to this day. See Roth v. United States, supra, at 354 U. S. 482-485.

"Our duty admits of no 'substitute for facing up to the tough individual problems of constitutional judgment involved in every obscenity case.' [Roth v. United States, supra, at 354 U. S. 498]; see Manual Enterprises, Inc. v. Day, 370 U. S. 478, 370 U. S. 488 (opinion of Harlan, J.) [omitted]."

Jacobellis v. Ohio, supra, at 378 U. S. 188 (opinion of BRENNAN, J.).

III

Under a National Constitution, fundamental First Amendment limitations on the powers of the States do not vary from community to community, but this does not mean that there are, or should or can be, fixed, uniform national standards of precisely what appeals to the "prurient interest" or is "patently offensive." These are essentially questions of fact, and our Nation is simply too big and too diverse for this Court to reasonably expect that such standards could be articulated for all 50 States in a single formulation, even assuming the prerequisite consensus exists. When triers of fact are asked to decide whether "the average person, applying contemporary community standards" would consider certain materials "prurient," it would be unrealistic to require that the answer be based on some abstract formulation. The adversary system, with lay jurors as the usual ultimate factfinders in criminal prosecutions, has historically permitted triers of fact to draw on the standards of their community, guided always by limiting instructions on the law. To require a State to structure obscenity proceedings around evidence of a national "community standard" would be an exercise in futility.

As noted before, this case was tried on the theory that the California obscenity statute sought to incorporate the tripartite test of Memoirs. This, a "national" standard of First Amendment protection enumerated by a plurality of this Court, was correctly regarded at the time of trial as limiting state prosecution under the controlling case law. The jury, however, was explicitly instructed that, in determining whether the "dominant theme of the material as a whole . . . appeals to the prurient interest," and, in determining whether the material "goes substantially beyond customary limits of candor and affronts contemporary community standards of decency," it was to apply "contemporary community standards of the State of California."

During the trial, both the prosecution and the defense assumed that the relevant "community standards" in making the factual determination of obscenity were those of the State of California, not some hypothetical standard of the entire United States of America. Defense counsel at trial never objected to the testimony of the State's expert on community standards [12] or to the instructions of the trial judge on "state-wide" standards. On appeal to the Appellate Department, Superior Court of California, County of Orange, appellant for the first time contended that application of state, rather than national, standards violated the First and Fourteenth Amendments.

We conclude that neither the State's alleged failure to offer evidence of "national standards," nor the trial court's charge that the jury consider state community standards, were constitutional errors. Nothing in the First Amendment requires that a jury must consider hypothetical and unascertainable "national standards" when attempting to determine whether certain materials are obscene as a matter of fact. Mr. Chief Justice Warren pointedly commented in his dissent in Jacobellis v. Ohio, supra, at 378 U. S. 200:

"It is my belief that, when the Court said in Roth that obscenity is to be defined by reference to 'community standards,' it meant community standards -- not a national standard, as is sometimes argued. I believe that there is no provable 'national standard.' . . . At all events, this Court has not been able to enunciate one, and it would be unreasonable to expect local courts to divine one."

It is neither realistic nor constitutionally sound to read the First Amendment as requiring that the people of Maine or Mississippi accept public depiction of conduct found tolerable in Las Vegas, or New York City. [13]

See Hoyt v. Minnesota, 399 U.S. at 524-525 (1970) (BLACKMUN, J., dissenting); Walker v. Ohio, 398 U.S. at 434 (1970) (BURGER, C.J., dissenting); id. at 434-435 (Harlan, J., dissenting); Cain v. Kentucky, 397 U. S. 319 (1970) (BURGER, C.J., dissenting); id. at 397 U. S. 319-320 (Harlan, J., dissenting); United States v. Groner, 479 F.2d at 581-583; O'Meara & Shaffer, Obscenity in The Supreme Court: A Note on Jacobellis v. Ohio, 40 Notre Dame Law. 1, 6-7 (1964). See also Memoirs v. Massachusetts, 383 U.S. at 383 U. S. 458 (Harlan, J., dissenting); Jacobellis v. Ohio, supra, at 378 U. S. 203-204 (Harlan, J., dissenting); Roth v. United States, supra, at 354 U. S. 505-506 (Harlan, J., concurring and dissenting). People in different States vary in their tastes and attitudes, and this diversity is not to be strangled by the absolutism of imposed uniformity. As the Court made clear in Mishkin v. New York, 383 U.S. at 383 U. S. 508-509, the primary concern with requiring a jury to apply the standard of "the average person, applying contemporary community standards" is to be certain that, so far as material is not aimed at a deviant group, it will be judged by its impact on an average person, rather than a particularly susceptible or sensitive person -- or indeed a totally insensitive one. See Roth v. United States, supra, at 354 U. S. 489. Cf. the now discredited test in Regina v. Hicklin, [1868] L.R. 3 Q.B. 360. We hold that the requirement that the jury evaluate the materials with reference to "contemporary standards of the State of California" serves this protective purpose and is constitutionally adequate. [14]

IV

The dissenting Justices sound the alarm of repression. But, in our view, to equate the free and robust exchange of ideas and political debate with commercial exploitation of obscene material demeans the grand conception of the First Amendment and its high purposes in the historic struggle for freedom. It is a "misuse of the great guarantees of free speech and free press. . . ." Breard v. Alexandria, 341 U.S. at 341 U. S. 645. The First Amendment protects works which, taken as a whole, have serious literary, artistic, political, or scientific value, regardless of whether the government or a majority of the people approve of the ideas these works represent.

"The protection given speech and press was fashioned to assure unfettered interchange of ideas for the bringing about of political and social changes desired by the people,"

Roth v. United States, supra, at 354 U. S. 484 (emphasis added). See Kois v. Wisconsin, 408 U.S. at 408 U. S. 230-232; Thornhill v. Alabama, 310 U.S. at 310 U. S. 101-102. But the public portrayal of hard-core sexual conduct for its own sake, and for the ensuing commercial gain, is a different matter. [15]

There is no evidence, empirical or historical, that the stern 19th century American censorship of public distribution and display of material relating to sex, see Roth v. United States, supra, at 354 U. S. 482-485, in any way limited or affected expression of serious literary, artistic, political, or scientific ideas. On the contrary, it is beyond any question that the era following Thomas Jefferson to Theodore Roosevelt was an "extraordinarily vigorous period" not just in economics and politics, but in belles lettres and in "the outlying fields of social and political philosophies." [16] We do not see the harsh hand of censorship of ideas -- good or bad, sound or unsound -- and "repression" of political liberty lurking in every state regulation of commercial exploitation of human interest in sex.

MR. JUSTICE BRENNAN finds "it is hard to see how state-ordered regimentation of our minds can ever be forestalled." Paris Adult Theatre I v. Slaton, post, at 413 U. S. 110 (BRENNAN, J., dissenting). These doleful anticipations assume that courts cannot distinguish commerce in ideas, protected by the First Amendment, from commercial exploitation of obscene material. Moreover, state regulation of hard-core pornography so as to make it unavailable to nonadults, a regulation which MR. JUSTICE BRENNAN finds constitutionally permissible, has all the elements of "censorship" for adults; indeed even more rigid enforcement techniques may be called for with such dichotomy of regulation. See Interstate Circuit, Inc. v. Dallas, 390 U.S. at 390 U. S. 690. [17] One can concede that the "sexual revolution" of recent years may have had useful byproducts in striking layers of prudery from a subject long irrationally kept from needed ventilation. But it does not follow that no regulation of patently offensive "hard core" materials is needed or permissible; civilized people do not allow unregulated access to heroin because it is a derivative of medicinal morphlne.

In sum, we (a) reaffirm the Roth holding that obscene material is not protected by the First Amendment; (b) hold that such material can be regulated by the States, subject to the specific safeguards enunciated above, without a showing that the material is "utterly without redeeming social value"; and (c) hold that obscenity is to be determined by applying "contemporary community standards," see Kois v. Wisconsin, supra, at 408 U. S. 230, and Roth v. United States, supra, at 354 U. S. 489, not "national standards." The judgment of the Appellate Department of the Superior Court, Orange County, California, is vacated and the case remanded to that court for further proceedings not inconsistent with the First Amendment standards established by this opinion. See United States v. 12 200-ft. Reels of Film, post at 413 U. S. 130 n. 7.

Vacated and remanded.

## Paris Adult Theatre I v. Slaton (June 21, 1973) [Notes omitted]

MR. CHIEF JUSTICE BURGER delivered the opinion of the Court.

Petitioners are two Atlanta, Georgia, movie theaters and their owners and managers, operating in the style of "adult" theaters. On December 28, 1970, respondents, the local state district attorney and the solicitor for the local state trial court, filed civil complaints in that court alleging that petitioners were exhibiting to the public for paid admission two allegedly obscene films, contrary to Georgia Code Ann. § 26-2101. [1] The two films in question, "Magic Mirror" and "It All Comes Out in the End," depict sexual conduct characterized by the Georgia Supreme Court as "hard core pornography" leaving "little to the imagination."

Respondents' complaints, made on behalf of the State of Georgia, demanded that the two films be declared obscene and that petitioners be enjoined from exhibiting the films. The exhibition of the films was not enjoined, but a temporary injunction was granted ex parte by the local trial court, restraining petitioners from destroying the films or removing them from the jurisdiction. Petitioners were further ordered to have one print each of the films in court on January 13, 1971, together with the proper viewing equipment.

On January 13, 1971, 15 days after the proceedings began, the films were produced by petitioners at a jury-waived trial. Certain photographs, also produced at trial, were stipulated to portray the single entrance to both Paris Adult Theatre I and Paris Adult Theatre II as it appeared at the time of the complaints. These photographs show a conventional, inoffensive theater entrance, without any pictures, but with signs indicating that the theaters exhibit "Atlanta's Finest Mature Feature Films." On the door itself is a sign saying: "Adult Theatre -- You must be 21 and able to prove it. If viewing the nude body offends you, Please Do Not Enter."

The two films were exhibited to the trial court. The only other state evidence was testimony by criminal investigators that they had paid admission to see the films and that nothing on the outside of the theater indicated the full nature of what was shown. In particular, nothing indicated that the films depicted -- as they did -- scenes of simulated fellatio, cunnilingus, and group sex intercourse. There was no evidence presented that minors had ever entered the theaters. Nor was there evidence presented that petitioners had a systematic policy of barring minors, apart from posting signs at the entrance. On April 12, 1971, the trial judge dismissed respondents' complaints. He assumed "that obscenity is established," but stated:

"It appears to the Court that the display of these films in a commercial theatre, when surrounded by requisite notice to the public of their nature and by reasonable protection against the exposure of these films to minors, is constitutionally permissible."

On appeal, the Georgia Supreme Court unanimously reversed. It assumed that the adult theaters in question barred minors and gave a full warning to the general public of the nature of the films shown, but held that the films were without protection under the First Amendment. Citing the opinion of this Court in United States v. Reidel, 402 U. S. 351 (1971), the Georgia court stated that "the sale and delivery of obscene material to willing adults is not protected under the first amendment." The Georgia court also held Stanley v. Georgia, 394 U. S. 557 (1969), to be inapposite, since it did not deal with "the commercial distribution of pornography, but with the right of Stanley to possess, in the privacy of his home, pornographic films." 228 Ga. 343, 345, 185 S.E.2d 768, 769 (1971). After viewing the films, the Georgia Supreme Court held that their exhibition should have been enjoined, stating:

"The films in this case leave little to the imagination. It is plain what they purport to depict, that is, conduct of the most salacious character. We hold that these films are also hard core pornography, and the showing of such films should have been enjoined, since their exhibition is not protected by the first amendment."

Id. at 347, 185 S.E.2d at 770.

I

It should be clear from the outset that we do not undertake to tell the States what they must do, but rather to define the area in which they may chart their own course in dealing with obscene material. This Court has consistently held that obscene material is not protected by the First Amendment as a limitation on the state police power by virtue of the Fourteenth Amendment. Miller v. California, ante at 413 U. S. 225; Kois v. Wisconsin, 408 U. S. 229, 408 U. S. 230 (1972); United States v. Reidel, supra, at 402 U. S. 354; Roth v. United States, 354 U. S. 476, 354 U. S. 485 (1957).

Georgia case law permits a civil injunction of the exhibition of obscene materials. See 1024 Peachtree Corp. v. Slaton, 228 Ga. 102, 184 S.E.2d 144 (1971); Walter v. Slaton, 227 Ga. 676, 182 S.E.2d 464 (1971); Evans Theatre Corp. v. Slaton, 227 Ga. 377, 180 S.E.2d 712 (1971). While this procedure is civil in nature, and does not directly involve the state criminal statute proscribing exhibition of obscene material, [2] the Georgia case law permitting civil injunction does adopt the definition of "obscene materials" used by the criminal statute. [3] Today, in Miller v. California, supra, we have sought to clarify the constitutional definition of obscene material subject to regulation by the States, and we vacate and remand this case for reconsideration in light of Miller.

This is not to be read as disapproval of the Georgia civil procedure employed in this case, assuming the use of a constitutionally acceptable standard for determining what is unprotected by the First Amendment. On the contrary, such a procedure provides an exhibitor or purveyor of materials the best possible notice, prior to any criminal indictments, as to whether the materials are unprotected by the First Amendment and subject to state regulation. [4] See Kingsley Books, Inc. v. Brown, 354 U. S. 436, 354 U. S. 441-444 (1957). Here, Georgia imposed no restraint on the exhibition of the films involved in this case until after a full adversary proceeding and a final judicial determination by the Georgia Supreme Court that the materials were constitutionally unprotected. [5] Thus, the standards of Blount v. Rizzi, 400 U. S. 410, 400 U. S. 417 (1971); Teitel Film Corp. v. Cusack, 390 U. S. 139, 390 U. S. 141-142 (1968); Freedman v. Maryland, 380 U. S. 51, 380 U. S. 559 (1965), and Kingsley Books, Inc. v. Brown, supra, at 354 U. S. 443-445, were met. Cf. United States v. Thirty-seven Photographs, 402 U. S. 363, 402 U. S. 367-369 (1971) (opinion of WHITE, J.).

Nor was it error to fail to require "expert" affirmative evidence that the materials were obscene when the materials themselves were actually placed in evidence. United States v. Groner, 479 F.2d 577, 579-586 (CA5 1973); id. at 586-588 (Ainsworth, J., concurring); id. at 586-589 (Clark, J., concurring); United States v. Wild, 422 1.2d 34, 35-36 (CA2 1969), cert. denied, 402 U.S. 986 (1971); Kahm v. United States, 300 F.2d 78, 84 (CA5), cert. denied, 369 U.S. 859 (1962); State v. Amato, 49 Wis.2d 638, 645, 183 N.W.2d 29, 32 (1971), cert. denied sub nom. Amato v. Wisconsin, 404 U.S. 1063 (1972). See Smith v. California, 361 U. S. 147, 361 U. S. 172 (1959) (Harlan, J., concurring and dissenting); United States v. Brown, 328 F.Supp. 196, 199 (ED Va.1971). The films, obviously, are the best evidence of what they represent. [6]

"In the cases in which this Court has decided obscenity questions since Roth, it has regarded the materials as sufficient in themselves for the determination of the question."

Ginzburg v. United States, 383 U. S. 463, 383 U. S. 465 (1966).

II

We categorically disapprove the theory, apparently adopted by the trial judge, that obscene, pornographic films acquire constitutional immunity from state regulation simply because they are exhibited for consenting adults only. This holding was properly rejected by the Georgia Supreme Court. Although we have often pointedly recognized the high importance of the state interest in regulating the exposure of obscene materials to juveniles and unconsenting adults, see Miller v. California, ante at 413 U. S. 18-20; Stanley v. Georgia, 394 U.S. at 394 U. S. 567; Redrup v. New York, 386 U. S. 767, 386 U. S. 769 (1967), this Court has never declared these to be the only legitimate state interests permitting regulation of obscene material. The States have a long-recognized legitimate interest in regulating the use of obscene material in local commerce and in all places of public accommodation, as long as these regulations do not run afoul of specific constitutional prohibitions. See United States v. Thirty-seven Photographs, supra, at 402 U. S. 376-377 (opinion of WHITE, J.); United States v. Reidel, 402 U.S. at 402 U. S. 354-

356. Cf. United States v. Thirty-seven Photographs, supra, at 402 U. S. 378 (STEWART, J., concurring).

"In an unbroken series of cases extending over a long stretch of this Court's history, it has been accepted as a postulate that 'the primary requirements of decency may be enforced against obscene publications.' [Near v. Minnesota, 283 U. S. 697, 283 U. S. 716 (1931)]."

Kingsley Books, Inc. v. Brown, supra, at 354 U. S. 440.

In particular, we hold that there are legitimate state interests at stake in stemming the tide of commercialized obscenity, even assuming it is feasible to enforce effective safeguards against exposure to juveniles and to passersby. [7]

Rights and interests "other than those of the advocates are involved." Breard v. Alexandria, 341 U. S. 622, 341 U. S. 642 (1951). These include the interest of the public in the quality of life and the total community environment, the tone of commerce in the great city centers, and, possibly, the public safety itself. The Hill-Link Minority Report of the Commission on Obscenity and Pornography indicates that there is at least an arguable correlation between obscene material and crime. [8] Quite apart from sex crimes, however, there remains one problem of large proportions aptly described by Professor Bickel:

"It concerns the tone of the society, the mode, or to use terms that have perhaps greater currency, the style and quality of life, now and in the future. A man may be entitled to read an obscene book in his room, or expose himself indecently there. . . . We should protect his privacy. But if he demands a right to obtain the books and pictures he wants in the market, and to foregather in public places -- discreet, if you will, but accessible to all -- with others who share his tastes, then to grant him his right is to affect the world about the rest of us, and to impinge on other privacies. Even supposing that each of us can, if he wishes, effectively avert the eye and stop the ear (which, in truth, we cannot), what is commonly read and seen and heard and done intrudes upon us all, want it or not."

22 The Public Interest 25-26 (Winter 1971). [9] (Emphasis added.) As Mr. Chief Justice Warren stated, there is a "right of the Nation and of the States to maintain a decent society . . .,"

Jacobellis v. Ohio, 378 U. S. 184, 378 U. S. 199 (1964) (dissenting opinion). [10] See Memoirs v. Massachusetts, 383 U. S. 413, 383 U. S. 457 (1966) (Harlan, J., dissenting); Beauharnais v. Illinois, 343 U. S. 250, 343 U. S. 256-257 (1952); Kovacs v. Cooper, 336 U. S. 77, 336 U. S. 86-88 (1949).

But, it is argued, there are no scientific data which conclusively demonstrate that exposure to obscene material adversely affects men and women or their society. It is urged on behalf of the petitioners that, absent such a demonstration, any kind of state regulation is "impermissible." We reject this argument. It is not for us to resolve empirical uncertainties underlying state legislation, save in the exceptional case where that legislation plainly impinges upon rights protected by the Constitution itself. [11] MR.

JUSTICE BRENNAN, speaking for the Court in Ginsberg v. New York, 390 U. S. 629, 390 U. S. 642-643 (1968), said: "We do not demand of legislatures scientifically certain criteria of legislation.' Noble State Bank v. Haskell, 219 U. S. 104, 219 U. S. 110." Although there is no conclusive proof of a connection between antisocial behavior and obscene material, the legislature of Georgia could quite reasonably determine that such a connection does or might exist. In deciding Roth, this Court implicitly accepted that a legislature could legitimately act on such a conclusion to protect "the social interest in order and morality." Roth v. United States, 354 U.S. at 354 U. S. 485, quoting Chaplinsky v. New Hampshire, 315 U. S. 568, 315 U. S. 572 (1942) (emphasis added in Roth). [12]

From the beginning of civilized societies, legislators and judges have acted on various unprovable assumptions. Such assumptions underlie much lawful state regulation of commercial and business affairs. See Ferguson v. Skrupa, 372 U. S. 726, 372 U. S. 730 (1963); Breard v. Alexandria, 341 U.S. at 341 U. S. 632-633, 341 U. S. 641-645; Lincoln Federal Labor Union v. Northwestern Iron Metal Co., 335 U. S. 525, 335 U. S. 536-537 (1949). The same is true of the federal securities and antitrust laws and a host of federal regulations. See SEC v. Capital Gains Research Bureau, Inc., 375 U. S. 180, 375 U. S. 186-195 (1963); American Power & Light Co. v. SEC, 329 U. S. 90, 329 U. S. 99-103 (1946); North American Co. v. SEC, 327 U. S. 686, 327 U. S. 705-707 (1946), and cases cited. See also Brooks v. United States, 267 U. S. 432, 267 U. S. 436-437 (1925), and Hoke v. United States, 227 U. S. 308, 227 U. S. 322 (1913). On the basis of these assumptions both Congress and state legislatures have, for example, drastically restricted associational rights by adopting antitrust laws, and have strictly regulated public expression by issuers of and dealers in securities, profit sharing "coupons," and "trading stamps," commanding what they must and must not publish and announce. See Sugar Institute, Inc. v. United States, 297 U. S. 553, 297 U. S. 597-602 (1936); Merrick v. N.W. Halsey & Co., 242 U. S. 568, 242 U. S. 584-589 (1917); Caldwell v. Sioux Falls Stock Yards Co., 242 U. S. 559, 242 U. S. 567-568 (1917); Hall v. Geiger-Jones Co., 242 U. S. 539, 242 U. S. 548-552 (1917); Tanner v. Little, 240 U. S. 369, 240 U. S. 383-386 (1916); Rast v. Van Deman Lewis Co., 240 U. S. 342, 240 U. S. 363-368 (1916). Understandably those who entertain an absolutist view of the First Amendment find it uncomfortable to explain why rights of association, speech, and press should be severely restrained in the marketplace of goods and money, but not in the marketplace of pornography.

Likewise, when legislatures and administrators act to protect the physical environment from pollution and to preserve our resources of forests, streams, and parks, they must act on such imponderables as the impact of a new highway near or through an existing park or wilderness area. See Citizens to Preserve Overton Park v. Volpe, 401 U. S. 402, 401 U. S. 417-420 (1971). Thus, § 18(a) of the Federal-Aid Highway Act of 1968, 23 U.S.C. § 138, and the Department of Transportation Act of 1966, as amended, 82 Stat. 824, 49 U.S.C. § 1653(f), have been described by Mr. Justice Black as

"a solemn determination of the highest law-making body of this Nation that the beauty and health-giving facilities of our parks are not to be taken away for public roads without hearings, factfindings, and policy determinations under the supervision of a Cabinet officer. . . ."

Citizens to Preserve Overton Park, supra, at 401 U. S. 421 (separate opinion joined by BRENNAN, J.). The fact that a congressional directive reflects unprovable assumptions about what is good for the people, including imponderable aesthetic assumptions, is not a sufficient reason to find that statute unconstitutional.

If we accept the unprovable assumption that a complete education requires the reading of certain books, see Board of Education v. Allen, 392 U. S. 236, 392 U. S. 245 (1968), and Johnson v. New York State Education Dept., 449 F.2d 871, 882-883 (CA2 1971) (dissenting opinion), vacated and remanded to consider mootness, 409 U. S. 75 (1972), id. at 777 (MARSHALL, J., concurring), and the well nigh universal belief that good books, plays, and art lift the spirit, improve the mind, enrich the human personality, and develop character, can we then say that a state legislature may not act on the corollary assumption that commerce in obscene books, or public exhibitions focused on obscene conduct, have a tendency to exert a corrupting and debasing impact leading to antisocial behavior? "Many of these effects may be intangible and indistinct, but they are nonetheless real." American Power & Light Co. v. SEC, supra, at 329 U. S. 103. Mr. Justice Cardozo said that all laws in Western civilization are "guided by a robust common sense. . . ." Steward Machine Co. v. Davis, 301 U. S. 548, 301 U. S. 590 (1937). The sum of experience, including that of the past two decades, affords an ample basis for legislatures to conclude that a sensitive, key relationship of human existence, central to family life, community welfare, and the development of human personality, can be debased and distorted by crass commercial exploitation of sex. Nothing in the Constitution prohibits a State from reaching such a conclusion and acting on it legislatively simply because there is no conclusive evidence or empirical data.

It is argued that individual "free will" must govern, even in activities beyond the protection of the First Amendment and other constitutional guarantees of privacy, and that government cannot legitimately impede an individual's desire to see or acquire obscene plays, movies, and books. We do indeed base our society on certain assumptions that people have the capacity for free choice. Most exercises of individual free choice -- those in politics, religion, and expression of idea are explicitly protected by the Constitution. Totally unlimited play for free will, however, is not allowed in our or any other society. We have just noted, for example, that neither the First Amendment nor "free will" precludes States from having "blue sky" laws to regulate what sellers of securities may write or publish about their wares. See supra at 413 U. S. 61-62. Such laws are to protect the weak, the uninformed, the unsuspecting, and the gullible from the exercise of their own volition. Nor do modern societies leave disposal of garbage and sewage up to the individual "free will," but impose regulation to protect both public health and the appearance of public places. States are told by some that they must await a "laissez-faire" market solution to the obscenity-pornography problem, paradoxically "by people who have never otherwise had a kind word to say for laissez-faire," particularly in solving urban, commercial, and environmental pollution problems. See I. Kristol, On the Democratic Idea in America 37 (1972).

The States, of course, may follow such a "laissez-faire" policy and drop all controls on commercialized obscenity, if that is what they prefer, just as they can ignore consumer protection in the marketplace, but nothing in the Constitution compels the States to do so with regard to matters falling within state jurisdiction. See United States v. Reidel, 402 U.S. at 402 U. S. 357; Memoirs v. Massachusetts, 383 U.S. at 383 U. S. 462 (WHITE, J., dissenting).

"We do not sit as a super-legislature to determine the wisdom, need, and propriety of laws that touch economic problems, business affairs, or social conditions."

Griswold v. Connecticut, 381 U. S. 479, 381 U. S. 482 (1965). See Ferguson v. Skrupa, 372 U.S. at 372 U. S. 731; Day-Brite Lighting, Inc. v. Missouri, 342 U. S. 421, 342 U. S. 423 (1952).

It is asserted, however, that standards for evaluating state commercial regulations are inapposite in the present context, as state regulation of access by consenting adults to obscene material violates the constitutionally protected right to privacy enjoyed by petitioners' customers. Even assuming that petitioners have vicarious standing to assert potential customers' rights, it is unavailing to compare a theater open to the public for a fee, with the private home of Stanley v. Georgia, 394 U.S. at 394 U. S. 568, and the marital bedroom of Griswold v. Connecticut, supra, at 381 U. S. 485-486. This Court, has, on numerous occasions, refused to hold that commercial ventures such as a motion-picture house are "private" for the purpose of civil rights litigation and civil rights statutes. See Sullivan v. Little Hunting Park, Inc., 396 U. S. 229, 396 U. S. 236 (1969); Daniel v. Paul, 395 U. S. 298, 395 U. S. 305-308 (1969); Blow v. North Carolina, 379 U. S. 684, 379 U. S. 685-686 (1965); Hamm v. Rock Hill, 379 U. S. 306, 379 U. S. 307-308 (1964); Heart of Atlanta Motel, Inc. v. United States, 379 U. S. 241, 379 U. S. 247, 379 U. S. 260-261 (1964). The Civil Rights Act of 1964 specifically defines motion picture houses and theaters as places of "public accommodation" covered by the Act as operations affecting commerce. 78 Stat. 243, 42 U.S.C. § § 2000a(b)(3), (c).

Our prior decisions recognizing a right to privacy guaranteed by the Fourteenth Amendment included

"only personal rights that can be deemed 'fundamental' or 'implicit in the concept of ordered liberty.' Palko v. Connecticut, 302 U. S. 319, 302 U. S. 325 (1937)."

Roe v. Wade, 410 U. S. 113, 410 U. S. 152 (1973). This privacy right encompasses and protects the personal intimacies of the home, the family, marriage, motherhood, procreation, and childrearing. Cf. Eisenstadt v. Baird, 405 U. S. 438, 405 U. S. 453-454 (1972); id. at 405 U. S. 460, 405 U. S. 463-465 (WHITE, J., concurring); Stanley v. Georgia, supra, at 394 U. S. 568; Loving v. Virginia, 388 U.S. 1, 388 U. S. 12 (1967); Griswold v. Connecticut, supra, at 381 U. S. 486; Prince v. Massachusetts, 321 U. S. 158, 321 U. S. 166 (1944); Skinner v. Oklahoma, 316 U. S. 535, 316 U. S. 541 (1942); Pierce v. Society of Sisters, 268 U. S. 510, 268 U. S. 535 (1925); Meyer v. Nebraska, 262 U. S. 390,

262 U. S. 399 (1923). Nothing, however, in this Court's decisions intimates that there is any "fundamental" privacy right "implicit in the concept of ordered liberty" to watch obscene movies in places of public accommodation.

If obscene material unprotected by the First Amendment, in itself, carried with it a "penumbra" of constitutionally protected privacy, this Court would not have found it necessary to decide Stanley on the narrow basis of the "privacy of the home," which was hardly more than a reaffirmation that "a man's home is his castle." Cf. Stanley v. Georgia, supra, at 394 U. S. 564. [13] Moreover, we have declined to equate the privacy of the home relied on in Stanley with a "zone" of "privacy" that follows a distributor or a consumer of obscene materials wherever he goes. See United States v. Orito, post at 413 U. S. 141-143; United States v. 12 200-ft. Reels of Film, post at 413 U. S. 126-129; United States v. Thirty-seven Photographs, 42 U.S. at 43 U. S. 376-377 (opinion of WHITE, J.); United States v. Reidel, supra, at 402 U. S. 355. The idea of a "privacy" right and a place of public accommodation are, in this context, mutually exclusive. Conduct or depictions of conduct that the state police power can prohibit on a public street do not become automatically protected by the Constitution merely because the conduct is moved to a bar or a "live" theater stage, any more than a "live" performance of a man and woman locked in a sexual embrace at high noon in Times Square is protected by the Constitution because they simultaneously engage in a valid political dialogue.

It is also argued that the State has no legitimate interest in "control [of] the moral content of a person's thoughts," Stanley v. Georgia, supra, at 394 U. S. 565, and we need not quarrel with this. But we reject the claim that the State of Georgia is here attempting to control the minds or thoughts of those who patronize theaters. Preventing unlimited display or distribution of obscene material, which by definition lacks any serious literary, artistic, political, or scientific value as communication, Miller v. California, ante at 413 U. S. 24, 413 U. S. 34, is distinct from a control of reason and the intellect. Cf. Kois v. Wisconsin, 408 U. S. 229 (1972); Roth v. United States, supra, at 354 U. S. 485-487; Thornhill v. Alabama, 310 U. S. 88, 310 U. S. 101-102 (1940); Finnis, "Reason and Passion": The Constitutional Dialectic of Free Speech and Obscenity, 116 U.Pa.L.Rev. 222, 229-230, 241-243 (1967). Where communication of ideas, protected by the First Amendment, is not involved, or the particular privacy of the home protected by Stanley, or any of the other "areas or zones" of constitutionally protected privacy, the mere fact that, as a consequence, some human "utterances" or. "thoughts" may be incidentally affected does not bar the State from acting to protect legitimate state interests. Cf. Roth v. United States, supra, at 354 U. S. 483, 485-487; Beauharnais v. Illinois, 343 U.S. at 343 U. S. 256-257. The fantasies of a drug addict are his own and beyond the reach of government, but government regulation of drug sales is not prohibited by the Constitution. Cf. United States v. Reidel, supra, at 402 U. S. 359-360 (Harlan, J., concurring).

Finally, petitioners argue that conduct which directly involves "consenting adults" only has, for that sole reason, a special claim to constitutional protection. Our

Constitution establishes a broad range of conditions on the exercise of power by the States, but for us to say that our Constitution incorporates the proposition that conduct involving consenting adults only is always beyond state regulation, [14] is a step we are unable to take. [15] Commercial exploitation of depictions, descriptions, or exhibitions of obscene conduct on commercial premises open to the adult public falls within a State's broad power to regulate commerce and protect the public environment. The issue in this context goes beyond whether someone, or even the majority, considers the conduct depicted as "wrong" or "sinful." The States have the power to make a morally neutral judgment that public exhibition of obscene material, or commerce in such material, has a tendency to injure the community as a whole, to endanger the public safety, or to jeopardize, in Mr. Chief Justice Warren's words, the States' "right . . . to maintain a decent society." Jacobellis v. Ohio, 378 U.S. at 378 U. S. 199 (dissenting opinion).

To summarize, we have today reaffirmed the basic holding of Roth v. United States, supra, that obscene material has no protection under the First Amendment. See Miller v. California, supra, and Kaplan v. California, post, p. 413 U. S. 115. We have directed our holdings, not at thoughts or speech, but at depiction and description of specifically defined sexual conduct that States may regulate within limits designed to prevent infringement of First Amendment rights. We have also reaffirmed the holdings of United States v. Reidel, supra, and United States v. Thirty-seven Photographs, supra, that commerce in obscene material is unprotected by any constitutional doctrine of privacy. United States v. Orito, post at 413 U. S. 141-143; United States v. 12 200-ft. Reels of Film, post at 413 U. S. 126-129. In this case, we hold that the States have a legitimate interest in regulating commerce in obscene material and in regulating exhibition of obscene material in places of public accommodation, including so-called "adult" theaters from which minors are excluded. In light of these holdings, nothing precludes the State of Georgia from the regulation of the allegedly obscene material exhibited in Paris Adult Theatre I or II, provided that the applicable Georgia law, as written or authoritatively interpreted by the Georgia courts, meets the First Amendment standards set forth in Miller v. California, ante at 413 U. S. 23-25. The judgment is vacated and the case remanded to the Georgia Supreme Court for further proceedings not inconsistent with this opinion and Miller v. California, supra. See United States v. 12 200-ft. Reels of Film, post at 413 U. S. 130 n. 7.

Vacated and remanded.

## Kaplan v. California (June 21, 1973)

MR. CHIEF JUSTICE BURGER delivered the opinion of the Court.

We granted certiorari to the Appellate Department of the Superior Court of California for the County of Los Angeles to review the petitioner's conviction for violation of California statutes regarding obscenity.

Petitioner was the proprietor of the Peek-A-Boo Bookstore, one of the approximately 250 "adult" bookstores in the city of Los Angeles, California. [1] On May

14, 1969, in response to citizen complaints, an undercover police officer entered the store and began to peruse several books and magazines. Petitioner advised the officer that the store "was not a library." The officer then asked petitioner if he had "any good sexy books." Petitioner replied that "all of our books are sexy" and exhibited a lewd photograph. At petitioner's recommendation, and after petitioner had read aloud a sample paragraph, the officer purchased the book Suite 69. On the basis of this sale, petitioner was convicted by a jury of violating California Penal Code § 311.2, [2] a misdemeanor.

The book, Suite 69, has a plain cover and contains no pictures. It is made up entirely of repetitive descriptions of physical, sexual conduct, "clinically" explicit and offensive to the point of being nauseous; there is only the most tenuous "plot." Almost every conceivable variety of sexual contact, homosexual and heterosexual, is described. Whether one samples every 5th, 10th, or 20th page, beginning at any point or page at random, the content is unvarying.

At trial, both sides presented testimony, by persons accepted to be "experts," as to the content and nature of the book. The book itself was received in evidence, and read, in its entirety, to the jury. Each juror inspected the book. But the State offered no "expert" evidence that the book was "utterly without socially redeeming value," or any evidence of "national standards."

On appeal, the Appellate Department of the Superior Court of California for the County of Los Angeles affirmed petitioner's conviction. Relying on the dissenting opinions in Jacobellis v. Ohio, 378 U. S. 184, 378 U. S. 199, 203 (1964), and MR. JUSTICE WHITE's dissent in Memoirs v. Massachusetts, 383 U. S. 413, 383 U. S. 462 (1966), it concluded that evidence of a "national" standard of obscenity was not required. It also decided that the State did not always have to present "expert" evidence that the book lacked "socially redeeming value," and that "[i]n light . . . of the circumstances surrounding the sale" and the nature of the book itself, there was sufficient evidence to sustain petitioner's conviction. Finally, the state court considered petitioner's argument that the book was not "obscene" as a matter of constitutional law. Pointing out that petitioner was arguing, in part, that all books were constitutionally protected in an absolute sense, it rejected that thesis. On "independent review," it concluded "Suite 69 appeals to a prurient interest in sex and is beyond the customary limits of candor within the State of California." It held that the book was not protected by the First Amendment. We agree.

This case squarely presents the issue of whether expression by words alone can be legally "obscene" in the sense of being unprotected by the First Amendment. [3] When the Court declared that obscenity is not a form of expression protected by the First Amendment, no distinction was made as to the medium of the expression. See Roth v. United States, 354 U. S. 476, 354 U. S. 481-485 (1957). Obscenity can, of course, manifest itself in conduct, in the pictorial representation of conduct, or in the written and oral description of conduct. The Court has applied similarly conceived First Amendment standards to moving pictures, to photographs, and to words in books. See Freedman v. Maryland, 380 U. S. 51, 380 U. S. 57 (1965); Jacobellis v. Ohio, supra, at 378 U. S. 187-188; Times Film Corp. v. Chicago, 365 U. S. 43, 365 U. S. 46 (1961); id. at 365 U. S. 51 (Warren, C.J., dissenting); Kingsley Pictures Corp. v. Regents, 360 U. S. 684, 360 U. S. 689-690 (1959); Superior Films, Inc. v. Dept. of Education, 346 U. S. 587, 346 U. S. 589 (1954) (DOUGLAS, J., concurring); Joseph Burstyn, Inc. v. Wilson, 343 U. S. 495, 343 U. S. 503 (1952).

Because of a profound commitment to protecting communication of ideas, any restraint on expression by way of the printed word or in speech stimulates a traditional and emotional response, unlike the response to obscene pictures of flagrant human conduct. A book seems to have a different and preferred place in our hierarchy of values, and so it should be. But this generalization, like so many, is qualified by the book's content. As with pictures, films, paintings, drawings, and engravings, both oral utterance and the printed word have First Amendment protection until they collide with the long-settled position of this Court that obscenity is not protected by the Constitution. Miller v. California, ante at 413 U. S. 23-25; Roth v. United States, supra, at 354 U. S. 483-485.

For good or ill, a book has a continuing life. It is passed hand to hand, and we can take note of the tendency of widely circulated books of this category to reach the impressionable young and have a continuing impact. [4] A State could reasonably regard the "hard core" conduct described by Suite 69 as capable of encouraging or causing antisocial behavior, especially in its impact on young people. States need not wait until behavioral experts or educators can provide empirical data before enacting controls of commerce in obscene materials unprotected by the First Amendment or by a constitutional right to privacy. We have noted the power of a legislative body to enact such regulatory laws on the basis of unprovable assumptions. See Paris Adult Theatre I v. Slaton, ante at 413 U. S. 60-63.

Prior to trial, petitioner moved to dismiss the complaint on the basis that sale of sexually oriented material to consenting adults is constitutionally protected. In connection with this motion only, the prosecution stipulated that it did not claim that petitioner either disseminated any material to minors or thrust it upon the general public. The trial court denied the motion. Today, this Court, in Paris Adult Theatre I v. Slaton, ante at 413 U. S. 68-69, reaffirms that commercial exposure and sale of obscene materials to anyone, including consenting adults, is subject to state regulation. See also United States v. Orito, post at 413 U. S. 141-144; United States v. 12 200-ft. Reels of Film, post at 413 U. S. 128; United States v. Thirty-seven Photographs, 402 U. S. 363, 402 U. S. 376 (1971) (opinion of WHITE, J.); United States v. Reidel, 402 U. S. 351, 402 U. S. 355-356 (1971). The denial of petitioner's motion was, therefore, not error.

At trial the prosecution tendered the book itself into evidence and also tendered, as an expert witness, a police officer in the vice squad. The officer testified to extensive experience with pornographic materials and gave his opinion that Suite 69, taken as a whole, predominantly appealed to the prurient interest of the average person in the State of California, "applying contemporary standards," and that the book went "substantially beyond the customary limits of candor" in the State of California. The witness explained specifically how the book did so, that it was a purveyor of perverted sex for its own sake. No "expert" state testimony was offered that the book was obscene under "national standards," or that the book was "utterly without redeeming social importance," despite "expert" defense testimony to the contrary.

In Miller v. California, ante, p. 413 U. S. 15, the Court today holds that the "contemporary community standards of the State of California,'" as opposed to "national standards," are constitutionally adequate to establish whether a work is obscene. We also reject in Paris Adult Theatre I v. Slaton, ante, p. 413 U. S. 49, any constitutional need for "expert" testimony on behalf of the prosecution, or for any other ancillary evidence of obscenity, once the allegedly obscene material itself is placed in evidence. Paris Adult Theatre I, ante at 413 U. S. 56. The defense should be free to introduce appropriate expert testimony, see Smith v. California, 361 U. S. 147, 361 U. S. 164-165 (1959) (Frankfurter, J., concurring), but in "the cases in which this Court has decided obscenity questions since Roth, it has regarded the materials as sufficient in themselves for the determination of the question." Ginzburg v. United States, 383 U. S. 463, 383 U. S. 465 (1966). See United States v. Groner, 479 F.2d 577, 579-586 (CA5 1973). On the record in this case, the prosecution's evidence was sufficient, as a matter of federal constitutional law, to support petitioner's conviction. [5]

Both Miller v. California, supra, and this case involve California obscenity statutes. The judgment of the Appellate Department of the Superior Court of California for the County of Los Angeles is vacated, and the case remanded to that court for further proceedings not inconsistent with this opinion, Miller v. California, supra, and Paris Adult Theatre I v. Slaton, supra. See United States v. 12 200-ft. Reels of Film, post at 413 U. S. 130 n. 7, decided today.

Vacated and remanded.

MR. JUSTICE DOUGLAS would vacate and remand for dismissal of the criminal complaint under which petitioner was found guilty because "obscenity" as defined by the California courts and by this Court is too vague to satisfy the requirements of due process. See Miller v. California, ante, p. 413 U. S. 37 (DOUGLAS, J., dissenting).

Notes

[1] The number of these stores was so estimated by both parties at oral argument. These stores purport to bar minors from the premises. In this case, there is no evidence that petitioner sold materials to juveniles. Cf. Miller v. California, ante at 413 U. S. 120.

[2] The California Penal Code § 311.2, at the time of the commission of the alleged offense, read in relevant part:

"(a) Every person who knowingly: sends or causes to be sent, or brings or causes to be brought, into this state for sale or distribution, or in this state prepares, publishes, prints, exhibits, distributes, or offers to distribute, or has in his possession with intent to distribute or to exhibit or offer to distribute, any obscene matter is guilty of a misdemeanor. . . ."

California Penal Code § 311, at the time of the commission of the alleged offense, provided as follows:

"As used in this chapter: "

"(a) 'Obscene' means that to the average person, applying contemporary standards, the predominant appeal of the matter taken as a whole, is to prurient interest, i.e., a shameful or morbid interest in nudity, sex, or excretion, which goes substantially beyond customary limits of candor in description or representation of such matters and is matter which is utterly without redeeming social importance."

"(b) 'Matter' means any book, magazine, newspaper, or other printed or written material or any picture, drawing, photograph, motion picture, or other pictorial representation or any statue or other figure, or any recording, transcription or mechanical, chemical or electrical reproduction or any other articles, equipment, machines or materials."

"(c) 'Person' means any individual, partnership, firm, association, corporation, or other legal entity."

"(d) 'Distribute' means to transfer possession of, whether with or without consideration."

"(e) 'Knowingly' means having knowledge that the matter is obscene."

[3] This Court, since Roth v. United States, 354 U. S. 476 (1957), has only once held books to be obscene. That case was Mishkin v. New York, 383 U. S. 502 (1966), and the books involved were very similar in content to Suite 69. But most of the Mishkin books, if not all, were illustrated. See id. at 383 U. S. 505, 383 U. S. 514-515. Prior to Roth, this court affirmed, by an equally divided court, a conviction for sale of an unillustrated book. Doubleday & Co., Inc. v. New York, 335 U.S. 848 (1948). This court has always rigorously scrutinized judgments involving books for possible violation of First Amendment rights, and has regularly reversed convictions on that basis. See Childs v. Oregon, 401 U.S. 1006 (1971); Walker v. Ohio, 398 U. S. 434 (1970); Keney v. New York, 388 U. S. 440 (1967); Friedman v. New York, 388 U. S. 441 (1967); Sheperd v. New York, 388 U. S. 444 (1967); Avansino v. New York, 388 U. S. 446 (1967); Corinth Publications, Inc. v. Wesberry, 388 U. S. 448 (1967); Books, Inc. v. United States, 388 U. S. 449 (1967); A Quantity of Books v. Kansas, 388 U. S. 452 (1967); Redrup v. New York, 386 U. S. 767 (1967); Memoirs v. Massachusetts, 383 U. S. 413 (1966); Tralins v. Gerstein, 378 U. S. 576 (1964); Grove Press, Inc. v. Gerstein, 378 U. S. 577 (1964); A Quantity of Books v. Kansas, 378 U. S. 205 (1964); Marcus v. Search Warrant, 367 U. S. 717 (1961); Smith v. California, 361 U. S. 147 (1959); Kingsley Books, Inc. v. Brown, 354 U. S. 436 (1957).

[4] See Paris Adult Theatre I v. Slaton, ante at 413 U. S. 58 n. 7; Report of the Commission on Obscenity and Pornography 401 (1970) (Hill-Link Minority Report).

[5] As the prosecution's introduction of the book itself into evidence was adequate, as a matter of federal constitutional law, to establish the book's obscenity, we

need not consider petitioner's claim that evidence of pandering was wrongly considered on appeal to support the jury finding of obscenity. Petitioner's additional claims that his conviction was affirmed on the basis of a "theory" of "pandering" not considered at trial and that he was subjected to retroactive application of a state statute are meritless on the record.

### US v. 12 200-Ft. Reels of Super 8mm. Film (June 21, 1973)

Mr. Chief Justice BURGER delivered the opinion of the Court.

We noted probable jurisdiction to review a summary decision of the United States District Court for the Central District of California holding that § 305(a) of the Tariff Act of 1930, 46 Stat. 688, as amended, 19 U.S.C. 1305(a) was 'unconstitutional on its face' and dismissing a forfeiture action brought under that statute. 1 The statute provides in pertinent part:

'All persons are prohibited from importing into the United States from any foreign country . . . any obscene book, pamphlet, paper, writing, advertisement, circular, print, picture, drawing, or other representation, figure, or image on or of paper or other material, or any cast, instrument, or other article which is obscene or immoral . . .. No such articles whether imported separately or contained in packages with other goods entitled to entry, shall be admitted to entry; and all such articles and, unless it appears to the satisfaction of the appropriate customs officer that the obscene or other prohibited articles contained in the package were inclosed therein without the knowledge or consent of the importer, owner, agent, or consignee, the entire contents of the package in which such articles are contained, shall be subject to seizure and forfeiture as hereinafter provided . . .. Provided further That the Secretary of the Treasury may, in his discretion, admit the so-called classics or books of recognized and established literary or scientific merit, but may, in his discretion, admit such classics or books only when imported for noncommercal purposes.'

On April 2, 1970, the claimant Paladini sought to carry movie films, color slides, photographs, and other printed and graphic material into the United States from Mexico. The materials were seized as being obscene by customs officers at a port of entry, Los Angeles Airport, and made the subject of a forfeiture action under 19 U.S.C. 1305(a). The District Court dismissed the Government's complaint, relying on the decision of a three-judge district court in United States v. Thirty-Seven Photographs, 309 F.Supp. 36 (CD Cal. 1970), which we later reversed, 402 U.S. 363, 91 S.Ct. 1400, 28 L.Ed.2d 822 (1971). That case concerned photographs concededly imported for commercial purposes. The narrow issue directly presented in this case, and not in Thirty Seven Photographs, is whether the United States may constitutionally prohibit importation of obscene material which the importer claims is for private, personal use and possession only. 2

Import restrictions and searches of persons or packages at the national borders rest on different considerations and different rules of constitutional law from domestic regulations. The Constitution gives Congress broad, comprehensive powers '(t)o regulate Commerce with foreign Nations.' Art. I, § 8, cl. 3. Historically such broad powers have been necessary to prevent smuggling and to prevent prohibited articles from entry. See United States v. Thirty-Seven Photographs, 402 U.S., at 376—377, 91 S.Ct., at 1408—1409 (opinion of White, J.); Carroll v. United States, 267 U.S. 132, 154, 45 S.Ct. 280, 285, 69 L.Ed. 543 (1925); Brolan v. United States, 236 U.S. 216, 218, 35 S.Ct. 285, 59 L.Ed. 544 (1915); Boyd v. United States, 116 U.S. 616, 623—624, 6 S.Ct. 524, 528—529, 29 L.Ed. 746 (1886); Alexander v. United States, 362 F.2d 379, 382 (CA9), cert. denied, 385 U.S. 977, 87 S.Ct. 519, 17 L.Ed.2d 439 (1966). The plenary power of Congress to regulate imports is illustrated in a holding of this Court which sustained the validity of an Act of Congress prohibiting the importation of 'any film or other pictorial representation of any prize fight . . . designed to be used or (that) may be used for purposes of public exhibition' 3 in view of 'the complete power of Congress over foreign commerce and its authority to prohibit the introduction of foreign articles . . .. Buttfield v. Stranahan, 192 U.S. 470 (24 S.Ct. 349, 48 L.Ed. 525); The Abby Dodge, 223 U.S. 166, 176 (32 S.Ct. 310, 56 L.Ed. 390). Brolan v. United States, 236 U.S. 216 (35 S.Ct. 285, 59 L.Ed. 544).' Weber v. Freed, 239 U.S. 325, 329, 36 S.Ct. 131, 132, 60 L.Ed. 308 (1915).

Claimant relies on the First Amendment and our decision in Stanley v. Georgia, 394 U.S. 557, 89 S.Ct. 1243, 22 L.Ed.2d 542 (1969). But it is now well established that obscene material is not protected by the First Amendment. Roth v. United States, 354 U.S. 476, 485, 77 S.Ct. 1304, 1309, 1 L.Ed.2d 1498 (1957), reaffirmed today in Miller v. California, 413 U.S. 15, at 23, 93 S.Ct. 2607, at 2614, 37 L.Ed.2d 419. As we have noted in United States v. Orito, 413 U.S. 139, at 141—143, 93 S.Ct. 2674, at 2677 2678, 37 L.Ed.2d 513, also decided today, Stanley depended, not on any First Amendment right to purchase or possess obscene materials, but on the right to privacy in the home. Three concurring Justices indicated that the case could have been disposed of on Fourth Amendment grounds without reference to the nature of the materials. Stanley v. Georgia, supra, 394 U.S., at 569, 89 S.Ct., at 1250 (Stewart, J., joined by Brennan and White, JJ., concurring).

In particular, claimant contends that, under Stanley, the right to possess obscene material in the privacy of the home creates a right to acquire it or import it from another country. This overlooks the explicitly narrow and precisely delineated privacy right on which Stanley rests. That holding reflects no more than what Mr. Justice Harlan characterized as the law's 'solicitude to protect the privacies of the life within (the home).' Poe v. Ullman, 367 U.S. 497, 551, 81 S.Ct. 1752, 1781, 6 L.Ed.2d 989 (1961) (dissenting opinion). 4 The seductive plausibility of single steps in a chain of evolutionary development of a legal rule is often not perceived until a third, fourth, or fifth 'logical' extension occurs. Each step, when taken, appeared a reasonable step in relation to that which preceded it, although the aggregate or end result is one that would never have been seriously considered in the first instance. 5 This kind of gestative propensity calls for the 'line drawing' familiar in the judicial, as in the legislative process: 'thus far but not beyond.' Perspectives may change, but our conclusion is that Stanley represents such a line of demarcation; and it is not unreasonable to assume that had it not been so delineated, Stanley would not be the law today. See United States v. Reidel, 402 U.S. 351, at 354—356, 91 S.Ct. 1410, at 1411—1413, 28 L.Ed.2d 813 (1971); id., at 357—360, 91 S.Ct., at 1413—1414 (Harlan, J., concurring). See also Miller v. United States, 431 F.2d 655, 657 (CA9 1970); United States v. Fragus, 428 F.2d 1211, 1213 (CA5 1970); United States v. Melvin, 419 F.2d 136, 139 (CA4 1969); Gable v. Jenkins, 309 F.Supp. 998, 1000—1001 (ND Ga.1969), aff'd, 397 U.S. 592, 90 S.Ct. 1351, 25 L.Ed.2d 595 (1970). Cf. Karalexis v. Byrne, 306 F.Supp. 1363, 1366 (D.Mass.1969), vacated on other grounds, 401 U.S. 216, 91 S.Ct. 777, 27 L.Ed.2d 792 (1971).

We are not disposed to extend the precise, carefully limited holding of Stanley to permit importation of admittedly obscene materials simply because it is imported for private use only. To allow such a claim would be not unlike compelling the Government to permit importation of prohibited or controlled drugs for private consumption as long as such drugs are not for public distribution or sale. We have already indicated that the protected right to possess obscene material in the privacy of one's home does not give rise to a correlative right to have someone sell or give it to others. United States v. Thirty-Seven Photographs, supra, 402 U.S., at 376, 91 S.Ct., at 1408 (opinion of White, J.), and United States v. Reidel, supra, 402 U.S., at 355, 91 S.Ct., at 1412. Nor is there any correlative right to transport obscene material in interstate commerce. United States v. Orito, supra, 413 U.S., at 142—144, 93 S.Ct., at 2677—2678. 6 It follows that Stanley does not permit one to go abroad and bring such material into the country for private purposes. 'Stanley's emphasis was on the freedom of thought and mind in the privacy of the home. But a port of entry is not a traveler's home.' United States v. Thirty-Seven Photographs, supra, 402 U.S., at 376, 91 S.Ct., at 1408 (opinion of White, J.).

This is not to say that Congress could not allow an exemption for private use, with or without appropriate guarantees such as bonding, or permit the transportation of obscene material under conditions insuring privacy. But Congress has not seen fit to do so, and the holding in Roth v. United States, supra, read with the narrow holding of Stanley v. Georgia, supra, does not afford a basis for claimant's arguments. The Constitution does not compel, and Congress has not authorized, an exception for private use of obscene material. See Paris Adult Theatre I v. Slaton, 413 U.S., at 64—69, 93 S.Ct., at 2638—2642; United States v. Reidel, supra, 402 U.S., at 357, 91 S.Ct., at 1413; A Book Named 'John Cleland's Memoirs of a Woman of Pleasure' v. Attorney General of Massachusetts, 383 U.S. 413, 462, 86 S.Ct. 975, 999, 16 L.Ed.2d 1 (1966) (White, J., dissenting).

The attack on the overbreadth of the statute is thus foreclosed, but, independently, we should note that it is extremely difficult to control the uses to which obscene material is put once it enters this country. Even single copies, represented to be for personal use, can be quickly and cheaply duplicated by modern technology thus facilitating wide-scale distribution. While it is true that a large volume of obscene material on microfilm could rather easily be smuggled into the United States by mail, or otherwise, and could be enlarged or reproduced for commercial purposes, Congress is not precluded from barring some avenues of illegal importation because avenues exist that are more difficult to regulate. See American Power & Light Co. v. SEC, 329 U.S. 90, 99–100, 67 S.Ct. 133, 139–140, 91 L.Ed. 103 (1946).

As this case came to us on the District Court's summary dismissal of the forfeiture action, no determination of the obscenity of the materials involved has been made. We have today arrived at standards for testing the constitutionality of state legislation regulating obscenity. See Miller v. California, supra, 413 U.S., at 23–25, 93 S.Ct., at 2614–2615. These standards are applicable to federal legislation. 7 The judgment of the District Court is vacated and the case is remanded for further proceedings consistent with this opinion, Miller v. California, supra, and United States v. Orito, supra, both decided today.

Vacated and remanded.

Notes

1. The United States brought this direct appeal under 28 U.S.C. 1252. See Clark v. Gabriel, 393 U.S. 256, 258, 89 S.Ct. 424, 426, 21 L.Ed.2d 418 (1968).

2. On the day the complaint was dismissed, claimant filed an affidavit with the District Court stating that none of the seized materials 'were imported by me for any commercial purpose but were intended to be used and possessed by me personally.' In conjunction with the Government's motion to stay the order of dismissal, denied below but granted by Mr. Justice Brennan, the Government conceded it had no evidence to contradict claimant's affidavit and did not 'contest the fact that this was a private importation.'

3. Act of July 31, 1912, c. 263, § 1, 37 Stat. 240.

4. Nor can claimant rely on any other sphere of constitutionally protected privacy, such as that which encompasses the intimate medical problems of family, marriage, and motherhood. See Paris Adult Theatre I v. Slaton, 413 U.S. 49, at 65–67, 93 S.Ct. 2628, at 2639–2640, 37 L.Ed.2d 446, and United States v. Orito, supra, 413 U.S., at 142–143, 93 S.Ct., at 2677–2678.

5. Mr. Justice Holmes had this kind of situation in mind when he said:

'All rights tend to declare themselves absolute to their logical extreme. Yet all in fact are limited by the neighborhood of principles of policy which are other than those on which the particular right is founded, and which become strong enough to hold their own when a certain point is reached.' Hudson County Water Co. v. McCarter, 209 U.S. 349, 355, 28 S.Ct. 529, 531, 52 L.Ed. 828 (1908).

6. In Caminetti v. United States, 242 U.S. 470, 37 S.Ct. 192, 61 L.Ed. 442 (1917), and Hoke v. United States, 227 U.S. 308, 33 S.Ct. 281, 57 L.Ed. 523 (1913), this Court upheld the 'so-called White Slave Traffic Act, which was construed to punish any person engaged in enticing a woman from one state to another for immoral ends, whether for commercial purposes or otherwise, . . . because it was intended to prevent the use of

interstate commerce to facilitate prostitution or concubinage, and other forms of immorality.' Brooks v. United States, 267 U.S. 432, 437, 45 S.Ct. 345, 346, 69 L.Ed. 699 (1925) (emphasis added).

7. We further note that, while we must leave to state courts the construction of state legislation, we do have a duty to authoritatively construe federal statutes where "a serious doubt of constitutionality is raised" and "a construction of the statute is fairly possible by which the question may be avoided." United States v. Thirty-Seven Photographs, 402 U.S. 363, 369, 91 S.Ct. 1400, 1404, 28 L.Ed.2d 822 (1971) (opinion of White, J.), quoting from Crowell v. Benson, 285 U.S. 22, 62, 52 S.Ct. 285, 296, 76 L.Ed. 598 (1932). If and when such a 'serious doubt' is raised as to the vagueness of the words 'obscene,' 'lewd,' 'lascivious,' 'filthy,' 'indecent,' or 'immoral' as used to describe regulated material in 19 U.S.C. 1305(a) and 18 U.S.C. § 1462, see United States v. Orito, supra, 413 U.S., at 140 n. 1, 93 S.Ct., at 2676 n. 1, we are prepared to construe such terms as limiting regulated material to patently offensive representations or descriptions ofthat specific 'hard core' sexual conduct given as examples in Miller v. California, supra, 413 U.S., at 25, 93 S.Ct., at 2615. See United States v. Thirty-Seven Photographs, supra, 402 U.S., at 369—374, 91 S.Ct., at 1404—1407 (opinion of White, J.). Of course, Congress could always define other specific 'hard core' conduct.

## US v. Orito (June 21, 1973)

MR. CHIEF JUSTICE BURGER delivered the opinion of the Court.

Appellee Orito was charged in the United States District Court for the Eastern District of Wisconsin with a violation of 18 U.S.C. 1462 [1] in that he did

"knowingly transport and carry in interstate commerce from San Francisco . . . to Milwaukee . . . by means of a common carrier, that is, Trans-World Airlines and North Central Airlines, copies of [specified] obscene, lewd, lascivious, and filthy materials. . . ."

The materials specified included some 83 reels of film, with as many as eight to 10 copies of some of the films. Appellee moved to dismiss the indictment on the ground that the statute violated his First and Ninth Amendment rights. [2] The District Court granted his motion, holding that the statute was unconstitutionally overbroad, since it failed to distinguish between "public" and "non-public" transportation of obscene material. The District Court interpreted this Court's decisions in Griswold v. Connecticut, 381 U. S. 479 (1965); Redrup v. New York, 386 U. S. 767 (1967); and Stanley v. Georgia, 394 U. S. 557 (1969), to establish the proposition that "non-public transportation" of obscene material was constitutionally protected. [3]

Although the District Court held the statute void on its face for overbreadth, it is not clear whether the statute was held to be overbroad because it covered transportation intended solely for the private use of the transporter, or because, regardless of the intended use of the material, the statute extended to "private carriage" or "nonpublic" transportation which, in itself, involved no risk of exposure to children or unwilling adults. The United States brought this direct appeal under former 18 U.S.C. § 3731 (1964 ed.) now amended, Pub.L. 91644, § 14(a), 84 Stat. 1890. See United States v. Spector, 343 U. S. 169, 343 U. S. 171 (1952).

The District Court erred in striking down 18 U.S.C. § 1462 and dismissing appellee's indictment on these "privacy" grounds. The essence of appellee's contentions is that Stanley has firmly established the right to possess obscene material in the privacy of the home, and that this creates a correlative right to receive it, transport it, or distribute it. We have rejected that reasoning. This case was decided by the District Court before our decisions in United States v. Thirty-seven Photographs, 402 U. S. 363 (1971), and United States v. Reidel, 402 U. S. 351 (1971). Those holdings negate the idea that some zone of constitutionally protected privacy follows such material when it is moved outside the home area protected by Stanley. [4] United States v. Thirty-seven Photographs, supra, at 402 U. S. 36 (opinion of WHITE, J.). United States v. Reidel, supra, at 402 U. S. 354-356. See United States v. Zacher, 332 F.Supp. 883, 885-886 (ED Wis.1971). But cf. United States v. Thirty-seven Photographs, supra, at 402 U. S. 379 (STEWART, J., concurring). The Constitution extends special safeguards to the privacy of the home, just as it protects other special privacy rights such as those of marriage, procreation, motherhood, childrearing, and education. See Eisenstadt v. Baird, 405 U. S. 438, 405 U. S. 453-454 (1972); Loving v. Virginia, 388 U. S. 1, 388 U. S. 12 (1967); Griswold v. Connecticut, supra, at 381 U. S. 486; Prince v. Massachusetts, 321 U. S. 158, 321 U. S. 166 (1944); Skinner v. Oklahoma, 316 U. S. 535, 316 U. S. 541 (1942); Pierce v. Society of Sisters, 268 U. S. 510, 268 U. S. 535 (1925). But viewing obscene films in a commercial theater open to the adult public, see Paris Adult Theatre I v. Slaton, ante at 413 U. S. 65-67, or transporting such films in common carriers in interstate commerce, has no claim to such special consideration. [5] It is hardly necessary to catalog the myriad activities that may be lawfully conducted within the privacy and confines of the home, but may be prohibited in public. The Court has consistently rejected constitutional protection for obscene material outside the home. See United States v. 12 200-ft. Reels of Film, ante at 413 U. S. 126-129; Miller v. California, ante at 413 U. S. 23; United States v. Reidel, supra, at 402 U. S. 354-356 (opinion of WHITE, J.); id. at 402 U. S. 357-360 (Harlan, J., concurring); Roth v. United States, 354 U. S. 476, 354 U. S. 484-485 (1957).

Given (a) that obscene material is not protected under the First Amendment, Miller v. California, supra; Roth v. United States, supra, (b) that the Government has a legitimate interest in protecting the public commercial environment by preventing such material from entering the stream of commerce, see Paris Adult Theatre I, ante at 413 U. S. 57-64, and (c) that no constitutionally protected privacy is involved, United States v. Thirty-seven Photographs, supra, at 402 U. S. 376 (opinion of WHITE, J.), we cannot say that the Constitution forbids comprehensive federal regulation of interstate transportation of obscene material merely because such transport may be by private carriage, or because the material is intended for the private use of the transporter. That the transporter has an abstract proprietary power to shield the obscene material from all others and to guard the material with the same privacy as in the home is not controlling. Congress may regulate on the basis of the natural tendency of material in the home being kept private and the contrary tendency once material leaves that area, regardless of a transporter's professed intent. Congress could reasonably determine such regulation to be necessary to effect permissible federal control of interstate commerce in obscene material, based as that regulation is on a legislatively determined risk of ultimate exposure to juveniles or to the public and the harm that exposure could cause. See Paris Adult Theatre I v. Slaton, ante at 413 U. S. 57-63. See also United States v. Alpers, 338 U. S. 680, 338 U. S. 681-685 (1950); Brooks v. United States, 267 U. S. 432, 267 U. S. 436-437 (1925); Weber v. Freed, 239 U. S. 325, 239 U. S. 329-330 (1915).

"The motive and purpose of a regulation of interstate commerce are matters for the legislative judgment upon the exercise of which the Constitution places no restriction and over which the courts are given no control. McCray v. United States, 195 U. S. 27; Sonzinsky v. United States, 300 U. S. 506, 300 U. S. 513 and cases cited."

United States v. Darby, 312 U. S. 100, 312 U. S. 115 (1941).

"It is sufficient to reiterate the well settled principle that Congress may impose relevant conditions and requirement on those who use the channels of interstate commerce in order that those channels will not become the means of promoting or spreading evil, whether of a physical, moral or economic nature."

North American Co. v. SEC, 327 U. S. 686, 327 U. S. 705 (1946). [6]

As this case came to us on the District Court's summary dismissal of the indictment, no determination of the obscenity of the material involved has been made. Today, for the first time since Roth v. United States, supra, we have arrived at standards accepted by a majority of this Court for distinguishing obscene material, unprotected by the First Amendment, from protected free speech. See Miller v. California, ante at 413 U. S. 23-25; United States v. 12 200-ft. Reels of Film, ante at 413 U. S. 130 n. 7. The decision of the District Court is therefore vacated and the case is remanded for reconsideration of the sufficiency of the indictment in light of Miller v. California, supra; United States v. 12 200-ft. Reels, supra; and this opinion.

Vacated and remanded.

Notes

[1] Title 18 U.S.C. § 1462 provides in pertinent part:

"Whoever brings into the United States, or any place subject to the jurisdiction thereof, or knowingly uses any express company or other common carrier, for carriage in interstate or foreign commerce --"

"(a) any obscene, lewd, lascivious, or filthy book, pamphlet, picture, motion-picture film, paper, letter, writing, print, or other matter of indecent character; . . ."

"* * * *"

"Shall be fined not more than $5,000 or imprisoned not more than five years, or both, for the first such offense and shall be fined not more than $10,000 or imprisoned not more than ten years, or both, for each such offense thereafter."

[2] Appellee also moved to dismiss the indictment on the grounds that 18 U.S.C. § 1462 does not require proof of scienter. That issue was not reached by the District Court, and is not before us now.

[3] The District Court stated:

"By analogy, it follows that with the right to read obscene matters comes the right to transport or to receive such material when done in a fashion that does not pander it or impose it upon unwilling adults or upon minors."

"* * * *"

"I find no meaningful distinction between the private possession which was held to be protected in Stanley and the non-public transportation which the statute at bar proscribes."

338 F.Supp. 308, 310 (1970).

[4] "These are the rights that appellant is asserting in the case before us. He is asserting the right to read or observe what he pleases -- the right to satisfy his intellectual and emotional needs in the privacy of his own home."

Stanley v. Georgia, 394 U. S. 557, 394 U. S. 565 (1969). (Emphasis added.)

[5] The Solicitor General indicates that the tariffs of most, if not all, common carriers include a right of inspection. Resorting to common carriers, like entering a place of public accommodation, does not involve the privacies associated with the home. See United States v. Thirty-seven Photographs, 402 U. S. 363, 402 U. S. 376 (1971) (opinion of WHITE, J.); United States v. Reidel, 402 U. S. 351, 402 U. S. 359-360 (1971) (Harlan, J., concurring); Poe v. Ullman, 367 U. S. 497, 367 U. S. 551-552 (1961) (Harlan, J., dissenting); Miller v. United States, 431 F.2d 655, 657 (CA9 1970); United States v. Melvin, 419 F.2d 136, 139 (CA4 1969).

[6] "Congress can certainly regulate interstate commerce to the extent of forbidding and punishing the use of such commerce as an agency to promote immorality, dishonesty or the spread of any evil or harm to the people of other States from the State of origin. In doing this, it is merely exercising the police power, for the benefit of the public, within the field of interstate commerce. . . . In the Lottery Case, 188 U. S. 321, it was held that Congress might pass a law punishing the transmission of lottery tickets from one State to another, in order to prevent the carriage of those tickets to be sold in other States and thus demoralize, through a spread of the gambling habit, individuals who were likely to purchase. . . . In Hoke v. United States, 227 U. S. 308 and Caminetti v. United States, 242 U. S. 470, the so-called White Slave Traffic Act, which was construed to punish any person engaged in enticing a woman from one State to another for immoral ends, whether for commercial purposes or otherwise, was valid because it was intended to prevent the use of interstate commerce to facilitate prostitution or concubinage, and other forms of immorality. . . . In Weber v. Freed, 239 U. S. 325, it was held that Congress had power to prohibit the importation of pictorial representations of prize fights designed for public exhibition, because of the demoralizing effect of such exhibitions in the State of

destination."

Brooks v. United States, 267 U. S. 432, 267 U. S. 436-437 (1925).

## Hamling v. US (June 24, 1974)

MR. JUSTICE REHNQUIST delivered the opinion of the Court.

On March 5, 1971, a grand jury in the United States District Court for the Southern District of California indicted petitioners William L. Hamling, Earl Kemp, Shirley R. Wright, David L. Thomas, Reed Enterprises, Inc., and Library Service, Inc., on 21 counts of an indictment charging use of the mails to carry an obscene book, The Illustrated Presidential Report of the Commission on Obscenity and Pornography, and an obscene advertisement, which gave information as to where, how, and from whom and by what means the Illustrated Report might be obtained, and of conspiracy to commit the above offenses, in violation of 18 U.S.C. §§ 2, 371, and 1461. [1] Prior to trial, petitioners moved to dismiss the indictment on the grounds that it failed to inform them of the charges, and that the grand jury had insufficient evidence before it to return an indictment and was improperly instructed on the law. Petitioners also challenged the petit jury panel and moved to strike the venire on the ground that there had been an unconstitutional exclusion of all persons under 25 years of age. The District Court denied all of these motions.

Following a jury trial, petitioners were convicted on 12 counts of mailing and conspiring to mail the obscene advertisement. [2] On appeal, the United States Court of Appeals for the Ninth Circuit affirmed. 481 F.2d 307 (1973). The jury was unable to reach a verdict with regard to the counts of the indictment which charged the mailing of the allegedly obscene Illustrated Report. [3] The advertisement found obscene is a single sheet brochure mailed to approximately 55,000 persons in various parts of the United States; one side of the brochure contains a collage of photographs from the Illustrated Report; the other side gives certain information and an order blank from which the Illustrated Report could be ordered.

The Court of Appeals accurately described the photographs in the brochure as follows:

"The folder opens to a full page splash of pictures portraying heterosexual and homosexual intercourse, sodomy and a variety of deviate sexual acts. Specifically, a group picture of nine persons, one male engaged in masturbation, a female masturbating two males, two couples engaged in intercourse in reverse fashion while one female participant engages in fellatio of a male; a second group picture of six persons, two males masturbating, two fellatrices practicing the act, each bearing a clear depiction of ejaculated seminal fluid on their faces; two persons with the female engaged in the act of fellatio and the male in female masturbation by hand; two separate pictures of males engaged in cunnilinction; a film strip of six frames depicting lesbian love scenes including a cunnilinguist in action and female masturbation with another's hand and a vibrator, and two frames, one depicting a woman mouthing the penis of a horse, and a second poising the same for entrance into her vagina."

481 F.2d at 316-317. [4]

The reverse side of the brochure contains a facsimile of the Illustrated Report's cover, and an order form for the Illustrated Report. It also contains the following language:

"THANKS A LOT, MR. PRESIDENT. A monumental work of research and investigation has now become a giant of a book. All the facts, all the statistics, presented in the best possible format . . . and . . . completely illustrated in black and white and full color. Every facet of the most controversial public report ever issued is covered in detail. "

"The book is a MUST for the research shelves of every library, public or private, seriously concerned with full intellectual freedom and adult selection."

"Millions of dollars in public funds were expended to determine the PRECISE TRUTH about eroticism in the United States today, yet every possible attempt to suppress this information was made from the very highest levels."

"Even the President dismissed the facts out of hand. The attempt to suppress this volume is an inexcusable insult directed at every adult in this country. Each individual MUST be allowed to make his own decision; the fact are inescapable. Many adults, MANY OF THEM, will do just that, after reading this REPORT. In a truly free society, a book like this wouldn't even be necessary."

The Court of Appeals indicated that the actual report of the Commission on Obscenity and Pornography is an official Government document printed by the United States Government Printing Office. The major difference between the Illustrated Report, charged to be obscene in the indictment, and the actual report is that the Illustrated Report contained illustrations, which the publishers of the Illustrated Report said were included

"'as examples of the type of subject matter discussed and the type of material shown to persons who were part of the research projects engaged in for the Commission as basis for their Report.'"

481 F.2d at 315.

The facts adduced at trial showed that postal patrons in various parts of the country received the brochure advertising the Illustrated Report. The mailings these persons received consisted of an outer envelope, an inner return envelope addressed to Library Service, Inc., at a post office box in San Diego, California, and the brochure itself, which also identified Library Service, Inc., at the same address, as the party responsible for the mailing. The outer envelopes bore a postmark that indicated they were mailed from North Hollywood, California, on or about January 12, 1971, and that the postage was affixed to the envelopes by a Pitney-Bowes meter number.

The mailing of these brochures was accomplished by petitioners through the use of other businesses. Approximately 55,000-58,000 of these brochures were placed in envelopes, and postage was affixed to them by one Richard and one Venita Harte, who operate the Academy Addressing and Mailing Service. The brochures and the Pitney-Bowes meter number with which they affixed the postage were supplied to them by one Bernard Lieterman of Regent House, Inc., of North Hollywood, California, who, on January 11, 1971, had paid the United States Postal Service to set $3,300 worth of postage on the meter number. Regent House was billed $541.15 by the Hartes for their services. Regent House, in turn, charged its services and costs for the postage and the Hartes' mailing service to Reed Enterprises, Inc., which paid the bill on January 19, 1971, with a check signed by petitioner Hamling.

Those individuals responding to the brochure would be sent copies of the Illustrated Report, which would be mailed with postage affixed by a second Pitney-Bowes meter number which was installed at Library Service, Inc., at the direction of an employee of Pitney-Bowes. The rental agreement for this meter was signed for Library Service by petitioner David Thomas, whom that employee identified as the person with whom he had dealt on the matter.

The evidence indicated that the individual petitioners were officers in the corporate petitioners, and also indicated that they were involved with selling the Illustrated Report, which entailed mailing out the advertising brochure.

Petitioner Hamling, as president of Reed Enterprises, Inc., signed the check on the corporation's behalf in payment to Regent House for the mailing of the advertisement. Petitioner Kemp was the editor of the Illustrated Report, and was vice-president of Library Service, Inc., and Greenleaf Classics, Inc., which is the publisher of the Illustrated Report. [5] He signed the application on behalf of Library Service, Inc., for the post office box in San Diego, which was the same post office box on the return envelope sent with the advertisement and on the advertisement itself. Petitioner Thomas signed the rental agreement for the postage meter which was used in affixing postage for sending copies of the Illustrated Report, and which Thomas directed to be installed at Library Service.

Petitioner Wright was the secretary of Reed Enterprises, Inc., and Greenleaf Classics, Inc. Wright assisted the postal superintendent in obtaining Kemp's signature on the application for the post office box in San Diego. Wright also received a memorandum from London Press, Inc., the printer of the Illustrated Report, addressed to her as representative of Reed Enterprises, Inc., confirming the shipment of 28,537 copies of the Illustrated Report. Various other corporate documents tended to show the individual petitioners' involvement with the corporate petitioners. Both the Government and the petitioners introduced testimony from various expert witnesses concerning the obscenity vel non of both the Illustrated Report and the brochure.

In affirming the convictions of these petitioners for the distribution of the obscene brochure, the Court of Appeal rejected various contention made by the petitioners. The Court of Appeals also rejected petitioners' petition for rehearing and suggestion for rehearing en banc. We granted certiorari, 414 U.S. 1143 (1974), and now affirm the judgment of the Court of Appeal.

I

These petitioners were convicted by a jury on December 23, 1971. App. 9. The Court of Appeals affirmed their convictions in an opinion filed on June 7, 1973. The Court of Appeals originally denied rehearing and suggestion for rehearing en banc on July 9, 1973. That order was withdrawn by the Court of Appeals to be reconsidered in light of this Court's decision, announced June 21, 1973, in Miller v. California, 413 U. S. 15, and related cases, [6] and was submitted to the en banc court by order dated August 20, 1973. [7] On August 22, 1973, the Court of Appeals entered an order denying the petition for rehearing and the suggestion for rehearing en banc.

The principal question presented by this case is what rules of law shall govern obscenity convictions that occurred prior to the date on which this Court's decision in Miller v. California, supra, and its companion cases were handed down, but which had not at that point become final. Petitioners mount a series of challenges to their convictions based upon the so-called Memoirs test for the proscription of obscenity. (Memoirs v. Massachusetts, 383 U. S. 413 (1966).) They also attack the judgments as failing to comply with the standards enunciated in the Miller cases, and conclude by challenging other procedural and evidentiary rulings of the District Court.

Questions as to the constitutionality of 18 U.S.C. § 1461, [8] the primary statute under which petitioners were convicted, were not strangers to this Court prior to the Miller decision. In Roth v. United States, 354 U. S. 476 (1957), the Court held that this statute did not offend the free speech and free press guarantees of the First Amendment, and that it did not deny the due process guaranteed by the Fifth Amendment because it was "too vague to support conviction for crime." Id. at 354 U. S. 480. That holding was reaffirmed in United States v. Reidel, 402 U. S. 351 (1971). See also Manual Enterprises, Inc. v. Day, 370 U. S. 478 (1962); Ginzburg v. United States, 383 U. S. 463 (1966). Prior to Miller, therefore, this Court had held that 18 U.S.C. § 1461,

"applied according to the proper standard for judging obscenity, do[es] not offend constitutional safeguards against convictions based upon protected material, or fail to give men in acting adequate notice of what is prohibited."

Roth v. United States, supra, at 354 U. S. 492.

These petitioners were tried and convicted under the definition of obscenity originally announced by the Court in Roth v. United States, supra, and significantly refined by the plurality opinion in Memoirs v. Massachusetts, supra. The Memoirs plurality held that, under the Roth definition

"as elaborated in subsequent cases, three elements must coalesce: it must be established that (a) the dominant theme of the material taken as a whole appeals to a prurient interest in sex; (b) the material is patently offensive because it affronts contemporary community standards relating to the description or representation of sexual matters; and (c) the material is utterly without redeeming social value."

Id. at 383 U. S. 418.

Petitioners make no contention that the instructions given by the District Court in this case were inconsistent with the test of the Memoirs plurality. They argue instead that the obscenity vel non of the brochure has not been established under the Memoirs test. The Court of Appeals ruled against petitioners on this score, concluding that the jury's finding that the brochure was obscene under the Memoirs plurality test was correct. Petitioners argue at length that their expert witnesses established that the brochure did not appeal to a prurient interest in sex, that it was not patently offensive, and that it had social value. Examining the record below, we find that the jury could constitutionally find the brochure obscene under the Memoirs test. Expert testimony is not necessary to enable the jury to judge the obscenity of material which, as here, has been placed into evidence. See Paris Adult Theatre I v. Slaton, 413 U. S. 49, 413 U. S. 56 (1973), Kaplan v. California, 413 U. S. 115, 413 U. S. 120-121 (1973); Ginzburg v. United States, supra, at 383 U. S. 465. In this case, both the Government and the petitioners introduced testimony through expert witnesses concerning the alleged obscenity of the brochure. The jury was not bound to accept the opinion of any expert in weighing the evidence of obscenity, and we conclude that its determination that the brochure was obscene was supported by the evidence and consistent with the Memoirs formulation of obscenity.

Petitioners nevertheless contend that, since the jury was unable to reach a verdict on the counts charging the obscenity vel non of the Illustrated Report itself, that report must be presumed to be nonobscene, and therefore protected by the First Amendment. From this premise they contend that, since the brochure fairly advertised the Illustrated Report, the brochure must also be nonobscene. The Court of Appeals rejected this contention, noting that "[t]he premise is false. The jury made no finding on the charged obscenity of the Report." 481 F.2d at 315. The jury in this case did not acquit the petitioners of the charges relating to the distribution of the allegedly obscene Illustrated Report. It instead was unable to reach a verdict on the counts charging the distribution of the Illustrated Report, and, accordingly, the District Court declared a mistrial as to those counts. App. 9-10. It has, of course, long been the rule that consistency in verdicts or judgments of conviction is not required. United States v. Dotterweich, 320 U. S. 277, 320 U. S. 279 (1943); Dunn v. United States, 284 U. S. 390, 284 U. S. 393 (1932).

"The mere fact juries may reach different conclusions as to the same material does not mean that constitutional rights are abridged. As this Court observed in Roth v. United States, 354 U.S. at 354 U. S. 492 n. 30,"

"it is common experience that different juries may reach different results under any criminal statute. That is one of the consequences we accept under our jury system. Cf. Dunlop v. United States, 165 U. S. 486, 165 U. S. 499-500."

Miller v. California, 413 U.S. at 413 U. S. 26 n. 9. The brochure in this case stands by itself, and must accordingly be judged. It is not, as petitioners suggest, inseparable from the Illustrated Report, and it cannot be seriously contended that an obscene advertisement could not be prepared for some type of nonobscene material. If consistency in jury verdicts as to the obscenity vel non of identical materials is not constitutionally required, Miller v. California, supra, the same is true a fortiori of verdicts as to separate materials, regardless of their similarities.

Our Miller decisions dealing with the constitutional aspects of obscenity prosecutions were announced after the petitioners had been found guilty by a jury, and their judgment of conviction affirmed by a panel of the Court of Appeals. Our prior decisions establish a general rule that a change in the law occurring after a relevant event in a case will be given effect while the case is on direct review. United States v. Schooner Peggy, 1 Cranch 103 (1801); Linkletter v. Walker, 381 U. S. 618, 381 U. S. 627 (1965); Bradley v. School Board of Richmond, 416 U. S. 696, 416 U. S. 711 (1974). Since the judgment in this case has not become final, we examine the judgment against petitioners in the light of the principles laid down in the Miller cases. While the language of 18 U.S.C. § 1461 has remained the same throughout this litigation, the statute defines an offense in terms of "obscenity," and this Court's decisions, at least since Roth v. United States, supra, indicate that there are constitutional limitations which must be borne in mind in defining that statutory term. Thus, any constitutional principle enunciated in Miller which would serve to benefit petitioners must be applied in their case.

Recognizing that the Memoirs plurality test had represented a sharp break with the test of obscenity as announced in Roth v. United States, supra, our decision in Miller v. California reformulated the test for the determination of obscenity vel non:

"The basic guidelines for the trier of fact must be: (a) whether 'the average person, applying contemporary community standards,' would find that the work, taken as a whole, appeals to the prurient interest . . .; (b) whether the work depicts or describes, in a patently offensive way, sexual conduct specifically defined by the applicable state law; and (c) whether the work, taken as a whole, lacks serious literary, artistic, political, or scientific value."

413 U.S. at 413 U. S. 24. The Court of Appeals held on rehearing that the Miller cases generally prescribed a more relaxed standard of review under the Federal Constitution for obscenity convictions, and that, therefore, petitioners could derive no benefit from the principles enunciated in those cases. See n 7, supra. Petitioners concede that this observation may be true in many particulars, but that, in at least two, it is not. They contend that the Miller treatment of the concept of "national standards" necessarily invalidates the District Court's charge to the jury in their case relating to the standard by which the question of obscenity was to be judged, and they further contend that the general language of 18 U.S.C. § 1461 is, in the light of the holding in the Miller cases, unconstitutionally vague.

A

The trial court instructed the jury that it was to judge the obscenity vel non of the brochure by reference to

"what is reasonably accepted according to the contemporary standards of the community as a whole. . . . Contemporary community standards means the standards generally held throughout this country concerning sex and matters pertaining to sex. This phrase means, as it has been aptly stated, the average conscience of the time, and the present critical point in the compromise between candor and shame, at which the community may have arrived here and now."

App. 241. Petitioners describe this as an instruction embodying the principle of "national standards" which, although it may have been proper under the law as it existed when they were tried, cannot be sustained under the law as laid down in Miller, where the Court stated:

"Nothing in the First Amendment requires that a jury must consider hypothetical and unascertainable 'national standards' when attempting to determine whether certain materials are obscene as a matter of fact."

413 U.S. at 413 U. S. 31-32.

Paradoxically, however, petitioners also contend that, in order to avoid serious constitutional questions, the standards in federal obscenity prosecutions must be national ones, relying on Manual Enterprises, Inc. v. Day, 370 U.S. at 370 U. S. 488 (opinion of Harlan, J.), and United States v. Palladino, 490 F.2d 499 (CA1 1974). Petitioners assert that our decisions in the two federal obscenity cases decided with Miller [9] indicate that this Court has not definitively decided whether the Constitution requires the use of nationwide standards in federal obscenity prosecutions.

We think that both of these contentions evidence a misunderstanding of our Miller holdings. Miller rejected the view that the First and Fourteenth Amendments require that the proscription of obscenity be based on uniform nationwide standards of what is obscene, describing such standards as "hypothetical and unascertainable," 413 U.S. at 413 U. S. 31. But, in so doing, the Court did not require as a constitutional matter the substitution of some smaller geographical area into the same sort of formula; the test was stated in terms of the understanding of "the average person, applying contemporary community standards." Id. at 413 U. S. 24. When this approach is coupled with the reaffirmation in Paris Adult Theatre I v. Slaton, 413 U.S. at 413 U. S. 56, of the rule that the prosecution need not, as a matter of constitutional law, produce "expert" witnesses to testify as to the obscenity of the material, the import of the quoted language from Miller becomes clear. A juror is entitled to draw on his own knowledge of the views of the average person in the community or vicinage from which he comes for making the required determination, just as he is entitled to draw on his knowledge of the propensities of a "reasonable" person in other areas of the law. Stone v. New York, C. & St. L.R. Co., 344 U. S. 407, 344 U. S. 409 (1953); Schulz v. Pennsylvania R. Co., 350 U. S. 523, 350 U. S. 525-526 (19.56). Our holding in Miller that California could constitutionally proscribe obscenity in terms of a "state-wide" standard did not mean that any such precise geographic area is required as a matter of constitutional law.

Our analysis in Miller of the difficulty in formulating uniform national standards of obscenity, and our emphasis on the ability of the juror to ascertain the sense of the "average person, applying contemporary community standards" without the benefit of expert evidence, clearly indicates that 18 U.S.C. § 1461 is not to be interpreted as requiring proof of the uniform national standards which were criticized in Miller. In

United States v. 12 200-ft. Reels of Film, 413 U. S. 123 (1973), a federal obscenity case decided with Miller, we said:

"We have today arrived at standards for testing the constitutionality of state legislation regulating obscenity. See Miller v. California, ante, at 413 U. S. 23-25. These standards are applicable to federal legislation."

Id. at 413 U. S. 129-130. Included in the pages referred to in Miller is the standard of "the average person, applying contemporary community standards." In view of our holding in 12 200-ft. Reels of Film, we hold that 18 U.S.C. § 1461 incorporates this test in defining obscenity.

The result of the Miller cases, therefore, as a matter of constitutional law and federal statutory construction, is to permit a juror sitting in obscenity cases to draw on knowledge of the community or vicinage from which he comes in deciding what conclusion "the average person, applying contemporary community standards" would reach in a given case. Since this case was tried in the Southern District of California, and presumably jurors from throughout that judicial district were available to serve on the panel which tried petitioners, it would be the standards of that "community" upon which the jurors would draw. But this is not to say that a district court would not be at liberty to admit evidence of standards existing in some place outside of this particular district if it felt such evidence would assist the jurors in the resolution of the issues which they were to decide.

Our Brother BRENNAN suggests in dissent that, in holding that a federal obscenity case may be tried on local community standards, we do violence both to congressional prerogative and to the Constitution. Both of these arguments are foreclosed by our decision last Term in United States v. 12 200-ft. Reels of Film, supra, that the Miller standards, including the "contemporary community standards" formulation, applied to federal legislation. The fact that distributors of allegedly obscene materials may be subjected to varying community standards in the various federal judicial districts into which they transmit the materials does not render a federal statute unconstitutional because of the failure of application of uniform national standards of obscenity. Those same distributors may be subjected to such varying degrees of criminal liability in prosecutions by the States for violations of state obscenity statutes; we see no constitutional impediment to a similar rule for federal prosecutions. In Miller v. California, 413 U.S. at 413 U. S. 32, we cited with approval Mr. Chief Justice Warren's statement:

"[W]hen the Court said in Roth that obscenity is to be defined by reference to 'community standards,' it meant community standards -- not a national standard, as is sometimes argued. I believe that there is no provable 'national standard,' and perhaps there should be none. At all events, this Court has not been able to enunciate one, and it would be unreasonable to expect local courts to divine one. It is said that such a 'community' approach may well result in material's being proscribed as obscene in one community but not in another, and, in all probability, that is true. But communities throughout the Nation are, in fact, diverse, and it must be remembered that, in cases such as this one, the Court is confronted with the task of reconciling conflicting rights of the diverse communities within our society and of individuals."

Jacobellis v. Ohio, 378 U. S. 184, 378 U. S. 200-201 (1964) (dissenting opinion).

Judging the instruction given by the District Court in this case by these principles, there is no doubt that its occasional references to the community standards of the "nation as a whole" delineated a wider geographical area than would be warranted by Miller, 12 200-ft. Reels of Film, and our construction of § 1461 herein, supra at 418 U. S. 105. Whether petitioners were materially prejudiced by those references is a different question. Certainly the giving of such an instruction does not render their convictions void as a matter of constitutional law. This Court has emphasized on more than one occasion that a principal concern in requiring that a judgment be made on the basis of "contemporary community standards" is to assure that the material is judged neither on the basis of each juror's personal opinion nor by its effect on a particularly sensitive or insensitive person or group. Miller v. California, supra, at 413 U. S. 33; Mishkin v. New York, 383 U. S. 502, 383 U. S. 508-509 (1966); Roth v. United States, 354 U.S. at 354 U. S. 489. The District Court's instruction in this case, including its reference to the standards of the "nation as a whole," undoubtedly accomplished this purpose.

We have frequently held that jury instructions are to be judged as a whole, rather than by picking isolated phrases from them. Boyd v. United States, 271 U. S. 104, 271 U. S. 107 (1926). In the unusual posture of this case, in which petitioners agree that the challenged instruction was proper at the time it was given by the District Court, but now seek to claim the benefit of a change in the law which casts doubt on the correctness of portions of it, we hold that reversal is required only where there is a probability that the excision of the references to the "nation as a whole" in the instruction dealing with community standards would have materially affected the deliberations of the jury. Cf. Namet v. United States, 373 U. S. 179, 373 U. S. 190-191 (1963); Lopez v. United States, 373 U. S. 427, 373 U. S. 436 (1963). Our examination of the record convinces us that such a probability does not exist in this case.

Our Brother BRENNAN takes us to task for reaching this conclusion, insisting that the District Court's instructions and its exclusion of the testimony of a witness, Miss Carlsen, who had assertedly conducted a survey of standards in the San Diego area require that petitioners be accorded a new trial. As we have noted, infra at 418 U. S. 124-125, the District Court has wide discretion in its determination to admit and exclude evidence, and this is particularly true in the case of expert testimony. Stillwell Mfg. Co. v. Phelps, 130 U. S. 520, 130 U. S. 527 (1889); Barnes v. Smith, 305 F.2d 226, 232 (CA10 1962); 2 J. Wigmore, Evidence § 561 (3d ed.1940). [10] But even assuming that the District Court may have erred in excluding the witness' testimony in light of the Miller cases, we think arguments made by petitioners' counsel urging the admission of the survey reemphasize the confusing and often gossamer distinctions between "national" standards and other types of standards. Petitioners' counsel, in urging the District Court to admit the survey, stated:

"We have already had experts who have testified, and expect to bring in others who have testified both for the prosecution and the defense that the material that they found was similar in all cities. . . ."

Tr. 3931.

"This witness can testify about experiences she had in one particular city. Whether this is or not a typical city is for the jury to decide."

Id. at 3932.

"Now this supports the national survey. It is not something that stands alone. The findings here are consistent with the national survey and as part of the overall picture, taking into account, of course, that this is something that has taken place after the national survey, which was about two years ago, that Dr. Abelson performed."

Id. at 3934-3935.

The District Court permitted Dr. Wilson, one of the four expert witnesses who testified on behalf of petitioners, to testify as to materials he found available in San Diego, as a result of having spent several days there. Id. at 3575. He was then asked by petitioners' counsel whether this material was "similar to or different than" the material found in other cities where he had also visited adult bookstores. The witness responded that he thought "essentially the same kinds of material are found throughout the United States." Id. at 3577. These statements, in colloquies between counsel and Dr. Wilson, only serve to confirm our conclusion that, while there may have been an error in the District Court's references to the "community standards of the nation as a whole" in its instructions, and in its stated reasons for excluding the testimony of Miss Carlsen, these errors do not require reversal under the standard previously enunciated. [11]

B

Petitioners next argue that, prior to our decision in Miller, 18 U.S.C. § 1461 did not contain in its language, nor had it been construed to apply to, the specific types of sexual conduct referred to in Miller, and therefore the section was unconstitutionally vague as applied to them in the prosecution of these cases. Such an argument, however, not only neglects this Court's decisions prior to Miller rejecting vagueness challenges to the federal statute, but also fundamentally misconceives the thrust of our decision in the Miller cases.

In Roth v. United States, 354 U.S. at 354 U. S. 491, we upheld the constitutionality of 18 U.S.C. § 1461 against a contention that it did "not provide reasonably ascertainable standards of guilt, and therefore violate[s] the constitutional requirements of due process." In noting that the federal obscenity statute made punishable the mailing of material that is "obscene, lewd, lascivious, or filthy . . . [and of] other publication[s] of an indecent character," the Court stated in Roth:

"Many decisions have recognized that these terms of obscenity statutes are not precise. This Court, however, has consistently held that lack of precision is not itself offensive to the requirements of due process. ' . . . [T]he Constitution does not require impossible standards;' all that is required is that the language 'conveys sufficiently definite warning as to the proscribed conduct when measured by common understanding and practices. . . .' United States v. Petrillo, 332 U. S. 1, 332 U. S. 7-8. These words, applied according to the proper standard for judging obscenity, already discussed, give adequate warning of the conduct proscribed and mark"

"... boundaries sufficiently distinct for judges and juries fairly to administer the law. . . . That there may be marginal cases in which it is difficult to determine the side of the line on which a particular fact situation falls is no sufficient reason to hold the language too ambiguous to define a criminal offense. . . ."

"Id. at 332 U. S. 7."

354 U.S. at 354 U. S. 491-492 (footnote omitted). Other decisions dealing with the pre-Miller constitutionality or interpretation of 18 U.S.C. § 1461 in other contexts have not retreated from the language of Roth. See, e.g., United States v. Reidel, 402 U. S. 351 (1971); Ginzburg v. United States, 383 U. S. 463 (1966); Manual Enterprises, Inc. v. Day, 370 U. S. 478 (1962). And as made clear by the opinion of Mr. Justice Harlan in Manual Enterprises, the language of 18 U.S.C. § 1461 had been, prior to the date of our decision in Miller, authoritatively construed in a manner consistent with Miller:

"The words of section 1461, 'obscene, lewd, lascivious, indecent, filthy or vile,' connote something that is portrayed in a manner so offensive as to make it unacceptable under current community mores. While in common usage the words have different shades of meaning, the statute since its inception has always been taken as aimed at obnoxiously debasing portrayals of sex. Although the statute condemns such material irrespective of the effect it may have upon those into whose hands it falls, the early case of United States v. Bennett, 24 Fed.Cas. 1093 (No. 14571), put a limiting gloss upon the statutory language: the statute reaches only indecent material which, as now expressed in Roth v. United States, supra, at 354 U. S. 489, 'taken as a whole, appeals to prurient interest.'"

370 U.S. at 370 U. S. 482-484 (footnotes omitted) (emphasis in original).

At no point does Miller or any of the other obscenity decisions decided last Term intimate that the constitutionality of pre-Miller convictions under statutes such as 18 U.S.C. § 1461 was to be cast in doubt. Indeed, the contrary is readily apparent from the opinions in those cases. We made clear in Miller, 413 U.S. at 413 U. S. 24 n. 6, that our decision was not intended to hold all state statutes inadequate, and we clearly recognized that existing statutes "as construed heretofore or hereafter, may well be adequate." That recognition is emphasized in our opinion in United States v. 12 200-ft. Reels of Film, 413 U. S. 123 (1973). That case had come to this Court on appeal from the District Court's dismissal of the Government's forfeiture action under 19 U.S.C. § 1305(a), which statute the District Court had found unconstitutional. In vacating the District Court's constitutional decision and remanding the case to the District Court for a determination of the obscenity vel non of the materials there involved, we stated:

"We further note that, while we must leave to state courts the construction of state legislation, we do have a duty to authoritatively construe federal statutes where "a serious doubt of constitutionality is raised" and "a construction of the statute is fairly possible by which the question may be avoided.'" United States v. Thirty-seven Photographs, 402 U. S. 363, 402 U. S. 369 (1971) (opinion of WHITE, J.), quoting from Crowell v. Benson, 285 U. S. 22, 285 U. S. 62 (1932). If and when such a "serious doubt" is raised as to the vagueness of the words "obscene," "lewd," "lascivious," "filthy," "indecent," or "immoral" as used to describe regulated material in 19 U.S.C. § 1305(a) and 18 U.S.C. § 1462, see United States v. Orito, [413 U.S.] at 413 U. S. 140 n. 1, we are prepared to construe such terms as limiting regulated material to patently offensive representations or descriptions of that specific "hard core" sexual conduct given as examples in Miller v. California, [413 U.S.] at 413 U. S. 25. See United States v. Thirty-seven Photographs, supra, at 402 U. S. 369-374 (opinion of WHITE, J.). Of course, Congress could always define other specific "hard core" conduct."

413 U.S. at 413 U. S. 130 n. 7. Miller undertook to set forth examples of the types of material which a statute might proscribe as portraying sexual conduct in a patently offensive way, 413 U.S. at 413 U. S. 25-26, and went on to say that no one could be prosecuted for the

"sale or exposure of obscene materials unless these materials depict or describe patently offensive 'hard core' sexual conduct specifically defined by the regulating state law, as written or construed."

Id. at 413 U. S. 27. As noted above, we indicated in United States v. 12 200-ft. Reels of Film, supra, at 413 U. S. 130 n. 7, that we were prepared to construe the generic terms in 18 U.S.C. § 1462 to be limited to the sort of "patently offensive representations or descriptions of that specific hard core' sexual conduct given as examples in Miller v. California." We now so construe the companion provision in 18 U.S.C. § 1461, the substantive statute under which this prosecution was brought. As so construed, we do not believe that petitioners' attack on the statute as unconstitutionally vague can be sustained.

Miller, in describing the type of material which might be constitutionally proscribed, 413 U.S. at 413 U. S. 25, was speaking in terms of substantive constitutional law of the First and Fourteenth Amendments. See Jenkins v. Georgia, post at 418 U. S. 160-161. While the particular descriptions there contained were not intended to be exhaustive, they clearly indicate that there is a limit beyond which neither legislative draftsmen nor juries may go in concluding that particular material is "patently offensive" within the meaning of the obscenity test set forth in the Miller cases. And while the Court in Miller did refer to "specific prerequisites" which "will provide fair notice to a dealer in such materials," 413 U.S. at 413 U. S. 27, the Court immediately thereafter quoted the language of the Court in Roth v. United States, 354 U.S. at 354 U. S. 491-492, concluding with these words:

"'That there may be marginal cases in which it is difficult to determine the side of the line on which a particular fact situation falls is no sufficient reason to hold the language too ambiguous to define a criminal offense. . . .'"

413 U.S. at 413 U. S. 28 n.10.

The Miller cases, important as they were in enunciating a constitutional test for obscenity to which a majority of the Court subscribed for the first time in a number of years, were intended neither as legislative drafting handbooks nor as manuals of jury instructions. Title 18 U.S.C. § 1461 had been held invulnerable to a challenge on the ground of unconstitutional vagueness in Roth; the language of Roth was repeated in Miller, along with a description of the types of material which could constitutionally be proscribed and the adjuration that such statutory proscriptions be made explicit either by their own language or by judicial construction; and United States v. 12 200-ft. Reels of Film, supra, made clear our willingness to construe federal statutes dealing with obscenity to be limited to material such as that described in Miller. It is plain from the Court of Appeals' description of the brochure involved here that it is a form of hard-core pornography well within the types of permissibly proscribed depictions described in Miller, and which we now hold § 1461 to cover. Whatever complaint the distributor of material which presented a more difficult question of obscenity vel non might have as to the lack of a previous limiting construction of 18 U.S.C. § 1461, these petitioners have none. See Dennis v. United States, 341 U. S. 494, 341 U. S. 511-515 (1951) (opinion of Vinson, C.J.).

Nor do we find merit in petitioners' contention that cases such as Bouie v. City of Columbia, 378 U. S. 347 (1964), require reversal of their convictions. The Court in Bouie held that, since the crime for which the petitioners there stood convicted was "not enumerated in the statute" at the time of their conduct, their conviction could not be sustained. Id. at 378 U. S. 363. The Court noted that

"a deprivation of the right of fair warning can result not only from vague statutory language, but also from an unforeseeable and retroactive judicial expansion of narrow and precise statutory language."

Id. at 378 U. S. 352. But the enumeration of specific categories of material in Miller which might be found obscene did not purport to make criminal, for the purpose of 18 U.S.C. § 1461, conduct which had not previously been thought criminal. That requirement instead added a "clarifying gloss" to the prior construction, and therefore made the meaning of the federal statute involved here "more definite" in its application to federal obscenity prosecutions. Bouie v. City of Columbia, supra, at 378 U. S. 353. Judged by both the judicial construction of § 1461 prior to Miller and by the construction of that section which we adopt today in the light of Miller, petitioners' claims of vagueness and lack of fair notice as to the proscription of the material which they were distributing must fail.

C

Petitioners' final Miller-based contention is that our rejection of the third part of the Memoirs test and our revision of that test in Miller indicate that 18 U.S.C. § 1461 was, at the time of their convictions, unconstitutionally vague for the additional reason that it provided insufficient guidance to them as to the proper test of "social value." But our opinion in Miller plainly indicates that we rejected the Memoirs "social value" formulation not because it was so vague as to deprive criminal defendants of adequate notice, but instead because it represented a departure from the definition of obscenity in Roth, and because in calling on the prosecution to "prove a negative," it imposed a "[prosecutorial] burden virtually impossible to discharge" and not constitutionally required. 413 U.S. at 413 U. S. 22. Since Miller permits the imposition of a lesser burden on the prosecution in this phase of the proof of obscenity than did Memoirs, and since the jury convicted these petitioners on the basis of an instruction concededly based on the Memoirs test, petitioners derive no benefit from the revision of that test in Miller.

II

Petitioners attack the sufficiency of the indictment under which they were charged for two reasons: first, that it charged them only in the statutory language of 18 U.S. C § 1461 which they contend was unconstitutionally vague as applied to them, and second, that the indictment failed to give them adequate notice of the charges against them. As noted above, however, at the time of petitioners' convictions, Roth v. United States had held that the language of § 1461 was not "too vague to support conviction for crime." 354 U.S. at 354 U. S. 480. See United States v. Reidel, 402 U.S. at 402 U. S. 354

Our prior cases indicate that an indictment is sufficient if it, first, contains the elements of the offense charged and fairly informs a defendant of the charge against which he must defend, and, second, enables him to plead an acquittal or conviction in bar of future prosecutions for the same offense. Hagner v. United States, 285 U. S. 427 (1932); United States v. Debrow, 346 U. S. 374 (1953). It is generally sufficient that an indictment set forth the offense in the words of the statute itself, as long as

"those words, of themselves, fully, directly, and expressly, without any uncertainty or ambiguity, set forth all the elements necessary to constitute the offence intended to be punished."

United States v. Carll, 105 U. S. 611 612 (1882).

"Undoubtedly the language of the statute may be used in the general description of an offence, but it must be accompanied with such a statement of the facts and circumstances as will inform the accused of the specific offence, coming under the general description, with which he is charged."

United States v. Hess, 124 U. S. 483, 124 U. S. 487 (1888).

Russell v. United States, 369 U. S. 749 (1962), relied upon by petitioners, does not require a finding that the indictment here is insufficient. In Russell, the indictment recited the proscription of 2 U.S.C. § 192, and charged that the defendants had refused to answer questions that "were pertinent to the question then under inquiry" by a committee of Congress. In holding that the indictment was insufficient because it did not state the subject which was under inquiry, this Court stated:

"[T]he very core of criminality under 2 U.S.C. § 192 is pertinency to the subject under inquiry of the questions which the defendant refused to answer. What the subject actually was, therefore, is central to every prosecution under the statute. Where guilt depends so crucially upon such a specific identification of fact, our cases have uniformly held that an indictment must do more than simply repeat the language of the criminal statute."

369 U.S. at 369 U. S. 764 (emphasis added).

The definition of obscenity, however, is not a question of fact, but one of law; the word "obscene," as used in 18 U.S.C. § 1461, is not merely a generic or descriptive term, but a legal term of art. See Roth v. United States, 354 U.S. at 354 U. S. 487-488; Manual Enterprises, Inc. v. Day, 370 U.S. at 370 U. S. 482-487 (opinion of Harlan, J.); United States v. Thevis, 484 F.2d 1149, 1152 (CA5 1973), cert. pending, No. 73-1075; United States v. Luros, 243 F.Supp. 160, 167 (ND Iowa), cert. denied, 382 U.S. 956 (1965). The legal definition of obscenity does not change with each indictment; it is a term sufficiently definite in legal meaning to give a defendant notice of the charge against him. Roth v. United States, supra, at 354 U. S. 491-492; Manual Enterprises, Inc. v. Day, supra, at 370 U. S. 482-487 (opinion of Harlan, J.). Since the various component part of the constitutional definition of obscenity need not be alleged in the indictment in order to establish its sufficiency, the indictment in this case was sufficient to adequately inform petitioners of the charges against them. [12]

Petitioners also contend that, in order for them to be convicted under 18 U.S.C. § 1461 for the crime of mailing obscene materials, the Government must prove that they knew the materials mailed were obscene. That statute provides in pertinent part that "[w]hoever knowingly use the mails for the mailing . . . of anything declared by this section . . . to be nonmailable . . ." is guilty of the proscribed offense. Consistent with the statute, the District Court instructed the jury, inter alia, that, in order to prove specific intent on the part of these petitioners, the Government had to demonstrate that petitioners

"knew the envelopes and packages containing the subject material were mailed or placed . . . in Interstate Commerce, and . . . that they had knowledge of the character of the materials."

App. 236. The District Court further instructed that the "[petitioners'] belief as to the obscenity or non-obscenity of the material is irrelevant." Ibid.

Petitioners contend that this instruction was improper, and that proof of scienter in obscenity prosecutions requires, "at the very least, proof both of knowledge of the contents of the material and awareness of the obscene character of the material." Brief for Petitioner Kemp 31-32. In support of this contention, petitioners urge, as they must, that we overrule our prior decision in Rosen v. United States, 161 U. S. 29 (1896). We decline that invitation, and hold that the District Court in this case properly instructed the jury on the question of scienter.

In Rosen v. United States, supra, this Court was faced with the question of whether, under a forerunner statute to the present 18 U.S.C. § 1461, see Rev.Stat. § 3893, 19 Stat. 90, c. 186, a charge of mailing obscene material mus be supported by evidence that a defendant "knew or believed that such [material] could be properly or justly characterized as obscene. . . ." 161 U.S. at 161 U. S. 41. The Court rejected this contention, stating:

"The statute is not to be so interpreted. The inquiry under the statute is whether the paper charged to have been obscene, lewd, and lascivious was, in fact, of that character, and if it was of that character and was deposited in the mail by one who knew or had notice at the time of its contents, the offence is complete, although the defendant himself did not regard the paper as one that the statute forbade to be carried in the mails. Congress did not intend that the question as to the character of the paper should depend upon the opinion or belief of the person who, with knowledge or notice of its contents, assumed the responsibility of putting it in the mails of the United States. The evils that Congress sought to remedy would continue and increase in volume if the belief of the accused as to what was obscene, lewd, and lascivious was recognized as the test for determining whether the statute has been violated."

Id. at 161 U. S. 41-42. Our subsequent cases have not retreated from this general rule, as a matter of either statutory or constitutional interpretation, nor have they purported to hold that the prosecution must prove a defendant's knowledge of the legal status of the materials he distributes.

In Smith v. California, 361 U. S. 147 (1959), this Court was faced with a challenge to the constitutionality of a Los Angeles ordinance which had been construed by the state courts as making the proprietor of a bookstore absolutely liable criminally for the mere possession in his store of a book later judicially determined to be obscene, even though he had no knowledge of the contents of the book. The Court held that the ordinance could not constitutionally eliminate altogether a scienter requirement, and that, in order to be constitutionally applied to a book distributor, it must be shown that he had "knowledge of the contents of the book." Id. at 361 U. S. 153. The Court further noted that

"[w]e need not and most definitely do not pass today on what sort of mental element is requisite to a constitutionally permissible prosecution of a bookseller for carrying an obscene book in stock."

Id. at 361 U. S. 154.

Smith does not support petitioners' claim in this case, since it dealt with an ordinance which totally dispensed with any proof of scienter on the part of the distributor of obscene material. Nor did the Court's decision in Manual Enterprises, Inc. v. Day, supra, also relied upon by petitioners, suggest otherwise. There Mr. Justice Harlan's opinion, recognizing that scienter was required for a criminal prosecution under 18 U.S.C. § 1461, rejected the Government's contention that such a requirement was unnecessary in an administrative determination by the Post Office Department that certain materials were nonmailable under that section. That opinion concluded that the obscene advertising proscription of the federal statute was not applicable in such an administrative determination unless the publisher of the materials knew that at least some of his advertisers were offering to sell obscene material. Such proof was deemed lacking, and therefore the publishers could not be administratively prohibited from mailing the publications. [13]

Significantly, a substantially similar claim to the instant one was rejected by this Court in Mishkin v. New York, 383 U. S. 502 (1966). In examining a New York statute, the Court there noted that the New York Court of Appeals had "authoritatively interpreted" the statutory provision to require the "vital element of scienter" and that it had defined the required mental element as follows:,

"'A reading of the [New York] statute . . . as a whole clearly indicates that only those who are in some manner aware of the character of the material they attempt to distribute should be punished. It is not innocent, but calculated purveyance of filth which is exorcised. . . .'"

Id. at 383 U. S. 510 (emphasis in original), quoting from People v. Finkelstein, 9 N.Y.2d 342, 344-345, 174 N.E.2d 470, 471 (1961). The Court emphasized that this construction of the New York statute "foreclosed" the defendant's challenge to the statute based on Smith v. California, supra, and stated:

"The Constitution requires proof of scienter to avoid the hazard of self-censorship of constitutionally protected material and to compensate for the ambiguities inherent in the definition of obscenity. The New York definition of the scienter required by [the New York statute] amply serves those ends, and therefore fully meets the demands of the Constitution. Cf. Roth v. United States, 354 U.S. at 354 U. S. 495-496 (WARREN, C.J., concurring)."

383 U.S. at 383 U. S. 511.

The Mishkin holding was reaffirmed in Ginsberg v. New York, 390 U. S. 629 (1968). There, the Court was again faced with the sufficiency of the scienter requirement of another New York statute, which proscribed the "knowing" distribution of obscene materials to minors. "Knowingly" was defined in the statute as "knowledge" of, or "reason to know" of, the character and content of the material. Citing Mishkin, and the New York Court of Appeals' construction of the other similar statutory language, the Court rejected the challenge to the scienter provision.

We think the "knowingly" language of 18 U.S.C. § 1461, and the instructions given by the District Court in this case satisfied the constitutional requirements of scienter. It is constitutionally sufficient that the prosecution show that a defendant had knowledge of the contents of the materials he distributed, and that he knew the character and nature of the materials. To require proof of a defendant's knowledge of the legal status of the materials would permit the defendant to avoid prosecution by simply claiming that he had not brushed up on the law. Such a formulation of the scienter requirement is required neither by the language of 18 U.S.C. § 1461 nor by the Constitution.

"Whenever the law draws a line, there will be cases very near each other on opposite sides. The precise course of the line may be uncertain, but no one can come near it without knowing that he does so, if he thinks, and if he does so, it is familiar to the criminal law to make him take the risk."

United States v. Wurzbach, 280 U. S. 396, 280 U. S. 399 (1930).

Petitioners also make a broad attack on the sufficiency of the evidence. The general rule of application is that "[t]he verdict of a jury must be sustained if there is substantial evidence, taking the view most favorable to the Government, to support it." Glasser v. United States, 315 U. S. 60, 315 U. S. 80 (1942). The primary responsibility for reviewing the sufficiency of the evidence to support a criminal conviction rests with the Court of Appeals, which in this case held that the Government had satisfied its burden. We agree. Based on the evidence before it, the jury was entitled to conclude that the individual petitioners, as corporate officials directly concerned with the activities of their organizations, were aware of the mail solicitation scheme, and of the contents of the brochure. The evidence is likewise sufficient to establish the existence of a conspiracy to mail the obscene brochure. The existence of an agreement may be shown by circumstances indicating that criminal defendants acted in concert to achieve a common goal. See, e.g., Blumenthal v. United States, 332 U. S. 539, 332 U. S. 556-558 (1947).

III

We turn now to petitioners' attack on certain evidentiary rulings of the District Court. Petitioners have very much the laboring oar in showing that such rulings constitute reversible error, since,

"in judicial trials, the whole tendency is to leave rulings as to the illuminating relevance of testimony largely to the discretion of the trial court that hears the evidence."

NLRB v. Donnelly Co., 330 U. S. 219, 330 U. S. 236 (1947); Michelson v. United States, 335 U. S. 469, 335 U. S. 480 (1948); Salem v. United States Lines Co., 370 U. S. 31, 370 U. S. 35 (1962).

Petitioners offered in evidence at trial three categories of allegedly comparable materials argued to be relevant to community standards: (1) materials which had received second-class mailing privileges; (2) materials which had previously been the subject of litigation and had been found to be "constitutionally protected"; and (3) materials openly available on the newsstands. The District Court, after examining the materials, refused to admit them into evidence on the grounds that "they tend to confuse the jury," and "would serve no probative value in comparison to the amount of confusion and deluge of material that could result therefrom." App. 158. The Court of Appeals concluded that the District Court was correct in rejecting the proffered evidence, stating that any abuse of discretion in refusing to admit the materials themselves had been "cured by the District Court's offer to entertain expert testimony with respect to the element to be shown for the advice of the jury." 481 F.2d at 320. Here, the District Court permitted four expert witnesses called by petitioners to testify extensively concerning the relevant community standards.

The defendant in an obscenity prosecution, just as a defendant in any other prosecution, is entitled to an opportunity to adduce relevant, competent evidence bearing on the issues to be tried. But the availability of similar materials on the newsstands of the community does not automatically make them admissible as tending to prove the nonobscenity of the materials which the defendant is charged with circulating. As stated by the Court of Appeals, the mere fact that materials similar to the brochure at issue here "are for sale and purchased at book stores around the country does not make them witnesses of virtue." Ibid. Or, as put by the Court of Appeals in United States v. Manarite, 448 F.2d 583 (CA2 1971):

"Mere availability of similar material, by itself, means nothing more than that other persons are engaged in similar activities."

Id. at 593.

Nor do we think the District Court erred in refusing petitioners' offer of a magazine which had received a second-class mailing privilege. [14] While federal law, see former 39 U.S.C. § 4354 (1964 ed.); 39 CFR Pt. 132 (1973), may lay down certain standards for the issuance of a second-class mailing permit, this Court has held that these standards give postal inspectors no power of censorship., Hannegan v. Esquire, Inc., 327 U. S. 146 (1946). The mere fact that a publication has acquired a second-class mailing privilege does not therefore create any presumption that it is not obscene.

Finally, we do not think the District Court abused its discretion in refusing to admit certain allegedly comparable materials, a film and two magazines, [15] which had been found to be nonobscene by this Court. See Pinkus v. Pitchess, 429 F.2d 416 (CA), aff'd sub nom. California v. Pinkus, 400 U.S. 922 (1970); Burgin v. South Carolina, 404 U.S. 806 (1971), rev'g 255 S.C. 237, 178 S.E.2d 325 (1970). A judicial determination that particular matters are not obscene does not necessarily make them relevant to the determination of the obscenity of other materials, much less mandate their admission into evidence.

Much of the material offered by petitioners was not of demonstrated relevance to the issues in this case. Such of it as may have been clearly relevant was subject to the District Court's observation that it would tend to create more confusion than enlightenment in the minds of the jury, and to the court's expressed willingness to permit the same material to be treated in the testimony of expert witnesses. The District Court retains considerable latitude even with admittedly relevant evidence in rejecting that which is cumulative, and in requiring that which is to be brought to the jury's attention to be done so in a manner least likely to confuse that body. We agree with the Court of Appeals that the District Court's discretion was not abused. [16]

Petitioners' second contention is that the District Court erred in instructing the jury as to the determination of the prurient appeal of the brochure. At the trial, the Government introduced, over petitioners' objection, testimony from an expert witness that the material in the Illustrated Report appealed to the prurient interest of various deviant sexual groups. [17] The testimony concerning the brochure was that it appealed to a prurient interest in general, and not specifically to some deviant group. Petitioners concede, however, that each of the pictures said to appeal to deviant groups did, in fact, appear in the brochure. [18] The District Court accordingly instructed the jury that, in deciding whether the predominant appeal of the Illustrated Report and the brochure was to a prurient interest in sex, it could consider whether some portions of those materials appealed to a prurient interest of a specifically defined deviant group as well as whether they appealed to the prurient interest of the average person. App. 239-241. The Court of Appeal found no error in the instruction, since it was "manifest that the District Court considered that some of the portrayals in the Brochure might be found to have a prurient appeal" to a deviant group. 481 F.2d at 321.

Petitioner contend that the District Court's instruction was improper because it allowed the jury to measure the brochure by its appeal to the prurient interest not only of the average person, but also of a clearly defined deviant group. Our decision in Mishkin v. New York, 383 U. S. 502 (1966), clearly indicates that, in measuring the prurient appeal of allegedly obscene materials, i.e., whether the "dominant theme of the material taken as a whole appeal to a prurient interest in sex," consideration may be given to the prurient appeal of the material to clearly defined deviant sexual groups. Petitioners appear to argue that, if some of the material appeals to the prurient interest of sexual deviants while other parts appeal to the prurient interest of the average person, a general finding that the material appeal to a prurient interest in sex is somehow precluded. But we stated in Mishkin v. New York:

"Where the material is designed for and primarily disseminated to a clearly defined deviant sexual group, rather than the public at large, the prurient appeal requirement of the Roth test is satisfied if the dominant theme of the material taken as a whole appeals to the prurient interest in sex of the members of that group. The reference to the 'average' or 'normal' person in Roth, 354 U.S. at 354 U. S. 489-490, does not foreclose this holding. . . . We adjust the prurient appeal requirement to social realities by permitting the appeal of this type of material to be assessed in terms of the sexual interests of its intended and probable recipient group; and since our holding require that the recipient group be defined with more specificity than in terms of sexually immature persons, it also avoids the inadequacy of the 'most susceptible person' facet of the [Rena v.] Hicklin [[1868] L.R. 3 Q.B. 360] test."

383 U.S. at 383 U. S. 508-509 (footnotes omitted). The District Court's instruction was consistent with this statement in Mishkin. The jury was instructed that it must find that the materials as a whole appealed generally to a prurient interest in sex. In making that determination, the jury was properly instructed that it should measure the prurient appeal of the materials as to all groups. Such an instruction was also consistent with our recent decision in the Miller cases. We stated in Miller:

"As the Court made clear in Mishkin v. New York, 383 U.S. at 383 U. S. 508-509, the primary concern with requiring a jury to apply the standard of 'the average person, applying contemporary community standards' is to be certain that, so far as material is not aimed at a deviant group, it will be judged by its impact on an average person, rather than a particularly susceptible or sensitive person -- or indeed a totally insensitive one."

413 U.S. at 413 U. S. 33 (emphasis added).

Finally, we similarly think petitioners' challenge to the pandering instruction given by the District Court is without merit. The District Court instructed the jurors that they must apply the three-part test of the plurality opinion in Memoirs v. Massachusetts, 383 U.S. at 383 U. S. 418, and then indicated that the jury could, in applying that test, if it found the case to be close, also consider whether the materials had been pandered, by looking to their "[m]anner of distribution, circumstances of production, sale, . . . advertising. . . . [and] editorial intent. . . ." App. 245. This instruction was given with respect to both the Illustrated Report and the brochure which advertised it, both of which were at issue in the trial.

Petitioners contend that the instruction was improper on the facts adduced below, and that it caused them to be "convicted" of pandering. Pandering was not charged in the indictment of the petitioners, but it is not, of course, an element of the offense of mailing obscene matter under 18 U.S.C. § 1461. The District Court's instruction was clearly consistent with our decision in Ginzburg v. United States, 383 U. S. 463 (1966), which held that evidence of pandering could be relevant in the determination of the obscenity of the materials at issue, as long as the proper constitutional definition of obscenity is applied. Nor does the enactment by Congress of 39 U.S.C. § 3008, enabling the Postal Service to cease forwarding pandering advertisements at the request of an addressee, authorize, as contended by petitioners, the pandering of obscene advertisements. That statute simply gives a postal recipient the means to insulate himself from advertisements which offer for sale matter "which the addressee in his sole discretion believes to be erotically arousing or sexually provocative," by instructing the Post Office to order the sender to refrain from mailing any further advertisements to him. See Rowan v. U.S. Post Office Dept., 397 U. S. 728 (1970). The statute does not purport to authorize the mailing of legally obscene pandering advertisements, which continues to be proscribed by 18 U.S.C. § 1461. See 39 U.S.C. § 3011(e).

IV

Petitioners' final contentions are directed at alleged procedural irregularities said to have occurred during the course of the trial.

They first contend that the District Court committed reversible error by denying their request to make additional objections to the court's instructions to the jury out of the presence of the jury. Prior to closing arguments and instructions to the jury, the parties had made a record with respect to the instructions which the Court indicated it would give. After argument and instructions, but before the jury had retired, petitioners' counsel approached the bench and requested that the jury be excused in order that he might present further objections to the charge. The court declined to excuse the jury, saying:

"You have made all the objections suitable that I can think of. I want to send this Jury out. If you want to make a statement, make a statement."

App. 257.

Petitioners contend that the court's refusal to excuse the jury violated the provisions of Fed.Rule Crim.Proc. 30, and requires reversal. Rule 30 provides:

"At the close of the evidence or at such earlier time during the trial as the court reasonably directs, any party may file written requests that the court instruct the jury on the law as set forth in the requests.

At the same time, copies of such requests shall be furnished to adverse parties. The court shall inform counsel of its propose action upon the requests prior to their arguments to the jury, but the court shall instruct the jury after the arguments are completed. No party may assign as error any portion of the charge or omission therefrom unless he objects thereto before the jury retires to consider its verdict, stating distinctly the matter to which he objects and the grounds of his objection. Opportunity shall be given to make the objection out of the hearing of the jury and, on request of any party, out of the presence of the jury."

(Emphasis added.)

Nothing in Rule 30 transfers from the district court to counsel the function of deciding at what point in the trial, consistent with established practice, counsel shall be given the opportunity required by Rule 30 to make a record on the instructions given by the court. But when counsel, at the close of the court's instruction to the jury, indicates that he wishes to make objections of a kind which could not previously have been brought to the court's attention, he runs the risk of waiving a claim of error under the fourth sentence of the Rule unless the court indicates that it will permit such objections to be made after the jury retires. Since the court here asked counsel for comments, and did not indicate that it would permit objections which could not have been previously formulated to be made after the jury retired, we agree with the Court of Appeals that the District Court erred in refusing to permit such objections to be made out of the presence of the jury. We also agree with the Court of Appeals' conclusion that such procedural error does not mandate reversal.

The courts of appeals have taken varying approaches to the question of when a failure to comply with the provisions of Rule 30 constitutes reversible error. [19] Some appear to have applied a general rule that such a violation is not reversible error unless the defendant demonstrates that he has been prejudiced. United States v. Hall, 200 F.2d 957 (CA2 1953); United States v. Titus, 221 F.2d 571 (CA2), cert. denied, 350 U.S. 832 (1955); United States v. Fernandez, 456 F.2d 638 (CA2 1972); Hodges v. United States, 243 F.2d 281 (CA5 1957); Sultan v. United States, 249 F.2d 385 (CA5 1957). Others appear to have adopted a rule whereby a violation is not reversible error where it affirmatively appears that the defendant was not prejudiced. United States v. Schartner, 426 F.2d 470 (CA3 1970); Lovely v. United States, 169 F.2d 386 (CA4 1948). At least one Court of Appeals appears to take the position that the failure to comply with Rule 30 is automatic grounds for reversal, regardless of attenuating circumstances. Hall v. United States, 378 F.2d 349 (CA10 1967).

The Court of Appeals in this case felt that the rule announced by the Third Circuit in United States v. Schartner, supra, was the appropriate one for application where Rule 30 has not been complied with. The court in Schartner held that a District Court's failure to comply with the "out of the presence of the jury" requirement of Rule 30, upon proper request by a party, constitutes reversible error "unless it be demonstrable on an examination of the whole record that the denial of the right did not prejudice" the defendant's case. 426 F.2d at 480. Applying that rule, the Court of Appeals here concluded that there was no prejudice to any of the petitioners as a result of the District Court's failure to comply with Rule 30.

The language in Rule 30 at issue here was added to that Rule by a 1966 amendment; prior to that time, the Rule had only provided that a party should be given the opportunity to make the objection out of the hearing of the jury. The significance of the change was not elaborated by the Advisory Committee in its note accompanying the Rule, which merely mentioned the change. Courts examining the Rule have found that it is principally designed to avoid the subtle psychological pressures upon the jurors which would arise if they were to view and hear defense counsel in a posture of apparent antagonism toward the judge. Lovely v. United States, supra, at 391; Hodges v. United States, supra, at 283-284; United States v. Schartner, supra, at 479. While that goal might be served in many cases by a sufficiently low-tone bench conference, the ultimate way to assure the goal is to comply with the Rule.

Petitioners urge that we adopt a strict approach and declare that any noncompliance with the Rule requires reversal. We think such an approach would be unduly mechanical, and would be inconsistent with interpretation in pari materia of Rule 30 and other relevant provisions of the Federal Rules of Criminal Procedure, since Rule 52(a) specifically provides that "[a]ny error, defect, irregularity or variance which does not affect substantial rights shall be disregarded." This provision suggests the soundness of an approach similar to that of the Court of Appeals here and the various other Courts of Appeals, supra, which have in some manner examined the prejudice to the defendant in deciding whether reversal is required where there is a failure to comply with Rule 30.

We conclude that the Court of Appeals did not err in refusing to reverse petitioners' convictions for the failure to comply with the provisions of Rule 30. The Court of Appeals felt that it should apply the somewhat stricter test of the Schartner case, supra; the court felt that "the rule of Fernandez, [456 F.2d 638 (CA2 1972),] places a burden upon a defendant in a criminal case that he may not be able to carry." 481 F.2d at 324. Applying the Schartner test, the Court of Appeals determined that there was no prejudice to petitioners from the failure to hold the instruction objection session out of the presence of the jury. Our independent examination of that bench conference convinces us that the holding of the Court of Appeals was correct. The bench conference was one of many at the trial, and there is no indication in the record that the discussion was heard by the jury. The colloquy between petitioners' counsel and the court concerned purely legal issues, App. 257-265, and the District Court had prior to that point indicated its rulings with respect to the instructions requested by counsel. We express no view, of course, as to whether a court of appeals may follow the apparently more lenient standard of requiring the defendant to demonstrate that he was prejudiced. See United States v. Fernandez, 456 F.2d at 643-644.

Petitioners' second procedural contention is that the trial jury was improperly constituted because an allegedly cognizable class of citizens, "young adults," which petitioners define as those between the ages of 18 and 24 years, were systematically excluded. [20] Petitioners therefore argue that the District Court abused its discretion in refusing to grant a continuance until a new jury, which would have presumably contained a greater ratio of young persons, was drawn.

At the time of petitioners' indictment and trial, the jury selection plan of the Southern District of California, adopted pursuant to 28 U.S.C. §§ 1863(b)(2) and (4), 82 Stat. 55, provided for the periodic emptying and refilling of the master jury wheel from voter registration lists. At that point, it had been slightly less than four years since the jury wheel in the District had last been filled. Petitioners' argument is that, because the jury wheel had last been filled in 1968, the youngest potential juror for their trial was at least 24 years old. The petitioner called as a witness the Clerk of the Southern District of California, who testified that, within one month, the master wheel would be refilled with the names of persons who then appeared on the voters' registration list, and that the master list would then contain the names of persons 21 years of age and over. Tr. 94-98. A 1972 amendment to 28 U.S.C. § 1863(b)(4) (1970 ed., Supp. II) provided that the periodic emptying and refilling of the master wheel should occur at specified intervals, "not [to] exceed four years." Pub.L. No. 9269, § 2, 86 Stat. 117. The District Court denied petitioners' motion to strike the venire, but stated that the evidence presented indicated that "it is time to change the jury master wheel." Tr. 93. The petitioners then moved for a continuance of approximately one month, so that their jury would be drawn from a master wheel that included the names of persons 21 years of age or over. Id. at 998. The District Court denied the motion.

The Court of Appeals assumed, without deciding, that the young do constitute a cognizable group or class, but concluded that petitioners had

"failed to show, let alone establish, a purposeful systematic exclusion of the members of that class whose names, but for such systematic exclusion, would otherwise be selected for the matter jury wheel,"

and therefore that the District Court's refusal to grant a continuance was not an abuse of discretion. 481 F.2d at 314. We agree with the Court of Appeals.

Petitioners do not cite case authority for the proposition that the young are an identifiable group entitled to a group-based protection under our prior cases, see Hernandez v. Texas, 347 U. S. 475, 347 U. S. 479-480 (1954); claims of exclusion of the young from juries have met with little success in the federal courts. [21] Assuming, as did the Court of Appeals, that the young are such a group, we do not believe that there is evidence in this case sufficient to make out a prima facie case of discrimination which would, in turn, place the burden on the Government to overcome it. The master wheel under the Southern District of California plan, as under plans in other judicial districts, is periodically emptied and then refilled with names from the available voter lists. Persons added to the voter lists subsequent to one filling of the jury wheel are therefore not added to the wheel until the next refilling. But some play in the joints of the jury selection process is necessary in order to accommodate the practical problems of judicial administration. Congress could reasonably adopt procedures which, while designed to assure that "an impartial jury [is] drawn from a cross-section of the community," Thiel v. Southern Pacific Co., 328 U. S. 217, 328 U. S. 220 (1946); Smith v. Texas, 311 U. S. 128, 311 U. S. 130 (1940), at the same time take into account practical problems in judicial administration. Unless we were to require the daily refilling of the jury wheel, Congress may necessarily conclude that some periodic delay in updating the wheel is reasonable to permit the orderly administration of justice. [22] Invariably, of course, as time goes on, the jury wheel will be more and more out of date, especially near the end of the statutorily prescribed time period for updating the wheel. But if the jury wheel is not discriminatory when completely updated at the time of each refilling, a prohibited "purposeful discrimination" does not arise near the end of the period simply because the young and other persons have belatedly become eligible for jury service by becoming registered voters. Whitus v. Georgia, 385 U. S. 545, 385 U. S. 551 (1967); see Avery v. Georgia, 345 U. S. 559 (1953); Alexander v. Louisiana, 405 U. S. 625 (1972). Since petitioners failed to establish a discriminatory exclusion of the young from their jury, the District Court properly exercised its discretion in refusing to grant petitioners' motion for a continuance.

Petitioners' third procedural contention is that the District Court erred in refusing to ask certain questions on voir dire concerning possible religious and other biases of the jurors. [23] Specifically, petitioners requested the court to ask questions as to whether the jurors' educational, political, and religious beliefs might affect their views on the question of obscenity. App. 781. The Court of Appeals concluded that the District Court's examination on the voir dire of the prospective jurors "was full, complete and . . . fair to the [petitioners] as contemplated by Rule 24(a), Federal Rules of Criminal Procedure." 481 F.2d at 314. Noting that petitioners had requested the submission of numerous questions to the petit panel, the Court of Appeals stated:

"The District Court asked many of the questions as submitted, many in altered and consolidated form, and declined to ask many others which were cumulative and argumentative. The handling of those questions not asked was clearly within the range of the District Court's discretion in the matter, and no clear abuse of the discretion nor prejudice to the [petitioners] has been shown."

Ibid.

We agree with the Court of Appeals. Federal Rule Crim.Proc. 24(a) permits a district court to conduct the voir dire examination, making such use of questions submitted by the parties as it deems proper. The District Court here asked questions similar to many of those submitted by petitioners, and its examination was clearly sufficient to test the qualifications and competency of the prospective jurors. Petitioners' reliance on this Court's decisions in Aldridge v. United States, 283 U. S. 308 (1931), and Ham v. South Carolina, 409 U. S. 524 (1973), is misplaced. Those cases held that, in certain situations, a judge must inquire into possible racial prejudices of the jurors in order to satisfy the demands of due process. But in Ham v. South Carolina, supra, we also rejected a claim that the trial judge had erred in refusing to ask the jurors about potential bias against beards, noting our inability "to constitutionally distinguish possible prejudice against beards from a host of other possible similar prejudices. . . ." Id. at 409 U. S. 528. Here, as in Ham, the trial judge made a general inquiry into the jurors' general views concerning obscenity. Failure to ask specific questions as to the possible effect of educational, political, and religious biases did "not reach the level of a constitutional violation," ibid., nor was it error requiring the exercise of our supervisory authority over the administration of justice in the federal courts. We hold that the District Court acted within its discretion in refusing to ask the questions.

The judgment of the Court of Appeals for the Ninth Circuit in this case is Affirmed.

Notes

[1] The indictment is reproduced in full at App. 14-31.

[2] Each petitioner was convicted on counts 1-5 and 7-13 of the indictment. App. 9. Petitioner Hamling was sentenced to imprisonment for one year on the conspiracy count, and consecutive to that, concurrent terms of three years each on the 11 substantive counts, and he was fined $32,000. Petitioner Kemp was sentenced to imprisonment for one year and one day on the conspiracy count, and consecutive to that, concurrent terms of two years each on the 11 substantive counts. Petitioners Wright and Thomas received suspended sentences of one and one-half years, and were placed on probation for five years. Petitioners Reed Enterprises, Inc., and Library Services, Inc., were fined $43,000 and $12,000, respectively.

[3] Those counts on which the jury was unable to reach a verdict and upon which a mistrial was declared were counts 15, 16, 17, 19, and 21. App. 10. After presentation of the Government's case, the District Court dismissed four of the substantive counts (6, 14, 18, and 20) for lack of proof. App. 7; Brief for United States 6 n. 4. The obscenity vel non of the Illustrated Report was thus not at issue in the Court of Appeals, nor is it at issue in this Court.

[4] The only printed words appearing on the interfold of pictures are:

"In the Katzman Studies (1970) for the Commission (see page 180), some 90 photographs were rated on five-point scales for 'obscene' and 'sexually stimulating' by the control group. Group activity scenes of the type here illustrated could have been part of the 90. Both these group sex pictures are from the Danish magazine Porno Club No. 3, supposedly this was filmed at a 'live show' night club in Copenhagen. There are many similar clubs."

[5] Greenleaf Classics, Inc., was also indicted, but was acquitted on the counts involving the brochure, including the conspiracy count. As mentioned above, the jury was unable to reach a verdict on the counts involving the Illustrated Report. See n 3, supra.

[6] Paris Adult Theatre I v. Slaton, 413 U. S. 49 (1973); Kaplan v. California, 413 U. S. 115 (1973); United States v. 12 200-ft. Reels of Film, 413 U. S. 123 (1973); United States v. Orito, 413 U. S. 139 (1973).

[7] Upon withdrawing the original order denying rehearing for reconsideration in light of Miller v. California, supra, and the related cases, the Court of Appeals stated (Pet. for Cert. App. 39-40):

"We heretofore determined that the evidence was abundantly sufficient to meet, and the District Court's jury instructions in full compliance with, the essential elements of the Roth-Memoirs test. United States v. One Reel of Film, et al., ___ F.2d ___ (1st Cir. July 16, 1973, No. 73-1181) at pages 5 and 7 of the slip opinion, in considering the same problem, succinctly states:"

" A fortiori, the more relaxed standards announced by the Supreme Court were met."

" [W]e see no possible reason to remand, especially as the Supreme Court has just addressed itself to the construction and adequacy of the federal statute involved. See United States v. 12 200-Ft. Reels of Super 8mm. Film, supra, 41 U.S.L.W. at 4963, n. 7.'"

[8] Title 18 U.S.C. . § 1461 provides in pertinent part:

"Every obscene, lewd, lascivious, indecent, filthy or vile article, matter, thing, device, or substance; and --"

"* * * *"

"Every written or printed card, letter, circular, book, pamphlet, advertisement, or notice of any kind giving information, directly or indirectly, where, or how, or from whom, or by what means any of such mentioned matters, articles, or things may be obtained or made. . . . "

"* * * *"

"Is declared to be nonmailable matter and shall not be conveyed in the mails or delivered from any post office or by any letter carrier."

"Whoever knowingly uses the mails for the mailing, carriage in the mails, or delivery of anything declared by this section or section 3001(e) of Title 39 to be nonmailable, or knowingly causes to be delivered by mail according to the direction thereon, or at the place at which it is directed to be delivered by the person to whom it is addressed, or knowingly takes any such thing from the mails for the purpose of circulating or disposing thereof, or of aiding in the circulation or disposition thereof, shall be fined not more than $5,000 or imprisoned not more than five years, or both, for the first such offense, and shall be fined not more than $10,000 or imprisoned not more than ten years, or both, for each such offense thereafter. . . ."

[9] United States v. Orito, 413 U. S. 139 (1973); United States v. 12 200-ft. Reels of Film, 413 U. S. 123 (173).

[10] The stated basis for the District Court's exclusion of the testimony of Miss Carlsen was that her survey was not framed in terms of "national" standards, but it is not at all clear that the District Court would have admitted her testimony had it been so

framed. "[A] specific objection sustained . . . is sufficient, though naming an untenable ground, if some other tenable one existed." 1 J. Wigmore, Evidence § 18, p. 32 (3d ed.1940), citing Kansas City S. R. Co. v. Jones, 241 U. S. 181 (1916). Miss Carlsen was a student at San Diego State University who worked part time at F. W. Woolworth, doing composition layouts of newspaper advertising for the company's store in Fashion Valley. She had undertaken a "Special Studies" course with her journalism professor, Mr. Haberstroh, who was also offered by petitioners as an expert witness at the trial. Miss Carlsen had circulated through the San Diego area and asked various persons at random whether they thought "adults should be able to buy and view this book and material." Tr. 3926.

[11] The sequence of events in this case is quite different from that, in Saunders v. Shaw, 244 U. S. 317 (1917), upon which our Brother BRENNAN relies. There, the Supreme Court of Louisiana directed the entry of judgment against an intervening defendant who had prevailed in the trial court, on the basis of testimony adduced merely as an offer of proof by the plaintiff, and to which the intervening defendant had therefore had no occasion to respond. Since the trial court had ruled that the issue to which plaintiff's proof was addressed was irrelevant, this Court reversed the Supreme Court of Louisiana in order that the intervening defendant might have an opportunity to controvert the plaintiff's proof. Here, petitioners were given full latitude in rebutting every factual issue dealt with in the Government's case, and no claim is made that the jury was permitted to rely on evidence introduced merely by way of offer of proof which was not subject to cross-examination or to contradiction by countervailing evidence offered by the petitioners. The present case seems to us much closer to Ginzburg v. United States, 383 U. S. 463 (1966), than to Saunders.

[12] Petitioners' further contention that our remand to the District Court in United States v. Orito, 413 U. S. 139 (1973), for reconsideration of the sufficiency of the indictment in light of Miller and United States v. 12 200-ft. Reels of Film, indicates that the sufficiency of their indictment is in question misses the mark. In Orito, we reviewed a District Court judgment which had dismissed an indictment under 18 U.S.C. § 1462, and held the statute unconstitutional. In upholding the statute and vacating the judgment of the District Court, we remanded the case for reconsideration of the indictment in light of Miller and 12 200-ft. Reels, which had, of course, enunciated new standards for state and federal obscenity prosecutions, and for reconsideration in light of our opinion reversing the District Court's holding that the statute was unconstitutional. Here, of course, the District Court and the Court of Appeals have already upheld both the sufficiency of the indictment and the constitutionality of 18 U.S.C. § 1461, and we agree with their rulings.

[13] MR. JUSTICE BRENNAN, joined by Mr. Chief Justice Warren and MR. JUSTICE DOUGLAS, concluded that 18 U.S.C. § 1461 does not authorize the Postmaster General to employ any administrative process of his own to close the mails to matter which, in his view, falls within the ban of that section. Manual Enterprises, Inc. v. Day, 370 U. S. 478, 370 U. S. 495-519 (1962) (separate opinion).

[14] The magazine offered was entitled Nude Living, No. 63. The foundation alleged for its admissibility was that it had received a second-class mailing privilege. App. 212-213.

[15] Brief for Petitioner Kemp 69.

[16] Other proffered materials, alleged to be comparable, included numerous magazines and films, and also the survey (see n 10, supra) conducted by the student at San Diego State University of the reactions of people in the San Diego area to the Illustrated Report and the brochure. Brief for Petitioner Kemp 64-71.

[17] Petitioners also contend that this evidence was at variance with the Government's answer to their Bill of Particulars. Brief for Petitioner Hamling 450. The Court of Appeals assumed, without deciding, that such evidence did constitute a variance, but concluded that

"such variance was in no wise a surprise or prejudice to the defendants, as their own expert opinion testimony interwove and covered the same field completely."

481 F.2d at 322. We agree with the Court of Appeals.

[18] Brief for Petitioner Hamling 49-50.

[19] Federal Rule Civ.Proc. 51 states that "[o]pportunity shall be given to make the objection out of the hearing of the jury." Though the "out of the presence of the jury" language is not contained in that Rule, the Advisory Committee's note attending Fed.Rule Crim.Proc. 30 states that it is to

"correspond to Rule 51 of the Federal Rules of Civil Procedure. . . . It seemed appropriate that, on a point such as instructions to juries there should be no difference in procedure between civil and criminal cases."

The Government argues that, in considering whether failure to comply with Fed.Rule Crim.Proc. 30 requires reversal, the appropriate test should be similar to the general standard of consideration where there is a failure to comply with Fed.Rule Civ.Proc. 51, i.e., reversal is required

"if there is reasonable basis for concluding that the colloquy had in the presence of the jury as a result of the judge's ignoring or denying a proper request was prejudicial."

Swain v. Boeing Airplane Co., 337 F.2d 940, 943 (CA2 1964), cert. denied, 380 U.S. 951 (1965). This approach was used by a panel of the Court of Appeal for the Second Circuit in a case involving failure to comply with Fed.Rule Crim.Proc. 30. United States v. Fernandez, 456 F.2d 638 (1972).

[20] In connection with their motion to strike the venire, petitioners introduced evidence which they contended established that

"young persons were a cognizable group, and that they were more tolerant than older persons in matters pertaining to the depiction of sexually explicit material."

Brief for Petitioner Hamling 88.

[21] See, e.g., United States v. Butera, 420 F.2d 564 (CA1 1970); United States v. Camara, 451 F.2d 1122 (CA1 1971); United States v. Gooding, 473 F.2d 425 (CA5 1973); United States v. Kuhn, 441 F.2d 179 (CA5 1971); United States v. Gast, 457 F.2d 141 (CA7,

cert. denied, 406 U.S. 969 (1972).

[22] Various delays in refilling jury wheels have been upheld by the federal courts. E.g., United States v. Pentado, 463 F.2d 355 (CA5 1972) (three years); United States v. Gooding, supra, (three years, four months); United States v. Kuhn, supra, (five years).

[23] Petitioners also contend that certain actions of the Government's attorney before the grand jury prejudiced that body against them. The Court of Appeals, in rejecting this contention, stated:

"The record before us is totally lacking of any evidence or showing of any kind that any member of the Grand Jury was biased or prejudiced in any degree against any of the [petitioners], except only a supposition as to how the members may have reacted upon a view of the Brochure and Report. The presumption of regularity which attaches to Grand Jury proceedings still abides. . . . [T]he assignment has no merit."

481 F.2d at 313 (citations omitted). We agree with the Court of Appeals.

## Jenkins v. Georgia (June 24, 1974)

MR. JUSTICE REHNQUIST delivered the opinion of the Court.

Appellant was convicted in Georgia of the crime of distributing obscene material. His conviction, in March 1972, was for showing the film "Carnal Knowledge" in a movie theater in Albany, Georgia. The jury that found appellant guilty was instructed on obscenity pursuant to the Georgia statute, which defines obscene material in language similar to that of the definition of obscenity set forth in this Court's plurality opinion in Memoirs v. Massachusetts, 383 U.S. 413, 418 (1966):

"Material is obscene if considered as a whole, applying community standards, its predominant appeal is to prurient interest, that is, a shameful or morbid interest in nudity, sex or excretion, and utterly without redeeming social value and if, in addition, it goes substantially beyond customary limits of candor in describing or representing such matters." Ga. Code Ann. 26-2101 (b) (1972). 1

We hold today in Hamling v. United States, ante, p. 87, that defendants convicted prior to the announcement of our Miller decisions but whose convictions were on direct appeal at that time should receive any benefit available to them from those decisions. We conclude here that the film "Carnal Knowledge" is not obscene under the constitutional standards announced in Miller v. California, 413 U.S. 15 (1973), and that the First and Fourteenth Amendments therefore require that the judgment of the Supreme Court of Georgia affirming appellant's conviction be reversed.

Appellant was the manager of the theater in which "Carnal Knowledge" was being shown. While he was exhibiting the film on January 13, 1972, local law enforcement officers seized it pursuant to a search warrant. Appellant was later charged by accusation, Ga. Code Ann. 27-704 (1972), with the offense of distributing obscene material. 2 After his trial in the Superior Court of Dougherty County, the jury, having seen the film and heard testimony, returned a general verdict of guilty on March 23, 1972. 3 Appellant was fined $750 and sentenced to 12 months' probation. He appealed to the Supreme Court of Georgia, which by a divided vote affirmed the judgment of conviction on July 2, 1973. That court stated that the definition of obscenity contained in the Georgia statute was "considerably more restrictive" than the new test set forth in the recent case of Miller v. California, supra, and that the First Amendment does not protect the commercial exhibition of "hard core" pornography. The dissenting Justices, in addition to other disagreements with the court, thought that "Carnal Knowledge" was entitled to the protection of the First and Fourteenth Amendments. Appellant then appealed to this Court and we noted probable jurisdiction, 414 U.S. 1090 (1973).

We agree with the Supreme Court of Georgia's implicit ruling that the Constitution does not require that juries be instructed in state obscenity cases to apply the standards of a hypothetical statewide community. Miller approved the use of such instructions; it did not mandate their use. What Miller makes clear is that state juries need not be instructed to apply "national standards." We also agree with the Supreme Court of Georgia's implicit approval of the trial court's instructions directing jurors to apply "community standards" without specifying what "community." Miller held that it was constitutionally permissible to permit juries to rely on the understanding of the community from which they came as to contemporary community standards, and the States have considerable latitude in framing statutes under this element of the Miller decision. A State may choose to define an obscenity offense in terms of "contemporary community standards" as defined in Miller without further specification, as was done here, or it may choose to define the standards in more precise geographic terms, as was done by California in Miller.

We now turn to the question of whether appellant's exhibition of the film was protected by the First and Fourteenth Amendments, a question which appellee asserts is not properly before us because appellant did not raise it on his state appeal. But whether or not appellant argued this constitutional issue below, it is clear that the Supreme Court of Georgia reached and decided it. That is sufficient under our practice. Raley v. Ohio, 360 U.S. 423, 436 (1959). We also note that the trial court instructed the jury on charges other than the distribution charge. 4 However, the jury returned a general verdict and appellee does not suggest that appellant's conviction can be sustained on these alternative grounds. Cf. Stromberg v. California, 283 U.S. 359, 367 -368 (1931).

There is little to be found in the record about the film "Carnal Knowledge" other than the film itself. 5 However, appellant has supplied a variety of information and critical commentary, the authenticity of which appellee does not dispute. The film appeared on many "Ten Best" lists for 1971, the year in which it was released. Many but not all of the reviews were favorable. We believe that the following passage from a review which appeared in the Saturday Review is a reasonably accurate description of the film:

"[It is basically a story] of two young college men, roommates and lifelong friends forever preoccupied with their sex lives. Both are first met as virgins. Nicholson is the more knowledgeable and attractive of the two; speaking colloquially, he is a burgeoning bastard. Art Garfunkel is his friend, the nice but troubled guy straight out of those early Feiffer cartoons, but real. He falls in love with the lovely Susan (Candice Bergen) and unknowingly shares her with his college buddy. As the `safer' one of the two, he is selected by Susan for marriage.

"The time changes. Both men are in their thirties, pursuing successful careers in New York. Nicholson has been running through an average of a dozen women a year but has never managed to meet the right one, the one with the full bosom, the good legs, the properly rounded bottom. More than that, each and every one is a threat to his malehood and peace of mind, until at last, in a bar, he finds Ann-Margret, an aging bachelor girl with striking cleavage and, quite obviously, something of a past. `Why don't we shack up?' she suggests. They do and a horrendous relationship ensues, complicated mainly by her paranoidal desire to marry. Meanwhile, what of Garfunkel? The sparks have gone out of his marriage, the sex has lost its savor, and Garfunkel tries once more. And later, even more foolishly, again." 6

Appellee contends essentially that under Miller the obscenity vel non of the film "Carnal Knowledge" was a question for the jury, and that the jury having resolved the question against appellant, and there being some evidence to support its findings, the judgment of conviction should be affirmed. We turn to the language of Miller to evaluate appellee's contention.

Miller states that the questions of what appeals to the "prurient interest" and what is "patently offensive" under the obscenity test which it formulates are "essentially questions of fact." 413 U.S., at 30 . "When triers of fact are asked to decide whether `the average person, applying contemporary community standards' would consider certain materials `prurient' it would be unrealistic to require that the answer be based on some abstract formulation . . . . To require a State to structure obscenity proceedings around evidence of a national `community standard' would be an exercise in futility." Ibid. We held in Paris Adult Theatre I v. Slaton, 413 U.S. 49 (1973), decided on the same day, that expert testimony as to obscenity is not necessary when the films at issue are themselves placed in evidence. Id., at 56.

But all of this does not lead us to agree with the Supreme Court of Georgia's apparent conclusion that the jury's verdict against appellant virtually precluded all further appellate review of appellant's assertion that his exhibition of the film was protected by the First and Fourteenth Amendments. Even though questions of appeal to the "prurient interest" or of patent offensiveness are "essentially questions of fact," it would be a serious misreading of Miller to conclude that juries have unbridled discretion in determining what is "patently offensive." Not only did we there say that "the First Amendment values applicable to the States through the Fourteenth Amendment are adequately protected by the ultimate power of appellate courts to conduct an independent review of constitutional claims when necessary," 413 U.S., at 25, but we made it plain that under that holding "no one will be subject to prosecution for the sale or exposure of obscene materials unless these materials depict or describe patently offensive `hard core' sexual conduct . . . ." Id., at 27.

We also took pains in Miller to "give a few plain examples of what a state statute could define for regulation under part (b) of the standard announced," that is, the requirement of patent offensiveness. Id., at 25. These examples included "representations or descriptions of ultimate sexual acts, normal or perverted, actual or simulated," and "representations or descriptions of masturbation, excretory functions, and lewd exhibition of the genitals." Ibid. While this did not purport to be an exhaustive catalog of what juries might find patently offensive, it was certainly intended to fix substantive constitutional limitations, deriving from the First Amendment, on the type of material subject to such a determination. It would be wholly at odds with this aspect of Miller to uphold an obscenity conviction based upon a defendant's depiction of a woman with a bare midriff, even though a properly charged jury unanimously agreed on a verdict of guilty.

Our own viewing of the film satisfies us that "Carnal Knowledge" could not be found under the Miller standards to depict sexual conduct in a patently offensive way. Nothing in the movie falls within either of the two examples given in Miller of material which may constitutionally be found to meet the "patently offensive" element of those standards, nor is there anything sufficiently similar to such material to justify similar treatment. While the subject matter of the picture is, in a broader sense, sex, and there are scenes in which sexual conduct including "ultimate sexual acts" is to be understood to be taking place, the camera does not focus on the bodies of the actors at such times. There is no exhibition whatever of the actors' genitals, lewd or otherwise, during these scenes. There are occasional scenes of nudity, but nudity alone is not enough to make material legally obscene under the Miller standards.

Appellant's showing of the film "Carnal Knowledge" is simply not the "public portrayal of hard core sexual conduct for its own sake, and for the ensuing commercial gain" which we said was punishable in Miller. Id., at 35. We hold that the film could not, as a matter of constitutional law, be found to depict sexual conduct in a patently offensive way, and that it is therefore not outside the protection of the First and Fourteenth Amendments because it is obscene. No other basis appearing in the record upon which the judgment of conviction can be sustained, we reverse the judgment of the Supreme Court of Georgia.

Reversed.

Notes

[1] Section 26 2101 is entitled "Distributing obscene materials." Subsection (a) of 26-2101 provides in relevant part: "A person commits the offense of distributing obscene materials when he . . . exhibits or otherwise disseminates to any person any obscene material of any description, knowing the obscene nature thereof . . . ." Subsection (c) of 26-2101 provides that "[material], not otherwise obscene, may be obscene under this

section if the distribution thereof . . . is a commercial exploitation of erotica solely for the sake of their prurient appeal." Subsection (d) provides that a first offense under the section shall be punished as a misdemeanor and that any subsequent offense shall be punished by one to five years' imprisonment and/or a fine not to exceed $5,000.

[2 ] The accusation, App. 8, charged appellant "with the offense of Distributing Obscene Material" for knowingly exhibiting a motion picture to the general public which contained conduct showing "(a) an act of sexual intercourse, (b) a lewd exposure of the sexual organs, (c) a lewd appearance in a state of partial or complete nudity, (d) a lewd caress or indecent fondling of another person" contrary to the laws of Georgia. The latter-quoted language appears in Ga. Code Ann. 26-2011, entitled "Public indecency," which makes performance of any of the listed acts in a public place a misdemeanor. Under Ga. Code Ann. 26-2105, it is a crime to exhibit a motion picture portraying acts which would constitute "public indecency" under 26-2011 if performed in a public place. Appellant's arrest warrant specified 26-2105 as the statute he was charged with violating. In view of our holding today, we need not reach appellant's contention that he was denied due process because the warrant specified only 26-2105, while the jury was allowed to convict under 26-2101. However, we note that appellant's demurrer to the accusation demonstrates his awareness that he was being charged with the 26-2101 offense, App. 9, and that he requested numerous instructions on obscenity, id., at 47-49.

[3 ] Appellant's trial jury was alternatively instructed under subsections (a) and (c) of 26-2101 (pandering), see n. 1, supra, and under 26-2105, see n. 2, supra.

[4 ] See n. 3, supra.

[5 ] Appellant testified that the film was "critically acclaimed as one of the ten best pictures of 1971 and Ann Margret has received an Academy Award nomination for her performance in the picture." He further testified that "Carnal Knowledge" had played in 29 towns in Georgia and that it was booked in 50 or 60 more theaters for spring and summer showing. App. 24.

[6 ] Review of "Carnal Knowledge" by Hollis Alpert, Saturday Review, July 3, 1971, p. 18.

## Southeastern Promotions, Ltd. v. Conrad (March 18, 1975)

MR. JUSTICE BLACKMUN delivered the opinion of the Court.

The issue in this case is whether First Amendment rights were abridged when respondents denied petitioner the use of a municipal facility in Chattanooga, Tenn., for the showing of the controversial rock musical "Hair." It is established, of course, that the Fourteenth Amendment has made applicable to the States the First Amendment's guarantee of free speech. Douglas v. City of Jeannette, 319 U. S. 157, 162 (1943).

I

Petitioner, Southeastern Promotions, Ltd., is a New York corporation engaged in the business of promoting and presenting theatrical productions for profit. On October

29, 1971, it applied for the use of the Tivoli, a privately owned Chattanooga theater under long-term lease to the city, to present "Hair" there for six days beginning November 23. This was to be a road company showing of the musical that had played for three years on Broadway, and had appeared in over 140 cities in the United States.[1]

Respondents are the directors of the Chattanooga Memorial Auditorium, a municipal theater.[2] Shortly after receiving Southeastern's application, the directors met, and, after a brief discussion, voted to reject it. None of them had seen the play or read the script, but they understood from outside reports that the musical, as produced elsewhere, involved nudity and obscenity on stage. Although no conflicting engagement was scheduled for the Tivoli, respondents determined that the production would not be "in the best interest of the community." Southeastern was so notified but no written statement of reasons was provided.

On November 1 petitioner, alleging that respondents' action abridged its First Amendment rights, sought a preliminary injunction from the United States District Court for the Eastern District of Tennessee. Respondents did not then file an answer to the complaint.[3] A hearing was held on November 4. The District Court took evidence as to the play's content, and respondent Conrad gave the following account of the board's decision:

"We use the general terminology in turning down the request for its use that we felt it was not in the best interest of the community and I can't speak beyond that. That was the board's determination.

"Now, I would have to speak for myself, the policy to which I would refer, as I mentioned, basically indicates that we will, as a board, allow those productions which are clean and healthful and culturally uplifting, or words to that effect. They are quoted in the original dedication booklet of the Memorial Auditorium." App. 25.[4]

The court denied preliminary relief, concluding that petitioner had failed to show that it would be irreparably harmed pending a final judgment since scheduling was "purely a matter of financial loss or gain" and was compensable.

Southeastern some weeks later pressed for a permanent injunction permitting it to use the larger auditorium, rather than the Tivoli, on Sunday, April 9, 1972. The District Court held three days of hearings beginning April 3. On the issue of obscenity vel non, presented to an advisory jury, it took evidence consisting of the full script and libretto, with production notes and stage instructions, a recording of the musical numbers, a souvenir program, and the testimony of seven witnesses who had seen the production elsewhere. The jury returned a verdict that "Hair" was obscene. The District Court agreed. It concluded that conduct in the production— group nudity and simulated sex—would violate city ordinances and state statutes[5] making public nudity and obscene acts criminal offenses.[6] This criminal conduct, the court reasoned, was neither speech nor symbolic speech, and was to be viewed separately from the musical's speech elements. Being pure conduct, comparable to rape or murder, it was not entitled to First Amendment protection. Accordingly, the court denied the injunction. 341 F. Supp. 465

(1972).

On appeal, the United States Court of Appeals for the Sixth Circuit, by a divided vote, affirmed. 486 F. 2d 894 (1973). The majority relied primarily on the lower court's reasoning. Neither the judges of the Court of Appeals nor the District Court saw the musical performed. Because of the First Amendment overtones, we granted certiorari. 415 U. S. 912 (1974).

Petitioner urges reversal on the grounds that (1) respondents' action constituted an unlawful prior restraint, (2) the courts below applied an incorrect standard for the determination of the issue of obscenity vel non, and (3) the record does not support a finding that "Hair" is obscene. We do not reach the latter two contentions, for we agree with the first. We hold that respondents' rejection of petitioner's application to use this public forum accomplished a prior restraint under a system lacking in constitutionally required minimal procedural safeguards. Accordingly, on this narrow ground, we reverse.

II

Respondents' action here is indistinguishable in its censoring effect from the official actions consistently identified as prior restraints in a long line of this Court's decisions. See Shuttlesworth v. Birmingham, 394 U. S. 147, 150-151 (1969); Staub v. City of Baxley, 355 U. S. 313, 322 (1958); Kunz v. New York, 340 U. S. 290, 293-294 (1951); Schneider v. State, 308 U. S. 147, 161-162 (1939); Lovell v. Griffin, 303 U. S. 444, 451-452 (1938). In these cases, the plaintiffs asked the courts to provide relief where public officials had forbidden the plaintiffs the use of public places to say what they wanted to say. The restraints took a variety of forms, with officials exercising control over different kinds of public places under the authority of particular statutes. All, however, had this in common: they gave public officials the power to deny use of a forum in advance of actual expression.

Invariably, the Court has felt obliged to condemn systems in which the exercise of such authority was not bounded by precise and clear standards. The reasoning has been, simply, that the danger of censorship and of abridgment of our precious First Amendment freedoms is too great where officials have unbridled discretion over a forum's use. Our distaste for censorship—reflecting the natural distaste of a free people— is deep-written in our law.

In each of the cited cases the prior restraint was embedded in the licensing system itself, operating without acceptable standards. In Shuttlesworth the Court held unconstitutional a Birmingham ordinance which conferred upon the city commission virtually absolute power to prohibit any "parade," "procession," or "demonstration" on streets or public ways. It ruled that "a law subjecting the exercise of First Amendment freedoms to the prior restraint of a license, without narrow, objective, and definite standards to guide the licensing authority, is unconstitutional." 394 U. S., at 150-151. In Hague v. CIO, 307 U. S. 496 (1939), a Jersey City ordinance that forbade public assembly in the streets or parks without a permit from the local director of safety, who was empowered to refuse the permit upon his opinion that he would thereby prevent " `riots, disturbances or disorderly assemblage,' " was held void on its face. Id., at 516 (opinion of Roberts, J.).

In Cantwell v. Connecticut, 310 U. S. 296 (1940), a unanimous Court held invalid an act which proscribed the solicitation of money or any valuable thing for "any alleged religious, charitable or philanthropic cause" unless that cause was approved by the secretary of the public welfare council. The elements of the prior restraint were clearly set forth:

"It will be noted, however, that the Act requires an application to the secretary of the public welfare council of the State; that he is empowered to determine whether the cause is a religious one, and that the issue of a certificate depends upon his affirmative action. If he finds that the cause is not that of religion, to solicit for it becomes a crime. He is not to issue a certificate as a matter of course. His decision to issue or refuse it involves appraisal of facts, the exercise of judgment, and the formation of an opinion." Id., at 305.

The elements of prior restraint identified in Cantwell and other cases were clearly present in the system by which the Chattanooga board regulated the use of its theaters. One seeking to use a theater was required to apply to the board. The board was empowered to determine whether the applicant should be granted permission —in effect, a license or permit—on the basis of its review of the content of the proposed production. Approval of the application depended upon the board's affirmative action. Approval was not a matter of routine; instead, it involved the "appraisal of facts, the exercise of judgment, and the formation of an opinion" by the board.[7]

The board's judgment effectively kept the musical off stage. Respondents did not permit the show to go on and rely on law enforcement authorities to prosecute for anything illegal that occurred. Rather, they denied the application in anticipation that the production would violate the law. See New York Times Co. v. United States, 403 U. S. 713, 735-738 (1971) (WHITE, J., concurring).

Respondents' action was no less a prior restraint because the public facilities under their control happened to be municipal theaters. The Memorial Auditorium and the Tivoli were public forums designed for and dedicated to expressive activities. There was no question as to the usefulness of either facility for petitioner's production. There was no contention by the board that these facilities could not accommodate a production of this size. None of the circumstances qualifying as an established exception to the doctrine of prior restraint was present. Petitioner was not seeking to use a facility primarily serving a competing use. See, e. g., Cameron v. Johnson, 390 U. S. 611 (1968); Adderley v. Florida, 385 U. S. 39 (1966); Brown v. Louisiana, 383 U. S. 131 (1966). Nor was rejection of the application based on any regulation of time, place, or manner related to the nature of the facility or applications from other users. See Cox v. New Hampshire, 312 U. S. 569, 574 (1941); Poulos v. New Hampshire, 345 U. S. 395, 408 (1953). No rights of individuals in surrounding areas were violated by noise or any other aspect of the production. See Kovacs v. Cooper, 336 U. S. 77 (1949). There was no captive audience. See Lehman v. City of Shaker Heights, 418 U. S. 298, 304, 306-308 (1974); Public

Utilities Comm'n v. Pollak, 343 U. S. 451, 467-468 (1952) (DOUGLAS, J., dissenting).

Whether petitioner might have used some other, privately owned, theater in the city for the production is of no consequence. There is reason to doubt on this record whether any other facility would have served as well as these, since none apparently had the seating capacity, acoustical features, stage equipment, and electrical service that the show required. Even if a privately owned forum had been available, that fact alone would not justify an otherwise impermissible prior restraint. "[O]ne is not to have the exercise of his liberty of expression in appropriate places abridged on the plea that it may be exercised in some other place." Schneider v. State, 308 U. S., at 163.

Thus, it does not matter for purposes of this case that the board's decision might not have had the effect of total suppression of the musical in the community. Denying use of the municipal facility under the circumstances present here constituted the prior restraint.[8]

That restraint was final. It was no mere temporary bar while necessary judicial proceedings were under way.[9]

Only if we were to conclude that live drama is unprotected by the First Amendment—or subject to a totally different standard from that applied to other forms of expression—could we possibly find no prior restraint here. Each medium of expression, of course, must be assessed for First Amendment purposes by standards suited to it, for each may present its own problems. Joseph Burstyn, Inc. v. Wilson, 343 U. S. 495, 503 (1952); see Red Lion Broadcasting Co. v. FCC, 395 U. S. 367 (1969). By its nature, theater usually is the acting out—or singing out— of the written word, and frequently mixes speech with live action or conduct. But that is no reason to hold theater subject to a drastically different standard. For, as was said in Burstyn, supra, at 503, when the Court was faced with the question of what First Amendment standard applies to films:

"[T]he basic principles of freedom of speech and the press, like the First Amendment's command, do not vary. Those principles, as they have frequently been enunciated by this Court, make freedom of expression the rule. There is no justification in this case for making an exception to that rule."

III

Labeling respondents' action a prior restraint does not end the inquiry. Prior restraints are not unconstitutional per se. Bantam Books, Inc. v. Sullivan, 372 U. S. 58, 70 n. 10 (1963). See Near v. Minnesota ex rel. Olson, 283 U. S. 697, 716 (1931); Times Film Corp. v. Chicago, 365 U. S. 43 (1961). We have rejected the contention that the First Amendment's protection "includes complete and absolute freedom to exhibit, at least once, any and every kind of motion picture . . . even if this film contains the basest type of pornography, or incitement to riot, or forceful overthrow of orderly government . . . ." Id., at 46-47.

Any system of prior restraint, however, "comes to this Court bearing a heavy presumption against its constitutional validity." Bantam Books, Inc. v. Sullivan, 372 U. S., at 70; New York Times Co. v. United States, 403 U. S., at 714; Organization for a Better

Austin v. Keefe, 402 U. S. 415, 419 (1971); Carroll v. Princess Anne, 393 U. S. 175, 181 (1968); Near v. Minnesota ex rel. Olson, 283 U. S., at 716. The presumption against prior restraints is heavier—and the degree of protection broader—than that against limits on expression imposed by criminal penalties. Behind the distinction is a theory deeply etched in our law: a free society prefers to punish the few who abuse rights of speech after they break the law than to throttle them and all others beforehand. It is always difficult to know in advance what an individual will say, and the line between legitimate and illegitimate speech is often so finely drawn that the risks of freewheeling censorship are formidable. See Speiser v. Randall, 357 U. S. 513 (1958).

In order to be held lawful, respondents' action, first, must fit within one of the narrowly defined exceptions to the prohibition against prior restraints, and, second, must have been accomplished with procedural safeguards that reduce the danger of suppressing constitutionally protected speech. Bantam Books, Inc. v. Sullivan, 372 U. S., at 71. We do not decide whether the performance of "Hair" fits within such an exception or whether, as a substantive matter, the board's standard for resolving that question was correct, for we conclude that the standard, whatever it may have been, was not implemented by the board under a system with appropriate and necessary procedural safeguards.

The settled rule is that a system of prior restraint "avoids constitutional infirmity only if it takes place under procedural safeguards designed to obviate the dangers of a censorship system." Freedman v. Maryland, 380 U. S. 51, 58 (1965). See United States v. Thirtyseven Photographs, 402 U. S. 363, 367 (1971); Blount v. Rizzi, 400 U. S. 410, 419-421 (1971); Teitel Film Corp. v. Cusack, 390 U. S. 139, 141-142 (1968). See also Heller v. New York, 413 U. S. 483, 489-490 (1973); Bantam Books, Inc. v. Sullivan, 372 U. S., at 70-71; Kingsley Books, Inc. v. Brown, 354 U. S. 436 (1957). In Freedman the Court struck down a state scheme for the licensing of motion pictures, holding "that, because only a judicial determination in an adversary proceeding ensures the necessary sensitivity to freedom of expression, only a procedure requiring a judicial determination suffices to impose a valid final restraint." 380 U. S., at 58. We held in Freedman, and we reaffirm here, that a system of prior restraint runs afoul of the First Amendment if it lacks certain safeguards: First, the burden of instituting judicial proceedings, and of proving that the material is unprotected, must rest on the censor. Second, any restraint prior to judicial review can be imposed only for a specified brief period and only for the purpose of preserving the status quo. Third, a prompt final judicial determination must be assured.

Although most of our cases have pertained to motion picture licensing or censorship, this Court has applied Freedman to the system by which federal customs agents seize imported materials, United States v. Thirty seven Photographs, supra, and to that by which postal officials restrict use of the mails, Blount v. Rizzi, supra. In Blount we held unconstitutional provisions of the postal laws designed to control use of the mails for commerce in obscene materials. The provisions enabled the Postmaster General to halt delivery of mail to an individual and prevent payment of money orders to him. The administrative order became effective without judicial approval, and the burden of obtaining judicial review was placed upon the user.

If a scheme that restricts access to the mails must furnish the procedural safeguards set forth in Freedman, no less must be expected of a system that regulates use of a public forum. Respondents here had the same powers of licensing and censorship exercised by postal officials in Blount, and by boards and officials in other cases.

The theory underlying the requirement of safeguards is applicable here with equal if not greater force. An administrative board assigned to screening stage productions —and keeping off stage anything not deemed culturally uplifting or healthful may well be less responsive than a court, an independent branch of government, to constitutionally protected interests in free expression.[10] And if judicial review is made unduly onerous, by reason of delay or otherwise, the board's determination in practice may be final.

Insistence on rigorous procedural safeguards under these circumstances is "but a special instance of the larger principle that the freedoms of expression must be ringed about with adequate bulwarks." Bantam Books, Inc. v. Sullivan, 372 U. S., at 66. Because the line between unconditionally guaranteed speech and speech that may be legitimately regulated is a close one, the "separation of legitimate from illegitimate speech calls for . . . sensitive tools." Speiser v. Randall, 357 U. S., at 525. The perils of prior restraint are well illustrated by this case, where neither the Board nor the lower courts could have known precisely the extent of nudity or simulated sex in the musical, or even that either would appear, before the play was actually performed.[11]

Procedural safeguards were lacking here in several respects. The board's system did not provide a procedure for prompt judicial review. Although the District Court commendably held a hearing on petitioner's motion for a preliminary injunction within a few days of the board's decision, it did not review the merits of the decision at that time. The question at the hearing was whether petitioner should receive preliminary relief. i. e., whether there was likelihood of success on the merits and whether petitioner would suffer irreparable injury pending full review. Effective review on the merits was not obtained until more than five months later. Throughout, it was petitioner, not the board, that bore the burden of obtaining judicial review. It was petitioner that had the burden of persuasion at the preliminary hearing if not at the later stages of the litigation. Respondents did not file a formal answer to the complaint for five months after petitioner sought review. During the time prior to judicial determination, the restraint altered the status quo. Petitioner was forced to forgo the initial dates planned for the engagement and to seek to schedule the performance at a later date. The delay and uncertainty inevitably discouraged use of the forum.

The procedural shortcomings that form the basis for our decision are unrelated to the standard that the board applied. Whatever the reasons may have been for the board's exclusion of the musical, it could not escape the obligation to afford appropriate procedural safeguards. We need not decide whether the standard of obscenity applied by respondents or the courts below was sufficiently precise or substantively correct, or whether the production is in fact obscene. See Hamling v. United States, 418 U. S. 87 (1974); Jenkins v. Georgia, 418 U. S. 153 (1974); Lewis v. City of New Orleans, 415 U. S. 130 (1974); Miller v. California, 413 U. S. 15 (1973); Gooding v. Wilson, 405 U. S. 518 (1972). The standard, whatever it may be, must be implemented under a system that assures prompt judicial review with a minimal restriction of First Amendment rights necessary under the circumstances.

Reversed.


Notes

[1] Twice previously, petitioner informally had asked permission to use the Tivoli, and had been refused. In other cities, it had encountered similar resistance and had successfully sought injunctions ordering local officials to permit use of municipal facilities. See Southeastern Promotions, Ltd. v. City of Mobile, 457 F. 2d 340 (CA5 1972); Southeastern Promotions, Ltd. v. City of West Palm Beach, 457 F. 2d 1016 (CA5 1972); Southeastern Promotions, Ltd. v. Oklahoma City, 459 F. 2d 282 (CA10 1972); Southeastern Promotions, Ltd. v. City of Charlotte, 333 F. Supp. 345 (WDNC 1971); Southeastern Promotions, Ltd. v. City of Atlanta, 334 F. Supp. 634 (ND Ga. 1971). See also P. B. I. C., Inc. v. Byrne, 313 F. Supp. 757 (Mass. 1970), vacated and remanded for further consideration, 413 U. S. 905 (1973). But see Southeastern Promotions, Ltd. v. Oklahoma City, Civil Action No. 72-105 (WD Okla. Mar. 27, 1972), rev'd, 459 F. 2d 282, supra.

The musical had been presented in two Tennessee cities, Memphis and Nashville.

[2] Code of the city of Chattanooga § 2-238. The board's members are appointed by the mayor and confirmed by the city's board of commissioners. § 2-237. The chairman, respondent Conrad, is commissioner of public utilities, grounds, and buildings. § 2-236.

[3] Neither did it file at that time a formal motion to dismiss. That motion was made later, on November 22, some time after the initial hearing. An answer was finally filed, pursuant to court order, on March 31, 1972.

[4] The Memorial Auditorium, completed in 1924, was dedicated to the memory of Chattanooga citizens who had "offered their lives" in World War I. The booklet referred to is entitled Souvenir of Dedication of Soldiers & Sailors Auditorium Chattanooga, Tenn. It contains the following:

"It will be [the board's] endeavor to make [the auditorium] the community center of Chattanooga; where civic, educational, religious, patriotic and charitable organizations and associations may have a common meeting place to discuss and further the upbuilding and general welfare of the city and surrounding territory.

"It will not be operated for profit, and no effort to obtain financial returns above the actual operating expenses will be permitted. Instead its purpose will be devoted for cultural advancement, and for clean, healthful, entertainment which will make for the upbuilding of a better citizenship." Exhibit 2, p. 40.

[5] Chattanooga Code:

"Sec. 6-4. Offensive, indecent entertainment.

"It shall be unlawful for any person to hold, conduct or carry on, or to cause or permit to be held, conducted or carried on any motion picture exhibition or entertainment of any sort which is offensive to decency, or which is of an obscene, indecent or immoral nature, or so suggestive as to be offensive to the moral sense, or which is calculated to incite crime or riot."

"Sec. 25-28. Indecent exposure and conduct.

"It shall be unlawful for any person in the city to appear in a public place in a state of nudity, or to bathe in such state in the daytime in the river or any bayou or stream within the city within sight of any street or occupied premises; or to appear in public in an indecent or lewd dress, or to do any lewd, obscene or indecent act in any public place."

Tennessee Code Ann. (Supp. 1971):

"39-1013. Sale or loan of material to minor—Indecent exhibits.—It shall be unlawful:

"(a) for any person knowingly to sell or loan for monetary consideration or otherwise exhibit or make available to a minor:

"(1) any picture, photograph, drawing, sculpture, motion picture film, or similar visual representation or image of a person or portion of the human body, which depicts nudity, sexual conduct, excess violence, or sado-masochistic abuse, and which is harmful to minors;

"(2) any book, pamphlet, magazine, printed matter, however reproduced, or sound recording, which contains any matter enumerated in paragraph (1) hereof above, or which contains explicit and detailed verbal descriptions or narrative accounts of sexual excitement, sexual conduct, excess violence, or sado-masochistic abuse, and which is harmful to minors;

"(b) for any person knowingly to exhibit to a minor for a monetary consideration, or knowingly to sell to a minor an admission ticket or pass or otherwise to admit a minor to premises whereon there is exhibited a motion picture, show or other presentation which, in whole or in part, depicts nudity, sexual conduct, excess violence, or sado-masochistic abuse, and which is harmful to minors."

"39-3003. Obscene material—Knowingly selling, distributing or exhibiting—Penalty.—It shall be a misdemeanor for any person to knowingly sell, distribute, display, exhibit, possess with the intent to sell, distribute, display or exhibit; or to publish, produce, or otherwise create with the intent to sell, distribute, display or exhibit any obscene material."

Subsequent to our grant of the petition for certiorari in this case, the Supreme Court of Tennessee held that § 39-3007 of the Tennessee Code, which defined "obscene material," as those words were used in § 39-3003 and related sections, was unconstitutional for failure to satisfy the specificity requirements of Miller v. California, 413 U. S. 15 (1973). Art Theater Guild, Inc. v. State ex rel. Rhodes, 510 S. W. 2d 258

(1974). Thereafter, a new obscenity statute, Acts 1974 (Adj. S), c. 510, was enacted by the Tennessee Legislature; § 14 of that act specifically repealed the above quoted § 39-3003.

[6] Respondents also contended that production of the musical would violate the standard lease that petitioner would be required to sign. The relevant provision of that lease reads:

"This agreement is made and entered into upon the following express covenants and conditions, all and every one of which the lessee hereby covenants and agrees to and with the lessor to keep and perform:

"1. That said lessee will comply with all laws of the United States and of the State of Tennessee, all ordinances of the City of Chattanooga, and all rules and requirements of the police and fire departments or other municipal authorities of the City of Chattanooga." Exhibit 3.

[7] With respect to petitioner's musical, respondents' determination was that the production would not be "in the best interest of the community." That determination may have been guided by other criteria: (1) their own requirement, in the words of respondent Conrad, that a production be "clean and healthful and culturally uplifting," App. 25: or (2) the provisions of the statutes and ordinances prohibiting public nudity and obscenity. Whether or not their exercise of discretion was sufficiently controlled by law, Shuttlesworth v. Birmingham, 394 U. S. 147 (1969), there can be no doubt that approval of an application required some judgment as to the content and quality of the production.

[8] Also important, though unessential to our conclusion, are the classificatory aspects of the board's decision. A licensing system need not effect total suppression in order to create a prior restraint. In Interstate Circuit v. Dallas, 390 U. S. 676, 688 (1968), it was observed that the evils attendant on prior restraint "are not rendered less objectionable because the regulation of expression is one of classification rather than direct suppression." In that case, the Court held that a prior restraint was created by a system whereby an administrative board in Texas classified films as "suitable for young persons" or "not suitable for young persons." The "not suitable" films were not suppressed, but exhibitors were required to have special licenses and to advertise their classification in order to show them. Similarly, in Bantam Books, Inc. v. Sullivan, 372 U. S. 58 (1963), the Court held that a system of "informal censorship" working by exhortation and advice sufficiently inhibited expression to constitute a prior restraint and warrant injunctive relief. There, the Court held unconstitutional a system in which a commission was charged with reviewing material "manifestly tending to the corruption of the youth"; it did not have direct regulatory or suppressing functions, but operated by persuasion and intimidation, and these informal methods were found effective.

In the present case, the board classified the musical as unfit for showing in municipal facilities. It did not make a point of publicizing its finding that "Hair" was not in the "best interest" of the public, but the classification stood as a warning to all concerned, private theater owners and general public alike. There is little in the record to indicate the extent to which the board's action may have affected petitioner's ability to obtain a theater and attract an audience. The board's classification, whatever the magnitude of its effect, was not unlike that in Interstate Circuit and Bantam Books.

[9] This case is clearly distinguishable from Heller v. New York, 413 U. S. 483 (1973). There, state authorities seized a copy of a film, temporarily, in order to preserve it as evidence. Id., at 490. The Court held that there was not "any form of `final restraint,' in the sense of being enjoined from exhibition or threatened with destruction." Ibid. Here, the board did not merely detain temporarily a copy of the script or libretto for the musical. Respondents reached a final decision to bar performance.

[10] See Monaghan, First Amendment "Due Process," 83 Harv. L. Rev. 518, 522-524 (1970); Emerson, The Doctrine of Prior Restraint, 20 Law & Contemp. Prob. 648, 656-659 (1955).

[11] There was testimony that the musical as performed differed "substantially" from the script, App. 79-80, and that the show was varied to fit the anticipated tastes of different audiences in different parts of the country. Id., at 93. The musical's nude scene, apparently the most controversial portion, was played under varying conditions. No actor was under contractual obligation to perform it, and the number doing so changed from one performance to another, as did the lighting, and the duration of the scene. Id., at 97-98, 23.

## Erznoznik v. City of Jacksonville (June 23, 1975)

MR. JUSTICE POWELL delivered the opinion of the Court.

This case presents a challenge to the facial validity of a Jacksonville, Fla., ordinance that prohibits showing films containing nudity by a drive-in movie theater when its screen is visible from a public street or place.

I

Appellant, Richard Erznoznik, is the manager of the University Drive-In Theatre in Jacksonville. On March 13, 1972, he was charged with violating § 330.313 of the municipal code for exhibiting a motion picture, visible from public streets, in which "female buttocks and bare breasts were shown." [1] The ordinance, adopted January 14, 1972, provides:

"330.313 Drive-In Theaters, Films Visible From Public Streets or Public Places. It shall be unlawful and it is hereby declared a public nuisance for any ticket seller, ticket taker, usher, motion picture projection machine operator, manager, owner, or any other person connected with or employed by any drive-in theater in the City to exhibit, or aid or assist in exhibiting, any motion picture, slide, or other exhibit in which the human male or female bare buttocks, human female bare breasts, or human bare pubic areas are shown, if such motion picture, slide, or other exhibit is visible from any public street or public place. Violation of this section shall be punishable as a Class C offense."

Appellant, with the consent of the city prosecutor, successfully moved to stay his prosecution so that the validity of the ordinance could be tested in a separate declaratory action. In that action, appellee, the city of Jacksonville, introduced evidence showing that the screen of appellant's theater is visible from two adjacent public streets and a nearby church parking lot. There was also testimony indicating that people had been observed watching films while sitting outside the theater in parked cars and in the grass.

The trial court upheld the ordinance as a legitimate exercise of the municipality's police power, and ruled that it did not infringe upon appellant's First Amendment rights. The District Court of Appeal, First District of Florida, affirmed, 288 So.2d 260 (1974), relying exclusively on Chemline, Inc. v. City of Grand Prairie, 364 F.2d 721 (CA5 1966), which had sustained a similar ordinance. [2] The Florida Supreme Court denied certiorari, three judges dissenting. 294 So.2d 93 (1974). We noted probable jurisdiction, [3] 419 U.S. 822 (1974), and now reverse.

II

Appellee concedes that its ordinance sweeps far beyond the permissible restraints on obscenity, see Miller v. California, 413 U. S. 15 (1973), and thus applies to films that are protected by the First Amendment. See Joseph Burstyn, Inc. v. Wilson, 343 U. S. 495 (1952); Jenkins v. Georgia, 418 U. S. 153 (1974). Nevertheless, it maintains that any movie containing nudity which is visible from a public place may be suppressed as a nuisance. Several theories are advanced to justify this contention.

A

Appellee's primary argument is that it may protect its citizens against unwilling exposure to materials that may be offensive. Jacksonville's ordinance, however, does not protect citizens from all movies that might offend; rather, it singles out films containing nudity, presumably because the lawmakers considered them especially offensive to passersby.

This Court has considered analogous issues -- pitting the First Amendment rights of speakers against the privacy rights of those who may be unwilling viewers or auditors -- in a variety of contexts. See, e.g., Kovacs v. Cooper, 336 U. S. 77 (1949); Breard v. Alexandria, 341 U. S. 622, 341 U. S. 641-645 (1951); Cohen v. California, 403 U. S. 15 (1971); Lehman v. City of Shaker Heights, 418 U. S. 298 (1974). See generally Haiman, Speech v. Privacy: Is There A Right Not To Be Spoken To?, 67 Nw.U.L.Rev. 153 (1972). Such cases demand delicate balancing because:

"In the [e] sphere of collision between claims of privacy and those of [free speech or] free press, the interests on both sides are plainly rooted in the traditions and significant concerns of our society. "

Cox Broadcasting Corp. v. Cohn, 420 U. S. 469, 420 U. S. 491 (1975).

Although each case ultimately must depend on its own specific facts, some general principles have emerged. A State or municipality may protect individual privacy by enacting reasonable time, place, and manner regulations applicable to all speech irrespective of content. See Kovacs v. Cooper, supra; Cox v. Louisiana, 379 U. S. 536, 379 U. S. 554 (1965); Adderley v. Florida, 385 U. S. 39 (1966). But when the government, acting as censor, undertakes selectively to shield the public from some kinds of speech on the ground that they are more offensive than others, the First Amendment strictly limits its power. See, e.g., Police Dept. of Chicago v. Mosley, 408 U. S. 92 (1972); Fowler v. Rhode Island, 345 U. S. 67 (1953); Kovacs v. Cooper, supra at 336 U. S. 97 (Jackson, J., concurring). Such selective restrictions have been upheld only when the speaker intrudes on the privacy of the home, see Rowan v. Post Office Dept., 397 U. S. 728 (1970), [4] or the degree of captivity makes it impractical for the unwilling viewer or auditor to avoid exposure. See Lehman v. City of Shaker Heights, supra. [5] As Mr. Justice Harlan cautioned:

"The ability of government, consonant with the Constitution, to shut off discourse solely to protect others from hearing it is . . . dependent upon a showing that substantial privacy interests are being invaded in an essentially intolerable manner. Any broader view of this authority would effectively empower a majority to silence dissidents simply as a matter of personal predilections."

Cohen v. California, 403 U.S. at 403 U. S. 21.

The plain, if at times disquieting, truth is that, in our pluralistic society, constantly proliferating new and ingenious forms of expression, "we are inescapably captive audiences for many purposes." Rowan v. Post Office Dept., supra, at 397 U. S. 736. Much that we encounter offends our esthetic, if not our political and moral, sensibilities. Nevertheless, the Constitution does not permit government to decide which types of otherwise protected speech are sufficiently offensive to require protection for the unwilling listener or viewer. Rather, absent the narrow circumstances described above, [6] the burden normally falls upon the viewer to "avoid further bombardment of [his] sensibilities simply by averting [his] eyes." Cohen v. California, supra, at 403 U. S. 21. See also Spence v. Washington, 418 U. S. 405, 418 U. S. 412 (1974).

The Jacksonville ordinance discriminates among movies solely on the basis of content. [7] Its effect is to deter drive-in theaters from showing movies containing any nudity, however innocent or even educational. [8] This discrimination cannot be justified as a means of preventing significant intrusions on privacy. The ordinance seeks only to keep these films from being seen from public streets and places where the offended viewer readily can avert his eyes. In short, the screen of a drive-in theater is not "so obtrusive as to make it impossible for an unwilling individual to avoid exposure to it." Redrup v. New York, 386 U. S. 767, 386 U. S. 769 (1967). Thus, we conclude that the limited privacy interest of persons on the public streets cannot justify this censorship of otherwise protected speech on the basis of its content. [9]

B

Appellee also attempts to support the ordinance as an exercise of the city's undoubted police power to protect children. Appellee maintains that, even though it cannot prohibit the display of films containing nudity to adults, the present ordinance is a reasonable means of protecting minors from this type of visual influence.

It is well settled that a State or municipality can adopt more stringent controls on communicative materials available to youths than on those available to adults. See, e.g.,

Ginsberg v. New York, 390 U. S. 629 (1968). Nevertheless, minors are entitled to a significant measure of First Amendment protection, See Tinker v. Des Moines School Dist., 393 U. S. 503 (1969), and only in relatively narrow and well defined circumstances may government bar public dissemination of protected materials to them. See, e.g., Interstate Circuit, Inc. v. City of Dallas, 390 U. S. 676 (1968); Rabeck v. New York, 391 U. S. 462 (1968).

In this case, assuming the ordinance is aimed at prohibiting youths from viewing the films, the restriction is broader than permissible. The ordinance is not directed against sexually explicit nudity, nor is it otherwise limited. Rather, it sweepingly forbids display of all films containing any uncovered buttocks or breasts, irrespective of context or pervasiveness. Thus it would bar a film containing a picture of a baby's buttocks, the nude body of a war victim, or scenes from a culture in which nudity is indigenous. The ordinance also might prohibit newsreel scenes of the opening of an art exhibit, as well as shots of bathers on a beach. Clearly all nudity cannot be deemed obscene, even as to minors. See Ginsberg v. New York, supra. [10] Nor can such a broad restriction be justified by any other governmental interest pertaining to minors. Speech that is neither obscene as to youths nor subject to some other legitimate proscription cannot be suppressed solely to protect the young from ideas or images that a legislative body thinks unsuitable or them. In most circumstances, [11] the values protected by the First Amendment are no less applicable when government seeks to control the flow of information to minors. See Tinker v. Des Moines School Dist., supra. Cf. West Virginia Bd. of Ed. v. Barnette, 319 U. S. 624 (1943). Thus, if Jacksonville's ordinance is intended to regulate expression accessible to minors, it is overbroad in its proscription. [12]

C

At oral argument, appellee, for the first time, sought to justify its ordinance as a traffic regulation. It claimed that nudity on a drive-in movie screen distracts passing motorists, thus slowing the flow of traffic and increasing the likelihood of accidents.

Nothing in the record or in the text of the ordinance suggests that it is aimed at traffic regulation. Indeed, the ordinance applies to movie screens visible from public places, as well as public streets, thus indicating that it is not a traffic regulation. But even if this were the purpose of the ordinance, it nonetheless would be invalid. By singling out movies containing even the most fleeting and innocent glimpses of nudity, the legislative classification is strikingly underinclusive. There is no reason to think that a wide variety of other scenes in the customary screen diet, ranging from soap opera to violence, would be any less distracting to the passing motorist.

This Court frequently has upheld underinclusive classifications on the sound theory that a legislature may deal with one part of a problem without addressing all of it. See, e.g., Williamson v. Lee Optical Co., 348 U. S. 483, 348 U. S. 488-489 (1955). This presumption of statutory validity, however, has less force when a classification turns on the subject matter of expression.

"[A]bove all else, the First Amendment means that government has no power to restrict expression because of its message, its ideas, its subject matter, or its content."

Police Dept. of Chicago v. Mosley, 408 U.S. at 408 U. S. 95. Thus, "under the Equal Protection Clause, not to mention the First Amendment itself," id. at 408 U. S. 96, even a traffic regulation cannot discriminate on the basis of content unless there are clear reasons for the distinctions. See also Cox v. Louisiana, 379 U. S. 559, 379 U. S. 581 (1965) (opinion of Black, J.). Cf. Williams v. Rhodes, 393 U. S. 23 (1968); Shapiro v. Thompson, 394 U. S. 618 (1969).

Appellee offers no justification, nor are we aware of any, for distinguishing movies containing nudity from all other movies in a regulation designed to protect traffic. Absent such a justification, the ordinance cannot be salvaged by this rationale. [13]

III

Even though none of the reasons advanced by appellee will sustain the Jacksonville ordinance, it remains for us to decide whether the ordinance should be invalidated on its face. This Court has long recognized that a demonstrably overbroad statute or ordinance may deter the legitimate exercise of First Amendment rights. Nonetheless, when considering a facial challenge, it is necessary to proceed with caution and restraint, as invalidation may result in unnecessary interference with a state regulatory program. In accommodating these competing interests, the Court has held that a state statute should not be deemed facially invalid unless it is not readily subject to a narrowing construction by the state courts, see Dombrowski v. Pfister, 380 U. S. 479, 380 U. S. 497 (1965), and its deterrent effect on legitimate expression is both real and substantial. See Broadrick v. Oklahoma, 413 U. S. 601, 413 U. S. 612-615 (1973). See generally Note, The First Amendment Overbreadth Doctrine, 83 Harv.L.Rev. 844 (1970).

In the present case, the possibility of a limiting construction appears remote. Appellee explicitly joined in this test of the facial validity of its ordinance by agreeing to stay appellant's prosecution. [14] Moreover, the ordinance, by its plain terms, is not easily susceptible of a narrowing construction. [15] Indeed, when the state courts were presented with this overbreadth challenge, they made no effort to restrict its application. Compare Coates v. City of Cincinnati, 402 U. S. 611, 402 U. S. 612-613 (1971), and Brandenburg v. Ohio, 395 U. S. 444, 395 U. S. 448-449 (1969), with Cox v. New Hampshire, 312 U. S. 569, 312 U. S. 575-576 (1941), and Chaplinsky v. New Hampshire, 315 U. S. 568, 315 U. S. 572-573 (1942). In these circumstances, particularly where, as here, appellee offers several distinct justifications for the ordinance in its broadest terms, there is no reason to assume that the ordinance can or will be decisively narrowed. See Gooding v. Wilson, 405 U. S. 518, 405 U. S. 520-527 (1972). Cf. Grayned v. City of Rockford, 408 U. S. 104, 408 U. S. 111-112 (1972); Time, Inc. v. Hill, 385 U. S. 374, 385 U. S. 397 (1967)

Moreover, the deterrent effect of this ordinance is both real and substantial. Since it applies specifically to all persons employed by or connected with drive-in theaters, the owners and operators of these theaters are faced with an unwelcome choice: to avoid prosecution of themselves and their employees, they must either restrict their movie offerings or construct adequate protective fencing which may be extremely expensive or even physically impracticable. [16] Cf. Lake Carriers' Assn. v. MacMillan, 406 U. S. 498, 406 U. S. 513 (1972) (POWELL, J., dissenting).

IV

In concluding that this ordinance is invalid, we do not deprecate the legitimate interests asserted by the city of Jacksonville. We hold only that the present ordinance does not satisfy the rigorous constitutional standards that apply when government attempts to regulate expression. Where First Amendment freedoms are at stake, we have repeatedly emphasized that precision of drafting and clarity of purpose are essential. These prerequisites are absent here. Accordingly, the judgment below is

Reversed.

Notes

[1] The movie, "Class of '74," had been rated "R" by the Motion Picture Association of America. An "R" rating indicates that youths may be admitted only when accompanied by a parent or guardian. See generally Friedman, The Motion Picture Rating System of 1968: A Constitutional Analysis of Self-Regulation by the Film Industry, 73 Col.L.Rev. 185 (1973). Although there is nothing in the record regarding the content of the movie, the parties agree that it includes pictures of uncovered female breasts and buttocks.

[2] The only other United States Court of Appeals to consider this question reached a contrary result. See Cinecom Theaters Midwest States, Inc. v. City of Fort Wayne, 473 F.2d 1297 (CA7 1973).

[3] A local ordinance is deemed a state statute for purposes of invoking this Court's jurisdiction under 28 U.S.C. § 1257(2). See King Mfg. Co. v. City Council of Augusta, 277 U. S. 100 (1928).

[4] Rowan involved a federal statute that permits a person receiving a "pandering advertisement" which he believes to be "erotically arousing or sexually provocative" to instruct the Postmaster General to inform the sender that such mail is not to be sent in the future. The Court upheld the statute, emphasizing that individual privacy is entitled to greater protection in the home than on the streets, and noting that "the right of every person to be let alone' must be placed in the scales with the right of others to communicate." See 397 U.S. at 397 U. S. 736-738.

[5] In Lehman, the Court sustained a municipality's policy of barring political advertisements while permitting nonpolitical advertisements on city buses. The issue was whether the city had created a "public forum," and thereby obligated itself to accept all advertising. While concluding that no public forum had been established, both the plurality and concurring opinions recognized that the degree of captivity and the resultant intrusion on privacy is significantly greater for a passenger on a bus than for a person on the street. See 418 U. S. 298, 418 U. S. 302-304 (opinion of BLACKMUN, J.), and id. at 418 U. S. 306-308 (DOUGLAS, J., concurring). See also Public Utilities

Comm'n v. Pollak, 343 U. S. 451, 343 U. S. 467 (1952) (DOUGLAS, J., dissenting).

[6] It has also been suggested that government may proscribe, by a properly framed law, "the willful use of scurrilous language calculated to offend the sensibilities of an unwilling audience." Rosenfeld v. New Jersey, 408 U. S. 901, 905 (1972) (POWELL, J., dissenting). Cf. Ginzburg v. United States, 383 U. S. 463 (1966). In such cases, the speaker may seek to "force public confrontation with the potentially offensive aspects of the work." Id. at 383 U. S. 470. It may not be the content of the speech as much as the deliberate "verbal [or visual] assault," Rosenfeld, supra at 906, that justifies proscription. See Redrup v. New York, 386 U. S. 767, 386 U. S. 769 (1967). In the present case, however, appellant is not trying to reach, much less shock, unwilling viewers. Appellant manages a commercial enterprise which depends for its success on paying customers, not on freeloading passersby. Presumably, where economically feasible, the screen of a drive-in theater will be shielded from those who do not pay.

[7] Scenes of nudity in a movie, like pictures of nude persons in a book, must be considered as a part of the whole work. See Miller v. California, 413 U. S. 15, 413 U. S. 24 (1973); Kois v. Wisconsin, 408 U. S. 229 (1972). In this respect, such nudity is distinguishable from the kind of public nudity traditionally subject to indecent exposure laws. See Roth v. United States, 354 U. S. 476, 354 U. S. 512 (1957) (DOUGLAS, J., dissenting) ("No one would suggest that the First Amendment permits nudity in public places"). Cf. United States v. O'Brien, 391 U. S. 367 (1968).

THE CHIEF JUSTICE's dissent, in response to this point, states that,

"[u]nlike persons reading books, passersby cannot consider fragments of drive-in movies as a part of the 'whole work' for the simple reason that they see, but do not hear, the performance. . . ."

Post at 422 U. S. 222 (emphasis in original). At issue here, however, is not the viewing rights of unwilling viewers, but rather the rights of those who operate drive-in theaters and the public that attends these establishments. The effect of the Jacksonville ordinance is to increase the cost of showing films containing nudity. See n 8, infra. In certain circumstances, theaters will avoid showing these movies rather than incur the additional costs. As a result, persons who want to see such films at drive-ins will be unable to do so. It is in this regard that a motion picture must be considered as a whole, and not as isolated fragments or scenes of nudity.

[8] Such a deterrent, although it might not result in total suppression of these movies, is a restraint on free expression. See Speiser v. Randall, 357 U. S. 513, 357 U. S. 518-519 (1958). The record does not indicate how much it would cost to block public view of appellant's theater. Such costs generally will vary with circumstances. In one case, the expense was estimated at approximately a quarter million dollars. See Olympic Drive-In Theatre, Inc. v. City of Paledale, 441 S.W.2d 5, 8 (Mo.1969).

[9] We are not concerned in this case with a properly drawn zoning ordinance restricting the location of drive-in theaters or with a nondiscriminatory nuisance ordinance designed to protect the privacy of persons in their homes from the visual and

audible intrusions of such theaters.

[10] In Ginsberg, the Court adopted a variation of the adult obscenity standards enunciated in Roth v. United States, 354 U. S. 476 (1957), and Memoirs v. Massachusetts, 383 U. S. 413 (1966) (plurality opinion). In Miller v. California, supra, we abandoned the Roth-Memoirs test for judging obscenity with respect to adults. We have not had occasion to decide what effect Miller will have on the Ginsberg formulation. It is clear, however, that, under any test of obscenity as to minors not all nudity would be proscribed. Rather, to be obscene, "such expression must be, in some significant way, erotic." Cohen v. California, 403 U. S. 15, 403 U. S. 20 (1971). See Paris Adult Theatre I v. Slaton, 413 U. S. 49, 413 U. S. 106-107 (1973) (BRENNAN, J., dissenting).

[11] The First Amendment rights of minors are not "coextensive with those. of adults." Tinker v. Des Moines School Dist., 393 U. S. 503, 393 U. S. 515 (1969) (STEWART, J., concurring).

"[A] State may permissibly determine that., at least in some precisely delineated areas, a child -- like someone in a captive audience -- is not possessed of that full capacity for individual choice which is the presupposition of First Amendment guarantees."

Ginsberg v. New York, 390 U. S. 629, 390 U. S. 649-650 (1968) (STEWART, J., concurring). In assessing whether a minor has the requisite capacity for individual choice, the age of the minor is a significant factor. See Rowan v. Post Office Dept., 397 U.S. at 397 U. S. 741 (BRENNAN, J., concurring).

[12] See 422 U. S. infra.

[13] This is not to say that a narrowly drawn nondiscriminatory traffic regulation requiring screening of drive-in movie theaters from the view of motorists would not be a reasonable exercise of police power. See Police Dept. of Chicago v. Mosley, 408 U. S. 92, 408 U. S. 98 (1972), and cases cited.

[14] In this respect, the present case arises in a posture that differs from most challenges to a statute or ordinance considered by this Court. Typically in such cases, the issue arises in a context where the statute or ordinance has been applied to allegedly unprotected activity. Thus, we are able to consider the constitutionality of the statute "as applied," as well as "on its face."

[15] The only narrowing construction which occurs to us would be to limit the ordinance to movies that are obscene as to minors. Neither appellee nor the Florida courts have suggested such a limitation, perhaps because a rewriting of the ordinance would be necessary to reach that result.

[16] In this case, appellant himself is a theater manager. Hence, the statute's deterrent effect acts upon him personally; he is not seeking to raise the hypothetical rights of others. See Breard v. Alexandria, 341 U. S. 622, 341 U. S. 641 (1951).

## Young v. American Mini Theatres, Inc. (June 24, 1976)

MR. JUSTICE STEVENS delivered the opinion of the Court. *

Zoning ordinances adopted by the city of Detroit differentiate between motion picture theaters which exhibit sexually explicit "adult" movies and those which do not. The principal question presented by this case is whether that statutory classification is unconstitutional because it is based on the content of communication protected by the First Amendment. 1

Effective November 2, 1972, Detroit adopted the ordinances challenged in this litigation. Instead of concentrating "adult" theaters in limited zones, these ordinances require that such theaters be dispersed. Specifically, an adult theater may not be located within 1,000 feet of any two other "regulated uses" or within 500 feet of a residential area. 2 The term "regulated uses" includes 10 different kinds of establishments in addition to adult theaters. 3

The classification of a theater as "adult" is expressly predicated on the character of the motion pictures which it exhibits. If the theater is used to present "material distinguished or characterized by an emphasis on matter depicting, describing or relating to `Specified Sexual Activities' or `Specified Anatomical Areas,'" 4 it is an adult establishment. 5

The 1972 ordinances were amendments to an "Anti-Skid Row Ordinance" which had been adopted 10 years earlier. At that time the Detroit Common Council made a finding that some uses of property are especially injurious to a neighborhood when they are concentrated in limited areas. 6 The decision to add adult motion picture theaters and adult book stores to the list of businesses which, apart from a special waiver, 7 could not be located within 1,000 feet of two other "regulated uses," was, in part, a response to the significant growth in the number of such establishments. 8 In the opinion of urban planners and real estate experts who supported the ordinances, the location of several such businesses in the same neighborhood tends to attract an undesirable quantity and quality of transients, adversely affects property values, causes an increase in crime, especially prostitution, and encourages residents and businesses to move elsewhere.

Respondents are the operators of two adult motion picture theaters. One, the Nortown, was an established theater which began to exhibit adult films in March 1973. The other, the Pussy Cat, was a corner gas station which was converted into a "mini theater," but denied a certificate of occupancy because of its plan to exhibit adult films. Both theaters were located within 1,000 feet of two other regulated uses and the Pussy Cat was less than 500 feet from a residential area. The respondents brought two separate actions against appropriate city officials, seeking a declaratory judgment that the ordinances were unconstitutional and an injunction against their enforcement. Federal jurisdiction was properly invoked 9 and the two cases were consolidated for decision. 10

The District Court granted defendants' motion for summary judgment. On the basis of the reasons stated by the city for adopting the ordinances, the court concluded that they represented a rational attempt to preserve the city's neighborhoods. 11 The court analyzed and rejected respondents' argument that the definition and waiver provisions in the ordinances were impermissibly vague; it held that the disparate treatment of adult theaters and other theaters was justified by a compelling state interest and therefore did not violate the Equal Protection Clause; 12 and finally it concluded that the regulation of the places where adult films could be shown did not violate the First Amendment. 13

The Court of Appeals reversed. American Mini Theaters, Inc. v. Gribbs, 518 F.2d 1014 (CA6 1975). The majority opinion concluded that the ordinances imposed a prior restraint on constitutionally protected communication and therefore "merely establishing that they were designed to serve a compelling public interest" provided an insufficient justification for a classification of motion picture theaters on the basis of the content of the materials they purvey to the public. 14 Relying primarily on Police Department of Chicago v. Mosley, 408 U.S. 92, the court held the ordinance invalid under the Equal Protection Clause. Judge Celebrezze, in dissent, expressed the opinion that the ordinance was a valid "`time, place and manner' regulation," rather than a regulation of speech on the basis of its content. 15

Because of the importance of the decision, we granted certiorari, 423 U.S. 911 .

As they did in the District Court, respondents contend (1) that the ordinances are so vague that they violate the Due Process Clause of the Fourteenth Amendment; (2) that they are invalid under the First Amendment as prior restraints on protected communication; and (3) that the classification of theaters on the basis of the content of their exhibitions violates the Equal Protection Clause of the Fourteenth Amendment. We consider their arguments in that order.

I

There are two parts to respondents' claim that the ordinances are too vague. They do not attack the specificity of the definition of "Specified Sexual Activities" or "Specified Anatomical Areas." They argue, however, that they cannot determine how much of the described activity may be permissible before the exhibition is "characterized by an emphasis" on such matter. In addition, they argue that the ordinances are vague because they do not specify adequate procedures or standards for obtaining a waiver of the 1,000-foot restriction.

We find it unnecessary to consider the validity of either of these arguments in the abstract. For even if there may be some uncertainty about the effect of the ordinances on other litigants, they are unquestionably applicable to these respondents. The record indicates that both theaters propose to offer adult fare on a regular basis. 16 Neither respondent has alleged any basis for claiming or anticipating any waiver of the restriction as applied to its theater. It is clear, therefore, that any element of vagueness in these ordinances has not affected these respondents. To the extent that their challenge is predicated on inadequate notice resulting in a denial of procedural due process under the Fourteenth Amendment, it must be rejected. Cf. Parker v. Levy, 417 U.S. 733, 754 -757.

Because the ordinances affect communication protected by the First Amendment, respondents argue that they may raise the vagueness issue even though there is no uncertainty about the impact of the ordinances on their own rights. On several occasions we have determined that a defendant whose own speech was unprotected had standing to challenge the constitutionality of a statute which purported to prohibit protected speech, or even speech arguably protected. 17 This exception from traditional rules of standing to raise constitutional issues has reflected the Court's judgment that the very existence of some statutes may cause persons not before the Court to refrain from engaging in constitutionally protected speech or expression. See Broadrick v. Oklahoma, 413 U.S. 601, 611 -614. The exception is justified by the overriding importance of maintaining a free and open market for the interchange of ideas. Nevertheless, if the statute's deterrent effect on legitimate expression is not "both real and substantial," and if the statute is "readily subject to a narrowing construction by the state courts," see Erznoznik v. City of Jacksonville, 422 U.S. 205, 216, the litigant is not permitted to assert the rights of third parties.

We are not persuaded that the Detroit zoning ordinances will have a significant deterrent effect on the exhibition of films protected by the First Amendment. As already noted, the only vagueness in the ordinances relates to the amount of sexually explicit activity that may be portrayed before the material can be said to be "characterized by an emphasis" on such matter. For most films the question will be readily answerable; to the extent that an area of doubt exists, we see no reason why the ordinances are not "readily subject to a narrowing construction by the state courts." Since there is surely a less vital interest in the uninhibited exhibition of material that is on the borderline between pornography and artistic expression than in the free dissemination of ideas of social and political significance, and since the limited amount of uncertainty in the ordinances is easily susceptible of a narrowing construction, we think this is an inappropriate case in which to adjudicate the `hypothetical claims of persons not before the Court.

The only area of protected communication that may be deterred by these ordinances comprises films containing material falling within the specific definitions of "Specified Sexual Activities" or "Specified Anatomical Areas." The fact that the First Amendment protects some, though not necessarily all, of that material from total suppression does not warrant the further conclusion that an exhibitor's doubts as to whether a borderline film may be shown in his theater, as well as in theaters licensed for adult presentations, involves the kind of threat to the free market in ideas and expression that justifies the exceptional approach to constitutional adjudication recognized in cases like Dombrowski v. Pfister, 380 U.S. 479 .

The application of the ordinances to respondents is plain; even if there is some area of uncertainty about their application in other situations, we agree with the District Court that respondents' due process argument must be rejected.

II

Petitioners acknowledge that the ordinances prohibit theaters which are not licensed as "adult motion picture theaters" from exhibiting films which are protected by the First Amendment. Respondents argue that the ordinances are therefore invalid as prior restraints on free speech.

The ordinances are not challenged on the ground that they impose a limit on the total number of adult theaters which may operate in the city of Detroit. There is no claim that distributors or exhibitors of adult films are denied access to the market or, conversely, that the viewing public is unable to satisfy its appetite for sexually explicit fare. Viewed as an entity, the market for this commodity is essentially unrestrained.

It is true, however, that adult films may only be exhibited commercially in licensed theaters. But that is also true of all motion pictures. The city's general zoning laws require all motion picture theaters to satisfy certain locational as well as other requirements; we have no doubt that the municipality may control the location of theaters as well as the location of other commercial establishments, either by confining them to certain specified commercial zones or by requiring that they be dispersed throughout the city. The mere fact that the commercial exploitation of material protected by the First Amendment is subject to zoning and other licensing requirements is not a sufficient reason for invalidating these ordinances.

Putting to one side for the moment the fact that adult motion picture theaters must satisfy a locational restriction not applicable to other theaters, we are also persuaded that the 1,000-foot restriction does not, in itself, create an impermissible restraint on protected communication. The city's interest in planning and regulating the use of property for commercial purposes is clearly adequate to support that kind of restriction applicable to all theaters within the city limits. In short, apart from the fact that the ordinances treat adult theaters differently from other theaters and the fact that the classification is predicated on the content of material shown in the respective theaters, the regulation of the place where such films may be exhibited does not offend the First Amendment. 18 We turn, therefore, to the question whether the classification is consistent with the Equal Protection Clause.

III

A remark attributed to Voltaire characterizes our zealous adherence to the principle that the government may not tell the citizen what he may or may not say. Referring to a suggestion that the violent overthrow of tyranny might be legitimate, he said: "I disapprove of what you say, but I will defend to the death your right to say it." 19 The essence of that comment has been repeated time after time in our decisions invalidating attempts by the government to impose selective controls upon the dissemination of ideas.

Thus, the use of streets and parks for the free expression of views on national affairs may not be conditioned upon the sovereign's agreement with what a speaker may intend to say. 20 Nor may speech be curtailed because it invites dispute, creates dissatisfaction with conditions the way they are, or even stirs people to anger. 21 The sovereign's agreement or disagreement with the content of what a speaker has to say may not affect the regulation of the time, place, or manner of presenting the speech.

If picketing in the vicinity of a school is to be allowed to express the point of view of labor, that means of expression in that place must be allowed for other points of view as well. As we said in Mosley:

"The central problem with Chicago's ordinance is that it describes permissible picketing in terms of its subject matter. Peaceful picketing on the subject of a school's labor-management dispute is permitted, but all other peaceful picketing is prohibited. The operative distinction is the message on a picket sign. But, above all else, the First Amendment means that government has no power to restrict expression because of its message, its ideas, its subject matter, or its content. Cohen v. California, 403 U.S. 15, 24 (1971); Street v. New York, 394 U.S. 576 (1969); New York Times Co. v. Sullivan, 376 U.S. 254, 269 -270 (1964), and cases cited; NAACP v. Button, 371 U.S. 415, 445 (1963); Wood v. Georgia, 370 U.S. 375, 388 -389 (1962); Terminiello v. Chicago, 337 U.S. 1, 4 (1949); De Jonge v. Oregon, 299 U.S. 353, 365 (1937). To permit the continued building of our politics and culture, and to assure self-fulfillment for each individual, our people are guaranteed the right to express any thought, free from government censorship. The essence of this forbidden censorship is content control. Any restriction on expressive activity because of its content would completely undercut the `profound national commitment to the principle that debate on public issue should be uninhibited, robust, and wide-open.' New York Times Co. v. Sullivan, supra, at 270.

"Necessarily, then under the Equal Protection Clause, not to mention the First Amendment itself, government may not grant the use of a forum to people whose views it finds acceptable, but deny use to those wishing to express less favored or more controversial views. And it may not select which issues are worth discussing or debating in public facilities. There is an `equality of status in the field of ideas,' and government must afford all points of view an equal opportunity to be heard. Once a forum is opened up to assembly or speaking by some groups, government may not prohibit others from assembling or speaking on the basis of what they intend to say. Selective exclusions from a public forum may not be based on content alone, and may not be justified by reference to content alone." 408 U.S., at 95 -96. (Footnote omitted.)

This statement, and others to the same effect, read literally and without regard for the facts of the case in which it was made, would absolutely preclude any regulation of expressive activity predicated in whole or in part on the content of the communication. But we learned long ago that broad statements of principle, no matter how correct in the context in which they are made, are sometimes qualified by contrary decisions before the absolute limit of the stated principle is reached. 22 When we review this Court's actual adjudications in the First Amendment area, we find this to have been the case with the stated principle that there may be no restriction whatever on expressive activity because of its content.

The question whether speech is, or is not, protected by the First Amendment often depends on the content of the speech. Thus, the line between permissible advocacy and impermissible incitation to crime or violence depends, not merely on the setting in which the speech occurs, but also on exactly what the speaker had to say. 23 Similarly, it is the content of the utterance that determines whether it is a protected epithet or an unprotected "fighting comment." 24 And in time of war "the publication of the sailing dates of transports or the number and location of troops" may unquestionably be restrained, see Near v. Minnesota ex rel. Olson, 283 U.S. 697, 716, although publication of news stories with a different content would be protected.

Even within the area of protected speech, a difference in content may require a different governmental response. In New York Times Co. v. Sullivan, 376 U.S. 254, we recognized that the First Amendment places limitations on the States' power to enforce their libel laws. We held that a public official may not recover damages from a critic of his official conduct without proof of "malice" as specially defined in that opinion. 25 Implicit in the opinion is the assumption that if the content of the newspaper article had been different - that is, if its subject matter had not been a public official - a lesser standard of proof would have been adequate.

In a series of later cases, in which separate individual views were frequently stated, the Court addressed the broad problem of when the New York Times standard of malice was required by the First Amendment. Despite a diversity of opinion on whether it was required only in cases involving public figures, or also in cases involving public issues, and on whether the character of the damages claim mattered, a common thread which ran through all the opinions was the assumption that the rule to be applied depended on the content of the communication. 26 But that assumption did not contradict the underlying reason for the rule which is generally described as a prohibition of regulation based on the content of protected communication. The essence of that rule is the need for absolute neutrality by the government; its regulation of communication may not be affected by sympathy or hostility for the point of view being expressed by the communicator. 27 Thus, although the content of a story must be examined to decide whether it involves a public figure or a public issue, the Court's application of the relevant rule may not depend on its favorable or unfavorable appraisal of that figure or that issue.

We have recently held that the First Amendment affords some protection to commercial speech. 28 We have also made it clear, however, that the content of a particular advertisement may determine the extent of its protection. A public rapid transit system may accept some advertisements and reject others. 29 A state statute may permit highway billboards to advertise business located in the neighborhood but not elsewhere, 30 and regulatory commissions may prohibit businessmen from making statements which, though literally true, are potentially deceptive. 31 The measure of constitutional protection to be afforded commercial speech will surely be governed largely by the content of the communication. 32

More directly in point are opinions dealing with the question whether the First Amendment prohibits the State and Federal Governments from wholly suppressing sexually oriented materials on the basis of their "obscene character." In Ginsberg v. New York, 390 U.S. 629, the Court upheld a conviction for selling to a minor magazines which were concededly not "obscene" if shown to adults. Indeed, the Members of the Court who would accord the greatest protection to such materials have repeatedly indicated that the State could prohibit the distribution or exhibition of such materials to juveniles and unconsenting adults. 33 Surely the First Amendment does not foreclose such a prohibition; yet it is equally clear that any such prohibition must rest squarely on an appraisal of the content of material otherwise within a constitutionally protected area.

Such a line may be drawn on the basis of content without violating the government's paramount obligation of neutrality in its regulation of protected communication. For the regulation of the places where sexually explicit films may be exhibited is unaffected by whatever social, political, or philosophical message a film may be intended to communicate; whether a motion picture ridicules or characterizes one point of view or another, the effect of the ordinances is exactly the same.

Moreover, even though we recognize that the First Amendment will not tolerate the total suppression of erotic materials that have some arguably artistic value, it is manifest that society's interest in protecting this type of expression is of a wholly different, and lesser, magnitude than the interest in untrammeled political debate that inspired Voltaire's immortal comment. Whether political oratory or philosophical discussion moves us to applaud or to despise what is said, every schoolchild can understand why our duty to defend the right to speak remains the same. But few of us would march our sons and daughters off to war to preserve the citizen's right to see "Specified Sexual Activities" exhibited in the theaters of our choice. Even though the First Amendment protects communication in this area from total suppression, we hold that the State may legitimately use the content of these materials as the basis for placing them in a different classification from other motion pictures.

The remaining question is whether the line drawn by these ordinances is justified by the city's interest in preserving the character of its neighborhoods. On this question we agree with the views expressed by District Judges Kennedy and Gubow. The record discloses a factual basis for the Common Council's conclusion that this kind of restriction will have the desired effect. 34 It is not our function to appraise the wisdom of its decision to require adult theaters to be separated rather than concentrated in the same areas. In either event, the city's interest in attempting to preserve the quality of urban life is one that must be accorded high respect. Moreover, the city must be allowed a reasonable opportunity to experiment with solutions to admittedly serious problems.

Since what is ultimately at stake is nothing more than a limitation on the place where adult films may be exhibited, 35 even though the determination of whether a particular film fits that characterization turns on the nature of its content, we conclude that the city's interest in the present and future character of its neighborhoods adequately supports its classification of motion pictures. We hold that the zoning ordinances requiring that adult motion picture theaters not be located within 1,000 feet of two other regulated uses does not violate the Equal Protection Clause of the Fourteenth Amendment.

The judgment of the Court of Appeals is

Reversed.

[*] Part III of this opinion is joined by only THE CHIEF JUSTICE, MR. JUSTICE

WHITE, and MR. JUSTICE REHNQUIST.

Notes

[1] "Congress shall make no law . . . abridging the freedom of speech, or of the press . . . ." This Amendment is made applicable to the States by the Due Process Clause of the Fourteenth Amendment. Edwards v. South Carolina, 372 U.S. 229 .

[2] The District Court held that the original form of the 500-foot restriction was invalid because it was measured from "any building containing a residential, dwelling or rooming unit." The city did not appeal from that ruling, but adopted an amendment prohibiting the operation of an adult theater within 500 feet of any area zoned for residential use. The amended restriction is not directly challenged in this litigation.

[3] In addition to adult motion picture theaters and "mini" theaters, which contain less than 50 seats, the regulated uses include adult bookstores; cabarets (group "D"); establishments for the sale of beer or intoxicating liquor for consumption on the premises; hotels or motels; pawnshops; pool or billiard halls; public lodging houses; secondhand stores; shoeshine parlors; and taxi dance halls.

[4] These terms are defined as follows:

"For the purpose of this Section, `Specified Sexual Activities' is defined as:

"1. Human Genitals in a state of sexual stimulation or arousal;

"2. Acts of human masturbation, sexual intercourse or sodomy;

"3. Fondling or other erotic touching of human genitals, public region, buttock or female breast.

"And `Specified Anatomical Areas' is defined as:

"1. Less than completely and opaquely covered: (a) human genitals, pubic region, (b) buttock, and (c) female breast below a point immediately above the top of the areola; and

"2. Human male genitals in a discernibly turgid state, even if completely and opaquely covered."

[5] There are three types of adult establishments - bookstores, motion picture theaters, and mini motion picture theaters - defined respectively as follows:

"Adult Book Store

"An establishment having as a substantial or significant portion of its stock in trade, books, magazines, and other periodicals which are distinguished or characterized by their emphasis on matter depicting, describing or relating to `Specified Sexual Activities' or `Specified Anatomical Areas,' (as defined below), or an establishment with a segment or section devoted to the sale or display of such material.

"Adult Motion Picture Theater

"An enclosed building with a capacity of 50 or more persons used for presenting material distinguished or characterized by an emphasis on matter depicting, describing or relating to `Specified Sexual Activities' or `Specified Anatomical Areas,' (as defined below) for observation by patrons therein.

"Adult Mini Motion Picture Theater

"An enclosed building with a capacity for less than 50 persons used for presenting material distinguished or characterized by an emphasis on matter depicting, describing or relating to `Specified Sexual Activities' or `Specified Anatomical Areas,' (as defined below), for observation by patrons therein."

[6 ] Section 66.000 of the Official Zoning Ordinance (1972) recited:

"In the development and execution of this Ordinance, it is recognized that there are some uses which, because of their very nature, are recognized as having serious objectionable operational characteristics, particularly when several of them are concentrated under certain circumstances thereby having a deleterious effect upon the adjacent areas. Special regulation of these uses is necessary to insure that these adverse effects will not contribute to the blighting or downgrading of the surrounding neighborhood. These special regulations are itemized in this section. The primary control or regulation is for the purpose of preventing a concentration of these uses in any one area (i. e. not more than two such uses within one thousand feet of each other which would create such adverse effects)."

[7 ] The ordinance authorizes the Zoning Commission to waive the 1,000-foot restriction if it finds:

"a) That the proposed use will not be contrary to the public interest or injurious to nearby properties, and that the spirit and intent of this Ordinance will be observed.

"b) That the proposed use will not enlarge or encourage the development of a `skid row' area.

"c) That the establishment of an additional regulated use in the area will not be contrary to any program of neigh[bor]hood conservation nor will it interfere with any program of urban renewal.

"d) That all applicable regulations of this Ordinance will be observed."

[8 ] A police department memorandum addressed to the assistant corporation counsel stated that since 1967 there had been an increase in the number of adult theaters in Detroit from 2 to 25, and a comparable increase in the number of adult book stores and other "adult-type business."

[9 ] Respondents alleged a claim for relief under 42 U.S.C. 1983, invoking the jurisdiction of the federal court under 28 U.S.C. 1343 (3).

[10 ] Both cases were decided in a single opinion filed jointly by Judge Kennedy and Judge Gubow. Nortown Theatre v. Gribbs, 373 F. Supp. 363 (ED Mich. 1974).

[11 ] "When, as here, the City has stated a reason for adopting an ordinance which is a subject of legitimate concern, that statement of purpose is not subject to attack.

"Nor may the Court substitute its judgment for that of the Common Council of the City of Detroit as to the methods adopted to deal with the City's legitimate concern to preserve neighborhoods, so long as there is some rational relationship between the objective of the Ordinance and the methods adopted." Id., at 367.

[12 ] "Because the Ordinances distinguish adult theaters and bookstores from

ordinary theaters and bookstores on the basis of the content of their respective wares, the classification is one which restrains conduct protected by the First Amendment. See Interstate Circuit, Inc. v. Dallas, 390 U.S. 676 . . . (1968). The appropriate standard for reviewing the classification, therefore, is a test of close scrutiny. Harper v. Virginia Board of Elections, 383 U.S. 663, 670 . . . (1966); NAACP v. Button, 371 U.S. 415, 438 . . . (1963). Under this test, the validity of the classification depends on whether it is necessary to further a compelling State interest.

"The compelling State interest which the Defendants point to as justifying the restrictions on locations of adult theaters and bookstores is the preservation of neighborhoods, upon which adult establishments have been found to have a destructive impact. The affidavit of Dr. Mel Ravitz clearly establishes that the prohibition of more than one regulated use within 1000 feet is necessary to promote that interest. This provision therefore does not offend the equal protection clause." Id., at 369.

[13 ] "Applying those standards to the instant case, the power to license and zone businesses and prohibit their location in certain areas is clearly within the constitutional power of the City. The government interest, i. e. the preservation and stabilization of neighborhoods in the City of Detroit, is unrelated to the suppression of free expression. First Amendment rights are indirectly related, but only in the sense that they cannot be freely exercised in specific locations. Plaintiffs would not contend that they are entitled to operate a theatre or bookstore, which are commercial businesses, in a residentially zoned area; nor could they claim the right to put on a performance for profit in a public street. Admittedly the regulation here is more restrictive, but it is of the same character." Id., at 371.

[14 ] "The City did not discharge its heavy burden of justifying the prior restraint which these ordinance undoubtedly impose by merely establishing that they were designed to serve a compelling public interest. Since fundamental rights are involved, the City had the further burden of showing that the method which it chose to deal with the problem at hand was necessary and that its effect on protected rights was only incidental. The City could legally regulate movie theaters and bookstores under its police powers by providing that such establishments be operated only in particular areas. . . . However, this ordinance selects for special treatment particular business enterprises which fall within the general business classifications permissible under zoning laws and classifies them as regulated uses solely by reference to the content of the constitutionally protected materials which they purvey to the public." 518 F.2d, at 1019-1020.

[15 ] He stated in part:

"I do not view the 1000-foot provision as a regulation of speech on the basis of its content. Rather, it is a regulation of the right to locate a business based on the side-effects of its location. The interest in preserving neighborhoods is not a subterfuge for censorship." Id., at 1023.

[16 ] Both complaints allege that only adults are admitted to these theaters. Nortown expressly alleges that it "desires to continue exhibiting adult-type motion

picture films at said theater." Neither respondent has indicated any plan to exhibit pictures even arguably outside the coverage of the ordinances.

[17 ] "Such claims of facial overbreadth have been entertained in cases involving statutes which, by their terms, seek to regulate `only spoken words.' Gooding v. Wilson, 405 U.S. 518, 520 (1972). See Cohen v. California, 403 U.S. 15 (1971); Street v. New York, 394 U.S. 576 (1969); Brandenburg v. Ohio, 395 U.S. 444 (1969); Chaplinsky v. New Hampshire, 315 U.S. 568 (1942). In such cases, it has been the judgment of this Court that the possible harm to society in permitting some unprotected speech to go unpunished is outweighed by the possibility that protected speech of others may be muted and perceived grievances left to fester because of the possible inhibitory effects of overly broad statutes. Overbreadth attacks have also been allowed where the Court thought rights of association were ensnared in statutes which, by their broad sweep, might result in burdening innocent associations. See Keyishian v. Board of Regents, 385 U.S. 589 (1967); United States v. Robel, 389 U.S. 258 (1967); Aptheker v. Secretary of State, 378 U.S. 500 (1964); Shelton v. Tucker, [ 364 U.S. 479 (1960)]. Facial overbreadth claims have also been entertained where statutes, by their terms, purport to regulate the time, place, and manner of expressive or communicative conduct, see Grayned v. City of Rockford, supra, at 114-121; Cameron v. Johnson, 390 U.S., at 617 -619; Zwickler v. Koota, 389 U.S. 241, 249 -250 (1967); Thornhill v. Alabama, 310 U.S. 88 (1940), and where such conduct has required official approval under laws that delegated standardless discretionary power to local functionaries, resulting in virtually unreviewable prior restraints on First Amendment rights. See Shuttlesworth v. Birmingham, 394 U.S. 147 (1969); Cox v. Louisiana, 379 U.S. 536, 553 -558 (1965); Kunz v. New York, 340 U.S. 290 (1951); Lovell v. Griffin, 303 U.S. 444 (1938)." Broadrick v. Oklahoma, 413 U.S. 601, 612 - 613.

[18 ] Reasonable regulations of the time, place, and manner of protected speech, where those regulations are necessary to further significant governmental interests, are permitted by the First Amendment. See, e. g., Kovacs v. Cooper, 336 U.S. 77 (limitation on use of sound trucks); Cox v. Louisiana, 379 U.S. 559 (ban on demonstrations in or near a courthouse with the intent to obstruct justice); Grayned v. City of Rockford, 408 U.S. 104 (ban on willful making, on grounds adjacent to a school, of any noise which disturbs the good order of the school session).

[19 ] S. Tallentyre, The Friends of Voltaire 199 (1907).

[20 ] See Hague v. CIO, 307 U.S. 496, 516 (opinion of Roberts, J.).

[21 ] Terminiello v. Chicago, 337 U.S. 1, 4 .

[22 ] See, e. g., Kastigar v. United States, 406 U.S. 441, 454 -455; United Gas Co. v. Continental Oil Co., 381 U.S. 392, 404 .

[23 ] See Bond v. Floyd, 385 U.S. 116, 133 -134; Harisiades v. Shaughnessy, 342 U.S. 580, 592; Musser v. Utah, 333 U.S. 95, 99 -101.

[24 ] In Chaplinsky v. New Hampshire, 315 U.S. 568, 574, we held that a statute punishing the use of "damned racketeer[s]" and "damned Facist[s]" did not unduly

impair liberty of expression.

[25 ] "Actual malice" is shown by proof that a statement was made "with knowledge that it was false or with reckless disregard of whether it was false or not." 376 U.S., at 280 .

[26 ] See, for example, the discussion of the "`public or general interest' test" for determining the applicability of the New York Times standard in Gertz v. Robert Welch, Inc., 418 U.S. 323, 346, and the reference, id., at 348, to a factual misstatement "whose content did not warn a reasonably prudent editor or broadcaster of its defamatory potential." The mere fact that an alleged defamatory statement is false does not, of course, place it completely beyond the protection of the First Amendment. "The First Amendment requires that we protect some falsehood in order to protect speech that matters." Id., at 341.

[27 ] Thus, Professor Kalven wrote in The Concept of the Public Forum: Cox v. Louisiana, 1965 Sup. Ct. Rev. 1, 29:

"[The Equal Protection Clause] is likely to provide a second line of defense for vigorous users of the public forum. If some groups are exempted from a prohibition on parades and pickets, the rationale for regulation is fatally impeached. The objection can then no longer be keyed to interferences with other uses of the public places, but would appear to implicate the kind of message that the groups were transmitting. The regulation would thus slip from the neutrality of time, place, and circumstance into a concern about content. The result is that equal-protection analysis in the area of speech issues would merge with considerations of censorship. And this is precisely what Mr. Justice Black argued in Cox:

"`But by specifically permitting picketing for the publication of labor union views, Louisiana is attempting to pick and choose among the views it is willing to have discussed on its streets. It is thus trying to prescribe by law what matters of public interest people it allows to assemble on its streets may and may not discuss. This seems to me to be censorship in a most odious form . . .' [ 379 U.S., at 581 ]."

[28 ] Virginia Pharmacy Board v. Virginia Consumer Council, 425 U.S. 748 .

[29 ] Lehman v. City of Shaker Heights, 418 U.S. 298 (product advertising accepted, while political cards rejected).

[30 ] Markham Advertising Co. v. State, 73 Wash. 2d 405, 439 P.2d 248 (1968), appeal dismissed for want of a substantial federal question, 393 U.S. 316 .

[31 ] In NLRB v. Gissel Packing Co., 395 U.S. 575, 617, the Court upheld a federal statute which balanced an employer's free speech right to communicate with his employees against the employees' rights to associate freely by providing that the expression of "`any views, argument, or opinion'" should not be "`evidence of an unfair labor practice,'" so long as such expression contains "`no threat of reprisal or force or promise of benefit'" which would involve interference, restraint, or coercion of employees in the exercise of their right to self-organization.

The power of the Federal Trade Commission to restrain misleading, as well as false, statements in labels and advertisements has long been recognized. See, e. g., Jacob Siegel Co. v. FTC, 327 U.S. 608; FTC v. National Comm'n on Egg Nutrition, 517 F.2d 485 (CA7 1975); E. F. Drew & Co. v. FTC, 235 F.2d 735, 740 (CA2 1956).

[32] As MR. JUSTICE STEWART pointed out in Virginia Pharmacy Board v. Virginia Consumer Council, supra, at 779 (concurring opinion), the "differences between commercial price and product advertising . . . and ideological communication" permits regulation of the former that the First Amendment would not tolerate with respect to the latter.

[33] In Paris Adult Theatre I v. Slaton, 413 U.S. 49, 73, MR. JUSTICE BRENNAN, in a dissent joined by MR. JUSTICE STEWART and MR. JUSTICE MARSHALL, explained his approach to the difficult problem of obscenity under the First Amendment:

"I would hold, therefore, that at least in the absence of distribution to juveniles or obtrusive exposure to unconsenting adults, the First and Fourteenth Amendments prohibit the State and Federal Governments from attempting wholly to suppress sexually oriented materials on the basis of their allegedly `obscene' contents. Nothing in this approach precludes those governments from taking action to serve what may be strong and legitimate interests through regulation of the manner of distribution of sexually oriented material." Id., at 113.

[34] The Common Council's determination was that a concentration of "adult" movie theaters causes the area to deteriorate and become a focus of crime, effects which are not attributable to theaters showing other types of films. It is this secondary effect which these zoning ordinances attempt to avoid, not the dissemination of "offensive" speech. In contrast, in Erznoznik v. City of Jacksonville, 422 U.S. 205, the justifications offered by the city rested primarily on the city's interest in protecting its citizens from exposure to unwanted, "offensive" speech. The only secondary effect relied on to support that ordinance was the impact on traffic - an effect which might be caused by a distracting open-air movie even if it did not exhibit nudity.

[35] The situation would be quite different if the ordinance had the effect of suppressing, or greatly restricting access to, lawful speech. Here, however, the District Court specifically found that "[t]he Ordinances do not affect the operation of existing establishments but only the location of new ones. There are myriad locations in the City of Detroit which must be over 1000 feet from existing regulated establishments. This burden on First Amendment rights is slight." 373 F. Supp., at 370.

It should also be noted that the definitions of "Specified Sexual Activities" and "Specified Anatomical Areas" in the zoning ordinances, which require an emphasis on such matter and primarily concern conduct, are much more limited than the terms of the public nuisance ordinance involved in Erznoznik, supra, which broadly prohibited scenes which could not be deemed inappropriate even for juveniles.

"The ordinance is not directed against sexually explicit nudity, nor is it otherwise limited. Rather, it sweepingly forbids display of all films containing any uncovered buttocks or breasts, irrespective of context or pervasiveness. Thus it would bar a film containing a picture of a baby's buttocks, the nude body of a war victim, or scenes from a culture in which nudity is indigenous. The ordinance also might prohibit newsreel scenes of the opening of an art exhibit as well as shots of bathers on a beach. Clearly all nudity cannot be deemed obscene even as to minors. See Ginsberg v. New York, supra. Nor can such a broad restriction be justified by any other governmental interest pertaining to minors. Speech that is neither obscene as to youths nor subject to some other legitimate proscription cannot be suppressed solely to protect the young from ideas or images that a legislative body thinks unsuitable for them." 422 U.S., at 213 -214.

Moreover, unlike the ordinances in this case, the Erznoznik ordinance singled out movies "containing even the most fleeting and innocent glimpses of nudity . . . ." Id., at 214.

The Court's opinion in Erznoznik presaged our holding today by nothing that the presumption of statutory validity "has less force when a classification turns on the subject matter of expression." Id., at 215. Respondents' position is that the presumption has no force, or more precisely, that any classification based on subject matter is absolutely prohibited.

## Splawn v. California (June 6, 1977)

MR. JUSTICE REHNQUIST delivered the opinion of the Court.

Petitioner Splawn was convicted in 1971 of the sale of two reels of obscene film, a misdemeanor violation of California Penal Code § 311.2 (West 1970). After the conviction was affirmed on appeal by the California First District Court of Appeal and the State Supreme Court denied review, this Court granted certiorari, vacated the judgment, and remanded for consideration in light of our decision in Miller v. California, 413 U. S. 15 (1973), which had set forth the standards by which the constitutionality of § 311.2 was to be determined. After the State Supreme Court ruled that the statute satisfied the requirements articulated in Miller, see Bloom v. Municipal Court, 16 Cal.3d 71, 545 P.2d 229 (1976), the Court of Appeal again affirmed the conviction and the California Supreme Court denied petitioner's motion for a hearing.

We again granted certiorari, 429 U.S. 997 (1976), to consider petitioner's assorted contentions that his conviction must be reversed because portions of the instructions given to the jury during his trial render his conviction violative of the First and Fourteenth Amendments. He claims that the instruction allowed the jury to convict him even though it might otherwise have found the material in question to have been protected under the Miller standards. He also contends that the same portions of the instructions render his conviction invalid by reason of the constitutional prohibition against ex post facto laws and the requirement of fair warning in the construction of a criminal statute enunciated in Bouie v. City of Columbia, 378 U. S. 347 (1964). We consider these contentions in light of the fact that petitioner has abandoned any claim that the material for the selling of which he was convicted could not be found to be obscene consistently with the First and Fourteenth Amendments, and any claim that the California statute under which he was convicted does not satisfy the requirements articulated in Miller, supra.

As it was understood by the California Court of Appeal, petitioner's challenge is leveled against the following portion of the instructions:

"In determining the question of whether the allegedly obscene matter is utterly without redeeming social importance, you may consider the circumstances of sale and distribution, and particularly whether such circumstances indicate that the matter was being commercially exploited by the defendants for the sake of its prurient appeal. Such evidence is probative with respect to the nature of the matter and can justify the conclusion that the matter is utterly without redeeming social importance. The weight, if any, such evidence is entitled [to] is a matter for you, the Jury, to determine."

"* * * *"

"Circumstances of production and dissemination are relevant to determining whether social importance claimed for material was, in the circumstances, pretense or reality. If you conclude that the purveyor's sole emphasis is in the sexually provocative aspect of the publication, that fact can justify the conclusion that the matter is utterly without redeeming social importance."

App. 38-39.

There is no doubt that, as a matter of First Amendment obscenity law, evidence of pandering to prurient interests in the creation, promotion, or dissemination of material is relevant in determining whether the material is obscene. Hamling v. United States, 418 U. S. 87, 418 U. S. 130 (1974); Ginzburg v. United States, 383 U. S. 463, 383 U. S. 470 (1966). This is so partly because, as the Court has pointed out before, the fact that the accused made such an appeal has a bearing on the ultimate constitutional tests for obscenity:

"The deliberate representation of petitioners' publications as erotically arousing,.for example, stimulated the reader to accept them as prurient; he looks for titillation, not for saving intellectual content. Similarly, such representation would tend to force public confrontation with the potentially offensive aspects of the work; the brazenness of such an appeal heightens the offensiveness of the publications to those who are offended by such material. And the circumstances of presentation and dissemination of material are equally relevant to determining whether social importance claimed for material in the courtroom was, in the circumstances, pretense or reality – whether it was the basis upon which it was traded in the marketplace or a spurious claim for litigation purposes."

Ibid.

Petitioner's interpretation of the challenged portions of the instructions in his case is that they permitted the jury to consider motives of commercial exploitation on the part of persons in the chain of distribution of the material other than himself. We upheld a similar instruction in Hamling, supra, however, wherein the jury was told that it could consider

"whether the materials had been pandered, by looking to their '[m]anner of distribution, circumstances of production, sale, . . . advertising . . . [, and] editorial intent. . . .' This instruction was given with respect to both the Illustrated Report and the brochure which advertised it, both of which were at issue in the trial."

418 U.S. at 418 U. S. 130.

Both Hamling and Ginzburg were prosecutions under federal obscenity statutes in federal courts, where our authority to review jury instructions is a good deal broader than is our power to upset state court convictions by reason of instructions given during the course of a trial. See Cupp v. Naughten, 414 U. S. 141 (1973); Henderson v. Kibbe, ante p. 431 U. S. 145. We can exercise the latter authority only if the instruction renders the subsequent conviction violative of the United States Constitution. Questions of what categories of evidence may be admissible and probative are otherwise for the courts of the States to decide. We think Hamling, supra, and Ginzburg, supra, rather clearly show that the instruction in question abridges no rights of petitioner under the First Amendment as made applicable to the States by the Fourteenth Amendment.

But petitioner contends that, even though this be so, the particular portions of the instructions of which he complains were given pursuant to a statute enacted after the conduct for which he was prosecuted. In his view, therefore, his conviction both violates the constitutional prohibition against ex post facto laws, See Calder v. Bull, 3 Dall. 386, 3 U. S. 390 (1798), and failed to give him constitutionally fair warning of the prohibited conduct with which he was charged. Bouie v. Columbia, supra. We find these contentions to be without merit, and we reject them.

The section of the California Penal Code defining the substantive misdemeanor with which petitioner was convicted, § 311.2, was in full force and effect at all times relevant to petitioner's conduct. California Penal Code § 311(a) (West 1970), which authorized the above-quoted instructions, was enacted after part of the conduct for which he was convicted but prior to his trial. That section, however, does not create any new substantive offense, but merely declares what type of evidence may be received and considered in deciding whether the matter in question was "utterly without redeeming social importance."

Petitioner's ex post facto argument is based on his reading of an earlier decision of the Supreme Court of California, People v. Noroff, 67 Cal.2d 791, 433 P.2d 479 (1967). His view is that, under that case, evidence such as was admitted here would not have been admissible at his trial on the substantive offense but for the enactment of § 311(a)(2). He claims that such a change in procedural rules governing his trial amounts to the enactment of an ex post facto law in violation of Art. I, § 9, cl. 3. The California Court of Appeal's opinion in this case rejected that contention, and since it is a contention which must in the last analysis turn on a proper reading of the California decisions, such a determination by the California Court of Appeal is entitled to great weight in evaluating petitioner's constitutional contentions.

The Court of Appeal, commenting on Noroff, said with respect to the California Supreme Court's decision in that case:

"The court did not, however, disapprove of any use of evidence of pandering for its probative value on the issue of whether the material was obscene. It merely rejected the concept of pandering of nonobscene material as a separate crime under the existing laws of California."

App. to Pet. for Cert. ix.

We accept this conclusion of the California Court of Appeal, and therefore find it unnecessary to determine whether if § 311(a)(2) had permitted the introduction of evidence which would have been previously excluded under California law, petitioner would have had a tenable claim under the Ex Post Facto Clause of the United States Constitution.

Bouie v. City of Columbia, supra, holds that the elements of a statutory offense may not be so changed by judicial interpretation as to deny to accused defendants fair warning of the crime prohibited. No such change in the interpretation of the elements of the substantive offense prohibited by California law took place here, and petitioner may therefore derive no benefit from Bouie.

We thus find no merit in petitioner's claims based on First and Fourteenth Amendment protection of nonobscene matter, the constitutional prohibition against ex post facto laws, or Bouie v. City of Columbia. We have considered petitioner's other claims, which appear to be variations on the same theme. and likewise reject them. The judgment of the California Court of Appeal is

Affirmed.

## Ward v. Illinois (June 9, 1977)

MR. JUSTICE WHITE delivered the opinion of the Court.

The principal issue in this case is the validity of the Illinois obscenity statute, considered in light of Miller v. California, 413 U.S. 15 (1973). There we reaffirmed numerous prior decisions declaring that "obscene material is unprotected by the First Amendment," id., at 23; but acknowledging "the inherent dangers of undertaking to regulate any form of expression," ibid., we recognized that official regulation must be limited to "works which depict or describe sexual conduct" and that such conduct "must be specifically defined by the applicable state law, as written or authoritatively construed." Id., at 24. Basic guidelines for the trier of fact, along with more specific suggestions, were then offered:

"The basic guidelines for the trier of fact must be:

(a) whether `the average person, applying contemporary community standards' would find that the work, taken as a whole, appeals to the prurient interest, Kois v. Wisconsin, [ 408 U.S. 229,] 230 [(1972)], quoting Roth v. United States, [ 354 U.S. 476,]

489 [(1957)]; (b) whether the work depicts or describes, in a patently offensive way, sexual conduct specifically defined by the applicable state law; and (c) whether the work, taken as a whole, lacks serious literary, artistic, political, or scientific value. We do not adopt as a constitutional standard the `utterly without redeeming social value' test of Memoirs v. Massachusetts, 383 U.S., at 419; that concept has never commanded the adherence of more than three Justices at one time. See supra, at 21. If a state law that regulates obscene material is thus limited, as written or construed, the First Amendment values applicable to the States through the Fourteenth Amendment are adequately protected by the ultimate power of appellate courts to conduct an independent review of constitutional claims when necessary. See Kois v. Wisconsin, supra, at 232; Memoirs v. Massachusetts, supra, at 459-460 (Harlan, J., dissenting); Jacobellis v. Ohio, 378 U.S., at 204 (Harlan, J., dissenting); New York Times Co. v. Sullivan, 376 U.S. 254, 284 -285 (1964); Roth v. United States, supra, at 497-498 (Harlan, J., concurring and dissenting).

"We emphasize that it is not our function to propose regulatory schemes for the States. That must await their concrete legislative efforts. It is possible, however, to give a few plain examples of what a state statute could define for regulation under part(b) of the standard announced in this opinion, supra:

"(a) Patently offensive representations or descriptions of ultimate sexual acts, normal or perverted, actual or simulated.

"(b) Patently offensive representations or descriptions of masturbation, excretory functions, and lewd exhibition of the genitals." Id., at 24-25. (Footnotes omitted.)

Illinois Rev. Stat., c. 38, 11-20 (a) (1) (1975), forbids the sale of obscene matter. Section 11-20(b) defines "obscene" as follows:

"A thing is obscene if, considered as a whole, its predominant appeal is to prurient interest, that is, a shameful or morbid interest in nudity, sex or excretion, and if it goes substantially beyond customary limits of candor in description or representation of such matters. A thing is obscene even though the obscenity is latent, as in the case of undeveloped photographs." 1

In October 1971 appellant Ward was charged in the State of Illinois with having sold two obscene publications in violation of 11-20 (a) (1). A jury was waived. At the bench trial the State's evidence consisted solely of the two publications - "Bizarre World" and "Illustrated Case Histories, a Study of Sado-Masochism" - and the testimony of the police officer who purchased them in Ward's store. Ward was found guilty, and in April 1972, he was sentenced to one day in jail and fined $200. His conviction was affirmed in the state appellate courts after this Court's decision in Miller. The Illinois Supreme Court expressly rejected his challenge to the constitutionality of the Illinois obscenity statute for failure to conform to the standards of Miller, as well as a claim that the two publications were not obscene. 63 Ill. 2d 437, 349 N. E. 2d 47 (1976). Ward appealed, and we noted probable jurisdiction, 429 U.S. 1037 (1977), to resolve a conflict with a decision of a three-judge District Court for the Northern District of Illinois. Eagle Books, Inc. v. Reinhard,

418 F. Supp. 345 (1976), appeal docketed, No. 76-366. We affirm.

As we read the questions presented by Ward, 2 they fairly subsume four issues. First, is the claim that Illinois has failed to comply with Miller's requirement that the sexual conduct that may not be depicted in a patently offensive way must be "specifically defined by the applicable state law as written or authoritatively construed," see supra, at 768, and that absent such compliance the Illinois law is unconstitutionally vague because it failed to give him notice that materials dealing with the kind of sexual conduct involved here could not legally be sold in the State. This claim is wholly without merit. As we shall see below, the State has complied with Miller, but even if this were not the case, appellant had ample guidance from the Illinois Supreme Court that his conduct did not conform to the Illinois law. Materials such as these, which by title or content may fairly be described as sado-masochistic, had been expressly held to violate the Illinois statute long before Miller and prior to the sales for which Ward was prosecuted.

In People v. Sikora, 32 Ill. 2d 260, 267-268, 204 N. E. 2d 768, 772-773 (1965), there are detailed recitations of the kind of sexual conduct depicted in the materials found to be obscene under the Illinois statute. These recitations included "sadism and masochism." 3 See also People v. DeVilbiss, 41 Ill. 2d 135, 142, 242 N. E. 2d 761, 765 (1968); 4 cf. Chicago v. Geraci, 46 Ill. 2d 576, 582-583, 264 N. E. 2d 153, 157 (1970). 5 The construction of the statute in Sikora gives detailed meaning to the Illinois law, is binding on us, and makes plain that 11-20 reaches the kind of sexual materials which we now have before us. If Ward cannot be convicted for selling these materials, it is for other reasons and not because the Illinois statute is vague and gave him no notice that the statute purports to ban the kind of materials he sold. The statute is not vague as applied to Ward's conduct.

Second, Ward appears to assert that sado-masochistic materials may not be constitutionally proscribed because they are not expressly included within the examples of the kinds of sexually explicit representations that Miller used to explicate the aspect of its obscenity definition dealing with patently offensive depictions of specifically defined sexual conduct. But those specifics were offered merely as "examples," 413 U.S., at 25; and, as later pointed out in Hamling v. United States, 418 U.S. 87, 114 (1974), they "were not intended to be exhaustive." Furthermore, there was no suggestion in Miller that we intended to extend constitutional protection to the kind of flagellatory materials that were among those held obscene in Mishkin v. New York, 383 U.S. 502, 505 -510 (1966). If the Mishkin publications remain unprotected, surely those before us today deal with a category of sexual conduct which, if obscenely described, may be proscribed by state law.

The third claim is simply that these materials are not obscene when examined under the three-part test of Miller. This argument is also foreclosed by Mishkin v. New York, supra, which came down the same day as Memoirs v. Massachusetts, 383 U.S. 413 (1966), and which employed the obscenity criteria announced by the latter case. See Marks v. United States, 430 U.S. 188, 194 (1977). The courts below examined the materials and found them obscene under the Illinois statute, which, as we shall see, infra, at 774-776, conforms to the standards set out in Miller, except that it retains the stricter Memoirs formulation of the "redeeming social value" factor. We have found no reason to differ with the Illinois courts.

Fourth, even assuming that the Illinois statute had been construed to overcome the vagueness challenge in this case and even assuming that the materials at issue here are not protected under Miller, there remains the claim that Illinois has failed to conform to the Miller requirement that a state obscenity law, as written or authoritatively construed, must state specifically the kinds of sexual conduct the description or representation of which the State intends to proscribe by its obscenity law. If Illinois has not complied with this requirement, its statute is arguably overbroad, unconstitutional on its face, and an invalid predicate for Ward's conviction.

As we see it, Illinois has not failed to comply with Miller, and its statute is not overbroad. People v. Ridens, 51 Ill. 2d 410, 282 N. E. 2d 691 (1972), vacated and remanded, 413 U.S. 912 (1973), involved a conviction under this same Illinois obscenity law. It was pending on our docket when our judgment and opinion in Miller issued. We vacated the Ridens judgment and remanded the case for further consideration in the light of Miller. On remand, the Illinois Supreme Court explained that originally 11-20 had provided the tests for obscenity found in Roth v. United States, 354 U.S. 476 (1957), and that it subsequently had been construed to incorporate the tripartite standard found in Memoirs v. Massachusetts, supra, including the requirement that the materials prohibited be "utterly without redeeming social value." People v. Ridens, 59 Ill. 2d 362, 321 N. E. 2d 264 (1974). The Illinois court then proceeded to "construe section 11-20 of the Criminal Code . . . to incorporate parts (a) and (b) of the Miller standards," id., at 373, 321 N. E. 2d, at 270, but to retain the "utterly without redeeming social value" standard of Memoirs in preference to the more relaxed criterion contained in part (c) of the Miller guidelines. Ridens' conviction was affirmed, and we denied certiorari. 6   421 U.S. 993 (1975).

Because the Illinois court did not go further and expressly describe the kinds of sexual conduct intended to be referred to under part (b) of the Miller guidelines, the issue is whether the Illinois obscenity law is open-ended and overbroad. As we understand the Illinois Supreme Court, however, the statute is not vulnerable in this respect. That court expressly incorporated into the statute part (b) of the guidelines, which requires inquiry "whether the work depicts or describes, in a patently offensive way, sexual conduct specifically defined by the applicable state law." 413 U.S., at 24 . The Illinois court thus must have been aware of the need for specificity and of the Miller Court's examples explaining the reach of part (b). See id., at 25. The Illinois court plainly intended to conform the Illinois law to part (b) of Miller, and there is no reason to doubt that, in incorporating the guideline as part of the law, the Illinois court intended as well to adopt the Miller examples, which gave substantive meaning to part (b) by indicating the kinds of materials within its reach. The alternative reading of the decision would lead us to the untenable conclusion that the Illinois Supreme Court chose to create a fatal flaw in its statute by refusing to take cognizance of the specificity requirement set down in Miller.

Furthermore, in a later case, People v. Gould, 60 Ill. 2d 159, 324 N. E. 2d 412 (1975), the Illinois Supreme Court quoted at length from Miller v. California, including the entire passage set out at the beginning of this opinion, supra, at 768-770 - a passage that contains the explanatory examples as well as the guidelines. It then stated that Ridens had construed the Illinois statute to include parts (a) and (b) of the Miller guidelines, and it expressly referred to the standards set out in the immediately preceding quotation from Miller. 60 Ill. 2d, at 164-165, 324 N. E. 2d, at 415. Because the quotation contained not only part (b) but the examples given to explain that part, it would be a needlessly technical and wholly unwarranted reading of the Illinois opinions to conclude that the state court did not adopt these explanatory examples as well as the guidelines themselves.

It might be argued that, whether or not the Illinois court adopted the Miller examples as part of its law, 11-20 nevertheless remains overbroad because the State has not provided an exhaustive list of the sexual conduct the patently offensive description of which may be held obscene under the statute. We agree with the Illinois Supreme Court, however, that "in order that a statute be held overbroad the overbreadth `must not only be real, but substantial as well, judged in relation to the statute's plainly legitimate sweep.' (Broadrick v. Oklahoma, 413 U.S. 601, 615 . . . .)" People v. Ridens, supra, at 372, 321 N. E. 2d, at 269. Since it is plain enough from its prior cases and from its response to Miller that the Illinois court recognizes the limitations on the kinds of sexual conduct which may not be represented or depicted under the obscenity laws, we cannot hold the Illinois statute to be unconstitutionally overbroad.

Given that Illinois has adopted Miller's explanatory examples, what the State has done in attempting to bring its statute in conformity with Miller is surely as much as this Court did in its post-Miller construction of federal obscenity statutes. In Hamling v. United States, 418 U.S., at 114, we construed 18 U.S.C. 1461, which prohibits the mailing of obscene matter, to be limited to "the sort of" patently offensive representations or descriptions of that specific hardcore sexual conduct given as examples in Miller. We have also indicated our approval of an identical approach with respect to the companion provisions of 18 U.S.C. 1462, which prohibits importation or transportation of obscene matter. See United States v. 12 200-Ft. Reels of Film, 413 U.S. 123, 130 n. 7 (1973).

Finding all four of Ward's claims to be without merit, we affirm the judgment of the Illinois Supreme Court.

So ordered.

Notes

[1 ] Section 11-20 (c) provides: "(c) Interpretation of Evidence. "Obscenity shall be judged with reference to ordinary adults, except that it shall be judged with reference to children or other specially susceptible audiences if it appears from the character of the material or the circumstances of its dissemination to be specially designed for or directed

to such an audience."

[2 ] The questions presented in Ward's Jurisdictional Statement 3 are (1) whether the provisions of 11-20, "on its face and as construed by the Illinois Supreme Court, are vague, indefinite, overbroad and uncertain, in violation of the free speech and press and due process provisions of the First and Fourteenth Amendments to the Constitution of the United States"; and (2) whether "the publications, `Bizarre World' and `Illustrated Case Histories, a Study of Sado-Masochism' are constitutionally protected, as a matter of law."

[3 ] The Illinois Supreme Court described the materials as follows, 32 Ill. 2d, at 267-268, 204 N. E. 2d, at 772-773: "`Lust Campus' by Andrew Shaw is a story of sexual adventures on a college campus `where even members of the faculty taught sin and evil.' The book describes homosexuals `necking' on a public beach; mutual masturbation; self fondling; a circle of persons engaged in oral-genital contact; rape; intercourse; lesbian intercourse; cunnilingus and flagellation; flagellation with barbed wire; an abortion with red-hot barbed wire; masturbation with a mirror reflection, and a transvestite episode. "`Passion Bride' by John Dexter described curricular and extracurricular sexual episodes that take place during a honeymoon on the French Riviera. The book describes masturbation; intercourse; a party between an old man and three prostitutes; attempted intercourse in a bath; lesbian foreplay; flagellation; rape ending in the death of the female from a broken back and intercourse ending in the broken back of the male participant. "`Crossroads of Lust' by Andrew Shaw describes the sexual adventures of various persons in a small town. There are numerous descriptions of intercourse; lesbian intercourse; oral-genital contact; and rape. A woman stabs a man in the course of intercourse, completing the act after he is dead. There are also three voyeurism scenes, two of which involve watching lesbian love play. The third is characterized by sadism and masochism."

[4 ] This case involved a local ordinance that the Illinois Supreme Court described as identical to the state statute. The court described the materials at issue: "The books are replete with accounts of homosexual acts, masturbation, flagellation, oral-genital acts, rape, voyeurism, masochism and sadism. These accounts can only appeal to the prurient interest, and clearly go beyond customary limits of candor in the kinds of conduct described and in the detail of description." 41 Ill. 2d, at 142, 242 N. E. 2d, at 765.

[5 ] The materials under scrutiny - also under a local ordinance - were described by the court: "The author's accounts of normal and abnormal sexual conduct, including sodomy, flagellation, masturbation, oral-genital contact, anal intercourse, lesbianism, and sadism and masochism, are vivid, intimately detailed, and explicit. (Cf. One, Inc. v. Olesen (1958), 355 U.S. 371 . . .)" 46 Ill. 2d, at 582-583, 264 N. E. 2d, at 157.

[6 ] Four Justices dissented, but waived the Rule of Four - that, if at least four Justices so request, the Court will give plenary consideration to a particular case. 421 U.S., at 994 n.

**National Socialist Party of America v. Village of Skokie (June 14, 1977)**

PER CURIAM.

On April 29, 1977, the Circuit Court of Cook County entered an injunction against petitioners. The injunction prohibited them from performing any of the following actions within the village of Skokie, Ill.: "[m]arching, walking or parading in the uniform of the National Socialist Party of America; [m]arching, walking or parading or otherwise displaying the swastika on or off their person; [d]istributing pamphlets or displaying any materials which incite or promote hatred against persons of Jewish faith or ancestry or hatred against persons of any faith or ancestry, race or religion." The Illinois Appellate Court denied an application for stay pending appeal. Applicants then filed a petition for a stay in the Illinois Supreme Court, together with a request for a direct expedited appeal to that court. The Illinois Supreme Court denied both the stay and leave for an expedited appeal. Applicants then filed an application for a stay with MR. JUSTICE STEVENS, as Circuit Justice, who referred the matter to the Court.

Treating the application as a petition for certiorari from the order of the Illinois Supreme Court, we grant certiorari and reverse the Illinois Supreme Court's denial of a stay. That order is a final judgment for purposes of our jurisdiction, since it involved a right "separable from, and collateral to" the merits, Cohen v. Beneficial Loan Corp., 337 U.S. 541, 546 (1949). See Abney v. United States, 431 U.S. 651 (1977); cf. Cox Broadcasting Corp. v. Cohn, 420 U.S. 469, 476 -487 (1975). It finally determined the merits of petitioners' claim that the outstanding injunction will deprive them of rights protected by the First Amendment during the period of appellate review which, in the normal course, may take a year or more to complete. If a State seeks to impose a restraint of this kind, it must provide strict procedural safeguards, Freedman v. Maryland, 380 U.S. 51 (1965), including immediate appellate review, see Nebraska Press Assn. v. Stuart, 423 U.S. 1319, 1327 (1975) (BLACKMUN, J., in chambers). Absent such review, the State must instead allow a stay. The order of the Illinois Supreme Court constituted a denial of that right.

Reversed and remanded for further proceedings not inconsistent with this opinion.

So ordered.

## Pinkus v. US (May 23, 1978)

MR. CHIEF JUSTICE BURGER delivered the opinion of the Court.

We granted certiorari in this case to decide whether the court's instructions in a trial for mailing obscene materials prior to 1973, and therefore tried under the Roth-Memoirs standards, could properly include children and sensitive persons within the definition of the community by whose standards obscenity is to be judged. We are also asked to determine whether the evidence supported a charge that members of deviant sexual groups may be considered in determining whether the materials appealed to prurient interest in sex; whether a charge of pandering was proper in light of the evidence; and whether comparison evidence proffered by petitioner should have been admitted on the issue of contemporary community standards.

Petitioner was convicted after a jury trial in United States District Court on 11 counts, charging that he had mailed obscene materials and advertising brochures for obscene materials in violation of 18 U.S.C. § 1461 (1976 ed.). [1] On appeal, his conviction was reversed on the grounds that the instructions to the jury defining obscenity had been cast under the standards established in Miller v. California, 413 U. S. 15 (1973), although the offenses charged occurred in 1971, when the standards announced in Roth v. United States, 354 U. S. 476 (1957), and particularized in Memoirs v. Massachusetts, 383 U. S. 413 (1966), were applicable. Accordingly, the case was remanded to the District Court for a new trial under the standards controlling in 1971. No. 73-2900 (CA9 Feb. 5, 1975, rehearing denied May 13, 1975); see Marks v. United States, 430 U. S. 188 (1977).

On retrial in 1976, petitioner was again convicted on the same 11 counts. He was sentenced to terms of four years' imprisonment on each count, the terms to be served concurrently, and fined $500 on each count, for a total fine of $5,500. The Court of Appeals affirmed. 551 F.2d 1155 (CA9 1977).

I

The evidence presented by the Government in its case in chief consisted of materials mailed by the petitioner, accompanied by a stipulation of facts which, among other things, recited that petitioner, knowing the contents of the mailings, [2] had "voluntarily and intentionally" used the mails on 11 occasions to deliver brochures illustrating sex books, magazines, and films, and to deliver a sex magazine (one count) and a sex film (one count), with the intention that these were for the personal use of the recipients. From the stipulation and the record, it appears undisputed that the recipients were adults who resided both within and without the State of California. Because of the basis of our disposition of this case, it is unnecessary for us to review the contents of the exhibits in detail.

The defense consisted of expert testimony and surveys offered to demonstrate that the materials did not appeal to prurient interest, were not in conflict with community standards, and had redeeming social value. Two films were proffered by the defense for the stated purpose of demonstrating that comparable material had received wide box office acceptance, thus demonstrating that the materials covered by the indictment were not obscene and complied with community standards.

As a rebuttal witness, the Government presented an expert who testified as to what some of the exhibits depicted and that, in his opinion, they appealed to the prurient interest of the average person and to that of members of particular deviant groups.

II

In this Court, as in the Court of Appeals, petitioner challenges four parts of the jury instructions and the trial court's rejection of the comparison films.

A. Instruction as to Children

Petitioner challenges that part of the jury instruction which read:

"In determining community standards, you are to consider the community as a whole, young and old, educated and uneducated, the religious and the irreligious, men, women and children, from all walks of life."

(Emphasis added.)

The Court of Appeals concluded that the inclusion of children was "unnecessary," and that it would "prefer that children be excluded from the court's [jury] instruction until the Supreme Court clearly indicates that inclusion is proper." 551 .2d at 1158. It correctly noted that this Court had been ambivalent on this point, having sustained the conviction in Roth, supra, where the instruction included children, and having intimated later in Ginzburg v. United States, 383 U. S. 463, 383 U. S. 465 n. 3 (1966), that it did not necessarily approve the inclusion of "children" as part of the community instruction. [3]

Reviewing the charge as a whole under the traditional standard of review, cogent arguments can be made that the inclusion of children was harmless error, see Hamling v. United States, 418 U. S. 87, 418 U. S. 107 (1974); however, the courts, the bar, and the public are entitled to greater clarity than is offered by the ambiguous comment in Ginzburg on this score. Since this is a federal prosecution under an Act of Congress, we elect to take this occasion to make clear that children are not to be included for these purposes as part of the "community" as that term relates to the "obscene materials" proscribed by 18 U.S.C. § 1461 (1976 ed.). Cf. Cupp v. Naughten, 414 U. S. 141, 414 U. S. 146 (1973).

Earlier in the same Term in which Roth was decided, the Court had reversed a conviction under a state statute which made criminal the dissemination of a book "found to have a potentially deleterious influence on youth." Butler v. Michigan, 352 U. S. 380, 352 U. S. 383 (1957). The statute was invalidated because its "incidence . . . is to reduce the adult population . . . to reading only what is fit for children." Ibid. The instruction given here, when read as a whole, did not have an effect so drastic as the Butler statute. But it may well be that a jury conscientiously striving to define the relevant community of persons, the "average person," Smith v. United States, 431 U. S. 291, 431 U. S. 304 (1977), by whose standards obscenity is to be judged, would reach a much lower "average" when children are part of the equation than it would if it restricted its consideration to the effect of allegedly obscene materials on adults. Cf. Ginsberg v. New York, 390 U. S. 629 (1968). There was no evidence that children were the intended recipients of the materials at issue here, or that petitioner had reason to know children were likely to receive the materials. Indeed, an affirmative representation was made that children were not involved in this case. [4] We therefore conclude it was error to instruct the jury that they were a part of the relevant community, and accordingly the conviction cannot stand.

B. Instruction as to Sensitive Persons

It does not follow, however, as petitioner contends, that the inclusion of "sensitive persons" in the charge advising the jury of whom the community consists was error. The District Court's charge was:

"Thus the brochures, magazines and film are not to be judged on the basis of your personal opinion. Nor are they to be judged by their effect on a particularly sensitive or insensitive person or group in the community. You are to judge these materials by the standard of the hypothetical average person in the community, but, in determining this average standard, you must include the sensitive and the insensitive, in other words, you must include everyone in the community."

(Emphasis added.)

Petitioner's reliance on passages from Miller, 413 U.S. at 413 U. S. 33, and Smith v. United States, supra at 431 U. S. 304, for the proposition that inclusion of sensitive persons in the relevant community was error is misplaced. In Miller, we said,

"[T]he primary concern with requiring a jury to apply the standard of 'the average person, applying contemporary community standards' is to be certain that, so far as material is not aimed at a deviant group, it will be judged by its impact on an average person, rather than a particularly susceptible or sensitive person -- or indeed a totally insensitive one. See Roth v. United States, supra at 354 U. S. 489."

This statement was essentially repeated in Smith:

"[T]he Court has held that § 1461 embodies a requirement that local, rather than national, standards should be applied. Hamling v. United States, supra. Similarly, obscenity is to be judged according to the average person in the community, rather than the most prudish or the most tolerant. Hamling v. United States, supra; Miller v. California, supra; Roth v. United States, 354 U. S. 476 (1957). Both of these substantive limitations are passed on to the jury in the form of instructions."

(Footnote omitted.)

The point of these passages was to emphasize what was an issue central to Roth, that

"judging obscenity by the effect of isolated passages upon the most susceptible persons, might well encompass material legitimately treating with sex, and so it must be rejected as unconstitutionally restrictive of the freedoms of speech and press."

354 U.S. at 354 U. S. 489. [5] But nothing in those opinions suggests that "sensitive" and "insensitive" persons, however defined, are to be excluded from the community as a whole for the purpose of deciding if materials are obscene. In the narrow and limited context of this case, the community includes all adults who constitute it, and a jury can consider them all in determining relevant community standards. The vice is in focusing upon the most susceptible or sensitive members when judging the obscenity of materials, not in including them along with all others in the community. See Mishkin v. New York, 383 U. S. 502, 383 U. S. 508-509 (1966).

Petitioner relies also on Hamling v. United States, 418 U. S. 87 (1974), to support his argument. Like Miller and Smith, supra, though, Hamling merely restated the by now familiar rule that jurors are not to base their decision about the materials on their "personal opinion, nor by its effect on a particularly sensitive or insensitive person or group." 418 U.S. at 418 U. S. 107. It is clear the trial court did not instruct the jury to focus on sensitive persons or groups. It explicitly said the jury should not use sensitive persons as a standard, and emphasized that, in determining the "average person" standard, the jury "must include the sensitive and the insensitive, in other words . . . everyone in the community."

The difficulty of framing charges in this area is well recognized. But the term "average person," as used in this charge, means what it usually means, and is no less clear than "reasonable person" used for generations in other contexts. Cf. Hamling . United States, supra at 418 U. S. 104-105. Cautionary instructions to avoid subjective personal and private views in determining community standards can do no more than tell the individual juror that, in evaluating the hypothetical "average person," he is to determine the collective view of the community, as best as it. can be done.

Simon E. Sobeloff, then Solicitor General, later Chief Judge of the United States Court of Appeals for the Fourth Circuit, very aptly stated the dilemma:

"Is the so-called definition of negligence really a definition? What could be fuzzier than the instruction to the jury that negligence is a failure to observe that care which would be observed by 'reasonable man' -- a chimerical creature conjured up to give an aura of definiteness where definiteness is not possible. . . . "

"Every man is likely to think of himself as the happy exemplification of 'the reasonable man;' and so the standard he adopts in order to fulfill the law's prescription will resemble himself, or what he thinks he is, or what he thinks he should be, even if he is not. All these shifts and variation of his personal norm will find reflection in the verdict. The whole business is necessarily equivocal. This we recognize, but we are reconciled to the impossibility of discovering any form of words that will ring with perfect clarity and be automatically self-executing. Alas, there is no magic push-button in this or in other branches of the law. [6]"

(Emphasis added.)

However one defines "sensitive" or "insensitive" persons, they are part of the community. The contention that the instruction was erroneous because it included sensitive persons is therefore without merit.

C. Instruction as to Deviant Groups

Challenge is made to the inclusion of "members of a deviant sexual group" in the charge, which recited:

"The first test to be applied, in determining whether a given picture is obscene, is whether the predominant theme or purpose of the picture, when viewed as a whole and not part by part, and when considered in relation to the intended and probable recipients, is an appeal to the prurient interest of the average person of the community as a whole or the prurient interest of members of a deviant sexual group at the time of mailing."

"* * * *"

"In applying this test, the question involved is not how the picture now impresses the individual juror, but rather, considering the intended and probable recipients, how the picture would have impressed the average person, or a member of a deviant sexual group at the time they received the picture."

Examination of some of the materials could lead to the reasonable conclusion that their prurient appeal would be more acute to persons of deviant persuasions, but it is equally clear they were intended to arouse the prurient interest of any reader or observer. Nothing prevents a court from giving an instruction on prurient appeal to deviant sexual groups as part of an instruction pertaining to appeal to the average person when the evidence, as here, would support such a charge. See Hamling v. United States, supra at 418 U. S. 128-130. Many of the exhibits depicted aberrant sexual activities. These depictions were generally provided along with or as a part of the materials which apparently were thought likely to appeal to the prurient interest in sex of nondeviant persons. One of the mailings even provided a list of deviant sexual groups which the recipient was asked to mark to indicate interest in receiving the type of materials thought appealing to that particular group.

Whether materials are obscene generally can be decided by viewing them; expert testimony is not necessary. Ginzburg v. United States, 383 U.S. at 383 U. S. 465; Hamling v. United States, supra at 418 U. S. 100; see Jacobellis v. Ohio, 378 U. S. 184, 378 U. S. 197 (1964) (STEWART, J., concurring). But petitioner claims that to support an instruction on appeal to the prurient interest of deviants, the prosecution must come forward with evidence to guide the jury in its deliberations, since jurors cannot be presumed to know the reaction of such groups to stimuli as they would that of the average person. Concededly, in the past, we have

"reserve[d] judgment . . . on the extreme case . . . where contested materials are directed at such a bizarre deviant group that the experience of the trier of fact would be plainly inadequate to judge whether the material appeals to the [particular] prurient interest."

Paris Adult Theatre I v. Slaton, 413 U. S. 49, 413 U. S. 56 n. 6 (1973). But here we are not presented with that "extreme" case, because the Government did, in fact, present expert testimony on rebuttal which, when combined with the exhibits themselves, sufficiently guided the jury. This instruction, therefore, was acceptable.

D. Instruction as to Pandering

Pandering is "the business of purveying textual or graphic matter openly advertised to appeal to the erotic interest of their customers." Ginzburg v. United States, supra at 383 U. S. 467, citing Roth v. United States, 354 U.S. at 354 U. S. 495-496 (Warren, C.J., concurring). We have held, and reaffirmed, that to aid a jury in its determination of whether materials are obscene, the methods of their creation, promotion, or dissemination are relevant. Splawn v. California, 431 U. S. 595, 431 U. S. 598 (1977); Hamling v. United States, 418 U.S. at 418 U. S. 130. In essence, the Court has considered motivation relevant to the ultimate evaluation if the prosecution offers evidence of motivation.

In this case, the trial judge gave a pandering instruction to which the jury could advert if it found "this to be a close case" under the three-part Roth-Memoirs test. This was not a so-called finding instruction which removed the jury's discretion; rather, it permitted the jury to consider the touting descriptions along with the materials themselves to determine whether they were intended to appeal to the recipient's prurient interest in sex, whether they were "commercial exploitation of erotica solely for the sake of their prurient appeal," Ginzburg, supra at 383 U. S. 466, if indeed the evidence admitted of any other purpose. And while it is true the Government offered no extensive evidence of the methods of production, editorial goals, if any, methods of operation, or means of delivery other than the mailings and the names, locations, and occupations of the recipients, the evidence was sufficient to trigger the Ginzburg pandering instruction.

E. Exclusion of Comparison Evidence

At trial, petitioner proffered, and the trial judge rejected, two films which were said to have had considerable popular and commercial success when displayed in Los Angeles and elsewhere around the country. He proffered this assertedly comparable material as evidence that materials as explicit as his had secured community tolerance. Apparently the theory was that display of such movies had altered the level of community tolerance.

On appeal, the Court of Appeals began an inquiry into whether the comparison evidence should have been admitted. It held that exclusion of the evidence was proper as to the printed materials, but it abandoned the inquiry when, in reliance on the so-called concurrent sentence doctrine, it concluded that, even if the comparison evidence had been improperly excluded as to the count involving petitioner's film, the sentence would not be affected. It therefore exercised its discretion not to pass on the admissibility of the comparison evidence, and hence did not review the conviction on the film count. [7]

However, the sentences on the 11 counts were not, in fact, fully concurrent; petitioner's 11 prison terms of four years each were concurrent, but the $500 fines on each of the counts were cumulative, totaling $5,500, so that a separate fine of $500 was imposed on the film count. Petitioner thus had at least a pecuniary interest in securing review of his conviction on each of the counts.

In light of our disposition of the case, the issue of admissibility of the comparison evidence is not before us, and we leave it to the Court of Appeals to decide whether or to what extent such evidence is relevant to a jury's evaluation of community standards.

Accordingly, the case is remanded to the Court of Appeals for further consideration consistent with this opinion.

Reversed and remanded.


Notes

[1] Title 18 U.S.C. § 1461 (1976 ed.) declares, in essence, that obscene materials are nonmailable and the Postal Service may not be used to convey them. It provides for fines and imprisonment upon conviction for its violation.

[2] Two of the 11 paragraphs of the stipulation, corresponding to the evidence relating to the 11 charges, do not recite that petitioner knew the contents of those two

particular mailings. Neither party has made an issue of this apparent oversight, and we believe it is without significance.

[3] Indeed, confusion over this issue might have been foreseen in light of Mr. Justice Harlan's separate opinion in Roth and its companion case, Alberts v. California. He observed that the correctness of the charge in Roth was not before the Court, but must be assumed correct. It was the constitutionality of the statute which was being decided. 354 U.S. at 354 U. S. 499 n. 1, 507 n. 8. Simultaneously, he said that he "agree[d] with the Court, of course, that the books must be judged as a whole and in relation to the normal adult reader," id. at 354 U. S. 502 (emphasis added; referring to Alberts), but the "charge [in Roth] fail[ed] to measure up to the standards which I understand the Court to approve. . . ." Id. at 354 U. S. 507.

The trial judge tried to accommodate petitioners demand that he be tried under Roth-Memoirs, and gave almost precisely the same instruction in this case as had apparently been approved in Roth.

[4] During voir dire, in response to a prospective juror's question, and after a bench conference with counsel for both sides, the District Judge said,

"[I]n no way does [the case] involve any distribution of material of any kind to children, and that the evidence will, that there will be a stipulation even that there has been no exposure of any of this evidence to children."

Though the stipulation did not specifically state no children were involved, it could be so inferred upon reading it. The Government does not contend otherwise.

[5] This rejected standard for judging obscenity was first articulated in The Queen v. Hicklin, [1868] L.R. 3 Q.B. 360.

[6] Sobeloff, Insanity and the Criminal Law: From McNaghten to Durham, and Beyond, 41 A.B.A.J. 793, 796 (1955).

[7] The validity of the concurrent sentence doctrine is not challenged here. See Benton v. Maryland, 395 U. S. 784, 395 U. S. 791 (1969).

## FCC v. Pacifica Foundation (July 3, 1978) [Appendix omitted]

MR. JUSTICE STEVENS delivered the opinion of the Court (Parts I, II, III, and IV-C) and an opinion in which THE CHIEF JUSTICE and MR. JUSTICE REHNQUIST joined (Parts IV-A and IV-B).

This case requires that we decide whether the Federal Communications Commission has any power to regulate a radio broadcast that is indecent but not obscene.

A satiric humorist named George Carlin recorded a 12-minute monologue entitled "Filthy Words" before a live audience in a California theater. He began by referring to his thoughts about "the words you couldn't say on the public, ah, airwaves, um, the ones you definitely wouldn't say, ever." He proceeded to list those words and repeat them over and over again in a variety of colloquialisms. The transcript of the recording, which is appended to this opinion, indicates frequent laughter from the audience.

At about 2 o'clock in the afternoon on Tuesday, October 30, 1973, a New York radio station, owned by respondent Pacifica Foundation, broadcast the "Filthy Words" monologue. A few weeks later a man, who stated that he had heard the broadcast while driving with his young son, wrote a letter complaining to the Commission. He stated that, although he could perhaps understand the "record's being sold for private use, I certainly cannot understand the broadcast of same over the air that, supposedly, you control."

The complaint was forwarded to the station for comment. In its response, Pacifica explained that the monologue had been played during a program about contemporary society's attitude toward language and that, immediately before its broadcast, listeners had been advised that it included "sensitive language which might be regarded as offensive to some." Pacifica characterized George Carlin as "a significant social satirist" who "like Twain and Sahl before him, examines the language of ordinary people. . . . Carlin is not mouthing obscenities, he is merely using words to satirize as harmless and essentially silly our attitudes towards those words." Pacifica stated that it was not aware of any other complaints about the broadcast.

On February 21, 1975, the Commission issued a declaratory order granting the complaint and holding that Pacifica "could have been the subject of administrative sanctions." 56 F. C. C. 2d 94, 99. The Commission did not impose formal sanctions, but it did state that the order would be "associated with the station's license file, and in the event that subsequent complaints are received, the Commission will then decide whether it should utilize any of the available sanctions it has been granted by Congress." 1

In its memorandum opinion the Commission stated that it intended to "clarify the standards which will be utilized in considering" the growing number of complaints about indecent speech on the airwaves. Id., at 94. Advancing several reasons for treating broadcast speech differently from other forms of expression, 2 the Commission found a power to regulate indecent broadcasting in two statutes: 18 U.S.C. 1464 (1976 ed.), which forbids the use of "any obscene, indecent, or profane language by means of radio communications," 3 and 47 U.S.C. 303 (g), which requires the Commission to "encourage the larger and more effective use of radio in the public interest." 4

The Commission characterized the language used in the Carlin monologue as "patently offensive," though not necessarily obscene, and expressed the opinion that it should be regulated by principles analogous to those found in the law of nuisance where the "law generally speaks to channeling behavior more than actually prohibiting it. . . . [T]he concept of `indecent' is intimately connected with the exposure of children to language that describes, in terms patently offensive as measured by contemporary community standards for the broadcast medium, sexual or excretory activities and organs, at times of the day when there is a reasonable risk that children may be in the audience." 56 F. C. C. 2d, at 98. 5

Applying these considerations to the language used in the monologue as broadcast by respondent, the Commission concluded that certain words depicted sexual and excretory activities in a patently offensive manner, noted that they "were broadcast at a time when children were undoubtedly in the audience (i. e., in the early afternoon)," and that the prerecorded language, with these offensive words "repeated over and over," was "deliberately broadcast." Id., at 99. In summary, the Commission stated: "We therefore hold that the language as broadcast was indecent and prohibited by 18 U.S.C. [] 1464." 6 Ibid.

After the order issued, the Commission was asked to clarify its opinion by ruling that the broadcast of indecent words as part of a live newscast would not be prohibited. The Commission issued another opinion in which it pointed out that it "never intended to place an absolute prohibition on the broadcast of this type of language, but rather sought to channel it to times of day when children most likely would not be exposed to it." 59 F. C. C. 2d 892 (1976). The Commission noted that its "declaratory order was issued in a specific factual context," and declined to comment on various hypothetical situations presented by the petition. 7 Id., at 893. It relied on its "long standing policy of refusing to issue interpretive rulings or advisory opinions when the critical facts are not explicitly stated or there is a possibility that subsequent events will alter them." Ibid.

The United States Court of Appeals for the District of Columbia Circuit reversed, with each of the three judges on the panel writing separately. 181 U.S. App. D.C. 132, 556 F.2d 9. Judge Tamm concluded that the order represented censorship and was expressly prohibited by 326 of the Communications Act. 8 Alternatively, Judge Tamm read the Commission opinion as the functional equivalent of a rule and concluded that it was "overbroad." 181 U.S. App. D.C., at 141, 556 F.2d, at 18. Chief Judge Bazelon's concurrence rested on the Constitution. He was persuaded that 326's prohibition against censorship is inapplicable to broadcasts forbidden by 1464. However, he concluded that 1464 must be narrowly construed to cover only language that is obscene or otherwise unprotected by the First Amendment. 181 U.S. App. D.C., at 140-153, 556 F.2d, at 24-30. Judge Leventhal, in dissent, stated that the only issue was whether the Commission could regulate the language "as broadcast." Id., at 154, 556 F.2d, at 31. Emphasizing the interest in protecting children, not only from exposure to indecent language, but also from exposure to the idea that such language has official approval, id., at 160, and n. 18, 556 F.2d, at 37, and n. 18, he concluded that the Commission had correctly condemned the daytime broadcast as indecent.

Having granted the Commission's petition for certiorari, 434 U.S. 1008, we must decide: (1) whether the scope of judicial review encompasses more than the Commission's determination that the monologue was indecent "as broadcast"; (2) whether the Commission's order was a form of censorship forbidden by 326; (3) whether the broadcast was indecent within the meaning of 1464; and (4) whether the order violates the First Amendment of the United States Constitution.

I

The general statements in the Commission's memorandum opinion do not change the character of its order. Its action was an adjudication under 5 U.S.C. 554 (e)

(1976 ed.); it did not purport to engage in formal rulemaking or in the promulgation of any regulations. The order "was issued in a specific factual context"; questions concerning possible action in other contexts were expressly reserved for the future. The specific holding was carefully confined to the monologue "as broadcast."

"This Court . . . reviews judgments, not statements in opinions." Black v. Cutter Laboratories, 351 U.S. 292, 297 . That admonition has special force when the statements raise constitutional questions, for it is our settled practice to avoid the unnecessary decision of such issues. Rescue Army v. Municipal Court, 331 U.S. 549, 568 -569. However appropriate it may be for an administrative agency to write broadly in an adjudicatory proceeding, federal courts have never been empowered to issue advisory opinions. See Herb v. Pitcairn, 324 U.S. 117, 126 . Accordingly, the focus of our review must be on the Commission's determination that the Carlin monologue was indecent as broadcast.

II

The relevant statutory questions are whether the Commission's action is forbidden "censorship" within the meaning of 47 U.S.C. 326 and whether speech that concededly is not obscene may be restricted as "indecent" under the authority of 18 U.S.C. 1464 (1976 ed.). The questions are not unrelated, for the two statutory provisions have a common origin. Nevertheless, we analyze them separately.

Section 29 of the Radio Act of 1927 provided:

"Nothing in this Act shall be understood or construed to give the licensing authority the power of censorship over the radio communications or signals transmitted by any radio station, and no regulation or condition shall be promulgated or fixed by the licensing authority which shall interfere with the right of free speech by means of radio communications. No person within the jurisdiction of the United States shall utter any obscene, indecent, or profane language by means of radio communication." 44 Stat. 1172.

The prohibition against censorship unequivocally denies the Commission any power to edit proposed broadcasts in advance and to excise material considered inappropriate for the airwaves. The prohibition, however, has never been construed to deny the Commission the power to review the content of completed broadcasts in the performance of its regulatory duties. 9

During the period between the original enactment of the provision in 1927 and its re-enactment in the Communications Act of 1934, the courts and the Federal Radio Commission held that the section deprived the Commission of the power to subject "broadcasting matter to scrutiny prior to its release," but they concluded that the Commission's "undoubted right" to take note of past program content when considering a licensee's renewal application "is not censorship." 10

Not only did the Federal Radio Commission so construe the statute prior to 1934; its successor, the Federal Communications Commission, has consistently interpreted the provision in the same way ever since. See Note, Regulation of Program Content by the FCC, 77 Harv. L. Rev. 701 (1964). And, until this case, the Court of Appeals for the District of Columbia Circuit has consistently agreed with this construction. 11 Thus, for example, in his opinion in Anti-Defamation League of B'nai B'rith v. FCC, 131 U.S. App. D.C. 146, 403 F.2d 169 (1968), cert. denied, 394 U.S. 930, Judge Wright forcefully pointed out that the Commission is not prevented from canceling the license of a broadcaster who persists in a course of improper programming. He explained:

"This would not be prohibited `censorship,' . . . any more than would the Commission's considering on a license renewal application whether a broadcaster allowed `coarse, vulgar, suggestive, double-meaning' programming; programs containing such material are grounds for denial of a license renewal." 131 U.S. App. D.C., at 150-151, n. 3. 403 F.2d, at 173-174, n. 3.

See also Office of Communication of United Church of Christ v. FCC, 123 U.S. App. D.C. 328, 359 F.2d 994 (1966).

Entirely apart from the fact that the subsequent review of program content is not the sort of censorship at which the statute was directed, its history makes it perfectly clear that it was not intended to limit the Commission's power to regulate the broadcast of obscene, indecent, or profane language. A single section of the 1927 Act is the source of both the anticensorship provision and the Commission's authority to impose sanctions for the broadcast of indecent or obscene language. Quite plainly, Congress intended to give meaning to both provisions. Respect for that intent requires that the censorship language be read as inapplicable to the prohibition on broadcasting obscene, indecent, or profane language.

There is nothing in the legislative history to contradict this conclusion. The provision was discussed only in generalities when it was first enacted. 12 In 1934, the anticensorship provision and the prohibition against indecent broadcasts were re-enacted in the same section, just as in the 1927 Act. In 1948, when the Criminal Code was revised to include provisions that had previously been located in other Titles of the United States Code, the prohibition against obscene, indecent, and profane broadcasts was removed from the Communications Act and re-enacted as 1464 of Title 18. 62 Stat. 769 and 866. That rearrangement of the Code cannot reasonably be interpreted as having been intended to change the meaning of the anticensorship provision. H. R. Rep. No. 304, 80th Cong., 1st Sess., A106 (1947). Cf. Tidewater Oil Co. v. United States, 409 U.S. 151, 162 .

We conclude, therefore, that 326 does not limit the Commission's authority to impose sanctions on licensees who engage in obscene, indecent, or profane broadcasting.

III

The only other statutory question presented by this case is whether the afternoon broadcast of the "Filthy Words" monologue was indecent within the meaning of 1464. 13 Even that question is narrowly confined by the arguments of the parties.

The Commission identified several words that referred to excretory or sexual activities or organs, stated that the repetitive, deliberate use of those words in an afternoon broadcast when children are in the audience was patently offensive, and held that the broadcast was indecent. Pacifica takes issue with the Commission's definition of indecency, but does not dispute the Commission's preliminary determination that each of the components of its definition was present. Specifically, Pacifica does not quarrel with the conclusion that this afternoon broadcast was patently offensive. Pacifica's claim that the broadcast was not indecent within the meaning of the statute rests entirely on the absence of prurient appeal.

The plain language of the statute does not support Pacifica's argument. The words "obscene, indecent, or profane" are written in the disjunctive, implying that each has a separate meaning. Prurient appeal is an element of the obscene, but the normal definition of "indecent" merely refers to nonconformance with accepted standards of morality. 14

Pacifica argues, however, that this Court has construed the term "indecent" in related statutes to mean "obscene," as that term was defined in Miller v. California, 413 U.S. 15 . Pacifica relies most heavily on the construction this Court gave to 18 U.S.C. 1461 in Hamling v. United States, 418 U.S. 87 . See also United States v. 12 200-ft. Reels of Film, 413 U.S. 123, 130 n. 7 (18 U.S.C. 1462) (dicta). Hamling rejected a vagueness attack on 1461, which forbids the mailing of "obscene, lewd, lascivious, indecent, filthy or vile" material. In holding that the statute's coverage is limited to obscenity, the Court followed the lead of Mr. Justice Harlan in Manual Enterprises, Inc. v. Day, 370 U.S. 478 . In that case, Mr. Justice Harlan recognized that 1461 contained a variety of words with many shades of meaning. 15 Nonetheless, he thought that the phrase "obscene, lewd, lascivious, indecent, filthy or vile," taken as a whole, was clearly limited to the obscene, a reading well grounded in prior judicial constructions: "[T]he statute since its inception has always been taken as aimed at obnoxiously debasing portrayals of sex." 370 U.S., at 483 . In Hamling the Court agreed with Mr. Justice Harlan that 1461 was meant only to regulate obscenity in the mails; by reading into it the limits set by Miller v. California, supra, the Court adopted a construction which assured the statute's constitutionality.

The reasons supporting Hamling's construction of 1461 do not apply to 1464. Although the history of the former revealed a primary concern with the prurient, the Commission has long interpreted 1464 as encompassing more than the obscene. 16 The former statute deals primarily with printed matter enclosed in sealed envelopes mailed from one individual to another; the latter deals with the content of public broadcasts. It is unrealistic to assume that Congress intended to impose precisely the same limitations on the dissemination of patently offensive matter by such different means. 17

Because neither our prior decisions nor the language or history of 1464 supports the conclusion that prurient appeal is an essential component of indecent language, we reject Pacifica's construction of the statute. When that construction is put to one side, there is no basis for disagreeing with the Commission's conclusion that indecent language was used in this broadcast.

IV

Pacifica makes two constitutional attacks on the Commission's order. First, it argues that the Commission's construction of the statutory language broadly encompasses so much constitutionally protected speech that reversal is required even if Pacifica's broadcast of the "Filthy Words" monologue is not itself protected by the First Amendment. Second, Pacifica argues that inasmuch as the recording is not obscene, the Constitution forbids any abridgment of the right to broadcast it on the radio.

A

The first argument fails because our review is limited to the question whether the Commission has the authority to proscribe this particular broadcast. As the Commission itself emphasized, its order was "issued in a specific factual context." 59 F. C. C. 2d, at 893. That approach is appropriate for courts as well as the Commission when regulation of indecency is at stake, for indecency is largely a function of context - it cannot be adequately judged in the abstract.

The approach is also consistent with Red Lion Broadcasting Co. v. FCC, 395 U.S. 367 . In that case the Court rejected an argument that the Commission's regulations defining the fairness doctrine were so vague that they would inevitably abridge the broadcasters' freedom of speech. The Court of Appeals had invalidated the regulations because their vagueness might lead to self-censorship of controversial program content. Radio Television News Directors Assn. v. United States, 400 F.2d 1002, 1016 (CA7 1968). This Court reversed. After noting that the Commission had indicated, as it has in this case, that it would not impose sanctions without warning in cases in which the applicability of the law was unclear, the Court stated:

"We need not approve every aspect of the fairness doctrine to decide these cases, and we will not now pass upon the constitutionality of these regulations by envisioning the most extreme applications conceivable, United States v. Sullivan, 332 U.S. 689, 694 (1948), but will deal with those problems if and when they arise." 395 U.S., at 396 .

It is true that the Commission's order may lead some broadcasters to censor themselves. At most, however, the Commission's definition of indecency will deter only the broadcasting of patently offensive references to excretory and sexual organs and activities. 18 While some of these references may be protected, they surely lie at the periphery of First Amendment concern. Cf. Bates v. State Bar of Arizona, 433 U.S. 350, 380 -381. Young v. American Mini Theatres, Inc., 427 U.S. 50, 61 . The danger dismissed so summarily in Red Lion, in contrast, was that broadcasters would respond to the vagueness of the regulations by refusing to present programs dealing with important social and political controversies. Invalidating any rule on the basis of its hypothetical application to situations not before the Court is "strong medicine" to be applied "sparingly and only as a last resort." Broadrick v. Oklahoma, 413 U.S. 601, 613 . We decline to administer that medicine to preserve the vigor of patently offensive sexual and excretory speech.

B

When the issue is narrowed to the facts of this case, the question is whether the

First Amendment denies government any power to restrict the public broadcast of indecent language in any circumstances. 19 For if the government has any such power, this was an appropriate occasion for its exercise.

The words of the Carlin monologue are unquestionably "speech" within the meaning of the First Amendment. It is equally clear that the Commission's objections to the broadcast were based in part on its content. The order must therefore fall if, as Pacifica argues, the First Amendment prohibits all governmental regulation that depends on the content of speech. Our past cases demonstrate, however, that no such absolute rule is mandated by the Constitution.

The classic exposition of the proposition that both the content and the context of speech are critical elements of First Amendment analysis is Mr. Justice Holmes' statement for the Court in Schenck v. United States, 249 U.S. 47, 52 :

"We admit that in many places and in ordinary times the defendants in saying all that was said in the circular would have been within their constitutional rights. But the character of every act depends upon the circumstances in which it is done. . . . The most stringent protection of free speech would not protect a man in falsely shouting fire in a theatre and causing a panic. It does not even protect a man from an injunction against uttering words that may have all the effect of force. . . . The question in every case is whether the words used are used in such circumstances and are of such a nature as to create a clear and present danger that they will bring about the substantive evils that Congress has a right to prevent."

Other distinctions based on content have been approved in the years since Schenck. The government may forbid speech calculated to provoke a fight. See Chaplinsky v. New Hampshire, 315 U.S. 568 . It may pay heed to the "`commonsense differences' between commercial speech and other varieties." Bates v. State Bar of Arizona, supra, at 381. It may treat libels against private citizens more severely than libels against public officials. See Gertz v. Robert Welch, Inc., 418 U.S. 323 . Obscenity may be wholly prohibited. Miller v. California, 413 U.S. 15 . And only two Terms ago we refused to hold that a "statutory classification is unconstitutional because it is based on the content of communication protected by the First Amendment." Young v. American Mini Theatres, Inc., supra, at 52.

The question in this case is whether a broadcast of patently offensive words dealing with sex and excretion may be regulated because of its content. 20 Obscene materials have been denied the protection of the First Amendment because their content is so offensive to contemporary moral standards. Roth v. United States, 354 U.S. 476 . But the fact that society may find speech offensive is not a sufficient reason for suppressing it. Indeed, if it is the speaker's opinion that gives offense, that consequence is a reason for according it constitutional protection. For it is a central tenet of the First Amendment that the government must remain neutral in the marketplace of ideas. 21 If there were any reason to believe that the Commission's characterization of the Carlin monologue as offensive could be traced to its political content - or even to the fact that it satirized contemporary attitudes about four-letter words 22 - First Amendment protection might be required. But that is simply not this case. These words offend for the same reasons that obscenity offends. 23 Their place in the hierarchy of First Amendment values was aptly sketched by Mr. Justice Murphy when he said: "[S]uch utterances are no essential part of any exposition of ideas, and are of such slight social value as a step to truth that any benefit that may be derived from them is clearly outweighed by the social interest in order and morality." Chaplinsky v. New Hampshire, 315 U.S., at 572 .

Although these words ordinarily lack literary, political, or scientific value, they are not entirely outside the protection of the First Amendment. Some uses of even the most offensive words are unquestionably protected. See, e. g., Hess v. Indiana, 414 U.S. 105 . Indeed, we may assume, arguendo, that this monologue would be protected in other contexts. Nonetheless, the constitutional protection accorded to a communication containing such patently offensive sexual and excretory language need not be the same in every context. 24 It is a characteristic of speech such as this that both its capacity to offend and its "social value," to use Mr. Justice Murphy's term, vary with the circumstances. Words that are commonplace in one setting are shocking in another. To paraphrase Mr. Justice Harlan, one occasion's lyric is another's vulgarity. Cf. Cohen v. California, 403 U.S. 15, 25 . 25

In this case it is undisputed that the content of Pacifica's broadcast was "vulgar," "offensive," and "shocking." Because content of that character is not entitled to absolute constitutional protection under all circumstances, we must consider its context in order to determine whether the Commission's action was constitutionally permissible.

C

We have long recognized that each medium of expression presents special First Amendment problems. Joseph Burstyn, Inc. v. Wilson, 343 U.S. 495, 502 -503. And of all forms of communication, it is broadcasting that has received the most limited First Amendment protection. Thus, although other speakers cannot be licensed except under laws that carefully define and narrow official discretion, a broadcaster may be deprived of his license and his forum if the Commission decides that such an action would serve "the public interest, convenience, and necessity." 26 Similarly, although the First Amendment protects newspaper publishers from being required to print the replies of those whom they criticize, Miami Herald Publishing Co. v. Tornillo, 418 U.S. 241, it affords no such protection to broadcasters; on the contrary, they must give free time to the victims of their criticism. Red Lion Broadcasting Co. v. FCC, 395 U.S. 367 .

The reasons for these distinctions are complex, but two have relevance to the present case. First, the broadcast media have established a uniquely pervasive presence in the lives of all Americans. Patently offensive, indecent material presented over the airwaves confronts the citizen, not only in public, but also in the privacy of the home, where the individual's right to be left alone plainly outweighs the First Amendment rights of an intruder. Rowan v. Post Office Dept., 397 U.S. 728 . Because the broadcast audience is constantly tuning in and out, prior warnings cannot completely protect the listener or viewer from unexpected program content. To say that one may avoid further offense by turning off the radio when he hears indecent language is like saying that the remedy for an assault is to run away after the first blow. One may hang up on an indecent phone call, but that option does not give the caller a constitutional immunity or avoid a harm that has already taken place. 27

Second, broadcasting is uniquely accessible to children, even those too young to read. Although Cohen's written message might have been incomprehensible to a first grader, Pacifica's broadcast could have enlarged a child's vocabulary in an instant. Other forms of offensive expression may be withheld from the young without restricting the expression at its source. Bookstores and motion picture theaters, for example, may be prohibited from making indecent material available to children. We held in Ginsberg v. New York, 390 U.S. 629, that the government's interest in the "well-being of its youth" and in supporting "parents' claim to authority in their own household" justified the regulation of otherwise protected expression. Id., at 640 and 639. 28 The case with which children may obtain access to broadcast material, coupled with the concerns recognized in Ginsberg, amply justify special treatment of indecent broadcasting.

It is appropriate, in conclusion, to emphasize the narrowness of our holding. This case does not involve a two-way radio conversation between a cab driver and a dispatcher, or a telecast of an Elizabethan comedy. We have not decided that an occasional expletive in either setting would justify any sanction or, indeed, that this broadcast would justify a criminal prosecution. The Commission's decision rested entirely on a nuisance rationale under which context is all-important. The concept requires consideration of a host of variables. The time of day was emphasized by the Commission. The content of the program in which the language is used will also affect the composition of the audience, 29 and differences between radio, television, and perhaps closed-circuit transmissions, may also be relevant. As Mr. Justice Sutherland wrote, a "nuisance may be merely a right thing in the wrong place, - like a pig in the parlor instead of the barnyard." Euclid v. Ambler Realty Co., 272 U.S. 365, 388 . We simply hold that when the Commission finds that a pig has entered the parlor, the exercise of its regulatory power does not depend on proof that the pig is obscene.

The judgment of the Court of Appeals is reversed.

It is so ordered.

Notes

[1 ] 56 F. C. C. 2d, at 99. The Commission noted:

"Congress has specifically empowered the FCC to (1) revoke a station's license (2) issue a cease and desist order, or (3) impose a monetary forfeiture for a violation of Section 1464, 47 U.S.C. [] 312 (a), 312 (b), 503 (b) (1) (E). The FCC can also (4) deny license renewal or (5) grant a short term renewal, 47 U.S.C. [] 307, 308." Id., at 96 n. 3.

[2 ] "Broadcasting requires special treatment because of four important considerations: (1) children have access to radios and in many cases are unsupervised by

parents; (2) radio receivers are in the home, a place where people's privacy interest is entitled to extra deference, see Rowan v. Post Office Dept., 397 U.S. 728 (1970); (3) unconsenting adults may tune in a station without any warning that offensive language is being or will be broadcast; and (4) there is a scarcity of spectrum space, the use of which the government must therefore license in the public interest. Of special concern to the Commission as well as parents is the first point regarding the use of radio by children." Id., at 97.

[3 ] Title 18 U.S.C. 1464 (1976 ed.) provides:

"Whoever utters any obscene, indecent, or profane language by means of radio communication shall be fined not more than $10,000 or imprisoned not more than two years, or both."

[4 ] Section 303 (g) of the Communications Act of 1934, 48 Stat. 1082, as amended, as set forth in 47 U.S.C. 303 (g), in relevant part, provides:

"Except as otherwise provided in this chapter, the Commission from time to time, as public convenience, interest, or necessity requires, shall -

. . . . .

"(g) . . . generally encourage the larger and more effective use of radio in the public interest."

[5 ] Thus, the Commission suggested, if an offensive broadcast had literary, artistic, political, or scientific value, and were preceded by warnings, it might not be indecent in the late evening, but would be so during the day, when children are in the audience. 56 F. C. C. 2d, at 98.

[6 ] Chairman Wiley concurred in the result without joining the opinion. Commissioners Reid and Quello filed separate statements expressing the opinion that the language was inappropriate for broadcast at any time. Id., at 102-103. Commissioner Robinson, joined by Commissioner Hooks, filed a concurring statement expressing the opinion: "[W]e can regulate offensive speech to the extent it constitutes a public nuisance. . . . The governing idea is that `indecency' is not an inherent attribute of words themselves; it is rather a matter of context and conduct. . . . If I were called on to do so, I would find that Carlin's monologue, if it were broadcast at an appropriate hour and accompanied by suitable warning, was distinguished by sufficient literary value to avoid being `indecent' within the meaning of the statute." Id., at 107-108, and n. 9.

[7 ] The Commission did, however, comment:

"`[I]n some cases, public events likely to produce offensive speech are covered live, and there is no opportunity for journalistic editing.' Under these circumstances we believe that it would be inequitable for us to hold a licensee responsible for indecent language. . . . We trust that under such circumstances a licensee will exercise judgment, responsibility, and sensitivity to the community's needs, interests and tastes." 59 F. C. C. 2d, at 893 n. 1.

[8 ] "Nothing in this Act shall be understood or construed to give the Commission the power of censorship over the radio communications or signals transmitted by any

radio station, and no regulation or condition shall be promulgated or fixed by the Commission which shall interfere with the right of free speech by means of radio communication." 48 Stat. 1091, 47 U.S.C. 326.

[9 ] Zechariah Chafee, defending the Commission's authority to take into account program service in granting licenses, interpreted the restriction on "censorship" narrowly: "This means, I feel sure, the sort of censorship which went on in the seventeenth century in England - the deletion of specific items and dictation as to what should go into particular programs." 2 Z. Chafee, Government and Mass Communications 641 (1947).

[10 ] In KFKB Broadcasting Assn. v. Federal Radio Comm'n, 60 App. D.C. 79, 47 F.2d 670 (1931), a doctor who controlled a radio station as well as a pharmaceutical association made frequent broadcasts in which he answered the medical questions of listeners. He often prescribed mixtures prepared by his pharmaceutical association. The Commission determined that renewal of the station's license would not be in the public interest, convenience, or necessity because many of the broadcasts served the doctor's private interests. In response to the claim that this was censorship in violation of 29 of the 1927 Act, the Court held:

"This contention is without merit. There has been no attempt on the part of the commission to subject any part of appellant's broadcasting matter to scrutiny prior to its release. In considering the question whether the public interest, convenience, or necessity will be served by a renewal of appellant's license, the commission has merely exercised its undoubted right to take note of appellant's past conduct, which is not censorship." 60 App. D.C., at 81, 47 F.2d, at 672.

In Trinity Methodist Church, South v. Federal Radio Comm'n, 61 App. D.C. 311, 62 F.2d 850 (1932), cert. denied, 288 U.S. 599, the station was controlled by a minister whose broadcasts contained frequent references to "pimps" and "prostitutes" as well as bitter attacks on the Roman Catholic Church. The Commission refused to renew the license, citing the nature of the broadcasts. The Court of Appeals affirmed, concluding the First Amendment concerns did not prevent the Commission from regulating broadcasts that "offend the religious susceptibilities of thousands . . . or offend youth and innocence by the free use of words suggestive of sexual immorality." 61 App. D.C., at 314, 62 F.2d, at 853. The court recognized that the licensee had a right to broadcast this material free of prior restraint, but "this does not mean that the government, through agencies established by Congress, may not refuse a renewal of license to one who has abused it." Id., at 312, 62 F.2d, at 851.

[11 ] See, e. g., Bay State Beacon, Inc. v. FCC, 84 U.S. App. D.C. 216, 171 F.2d 826 (1948); Idaho Microwave, Inc. v. FCC, 122 U.S. App. D.C. 253, 352 F.2d 729 (1965); National Assn. of Theatre Owners v. FCC, 136 U.S. App. D.C. 352, 420 F.2d 194 (1969), cert. denied, 397 U.S. 922 .

[12 ] See, e. g., 67 Cong. Rec. 12615 (1926) (remarks of Sen. Dill); id., at 5480 (remarks of Rep. White); 68 Cong. Rec. 2567 (1927) (remarks of Rep. Scott); Hearings on

S. 1 and S. 1754 before the Senate Committee on Interstate Commerce, 69th Cong., 1st Sess., 121 (1926); Hearings on H. R. 5589 before the House Committee on the Merchant Marine and Fisheries, 69th Cong., 1st Sess., 26 and 40 (1926). See also Hearings on H. R. 8825 before the House Committee on the Merchant Marine and Fisheries, 70th Cong., 1st Sess., passim (1928).

[13 ] In addition to 1464, the Commission also relied on its power to regulate in the public interest under 47 U.S.C. 303 (g). We do not need to consider whether 303 may have independent significance in a case such as this. The statutes authorizing civil penalties incorporate 1464, a criminal statute. See 47 U.S.C. 312 (a) (6), 312 (b) (2), and 503 (b) (1) (E) (1970 ed. and Supp. V). But the validity of the civil sanctions is not linked to the validity of the criminal penalty. The legislative history of the provisions establishes their independence. As enacted in 1927 and 1934, the prohibition on indecent speech was separate from the provisions imposing civil and criminal penalties for violating the prohibition. Radio Act of 1927, 14, 29, and 33, 44 Stat. 1168 and 1173; Communications Act of 1934, 312, 326, and 501, 48 Stat. 1086, 1091, and 1100, 47 U.S.C. 312, 326, and 501 (1970 ed. and Supp. V). The 1927 and 1934 Acts indicated in the strongest possible language that any invalid provision was separable from the rest of the Act. Radio Act of 1927, 38, 44 Stat. 1174; Communications Act of 1934, 608, 48 Stat. 1105, 47 U.S.C. 608. Although the 1948 codification of the criminal laws and the addition of new civil penalties changes the statutory structure, no substantive change was apparently intended. Cf. Tidewater Oil Co. v. United States, 409 U.S. 151, 162 . Accordingly, we need not consider any question relating to the possible application of 1464 as a criminal statute.

[14 ] Webster defines the term as "a: altogether unbecoming: contrary to what the nature of things or what circumstances would dictate as right or expected or appropriate: hardly suitable: UNSEEMLY . . . b: not conforming to generally accepted standards of morality: . . . ." Webster's Third New International Dictionary (1966).

[15 ] Indeed, at one point, he used "indecency" as a shorthand term for "patent offensiveness," 370 U.S., at 482, a usage strikingly similar to the Commission's definition in this case. 56 F. C. C. 2d, at 98.

[16 ] "`[W]hile a nudist magazine may be within the protection of the First Amendment . . . the televising of nudes might well raise a serious question of programming contrary to 18 U.S.C. 1464. . . . Similarly, regardless of whether the "4-letter words" and sexual description, set forth in "lady Chatterly's Lover," (when considered in the context of the whole book) make the book obscene for mailability purposes, the utterance of such words or the depiction of such sexual activity on radio or TV would raise similar public interest and section 1464 questions.'" En banc Programing Inquiry, 44 F. C. C. 2303, 2307 (1960). See also In re WUHYFM, 24 F. C. C. 2d 408, 412 (1970); In re Sonderling Broadcasting Corp., 27 R. R. 2d 285, on reconsideration, 41 F. C. C. 2d 777 (1973), aff'd on other grounds sub nom. Illinois Citizens Committee for Broadcasting v. FCC, 169 U.S. App. D.C. 166, 515 F.2d 397 (1974); In re Mile High Stations, Inc., 28 F. C. C. 795 (1960); In re Palmetto Broadcasting Co., 33 F. C. C. 250 (1962), reconsideration

denied, 34 F. C. C. 101 (1963), aff'd on other grounds sub nom. Robinson v. FCC, 118 U.S. App. D.C. 144, 334 F.2d 534 (1964), cert. denied, 379 U.S. 843 .

[17 ] This conclusion is reinforced by noting the different constitutional limits on Congress' power to regulate the two different subjects. Use of the postal power to regulate material that is not fraudulent or obscene raises "grave constitutional questions." Hannegan v. Esquire, Inc., 327 U.S. 146, 156 . But it is well settled that the First Amendment has a special meaning in the broadcasting context. See, e. g., FCC v. National Citizens Committee for Broadcasting, 436 U.S. 775; Red Lion Broadcasting Co. v. FCC, 395 U.S. 367; Columbia Broadcasting System, Inc. v. Democratic National Committee, 412 U.S. 94 . For this reason, the presumption that Congress never intends to exceed constitutional limits, which supported Hamling's narrow reading of 1461, does not support a comparable reading of 1464.

[18 ] A requirement that indecent language be avoided will have its primary effect on the form, rather than the content, of serious communication. There are few, if any, thoughts that cannot be expressed by the use of less offensive language.

[19 ] Pacifica's position would, of course, deprive the Commission of any power to regulate erotic telecasts unless they were obscene under Miller v. California, 413 U.S. 15 . Anything that could be sold at a newsstand for private examination could be publicly displayed on television.

We are assured by Pacifica that the free play of market forces will discourage indecent programming. "Smut may," as Judge Leventhal put it, "drive itself from the market and confound Gresham," 181 U.S. App. D.C., at 158, 556 F.2d, at 35; the prosperity of those who traffic in pornographic literature and films would appear to justify skepticism.

[20 ] Although neither MR. JUSTICE POWELL nor MR. JUSTICE BRENNAN directly confronts this question, both have answered it affirmatively, the latter explicitly, post, at 768 n. 3, and the former implicitly by concurring in a judgment that could not otherwise stand.

[21 ] See, e. g., Madison School District v. Wisconsin Employment Relations Comm'n, 429 U.S. 167, 175 -176; First National Bank of Boston v. Bellotti, 435 U.S. 765 .

[22 ] The monologue does present a point of view; it attempts to show that the words it uses are "harmless" and that our attitudes toward them are "essentially silly." See supra, at 730. The Commission objects, not to this point of view, but to the way in which it is expressed. The belief that these words are harmless does not necessarily confer a First Amendment privilege to use them while proselytizing, just as the conviction that obscenity is harmless does not license one to communicate that conviction by the indiscriminate distribution of an obscene leaflet.

[23 ] The Commission stated: "Obnoxious, gutter language describing these matters has the effect of debasing and brutalizing human beings by reducing them to their mere bodily functions . . . ." 56 F. C. C. 2d, at 98. Our society has a tradition of performing certain bodily functions in private, and of severely limiting the public

exposure or discussion of such matters. Verbal or physical acts exposing those intimacies are offensive irrespective of any message that may accompany the exposure.

[24 ] With respect to other types of speech, the Court has tailored its protection to both the abuses and the uses to which it might be put. See, e. g., New York Times Co. v. Sullivan, 376 U.S. 254 (special scienter rules in libel suits brought by public officials); Bates v. State Bar of Arizona, 433 U.S. 350 (government may strictly regulate truthfulness in commercial speech). See also Young v. American Mini Theatres, Inc., 427 U.S. 50, 82 n. 6 (POWELL, J., concurring).

[25 ] The importance of context is illustrated by the Cohen case. That case arose when Paul Cohen entered a Los Angeles courthouse wearing a jacket emblazoned with the words "Fuck the Draft." After entering the courtroom, he took the jacket off and folded it. 403 U.S., at 19 n. 3. So far as the evidence showed, no one in the courthouse was offended by his jacket. Nonetheless, when he left the courtroom, Cohen was arrested, convicted of disturbing the peace, and sentenced to 30 days in prison.

In holding that criminal sanctions could not be imposed on Cohen for his political statement in a public place, the Court rejected the argument that his speech would offend unwilling viewers; it noted that "there was no evidence that persons powerless to avoid [his] conduct did in fact object to it." Id., at 22. In contrast, in this case the Commission was responding to a listener's strenuous complaint, and Pacifica does not question its determination that this afternoon broadcast was likely to offend listeners. It should be noted that the Commission imposed a far more moderate penalty on Pacifica than the state court imposed on Cohen. Even the strongest civil penalty at the Commission's command does not include criminal prosecution. See n. 1, supra.

[26 ] 47 U.S.C. 309 (a), 312 (a) (2); FCC v. WOKO, Inc., 329 U.S. 223, 229 . Cf. Shuttlesworth v. Birmingham, 394 U.S. 147; Staub v. Baxley, 355 U.S. 313 .

[27 ] Outside the home, the balance between the offensive speaker and the unwilling audience may sometimes tip in favor of the speaker, requiring the offended listener to turn away. See Erznoznik v. Jacksonville, 422 U.S. 205 . As we noted in Cohen v. California:

"While this Court has recognized that government may properly act in many situations to prohibit intrusion into the privacy of the home of unwelcome views and ideas which cannot be totally banned from the public dialogue . . ., we have at the same time consistently stressed that `we are often "captives" outside the sanctuary of the home and subject to objectionable speech.'" 403 U.S., at 21 .

The problem of harassing phone calls is hardly hypothetical. Congress has recently found it necessary to prohibit debt collectors from "plac[ing] telephone calls without meaningful disclosure of the caller's identity"; from "engaging any person in telephone conversation repeatedly or continuously with intent to annoy, abuse, or harass any person at the called number"; and from "us[ing] obscene or profane language or language the natural consequence of which is to abuse the hearer or reader." Consumer Credit Protection Act Amendments, 91 Stat. 877, 15 U.S.C. 1692d (1976 ed., Supp. II).

[28 ] The Commission's action does not by any means reduce adults to hearing only what is fit for children. Cf. Butler v. Michigan, 352 U.S. 380, 383 . Adults who feel the need may purchase tapes and records or go to theaters and nightclubs to hear these words. In fact, the Commission has not unequivocally closed even broadcasting to speech of this sort; whether broadcast audiences in the late evening contain so few children that playing this monologue would be permissible is an issue neither the Commission nor this Court has decided.

[29 ] Even a prime-time recitation of Geoffrey Chaucer's Miller's Tale would not be likely to command the attention of many children who are both old enough to understand and young enough to be adversely affected by passages such as: "And prively he caughte hire by the queynte." The Canterbury Tales, Chaucer's Complete Works (Cambridge ed. 1933), p. 58, l. 3276.

## Schad v. Borough of Mount Ephraim (June 1, 1981)

JUSTICE WHITE delivered the opinion of the Court.

In 1973, appellants began operating an adult bookstore in the commercial zone in the Borough of Mount Ephraim in Camden County, N.J. The store sold adult books, magazines, and films. Amusement licenses shortly issued permitting the store to install coin-operated devices by virtue of which a customer could sit in a booth, insert a coin, and watch an adult film. In 1976, the store introduced an additional coin-operated mechanism permitting the customer to watch a live dancer, usually nude, performing behind a glass panel. Complaints were soon filed against appellants charging that the bookstore's exhibition of live dancing violated § 99-15B of Mount Ephraim's zoning ordinance, which described the permitted uses in a commercial zone, [n1] in which the store was located, as follows:

B. Principal permitted uses on the land and in buildings.

(1) Offices and banks; taverns; restaurants and luncheonettes for sit-down dinners only and with no drive-in facilities; automobile sales; retail stores, such as but not limited to food, wearing apparel, millinery, fabrics, hardware, lumber, jewelry, paint, wallpaper, appliances, flowers, gifts, books, stationery, pharmacy, liquors, cleaners, novelties, hobbies and toys; repair shops for shoes, jewels, clothes and appliances; barbershops and beauty salons; cleaners and laundries; pet stores; and nurseries. Offices may, in addition, be permitted to a group of four (4) stores or more without additional parking, provided the offices do not exceed the equivalent of twenty percent (20%) of the gross floor area of the stores.

(2) Motels.

Mount Ephraim Code § 99-15B(1), (2) (1979). [n2] Section 99 of the Borough's code provided that "[a]ll uses not expressly permitted in this chapter are prohibited."

Appellants were found guilty in the Municipal Court, and fines were imposed. Appeal was taken to the Camden County Court, where a trial de novo was held on the record made in the Municipal Court and appellants were again found guilty. The County Court first rejected appellants' claim that the ordinance was being selectively and improperly enforced against them because other establishments offering live entertainment were permitted in the commercial zones. [n3] Those establishments, the court held, were permitted, nonconforming uses that had existed prior to the passage of the ordinance. In response to appellants' defense based on the First and Fourteenth Amendments, the court recognized that "live nude dancing is protected by the First Amendment," but was of the view that "First Amendment guarantees are not involved," since the case "involves solely a zoning ordinance" under which "[l]ive entertainment is simply not a permitted use in any establishment" whether the entertainment is a nude dance or some other form of live presentation. App. to Juris. Statement 8a, 12a. Reliance was placed on the statement in Young v. American Mini Theatres, Inc., 427 U.S. 50, 62 (1976), that

[t]he mere fact that the commercial exploitation of material protected by the First Amendment is subject to zoning and other licensing requirements is not a sufficient reason for invalidating these ordinances.

The Appellate Division of the Superior Court of New Jersey affirmed appellants' convictions in a per curiam opinion "essentially for the reasons" given by the County Court. App. to Juris.Statement 14a. The Supreme Court of New Jersey denied further review. Id. at 17a, 18a.

Appellants appealed to this Court. Their principal claim is that the imposition of criminal penalties under an ordinance prohibiting all live entertainment, including nonobscene, nude dancing, violated their rights of free expression guaranteed by the First and Fourteenth Amendments of the United States Constitution. [n4] We noted probable jurisdiction, 449 U.S. 897 (1980), and now set aside appellants' convictions.

I

As the Mount Ephraim Code has been construed by the New Jersey courts -- a construction that is binding upon us -- "live entertainment," including nude dancing, is "not a permitted use in any establishment" in the Borough of Mount Ephraim. App. to Juris.Statement 12a. By excluding live entertainment throughout the Borough, the Mount Ephraim ordinance prohibits a wide range of expression that has long been held to be within the protections of the First and Fourteenth Amendments. Entertainment, as well as political and ideological speech, is protected; motion pictures, programs broadcast by radio and television, and live entertainment such as musical and dramatic works, fall within the First Amendment guarantee. Joseph Burstyn, Inc. v. Wilson, 343 U.S. 495 (1952); Schacht v. United States, 398 U.S. 58 (1970); Jenkins v. Georgia, 418 U.S. 153 (1974); Southeastern Promotions, Ltd. v. Conrad, 420 U.S. 546 (1975); Erznoznik v. City of Jacksonville, 422 U.S. 205 (1975); Doran v. Salem Inn, Inc., 422 U.S. 922 (1975). See also California v. LaRue, 409 U.S. 109, 118 (1972); Young v. American Mini Theatres, Inc., supra, at 61, 62. Nor may an entertainment program be prohibited solely because it displays the nude human figure. "[N]udity alone" does not place otherwise protected material outside the mantle of the First Amendment. Jenkins v. Georgia, supra, at 161; Southeastern Promotions, Ltd. v. Conrad, supra; Erznoznik v. City of Jacksonville, supra, at 211-212, 213. Furthermore, as the state courts in this case recognized, nude dancing is not without its First Amendment protections from official regulation. Doran v. Salem Inn, Inc., supra; Southeastern Promotions, Ltd. v. Conrad, supra; California v. LaRue, supra.

Whatever First Amendment protection should be extended to nude dancing, live or on film, however, the Mount Ephraim ordinance prohibits all live entertainment in the Borough: no property in the Borough may be principally used for the commercial production of plays, concerts, musicals, dance, or any other form of live entertainment. [n5] Because appellants' claims are rooted in the First Amendment, they are entitled to rely on the impact of the ordinance on the expressive activities of others as well as their own.

Because overbroad laws, like vague ones, deter privileged activit[ies], our cases firmly establish appellant's standing to raise an overbreadth challenge.

Grayned v. City of Rockford, 408 U.S. 104, 114 (1972).

II

The First Amendment requires that there be sufficient justification for the exclusion of a broad category of protected expression as one of the permitted commercial uses in the Borough. The justification does not appear on the face of the ordinance, since the ordinance itself is ambiguous with respect to whether live entertainment is permitted: § 99-15B purports to specify only the "principal" permitted uses in commercial establishments, and its listing of permitted retail establishments is expressly nonexclusive; yet, § 99 declares that all uses not expressly permitted are forbidden. [n6] The state courts at least partially resolved the ambiguity by declaring live entertainment to be an impermissible commercial use. In doing so, the County Court, whose opinion was adopted by the Appellate Division of the Superior Court, sought to avoid or to meet the First Amendment issue only by declaring that the restriction on the use of appellants' property was contained in a zoning ordinance that excluded all live entertainment from the Borough, including live nude dancing.

The power of local governments to zone and control land use is undoubtedly broad, and its proper exercise is an essential aspect of achieving a satisfactory quality of life in both urban and rural communities. But the zoning power is not infinite and unchallengeable; it "must be exercised within constitutional limits." Moore v. East Cleveland, 431 U.S. 494, 514 (1977) (STEVENS, J., concurring in judgment). Accordingly, it is subject to judicial review; and as is most often the case, the standard of review is determined by the nature of the right assertedly threatened or violated, rather than by the power being exercised or the specific limitation imposed. Thomas v. Collins, 323 U.S. 516, 529-530 (1945).

Where property interests are adversely affected by zoning, the courts generally have emphasized the breadth of municipal power to control land use, and have sustained the regulation if it is rationally related to legitimate state concerns and does not deprive the owner of economically viable use of his property. Agins v. City of Tiburon, 447 U.S. 255, 260 (1980); Village of Belle Terre v. Boraas, 416 U.S. 1 (1974); Euclid v. Ambler Realty Co., 272 U.S. 365, 395 (1926). But an ordinance may fail even under that limited standard of review. Moore v. East Cleveland, supra, at 520 (STEVENS, J., concurring in judgment); Nectow v. Cambridge, 277 U.S. 183 (1928).

Beyond that, as is true of other ordinances, when a zoning law infringes upon a protected liberty, it must be narrowly drawn and must further a sufficiently substantial government interest. [n7] In Schneider v. State, 308 U.S. 147 (1939), for example, the Court recognized its obligation to assess the substantiality of the justification offered for a regulation that significantly impinged on freedom of speech:

Mere legislative preferences or beliefs respecting matters of public convenience may well support regulation directed at other personal activities, but be insufficient to justify such as diminishes the exercise of rights so vital to the maintenance of democratic institutions. And so, as cases arise, the delicate and difficult task falls upon the courts to weigh the circumstances and to appraise the substantiality of the reasons advanced in support of the regulation of the free enjoyment of [First Amendment] rights.

Id. at 161. [n8] Similarly, in Village of Schaumburg v. Citizens for a Better Environment, 444 U.S. 620, 637 (1980), [n9] it was emphasized that the Court must not only assess the substantiality of the governmental interests asserted, but also determine whether those interests could be served by means that would be less intrusive on activity protected by the First Amendment:

The Village may serve its legitimate interests, but it must do so by narrowly drawn regulations designed to serve those interests without unnecessarily interfering with First Amendment freedoms. Hynes v. Mayor of Oradell, 425 U.S. at 620; First National Bank of Boston v. Bellotti, 435 U.S. 765, 786 (1978). "Broad prophylactic rules in the area of free expression are suspect. Precision of regulation must be the touchstone. . . ." NAACP v. Button, 371 U.S. 415, 438 (1963).

JUSTICE POWELL said much the same thing in addressing the validity of a zoning ordinance in Moore v. East Cleveland, 431 U.S. at 499: when the government intrudes on one of the liberties protected by the Due Process Clause of the Fourteenth Amendment,

this Court must examine carefully the importance of the governmental interests advanced and the extent to which they are served by the challenged regulation.

Because the ordinance challenged in this case significantly limits communicative activity within the Borough, we must scrutinize both the interests advanced by the Borough to justify this limitation on protected expression and the means chosen to further those interests.

As an initial matter, this case is not controlled by Young v. American Mini Theatres, Inc., the decision relied upon by the Camden County Court. Although the Court there stated that a zoning ordinance is not invalid merely because it regulates activity protected under the First Amendment, it emphasized that the challenged restriction on the location of adult movie theaters imposed a minimal burden on protected speech. 427 U.S. at 62. The restriction did not affect the number of adult movie theaters that could operate in the city; it merely dispersed them. The Court did not imply that a municipality could ban all adult theaters -- much less all live entertainment or all nude dancing -- from its commercial districts city-wide. [n10] Moreover, it was emphasized in that case that the evidence presented to the Detroit Common Council indicated that the concentration of adult movie theaters in limited areas led to deterioration of surrounding neighborhoods, [n11] and it was concluded that the city had justified the incidental burden on First Amendment interests resulting from merely dispersing, but not excluding, adult theaters.

In this case, however, Mount Ephraim has not adequately justified its substantial restriction of protected activity. [n12] None of the justifications asserted in this Court was articulated by the state courts, and none of them withstands scrutiny. First, the Borough contends that permitting live entertainment would conflict with its plan to create a commercial area that caters only to the "immediate needs" of its residents and that would enable them to purchase at local stores the few items they occasionally forgot to buy outside the Borough. [n13] No evidence was introduced below to support this assertion, and it is difficult to reconcile this characterization of the Borough's commercial zones with the provisions of the ordinance. Section 99-15A expressly states that the purpose of creating commercial zones was to provide areas for "local and regional commercial operations." (Emphasis added.) The range of permitted uses goes far beyond providing for the "immediate needs" of the residents. Motels, hardware stores, lumber stores, banks, offices, and car showrooms are permitted in commercial zones. The list of permitted "retail store" is nonexclusive, and it includes such services as beauty salons, barbershops, cleaners, and restaurants. Virtually the only item or service that may not be sold in a commercial zone is entertainment, or at least live entertainment. [n14] The Borough's first justification is patently insufficient.

Second, Mount Ephraim contends that it may selectively exclude commercial live entertainment from the broad range of commercial uses permitted in the Borough for reasons normally associated with zoning in commercial districts, that is, to avoid the problems that may be associated with live entertainment, such as parking, trash, police protection, and medical facilities. The Borough has presented no evidence, and it is not immediately apparent as a matter of experience, that live entertainment poses problems of this nature more significant than those associated with various permitted uses; nor does it appear that the Borough's zoning authority has arrived at a defensible conclusion that unusual problems are presented by live entertainment. Cf. Young v. American Mini Theatres, Inc., 427 U.S. at 54-55, and n. 6. [n15] We do not find it self-evident that a theater, for example, would create greater parking problems than would a restaurant. [n16] Even less apparent is what unique problems would be posed by exhibiting live nude dancing in connection with the sale of adult books and films, particularly since the bookstore is licensed to exhibit nude dancing on films. It may be that some forms of live entertainment would create problems that are not associated with the commercial uses presently permitted in Mount Ephraim. Yet this ordinance is not narrowly drawn to respond to what might be the distinctive problems arising from certain types of live entertainment, and it is not clear that a more selective approach would fail to address those unique problems if any there are. The Borough has not established that its interests could not be met by restrictions that are less intrusive on protected forms of expression.

The Borough also suggests that § 99-15B is a reasonable "time, place, and manner" restriction; yet it does not identify the municipal interests making it reasonable to exclude all commercial live entertainment but to allow a variety of other commercial uses in the Borough. [n17] In Grayned v. City of Rockford, 408 U.S. 104 (1972), we stated:

The nature of a place, "the pattern of its normal activities, dictate the kinds of regulations of time, place, and manner that are reasonable." . . . The crucial question is whether the manner of expression is basically incompatible with the normal activity of a particular place at a particular time. Our cases make clear that, in assessing the reasonableness of a regulation, we must weigh heavily the fact that communication is involved; the regulation must be narrowly tailored to further the State's legitimate interest.

Id. at 116-117 (footnotes omitted). Thus, the initial question in determining the validity of the exclusion as a time, place, and manner restriction is whether live entertainment is "basically incompatible with the normal activity [in the commercial zones]." As discussed above, no evidence has been presented to establish that live entertainment is incompatible with the uses presently permitted by the Borough. Mount Ephraim asserts that it could have chosen to eliminate all commercial uses within its boundaries. Yet we must assess the exclusion of live entertainment in light of the commercial uses Mount Ephraim allows, not in light of what the Borough might have done. [n18]

To be reasonable, time, place, and manner restrictions not only must serve significant state interests, but also must leave open adequate alternative channels of communication. Grayned v. City of Rockford, supra, at 116, 118; Kovacs v. Cooper, 336 U.S. 77, 85-87 (1949); see also Consolidated Edison Co. v. Public Service Comm'n of New York, 447 U.S. 530, 535 (1980); Virginia Pharmacy Board v. Virginia Citizens Consumer Council, 425 U.S. 748, 771 (1976). Here, the Borough totally excludes all live entertainment, including nonobscene nude dancing that is otherwise protected by the First Amendment. As we have observed, Young v. American Mini Theatres, Inc., supra, did not purport to approve the total exclusion from the city of theaters showing adult, but not obscene, materials. It was carefully noted in that case that the number of regulated establishments was not limited and that "[t]he situation would be quite different if the ordinance had the effect of suppressing, or greatly restricting access to, lawful speech." 427 U.S. at 71, n. 35.

The Borough nevertheless contends that live entertainment in general and nude dancing in particular are amply available in close-by areas outside the limits of the Borough. Its position suggests the argument that, if there were countywide zoning, it would be quite legal to allow live entertainment in only selected areas of the county and to exclude it from primarily residential communities, such as the Borough of Mount Ephraim. This may very well be true, but the Borough cannot avail itself of that argument in this case. There is no county-wide zoning in Camden County, and Mount Ephraim is free under state law to impose its own zoning restrictions, within constitutional limits. Furthermore, there is no evidence in this record to support the proposition that the kind of entertainment appellants wish to provide is available in reasonably nearby areas. The courts below made no such findings; and at least in their absence, the ordinance excluding live entertainment from the commercial zone cannot constitutionally be applied to appellants so as to criminalize the activities for which they have been fined. "[O]ne is not to have the exercise of his liberty of expression in appropriate places abridged on the plea that it may be exercised in some other place." Schneider v. State, 308 U.S. at 163.

Accordingly, the convictions of these appellants are infirm, and the judgment of the Appellate Division of the Superior Court of New Jersey is reversed and the case is remanded for further proceedings not inconsistent with this opinion.

So ordered.

Notes

1. The zoning ordinance establishes three types of zones. The "R-1" residential district is zoned for single-family dwellings. The "R-2" residential district is zoned for single-family dwellings, townhouses, and garden apartments. The "C" district is zoned for commercial use, as specified in § 99-15 of the Mount Ephraim Code. See Mount Ephraim Code § 99-7 (1979).

2. Section 99-15A states the purpose of the commercial zone:

A. Purpose. The purpose of this district is to provide areas for local and regional commercial operations. The zone district pattern recognizes the strip commercial pattern which exists along Kings Highway and the Black Horse Pike. It is intended, however, to encourage such existing uses and any new uses or redevelopment to improve upon the zoning districts of greater depth by encouraging shopping center type development with buildings related to each other in design, landscaping and site planning and by requiring off-street parking, controlled ingress and egress, greater building setbacks, buffer areas along property lines adjacent to residential uses, and a concentration of commercial uses into fewer locations to eliminate the strip pattern.

3. The building inspector, who is responsible for enforcing the zoning ordinance, testified that three establishments located in commercial zones of the Borough offered live music. However, he stated that they were permitted to do so only because this use of the premises preceded the enactment of the zoning ordinance, and thus qualified as a "nonconforming" use under the ordinance. Munic. Ct. Tr. 21-25, 35-36, 559.

The Police Chief also testified. He stated that he knew of no live entertainment in the commercial zones other than that offered by appellants and by the three establishments mentioned by the building inspector. Id. at 67.

4. Appellants also contend that the zoning ordinance, as applied to them, violates due process and equal protection, since the Borough has acted arbitrarily and irrationally in prohibiting booths in which customers can view live nude dancing while permitting coin-operated movie booths. Since we sustain appellants' First Amendment challenge to the ordinance, we do not address these additional claims.

5. The Borough's counsel asserted at oral argument that the ordinance would not prohibit noncommercial live entertainment, such as singing Christmas carols at an office party. Tr. of Oral Arg. 33. Apparently a high school could perform a play if it did not charge admission. However, the ordinance prohibits the production of plays in commercial theaters. Id. at 34.

6. Service stations are not listed as principal permitted uses in § 99-15B. However, both § 99-15E ("Area and yard requirements") and § 99-15F ("Minimum off-street parking") specifically refer to service stations, and § 99-15J limits the construction or expansion of service stations in a designated area of the commercial district. Service stations would thus appear to be permitted uses even though not expressly listed in § 915B.

Various official views have been expressed as to what extent entertainment is excluded from the commercial zone. At the initial evidentiary hearing, the prosecutor suggested that the ordinance only banned "live entertainment" in commercial establishments. Munic. Ct. Tr. 49 (emphasis added). By contrast, the building inspector for the Borough stated that there was no basis for distinguishing between live entertainment and other entertainment under the ordinance. Id. at 20, 50. Before this Court, the Borough asserted in its brief that the ordinance "does not prohibit all entertainment, but only live entertainment," Brief for Appellee 21, yet counsel for the Borough stated during oral argument that the ordinance prohibits commercial establishments from offering any entertainment. Tr. of Oral Arg. 40. The County Court ruled that "live entertainment" is not a permitted use under § 99-15B, but it did not consider whether nonlive entertainment might be a permitted use. At oral argument, counsel for appellants referred to a movie theater in the Borough, Tr. of Oral Arg. 9, but counsel for the Borough explained that it is permitted only because it is a nonconforming use. Id. at 28, 340.

7. In Village of Belle Terre v. Boraas, 416 U.S. 1 (1974), the Court upheld a zoning ordinance that restricted the use of land to "one-family" dwellings. The Court concluded that the municipality's definition of a "family" (no more than two unrelated persons) did not burden any fundamental right guaranteed by the Constitution. Id. at 7. Thus, it merely had to bear a rational relationship to permissible state objective. Id. at 8. JUSTICE MARSHALL dissented, asserting that the ordinance impinged on fundamental personal rights:

[Thus,] it can withstand constitutional scrutiny only upon a clear showing that the burden imposed is necessary to protect a compelling and substantial governmental interest. . . . [T]he onus of demonstrating that no less intrusive means will adequately protect the compelling state interest, and that the challenged statute is sufficiently narrowly drawn, is upon the party seeking to justify the burden.

Id. at 18 (citation omitted).

Moore v. East Cleveland, 431 U.S. 494 (1977), like Belle Terre, involved an ordinance that limited the occupancy of each dwelling to a single family. Unlike the ordinance challenged in Belle Terre, however, this ordinance defined "family" in a manner that prevented certain relatives from living together. JUSTICE POWELL, joined by three other Justices, concluded that the ordinance impermissibly impinged upon protected liberty interests. 431 U.S. at 499. JUSTICE STEVENS concluded that the ordinance did not even survive the Euclid test. 431 U.S. at 520-521. The dissenting opinions did not contend that zoning ordinances must always be deferentially reviewed. Rather, the dissenting Justices who addressed the issue rejected the view that the ordinance impinged upon interests that required heightened protection under the Due Process Clause. Id. at 537 (STEWART, J., joined by REHNQUIST, J., dissenting), id. at 549 (WHITE, J., dissenting).

Even where a challenged regulation restricts freedom of expression only incidentally or only in a small number of cases, we have scrutinized the governmental interest furthered by the regulation and have stated that the regulation must be narrowly drawn to avoid unnecessary intrusion on freedom of expression. See United States v. O'Brien, 391 U.S. 367, 376-377 (1968).

8. Several municipalities argued in Schneider that their anti-leafletting ordinances were designed to prevent littering of the streets. The Court did not deny that the ordinances would further that purpose, but it concluded that the cities' interest in preventing littering was not sufficiently strong to justify the limitation on First Amendment rights. The Court pointed out that the cities were free to pursue other methods of preventing littering, such as punishing those who actually threw papers on the streets. 308 U.S. at 162.

9. Village of Schaumburg invalidated on First Amendment grounds a municipal ordinance prohibiting the solicitation of contributions by charitable organizations that did not use at least 75% of their receipts for "charitable purposes." Although recognizing that the Village had substantial interests "'in protecting the public from fraud, crime, and undue annoyance,'" 444 U.S. at 636, we found these interests were

only peripherally promoted by the 75-percent requirement and could be sufficiently served by measures less destructive of First Amendment interests.

Ibid.

10. JUSTICE STEVENS relied on the District Court's finding that compliance with the challenged ordinances would only impose a slight burden on First Amendment rights, since there were "myriad locations" within the city where new adult movie theaters could be located in compliance with the ordinances. 427 U.S. at 71, n. 35.

Similarly, JUSTICE POWELL's concurring opinion stressed that the effect of the challenged ordinance on First Amendment interests was "incidental and minimal." Id. at 78. We did not suggest that a municipality could validly exclude theaters from its commercial zones if it had included other businesses presenting similar problems. Although he regarded the burden imposed by the ordinance as minimal, JUSTICE POWELL examined the city's justification for the restriction before he concluded that the ordinance was valid. Id. at 82, and n. 5. Emphasizing that the restriction was tailored to the particular problem identified by the city council, he acknowledged that

[t]he case would have present[ed] a different situation had Detroit brought within the ordinance types of theaters that had not been shown to contribute to the deterioration of surrounding areas.

Id. at 82.

11. Id. at 71, and n. 34 (opinion of STEVENS, J.); id. at 82, n. 5 (POWELL, J., concurring).

12. If the New Jersey courts had expressly interpreted this ordinance as banning all entertainment, we would reach the same result.

13. Mount Ephraim's counsel stated in this Court that these stores were available "[i]f you come home at night and you forgot to buy your bread, your milk, your gift." Tr. of Oral Arg. 40.

14. At present, this effect is somewhat lessened by the presence of at least three establishments that are permitted to offer live entertainment as a nonconforming use. See n. 3, supra. These uses apparently may continue indefinitely, since the Mount Ephraim Code does not require nonconforming uses to be terminated within a specified period of time. See Mount Ephraim Code § 99-24 (1979). The Borough's decision to permit live entertainment as a nonconforming use only undermines the Borough's contention that live entertainment poses inherent problems that justify its exclusion .

15. The Borough also speculates that it may have concluded that live nude dancing is undesirable. Brief for Appellee 20. It is noted that in California v. LaRue, 409 U.S. 109 (1972), this Court identified a number of problems that California sought to eliminate by prohibiting certain explicitly sexual entertainment in bars and in nightclubs licensed to serve liquor. This speculation lends no support to the challenged ordinance. First, § 99-15B excludes all live entertainment, not just live nude dancing. Even if Mount Ephraim might validly place restrictions on certain forms of live nude dancing under a narrowly drawn ordinance, this would not justify the exclusion of all live entertainment or, insofar as this record reveals, even the nude dancing involved in this case. Second, the regulation challenged in California v. LaRue was adopted only after the Department of Alcoholic Beverage Control had determined that significant problems were linked to the activity that was later regulated. Third, in California v. LaRue, the Court relied heavily on the State's power under the Twenty-first Amendment. Cf. Doran v. Salem Inn, Inc., 422 U.S. 922 (1975).

16. Mount Ephraim has responded to the parking problems presented by the uses that are permitted in commercial zones by requiring that each type of commercial

establishment provide a specified amount of parking. See Mount Ephraim Code §§ 99-15F (1979).

17. Mount Ephraim argued in its brief that nonlive entertainment is an adequate substitute for live entertainment. Brief for Appellee 221. This contention was apparently abandoned at oral argument, since the Borough's counsel stated that the ordinance bans all commercial entertainment. At any rate, the argument is an inadequate response to the fact that live entertainment, which the ordinance bans, is protected by the First Amendment.

18. Thus, our decision today does not establish that every unit of local government entrusted with zoning responsibilities must provide a commercial zone in which live entertainment is permitted.

## New York State Liquor Authority v. Bellanca (June 22, 1981)

PER CURIAM.

The question presented in this case is the power of a State to prohibit topless dancing in an establishment licensed by the State to serve liquor. In 1977, the State of New York amended its Alcoholic Beverage Control Law to prohibit nude dancing in establishments licensed by the State to sell liquor for on-premises consumption. N.Y.Alco.Bev.Cont.Law, § 106, subd. 6-a (McKinney Supp.1980-1981). [1] The statute does not provide for criminal penalties, but its violation may cause an establishment to lose its liquor license.

Respondents, owners of nightclubs, bars, and restaurants which had for a number of years offered topless dancing, brought a declaratory judgment action in state court, alleging that the statute violates the First Amendment of the United States Constitution insofar as it prohibits all topless dancing in all licensed premises. The New York Supreme Court declared the statute unconstitutional, and the New York Court of Appeals affirmed by a divided vote. 50 N.Y.2d 524, 407 N.E.2d 460. It reasoned that topless dancing was a form of protected expression under the First Amendment, and that the State had not demonstrated a need for prohibiting "licensees from presenting nonobscene topless dancing performances to willing customers. . . ." Id. at 529, 407 N.E.2d at 463. The dissent contended that the statute was well within the State's power, conferred by the Twenty-first Amendment, to regulate the sale of liquor within its boundaries. [2] We agree with the reasoning of the dissent, and now reverse the decision of the New York Court of Appeals.

This Court has long recognized that a State has absolute power under the Twenty-first Amendment to prohibit totally the sale of liquor within its boundaries. Ziffrin, Inc. v. Reeves, 308 U. S. 132, 308 U. S. 138 (1939). It is equally well established that a State has broad power under the Twenty-first Amendment to regulate the times, places, and circumstances under which liquor may be sold. In California v. LaRue, 409 U. S. 109 (1972), we upheld the facial constitutionality of a statute prohibiting acts of "gross sexuality," including the display of the genitals and live or filmed performances of sexual acts, in establishments licensed by the State to serve liquor. Although we recognized that not all of the prohibited acts would be found obscene and were therefore entitled to some measure of First Amendment protection, we reasoned that the statute was within the State's broad power under the Twenty-first Amendment to regulate the sale of liquor.

In Doran v. Salem Inn, Inc., 422 U. S. 922 (1975), we considered a First Amendment challenge to a local ordinance which prohibited females from appearing topless not just in bars, but "any public place." Though we concluded that the District Court had not abused its discretion in granting a preliminary injunction against enforcement of the ordinance, that decision does not limit our holding in LaRue. First, because Doran arose in the context of a preliminary injunction, we limited our standard of review to whether the District Court abused its discretion in concluding that plaintiffs were likely to prevail on the merits of their claim, not whether the ordinance actually violated the First Amendment. Thus, the decision may not be considered a "final judicial decision based on the actual merits of the controversy." University of Texas v. Camenisch, 451 U. S. 390, 451 U. S. 396 (1981). Second, the ordinance was far broader than the ordinance involved either in LaRue or here, since it proscribed conduct at "any public place," a term that "could include the theater, town hall, opera place, as well as a public market place, street or any place of assembly, indoors or outdoors.'" 422 U.S. at 422 U. S. 933 (quoting Salem. Inn, Inc. v. Frank, 364 F.Supp. 478, 483 (EDNY 1973)). Here, in contrast, the State has not attempted to ban topless dancing in "any public place": as in LaRue, the statute's prohibition applies only to establishments which are licensed by the State to serve liquor. Indeed, we explicitly recognized in Doran that a more narrowly drawn statute would survive judicial scrutiny:

"Although the customary 'barroom' type of nude dancing may involve only the barest minimum of protected expression, we recognized in California v. LaRue, 409 U.S. 109, 409 U. S. 118 (1972), that this form of entertainment might be entitled to First and Fourteenth Amendment protection under some circumstances. In LaRue, however, we concluded that the broad powers of the States to regulate the sale of liquor, conferred by the Twenty-first Amendment, outweighed any First Amendment interest in nude dancing, and that a State could therefore ban such dancing as part of its liquor license control program."

422 U.S. at 422 U. S. 932-933.

Judged by the standards announced in LaRue and Doran, the statute at issue here is not unconstitutional. What the New York Legislature has done in this case is precisely what this Court in Doran has said a State may do. Pursuant to its power to regulate the sale of liquor within its boundaries, it has banned topless dancing in establishments granted a license to serve liquor. The State's power to ban the sale of alcoholic beverages entirely includes the lesser power to ban the sale of liquor on premises where topless dancing occurs.

Respondents nonetheless insist that LaRue is distinguishable from this case, since the statute there prohibited acts of "gross sexuality" and was well supported by legislative findings demonstrating a need for the rule. They argue that the statute here is unconstitutional as applied to topless dancing because there is no legislative finding that topless dancing poses anywhere near the problem posed by acts of "gross sexuality." But even if explicit legislative findings were required to uphold the constitutionality of this statute as applied to topless dancing, those findings exist in this case. The purposes of the statute have been set forth in an accompanying legislative memorandum, New York State Legislative Annual 150 (1977).

"Nudity is the kind of conduct that is a proper subject for legislative action, as well as regulation by the State Liquor Authority as a phase of liquor licensing. It has long been held that sexual acts and performances may constitute disorderly behavior within the meaning of the Alcoholic Beverage Control Law. . . . "

"Common sense indicates that any form of nudity coupled with alcohol in a public place begets undesirable behavior. This legislation prohibiting nudity in public will, once and for all, outlaw conduct which is now quite out of hand."

In short, the elected representatives of the State of New York have chosen to avoid the disturbances associated with mixing alcohol and nude dancing by means of a reasonable restriction upon establishments which sell liquor for on-premises consumption. Given the "added presumption in favor of the validity of the state regulation" conferred by the Twenty-first Amendment, California v. LaRue, 409 U.S. at 409 U. S. 118, we cannot agree with the New York Court of Appeals that the statute violates the United States Constitution. Whatever artistic or communicative value may attach to topless dancing is overcome by the State's exercise of its broad powers arising under the Twenty-first Amendment. Although some may quarrel with the wisdom of such legislation, and may consider topless dancing a harmless diversion, the Twenty-first Amendment makes that a policy judgment for the state legislature, not the courts.

Accordingly the petition for certiorari is granted, the judgment of the New York Court of Appeals is reversed, and the case is remanded for further proceedings not inconsistent with this opinion.

It is so ordered.

Notes

[1] The statute provides:

"No retail licensee for on-premises consumption shall suffer or permit any person to appear on licensed premises in such manner or attire as to expose to view any portion of the pubic area, anus, vulva or genitals, or any simulation thereof, nor shall suffer or permit any female to appear on licensed premises in such manner or attire as to expose to view any portion of the breast below the top of the areola, or any simulation thereof."

[2] The Twenty-first Amendment provides in relevant part that

"[t]he transportation or importation into any State, Territory, or possession of the United States for delivery or use therein of intoxicating liquors, in violation of the laws thereof, is hereby prohibited."

## New York v. Ferber (July 2, 1982)

JUSTICE WHITE delivered the opinion of the Court.

At issue in this case is the constitutionality of a New York criminal statute which prohibits persons from knowingly promoting sexual performances by children under the age of 16 by distributing material which depicts such performances.

I

In recent years, the exploitive use of children in the production of pornography has become a serious national problem. [1] The Federal Government and 47 States have sought to combat the problem with statutes specifically directed at the production of child pornography. At least half of such statutes do not require that the materials produced be legally obscene. Thirty-five States and the United States Congress have also passed legislation prohibiting the distribution of such materials; 20 States prohibit the distribution of material depicting children engaged in sexual conduct without requiring that the material be legally obscene. [2]

New York is one of the 20. In 1977, the New York Legislature enacted Article 263 of its Penal Law. N.Y.Penal Law, Art. 263 (McKinney 1980). Section 263.05 criminalizes as a class C felony the use of a child in a sexual performance:

"A person is guilty of the use of a child in a sexual performance if knowing the character and content thereof he employs, authorizes or induces a child less than sixteen years of age to engage in a sexual performance or being a parent, legal guardian or custodian of such child, he consents to the participation by such child in a sexual performance."

A "[s]exual performance" is defined as "any performance or part thereof which includes sexual conduct by a child less than sixteen years of age." § 263.00(1). "Sexual conduct" is in turn defined in § 263.00(3):

"'Sexual conduct' means actual or simulated sexual intercourse, deviate sexual intercourse, sexual bestiality, masturbation, sado-masochistic abuse, or lewd exhibition of the genitals."

A performance is defined as "any play, motion picture, photograph or dance" or "any other visual representation exhibited before an audience." § 263.00(4).

At issue in this case is § 263.15, defining a class D felony: [3]

"A person is guilty of promoting a sexual performance by a child when, knowing the character and content thereof, he produces, directs or promotes any performance which includes sexual conduct by a child less than sixteen years of age."

To "promote" is also defined:

"'Promote' means to procure, manufacture, issue, sell, give, provide, lend, mail, deliver, transfer, transmute, publish, distribute, circulate, disseminate, present, exhibit or advertise, or to offer or agree to do the same."

§ 263.00(5). A companion provision bans only the knowing dissemination of obscene material. § 263.10.

This case arose when Paul Ferber, the proprietor of a Manhattan bookstore specializing in sexually oriented products, sold two films to an undercover police officer. The films are devoted almost exclusively to depicting young boys masturbating. Ferber was indicted on two counts of violating § 263.10 and two counts of violating § 263.15, the two New York laws controlling dissemination of child pornography. [4] After a jury trial, Ferber was acquitted of the two counts of promoting an obscene sexual performance, but found guilty of the two counts under § 263.15, which did not require proof that the films were obscene. Ferber's convictions were affirmed without opinion by the Appellate Division of the New York State Supreme Court. 74 App.Div.2d 558, 424 N.Y.S.2d 967 (1980).

The New York Court of Appeals reversed, holding that § 263.15 violated the First Amendment. 52 N.Y.2d 674, 422 N.E.2d 523 (1981). The court began by noting that, in light of § 263.10's explicit inclusion of an obscenity standard, § 263.15 could not be construed to include such a standard. Therefore,

"the statute would . . . prohibit the promotion of materials which are traditionally entitled to constitutional protection from government interference under the First Amendment."

52 N.Y.2d at 678, 422 N.E.2d at 525. Although the court recognized the State's "legitimate interest in protecting the welfare of minors" and noted that this "interest may transcend First Amendment concerns," id. at 679, 422 N.E.2d at 525-526, it nevertheless found two fatal defects in the New York statute. Section 263.15 was underinclusive because it discriminated against visual portrayals of children engaged in sexual activity by not also prohibiting the distribution of films of other dangerous activity. It was also overbroad because it prohibited the distribution of materials produced outside the State, as well as materials, such as medical books and educational sources, which "deal with adolescent sex in a realistic but nonobscene manner." 52 N.Y.2d at 681, 422 N.E.2d at 526. Two judges dissented. We granted the State's petition for certiorari, 454 U.S. 1052 (1981), presenting the single question:

"To prevent the abuse of children who are made to engage in sexual conduct for commercial purposes, could the New York State Legislature, consistent with the First Amendment, prohibit the dissemination of material which shows children engaged in sexual conduct, regardless of whether such material is obscene?"

II

The Court of Appeals proceeded on the assumption that the standard of obscenity incorporated in § 263.10, which follows the guidelines enunciated in Miller v. California, 413 U. S. 15 (1973), [5] constitutes the appropriate line dividing protected from unprotected expression by which to measure a regulation directed at child pornography. It was on the premise that "nonobscene adolescent sex" could not be singled out for special treatment that the court found § 263.15 "strikingly underinclusive." Moreover, the assumption that the constitutionally permissible regulation of pornography could not be more extensive with respect to the distribution of material depicting children may also have led the court to conclude that a narrowing construction of § 263.15 was unavailable.

The Court of Appeals' assumption was not unreasonable in light of our decisions. This case, however, constitutes our first examination of a statute directed at and limited to depictions of sexual activity involving children. We believe our inquiry should begin with the question of whether a State has somewhat more freedom in proscribing works which portray sexual acts or lewd exhibitions of genitalia by children.

A

In Chaplinsky v. New Hampshire, 315 U. S. 568 (1942), the Court laid the foundation for the excision of obscenity from the realm of constitutionally protected expression:

"There are certain well-defined and narrowly limited classes of speech, the prevention and punishment of which have never been thought to raise any Constitutional problem. These include the lewd and obscene. . . . It has been well observed that such utterances are no essential part of any exposition of ideas, and are of such slight social value as a step to truth that any benefit that may be derived from them is clearly outweighed by the social interest in order and morality."

Id. at 315 U. S. 571-572 (footnotes omitted).

Embracing this judgment, the Court squarely held in Roth v. United States, 354 U. S. 476 (1957), that "obscenity is not within the area of constitutionally protected speech or press." Id. at 354 U. S. 485. The Court recognized that "rejection of obscenity as utterly without redeeming social importance" was implicit in the history of the First Amendment: the original States provided for the prosecution of libel, blasphemy, and profanity, and the

"universal judgment that obscenity should be restrained [is] reflected in the international agreement of over 50 nations, in the obscenity laws of all of the 48 states, and in the 20 obscenity laws enacted by Congress from 1842 to 1956."

Id. at 354 U. S. 484-485 (footnotes omitted).

Roth was followed by 15 years during which this Court struggled with "the intractable obscenity problem." Interstate Circuit, Inc. v. Dallas, 390 U. S. 676, 390 U. S. 704 (1968) (opinion of Harlan, J.). See, e.g., Redrup v. New York, 386 U. S. 767 (1967). Despite considerable vacillation over the proper definition of obscenity, a majority of the Members of the Court remained firm in the position that

"the States have a legitimate interest in prohibiting dissemination or exhibition of obscene material when the mode of dissemination carries with it a significant danger of offending the sensibilities of unwilling recipients or of exposure to juveniles."

Miller v. California, supra, at 413 U. S. 119 (footnote omitted); Stanley v. Georgia, 394 U. S. 557, 394 U. S. 567 (1969); Ginsberg v. New York, 390 U. S. 629, 390 U. S. 637-643 (1968); Interstate Circuit, Inc. v. Dallas, supra, at 390 U. S. 690; Redrup v. New York, supra, at 386 U. S. 769; Jacobellis v. Ohio, 378 U. S. 184, 378 U. S. 195 (1964).

Throughout this period, we recognized "the inherent dangers of undertaking to regulate any form of expression." Miller v. California, supra, at 413 U. S. 23. Consequently, our difficulty was not only to assure that statutes designed to regulate obscene materials sufficiently defined what was prohibited, but also to devise substantive limits on what fell within the permissible scope of regulation. In Miller v. California, supra, a majority of the Court agreed that a

"state offense must also be limited to works which, taken as a whole, appeal to the prurient interest in sex, which portray sexual conduct in a patently offensive way, and which, taken as a whole, do not have serious literary, artistic, political, or scientific value."

Id. at 413 U. S. 24. Over the past decade, we have adhered to the guidelines expressed in Miller, [6] which subsequently has been followed in the regulatory schemes of most States. [7]

B

The Miller standard, like its predecessors, was an accommodation between the State's interests in protecting the "sensibilities of unwilling recipients" from exposure to pornographic material and the dangers of censorship inherent in unabashedly content-based laws. Like obscenity statutes, laws directed at the dissemination of child pornography run the risk of suppressing protected expression by allowing the hand of the censor to become unduly heavy. For the following reasons, however, we are persuaded that the States are entitled to greater leeway in the regulation of pornographic depictions of children.

First. It is evident beyond the need for elaboration that a State's interest in "safeguarding the physical and psychological wellbeing of a minor" is "compelling." Globe Newspaper Co. v. Superior Court, 457 U. S. 596, 457 U. S. 607 (1982). "A democratic society rests, for its continuance, upon the healthy, well-rounded growth of young people into full maturity as citizens." Prince v. Massachusetts, 321 U. S. 158, 321 U. S. 168 (1944). Accordingly, we have sustained legislation aimed at protecting the physical and emotional wellbeing of youth even when the laws have operated in the sensitive area of constitutionally protected rights. In Prince v. Massachusetts, supra, the Court held that a statute prohibiting use of a child to distribute literature on the street was valid notwithstanding the statute's effect on a First Amendment activity. In Ginsberg v. New York, supra, we sustained a New York law protecting children from exposure to nonobscene literature. Most recently, we held that the Government's interest in the "wellbeing of its youth" justified special treatment of indecent broadcasting received by adults as well as children. FCC v. Pacifica Foundation, 438 U. S. 726 (1978).

The prevention of sexual exploitation and abuse of children constitutes a government objective of surpassing importance. The legislative findings accompanying passage of the New York laws reflect this concern:

"[T]here has been a proliferation of exploitation of children as subjects in sexual performances. The care of children is a sacred trust and should not be abused by those who seek to profit through a commercial network based upon the exploitation of children.

The public policy of the state demands the protection of children from exploitation through sexual performances."

1977 N.Y.Laws, ch. 910, § 1. [8]

We shall not second-guess this legislative judgment. Respondent has not intimated that we do so. Suffice it to say that virtually all of the States and the United States have passed legislation proscribing the production of or otherwise combating "child pornography." The legislative judgment, as well as the judgment found in the relevant literature, is that the use of children as subjects of pornographic materials is harmful to the physiological, emotional, and mental health of the child. [9] That judgment, we think, easily passes muster under the First Amendment.

Second. The distribution of photographs and films depicting sexual activity by juveniles is intrinsically related to the sexual abuse of children in at least two ways. First, the materials produced are a permanent record of the children's participation and the harm to the child is exacerbated by their circulation. [10] Second, the distribution network for child pornography must be closed if the production of material which requires the sexual exploitation of children is to be effectively controlled. Indeed, there is no serious contention that the legislature was unjustified in believing that it is difficult, if not impossible, to halt the exploitation of children by pursuing only those who produce the photographs and movies. While the production of pornographic materials is a low profile, clandestine industry, the need to market the resulting products requires a visible apparatus of distribution. The most expeditious, if not the only practical, method of law enforcement may be to dry up the market for this material by imposing severe criminal penalties on persons selling, advertising, or otherwise promoting the product. Thirty-five States and Congress have concluded that restraints on the distribution of pornographic materials are required in order to effectively combat the problem, and there is a body of literature and testimony to support these legislative conclusions. [11] Cf. United States v. Darby, 312 U. S. 100 (1941) (upholding federal restrictions on sale of goods manufactured in violation of Fair Labor Standards Act).

Respondent does not contend that the State is unjustified in pursuing those who distribute child pornography. Rather, he argues that it is enough for the State to prohibit the distribution of materials that are legally obscene under the Miller test. While some States may find that this approach properly accommodates its interests, it does not follow that the First Amendment prohibits a State from going further. The Miller standard, like all general definitions of what may be banned as obscene, does not reflect the State's particular and more compelling interest in prosecuting those who promote the sexual exploitation of children. Thus, the question under the Miller test of whether a work, taken as a whole, appeals to the prurient interest of the average person bears no connection to the issue of whether a child has been physically or psychologically harmed in the production of the work. Similarly, a sexually explicit depiction need not be "patently offensive" in order to have required the sexual exploitation of a child for its production. In addition, a work which, taken on the whole, contains serious literary, artistic, political, or scientific value may nevertheless embody the hardest core of child pornography. "It is irrelevant to the child [who has been abused] whether or not the material . . . has a literary, artistic, political or social value." Memorandum of Assemblyman Lasher in Support of § 263.15. We therefore cannot conclude that the Miller standard is a satisfactory solution to the child pornography problem. [12]

Third. The advertising and selling of child pornography provide an economic motive for, and are thus an integral part of, the production of such materials, an activity illegal throughout the Nation. [13]

"It rarely has been suggested that the constitutional freedom for speech and press extends its immunity to speech or writing used as an integral part of conduct in violation of a valid criminal statute."

Giboney v. Empire Storage & Ice Co., 336 U. S. 490, 336 U. S. 498 (1949). [14] We note that, were the statutes outlawing the employment of children in these films and photographs fully effective, and the constitutionality of these laws has not been questioned, the First Amendment implications would be no greater than that presented by laws against distribution: enforceable production laws would leave no child pornography to be marketed. [15]

Fourth. The value of permitting live performances and photographic reproductions of children engaged in lewd sexual conduct is exceedingly modest, if not de minimis. We consider it unlikely that visual depictions of children performing sexual acts or lewdly exhibiting their genitals would often constitute an important and necessary part of a literary performance or scientific or educational work. As a state judge in this case observed, if it were necessary for literary or artistic value, a person over the statutory age who perhaps looked younger could be utilized. [16] Simulation outside of the prohibition of the statute could provide another alternative. Nor is there any question here of censoring a particular literary theme or portrayal of sexual activity. The First Amendment interest is limited to that of rendering the portrayal somewhat more "realistic" by utilizing or photographing children.

Fifth. Recognizing and classifying child pornography as a category of material outside the protection of the First Amendment is not incompatible with our earlier decisions. "The question whether speech is, or is not, protected by the First Amendment often depends on the content of the speech." Young v. American Mini Theatres, Inc., 427 U. S. 50, 427 U. S. 66 (1976) (opinion of STEVENS, J., joined by BURGER, C.J., and WHITE and REHNQUIST JJ.). See also FCC v. Pacifica Foundation, 438 U. S. 726, 438 U. S. 742-748 (1978) (opinion of STEVENS, J., joined by BURGER, C.J., and REHNQUIST, J.). "[I]t is the content of [an] utterance that determines whether it is a protected epithet or an unprotected fighting comment.'" Young v. American Mini Theatres, Inc., supra, at 427 U. S. 66. See Chaplinsky v. New Hampshire, 315 U. S. 568 (1942). Leaving aside the special considerations when public officials are the target, New York Times Co. v. Sullivan, 376 U. S. 254 (1964), a libelous publication is not protected by the Constitution. Beauharnais v. Illinois, 343 U. S. 250 (1952). Thus, it is not rare that a content-based classification of speech has been accepted because it may be appropriately generalized that within the confines of the given classification, the evil to be restricted so overwhelmingly outweighs the expressive interests, if any, at stake, that no process of case-by-case adjudication is required. When a definable class of material, such as that covered by § 263.15, bears so heavily and pervasively on the welfare of children engaged in its production, we think the balance of competing interests is clearly struck, and that it is permissible to consider these materials as without the protection of the First Amendment.

C

There are, of course, limits on the category of child pornography which, like obscenity, is unprotected by the First Amendment. As with all legislation in this sensitive area, the conduct to be prohibited must be adequately defined by the applicable state law, as written or authoritatively construed. Here the nature of the harm to be combated requires that the state offense be limited to works that visually depict sexual conduct by children below a specified age. [17] The category of "sexual conduct" proscribed must also be suitably limited and described.

The test for child pornography is separate from the obscenity standard enunciated in Miller, but may be compared to it for the purpose of clarity. The Miller formulation is adjusted in the following respects: a trier of fact need not find that the material appeals to the prurient interest of the average person; it is not required that sexual conduct portrayed be done so in a patently offensive manner; and the material at issue need not be considered as a whole. We note that the distribution of descriptions or other depictions of sexual conduct, not otherwise obscene, which do not involve live performance or photographic or other visual reproduction of live performances, retains First Amendment protection. As with obscenity laws, criminal responsibility may not be imposed without some element of scienter on the part of the defendant. Smith v. California, 361 U. S. 147 (1959); Hamling v. United States, 418 U. S. 87 (1974).

D

Section 263.15's prohibition incorporates a definition of sexual conduct that comports with the above-stated principles. The forbidden acts to be depicted are listed with sufficient precision and represent the kind of conduct that, if it were the theme of a work, could render it legally obscene:

"actual or simulated sexual intercourse, deviate sexual intercourse, sexual bestiality, masturbation, sado-masochistic abuse, or lewd exhibition of the genitals."

§ 263.00(3). The term "lewd exhibition of the genitals" is not unknown in this area and, indeed, was given in Miller as an example of a permissible regulation. 413 U.S. at 413 U. S. 25. A performance is defined only to include live or visual depictions: "any play, motion picture, photograph or dance . . . [or] other visual representation exhibited before an audience." § 263.00(4). Section 263.15 expressly includes a scienter requirement.

We hold that § 263.15 sufficiently describes a category of material the production and distribution of which is not entitled to First Amendment protection. It is therefore clear that there is nothing unconstitutionally "underinclusive" about a statute that singles out this category of material for proscription. [18] It also follows that the State is not barred by the First Amendment from prohibiting the distribution of unprotected materials produced outside the State. [19]

### III

It remains to address the claim that the New York statute is unconstitutionally overbroad because it would forbid the distribution of material with serious literary, scientific, or educational value or material which does not threaten the harms sought to be combated by the State. Respondent prevailed on that ground below, and it is to that issue that we now turn.

The New York Court of Appeals recognized that overbreadth scrutiny has been limited with respect to conduct-related regulation, Broadrick v. Oklahoma, 413 U. S. 601 (1973), but it did not apply the test enunciated in Broadrick because the challenged statute, in its view, was directed at "pure speech." The court went on to find that § 263.15 was fatally overbroad:

"[T]he statute would prohibit the showing of any play or movie in which a child portrays a defined sexual act, real or simulated, in a nonobscene manner. It would also prohibit the sale, showing, or distributing of medical or educational materials containing photographs of such acts.

Indeed, by its terms, the statute would prohibit those who oppose such portrayals from providing illustrations of what they oppose."

52 N.Y.2d at 678, 422 N.E.2d at 525.

While the construction that a state court gives a state statute is not a matter subject to our review, Wainwright v. Stone, 414 U. S. 21, 414 U. S. 22-23 (1973); Gooding v. Wilson, 405 U. S. 518, 405 U. S. 520 (1972), this Court is the final arbiter of whether the Federal Constitution necessitated the invalidation of a state law. It is only through this process of review that we may correct erroneous applications of the Constitution that err on the side of an overly broad reading of our doctrines and precedents, as well as state court decisions giving the Constitution too little shrift. A state court is not free to avoid a proper facial attack on federal constitutional grounds. Bigelow v. Virginia, 421 U. S. 809, 421 U. S. 817 (1975). By the same token, it should not be compelled to entertain an overbreadth attack when not required to do so by the Constitution.

### A

The traditional rule is that a person to whom a statute may constitutionally be applied may not challenge that statute on the ground that it may conceivably be applied unconstitutionally to others in situations not before the Court. Broadrick v. Oklahoma, supra, at 413 U. S. 610; United States v. Raines, 362 U. S. 17, 362 U. S. 21 (1960); Carmichael v. Southern Coal & Coke Co., 301 U. S. 495, 301 U. S. 513 (1937); Yazoo & M. V. R. Co. v. Jackson Vinegar Co., 226 U. S. 217, 226 U. S. 219-220 (1912). In Broadrick, we recognized that this rule reflects two cardinal principles of our constitutional order: the personal nature of constitutional rights, McGowan v. Maryland, 366 U. S. 420, 366 U. S. 429 (1961), and prudential limitations on constitutional adjudication. [20] In United States v. Raines, supra, at 362 U. S. 21, we noted the "incontrovertible proposition" that it

"'would indeed be undesirable for this Court to consider every conceivable situation which might possibly arise in the application of complex and comprehensive legislation,'"

(quoting Barrows v. Jackson, 346 U. S. 249, 346 U. S. 256 (1953)). By focusing on the factual situation before us, and similar cases necessary for development of a constitutional rule, [21] we face "flesh-and-blood" [22] legal problems with data "relevant and adequate to an informed judgment." [23] This practice also fulfills a valuable institutional purpose: it allows state courts the opportunity to construe a law to avoid constitutional infirmities.

What has come to be known as the First Amendment overbreadth doctrine is one of the few exceptions to this principle, and must be justified by "weighty countervailing policies." United States v. Raines, supra, at 362 U. S. 223. The doctrine is predicated on the sensitive nature of protected expression:

"persons whose expression is constitutionally protected may well refrain from exercising their rights for fear of criminal sanctions by a statute susceptible of application to protected expression."

Village of Schaumburg v. Citizens for a Better Environment, 444 U. S. 620, 444 U. S. 634 (1980); Gooding v. Wilson, supra, at 405 U. S. 521. It is for this reason that we have allowed persons to attack overly broad statutes even though the conduct of the person making the attack is clearly unprotected, and could be proscribed by a law drawn with the requisite specificity. Dombrowski v. Pfister, 380 U. S. 479, 380 U. S. 486 (1965); Thornhill v. Alabama, 310 U. S. 88, 310 U. S. 97-98 (1940); United States v. Raines, supra, at 362 U. S. 21-22; Gooding v. Wilson, supra, at 405 U. S. 521.

The scope of the First Amendment overbreadth doctrine, like most exceptions to established principles, must be carefully tied to the circumstances in which facial invalidation of a statute is truly warranted. Because of the wide-reaching effects of striking down a statute on its face at the request of one whose own conduct may be punished despite the First Amendment, we have recognized that the overbreadth doctrine is "strong medicine," and have employed it with hesitation, and then "only as a last resort." Broadrick, 413 U.S. at 413 U. S. 613. We have, in consequence, insisted that the overbreadth involved be "substantial" before the statute involved will be invalidated on its face. [24]

In Broadrick, we explained the basis for this requirement:

"[T]he plain import of our cases is, at the very least, that facial overbreadth adjudication is an exception to our traditional rules of practice, and that its function, a limited one at the outset, attenuates as the otherwise unprotected behavior that it forbids the State to sanction moves from 'pure speech' toward conduct, and that conduct -- even if expressive -- falls within the scope of otherwise valid criminal laws that reflect legitimate state interests in maintaining comprehensive controls over harmful, constitutionally unprotected conduct. Although such laws, if too broadly worded, may deter protected speech to some unknown extent, there comes a point where that effect -- at best a prediction -- cannot, with confidence, justify invalidating a statute on its face, and so prohibiting a State from enforcing the statute against conduct that is admittedly within its power to proscribe. Cf. Aldelman v. United States, 394 U. S. 165, 394 U. S. 174-175 (1969)."

Id. at 413 U. S. 615. We accordingly held that,

"particularly where conduct, and not merely speech, is involved, we believe that the overbreadth of a statute must not only be real, but substantial as well, judged in relation to the statute's plainly legitimate sweep."

Ibid. [25]

Broadrick examined a regulation involving restrictions on political campaign activity, an area not considered "pure speech," and thus it was unnecessary to consider the proper overbreadth test when a law arguably reaches traditional forms of expression such as books and films. As we intimated in Broadrick, the requirement of substantial overbreadth extended "at the very least" to cases involving conduct plus speech. This case, which poses the question squarely, convinces us that the rationale of Broadrick is sound, and should be applied in the present context involving the harmful employment of children to make sexually explicit materials for distribution.

The premise that a law should not be invalidated for overbreadth unless it reaches a substantial number of impermissible applications is hardly novel. On most occasions involving facial invalidation, the Court has stressed the embracing sweep of the statute over protected expression. [26]

Indeed, JUSTICE BRENNAN observed in his dissenting opinion in Broadrick:

"We have never held that a statute should be held invalid on its face merely because it is possible to conceive of a single impermissible application, and in that sense, a requirement of substantial overbreadth is already implicit in the doctrine."

Id. at 413 U. S. 630. The requirement of substantial overbreadth is directly derived from the purpose and nature of the doctrine. While a sweeping statute, or one incapable of limitation, has the potential to repeatedly chill the exercise of expressive activity by many individuals, the extent of deterrence of protected speech can be expected to decrease with the declining reach of the regulation. [27] This observation appears equally applicable to the publication of books and films as it is to activities, such as picketing or participation in election campaigns, which have previously been categorized as involving conduct plus speech. We see no appreciable difference between the position of a publisher or bookseller in doubt as to the reach of New York's child pornography law and the situation faced by the Oklahoma state employees with respect to that State's restriction on partisan political activity. Indeed, it could reasonably be argued that the bookseller, with an economic incentive to sell materials that may fall within the statute's scope, may be less likely to be deterred than the employee who wishes to engage in political campaign activity. Cf. Bates v. State Bar of Arizona, 433 U. S. 350, 433 U. S. 380-381 (1977) (overbreadth analysis inapplicable to commercial speech).

This requirement of substantial overbreadth may justifiably be applied to statutory challenges which arise in defense of a criminal prosecution as well as civil enforcement or actions seeking a declaratory judgment. Cf. Parker v. Levy, 417 U. S. 733, 417 U. S. 760 (1974). Indeed, the Court's practice when confronted with ordinary criminal laws that are sought to be applied against protected conduct is not to invalidate the law in toto, but rather to reverse the particular conviction. Cantwell v. Connecticut, 310 U. S. 296 (1940); Edwards v. South Carolina, 372 U. S. 229 (1973). We recognize, however, that the penalty to be imposed is relevant in determining whether demonstrable overbreadth is substantial. We simply hold that the fact that a criminal prohibition is involved does not obviate the need for the inquiry or a priori warrant a finding of substantial overbreadth.

Applying these principles, we hold that § 263.15 is not substantially overbroad. We consider this the paradigmatic case of a state statute whose legitimate reach dwarfs its arguably impermissible applications. New York, as we have held, may constitutionally prohibit dissemination of material specified in § 263.15. While the reach of the statute is directed at the hard core of child pornography, the Court of Appeals was understandably concerned that some protected expression, ranging from medical textbooks to pictorials in the National Geographic would fall prey to the statute. How often, if ever, it may be necessary to employ children to engage in conduct clearly within the reach of § 263.15 in order to produce educational, medical, or artistic works cannot be known with certainty. Yet we seriously doubt, and it has not been suggested, that these arguably impermissible applications of the statute amount to more than a tiny fraction of the materials within the statute's reach. Nor will we assume that the New York courts will widen the possibly invalid reach of the statute by giving an expansive construction to the proscription on "lewd exhibition[s] of the genitals." Under these circumstances, § 263.15 is

"not substantially overbroad, and . . . whatever overbreadth may exist should be cured through case-by-case analysis of the fact situations to which its sanctions, assertedly, may not be applied."

Broadrick v. Oklahoma, 413 U.S. at 413 U. S. 615-616.

IV

Because § 263.15 is not substantially overbroad, it is unnecessary to consider its application to material that does not depict sexual conduct of a type that New York may restrict consistent with the First Amendment. As applied to Paul Ferber and to others who distribute similar material, the statute does not violate the First Amendment as applied to the States through the Fourteenth. [28] The judgment of the New York Court of Appeals is reversed, and the case is remanded to that court for further proceedings not inconsistent with this opinion.

So ordered.

Notes

[1] "[C]hild pornography and child prostitution have become highly organized, multimillion dollar industries that operate on a nationwide scale." S. Rep. No. 95-438, p. 5 (1977). One researcher has documented the existence of over 260 different magazines which depict children engaging in sexually explicit conduct. Ibid. "Such magazines depict children, some as young as three to five years of age . . . . The activities featured range from lewd poses to intercourse, fellatio, cunnilingus, masturbation, rape, incest and sado-masochism." Id., at 6. In Los Angeles alone, police reported that 30,000 children have been sexually exploited. Sexual Exploitation of Children, Hearings before the Subcommittee on Select Education of the House Committee on Education and Labor, 95th Cong., 1st Sess., 41-42 (1977).

[2] In addition to New York, 19 States have prohibited the dissemination of material depicting children engaged in sexual conduct regardless of whether the material is obscene. Ariz. Rev. Stat. Ann. § 13-3553 (Supp. 1981-1982); Colo. Rev. Stat. § 18-6-403 (Supp. 1981); Del. Code Ann., Tit. 11, §§ 1108, 1109 (1979); Fla. Stat. § 847.014 (1981); Haw. Rev. Stat. § 707-751 (Supp. 1981); Ky. Rev. Stat. §§ 531.320, 531.340-531.360 (Supp. 1980); La. Rev. Stat. Ann. § 14:81.1(A)(3) (West Supp. 1982); Mass. Gen. Laws Ann., ch. 272, § 29A (West Supp. 1982-1983); Mich. Comp. Laws Ann. § 750.145c(3) (1982-1983); Miss. Code Ann. § 97-5-33(4) (Supp. 1981); Mont. Code Ann. § 45-5-625 (1981); N. J. Stat. Ann. § 2C:24-4(b)(5) (West 1981); Okla. Stat., Tit. 21, § 1021.2 (1981); Pa. Stat. Ann., Tit. 18, § 6312(c) (Purdon 1982-1983); R. I. Gen. Laws § 11-9-1.1 (1981); Tex. Penal Code Ann. § 43.25 (1982); Utah Code Ann. § 76-10-1206.5(3) (Supp. 1981); W. Va. Code § 61-8C-3 (Supp. 1981); Wis. Stat. § 940.203(4) (1979-1980).

Fifteen States prohibit the dissemination of such material only if it is obscene. Ala. Code §§ 13-7-231, 13-7-232 (Supp. 1981); Ark. Stat. Ann. § 41-4204 (Supp. 1981); Cal. Penal Code Ann. § 311.2(b) (West Supp. 1982) (general obscenity statute); Ill. Rev. Stat., ch. 38, ¶ 11-20a(b)(1) (1979); Ind. Code § 35-30-10.1-2 (1979); Me. Rev. Stat. Ann., Tit. 17, § 2923(1) (Supp. 1981-1982); Minn. Stat. §§ 617.246(3) and (4) (1980); Neb. Rev. Stat. § 28-1463(2) (1979); N. H. Rev. Stat. Ann. § 650:2(11) (Supp. 1981); N. D. Cent. Code § 12.1-27.1-01 (1976) (general obscenity statute); Ohio Rev. Code Ann. § 2907.321(A) (1982); Ore. Rev. Stat. § 163.485 (1981); S. D. Codified Laws §§ 22-22-24, 22-22-25 (1979); Tenn. Code Ann. § 39-1020 (Supp. 1981); Wash. Rev. Code § 9.68A.030 (1981). The federal statute also prohibits dissemination only if the material is obscene. 18 U. S. C. § 2252(a) (1976 ed., Supp. IV). Two States prohibit dissemination only if the material is obscene as to minors. Conn. Gen. Stat. § 53a-196b (1981); Va. Code § 18.2-374.1 (1982).

Twelve States prohibit only the use of minors in the production of the material. Alaska Stat. Ann. § 11.41.455 (1978); Ga. Code § 26-9943a(b) (1978); Idaho Code § 44-1306 (1977); Iowa Code § 728.12 (1981); Kan. Stat. Ann. § 21-3516 (1981); Md. Ann. Code, Art. 27, § 419A (Supp. 1981); Mo. Rev. Stat. § 568.060(1)(b) (1978); Nev. Rev. Stat. § 200.509 (1981); N. M. Stat. Ann. § 30-6-1 (Supp. 1982); N. C. Gen. Stat. § 14-190.6 (1981); S. C. Code § 16-15-380 (Supp. 1981); Wyo. Stat. § 14-3-102(a)(v)(E) (1978).

[3] Class D felonies carry a maximum punishment of imprisonment for up to seven years as to individuals, and as to corporations a fine of up to $10,000. N. Y. Penal Law §§ 70.00, 80.10 (McKinney 1975). Respondent Ferber was sentenced to 45 days in prison.

[4] A state judge rejected Ferber's First Amendment attack on the two sections in denying a motion to dismiss the indictment. 96 Misc. 2d 669, 409 N. Y. S. 2d 632 (1978).

[5] N. Y. Penal Law § 235.00(1) (McKinney 1980); People v. Illardo, 48 N. Y. 2d 408, 415, and n. 3, 399 N. E. 2d 59, 62-63, and n. 3 (1979).

[6] Hamling v. United States, 418 U. S. 87 (1974); Jenkins v. Georgia, 418 U. S. 153 (1974); Ward v. Illinois, 431 U. S. 767 (1977); Marks v. United States, 430 U. S. 188 (1977); Pinkus v. United States, 436 U. S. 293 (1978).

[7] Thirty-seven States and the District of Columbia have either legislatively adopted or judicially incorporated the Miller test for obscenity. Ala. Code § 13A-12-150 (Supp. 1981); Ariz. Rev. Stat. Ann. § 13-3501(2) (1978); Ark. Stat. Ann. § 41-3502(6) (Supp. 1981); Colo. Rev. Stat. § 18-7-101(2) (Supp. 1981); Del. Code Ann., Tit. 11, § 1364 (1979); Lakin v. United States, 363 A. 2d 990 (D. C. 1976); Ga. Code § 26-2101(b) (1978); Haw. Rev. Stat. § 712-1210(6) (Supp. 1981); Idaho Code § 18-4101(A) (1979); Iowa Code § 728.4 (1981) (only child pornography covered); Ind. Code § 35-30-10.1-1(c) (1979); Kan. Stat. Ann. § 21-4301 (2)(a) (1981); Ky. Rev. Stat. § 531.010(3) (1975); La. Rev. Stat. Ann. §§ 14:106(A)(2) and (A)(3) (West Supp. 1982); Ebert v. Maryland State Bd. of Censors, 19 Md. App. 300, 313 A. 2d 536 (1973); Mass. Gen. Laws Ann., ch. 272, § 31 (West Supp. 1982-1983); People v. Neumayer, 405 Mich. 341, 275 N. W. 2d 230 (1979); State v. Welke, 298 Minn. 402, 216 N. W. 2d 641 (1974); Mo. Rev. Stat. § 573.010(1) (1978); Neb. Rev. Stat. § 28-807(9) (1979); Nev. Rev. Stat. § 201.235 (1981); N. H. Rev. Stat. Ann. § 650:1(IV) (Supp. 1981); N. J. Stat. Ann. § 2C:34-2 (West 1981); N. Y. Penal Law § 235.00(1) (McKinney 1980); N. C. Gen. Stat. § 14-190.1(b) (1981); N. D. Cent. Code § 12.1-27.1-01(4) (1976); State v. Burgun, 56 Ohio St. 2d 354, 384 N. E. 2d 255 (1978); McCrary v. State, 533 P. 2d 629 (Okla. Crim. App. 1974); Ore. Rev. Stat. § 167.087(2) (1981); Pa. Stat. Ann., Tit. 18, § 5903(b) (Purdon Supp. 1982-1983); R. I. Gen. Laws § 11-31-1 (1981); S. C. Code § 16-15-260(a) (Supp. 1981); S. D. Codified Laws § 22-24-27(10) (1979); Tenn. Code Ann. § 39-3001(1) (Supp. 1981); Tex. Penal Code Ann. § 43.21(a) (1982); Utah Code Ann. § 76-10-1203(1) (1978); Va. Code § 18.2-372 (1982); 1982 Wash. Laws., ch. 184, § 1(2).

Four States continue to follow the test approved in Memoirs v. Massachusetts, 383 U. S. 413 (1966). Cal. Penal Code Ann. § 311(a) (West Supp. 1982); Conn. Gen. Stat. § 53a-193 (1981); Fla. Stat. § 847.07 (1981); Ill. Rev. Stat., ch. 38, ¶ 11-20(b) (1979). Five States regulate only the distribution of pornographic material to minors. Me. Rev. Stat. Ann., Tit. 17, § 2911 (Supp. 1981-1982); Mont. Code Ann. § 45-8-201 (1981); N. M. Stat. Ann. § 30-37-2 (Supp. 1982); Vt. Stat. Ann., Tit. 13, § 2802 (1974); W. Va. Code § 61-8A-2 (1977). Three state obscenity laws do not fall into any of the above categories. Miss. Code Ann. § 97-29-33 (1973), declared invalid in ABC Interstate Theatres, Inc. v. State, 325 So.

2d 123 (Miss. 1976); Wis. Stat. § 944.21(1)(a) (1979-1980), declared invalid in State v. Princess Cinema of Milwaukee, Inc., 96 Wis. 2d 646, 292 N. W. 2d 807 (1980); Wyo. Stat. § 6-5-303 (1977). Alaska has no current state obscenity law.

A number of States employ a different obscenity standard with respect to material distributed to children. See, e. g., Fla. Stat. § 847.0125 (1981).

[8] In addition, the legislature found "the sale of these movies, magazines and photographs depicting the sexual conduct of children to be so abhorrent to the fabric of our society that it urge[d] law enforcement officers to aggressively seek out and prosecute . . . the peddlers . . . of this filth by vigorously applying the sanctions contained in this act." 1977 N. Y. Laws, ch. 910, § 1.

[9] "[T]he use of children as . . . subjects of pornographic materials is very harmful to both the children and the society as a whole." S. Rep. No. 95-438, p. 5 (1977). It has been found that sexually exploited children are unable to develop healthy affectionate relationships in later life, have sexual dysfunctions, and have a tendency to become sexual abusers as adults. Schoettle, Child Exploitation: A Study of Child Pornography, 19 J. Am. Acad. Child Psychiatry 289, 296 (1980) (hereafter cited as Child Exploitation); Schoettle, Treatment of the Child Pornography Patient, 137 Am. J. Psychiatry 1109, 1110 (1980); Densen-Gerner, Child Prostitution and Child Pornography: Medical, Legal, and Societal Aspects of the Commercial Exploitation of Children, reprinted in U. S. Dept. of Health and Human Services, Sexual Abuse of Children: Selected Readings 77, 80 (1980) (hereafter cited as Commercial Exploitation) (sexually exploited children pre-disposed to self-destructive behavior such as drug and alcohol abuse or prostitution). See generally Burgess & Holmstrom, Accessory-to-Sex: Pressure, Sex, and Secrecy, in A. Burgess, A. Groth, L. Holmstrom, & S. Sgroi, Sexual Assault of Children and Adolescents 85, 94 (1978); V. De Francis, Protecting the Child Victim of Sex Crimes Committed by Adults 169 (1969); Ellerstein & Canavan, Sexual Abuse of Boys, 134 Am. J. Diseases of Children 255, 256-257 (1980); Finch, Adult Seduction of the Child: Effects on the Child, Medical Aspects of Human Sexuality 170, 185 (Mar. 1973); Groth, Sexual Trauma in the Life Histories of Rapists and Child Molesters, 4 Victimology 10 (1979). Sexual molestation by adults is often involved in the production of child sexual performances. Sexual Exploitation of Children, A Report to the Illinois General Assembly by the Illinois Legislative Investigating Commission 30-31 (1980). When such performances are recorded and distributed, the child's privacy interests are also invaded. See n. 10, infra.

[10] As one authority has explained:

"[P]ornography poses an even greater threat to the child victim than does sexual abuse or prostitution. Because the child's actions are reduced to a recording, the pornography may haunt him in future years, long after the original misdeed took place. A child who has posed for a camera must go through life knowing that the recording is circulating within the mass distribution system for child pornography." Shouvlin, Preventing the Sexual Exploitation of Children: A Model Act, 17 Wake Forest L. Rev. 535,

545 (1981).

See also Child Exploitation 292 ("[I]t is the fear of exposure and the tension of keeping the act secret that seem to have the most profound emotional repercussions"); Note, Protection of Children from Use in Pornography: Toward Constitutional and Enforceable Legislation, 12 U. Mich. J. Law Reform 295, 301 (1979) (hereafter cited as Use in Pornography) (interview with child psychiatrist) ("The victim's knowledge of publication of the visual material increases the emotional and psychic harm suffered by the child").

Thus, distribution of the material violates "the individual interest in avoiding disclosure of personal matters." Whalen v. Roe, 429 U. S. 589, 599 (1977). Respondent cannot undermine the force of the privacy interests involved here by looking to Cox Broadcasting Corp. v. Cohn, 420 U. S. 469 (1975), and Smith v. Daily Mail Publishing Co., 443 U. S. 97 (1979), cases protecting the right of newspapers to publish, respectively, the identity of a rape victim and a youth charged as a juvenile offender. Those cases only stand for the proposition that "if a newspaper lawfully obtains truthful information about a matter of public significance then state officials may not constitutionally punish publication of the information, absent a need . . . of the highest order." Id., at 103.

[11] See Sexual Exploitation of Children, Hearings before the Subcommittee on Crime of the House Judiciary Committee, 95th Cong., 1st Sess., 34 (1977) (statement of Charles Rembar) ("It is an impossible prosecutorial job to try to get at the acts themselves"); id., at 11 (statement of Frank Osanka, Professor of Social Justice and Sociology) ("[W]e have to be very careful . . . that we don't take comfort in the existence of statutes that are on the books in the connection with the use of children in pornography. . . . There are usually no witnesses to these acts of producing pornography"); id., at 69 (statement of Investigator Lloyd Martin, Los Angeles Police Department) (producers of child pornography use false names making difficult the tracing of material back from distributor). See also L. Tribe, American Constitutional Law 666, n. 62 (1978); Note, Child Pornography: A New Role for the Obscenity Doctrine, 1978 U. Ill. Law Forum 711, 716, n. 29; Use in Pornography 315 ("passage of criminal laws aimed at producers without similar regulation of distributors will arguably shift the production process further underground").

[12] In addition, legal obscenity under Miller is a function of "contemporary community standards." 413 U. S., at 24. "It is neither realistic nor constitutionally sound to read the First Amendment as requiring that the people of Maine or Mississippi accept public depiction of conduct found tolerable in Las Vegas, or New York City." Id., at 32. It would be equally unrealistic to equate a community's toleration for sexually oriented material with the permissible scope of legislation aimed at protecting children from sexual exploitation. Furthermore, a number of States rely on stricter obscenity tests, see n. 7, supra, under which successful prosecution for child pornography may be even more difficult.

[13] One state committee studying the problem declared: "The act of selling these

materials is guaranteeing that there will be additional abuse of children." Texas House Select Committee on Child Pornography: Its Related Causes and Control 132 (1978). See also Commercial Exploitation 80 ("Printed materials cannot be isolated or removed from the process involved in developing them").

[14] In Giboney, a unanimous Court held that labor unions could be restrained from picketing a firm in support of a secondary boycott which a State had validly outlawed. In Pittsburgh Press Co. v. Pittsburgh Comm'n on Human Relations, 413 U. S. 376 (1973), the Court allowed an injunction against a newspaper's furtherance of illegal sex discrimination by placing of job advertisements in gender-designated columns. The Court stated:

"Any First Amendment interest which might be served by advertising an ordinary commercial proposal and which might arguably outweigh the governmental interest supporting the regulation is altogether absent when the commercial activity itself is illegal and the restriction on advertising is incidental to a valid limitation on economic activity." Id., at 389.

[15] In this connection we note that 18 U. S. C. § 2251 (1976 ed., Supp. IV), making it a federal offense for anyone to use children under the age of 16 in the production of pornographic materials, embraces all "sexually explicit conduct" without imposing an obscenity test. In addition, half of the state laws imposing criminal liability on the producer do not require the visual material to be legally obscene. Use in Pornography 307-308.

[16] 96 Misc. 2d, at 676, 409 N. Y. S. 2d, at 637. This is not merely a hypothetical possibility. See Brief for Petitioner 25 and examples cited therein.

[17] Sixteen States define a child as a person under age 18. Four States define a child as under 17 years old. The federal law and 16 States, including New York, define a child as under 16. Illinois and Nebraska define a child as a person under age 16 or who appears as a prepubescent. Ill. Rev. Stat., ch. 38, ¶ 11-20a(a)(1)(A) (1979); Neb. Rev. Stat. § 28-1463 (1979). Indiana defines a child as one who is or appears to be under 16. Ind. Code. §§ 35-30-10.1-2, 35-30-10.1-3 (1979). Kentucky provides for two age classifications (16 and 18) and varies punishment according to the victim's age. Ky. Rev. Stat. §§ 531.300-531.370 (Supp. 1980). See Use in Pornography 307, n. 71 (collecting statutes).

[18] Erznoznik v. City of Jacksonville, 422 U. S. 205 (1975), relied upon by the Court of Appeals, struck down a law against drive-in theaters showing nude scenes if movies could be seen from a public place. Since nudity, without more is protected expression, id., at 213, we proceeded to consider the underinclusiveness of the ordinance. The Jacksonville ordinance impermissibly singled out movies with nudity for special treatment while failing to regulate other protected speech which created the same alleged risk to traffic. Today, we hold that child pornography as defined in § 263.15 is unprotected speech subject to content-based regulation. Hence, it cannot be underinclusive or unconstitutional for a State to do precisely that.

[19] It is often impossible to determine where such material is produced. The

Senate Report accompanying federal child pornography legislation stressed that "it is quite common for photographs or films made in the United States to be sent to foreign countries to be reproduced and then returned to this country in order to give the impression of foreign origin." S. Rep. No. 95-438, p. 6 (1977). In addition, States have not limited their distribution laws to material produced within their own borders because the maintenance of the market itself "leaves open the financial conduit by which the production of such material is funded and materially increases the risk that [local] children will be injured." 52 N. Y. 2d 674, 688, 422 N. E. 2d 523, 531 (1981) (Jasen, J., dissenting).

[20] In addition to prudential restraints, the traditional rule is grounded in Art. III limits on the jurisdiction of federal courts to actual cases and controversies.

"This Court, as is the case with all federal courts, `has no jurisdiction to pronounce any statute, either of a State or of the United States, void, because irreconcilable with the Constitution, except as it is called upon to adjudge the legal rights of litigants in actual controversies. In the exercise of that jurisdiction, it is bound by two rules, to which it has rigidly adhered, one, never to anticipate a question of constitutional law in advance of the necessity of deciding it; the other never to formulate a rule of constitutional law broader than is required by the precise facts to which it is to be applied.' Liverpool, New York & Philadelphia S.S. Co. v. Commissioners of Emigration, 113 U. S. 33, 39." United States v. Raines, 362 U. S. 17, 21 (1960).

[21] Overbreadth challenges are only one type of facial attack. A person whose activity may be constitutionally regulated nevertheless may argue that the statute under which he is convicted or regulated is invalid on its face. See, e. g., Terminiello v. City of Chicago, 337 U. S. 1, 5 (1949). See generally Monaghan, Overbreadth, 1981 S. Ct. Rev. 1, 10-14.

[22] A. Bickel, The Least Dangerous Branch 115-116 (1962).

[23] Frankfurter & Hart, The Business of the Supreme Court at October Term, 1934, 49 Harv. L. Rev. 68, 95-96 (1935).

[24] When a federal court is dealing with a federal statute challenged as overbroad, it should, of course, construe the statute to avoid constitutional problems, if the statute is subject to such a limiting construction. Crowell v. Benson, 285 U. S. 22, 62 (1932). Accord, e. g., Haynes v. United States, 390 U. S. 85, 92 (1968) (dictum); Schneider v. Smith, 390 U. S. 17, 27 (1968); United States v. Rumely, 345 U. S. 41, 45 (1953); Ashwander v. TVA, 297 U. S. 288, 348 (1936) (Brandeis, J., concurring). Furthermore, if the federal statute is not subject to a narrowing construction and is impermissibly overbroad, it nevertheless should not be stricken down on its face; if it is severable, only the unconstitutional portion is to be invalidated. United States v. Thirty-seven Photographs, 402 U. S. 363 (1971).

A state court is also free to deal with a state statute in the same way. If the invalid reach of the law is cured, there is no longer reason for proscribing the statute's application to unprotected conduct. Here, of course, we are dealing with a state statute on direct review of a state-court decision that has construed the statute. Such a construction is binding on us.

[25] Parker v. Levy, 417 U. S. 733, 760 (1974) ("This Court has . . . repeatedly expressed its reluctance to strike down a statute on its face where there were a substantial number of situations to which it might be validly applied. Thus, even if there are marginal applications in which a statute would infringe on First Amendment values, facial invalidation is inappropriate if the `remainder of the statute . . . covers a whole range of easily identifiable and constitutionally proscribable . . . conduct . . . .' CSC v. Letter Carriers, 413 U. S. 548, 580-581 (1973)"). See Bogen, First Amendment Ancillary Doctrines, 37 Md. L. Rev. 679, 712-714 (1978); Note, The First Amendment Overbreadth Doctrine, 83 Harv. L. Rev. 844, 860-861 (1970).

[26] In Gooding v. Wilson, 405 U. S. 518, 519, 527 (1972), the Court's invalidation of a Georgia statute making it a misdemeanor to use "`opprobrious words or abusive language, tending to cause a breach of the peace'" followed from state judicial decisions indicating that "merely to speak words offensive to some who hear them" could constitute a "breach of the peace." Cases invalidating laws requiring members of a "subversive organization" to take a loyalty oath, Baggett v. Bullitt, 377 U. S. 360 (1964), or register with the government, Dombrowski v. Pfister, 380 U. S. 479 (1965), can be explained on the basis that the laws involved, unlike § 263.15, defined no central core of constitutionally regulable conduct; the entire scope of the laws was subject to the uncertainties and vagaries of prosecutorial discretion. See also Bigelow v. Virginia, 421 U. S. 809, 817 (1975) ("the facts of this case well illustrate `the statute's potential for sweeping and improper applications'") (citation omitted); NAACP v. Button, 371 U. S. 415, 433 (1963) ("We read the decree of the Virginia Supreme Court of Appeals . . . as proscribing any arrangement by which prospective litigants are advised to seek the assistance of particular attorneys"); Thornhill v. Alabama, 310 U. S. 88, 97 (1940) (the statute "does not aim specifically at evils within the allowable area of state control but, on the contrary, sweeps within its ambit other activities that in ordinary circumstances constitute an exercise of freedom of speech or of the press").

[27] "A substantial overbreadth rule is implicit in the chilling effect rationale.. . . [T]he presumption must be that only substantially overbroad laws set up the kind and degree of chill that is judicially cognizable." Moreover, "[w]ithout a substantial overbreadth limitation, review for overbreadth would be draconian indeed. It is difficult to think of a law that is utterly devoid of potential for unconstitutionality in some conceivable application." Note, 83 Harv. L. Rev., supra n. 25, at 859, and n. 61.

[28] There is no argument that the films sold by respondent do not fall squarely within the category of activity we have defined as unprotected. Therefore, no independent examination of the material is necessary to assure ourselves that the judgment here "does not constitute a forbidden intrusion on the field of free expression." New York Times Co. v. Sullivan, 376 U. S. 254, 285 (1964).

## Brockett v. Spokane Arcades, Inc. (June 19, 1985)

JUSTICE WHITE delivered the opinion of the Court.

The question in these cases is whether the Court of Appeals for the Ninth Circuit erred in invalidating in its entirety a Washington statute aimed at preventing and punishing the publication of obscene materials.

I

On April 1, 1982, the Washington state moral nuisance law became effective. Wash. Rev. Code 7.48A.010-7.48A.900 (1983). 1 It sets forth a comprehensive scheme establishing criminal and civil penalties for those who deal in obscenity or prostitution. The statute declares to be a "moral nuisance" any place "where lewd films are publicly exhibited as a regular course of business" and any place of business "in which lewd publications constitute a principal part of the stock in trade." 7.48A.020(1), (3). Subsection (2) of the "Definitions" section of the statute provides that "lewd matter" is synonymous with "obscene matter," and defines these terms to mean any matter:

"(a) Which the average person, applying contemporary community standards, would find, when considered as a whole, appeals to the prurient interest; and

"(b) Which explicitly depicts or describes patently offensive representations or descriptions of:

"(i) Ultimate sexual acts, normal or perverted, actual or simulated; or

"(ii) Masturbation, fellatio, cunnilingus, bestiality, excretory functions, or lewd exhibition of the genitals or genital area; or

"(iii) Violent or destructive sexual acts, including but not limited to human or animal mutilation, dismemberment, rape or torture; and

"(c) Which, when considered as a whole, and in the context in which it is used, lacks serious literary, artistic, political, or scientific value." 7.48A.010(2).

The word "prurient," as used in subsection (2)(a), is defined in subsection (8) to mean "that which incites lasciviousness or lust." 7.48A.010(8).

On April 5, four days after the effective date of the statute, appellees - various individuals and corporations who purvey sexually oriented books and movies to the adult public 2 - challenged the constitutionality of the statute in Federal District Court, seeking injunctive and declaratory relief. One of their assertions was that the statute's definition of "prurient" to include "that which incites . . . lust" was unconstitutionally overbroad because it reached material that aroused only a normal, healthy interest in sex and that the statute was therefore to be declared invalid on its face. 3 Appellees alleged that the sexually oriented films and books they sold were protected by the First Amendment, and that the state authorities would enforce the new legislation against them unless restrained by the Court. App. 33. On April 13, the District Court for the Eastern District of Washington issued a preliminary injunction against enforcement of the statute. Id., at 35.

After trial, the District Court rejected all of appellees' constitutional challenges to the validity of the statute. 544 F. Supp. 1034 (1982). 4 A divided panel of the Court of

Appeals for the Ninth Circuit reversed. 725 F.2d 482 (1984). It first held that a facial challenge to the allegedly overbroad statute was appropriate despite the fact that the law had not yet been authoritatively interpreted or enforced. This was necessary when First Amendment rights were at stake lest the very existence of the statute have a chilling effect on protected expression. The Court of Appeals acknowledged that facial invalidation required "substantial overbreadth," Broadrick v. Oklahoma, 413 U.S. 601 (1973), but concluded that the requirement applies only when the challenged statute regulates conduct, as opposed to "pure speech." 725 F.2d, at 487. Nor did the court find this to be an appropriate case for abstention. See Railroad Comm'n v. Pullman Co., 312 U.S. 496 (1941).

Reaching the merits, the Court of Appeals held that by including "lust" in its definition of "prurient," the Washington state legislature had intended the statute to reach material that merely stimulated normal sexual responses, material that it considered to be constitutionally protected. Because in its view the statute did not lend itself to a saving construction by a state court and any application of the statute would depend on a determination of obscenity by reference to the "unconstitutionally overbroad" definition, the Court of Appeals declared the statute as a whole to be null and void. 5

The defendant state and county officials separately appealed to this Court. We noted probable jurisdiction in both cases, 469 U.S. 813 (1984). 6

II

The Court of Appeals was of the view that neither Roth v. United States, 354 U.S. 476 (1957), nor later cases should be read to include within the definition of obscenity those materials that appeal to only normal sexual appetites. Roth held that the protection of the First Amendment did not extend to obscene speech, which was to be identified by inquiring "whether to the average person, applying contemporary community standards, the dominant theme of the material taken as a whole appeals to prurient interest." Id., at 489 (footnote omitted). Earlier in its opinion, id., at 487, n. 20, the Court had defined "material which deals with sex in a manner appealing to prurient interest" as:

"I. e., material having a tendency to excite lustful thoughts. Webster's New International Dictionary (Unabridged, 2d ed., 1949) defines prurient, in pertinent part, as follows:

"`. . . Itching; longing; uneasy with desire or longing; of persons, having itching, morbid, or lascivious longings; of desire, curiosity, or propensity, lewd. . . .'

"Pruriency is defined, in pertinent part, as follows:

"`. . . Quality of being prurient; lascivious desire or thought. . . .'

"See also Mutual Film Corp. v. Industrial Comm'n, 236 U.S. 230, 242, where this Court said as to motion pictures: `. . . They take their attraction from the general interest, eager and wholesome it may be, in their subjects, but a prurient interest may be excited and appealed to. . . .' (Emphasis added.)

"We perceive no significant difference between the meaning of obscenity developed in the case law and the definition of the A. L. I., Model Penal Code, 207.10(2) (Tent. Draft No. 6, 1957), viz.:

"`. . . A thing is obscene if, considered as a whole, its predominant appeal is to prurient interest, i. e., a shameful or morbid interest in nudity, sex, or excretion, and if it goes substantially beyond customary limits of candor in description or representation of such matters. . . .' See Comment, id., at 10, and the discussion at page 29 et seq."

Under Roth, obscenity was equated with prurience and was not entitled to First Amendment protection. Nine years later, however, the decision in Memoirs v. Massachusetts, 383 U.S. 413 (1966), established a much more demanding three-part definition of obscenity, a definition that was in turn modified in Miller v. California, 413 U.S. 15 (1973). 7 The Miller guidelines for identifying obscenity are:

"(a) whether `the average person, applying contemporary community standards' would find that the work, taken as a whole, appeals to the prurient interest, Kois v. Wisconsin, [408 U.S.,] at 230, quoting Roth v. United States, supra, at 489; (b) whether the work depicts or describes, in a patently offensive way, sexual conduct specifically defined by the applicable state law; and (c) whether the work, taken as a whole, lacks serious literary, artistic, political, or scientific value." Id., at 24.

Miller thus retained, as had Memoirs, the Roth formulation as the first part of this test, without elaborating on or disagreeing with the definition of "prurient interest" contained in the Roth opinion.

The Court of Appeals was aware that Roth had indicated in footnote 20 that material appealing to the prurient interest was "material having a tendency to excite lustful thoughts" but did not believe that Roth had intended to characterize as obscene material that provoked only normal, healthy sexual desires. We do not differ with that view. As already noted, material appealing to the "prurient interest" was itself the definition of obscenity announced in Roth; and we are quite sure that by using the words "lustful thoughts" in footnote 20, the Court was referring to sexual responses over and beyond those that would be characterized as normal. At the end of that footnote, as the Court of Appeals observed, the Roth opinion referred to the Model Penal Code definition of obscenity - material whose predominate appeal is to "a shameful or morbid interest in nudity, sex, or excretion" and indicated that it perceived no significant difference between that definition and the meaning of obscenity developed in the case law. This effectively negated any inference that "lustful thoughts" as used earlier in the footnote was limited to or included normal sexual responses. 8 It would require more than the possible ambiguity in footnote 20 to lead us to believe that the Court intended to characterize as obscene and exclude from the protection of the First Amendment any and all speech that aroused any sexual responses, whether normal or morbid.

Appellants urge that because Roth defined prurience in terms of lust, the Washington obscenity statute cannot be faulted for defining "prurient" as that which "incites lasciviousness or lust." Whatever Roth meant by "lustful thoughts" - and the State agrees that the Court did not intend to include materials that provoked only normal sexual reactions - that meaning should be attributed to the term "lust" appearing in the state law. On this basis, the State submits that the statute cannot be unconstitutional for defining prurience in this manner.

The Court of Appeals rejected this view, holding that the term "lust" had acquired a far broader meaning since Roth was decided in 1957. The word had come to be understood as referring to a "healthy, wholesome, human reaction common to millions of well-adjusted persons in our society," rather than to any shameful or morbid desire. 725 F.2d, at 490. Construed in this way, the statutory definition of prurience would include within the first part of the Miller definition of obscenity material that is constitutionally protected by the First Amendment: material that, taken as a whole, does no more than arouse, "good, old fashioned, healthy" interest in sex. Id., at 492. The statute, the Court of Appeals held, was thus overbroad and invalid on its face.

Appellants fault the Court of Appeals for construing the statute in this manner. Normally, however we defer to the construction of a state statute given it by the lower federal courts. Chardon v. Fumero Soto, 462 U.S. 650, 654 -655, n. 5 (1983); Haring v. Prosise, 462 U.S. 306, 314, n. 8 (1983); Pierson v. Ray, 386 U.S. 547, 558, n. 12 (1967); General Box Co. v. United States, 351 U.S. 159, 165 (1956). We do so not only to "render unnecessary review of their decisions in this respect," Cort v. Ash, 422 U.S. 66, 73, n. 6 (1975), but also to reflect our belief that district courts and courts of appeals are better schooled in and more able to interpret the laws of their respective States. See Bishop v. Wood, 426 U.S. 341, 345 -346 (1976); Gooding v. Wilson, 405 U.S. 518, 524, and n. 2 (1972). The rule is not ironclad, however, and we surely have the authority to differ with the lower federal courts as to the meaning of a state statute. 9 It may also be that, other things being equal, this would not be a case for deferring to the Court of Appeals. 10 But we pretermit this issue, for the Court of Appeals fell into another error when it invalidated the statute on its face because of its "unconstitutionally overbroad" definition of obscenity.

III

Appellants insist that the error was in finding any invalidity in the statute, even accepting the court's construction of the word "lust." To be obscene under Miller, a publication must, taken as a whole, appeal to the prurient interest, must contain patently offensive depictions or descriptions of specified sexual conduct, and on the whole have no serious literary, artistic, political, or scientific value. Appellants submit that the latter two Miller guidelines, which the Washington statute faithfully follows, will completely cure any overbreadth that may inhere in the statute's definition of prurience as construed by the Court of Appeals. We are not at all confident that this would always be the case. It could be that a publication that on the whole arouses normal sexual responses would be declared obscene because it contains an isolated example of conduct required by the second guideline and because it also fails to have the redeeming value required by the third. Under the existing case law, material of that kind is not without constitutional protection. 11

Facial invalidation of the statute was nevertheless improvident. We call to mind two of the cardinal rules governing the federal courts: "`[o]ne, never to anticipate a question of constitutional law in advance of the necessity of deciding it; the other never to formulate a rule of constitutional law broader than is required by the precise facts to which it is to be applied.'" United States v. Raines, 362 U.S. 17, 21 (1960), quoting Liverpool, New York & Philadelphia S. S. Co. v. Commissioners of Emigration, 113 U.S. 33, 39 (1885). Citing a long line of cases, Raines also held that "[k]indred to these rules is the rule that one to whom application of a statute is constitutional will not be heard to attack the statute on the ground that impliedly it might also be taken as applying to other persons or other situations in which its application might be unconstitutional." These guideposts are at the bottom of the "elementary principle that the same statute may be in part constitutional and in part unconstitutional, and that if the parts are wholly independent of each other, that which is constitutional may stand while that which is unconstitutional will be rejected." Allen v. Louisiana, 103 U.S. 80, 83 -84 (1881), quoted with approval in Field v. Clark, 143 U.S. 649, 695 -696 (1892). Absent "weighty countervailing" circumstances, Raines, supra, at 22, this is the course that the Court has adhered to. Reagan v. Farmers' Loan & Trust Co., 154 U.S. 362, 395 -396 (1894); Champlin Refining Co. v. Corporation Comm'n, 286 U.S. 210, 234 -235 (1932); Watson v. Buck, 313 U.S. 387, 395 -396 (1941); Buckley v. Valeo, 424 U.S. 1, 108 (1976). Just this Term, in Tennessee v. Garner, 471 U.S. 1 (1985), we held unconstitutional a state statute authorizing the use of deadly force against fleeing suspects, not on its face, but only insofar as it authorized the use of lethal force against unarmed and nondangerous suspects.

Nor does the First Amendment involvement in this case render inapplicable the rule that a federal court should not extend its invalidation of a statute further than necessary to dispose of the case before it. Buckley v. Valeo, supra, illustrates as much. So does Cantwell v. Connecticut, 310 U.S. 296 (1940), where the Court did not invalidate the state offense of "breach of the peace" on its face but only to the extent that it was construed and applied to prevent the peaceful distribution of religious literature on the streets. In Marsh v. Alabama, 326 U.S. 501 (1946), the Court struck down a state trespass law only "[i]nsofar as the State has attempted to impose criminal punishment" on those distributing literature on the streets of a company town. Id., at 509. NAACP v. Button, 371 U.S. 415 (1963), did not facially invalidate the State's rules against solicitation by attorneys but only as they were sought to be applied to the activities of the NAACP involved in that case. Id., at 419, 439. More recently, in United States v. Grace, 461 U.S. 171 (1983), we declined to invalidate on its face a federal statute prohibiting demonstrations on the Supreme Court grounds and confined our holding to the invalidity of the statute as applied to picketing on the public sidewalks surrounding the building. Id., at 175.

For its holding that in First Amendment cases an overbroad statute must be stricken down on its face, the Court of Appeals relied on that line of cases exemplified by

Thornhill v. Alabama, 310 U.S. 88 (1940), and more recently by Village of Schaumburg v. Citizens for a Better Environment, 444 U.S. 620 (1980). In those cases, an individual whose own speech or expressive conduct may validly be prohibited or sanctioned is permitted to challenge a statute on its face because it also threatens others not before the court - those who desire to engage in legally protected expression but who may refrain from doing so rather than risk prosecution or undertake to have the law declared partially invalid. If the overbreadth is "substantial," 12 the law may not be enforced against anyone, including the party before the court, until it is narrowed to reach only unprotected activity, whether by legislative action or by judicial construction or partial invalidation. Broadrick v. Oklahoma, 413 U.S. 601 (1973).

It is otherwise where the parties challenging the statute are those who desire to engage in protected speech that the overbroad statute purports to punish, or who seek to publish both protected and unprotected material. There is then no want of a proper party to challenge the statute, no concern that an attack on the statute will be unduly delayed or protected speech discouraged. The statute may forthwith be declared invalid to the extent that it reaches too far, but otherwise left intact.

The cases before us are ones governed by the normal rule that partial, rather than facial, invalidation is the required course. The Washington statute was faulted by the Court of Appeals only because it reached material that incited normal as well as unhealthy interest in sex, and appellees, or some of them, desiring to publish this sort of material, claimed that they faced punishment if they did so. Unless there are countervailing considerations, the Washington law should have been invalidated only insofar as the word "lust" is to be understood as reaching protected materials.

The Court of Appeals was of the view that the term "lust" did not lend itself to a limiting construction and that it would not be feasible to separate its valid and invalid applications. Even accepting the Court of Appeals' construction of "lust," however, we are unconvinced that the identified overbreadth is incurable and would taint all possible applications of the statute, as was the case in Secretary of State of Maryland v. Joseph H. Munson Co., 467 U.S. 947 (1984). See also City Council of Los Angeles v. Taxpayers for Vincent, 466 U.S. 789, 796 -799, and nn. 12-16 (1984). If, as we have held, prurience may be constitutionally defined for the purposes of identifying obscenity as that which appeals to a shameful or morbid interest in sex, Roth v. United States, 354 U.S. 476 (1957), it is equally certain that if the statute at issue here is invalidated only insofar as the word "lust" is taken to include normal interest in sex, the statute would pass constitutional muster and would validly reach the whole range of obscene publications. Furthermore, had the Court of Appeals thought that "lust" refers only to normal sexual appetites, it could have excised the word from the statute entirely, since the statutory definition of prurience referred to "lasciviousness" as well as "lust." Even if the statute had not defined prurience at all, there would have been no satisfactory ground for striking the statute down in its entirety because of invalidity in all of its applications. 13

Partial invalidation would be improper if it were contrary to legislative intent in the sense that the legislature had passed an inseverable Act or would not have passed it had it known the challenged provision was invalid. But here the statute itself contains a severability clause; 14 and under Washington law, a statute is not to be declared unconstitutional in its entirety unless "the invalid provisions are unseverable and it cannot reasonably be believed that the legislature would have passed the one without the other, or unless the elimination of the invalid part would render the remainder of the act incapable of accomplishing the legislative purposes." State v. Anderson, 81 Wash. 2d 234, 236, 501 P.2d 184, 185-186 (1972). 15 It would be frivolous to suggest, and no one does, that the Washington Legislature, if it could not proscribe materials that appealed to normal as well as abnormal sexual appetites, would have refrained from passing the moral nuisance statute. And it is quite evident that the remainder of the statute retains its effectiveness as a regulation of obscenity. In these circumstances, the issue of severability is no obstacle to partial invalidation, which is the course the Court of Appeals should have pursued.

The judgment of the Court of Appeals is accordingly reversed, and the case is remanded for further proceedings consistent with this opinion.

So ordered.


Notes

[1] An earlier moral nuisance law, Wash. Rev. Code 7.48.052 et seq. (1983), adopted as an initiative measure in 1977, was struck down as an impermissible prior restraint. See Spokane Arcades, Inc. v. Brockett, 631 F.2d 135 (CA9 1980), summarily aff'd, 454 U.S. 1022 (1981).

[2] Seven separate suits were originally filed in the District Court for the Eastern District of Washington, where they were consolidated.

[3] Appellees also challenged the Washington statute's paraphrasing of the second and third parts of the test set forth in Miller v. California, 413 U.S. 15 (1973). See infra, at 497. The District Court rejected these attacks, and the Court of Appeals did not address them. Appellees have not renewed these claims in this Court.

[4] The District Court stayed its judgment to allow appellees to seek a stay pending appeal from the Court of Appeals, which the Court of Appeals subsequently granted. 725 F.2d 482, 485 (1984). Thus, the statute was not enforced pending appeal.

[5] Having struck down the statute in toto on overbreadth grounds, the Court of Appeals nevertheless went on to conclude that the statute's civil fine provisions were constitutionally invalid, on the theory that "the legislature will undoubtedly try again." 725 F.2d, at 493. This part of the opinion was obviously unnecessary to the Court of Appeals' holding, and in view of our disposition of this case, will require reconsideration on remand.

[6] Because there are no significant differences between the two cases, we do not distinguish between them in our discussion.

[7] The basic difference between the Memoirs test and the Miller test was the

Memoirs requirement that in order to be judged obscene, a work must be "utterly without redeeming social value." 383 U.S., at 418. Miller settled on the formulation, "whether the work, taken as a whole, lacks serious literary, artistic, political, or scientific value." 413 U.S., at 24 .

[8 ] This conclusion is bolstered by a subsequent footnote, 354 U.S., at 489, n. 26, referring to a number of cases defining obscenity in terms of "lust" or "lustful." See Parmelee v. United States, 72 App. D.C. 203, 210, 113 F.2d 729, 736 (1940) (material is protected if "the erotic matter is not introduced to promote lust"); United States v. Dennett, 39 F.2d 564, 569 (CA2 1930) (sex education pamphlet not obscene because tendency is to "rationalize and dignify [sex] emotions rather than to arouse lust"); United States v. One Book Called "Ulysses," 5 F. Supp. 182, 184 (SDNY 1933), aff'd, 72 F.2d 705 (CA2 1934) (meaning of the word "obscene" is "[t]ending to stir the sex impulses or to lead to sexually impure and lustful thoughts"); Commonwealth v. Isenstadt, 318 Mass. 543, 549-550, 62 N. E. 2d 840, 844 (1945) (material is obscene if it has "a substantial tendency to deprave or corrupt its readers by inciting lascivious thoughts or arousing lustful desire"); Missouri v. Becker, 364 Mo. 1079, 1085, 272 S. W. 2d 283, 286 (1954) (materials are obscene if they "incite lascivious thoughts, arouse lustful desire"); Adams Theatre Co. v. Keenan, 12 N. J. 267, 272, 96 A. 2d 519, 521 (1953) (BRENNAN, J.) (question is whether "dominant note of the presentation is erotic allurement `tending to excite lustful and lecherous desire'").

[9 ] The Court has stated that it will defer to lower courts on state-law issues unless there is "plain" error, Palmer v. Hoffman, 318 U.S. 109, 118 (1943); the view of the lower court is "clearly wrong," The Tungus v. Skovgaard, 358 U.S. 588, 596 (1959); or the construction is "clearly erroneous," United States v. Durham Lumber Co., 363 U.S. 522, 527 (1960), or "unreasonable," Propper v. Clark, 337 U.S. 472, 486 -487 (1949). On occasion, then, the Court has refused to follow the views of a lower federal court on an issue of state law. In Cole v. Richardson, 405 U.S. 676, 683 -684 (1972), e. g., we refused to accept a three-judge District Court's construction of a single statutory word based on the dictionary definition of that language where more reliable indicia of the legislative intent were available.

[10 ] Appellants make a strong argument that the Court of Appeals erred in construing the Washington statute. The Court of Appeals relied on dictionary definitions of "prurient" and "lust," saying that the most recent edition of Webster's Third New International Dictionary (Unabridged, 4th ed. 1976) did not include the word "lust" in its definition of "prurient." But neither did the edition of Webster cited by the Roth court. Webster's Second Edition defined "lust" as (excluding the obsolete meanings):

"sensuous desire; bodily appetite; specif. and most commonly, sexual desire, as a violent or degrading passion." Webster's New International Dictionary (Unabridged, 2d ed., 1949).

Furthermore, and of some significance, the word "lust" is defined in Webster's Third New International (Unabridged, 5th ed., 1981) in pertinent part as follows:

"1 obs. a: PLEASURE, GRATIFICATION, DELIGHT . . . b: personal inclination: WISH, WHIM . . . c: VIGOR, FERTILITY . . . 2: sexual desire esp. of a violent self-indulgent character: LECHERY, LASCIVIOUSNESS . . . 3 a: an intense longing: CRAVING . . . b: EAGERNESS, ENTHUSIASM."

[11 ] Roth specifically rejected a standard of obscenity that "allowed material to be judged merely by the effect of an isolated excerpt upon particularly susceptible persons." 354 U.S., at 488 -489 (discussing Queen v. Hicklin, 1868. L. R. 3 Q. B. 360).

[12 ] The Court of Appeals erred in holding that the Broadrick v. Oklahoma, 413 U.S. 601 (1973), substantial overbreadth requirement is inapplicable where pure speech rather than conduct is at issue. New York v. Ferber, 458 U.S. 747, 772 (1982), specifically held to the contrary. Because of our disposition of these cases, we do not address the issue whether the overbreadth of the Washington statute, in relation to its legitimate reach, is substantial and warrants a declaration of facial invalidity. See Secretary of State of Maryland v. Joseph H. Munson Co., 467 U.S. 947, 964 -965 (1984); CSC v. Letter Carriers, 413 U.S. 548, 580 -581 (1973).

[13 ] According to appellees, the vast majority of state statutes either leave the word "prurient" undefined or adopt a definition using the words "shameful or morbid." Brief for Appellees 26-27. One State, New Hampshire, defines prurient interest as "an interest in lewdness or lascivious thoughts." N. H. Rev. Stat. Ann. 650:(1)(I)-(IV)(a) (Supp. 1983). Mississippi is apparently the only State other than Washington to use the word "lust" in its definition of "prurient." Miss. Code Ann. 97-29-103(1)(a) (Supp. 1984) ("a lustful, erotic, shameful, or morbid interest in nudity, sex or excretion"). The District Court for the Northern District of Mississippi has issued a preliminary injunction against enforcement of the statute, partly on the ground that "[t]he inclusion of the terms lustful and erotic [in the definition of prurient] would permit the application of the statute to arguably protected materials." Goldstein v. Allain, 568 F. Supp. 1377, 1385 (1983), appeal stayed pending trial on the merits, Case No. 83-4452 (CA5, June 20, 1984).

Some lower courts considering the issue have used the words "shameful or morbid" in describing the "prurient interest" that distinguishes obscene materials. See, e. g., Red Bluff Drive-In, Inc. v. Vance, 648 F.2d 1020, 1026 (CA5 1981), cert. denied sub nom. Theatres West, Inc. v. Holmes, 455 U.S. 913 (1982); Leach v. American Booksellers Assn., Inc., 582 S. W. 2d 738, 749-750 (Tenn. 1979). Others, however, have used "lust" in connection with definitions of "prurient," reading the word as connoting a sense of shame or debasement, or relying on its use in Roth. See, e. g., United States v. 35 MM. Motion Picture Film Entitled "Language of Love," 432 F.2d 705, 711-712 (CA2 1970); Childs v. Oregon, 431 F.2d 272, 275 (CA9 1970); Flying Eagle Publications, Inc. v. United States, 273 F.2d 799, 803 (CA1 1960).

An obscenity statute that leaves the word "prurient" undefined, or rather, defined only by case law has been sustained. See Red Bluff Drive-In, Inc. v. Vance, supra, at 1026. See also Ward v. Illinois, 431 U.S. 767, 775 (1977) (state obscenity statute not overbroad for failure to expressly describe the kinds of sexual conduct intended to be referred to under part (b) of Miller guidelines, where state court had construed statute to incorporate the examples of sexual conduct mentioned in Miller). A predecessor of the Washington statute at issue here similarly used the word "prurient" without defining it. Wash. Rev. Code 7.48.050 et seq. (1983). The Court of Appeals for the Ninth Circuit struck down the statute on other grounds, but apparently the use of the word "prurient" was not challenged. See Spokane Arcades v. Brockett, 631 F.2d, at 136, n. 1. An earlier predecessor statute used only the word "obscene," without any further definition whatsoever. The Washington Supreme Court construed the statute to incorporate the Roth-Miller test, saving it from unconstitutional vagueness. See State v. J-R Distributors, Inc., 82 Wash. 2d 584, 602-603, 512 P.2d 1049, 1061 (1973). The evident likelihood that the Washington courts would construe the instant statute to conform with the Miller standards also counsels against facial invalidation in this case. Cf. Time, Inc. v. Hill, 385 U.S. 374 (1967).

[14 ] "If any provision of this act or its application to any person or circumstance is held invalid, the remainder of the act or the application of the provision to other persons or circumstances is not affected." Wash. Rev. Code 7.48A.900 (1983).

[15 ] This standard is similar to that which we would apply in determining the severability of a federal statute: "`Unless it is evident that the Legislature would not have enacted those provisions which are within its power, independently of that which is not, the invalid part may be dropped if what is left is fully operative as a law.'" See Buckley v. Valeo, 424 U.S. 1, 108 -109 (1976), quoting Champlin Refining Co. v. Corporation Comm'n, 286 U.S. 210, 234 (1932).

## Renton v. Playtime Theatres, Inc. (February 25, 1986)

JUSTICE REHNQUIST delivered the opinion of the Court.

This case involves a constitutional challenge to a zoning ordinance, enacted by appellant city of Renton, Washington, that prohibits adult motion picture theaters from locating within 1,000 feet of any residential zone, single- or multiple-family dwelling, church, park, or school. Appellees, Playtime Theatres, Inc., and Sea-First Properties, Inc., filed an action in the United States District Court for the Western District of Washington seeking a declaratory judgment that the Renton ordinance violated the First and Fourteenth Amendments and a permanent injunction against its enforcement. The District Court ruled in favor of Renton and denied the permanent injunction, but the Court of Appeals for the Ninth Circuit reversed and remanded for reconsideration. 748 F.2d 527 (1984). We noted probable jurisdiction, 471 U.S. 1013 (1985), and now reverse the judgment of the Ninth Circuit. 1

In May 1980, the Mayor of Renton, a city of approximately 32,000 people located just south of Seattle, suggested to the Renton City Council that it consider the advisability of enacting zoning legislation dealing with adult entertainment uses. No such uses existed in the city at that time. Upon the Mayor's suggestion, the City Council referred the matter to the city's Planning and Development Committee. The Committee held public hearings, reviewed the experiences of Seattle and other cities, and received a report from the City Attorney's Office advising as to developments in other cities. The City Council, meanwhile, adopted Resolution No. 2368, which imposed a moratorium on the licensing of "any business . . . which . . . has as its primary purpose the selling, renting or showing of sexually explicit materials." App. 43. The resolution contained a clause explaining that such businesses "would have a severe impact upon surrounding businesses and residences." Id., at 42.

In April 1981, acting on the basis of the Planning and Development Committee's recommendation, the City Council enacted Ordinance No. 3526. The ordinance prohibited any "adult motion picture theater" from locating within 1,000 feet of any residential zone, single- or multiple-family dwelling, church, or park, and within one mile of any school. App. to Juris. Statement 79a. The term "adult motion picture theater" was defined as "[a]n enclosed building used for presenting motion picture films, video cassettes, cable television, or any other such visual media, distinguished or characteri[zed] by an emphasis on matter depicting, describing or relating to `specified sexual activities' or `specified anatomical areas' . . . for observation by patrons therein." Id., at 78a.

In early 1982, respondents acquired two existing theaters in downtown Renton, with the intention of using them to exhibit feature-length adult films. The theaters were located within the area proscribed by Ordinance No. 3526. At about the same time, respondents filed the previously mentioned lawsuit challenging the ordinance on First and Fourteenth Amendment grounds, and seeking declaratory and injunctive relief. While the federal action was pending, the City Council amended the ordinance in several respects, adding a statement of reasons for its enactment and reducing the minimum distance from any school to 1,000 feet.

In November 1982, the Federal Magistrate to whom respondents' action had been referred recommended the entry of a preliminary injunction against enforcement of the Renton ordinance and the denial of Renton's motions to dismiss and for summary judgment. The District Court adopted the Magistrate's recommendations and entered the preliminary injunction, and respondents began showing adult films at their two theaters in Renton. Shortly thereafter, the parties agreed to submit the case for a final decision on whether a permanent injunction should issue on the basis of the record as already developed.

The District Court then vacated the preliminary injunction, denied respondents' requested permanent injunction, and entered summary judgment in favor of Renton. The court found that the Renton ordinance did not substantially restrict First Amendment interests, that Renton was not required to show specific adverse impact on Renton from the operation of adult theaters but could rely on the experiences of other cities, that the purposes of the ordinance were unrelated to the suppression of speech, and that the restrictions on speech imposed by the ordinance were no greater than necessary to further the governmental interests involved. Relying on Young v. American Mini

Theatres, Inc., 427 U.S. 50 (1976), and United States v. O'Brien, 391 U.S. 367 (1968), the court held that the Renton ordinance did not violate the First Amendment.

The Court of Appeals for the Ninth Circuit reversed. The Court of Appeals first concluded, contrary to the finding of the District Court, that the Renton ordinance constituted a substantial restriction on First Amendment interests. Then, using the standards set forth in United States v. O'Brien, supra, the Court of Appeals held that Renton had improperly relied on the experiences of other cities in lieu of evidence about the effects of adult theaters on Renton, that Renton had thus failed to establish adequately the existence of a substantial governmental interest in support of its ordinance, and that in any event Renton's asserted interests had not been shown to be unrelated to the suppression of expression. The Court of Appeals remanded the case to the District Court for reconsideration of Renton's asserted interests.

In our view, the resolution of this case is largely dictated by our decision in Young v. American Mini Theatres, Inc., supra. There, although five Members of the Court did not agree on a single rationale for the decision, we held that the city of Detroit's zoning ordinance, which prohibited locating an adult theater within 1,000 feet of any two other "regulated uses" or within 500 feet of any residential zone, did not violate the First and Fourteenth Amendments. Id., at 72-73 (plurality opinion of STEVENS, J., joined by BURGER, C. J., and WHITE and REHNQUIST, JJ.); id., at 84 (POWELL, J., concurring). The Renton ordinance, like the one in American Mini Theatres, does not ban adult theaters altogether, but merely provides that such theaters may not be located within 1,000 feet of any residential zone, single- or multiple-family dwelling, church, park, or school. The ordinance is therefore properly analyzed as a form of time, place, and manner regulation. Id., at 63, and n. 18; id., at 78-79 (POWELL, J., concurring).

Describing the ordinance as a time, place, and manner regulation is, of course, only the first step in our inquiry. This Court has long held that regulations enacted for the purpose of restraining speech on the basis of its content presumptively violate the First Amendment. See Carey v. Brown, 447 U.S. 455, 462 -463, and n. 7 (1980); Police Dept. of Chicago v. Mosley, 408 U.S. 92, 95, 98-99 (1972). On the other hand, so-called "content-neutral" time, place, and manner regulations are acceptable so long as they are designed to serve a substantial governmental interest and do not unreasonably limit alternative avenues of communication. See Clark v. Community for Creative Non-Violence, 468 U.S. 288, 293 (1984); City Council of Los Angeles v. Taxpayers for Vincent, 466 U.S. 789, 807 (1984); Heffron v. International Society for Krishna Consciousness, Inc., 452 U.S. 640, 647 -648 (1981).

At first glance, the Renton ordinance, like the ordinance in American Mini Theatres, does not appear to fit neatly into either the "content-based" or the "content-neutral" category. To be sure, the ordinance treats theaters that specialize in adult films differently from other kinds of theaters. Nevertheless, as the District Court concluded, the Renton ordinance is aimed not at the content of the films shown at "adult motion picture theatres," but rather at the secondary effects of such theaters on the surrounding community. The District Court found that the City Council's "predominate concerns" were with the secondary effects of adult theaters, and not with the content of adult films themselves. App. to Juris. Statement 31a (emphasis added). But the Court of Appeals, relying on its decision in Tovar v. Billmeyer, 721 F.2d 1260, 1266 (CA9 1983), held that this was not enough to sustain the ordinance. According to the Court of Appeals, if "a motivating factor" in enacting the ordinance was to restrict respondents' exercise of First Amendment rights the ordinance would be invalid, apparently no matter how small a part this motivating factor may have played in the City Council's decision. 748 F.2d, at 537 (emphasis in original). This view of the law was rejected in United States v. O'Brien, 391 U.S., at 382 -386, the very case that the Court of Appeals said it was applying:

"It is a familiar principle of constitutional law that this Court will not strike down an otherwise constitutional statute on the basis of an alleged illicit legislative motive. . . .

. . . . .

". . . What motivates one legislator to make a speech about a statute is not necessarily what motivates scores of others to enact it, and the stakes are sufficiently high for us to eschew guesswork." Id., at 383-384.

The District Court's finding as to "predominate" intent, left undisturbed by the Court of Appeals, is more than adequate to establish that the city's pursuit of its zoning interests here was unrelated to the suppression of free expression. The ordinance by its terms is designed to prevent crime, protect the city's retail trade, maintain property values, and generally "protec[t] and preserv[e] the quality of [the city's] neighborhoods, commercial districts, and the quality of urban life," not to suppress the expression of unpopular views. See App. to Juris. Statement 90a. As JUSTICE POWELL observed in American Mini Theatres, "[i]f [the city] had been concerned with restricting the message purveyed by adult theaters, it would have tried to close them or restrict their number rather than circumscribe their choice as to location." 427 U.S., at 82, n. 4.

In short, the Renton ordinance is completely consistent with our definition of "content-neutral" speech regulations as those that "are justified without reference to the content of the regulated speech." Virginia Pharmacy Board v. Virginia Citizens Consumer Council, Inc., 425 U.S. 748, 771 (1976) (emphasis added); Community for Creative Non-Violence, supra, at 293; International Society for Krishna Consciousness, supra, at 648. The ordinance does not contravene the fundamental principle that underlies our concern about "content-based" speech regulations: that "government may not grant the use of a forum to people whose views it finds acceptable, but deny use to those wishing to express less favored or more controversial views." Mosley, supra, at 95-96.

It was with this understanding in mind that, in American Mini Theatres, a majority of this Court decided that, at least with respect to businesses that purvey sexually explicit materials, 2 zoning ordinances designed to combat the undesirable secondary effects of such businesses are to be reviewed under the standards applicable to "content-neutral" time, place, and manner regulations. JUSTICE STEVENS, writing for the plurality, concluded that the city of Detroit was entitled to draw a distinction between adult theaters and other kinds of theaters "without violating the government's paramount obligation of neutrality in its regulation of protected communication," 427 U.S., at 70, noting that "[i]t is th[e] secondary effect which these zoning ordinances attempt to avoid, not the dissemination of `offensive' speech," id., at 71, n. 34. JUSTICE POWELL, in concurrence, elaborated:

"[The] dissent misconceives the issue in this case by insisting that it involves an impermissible time, place, and manner restriction based on the content of expression. It involves nothing of the kind. We have here merely a decision by the city to treat certain movie theaters differently because they have markedly different effects upon their surroundings. . . . Moreover, even if this were a case involving a special governmental response to the content of one type of movie, it is possible that the result would be supported by a line of cases recognizing that the government can tailor its reaction to different types of speech according to the degree to which its special and overriding interests are implicated. See, e. g., Tinker v. Des Moines School Dist., 393 U.S. 503, 509 - 511 (1969); Procunier v. Martinez, 416 U.S. 396, 413 -414 (1974); Greer v. Spock, 424 U.S. 828, 842 -844 (1976) (POWELL, J., concurring); cf. CSC v. Letter Carriers, 413 U.S. 548 (1973)." Id., at 82, n. 6.

The appropriate inquiry in this case, then, is whether the Renton ordinance is designed to serve a substantial governmental interest and allows for reasonable alternative avenues of communication. See Community for Creative Non-Violence, 468 U.S., at 293; International Society for Krishna Consciousness, 452 U.S., at 649, 654. It is clear that the ordinance meets such a standard. As a majority of this Court recognized in American Mini Theatres, a city's "interest in attempting to preserve the quality of urban life is one that must be accorded high respect." 427 U.S., at 71 (plurality opinion); see id., at 80 (POWELL, J., concurring) ("Nor is there doubt that the interests furthered by this ordinance are both important and substantial"). Exactly the same vital governmental interests are at stake here.

The Court of Appeals ruled, however, that because the Renton ordinance was enacted without the benefit of studies specifically relating to "the particular problems or needs of Renton," the city's justifications for the ordinance were "conclusory and speculative." 748 F.2d, at 537. We think the Court of Appeals imposed on the city an unnecessarily rigid burden of proof. The record in this case reveals that Renton relied heavily on the experience of, and studies produced by, the city of Seattle. In Seattle, as in Renton, the adult theater zoning ordinance was aimed at preventing the secondary effects caused by the presence of even one such theater in a given neighborhood. See Northend Cinema, Inc. v. Seattle, 90 Wash. 2d 709, 585 P.2d 1153 (1978). The opinion of the Supreme Court of Washington in Northend Cinema, which was before the Renton City Council when it enacted the ordinance in question here, described Seattle's experience as follows:

"The amendments to the City's zoning code which are at issue here are the culmination of a long period of study and discussion of the problems of adult movie theaters in residential areas of the City. . . . [T]he City's Department of Community Development made a study of the need for zoning controls of adult theaters . . . . The study analyzed the City's zoning scheme, comprehensive plan, and land uses around existing adult motion picture theaters. . . ." Id., at 711, 585 P.2d, at 1155.

"[T]he [trial] court heard extensive testimony regarding the history and purpose of these ordinances. It heard expert testimony on the adverse effects of the presence of adult motion picture theaters on neighborhood children and community improvement efforts. The court's detailed findings, which include a finding that the location of adult theaters has a harmful effect on the area and contribute to neighborhood blight, are supported by substantial evidence in the record." Id., at 713, 585 P.2d, at 1156.

"The record is replete with testimony regarding the effects of adult movie theater locations on residential neighborhoods." Id., at 719, 585 P.2d, at 1159.

We hold that Renton was entitled to rely on the experiences of Seattle and other cities, and in particular on the "detailed findings" summarized in the Washington Supreme Court's Northend Cinema opinion, in enacting its adult theater zoning ordinance. The First Amendment does not require a city, before enacting such an ordinance, to conduct new studies or produce evidence independent of that already generated by other cities, so long as whatever evidence the city relies upon is reasonably believed to be relevant to the problem that the city addresses. That was the case here. Nor is our holding affected by the fact that Seattle ultimately chose a different method of adult theater zoning than that chosen by Renton, since Seattle's choice of a different remedy to combat the secondary effects of adult theaters does not call into question either Seattle's identification of those secondary effects or the relevance of Seattle's experience to Renton.

We also find no constitutional defect in the method chosen by Renton to further its substantial interests. Cities may regulate adult theaters by dispersing them, as in Detroit, or by effectively concentrating them, as in Renton. "It is not our function to appraise the wisdom of [the city's] decision to require adult theaters to be separated rather than concentrated in the same areas. . . . [T]he city must be allowed a reasonable opportunity to experiment with solutions to admittedly serious problems." American Mini Theatres, 427 U.S., at 71 (plurality opinion). Moreover, the Renton ordinance is "narrowly tailored" to affect only that category of theaters shown to produce the unwanted secondary effects, thus avoiding the flaw that proved fatal to the regulations in Schad v. Mount Ephraim, 452 U.S. 61 (1981), and Erznoznik v. City of Jacksonville, 422 U.S. 205 (1975).

Respondents contend that the Renton ordinance is "underinclusive," in that it fails to regulate other kinds of adult businesses that are likely to produce secondary effects similar to those produced by adult theaters. On this record the contention must fail. There is no evidence that, at the time the Renton ordinance was enacted, any other adult business was located in, or was contemplating moving into, Renton. In fact,

Resolution No. 2368, enacted in October 1980, states that "the City of Renton does not, at the present time, have any business whose primary purpose is the sale, rental, or showing of sexually explicit materials." App. 42. That Renton chose first to address the potential problems created by one particular kind of adult business in no way suggests that the city has "singled out" adult theaters for discriminatory treatment. We simply have no basis on this record for assuming that Renton will not, in the future, amend its ordinance to include other kinds of adult businesses that have been shown to produce the same kinds of secondary effects as adult theaters. See Williamson v. Lee Optical Co., 348 U.S. 483, 488 -489 (1955).

Finally, turning to the question whether the Renton ordinance allows for reasonable alternative avenues of communication, we note that the ordinance leaves some 520 acres, or more than five percent of the entire land area of Renton, open to use as adult theater sites. The District Court found, and the Court of Appeals did not dispute the finding, that the 520 acres of land consists of "[a]mple, accessible real estate," including "acreage in all stages of development from raw land to developed, industrial, warehouse, office, and shopping space that is crisscrossed by freeways, highways, and roads." App. to Juris. Statement 28a.

Respondents argue, however, that some of the land in question is already occupied by existing businesses, that "practically none" of the undeveloped land is currently for sale or lease, and that in general there are no "commercially viable" adult theater sites within the 520 acres left open by the Renton ordinance. Brief for Appellees 34-37. The Court of Appeals accepted these arguments, 3 concluded that the 520 acres was not truly "available" land, and therefore held that the Renton ordinance "would result in a substantial restriction" on speech. 748 F.2d, at 534.

We disagree with both the reasoning and the conclusion of the Court of Appeals. That respondents must fend for themselves in the real estate market, on an equal footing with other prospective purchasers and lessees, does not give rise to a First Amendment violation. And although we have cautioned against the enactment of zoning regulations that have "the effect of suppressing, or greatly restricting access to, lawful speech," American Mini Theatres, 427 U.S., at 71, n. 35 (plurality opinion), we have never suggested that the First Amendment compels the Government to ensure that adult theaters, or any other kinds of speech-related businesses for that matter, will be able to obtain sites at bargain prices. See id., at 78 (POWELL, J., concurring) ("The inquiry for First Amendment purposes is not concerned with economic impact"). In our view, the First Amendment requires only that Renton refrain from effectively denying respondents a reasonable opportunity to open and operate an adult theater within the city, and the ordinance before us easily meets this requirement.

In sum, we find that the Renton ordinance represents a valid governmental response to the "admittedly serious problems" created by adult theaters. See id., at 71 (plurality opinion). Renton has not used "the power to zone as a pretext for suppressing expression," id., at 84 (POWELL, J., concurring), but rather has sought to make some areas available for adult theaters and their patrons, while at the same time preserving the quality of life in the community at large by preventing those theaters from locating in other areas. This, after all, is the essence of zoning. Here, as in American Mini Theatres, the city has enacted a zoning ordinance that meets these goals while also satisfying the dictates of the First Amendment. 4 The judgment of the Court of Appeals is therefore

      Reversed.


    Notes

    [1] This appeal was taken under 28 U.S.C. 1254(2), which provides this Court with appellate jurisdiction at the behest of a party relying on a state statute or local ordinance held unconstitutional by a court of appeals. As we have previously noted, there is some question whether jurisdiction under 1254(2) is available to review a nonfinal judgment. See South Carolina Electric & Gas Co. v. Flemming, 351 U.S. 901 (1956); Slaker v. O'Connor, 278 U.S. 188 (1929). But see Chicago v. Atchison, T. & S. F. R. Co., 357 U.S. 77, 82 -83 (1958).

    The present appeal seeks review of a judgment remanding the case to the District Court. We need not resolve whether this appeal is proper under 1254(2), however, because in any event we have certiorari jurisdiction under 28 U.S.C. 2103. As we have previously done in equivalent situations, see El Paso v. Simmons, 379 U.S. 497, 502 -503 (1965); Doran v. Salem Inn, Inc., 422 U.S. 922, 927 (1975), we dismiss the appeal and, treating the papers as a petition for certiorari, grant the writ of certiorari. Henceforth, we shall refer to the parties as "petitioners" and "respondents."

    [2] See American Mini Theatres, 427 U.S., at 70 (plurality opinion) ("[I]t is manifest that society's interest in protecting this type of expression is of a wholly different, and lesser, magnitude than the interest in untrammeled political debate . . .").

    [3] The Court of Appeals' rejection of the District Court's findings on this issue may have stemmed in part from the belief, expressed elsewhere in the Court of Appeals' opinion, that, under Bose Corp. v. Consumers Union of United States, Inc., 466 U.S. 485 (1984), appellate courts have a duty to review de novo all mixed findings of law and fact relevant to the application of First Amendment principles. See 748 F.2d 527, 535 (1984). We need not review the correctness of the Court of Appeals' interpretation of Bose Corp., since we determine that, under any standard of review, the District Court's findings should not have been disturbed.

    [4] Respondents argue, as an "alternative basis" for affirming the decision of the Court of Appeals, that the Renton ordinance violates their rights under the Equal Protection Clause of the Fourteenth Amendment. As should be apparent from our preceding discussion, respondents can fare no better under the Equal Protection Clause than under the First Amendment itself. See Young v. American Mini Theatres, Inc., 427 U.S., at 63 -73.

    Respondents also argue that the Renton ordinance is unconstitutionally vague. More particularly, respondents challenge the ordinance's application to buildings "used" for presenting sexually explicit films, where the term "used" describes "a continuing course of conduct of exhibiting [sexually explicit films] in a manner which appeals to a prurient interest." App. to Juris. Statement 96a. We reject respondents' "vagueness" argument for the same reasons that led us to reject a similar challenge in American Mini Theatres, supra. There, the Detroit ordinance applied to theaters "used to present material distinguished or characterized by an emphasis on [sexually explicit matter]." Id., at 53. We held that "even if there may be some uncertainty about the effect of the ordinances on other litigants, they are unquestionably applicable to these respondents." Id., at 58-59. We also held that the Detroit ordinance created no "significant deterrent effect" that might justify invocation of the First Amendment "overbreadth" doctrine. Id., at 59-61.

## Bethel School District No. 403 v. Fraser (July 7, 1986)

CHIEF JUSTICE BURGER delivered the opinion of the Court.

We granted certiorari to decide whether the First Amendment prevents a school district from disciplining a high school student for giving a lewd speech at a school assembly.

I

A

On April 26, 1983, respondent Matthew N. Fraser, a student at Bethel High School in Pierce County, Washington, delivered a speech nominating a fellow student for student elective office. Approximately 600 high school students, many of whom were 14-year-olds, attended the assembly. Students were required to attend the assembly or to report to the study hall. The assembly was part of a school-sponsored educational program in self-government. Students who elected not to attend the assembly were required to report to study hall. During the entire speech, Fraser referred to his candidate in terms of an elaborate, graphic, and explicit sexual metaphor.

Two of Fraser's teachers, with whom he discussed the contents of his speech in advance, informed him that the speech was "inappropriate and that he probably should not deliver it," App. 30, and that his delivery of the speech might have "severe consequences." Id. at 61.

During Fraser's delivery of the speech, a school counselor observed the reaction of students to the speech. Some students hooted and yelled; some by gestures graphically simulated the sexual activities pointedly alluded to in respondent's speech. Other students appeared to be bewildered and embarrassed by the speech. One teacher reported that, on the day following the speech, she found it necessary to forgo a portion of the scheduled class lesson in order to discuss the speech with the class. Id. at 41-44.

A Bethel High School disciplinary rule prohibiting the use of obscene language in the school provides:

Conduct which materially and substantially interferes with the educational process is prohibited, including the use of obscene, profane language or gestures.

The morning after the assembly, the Assistant Principal called Fraser into her office and notified him that the school considered his speech to have been a violation of this rule. Fraser was presented with copies of five letters submitted by teachers, describing his conduct at the assembly; he was given a chance to explain his conduct and he admitted to having given the speech described and that he deliberately used sexual innuendo in the speech. Fraser was then informed that he would be suspended for three days, and that his name would be removed from the list of candidates for graduation speaker at the school's commencement exercises.

Fraser sought review of this disciplinary action through the School District's grievance procedures. The hearing officer determined that the speech given by respondent was "indecent, lewd, and offensive to the modesty and decency of many of the students and faculty in attendance at the assembly." The examiner determined that the speech fell within the ordinary meaning of "obscene," as used in the disruptive conduct rule, and affirmed the discipline in its entirety. Fraser served two days of his suspension, and was allowed to return to school on the third day.

B

Respondent, by his father as guardian ad litem, then brought this action in the United States District Court for the Western District of Washington. Respondent alleged a violation of his First Amendment right to freedom of speech, and sought both injunctive relief and monetary damages under 42 U.S.C. § 1983. The District Court held that the school's sanctions violated respondent's right to freedom of speech under the First Amendment to the United States Constitution, that the school's disruptive conduct rule is unconstitutionally vague and overbroad, and that the removal of respondent's name from the graduation speaker's list violated the Due Process Clause of the Fourteenth Amendment because the disciplinary rule makes no mention of such removal as a possible sanction. The District Court awarded respondent $278 in damages, $12,750 in litigation costs and attorney's fees, and enjoined the School District from preventing respondent from speaking at the commencement ceremonies. Respondent, who had been elected graduation speaker by a write-in vote of his classmates, delivered a speech at the commencement ceremonies on June 8, 1983.

The Court of Appeals for the Ninth Circuit affirmed the judgment of the District Court, 755 F.2d 1356 (1985), holding that respondent's speech was indistinguishable from the protest armband in Tinker v. Des Moines Independent Community School Dist., 393 U.S. 503 (1969). The court explicitly rejected the School District's argument that the speech, unlike the passive conduct of wearing a black armband, had a disruptive effect on the educational process. The Court of Appeals also rejected the School District's argument that it had an interest in protecting an essentially captive audience of minors from lewd and indecent language in a setting sponsored by the school, reasoning that the School District's "unbridled discretion" to determine what discourse is "decent" would "increase the risk of cementing white, middle-class standards for determining what is acceptable and proper speech and behavior in our public schools." 755 F.2d at 1363. Finally, the Court of Appeals rejected the School District's argument that, incident to its responsibility for the school curriculum, it had the power to control the language used to express ideas during a school-sponsored activity.

We granted certiorari, 474 U.S. 814 (1985). We reverse.

II

This Court acknowledged in Tinker v. Des Moines Independent Community School Dist., supra, that students do not "shed their constitutional rights to freedom of speech or expression at the schoolhouse gate." Id. at 506. The Court of Appeals read that case as precluding any discipline of Fraser for indecent speech and lewd conduct in the school assembly. That court appears to have proceeded on the theory that the use of lewd and obscene speech in order to make what the speaker considered to be a point in a nominating speech for a fellow student was essentially the same as the wearing of an armband in Tinker as a form of protest or the expression of a political position.

The marked distinction between the political "message" of the armbands in Tinker and the sexual content of respondent's speech in this case seems to have been given little weight by the Court of Appeals. In upholding the students' right to engage in a nondisruptive, passive expression of a political viewpoint in Tinker, this Court was careful to note that the case did "not concern speech or action that intrudes upon the work of the schools or the rights of other students." Id. at 508.

It is against this background that we turn to consider the level of First Amendment protection accorded to Fraser's utterances and actions before an official high school assembly attended by 600 students.

III

The role and purpose of the American public school system were well described by two historians, who stated:

[P]ublic education must prepare pupils for citizenship in the Republic. . . . It must inculcate the habits and manners of civility as values in themselves conducive to happiness and as indispensable to the practice of self-government in the community and the nation.

C. Beard & M. Beard, New Basic History of the United States 228 (1968). In Ambach v. Norwick, 441 U.S. 68, 76-77 (1979), we echoed the essence of this statement of the objectives of public education as the "inculcat[ion of] fundamental values necessary to the maintenance of a democratic political system."

These fundamental values of "habits and manners of civility" essential to a democratic society must, of course, include tolerance of divergent political and religious views, even when the views expressed may be unpopular. But these "fundamental values" must also take into account consideration of the sensibilities of others, and, in the case of a school, the sensibilities of fellow students. The undoubted freedom to advocate unpopular and controversial views in schools and classrooms must be balanced against the society's countervailing interest in teaching students the boundaries of socially appropriate behavior. Even the most heated political discourse in a democratic society requires consideration for the personal sensibilities of the other participants and audiences.

In our Nation's legislative halls, where some of the most vigorous political debates in our society are carried on, there are rules prohibiting the use of expressions offensive to other participants in the debate. The Manual of Parliamentary Practice, drafted by Thomas Jefferson and adopted by the House of Representatives to govern the proceedings in that body, prohibits the use of "impertinent" speech during debate, and likewise provides that "[n]o person is to use indecent language against the proceedings of the House." Jefferson's Manual of Parliamentary Practice §§ 359, 360, reprinted in Manual and Rules of House of Representatives, H.R. Doc. No. 97-271, pp. 158-159 (1982); see id. at 111, n. a (Jefferson's Manual governs the House in all cases to which it applies). The Rules of Debate applicable in the Senate likewise provide that a Senator may be called to order for imputing improper motives to another Senator or for referring offensively to any state. See Senate Procedure, S. Doc. No. 97-2, Rule XIX, pp. 568-569, 588-591 (1981). Senators have been censured for abusive language directed at other Senators. See Senate Election, Expulsion and Censure Cases from 1793 to 1972, S.Doc. No. 92-7, pp. 95-98 (1972) (Sens. McLaurin and Tillman); id. at 152-153 (Sen. McCarthy). Can it be that what is proscribed in the halls of Congress is beyond the reach of school officials to regulate?

The First Amendment guarantees wide freedom in matters of adult public discourse. A sharply divided Court upheld the right to express an antidraft viewpoint in a public place, albeit in terms highly offensive to most citizens. See Cohen v. California, 403 U.S. 15"] 403 U.S. 15 (1971). It does not follow, however, that, simply because the use of an offensive form of expression may not be prohibited to adults making what the speaker considers a political point, the same latitude must be permitted to children in a public school. In 403 U.S. 15 (1971). It does not follow, however, that, simply because the use of an offensive form of expression may not be prohibited to adults making what the speaker considers a political point, the same latitude must be permitted to children in a public school. In New Jersey v. T.L.O., 469 U.S. 325, 340-342 (1985), we reaffirmed that the constitutional rights of students in public school are not automatically coextensive with the rights of adults in other settings. As cogently expressed by Judge Newman, "the First Amendment gives a high school student the classroom right to wear Tinker's armband, but not Cohen's jacket." Thomas v. Board of Education, Granville Central School Dist., 607 F.2d 1043, 1057 (CA2 1979) (opinion concurring in result).

Surely it is a highly appropriate function of public school education to prohibit the use of vulgar and offensive terms in public discourse. Indeed, the "fundamental values necessary to the maintenance of a democratic political system" disfavor the use of terms of debate highly offensive or highly threatening to others. Nothing in the Constitution prohibits the states from insisting that certain modes of expression are inappropriate and subject to sanctions. The inculcation of these values is truly the "work of the schools."

Tinker, 393 U.S. at 508; see Ambach v. Norwick, supra. The determination of what manner of speech in the classroom or in school assembly is inappropriate properly rests with the school board.

The process of educating our youth for citizenship in public schools is not confined to books, the curriculum, and the civics class; schools must teach by example the shared values of a civilized social order. Consciously or otherwise, teachers -- and indeed the older students -- demonstrate the appropriate form of civil discourse and political expression by their conduct and deportment in and out of class. Inescapably, like parents, they are role models. The schools, as instruments of the state, may determine that the essential lessons of civil, mature conduct cannot be conveyed in a school that tolerates lewd, indecent, or offensive speech and conduct such as that indulged in by this confused boy.

The pervasive sexual innuendo in Fraser's speech was plainly offensive to both teachers and students -- indeed, to any mature person. By glorifying male sexuality, and in its verbal content, the speech was acutely insulting to teenage girl students. See App. 77-81. The speech could well be seriously damaging to its less mature audience, many of whom were only 14 years old and on the threshold of awareness of human sexuality. Some students were reported as bewildered by the speech and the reaction of mimicry it provoked.

This Court's First Amendment jurisprudence has acknowledged limitations on the otherwise absolute interest of the speaker in reaching an unlimited audience where the speech is sexually explicit and the audience may include children. In Ginsberg v. New York, 390 U.S. 629 (1968), this Court upheld a New York statute banning the sale of sexually oriented material to minors, even though the material in question was entitled to First Amendment protection with respect to adults. And in addressing the question whether the First Amendment places any limit on the authority of public schools to remove books from a public school library, all Members of the Court, otherwise sharply divided, acknowledged that the school board has the authority to remove books that are vulgar. Board of Education v. Pico, 457 U.S. 853, 871-872 (1982) (plurality opinion); id. at 879-881 (BLACKMUN, J., concurring in part and in judgment); id. at 918-920 (REHNQUIST, J., dissenting). These cases recognize the obvious concern on the part of parents, and school authorities acting in loco parentis, to protect children especially in a captive audience -- from exposure to sexually explicit, indecent, or lewd speech.

We have also recognized an interest in protecting minors from exposure to vulgar and offensive spoken language. In FCC v. Pacifica Foundation, 438 U.S. 726 (1978), we dealt with the power of the Federal Communications Commission to regulate a radio broadcast described as "indecent but not obscene." There the Court reviewed an administrative condemnation of the radio broadcast of a self-styled "humorist" who described his own performance as being in "the words you couldn't say on the public, ah, airwaves, um, the ones you definitely wouldn't say ever." Id. at 729; see also id. at 751-755 (Appendix to opinion of the Court). The Commission concluded that "certain words depicted sexual and excretory activities in a patently offensive manner, [and] noted that they 'were broadcast at a time when children were undoubtedly in the audience.'" The Commission issued an order declaring that the radio station was guilty of broadcasting indecent language in violation of 18 U.S.C. § 1464. 438 U.S. at 732. The Court of Appeals set aside the Commission's determination, and we reversed, reinstating the Commission's citation of the station. We concluded that the broadcast was properly considered "obscene, indecent, or profane" within the meaning of the statute. The plurality opinion went on to reject the radio station's assertion of a First Amendment right to broadcast vulgarity:

> These words offend for the same reasons that obscenity offends. Their place in the hierarchy of First Amendment values was aptly sketched by Mr. Justice Murphy when he said:

> [S]uch utterances are no essential part of any exposition of ideas, and are of such slight social value as a step to truth that any benefit that may be derived from them is clearly outweighed by the social interest in order and morality.

> Chaplinsky v. New Hampshire, 315 U.S. at 572.

> Id. at 746.

We hold that petitioner School District acted entirely within its permissible authority in imposing sanctions upon Fraser in response to his offensively lewd and indecent speech. Unlike the sanctions imposed on the students wearing armbands in Tinker, the penalties imposed in this case were unrelated to any political viewpoint. The First Amendment does not prevent the school officials from determining that to permit a vulgar and lewd speech such as respondent's would undermine the school's basic educational mission. A high school assembly or classroom is no place for a sexually explicit monologue directed towards an unsuspecting audience of teenage students. Accordingly, it was perfectly appropriate for the school to disassociate itself to make the point to the pupils that vulgar speech and lewd conduct is wholly inconsistent with the "fundamental values" of public school education. Justice Black, dissenting in Tinker, made a point that is especially relevant in this case:

> I wish therefore, . . . to disclaim any purpose . . . to hold that the Federal Constitution compels the teachers, parents, and elected school officials to surrender control of the American public school system to public school students.

> 393 U.S. at 526.

IV

Respondent contends that the circumstances of his suspension violated due process because he had no way of knowing that the delivery of the speech in question would subject him to disciplinary sanctions. This argument is wholly without merit. We have recognized that

> maintaining security and order in the schools requires a certain degree of flexibility in school disciplinary procedures, and we have respected the value of preserving the informality of the student-teacher relationship.

New Jersey v. T.L.O., 469 U.S. at 340. Given the school's need to be able to impose disciplinary sanctions for a wide range of unanticipated conduct disruptive of the educational process, the school disciplinary rules need not be as detailed as a criminal code, which imposes criminal sanctions. Cf. Arnett v. Kennedy, 416 U.S. 134, 161 (1974) (REHNQUIST, J., concurring). Two days' suspension from school does not rise to the level of a penal sanction calling for the full panoply of procedural due process protections applicable to a criminal prosecution. Cf. Goss v. Lopez, 419 U.S. 565 (1975). The school disciplinary rule proscribing "obscene" language and the prespeech admonitions of teachers gave adequate warning to Fraser that his lewd speech could subject him to sanctions. [*]

The judgment of the Court of Appeals for the Ninth Circuit is
Reversed.

* Petitioners also challenge the ruling of the District Court that the removal of Fraser's name from the ballot for graduation speaker violated his due process rights because that sanction was not indicated as a potential punishment in the school's disciplinary rules. We agree with the Court of Appeals that this issue has become moot, since the graduation ceremony has long since passed and Fraser was permitted to speak in accordance with the District Court's injunction. No part of the damages award was based upon the removal of Fraser's name from the list, since damages were based upon the loss of two days' schooling.

## Pope v. Illinois (May 4, 1987) [Notes omitted]

JUSTICE WHITE delivered the opinion of the Court.

In Miller v. California, 413 U.S. 15 (1973), the Court set out a tripartite test for judging whether material is obscene. The third prong of the Miller test requires the trier of fact to determine "whether the work, taken as a whole, lacks serious literary, artistic, political, or scientific value." Id., at 24. The issue in this case is whether, in a prosecution for the sale of allegedly obscene materials, the jury may be instructed to apply community standards in deciding the value question.

I

On July 21, 1983, Rockford, Illinois, police detectives purchased certain magazines from the two petitioners, each of whom was an attendant at an adult bookstore. Petitioners were subsequently charged separately with the offense of "obscenity" for the sale of these magazines. Each petitioner moved to dismiss the charges against him on the ground that the then-current version of the Illinois obscenity statute, Ill. Rev. Stat., ch. 38, § 11-20 (1983), violated the First and Fourteenth Amendments to the United States Constitution. Both petitioners argued, among other things, that the statute was unconstitutional in failing to require that the value question be judged "solely on an objective basis as opposed to reference [sic] to contemporary community standards." App. 8, 22. 1 Both trial courts rejected this contention and instructed the respective juries to judge whether the material was obscene by determining how it would be viewed by ordinary adults in the whole State of Illinois. 2 Both petitioners were found guilty, and both appealed to the Illinois Appellate Court, Second District. That court also rejected petitioners' contention that the issue of value must be determined on an objective basis and not by reference to contemporary community standards. 138 Ill. App. 3d 726, 486 N. E. 2d 350 (1985); 138 Ill. App. 3d 595, 486 N. E. 2d 345 (1985). The Illinois Supreme Court denied review, and we granted certiorari, 479 U.S. 812 (1986).

## II

There is no suggestion in our cases that the question of the value of an allegedly obscene work is to be determined by reference to community standards. Indeed, our cases are to the contrary. Smith v. United States, 431 U.S. 291 (1977), held that, in a federal prosecution for mailing obscene materials, the first and second prongs of the Miller test - appeal to prurient interest and patent offensiveness - are issues of fact for the jury to determine applying contemporary community standards. The Court then observed that, unlike prurient appeal and patent offensiveness, "[l]iterary, artistic, political, or scientific value . . . is not discussed in Miller in terms of contemporary community standards." Id., at 301 (citing F. Schauer, The Law of Obscenity 123-124 (1976)). This comment was not meant to point out an oversight in the Miller opinion, but to call attention to and approve a deliberate choice.

In Miller itself, the Court was careful to point out that "[t]he First Amendment protects works which, taken as a whole, have serious literary, artistic, political, or scientific value, regardless of whether the government or a majority of the people approve of the ideas these works represent." 413 U.S., at 34 . Just as the ideas a work represents need not obtain majority approval to merit protection, neither, insofar as the First Amendment is concerned, does the value of the work vary from community to community based on the degree of local acceptance it has won. The proper inquiry is not whether an ordinary member of any given community would find serious literary, artistic, political, or scientific value in allegedly obscene material, but whether a reasonable person would find such value in the material, taken as a whole. 3 The instruction at issue in this case was therefore unconstitutional.

## III

The question remains whether the convictions should be reversed outright or are subject to salvage if the erroneous instruction is found to be harmless error. Petitioners contend that the statute is invalid on its face and that the convictions must necessarily be reversed because, as we understand it, the State should not be allowed to preserve any conviction under a law that poses a threat to First Amendment values. But the statute under which petitioners were convicted is no longer on the books; it has been repealed and replaced by a statute that does not call for the application of community standards to the value question. 4 Facial invalidation of the repealed statute would not serve the purpose of preventing future prosecutions under a constitutionally defective standard. Cf., e. g., Secretary of State of Maryland v. Joseph H. Munson Co., 467 U.S. 947, 964 -

968, and n. 13 (1984). And if we did facially invalidate the repealed statute and reverse petitioners' convictions, petitioners could still be retried under that statute, provided that the erroneous instruction was not repeated, because petitioners could not plausibly claim that the repealed statute failed to give them notice that the sale of obscene materials would be prosecuted. See Dombrowski v. Pfister, 380 U.S. 479, 491, n. 7 (1965); United States v. Thirty-seven Photographs, 402 U.S. 363, 375, n. 3 (1971). Under these circumstances, we see no reason to require a retrial if it can be said beyond a reasonable doubt that the jury's verdict in this case was not affected by the erroneous instruction.

The situation here is comparable to that in Rose v. Clark, 478 U.S. 570 (1986). In Rose, the jury in a murder trial was incorrectly instructed on the element of malice, 5 yet the Court held that a harmless-error inquiry was appropriate. The Court explained that in the absence of error that renders a trial fundamentally unfair, such as denial of the right to counsel or trial before a financially interested judge, a conviction should be affirmed "[w]here a reviewing court can find that the record developed at trial established guilt beyond a reasonable doubt . . . ." Id., at 579. The error in Rose did not entirely preclude the jury from considering the element of malice, id., at 580, n. 8, and the fact that the jury could conceivably have had the impermissible presumption in mind when it considered the element of malice was not a reason to retry the defendant if the facts that the jury necessarily found established guilt beyond a reasonable doubt. 6 The Court said: "When a jury is instructed to presume malice from predicate facts, it still must find the existence of those facts beyond reasonable doubt. Connecticut v. Johnson, 460 U.S. 73, 96 -97 (1983) (POWELL, J., dissenting). In many cases, the predicate facts conclusively establish intent, so that no rational jury could find that the defendant committed the relevant criminal act but did not intend to cause injury." Id., at 580-581.

Similarly, in the present cases the jurors were not precluded from considering the question of value: they were informed that to convict they must find, among other things, that the magazines petitioners sold were utterly without redeeming social value. While it was error to instruct the juries to use a state community standard in considering the value question, if a reviewing court concludes that no rational juror, if properly instructed, could find value in the magazines, the convictions should stand. 7

Although we plainly have the authority to decide whether, on the facts of a given case, a constitutional error was harmless under the standard of Chapman v. California, 386 U.S. 18 (1967), we do so sparingly. Rose v. Clark, supra, at 584. In this case the Illinois Appellate Court has not considered the harmless-error issue. We therefore vacate its judgment and remand so that it may do so.

It is so ordered.

## Hazelwood School District v. Kuhlmeier (Jan 13, 1988) [Notes omitted]

JUSTICE WHITE delivered the opinion of the Court.

This case concerns the extent to which educators may exercise editorial control over the contents of a high school newspaper produced as part of the school's journalism curriculum.

I

Petitioners are the Hazelwood School District in St. Louis County, Missouri; various school officials; Robert Eugene Reynolds, the principal of Hazelwood East High School; and Howard Emerson, a teacher in the school district. Respondents are three former Hazelwood East students who were staff members of Spectrum, the school newspaper. They contend that school officials violated their First Amendment rights by deleting two pages of articles from the May 13, 1983, issue of Spectrum.

Spectrum was written and edited by the Journalism II class at Hazelwood East. The newspaper was published every three weeks or so during the 1982-1983 school year. More than 4,500 copies of the newspaper were distributed during that year to students, school personnel, and members of the community.

The Board of Education allocated funds from its annual budget for the printing of Spectrum. These funds were supplemented by proceeds from sales of the newspaper. The printing expenses during the 1982-1983 school year totaled $4,668.50; revenue from sales was $1,166.84. The other costs associated with the newspaper - such as supplies, textbooks, and a portion of the journalism teacher's salary - were borne entirely by the Board.

The Journalism II course was taught by Robert Stergos for most of the 1982-1983 academic year. Stergos left Hazelwood East to take a job in private industry on April 29, 1983, when the May 13 edition of Spectrum was nearing completion, and petitioner Emerson took his place as newspaper adviser for the remaining weeks of the term.

The practice at Hazelwood East during the spring 1983 semester was for the journalism teacher to submit page proofs of each Spectrum issue to Principal Reynolds for his review prior to publication. On May 10, Emerson delivered the proofs of the May 13 edition to Reynolds, who objected to two of the articles scheduled to appear in that edition. One of the stories described three Hazelwood East students' experiences with pregnancy; the other discussed the impact of divorce on students at the school.

Reynolds was concerned that, although the pregnancy story used false names "to keep the identity of these girls a secret," the pregnant students still might be identifiable from the text. He also believed that the article's references to sexual activity and birth control were inappropriate for some of the younger students at the school. In addition, Reynolds was concerned that a student identified by name in the divorce story had complained that her father "wasn't spending enough time with my mom, my sister and I" prior to the divorce, "was always out of town on business or out late playing cards with the guys," and "always argued about everything" with her mother. App. to Pet. for Cert. 38. Reynolds believed that the student's parents should have been given an opportunity to respond to these remarks or to consent to their publication. He was unaware that Emerson had deleted the student's name from the final version of the article.

Reynolds believed that there was no time to make the necessary changes in the stories before the scheduled press run and that the newspaper would not appear before the end of the school year if printing were delayed to any significant extent. He concluded that his only options under the circumstances were to publish a four-page newspaper instead of the planned six-page newspaper, eliminating the two pages on which the offending stories appeared, or to publish no newspaper at all. Accordingly, he directed Emerson to withhold from publication the two pages containing the stories on pregnancy and divorce. 1 He informed his superiors of the decision, and they concurred.

Respondents subsequently commenced this action in the United States District Court for the Eastern District of Missouri seeking a declaration that their First Amendment rights had been violated, injunctive relief, and monetary damages. After a bench trial, the District Court denied an injunction, holding that no First Amendment violation had occurred. 607 F. Supp. 1450 (1985).

The District Court concluded that school officials may impose restraints on students' speech in activities that are "`an integral part of the school's educational function'" - including the publication of a school-sponsored newspaper by a journalism class - so long as their decision has "`a substantial and reasonable basis.'" Id., at 1466 (quoting Frasca v. Andrews, 463 F. Supp. 1043, 1052 (EDNY 1979)). The court found that Principal Reynolds' concern that the pregnant student's anonymity would be lost and their privacy invaded was "legitimate and reasonable," given "the small number of pregnant students at Hazelwood East and several identifying characteristics that were disclosed in the article." 607 F. Supp., at 1466. The court held that Reynolds' action was also justified "to avoid the impression that [the school] endorses the sexual norms of the subjects" and to shield younger students from exposure to unsuitable material. Ibid. The deletion of the article on divorce was seen by the court as a reasonable response to the invasion of privacy concerns raised by the named student's remarks. Because the article did not indicate that the student's parents had been offered an opportunity to respond to her allegations, said the court, there was cause for "serious doubt that the article complied with the rules of fairness which are standard in the field of journalism and which were covered in the textbook used in the Journalism II class." Id., at 1467. Furthermore, the court concluded that Reynolds was justified in deleting two full pages of the newspaper, instead of deleting only the pregnancy and divorce stories or requiring that those stories be modified to address his concerns, based on his "reasonable belief that he had to make an immediate decision and that there was no time to make modifications to the articles in question." Id., at 1466.

The Court of Appeals for the Eighth Circuit reversed. 795 F.2d 1368 (1986). The court held at the outset that Spectrum was not only "a part of the school adopted curriculum," id., at 1373, but also a public forum, because the newspaper was "intended to be and operated as a conduit for student viewpoint." Id., at 1372. The court then concluded that Spectrum's status as a public forum precluded school officials from censoring its contents except when "`necessary to avoid material and substantial interference with school work or discipline . . . or the rights of others.'" Id., at 1374 (quoting Tinker v. Des Moines Independent Community School Dist., 393 U.S. 503, 511 (1969)).

The Court of Appeals found "no evidence in the record that the principal could have reasonably forecast that the censored articles or any materials in the censored articles would have materially disrupted classwork or given rise to substantial disorder in the school." 795 F.2d, at 1375. School officials were entitled to censor the articles on the ground that they invaded the rights of others, according to the court, only if publication of the articles could have resulted in tort liability to the school. The court concluded that no tort action for libel or invasion of privacy could have been maintained against the school by the subjects of the two articles or by their families. Accordingly, the court held that school officials had violated respondents' First Amendment rights by deleting the two pages of the newspaper.

We granted certiorari, 479 U.S. 1053 (1987), and we now reverse.

II

Students in the public schools do not "shed their constitutional rights to freedom of speech or expression at the schoolhouse gate." Tinker, supra, at 506. They cannot be punished merely for expressing their personal views on the school premises - whether "in the cafeteria, or on the playing field, or on the campus during the authorized hours," 393 U.S., at 512 -513 - unless school authorities have reason to believe that such expression will "substantially interfere with the work of the school or impinge upon the rights of other students." Id., at 509.

We have nonetheless recognized that the First Amendment rights of students in the public schools "are not automatically coextensive with the rights of adults in other settings," Bethel School District No. 403 v. Fraser, 478 U.S. 675, 682 (1986), and must be "applied in light of the special characteristics of the school environment." Tinker, supra, at 506; cf. New Jersey v. T. L. O., 469 U.S. 325, 341 -343 (1985). A school need not tolerate student speech that is inconsistent with its "basic educational mission," Fraser, supra, at 685, even though the government could not censor similar speech outside the school. Accordingly, we held in Fraser that a student could be disciplined for having delivered a speech that was "sexually explicit" but not legally obscene at an official school assembly, because the school was entitled to "disassociate itself" from the speech in a manner that would demonstrate to others that such vulgarity is "wholly inconsistent with the `fundamental values' of public school education." 478 U.S., at 685 -686. We thus recognized that "[t]he determination of what manner of speech in the classroom or in school assembly is inappropriate properly rests with the school board," id., at 683, rather than with the federal courts. It is in this context that respondents' First Amendment claims must be considered.

A

We deal first with the question whether Spectrum may appropriately be characterized as a forum for public expression. The public schools do not possess all of the attributes of streets, parks, and other traditional public forums that "time out of mind, have been used for purposes of assembly, communicating thoughts between citizens, and discussing public questions." Hague v. CIO, 307 U.S. 496, 515 (1939). Cf. Widmar v. Vincent, 454 U.S. 263, 267 -268, n. 5 (1981). Hence, school facilities may be deemed to be public forums only if school authorities have "by policy or by practice" opened those facilities "for indiscriminate use by the general public," Perry Education Assn. v. Perry Local Educators' Assn., 460 U.S. 37, 47 (1983), or by some segment of the public, such as student organizations. Id., at 46, n. 7 (citing Widmar v. Vincent). If the facilities have instead been reserved for other intended purposes, "communicative or otherwise," then no public forum has been created, and school officials may impose reasonable restrictions on the speech of students, teachers, and other members of the school community. 460 U.S., at 46, n. 7. "The government does not create a public forum by inaction or by permitting limited discourse, but only by intentionally opening a nontraditional forum for public discourse." Cornelius v. NAACP Legal Defense & Educational Fund, Inc., 473 U.S. 788, 802 (1985).

The policy of school officials toward Spectrum was reflected in Hazelwood School Board Policy 348.51 and the Hazelwood East Curriculum Guide. Board Policy 348.51 provided that "[s]chool sponsored publications are developed within the adopted curriculum and its educational implications in regular classroom activities." App. 22. The Hazelwood East Curriculum Guide described the Journalism II course as a "laboratory situation in which the students publish the school newspaper applying skills they have learned in Journalism I." Id., at 11. The lessons that were to be learned from the Journalism II course, according to the Curriculum Guide, included development of journalistic skills under deadline pressure, "the legal, moral, and ethical restrictions imposed upon journalists within the school community," and "responsibility and acceptance of criticism for articles of opinion." Ibid. Journalism II was taught by a faculty member during regular class hours. Students received grades and academic credit for their performance in the course.

School officials did not deviate in practice from their policy that production of Spectrum was to be part of the educational curriculum and a "regular classroom activit[y]." The District Court found that Robert Stergos, the journalism teacher during most of the 1982-1983 school year, "both had the authority to exercise and in fact exercised a great deal of control over Spectrum." 607 F. Supp., at 1453. For example, Stergos selected the editors of the newspaper, scheduled publication dates, decided the number of pages for each issue, assigned story ideas to class members, advised students on the development of their stories, reviewed the use of quotations, edited stories, selected and edited the letters to the editor, and dealt with the printing company. Many of these decisions were made without consultation with the Journalism II students. The District Court thus found it "clear that Mr. Stergos was the final authority with respect to almost every aspect of the production and publication of Spectrum, including its content." Ibid. Moreover, after each Spectrum issue had been finally approved by Stergos or his successor, the issue still had to be reviewed by Principal Reynolds prior to publication.

Respondents' assertion that they had believed that they could publish "practically anything" in Spectrum was therefore dismissed by the District Court as simply "not credible." Id., at 1456. These factual findings are amply supported by the record, and were not rejected as clearly erroneous by the Court of Appeals.

The evidence relied upon by the Court of Appeals in finding Spectrum to be a public forum, see 795 F.2d, at 1372-1373, is equivocal at best. For example, Board Policy 348.51, which stated in part that "[s]chool sponsored student publications will not restrict free expression or diverse viewpoints within the rules of responsible journalism," also stated that such publications were "developed within the adopted curriculum and its educational implications." App. 22. One might reasonably infer from the full text of Policy 348.51 that school officials retained ultimate control over what constituted "responsible journalism" in a school-sponsored newspaper. Although the Statement of Policy published in the September 14, 1982, issue of Spectrum declared that "Spectrum, as a student-press publication, accepts all rights implied by the First Amendment," this statement, understood in the context of the paper's role in the school's curriculum, suggests at most that the administration will not interfere with the students' exercise of those First Amendment rights that attend the publication of a school-sponsored newspaper. It does not reflect an intent to expand those rights by converting a curricular newspaper into a public forum. 2 Finally, that students were permitted to exercise some authority over the contents of Spectrum was fully consistent with the Curriculum Guide objective of teaching the Journalism II students "leadership responsibilities as issue and page editors." App. 11. A decision to teach leadership skills in the context of a classroom activity hardly implies a decision to relinquish school control over that activity. In sum, the evidence relied upon by the Court of Appeals fails to demonstrate the "clear intent to create a public forum," Cornelius, 473 U.S., at 802, that existed in cases in which we found public forums to have been created. See id., at 802-803 (citing Widmar v. Vincent, 454 U.S., at 267; Madison School District v. Wisconsin Employment Relations Comm'n, 429 U.S. 167, 174, n. 6 (1976); Southeastern Promotions, Ltd. v. Conrad, 420 U.S. 546, 555 (1975)). School officials did not evince either "by policy or by practice," Perry Education Assn., 460 U.S., at 47, any intent to open the pages of Spectrum to "indiscriminate use," ibid., by its student reporters and editors, or by the student body generally. Instead, they "reserve[d] the forum for its intended purpos[e]," id., at 46, as a supervised learning experience for journalism students. Accordingly, school officials were entitled to regulate the contents of Spectrum in any reasonable manner. Ibid. It is this standard, rather than our decision in Tinker, that governs this case.

B

The question whether the First Amendment requires a school to tolerate particular student speech - the question that we addressed in Tinker - is different from the question whether the First Amendment requires a school affirmatively to promote particular student speech. The former question addresses educators' ability to silence a student's personal expression that happens to occur on the school premises. The latter question concerns educators' authority over school-sponsored publications, theatrical productions, and other expressive activities that students, parents, and members of the public might reasonably perceive to bear the imprimatur of the school. These activities may fairly be characterized as part of the school curriculum, whether or not they occur in a traditional classroom setting, so long as they are supervised by faculty members and designed to impart particular knowledge or skills to student participants and audiences. 3

Educators are entitled to exercise greater control over this second form of student expression to assure that participants learn whatever lessons the activity is designed to teach, that readers or listeners are not exposed to material that may be inappropriate for their level of maturity, and that the views of the individual speaker are not erroneously attributed to the school. Hence, a school may in its capacity as publisher of a school newspaper or producer of a school play "disassociate itself," Fraser, 478 U.S., at 685, not only from speech that would "substantially interfere with [its] work . . . or impinge upon the rights of other students," Tinker, 393 U.S., at 509, but also from speech that is, for example, ungrammatical, poorly written, inadequately researched, biased or prejudiced, vulgar or profane, or unsuitable for immature audiences. 4 A school must be able to set high standards for the student speech that is disseminated under its auspices - standards that may be higher than those demanded by some newspaper publishers or theatrical producers in the "real" world - and may refuse to disseminate student speech that does not meet those standards. In addition, a school must be able to take into account the emotional maturity of the intended audience in determining whether to disseminate student speech on potentially sensitive topics, which might range from the existence of Santa Claus in an elementary school setting to the particulars of teenage sexual activity in a high school setting. A school must also retain the authority to refuse to sponsor student speech that might reasonably be perceived to advocate drug or alcohol use, irresponsible sex, or conduct otherwise inconsistent with "the shared values of a civilized social order," Fraser, supra, at 683, or to associate the school with any position other than neutrality on matters of political controversy. Otherwise, the schools would be unduly constrained from fulfilling their role as "a principal instrument in awakening the child to cultural values, in preparing him for later professional training, and in helping him to adjust normally to his environment." Brown v. Board of Education, 347 U.S. 483, 493 (1954).

Accordingly, we conclude that the standard articulated in Tinker for determining when a school may punish student expression need not also be the standard for determining when a school may refuse to lend its name and resources to the dissemination of student expression. 5 Instead, we hold that educators do not offend the First Amendment by exercising editorial control over the style and content of student speech in school-sponsored expressive activities so long as their actions are reasonably related to legitimate pedagogical concerns. 6

This standard is consistent with our oft-expressed view that the education of the Nation's youth is primarily the responsibility of parents, teachers, and state and local school officials, and not of federal judges. See, e. g., Board of Education of Hendrick

Hudson Central School Dist. v. Rowley, 458 U.S. 176, 208 (1982); Wood v. Strickland, 420 U.S. 308, 326 (1975); Epperson v. Arkansas, 393 U.S. 97, 104 (1968). It is only when the decision to censor a school-sponsored publication, theatrical production, or other vehicle of student expression has no valid educational purpose that the First Amendment is so "directly and sharply implicate[d]," ibid., as to require judicial intervention to protect students' constitutional rights. 7

III

We also conclude that Principal Reynolds acted reasonably in requiring the deletion from the May 13 issue of Spectrum of the pregnancy article, the divorce article, and the remaining articles that were to appear on the same pages of the newspaper.

The initial paragraph of the pregnancy article declared that "[a]ll names have been changed to keep the identity of these girls a secret." The principal concluded that the students' anonymity was not adequately protected, however, given the other identifying information in the article and the small number of pregnant students at the school. Indeed, a teacher at the school credibly testified that she could positively identify at least one of the girls and possibly all three. It is likely that many students at Hazelwood East would have been at least as successful in identifying the girls. Reynolds therefore could reasonably have feared that the article violated whatever pledge of anonymity had been given to the pregnant students. In addition, he could reasonably have been concerned that the article was not sufficiently sensitive to the privacy interests of the students' boyfriends and parents, who were discussed in the article but who were given no opportunity to consent to its publication or to offer a response. The article did not contain graphic accounts of sexual activity. The girls did comment in the article, however, concerning their sexual histories and their use or nonuse of birth control. It was not unreasonable for the principal to have concluded that such frank talk was inappropriate in a school-sponsored publication distributed to 14-year-old freshmen and presumably taken home to be read by students' even younger brothers and sisters.

The student who was quoted by name in the version of the divorce article seen by Principal Reynolds made comments sharply critical of her father. The principal could reasonably have concluded that an individual publicly identified as an inattentive parent - indeed, as one who chose "playing cards with the guys" over home and family - was entitled to an opportunity to defend himself as a matter of journalistic fairness. These concerns were shared by both of Spectrum's faculty advisers for the 1982-1983 school year, who testified that they would not have allowed the article to be printed without deletion of the student's name. 8

Principal Reynolds testified credibly at trial that, at the time that he reviewed the proofs of the May 13 issue during an extended telephone conversation with Emerson, he believed that there was no time to make any changes in the articles, and that the newspaper had to be printed immediately or not at all. It is true that Reynolds did not verify whether the necessary modifications could still have been made in the articles, and that Emerson did not volunteer the information that printing could be delayed until the changes were made. We nonetheless agree with the District Court that the decision to excise the two pages containing the problematic articles was reasonable given the particular circumstances of this case. These circumstances included the very recent replacement of Stergos by Emerson, who may not have been entirely familiar with Spectrum editorial and production procedures, and the pressure felt by Reynolds to make an immediate decision so that students would not be deprived of the newspaper altogether.

In sum, we cannot reject as unreasonable Principal Reynolds' conclusion that neither the pregnancy article nor the divorce article was suitable for publication in Spectrum. Reynolds could reasonably have concluded that the students who had written and edited these articles had not sufficiently mastered those portions of the Journalism II curriculum that pertained to the treatment of controversial issues and personal attacks, the need to protect the privacy of individuals whose most intimate concerns are to be revealed in the newspaper, and "the legal, moral, and ethical restrictions imposed upon journalists within [a] school community" that includes adolescent subjects and readers. Finally, we conclude that the principal's decision to delete two pages of Spectrum, rather than to delete only the offending articles or to require that they be modified, was reasonable under the circumstances as he understood them. Accordingly, no violation of First Amendment rights occurred. 9

The judgment of the Court of Appeals for the Eighth Circuit is therefore
Reversed.

## Fort Wayne Books, Inc. v. Indiana (February 21, 1989)

JUSTICE WHITE delivered the opinion of the Court.**

We have before us two decisions of the Indiana courts, involving the application of that State's Racketeer Influenced and Corrupt Organizations (RICO) and Civil Remedies for Racketeering Activity (CRRA) Acts to cases involving bookstores containing allegedly obscene materials.

I

The two causes before us arise from wholly unrelated incidents.

A

Petitioner in No. 87-470, Fort Wayne Books, Inc., and two other corporations [1] each operated an "adult bookstore" in Fort Wayne, Indiana. On March 19, 1984, the State of Indiana and a local prosecutor, respondents here, filed a civil action against the three corporations and certain of their employees alleging that defendants had engaged in a pattern of racketeering activity by repeatedly violating the state laws barring the distribution of obscene books and films, thereby violating the State's RICO law. [2] The complaint recited 39 criminal convictions for selling obscene publications from the three stores. App. 9-37. It was also alleged that there were currently other obscene materials available for sale in the stores. Id. at 37-44. The proceeds from the sales of obscene materials, it was alleged, were being used to operate and maintain the bookstores. Respondents sought civil injunctive relief to bar further racketeering violations, invoking the State's CRRA statute, Ind.Code § 34-4-30.5-1 et seq. (1988). Among the remedies requested in the complaint was forfeiture of all of Fort Wayne Books' property, real and personal, that "was used in the course of, intended for use in the course of, derived from, or realized through" petitioner's "racketeering activity." App. 47. Such forfeiture is authorized by the CRRA statute. Ind.Code § 34-4-30.5-3(a) (1988).

Respondents also moved, in a separate "Verified Petition for Seizure of Property Subject to Forfeiture," for the particular judicial order that is the subject of our consideration here. Specifically, respondents asked the Allen County Circuit Court "to immediately seize . . . all property subject to forfeiture' as set forth in [the CRRA] complaint." App. 51. Such pretrial seizures are authorized under Ind.Code § 34-4-30.5-3(b) (1988), which empowers prosecutors bringing CRRA actions to move for immediate seizure of the property subject to forfeiture, and permits courts to issue seizure orders "upon a showing of probable cause to believe that a violation of [the State's RICO law] involving the property in question has occurred." The seizure petition was supported by an affidavit executed by a local police officer, recounting the 39 criminal convictions involving the defendants, further describing various other books and films available for sale at petitioner's bookstores and believed by affiant to be obscene, and alleging a conspiracy among several of petitioner's employees and officers who had previous convictions for obscenity offenses. App. 55-78.

The trial court, ex parte, heard testimony in support of the petition and had supporting exhibits before it. On the same day, the court entered an order finding that probable cause existed to conclude that Fort Wayne Books was violating the State RICO law, and directing the immediate seizure of the real estate, publications, and other personal property comprising each of the three bookstores operated by the corporate defendants. Id. at 81-83. The court's order authorized the county sheriff to padlock the stores. This was done, and a few days later, the contents of the stores were hauled away by law enforcement officials. No trial date on the CRRA complaint was ever set.

Following the March, 1984, seizure of the bookstores, Fort Wayne Books sought to vacate the ex parte seizure order. An adversarial hearing on a motion to vacate the order based on federal constitutional grounds failed to yield relief. Other efforts to obtain some measure of relief also failed. The trial court did, however, certify the constitutional issues to the Indiana Court of Appeals. In June, 1985, that court held that the relevant RICO/CRRA provisions were violative of the United States Constitution. 4447 Corp. v. Goldsmith, 479 N.E.2d 578 (Ind.App.). [3] The Indiana Supreme Court reversed, upholding the constitutionality of the CRRA statute as a general proposition and the pretrial seizure of Fort Wayne Books' store as a specific matter. 4447 Corp. v. Goldsmith, 504 N.E.2d 559 (1987).

We granted Fort Wayne's petition for certiorari, 485 U.S. 933 (1988), for the purpose of considering the substantial constitutional issues raised by the pretrial seizure.

396

B

In No. 87-614, an investigation of adult bookstores in Howard County, Indiana, led prosecutors there, in April, 1985, to charge petitioner Sappenfield with six counts of distribution of obscene matter, in violation of Ind.Code § 35-49-3-1 (1988). In addition, employing the 1984 amendments to the Indiana RICO statute discussed above, prosecutors used these alleged predicate acts of obscenity as a basis for filing two charges of RICO violations against petitioner. App. 142-143, 148-149. The obscenity charges were Class A misdemeanors under Indiana law, the racketeering offenses Class C felonies.

The trial court dismissed the two RICO counts on the ground that the RICO statute was unconstitutionally vague as applied to obscenity predicate offenses. The Indiana Court of Appeals reversed, and reinstated the charges against petitioner. Relying on the Indiana Supreme Court's opinion under review here in No. 87-40, 4447 Corp. v. Goldsmith, supra, the Court of Appeals held that "Indiana's RICO statute is not unconstitutional as applied to the State's obscenity statute." 505 N.E.2d 504, 506 (1987). The Indiana Supreme Court declined to review this holding of the Indiana Court of Appeals.

We granted certiorari, 485 U.S. 933 (1988), and consolidated this case with No. 87-470, to consider the common and separate issues presented by both cases.

II

Since it involves challenges to the constitutionality of the Indiana RICO statute, we deal first with No. 87-614.

As noted above, petitioner was charged with six substantive obscenity violations and two RICO offenses. App. 138-149. Petitioner challenged only the latter charges, raising no objection to the obscenity indictments. Id. at 150. He makes no claim here that the Constitution bars a criminal prosecution for distributing obscene materials. [4] Rather, petitioner's claim is that certain particulars of the Indiana RICO law render the prosecution of petitioner under that statute unconstitutional. Petitioner advances several specific attacks on the RICO statute.

A

Before we address the merits of petitioner's claims, we must first consider our jurisdiction to hear this case. The relevant statute, 28 U.S.C. § 1257, limits our review to "[f]inal judgments or decrees" of the state courts. The general rule is that finality in the context of a criminal prosecution is defined by a judgment of conviction and the imposition of a sentence. See Parr v. United States, 351 U. S. 513, 351 U. S. 518 (1956); Berman v. United States, 302 U. S. 211, 302 U. S. 212 (1937). Since neither is present here, we would usually conclude that the judgment below is not final, and is hence unreviewable.

There are, however, exceptions to the general rule. See Cox Broadcasting Corp. v. Cohn, 420 U. S. 469 (1975). Cox identified four categories of cases in which a judgment is final even though further proceedings are pending in the state courts. This case fits within the fourth category of cases described in Cox:

"[W]here the federal issue has been finally decided in the state courts with further proceedings pending in which the party seeking review here might prevail on the merits on nonfederal grounds, thus rendering unnecessary review of the federal issue by this Court, and where reversal of the state court on the federal issue would be preclusive of any further litigation on the relevant cause of action . . . in the state court proceedings still to come. In these circumstances, if a refusal immediately to review the state court decision might seriously erode federal policy, the Court has entertained and decided the federal issue, which itself has been finally determined by the state courts for the purposes of the state litigation."

Id. at 420 U. S. 482-483.

This case clearly satisfies the first sentence of the above-cited passage: petitioner could well prevail on nonfederal grounds at a subsequent trial, and reversal of the Indiana Court of Appeals' holding would bar further prosecution on the RICO counts at issue here. Thus, the only debatable question is whether a refusal to grant immediate review of petitioner's claims "might seriously erode federal policy." Ibid.

Adjudicating the proper scope of First Amendment protections has often been recognized by this Court as a "federal policy" that merits application of an exception to the general finality rule. See, e.g., National Socialist Party of America v. Skokie, 432 U. S. 43, 432 U. S. 44 (1977) (per curiam); Miami Herald Publishing Co. v. Tornillo, 418 U. S. 241, 418 U. S. 246-247 (1974). Petitioner's challenge to the constitutionality of the use of RICO statutes to criminalize patterns of obscenity offenses calls into question the legitimacy of the law enforcement practices of several States, as well as the Federal Government. [5]

Resolution of this important issue of the possible limits the First Amendment places on state and federal efforts to control organized crime should not remain in doubt.

"Whichever way we were to decide on the merits, it would be intolerable to leave unanswered, under these circumstances, an important question of freedom of the press under the First Amendment; an uneasy and unsettled constitutional posture [of the state statute in question] could only further harm the operation of a free press."

Tornillo, supra, at 418 U. S. 247, n. 6.

JUSTICE O'CONNOR contends that a contrary result is counseled here by our decision in Flynt v. Ohio, 451 U. S. 619 (1981) (per curiam). Post at 489 U. S. 69-70. But as the Court understood it,

"[t]he question presented for review [in Flynt was] whether, on [that] record, the decision to prosecute petitioners was selective or discriminatory in violation of the Equal Protection Clause."

Flynt, supra, at 451 U. S. 622 (emphasis added). The claim before us in Flynt was not a First Amendment claim, but rather an equal protection claim (albeit one in the context of a trial raising First Amendment issues). As a result, Cox's fourth exception was held to be inapplicable in that case. Though the dissenters in Flynt disagreed with the premise of the Court's holding, and contended that that case was a First Amendment dispute that demanded immediate attention under Cox's fourth exception, see 451 U.S. at 451 U. S. 623 (Stewart, J., dissenting); id. at 451 U. S. 623-624 (STEVENS, J., dissenting), the fact is that no Member of the Court concluded in Flynt -- as JUSTICE O'CONNOR does today -- that where an important First Amendment claim is before us, the Court should refuse to invoke Cox's fourth exception and hold that we have no authority to address the issue.

Consequently, we conclude that this case, which clearly involves a First Amendment challenge to the facial validity of the Indiana RICO statute, merits review under the fourth exception recognized by Cox to the finality rule.

B

Petitioner's broadest contention is that the Constitution forbids the use of obscenity violations as predicate acts for a RICO conviction. Petitioner's argument in this regard is twofold: first, that the Indiana RICO law, as applied to an "enterprise" that has allegedly distributed obscene materials, is unconstitutionally vague; and second, that the potential punishments available under the RICO law are so severe that the statute lacks a "necessary sensitivity to first amendment rights," Brief for Petitioner in No. 87-614, p. 23. We consider each of these arguments in turn.

(1)

The "racketeering activities" forbidden by the Indiana RICO law are a "pattern" of multiple violations of certain substantive crimes, of which distributing obscenity (Ind.Code § 35-49-3-1) is one. Ind.Code § 35-45-6-1 (1988). Thus, the RICO statute at issue wholly incorporates the state obscenity law by reference.

Petitioner argues that the "inherent vagueness" of the standards established by Miller v. California, 413 U. S. 15 (1973), are at the root of his objection to any RICO prosecution based on predicate acts of obscenity. Brief for Petitioner in No. 87-614, pp. 24-33. Yet this is nothing less than an invitation to overturn Miller -- an invitation that we reject. And we note that the Indiana obscenity statute, Ind.Code § 35-49-1-1 et seq. (1988), is closely tailored to conform to the Miller standards. Cf. Sedelbauer v. State, 428 N.E.2d 206, 210-211 (Ind.1981), cert. denied, 455 U. S. 1035 (1982). [6] Moreover, petitioner's motion to dismiss the RICO charges in the trial court rested on the alleged vagueness of that statute, and not any alleged defect in the underlying obscenity law. See App. 150-151, 161-167.

We find no merit in petitioner's claim that the Indiana RICO law is unconstitutionally vague as applied to obscenity predicate offenses. Given that the RICO statute totally encompasses the obscenity law, if the latter is not unconstitutionally vague, the former cannot be vague either. At petitioner's forthcoming trial, the prosecution will have to prove beyond a reasonable doubt each element of the alleged RICO offense, including the allegation that petitioner violated (or attempted or conspired to violate) the Indiana obscenity law. Cf. Ind.Code § 35-45-6-1 (1988); 504 N.E.2d at 566. Thus, petitioner cannot be convicted of violating the RICO law without first being "found guilty" of two counts of distributing (or attempting to, or conspiring to, distribute) obscene materials.

It is true, as petitioner argues, Brief for Petitioner in No. 87-614, pp. 16-18, that the punishments available in a RICO prosecution are different from those for obscenity violations. But we fail to see how this difference renders the RICO statute void for vagueness. [7]

(2)

Petitioner's next contention rests on the difference between the sanctions imposed on obscenity law violators and those imposed on convicted "racketeers": the sanctions imposed on RICO violators are so "draconian" that they have an improper chilling effect on First Amendment freedoms, petitioner contends. See id. at 12, 17. The use of such "heavy artillery" from the "war on crime" against obscenity is improper, petitioner argues, and therefore, obscenity offenses should not be permitted to be used as predicate acts for RICO purposes.

It is true that the criminal penalties for a RICO violation under Indiana law, a Class C felony, are more severe than those authorized for an obscenity offense, a Class A misdemeanor. Specifically, if petitioner is found guilty of the two RICO counts against him, he faces a maximum sentence of 10 years in prison and a $20,000 fine; if petitioner were convicted instead of only the six predicate obscenity offenses charged in the indictments, the maximum punishment he could face would be six years in jail and $30,000 in fines. Compare Ind.Code § 35-50-2-6 (1988), with Ind.Code § 35-50-3-2 (1988). While the RICO punishment is obviously greater than that for obscenity violations, we do not perceive any constitutionally significant difference between the two potential punishments. [8] Indeed, the Indiana RICO provisions in this respect function quite similarly to an enhanced sentencing scheme for multiple obscenity violations. As such, "[i]t is not for this Court . . . to limit the State in resorting to various weapons in the armory of the law." Kingsley Books, Inc. v. Brown, 354 U. S. 436, 354 U. S. 441 (1957).

It may be true that the stiffer RICO penalties will provide an additional deterrent to those who might otherwise sell obscene materials; perhaps this means -- as petitioner suggests, Brief for Petitioner in No. 87-614, pp. 20-22 -- that some cautious booksellers will practice self-censorship and remove First Amendment protected materials from their shelves. But deterrence of the sale of obscene materials is a legitimate end of state anti-obscenity laws, and our cases have long recognized the practical reality that

"any form of criminal obscenity statute applicable to a bookseller will induce some tendency to self-censorship and have some inhibitory effect on the dissemination of material not obscene."

Smith v. California, 361 U. S. 147, 361 U. S. 154-155 (1959). Cf. also Arcara v. Cloud Books, Inc., 478 U. S. 697, 478 U. S. 706 (1986). The mere assertion of some possible self-censorship resulting from a statute is not enough to render an anti-obscenity law unconstitutional under our precedents.

Petitioner further raises the question whether the civil sanctions available against RICO violations -- under the CRRA statute -- are so severe as to render the RICO statute itself unconstitutional. See, e.g., Brief for Petitioner in No. 87-614, pp. 22-23. However, this contention is not ripe, since the State has not sought any civil penalties in this case. These claims can only be reviewed when (or if) such remedies are enforced against petitioner.

Consequently, we find no constitutional bar to the State's inclusion of substantive obscenity violations among the predicate offenses under its RICO statute.

C

Finally, petitioner advances two narrower objections to the application of the Indiana RICO statute in obscenity-related prosecutions.

(1)

First, petitioner contends that, even if the statute is constitutional on its face,

"the First Amendment . . . requires that predicate obscenity offenses must be affirmed convictions on successive dates . . . in the same jurisdiction as that where the RICO charge is brought."

Id. at 33.

We find no constitutional basis for the claim that the alleged predicate acts used in a RICO/obscenity prosecution must be "affirmed convictions." We rejected a like contention, albeit in dicta, when considering a case under the Federal RICO statute. See Sedima, S. P. R. L. v. Imrex Co., 473 U. S. 479, 473 U. S. 488 (1985). We see no reason for a different rule where the alleged predicate acts are obscenity. As long as the standard of proof is the proper one with respect to all of the elements of the RICO allegation -- including proof, beyond a reasonable doubt, of the requisite number of constitutionally proscribable predicate acts -- all of the relevant constitutional requirements have been met. The analogy suggested by the United States in its amicus brief is apt:

"This Court has never required a State to fire warning shots, in the form of misdemeanor prosecutions, before it may bring felony charges for distributing obscene materials."

Brief for United States as Amicus Curiae 16. We likewise decline to impose such a "warning shot" requirement here.

The second aspect of this claim -- that all of the predicate offenses charged must have occurred in the jurisdiction where the RICO indictment is brought -- also lacks merit. This contention must be rejected in this case, if for no other reason than the fact that all of petitioner's alleged predicate acts of distributing obscenity did take place in the same jurisdiction (Howard County) where the RICO prosecution was initiated; petitioner lacks standing to advance this claim on these facts. See App. 138-149. More significantly, petitioner's suggestion fails because such a rule would essentially turn the RICO statute on its head: barring RICO prosecutions of large national enterprises that commit single predicate offenses in numerous jurisdictions, for example.

Of course, petitioner is correct when he argues that "community standards" may vary from jurisdiction to jurisdiction where different predicate obscenity offenses allegedly were committed. But as long as, for example, each previous obscenity conviction was measured by the appropriate community's standard, we see no reason why the RICO prosecution -- alleging a pattern of such violations -- may take place only in a jurisdiction where two or more such offenses have occurred. Cf. Smith v. United States, 431 U. S. 291, 431 U. S. 306-309 (1977).

(2)

Second, petitioner contends that he should have been provided with a prompt adversarial hearing, shortly after his arrest, on the question of the obscenity of the materials he allegedly distributed. Brief for Petitioner in No. 87-614, pp. 36-37.

This contention lacks merit for several reasons. First, it does not appear that petitioner requested such a hearing below. See App. 135-137. Second, unlike No. 87-470, in this case, there was no seizure of any books or films owned by petitioner. The only expressive materials "seized" by Howard County officials in this case were a few items purchased by police officers in connection with their investigation of petitioner's stores. See id. at 138-147. We have previously rejected the argument that such purchases trigger constitutional concerns. See Maryland v. Macon, 472 U. S. 463, 472 U. S. 468-471 (1985).

We consequently affirm the judgment in No. 87-614.

III

We reverse, however, the judgment in No. 87-470 sustaining the pretrial seizure order.

In a line of cases dating back to Marcus v. Search Warrant, 367 U. S. 717 (1961), this Court has repeatedly held that rigorous procedural safeguards must be employed before expressive materials can be seized as "obscene." In Marcus, and again in A Quantity of Books v. Kansas, 378 U. S. 205 (1964), the Court invalidated large-scale confiscations of books and films, where numerous copies of selected books were seized without a prior adversarial hearing on their obscenity. In those cases, and the ones that immediately came after them, the Court established that pretrial seizures of expressive materials could only be undertaken pursuant to a "procedure designed to focus searchingly on the question of obscenity.'" Id. at 378 U. S. 210 (quoting Marcus, supra, at 367 U. S. 732). See also e.g., Lee Art Theatre, Inc. v. Virginia, 392 U. S. 636 (1968).

We refined that approach further in our subsequent decisions. Most importantly, in Heller v. New York, 413 U. S. 483, 413 U. S. 492 (1973), the Court noted that

"seizing films to destroy them or to block their distribution or exhibition is a very different matter from seizing a single copy of a film for the bona fide purpose of preserving it as evidence in a criminal proceeding."

As a result, we concluded that, until there was a "judicial determination of the obscenity issue in an adversary proceeding," exhibition of a film could not be restrained by seizing all the available copies of it. Id. at 413 U. S. 492-493. The same is obviously true for books or any other expressive materials. While a single copy of a book or film may be seized and retained for evidentiary purposes based on a finding of probable cause, the publication may not be taken out of circulation completely until there has been a determination of obscenity after an adversary hearing. Ibid.; see New York v. P. J. Video,

Inc., 475 U. S. 868, 475 U. S. 874-876 (1986).

Thus, while the general rule under the Fourth Amendment is that any and all contraband, instrumentalities, and evidence of crimes may be seized on probable cause (and even without a warrant in various circumstances), it is otherwise when materials presumptively protected by the First Amendment are involved. Lo-Ji Sales, Inc. v. New York, 442 U. S. 319, 442 U. S. 326, n. 5 (1979). It is

"[t]he risk of prior restraint, which is the underlying basis for the special Fourth Amendment protections accorded searches for and seizure of First Amendment materials"

that motivates this rule. Maryland v. Macon, supra, at 472 U. S. 470. These same concerns render invalid the pretrial seizure at issue here. [9]

In its decision below, the Indiana Supreme Court did not challenge our precedents or the limitations on seizures that our decisions in this area have established. Rather, the court found those rules largely inapplicable in this case. 504 N.E.2d at 564-567. The court noted that the alleged predicate offenses included 39 convictions for violating the State's obscenity laws, [10] and observed that the pretrial seizures (which were made in strict accordance with Indiana law) were not based on the nature or suspected obscenity of the contents of the items seized, but upon the neutral ground that the sequestered property represented assets used and acquired in the course of racketeering activity.

"The remedy of forfeiture is intended not to restrain the future distribution of presumptively protected speech, but rather to disgorge assets acquired through racketeering activity. Stated simply, it is irrelevant whether assets derived from an alleged violation of the RICO statute are or are not obscene."

Id. at 565. The court also specifically rejected petitioner's claim that the legislative inclusion of violations of obscenity laws as a form of racketeering activity was "merely a semantic device intended to circumvent well-established First Amendment doctrine." Id. at 564. The assets seized were subject to forfeiture "if the elements of a pattern of racketeering activity are shown," ibid.; there being probable cause to believe this was the case here, the pretrial seizure was permissible, the Indiana Supreme Court concluded.

We do not question the holding of the court below that adding obscenity law violations to the list of RICO predicate crimes was not a mere ruse to sidestep the First Amendment. And, for the purpose of disposing of this case, we assume without deciding that bookstores and their contents are forfeitable (like other property such as a bank account or a yacht) when it is proved that these items are property actually used in, or derived from, a pattern of violations of the State's obscenity laws. [11] Even with these assumptions, though, we find the seizure at issue here unconstitutional. It is incontestable that these proceedings were begun to put an end to the sale of obscenity at the three bookstores named in the complaint, and hence we are quite sure that the special rules applicable to removing First Amendment materials from circulation are relevant here. This includes specifically the admonition that probable cause to believe that there are valid grounds for seizure is insufficient to interrupt the sale of presumptively protected books and films.

Here there was not -- and has not been -- any determination that the seized items were "obscene," or that a RICO violation has occurred. True, the predicate crimes on which the seizure order was based had been adjudicated, and are unchallenged. But the petition for seizure and the hearing thereon were aimed at establishing no more than probable cause to believe that a RICO violation had occurred, and the order for seizure recited no more than probable cause in that respect. As noted above, our cases firmly hold that mere probable cause to believe a legal violation has transpired is not adequate to remove books or films from circulation. See, e.g., New York v. P. J. Video, Inc., supra; Heller v. New York, 413 U. S. 483 (1973). The elements of a RICO violation other than the predicate crimes remain to be established in this case, e.g., whether the obscenity violations by the three corporations or their employees established a pattern of racketeering activity, and whether the assets seized were forfeitable under the State's CRRA statute. Therefore, the pretrial seizure at issue here was improper.

The fact that respondent's motion for seizure was couched as one under the Indiana RICO law -- instead of being brought under the substantive obscenity statute -- is unavailing. As far back as the decision in Near v. Minnesota ex rel. Olson, 283 U. S. 697, 283 U. S. 720-721 (1931), this Court has recognized that the way in which a restraint on speech is "characterized" under state law is of little consequence. See also Schad v. Mount Ephraim, 452 U. S. 61, 452 U. S. 67-68 (1981); Southeastern Promotions, Ltd. v. Conrad, 420 U. S. 546, 420 U. S. 552-555 (1975). For example, in Vance v. Universal Amusement Co., 445 U. S. 308 (1980) (per curiam), we struck down a prior restraint placed on the exhibitions of films under a Texas "public nuisance" statute, finding that its failure to comply with our prior case law in this area was a fatal defect. Cf. also Arcara v. Cloud Books, Inc., 478 U.S. at 478 U. S. 708 (O'CONNOR, J., concurring) (noting that, if a "city were to use a nuisance statute as a pretext for closing down a bookstore because it sold indecent books . . . the case would clearly implicate First Amendment concerns and require analysis under the appropriate First Amendment standard of review"). While we accept the Indiana Supreme Court's finding that Indiana's RICO law is not "pretextual" as applied to obscenity offenses, it is true that the State cannot escape the constitutional safeguards of our prior cases by merely recategorizing a pattern of obscenity violations as "racketeering."

At least where the RICO violation claimed is a pattern of racketeering that can be established only by rebutting the presumption that expressive materials are protected by the First Amendment, [12] that presumption is not rebutted until the claimed justification for seizing books or other publications is properly established in an adversary proceeding. Here, literally thousands of books and films were carried away and taken out of circulation by the pretrial order. See App. 87; Record 601-627. Yet it remained to be proved whether the seizure was actually warranted under the Indiana CRRA and RICO statutes. If we are to maintain the regard for First Amendment values expressed in our prior decisions dealing with interrupting the flow of expressive materials, the judgment of the Indiana Court must be reversed. [13]

IV

For the reasons given above, the judgment in No. 87-470 is reversed, and the case is remanded for further proceedings. The judgment in No. 87-614 is affirmed, and it too is remanded for further proceedings.

It is so ordered.

Notes

[1] In addition to petitioner Fort Wayne Books, Inc., the Fort Wayne proceedings involved Cinema Blue of Fort Wayne, Inc., and Erotica House Bookstore, Inc. See App. 7.

These other entities did not seek certiorari or enter an appearance in this Court. We therefore deal only with the claims and issues raised by Fort Wayne Books, Inc.

[2] A 1984 amendment to the state RICO law had added obscenity violations to the list of predicate offenses deemed to constitute "racketeering activity" under Indiana law. See Ind.Code § 35-45-6-1 (1988).

[3] The Indiana Court of Appeals had consolidated the Fort Wayne Books case with another case arising from a CRRA action brought in Indianapolis, 4447 Corp. v. Goldsmith. The Indiana Supreme Court also heard these cases on a consolidated basis, issuing a single judgment upholding both seizures.

Only Fort Wayne Books, Inc., petitioned for review of the decision below. See Pet. for Cert. in No. 87-470, p. iv. Officials of the 4447 Corporation have never expressed any interest in the proceedings here, and several factual aspects of that case brought to our attention during Argument, see Tr. of Oral Arg. 53, suggest that it may be moot. In any event, we address only the claims and issues presented by Fort Wayne Books, Inc.

[4] The constitutionality of criminal sanctions against those who distribute obscene materials is well established by our prior cases. See, e.g., Pinkus v. United States, 436 U. S. 293, 436 U. S. 303-304 (1978); Splawn v. California, 431 U. S. 595, 431 U. S. 597-599 (1977); Miller v. California, 413 U. S. 15, 413 U. S. 23-26 (1973); Kingsley Books, Inc. v. Brown, 354 U. S. 436, 354 U. S. 441 (1957).

[5] The Federal RICO statute also permits prosecutions for a pattern of obscenity violations, in a manner quite similar to the Indiana law under review here. See 18 U.S.C. § 1961(1) (1982 ed., Supp. IV). Thus, the "outcome of this case may . . . determine the constitutionality of using obscenity crimes as predicate acts in the federal RICO statute." See Brief for United States as Amicus Curiae 2.

In addition, several States have followed Congress' lead, and have added obscenity-related offenses to the list of predicate offenses that can give rise to violations of their state RICO laws. See, e.g., Ariz.Rev.Stat.Ann. § 13-2301 (Supp.1988-1989); Ind.Code § 35-45-6-1 (1988); Ga.Code Ann. § 16-14-3(3)(A)(xii) (1988); Conn.Gen.Stat. § 53-394 (1985); Cal.Penal Code Ann. § 186.2(a)(19) (West 1988).

[6] The definition of obscenity found in the relevant statute provides that a book or film (a "matter," in the law's parlance) is obscene if:

"(1) the average person, applying contemporary community standards, finds that the dominant theme of the matter or performance, taken as a whole, appeals to the prurient interest in sex;"

"(2) the matter or performance depicts or describes, in a patently offensive way, sexual conduct; and"

"(3) the matter or performance, taken as a whole, lacks serious literary artistic, political, or scientific value."

Ind.Code § 35-49-2-1 (1988). Cf. Pope v. Illinois, 481 U. S. 497, 481 U. S. 501-502, n. 4 (1987); Miller v. California, 413 U.S. at 413 U. S. 25-26.

[7] Indeed, because the scope of the Indiana RICO law is more limited than the scope of the State's obscenity statute -- with obscenity-related RICO prosecutions possible only where one is guilty of a "pattern" of obscenity violations -- it would seem that the RICO statute is inherently less vague than any state obscenity law: a prosecution under the RICO law will be possible only where all the elements of an obscenity offense are present, and then some.

[8] We have in the past upheld the constitutionality of statutes that provide criminal penalties for obscenity offenses that are not significantly different from those provided in the Indiana RICO law. See, e.g., Smith v. United States, 431 U. S. 291, 431 U. S. 296, n. 3 (1977) (5-year prison term and $5,000 fine for first offense; 10-year term and $10,000 fine for each subsequent violation); Ginzburg v. United States, 383 U. S. 463, 383 U. S. 464-465, n. 2 (1966) (5-year prison term and $5,000 fine).

[9] Following its ruling for petitioner, the Indiana Court of Appeals certified two questions for review to the Indiana Supreme Court:

"(a) Does the application for seizure upon probable cause shown ex parte as provided for by I.C. 34-4-30.5-3(b) violate due process guarantees provided by the Indiana and United States Constitutions."

"(b) Is the Order of seizure issued March 19, 1984, which is based upon enumerated criminal convictions, a violation of the First Amendment."

Record 700.

The Indiana Supreme Court answered both of these questions in the negative. 4447 Corp. v. Goldsmith, 504 N.E. 559, 566-567 (1987). Because we dispose of petitioner's claims on First Amendment grounds, we need not reach any due process questions that may be involved in this case.

[10] Respondent suggested at argument, see Tr. of Oral Arg. 43, 53, that the fact that petitioner (and/or those employed by petitioner) had numerous prior convictions for obscenity offenses sufficed to justify this pretrial seizure even if it were otherwise impermissible. But the state trial court did not purport to impose the seizure as a punishment for the past criminal acts (even if such a punishment were permissible under the First Amendment). Instead, as noted above, the seizure was undertaken to prevent

future violations of Indiana's RICO laws; as a prospective, pretrial seizure, it was required to comply with the Marcus v. Search Warrant, 367 U. S. 717 (1961), line of cases, which (as we explain below) it did not.

[11] Contrary to petitioner's urging, see Brief for Petitioner in No. 87-470, pp. 44-45, we do not reach the question of the constitutionality of post-trial forfeiture -- or any other civil post-trial sanction authorized by the Indiana RICO/CRRA laws -- in this context. The case before us does not involve such a forfeiture, and we see no reason to depart from our usual practice of deciding only "concrete legal issues, presented in actual cases. . . ." See Public Workers v. Mitchell, 330 U. S. 75, 330 U. S. 89 (1947); see also Electric Bond & Share Co. v. SEC, 303 U. S. 419, 303 U. S. 443 (1938).

[12] We do not hold today that the pretrial seizure of petitioner's nonexpressive property was invalid. Petitioner did not challenge this aspect of the seizure here.

[13] Although it is of no direct significance, we note that the Federal Government -- which has a RICO statute similar to Indiana's, 18 U.S.C. § 1961 et seq. -- does not pursue pretrial seizure of expressive materials in its RICO actions against "adult bookstores" or like operations. See Brief for United States as Amicus Curiae 15, n. 12; cf. United States v. Pryba, 674 F.Supp. 1504, 1508, n. 16 (ED Va.1987).

## Texas v. Johnson (June 21, 1989)

JUSTICE BRENNAN delivered the opinion of the Court.

After publicly burning an American flag as a means of political protest, Gregory Lee Johnson was convicted of desecrating a flag in violation of Texas law. This case presents the question whether his conviction is consistent with the First Amendment. We hold that it is not.

I

While the Republican National Convention was taking place in Dallas in 1984, respondent Johnson participated in a political demonstration dubbed the "Republican War Chest Tour." As explained in literature distributed by the demonstrators and in speeches made by them, the purpose of this event was to protest the policies of the Reagan administration and of certain Dallas-based corporations. The demonstrators marched through the Dallas streets, chanting political slogans and stopping at several corporate locations to stage "die-ins" intended to dramatize the consequences of nuclear war. On several occasions they spray-painted the walls of buildings and overturned potted plants, but Johnson himself took no part in such activities. He did, however, accept an American flag handed to him by a fellow protestor who had taken it from a flagpole outside one of the targeted buildings.

The demonstration ended in front of Dallas City Hall, where Johnson unfurled the American flag, doused it with kerosene, and set it on fire. While the flag burned, the protestors chanted, "America, the red, white, and blue, we spit on you." After the demonstrators dispersed, a witness to the flag burning collected the flag's remains and buried them in his backyard. No one was physically injured or threatened with injury, though several witnesses testified that they had been seriously offended by the flag burning.

Of the approximately 100 demonstrators, Johnson alone was charged with a crime. The only criminal offense with which he was charged was the desecration of a venerated object in violation of Tex.Penal Code Ann. § 42.09(a)(3) (1989). [n1] After a trial, he was convicted, sentenced to one year in prison, and fined $2,000. The Court of Appeals for the Fifth District of Texas at Dallas affirmed Johnson's conviction, 706 S.W.2d 120 (1986), but the Texas Court of Criminal Appeals reversed, 755 S.W.2d 92 (1988), holding that the State could not, consistent with the First Amendment, punish Johnson for burning the flag in these circumstances.

The Court of Criminal Appeals began by recognizing that Johnson's conduct was symbolic speech protected by the First Amendment:

Given the context of an organized demonstration, speeches, slogans, and the distribution of literature, anyone who observed appellant's act would have understood the message that appellant intended to convey. The act for which appellant was convicted was clearly "speech" contemplated by the First Amendment.

Id. at 95. To justify Johnson's conviction for engaging in symbolic speech, the State asserted two interests: preserving the flag as a symbol of national unity and preventing breaches of the peace. The Court of Criminal Appeals held that neither interest supported his conviction.

Acknowledging that this Court had not yet decided whether the Government may criminally sanction flag desecration in order to preserve the flag's symbolic value, the Texas court nevertheless concluded that our decision in West Virginia Board of Education v. Barnette, 319 U.S. 624 (1943), suggested that furthering this interest by curtailing speech was impermissible. "Recognizing that the right to differ is the centerpiece of our First Amendment freedoms," the court explained,

a government cannot mandate by fiat a feeling of unity in its citizens. Therefore, that very same government cannot carve out a symbol of unity and prescribe a set of approved messages to be associated with that symbol when it cannot mandate the status or feeling the symbol purports to represent.

755 S.W.2d at 97. Noting that the State had not shown that the flag was in "grave and immediate danger," Barnette, supra, at 639, of being stripped of its symbolic value, the Texas court also decided that the flag's special status was not endangered by Johnson's conduct. 755 S.W.2d at 97.

As to the State's goal of preventing breaches of the peace, the court concluded that the flag desecration statute was not drawn narrowly enough to encompass only those flag burnings that were likely to result in a serious disturbance of the peace. And in fact, the court emphasized, the flag burning in this particular case did not threaten such a reaction. "'Serious offense' occurred," the court admitted,

but there was no breach of peace, nor does the record reflect that the situation was potentially explosive. One cannot equate "serious offense" with incitement to breach the peace.

Id. at 96. The court also stressed that another Texas statute, Tex.Penal Code Ann. § 42.01 (1989), prohibited breaches of the peace. Citing Boos v. Barry, 485 U.S. 312 (1988), the court decided that § 42.01 demonstrated Texas' ability to prevent disturbances of the peace without punishing this flag desecration. 755 S.W.2d at 96.

Because it reversed Johnson's conviction on the ground that § 42.09 was unconstitutional as applied to him, the state court did not address Johnson's argument that the statute was, on its face, unconstitutionally vague and overbroad. We granted certiorari, 488 U.S. 907 (1988), and now affirm.

II

Johnson was convicted of flag desecration for burning the flag, rather than for uttering insulting words. [n2] This fact somewhat complicates our consideration of his conviction under the First Amendment. We must first determine whether Johnson's burning of the flag constituted expressive conduct, permitting him to invoke the First Amendment in challenging his conviction. See, e.g., Spence v. Washington, 418 U.S. 405, 409-411 (1974). If his conduct was expressive, we next decide whether the State's regulation is related to the suppression of free expression. See, e.g., United States v. O'Brien, 391 U.S. 367, 377 (1968); Spence, supra, at 414, n. 8. If the State's regulation is not related to expression, then the less stringent standard we announced in United States v. O'Brien for regulations of noncommunicative conduct controls. See O'Brien, supra, at 377. If it is, then we are outside of O'Brien's test, and we must ask whether this interest justifies Johnson's conviction under a more demanding standard. [n3] See Spence, supra, at 411. A third possibility is that the State's asserted interest is simply not implicated on these facts, and, in that event, the interest drops out of the picture. See 418 U.S. at 414, n. 8.

The First Amendment literally forbids the abridgment only of "speech," but we have long recognized that its protection does not end at the spoken or written word. While we have rejected

the view that an apparently limitless variety of conduct can be labeled "speech" whenever the person engaging in the conduct intends thereby to express an idea,

United States v. O'Brien, supra, at 376, we have acknowledged that conduct may be "sufficiently imbued with elements of communication to fall within the scope of the First and Fourteenth Amendments," Spence, supra, at 409.

In deciding whether particular conduct possesses sufficient communicative elements to bring the First Amendment into play, we have asked whether

[a]n intent to convey a particularized message was present, and [whether] the likelihood was great that the message would be understood by those who viewed it.

418 U.S. at 410-411. Hence, we have recognized the expressive nature of students' wearing of black armbands to protest American military involvement in Vietnam, Tinker v. Des Moines Independent Community School Dist., 393 U.S. 503, 505 (1969); of a sit-in

by blacks in a "whites only" area to protest segregation, Brown v. Louisiana, 383 U.S. 131, 141-142 (1966); of the wearing of American military uniforms in a dramatic presentation criticizing American involvement in Vietnam, Schacht v. United States, 398 U.S. 58 (1970); and of picketing about a wide variety of causes, see, e.g., Food Employees v. Logan Valley Plaza, Inc., 391 U.S. 308, 313-314 (1968); United States v. Grace, 461 U.S. 171, 176 (1983).

Especially pertinent to this case are our decisions recognizing the communicative nature of conduct relating to flags. Attaching a peace sign to the flag, Spence, supra, at 418 U.S. 409"]409-410; refusing to salute the flag, Barnette, 319 U.S. at 632; and displaying a red flag, 409-410; refusing to salute the flag, Barnette, 319 U.S. at 632; and displaying a red flag, Stromberg v. California, 283 U.S. 359, 368-369 (1931), we have held, all may find shelter under the First Amendment. See also Smith v. Goguen, 415 U.S. 566, 588 (1974) (WHITE, J., concurring in judgment) (treating flag "contemptuously" by wearing pants with small flag sewn into their seat is expressive conduct). That we have had little difficulty identifying an expressive element in conduct relating to flags should not be surprising. The very purpose of a national flag is to serve as a symbol of our country; it is, one might say, "the one visible manifestation of two hundred years of nationhood." Id. at 603 (REHNQUIST, J., dissenting). Thus, we have observed:

[T]he flag salute is a form of utterance. Symbolism is a primitive but effective way of communicating ideas. The use of an emblem or flag to symbolize some system, idea, institution, or personality, is a shortcut from mind to mind. Causes and nations, political parties, lodges and ecclesiastical groups seek to knit the loyalty of their followings to a flag or banner, a color or design.

Barnette, supra, at 632. Pregnant with expressive content, the flag as readily signifies this Nation as does the combination of letters found in "America."

We have not automatically concluded, however, that any action taken with respect to our flag is expressive. Instead, in characterizing such action for First Amendment purposes, we have considered the context in which it occurred. In Spence, for example, we emphasized that Spence's taping of a peace sign to his flag was "roughly simultaneous with and concededly triggered by the Cambodian incursion and the Kent State tragedy." 418 U.S. at 410. The State of Washington had conceded, in fact, that Spence's conduct was a form of communication, and we stated that "the State's concession is inevitable on this record." Id. at 409.

The State of Texas conceded for purposes of its oral argument in this case that Johnson's conduct was expressive conduct, Tr. of Oral Arg. 4, and this concession seems to us as prudent as was Washington's in Spence. Johnson burned an American flag as part -- indeed, as the culmination -- of a political demonstration that coincided with the convening of the Republican Party and its renomination of Ronald Reagan for President. The expressive, overtly political nature of this conduct was both intentional and overwhelmingly apparent. At his trial, Johnson explained his reasons for burning the flag as follows:

The American Flag was burned as Ronald Reagan was being renominated as President. And a more powerful statement of symbolic speech, whether you agree with it or not, couldn't have been made at that time. It's quite a just position [juxtaposition]. We had new patriotism and no patriotism.

5 Record 656. In these circumstances, Johnson's burning of the flag was conduct "sufficiently imbued with elements of communication," Spence, 418 U.S. at 409, to implicate the First Amendment.

III

The government generally has a freer hand in restricting expressive conduct than it has in restricting the written or spoken word. See O'Brien, 391 U.S. at 376-377; Clark v. Community for Creative Non-Violence, 468 U.S. 288, 293 (1984); Dallas v. Stanglin, 490 U.S. 19, 25 (1989). It may not, however, proscribe particular conduct because it has expressive elements.

[W]hat might be termed the more generalized guarantee of freedom of expression makes the communicative nature of conduct an inadequate basis for singling out that conduct for proscription. A law directed at the communicative nature of conduct must, like a law directed at speech itself, be justified by the substantial showing of need that the First Amendment requires.

Community for Creative Non-Violence v. Watt, 227 U.S.App.D.C. 19, 55-56, 703 F.2d 586, 622-623 (1983) (Scalia, J., dissenting) (emphasis in original), rev'd sub nom. Clark v. Community for Creative Non-Violence, supra. It is, in short, not simply the verbal or nonverbal nature of the expression, but the governmental interest at stake, that helps to determine whether a restriction on that expression is valid.

Thus, although we have recognized that, where

"speech" and "nonspeech" elements are combined in the same course of conduct, a sufficiently important governmental interest in regulating the nonspeech element can justify incidental limitations on First Amendment freedoms,

O'Brien, supra, at 376, we have limited the applicability of O'Brien's relatively lenient standard to those cases in which "the governmental interest is unrelated to the suppression of free expression." Id. at 377; see also Spence, 418 U.S. at 414, n. 8. In stating, moreover, that O'Brien's test "in the last analysis is little, if any, different from the standard applied to time, place, or manner restrictions," Clark, supra, at 298, we have highlighted the requirement that the governmental interest in question be unconnected to expression in order to come under O'Brien's less demanding rule.

In order to decide whether O'Brien's test applies here, therefore, we must decide whether Texas has asserted an interest in support of Johnson's conviction that is unrelated to the suppression of expression. If we find that an interest asserted by the State is simply not implicated on the facts before us, we need not ask whether O'Brien's test applies. See Spence, supra, at 414, n. 8. The State offers two separate interests to justify this conviction: preventing breaches of the peace and preserving the flag as a symbol of nationhood and national unity. We hold that the first interest is not implicated on this record, and that the second is related to the suppression of expression.

A

Texas claims that its interest in preventing breaches of the peace justifies Johnson's conviction for flag desecration. [n4] However, no disturbance of the peace actually occurred or threatened to occur because of Johnson's burning of the flag. Although the State stresses the disruptive behavior of the protestors during their march toward City Hall, Brief for Petitioner 34-36, it admits that "no actual breach of the peace occurred at the time of the flagburning or in response to the flagburning." Id. at 34. The State's emphasis on the protestors' disorderly actions prior to arriving at City Hall is not only somewhat surprising, given that no charges were brought on the basis of this conduct, but it also fails to show that a disturbance of the peace was a likely reaction to Johnson's conduct. The only evidence offered by the State at trial to show the reaction to Johnson's actions was the testimony of several persons who had been seriously offended by the flag burning. Id. at 6-7.

The State's position, therefore, amounts to a claim that an audience that takes serious offense at particular expression is necessarily likely to disturb the peace, and that the expression may be prohibited on this basis. [n5] Our precedents do not countenance such a presumption. On the contrary, they recognize that a principal

function of free speech under our system of government is to invite dispute. It may indeed best serve its high purpose when it induces a condition of unrest, creates dissatisfaction with conditions as they are, or even stirs people to anger.

Terminiello v. Chicago, 337 U.S. 1, 4 (1949). See also Cox v. Louisiana, 379 U.S. 536, 551 (1965); Tinker v. Des Moines Independent Community School Dist., 393 U.S. at 508-509; Coates v. Cincinnati, 402 U.S. 611, 615 (1971); Hustler Magazine, Inc. v. Falwell, 485 U.S. 46, 55-56 (1988). It would be odd indeed to conclude both that "if it is the speaker's opinion that gives offense, that consequence is a reason for according it constitutional protection," FCC v. Pacifica Foundation, 438 U.S. 726, 745 (1978) (opinion of STEVENS, J.), and that the Government may ban the expression of certain disagreeable ideas on the unsupported presumption that their very disagreeableness will provoke violence.

Thus, we have not permitted the government to assume that every expression of a provocative idea will incite a riot, but have instead required careful consideration of the actual circumstances surrounding such expression, asking whether the expression "is directed to inciting or producing imminent lawless action and is likely to incite or produce such action." Brandenburg v. Ohio, 395 U.S. 444, 447 (1969) (reviewing circumstances surrounding rally and speeches by Ku Klux Klan). To accept Texas' arguments that it need only demonstrate "the potential for a breach of the peace," Brief for Petitioner 37, and that every flag burning necessarily possesses that potential, would be to eviscerate our holding in Brandenburg. This we decline to do.

Nor does Johnson's expressive conduct fall within that small class of "fighting words" that are "likely to provoke the average person to retaliation, and thereby cause a breach of the peace." Chaplinsky v. New Hampshire, 315 U.S. 568, 574 (1942). No reasonable onlooker would have regarded Johnson's generalized expression of dissatisfaction with the policies of the Federal Government as a direct personal insult or an invitation to exchange fisticuffs. See id. at 572-573; Cantwell v. Connecticut, 310 U.S. 296, 309 (1940); FCC v. Pacifica Foundation, supra, at 745 (opinion of STEVENS, J.).

We thus conclude that the State's interest in maintaining order is not implicated on these facts. The State need not worry that our holding will disable it from preserving the peace. We do not suggest that the First Amendment forbids a State to prevent "imminent lawless action." Brandenburg, supra, at 447. And, in fact, Texas already has a statute specifically prohibiting breaches of the peace, Tex.Penal Code Ann. § 42.01 (1989), which tends to confirm that Texas need not punish this flag desecration in order to keep the peace. See Boos v. Barry, 485 U.S. at 327-329.

B

The State also asserts an interest in preserving the flag as a symbol of nationhood and national unity. In Spence, we acknowledged that the government's interest in preserving the flag's special symbolic value "is directly related to expression in the context of activity" such as affixing a peace symbol to a flag. 418 U.S. at 414, n. 8. We are equally persuaded that this interest is related to expression in the case of Johnson's burning of the flag. The State, apparently, is concerned that such conduct will lead people to believe either that the flag does not stand for nationhood and national unity, but instead reflects other, less positive concepts, or that the concepts reflected in the flag do not in fact exist, that is, that we do not enjoy unity as a Nation. These concerns blossom only when a person's treatment of the flag communicates some message, and thus are related "to the suppression of free expression" within the meaning of O'Brien. We are thus outside of O'Brien's test altogether.

IV

It remains to consider whether the State's interest in preserving the flag as a symbol of nationhood and national unity justifies Johnson's conviction.

As in Spence, "[w]e are confronted with a case of prosecution for the expression of an idea through activity," and "[a]ccordingly, we must examine with particular care the interests advanced by [petitioner] to support its prosecution." 418 U.S. at 418 U.S. 411"]411. Johnson was not, we add, prosecuted for the expression of just any idea; he was prosecuted for his expression of dissatisfaction with the policies of this country, expression situated at the core of our First Amendment values. See, e.g., Boos v. Barry, supra, at 318; 411. Johnson was not, we add, prosecuted for the expression of just any idea; he was prosecuted for his expression of dissatisfaction with the policies of this country, expression situated at the core of our First Amendment values. See, e.g., Boos v. Barry, supra, at 318; Frisby v. Schultz, 487 U.S. 474, 479 (1988).

Moreover, Johnson was prosecuted because he knew that his politically charged expression would cause "serious offense." If he had burned the flag as a means of disposing of it because it was dirty or torn, he would not have been convicted of flag desecration under this Texas law: federal law designates burning as the preferred means of disposing of a flag "when it is in such condition that it is no longer a fitting emblem for display," 36 U.S.C. § 176(k), and Texas has no quarrel with this means of disposal. Brief for Petitioner 45. The Texas law is thus not aimed at protecting the physical integrity of the flag in all circumstances, but is designed instead to protect it only against impairments that would cause serious offense to others. [n6] Texas concedes as much:

Section 42.09(b) reaches only those severe acts of physical abuse of the flag carried out in a way likely to be offensive. The statute mandates intentional or knowing abuse, that is, the kind of mistreatment that is not innocent, but rather is intentionally designed to seriously offend other individuals.

Id. at 44.

Whether Johnson's treatment of the flag violated Texas law thus depended on the likely communicative impact of his expressive conduct. [n7] Our decision in Boos v. Barry, supra, tells us that this restriction on Johnson's expression is content-based. In Boos, we considered the constitutionality of a law prohibiting

the display of any sign within 500 feet of a foreign embassy if that sign tends to bring that foreign government into "public odium" or "public disrepute."

Id. at 315. Rejecting the argument that the law was content-neutral because it was justified by "our international law obligation to shield diplomats from speech that offends their dignity," id. at 320, we held that "[t]he emotive impact of speech on its audience is not a 'secondary effect'" unrelated to the content of the expression itself. Id. at 321 (plurality opinion); see also id. at 334 (BRENNAN, J., concurring in part and concurring in judgment).

According to the principles announced in Boos, Johnson's political expression was restricted because of the content of the message he conveyed. We must therefore subject the State's asserted interest in preserving the special symbolic character of the flag to "the most exacting scrutiny." Boos v. Barry, 485 U.S. at 321. [n8]

Texas argues that its interest in preserving the flag as a symbol of nationhood and national unity survives this close analysis. Quoting extensively from the writings of this Court chronicling the flag's historic and symbolic role in our society, the State emphasizes the "'special place'" reserved for the flag in our Nation. Brief for Petitioner 22, quoting Smith v. Goguen, 415 U.S. at 601 (REHNQUIST, J., dissenting). The State's argument is not that it has an interest simply in maintaining the flag as a symbol of something, no matter what it symbolizes; indeed, if that were the State's position, it would be difficult to see how that interest is endangered by highly symbolic conduct such as Johnson's. Rather, the State's claim is that it has an interest in preserving the flag as a symbol of nationhood and national unity, a symbol with a determinate range of meanings. Brief for Petitioner 20-24. According to Texas, if one physically treats the flag in a way that would tend to cast doubt on either the idea that nationhood and national unity are the flag's referents or that national unity actually exists, the message conveyed thereby is a harmful one, and therefore may be prohibited. [n9]

If there is a bedrock principle underlying the First Amendment, it is that the government may not prohibit the expression of an idea simply because society finds the idea itself offensive or disagreeable. See, e.g., Hustler Magazine v. Falwell, 485 U.S. at 55-56; City Council of Los Angeles v. Taxpayers for Vincent, 466 U.S. 789, 804 (1984); Bolger v. Youngs Drug Products Corp., 463 U.S. 60, 65, 72 (1983); Carey v. Brown, 447 U.S. 455, 462-463 (1980); FCC v. Pacifica Foundation, 438 U.S. at 745-746; Young v. American Mini Theatres, Inc., 427 U.S. 50, 63-65, 67-68 (1976) (plurality opinion); Buckley v. Valeo, 424 U.S. 1, 16-17 (1976); Grayned v. Rockford, 408 U.S. 104, 115 (1972); Police Dept. of Chicago v. Mosley, 408 U.S. 92, 95 (1972); Bachellar v. Maryland, 397 U.S. 564, 567 (1970); O'Brien, 391 U.S. at 382; Brown v. Louisiana, 383 U.S. at 142-143; Stromberg v. California, 283 U.S. at 368-369.

We have not recognized an exception to this principle even where our flag has been involved. In Street v. New York, 394 U.S. 576 (1969), we held that a State may not criminally punish a person for uttering words critical of the flag. Rejecting the argument that the conviction could be sustained on the ground that Street had "failed to show the respect for our national symbol which may properly be demanded of every citizen," we concluded that

the constitutionally guaranteed "freedom to be intellectually . . . diverse or even contrary," and the "right to differ as to things that touch the heart of the existing order," encompass the freedom to express publicly one's opinions about our flag, including those opinions which are defiant or contemptuous.

Id. at 593, quoting Barnette, 319 U.S. at 642. Nor may the government, we have held, compel conduct that would evince respect for the flag.

To sustain the compulsory flag salute, we are required to say that a Bill of Rights which guards the individual's right to speak his own mind left it open to public authorities to compel him to utter what is not in his mind.

Id. at 634.

In holding in Barnette that the Constitution did not leave this course open to the government, Justice Jackson described one of our society's defining principles in words deserving of their frequent repetition:

If there is any fixed star in our constitutional constellation, it is that no official, high or petty, can prescribe what shall be orthodox in politics, nationalism, religion, or other matters of opinion or force citizens to confess by word or act their faith therein.

Id. at 642. In Spence, we held that the same interest asserted by Texas here was insufficient to support a criminal conviction under a flag-misuse statute for the taping of a peace sign to an American flag.

Given the protected character of [Spence's] expression and in light of the fact that no interest the State may have in preserving the physical integrity of a privately owned flag was significantly impaired on these facts,

we held, "the conviction must be invalidated." 418 U.S. at 415. See also Goguen, 415 U.S. at 588 (WHITE, J., concurring in judgment) (to convict person who had sewn a flag onto the seat of his pants for "contemptuous" treatment of the flag would be "[t]o convict not to protect the physical integrity or to protect against acts interfering with the proper use of the flag, but to punish for communicating ideas unacceptable to the controlling majority in the legislature").

In short, nothing in our precedents suggests that a State may foster its own view of the flag by prohibiting expressive conduct relating to it. [n10] To bring its argument outside our precedents, Texas attempts to convince us that, even if its interest in preserving the flag's symbolic role does not allow it to prohibit words or some expressive conduct critical of the flag, it does permit it to forbid the outright destruction of the flag. The State's argument cannot depend here on the distinction between written or spoken words and nonverbal conduct. That distinction, we have shown, is of no moment where the nonverbal conduct is expressive, as it is here, and where the regulation of that conduct is related to expression, as it is here. See supra at 402-403. In addition, both Barnette and Spence involved expressive conduct, not only verbal communication, and both found that conduct protected.

Texas' focus on the precise nature of Johnson's expression, moreover, misses the point of our prior decisions: their enduring lesson, that the government may not prohibit expression simply because it disagrees with its message, is not dependent on the particular mode in which one chooses to express an idea. [n11] If we were to hold that a State may forbid flag burning wherever it is likely to endanger the flag's symbolic role, but allow it wherever burning a flag promotes that role -- as where, for example, a person ceremoniously burns a dirty flag -- we would be saying that when it comes to impairing the flag's physical integrity, the flag itself may be used as a symbol -- as a substitute for the written or spoken word or a "short cut from mind to mind" -- only in one direction. We would be permitting a State to "prescribe what shall be orthodox" by saying that one may burn the flag to convey one's attitude toward it and its referents only if one does not endanger the flag's representation of nationhood and national unity.

We never before have held that the Government may ensure that a symbol be used to express only one view of that symbol or its referents. Indeed, in Schacht v. United States, we invalidated a federal statute permitting an actor portraying a member of one of our armed forces to "'wear the uniform of that armed force if the portrayal does not tend to discredit that armed force.'" 398 U.S. at 60, quoting 10 U.S.C. § 772(f). This proviso, we held,

which leaves Americans free to praise the war in Vietnam but can send persons like Schacht to prison for opposing it, cannot survive in a country which has the First Amendment.

Id. at 63.

We perceive no basis on which to hold that the principle underlying our decision in Schacht does not apply to this case. To conclude that the government may permit designated symbols to be used to communicate only a limited set of messages would be to enter territory having no discernible or defensible boundaries. Could the government, on this theory, prohibit the burning of state flags? Of copies of the Presidential seal? Of the Constitution? In evaluating these choices under the First Amendment, how would we decide which symbols were sufficiently special to warrant this unique status? To do so, we would be forced to consult our own political preferences, and impose them on the citizenry, in the very way that the First Amendment forbids us to do. See Carey v. Brown, 447 U.S. at 466-467.

There is, moreover, no indication -- either in the text of the Constitution or in our cases interpreting it -- that a separate juridical category exists for the American flag alone. Indeed, we would not be surprised to learn that the persons who framed our Constitution and wrote the Amendment that we now construe were not known for their reverence for the Union Jack. The First Amendment does not guarantee that other concepts virtually sacred to our Nation as a whole -- such as the principle that discrimination on the basis of race is odious and destructive -- will go unquestioned in the marketplace of ideas. See Brandenburg v. Ohio, 395 U.S. 444 (1969). We decline, therefore, to create for the flag an exception to the joust of principles protected by the First Amendment.

It is not the State's ends, but its means, to which we object. It cannot be gainsaid that there is a special place reserved for the flag in this Nation, and thus we do not doubt that the government has a legitimate interest in making efforts to "preserv[e] the national flag as an unalloyed symbol of our country." Spence, 418 U.S. at 412. We reject the suggestion, urged at oral argument by counsel for Johnson, that the government lacks "any state interest whatsoever" in regulating the manner in which the flag may be displayed. Tr. of Oral Arg. 38. Congress has, for example, enacted precatory regulations describing the proper treatment of the flag, see 36 U.S.C. §§ 173-177, and we cast no doubt on the legitimacy of its interest in making such recommendations. To say that the government has an interest in encouraging proper treatment of the flag, however, is not to say that it may criminally punish a person for burning a flag as a means of political protest.

National unity as an end which officials may foster by persuasion and example is not in question. The problem is whether, under our Constitution, compulsion as here employed is a permissible means for its achievement.

Barnette, 319 U.S. at 640.

We are fortified in today's conclusion by our conviction that forbidding criminal punishment for conduct such as Johnson's will not endanger the special role played by our flag or the feelings it inspires. To paraphrase Justice Holmes, we submit that nobody can suppose that this one gesture of an unknown man will change our Nation's attitude towards its flag. See Abrams v. United States, 250 U.S. 616, 628 (1919) (Holmes, J., dissenting). Indeed, Texas' argument that the burning of an American flag "'is an act having a high likelihood to cause a breach of the peace,'" Brief for Petitioner 31, quoting Sutherland v. DeWulf, 323 F.Supp. 740, 745 (SD Ill.1971) (citation omitted), and its statute's implicit assumption that physical mistreatment of the flag will lead to "serious offense," tend to confirm that the flag's special role is not in danger; if it were, no one would riot or take offense because a flag had been burned.

We are tempted to say, in fact, that the flag's deservedly cherished place in our community will be strengthened, not weakened, by our holding today. Our decision is a reaffirmation of the principles of freedom and inclusiveness that the flag best reflects, and of the conviction that our toleration of criticism such as Johnson's is a sign and source of our strength. Indeed, one of the proudest images of our flag, the one immortalized in our own national anthem, is of the bombardment it survived at Fort McHenry. It is the Nation's resilience, not its rigidity, that Texas sees reflected in the flag -- and it is that resilience that we reassert today.

The way to preserve the flag's special role is not to punish those who feel differently about these matters. It is to persuade them that they are wrong.

To courageous, self-reliant men, with confidence in the power of free and fearless reasoning applied through the processes of popular government, no danger flowing from speech can be deemed clear and present unless the incidence of the evil apprehended is so imminent that it may befall before there is opportunity for full discussion. If there be time to expose through discussion the falsehood and fallacies, to avert the evil by the processes of education, the remedy to bee applied is more speech, not enforced silence.

Whitney v. California, 274 U.S. 357, 377 (1927) (Brandeis, J., concurring). And, precisely because it is our flag that is involved, one's response to the flag-burner may exploit the uniquely persuasive power of the flag itself. We can imagine no more appropriate response to burning a flag than waving one's own, no better way to counter a flag burner's message than by saluting the flag that burns, no surer means of preserving the dignity even of the flag that burned than by -- as one witness here did -- according its remains a respectful burial. We do not consecrate the flag by punishing its desecration, for in doing so we dilute the freedom that this cherished emblem represents.

V

Johnson was convicted for engaging in expressive conduct. The State's interest in preventing breaches of the peace does not support his conviction, because Johnson's conduct did not threaten to disturb the peace. Nor does the State's interest in preserving the flag as a symbol of nationhood and national unity justify his criminal conviction for engaging in political expression. The judgment of the Texas Court of Criminal Appeals is therefore

Affirmed.

Notes

1. Tex.Penal Code Ann. § 42.09 (1989) provides in full:

§ 42.09. Desecration of Venerated Object

(a) A person commits an offense if he intentionally or knowingly desecrates:

(1) a public monument;

(2) a place of worship or burial; or

(3) a state or national flag.

(b) For purposes of this section, "desecrate" means deface, damage, or otherwise physically mistreat in a way that the actor knows will seriously offend one or more persons likely to observe or discover his action.

(c) An offense under this section is a Class A misdemeanor.

2. Because the prosecutor's closing argument observed that Johnson had led the protestors in chants denouncing the flag while it burned, Johnson suggests that he may have been convicted for uttering critical words, rather than for burning the flag. Brief for Respondent 33-34. He relies on Street v. New York, 394 U.S. 576, 578 (1969), in which we reversed a conviction obtained under a New York statute that prohibited publicly defying or casting contempt on the flag "either by words or act" because we were persuaded that the defendant may have been convicted for his words alone. Unlike the law we faced in Street, however, the Texas flag desecration statute does not on its face permit conviction for remarks critical of the flag, as Johnson himself admits. See Brief for Respondent 34. Nor was the jury in this case told that it could convict Johnson of flag desecration if it found only that he had uttered words critical of the flag and its referents.

Johnson emphasizes, though, that the jury was instructed -- according to Texas' law of parties -- that

"a person is criminally responsible for an offense committed by the conduct of another if acting with intent to promote or assist the commission of the offense, he solicits, encourages, directs, aids, or attempts to aid the other person to commit the offense."

Brief for Respondent 2, n. 2, quoting 1 Record 49. The State offered this instruction because Johnson's defense was that he was not the person who had burned the flag. Johnson did not object to this instruction at trial, and although he challenged it on direct appeal, he did so only on the ground that there was insufficient evidence to support it. 706 S.W.2d 120, 124 (Tex.App.1986). It is only in this Court that Johnson has argued that the law-of-parties instruction might have led the jury to convict him for his words alone. Even if we were to find that this argument is properly raised here, however, we would conclude that it has no merit in these circumstances. The instruction would not have permitted a conviction merely for the pejorative nature of Johnson's words, and those words themselves did not encourage the burning of the flag, as the instruction seems to require. Given the additional fact that "the bulk of the State's argument was premised on Johnson's culpability as a sole actor," ibid., we find it too unlikely that the jury convicted Johnson on the basis of this alternative theory to consider reversing his conviction on this ground.

3. Although Johnson has raised a facial challenge to Texas' flag desecration statute, we choose to resolve this case on the basis of his claim that the statute, as applied to him, violates the First Amendment. Section 42.09 regulates only physical conduct with respect to the flag, not the written or spoken word, and although one violates the statute only if one "knows" that one's physical treatment of the flag "will seriously offend one or more persons likely to observe or discover his action," Tex.Penal Code Ann. § 42.09(b)

(1989), this fact does not necessarily mean that the statute applies only to expressive conduct protected by the First Amendment. Cf. Smith v. Goguen, 415 U.S. 566, 588 (1974) (WHITE, J., concurring in judgment) (statute prohibiting "contemptuous" treatment of flag encompasses only expressive conduct). A tired person might, for example, drag a flag through the mud, knowing that this conduct is likely to offend others, and yet have no thought of expressing any idea; neither the language nor the Texas courts' interpretations of the statute precludes the possibility that such a person would be prosecuted for flag desecration. Because the prosecution of a person who had not engaged in expressive conduct would pose a different case, and because this case may be disposed of on narrower grounds, we address only Johnson's claim that § 42.09, as applied to political expression like his, violates the First Amendment.

4. Relying on our decision in Boos v. Barry, 485 U.S. 312"] 485 U.S. 312 (1988), Johnson argues that this state interest is related to the suppression of free expression within the meaning of 485 U.S. 312 (1988), Johnson argues that this state interest is related to the suppression of free expression within the meaning of United States v. O'Brien, 391 U.S. 367 (1968). He reasons that the violent reaction to flag burnings feared by Texas would be the result of the message conveyed by them, and that this fact connects the State's interest to the suppression of expression. Brief for Respondent 12, n. 11. This view has found some favor in the lower courts. See Monroe v. State Court of Fulton County, 739 F.2d 568 574-575 (CA11 1984). Johnson's theory may overread Boos insofar as it suggests that a desire to prevent a violent audience reaction is "related to expression" in the same way that a desire to prevent an audience from being offended is "related to expression." Because we find that the State's interest in preventing breaches of the peace is not implicated on these facts, however, we need not venture further into this area.

5. There is, of course, a tension between this argument and the State's claim that one need not actually cause serious offense in order to violate § 42.09. See Brief for Petitioner 44.

6. Cf. Smith v. Goguen, 415 U.S. at 590-591 (BLACKMUN, J., dissenting) (emphasizing that lower court appeared to have construed state statute so as to protect physical integrity of the flag in all circumstances); id. at 597-598 (REHNQUIST, J., dissenting) (same).

7. Texas suggests that Johnson's conviction did not depend on the onlookers' reaction to the flag burning, because § 42.09 is violated only when a person physically mistreats the flag in a way that he "knows will seriously offend one or more persons likely to observe or discover his action." Tex.Penal Code Ann. § 42.09(b) (1969) (emphasis added). "The 'serious offense' language of the statute," Texas argues, "refers to an individual's intent and to the manner in which the conduct is effectuated, not to the reaction of the crowd." Brief for Petitioner 44. If the statute were aimed only at the actor's intent, and not at the communicative impact of his actions, however, there would be little reason for the law to be triggered only when an audience is "likely" to be present. At Johnson's trial, indeed, the State itself seems not to have seen the distinction between

knowledge and actual communicative impact that it now stresses: it proved the element of knowledge by offering the testimony of persons who had in fact been seriously offended by Johnson's conduct. Id. at 6-7. In any event, we find the distinction between Texas' statute and one dependent on actual audience reaction too precious to be of constitutional significance. Both kinds of statutes clearly are aimed at protecting onlookers from being offended by the ideas expressed by the prohibited activity.

8. Our inquiry is, of course, bounded by the particular facts of this case and by the statute under which Johnson was convicted. There was no evidence that Johnson himself stole the flag he burned, Tr. of Oral Arg. 17, nor did the prosecution or the arguments urged in support of it depend on the theory that the flag was stolen. Ibid. Thus, our analysis does not rely on the way in which the flag was acquired, and nothing in our opinion should be taken to suggest that one is free to steal a flag so long as one later uses it to communicate an idea. We also emphasize that Johnson was prosecuted only for flag desecration -- not for trespass, disorderly conduct, or arson.

9. Texas claims that "Texas is not endorsing, protecting, avowing or prohibiting any particular philosophy." Brief for Petitioner 29. If Texas means to suggest that its asserted interest does not prefer Democrats over Socialists, or Republicans over Democrats, for example, then it is beside the point, for Johnson does not rely on such an argument. He argues instead that the State's desire to maintain the flag as a symbol of nationhood and national unity assumes that there is only one proper view of the flag. Thus, if Texas means to argue that its interest does not prefer any viewpoint over another, it is mistaken; surely one's attitude toward the flag and its referents is a viewpoint.

10. Our decision in Halter v. Nebraska, 205 U.S. 34 (1907), addressing the validity of a state law prohibiting certain commercial uses of the flag, is not to the contrary. That case was decided "nearly 20 years before the Court concluded that the First Amendment applies to the States by virtue of the Fourteenth Amendment." Spence v. Washington, 418 U.S. 405, 413, n. 7 (1974). More important, as we continually emphasized in Halter itself, that case involved purely commercial, rather than political, speech. 205 U.S. at 38, 41, 42, 45.

Nor does San Francisco Arts & Athletics, Inc. v. United States Olympic Committee, 483 U.S. 522, 524 (1987), addressing the validity of Congress' decision to "authoriz[e] the United States Olympic Committee to prohibit certain commercial and promotional uses of the word 'Olympic,'" relied upon by THE CHIEF JUSTICE's dissent, post at 429, even begin to tell us whether the government may criminally punish physical conduct towards the flag engaged in as a means of political protest.

11. THE CHIEF JUSTICE's dissent appears to believe that Johnson's conduct may be prohibited and, indeed, criminally sanctioned, because "his act . . . conveyed nothing that could not have been conveyed and was not conveyed just as forcefully in a dozen different ways." Post at 431. Not only does this assertion sit uneasily next to the dissent's quite correct reminder that the flag occupies a unique position in our society -- which demonstrates that messages conveyed without use of the flag are not "just as forcefu[l]"

as those conveyed with it -- but it also ignores the fact that, in Spence, supra, we "rejected summarily" this very claim. See 418 U.S. at 411, n. 4.

## Florida Star v. B.J.F. (June 21, 1989)

JUSTICE MARSHALL delivered the opinion of the Court.

Florida Stat. § 794.03 (1987) makes it unlawful to "print, publish, or broadcast . . . in any instrument of mass communication" the name of the victim of a sexual offense. [1] Pursuant to this statute, appellant The Florida Star was found civilly liable for publishing the name of a rape victim which it had obtained from a publicly released police report. The issue presented here is whether this result comports with the First Amendment. We hold that it does not.

I

The Florida Star is a weekly newspaper which serves the community of Jacksonville, Florida, and which has an average circulation of approximately 18,000 copies. A regular feature of the newspaper is its "Police Reports" section.

That section, typically two to three pages in length, contains brief articles describing local criminal incidents under police investigation.

On October 20, 1983, appellee B.J.F. [2] reported to the Duval County, Florida, Sheriff's Department (the Department) that she had been robbed and sexually assaulted by an unknown assailant. The Department prepared a report on the incident which identified B.J.F. by her full name. The Department then placed the report in its pressroom. The Department does not restrict access either to the pressroom or to the reports made available therein.

A Florida Star reporter-trainee sent to the pressroom copied the police report verbatim, including B.J.F.'s full name, on a blank duplicate of the Department's forms. A Florida Star reporter then prepared a one-paragraph article about the crime, derived entirely from the trainee's copy of the police report. The article included B.J.F.'s full name. It appeared in the "Robberies" subsection of the "Police Reports" section on October 29, 1983, one of fifty-four police blotter stories in that day's edition. The article read:

"[B.J.F.] reported on Thursday, October 20, she was crossing Brentwood Park, which is in the 500 block of Golfair Boulevard, enroute to her bus stop, when an unknown black man ran up behind the lady and placed a knife to her neck and told her not to yell. The suspect then undressed the lady and had sexual intercourse with her before fleeing the scene with her 60 cents, Timex watch and gold necklace. Patrol efforts have been suspended concerning this incident because of a lack of evidence.

In printing B.J.F.'s full name, The Florida Star violated its internal policy of not publishing the names of sexual offense victims."

On September 26, 1984, B.J.F. filed suit in the Circuit Court of Duval County against the Department and The Florida Star, alleging that these parties negligently violated § 794.03. See n 1, supra. Before trial, the Department settled with B.J.F. for $2,500. The Florida Star moved to dismiss, claiming, inter alia, that imposing civil sanctions on the newspaper pursuant to § 794.03 violated the First Amendment. The trial judge rejected the motion. App. 4.

At the ensuing day-long trial, B.J.F. testified that she had suffered emotional distress from the publication of her name. She stated that she had heard about the article from fellow workers and acquaintances; that her mother had received several threatening phone calls from a man who stated that he would rape B.J.F. again; and that these events had forced B.J.F. to change her phone number and residence, to seek police protection, and to obtain mental health counseling. In defense, The Florida Star put forth evidence indicating that the newspaper had learned B.J.F.'s name from the incident report released by the Department, and that the newspaper's violation of its internal rule against publishing the names of sexual offense victims was inadvertent.

At the close of B.J.F.'s case, and again at the close of its defense, The Florida Star moved for a directed verdict. On both occasions, the trial judge denied these motions. He ruled from the bench that § 794.03 was constitutional because it reflected a proper balance between the First Amendment and privacy rights, as it applied only to a narrow set of "rather sensitive . . . criminal offenses." App. 18-19 (rejecting first motion); see id. at 32-33 (rejecting second motion). At the close of the newspaper's defense, the judge granted B.J.F.'s motion for a directed verdict on the issue of negligence, finding the newspaper per se negligent based upon its violation of § 794.03. Id. at 33. This ruling left the jury to consider only the questions of causation and damages. The judge instructed the jury that it could award B.J.F. punitive damages if it found that the newspaper had "acted with reckless indifference to the rights of others." Id. at 35. The jury awarded B.J.F. $75,000 in compensatory damages and $25,000 in punitive damages. Against the actual damages award, the judge set off B.J.F.'s settlement with the Department.

The First District Court of Appeal affirmed in a three-paragraph per curiam opinion. 499 So.2d 883 (1986). In the paragraph devoted to The Florida Star's First Amendment claim, the court stated that the directed verdict for B.J.F. had been properly entered because, under § 794.03, a rape victim's name is "of a private nature and not to be published as a matter of law." Id. at 884, citing Doe v. Sarasota-Bradenton Florida Television Co., 436 So.2d 328, 330 (Fla.App.1983) (footnote omitted). [3] The Supreme Court of Florida denied discretionary review.

The Florida Star appealed to this Court. [4] We noted probable jurisdiction, 488 U.S. 887 (1988), and now reverse.

II

The tension between the right which the First Amendment accords to a free press, on the one hand, and the protections which various statutes and common law doctrines accord to personal privacy against the publication of truthful information, on the other, is a subject we have addressed several times in recent years. Our decisions in cases involving government attempts to sanction the accurate dissemination of information as invasive of privacy have not, however, exhaustively considered this conflict. On the contrary, although our decisions have without exception upheld the press' right to publish, we have emphasized each time that we were resolving this conflict only as it arose in a discrete factual context. [5]

The parties to this case frame their contentions in light of a trilogy of cases which have presented, in different contexts, the conflict between truthful reporting and state-protected privacy interests. In Cox Broadcasting Corp. v. Cohn, 420 U. S. 469 (1975), we found unconstitutional a civil damages award entered against a television station for broadcasting the name of a rape-murder victim which the station had obtained from courthouse records. In Oklahoma Publishing Co. v. Oklahoma County District Court, 430 U. S. 308 (1977), we found unconstitutional a state court's pretrial order enjoining the media from publishing the name or photograph of an 11-year-old boy in connection with a juvenile proceeding involving that child which reporters had attended. Finally, in Smith v. Daily Mail Publishing Co., 443 U. S. 97 (1979), we found unconstitutional the indictment of two newspapers for violating a state statute forbidding newspapers to publish, without written approval of the juvenile court, the name of any youth charged as a juvenile offender. The papers had learned about a shooting by monitoring a police band radio frequency, and had obtained the name of the alleged juvenile assailant from witnesses, the police, and a local prosecutor.

Appellant takes the position that this case is indistinguishable from Cox Broadcasting. Brief for Appellant 8. Alternatively, it urges that our decisions in the above trilogy, and in other cases in which we have held that the right of the press to publish truth overcame asserted interests other than personal privacy, [6] can be distilled to yield a broader First Amendment principle that the press may never be punished, civilly or criminally, for publishing the truth. Id. at 19. Appellee counters that the privacy trilogy is inapposite, because in each case the private information already appeared on a "public record," Brief for Appellee 12, 24, 25, and because the privacy interests at stake were far less profound than in the present case. See, e.g., id. at 34. In the alternative, appellee urges that Cox Broadcasting be overruled and replaced with a categorical rule that publication of the name of a rape victim never enjoys constitutional protection. Tr. of Oral Arg. 44.

We conclude that imposing damages on appellant for publishing B.J.F.'s name violates the First Amendment, although not for either of the reasons appellant urges. Despite the strong resemblance this case bears to Cox Broadcasting, that case cannot fairly be read as controlling here. The name of the rape victim in that case was obtained from courthouse records that were open to public inspection, a fact which JUSTICE WHITE'S opinion for the Court repeatedly noted. 420 U.S. at 420 U. S. 492 (noting "special protected nature of accurate reports of judicial proceedings") (emphasis added); see also id. at 420 U. S. 493, 420 U. S. 496. Significantly, one of the reasons we gave in Cox Broadcasting for invalidating the challenged damages award was the important role the press plays in subjecting trials to public scrutiny and thereby helping guarantee their fairness. Id. at 420 U. S. 492-493. [7] That role is not directly compromised where, as here, the information in question comes from a police report prepared and disseminated at a time at which not only had no adversarial criminal proceedings begun, but no suspect had been identified.

Nor need we accept appellant's invitation to hold broadly that truthful publication may never be punished consistent with the First Amendment. Our cases have carefully eschewed reaching this ultimate question, mindful that the future may bring scenarios which prudence counsels our not resolving anticipatorily. See, e.g., Near v. Minnesota ex rel. Olson, 283 U. S. 697, 283 U. S. 716 (1931) (hypothesizing "publication of the sailing dates of transports or the number and location of troops"); see also Garrison v. Louisiana, 379 U. S. 64, 379 U. S. 72, n. 8, 379 U. S. 74 (1964) (endorsing absolute defense of truth "where discussion of public affairs is concerned," but leaving unsettled the constitutional implications of truthfulness "in the discrete area of purely private libels"); Landmark Communications, Inc. v. Virginia, 435 U. S. 829, 435 U. S. 838 (1978); Time, Inc. v. Hill, 385 U. S. 374, 385 U. S. 383, n. 7 (1967). Indeed, in Cox Broadcasting, we pointedly refused to answer even the less sweeping question "whether truthful publications may ever be subjected to civil or criminal liability" for invading "an area of privacy" defined by the State. 420 U.S. at 420 U. S. 491. Respecting the fact that press freedom and privacy rights are both "plainly rooted in the traditions and significant concerns of our society," we instead focused on the less sweeping issue

"whether the State may impose sanctions on the accurate publication of the name of a rape victim obtained from public records -- more specifically, from judicial records which are maintained in connection with a public prosecution and which themselves are open to public inspection."

Ibid. We continue to believe that the sensitivity and significance of the interests presented in clashes between First Amendment and privacy rights counsel relying on limited principles that sweep no more broadly than the appropriate context of the instant case.

In our view, this case is appropriately analyzed with reference to such a limited First Amendment principle. It is the one, in fact, which we articulated in Daily Mail in our synthesis of prior cases involving attempts to punish truthful publication:

"[I]f a newspaper lawfully obtains truthful information about a matter of public significance, then state officials may not constitutionally punish publication of the information, absent a need to further a state interest of the highest order."

443 U.S. at 443 U. S. 103. According the press the ample protection provided by that principle is supported by at least three separate considerations, in addition to, of course, the overarching "public interest, secured by the Constitution, in the dissemination of truth.'" Cox Broadcasting, supra, at 420 U. S. 491, quoting Garrison, supra, at 379 U. S. 73 (footnote omitted). The cases on which the Daily Mail synthesis relied demonstrate these considerations.

First, because the Daily Mail formulation only protects the publication of information which a newspaper has "lawfully obtain[ed]," 443 U.S. at 443 U. S. 103, the government retains ample means of safeguarding significant interests upon which publication may impinge, including protecting a rape victim's anonymity. To the extent sensitive information rests in private hands, the government may under some circumstances forbid its nonconsensual acquisition, thereby bringing outside of the Daily Mail principle the publication of any information so acquired. To the extent sensitive information is in the government's custody, it has even greater power to forestall or mitigate the injury caused by its release. The government may classify certain information, establish and enforce procedures ensuring its redacted release, and extend a damages remedy against the government or its officials where the government's mishandling of sensitive information leads to its dissemination. Where information is entrusted to the government, a less drastic means than punishing truthful publication almost always exists for guarding against the dissemination of private facts. See, e.g., Landmark Communications, supra, at 435 U. S. 845 ("[M]uch of the risk [from disclosure of sensitive information regarding judicial disciplinary proceedings] can be eliminated through careful internal procedures to protect the confidentiality of Commission proceedings"); Oklahoma Publishing, 430 U.S. at 430 U. S. 311 (noting trial judge's failure to avail himself of the opportunity, provided by a state statute, to close juvenile hearing to the public, including members of the press, who later broadcast juvenile defendant's name); Cox Broadcasting, supra, at 420 U. S. 496 ("If there are privacy interests to be protected in judicial proceedings, the States must respond by means which avoid public documentation or other exposure of private information"). [8]

A second consideration undergirding the Daily Mail principle is the fact that punishing the press for its dissemination of information which is already publicly available is relatively unlikely to advance the interests in the service of which the State seeks to act. It is not, of course, always the case that information lawfully acquired by the press is known, or accessible, to others. But where the government has made certain information publicly available, it is highly anomalous to sanction persons other than the source of its release. We noted this anomaly in Cox Broadcasting:

"By placing the information in the public domain on official court records, the State must be presumed to have concluded that the public interest was thereby being served."

420 U.S. at 420 U. S. 495. The Daily Mail formulation reflects the fact that it is a limited set of cases indeed where, despite the accessibility of the public to certain information, a meaningful public interest is served by restricting its further release by other entities, like the press. As Daily Mail observed in its summary of Oklahoma Publishing,

"once the truthful information was 'publicly revealed' or 'in the public domain,' the court could not constitutionally restrain its dissemination."

443 U.S. at 443 U. S. 103.

A third and final consideration is the "timidity and self-censorship" which may result from allowing the media to be punished for publishing certain truthful information. Cox Broadcasting, supra, at 420 U. S. 496. Cox Broadcasting noted this concern with overdeterrence in the context of information made public through official court records, but the fear of excessive media self-suppression is applicable as well to other information released, without qualification, by the government. A contrary rule, depriving protection to those who rely on the government's implied representations of the lawfulness of dissemination, would force upon the media the onerous obligation of sifting through government press releases, reports, and pronouncements to prune out material arguably unlawful for publication. This situation could inhere even where the newspaper's sole object was to reproduce, with no substantial change, the government's rendition of the event in question.

Applied to the instant case, the Daily Mail principle clearly commands reversal. The first inquiry is whether the newspaper "lawfully obtain[ed] truthful information about a matter of public significance." 443 U.S. at 443 U. S. 103. It is undisputed that the news article describing the assault on B.J.F. was accurate. In addition, appellant lawfully obtained B.J.F.'s name. Appellee's argument to the contrary is based on the fact that under Florida law, police reports which reveal the identity of the victim of a sexual offense are not among the matters of "public record" which the public, by law, is entitled to inspect. Brief for Appellee 17-18, citing Fla.Stat. § 119.07(3)(h) (1983). But the fact that state officials are not required to disclose such reports does not make it unlawful for a newspaper to receive them when furnished by the government. Nor does the fact that the Department apparently failed to fulfill its obligation under § 794.03 not to "cause or allow to be . . . published" the name of a sexual offense victim make the newspaper's ensuing receipt of this information unlawful. Even assuming the Constitution permitted a State to proscribe receipt of information, Florida has not taken this step. It is, clear, furthermore, that the news article concerned "a matter of public significance," 443 U.S. at 443 U. S. 103, in the sense in which the Daily Mail synthesis of prior cases used that term. That is, the article generally, as opposed to the specific identity contained within it, involved a matter of paramount public import: the commission, and investigation, of a violent crime which had been reported to authorities. See Cox Broadcasting, supra, (article identifying victim of rape-murder); Oklahoma Publishing Co. v. Oklahoma County District Court, 430 U. S. 308 (1977) (article identifying juvenile alleged to have committed murder); Daily Mail, supra, (same); cf. Landmark Communications, Inc. v. Virginia, 435 U.S. 435 U. S. 829 (1978) (article identifying judges whose conduct was being investigated).

The second inquiry is whether imposing liability on appellant pursuant to § 794.03 serves "a need to further a state interest of the highest order." Daily Mail, 443 U.S. at 443 U. S. 103. Appellee argues that a rule punishing publication furthers three closely related interests: the privacy of victims of sexual offenses; the physical safety of such victims, who may be targeted for retaliation if their names become known to their assailants; and the goal of encouraging victims of such crimes to report these offenses without fear of exposure. Brief for Appellee 29-30.

At a time in which we are daily reminded of the tragic reality of rape, it is undeniable that these are highly significant interests, a fact underscored by the Florida Legislature's explicit attempt to protect these interests by enacting a criminal statute prohibiting much dissemination of victim identities. We accordingly do not rule out the possibility that, in a proper case, imposing civil sanctions for publication of the name of a rape victim might be so overwhelmingly necessary to advance these interests as to satisfy the Daily Mail standard. For three independent reasons, however, imposing liability for publication under the circumstances of this case is too precipitous a means of advancing these interests to convince us that there is a "need" within the meaning of the Daily Mail formulation for Florida to take this extreme step. Cf. Landmark Communications, supra, (invalidating penalty on publication despite State's expressed interest in nondissemination, reflected in statute prohibiting unauthorized divulging of names of judges under investigation).

First is the manner in which appellant obtained the identifying information in question. As we have noted, where the government itself provides information to the media, it is most appropriate to assume that the government had, but failed to utilize, far more limited means of guarding against dissemination than the extreme step of punishing truthful speech. That assumption is richly borne out in this case. B.J.F.'s identity would never have come to light were it not for the erroneous, if inadvertent, inclusion by the Department of her full name in an incident report made available in a pressroom open to the public. Florida's policy against disclosure of rape victims' identities, reflected in § 794.03, was undercut by the Department's failure to abide by this policy. Where, as here, the government has failed to police itself in disseminating information, it is clear under Cox Broadcasting, Oklahoma Publishing, and Landmark Communications that the imposition of damages against the press for its subsequent publication can hardly be said to be a narrowly tailored means of safeguarding anonymity. See supra at 491 U. S. 534-535. Once the government has placed such information in the public domain, "reliance must rest upon the judgment of those who decide what to publish or broadcast," Cox Broadcasting, 420 U.S. at 420 U. S. 496, and hopes for restitution must rest upon the willingness of the government to compensate victims for their loss of privacy and to protect them from the other consequences of its mishandling of the information which these victims provided in confidence.

That appellant gained access to the information in question through a government news release makes it especially likely that, if liability were to be imposed, self-censorship would result. Reliance on a news release "is a paradigmatically routine newspaper reporting techniqu[e]." Daily Mail, 443 U.S. at 443 U. S. 103. The government's issuance of such a release, without qualification, can only convey to recipients that the government considered dissemination lawful, and indeed expected the recipients to disseminate the information further. Had appellant merely reproduced the news release prepared and released by the Department, imposing civil damages would surely violate the First Amendment. The fact that appellant converted the police report into a news story by adding the linguistic connecting tissue necessary to transform the report's facts into full sentences cannot change this result.

A second problem with Florida's imposition of liability for publication is the broad sweep of the negligence per se standard applied under the civil cause of action implied from § 794.03. Unlike claims based on the common law tort of invasion of privacy, see Restatement (Second) of Torts § 652D (1977), civil actions based on § 794.03 require no case-by-case findings that the disclosure of a fact about a person's private life was one that a reasonable person would find highly offensive. On the contrary, under the per se theory of negligence adopted by the courts below, liability follows automatically from publication. This is so regardless of whether the identity of the victim is already known throughout the community; whether the victim has voluntarily called public attention to the offense; or whether the identity of the victim has otherwise become a reasonable subject of public concern -- because, perhaps, questions have arisen whether the victim fabricated an assault by a particular person. Nor is there a scienter requirement of any kind under § 794.03, engendering the perverse result that truthful publications challenged pursuant to this cause of action are less protected by the First Amendment than even the least protected defamatory falsehoods: those involving purely private figures, where liability is evaluated under a standard, usually applied by a jury, of ordinary negligence. See Gertz v Robert Welch, Inc., 418 U. S. 323 (1974). We have previously noted the impermissibility of categorical prohibitions upon media access where important First Amendment interests are at stake. See Globe Newspaper Co. v. Superior Court of Norfolk County, 457 U. S. 596, 457 U. S. 608 (1982) (invalidating state statute providing for the categorical exclusion of the public from trials of sexual offenses involving juvenile victims). More individualized adjudication is no less indispensable where the State, seeking to safeguard the anonymity of crime victims, sets its face against publication of their names.

Third, and finally, the facial underinclusiveness of § 794.03 raises serious doubts about whether Florida is, in fact, serving, with this statute, the significant interests which appellee invokes in support of affirmance. Section 794.03 prohibits the publication of identifying information only if this information appears in an "instrument of mass communication," a term the statute does not define. Section 794.03 does not prohibit the spread by other means of the identities of victims of sexual offenses. An individual who maliciously spreads word of the identity of a rape victim is thus not covered, despite the fact that the communication of such information to persons who live near, or work with, the victim may have consequences as devastating as the exposure of her name to large numbers of strangers. See Tr. of Oral Arg. 49-50 (appellee acknowledges that § 794.03 would not apply to "the backyard gossip who tells 50 people that don't have to know").

When a State attempts the extraordinary measure of punishing truthful publication in the name of privacy, it must demonstrate its commitment to advancing this interest by applying its prohibition evenhandedly, to the small-time disseminator as well as the media giant. Where important First Amendment interests are at stake, the mass scope of disclosure is not an acceptable surrogate for injury. A ban on disclosures effected by "instrument[s] of mass communication" simply cannot be defended on the ground that partial prohibitions may effect partial relief. See Daily Mail, 443 U.S. at 443 U. S. 104-105 (statute is insufficiently tailored to interest in protecting anonymity where it restricted only newspapers, not the electronic media or other forms of publication, from identifying juvenile defendants); id. at 443 U. S. 110 (REHNQUIST, J., concurring in judgment) (same); cf. Arkansas Writers' Project, Inc. v. Ragland, 481 U. S. 221, 481 U. S. 229 (1987); Minneapolis Star & Tribune Co. v. Minnesota Comm'r of Revenue, 460 U. S. 575, 460 U. S. 585 (1983). Without more careful and inclusive precautions against alternative forms of dissemination, we cannot conclude that Florida's selective ban on publication by the mass media satisfactorily accomplishes its stated purpose. [9]

III

Our holding today is limited. We do not hold that truthful publication is automatically constitutionally protected, or that there is no zone of personal privacy within which the State may protect the individual from intrusion by the press, or even that a State may never punish publication of the name of a victim of a sexual offense. We hold only that, where a newspaper publishes truthful information which it has lawfully obtained, punishment may lawfully be imposed, if at all, only when narrowly tailored to a state interest of the highest order, and that no such interest is satisfactorily served by imposing liability under § 794.03 to appellant under the facts of this case. The decision below is therefore

Reversed.

Notes

[1] The statute provides in its entirety:

"Unlawful to publish or broadcast information identifying sexual offense victim. -- No person shall print, publish, or broadcast, or cause or allow to be printed, published, or broadcast, in any instalment of mass communication the name, address, or other identifying fact or information of the victim of any sexual offense within this chapter. An offense under this section shall constitute a misdemeanor of the second degree, punishable as provided in § 775.082, § 775.083, or § 775.084."

Fla.Stat. § 794.03 (1987).

[2] In filing this lawsuit, appellee used her full name in the caption of the case. On appeal, the Florida District Court of Appeal sua sponte revised the caption, stating that it would refer to the appellee by her initials, "in order to preserve [her] privacy interests." 499 So.2d 883, 883, n. (1986). Respecting those interests, we, too, refer to appellee by her initials, both in the caption and in our discussion.

[3] In Doe v. Sarasota-Bradenton Florida Television Co., 436 So.2d at 329, the Second District Court of Appeal upheld the dismissal on First Amendment grounds of a rape victim's damage claim against a Florida television station which had broadcast portions of her testimony at her assailant's trial. The court reasoned that, as in Cox

Broadcasting Corp. v. Cohn, 420 U. S. 469 (1975), the information in question "was readily available to the public, through the vehicle of a public trial." 436 So.2d at 330. The court stated, however, that § 794.03 could constitutionally be applied to punish publication of a sexual offense victim's name or other identifying information where it had not yet become "part of an open public record" by virtue of being revealed in "open, public judicial proceedings." Ibid., citing Fla.Op.Atty.Gen. 075-203 (1975).

[4] Before noting probable jurisdiction, we certified to the Florida Supreme Court the question whether it had possessed jurisdiction when it declined to hear the newspaper's case. 484 U.S. 984 (1987). The State Supreme Court answered in the affirmative. 530 So.2d 286, 287 (1988).

[5] The somewhat uncharted state of the law in this area thus contrasts markedly with the well mapped area of defamatory falsehoods, where a long line of decisions has produced relatively detailed legal standards governing the multifarious situations in which individuals aggrieved by the dissemination of damaging untruths seek redress. See, e.g., New York Times Co. v. Sullivan, 376 U. S. 254 (1964); Garrison v. Louisiana, 379 U. S. 64 (1964); Henry v. Collins, 380 U. S. 356 (1965); Rosenblatt v. Baer, 383 U. S. 75 (1966); Time, Inc. v. Hill, 385 U. S. 374 (1967); Greenbelt Cooperative Publishing Assn., Inc. v. Bresler, 398 U. S. 6 (1970); Monitor Patriot Co. v. Roy, 401 U. S. 265 (1971); Time, Inc. v. Pape, 401 U. S. 279 (1971); Rosenbloom v. Metromedia, Inc., 403 U. S. 29 (1971); Gertz v. Robert Welch, Inc., 418 U. S. 323 (1974); Herbert v. Lando, 441 U. S. 153 (1979); Hutchinson v. Proxmire, 443 U. S. 111 (1979); Dun & Bradstreet, Inc. v. Greenmoss Builders, Inc., 472 U. S. 749 (1985); Philadelphia Newspapers, Inc. v. Hepps, 475 U. S. 767 (1986); Anderson v. Liberty Lobby, Inc., 477 U. S. 242 (1986).

[6] See, e.g., Landmark Communications, Inc. v. Virginia, 435 U. S. 829 (1978) (interest in confidentiality of judicial disciplinary proceedings); Bates v. State Bar of Arizona, 433 U. S. 350 (1977) (interest in maintaining professionalism of attorneys); Nebraska Press Assn. v. Stuart, 427 U. S. 539 (1976) (interest in accused's right to fair trial); Virginia Pharmacy Bd. v. Virginia Citizens Consumer Council, Inc., 425 U. S. 748 (1976) (interest in maintaining professionalism of licensed pharmacists); New York Times Co. v. United States, 403 U. S. 713 (1971) (interest in national security); Garrison, supra, (interest in public figure's reputation).

[7] We also recognized that privacy interests fade once information already appears on the public record, 420 U.S. at 420 U. S. 494-495, and that making public records generally available to the media while allowing their publication to be punished if offensive would invite "self-censorship and very likely lead to the suppression of many items that . . . should be made available to the public." Id. at 420 U. S. 496.

[8] The Daily Mail principle does not settle the issue whether, in cases where information has been acquired unlawfully by a newspaper or by a source, government may ever punish not only the unlawful acquisition, but the ensuing publication as well. This issue was raised, but not definitively resolved, in New York Times Co. v. United States, 403 U. S. 713 (1971), and reserved in Landmark Communications, 435 U.S. at 435

U. S. 837. We have no occasion to address it here.

[9] Having concluded that imposing liability on appellant pursuant to § 794.03 violates the First Amendment, we have no occasion to address appellant's subsidiary arguments that the imposition of punitive damages for publication independently violated the First Amendment, or that § 794.03 functions as an impermissible prior restraint. See Smith v. Daily Mail Publishing Co., 443 U. S. 97, 443 U. S. 101-102 (1979).

## Sable Communications of California v. FCC (June 23, 1989)

JUSTICE WHITE delivered the opinion of the Court.

The issue before us is the constitutionality of § 223(b) of the Communications Act of 1934. 47 U.S.C. § 223(b). The statute, as amended in 1988, imposes an outright ban on indecent as well as obscene interstate commercial telephone messages. The District Court upheld the prohibition against obscene interstate telephone communications for commercial purposes, but enjoined the enforcement of the statute insofar as it applied to indecent messages. We affirm the District Court in both respects.

I

In 1983, Sable Communications, Inc., a Los Angeles-based affiliate of Carlin Communications, Inc., began offering sexually oriented prerecorded telephone messages [1] (popularly known as "dial-a-porn") through the Pacific Bell telephone network. In order to provide the messages, Sable arranged with Pacific Bell to use special telephone lines, designed to handle large volumes of calls simultaneously. Those who called the adult message number were charged a special fee. The fee was collected by Pacific Bell and divided between the phone company and the message provider. Callers outside the Los Angeles metropolitan area could reach the number by means of a long-distance toll call to the Los Angeles area code.

In 1988, Sable brought suit in District Court seeking declaratory and injunctive relief against enforcement of the recently amended § 223(b). The 1988 amendments to the statute imposed a blanket prohibition on indecent as well as obscene interstate commercial telephone messages. Sable brought this action to enjoin the FCC and the Justice Department from initiating any criminal investigation or prosecution, civil action or administrative proceeding under the statute. Sable also sought a declaratory judgment, challenging the indecency and the obscenity provisions of the amended § 223(b) as unconstitutional, chiefly under the First and Fourteenth Amendments to the Constitution.

The District Court found that a concrete controversy existed, and that Sable met the irreparable injury requirement for issuance of a preliminary injunction under Elrod v. Burns, 427 U. S. 347, 427 U. S. 373 (1976). 692 F.Supp. 1208, 1209 (CD Cal.1988). The District Court denied Sable's request for a preliminary injunction against enforcement of the statute's ban on obscene telephone messages, rejecting the argument that the statute was unconstitutional because it created a national standard of obscenity. The District

Court, however, struck down the "indecent speech" provision of § 223(b), holding that, in this respect, the statute was overbroad and unconstitutional, and that this result was consistent with FCC v. Pacifica Foundation, 438 U. S. 726 (1978).

"While the government unquestionably has a legitimate interest in, e.g., protecting children from exposure to indecent dial-a-porn messages, § 223(b) is not narrowly drawn to achieve any such purpose. Its flat-out ban of indecent speech is contrary to the First Amendment."

692 F.Supp. at 1209. Therefore, the Court issued a preliminary injunction prohibiting enforcement of § 223(b) with respect to any communication alleged to be "indecent."

We noted probable jurisdiction on Sable's appeal of the obscenity ruling (No. 88-515); we also noted probable jurisdiction on the federal parties' cross-appeal of the preliminary injunction holding the statute unconstitutional with respect to its ban on indecent speech (No. 88-525). 488 U.S. 1003 (1989). [2]

II

While dial-a-porn services are a creature of this decade, the medium, in its brief history, has been the subject of much litigation and the object of a series of attempts at regulation. [3]

The first litigation involving dial-a-porn was brought under 82 Stat. 112, 47 U.S.C. § 223, which proscribed knowingly "permitting a telephone under [one's] control" to be used to make "any comment, request, suggestion or proposal which is obscene, lewd, lascivious, filthy, or indecent." However, the FCC concluded in an administrative action that the existing law did not cover dial-a-porn. In re Application for Review of Complaint Filed by Peter F. Cohalan, FCC File No. E-83-14 (memorandum opinions and orders adopted May 13, 1983).

In reaction to that FCC determination, Congress made its first effort explicitly to address "dial-a-porn" when it added a subsection 223(b) to the 1934 Communications Act. The provision, which was the predecessor to the amendment at issue in this case, pertained directly to sexually oriented commercial telephone messages, and sought to restrict the access of minors to dial-a-porn. The relevant provision of the Act, Federal Communications Commission Authorization Act of 1983, Pub. L. 98-214, § 8(b), 97 Stat. 1470, made it a crime to use telephone facilities to make "obscene or indecent" interstate telephone communications "for commercial purposes to any person under eighteen years of age or to any other person without that person's consent." 47 U.S.C. § 223(b)(1) (A) (1982 ed., Supp. IV). The statute criminalized commercial transmission of sexually oriented communications to minors, and required the FCC to promulgate regulations laying out the means by which dial-a-porn sponsors could screen out underaged callers. § 223(b)(2). The enactment provided that it would be a defense to prosecution that the defendant restricted access to adults only, in accordance with procedures established by the FCC. The statute did not criminalize sexually oriented messages to adults, whether the messages were obscene or indecent.

The FCC initially promulgated regulations that would have established a defense to message providers operating only between the hours of 9 p.m. and 8 a.m. Eastern Time (time channeling) and to providers requiring payment by credit card (screening) before transmission of the dial-a-porn message. Restrictions on Obscene or Indecent Telephone Message Services, 47 CFR § 64.201 (1988). In Carlin Communications, Inc. v. FCC, 749 F.2d 113 (CA2 1984) (Carlin I), the Court of Appeals for the Second Circuit set aside the time channeling regulations and remanded to the FCC to examine other alternatives, concluding that the operating hours requirement was "both overinclusive and underinclusive" because it denied "access to adults between certain hours, but not to youths who can easily pick up a private or public telephone and call dial-a-porn during the remaining hours." Id. at 121. The Court of Appeals did not reach the constitutionality of the underlying legislation.

In 1985, the FCC promulgated new regulations which continued to permit credit card payment as a defense to prosecution. Instead of time restrictions, however, the Commission added a defense based on use of access codes (user identification codes). Thus, it would be a defense to prosecution under § 223(b) if the defendant, before transmission of the message, restricted customer access by requiring either payment by credit card or authorization by access or identification code. 50 Fed.Reg. 42699, 42705 (1985). The regulations required each dial-a-porn vendor to develop an identification code data base and implementation scheme. Callers would be required to provide an access number for identification (or a credit card) before receiving the message. The access code would be received through the mail after the message provider reviewed the application and concluded, through a written age ascertainment procedure, that the applicant was at least 18 years of age. The FCC rejected a proposal for "exchange blocking" which would block or screen telephone numbers at the customer's premises or at the telephone company offices. In Carlin Communications, Inc. v. FCC, 787 F.2d 846 (CA2 1986) (Carlin II), the Court of Appeals set aside the new regulations because of the FCC's failure adequately to consider customer premises blocking. Again, the constitutionality of the underlying legislation was not addressed.

The FCC then promulgated a third set of regulations, which again rejected customer premises blocking, but added to the prior defenses of credit card payment and access code use a third defense: message scrambling. 52 Fed.Reg. 17760 (1987). Under this system, providers would scramble the message, which would then be unintelligible without the use of a descrambler, the sale of which would be limited to adults. On January 15, 1988, in Carlin Communications, Inc. v. FCC, 837 F.2d 546 (Carlin III), cert. denied, 488 U.S. 924 (1988), the Court of Appeals for the Second Circuit held that the new regulations, which made access codes, along with credit card payments and scrambled messages, defenses to prosecution under § 223(b) for dial-a-porn providers, were supported by the evidence, had been properly arrived at, and were a "feasible and effective way to serve" the "compelling state interest" in protecting minors, 837 F.2d at 555; but the Court directed the FCC to reopen proceedings if a less restrictive technology became available. The Court of Appeals, however, this time reaching the constitutionality of the statute, invalidated § 223(b) insofar as it sought to apply to nonobscene speech. Id. at 560, 561.

Thereafter, in April 1988, Congress amended § 223(b) of the Communications Act to prohibit indecent as well as obscene interstate commercial telephone communications directed to any person, regardless of age. The amended statute, which took effect on July 1, 1988, also eliminated the requirement that the FCC promulgate regulations for restricting access to minors, since a total ban was imposed on dial-a-porn, making it illegal for adults, as well as children, to have access to the sexually explicit messages, Pub. L. 100297, 102 Stat. 424. [4] It was this version of the statute that was in effect when Sable commenced this action. [5]

III

In the ruling at issue in No. 88-515, the District Court upheld § 223(b)'s prohibition of obscene telephone messages as constitutional. We agree with that judgment. In contrast to the prohibition on indecent communications, there is no constitutional barrier to the ban on obscene dial-a-porn recordings. We have repeatedly held that the protection of the First Amendment does not extend to obscene speech. See, e.g., Paris Adult Theatre I v. Slatorn, 413 U. S. 49, 413 U. S. 69 (1973). The cases before us today do not require us to decide what is obscene or what is indecent, but rather to determine whether Congress is empowered to prohibit transmission of obscene telephonic communications.

In its facial challenge to the statute, Sable argues that the legislation creates an impermissible national standard of obscenity, and that it places message senders in a "double bind" by compelling them to tailor all their messages to the least tolerant community. [6]

We do not read § 223(b) as contravening the "contemporary community standards" requirement of Miller v. California, 413 U. S. 15 (1973). Section 223(b) no more establishes a "national standard" of obscenity than do federal statutes prohibiting the mailing of obscene materials, 18 U.S.C. § 1461, see Hamling v. United States, 418 U. S. 87 (1974), or the broadcasting of obscene messages, 18 U.S.C. § 1464. In United States v. Reidel, 402 U. S. 351 (1971), we said that Congress could prohibit the use of the mails for commercial distribution of materials properly classifiable as obscene, even though those materials were being distributed to willing adults who stated that they were adults. Similarly, we hold today that there is no constitutional stricture against Congress' prohibiting the interstate transmission of obscene commercial telephone recordings.

We stated in United States v. 12 200-ft. Reels of Film, 413 U. S. 123 (1973), that the Miller standards, including the "contemporary community standards" formulation, apply to federal legislation. As we have said before, the fact that

"distributors of allegedly obscene materials may be subjected to varying community standards in the various federal judicial districts into which they transmit the materials does not render a federal statute unconstitutional because of the failure of application of uniform national standards of obscenity."

Hamling v. United States, supra, at 418 U. S. 106.

Furthermore, Sable is free to tailor its messages, on a selective basis, if it so chooses, to the communities it chooses to serve. While Sable may be forced to incur some costs in developing and implementing a system for screening the locale of incoming calls, there is no constitutional impediment to enacting a law which may impose such costs on a medium electing to provide these messages. Whether Sable chooses to hire operators to determine the source of the calls or engages with the telephone company to arrange for the screening and blocking of out-of-area calls or finds another means for providing messages compatible with community standards is a decision for the message provider to make. There is no constitutional barrier under Miller to prohibiting communications that are obscene in some communities under local standards, even though they are not obscene in others. If Sable's audience is comprised of different communities with different local standards, Sable ultimately bears the burden of complying with the prohibition on obscene messages.

IV

In No. 88-525, the District Court concluded that, while the Government has a legitimate interest in protecting children from exposure to indecent dial-a-porn messages, § 223(b) was not sufficiently narrowly drawn to serve that purpose, and thus violated the First Amendment. We agree.

Sexual expression which is indecent but not obscene is protected by the First Amendment; and the federal parties do not submit that the sale of such materials to adults could be criminalized solely because they are indecent. The Government may, however, regulate the content of constitutionally protected speech in order to promote a compelling interest if it chooses the least restrictive means to further the articulated interest. We have recognized that there is a compelling interest in protecting the physical and psychological wellbeing of minors. This interest extends to shielding minors from the influence of literature that is not obscene by adult standards. Ginsberg v. New York, 390 U. S. 629, 390 U. S. 639-640 (1968); New York v. Ferber, 458 U. S. 747, 458 U. S. 756-757 (1982). The Government may serve this legitimate interest, but, to withstand constitutional scrutiny,

"it must do so by narrowly drawn regulations designed to serve those interests without unnecessarily interfering with First Amendment freedoms. Hynes v. Mayor of Oradell, 425 U.S. at 425 U. S. 620; First National Ban.k of Boston v. Bellotti, 435 U. S. 765, 435 U. S. 786 (1978)."

Schaumburg v. Citizens for a Better Environment, 444 U. S. 620, 444 U. S. 637 (1980). It is not enough to show that the Government's ends are compelling; the means must be carefully tailored to achieve those ends.

In Butler v. Michigan, 352 U. S. 380 (1957), a unanimous Court reversed a conviction under a statute which made it an offense to make available to the general public materials found to have a potentially harmful influence on minors. The Court found the law to be insufficiently tailored, since it denied adults their free speech rights by allowing them to read only what was acceptable for children. As Justice Frankfurter said in that case, "Surely this is to burn the house to roast the pig." Id. at 352 U. S. 383. In our judgment, this case, like Butler, presents us with "legislation not reasonably restricted to the evil with which it is said to deal." Ibid.

In attempting to justify the complete ban and criminalization of the indecent commercial telephone communications with adults as well as minors, the federal parties rely on FCC v. Pacifica Foundation, 438 U. S. 726 (1978), a case in which the Court considered whether the FCC has the power to regulate a radio broadcast that is indecent but not obscene. In an emphatically narrow holding, the Pacifica Court concluded that special treatment of indecent broadcasting was justified.

Pacifica is readily distinguishable from this case, most obviously because it did not involve a total ban on broadcasting indecent material. The FCC rule was not

"'intended to place an absolute prohibition on the broadcast of this type of language, but rather sought to channel it to times of day when children most likely would not be exposed to it.'"

Pacifica, supra, at 438 U. S. 733, quoting Pacifica Foundation, 59 F.C.C.2d 892 (1976). The issue of a total ban was not before the Court. 438 U.S. at 438 U. S. 750, n. 28.

The Pacifica opinion also relied on the "unique" attributes of broadcasting, noting that broadcasting is "uniquely pervasive," can intrude on the privacy of the home without prior warning as to program content, and is "uniquely accessible to children, even those too young to read." Id. at 438 U. S. 748-749. The private commercial telephone communications at issue here are substantially different from the public radio broadcast at issue in Pacifica. In contrast to public displays, unsolicited mailings, and other means of expression which the recipient has no meaningful opportunity to avoid, the dial-it medium requires the listener to take affirmative steps to receive the communication. There is no "captive audience" problem here; callers will generally not be unwilling listeners. The context of dial-in services, where a caller seeks and is willing to pay for the communication, is manifestly different from a situation in which a listener does not want the received message. Placing a telephone call is not the same as turning on a radio and being taken by surprise by an indecent message. Unlike an unexpected outburst on a radio broadcast, the message received by one who places a call to a dial-a-porn service is not so invasive or surprising that it prevents an unwilling listener from avoiding exposure to it.

The Court in Pacifica was careful "to emphasize the narrowness of [its] holding." Id. at 438 U. S. 750. As we did in Bolger v. Youngs Drug Products Corp., 463 U. S. 60 (1983), we distinguish Pacifica from the cases before us and reiterate that "the government may not reduce the adult population . . . to . . . only what is fit for children.'" 463 U.S. at 463 U. S. 73, quoting Butler v. Michigan, supra, at 352 U. S. 383.

The federal parties nevertheless argue that the total ban on indecent commercial telephone communications is justified because nothing less could prevent children from gaining access to such messages. We find the argument quite unpersuasive. The FCC, after lengthy proceedings, determined that its credit card, access code, and scrambling rules were a satisfactory solution to the problem of keeping indecent dial-a-porn messages out of the reach of minors. The Court of Appeals, after careful consideration, agreed that these rules represented a "feasible and effective" way to serve the Government's compelling interest in protecting children. 837 F.2d at 555.

The federal parties now insist that the rules would not be effective enough -- that enterprising youngsters could and would evade the rules and gain access to communications from which they should be shielded. There is no evidence in the record before us to that effect, nor could there be, since the FCC's implementation of § 223(b) prior to its 1988 amendment has never been tested over time. In this respect, the federal parties assert that, in amending § 223(b) in 1988, Congress expressed its view that there was not a sufficiently effective way to protect minors short of the total ban that it enacted. The federal parties claim that we must give deference to that judgment.

To the extent that the federal parties suggest that we should defer to Congress' conclusion about an issue of constitutional law, our answer is that, while we do not ignore it, it is our task, in the end, to decide whether Congress has violated the Constitution. This is particularly true where the Legislature has concluded that its product does not violate the First Amendment. "Deference to a legislative finding cannot limit judicial inquiry when First Amendment rights are at stake." Landmark Communications, Inc. v. Virginia, 435 U. S. 829, 435 U. S. 843 (1978). The federal parties, however, also urge us to defer to the factual findings by Congress relevant to resolving the constitutional issue; they rely on Walters v. National Association of Radiation Survivors, 473 U. S. 305, 473 U. S. 331, n. 12 (1985), and Rostker v. Goldberg, 453 U. S. 57, 453 U. S. 72-73 (1981). Beyond the fact that whatever deference is due legislative findings would not foreclose our independent judgment of the facts bearing on an issue of constitutional law, our answer is that the congressional record contains no legislative findings that would justify us in concluding that there is no constitutionally acceptable less restrictive means, short of a total ban, to achieve the Government's interest in protecting minors.

There is no doubt Congress enacted a total ban on both obscene and indecent telephone communications. But aside from conclusory statements during the debates by proponents of the bill, [7] as well as similar assertions in hearings on a substantially identical bill the year before, H. R. 1786, [8] that under the FCC regulations minors could still have access to dial-a-porn messages, the congressional record presented to us contains no evidence as to how effective or ineffective the FCC's most recent regulations were or might prove to be. It may well be that there is no fail-safe method of guaranteeing that never will a minor be able to access the dial-a-porn system. The bill that was enacted, however, was introduced on the floor; nor was there a committee report on the bill from which the language of the enacted bill was taken. No Congressman or Senator purported to present a considered judgment with respect to how often or to what extent minors could or would circumvent the rules and have access to dial-a-porn messages. On the other hand, in the hearings on H.R. 1786, the Committee heard testimony from the FCC and other witnesses that the FCC rules would be effective, and should be tried out in practice. [9] Furthermore, at the conclusion of the hearing, the Chairman of the Subcommittee suggested consultation looking toward

"drafting a piece of legislation that will pass constitutional muster, while at the same time providing for the practical relief which families and groups are looking for."

Hearings at 235. The bill never emerged from Committee.

For all we know from this record, the FCC's technological approach to restricting dial-a-porn messages to adults who seek them would be extremely effective, and only a few of the most enterprising and disobedient young people would manage to secure access to such messages. [10] If this is the case, it seems to us that § 223(b) is not a narrowly tailored effort to serve the compelling interest of preventing minors from being exposed to indecent telephone messages. Under our precedents, § 223(b), in its present form, has the invalid effect of limiting the content of adult telephone conversations to that which is suitable for children to hear. It is another case of "burn[ing] up the house to roast the pig." Butler v. Michigan, 352 U.S. at 352 U. S. 383.

Because the statute's denial of adult access to telephone messages which are indecent but not obscene far exceeds that which is necessary to limit the access of minors to such messages, we hold that the ban does not survive constitutional scrutiny.

Accordingly, we affirm the judgment of the District Court in Nos. 88-515 and 88-525.

It is so ordered.

Notes

[1] A typical prerecorded message lasts anywhere from 30 seconds to two minutes, and may be called by up to 50,000 people hourly through a single telephone number. Comment, Telephones, Sex and the First Amendment, 33 UCLA L.Rev. 1221, 1223 (1986).

[2] Sable appealed the District Court ruling to the Court of Appeals for the Ninth Circuit, concurrently filing an emergency motion for an injunction pending appeal. The District Court entered an order temporarily enjoining the FCC from enforcing the statute during the pendency of the appeal. After the federal parties filed their notice of appeal to this Court from the District Court's grant of the preliminary injunction as to "indecent" communication, the Court of Appeals for the Ninth Circuit entered an order directing Sable either to file a motion for voluntary dismissal or to show cause why the appeal should not be dismissed for lack of jurisdiction. Sable filed an ex parte application to this Court for an injunction pending appeal, as well as a return on the Court of Appeals' order to show cause. The Court of Appeals entered an order dismissing the appeal, since the filing of a direct appeal by the FCC had the effect of transferring Sable's appeal to this Court.

[3] Dial-a-porn is big business. The dial-a-porn service in New York City alone

received six to seven million calls a month for the 6-month period ending in April, 1985. Carlin Communications, Inc. v. FCC, 787 F.2d 846, 848 (CA2 1986).

[4] "(b)(1) Whoever knowingly -- "

"(A) in the District of Columbia or in interstate .or foreign communication, by means of telephone, makes (directly or by recording device) any obscene or indecent communication for commercial purposes to any person, regardless of whether the maker of such communication placed the call; or"

"(B) permits any telephone facility under such person's control to be used for an activity prohibited by subparagraph (A),"

"shall be fined not more than $50,000 or imprisoned not more than six months, or both."

[5] After Sable and the federal parties filed their jurisdictional statements with this Court, but before we noted probable jurisdiction, § 223(b) was again revised by Congress in § 7524 of the Child Protection and Obscenity Enforcement Act of 1988, § 7524, 102 Stat. 4502, which was enacted as Title VII, Subtitle N, of the Anti-Drug Abuse Act of 1988, Pub. L. 100690 (to be codified at 47 U.S.C. § 223(b)). This most recent legislation, signed into law on November 18, 1988, places the prohibition against obscene commercial telephone messages in a subsection separate from that containing the prohibition against indecent messages. In addition, under the new law, the prohibition against obscene or indecent telephone messages is enforceable only through criminal penalties, and no longer through administrative proceedings by the FCC.

Section 223(b) of the Communications Act of 1934, as amended by Section 7524 of the Child Protection and Obscenity Enforcement Act of 1988, states in pertinent part:

"(b)(1) Whoever knowingly -- "

"(A) in the District of Columbia or in interstate or foreign communication, by means of telephone, makes (directly or by recording device) any obscene communication for commercial purposes to any person, regardless of whether the maker of such communication placed the call; or"

"(B) permits any telephone facility under such person's control to be used for an activity prohibited by clause (i),"

"shall be fined in accordance with title 18 of the United States Code, or imprisoned not more than two years, or both."

"(2) Whoever knowingly -- "

"(A) in the District of Columbia or in interstate or foreign communication, by means of telephone, makes (directly or by recording device) any indecent communication for commercial purposes to any person, regardless of whether the maker of such communication placed the call; or"

"(B) permits any telephone facility under such person's control to be used for an activity prohibited by clause (i),"

"shall be fined not more than $50,000 or imprisoned not more than six months, or both."

102 Stat. 4502.

Since the substantive prohibitions under this amendment remain the same, this case is not moot.

[6] In its jurisdictional statement, Sable also argued that the prohibition on obscene calls is not severable from the ban on indecent messages. This last claim was not renewed in Sable's brief on the merits, presumably as a result of the subsequent modification of the statute in which Congress specifically placed the ban on obscene commercial telephone messages in a subsection separate from the prohibition against indecent messages. Thus, the severability question is no longer before us.

[7] See e.g., 134 Cong.Rec. 7331 (1988) (statement of Rep. Bliley); id. at 7336 (statement of Rep. Coats); id. at 7330 (statement of Rep. Hall); id. at 7599 (statement of Sen. Hatch).

[8] Telephone Decency Act of 1987: Hearing on H. R. 1786 before the Subcommittee on Telecommunications and Finance of the House Committee on Energy and Commerce, 100th Cong., 1st Sess., 2, 15 (1987) (Rep. Bliley) (Hearings); id. at 18 (Rep. Coats); id. at 20 (Rep. Tauke).

These hearings were held while Carlin III was pending before the Court of Appeals for the Second Circuit.

[9] See, e.g., Hearings, at 129, 130, 132-133, 195-196, 198-200, 230-231.

[10] In the Hearings on H. R. 1786, id. at 231-232, the following colloquy occurred between Congressman Nielson and Mr. Ward, a United States attorney interested in § 223(b) prosecutions:

"Mr. NIELSON. Let me ask the question I asked the previous panel. Do any of the current alternatives by the FCC -- that is the access codes, the credit cards, or the scrambling -- do any of those provide a foolproof way of limiting dial-a-porn access to adults only? Either of you."

"Mr. WARD. I think that -- it's not foolproof, but I think the access code requirement and the screening option both provide the means of dramatically reducing the number of calls from minors in the United States, almost eliminating them. So I think that it would be a very effective way to do it."

"Mr. NIELSON. But not foolproof?"

"Mr. WARD. Not absolutely foolproof."

## Osborne v. Ohio (April 18, 1990)

Justice WHITE delivered the opinion of the Court.

In order to combat child pornography, Ohio enacted Rev.Code Ann. § 2907.323(A)(3) (Supp.1989), which provides in pertinent part:

(A) No person shall do any of the following:

* * * *

(3) Possess or view any material or performance that shows a minor who is not

the person's child or ward in a state of nudity, unless one of the following applies:

(a) The material or performance is sold, disseminated, displayed, possessed, controlled, brought or caused to be brought into this state, or presented for a bona fide artistic, medical, scientific, educational, religious, governmental, judicial, or other proper purpose, by or to a physician, psychologist, sociologist, scientist, teacher, person pursuing bona fide studies or research, librarian, clergyman, prosecutor, judge, or other person having a proper interest in the material or performance.

(b) The person knows that the parents, guardian, or custodian has consented in writing to the photographing or use of the minor in a state of nudity and to the manner in which the material or performance is used or transferred.

Petitioner, Clyde Osborne, was convicted of violating this statute and sentenced to six months in prison after the Columbus, Ohio, police, pursuant to a valid search, found four photographs in Osborne's home. Each photograph depicts a nude male adolescent posed in a sexually explicit position. [n1]

The Ohio Supreme Court affirmed Osborne's conviction after an intermediate appellate court did the same. State v. Young, 37 Ohio St.3d 249, 525 N.E.2d 1363 (1988). Relying on one of its earlier decisions, the Court first rejected Osborne's contention that the First Amendment prohibits the States from proscribing the private possession of child pornography.

Next, the Court found that § 2907.323(A)(3) is not unconstitutionally overbroad. In so doing, the Court, relying on the statutory exceptions, read § 2907.323(A)(3) as only applying to depictions of nudity involving a lewd exhibition or graphic focus on a minor's genitals. The Court also found that scienter is an essential element of a § 2907.323(A)(3) offense. Osborne objected that the trial judge had not insisted that the government prove lewd exhibition and scienter as elements of his crime. The Ohio Supreme Court rejected these contentions because Osborne had failed to object to the jury instructions given at his trial and the Court did not believe that the failures of proof amounted to plain error. [n2]

The Ohio Supreme Court denied a motion for rehearing, and granted a stay pending appeal to this Court. We noted probable jurisdiction last June. 492 U.S. 904.

I

The threshold question in this case is whether Ohio may constitutionally proscribe the possession and viewing of child pornography or whether, as Osborne argues, our decision in Stanley v. Georgia, 394 U.S. 557 (1969), compels the contrary result. In Stanley, we struck down a Georgia law outlawing the private possession of obscene material. We recognized that the statute impinged upon Stanley's right to receive information in the privacy of his home, and we found Georgia's justifications for its law inadequate. Id. at 564-568. [n3]

Stanley should not be read too broadly. We have previously noted that Stanley was a narrow holding, see United States v. 12 200-ft. Reels of Film, 413 U.S. 123, 127 (1973), and, since the decision in that case, the value of permitting child pornography has been characterized as "exceedingly modest, if not de minimis." New York v. Ferber, 458 U.S. 747, 762 (1982). But assuming, for the sake of argument, that Osborne has a First Amendment interest in viewing and possessing child pornography, we nonetheless find this case distinct from Stanley because the interests underlying child pornography prohibitions far exceed the interests justifying the Georgia law at issue in Stanley. Every court to address the issue has so concluded. See e.g., People v. Geever, 122 Ill.2d 313, 327-328, 119 Ill.Dec. 341, 347-348, 522 N.E.2d 1200, 1206-1207 (1988); Felton v. State, 526 So.2d 635, 637 (Ala.Ct.Crim.App.), aff'd, sub nom. Ex parte Felton, 526 So.2d 638, 641 (Ala.1988); State v. Davis, 53 Wash.App. 502, 505, 768 P.2d 499, 501 (1989); Savery v. Texas, 767 S.W.2d 242, 245 (Tex.App.1989); United States v. Boffardi, 684 F.Supp. 1263, 1267 (SDNY 1988).

In Stanley, Georgia primarily sought to proscribe the private possession of obscenity because it was concerned that obscenity would poison the minds of its viewers. 394 U.S. at 565. [n4] We responded that

[w]hatever the power of the state to control public dissemination of ideas inimical to the public morality, it cannot constitutionally premise legislation on the desirability of controlling a person's private thoughts.

Id. at 566. The difference here is obvious: the State does not rely on a paternalistic interest in regulating Osborne's mind. Rather, Ohio has enacted § 2907.323(A)(3) in order to protect the victims of child pornography; it hopes to destroy a market for the exploitative use of children.

It is evident beyond the need for elaboration that a State's interest in "safeguarding the physical and psychological wellbeing of a minor" is "compelling." . . . The legislative judgment, as well as the judgment found in relevant literature, is that the use of children as subjects of pornographic materials is harmful to the physiological, emotional, and mental health of the child. That judgment, we think, easily passes muster under the First Amendment.

Ferber, 458 U.S. at 756-758 (citations omitted). It is also surely reasonable for the State to conclude that it will decrease the production of child pornography if it penalizes those who possess and view the product, thereby decreasing demand. In Ferber, where we upheld a New York statute outlawing the distribution of child pornography, we found a similar argument persuasive:

[t]he advertising and selling of child pornography provide an economic motive for, and are thus an integral part of, the production of such materials, an activity illegal throughout the Nation.

It rarely has been suggested that the constitutional freedom for speech and press extends its immunity to speech or writing used as an integral part of conduct in violation of a valid criminal statute.

Id. at 761-762, quoting Giboney v. Empire Storage & Ice Co., 336 U.S. 490 (1949).

Osborne contends that the State should use other measures, besides penalizing possession, to dry up the child pornography market. Osborne points out that, in Stanley, we rejected Georgia's argument that its prohibition on obscenity possession was a necessary incident to its proscription on obscenity distribution. 394 U.S. at 567-568. This holding, however, must be viewed in light of the weak interests asserted by the State in that case. Stanley itself emphasized that we did not

mean to express any opinion on statutes making criminal possession of other types of printed, filmed, or recorded materials. . . . In such cases, compelling reasons may exist for overriding the right of the individual to possess those materials.

Id. at 568, n. 11. [n5]

Given the importance of the State's interest in protecting the victims of child pornography, we cannot fault Ohio for attempting to stamp out this vice at all levels in the distribution chain. According to the State, since the time of our decision in Ferber, much of the child pornography market has been driven underground; as a result, it is now difficult, if not impossible, to solve the child pornography problem by only attacking production and distribution. Indeed, 19 States have found it necessary to proscribe the possession of this material. [n6]

Other interests also support the Ohio law. First, as Ferber recognized, the materials produced by child pornographers permanently record the victim's abuse. The pornography's continued existence causes the child victims continuing harm by haunting the children in years to come. 458 U.S. at 759. The State's ban on possession and viewing encourages the possessors of these materials to destroy them. Second, encouraging the destruction of these materials is also desirable because evidence suggests that pedophiles use child pornography to seduce other children into sexual activity. [n7]

Given the gravity of the State's interests in this context, we find that Ohio may constitutionally proscribe the possession and viewing of child pornography.

II

Osborne next argues that, even if the State may constitutionally ban the possession of child pornography, his conviction is invalid because § 2907.323(A)(3) is unconstitutionally overbroad in that it criminalizes an intolerable range of constitutionally protected conduct. [n8] In our previous decisions discussing the First Amendment overbreadth doctrine, we have repeatedly emphasized that, where a statute regulates expressive conduct, the scope of the statute does not render it unconstitutional unless its overbreadth is not only "real, but substantial as well, judged in relation to the statute's plainly legitimate sweep." Broadrick v. Oklahoma, 413 U.S. 601, 615 (1973). Even where a statute at its margins infringes on protected expression,

facial invalidation is inappropriate if the "remainder of the statute . . . covers a whole range of easily identifiable and constitutionally proscribable . . . conduct. . . ."

New York v. Ferber, 458 U.S. at 770, n. 25.

The Ohio statute, on its face, purports to prohibit the possession of "nude" photographs of minors. We have stated that depictions of nudity, without more, constitute protected expression. See Ferber, supra, at 765, n. 18. Relying on this observation, Osborne argues that the statute, as written, is substantially overbroad. We are sceptical of this claim because, in light of the statute's exemptions and "proper purposes" provisions, the statute may not be substantially overbroad under our cases. [n9] However that may be, Osborne's overbreadth challenge, in any event, fails because the statute, as construed by the Ohio Supreme Court on Osborne's direct appeal, plainly survives overbreadth scrutiny. Under the Ohio Supreme Court reading, the statute prohibits

the possession or viewing of material or performance of a minor who is in a state of nudity, where such nudity constitutes a lewd exhibition or involves a graphic focus on the genitals, and where the person depicted is neither the child nor the ward of the person charged.

37 Ohio St.3d at 252, 525 N.E.2d at 1368. [n10] By limiting the statute's operation in this manner, the Ohio Supreme Court avoided penalizing persons for viewing or possessing innocuous photographs of naked children. We have upheld similar language against overbreadth challenges in the past. In Ferber, we affirmed a conviction under a New York statute that made it a crime to promote the "'lewd exhibition of [a child's] genitals.'" 458 U.S. at 751. We noted that

[t]he term "lewd exhibition of the genitals" is not unknown in this area and, indeed, was given in Miller [v. California, 413 U.S. 15 (1973)] as an example of a permissible regulation.

Id. at 765. [n11]

The Ohio Supreme Court also concluded that the State had to establish scienter in order to prove a violation of § 2907.323(A)(3) based on the Ohio default statute specifying that recklessness applies when another statutory provision lacks an intent specification. See n. 9, supra. The statute on its face lacks a mens rea requirement, but that omission brings into play and is cured by another law that plainly satisfies the requirement laid down in Ferber that prohibitions on child pornography include some element of scienter. 458 U.S. at 765.

Osborne contends that it was impermissible for the Ohio Supreme Court to apply its construction of § 2907.323(A)(3) to him -- i.e., to rely on the narrowed construction of the statute when evaluating his overbreadth claim. Our cases, however, have long held that a statute as construed

may be applied to conduct occurring prior to the construction, provided such application affords fair warning to the defendan[t].

Dombrowski v. Pfister, 380 U.S. 479, 491, n. 7 (citations omitted). [n12] In Hamling v. United States, 418 U.S. 87 (1974), for example, we reviewed the petitioners' convictions for mailing and conspiring to mail an obscene advertising brochure under 18 U.S.C. § 1461. That statute makes it a crime to mail an "obscene, lewd, lascivious, indecent, filthy or vile article, matter, thing, device, or substance." In Hamling, for the first time, we construed the term "obscenity" as used in § 1461

to be limited to the sort of "patently offensive representations or depictions of that specific 'hard core' sexual conduct given as examples in Miller v. California."

In light of this construction, we rejected the petitioners' facial challenge to the statute as written, and we affirmed the petitioners' convictions under the section after finding that the petitioners had fair notice that their conduct was criminal. 418 U.S. at 114-116.

Like the Hamling petitioners, Osborne had notice that his conduct was proscribed. It is obvious from the face of § 2907.323(A)(3) that the goal of the statute is to eradicate child pornography. The provision criminalizes the viewing and possessing of material depicting children in a state of nudity for other than "proper purposes." The provision appears in the "Sex Offenses" chapter of the Ohio Code. Section 2907.323 is preceded by § 2907.322, which proscribes "[p]andering sexually oriented matter involving a minor," and followed by § 2907.33, which proscribes "[d]eception to obtain matter harmful to juveniles." That Osborne's photographs of adolescent boys in sexually explicit situations constitute child pornography hardly needs elaboration. Therefore, although § 2907.323(A)(3), as written, may have been imprecise at its fringes, someone in Osborne's position would not be surprised to learn that his possession of the four photographs at issue in this case constituted a crime.

Because Osborne had notice that his conduct was criminal, his case differs from three cases upon which he relies: Bouie v. City of Columbia, 378 U.S. 347 (1964), Rabe v. Washington, 405 U.S. 313 (1972), and Marks v. United States, 430 U.S. 188 (1977). In Bouie, the petitioners had refused to leave a restaurant after being asked to do so by the restaurant's manager. Although the manager had not objected when the petitioners entered the restaurant, the petitioners were convicted of violating a South Carolina trespass statute proscribing "'entry upon the lands, of another . . . after notice from the owner or tenant prohibiting such entry.'" 378 U.S. at 349. Affirming the convictions, the South Carolina Supreme Court construed the trespass law as also making it a crime for an individual to remain on another's land after being asked to leave. We reversed the convictions on due process grounds, because the South Carolina Supreme Court's expansion of the statute was unforeseeable and therefore the petitioners had no reason to suspect that their conduct was criminal. Id. at 350-352.

Likewise, in Rabe v. Washington, supra, the petitioner had been convicted of violating a Washington obscenity statute that, by its terms, did not proscribe the defendant's conduct. On petitioner's appeal, the Washington Supreme Court nevertheless affirmed the petitioner's conviction after construing the Washington obscenity statute to reach the petitioner. We overturned the conviction because the Washington Supreme Court's broadening of the statute was unexpected; therefore the petitioner had no warning that his actions were proscribed. Id. at 315.

And in Marks v. United States, supra, we held that the retroactive application of the obscenity standards announced in Miller v. California, 413 U.S. 15 (1973), to the potential detriment of the petitioner, violated the Due Process Clause because, at the time that the defendant committed the challenged conduct, our decision in Memoirs v. Massachusetts, 383 U.S. 413 (1966), provided the governing law. The defendant could not suspect that his actions would later become criminal when we expanded the range of constitutionally proscribable conduct in Miller.

Osborne suggests that our decision here is inconsistent with Shuttlesworth v. Birmingham, 382 U.S. 87 (1965); we disagree. In Shuttlesworth, the defendant had been convicted of violating an Alabama statute that, when read literally, provided that "a person may stand on a public sidewalk in Birmingham only at the whim of any police officer of that city." Id. at 90. We stated that "[t]he constitutional vice of so broad a provision needs no demonstration." Ibid. As subsequently construed by the Alabama Supreme Court, however, the statute merely made it criminal for an individual that was blocking free passage along a public street to disobey a police officer's order to move. We noted that

[i]t is our duty, of course, to accept this state judicial construction of the ordinance. . . . As so construed, we cannot say that the ordinance is unconstitutional, though it requires no great feat of imagination to envisage situations in which such an ordinance might be unconstitutionally applied.

Id. at 91. We nevertheless reversed the defendant's conviction because it was not clear that the state had convicted the defendant under the statute as construed, rather than as written. Id. at 91-92. [n13] Shuttlesworth, then stands for the proposition that, where a State Supreme Court narrows an unconstitutionally overbroad statute, the State must ensure that defendants are convicted under the statute as it is subsequently construed, and not as it was originally written; this proposition in no way conflicts with our holding in this case.

Finally, despite Osborne's contention to the contrary, we do not believe that Massachusetts v. Oakes, 491 U.S. 576 (1989), supports his theory of this case. In Oakes, the petitioner challenged a Massachusetts pornography statute as overbroad; since the time of the defendant's alleged crime, however, the state had substantially narrowed the statute through a subsequent legislative enactment -- an amendment to the statute. In a separate opinion, five Justices agreed that the state legislature could not cure the potential overbreadth problem through the subsequent legislative action; the statute was void as written. Id. at 585-586.

Osborne contends that Oakes stands for a similar but distinct proposition that, when faced with a potentially overinclusive statute, a court may not construe the statute to avoid overbreadth problems and then apply the statute, as construed, to past conduct. The implication of this argument is that, if a statute is overbroad as written, then the statute is void and incurable. As a result, when reviewing a conviction under a potentially overbroad statute, a court must either affirm or strike down the statute on its face, but the court may not, as the Ohio Supreme Court did in this case, narrow the statute, affirm on the basis of the narrowing construction, and leave the statute in full force. We disagree.

First, as indicated by our earlier discussion, if we accepted this proposition, it would require a radical reworking of our law. Courts routinely construe statutes so as to avoid the statutes' potentially overbroad reach, apply the statute in that case, and leave the statute in place. In Roth v. United States, 354 U.S. 476 (1957), for example, the court construed the open-ended terms used in 18 U.S.C. § 1461 which prohibits the mailing of material that is "obscene, lewd, lascivious, indecent, filthy or vile." Justice Harlan characterized Roth in this way:

The words of § 1461, "obscene, lewd, lascivious, indecent, filthy or vile," connote something that is portrayed in manner so offensive as to make is unacceptable under current community mores. While in common usage the words have different shades of meaning, the statute since its inception has always been taken as aimed at obnoxiously debasing portrayals of sex. Although the statute condemns such material irrespective of the effect it may have upon those into whose hands it falls, the early case of United States v. Bennet, 24 Fed.Cas. 1093 (No. 14571), put a limiting gloss upon the statutory language: the statute reaches only indecent material which, as now expressed in Roth v. United States, supra, at 489 "taken as a whole appeals to prurient interest." Manuel Enterprises v. Day, 370 U.S. 478, 482-484 (1962) (footnotes omitted); (emphasis in original).

See also Hamling, 418 U.S. at 112 (quoting the above). The petitioner's conviction was affirmed in Roth, and federal obscenity law was left in force. 354 U.S. at 494. [n14] We, moreover, have long respected the state Supreme Courts' ability to narrow state statutes so as to limit the statute's scope to unprotected conduct. See, e.g., Ginsberg v. New York, 390 U.S. 629 (1968).

Second, we do not believe that Oakes compels the proposition that Osborne urges us to accept. In Oakes, Justice SCALIA, writing for himself and four others, reasoned that

The overbreadth doctrine serves to protect constitutionally legitimate speech not merely ex post that is, after the offending statute is enacted, but also ex ante that is, when the legislature is contemplating what sort of statute to enact. If the promulgation of overbroad laws affecting speech was cost free . . . that is, if no conviction of constitutionally proscribable conduct would be lost so long as the offending statute was narrowed before the final appeal, . . . then legislatures would have significantly reduced incentive to stay within constitutional bounds in the first place. When one takes account of those overbroad statutes that are never challenged, and of the time that elapses before the ones that are challenged are amended to come within constitutional bounds, a substantial amount of legitimate speech would be "chilled." . . .

491 U.S. at 586 (emphasis in original). In other words, five of the Oakes Justices feared that, if we allowed a legislature to correct its mistakes without paying for them (beyond the inconvenience of passing a new law), we would decrease the legislature's incentive to draft a narrowly tailored law in the first place.

Legislators who know they can cure their own mistakes by amendment without significant cost may not be as careful to avoid drafting overbroad statutes as they might otherwise be. But a similar effect will not be likely if a judicial construction of a statute to eliminate overbreadth is allowed to be applied in the case before the Court. This is so primarily because the legislatures cannot be sure that the statute, when examined by a court, will be saved by a narrowing construction rather than invalidated for overbreadth.

In the latter event, there could be no convictions under that law even of those whose own conduct is unprotected by the First Amendment. Even if construed to obviate overbreadth, applying the statute to pending cases might be barred by the Due Process Clause. Thus, careless drafting cannot be considered to be cost-free based on the power of the courts to eliminate overbreadth by statutory construction.

There are also other considerations. Osborne contends that, when courts construe statutes so as to eliminate overbreadth, convictions of those found guilty of unprotected conduct covered by the statute must be reversed, and any further convictions for prior reprehensible conduct are barred. [n15] Furthermore, because he contends that overbroad laws implicating First Amendment interests are nullities, and incapable of valid application from the outset, this would mean that judicial construction could not save the statute, even as applied to subsequent conduct unprotected by the First Amendment. The overbreadth doctrine, as we have recognized, is indeed "strong medicine," Broadrick v. Oklahoma, 413 U.S. at 613, and requiring that statutes be facially invalidated whenever overbreadth is perceived would very likely invite reconsideration or redefinition of the doctrine in a way that would not serve First Amendment interests. [n16]

### III

Having rejected Osborne's Stanley and overbreadth arguments, we now reach Osborne's final objection to his conviction: his contention that he was denied due process because it is unclear that his conviction was based on a finding that each of the elements of § 2907.323(A)(3) was present. [n17] According to the Ohio Supreme Court, in order to secure a conviction under § 2907.323(A)(3), the State must prove both scienter and that the defendant possessed material depicting a lewd exhibition or a graphic focus on genitals. The jury in this case was not instructed that it could convict Osborne only for conduct that satisfied these requirements.

The State concedes the omissions in the jury instructions, but argues that Osborne waived his right to assert this due process challenge because he failed to object when the instructions were given at his trial. The Ohio Supreme Court so held, citing Ohio law. The question before us now, therefore, is whether we are precluded from reaching Osborne's due process challenge because counsel's failure to comply with the procedural rule constitutes an independent state law ground adequate to support the result below. We have no difficulty agreeing with the State that Osborne's counsel's failure to urge that the court instruct the jury on scienter constitutes an independent and adequate state law ground preventing us from reaching Osborne's due process contention on that point. Ohio law states that proof of scienter is required in instances, like the present one, where a criminal statute does not specify the applicable mental state. See n. 9, supra. The state procedural rule, moreover, serves the State's important interest in ensuring that counsel do their part in preventing trial courts from providing juries with erroneous instructions.

With respect to the trial court's failure to instruct on lewdness, however, we reach a different conclusion: based upon our review of the record, we believe that counsel's failure to object on this point does not prevent us from considering Osborne's constitutional claim. Osborne's trial was brief: the State called only the two arresting officers to the stand; the defense summoned only Osborne himself. Right before trial, Osborne's counsel moved to dismiss the case, contending that § 2907.323(A)(3) is unconstitutionally overbroad. Counsel stated:

I'm filing a motion to dismiss based on the fact that [the] statute is void for vagueness, overbroad . . . The statute's overbroad because . . . a person couldn't have pictures of his own grandchildren; probably couldn't even have nude photographs of himself.

Judge, if you had some nude photos of yourself when you were a child, you would probably be violating the law. . . .

     * * * *

So grandparents, neighbors, or other people who happen to view the photograph are criminally liable under the statute. And on that basis, I'm going to ask the Court to dismiss the case.

Tr. 3-4. The prosecutor informed the trial judge that a number of Ohio state courts had recently rejected identical motions challenging § 2907.323(A)(3). Tr. 5-6. The court then overruled the motion. Id. at 7. Immediately thereafter, Osborne's counsel proposed various jury instructions. Ibid.

Given this sequence of events, we believe that we may reach Osborne's due process claim, because we are convinced that Osborne's attorney pressed the issue of the State's failure of proof on lewdness before the trial court and, under the circumstances, nothing would be gained by requiring Osborne's lawyer to object a second time, specifically to the jury instructions. The trial judge, in no uncertain terms, rejected counsel's argument that the statute, as written, was overbroad. The State contends that counsel should then have insisted that the court instruct the jury on lewdness because, absent a finding that this element existed, a conviction would be unconstitutional. Were we to accept this position, we would "'force resort to an arid ritual of meaningless form,' . . . and would further no perceivable state interest."

James v. Kentucky, 466 U.S. 341, 349 (1984), quoting Staub v. City of Baxley, 355 U.S. 313, 320 (1958), and citing Henry [ 495 U.S. 125] v. Mississippi, 379 U.S. 443, 448-449 (1965). As Justice Holmes warned us years ago,

[w]hatever springs the State may set for those who are endeavoring to assert rights that the State confers, the assertion of federal rights, when plainly and reasonably made, is not to be defeated under the name of local practice.

Davis v. Wechsler, 263 U.S. 22, 24 (1923).

Our decision here is analogous to our decision in Douglas v. Alabama, 380 U.S. 415 (1965). In that case, the Alabama Supreme Court had held that a defendant had waived his confrontation clause objection to the reading into evidence of a confession that he had given. Although not following the precise procedure required by Alabama law,

[n18] the defendant had unsuccessfully objected to the prosecution's use of the confession. We followed "our consistent holdings that the adequacy of state procedural bars to the assertion of federal questions is itself a federal question," and stated that,

[i]n determining the sufficiency of objections, we have applied the general principle that an objection which is ample and timely to bring the alleged federal error to the attention of the trial court and enable it to take appropriate corrective action is sufficient to serve legitimate state interests, and therefore sufficient to preserve the claim for review here.

Id. at 422. Concluding that "[n]o legitimate state interest would have been served by requiring repetition of a patently futile objection," we held that the Alabama procedural ruling did not preclude our consideration of the defendant's constitutional claim. Id. at 421-422. We reach a similar conclusion in this case.

IV

To conclude, although we find Osborne's First Amendment arguments unpersuasive, we reverse his conviction and remand for a new trial in order to ensure that Osborne's conviction stemmed from a finding that the State had proved each of the elements of § 2907.323(A)(3).

So ordered.

Notes

1. Osborne contends that the subject in all of the pictures is the same boy; Osborne testified at trial that he was told that the youth was fourteen at the time that the photographs were taken. App. 16. The government maintains that three of the pictures are of one boy, and one of the pictures is of another. Three photographs depict the same boy in different positions: sitting with his legs over his head and his anus exposed; lying down with an erect penis and with an electrical object in his hand; and lying down with a plastic object which appears to be inserted in his anus. The fourth photograph depicts a nude standing boy; it is unclear whether this subject is the same boy photographed in the other pictures, because the photograph only depicts the boy's torso.

2. Osborne also unsuccessfully raised a number of other challenges that are not at issue before this Court.

3. We have since indicated that our decision in Stanley was "firmly grounded in the First Amendment." Bowers v. Hardwick, 478 U.S. 186, 195 (1986).

4. Georgia also argued that its ban on possession was a necessary complement to its ban on distribution (see discussion infra, at 110), and that the possession law benefited the public because, according to the state, exposure to obscene material might lead to deviant sexual behavior or crimes of sexual violence. 394 U.S. at 566. We found a lack of empirical evidence supporting the latter claim, and stated that "'[a]mong free men, the deterrents ordinarily to be applied to prevent crime are education and punishment for violations of the law. . . .'" Id. at 566-567 (citation omitted).

5. As the dissent notes, see post at 141, the Stanley Court cited illicit possession of

defense information as an example of the type of offense for which compelling state interests might justify a ban on possession. Stanley, however, did not suggest that this crime exhausted the entire category of proscribable offenses.

6. Ala.Code § 13A-12-192 (1988); Ariz.Rev.Stat. Ann. § 13-3553 (1989); Colo.Rev.Stat. § 18-6-403 (Supp.1989); Fla.Stat. § 827.071 (1989); Ga.Code Ann. § 16-12-100 (1989); Idaho Code § 18-1507 (1987); Ill.Rev.Stat., ch. 38, 11-20.1 (1987); Kans.Stat.Ann. § 21-3516 (Supp.1989); Minn.Stat. § 617.247 (1988); Mo.Rev.Stat. § 573.037 (Supp.1989); Neb.Rev.Stat. § 28-809 (1989); Nev.Rev.Stat. § 200.730 (1987); Ohio Rev.Code Ann. §§ 2907.322 and 2907.323 (Supp.1989); Okla.Stat., Tit. 21, § 1021.2 (Supp.1989); S.D.Comp.Laws Ann. § 22-22-23, 22-22-23.1 (1988); Tex.Penal Code Ann. § 43.26 (1989 and Supp. 1989-1990); Utah Code Ann. § 76-5a-3(1)(a) (Supp.1989), Wash. Rev.Code § 9.68A.070 (1989); W.Va.Code § 61-8C-3 (1989).

7. The Attorney General's Commission on Pornography, for example, states that

Child pornography is often used as part of a method of seducing child victims. A child who is reluctant to engage in sexual activity with an adult or to pose for sexually explicit photos can sometimes be convinced by viewing other children having "fun" participating in the activity.

1 Attorney General's Commission on Pornography, Final Report 649 (1986) (footnotes omitted). See also D. Campagna and D. Poffenberger, Sexual Trafficking in Children 118 (1988), S. O'Brien, Child Pornography 89 (1983).

8. In the First Amendment context, we permit defendants to challenge statutes on overbreadth grounds regardless of whether the individual defendant's conduct is constitutionally protected.

The First Amendment doctrine of substantial overbreadth is an exception to the general rule that a person to whom a statute may be constitutionally applied cannot challenge the statute on the ground that it may be unconstitutionally applied to others.

Massachussets v. Oakes, 491 U.S. 576, 581 (1989).

9. The statute applies only where an individual possesses or views the depiction of a minor "who is not the person's child or ward." The State, moreover, does not impose criminal liability if either

[t]he material or performance is sold, disseminated, displayed, possessed, controlled, brought or caused to be brought into this state, or presented for a bona fide artistic, medical, scientific, educational, religious, governmental, judicial, or other proper purpose, by or to a physician, psychologist, sociologist, scientist, teacher, person pursuing bona fide studies or research, librarian, clergyman, prosecutor, judge, or other person having a proper interest in the material or performance,

or

[t]he person knows that the parents, guardian, or custodian has consented in writing to the photographing or use of the minor in a state of nudity and to the manner in which the material or performance is used or transferred.

It is true that, despite the statutory exceptions, one might imagine circumstances in which the statute, by its terms, criminalizes constitutionally protected conduct. If, for example, a parent gave a family friend a picture of the parent's infant taken while the infant was unclothed, the statute would apply. But, given the broad statutory exceptions and the prevalence of child pornography, it is far from clear that the instances where the statute applies to constitutionally protected conduct are significant enough to warrant a finding that the statute is overbroad. Cf. Oakes, supra, at 589-590 (Opinion of SCALIA, J., joined by BLACKMUN, J., concurring judgment in part and dissenting in part).

Nor do we find very persuasive Osborne's contention that the statute is unconstitutionally overbroad because it applies in instances where viewers or possessors lack scienter. Although § 2907.323(A)(3) does not specify a mental state, Ohio law provides that recklessness is the appropriate mens rea where a statute "neither specifies culpability nor plainly indicates a purpose to impose strict liability." Ohio Rev.Stat. Ann. § 2901.21(B) (1987).

We also do not find any merit to Osborne's claim that § 2907.323(A)(3) is unconstitutionally vague because it does not define the term "minor." Under Ohio law, a minor is anyone under eighteen years of age. Ohio Rev.Code Ann. § 3109.01 (1989).

10. The Ohio Court reached this conclusion because,

when the "proper purposes" exceptions set forth in R.C. 2907.323(A)(3)(a) and (b) are considered, the scope of the prohibited conduct narrows significantly. The clear purpose of these exceptions . . . is to sanction the possession or viewing of material depicting nude minors where that conduct is morally innocent. Thus, the only conduct prohibited by the statute is conduct which is not morally innocent, i.e., the possession or viewing of the described material for prurient purposes. So construed, the statute's proscription is not so broad as to outlaw all depictions of minors in a state of nudity, but rather only those depictions which constitute child pornography.

37 Ohio St.3d at 251-252, 525 N.E.2d at 1367-1368 (emphasis in original).

11. The statute upheld against an overbreadth challenge in Ferber was, moreover, arguably less narrowly tailored than the statute challenged in this case, because, unlike § 2907.323(A)(3), the New York law did not provide a broad range of exceptions to the general prohibition on lewd exhibition of the genitals. Despite this lack of exceptions, we upheld the New York law, reasoning that

[h]ow often, if ever, it may be necessary to employ children to engage in conduct clearly within the reach of [the statute] in order to produce educational, medical, or artistic works cannot be known with certainty. Yet we seriously doubt, and it has not been suggested, that these arguably impermissible applications of the statute amount to more than a tiny fraction of the materials within the statute's reach.

458 U.S. at 773.

Justice BRENNAN distinguishes the Ohio statute, as construed, from the statute upheld in Ferber on the ground that the Ohio statute proscribes "'lewd exhibitions of nudity,' rather than 'lewd exhibitions of the genitals.'" See post at 129 (emphasis in original). He notes that Ohio defines nudity to include depictions of pubic areas, buttocks, the female breast, and covered male genitals "in a discernibly turgid state." Post at 130. We do not agree that this distinction between body areas and specific body parts is constitutionally significant: the crucial question is whether the depiction is lewd, not whether the depiction happens to focus on the genitals or the buttocks. In any event, however, Osborne would not be entitled to relief. The context of the opinion indicates that the Ohio Supreme Court believed that "the term 'nudity,' as used in R.C. 2907.323(A)(3), refers to a lewd exhibition of the genitals." State v. Young, 37 Ohio St.3d 249, 258, 525 N.E.2d 1363, 1373 (1988).

We do not concede, as Justice BRENNAN suggests, see post at 131, n. 5, that the statute, as construed, might proscribe a family friend's possession of an innocuous picture of an unclothed infant. We acknowledge (see n. 9, supra, ) that the statute, as written, might reach such conduct, but, as construed, the statute would surely not apply, because the photograph would not involve a "lewd exhibition or graphic focus on the genitals" of the child.

12. This principle, of course, accords with the rationale underlying overbreadth challenges. We normally do not allow a defendant to challenge a law as it is applied to others. In the First Amendment context, however, we have said that,

[b]ecause of the sensitive nature of constitutionally protected expression, we have not required that all those subject to overbroad regulations risk prosecution to test their rights. For free expression -- of transcendent value to all society, and not merely to those exercising their rights -- might be the loser.

Dombrowski, 380 U.S. at 486. But once a statute is authoritatively construed, there is no longer any danger that protected speech will be deterred, and therefore no longer any reason to entertain the defendant's challenge to the statute on its face.

13. In Shuttlesworth, we also overturned the defendant's conviction for violating another part of the same Alabama statute because that provision had been interpreted as criminalizing an individual's failure to follow a policeman's directions when the policeman was directing traffic, and the crime alleged in Shuttlesworth had nothing to do with motor traffic. 382 U.S. at 93-95.

14. Buckley v. Valeo, 424 U.S. 1, 76-80 (1976), is another landmark case where a law was construed to avoid potential overbreadth problems, and left in place. Section 304(e) of the Federal Election Campaign Act, 2 U.S.C. § 434(e) (1976 ed.), imposes certain reporting requirements on "[e]very person . . . who makes contributions or independent expenditures" exceeding $100 "other than by contribution to a political committee or candidate." We stated that,

[t]o insure that the reach of § 434(e) is not impermissibly broad, we construe "expenditure" for purposes of that section . . . to reach only funds used for communications that expressly advocate the election or defeat of a clearly identified candidate.

The section was upheld as construed. 424 U.S. at 80 (footnote omitted).

15. Under Osborne's submission, even where the construction eliminating

overbreadth occurs in a civil case, the statute could not be applied to conduct occurring prior to the decision; for, although plainly within reach of the terms of the statute and plainly not otherwise protected by the First Amendment, until the statute was narrowed to comply with the Amendment, the conduct was not illegal.

16. In terms of applying a ruling to pending cases, we see no difference of constitutional import between a court's affirming a conviction after construing a statute to avoid facial invalidation on the ground of overbreadth and affirming a conviction after rejecting a claim that the conduct at issue is not within the terms of the statute. In both situations, the Due Process Clause would require fair warning to the defendant that the statutory proscription, as construed, covers his conduct. But even with the due process limitation, courts repeatedly affirm convictions after rejecting nonfrivolous claims that the conduct at issue is not forbidden by the terms of the statute. As argued earlier, there is no doubt whatsoever that Osborne's conduct is proscribed by the terms of the child pornography statute involved here.

17. [T]he Due Process Clause protects the accused against conviction except upon proof beyond a reasonable doubt of every fact necessary to constitute the crime with which he is charged.

In Re Winship, 397 U.S. 358, 364 (1970).

18. The Alabama court had stated:

"There must be a ruling sought and acted on before the trial judge can be put in error. Here there was no ruling asked or invoked as to the questions embracing the alleged confession."

380 U.S. at 421 (citation omitted).

## Barnes v. Glen Theatre, Inc. (June 21, 1991)

Chief Justice Rehnquist delivered the opinion of the Court.

Respondents are two establishments in South Bend, Indiana, that wish to provide totally nude dancing as entertainment, and individual dancers who are employed at these establishments. They claim that the First Amendment's guarantee of freedom of expression prevents the State of Indiana from enforcing its public indecency law to prevent this form of dancing. We reject their claim.

The facts appear from the pleadings and findings of the District Court, and are uncontested here. The Kitty Kat Lounge, Inc. (Kitty Kat) is located in the city of South Bend. It sells alcoholic beverages and presents "go-go dancing." Its proprietor desires to present "totally nude dancing," but an applicable Indiana statute regulating public nudity requires that the dancers wear "pasties" and a "G-string" when they dance. The dancers are not paid an hourly wage, but work on commission. They receive a 100 percent commission on the first $60 in drink sales during their performances. Darlene Miller, one of the respondents in the action, had worked at the Kitty Kat for about two years at the time this action was brought. Miller wishes to dance nude because she believes she would make more money doing so.

Respondent Glen Theatre, Inc., is an Indiana corporation with a place of business in South Bend. Its primary business is supplying so-called adult entertainment through written and printed materials, movie showings, and live entertainment at an enclosed "bookstore." The live entertainment at the "bookstore" consists of nude and seminude performances and showings of the female body through glass panels. Customers sit in a booth and insert coins into a timing mechanism that permits them to observe the live nude and seminude dancers for a period of time. One of Glen Theatre's dancers, Gayle Ann Marie Sutro, has danced, modeled, and acted professionally for more than 15 years, and in addition to her performances at the Glen Theatre, can be seen in a pornographic movie at a nearby theater. App. to Pet. for Cert. 131-133.

Respondents sued in the United States District Court for the Northern District of Indiana to enjoin the enforcement of the Indiana public indecency statute, Ind. Code 35-45-4-1 (1988), asserting that its prohibition against complete nudity in public places violated the First Amendment. The District Court originally granted respondents' prayer for an injunction, finding that the statute was facially overbroad. The Court of Appeals for the Seventh Circuit reversed, deciding that previous litigation with respect to the statute in the Supreme Court of Indiana and this Court precluded the possibility of such a challenge, [n.1] and remanded to the District Court in order for the plaintiffs to pursue their claim that the statute violated the First Amendment as applied to their dancing. Glen Theatre, Inc. v. Pearson, 802 F. 2d 287, 288290 (1986). On remand, the District Court concluded that "the type of dancing these plaintiffs wish to perform is not expressive activity protected by the Constitution of the United States," and rendered judgment in favor of the defendants. Glen Theatre, Inc. v. Civil City of South Bend, 695 F. Supp. 414, 419 (ND Ind. 1988). The case was again appealed to the Seventh Circuit, and a panel of that court reversed the District Court, holding that the nude dancing involved here was expressive conduct protected by the First Amendment. Miller v. Civil City of South Bend, 887 F. 2d 826 (CA7 1989). The Court of Appeals then heard the case en banc, and the court rendered a series of comprehensive and thoughtful opinions. The majority concluded that non obscene nude dancing performed for entertainment is expression protected by the First Amendment, and that the public indecency statute was an improper infringement of that expressive activity because its purpose was to prevent the message of eroticism and sexuality conveyed by the dancers. Miller v. Civil City of South Bend, 904 F. 2d 1081 (CA7 1990). We granted certiorari, 498 U. S. — (1990), and now hold that the Indiana statutory requirement that the dancers in the establishments involved in this case must wear pasties and a G-string does not violate the First Amendment.

Several of our cases contain language suggesting that nude dancing of the kind involved here is expressive conduct protected by the First Amendment. In Doran v. Salem Inn, Inc., 422 U.S. 922, 932 (1975), we said: "[A]lthough the customary `barroom' type of nude dancing may involve only the barest minimum of protected expression, we recognized in California v. LaRue, 409 U.S. 109, 118 (1972), that this form of entertainment might be entitled to First and Fourteenth Amendment protection under some circumstances." In Schad v. Borough of Mount Ephraim, 452 U.S. 61, 66 (1981), we said that "[f]urthermore, as the state courts in this case recognized, nude dancing is not without its First Amendment protections from official regulation" (citations omitted). These statements support the conclusion of the Court of Appeals that nude dancing of the kind sought to be performed here is expressive conduct within the outer perimeters of the First Amendment, though we view it as only marginally so. This, of course, does not end our inquiry. We must determine the level of protection to be afforded to the expressive conduct at issue, and must determine whether the Indiana statute is an impermissible infringement of that protected activity.

Indiana, of course, has not banned nude dancing as such, but has proscribed public nudity across the board. The Supreme Court of Indiana has construed the Indiana statute to preclude nudity in what are essentially places of public accommodation such as the Glen Theatre and the Kitty Kat Lounge. In such places, respondents point out, minors are excluded and there are no non-consenting viewers. Respondents contend that while the state may license establishments such as the ones involved here, and limit the geographical area in which they do business, it may not in any way limit the performance of the dances within them without violating the First Amendment. The petitioner contends, on the other hand, that Indiana's restriction on nude dancing is a valid "time, place or manner" restriction under cases such as Clark v. Community for Creative Non-Violence, 468 U.S. 288 (1984).

The "time, place, or manner" test was developed for evaluating restrictions on expression taking place on public property which had been dedicated as a "public forum," Ward v. Rock Against Racism, 491 U.S. 781, 791 (1989), although we have on at least one occasion applied it to conduct occurring on private property. See Renton v. Playtime Theatres, Inc., 475 U.S. 41 (1986). In Clark we observed that this test has been interpreted to embody much the same standards as those set forth in United States v. O'Brien, 391 U.S. 367 (1968), and we turn, therefore, to the rule enunciated in O'Brien.

O'Brien burned his draft card on the steps of the South Boston courthouse in the presence of a sizable crowd, and was convicted of violating a statute that prohibited the knowing destruction or mutilation of such a card. He claimed that his conviction was contrary to the First Amendment because his act was "symbolic speech" — expressive conduct. The court rejected his contention that symbolic speech is entitled to full First Amendment protection, saying:

"[E]ven on the assumption that the alleged communicative element in O'Brien's conduct is sufficient to bring into play the First Amendment, it does not necessarily follow that the destruction of a registration certificate is constitutionally protected activity. This Court has held that when `speech' and `nonspeech' elements are combined in the same course of conduct, a sufficiently important governmental interest in regulating the nonspeech element can justify incidental limitations on First Amendment freedoms. To characterize the quality of the governmental interest which must appear, the Court has employed a variety of descriptive terms: compelling; substantial; subordinating; paramount; cogent; strong. Whatever imprecision inheres in these terms, we think it clear that a government regulation is sufficiently justified if it is within the constitutional power of the Government; if it furthers an important or substantial governmental interest; if the governmental interest is unrelated to the suppression of free expression; and if the incidental restriction on alleged First Amendment freedoms is no greater than is essential to the furtherance of that interest." Id., at 376-377 (footnotes omitted).

Applying the four-part O'Brien test enunciated above, we find that Indiana's public indecency statute is justified despite its incidental limitations on some expressive activity. The public indecency statute is clearly within the constitutional power of the State and furthers substantial governmental interests. It is impossible to discern, other than from the text of the statute, exactly what governmental interest the Indiana legislators had in mind when they enacted this statute, for Indiana does not record legislative history, and the state's highest court has not shed additional light on the statute's purpose. Nonetheless, the statute's purpose of protecting societal order and morality is clear from its text and history. Public indecency statutes of this sort are of ancient origin, and presently exist in at least 47 States. Public indecency, including nudity, was a criminal offense at common law, and this Court recognized the common-law roots of the offense of "gross and open indecency" in Winters v. New York, 333 U.S. 507, 515 (1948). Public nudity was considered an act malum en se. Le Roy v. Sidley, 1 Sid. 168, 82 Eng. Rep. 1036 (K. B. 1664). Public indecency statutes such as the one before us reflect moral disapproval of people appearing in the nude among strangers in public places.

This public indecency statute follows a long line of earlier Indiana statutes banning all public nudity. The history of Indiana's public indecency statute shows that it predates barroom nude dancing and was enacted as a general prohibition. At least as early as 1831, Indiana had a statute punishing "open and notorious lewdness, or . . . any grossly scandalous and public indecency." Rev. Laws of Ind., ch. 26, 60 (1831); Ind. Rev. Stat., ch. 53, 81 (1834). A gap during which no statute was in effect was filled by the Indiana Supreme Court in Ardery v. State, 56 Ind. 328 (1877), which held that the court could sustain a conviction for exhibition of "privates" in the presence of others. The court traced the offense to the Bible story of Adam and Eve. Id., at 329-330. In 1881, a statute was enacted that would remain essentially unchanged for nearly a century:

"Whoever, being over fourteen years of age, makes an indecent exposure of his person in a public place, or in any place where there are other persons to be offended or annoyed thereby, . . . is guilty of public indecency . . . ." 1881 Ind. Acts, ch. 37, 90.

The language quoted above remained unchanged until it was simultaneously repealed and replaced with the present statute in 1976. 1976 Ind. Acts, Pub. L. 148, Art. 45, ch. 4, 1. [n.2] This and other public indecency statutes were designed to protect morals and public order. The traditional police power of the States is defined as the authority to provide for the public health, safety, and morals, and we have upheld such a basis for legislation. In Paris Adult Theatre I v. Slaton, 413 U.S. 49, 61 (1973), we said:

"In deciding Roth [v. United States, 354 U.S. 476 (1957)], this Court implicitly accepted that a legislature could legitimately act on such a conclusion to protect `the social interest in order and morality.' [Id.], at 485." (Emphasis omitted.)

And in Bowers v. Hardwick, 478 U.S. 186, 196 (1986), we said:

"The law, however, is constantly based on notions of morality, and if all laws representing essentially moral choices are to be invalidated under the Due Process Clause, the courts will be very busy indeed."

Thus, the public indecency statute furthers a substantial government interest in protecting order and morality.

This interest is unrelated to the suppression of free expression. Some may view restricting nudity on moral grounds as necessarily related to expression. We disagree. It can be argued, of course, that almost limitless types of conduct — including appearing in the nude in public — are "expressive," and in one sense of the word this is true. People who go about in the nude in public may be expressing something about themselves by so doing. But the court rejected this expansive notion of "expressive conduct" in O'Brien, saying:

"We cannot accept the view that an apparently limitless variety of conduct can be labelled `speech' whenever the person engaging in the conduct intends thereby to express an idea." 391 U. S. at 376.

And in Dallas v. Stanglin, 490 U.S. 19, we further observed:

"It is possible to find some kernel of expression in almost every activity a person undertakes — for example, walking down the street or meeting one's friends at a shopping mall — but such a kernel is not sufficient to bring the activity within the protection of the First Amendment. We think the activity of these dance-hall patrons coming together to engage in recreational dancing — is not protected by the First Amendment." 490 U.S. 19, 25.

Respondents contend that even though prohibiting nudity in public generally may not be related to suppressing expression, prohibiting the performance of nude dancing is related to expression because the state seeks to prevent its erotic message. Therefore, they reason that the application of the Indiana statute to the nude dancing in this case violates the First Amendment, because it fails the third part of the O'Brien test, viz: the governmental interest must be unrelated to the suppression of free expression.

But we do not think that when Indiana applies its statute to the nude dancing in these nightclubs it is proscribing nudity because of the erotic message conveyed by the dancers. Presumably numerous other erotic performances are presented at these establishments and similar clubs without any interference from the state, so long as the performers wear a scant amount of clothing. Likewise, the requirement that the dancers don pasties and a G-string does not deprive the dance of whatever erotic message it conveys; it simply makes the message slightly less graphic. The perceived evil that

Indiana seeks to address is not erotic dancing, but public nudity. The appearance of people of all shapes, sizes and ages in the nude at a beach, for example, would convey little if any erotic message, yet the state still seeks to prevent it. Public nudity is the evil the state seeks to prevent, whether or not it is combined with expressive activity.

This conclusion is buttressed by a reference to the facts of O'Brien. An act of Congress provided that anyone who knowingly destroyed a selective service registration certificate committed an offense. O'Brien burned his certificate on the steps of the South Boston Courthouse to influence others to adopt his anti-war beliefs. This Court upheld his conviction, reasoning that the continued availability of issued certificates served a legitimate and substantial purpose in the administration of the selective service system. O'Brien's deliberate destruction of his certificate frustrated this purpose and "for this non-communicative aspect of his conduct, and for nothing else, he was convicted." 391 U. S., at 302. It was assumed that O'Brien's act in burning the certificate had a communicative element in it sufficient to bring into play the First Amendment, 391 U. S., at 376, but it was for the noncommunicative element that he was prosecuted. So here with the Indiana statute; while the dancing to which it was applied had a communicative element, it was not the dancing that was prohibited, but simply its being done in the nude. The fourth part of the O'Brien test requires that the incidental restriction on First Amendment freedom be no greater than is essential to the furtherance of the governmental interest. As indicated in the discussion above, the governmental interest served by the text of the prohibition is societal disapproval of nudity in public places and among strangers. The statutory prohibition is not a means to some greater end, but an end in itself. It is without cavil that the public indecency statute is "narrowly tailored;" Indiana's requirement that the dancers wear at least pasties and a Gstring is modest, and the bare minimum necessary to achieve the state's purpose.

The judgment of the Court of Appeals accordingly is

Notes

1 The Indiana Supreme Court appeared to give the public indecency stat- ute a limiting construction to save it from a facial overbreadth attack:

"There is no right to appear nude in public. Rather, it may be con- stitutionally required to tolerate or to allow some nudity as a part of some larger form of expression meriting protection, when the commu- nication of ideas is involved." State v. Baysinger, 272 Ind. 236, 247, 397 N. E. 2d 580, 587 (1979) (emphasis added) appeals dism'd sub nom. Clark v. Indiana, 446 U.S. 931, and Dove v. Indiana, 449 U.S. 806 (1980).

Five years after Baysinger, however, the Indiana Supreme Court re- versed a decision of the Indiana Court of Appeals holding that the statute did "not apply to activity such as the theatrical appearances involved herein, which may not be prohibited absent a finding of obscenity," in a case involving a partially nude dance in the "Miss Erotica of Fort Wayne" contest. Erhardt v. State, 468 N. E. 2d 224 (Ind. 1984). The Indiana Supreme Court did not discuss the constitutional issues beyond a cursory comment that the statute had been upheld against constitutional attack in Baysinger, and Erhardt's conduct fell within the statutory prohibition. Justice Hunter dissented, arguing that "a public indecency statute which prohibits nudity in any public place is unconstitutionally overbroad. My reasons for so concluding have already been articulated in State v. Bay singer, (1979) 272 Ind. 236, 397 N. E. 2d 580 (Hunter and DeBruler, JJ., dissenting)." Id., at 225-226. Justice DeBruler expressed similar views in his dissent in Erhardt. Ibid. Therefore, the Indiana Supreme Court did not affirmatively limit the reach of the statute in Baysinger, but merely said that to the extent the First Amendment would require it, the statute might be unconstitutional as applied to some activities.

2 Indiana Code 35-45-4-1 (1988) provides:

"Public Indecency

"Sec. 1. (a) A person who knowingly or intentionally, in a public place:

"(1) engages in sexual intercourse;

"(2) engages in deviate sexual conduct;

"(3) appears in a state of nudity; or

"(4) fondles the genitals of himself or another person;

commits public indecency, a Class A misdemeanor.

"(b) `Nudity' means the showing of the human male or female genitals, pubic area, or buttocks with less than a fully opaque covering, the showing of the female breast with less than a fully opaque covering of any part of the nipple, or the showing of the covered male genitals in a discernibly turgid state."

## R. A. V. v. City of St. Paul (June 22, 1992)

Justice Scalia delivered the opinion of the Court.

In the predawn hours of June 21, 1990, petitioner and several other teenagers allegedly assembled a crudely made cross by taping together broken chair legs. They then allegedly burned the cross inside the fenced yard of a black family that lived across the street from the house where petitioner was staying. Although this conduct could have been punished under any of a number of laws, [n.1] one of the two provisions under which respondent city of St. Paul chose to charge petitioner (then a juvenile) was the St. Paul Bias Motivated Crime Ordinance, St. Paul, Minn. Legis. Code § 292.02 (1990), which provides:

"Whoever places on public or private property a symbol, object, appellation, characterization or graffiti, including, but not limited to, a burning cross or Nazi swastika, which one knows or has reasonable grounds to know arouses anger, alarm or resentment in others on the basis of race, color, creed, religion or gender commits disorderly conduct and shall be guilty of a misdemeanor."

Petitioner moved to dismiss this count on the ground that the St. Paul ordinance was substantially overbroad and impermissibly content based and therefore facially invalid under the First Amendment. [n.2] The trial court granted this motion, but the

Minnesota Supreme Court reversed. That court rejected petitioner's overbreadth claim because, as construed in prior Minnesota cases, see, e. g., In re Welfare of S. L. J., 263 N. W. 2d 412 (Minn. 1978), the modifying phrase "arouses anger, alarm or resentment in others" limited the reach of the ordinance to conduct that amounts to "fighting words," i. e., "conduct that itself inflicts injury or tends to incite immediate violence . . .," In re Welfare of R. A. V., 464 N. W. 2d 507, 510 (Minn. 1991) (citing Chaplinsky v. New Hampshire, 315 U.S. 568, 572 (1942)), and therefore the ordinance reached only expression "that the first amendment does not protect." 464 N. W. 2d, at 511. The court also concluded that the ordinance was not impermissibly content based because, in its view, "the ordinance is a narrowly tailored means toward accomplishing the compelling governmental interest in protecting the community against bias motivated threats to public safety and order." Ibid. We granted certiorari, 501 U. S. ___ (1991).

In construing the St. Paul ordinance, we are bound by the construction given to it by the Minnesota court. Posadas de Puerto Rico Associates v. Tourism Co. of Puerto Rico, 478 U.S. 328, 339 (1986); New York v. Ferber, 458 U.S. 747,769, n. 24 (1982); Terminiello v. Chicago, 337 U.S. 1, 4 (1949). Accordingly, we accept the Minnesota Supreme Court's authoritative statement that the ordinance reaches only those expressions that constitute "fighting words" within the meaning of Chaplinsky. 464 N. W. 2d, at 510-511. Petitioner and his amici urge us to modify the scope of the Chaplinsky formulation, thereby invalidating the ordinance as "substantially overbroad," Broadrick v. Oklahoma, 413 U.S. 601, 610 (1973). We find it unnecessary to consider this issue. Assuming, arguendo, that all of the expression reached by the ordinance is proscribable under the "fighting words" doctrine, we nonetheless conclude that the ordinance is facially unconstitutional in that it prohibits otherwise permitted speech solely on the basis of the subjects the speech addresses. [n.3]

The First Amendment generally prevents government from proscribing speech, see, e. g., Cantwell v. Connecticut, 310 U.S. 296, 309-311 (1940), or even expressive conduct, see, e. g., Texas v. Johnson, 491 U.S. 397, 406 (1989), because of disapproval of the ideas expressed. Content based regulations are presumptively invalid. Simon & Schuster, Inc. v. Members of N. Y. State Crime Victims Bd., 502 U. S. ___, ___ (1991) (slip op., at 8-9); id., at ___ (Kennedy, J., concurring in judgment) (slip op., at 3-4); Consolidated Edison Co. of N. Y. v. Public Serv. Comm'n of N. Y., 447 U.S. 530, 536 (1980); Police Dept. of Chicago v. Mosley, 408 U.S. 92, 95 (1972). From 1791 to the present, however, our society, like other free but civilized societies, has permitted restrictions upon the content of speech in a few limited areas, which are "of such slight social value as a step to truth that any benefit that may be derived from them is clearly outweighed by the social interest in order and morality." Chaplinsky, supra, at 572. We have recognized that "the freedom of speech" referred to by the First Amendment does not include a freedom to disregard these traditional limitations. See, e. g., Roth v. United States, 354 U.S. 476 (1957) (obscenity); Beauharnais v. Illinois, 343 U.S. 250 (1952) (defamation); Chaplinsky v. New Hampshire, supra, ("fighting words"); see generally

Simon & Schuster, supra, at ____ (Kennedy, J., concurring in judgment) (slip op., at 4). Our decisions since the 1960's have narrowed the scope of the traditional categorical exceptions for defamation, see New York Times Co. v.Sullivan, 376 U.S. 254 (1964); Gertz v. Robert Welch, Inc., 418 U.S. 323 (1974); see generally Milkovich v. Lorain Journal Co., 497 U.S. 1, 13-17 (1990), and for obscenity, see Miller v. California, 413 U.S. 15 (1973), but a limited categorical approach has remained an important part of our First Amendment jurisprudence.

We have sometimes said that these categories of expression are "not within the area of constitutionally protected speech," Roth, supra, at 483; Beauharnais, supra, at 266; Chaplinsky, supra, at 571-572, or that the "protection of the First Amendment does not extend" to them, Bose Corp. v. Consumers Union of United States, Inc., 466 U.S. 485, 504 (1984); Sable Communications of Cal., Inc. v. FCC, 492 U.S. 115, 124 (1989). Such statements must be taken in context, however, and are no more literally true than is the occasionally repeated shorthand characterizing obscenity "as not being speech at all," Sunstein, Pornography and the First Amendment, 1986 Duke L. J. 589, 615, n. 146. What they mean is that these areas of speech can, consistently with the First Amendment, be regulated because of their constitutionally proscribable content (obscenity, defamation, etc.)--not that they are categories of speech entirely invisible to the Constitution, so that they may be made the vehicles for content discrimination unrelated to their distinctively proscribable content. Thus, the government may proscribe libel; but it may not make the further content discrimination of proscribing only libel critical of the government. We recently acknowledged this distinction in Ferber, 458 U. S., at 763, where, in upholding New York's child pornography law, we expressly recognized that there was no "question here of censoring a particular literary theme . . . ." See also id., at 775 (O'Connor, J., concurring) ("As drafted, New York's statute does not attempt to suppress the communication of particular ideas").

Our cases surely do not establish the proposition that the First Amendment imposes no obstacle whatsoever to regulation of particular instances of such proscribable expression, so that the government "may regulate [them] freely," post, at 4 (White, J., concurring in judgment). That would mean that a city council could enact an ordinance prohibiting only those legally obscene works that contain criticism of the city government or, indeed, that do not include endorsement of the city government. Such a simplistic, all or nothing at all approach to First Amendment protection is at odds with common sense and with our jurisprudence as well. [n.4] It is not true that "fighting words" have at most a "*de minimis*" expressive content, ibid., or that their content is in all respects "worthless and undeserving of constitutional protection," post, at 6; sometimes they are quite expressive indeed. We have not said that they constitute "no part of the expression of ideas," but only that they constitute "no essential part of any exposition of ideas." Chaplinsky, 315 U. S., at 572 (emphasis added).

The proposition that a particular instance of speech can be proscribable on the basis of one feature (e. g., obscenity) but not on the basis of another (e. g., opposition to the city government) is commonplace, and has found application in many contexts. We have long held, for example, that nonverbal expressive activity can be banned because of the action it entails, but not because of the ideas it expresses--so that burning a flag in violation of an ordinance against outdoor fires could be punishable, whereas burning a flag in violation of an ordinance against dishonoring the flag is not. See Johnson, 491 U. S., at 406-407. See also Barnes v. Glen Theatre, Inc., 501 U. S. ___, ___ ___ (1991) (plurality) (slip op., at 4-6); id., at ___ ___ (Scalia, J., concurring in judgment) (slip op., at 5-6); id., at ___ ___ (Souter, J., concurring in judgment) (slip op., at 1-2); United States v. O'Brien, 391 U.S. 367, 376-377 (1968). Similarly, we have upheld reasonable "time, place, or manner" restrictions, but only if they are "justified without reference to the content of the regulated speech." Ward v. Rock Against Racism, 491 U.S. 781, 791 (1989) (internal quotation marks omitted); see also Clark v. Community for Creative Non Violence, 468 U.S. 288, 298 (1984) (noting that the O'Brien test differs little from the standard applied to time, place, or manner restrictions). And just as the power to proscribe particular speech on the basis of a noncontent element (e. g., noise) does not entail the power to proscribe the same speech on the basis of a content element; so also, the power to proscribe it on the basis of one content element (e. g., obscenity) does not entail the power to proscribe it on the basis of other content elements.

In other words, the exclusion of "fighting words" from the scope of the First Amendment simply means that, for purposes of that Amendment, the unprotected features of the words are, despite their verbal character, essentially a "nonspeech" element of communication. Fighting words are thus analogous to a noisy sound truck: Each is, as Justice Frankfurter recognized, a "mode of speech," Niemotko v. Maryland, 340 U.S. 268, 282 (1951) (Frankfurter, J., concurring in result); both can be used to convey an idea; but neither has, in and of itself, a claim upon the First Amendment. As with the sound truck, however, so also with fighting words: The government may not regulate use based on hostility--or favoritism--towards the underlying message expressed. Compare Frisby v. Schultz, 487 U.S. 474 (1988) (upholding, against facial challenge, a content neutral ban on targeted residential picketing) with Carey v. Brown, 447 U.S. 455 (1980) (invalidating a ban on residential picketing that exempted labor picketing). [n.5]

The concurrences describe us as setting forth a new First Amendment principle that prohibition of constitutionally proscribable speech cannot be "underinclusiv[e]," post, at 6 (White, J., concurring in judgment)--a First Amendment "absolutism" whereby "within a particular `proscribable' category of expression, . . . a government must either pro scribe all speech or no speech at all," post, at 4 (Stevens, J., concurring in judgment). That easy target is of the concurrences' own invention. In our view, the First Amendment imposes not an "underinclusiveness" limitation but a "content discrimination" limitation upon a State's prohibition of proscribable speech. There is no problem whatever, for example, with a State's prohibiting obscenity (and other forms of proscribable expression) only in certain media or markets, for although that prohibition would be "underinclusive," it would not discriminate on the basis of content. See, e. g., Sable Communications, 492 U. S., at 124-126 (upholding 47 U.S.C. § 223(b)(1) (1988), which prohibits obscene telephone communications).

Even the prohibition against content discrimination that we assert the First Amendment requires is not absolute. It applies differently in the context of proscribable speech than in the area of fully protected speech. The rationale of the general prohibition, after all, is that content discrimination "rais[es] the specter that the Government may effectively drive certain ideas or viewpoints from the marketplace," Simon & Schuster, 502 U. S., at ___ (slip op., at 9); Leathers v. Medlock, 499 U. S. ___, ___ (1991); FCC v. League of Women Voters of California, 468 U.S. 364, 383-384 (1984); Consolidated Edison Co., 447 U. S., at 536; Police Dept. of Chicago v. Mosley, 408 U. S., at 95-98. But content discrimination among various instances of a class of proscribable speech often does not pose this threat.

When the basis for the content discrimination consists entirely of the very reason the entire class of speech at issue is proscribable, no significant danger of idea or viewpoint discrimination exists. Such a reason, having been adjudged neutral enough to support exclusion of the entire class of speech from First Amendment protection, is also neutral enough to form the basis of distinction within the class. To illustrate: A State might choose to prohibit only that obscenity which is the most patently offensive in its prurience--i. e., that which involves the most lascivious displays of sexual activity. But it may not prohibit, for example, only that obscenity which includes offensive political messages. See Kucharek v. Hanaway, 902 F. 2d 513, 517 (CA7 1990), cert. denied, 498 U. S. ___ (1991). And the Federal Government can criminalize only those threats of violence that are directed against the President, see 18 U.S.C. § 871--since the reasons why threats of violence are outside the First Amendment (protecting individuals from the fear of violence, from the disruption that fear engenders, and from the possibility that the threatened violence will occur) have special force when applied to the person of the President. See Watts v. United States, 394 U.S. 705, 707 (1969) (upholding the facial validity of § 871 because of the "overwhelmin[g] interest in protecting the safety of [the] Chief Executive and in allowing him to perform his duties without interference from threats of physical violence"). But the Federal Government may not criminalize only those threats against the President that mention his policy on aid to inner cities. And to take a final example (one mentioned by Justice Stevens, post, at 6-7), a State may choose to regulate price advertising in one industry but not in others, because the risk of fraud (one of the characteristics of commercial speech that justifies depriving it of full First Amendment protection, see Virginia Pharmacy Bd. v. Virginia Citizens Consumer Council, Inc., 425 U.S. 748, 771-772 (1976)) is in its view greater there. Cf. Morales v. Trans World Airlines, Inc., 504 U. S. ___ (1992) (state regulation of airline advertising); Ohralik v. Ohio State Bar Assn., 436 U.S. 447 (1978) (state regulation of lawyer advertising). But a State may not prohibit only that commercial advertising that depicts men in a demeaning fashion, see, e. g., L. A. Times, Aug. 8, 1989, section 4, p. 6, col. 1.

Another valid basis for according differential treatment to even a content defined subclass of proscribable speech is that the subclass happens to be associated with particular "secondary effects" of the speech, so that the regulation is%justified without reference to the content of the . . . speech," Renton v. Playtime Theatres, Inc., 475 U.S. 41, 48 (1986) (quoting, with emphasis, Virginia Pharmacy Bd., supra, at 771); see also Young v. American Mini Theatres, Inc., 427 U.S. 50, 71, n. 34 (1976) (plurality); id., at 80-82 (Powell, J., concurring); Barnes, 501 U. S., at ____ ____ (Souter, J., concurring in judgment) (slip op., at 3-7). A State could, for example, permit all obscene live performances except those involving minors. Moreover, since words can in some circumstances violate laws directed not against speech but against conduct (a law against treason, for example, is violated by telling the enemy the nation's defense secrets), a particular content based subcategory of a proscribable class of speech can be swept up incidentally within the reach of a statute directed at conduct rather than speech. See id., at ____ (plurality) (slip op., at 4); id., at ____ (Scalia, J., concurring in judgment) (slip op., at 5-6); id., at ____ (Souter, J., concurring in judgment) (slip op., at 1-2); FTC v. Superior Court Trial Lawyers Assn., 493 U.S. 411, 425-432 (1990); O'Brien, 391 U. S., at 376-377. Thus, for example, sexually derogatory "fighting words," among other words, may produce a violation of Title VII's general prohibition against sexual discrimination in employment practices, 42 U.S.C. § 2000e 2; 29 CFR § 1604.11 (1991). See also 18 U.S.C. § 242; 42 U.S.C. §§ 1981 1982. Where the government does not target conduct on the basis of its expressive content, acts are not shielded from regulation merely because they express a discriminatory idea or philosophy.

These bases for distinction refute the proposition that the selectivity of the restriction is "even arguably `conditioned upon the sovereign's agreement with what a speaker may intend to say.' " Metromedia, Inc. v. San Diego, 453 U.S. 490, 555 (1981) (Stevens, J., dissenting in part) (citation omitted). There may be other such bases as well. Indeed, to validate such selectivity (where totally proscribable speech is at issue) it may not even be necessary to identify any particular "neutral" basis, so long as the nature of the content discrimination is such that there is no realistic possibility that official suppression of ideas is afoot. (We cannot think of any First Amendment interest that would stand in the way of a State's prohibiting only those obscene motion pictures with blue eyed actresses.) Save for that limitation, the regulation of "fighting words," like the regulation of noisy speech, may address some offensive instances and leave other, equally offensive, instances alone. See Posadas de Puerto Rico, 478 U. S., at 342-343. [n.6]

Applying these principles to the St. Paul ordinance, we conclude that, even as narrowly construed by the Minnesota Supreme Court, the ordinance is facially unconstitutional. Although the phrase in the ordinance, "arouses anger, alarm or resentment in others," has been limited by the Minnesota Supreme Court's construction to reach only those symbols or displays that amount to "fighting words," the remaining, unmodified terms make clear that the ordinance applies only to "fighting words" that insult, or provoke violence, "on the basis of race, color, creed, religion or gender."

Displays containing abusive invective, no matter how vicious or severe, are permissible unless they are addressed to one of the specified disfavored topics. Those who wish to use "fighting words" in connection with other ideas--to express hostility, for example, on the basis of political affiliation, union membership, or homosexuality--are not covered. The First Amendment does not permit St. Paul to impose special prohibitions on those speakers who express views on disfavored subjects. See Simon & Schuster, 502 U. S., at ____ (slip op., at 8-9); Arkansas Writers' Project, Inc. v. Ragland, 481 U.S. 221, 229-230 (1987).

In its practical operation, moreover, the ordinance goes even beyond mere content discrimination, to actual viewpoint discrimination. Displays containing some words--odious racial epithets, for example--would be prohibited to proponents of all views. But "fighting words" that do not themselves invoke race, color, creed, religion, or gender--aspersions upon a person's mother, for example--would seemingly be usable ad libitum in the placards of those arguing in favor of racial, color, etc. tolerance and equality, but could not be used by that speaker's opponents. One could hold up a sign saying, for example, that all "anti Catholic bigots" are misbegotten; but not that all "papists" are, for that would insult and provoke violence "on the basis of religion." St. Paul has no such authority to license one side of a debate to fight freestyle, while requiring the other to follow Marquis of Queensbury Rules.

What we have here, it must be emphasized, is not a prohibition of fighting words that are directed at certain persons or groups (which would be facially valid if it met the requirements of the Equal Protection Clause); but rather, a prohibition of fighting words that contain (as the Minnesota Supreme Court repeatedly emphasized) messages of "bias motivated" hatred and in particular, as applied to this case, messages "based on virulent notions of racial supremacy." 464 N. W. 2d, at 508, 511. One must wholeheartedly agree with the Minnesota Supreme Court that "[i]t is the responsibility, even the obligation, of diverse communities to confront such notions in whatever form they appear," ibid., but the manner of that confrontation cannot consist of selective limitations upon speech. St. Paul's brief asserts that a general "fighting words" law would not meet the city's needs because only a content specific measure can communicate to minority groups that the "group hatred" aspect of such speech "is not condoned by the majority." Brief for Respondent 25. The point of the First Amendment is that majority preferences must be expressed in some fashion other than silencing speech on the basis of its content.

Despite the fact that the Minnesota Supreme Court and St. Paul acknowledge that the ordinance is directed at expression of group hatred, Justice Stevens suggests that this "fundamentally misreads" the ordinance. Post, at 18-19. It is directed, he claims, not to speech of a particular content, but to particular "injur[ies]" that are "qualitatively different" from other injuries. Post, at 9. This is word play. What makes the anger, fear, sense of dishonor, etc. produced by violation of this ordinance distinct from the anger, fear, sense of dishonor, etc. produced by other fighting words is nothing other than the fact that it is caused by a distinctive idea, conveyed by a distinctive message. The First

Amendment cannot be evaded that easily. It is obvious that the symbols which will arouse "anger, alarm or resentment in others on the basis of race, color, creed, religion or gender" are those symbols that communicate a message of hostility based on one of these characteristics. St. Paul concedes in its brief that the ordinance applies only to "racial, religious, or gender specific symbols" such as "a burning cross, Nazi swastika or other instrumentality of like import." Brief for Respon dent 8. Indeed, St. Paul argued in the Juvenile Court that%[t]he burning of a cross does express a message and it is, in fact, the content of that message which the St. Paul Ordinance attempts to legislate." Memorandum from the Ramsey County Attorney to the Honorable Charles A. Flinn, Jr., dated July 13, 1990, in In re Welfare of R. A. V., No. 89-D%1231 (Ramsey Cty. Juvenile Ct.), p. 1, reprinted in App. to Brief for Petitioner C 1.

The content based discrimination reflected in the St. Paul ordinance comes within neither any of the specific exceptions to the First Amendment prohibition we discussed earlier, nor within a more general exception for content discrimination that does not threaten censorship of ideas. It assuredly does not fall within the exception for content discrimination based on the very reasons why the particular class of speech at issue (here, fighting words) is proscribable. As explained earlier, see supra, at 8, the reason why fighting words are categorically excluded from the protection of the First Amendment is not that their content communicates any particular idea, but that their content embodies a particularly intolerable (and socially unnecessary) mode of expressing whatever idea the speaker wishes to convey. St. Paul has not singled out an especially offensive mode of expression--it has not, for example, selected for prohibition only those fighting words that communicate ideas in a threatening (as opposed to a merely obnoxious) manner. Rather, it has proscribed fighting words of whatever manner that communicate messages of racial, gender, or religious intolerance. Selectivity of this sort creates the possibility that the city is seeking to handicap the expression of particular ideas. That possibility would alone be enough to render the ordinance presumptively invalid, but St. Paul's comments and concessions in this case elevate the possibility to a certainty.

St. Paul argues that the ordinance comes within another of the specific exceptions we mentioned, the one that allows content discrimination aimed only at the "secondary effects" of the speech, see Renton v. Playtime Theatres, Inc., 475 U.S. 41 (1986). According to St. Paul, the ordinance is intended, "not to impact on [sic] the right of free expression of the accused," but rather to "protect against the victimization of a person or persons who are particularly vulnerable because of their membership in a group that historically has been discriminated against." Brief for Respondent 28. Even assuming that an ordinance that completely proscribes, rather than merely regulates, a specified category of speech can ever be considered to be directed only to the secondary effects of such speech, it is clear that the St. Paul ordinance is not directed to secondary effects within the meaning of Renton. As we said in Boos v. Barry, 485 U.S. 312 (1988), "[l]isteners' reactions to speech are not the type of `secondary effects' we referred to in

Renton." Id., at 321. "The emotive impact of speech on its audience is not a `secondary effect.' " Ibid. See also id., at 334 (opinion of Brennan, J.). [n.7]

It hardly needs discussion that the ordinance does not fall within some more general exception permitting all selectivity that for any reason is beyond the suspicion of official suppression of ideas. The statements of St. Paul in this very case afford ample basis for, if not full confirmation of, that suspicion.

Finally, St. Paul and its amici defend the conclusion of the Minnesota Supreme Court that, even if the ordinance regulates expression based on hostility towards its protected ideological content, this discrimination is nonetheless justified because it is narrowly tailored to serve compelling state interests. Specifically, they assert that the ordinance helps to ensure the basic human rights of members of groups that have historically been subjected to discrimination, including the right of such group members to live in peace where they wish. We do not doubt that these interests are compelling, and that the ordinance can be said to promote them. But the "danger of censorship" presented by a facially content based statute, Leathers v. Medlock, 499 U. S. ___, ___ (1991) (slip op., at 8), requires that that weapon be employed only where it is "necessary to serve the asserted [compelling] interest," Burson v. Freeman, 504 U. S. ___, ___ (1992) (plurality) (slip op., at 8) (emphasis added); Perry Education Assn. v. Perry Local Educators' Assn., 460 U.S. 37, 45 (1983). The existence of adequate content neutral alternatives thus "undercut[s] significantly" any defense of such a statute, Boos v. Barry, supra, at 329, casting considerable doubt on the government's protestations that "the asserted justification is in fact an accurate description of the purpose and effect of the law," Burson, supra, at ___ (Kennedy, J., concurring) (slip op., at 2). See Boos, supra, at 324-329; cf. Minneapolis Star & Tribune Co. v. Minnesota Comm'r of Revenue, 460 U.S. 575, 586-587 (1983). The dispositive question in this case, therefore, is whether content discrimination is reasonably necessary to achieve St. Paul's compelling interests; it plainly is not. An ordinance not limited to the favored topics, for example, would have precisely the same beneficial effect. In fact the only interest distinctively served by the content limitation is that of displaying the city council's special hostility towards the particular biases thus singled out. [n.8] That is precisely what the First Amendment forbids. The politicians of St. Paul are entitled to express that hostility--but not through the means of imposing unique limitations upon speakers who (however benightedly) disagree.

\* \* \*

Let there be no mistake about our belief that burning a cross in someone's front yard is reprehensible. But St. Paul has sufficient means at its disposal to prevent such behavior without adding the First Amendment to the fire.

The judgment of the Minnesota Supreme Court is reversed, and the case is remanded for proceedings not inconsistent with this opinion.

It is so ordered.

Notes

1 The conduct might have violated Minnesota statutes carrying significant penalties. See, e. g., Minn. Stat. § 609.713(1) (1987) (providing for up to five years in prison for terroristic threats); § 609.563 (arson) (providing for up to five years and a $10,000 fine, depending on the value of the property intended to be damaged); § 606.595 (Supp. 1992) (criminal damage to property) (providing for up to one year and a $3,000 fine, depending upon the extent of the damage to the property).

2 Petitioner has also been charged, in Count I of the delinquency petition, with a violation of Minn. Stat. § 609.2231(4) (Supp. 1990) (racially motivated assaults). Petitioner did not challenge this count.

3 Contrary to Justice White's suggestion, post, at 1-2, petitioner's claim is "fairly included" within the questions presented in the petition for certiorari, see this Court's Rule 14.1(a). It was clear from the petition and from petitioner's other filings in this Court (and in the courts below) that his assertion that the St. Paul ordinance "violat[es] overbreadth . . . principles of the First Amendment," Pet. for Cert. i, was not just a technical "overbreadth" claim--i. e., a claim that the ordinance violated the rights of too many third parties--but included the contention that the ordinance was "overbroad" in the sense of restricting more speech than the Constitution permits, even in its application to him, because it is content based. An important component of petitioner's argument is, and has been all along, that narrowly construing the ordinance to cover only "fighting words" cannot cure this fundamental defect. Id., at 12, 14, 15-16. In his briefs in this Court, petitioner argued that a narrowing construction was ineffective because (1) its boundaries were vague, Brief for Petitioner 26, and because (2) denominating particular expression a "fighting word" because of the impact of its ideological content upon the audience is inconsistent with the First Amendment, Reply Brief for Petitioner 5; id., at 13 ("[The ordinance] is overbroad, viewpoint discriminatory and vague as `narrowly construed' ") (emphasis added). At oral argument, counsel for Petitioner reiterated this second point: "It is . . . one of my positions, that in [punishing only some fighting words and not others], even though it is a subcategory, technically, of unprotected conduct, [the ordinance] still is picking out an opinion, a disfavored message, and making that clear through the State." Tr. of Oral Arg. 8. In resting our judgment upon this contention, we have not departed from our criteria of what is "fairly included" within the petition. See Arkansas Electric Cooperative Corp. v. Arkansas Pub. Serv. Comm'n, 461 U.S. 375, 382, n. 6 (1983); Brown v. Socialist Workers '74 Campaign Comm., 459 U.S. 87, 94, n. 9 (1982); Eddings v. Oklahoma, 455 U.S. 104, 113, n. 9 (1982); see generally R. Stern, E. Gressman, & S. Shapiro, Supreme Court Practice 361 (6th ed. 1986).

4 Justice White concedes that a city council cannot prohibit only those legally obscene works that contain criticism of the city government, post, at 11, but asserts that to be the consequence, not of the First Amendment, but of the Equal Protection Clause. Such content based discrimination would not, he asserts, "be rationally related to a legitimate government interest," ibid. But of course the only reason that government

interest is not a "legitimate" one is that it violates the First Amendment. This Court itself has occasionally fused the First Amendment into the Equal Protection Clause in this fashion, but at least with the acknowledgment (which Justice White cannot afford to make) that the First Amendment underlies its analysis. See Police Dept. of Chicago v. Mosley, 408 U.S. 92, 95 (1972) (ordinance prohibiting only nonlabor picketing violated the Equal Protection Clause because there was no "appropriate governmental interest" supporting the distinction inasmuch as "the First Amendment means that government has no power to restrict expression because of its message, its ideas, its subject matter, or its content"); Carey v. Brown, 447 U.S. 455 (1980). See generally Simon & Schuster, Inc. v. Members of N. Y. State Crime Victims Bd., 502 U. S. ____, ____ (1991) (Kennedy, J., concurring in judgment) (slip op., at 2-3).

Justice Stevens seeks to avoid the point by dismissing the notion of obscene anti-government speech as "fantastical," post, at 3, apparently believing that any reference to politics prevents a finding of obscenity. Unfortunately for the purveyors of obscenity, that is obviously false. A shockingly hard core pornographic movie that contains a model sporting a political tattoo can be found, "taken as a whole [to] lac[k] serious literary, artistic, political, or scientific value," Miller v. California, 413 U.S. 15, 24 (1973) (emphasis added). Anyway, it is easy enough to come up with other illustrations of a content based restriction upon "unprotected speech" that is obviously invalid: the anti government libel illustration mentioned earlier, for one. See supra, at 5. And of course the concept of racist fighting words is, unfortunately, anything but a "highly speculative hypothetica[l]," post, at 4.

5 Although Justice White asserts that our analysis disregards "established principles of First Amendment law," post, at 19, he cites not a single case (and we are aware of none) that even involved, much less considered and resolved, the issue of content discrimination through regulation of "unprotected" speech--though we plainly recognized that as an issue in Ferber. It is of course contrary to all traditions of our jurisprudence to consider the law on this point conclusively resolved by broad language in cases where the issue was not presented or even envisioned.

6 Justice Stevens cites a string of opinions as supporting his assertion that "selective regulation of speech based on content" is not presumptively invalid. Post, at 6-7. Analysis reveals, however, that they do not support it. To begin with, three of them did not command a majority of the Court, Young v. American Mini Theatres, Inc., 427 U.S. 50, 63-73 (1976) (plurality); FCC v. Pacifica Foundation, 438 U.S. 726, 744-748 (1978) (plurality); Lehman v. City of Shaker Heights, 418 U.S. 298 (1974) (plurality), and two others did not even discuss the First Amendment, Morales v. Trans World Airlines, Inc., 504 U. S. ____ (1992); Jacob Siegel Co. v. FTC, 327 U.S. 608 (1946). In any event, all that their contents establish is what we readily concede: that presumptive invalidity does not mean invariable invalidity, leaving room for such exceptions as reasonable and viewpoint neutral content based discrimination in nonpublic forums, see Lehman, supra, at 301-304; see also Cornelius v. NAACP Legal Defense & Educational Fund, Inc., 473 U.S. 788,

806 (1985), or with respect to certain speech by government employees, see Broadrick v. Oklahoma, 413 U.S. 601 (1973); see also CSC v. Letter Carriers, 413 U.S. 548, 564-567 (1973).

7 St. Paul has not argued in this case that the ordinance merely regulates that subclass of fighting words which is most likely to provoke a violent response. But even if one assumes (as appears unlikely) that the categories selected may be so described, that would not justify selective regulation under a "secondary effects" theory. The only reason why such expressive conduct would be especially correlated with violence is that it conveys a particularly odious message; because the "chain of causation" thus necessarily "run[s] through the persuasive effect of the expressive component" of the conduct, Barnes v. Glen Theatre, 501 U. S. ____, ____ (1991) (Souter, J., concurring in judgment) (slip op., at 6), it is clear that the St. Paul ordinance regulates on the basis of the "primary" effect of the speech--i. e., its persuasive (or repellant) force.

8 A plurality of the Court reached a different conclusion with regard to the Tennessee anti electioneering statute considered earlier this Termin Burson v. Freeman, 504 U. S. ____ (1992). In light of the "logical connection" between electioneering and the State's compelling interest in preventing voter intimidation and election fraud--an inherent connection borne out by a "long history" and a "wide spread and time tested consensus," id., at ____ ____ (slip op., at 14-19)--the plurality concluded that it was faced with one of those "rare case[s]" in which the use of a facially content based restriction was justified by interests unrelated to the suppression of ideas, id., at ____ (slip op., at 19); see also id., at ____ (Kennedy, J., concurring) (slip op., at 3). Justice White and Justice Stevens are therefore quite mistaken when they seek to convert the Burson plurality's passing comment that "[t]he First Amendment does not require States to regulate for problems that do not exist," id., at ____ (slip op., at 16), into endorsement of the revolutionary proposition that the suppression of particular ideas can be justified when only those ideas have been a source of trouble in the past. Post, at 10 (White, J.); post, at 19 (Stevens, J.).

## US v. X-Citement Video, Inc. (November 29, 1994)

Chief Justice Rehnquist delivered the opinion of the Court.

The Protection of Children Against Sexual Exploitation Act of 1977, as amended, prohibits the interstate transportation, shipping, receipt, distribution or reproduction of visual depictions of minors engaged in sexually explicit conduct. 18 U.S.C. § 2252. The Court of Appeals for the Ninth Circuit reversed the conviction of respondents for violation of this Act. It held that the Act did not require that the defendant know that one of the performers was a minor, and that it was therefore facially unconstitutional. We conclude that the Act is properly read to include such a requirement.

Rubin Gottesman owned and operated X Citement Video, Inc. Undercover police posed as pornography retailers and targeted X Citement Video for investigation. During the course of the sting operation, the media exposed Traci Lords for her roles in pornographic films while under the age of 18. Police Officer Steven Takeshita expressed an interest in obtaining Traci Lords tapes. Gottesman complied, selling Takeshita 49 videotapes featuring Lords before her 18th birthday. Two months later, Gottesman shipped eight tapes of the underage Traci Lords to Takeshita in Hawaii.

These two transactions formed the basis for a federal indictment under the child pornography statute. The indictment charged respondents with one count each of violating 18 U.S.C. §§ 2252(a)(1) and (a)(2), along with one count of conspiracy to do the same under 18 U.S.C. § 371. [n.1] Evidence at trial suggested that Gottesman had full awareness of Lords' underage performances. United States v. Gottesman, No. CR 88-295KN, Findings of Fact ¶ 7 (CD Cal., Sept. 20, 1989), App. to Pet. for Cert. A 39 ("Defendants knew that Traci Lords was underage when she made the films defendant's [sic] transported or shipped in interstate commerce"). The District Court convicted respondents of all three counts. On appeal, Gottesman argued inter alia that the Act was facially unconstitutional because it lacked a necessary scienter requirement and was unconstitutional as applied because the tapes at issue were not child pornography. The Ninth Circuit remanded to the District Court for reconsideration in light of United States v. Thomas, 893 F. 2d 1066 (CA9), cert. denied, 498 U.S. 826 (1990). In that case, the Ninth Circuit had held §2252 did not contain a scienter requirement, but had not reached the constitutional questions. On remand, the District Court refused to set aside the judgment of conviction.

On appeal for the second time, Gottesman reiterated his constitutional arguments. This time, the court reached the merits of his claims and, by a divided vote, found §2252 facially unconstitutional. The court first held that 18 U.S.C. § 2256 met constitutional standards in setting the age of minority at age 18, substituting lascivious for lewd, and prohibiting actual or simulated bestiality and sadistic or masochistic abuse. 982 F. 2d1285, 1288-1289 (CA9 1992). It then discussed §2252, noting it was bound by its conclusion in Thomas to construe the Act as lacking a scienter requirement for the age of minority. The court concluded that case law from this Court required that the defendant must have knowledge at least of the nature and character of the materials. 982 F. 2d, at 1290, citing Smith v. California, 361 U.S. 147 (1959); New York v. Ferber, 458 U.S. 747 (1982); and Hamling v. United States, 418 U.S. 87 (1974). The court extended these cases to hold that the First Amendment requires that the defendant possess knowledge of the particular fact that one performer had not reached the age of majority at the time the visual depiction was produced. 982 F. 2d at 1291. Because the court found the statute did not require such a showing, it reversed respondents' convictions. We granted certiorari, 510 U. S. -- (1994), and now reverse.

Title 18 U.S.C. § 2252 (1988 ed. and Supp. V) provides, in relevant part:

"(a) Any person who-

"(1) knowingly transports or ships in interstate or foreign commerce by any means including by computer or mails, any visual depiction, if-

"(A) the producing of such visual depiction involves the use of a minor engaging in sexually explicit conduct; and

"(B) such visual depiction is of such conduct;

"(2) knowingly receives, or distributes, any visual depiction that has been mailed, or has been shipped or transported in interstate or foreign commerce, or which contains materials which have been mailed or so shipped or transported, by any means including by computer, or knowingly reproduces any visual depiction for distribution ininterstate or foreign commerce or through the mails, if-

"(A) the producing of such visual depiction involves the use of a minor engaging in sexually explicit conduct; and

"(B) such visual depiction is of such conduct;

. . . . .

shall be punished as provided in subsection (b) of this section.

The critical determination which we must make is whether the term "knowingly" in subsections (1) and (2) modifies the phrase "the use of a minor" in subsections (1)(A) and (2)(A). The most natural grammatical reading, adopted by the Ninth Circuit, suggests that the term "knowingly" modifies only the surrounding verbs: transports, ships, receives, distributes, or reproduces. Under this construction, the word "knowingly" would not modify the elements of the minority of the performers, or the sexually explicit nature of the material, because they are set forth in independent clauses separated by interruptive punctuation. But we do not think this is the end of the matter, both because of anomalies which result from this construction, and because of the respective presumptions that some form of scienter is to be implied in a criminal statute even if not expressed, and that a statute is to be construed where fairly possible so as to avoid substantial constitutional questions.

If the term "knowingly" applies only to the relevant verbs in §2252 -- transporting, shipping, receiving, distributing and reproducing -- we would have to conclude that Congress wished to distinguish between someone who knowingly transported a particular package of film whose contents were unknown to him, and someone who unknowingly transported that package. It would seem odd, to say the least, that Congress distinguished between someone who inadvertently dropped an item into the mail without realizing it, and someone who consciously placed the same item in the mail, but was nonetheless unconcerned about whether the person had any knowledge of the prohibited contents of the package.

Some applications of respondents' position would produce results that were not merely odd, but positively absurd. If we were to conclude that "knowingly" only modifies the relevant verbs in §2252, we would sweep within the ambit of the statute actors who had no idea that they were even dealing with sexually explicit material. For instance, a retail druggist who returns an uninspected roll of developed film to a customer "knowingly distributes" a visual depiction and would be criminally liable if it were later discovered that the visual depiction contained images of children engaged in sexually explicit conduct. Or, a new resident of an apartment might receive mail for the prior resident and store the mail unopened. If the prior tenant had requested delivery of materials covered by §2252, his residential successor could be prosecuted for "knowing receipt" of such materials. Similarly, a Federal Express courier who delivers a box in which the shipper has declared the contents to be "film" "knowingly transports" such film. We do not assume that Congress, in passing laws, intended such results. Public Citizen v. Department of Justice, 491 U.S. 440, 453-455 (1989); United States v. Turkette, 452 U.S. 576, 580 (1981).

Our reluctance to simply follow the most grammatical reading of the statute is heightened by our cases interpreting criminal statutes to include broadly applicable scienter requirements, even where the statute by its terms does not contain them. The landmark opinion in Morissette v. United States, 342 U.S. 246 (1952), discussed the common law history of mens rea as applied to the elements of the federal embezzlement statute. That statute read: "Whoever embezzles, steals, purloins, or knowingly converts to his use or the use of another, or without authority, sells, conveys or disposes of any record, voucher, money, or thing of value of the United States . . . [s]hall be fined." 18 U.S.C. § 641 cited in Morissette, 342 U. S., at 248, n. 2. Perhaps even more obviously than in the statute presently before us, the word "knowingly" in its isolated position suggested that it only attached to the verb "converts," and required only that the defendant intentionally assume dominion over the property. But the Court used the background presumption of evil intent to conclude that the term "knowingly" also required that the defendant have knowledge of the facts that made the taking a conversion -- i.e., that the property belonged to the United States. Id., at 271. See also United States v. United States Gypsum Co., 438 U.S. 422, 438 (1978) ("[F]ar more than the simple omission of the appropriate phrase from the statutory definition is necessary to justify dispensing with an intent requirement").

Liparota v. United States, 471 U.S. 419 (1985), posed a challenge to a federal statute prohibiting certain actions with respect to food stamps. The statute's use of "knowingly" could be read only to modify "uses, transfers, acquires, alters, or possesses" or it could be read also to modify "in any manner not authorized by [the statute]." Noting that neither interpretation posed constitutional problems, id., at 424, n. 6, the Court held the scienter requirement applied to both elements by invoking the background principle set forth in Morissette. In addition, the Court was concerned with the broader reading which would "criminalize a broad range of apparently innocent conduct." 471 U. S., at 426. Imposing criminal liability on an unwitting food stamp recipient who purchased groceries at a store that inflated its prices to such purchasers struck the Court as beyond the intended reach of the statute.

The same analysis drove the recent conclusion in Staples v. United States, 511 U. S. -- (1994), that to be criminally liable a defendant must know that his weapon possessed automatic firing capability so as to make it a machine gun as defined by the National Firearms Act. Congress had not expressly imposed any mens rea requirement in the provision criminalizing the possession of a firearm in the absence of proper registration. 26 U.S.C. § 5861(d). The Court first rejected the argument that the statute described a public welfare offense, traditionally excepted from the background principle favoring scienter. Morissette, supra, at 255. The Court then expressed concern with a statutory reading that would criminalize behavior that a defendant believed fell within "a long tradition of widespread lawful gun ownership by private individuals." Staples, 511 U. S., at -- (slip op., at 10). The Court also emphasized the harsh penalties attaching to violations of the statute as a "significant consideration in determining whether the statute should be construed as dispensing with mens rea." Id., at -- (slip op., at 16).

Applying these principles, we think the Ninth Circuit's plain language reading of §2252 is not so plain. First, §2252 is not a public welfare offense. Persons do not harbor settled expectations that the contents of magazines and film are generally subject to stringent public regulation. In fact, First Amendment constraints presuppose the opposite view. Rather, the statute is more akin to the common law offenses against the "state, person, property, or public morals," Morissette, supra, at 255, that presume a scienter requirement in the absence of express contrary intent. [n.2] Second, Staples' concern with harsh penalties looms equally large respecting §2252: violations are punishable by up to 10 years in prison as well as substantial fines and forfeiture. 18 U.S.C. §§ 2252(b), 2253, 2254. See also Morissette, supra, at 260.

Morissette, reinforced by Staples, instructs that the presumption in favor of a scienter requirement should apply to each of the statutory elements which criminalize otherwise innocent conduct. Staples held that the features of a gun as technically described by the firearm registration act was such an element. Its holding rested upon "the nature of the particular device or substance Congress has subjected to regulation and the expectations that individuals may legitimately have in dealing with the regulated items." Staples, supra, at -- (slip op., at 20). Age of minority in §2252 indisputably possesses the same status as an elemental fact because non obscene, sexually explicit materials involving persons over the age of 17 are protected by the First Amendment. Alexander v. United States, 509 U. S. -- (1993) (slip op., at 4-5); Sable Communications of California, Inc. v. Federal Communications Commission, 492 U.S. 115, 126 (1989); FW/PBS, Inc. v. Dallas, 493 U.S. 215, 224 (1990); Smith v. California, 361 U. S., at 152. [n.3] In the light of these decisions, one would reasonably expect to be free from regulation when trafficking in sexually explicit, though not obscene, materials involving adults. Therefore, the age of the performers is the crucial element separating legal innocence from wrongful conduct.

The legislative history of the statute evolved over a period of years, and perhaps for that reason speaks somewhat indistinctly to the question whether "knowingly" in the statute modifies the elements of (1)(A) and (2)(A)--that the visual depiction involves the use of a minor engaging in sexually explicit conduct--or merely the verbs "transport or ship" in (1) and "receive or distribute . . . [or] reproduce" in (2). In 1959 we held in Smith v. California, supra, that a California statute which dispensed with any mens rea requirement as to the contents of an obscene book would violate the First Amendment. Id., at 154. When Congress began dealing with child pornography in 1977, the content of the legislative debates suggest that it was aware of this decision. See, e.g., 123 Cong. Rec. 30935 (1977) ("It is intended that they have knowledge of the type of material . . . proscribed by this bill. The legislative history should be clear on that so as to remove any chance it will lead into constitutional problems"). Even if that were not the case, we do not impute to Congress an intent to pass legislation that is inconsistent with the Constitution as construed by this Court. Yates v. United States, 354 U.S. 298, 319 (1957) ("In [construing thestatute] we should not assume that Congress chose to disregard a constitutional danger zone so clearly marked"). When first passed, §2252 punished one who "knowingly transports or ships in interstate or foreign commerce or mails, for the purpose of sale or distribution for sale, any obscene visual or print medium" if it involved the use of a minor engaged in sexually explicit conduct. Pub. L. 95-225, 92 Stat. 7 (emphasis added). Assuming awareness of Smith, at a minimum, "knowingly" was intended to modify "obscene" in the 1978 version.

In 1984, Congress amended the statute to its current form, broadening its application to those sexually explicit materials that, while not obscene as defined by Miller v. California, 413 U.S. 15 (1973), [n.4] could be restricted without violating the First Amendment as explained by New York v. Ferber, 458 U.S. 747 (1982). When Congress eliminated the adjective "obscene," all of the elements defining the character and content of the materials at issue were relegated to subsections (1)(a) and (2)(a). In this effort to expand the child pornography statute to its full constitutional limits, Congress nowhere expressed an intent to eliminate the mens rea requirement that had previously attached to the character and content of the material through the word obscene.

The committee reports and legislative debate speak more opaquely as to the desire of Congress for a scienter requirement with respect to the age of minority. An early form of the proposed legislation, S. 2011, was rejected principally because it failed to distinguishbetween obscene and non obscene materials. S. Rep. No. 95-438, p. 12 (1977). In evaluating the proposal, the Justice Department offered its thoughts:

"[T]he word 'knowingly' in the second line of section 2251 is unnecessary and should be stricken. . . . Unless 'knowingly' is deleted here, the bill might be subject to an interpretation requiring the Government to prove the defendant's knowledge of everything that follows 'knowingly', including the age of the child. We assume it is not the intention of the drafters to require the Government to prove that the defendant knew the child was under age sixteen but merely to prove that the child was, in fact, less than age sixteen. . . .

"On the other hand, the use of the word 'knowingly' in subsection 2252(a)(1) is appropriate to make it clear that the bill does not apply to common carriers or other innocent transporters who have no knowledge of the nature or character of the material they are transporting. To clarify the situation, the legislative history might reflect that the defendant's knowledge of the age of the child is not an element of the offense but that the bill is not intended to apply to innocent transportation with no knowledge of the nature or character of the material involved." Id., at 28-29 (emphasis added).

Respondents point to this language as an unambiguous revelation that Congress omitted a scienter requirement. But the bill eventually reported by the Senate Judiciary Committee adopted some, but not all of the Department's suggestions; most notably, it restricted the prohibition in §2251 to obscene materials. Id., at 2. The Committee did not make any clarification with respect to scienter as to the age of minority. In fact, the version reported by the committee eliminated §2252altogether. Ibid. At that juncture, Senator Roth introduced an amendment which would be another precursor of §2252. In one paragraph, the amendment forbade any person to "knowingly transport [or] ship . . . [any] visual medium depicting a minor engaged in sexually explicit conduct." 123 Cong. Rec. 33047 (1977). In an exchange during debate, Senator Percy inquired:

"Would this not mean that the distributor or seller must have either first, actual knowledge that the materials do contain child pornographic depictions or, second, circumstances must be such that he should have had such actual knowledge, and that mere inadvertence or negligence would not alone be enough to render his actions unlawful?" Id., at 33050.

Senator Roth replied:

"That is absolutely correct. This amendment, limited as it is by the phrase 'knowingly,' insures that only those sellers and distributors who are consciously and deliberately engaged in the marketing of child pornography . . . are subject to prosecution . . . ." Ibid.

The parallel House bill did not contain a comparable provision to §2252 of the Senate bill, and limited §2251 prosecutions to obscene materials. The Conference Committee adopted the substance of the Roth Amendment in large part, but followed the House version by restricting the proscribed depictions to obscene ones. The new bill did restructure the §2252 provision somewhat, setting off the age of minority requirement in a separate sub clause. S. Conf. Rep. No. 95-601, p. 2 (1977). Most importantly, the new bill retained the adverb "knowingly" in §2252 while simultaneouslydeleting the word "knowingly" from §2251(a). The Conference Committee explained the deletion in §2251(a) as reflecting an "intent that it is not a necessary element of a prosecution that the defendant knew the actual age of the child." Id., at 5. [n.5] Respondents point to the appearance of knowingly in §2251(c) and argue that §2252 ought to be read like §2251. But this argument depends on the conclusion that §2252(c) does not include a knowing requirement, a premise that respondents fail to support. Respondents offer in support of their premise only the legislative history discussing an intent to exclude a scienter requirement from §2251(a). Because §§2251(a) and 2251(c) were passed at different times and contain different wording, the intent to exclude scienter from §2251(a) does not imply an intent to exclude scienter from §2251(c). [n.6]

The legislative history can be summarized by saying that it persuasively indicates that Congress intended that the term "knowingly" apply to the requirement that the depiction be of sexually explicit conduct; it is a good deal less clear from the Committee Reports and floor debates that Congress intended that the requirement extend also to the age of the performers. But, turning once again to the statute itself, if the term "knowingly" applies to the sexually explicit conduct depicted, it is emancipated from merely modifying the verbs in subsections (1) and (2). And as a matter of grammar it is difficult to conclude that the word "knowingly" modifies one of the elements in (1)(A) and (2)(A), but not the other.

A final canon of statutory construction supports the reading that the term "knowingly" applies to both elements. Cases such as Ferber, 458 U. S., at 765 ("As with obscenity laws, criminal responsibility may not be imposed without some element of scienter on the part of the defendant"); Smith v. California, 361 U.S. 147 (1959); Hamling v. United States, 418 U.S. 87 (1974); and Osborne v. Ohio, 495 U.S. 103, 115 (1990), suggest that a statute completely bereft of a scienter requirement as to the age of the performers would raise serious constitutional doubts. It is therefore incumbent upon us to read the statute to eliminate those doubts so long as such a reading is not plainly contrary to the intent of Congress. Edward J. DeBartolo Corp. v. Florida GulfCoast Building & Construction Trades Council, 485 U.S. 568, 575 (1988).

For all of the foregoing reasons, we conclude that the term "knowingly" in §2252 extends both to the sexually explicit nature of the material and to the age of the performers.

As an alternative grounds for upholding the reversal of their convictions, respondents reiterate their constitutional challenge to 18 U.S.C. § 2256. These claims were not encompassed in the question on which this Court granted certiorari, but a prevailing party, without cross petitioning, is "entitled under our precedents to urge any grounds which would lend support to the judgment below." Dayton Bd. of Ed. v. Brinkman, 433 U.S. 406, 419 (1977). Respondents argue that section 2256 is unconstitutionally vague and overbroad because it makes the age of majority 18, rather than 16 as did the New York statute upheld in New York v. Ferber, supra, and because Congress replaced the term "lewd" with the term "lascivious" in defining illegal exhibition of the genitals of children. We regard these claims as insubstantial, and reject them for the reasons stated by the Court of Appeals in its opinion in this case.

Respondents also argued below that their indictment was fatally defective because it did not contain a scienter requirement on the age of minority. The Court of Appeals did not reach this issue because of its determination that §2252 was unconstitutional on its face, and we decline to decide it here.

The judgment of the Court of Appeals is
Reversed.


Notes
1 The indictment also charged six counts of violating federal obscenity statutes and two racketeering counts involving the same. Respondents were acquitted of these

charges.

2 Morissette's treatment of the common law presumption of mens rea recognized that the presumption expressly excepted "sex offenses, such as rape, in which the victim's actual age was determinative despite defendant's reasonable belief that the girl hadreached the age of consent." 342 U. S. at 251, n. 8. But as in the criminalization of pornography production at 18 U.S.C. § 2251 see infra, at 12 n. 5, the perpetrator confronts the underage victim personally and may reasonably be required to ascertain that victim's age. The opportunity for reasonable mistake as to age increases significantly once the victim is reduced to a visual depiction, unavailable for questioning by the distributor or receiver. Thus we do not think the common law treatment of sex offenses militates against our construction of the present statute.

3 In this regard, age of minority is not a "jurisdictional fact" that enhances an offense otherwise committed with an evil intent. See, e.g., United States v. Feola, 420 U.S. 671 (1975). There, the Courtdid not require knowledge of "jurisdictional facts"--that the target of an assault was a federal officer. Criminal intent serves to separate those who understand the wrongful nature of their act from those who do not, but does not require knowledge of the precise consequences that may flow from that act once aware that the act is wrongful. Id., at 685. Cf. Hamling v. United States, 418 U.S. 87, 120 (1974) (knowledge that the materials at issue are legally obscene not required).

4 The Miller test for obscenity asks whether the work, taken as a whole, "appeals to the prurient interest," "depicts or describes [sexual conduct] in a patently offensive way," and "lacks serious literary, artistic, political, or scientific value." Miller, 413 U. S., at 24.

5 The difference in congressional intent with respect to §2251 versus §2252 reflects the reality that producers are more conveniently able to ascertain the age of performers. It thus makes sense to impose the risk of error on producers. United States v. United States District Court for Central District of California, 858 F. 2d 534, 543, n. 6 (CA9 1988). Although producers may be convicted under §2251(a) without proof they had knowledge of age, Congress has independently required both primary and secondary producers to record the ages of performers with independent penalties for failure to comply. 18 U.S.C. §§ 2257(a) and (i) (1988 ed. and Supp. V); American Library Assn. v. Reno, 33 F. 3d 78 (CADC 1994).

6 Congress amended §2251 to insert subsection (c) in 1986. Pub. L. 99-628, 100 Stat. 3510. That provision created new offenses relating to the advertising of the availability of child pornography or soliciting children to participate in such depictions. The legislative history of §2251(c) does address the scienter requirement: "The government must prove that the defendant knew the character of the visual depictions as depicting a minor engaging in sexually explicit conduct, but need not prove that the defendant actually knew the person depicted was in fact under 18 years of age or that the depictions violated Federal law." H. Rep. No. 99-910, p. 6 (1986). It may be argued that since the House Committee Report rejects any requirement of scienter as to the age of

minority for §2251(c), the House Committee thought that there was no such requirement in §2252. But the views of one Congress as to the meaning of an act passed by an earlier Congress are not ordinarily of great weight, United States v. Clark, 445 U.S. 23, 33, n. 9 (1980), citing United States v. Southwestern Cable Co., 392 U.S. 157, 170 (1968), and the views of the committee of one House of another Congress are of even less weight. Pierce v. Underwood, 487 U.S. 552, 566 (1988).

## Hurley v. Irish-American Gay, Group of Boston (June 19, 1995)

Justice Souter delivered the opinion of the Court.

March 17 is set aside for two celebrations in South Boston. As early as 1737, some people in Boston observed the feast of the apostle to Ireland, and since 1776 the day has marked the evacuation of royal troops and Loyalists from the city, prompted by the guns captured at Ticonderoga and set up on Dorchester Heights under General Washington's command. Washington himself reportedly drew on the earlier tradition in choosing "St. Patrick" as the response to "Boston," the password used in the colonial lines on evacuation day. See J. Crimmins, St. Patrick's Day: Its Celebration in New York and other American Places, 1737-1845, pp. 15, 19 (1902); see generally 1 H.S. Commager & R. Morris, The Spirit of 'Seventy Six 138-183 (1958); The American Book of Days 262-265 (J. Hatch ed., 3d ed. 1978). Although the General Court of Massachusetts did not officially designate March 17 as Evacuation Day until 1938, see Mass. Gen. Laws §6:12K (1992), the City Council of Boston had previously sponsored public celebrations of Evacuation Day, including notable commemorations on the centennial in 1876, and on the 125th anniversary in 1901, with its parade, salute, concert, and fireworks display. See Celebration of the Centennial Anniversary of the Evacuation of Boston by the British Army (G. Ellis ed. 1876); Irish American Gay, Lesbian and Bisexual Group of Boston v. City of Boston et al., Civ. Action No. 92-1516 (Super. Ct., Mass., Dec. 15, 1993), reprinted in App. to Pet. for Cert. B1, B8-B9.

The tradition of formal sponsorship by the city came to an end in 1947, however, when Mayor James Michael Curley himself granted authority to organize and conduct the St. Patrick's Day Evacuation Day Parade to the petitioner South Boston Allied War Veterans Council, an unincorporated association of individuals elected from various South Boston veterans groups. Every year since that time, the Council has applied for and received a permit for the parade, which at times has included as many as 20,000 marchers and drawn up to 1 million watchers. No other applicant has ever applied for that permit. Id., at B9. Through 1992, the city allowed the Council to use the city's official seal, and provided printing services as well as direct funding.

1992 was the year that a number of gay, lesbian, and bisexual descendants of the Irish immigrants joined together with other supporters to form the respondent organization, GLIB, to march in the parade as a way to express pride in their Irish heritage as openly gay, lesbian, and bisexual individuals, to demonstrate that there are such men and women among those so descended, and to express their solidarity with like individuals who sought to march in New York's St. Patrick's Day Parade. Id., at B3; App. 51. Although the Council denied GLIB's application to take part in the 1992 parade, GLIB obtained a state court order to include its contingent, which marched "uneventfully" among that year's 10,000 participants and 750,000 spectators. App. to Pet. for Cert. B3, and n. 4.

In 1993, after the Council had again refused to admit GLIB to the upcoming parade, the organization and some of its members filed this suit against the Council, the individual petitioner John J. "Wacko" Hurley, and the City of Boston, alleging violations of the State and Federal Constitutions and of the state public accommodations law, which prohibits "any distinction, discrimination or restriction on account of . . . sexual orientation . . . relative to the admission of any person to, or treatment in any place of public accommodation, resort or amusement." Mass. Gen. Laws §272:98. After finding that "[f]or at least the past 47 years, the Parade has traveled the same basic route along the public streets of South Boston, providing entertainment, amusement, and recreation to participants and spectators alike," App. to Pet. for Cert. B5-B6, the state trial court ruled that the parade fell within the statutory definition of a public accommodation, which includes "any place . . . which is open to and accepts or solicits the patronage of the general public and, without limiting the generality of this definition, whether or not it be . . . (6) a boardwalk or other public highway [or] . . . (8) a place of public amusement, recreation, sport, exercise or entertainment," Mass. Gen. Laws §272:92A. The court found that the Council had no written criteria and employed no particular procedures for admission, voted on new applications in batches, had occasionally admitted groups who simply showed up at the parade without having submitted an application, and did "not generally inquire into the specific messages or views of each applicant." App. to Pet. for Cert. B8-B9. The court consequently rejected the Council's contention that the parade was "private" (in the sense of being exclusive), holding instead that "the lack of genuine selectivity in choosing participants and sponsors demonstrates that the Parade is a public event." Id., at B6. It found the parade to be "eclectic," containing a wide variety of "patriotic, commercial, political, moral, artistic, religious, athletic, public service, trade union, and eleemosynary themes," as well as conflicting messages. Id., at B24. While noting that the Council had indeed excluded the Ku Klux Klan and ROAR (an antibusing group), id., at B7, it attributed little significance to these facts, concluding ultimately that "[t]he only common theme among the participants and sponsors is their public involvement in the Parade," id., at B24.

The court rejected the Council's assertion that the exclusion of "groups with sexual themes merely formalized [the fact] that the Parade expresses traditional religious and social values," id., at B3, and found the Council's "final position [to be] that GLIB would be excluded because of its values and its message, i.e., its members' sexual orientation," id., at B4, n. 5, citing Tr. of Closing Arg. 43, 51-52 (Nov. 23, 1993). This position, in the court's view, was not only violative of the public accommodations law but "paradoxical" as well, since "a proper celebration of St. Patrick's and Evacuation Day requires diversity and inclusiveness." App. to Pet. for Cert. B24. The court rejected the notion that GLIB's admission would trample on the Council's First Amendment rights since the court understood that constitutional protection of any interest in expressive association would "requir[e] focus on a specific message, theme, or group" absent from the parade. Ibid. "Given the [Council's] lack of selectivity in choosing participants and failure to circumscribe the marchers' message," the court found it "impossible to discern any specific expressive purpose entitling the Parade to protection under the First Amendment." Id., at B25. It concluded that the parade is "not an exercise of [the Council's] constitutionally protected right of expressive association," but instead "an open recreational event that is subject to the public accommodations law." Id., at B27.

The court held that because the statute did not mandate inclusion of GLIB but only prohibited discrimination based on sexual orientation, any infringement on the Council's right to expressive association was only "incidental" and "no greater than necessary to accomplish the statute's legitimate purpose" of eradicating discrimination. Id., at B25, citing Roberts v. United States Jaycees, 468 U.S. 609, 628-629 (1984). Accordingly, it ruled that "GLIB is entitled to participate in the Parade on the same terms and conditions as other participants." Id., at B27. [n.1]

The Supreme Judicial Court of Massachusetts affirmed, seeing nothing clearly erroneous in the trial judge's findings that GLIB was excluded from the parade based on the sexual orientation of its members, that it was impossible to detect an expressive purpose in the parade, that there was no state action, and that the parade was a public accommodation within the meaning of §272:92A. Irish American Gay, Lesbian and Bisexual Group of Boston v. Boston, 418 Mass. 238, 242-248, 636N. E. 2d 1293, 1295-1298 (1994). [n.2] Turning to petitioners' First Amendment claim that application of the public accommodations law to the parade violated their freedom of speech (as distinguished from their right to expressive association, raised in the trial court), the court's majority held that it need not decide on the particular First Amendment theory involved "because, as the [trial] judge found, it is `impossible to discern any specific expressive purpose entitling the parade to protection under the First Amendment.' " Id., at 249, 636 N. E. 2d, at 1299 (footnote omitted). The defendants had thus failed at the trial level "to demonstrate that the parade truly was an exercise of . . . First Amendment rights," id., at 250, 636 N. E. 2d, at 1299, citing Clark v. Community for Creative Non Violence, 468 U.S. 288, 293, n. 5 (1984), and on appeal nothing indicated to the majority of the Supreme Judicial Court that the trial judge's assessment of the evidence on this point was clearly erroneous, ibid. The court rejected petitioners' further challenge to the law as overbroad, holding that it does not, on its face, regulate speech, does not let public officials examine the content of speech, and would not be interpreted as reaching speech. Id., at 251-252, 636 N. E. 2d, at 1300. Finally, the court rejected the challenge that the public accommodations law was unconstitutionally vague, holding that this case did not present an issue of speech and that the law gave persons of ordinary intelligence a reasonable opportunity to know what was prohibited. Id., at 252, 636 N. E. 2d, at 1300-1301.

Justice Nolan dissented. In his view, the Council "does not need a narrow or distinct theme or message in its parade for it to be protected under the First Amendment." Id., at 256, 636 N. E. 2d, at 1303. First, he wrote, even if the parade had no message at all, GLIB's particular message could not be forced upon it. Id., at 257, 636 N. E. 2d, at 1303, citing Wooley v. Maynard, 430 U.S. 705, 717 (1977) (state requirement to display "Live Free or Die" on license plates violates First Amendment). Second, according to Justice Nolan, the trial judge clearly erred in finding the parade devoid of expressive purpose. Ibid. He would have held that the Council, like any expressive association, cannot be barred from excluding applicants who do not share the views the Council wishes to advance. Id., at 257-259, 636 N. E. 2d, at 1303-1304, citing Roberts v. United States Jaycees, 468 U.S. 609 (1984). Under either a pure speech or associational theory, the State's purpose of eliminating discrimination on the basis of sexual orientation, according to the dissent, could be achieved by more narrowly drawn means, such as ordering admission of individuals regardless of sexual preference, without taking the further step of prohibiting the Council from editing the views expressed in their parade. Id., at 256, 258, 636 N. E. 2d, at 1302, 1304. In Justice Nolan's opinion, because GLIB's message was separable from the status of its members, such a narrower order would accommodate the State's interest without the likelihood of infringing on the Council's First Amendment rights. Finally, he found clear error in the trial judge's equation of exclusion on the basis of GLIB's message with exclusion on the basis of its members' sexual orientation. To the dissent this appeared false in the light of "overwhelming evidence" that the Council objected to GLIB on account of its message and a dearth of testimony or documentation indicating that sexual orientation was the bar to admission. Id., at 260, 636 N. E. 2d, at 1304. The dissent accordingly concluded that the Council had not even violated the State's public accommodations law.

We granted certiorari to determine whether the requirement to admit a parade contingent expressing a message not of the private organizers' own choosing violates the First Amendment. 513 U. S. ____ (1995). We hold that it does and reverse.

Given the scope of the issues as originally joined in this case, it is worth noting some that have fallen aside in the course of the litigation, before reaching us. Although the Council presents us with a First Amendment claim, respondents do not. Neither do they press a claim that the Council's action has denied them equal protection of the laws in violation of the Fourteenth Amendment. While the guarantees of free speech and equal protection guard only against encroachment by the government and "erec[t] no shield against merely private conduct," Shelley v. Kraemer, 334 U.S. 1, 13 (1948); see Hudgens v. NLRB, 424 U.S. 507, 513 (1976), respondents originally argued that the Council's conduct was not purely private, but had the character of state action. The trial court's review of the city's involvement led it to find otherwise, however, and although the Supreme Judicial Court did not squarely address the issue, it appears to have affirmed the trial court's decision on that point as well as the others. In any event, respondents have not brought that question up either in a cross petition for certiorari or in their briefs filed in this Court. When asked at oral argument whether they challenged the conclusion by the Massachusetts' courts that no state action is involved in the parade, respondents' counsel answered that they "do not press that issue here." Tr. of Oral Arg. 22. In this Court, then, their claim for inclusion in the parade rests solely on the Massachusetts public accommodations law.

There is no corresponding concession from the other side, however, and certainly not to the state courts' characterization of the parade as lacking the element of expression for purposes of the First Amendment. Accordingly, our review of petitioners' claim that their activity is indeed in the nature of protected speech carries with it a constitutional duty to conduct an independent examination of the record as a whole, without deference to the trial court. See Bose Corp. v. Consumers Union of United States, Inc., 466 U.S. 485, 499 (1984). The "requirement of independent appellate review . . . is a rule of federal constitutional law," id., at 510, which does not limit our deference to a trial court on matters of witness credibility, Harte Hanks Communications, Inc. v. Connaughton, 491 U.S. 657, 688 (1989), but which generally requires us to "review the finding of facts by a State court . . . where a conclusion of law as to a Federal right and a finding of fact are so intermingled as to make it necessary, in order to pass upon the Federal question, to analyze the facts," Fiske v. Kansas, 274 U.S. 380, 385-386 (1927). See also Niemotko v. Maryland, 340 U.S. 268, 271 (1951); Jacobellis v. Ohio, 378 U.S. 184, 189 (1964) (opinion of Brennan, J.). This obligation rests upon us simply because the reaches of the First Amendment are ultimately defined by the facts it is held to embrace, and we must thus decide for ourselves whether a given course of conduct falls on the near or far side of the line of constitutional protection. See Bose Corp., supra, at 503. Even where a speech case has originally been tried in a federal court, subject to the provision of Federal Rule of Civil Procedure 52(a) that "[f]indings of fact . . . shall not be set aside unless clearly erroneous," we are obliged to make a fresh examination of crucial facts. Hence, in this case, though we are confronted with the state courts' conclusion that the factual characteristics of petitioners' activity place it within the vast realm of non expressive conduct, our obligation is to " `make an independent examination of the whole record,' . . . so as to assure ourselves that th[is] judgment does not constitute a forbidden intrusion on the field of free expression." New York Times Co. v. Sullivan, 376 U.S. 254, 285 (1964) (footnote omitted), quoting Edwards v. South Carolina, 372 U.S. 229, 235 (1963).

If there were no reason for a group of people to march from here to there except to reach a destination, they could make the trip without expressing any message beyond the fact of the march itself. Some people might call such a procession a parade, but it would not be much of one. Real "[p]arades are public dramas of social relations, and in them performers define who can be a social actor and what subjects and ideas are available for communication and consideration." S. Davis, Parades and Power: Street Theatre in Nineteenth Century Philadelphia 6 (1986). Hence, we use the word "parade" to indicate marchers who are making some sort of collective point, not just to each other but to bystanders along the way. Indeed a parade's dependence on watchers is so extreme that nowadays, as with Bishop Berkeley's celebrated tree, "if a parade or demonstration receives no media coverage, it may as well not have happened." Id., at 171. Parades are thus a form of expression, not just motion, and the inherent expressiveness of marching to make a point explains our cases involving protest marches. In Gregory v. Chicago, 394 U.S. 111, 112 (1969), for example, petitioners had taken part in a procession to express their grievances to the city government, and we held that such a "march, if peaceful and orderly, falls well within the sphere of conduct protected by the First Amendment." Similarly, in Edwards v. South Carolina, 372 U.S. 229, 235 (1963), where petitioners had joined in a march of protest and pride, carrying placards and singing The Star Spangled Banner, we held that the activities "reflect an exercise of these basic constitutional rights in their most pristine and classic form." Accord, Shuttlesworth v. Birmingham, 394 U.S. 147, 152 (1969).

The protected expression that inheres in a parade is not limited to its banners and songs, however, for the Constitution looks beyond written or spoken words as mediums of expression. Noting that "[s]ymbolism is a primitive but effective way of communicating ideas," West Virginia Bd. of Ed. v. Barnette, 319 U.S. 624, 632 (1943), our cases have recognized that the First Amendment shields such acts as saluting a flag (and refusing to do so), id., at 632, 642, wearing an arm band to protest a war, Tinker v. Des Moines Independent Community School Dist., 393 U.S. 503, 505-506 (1969), displaying a red flag, Stromberg v. California, 283 U.S. 359, 369 (1931), and even "[m]arching, walking or parading" in uniforms displaying the swastika, National Socialist Party of America v. Skokie, 432 U.S. 43 (1977). As some of these examples show, a narrow, succinctly articulable message is not a condition of constitutional protection, which if confined to expressions conveying a "particularized message," cf. Spence v. Washington, 418 U.S. 405, 411 (1974) (per curiam), would never reach the unquestionably shielded painting of Jackson Pollock, music of Arnold Schönberg, or Jabberwocky verse of Lewis Carroll.

Not many marches, then, are beyond the realm of expressive parades, and the South Boston celebration is not one of them. Spectators line the streets; people march in costumes and uniforms, carrying flags and banners with all sorts of messages (e.g., "England get out of Ireland," "Say no to drugs"); marching bands and pipers play, floats are pulled along, and the whole show is broadcast over Boston television. See Record, Exh. 84 (video). To be sure, we agree with the state courts that in spite of excluding some applicants, the Council is rather lenient in admitting participants. But a private speaker does not forfeit constitutional protection simply by combining multifarious voices, or by failing to edit their themes to isolate an exact message as the exclusive subject matter of the speech. Nor, under our precedent, does First Amendment protection require a speaker to generate, as an original matter, each item featured in the communication. Cable operators, for example, are engaged in protected speech activities even when they only select programming originally produced by others. Turner Broadcasting System, Inc. v. FCC, 512 U. S. ___, ___ (1994) (slip op., at 11) ("Cable programmers and cable operators engage in and transmit speech, and they are entitled to the protection of the speech and press provisions of the First Amendment"). For that matter, the presentation of an edited compilation of speech generated by other persons is a staple of most newspapers' opinion pages, which, of course, fall squarely within the core of First Amendment security, Miami Herald Publishing Co. v. Tornillo, 418 U.S. 241, 258 (1974), as does even the simple selection of a paid noncommercial advertisement for inclusion in a daily paper, see New York Times, 376 U. S., at 265-266. The selection of contingents to make a parade is entitled to similar protection.

Respondents' participation as a unit in the parade was equally expressive. GLIB was formed for the very purpose of marching in it, as the trial court found, in order to celebrate its members' identity as openly gay, lesbian, and bisexual descendants of the Irish immigrants, to show that there are such individuals in the community, and to support the like men and women who sought to march in the New York parade. App. to Pet. for Cert. B3. The organization distributed a fact sheet describing the members' intentions, App. A51, and the record otherwise corroborates the expressive nature of GLIB's participation, see Record, Exh. 84; App. A67 (photograph). In 1993, members of GLIB marched behind a shamrock strewn banner with the simple inscription "Irish American Gay, Lesbian and Bisexual Group of Boston." GLIB understandably seeks to communicate its ideas as part of the existing parade, rather than staging one of its own.

The Massachusetts public accommodations law under which respondents brought suit has a venerable history. At common law, innkeepers, smiths, and others who "made profession of a public employment," were prohibited from refusing, without good reason, to serve a customer. Lane v. Cotton, 12 Mod. 472, 484-485, 88 Eng. Rep. 1458, 1464-1465 (K.B. 1701) (Holt, C. J.); see Bell v. Maryland, 378 U.S. 226, 298, n. 17 (1964) (Goldberg, J., concurring); Lombard v. Louisiana, 373 U.S. 267, 277 (1963) (Douglas, J., concurring). As one of the 19th century English judges put it, the rule was that "[t]he innkeeper is not to select his guests[;] [h]e has no right to say to one, you shall come into my inn, and to another you shall not, as every one coming and conducting himself in a proper manner has a right to be received; and for this purpose innkeepers are a sort of public servants." Rex v. Ivens, 7 Car. & P. 213, 219, 173 Eng. Rep. 94, 96 (N.P. 1835); M. Konvitz & T. Leskes, A Century of Civil Rights 160 (1961).

After the Civil War, the Commonwealth of Massachusetts was the first State to codify this principle to ensure access to public accommodations regardless of race. See Act Forbidding Unjust Discrimination on Account of Color or Race, 1865 Mass. Acts, ch. 277 (May 16, 1865); Konvitz & Leskes, supra, at 155-56; L.G. Lerman & A. Sanderson, Discrimination in Access to Public Places: A Survey of State and Federal Public Accommodations Laws, 7 N. Y. U. Rev. L. & Soc. Change 215, 238 (1978); F. Fox, Discrimination and Antidiscrimination in Massachusetts Law, 44 B. U. L. Rev. 30, 58 (1964). In prohibiting discrimination "in any licensed inn, in any public place of amusement, public conveyance or public meeting," 1865 Mass. Acts, ch. 277, §1, the original statute already expanded upon the common law, which had not conferred any right of access to places of public amusement, Lerman & Anderson, supra, at 248. As with many public accommodations statutes across the Nation, the legislature continued to broaden the scope of legislation, to the point that the law today prohibits discrimination on the basis of "race, color, religious creed, national origin, sex, sexual orientation . . ., deafness, blindness or any physical or mental disability or ancestry" in "the admission of any person to, or treatment in any place of public accommodation, resort or amusement." Mass. Gen. Laws §272:98. Provisions like these are well within the State's usual power to enact when a legislature has reason to believe that a given group is the target of discrimination, and they do not, as a general matter, violate the First or Fourteenth Amendments. See, e.g., New York State Club Assn., Inc. v. City of New York, 487 U.S. 1, 11-16 (1988); Roberts v. United States Jaycees, 468 U.S. 609, 624-626 (1984); Heart of Atlanta Motel, Inc. v. United States, 379 U.S. 241, 258-262 (1964). Nor is this statute unusual in any obvious way, since it does not, on its face, target speech or discriminate on the basis of its content, the focal point of its prohibition being rather on the act of discriminating against individuals in the provision of publicly available goods, privileges, and services on the proscribed grounds.

In the case before us, however, the Massachusetts law has been applied in a peculiar way. Its enforcement does not address any dispute about the participation of openly gay, lesbian, or bisexual individuals in various units admitted to the parade. The petitioners disclaim any intent to exclude homosexuals as such, and no individual member of GLIB claims to have been excluded from parading as a member of any group that the Council has approved to march. Instead, the disagreement goes to the admission of GLIB as its own parade unit carrying its own banner. See App. to Pet. for Cert. B26-B27, and n. 28. Since every participating unit affects the message conveyed by the private organizers, the state courts' application of the statute produced an order essentially requiring petitioners to alter the expressive content of their parade. Although the state courts spoke of the parade as a place of public accommodation, see, e.g., 418 Mass., at 247-248, 636 N. E. 2d, at 1297-1298, once the expressive character of both the parade and the marching GLIB contingent is understood, it becomes apparent that the state courts' application of the statute had the effect of declaring the sponsors' speech itself to be the public accommodation. Under this approach any contingent of protected individuals with a message would have the right to participate in petitioners' speech, so that the communication produced by the private organizers would be shaped by all those protected by the law who wished to join in with some expressive demonstration of their own. But this use of the State's power violates the fundamental rule of protection under the First Amendment, that a speaker has the autonomy to choose the content of his own message.

"Since all speech inherently involves choices of what to say and what to leave unsaid," Pacific Gas & Electric Co. v. Public Utilities Comm'n of Cal., 475 U.S. 1, 11 (1986) (plurality opinion) (emphasis in original), one important manifestation of the principle of free speech is that one who chooses to speak may also decide "what not to say," id., at 16. Although the State may at times "prescribe what shall be orthodox in commercial advertising" by requiring the dissemination of "purely factual and uncontroversial information," Zauderer v. Office of Disciplinary Counsel of Supreme Court of Ohio, 471 U.S. 626, 651 (1985); see Pittsburgh Press Co. v. Pittsburgh Comm'n on Human Relations, 413 U.S. 376, 386-387 (1973), outside that context it may not compel affirmance of a belief with which the speaker disagrees, see Barnette, 319 U. S., at 642. Indeed this general rule, that the speaker has the right to tailor the speech, applies not only to expressions of value, opinion, or endorsement, but equally to statements of fact the speaker would rather avoid, McIntyre v. Ohio Elections Comm'n, 514 U. S. ____, ____ (1995) (slip op., at 6-7); Riley v. National Federation of Blind of N.C., Inc., 487 U.S. 781, 797-798 (1988), subject, perhaps, to the permissive law of defamation, New York Times, 376 U.S. 254; Gertz v. Robert Welch, Inc., 418 U.S. 323, 347-349 (1974); Hustler Magazine, Inc. v. Falwell, 485 U.S. 46 (1988). Nor is the rule's benefit restricted to the press, being enjoyed by business corporations generally and by ordinary people engaged in unsophisticated expression as well as by professional publishers. Its point is simply the point of all speech protection, which is to shield just those choices of content that in someone's eyes are misguided, or even hurtful. See Brandenburg v. Ohio, 395 U.S. 444 (1969); Terminiello v. Chicago, 337 U.S. 1 (1949).

Petitioners' claim to the benefit of this principle of autonomy to control one's own speech is as sound as the South Boston parade is expressive. Rather like a composer, the Council selects the expressive units of the parade from potential participants, and though the score may not produce a particularized message, each contingent's expression in the Council's eyes comports with what merits celebration on that day. Even if this view gives the Council credit for a more considered judgment than it actively made, the Council clearly decided to exclude a message it did not like from the communication it chose to make, and that is enough to invoke its right as a private speaker to shape its expression by speaking on one subject while remaining silent on another. The message it disfavored is not difficult to identify. Although GLIB's point (like the Council's) is not wholly articulate, a contingent marching behind the organization's banner would at least bear witness to the fact that some Irish are gay, lesbian, or bisexual, and the presence of the organized marchers would suggest their view that people of their sexual orientations have as much claim to unqualified social acceptance as heterosexuals and indeed as members of parade units organized around other identifying characteristics. The parade's organizers may not believe these facts about Irish sexuality to be so, or they may object to unqualified social acceptance of gays and lesbians or have some other reason for wishing to keep GLIB's message out of the parade. But whatever the reason, it boils down to the choice of a speaker not to propound a particular point of view, and that choice is presumed to lie beyond the government's power to control.

Respondents argue that any tension between this rule and the Massachusetts law falls short of unconstitutionality, citing the most recent of our cases on the general subject of compelled access for expressive purposes, Turner Broadcasting, 512 U. S. ____. There we reviewed regulations requiring cable operators to set aside channels for designated broadcast signals, and applied only intermediate scrutiny. Id., at ____ (slip op., at 38). Respondents contend on this authority that admission of GLIB to the parade would not threaten the core principle of speaker's autonomy because the Council, like a cable operator, is merely "a conduit" for the speech of participants in the parade "rather than itself a speaker." Brief for Respondent 21. But this metaphor is not apt here, because GLIB's participation would likely be perceived as having resulted from the Council's customary determination about a unit admitted to the parade, that its message was worthy of presentation and quite possibly of support as well. A newspaper, similarly, "is more than a passive receptacle or conduit for news, comment, and advertising," and we have held that "[t]he choice of material . . . and the decisions made as to limitations on the size and content . . . and treatment of public issues . . . .--whether fair or unfair-- constitute the exercise of editorial control and judgment" upon which the State can not intrude. Tornillo, 418 U. S., at 258. Indeed, in Pacific Gas & Electric, we invalidated coerced access to the envelope of a private utility's bill and newsletter because the utility "may be forced either to appear to agree with [the intruding leaflet] or to respond." 475 U. S., at 15 (plurality) (citation omitted). The plurality made the further point that if "the government [were] freely able to compel . . . speakers to propound political messages with which they disagree, . . . protection [of a speaker's freedom] would be empty, for the government could require speakers to affirm in one breath that which they deny in the next." Id., at 16. Thus, when dissemination of a view contrary to one's own is forced upon a speaker intimately connected with the communication advanced, the speaker's right to autonomy over the message is compromised.

In Turner Broadcasting, we found this problem absent in the cable context, because "[g]iven cable's long history of serving as a conduit for broadcast signals, there appears little risk that cable viewers would assume that the broadcast stations carried on a cable system convey ideas or messages endorsed by the cable operator." 512 U. S., at ____ (slip op., at 31). We stressed that the viewer is frequently apprised of the identity of the broadcaster whose signal is being received via cable and that it is "common practice for broadcasters to disclaim any identity of viewpoint between the management and the speakers who use the broadcast facility." Ibid. (slip op., at 31) (citation omitted); see id., at ____ (slip op., at 11) (O'Connor, J., concurring in part and dissenting in part) (noting that Congress "might . . . conceivably obligate cable operators to act as common carriers for some of their channels").

Parades and demonstrations, in contrast, are not understood to be so neutrally presented or selectively viewed. Unlike the programming offered on various channels by a cable network, the parade does not consist of individual, unrelated segments that happen to be transmitted together for individual selection by members of the audience. Although each parade unit generally identifies itself, each is understood to contribute something to a common theme, and accordingly there is no customary practice whereby private sponsors disavow "any identity of viewpoint" between themselves and the selected participants. Practice follows practicability here, for such disclaimers would be quite curious in a moving parade. Cf. Prune Yard Shopping Center v. Robins, 447 U.S. 74, 87 (1980) (owner of shopping mall "can expressly disavow any connection with the message by simply posting signs in the area where the speakers or handbillers stand"). Without deciding on the precise significance of the likelihood of misattribution, it nonetheless becomes clear that in the context of an expressive parade, as with a protest march, the parade's overall message is distilled from the individual presentations along the way, and each unit's expression is perceived by spectators as part of the whole.

An additional distinction between Turner Broadcasting and this case points to the fundamental weakness of any attempt to justify the state court order's limitation on the Council's autonomy as a speaker. A cable is not only a conduit for speech produced by others and selected by cable operators for transmission, but a franchised channel giving monopolistic opportunity to shut out some speakers. This power gives rise to the government's interest in limiting monopolistic autonomy in order to allow for the survival of broadcasters who might otherwise be silenced and consequently destroyed. The government's interest in Turner Broadcasting was not the alteration of speech, but the survival of speakers. In thus identifying an interest going beyond abridgment of speech itself, the defenders of the law at issue in Turner Broadcasting addressed the threshold requirement of any review under the Speech Clause, whatever the ultimate level of scrutiny, that a challenged restriction on speech serve a compelling, or at least important, governmental object, see, e.g., Pacific Gas & Electric, supra, at 19; Turner Broadcasting, supra, at ____ (slip op., at 38); United States v. O'Brien, 391 U.S. 367, 377 (1968).

In this case, of course, there is no assertion comparable to the Turner Broadcasting claim that some speakers will be destroyed in the absence of the challenged law. True, the size and success of petitioners' parade makes it an enviable vehicle for the dissemination of GLIB's views, but that fact, without more, would fall far short of supporting a claim that petitioners enjoy an abiding monopoly of access to spectators. See App. to Pet. for Cert. B9; Brief for Respondents 10 (citing trial court's finding that no other applicant has applied for the permit). Considering that GLIB presumably would have had a fair shot (under neutral criteria developed by the city) at obtaining a parade permit of its own, respondents have not shown that petitioners enjoy the capacity to "silence the voice of competing speakers," as cable operators do with respect to program providers who wish to reach subscribers, Turner Broadcasting, supra, at ____ (slip op., at 32). Nor has any other legitimate interest been identified in support of applying the Massachusetts statute in this way to expressive activity like the parade.

The statute, Mass. Gen. Laws §272:98, is a piece of protective legislation that announces no purpose beyond the object both expressed and apparent in its provisions, which is to prevent any denial of access to (or discriminatory treatment in) public accommodations on proscribed grounds, including sexual orientation. On its face, the object of the law is to ensure by statute for gays and lesbians desiring to make use of public accommodations what the old common law promised to any member of the public wanting a meal at the inn, that accepting the usual terms of service, they will not be turned away merely on the proprietor's exercise of personal preference. When the law is applied to expressive activity in the way it was done here, its apparent object is simply to require speakers to modify the content of their expression to whatever extent beneficiaries of the law choose to alter it with messages of their own. But in the absence of some further, legitimate end, this object is merely to allow exactly what the general rule of speaker's autonomy forbids.

It might, of course, have been argued that a broader objective is apparent: that the ultimate point of forbidding acts of discrimination toward certain classes is to produce a society free of the corresponding biases. Requiring access to a speaker's message would thus be not an end in itself, but a means to produce speakers free of the biases, whose expressive conduct would be at least neutral toward the particular classes, obviating any future need for correction. But if this indeed is the point of applying the state law to expressive conduct, it is a decidedly fatal objective. Having availed itself of the public thoroughfares "for purposes of assembly [and] communicating thoughts between citizens," the Council is engaged in a use of the streets that has "from ancient times, been a part of the privileges, immunities, rights, and liberties of citizens." Hague v. Committee for Industrial Organization, 307 U.S. 496, 515 (1939) (opinion of Roberts, J.). Our tradition of free speech commands that a speaker who takes to the street corner to express his views in this way should be free from interference by the State based on the content of what he says. See, e.g., Police Department of Chicago v. Mosley, 408 U.S. 92, 95 (1972); cf. H. Kalven, Jr., A Worthy Tradition 6-19 (1988); O. Fiss, Free Speech and Social Structure, 71 Iowa L. Rev. 1405, 1408-1409 (1986). The very idea that a noncommercial speech restriction be used to produce thoughts and statements acceptable to some groups or, indeed, all people, grates on the First Amendment, for it amounts to nothing less than a proposal to limit speech in the service of orthodox expression. The Speech Clause has no more certain antithesis. See, e.g., Barnette, 319 U. S., at 642; Pacific Gas & Electric, 475 U. S., at 20. While the law is free to promote all sorts of conduct in place of harmful behavior, it is not free to interfere with speech for no better reason than promoting an approved message or discouraging a disfavored one, however enlightened either purpose may strike the government.

Far from supporting GLIB, then, Turner Broadcasting points to the reasons why the present application of the Massachusetts law can not be sustained. So do the two other principal authorities GLIB has cited. In PruneYard, 447 U.S. 74, to be sure, we sustained a state law requiring the proprietors of shopping malls to allow visitors to solicit signatures on political petitions without a showing that the shopping mall owners would otherwise prevent the beneficiaries of the law from reaching an audience. But we found in that case that the proprietors were running "a business establishment that is open to the public to come and go as they please," that the solicitations would "not likely be identified with those of the owner," and that the proprietors could "expressly disavow any connection with the message by simply posting signs in the area where the speakers or handbillers stand." Id., at 87. Also, in Pacific Gas & Electric, supra, at 12, we noted that PruneYard did not involve "any concern that access to this area might affect the shopping center owner's exercise of his own right to speak: the owner did not even allege that he objected to the content of the pamphlets . . . ." The principle of speaker's autonomy was simply not threatened in that case.

New York State Club Association is also instructive by the contrast it provides. There, we turned back a facial challenge to a state antidiscrimination statute on the assumption that the expressive associational character of a dining club with over 400 members could be sufficiently attenuated to permit application of the law even to such a private organization, but we also recognized that the State did not prohibit exclusion of those whose views were at odds with positions espoused by the general club memberships. 487 U. S., at 13; see also Roberts, 468 U. S., at 627. In other words, although the association provided public benefits to which a State could ensure equal access, it was also engaged in expressive activity; compelled access to the benefit, which was upheld, did not trespass on the organization's message itself. If we were to analyze this case strictly along those lines, GLIB would lose. Assuming the parade to be large enough and a source of benefits (apart from its expression) that would generally justify a mandated access provision, GLIB could nonetheless be refused admission as an expressive contingent with its own message just as readily as a private club could exclude an applicant whose manifest views were at odds with a position taken by the club's existing members.

Our holding today rests not on any particular view about the Council's message but on the Nation's commitment to protect freedom of speech. Disapproval of a private speaker's statement does not legitimize use of the Commonwealth's power to compel the speaker to alter the message by including one more acceptable to others. Accordingly, the judgment of the Supreme Judicial Court is reversed and the case remanded for proceedings not inconsistent with this opinion.

It is so ordered.

Notes

1 The court dismissed the public accommodations law claim against the city because it found that the city's actions did not amount to inciting or assisting in the Council's violations of §272:98. App. to Pet. for Cert. B12-B13. It also dismissed respondents' First and Fourteenth Amendment challenge against the Council for want of state action triggering the proscriptions of those Amendments. Id., at B14-B22. Finally, the court did not reach the state constitutional questions, since respondents had apparently assumed in their arguments that those claims, too, depended for their success upon a finding of state action and because of the court's holding that the public accommodation statutes apply to the parade. Id., at B22.

2 Since respondents did not cross appeal the dismissal of their claims against the city, the Supreme Judicial Court declined to reach those claims. 418 Mass., at 245, n. 12, 636 N. E. 2d, at 1297.

## Brown v. Hot, Sexy and Safer Productions, Inc. (First Circuit) (Oct 23, 1995) [Notes omitted]

Before TORRUELLA, Chief Judge, STAHL, Circuit Judge, and DOMINGUEZ,[*] District Judge.

TORRUELLA, Chief Judge.

The plaintiffs are two minors and their parents. The minors allege that they were compelled to attend an indecent AIDS and sex education program conducted at their public high school by defendant Hot, Sexy and Safer Productions ("Hot, Sexy, and Safer"). Plaintiffs allege, inter alia, that the compelled attendance deprived the minors of their privacy rights and their right to an educational environment free from sexual harassment. The district court granted the defendants' motion to dismiss under Federal Rule of Civil Procedure 12(b)(6). We affirm.

BACKGROUND

The plaintiffs are Chelmsford High School students Jason P. Mesiti ("Mesiti") and Shannon Silva ("Silva"), and their parents Ronald and Suzanne Brown ("the Browns"), and Carol and Richard Dubreuil ("the Dubreuils"). The plaintiffs' complaint alleges the following facts, which we take as true for purposes of this appeal. On April 8, 1992, Mesiti and Silva attended a mandatory, school-wide "assembly" at Chelmsford High School. Both students were fifteen years old at the time. The assembly consisted of a ninety-minute presentation characterized by the defendants as an AIDS awareness program (the "Program"). The Program was staged by defendant Suzi Landolphi ("Landolphi"), contracting through defendant Hot, Sexy, and Safer, Inc., a corporation wholly owned by Landolphi.

Plaintiffs allege that Landolphi gave sexually explicit monologues and participated in sexually suggestive skits with several minors chosen from the audience. Specifically, the complaint alleges that Landolphi: 1) told the students that they were going to have a "group sexual experience, with audience participation"; 2) used profane, lewd, and lascivious language to describe body parts and excretory functions; 3) advocated and approved oral sex, masturbation, homosexual sexual activity, and condom use during promiscuous premarital sex; 4) simulated masturbation; 5) characterized the loose pants worn by one minor as "erection wear"; 6) referred to being in "deep sh —" after anal sex; 7) had a male minor lick an oversized condom with her, after which she had a female minor pull it over the male minor's entire head and blow it up; 8) encouraged a male minor to display his "orgasm face" with her for the camera; 9) informed a male minor that he was not having enough orgasms; 10) closely inspected a minor and told him he had a "nice butt"; and 11) made eighteen references to orgasms, six references to male genitals, and eight references to female genitals.

Plaintiffs maintain that the sexually explicit nature of Landolphi's speech and behavior humiliated and intimidated Mesiti and Silva. Moreover, many students copied Landolphi's routines and generally displayed overtly sexual behavior in the weeks following the Program, allegedly exacerbating the minors' harassment. The complaint does not allege that either of the minor plaintiffs actually participated in any of the skits, or were the direct objects of any of Landolphi's comments.

The complaint names eight co-defendants along with Hot, Sexy, and Safer, and Landolphi, alleging that each played some role in planning, sponsoring, producing, and compelling the minor plaintiffs' attendance at the Program. In March 1992, defendant Judith Hass ("Hass"), then chairperson of the Chelmsford Parent Teacher Organization (the "PTO"), initiated negotiations with Hot, Sexy, and Safer. Hass and defendant Michael Gilchrist, M.D., also a member of the PTO, as well as the school physician, viewed a promotional videotape of segments of Landolphi's past performances and then recommended the Program to the school administration. On behalf of defendant Chelmsford School Committee (the "School Committee"), Hass executed an agreement with Hot, Sexy, and Safer, and authorized the release of $1,000 of Chelmsford school funds to pay Landolphi's fee.

The complaint also names as defendants two other members of the School Committee, Wendy Marcks and Mary E. Frantz, as well as the Superintendent and Assistant Superintendent of the Chelmsford Public Schools, Richard H. Moser, and David S. Troughton, and the Principal of Chelmsford High School, George J. Betses. Plaintiffs allege that all the defendants participated in the decisions to hire Landolphi, and to compel the students to attend the Program. All the defendants were physically present during the Program.

A school policy adopted by the School Committee required "[p]ositive subscription, with written parental permission" as a prerequisite to "instruction in human sexuality." The plaintiffs allege, however, that the parents were not given advance notice of the content of the Program or an opportunity to excuse their children from attendance at the assembly.

The district court granted defendants' motion to dismiss plaintiffs' complaint, pursuant to Federal Rule of Civil Procedure 12(b)(6), for failure to state a claim upon which relief may be granted, and also dismissed the state law claims under the supplemental jurisdiction principles of 28 U.S.C. § 1367.[1] The district court deferred entry of final judgment, giving plaintiffs leave to file an amended complaint curative of the deficiencies by February 10, 1995. Plaintiffs failed to do so, and final judgment was entered on March 3, 1995, dismissing their claims.

STANDARD OF REVIEW

We exercise de novo review over a district court's dismissal of a claim under Rule 12(b)(6). Vartanian v. Monsanto Co., 14 F.3d 697, 700 (1st Cir.1994); Kale v. Combined Ins. Co. of America, 924 F.2d 1161, 1165 (1st Cir.1991). We accept the allegations of the complaint as true, and determine whether, under any theory, the allegations are sufficient to state a cause of action in accordance with the law. Vartanian, 14 F.3d at 700; Knight v. Mills, 836 F.2d 659 (1st Cir.1987). Although our review is plenary, an appeal is not an opportunity to conjure new arguments not raised before the district court. McCoy v. Massachusetts Inst. of Tech., 950 F.2d 13, 22 (1st Cir.1991), cert. denied, 504 U.S. 910, 112 S.Ct. 1939, 118 L.Ed.2d 545 (1992). In addition, "[b]ecause only well pleaded facts are taken as true, we will not accept a complainant's unsupported conclusions or interpretations of law." Washington Legal Found. v. Massachusetts Bar Found., 993 F.2d 962, 971 (1st Cir.1993) (citations omitted). We may affirm a district court's dismissal order under any independently sufficient grounds. Id.

DISCUSSION

The plaintiffs seek both declaratory and monetary relief, alleging that the school sponsored program deprived the minor plaintiffs of: (1) their privacy rights under the First and Fourteenth Amendments; (2) their substantive due process rights under the First and Fourteenth Amendments; (3) their procedural due process rights under the Fourteenth Amendment; and (4) their First Amendment rights under the Free Exercise Clause (in conjunction with a deprivation of the parent plaintiffs' right to direct and control the upbringing of their children). Plaintiffs also allege that the Program created a sexually hostile educational environment in violation of Title IX of the Education Amendments of 1972, 20 U.S.C. § 1681 et seq.[2]

As an initial matter, we briefly address defendants' assertion of the defense of qualified immunity. Plaintiffs seek monetary damages under 42 U.S.C. § 1983,[3] and defendants assert the affirmative defense of qualified immunity, which shields public officials performing discretionary functions from liability for civil damages "insofar as their conduct does not violate clearly established statutory or constitutional rights of which a reasonable person would have known." Harlow v. Fitzgerald, 457 U.S. 800, 818, 102 S.Ct. 2727, 2738, 73 L.Ed.2d 396 (1982). A right is "clearly established" if, at the time of the alleged violation, "[t]he contours of the right [are] sufficiently clear that a reasonable official would understand that what he is doing violates that right." Anderson v. Creighton, 483 U.S. 635, 640, 107 S.Ct. 3034, 3039, 97 L.Ed.2d 523 (1987). "[T]he relevant question is whether a reasonable official could have believed his actions were lawful in light of clearly established law and the information the official possessed at the time of his allegedly unlawful conduct." Singer v. Maine, 49 F.3d 837, 844 (1st Cir.1995) (citations omitted).

The Supreme Court has explained that: "A necessary concomitant to the determination of whether the constitutional right asserted by a plaintiff is `clearly established' at the time the defendant acted is the determination of whether the plaintiff has asserted a violation of a constitutional right at all." Siegert v. Gilley, 500 U.S. 226, 232, 111 S.Ct. 1789, 1793, 114 L.Ed.2d 277 (1991). Therefore, "before even reaching qualified immunity, a court of appeals must ascertain whether the appellants have asserted a violation of a constitutional right at all." Watterson v. Page, 987 F.2d 1, 7 (1st

Cir.1993); Singer, 49 F.3d at 844. Thus, as a predicate to the objective reasonableness inquiry, "a plaintiff must establish that a particular defendant violated the plaintiff's federally protected rights." Singer, 49 F.3d at 844 (citations omitted).

Accordingly, we first address each of the plaintiffs' claims to determine whether it states a cause of action under federal law. If any of the claims meet this threshold requirement, we will then proceed to the issue of qualified immunity.

I. Privacy Rights and Substantive Due Process

The Fourteenth Amendment provides that "[n]o State shall ... deprive any person of life liberty or property without due process of law." U.S. Const. amend XIV. The substantive component of due process protects against "certain government actions regardless of the fairness of the procedures used to implement them." Daniels v. Williams, 474 U.S. 327, 331, 106 S.Ct. 662, 665, 88 L.Ed.2d 662 (1986). See also Pittsley v. Warish, 927 F.2d 3, 6 (1st Cir.1991) (comparing substantive due process to procedural due process) (citing Monroe v. Pape, 365 U.S. 167, 171-72, 81 S.Ct. 473, 475-76, 5 L.Ed.2d 492 (1961)). There are two theories under which a plaintiff may bring a substantive due process claim. Under the first, a plaintiff must demonstrate a deprivation of an identified liberty or property interest protected by the Fourteenth Amendment. Pittsley, 927 F.2d at 6 (citing Meyer v. Nebraska, 262 U.S. 390, 399, 43 S.Ct. 625, 626-27, 67 L.Ed. 1042 (1923)). Under the second, a plaintiff is not required to prove the deprivation of a specific liberty or property interest, but, rather, he must prove that the state's conduct "shocks the conscience." Id. at 6 (quoting Rochin v. California, 342 U.S. 165, 172, 72 S.Ct. 205, 209-10, 96 L.Ed. 183 (1952)). Plaintiffs contend that compelling the minors' attendance at the Program constitutes a substantive due process violation under both tests.

A. Conscience Shocking Behavior

Plaintiffs' claim that the defendants engaged in conscience shocking behavior when they compelled the minor plaintiffs to attend the Program. The Supreme Court set the standard for analyzing claims of conscience shocking behavior in Rochin. In that case, the Court held that the government could not use evidence obtained by pumping a defendant's stomach against his will because the state actor's conduct was so egregious that it "shock[ed] the conscience" and offended even "hardened sensibilities." Rochin, 342 U.S. at 172, 72 S.Ct. at 210. The Court explained that the stomach pumping employed by the state was "too close to the rack and screw to permit of constitutional differentiation." Id.

Similarly, we have found "conscience shocking" conduct only where the state actors engaged in "extreme or intrusive physical conduct." Souza v. Pina, 53 F.3d 423, 427 (1st Cir.1995); Harrington v. Almy, 977 F.2d 37, 43-44 (1st Cir.1992) (reasonable fact-finder could find "conscience shocking" conduct where a police officer charged with child abuse was required to take a penile plethysmograph[4] as a condition of his reinstatement). See also García v. Miera, 817 F.2d 650, 655 (10th Cir.1987) (corporal punishment of students may "shock the conscience" if it "caused injury so severe, was so disproportionate to the need presented, and was so inspired by malice or sadism ... that it amounted to a brutal and inhumane abuse of official power") (quoting Hall v. Tawney, 621 F.2d 607, 613 (4th Cir.1980)).

Although we have not foreclosed the possibility that words or verbal harassment may constitute "conscious shocking" behavior in violation of substantive due process rights, see Souza, 53 F.3d at 427; Pittsley, 927 F.2d at 6, our review of the caselaw indicates that the threshold for alleging such claims is high and that the facts alleged here do not rise to that level.

In Souza, the plaintiff alleged that the prosecutor had caused the suicide of her son by conducting press conferences in which he encouraged the media to link the son to a string of serial murders. The plaintiff further alleged that the prosecutor knew of her son's suicidal tendencies and should have known that he would take his own life as a result of the accusations. Although we "pause[d] to make clear that we do not condone the conduct alleged by Souza," we nevertheless found that the conduct was not "conscience shocking." Souza, 53 F.3d at 424-27.

In Pittsley, police officers told two young children — ages four and ten — that "if we ever see your father on the street again, you'll never see him again." Pittsley, 927 F.2d at 5. When the police subsequently arrested the children's father, they "use[d] vulgar language" and refused to let the children give their father a hug and kiss goodbye. Id. In affirming the directed verdicts for defendants, we explained: "As despicable and wrongful as it may have been, the single threat made by the officers is not sufficient to `shock the conscience.'" Id. at 7.

The facts alleged at bar are less severe than those found insufficient in Souza and Pittsley. The minor teenagers in this case were compelled to attend a sexually explicit AIDS awareness assembly without prior parent approval. While the defendants' failure to provide opt-out procedures may have displayed a certain callousness towards the sensibilities of the minors, their acts do not approach the mean-spirited brutality evinced by the defendants in Souza and Pittsley. We accordingly hold that the acts alleged here, taken as true, do not constitute conscience shocking and thus fail to state a claim under Rochin.

B. Protected Liberty Interests

The Supreme Court has held that the Fourteenth Amendment encompasses a privacy right that protects against significant government intrusions into certain personal decisions. See Roe v. Wade, 410 U.S. 113, 152, 93 S.Ct. 705, 726, 35 L.Ed.2d 147 (1973). This right of privacy "has some extension to activities relating to marriage, procreation, contraception, family relationships, and child rearing and education." Id. (citations omitted). Nevertheless, the Supreme Court has explained that only those rights that "can be deemed `fundamental' or `implicit in the concept of ordered liberty' are included in this guarantee of personal privacy." Id. (quoting Palko v. Connecticut, 302 U.S. 319, 325, 58 S.Ct. 149, 151-52, 82 L.Ed. 288 (1937)). Regulations limiting these "fundamental rights" may be justified "only by a `compelling state interest' ... [and] must be narrowly drawn to express only the legitimate interests at stake." Id. (citations omitted).

1. Right to Rear Children

Parent-plaintiffs allege that the defendants violated their privacy right to direct the upbringing of their children and educate them in accord with their own views. This, they maintain, is a constitutionally protected "fundamental right" and thus can only be infringed upon a showing of a "compelling state interest" that cannot be achieved by any less restrictive means.

The genesis of the right claimed here can be found in Meyer v. Nebraska, 262 U.S. 390, 43 S.Ct. 625, 67 L.Ed. 1042 (1923), and Pierce v. Society of Sisters, 268 U.S. 510, 535, 45 S.Ct. 571, 573-74, 69 L.Ed. 1070 (1925). In Meyer, the Court struck down a state law forbidding instruction in certain foreign languages in part because it arbitrarily interfered with the "right of parents" to procure such instruction for their children. Meyer, 262 U.S. at 400, 43 S.Ct. at 627. In so holding, the Court stated:

While this Court has not attempted to define with exactness the liberty [guaranteed by the due process clause of the Fourteenth Amendment], the term has received much consideration and some of the included things have been definitely stated. Without doubt, it denotes not merely freedom from bodily restraint but also the right of the individual to contract, to engage in any of the common occupations of life, to acquire useful knowledge, to marry, to establish a home and bring up children, to worship God according to the dictates of his own conscience, and generally to enjoy those privileges long recognized at common law as essential to the orderly pursuit of happiness by free men.

Id. at 399, 43 S.Ct. at 626.

Two years later the Court in Pierce struck down a state statute requiring public school attendance — and thus precluding attendance at parochial schools — because it "unreasonably interfere[d] with the liberty of parents or guardians to direct the upbringing and education of children under their control." 268 U.S. at 534-35, 45 S.Ct. at 573-74. The Meyer and Pierce decisions have since been interpreted by the Court as recognizing that, under our Constitutional scheme, "the custody, care and nurture of the child reside first in the parents." Prince v. Massachusetts, 321 U.S. 158, 166, 64 S.Ct. 438, 442, 88 L.Ed. 645 (1944); see Wisconsin v. Yoder, 406 U.S. 205, 232-33, 92 S.Ct. 1526, 1541-42, 32 L.Ed.2d 15 (1972).

Nevertheless, the Meyer and Pierce cases were decided well before the current "right to privacy" jurisprudence was developed, and the Supreme Court has yet to decide whether the right to direct the upbringing and education of one's children is among those fundamental rights whose infringement merits heightened scrutiny. We need not decide here whether the right to rear one's children is fundamental because we find that, even if it were, the plaintiffs have failed to demonstrate an intrusion of constitutional magnitude on this right.[5]

The Meyer and Pierce cases, we think, evince the principle that the state cannot prevent parents from choosing a specific educational program — whether it be religious instruction at a private school or instruction in a foreign language. That is, the state does not have the power to "standardize its children" or "foster a homogenous people" by completely foreclosing the opportunity of individuals and groups to choose a different path of education. Meyer, 262 U.S. at 402, 43 S.Ct. at 627-28, discussed in, Tribe, supra, § 15-6 at 1319. We do not think, however, that this freedom encompasses a fundamental constitutional right to dictate the curriculum at the public school to which they have chosen to send their children. See Rotunda & Nowak, supra, § 18.28 n. 25. We think it is fundamentally different for the state to say to a parent, "You can't teach your child German or send him to a parochial school," than for the parent to say to the state, "You can't teach my child subjects that are morally offensive to me." The first instance involves the state proscribing parents from educating their children, while the second involves parents prescribing what the state shall teach their children. If all parents had a fundamental constitutional right to dictate individually what the schools teach their children, the schools would be forced to cater a curriculum for each student whose parents had genuine moral disagreements with the school's choice of subject matter. We cannot see that the Constitution imposes such a burden on state educational systems, and accordingly find that the rights of parents as described by Meyer and Pierce do not encompass a broad-based right to restrict the flow of information in the public schools.[6]

2. Right to be Free from Offensive Speech

The minor plaintiffs maintain that the defendants' conduct violated their privacy right to be free from "exposure to vulgar and offensive language and obnoxiously debasing portrayals of human sexuality." Plaintiffs cite no cases — and we have found none — indicating that such a fundamental privacy right exists. Rather, they attempt to extract the claimed privacy right from the Supreme Court's First Amendment cases which uphold the state's limited power to regulate or discipline speech to protect minors from offensive or vulgar speech. See Bethel Sch. Dist. No. 403 v. Fraser, 478 U.S. 675, 685, 106 S.Ct. 3159, 3165, 92 L.Ed.2d 549 (1986) (cited for the proposition that "[a] high school assembly or classroom is no place for a sexually explicit monologue directed towards an unsuspecting audience of teenage students"); FCC v. Pacifica Found., 438 U.S. 726, 98 S.Ct. 3026, 57 L.Ed.2d 1073 (1978). We agree with the district court that these cases "do not create a private cause of action against state officials for exposure" to patently offensive language.[7]

II. Procedural Due Process

The plaintiffs' third claim alleges that their procedural due process rights under the Fourteenth Amendment were violated when the defendants compelled the minor plaintiffs to attend the Program without giving the parents advance notice and an opportunity to opt out of attending.

"In procedural due process claims, the deprivation by state action of a constitutionally protected interest in `life, liberty, or property' is not in itself unconstitutional; what is unconstitutional is the deprivation of such an interest without due process of law." Zinermon v. Burch, 494 U.S. 113, 125, 110 S.Ct. 975, 108 L.Ed.2d 100 (1990) (quoting Parratt v. Taylor, 451 U.S. 527, 537, 101 S.Ct. 1908, 1913-14, 68 L.Ed.2d

420 (1981)). Application of this prohibition requires a well settled two-stage analysis. We first decide whether the asserted individual interests are encompassed within the Fourteenth Amendment's protection of "life, liberty or property." If protected interests are implicated, we then must decide what procedures constitute "due process of law." Ingraham v. Wright, 430 U.S. 651, 672, 97 S.Ct. 1401, 1413, 51 L.Ed.2d 711 (1977) (citations omitted). Protected liberty interests may arise from two sources — the Due Process Clause itself and the laws of the states. Kentucky Dept. of Corrections v. Thompson, 490 U.S. 454, 460, 109 S.Ct. 1904, 1908, 104 L.Ed.2d 506 (1989) (citations omitted).

The liberty preserved from deprivation without due process includes the right "generally to enjoy those privileges long recognized at common law as essential to the orderly pursuit of happiness by free men." Meyer, 262 U.S. at 399, 43 S.Ct. at 626. As previously discussed, however, the liberty protected by the Fourteenth Amendment does not encompass a right to be free from exposure to speech which one regards as offensive. Thus, the plaintiffs' asserted liberty interest, if one exists, must derive from state law.

The plaintiffs contend that state law and the School Committee's policy on "Sex Education" (the "Sex Education Policy") confers a protected liberty interest, and that the defendants' actions deprived them of it without due process. Specifically, the complaint alleges that the defendants failed to follow the school's Sex Education Policy, which provides:

The Committee believes that the public schools can best transmit information on human sexuality to students in the context of the health education continuum. Therefore, information and instructional tools appropriate to the age group will be used to include instruction in human sexuality in the curricular offerings on health. Positive subscription, with written parental permission, will be a prerequisite to enrolling.

(Emphasis added.) The complaint further alleges that the parents were not given advance notice of the contents of the Program or an opportunity to opt out.

Defendants concede for the purposes of their motion that the Sex Education Policy confers a liberty interest in freedom from exposure to the content of the Program and in being afforded an opportunity to opt out.[8] They argue, however, that the plaintiffs still fail to state a claim because the violation of the Sex Education Policy was a "random and unauthorized" act within the confines of the Parratt-Hudson doctrine. Hudson v. Palmer, 468 U.S. 517, 104 S.Ct. 3194, 82 L.Ed.2d 393 (1984); Parratt, 451 U.S. at 527, 101 S.Ct. at 1909. The plaintiffs maintain that their claim is more akin to that stated in Zinermon, and is thus outside the scope of the Parratt-Hudson doctrine.

In Parratt, a state prisoner brought a § 1983 action because prison employees had negligently lost materials he had ordered by mail. The Supreme Court ruled that the prisoner's post-deprivation tort remedy was all the process that was due because the state could not have provided any predeprivation procedural safeguard to address the risk of this kind of random and unauthorized deprivation. Parratt, 451 U.S. at 541, 101 S.Ct. at 1916. As the Court explained, "the loss is not a result of some established state procedure and the State cannot predict precisely when the loss will occur. It is difficult to conceive of how the State could provide a meaningful hearing before the deprivation takes place." Id. In Hudson, the Supreme Court extended this reasoning to intentional deprivations of property, explaining that "[t]he state can no more anticipate the random and unauthorized intentional conduct of its employees than it can similar negligent conduct." Hudson, 468 U.S. at 533, 104 S.Ct. at 3203.

Parratt and Hudson preclude § 1983 claims for the "random and unauthorized" conduct of state officials because the state cannot "anticipate and control [such conduct] in advance." Zinermon, 494 U.S. at 130, 110 S.Ct. at 985. In addition, the Court has made clear that unauthorized deprivations of property by state employees do not constitute due process violations under the Fourteenth Amendment so long as meaningful postdeprivation remedies are available. Id. at 128-30, 110 S.Ct. at 984-86. Moreover, the Court has emphasized that "no matter how significant the private interest at stake and the risk of its erroneous deprivation, the State cannot be required constitutionally to do the impossible by providing predeprivation process." Id. at 129, 110 S.Ct. at 985 (citations omitted). Therefore, "the proper inquiry under Parratt is whether the state is in a position to provide for predeprivation process." Id. at 130, 110 S.Ct. at 985-86 (quotation omitted).

Zinermon involved a due process claim against the state doctors who admitted the plaintiff Burch as a "voluntary" mental patient. Burch alleged that he was incompetent at the time of his admission and should have been afforded the protections provided by the involuntary placement procedure. Although the Court found that Parratt-Hudson doctrine applied to deprivations of liberty, it nevertheless concluded that Burch had failed to state a viable § 1983 claim. Id. at 131-32, 110 S.Ct. at 986-87.

The court found that Burch's claim was not controlled by Parratt and Hudson for three basic reasons. First, the Court explained that the timing of Burch's deprivation of liberty was more predictable than in Parratt and Hudson. As the Court explained, "it is hardly unforeseeable that a person requesting treatment for mental illness might be incapable of informed consent." Id. at 136, 110 S.Ct. at 989. Thus, "[a]ny erroneous deprivation will occur, if at all, at a specific, predictable point in the admission process." Id. Second, the Court found that the state could have provided meaningful predeprivation process and possibly averted the deprivation Burch alleged. Third, the Court found that because the state had delegated the hospital officials broad authority to "effect the very deprivation complained of here," their conduct could not be characterized as "unauthorized" in the same sense as the destruction of the prisoners' property in Parratt and Hudson.

The Parratt-Hudson-Zinermon trilogy "requires that courts scrutinize carefully the assertion by state officials that their conduct is `random and unauthorized' ... where such a conclusion limits the procedural due process inquiry under § 1983 to the question of the adequacy of state postdeprivation remedies." Lowe v. Scott, 959 F.2d 323, 341 (1st Cir.1992).[9] Our examination here leads us to agree with the district court that the plaintiffs' claim falls within the Parratt-Hudson doctrine.

The plaintiffs have not alleged any facts that would bring their claim within the scope of Zinermon. They point to no facts suggesting that the state could have predicted the defendants' failure to give the required notice and opt-out opportunity, nor do they suggest any reasonable additional predeprivation procedures which would have meaningfully reduced the risk of the due process violation alleged.

The plaintiffs contend that the deprivation cannot be characterized as "random and unauthorized" because the performance was planned well in advance. This contention ignores both the nature of the deprivation and the relevant caselaw. The deprivation alleged here is not the staging of the Program itself, but rather the defendants' failure to follow the procedures mandated by the Sex Education Policy. Moreover, the Supreme Court has established that the Parratt-Hudson doctrine applies to both negligent and intentional tortious acts of state actors, explaining that "it would be absurd to suggest that the State hold a hearing to determine whether a [state official] should engage in such conduct." Hudson, 468 U.S. at 533, 104 S.Ct. at 3203-04. That reasoning is applicable here. The plaintiffs have not alleged any facts from which a court could reasonably infer that any defendant was vested with "the power and authority to effect the very deprivation complained of here." Zinermon, 494 U.S. at 138, 110 S.Ct. at 990.[10] Rather, the Sex Education Policy states that "[p]ositive subscription, with parental permission, will be a prerequisite to enrolling," and, accordingly, vested no discretion in school officials. We therefore conclude that the failure to follow the Sex Education Policy was a "random and unauthorized" act within the confines of the Parratt-Hudson doctrine.

The second stage of a Parratt-Hudson analysis looks to whether the state has provided adequate postdeprivation remedies. Lowe, 959 F.2d at 340 (discussing Parratt, 451 U.S. at 527, 101 S.Ct. at 1909). The plaintiffs did not argue to the district court that the state remedies were inadequate, relying instead on their belief that Zinermon was controlling. On appeal, they do no more than state baldly that "[n]o post-deprivation procedures can undo the damaging influences which were impressed on the students during the performance." Accordingly, we deem this point waived for appellate review, see United States v. Zannino, 895 F.2d 1, 17 (1st Cir.), cert. denied, 494 U.S. 1082, 110 S.Ct. 1814, 108 L.Ed.2d 944 (1990) (discussing the "settled appellate rule that issues adverted to in a perfunctory manner, unaccompanied by some effort at developed argumentation, are deemed waived"), and therefore find that the plaintiffs have failed to state a procedural due process claim.

III. Free Exercise Clause

Plaintiffs' fourth claim seeks both monetary and declaratory relief, alleging that the defendants' endorsement and encouragement of sexual promiscuity at a mandatory assembly "imping[ed] on their sincerely held religious values regarding chastity and morality," and thereby violated the Free Exercise Clause of the First Amendment.

In Employment Div., Oregon Dep't of Human Resources v. Smith, 494 U.S. 872, 110 S.Ct. 1595, 108 L.Ed.2d 876 (1990), the Supreme Court addressed a free exercise challenge to a facially neutral and generally applicable criminal statute. The Court held that the compelling interest test did not apply to free exercise challenges to "generally applicable prohibitions of socially harmful conduct." Id. at 882-85, 110 S.Ct. at 1601-04. The Court explained that the First Amendment was not offended by neutral, generally applicable laws, unless burdening religion was the object of the law. Id. at 878-82, 110 S.Ct. at 1599-1602.

In 1994, Congress enacted the Religious Freedom Restoration Act ("RFRA"), 42 U.S.C. § 2000bb, in response to the Supreme Court's decision in Smith. RFRA states, in relevant part:

(a) In General — Government shall not substantially burden a person's exercise of religion even if the burden results from a rule of general applicability, except as provided in subsection (b) of this section.

(b) Exception — Government may substantially burden a person's exercise of religion only if it demonstrates that application of the burden to the person —

(1) is in furtherance of a compelling governmental interest; and

(2) is the least restrictive means of furthering that compelling governmental interest.

Id. RFRA states that it was enacted to bring the law back to its pre-Smith state. Id.

The plaintiffs' Free Exercise challenge raises two complex constitutional issues. The threshold issue is whether the Free Exercise Clause even applies to public education.[11] If indeed the Free Exercise Clause applies to the plaintiffs' claim, the question would then be whether their free exercise rights were violated by the compulsory attendance at the Program. Because the Program was staged in 1992, and RFRA was enacted in 1994, however, a cause of action under RFRA exists only if the statute applies retroactively. For the reasons stated below, we conclude that RFRA does not apply retroactively to plaintiffs' claim for monetary damages.

The Supreme Court has explained that courts should "decline[] to give retroactive effect to statutes burdening private rights unless Congress ha[s] made clear its intent." Landgraf v. USI Film Products, ____ U.S. ____, ____, 114 S.Ct. 1483, 1499, 128 L.Ed.2d 229 (1994). Such an intent will not be inferred where the statute "lacks `clear, strong, and imperative' language requiring retroactive application." Id. (citing United States v. Heth, 7 U.S. (3 Cranch) 399, 413, 2 L.Ed. 479 (1806)). "The presumption against statutory retroactivity has consistently been explained by reference to the unfairness of imposing new burdens on persons after the fact." Id. at ____, 114 S.Ct. at 1500.

RFRA states that it "applies to all Federal and State law, whether statutory or otherwise, and whether adopted before or after the enactment of this Act." 42 U.S.C. § 2000bb. The statute was enacted to "restore the compelling interest test" and provide judicial relief to persons "whose religious exercise has been burdened in violation of this section." Id. While RFRA clearly provides access to declaratory and injunctive relief against all laws burdening the free exercise of religion, we think it lacks the "clear, strong, and imperative" language necessary to create a retroactive cause of action for monetary damages.

We have found no decisions in which a plaintiff was awarded damages under RFRA for conduct occurring before the statute's enactment. Rather, the decisions in which RFRA has been found retroactive considered only the issue of whether to grant injunctive relief, as opposed to an award of monetary damages. See, e.g., Werner v. McCotter, 49 F.3d 1476, 1479-80 (10th Cir. 1995); Brown-El v. Harris, 26 F.3d 68, 69 (8th Cir.1994) (dicta); Boone v. Commissioner of Prisons, No. 93-5074, 1994 WL 383590, 1994 U.S.Dist. LEXIS 10027 (E.D.Pa. July 21, 1994); Rust v. Clarke, 851 F.Supp. 377, 380 (D.Neb.1994) (dicta); Allah v. Menei, 844 F.Supp. 1056, 1061 at n. 15 (E.D.Pa.1994); Lawson v. Dugger, 844 F.Supp. 1538, 1542 (S.D.Fla.1994). Equitable relief, however, is prospective rather than retroactive, even when it applies to conduct occurring before a statute's enactment. See Landgraf, ____ U.S. at ____, 114 S.Ct. at 1500. We therefore find that the cases purportedly addressing retroactivity do not support a finding that Congress intended to create a retroactive cause of action for monetary damages under RFRA. Accordingly, the plaintiffs' claim must be addressed under Smith, the law in effect at the time of the defendants' actions.[12]

The Supreme Court has explained that a "law that is neutral and of general applicability need not be justified by a compelling governmental interest even if the law has the incidental effect of burdening a particular religious practice." Church of the Lukumi Babalu Aye, Inc. v. City of Hialeah, ____ U.S. ____, ____, 113 S.Ct. 2217, 2226-27, 124 L.Ed.2d 472 (1993) (citing Smith, 494 U.S. at 872, 110 S.Ct. at 1596-97). The plaintiffs do not allege, nor is it apparent from their claim, that the compulsory attendance at the Program was anything but a neutral requirement that applied generally to all students. Cf. Id. (where city ordinance violated Free Exercise clause because it targeted the ritual slaughter of animals only by religious groups).

Rather, plaintiffs allege that their case falls within the "hybrid" exception recognized by Smith for cases that involve "the Free Exercise Clause in conjunction with other constitutional protections." Smith, 494 U.S. at 881 & n. 1, 110 S.Ct. at 1601 & n. 1. The most relevant of the so-called hybrid cases is Wisconsin v. Yoder, 406 U.S. 205, 232-33, 92 S.Ct. 1526, 1541-42, 32 L.Ed.2d 15 (1972), in which the Court invalidated a compulsory school attendance law as applied to Amish parents who refused on religious grounds to send their children to school. In so holding, the Court explained that

Pierce stands as a charter of the rights of parents to direct the religious upbringing of their children. And, when combined with a free exercise claim of the nature revealed by this record, more than merely a "reasonable relation to some purpose within the competency of the State" is required to sustain the validity of the State's requirement under the First Amendment.

Id. at 232-33, 92 S.Ct. at 1542 (discussing Pierce, 268 U.S. 510, 45 S.Ct. 571). We find that the plaintiffs allegations do not bring them within the sweep of Yoder for two distinct reasons.

First, as we explained, the plaintiffs' allegations of interference with family relations and parental prerogatives do not state a privacy or substantive due process claim. Their free exercise challenge is thus not conjoined with an independently protected constitutional protection. Second, their free exercise claim is qualitatively distinguishable from that alleged in Yoder. As the Court in Yoder emphasized:

the Amish in this case have convincingly demonstrated the sincerity of their religious beliefs, the interrelationship of belief with their mode of life, the vital role that belief and daily conduct play in the continued survival of Old Order Amish communities and their religious organization, and the hazards presented by the State's enforcement of a Statute generally valid as to others.

Id. at 235, 92 S.Ct. at 1543. Here, the plaintiffs do not allege that the one-time compulsory attendance at the Program threatened their entire way of life. Accordingly, the plaintiffs' free exercise claim for damages was properly dismissed.

The plaintiffs also seek a declaratory judgment concerning the alleged infringement of their Free Exercise Rights. The standing requirement of Article III necessitates that the claimant "allege personal injury fairly traceable to the defendant's allegedly unlawful conduct and likely to be addressed by the requested relief." Allen v. Wright, 468 U.S. 737, 751, 104 S.Ct. 3315, 3324, 82 L.Ed.2d 556 (1984). The Supreme Court has made clear that past exposure to harm will not in and of itself confer standing upon a litigant to obtain equitable relief "[a]bsent a sufficient likelihood that he will again be wronged in a similar way." City of Los Angeles v. Lyons, 461 U.S. 95, 104-06, 111, 103 S.Ct. 1660, 1666-67, 1670, 75 L.Ed.2d 675 (1983). See also American Postal Workers Union v. Frank, 968 F.2d 1373, 1374-76 (1st Cir.1992). Here, the plaintiffs do not allege (nor does it appear) that they are likely to again be subject to school activities that allegedly violate their Free Exercise Rights. We accordingly lack jurisdiction over the claim for declaratory relief and conclude that it also was properly dismissed.

IV. Sexual Harassment

The plaintiffs' fifth claim alleges that the defendants engaged in sexual harassment by creating a sexually hostile environment, in violation of Title IX of the Education Amendments of 1972. Title IX provides in relevant part:

No person in the United States shall, on the basis of sex, be excluded from participation in, be denied the benefits of, or be subjected to discrimination under any education program or activity receiving Federal financial assistance....

20 U.S.C. § 1681. Because the relevant caselaw under Title IX is relatively sparse, we apply Title VII caselaw by analogy. See Franklin v. Gwinnett County Pub. Schs., 503 U.S. 60, 73-75, 112 S.Ct. 1028, 1037, 117 L.Ed.2d 208 (1990); Lipsett v. University of Puerto Rico, 864 F.2d 881, 899 (1st Cir.1988).

Title VII, and thus Title IX, "strike at the entire spectrum of disparate treatment of men and women," including conduct having the purpose or effect of unreasonably interfering with an individual's performance or creating an intimidating, hostile or offensive environment. Meritor Sav. Bank, FSB v. Vinson, 477 U.S. 57, 64-65, 106 S.Ct.

2399, 2404-05, 91 L.Ed.2d 49 (1986); Lipsett, 864 F.2d at 899. As the Supreme Court explained:

> Sexual harassment which creates a hostile or offensive environment for members of one sex is every bit the arbitrary barrier to sexual equality at the workplace that racial harassment is to racial equality. Surely, a requirement that a man or woman run a gauntlet of sexual abuse in return for the privilege of being allowed to work and make a living can be as demeaning and disconcerting as the harshest of racial epithets.

Meritor, 477 U.S. at 67, 106 S.Ct. at 2405 (quoting Henson v. Dundee, 682 F.2d 897, 902 (1982)).

The elements a plaintiff must prove to succeed in such type of sexual harassment claim are: (i) that he/she is a member of a protected class; (ii) that he/she was subject to unwelcome sexual harassment; (iii) that the harassment was based upon sex; (iv) that the harassment was sufficiently severe or pervasive so as to alter the conditions of plaintiff's education and create an abusive educational environment; and (v) that some basis for employer liability has been established. Id. at 66-73, 106 S.Ct. at 2405-09. See also Harris v. Forklift Sys. Inc., ____ U.S. ____, 114 S.Ct. 367, 126 L.Ed.2d 295 (1993); Lipsett, 864 F.2d at 898-901.

Title IX is violated "[w]hen the [educational environment] is permeated with `discriminatory intimidation, ridicule, and insult' that is `sufficiently severe or pervasive to alter the conditions of the victim's employment and create an abusive ... environment.'" Harris, ____ U.S. at ____, 114 S.Ct. at 370 (quoting Meritor, 477 U.S. at 64-65, 106 S.Ct. at 2404-05 (1986)); Lipsett, 864 F.2d at 898. While a court must consider all of the circumstances in determining whether a plaintiff has established that an environment is hostile or abusive, it must be particularly concerned with (1) the frequency of the discriminatory conduct; (2) its severity; (3) whether it is physically threatening or humiliating rather than a mere offensive utterance; and (4) whether it unreasonably interferes with an employee's work performance. See Harris, ____ U.S. at ____, 114 S.Ct. at 371. Although the presence or absence of psychological harm or an unreasonable effect on work performance are relevant, no single factor is required. See id.

The Court has explained that the relevant factors must be viewed both objectively and subjectively. See id. at ____, 114 S.Ct. at 370. If the conduct is not so severe or pervasive that a reasonable person would find it hostile or abusive, it is beyond Title IX's purview. See id. Similarly, if the plaintiff does not subjectively perceive the environment to be abusive, the conduct has not actually altered the conditions of her employment, and there is no Title IX violation. See id. Thus, the court must consider not only the actual effect of the harassment on the plaintiff, but also the effect such conduct would have on a reasonable person in the plaintiff's position.

Turning to the case at bar, we find that the facts alleged here are insufficient to state a claim for sexual harassment under a hostile environment theory. The plaintiffs' allegations are weak on every one of the Harris factors, and when considered in sum, are clearly insufficient to establish the existence of an objectively hostile or abusive environment. First, plaintiffs cannot claim that the offensive speech occurred frequently, as they allege only a one-time exposure to the comments.[13]

We also think that the plaintiffs' allegations do not establish that Landolphi's comments were so severe as to create an objectively hostile environment. This finding is based on both the context and content of her remarks. The remarks were given to the entire ninth and tenth grades at what the defendants labelled an "AIDS awareness program." Significantly, the plaintiffs do not allege that they were required to participate in any of the offensive skits or that they were the direct objects of Landolphi's sexual comments.

Moreover, during his introductory remarks, defendant Gilchrist advised students that the purpose of the Program was to educate them about the dangers of sexual activity, stating:

We [] see young people in their twenties who are infected with the AIDS virus.... It means they caught the virus when they were in high school, and will be dead before they are thirty years old. That's why the doctors are scared, and they want you to hear the message.

Now, sometimes to hear a message, it takes a special messenger. And today, we have a very special messenger, who uses probably one of the most effective forms of communication — humor. I want you to listen carefully. Enjoy it, but also remember the message.

Similarly, Landolphi stated in her opening remarks that "[w]e're going to talk about AIDS, but not in the usual way." These prefaces framed the Program in such a way that an objective person would understand that Landolphi's allegedly vulgar sexual commentary was intended to educate the students about the AIDS virus rather than to create a sexually hostile environment.

These introductions also belie the plaintiffs' claim that Landolphi's speech was physically threatening and humiliating, rather than a mere offensive utterance. Landolphi's remarks were not directed specifically at the plaintiffs and were couched in an attempt to use humor to educate the students on sex and the AIDS virus. In this context, while average high school students might have been offended by the graphic sexual discussions alleged here, Landolphi's remarks could not reasonably be considered physically threatening or humiliating so as to create a hostile environment.

Similarly, the plaintiffs' allegations establish that the Program did not significantly alter their educational environment from an objective standpoint. The Program consisted of two ninety-minute sex-education presentations, and although the plaintiffs allege that "coarse jesting, sexual innuendo, and overtly sexual behavior took place for the weeks following the Program," they fail to explain how the coarse jesting and overtly sexual behavior "create[d] an atmosphere so infused with hostility toward members of one sex that [it] alter[ed] the [educational environment] for them." Lipsett, 864 F.2d at 897. In fact, they allege that the offensive behavior was visited on "those students," regardless of gender, "who were not inclined to accept `the message' about human sexuality." If anything, then, they allege discrimination based upon the basis of viewpoint, rather than on the basis of gender, as required by Title IX. We therefore find that their claim under Title IX fails.

CONCLUSION

We have considered the other claims of the plaintiffs and find them similarly without merit.

Affirmed.


## Denver Area Educ. Telecommunications Consortium v. FCC (June 28, 1996)

Justice Breyer announced the judgment of the Court and delivered the opinion of the Court with respect to Part III, an opinion with respect to Parts I, II, and V, in which Justice Stevens, Justice O'Connor, and Justice Souter join, and an opinion with respect to Parts IV and VI, in which Justice Stevens and Justice Souter join.

These cases present First Amendment challenges to three statutory provisions that seek to regulate the broadcasting of "patently offensive" sex related material on cable television. Cable Television Consumer Protection and Competition Act of 1992 (1992 Act or Act), 106 Stat. 1486, §§10(a), 10(b), and 10(c), 47 U.S.C. §§ 532(h), 532(j), and note following §531. The provisions apply to programs broadcast over cable on what are known as "leased access channels" and "public, educational, or governmental channels." Two of the provisions essentially permit a cable system operator to prohibit the broadcasting of "programming" that the "operator reasonably believes describes or depicts sexual or excretory activities or organs in a patently offensive manner." 1992 Act, §10(a); see §10(c). See also In re Implementation of Section 10 of the Cable Consumer Protection and Competition Act of 1992: Indecent Programming and Other Types of Materials on Cable Access Channels, First Report and Order, 8 FCC Rcd 998 (1993) (First Report and Order); In re Implementation of Section 10 of the Cable Consumer Protection and Competition Act of 1992, Indecent Programming and Other Types of Materials on Cable Access Channels, Second Report and Order, 8 FCC Rcd 2638 (1993) (Second Report and Order). The remaining provision requires cable system operators to segregate certain "patently offensive" programming, to place it on a single channel, and to block that channel from viewer access unless the viewer requests access in advance and in writing. 1992 Act, §10(b); 47 CFR § 76.701(g) (1995).

We conclude that the first provision--that permits the operator to decide whether or not to broadcast such programs on leased access channels--is consistent with the First Amendment. The second provision, that requires leased channel operators to segregate and to block that programming, and the third provision, applicable to public, educational, and governmental channels, violate the First Amendment, for they are not appropriately tailored to achieve the basic, legitimate objective of protecting children from exposure to "patently offensive" material.

Cable operators typically own a physical cable network used to convey programming over several dozen cable channels into subscribers' houses. Program sources vary from channel to channel. Most channels carry programming produced by independent firms, including "many national and regional cable programming networks that have emerged in recent years," Turner Broadcasting System, Inc. v. FCC, 512 U. S. ___, ___ (1994) (slip op., at 3), as well as some programming that the system operator itself (or an operator affiliate) may provide. Other channels may simply retransmit through cable the signals of over the air broadcast stations. Id., at ___ (slip op., at 3-4). Certain special channels here at issue, called "leased channels" and "public, educational, or governmental channels," carry programs provided by those to whom the law gives special cable system access rights.

A "leased channel" is a channel that federal law requires a cable system operator to reserve for commercial lease by unaffiliated third parties. About 10 to 15 percent of a cable system's channels would typically fall into this category. See 47 U.S.C. § 532(b). "[P]ublic, educational, or governmental channels" (which we shall call "public access" channels) are channels that, over the years, local governments have required cable system operators to set aside for public, educational, or governmental purposes as part of the consideration an operator gives in return for permission to install cables under city streets and to use public rights of way. See §531; see also H. R. Rep. No. 98-934, p. 30 (1984) (authorizing local authorities to require creation of public access channels). Between 1984 and 1992 federal law (as had much pre-1984 state law, in respect to public access channels) prohibited cable system operators from exercising any editorial control over the content of any program broadcast over either leased or public access channels. See 47 U.S.C. §§ 531(e) (public access), 532(c)(2) (leased access).

In 1992, in an effort to control sexually explicit programming conveyed over access channels, Congress enacted the three provisions before us. The first two provisions relate to leased channels. The first says:

"This subsection shall permit a cable operator to enforce prospectively a written and published policy of prohibiting programming that the cable operator reasonably believes describes or depicts sexual or excretory activities or organs in a patently offensive manner as measured by contemporary community standards." 1992 Act, §10(a)(2), 106 Stat. 1486.

The second provision applicable only to leased channels requires cable operators to segregate and to block similar programming if they decide to permit, rather than to prohibit, its broadcast. The provision tells the Federal Communications Commission (FCC or Commission) to promulgate regulations that will (a) require "programmers to inform cable operators if the program[ming] would be indecent as defined by Commission regulations"; (b) require "cable operators to place" such material "on a single channel"; and (c) require "cable operators to block such single channel unless the subscriber requests access to such channel in writing." 1992 Act, §10(b)(1). The Commission issued regulations defining the material at issue in terms virtually identical to those we have already set forth, namely as descriptions or depictions of "sexual or excretory activities or organs in a patently offensive manner" as measured by the cable viewing community. First Report and Order, ¶¶33-38, 8 FCC Rcd, at 1003-1004. The regulations require the cable operators to place this material on a single channel and to block it (say, by scrambling). They also require the system operator to provide access to the blocked channel "within 30 days" of a subscriber's written request for access and to re block it within 30 days of a subscriber's request to do so. 47 CFR § 76.701(c) (1995).

The third provision is similar to the first provision, but applies only to public access channels. The relevant statutory section instructs the FCC to promulgate regulations that will

"enable a cable operator of a cable system to prohibit the use, on such system, of any channel capacity of any public, educational, or governmental access facility for any programming which contains obscene material, sexually explicit conduct, or material soliciting or promoting unlawful conduct." 1992 Act, §10(c), ibid.

The FCC, carrying out this statutory instruction, promulgated regulations defining "sexually explicit" in language almost identical to that in the statute's leased channel provision, namely as descriptions or depictions of "sexual or excretory activities or organs in a patently offensive manner" as measured by the cable viewing community. See 47 CFR § 76.702 (1995) (incorporating definition from 47 CFR § 76.701(g)).

The upshot is, as we said at the beginning, that the federal law before us (the statute as implemented through regulations) now permits cable operators either to allow or to forbid the transmission of "patently offensive" sex related materials over both leased and public access channels, and requires those operators, at a minimum, to segregate and to block transmission of that same material on leased channels.

Petitioners, claiming that the three statutory provisions, as implemented by the Commission regulations, violate the First Amendment, sought judicial review of the Commission's First Report and Order and its Second Report and Order in the United States Court of Appeals for the District of Columbia Circuit. A panel of that Circuit agreed with petitioners that the provisions violated the First Amendment. Alliance for Community Media v. FCC, 10 F. 3d 812 (1993). The entire Court of Appeals, however, heard the case en banc and reached the opposite conclusion. It held all three statutory provisions (as implemented) were consistent with the First Amendment. Alliance for Community Media v. FCC, 56 F. 3d 105 (1995). Four of the eleven en banc appeals court judges dissented. Two of the dissenting judges concluded that all three provisions violated the First Amendment. Two others thought that either one, or two, but not all three of the provisions, violated the First Amendment. We granted certiorari to review the en banc Court's First Amendment determinations.

We turn initially to the provision that permits cable system operators to prohibit "patently offensive" (or "indecent") programming transmitted over leased access channels. 1992 Act, §10(a). The Court of Appeals held that this provision did not violate the First Amendment because the First Amendment prohibits only "Congress" (and, through the Fourteenth Amendment, a "State"), not private individuals, from "abridging the freedom of speech." Although the court said that it found no "state action," 56 F. 3d, at 113, it could not have meant that phrase literally, for, of course, petitioners attack (as "abridg[ing] . . . speech") a congressional statute--which, by definition, is an Act of "Congress." More likely, the court viewed this statute's "permissive" provisions as not themselves restricting speech, but, rather, as simply reaffirming the authority to pick and choose programming that a private entity, say, a private broadcaster, would have had in the absence of intervention by any federal, or local, governmental entity.

We recognize that the First Amendment, the terms of which apply to governmental action, ordinarily does not itself throw into constitutional doubt the decisions of private citizens to permit, or to restrict, speech--and this is so ordinarily even where those decisions take place within the framework of a regulatory regime such as broadcasting. Were that not so, courts might have to face the difficult, and potentially restrictive, practical task of deciding which, among any number of private parties involved in providing a program (for example, networks, station owners, program editors, and program producers), is the "speaker" whose rights may not be abridged, and who is the speech restricting "censor." Furthermore, as this Court has held, the editorial function itself is an aspect of "speech," see Turner, 512 U. S., at ___ (slip op., at 11-12), and a court's decision that a private party, say, the station owner, is a "censor," could itself interfere with that private "censor's" freedom to speak as an editor. Thus, not surprisingly, this Court's First Amendment broadcasting cases have dealt with governmental efforts to restrict, not governmental efforts to provide or to maintain, a broadcaster's freedom to pick and to choose programming. Columbia Broadcasting System, Inc. v. Democratic National Committee, 412 U.S. 94 (1973) (striking restrictions on broadcaster's ability to refuse to carry political advertising); Red Lion Broadcasting Co. v. FCC, 395 U.S. 367 (1969) (upholding restrictions on editorial authority); FCC v. League of Women Voters of Cal., 468 U.S. 364 (1984) (striking restrictions); cf. Consolidated Edison Co. of N. Y. v. Public Serv. Comm'n of N. Y., 447 U.S. 530 (1980) (striking ban on political speech by public utility using its billing envelopes as a broadcast medium); Central Hudson Gas & Elec. Corp. v. Public Serv. Comm'n of N. Y., 447 U.S. 557 (1980) (striking restriction on public utility advertising).

Nonetheless, petitioners, while conceding that this is ordinarily so, point to circumstances that, in their view, make the analogy with private broadcasters inapposite and make this case a special one, warranting a different constitutional result. As a practical matter, they say, cable system operators have considerably more power to-censor" program viewing than do broadcasters, for individual communities typically have only one cable system, linking broadcasters and other program providers with each community's many subscribers. See Turner, supra, at ___ (slip op., at 8) (only one cable system in most communities; nationally more than 60% of homes subscribe to cable, which then becomes the primary or sole source of video programming in the overwhelming majority of these homes). Moreover, concern about system operators' exercise of this considerable power originally led government--local and federal--to insist that operators provide leased and public access channels free of operator editorial control. H. R. Rep. No. 98-934, at 30-31. To permit system operators to supervise programming on leased access channels will create the very private censorship risk that this anticensorship effort sought to avoid. At the same time, petitioners add, cable systems have two relevant special characteristics. They are unusually involved with government, for they depend upon government permission and government facilities (streets, rights of way) to string the cable necessary for their services. And in respect to leased channels, their speech interests are relatively weak because they act less like editors, such as newspapers or television broadcasters, than like common carriers, such as telephone companies.

Under these circumstances, petitioners conclude, Congress' "permissive" law, in actuality, will "abridge" their free speech. And this Court should treat that law as a congressionally imposed, content based, restriction unredeemed as a properly tailored effort to serve a "compelling interest." See Simon & Schuster, Inc. v. Members of N. Y. State Crime Victims Bd., 502 U.S. 105, 118 (1991); Sable Communications of Cal., Inc. v. FCC, 492 U.S. 115, 126 (1989). They further analogize the provisions to constitutionally forbidden content based restrictions upon speech taking place in "public forums" such as public streets, parks, or buildings dedicated to open speech and communication. See Cornelius v. NAACP Legal Defense & Ed. Fund, Inc., 473 U.S. 788, 802 (1985); Perry Ed. Assn. v. Perry Local Educators' Assn., 460 U.S. 37, 45 (1983); see also H. R. Rep. No. 98-934, supra, at 30 (identifying public access channels as the electronic equivalent of a "speaker's soap box"). And, finally, petitioners say that the legal standard the law contains (the "patently offensive" standard) is unconstitutionally vague. See, e.g., Interstate Circuit, Inc. v. Dallas, 390 U.S. 676 (1968) (rejecting censorship ordinance as vague, even though it was intended to protect children).

Like the petitioners, Justices Kennedy and Thomas would have us decide this case simply by transferring and applying literally categorical standards this Court has developed in other contexts. For Justice Kennedy, leased access channels are like a common carrier, cablecast is a protected medium, strict scrutiny applies, §10(a) fails this test, and, therefore, §10(a) is invalid. Post, at 17-20, 27-30. For Justice Thomas, the case is simple because the cable operator who owns the system over which access channels are broadcast, like a bookstore owner with respect to what it displays on the shelves, has a predominant First Amendment interest. Post, at 6-7, 12-13. Both categorical approaches suffer from the same flaws: they import law developed in very different contexts into a new and changing environment, and they lack the flexibility necessary to allow government to respond to very serious practical problems without sacrificing the free exchange of ideas the First Amendment is designed to protect.

The history of this Court's First Amendment jurisprudence, however, is one of continual development, as the Constitution's general command that "Congress shall make no law . . . abridging the freedom of speech, or of the press," has been applied to new circumstances requiring different adaptations of prior principles and precedents. The essence of that protection is that Congress may not regulate speech except in cases of extraordinary need and with the exercise of a degree of care that we have not elsewhere required. See, e.g., Schenck v. United States, 249 U.S. 47, 51-52 (1919); Abrams v. United States, 250 U.S. 616, 627-628 (1919) (Holmes, J., dissenting); West Viginia Bd. of Ed. v. Barnette, 319 U.S. 624, 639 (1943); Texas v. Johnson, 491 U.S. 397, 418-420 (1989). At the same time, our cases have not left Congress or the States powerless to address the most serious problems. See, e.g., Chaplinsky v. New Hampshire, 315 U.S. 568 (1942); Young v. American Mini Theaters, Inc. 427 U.S. 50 (1976); FCC v. Pacifica Foundation, 438 U.S. 726 (1978).

Over the years, this Court has restated and refined these basic First Amendment principles, adopting them more particularly to the balance of competing interests and the special circumstances of each field of application. See, e.g., New York Times Co. v. Sullivan, 376 U.S. 254 (1964) (allowing criticism of public officials to be regulated by civil libel only if the plaintiff shows actual malice); Gertz v. Robert Welch, Inc., 418 U.S. 323 (1974) (allowing greater regulation of speech harming individuals who are not public officials, but still requiring a negligence standard); Red Lion Broadcasting Co. v. FCC, 395 U.S. 367 (1969) (employing highly flexible standard in response to the scarcity problem unique to over the air broadcast); Arkansas Writers' Project, Inc. v. Ragland, 481 U.S. 221, 231-232 (1987) (requiring "compelling state interest" and a "narrowly drawn" means in context of differential taxation of media); Sable, supra, at 126, 131 (applying "compelling interest," "least restrictive means," and "narrowly tailored" requirements to indecent telephone communications); Turner, 512 U. S., at ___ (slip op., at 16) (using "heightened scrutiny" to address content neutral regulations of cable system broadcasts); Central Hudson Gas & Elec. Corp., 447 U. S., at 566 (restriction on commercial speech cannot be "more extensive than is necessary" to serve a "substantial" government interest).

This tradition teaches that the First Amendment embodies an overarching commitment to protect speech from Government regulation through close judicial scrutiny, thereby enforcing the Constitution's constraints, but without imposing judicial formulae so rigid that they become a straight jacket that disables Government from responding to serious problems. This Court, in different contexts, has consistently held that the Government may directly regulate speech to address extraordinary problems, where its regulations are appropriately tailored to resolve those problems without imposing an unnecessarily great restriction on speech. Justices Kennedy and Thomas would have us further declare which, among the many applications of the general approach that this Court has developed over the years, we are applying here. But no definitive choice among competing analogies (broadcast, common carrier, bookstore) allows us to declare a rigid single standard, good for now and for all future media and purposes. That is not to say that we reject all the more specific formulations of the standard--they appropriately cover the vast majority of cases involving Government regulation of speech. Rather, aware as we are of the changes taking place in the law, the technology, and the industrial structure, related to telecommunications, see, e.g., Telecommunications Act of 1996, 110 Stat. 56; S. Rep. No. 104-23 (1995); H. R. Rep. No. 104-204 (1995), we believe it unwise and unnecessary definitively to pick one analogy or one specific set of words now. See Columbia Broadcasting, 412 U. S., at 102 ("The problems of regulation are rendered more difficult because the broadcast industry is dynamic in terms of technological change; solutions adequate a decade ago are not necessarily so now, and those acceptable today may well be outmoded 10 years hence"); Pacifica, supra, at 748 ("We have long recognized that each medium of expression presents special First Amendment problems.") We therefore think it premature to answer the broad questions that Justices Kennedy and Thomas raise in their efforts to find a definitive analogy, deciding, for example, the extent to which private property can be designated a public forum, compare post, at 14-16 (Kennedy, J., concurring in part and dissenting in part), with post, at 15-19 (Thomas, J., dissenting in part and concurring in judgment); whether public access channels are a public forum, post, at 12-13 (Kennedy J.); whether the Government's viewpoint neutral decision to limit a public forum is subject to the same scrutiny as a selective exclusion from a pre-existing public forum, post, at 20-25 (Kennedy, J.); whether exclusion from common carriage must for all purposes be treated like exclusion from a public forum, post, at 18-19 (Kennedy, J.); and whether the interests of the owners of communications media always subordinate the interests of all other users of a medium, post, at 6-7 (Thomas, J.).

Rather than decide these issues, we can decide this case more narrowly, by closely scrutinizing §10(a) to assure that it properly addresses an extremely important problem, without imposing, in light of the relevant interests, an unnecessarily great restriction on speech. The importance of the interest at stake here--protecting children from exposure to patently offensive depictions of sex; the accommodation of the interests of programmers in maintaining access channels and of cable operators in editing the contents of their channels; the similarity of the problem and its solution to those at issue in Pacifica, supra; and the flexibility inherent in an approach that permits private cable operators to make editorial decisions, lead us to conclude that §10(a) is a sufficiently tailored response to an extraordinarily important problem.

First, the provision before us comes accompanied with an extremely important justification, one that this Court has often found compelling--the need to protect children from exposure to patently offensive sex related material. Sable Communications, 492 U. S., at 126; Ginsberg v. New York, 390 U.S. 629, 639-640 (1968); New York v. Ferber, 458 U.S. 747, 756-757 (1982).

Second, the provision arises in a very particular context--congressional permission for cable operators to regulate programming that, but for a previous Act of Congress, would have had no path of access to cable channels free of an operator's control. The First Amendment interests involved are therefore complex, and involve a balance between those interests served by the access requirements themselves (increasing the availability of avenues of expression to programmers who otherwise would not have them), H. R. Rep. No. 98-934, pp. 31-36 (1984), and the disadvantage to the First Amendment interests of cable operators and other programmers (those to whom the cable operator would have assigned the channels devoted to access). See Turner, 512 U. S., at ___ (slip op., at 11-12).

Third, the problem Congress addressed here is remarkably similar to the problem addressed by the FCC in Pacifica, and the balance Congress struck is commensurate with the balance we approved there. In Pacifica this Court considered a governmental ban of a radio broadcast of "indecent" materials, defined in part, like the provisions before us, to include

" `language that describes, in terms patently offensive as measured by contemporary community standards for the broadcast medium, sexual or excretory activities and organs, at times of the day when there is a reasonable risk that children may be in the audience.' " 438 U. S., at 732 (quoting 56F. C. C. 2d 94, 98 (1975)).

The Court found this ban constitutionally permissible primarily because "broadcasting is uniquely accessible to children" and children were likely listeners to the program there at issue--an afternoon radio broadcast. Id., at 749-750. In addition, the Court wrote, "the broadcast media have established a uniquely pervasive presence in the lives of all Americans," id., at 748, "[p]atently offensive, indecent material . . . confronts the citizen, not only in public, but also in the privacy of the home," generally without sufficient prior warning to allow the recipient to avert his or her eyes or ears, ibid.; and "[a]dults who feel the need may purchase tapes and records or go to theaters and nightclubs" to hear similar performances. Id., at 750, n. 28.

All these factors are present here. Cable television broadcasting, including access channel broadcasting, is as "accessible to children" as over the air broadcasting, if not more so. See Heeter, Greenberg, Baldwin, Paugh, Srigley, & Atkin, Parental Influences on Viewing Style, in Cableviewing 140 (C. Heeter & B. Greenberg eds. 1988) (children spend more time watching television and view more channels than do their parents, whether their household subscribes to cable or receives television over the air). Cable television systems, including access channels, "have established a uniquely pervasive presence in the lives of all Americans." Pacifica, supra, at 748. See Jost, The Future of Television, 4 The CQ Researcher 1131, 1146 (Dec. 23, 1994) (63% of American homes subscribe to cable); Greenberg, Heeter, D'Alessio, & Sipes, Cable and Noncable Viewing Style Comparisons, in Cableviewing, at 207 (cable households spend more of their day, on average, watching television, and will watch more channels, than households without cable service). "Patently offensive" material from these stations can "confron[t] the citizen" in the "privacy of the home," Pacifica, supra, at 748, with little or no prior warning. Cableviewing, at 217-218 (while cable subscribers tend to use guides more than do broadcast viewers, there was no difference among these groups in the amount of viewing that was planned, and, in fact, cable subscribers tended to sample more channels before settling on a program, thereby making them more, not less, susceptible to random exposure to unwanted materials). There is nothing to stop "adults who feel the need" from finding similar programming elsewhere, say, on tape or in theaters. In fact, the power of cable systems to control home program viewing is not absolute. Over the air broadcasting and direct broadcast satellites already provide alternative ways for programmers to reach the home, and are likely to do so to a greater extent in the near future. See generally Telecommunications Act of 1996, 110 Stat. 56, §§201 (advanced television services), 205 (direct broadcast satellite), 302 (video programming by telephone companies), and 304 (availability of navigation devices to enhance multichannel programming); L. Johnson, Toward Competition in Cable Television (1994).

Fourth, the permissive nature of §10(a) means that it likely restricts speech less than, not more than, the ban at issue in Pacifica. The provision removes a restriction as to some speakers--namely, cable operators. See supra, at 13. Moreover, although the provision does create a risk that a program will not appear, that risk is not the same as the certainty that accompanies a governmental ban. In fact, a glance at the programming that cable operators allow on their own (nonaccess) channels suggests that this distinction is not theoretical, but real. See App. 393 (regular channel broadcast of Playboy and "Real Sex" programming). Finally, the provision's permissive nature brings with it a flexibility that allows cable operators, for example, not to ban broadcasts, but, say, to rearrange broadcast times, better to fit the desires of adult audiences while lessening the risks of harm to children. See First Report and Order ¶31, 8 FCC Rcd, at 1003 (interpreting the Act's provisions to allow cable operators broad discretion over what to do with offensive materials). In all these respects, the permissive nature of the approach taken by Congress renders this measure appropriate as a means of achieving the underlying purpose of protecting children.

Of course, cable system operators may not always rearrange or reschedule patently offensive programming. Sometimes, as petitioners fear, they may ban the programming instead. But the same may be said of Pacifica's ban. In practice, the FCC's daytime broadcast ban could have become a total ban, depending upon how private operators (programmers, station owners, networks) responded to it. They would have had to decide whether to reschedule the daytime show for nighttime broadcast in light of comparative audience demand and a host of other practical factors that similarly would determine the practical outcomes of the provisions before us. The upshot, in both cases, must be uncertainty as to practical consequences--of the governmental ban in the one case and of the permission in the other. That common uncertainty makes it difficult to say the provision here is, in any respect, more restrictive than the order in Pacifica. At the same time, in the respects we discussed, the provision is significantly less restrictive.

The existence of this complex balance of interests persuades us that the permissive nature of the provision, coupled with its viewpoint neutral application, is a constitutionally permissible way to protect children from the type of sexual material that concerned Congress, while accommodating both the First Amendment interests served by the access requirements and those served in restoring to cable operators a degree of the editorial control that Congress removed in 1984.

Our basic disagreement with Justice Kennedy is narrow. Like him, we believe that we must scrutinize §10(a) with the greatest care. Like Justices Kennedy and Thomas, we believe that the interest of protecting children that §10(a) purports to serve is compelling. But we part company with Justice Kennedy on two issues. First, Justice Kennedy's focus on categorical analysis forces him to disregard the cable system operators' interests. Post, at 27-28. We, on the other hand, recognize that in the context of cable broadcast that involves an access requirement (here, its partial removal), and unlike in most cases where we have explicitly required "narrow tailoring," the expressive interests of cable operators do play a legitimate role. Cf. Turner, 512 U. S., at __%__ (slip op., at 11-12). While we cannot agree with Justice Thomas that everything turns on the rights of the cable owner, see post, at 12-13, we also cannot agree with Justice Kennedy that we must ignore the expressive interests of cable operators altogether. Second, Justice Kennedy's application of a very strict "narrow tailoring" test depends upon an analogy with a category ("the public forum cases"), which has been distilled over time from the similarities of many cases. Rather than seeking an analogy to a category of cases, however, we have looked to the cases themselves. And, as we have said, we found that Pacifica provides the closest analogy and lends considerable support to our conclusion.

Petitioners and Justice Kennedy, see post, at 19, 25, argue that the opposite result is required by two other cases: Sable Communications of Cal., Inc. v. FCC, 492 U.S. 115 (1989), a case in which this Court found unconstitutional a statute that banned "indecent" telephone messages, and Turner, in which this Court stated that cable broadcast receives full First Amendment protection. See Turner, supra, at __ (slip op., at 12-16). The ban at issue in Sable, however, was not only a total governmentally imposed ban on a category of communications, but also involved a communications medium, telephone service, that was significantly less likely to expose children to the banned material, was less intrusive, and allowed for significantly more control over what comes into the home than either broadcasting or the cable transmission system before us. See 492 U. S., at 128. The Court's distinction in Turner, furthermore, between cable and broadcast television, relied on the inapplicability of the spectrum scarcity problem to cable. See 512 U. S., at ____, (slip op., at 12-16). While that distinction was relevant in Turner to the justification for structural regulations at issue there (the "must carry" rules), it has little to do with a case that involves the effects of television viewing on children. Those effects are the result of how parents and children view television programming, and how pervasive and intrusive that programming is. In that respect, cable and broadcast television differ little, if at all. See supra, at 14-15. Justice Kennedy would have us decide that all common carriage exclusions are subject to the highest scrutiny, see post, at 18-21, and then decide the case on the basis of categories that provide imprecise analogies rather than on the basis of a more contextual assessment, consistent with our First Amendment tradition, of assessing whether Congress carefully and appropriately addressed a serious problem.

The petitioners also rely on this Court's "public forum" cases. They point to Perry

Ed. Assn. v. Perry Local Educators' Assn., 460 U. S., at 45, a case in which this Court said that "public forums" are "places" that the government "has opened for use by the public as a place for expressive activity," or which "by long tradition . . . have been devoted to assembly and debate." Id., at 45. See also Cornelius v. NAACP Legal Defense & Ed. Fund, Inc., 473 U. S., at 801 (assuming public forums may include "private property dedicated to public use"). They add that the government cannot "enforce a content based exclusion" from a public forum unless "necessary to serve a compelling state interest" and "narrowly drawn." Perry, supra, at 45. They further argue that the statute's permissive provisions unjustifiably exclude material, on the basis of content, from the "public forum" that the government has created in the form of access channels. Justice Kennedy adds by analogy that the decision to exclude certain content from common carriage is similarly subject to strict scrutiny, and here does not satisfy that standard of review. See post, at 18-21.

For three reasons, however, it is unnecessary, indeed, unwise, for us definitively to decide whether or how to apply the public forum doctrine to leased access channels. First, while it may be that content based exclusions from the right to use common carriers could violate the First Amendment, see post, at 18-21 (Kennedy, J.), it is not at all clear that the public forum doctrine should be imported wholesale into the area of common carriage regulation. As discussed above, we are wary of the notion that a partial analogy in one context, for which we have developed doctrines, can compel a full range of decisions in such a new and changing area. See supra, at 9-12. Second, it is plain from this Court's cases that a public forum "may be created for a limited purpose." Perry, supra, at 46, n. 7; see also Cornelius, supra, at 802 ("[T]he government `is not required to indefinitely retain the open character of the facility' ") (quoting Perry, supra, at 46). Our cases have not yet determined, however, that the Government's decision to dedicate a public forum to one type of content or another is necessarily subject to the highest level of scrutiny. Must a local government, for example, show a compelling state interest if it builds a band shell in the park and dedicates it solely to classical music (but not to jazz)? The answer is not obvious. Cf. Perry, supra, at 46, n. 7. But, at a minimum, this case does not require us to answer it. Finally, and most important, the effects of Congress' decision on the interests of programmers, viewers, cable operators, and children are the same, whether we characterize Congress' decision as one that limits access to a public forum, discriminates in common carriage, or constrains speech because of its content. If we consider this particular limitation of indecent television programming acceptable as a constraint on speech, we must no less accept the limitation it places on access to the claimed public forum or on use of a common carrier.

Consequently, if one wishes to view the permissive provisions before us through a "public forum" lens, one should view those provisions as limiting the otherwise totally open nature of the forum that leased access channels provide for communication of other than patently offensive sexual material--taking account of the fact that the limitation was imposed in light of experience gained from maintaining a totally open "forum." One must still ask whether the First Amendment forbids the limitation. But unless a label alone were to make a critical First Amendment difference (and we think here it does not), the features of this case that we have already discussed--the government's interest in protecting children, the "permissive" aspect of the statute, and the nature of the medium--sufficiently justify the "limitation" on the availability of this forum.

Finally, petitioners argue that the definition of the materials subject to the challenged provisions is too vague, thereby granting cable system operators too broad a program screening authority. Cf. Hoffman Estates v. Flipside, Hoffman Estates, Inc., 455 U.S. 489, 498 (1982) (citing Grayned v. Rockford, 408 U.S. 104, 108-109 (1972)) (vague laws may lead to arbitrary enforcement); Dombrowski v. Pfister, 380 U.S. 479, 486-487 (1965) (uncertainty may perniciously chill speech). That definition, however, uses language similar to language previously used by this Court for roughly similar purposes.

The provisions, as augmented by FCC regulations, permit cable system operators to prohibit

"programming that the cable operator reasonably believes describes or depicts sexual or excretory activities or organs in a patently offensive manner as measured by contemporary community standards." 1992 Act, §10(a), 106 Stat. 1486.

See also 47 CFR § 76.702 (1995) (reading approximately the same definition into §10(c)). This language is similar to language adopted by this Court in Miller v. California, 413 U.S. 15, 24 (1973) as a "guidelin[e]" for identifying materials that states may constitutionally regulate as obscene. In Miller, the Court defined obscene sexual material (material that lacks First Amendment protection) in terms of

"(a) whether the average person, applying contemporary community standards would find that the work, taken as a whole, appeals to the prurient interest . . .; (b) whether the work depicts or describes, in a patently offensive way, sexual conduct specifically defined by the applicable state law; and (c) whether the work, taken as a whole, lacks serious literary, artistic, political, or scientific value." Ibid. (emphasis added; internal quotation marks omitted).

The language, while vague, attempts to identify the category of materials that Justice Stewart thought could be described only in terms of "I know it when I see it." Jacobellis v. Ohio, 378 U.S. 184, 197 (1964) (Stewart, J., concurring). In §10(a) and the FCC regulations, without Miller's qualifiers, the language would seem to refer to material that would be offensive enough to fall within that category but for the fact that the material also has "serious literary, artistic, political or scientific value" or nonprurient purposes.

This history suggests that the statute's language aims at the kind of programming to which its sponsors referred--pictures of oral sex, bestiality, and rape, see 138 Cong. Rec. S642, S646 (Jan. 30, 1992) (statement of Sen. Helms)--and not at scientific or educational programs (at least unless done with a highly unusual lack of concern for viewer reaction). Moreover, as this Court pointed out in Pacifica, what is "patently offensive" depends on context (the kind of program on which it appears), degree (not "an occasional expletive"), and time of broadcast (a "pig" is offensive in "the parlor" but not the "barnyard"). 438 U. S., at 748, 750. Programming at two o'clock in the morning is seen by a basically adult audience and the "patently offensive" must be defined with that fact in mind.

Further, the statute protects against overly broad application of its standards insofar as it permits cable system operators to screen programs only pursuant to a "written and published policy." 1992 Act, §10(a), 106 Stat. 1486. A cable system operator would find it difficult to show that a leased access program prohibition reflects a rational "policy" if the operator permits similarly "offensive" programming to run elsewhere on its system at comparable times or in comparable ways. We concede that the statute's protection against overly broad application is somewhat diminished by the fact that it permits a cable operator to ban programming that the operator "reasonably believes" is patently offensive. Ibid. (emphasis added). But the "reasonabl[e] belie[f]" qualifier here, as elsewhere in the law, seems designed not to expand the category at which the law aims, but, rather, to provide a legal excuse, for (at least) one honest mistake, from liability that might otherwise attach. Cf. Waters v. Churchill, 511 U. S. ___, ___ (1994) (slip op., at 1) (Souter, J., concurring) (public employer's reasonable belief that employee engaged in unprotected speech excuses liability); United States v. United States Gypsum Co., 438 U. S. 422, 453-455, and n. 29 (1978) (" `meeting competition' " defense in antitrust based on reasonable belief in the necessity to meet competition); Pierson v. Ray, 386 U.S. 547, 555-557 (1967) (police officer has defense to constitutional claim, as did officers of the peace at common law in actions for false arrest, when the officer reasonably believed the statute whose violation precipitated the arrest was valid). And the contours of the shield-- reasonableness--constrain the discretion of the cable operator as much as they protect it. If, for example, a court had already found substantially similar programming to be beyond the pale of "patently offensive" material, or if a local authority overseeing the local public, governmental, or educational channels had indicated that materials of the type that the cable operator decides to ban were not "patently offensive" in that community, then the cable operator would be hard pressed to claim that the exclusion of the material was "reasonable." We conclude that the statute is not impermissibly vague.

For the reasons discussed, we conclude that §10(a) is consistent with the First Amendment.

The statute's second provision significantly differs from the first, for it does not simply permit, but rather requires, cable system operators to restrict speech--by segregating and blocking "patently offensive" sex related material appearing on leased channels (but not on other channels). 1992 Act, §10(b). In particular, as previously mentioned, see supra, at 4-5, this provision and its implementing regulations require cable system operators to place "patently offensive" leased channel programming on a separate channel; to block that channel; to unblock the channel within 30 days of a subscriber's written request for access; and to reblock the channel within 30 days of a subscriber's request for reblocking. 1992 Act, §10(b); 47 CFR §§ 76.701(b), (c), (g) (1995). Also, leased channel programmers must notify cable operators of an intended "patently offensive" broadcast up to 30 days before its scheduled broadcast date. §§76.701(d), (g).

These requirements have obvious restrictive effects. The several up to 30 day delays, along with single channel segregation, mean that a subscriber cannot decide to watch a single program without considerable advance planning and without letting the "patently offensive" channel in its entirety invade his household for days, perhaps weeks, at a time. These restrictions will prevent programmers from broadcasting to viewers who select programs day by day (or, through "surfing," minute by minute); to viewers who would like occasionally to watch a few, but not many, of the programs on the "patently offensive" channel; and to viewers who simply tend to judge a program's value through channel reputation, i.e., by the company it keeps. Moreover, the "written notice" requirement will further restrict viewing by subscribers who fear for their reputations should the operator, advertently or inadvertently, disclose the list of those who wish to watch the "patently offensive" channel. Cf. Lamont v. Postmaster General, 381 U.S. 301, 307 (1965) (finding unconstitutional a requirement that recipients of Communist literature notify the Post-Office that they wish to receive it). Further, the added costs and burdens that these requirements impose upon a cable system operator may encourage that operator to ban programming that the operator would otherwise permit to run, even if only late at night.

The Government argues that, despite these adverse consequences, the "segregate and block" requirements are lawful because they are "the least restrictive means of realizing" a "compelling interest," namely "protecting the physical and psychological well being of minors." See Brief for Federal Respondents 11 (quoting Sable, 492U. S., at 126). It adds that, in any event, the First Amendment, as applied in Pacifica, "does not require that regulations of indecency on television be subject to the strictest" First Amendment "standard of review." Ibid.

We agree with the Government that protection of children is a "compelling interest." See supra, at 10. But we do not agree that the "segregate and block" requirements properly accommodate the speech restrictions they impose and the legitimate objective they seek to attain. Nor need we here determine whether, or the extent to which, Pacifica does, or does not, impose some lesser standard of review where indecent speech is at issue, compare 438 U. S., at 745-748 (opinion of Stevens, J.) (indecent materials enjoy lesser First Amendment protection), with id., at 761-762 (Powell, J., concurring in part and concurring in judgment) (refusing to accept a lesser standard for nonobscene, indecent material). That is because once one examines this governmental restriction, it becomes apparent that, not only is it not a "least restrictive alternative," and is not "narrowly tailored" to meet its legitimate objective, it also seems considerably "more extensive than necessary." That is to say, it fails to satisfy this Court's formulations of the First Amendment's "strictest," as well as its somewhat less "strict," requirements. See, e.g., Sable, 492 U. S., at 126 ("compelling interest" and "least restrictive means" requirements applied to indecent telephone communications); id., at 131 (requiring "narrowly tailored" law); Turner, 512 U. S., at ____ (slip op., at 16) (using "heightened scrutiny" to address content neutral structural regulations of cable systems); id., at ____ (slip op., at 38) (quoting " `no greater than . . . essential' " language from United States v. O'Brien, 391 U.S. 367, 377 (1968), as an example of "heightened," less than strictest, First Amendment scrutiny); Central Hudson, 447 U. S., at 566 (restriction on commercial speech cannot be "more extensive than is necessary"); Florida Bar v. Went For It, Inc., 515 U. S. ____, ____ (1995) (slip op., at 5) (restriction must be "narrowly drawn"); id., at 14 (there must be a "reasonable" "fit" with the objective that legitimates speech restriction). The provision before us does not reveal the caution and care that the standards underlying these various verbal formulas impose upon laws that seek to reconcile the critically important interest in protecting free speech with very important, or even compelling, interests that sometimes warrant restrictions.

Several circumstances lead us to this conclusion. For one thing, the law, as recently amended, uses other means to protect children from similar "patently offensive" material broadcast on unleased cable channels, i.e., broadcast over any of a system's numerous ordinary, or public access, channels. The law, as recently amended, requires cable operators to "scramble or . . . block" such programming on any (unleased) channel "primarily dedicated to sexually oriented programming." Telecommunications Act of 1996, §505, 110 Stat. 136 (emphasis added). In addition, cable operators must honor a subscriber's request to block any, or all, programs on any channel to which he or she does not wish to subscribe. §504, ibid. And manufacturers, in the future, will have to make television sets with a so called "V chip"--a device that will be able automatically to identify and block sexually explicit or violent programs. §551, id., at 139-142.

Although we cannot, and do not, decide whether the new provisions are themselves lawful (a matter not before us), we note that they are significantly less restrictive than the provision here at issue. They do not force the viewer to receive (for days or weeks at a time) all "patently offensive" programming or none; they will not lead the viewer automatically to judge the few by the reputation of the many; and they will not automatically place the occasional viewer's name on a special list. They therefore inevitably lead us to ask why, if they adequately protect children from "patently offensive" material broadcast on ordinary channels, they would not offer adequate protection from similar leased channel broadcasts as well? Alternatively, if these provisions do not adequately protect children from "patently offensive" material broadcast on ordinary channels, how could one justify more severe leased channel restrictions when (given ordinary channel programming) they would yield so little additional protection for children?

The record does not answer these questions. It does not explain why, under the new Act, blocking alone--without written access requests--adequately protects children from exposure to regular sex dedicated channels, but cannot adequately protect those children from programming on similarly sex dedicated channels that are leased. It does not explain why a simple subscriber blocking request system, perhaps a phone call based system, would adequately protect children from "patently offensive" material broadcast on ordinary non sex dedicated channels (i.e., almost all channels) but a far more restrictive segregate/block/written access system is needed to protect children from similar broadcasts on what (in the absence of the segregation requirement) would be non sex dedicated channels that are leased. Nor is there any indication Congress thought the new ordinary channel protections less than adequate.

The answers to the questions are not obvious. We have no empirical reason to believe, for example, that sex dedicated channels are all (or mostly) leased channels, or that "patently offensive" programming on non sex dedicated channels is found only (or mostly) on leased channels. To the contrary, the parties' briefs (and major city television guides) provide examples of what seems likely to be such programming broadcast over both kinds of channels.

We recognize, as the Solicitor General properly points out, that Congress need not deal with every problem at once. Cf. Semler v. Oregon Bd. of Dental Examiners, 294 U.S. 608, 610 (1935) (the legislature need not "strike at all evils at the same time"); and Congress also must have a degree of leeway in tailoring means to ends. Columbia Broadcasting, 412 U. S., at 102-103. But in light of the 1996 statute, it seems fair to say that Congress now has tried to deal with most of the problem. At this point, we can take Congress' different, and significantly less restrictive, treatment of a highly similar problem at least as some indication that more restrictive means are not "essential" (or will not prove very helpful). Cf. Boos v. Barry, 485 U.S. 312, 329 (1988) (existence of a less restrictive statute suggested that a challenged ordinance, aimed at the same problem, was overly restrictive).

The record's description and discussion of a different alternative--the "lockbox"-- leads, through a different route, to a similar conclusion. The Cable Communications Policy Act of 1984 required cable operators to provide

"upon the request of a subscriber, a device by which the subscriber can prohibit viewing of a particular cable service during periods selected by the subscriber." 47 U.S.C. § 544(d)(2).

This device--the "lockbox"--would help protect children by permitting their parents to "lock out" those programs or channels that they did not want their children to see. See FCC 85-179, ¶132, 50 Fed. Reg. 18637, 18655 (1985) ("[T]he provision for lockboxes largely disposes of issues involving the Commission's standard for indecency"). The FCC, in upholding the "segregate and block" provisions said that lockboxes protected children (including, say, children with inattentive parents) less effectively than those provisions. See First Report and Order ¶¶14-15, 8 FCC Rcd, at 1000. But it is important to understand why that is so.

The Government sets forth the reasons as follows:

"In the case of lockboxes, parents would have to discover that such devices exist; find out that their cable operators offer them for sale; spend the time and money to buy one; learn how to program the lockbox to block undesired programs; and, finally, exercise sufficient vigilance to ensure that they have, indeed, locked out whatever indecent programming they do not wish their children to view." Brief for Federal Respondents 37.

We assume the accuracy of this statement. But, the reasons do not show need for a provision as restrictive as the one before us. Rather, they suggest a set of provisions very much like those that Congress placed in the 1996 Act.

No provision, we concede, short of an absolute ban, can offer certain protection against assault by a determined child. We have not, however, generally allowed this fact alone to justify " ` "reduc[ing] the adult population . . . to . . . only what is fit for children." ' " Sable, 492 U. S., at 128 (quoting Bolger v. Youngs Drug Products Corp., 463 U.S. 60, 73 (1983), in turn quoting Butler v. Michigan, 352 U.S. 380, 383 (1957)); see Sable, supra, at 130, and n. 10. But, leaving that problem aside, the Solicitor General's list of practical difficulties would seem to call, not for "segregate and block" requirements, but, rather, for informational requirements, for a simple coding system, for readily available blocking equipment (perhaps accessible by telephone), for imposing cost burdens upon system operators (who may spread them through subscription fees); or perhaps even for a system that requires lockbox defaults to be set to block certain channels (say, sex dedicated channels). These kinds of requirements resemble those that Congress has recently imposed upon all but leased channels. For that reason, the "lockbox" description and the discussion of its frailties reinforces our conclusion that the leased channel provision is overly restrictive when measured against the benefits it is likely to achieve. (We add that the record's discussion of the "lockbox" does not explain why the law now treats leased channels more restrictively than ordinary channels.)

There may, of course, be other explanations. Congress may simply not have bothered to change the leased channel provisions when it introduced a new system for other channels. But responses of this sort, like guesses about the comparative seriousness of the problem, are not legally adequate. In other cases, where, as here, the record before Congress or before an agency provides no convincing explanation, this Court has not been willing to stretch the limits of the plausible, to create hypothetical nonobvious explanations in order to justify laws that impose significant restrictions upon speech. See, e.g., Sable, supra, at 130 ("[T]he congressional record presented to us contains no evidence as to how effective or ineffective the FCC's most recent regulations were or might prove to be"); Simon & Schuster, 502 U. S., at 120; Minneapolis Star & Tribune Co. v. Minnesota Comm'r of Revenue, 460 U.S. 575, 585-586 (1983); Arkansas Writers' Project, Inc. v. Ragland, 481 U.S. 221, 231-232 (1987).

Consequently, we cannot find that the "segregate and block" restrictions on speech are a narrowly, or reasonably, tailored effort to protect children. Rather, they are overly restrictive, "sacrific[ing]" important First Amendment interests for too "speculative a gain." Columbia Broadcasting, 412 U. S., at 127; see League of Women Voters, 468 U. S., at 397. For that reason they are not consistent with the First Amendment.

The statute's third provision, as implemented by FCC regulation, is similar to its first provision, in that it too permits a cable operator to prevent transmission of "patently offensive" programming, in this case on public access channels. 1992 Act, §10(c); 47 CFR § 76.702 (1995). But there are four important differences.

The first is the historical background. As Justice Kennedy points out, see post, at 9-12, cable operators have traditionally agreed to reserve channel capacity for public, governmental, and educational channels as part of the consideration they give municipalities that award them cable franchises. See H. R. Rep. No. 98-934, at 30. In the terms preferred by Justice Thomas, see post, at 17-18, the requirement to reserve capacity for public access channels is similar to the reservation of a public easement, or a dedication of land for streets and parks, as part of a municipality's approval of a subdivision of land. Cf. post, at 15-16 (Kennedy, J.). Significantly, these are channels over which cable operators have not historically exercised editorial control. H. R. Rep. No. 98-934, supra, at 30. Unlike §10(a) therefore, §10(c) does not restore to cable operators editorial rights that they once had, and the countervailing First Amendment interest is nonexistent, or at least much diminished. See also post, at 13-15 (Kennedy, J.).

The second difference is the institutional background that has developed as a result of the historical difference. When a "leased channel" is made available by the operator to a private lessee, the lessee has total control of programming during the leased time slot. See 47 U.S.C. § 532(c)(2). Public access channels, on the other hand, are normally subject to complex supervisory systems of various sorts, often with both public and private elements. See §531(b) (franchising authorities "may require rules and procedures for the use of the [public access] channel capacity"). Municipalities generally provide in their cable franchising agreements for an access channel manager, who is most commonly a nonprofit organization, but may also be the municipality, or, in some instances, the cable system owner. See D. Brenner, M. Price, & M. Myerson, Cable Television and Other Nonbroadcast Video ¶6.04[7] (1993); P. Aufderheide, Public Access Cable Programming, Controversial Speech, and Free Expression (1992) (hereinafter Aufderheide), reprinted in App. 61, 63 (surveying 61 communities; the access manager was: a nonprofit organization in 41, a local government official in 12, the cable operator in 5, and an unidentified entity in 3); D. Agosta, C. Rogoff, & A. Norman, The Participate Report: A Case Study of Public Access Cable Television in New York State 28 (1990), attached as Exh. K to Joint Comments for the Alliance for Community Media et al., filed with the FCC under MM Docket No. 92-258 (materials so filed hereinafter FCC Record) ("In 88% [of New York public access systems] access channels were programmed jointly between the cable operator and another institution such as a university, library, or non profit access organization"); Agosta, at 28-32, FCC Record; Comments of National Cable Television Association Inc., at 14, FCC Record ("Operators often have no involvement in PEG channels that are run by local access organizations"). Access channel activity and management are partly financed with public funds--through franchise fees or other payments pursuant to the franchise agreement, or from general municipal funds, see Brenner, ¶6.04[3][c]; Aufderheide, App. 59-60--and are commonly subject to supervision by a local supervisory board. See, e.g., D. C. Code Ann. §43-1829 (1990 and Supp. 1996);

Lynchburg City Code §12.1-44(d)(2) (1988).

This system of public, private, and mixed nonprofit elements, through its supervising boards and nonprofit or governmental access managers, can set programming policy and approve or disapprove particular programming services. And this system can police that policy by, for example, requiring indemnification by programmers, certification of compliance with local standards, time segregation, adult content advisories, or even by prescreening individual programs. See Second Report and Order, 8 FCC Rcd, ¶26 ("[F]rom the comments received, it appears that a number of access organizations already have in place procedures that require certification statements [of compliance with local standards], or their equivalent, from access programmers"); Comments of the Boston Community Access and Programming Foundation, App. 163-164; Aufderheide, App. 69-71; Comments of Metropolitan Area Communications Commission, at 2, FCC Record; Reply Comments of Waycross Community Television, at 4-6, FCC Record; Reply Comments of Columbus Community Cable Access, Inc., App. 329; Reply Comments of the City of St. Paul, App. 318, 325; Reply Comments of Erik Mollberg, Public Access Coordinator, Ft. Wayne, Ind., at 3, FCC Record; Comments of Defiance Community Television, at 3, FCC Record; Comments of Nutmeg Public Access Television, Inc., at 3-4, FCC Record. Whether these locally accountable bodies prescreen programming, promulgate rules for the use of public access channels, or are merely available to respond when problems arise, the upshot is the same: there is a locally accountable body capable of addressing the problem, should it arise, of patently offensive programming broadcast to children, making it unlikely that many children will in fact be exposed to programming considered patently offensive in that community. See 56 F. 3d, at 127-128; Second Report and Order, supra, ¶26.

Third, the existence of a system aimed at encouraging and securing programming that the community considers valuable strongly suggests that a "cable operator's veto" is less likely necessary to achieve the statute's basic objective, protecting children, than a similar veto in the context of leased channels. Of course, the system of access managers and supervising boards can make mistakes, which the operator might in some cases correct with its veto power. Balanced against this potential benefit, however, is the risk that the veto itself may be mistaken; and its use, or threatened use, could prevent the presentation of programming, that, though borderline, is not "patently offensive" to its targeted audience. See Aufderheide, App. 64-66 (describing the programs that were considered borderline by access managers, including sex education, health education, broadcasts of politically marginal groups, and various artistic experiments). And this latter threat must bulk large within a system that already has publicly accountable systems for maintaining responsible programs.

Finally, our examination of the legislative history and the record before us is consistent with what common sense suggests, namely that the public/nonprofit programming control systems now in place would normally avoid, minimize, or eliminate any child related problems concerning "patently offensive" programming. We have found anecdotal references to what seem isolated instances of potentially indecent programming, some of which may well have occurred on leased, not public access channels. See 138 Cong. Rec. S642, S650 (Jan. 30, 1992) (statement of Sen. Wirth) (mentioning "abuses" on Time Warner's New York City channel); but see Comments of Manhattan Neighborhood Network, App. 235, 238 (New York access manager noting that leased, not public access channels, regularly carry sexually explicit programming in New York, and that no commercial programs or advertising are allowed on public access channels); Brief for Time Warner Cable as Amicus Curiae 2-3 (indicating that relevant "abuses" likely occurred on leased channels). See also 138 Cong. Rec., at S649 (Jan. 30, 1992) (statement of Sen. Fowler) (describing solicitation of prostitution); id., at S646 (statement of Sen. Helms) (identifying newspaper headline referring to mayor's protest of a "strip act"); 56 F. 3d, at 117-118 (recounting comments submitted to the FCC describing three complaints of offensive programming); Letter from Mayor of Rancho Palos Verdes, FCC Record; Resolution of San Antonio City Council, No. 92-49-40, FCC Record.

But these few examples do not necessarily indicate a significant nationwide pattern. See 56 F. 3d, at 127-128 (public access channels "did not pose dangers on the order of magnitude of those identified on leased access channels," and "local franchising authorities could respond" to such problems "by issuing `rules and procedures' or other `requirements' "). The Commission itself did not report any examples of "indecent" programs on public access channels. See Second Report and Order, 8 FCC Rcd 2638 (1993); see also Comments of Boston Community Access and Programming Foundation, App. 162-163 (noting that the FCC's Notice of Proposed Rulemaking, 7 FCC Rcd 7709 (1992) did not identify any "inappropriate" programming that actually exists on public access channels). Moreover, comments submitted to the FCC undermine any suggestion that prior to 1992 there were significant problems of indecent programming on public access channels. See Agosta, at 10, 28, FCC Record (surveying 76 public access systems in New York over two years, and finding "only two examples of controversial programming, and both had been settled by the producers and the access channel"); Reply Comments of Staten Island Community Television, at 2, FCC Record ("Our access channels have been on the air since 1986 without a single incident which would be covered by Section 10 of the new law"); Reply Comments of Waycross Community Television, at 2, FCC Record ("[I]ndecent and obscene programs . . . [have] never been cablecast through Waycross Community Television during our entire ten year programming history"); Reply Comments of Cambridge Community Television, App. 314 ("In Cambridge less than one hour out of 15,000 hours of programming CCTV has run in the past five year[s] may have been affected by the Act"); ibid. ("CCTV feels that there simply is not a problem which needs to be fixed"); Reply Comments of Columbus Community Cable Access, Inc., App. 329 ("ACTV is unaware of any actions taken by the cable operators under [a local law authorizing them to prohibit "legally obscene matter"] within the last 10 years"); Reply Comments of Cincinnati Community Video, Inc., App., at 316 ("[I]n 10 years of access operations with over 30,000 access programs cablecast not a single obscenity violation has ever occurred"); Comments of Defiance Community Television, at 2-3, FCC Record (in eight years of operation, "there has never been a serious problem with the content of programming on the channel").

At most, we have found borderline examples as to which people's judgment may differ, perhaps acceptable in some communities but not others, of the type that petitioners fear the law might prohibit. See, e.g., Aufderheide, App. 64-66; Brief for Petitioners in No. 95-124, p. 7 (describing depiction of a self help gynecological examination); Comments of Time Warner Entertainment Co., App. 252 (describing an Austin, Tex., program from that included "nude scenes from a movie," and an Indianapolis, Ind., "safe sex" program). It is difficult to see how such borderline examples could show a compelling need, nationally, to protect children from significantly harmful materials. Compare 138 Cong. Rec., at S646 (Jan. 30, 1992) (statement of Sen. Helms) (justifying regulation of leased access channels in terms of programming that depicts "bestiality" and "rape"). In the absence of a factual basis substantiating the harm and the efficacy of its proposed cure, we cannot assume that the harm exists or that the regulation redresses it. See Turner, 512 U. S. ____, ____ (slip op. at 40-41).

The upshot, in respect to the public access channels, is a law that could radically change present programming related relationships among local community and nonprofit supervising boards and access managers, which relationships are established through municipal law, regulation, and contract. In doing so, it would not significantly restore editorial rights of cable operators, but would greatly increase the risk that certain categories of programming (say, borderline offensive programs) will not appear. At the same time, given present supervisory mechanisms, the need for this particular provision, aimed directly at public access channels, is not obvious. Having carefully reviewed the legislative history of the Act, the proceedings before the FCC, the record below, and the submissions of the parties and amici here, we conclude that the Government cannot sustain its burden of showing that §10(c) is necessary to protect children or that it is appropriately tailored to secure that end. See, e.g., Columbia Broadcasting, 412 U. S., at 127; League of Women Voters, 468 U. S., at 398-399; Sable, 492 U. S., at 126. Consequently, we find that this third provision violates the First Amendment.

Finally, we must ask whether §10(a) is severable from the two other provisions. The question is one of legislative intent: Would Congress still "have passed" §10(a) "had it known" that the remaining "provision[s were] invalid"? Brockett v. Spokane Arcades, Inc., 472 U.S. 491, 506 (1985). If so, we need not invalidate all three provisions. New York v. Ferber, 458 U. S., at 769, n. 24 (citing United States v. Thirty seven Photographs, 402 U.S. 363 (1971)).

Although the 1992 Act contains no express "severability clause," we can find the Act's "severability" intention in its structure and purpose. It seems fairly obvious Congress would have intended its permissive "leased access" channels provision, §10(a), to stand irrespective of §10(c)'s legal fate. That is because the latter provision concerns only public, educational, and governmental channels. Its presence had little, if any, effect upon "leased access" channels; hence its absence in respect to those channels could not make a significant difference.

The "segregate and block" requirement's invalidity does make a difference, however, to the effectiveness of the permissive "leased access" provision, §10(a). Together they told the cable system operator: "either ban a `patently offensive' program or `segregate and block' it." Without the "segregate and block" provision, cable operators are afforded broad discretion over what to do with a patently offensive program, and because they will no longer bear the costs of segregation and blocking if they refuse to ban such programs, cable operators may choose to ban fewer programs.

Nonetheless, this difference does not make the two provisions unseverable. Without the "segregate and block" provision, the law simply treats leased channels (in respect to patently offensive programming) just as it treats all other channels. And judging by the absence of similar segregate and block provisions in the context of these other channels, Congress would probably have thought that §10(a), standing alone, was an effective (though, perhaps, not the most effective) means of pursuing its objective. Moreover, we can find no reason why, in light of Congress' basic objective (the protection of children), Congress would have preferred no provisions at all to the permissive provision standing by itself. That provision, capable of functioning on its own, still helps to achieve that basic objective. Consequently, we believe the valid provision is severable from the others.

For these reasons, the judgment of the Court of Appeals is affirmed insofar as it upheld §10(a); the judgment of the Court of Appeals is reversed insofar as it upheld §10(b) and §10(c).

It is so ordered.

## Reno v. American Civil Liberties Union (June 26, 1997)

Justice Stevens delivered the opinion of the Court.

At issue is the constitutionality of two statutory provisions enacted to protect minors from "indecent" and "patently offensive" communications on the Internet. Notwithstanding the legitimacy and importance of the congressional goal of protecting children from harmful materials, we agree with the three judge District Court that the statute abridges "the freedom of speech" protected by the First Amendment. [n.1]

The District Court made extensive findings of fact, most of which were based on a detailed stipulation prepared by the parties. See 929 F. Supp. 824, 830-849 (ED Pa. 1996). [n.2] The findings describe the character and the dimensions of the Internet, the availability of sexually explicit material in that medium, and the problems confronting age verification for recipients of Internet communications. Because those findings provide the underpinnings for the legal issues, we begin with a summary of the undisputed facts.

The Internet

The Internet is an international network of interconnected computers. It is the outgrowth of what began in 1969 as a military program called "ARPANET," [n.3] which was designed to enable computers operated by the military, defense contractors, and universities conducting defense related research to communicate with one another by redundant channels even if some portions of the network were damaged in a war. While the ARPANET no longer exists, it provided an example for the development of a number of civilian networks that, eventually linking with each other, now enable tens of millions of people to communicate with one another and to access vast amounts of information from around the world. The Internet is "a unique and wholly new medium of worldwide human communication." [n.4]

The Internet has experienced "extraordinary growth." [n.5] The number of "host" computers--those that store information and relay communications--increased from about 300 in 1981 to approximately 9, 400,000 by the time of the trial in 1996. Roughly 60% of these hosts are located in the United States. About 40 million people used the Internet at the time of trial, a number that is expected to mushroom to 200 million by 1999.

Individuals can obtain access to the Internet from many different sources, generally hosts themselves or entities with a host affiliation. Most colleges and universities provide access for their students and faculty; many corporations provide their employees with access through an office network; many communities and local libraries provide free access; and an increasing number of storefront "computer coffee shops" provide access for a small hourly fee. Several major national "online services" such as America Online, CompuServe, the Microsoft Network, and Prodigy offer access to their own extensive proprietary networks as well as a link to the much larger resources of the Internet. These commercial online services had almost 12 million individual subscribers at the time of trial.

Anyone with access to the Internet may take advantage of a wide variety of communication and information retrieval methods. These methods are constantly evolving and difficult to categorize precisely. But, as presently constituted, those most relevant to this case are electronic mail ("e mail"), automatic mailing list services ("mail exploders," sometimes referred to as "listservs"), "newsgroups," "chat rooms," and the "World Wide Web." All of these methods can be used to transmit text; most can transmit sound, pictures, and moving video images. Taken together, these tools constitute a unique medium--known to its users as "cyberspace"--located in no particular geographical location but available to anyone, anywhere in the world, with access to the Internet.

E mail enables an individual to send an electronic message--generally akin to a note or letter--to another individual or to a group of addressees. The message is generally stored electronically, sometimes waiting for the recipient to check her "mailbox" and sometimes making its receipt known through some type of prompt. A mail exploder is a sort of e mail group. Subscribers can send messages to a common e mail address, which then forwards the message to the group's other subscribers. Newsgroups also serve groups of regular participants, but these postings may be read by others as well. There are thousands of such groups, each serving to foster an exchange of information or opinion on a particular topic running the gamut from, say, the music of Wagner to Balkan politics to AIDS prevention to the Chicago Bulls. About 100,000 new messages are posted every day. In most newsgroups, postings are automatically purged at regular intervals. In addition to posting a message that can be read later, two or more individuals wishing to communicate more immediately can enter a chat room to engage in real time dialogue--in other words, by typing messages to one another that appear almost immediately on the others' computer screens. The District Court found that at any given time "tens of thousands of users are engaging in conversations on a huge range of subjects." [n.6] It is "no exaggeration to conclude that the content on the Internet is as diverse as human thought." [n.7]

The best known category of communication over the Internet is the World Wide Web, which allows users to search for and retrieve information stored in remote computers, as well as, in some cases, to communicate back to designated sites. In concrete terms, the Web consists of a vast number of documents stored in different computers all over the world. Some of these documents are simply files containing information. However, more elaborate documents, commonly known as Web "pages," are also prevalent. Each has its own address--"rather like a telephone number." [n.8] Web pages frequently contain information and sometimes allow the viewer to communicate with the page's (or "site's") author. They generally also contain "links" to other documents created by that site's author or to other (generally) related sites. Typically, the links are either blue or underlined text--sometimes images.

Navigating the Web is relatively straightforward. A user may either type the address of a known page or enter one or more keywords into a commercial "search engine" in an effort to locate sites on a subject of interest. A particular Web page may contain the information sought by the "surfer," or, through its links, it may be an avenue to other documents located anywhere on the Internet. Users generally explore a given Web page, or move to another, by clicking a computer "mouse" on one of the page's icons or links. Access to most Web pages is freely available, but some allow access only to those who have purchased the right from a commercial provider. The Web is thus comparable, from the readers' viewpoint, to both a vast library including millions of readily available and indexed publications and a sprawling mall offering goods and services.

From the publishers' point of view, it constitutes a vast platform from which to address and hear from a world wide audience of millions of readers, viewers, researchers, and buyers. Any person or organization with a computer connected to the Internet can "publish" information. Publishers include government agencies, educational institutions, commercial entities, advocacy groups, and individuals. [n.9] Publishers may either make their material available to the entire pool of Internet users, or confine access to a selected group, such as those willing to pay for the privilege. "No single organization controls any membership in the Web, nor is there any centralized point from which individual Web sites or services can be blocked from the Web." [n.10]

Sexually Explicit Material

Sexually explicit material on the Internet includes text, pictures, and chat and "extends from the modestly titillating to the hardest core." [n.11] These files are created, named, and posted in the same manner as material that is not sexually explicit, and may be accessed either deliberately or unintentionally during the course of an imprecise search. "Once a provider posts its content on the Internet, it cannot prevent that content from entering any community." [n.12] Thus, for example,

"when the UCR/California Museum of Photography posts to its Web site nudes by Edward Weston and Robert Mapplethorpe to announce that its new exhibit will travel to Baltimore and New York City, those images are available not only in Los Angeles, Baltimore, and New York City, but also in Cincinnati, Mobile, or Beijing--wherever Internet users live. Similarly, the safer sex instructions that Critical Path posts to its Web site, written in street language so that the teenage receiver can understand them, are available not just in Philadelphia, but also in Provo and Prague." [n.13]

Some of the communications over the Internet that originate in foreign countries are also sexually explicit. [n.14]

Though such material is widely available, users seldom encounter such content accidentally. "A document's title or a description of the document will usually appear before the document itself . . . and in many cases the user will receive detailed information about a site's content before he or she need take the step to access the document. Almost all sexually explicit images are preceded by warnings as to the content." [n.15] For that reason, the "odds are slim" that a user would enter a sexually explicit site by accident. [n.16] Unlike communications received by radio or television, "the receipt of information on the Internet requires a series of affirmative steps more deliberate and directed than merely turning a dial. A child requires some sophistication and some ability to read to retrieve material and thereby to use the Internet unattended." [n.17]

Systems have been developed to help parents control the material that may be available on a home computer with Internet access. A system may either limit a computer's access to an approved list of sources that have been identified as containing no adult material, it may block designated inappropriate sites, or it may attempt to block messages containing identifiable objectionable features. "Although parental control software currently can screen for certain suggestive words or for known sexually explicit sites, it cannot now screen for sexually explicit images." [n.18] Nevertheless, the evidence indicates that "a reasonably effective method by which parents can prevent their children from accessing sexually explicit and other material which parents may believe is inappropriate for their children will soon be available." [n.19]

Age Verification

The problem of age verification differs for different uses of the Internet. The District Court categorically determined that there "is no effective way to determine the identity or the age of a user who is accessing material through e mail, mail exploders, newsgroups or chat rooms." [n.20] The Government offered no evidence that there was a reliable way to screen recipients and participants in such fora for age. Moreover, even if it were technologically feasible to block minors' access to newsgroups and chat rooms containing discussions of art, politics or other subjects that potentially elicit "indecent" or "patently offensive" contributions, it would not be possible to block their access to that material and "still allow them access to the remaining content, even if the overwhelming majority of that content was not indecent." [n.21]

Technology exists by which an operator of a Web site may condition access on the verification of requested information such as a credit card number or an adult password. Credit card verification is only feasible, however, either in connection with a commercial transaction in which the card is used, or by payment to a verification agency. Using credit card possession as a surrogate for proof of age would impose costs on non commercial Web sites that would require many of them to shut down. For that reason, at the time of the trial, credit card verification was "effectively unavailable to a substantial number of Internet content providers." Id., at 846 (finding 102). Moreover, the imposition of such a requirement "would completely bar adults who do not have a credit card and lack the resources to obtain one from accessing any blocked material." [n.22]

Commercial pornographic sites that charge their users for access have assigned them passwords as a method of age verification. The record does not contain any evidence concerning the reliability of these technologies. Even if passwords are effective for commercial purveyors of indecent material, the District Court found that an adult password requirement would impose significant burdens on noncommercial sites, both because they would discourage users from accessing their sites and because the cost of creating and maintaining such screening systems would be "beyond their reach." [n.23]

In sum, the District Court found:

"Even if credit card verification or adult password verification were implemented, the Government presented no testimony as to how such systems could ensure that the user of the password or credit card is in fact over 18. The burdens imposed by credit card verification and adult password verification systems make them effectively unavailable to a substantial number of Internet content providers." Ibid. (finding 107).

The Telecommunications Act of 1996, Pub. L. 104-104, 110 Stat. 56, was an unusually important legislative enactment. As stated on the first of its 103 pages, its primary purpose was to reduce regulation and encourage "the rapid deployment of new telecommunications technologies." The major components of the statute have nothing to do with the Internet; they were designed to promote competition in the local telephone service market, the multichannel video market, and the market for over the air broadcasting. The Act includes seven Titles, six of which are the product of extensive committee hearings and the subject of discussion in Reports prepared by Committees of the Senate and the House of Representatives. By contrast, Title V--known as the "Communications Decency Act of 1996" (CDA)--contains provisions that were either added in executive committee after the hearings were concluded or as amendments offered during floor debate on the legislation. An amendment offered in the Senate was the source of the two statutory provisions challenged in this case. [n.24] They are informally described as the "indecent transmission" provision and the "patently offensive display" provision. [n.25]

The first, 47 U. S. C. A. §223(a) (Supp. 1997), prohibits the knowing transmission of obscene or indecent messages to any recipient under 18 years of age. It provides in pertinent part:

"(a) Whoever--

"(1) in interstate or foreign communications--

. . . . .

"(B) by means of a telecommunications device knowingly--

"(i) makes, creates, or solicits, and

"(ii) initiates the transmission of,

"any comment, request, suggestion, proposal, image, or other communication which is obscene or indecent, knowing that the recipient of the communication is under 18 years of age, regardless of whether the maker of such communication placed the call or initiated the communication;

. . . . .

"(2) knowingly permits any telecommunications facility under his control to be used for any activity prohibited by paragraph (1) with the intent that it be used for such activity,

"shall be fined under Title 18, or imprisoned not more than two years, or both."

The second provision, §223(d), prohibits the knowing sending or displaying of patently offensive messages in a manner that is available to a person under 18 years of age. It provides:

"(d) Whoever--

"(1) in interstate or foreign communications knowingly--

"(A) uses an interactive computer service to send to a specific person or persons under 18 years of age, or

"(B) uses any interactive computer service to display in a manner available to a person under 18 years of age,

"any comment, request, suggestion, proposal, image, or other communication that, in context, depicts or describes, in terms patently offensive as measured by contemporary community standards, sexual or excretory activities or organs, regardless of whether the user of such service placed the call or initiated the communication; or

"(2) knowingly permits any telecommunications facility under such person's control to be used for an activity prohibited by paragraph (1) with the intent that it be used for such activity,

"shall be fined under Title 18, or imprisoned not more than two years, or both."

The breadth of these prohibitions is qualified by two affirmative defenses. See

§223(e)(5). [n.26] One covers those who take "good faith, reasonable, effective, and appropriate actions" to restrict access by minors to the prohibited communications. §223(e)(5)(A). The other covers those who restrict access to covered material by requiring certain designated forms of age proof, such as a verified credit card or an adult identification number or code. §223(e)(5)(B).

On February 8, 1996, immediately after the President signed the statute, 20 plaintiffs [n.27] filed suit against the Attorney General of the United States and the Department of Justice challenging the constitutionality of §§223(a)(1) and 223(d). A week later, based on his conclusion that the term "indecent" was too vague to provide the basis for a criminal prosecution, District Judge Buckwalter entered a temporary restraining order against enforcement of §223(a)(1)(B)(ii) insofar as it applies to indecent communications. A second suit was then filed by 27 additional plaintiffs, [n.28] the two cases were consolidated, and a three judge District Court was convened pursuant to §561 of the Act. [n.29] After an evidentiary hearing, that Court entered a preliminary injunction against enforcement of both of the challenged provisions. Each of the three judges wrote a separate opinion, but their judgment was unanimous.

Chief Judge Sloviter doubted the strength of the Government's interest in regulating "the vast range of online material covered or potentially covered by the CDA," but acknowledged that the interest was "compelling" with respect to some of that material. 929 F. Supp., at 853. She concluded, nonetheless, that the statute "sweeps more broadly than necessary and thereby chills the expression of adults" and that the terms "patently offensive" and "indecent" were "inherently vague." Id., at 854. She also determined that the affirmative defenses were not "technologically or economically feasible for most providers," specifically considering and rejecting an argument that providers could avoid liability by "tagging" their material in a manner that would allow potential readers to screen out unwanted transmissions. Id., at 856. Chief Judge Sloviter also rejected the Government's suggestion that the scope of the statute could be narrowed by construing it to apply only to commercial pornographers. Id., at 854-855.

Judge Buckwalter concluded that the word "indecent" in §223(a)(1)(B) and the terms "patently offensive" and "in context" in §223(d)(1) were so vague that criminal enforcement of either section would violate the "fundamental constitutional principle" of "simple fairness," id., at 861, and the specific protections of the First and Fifth Amendments, id., at 858. He found no statutory basis for the Government's argument that the challenged provisions would be applied only to "pornographic" materials, noting that, unlike obscenity, "indecency has not been defined to exclude works of serious literary, artistic, political or scientific value." Id., at 863. Moreover, the Government's claim that the work must be considered patently offensive "in context" was itself vague because the relevant context might "refer to, among other things, the nature of the communication as a whole, the time of day it was conveyed, the medium used, the identity of the speaker, or whether or not it is accompanied by appropriate warnings." Id., at 864. He believed that the unique nature of the Internet aggravated the vagueness of the statute. Id., at 865, n. 9.

Judge Dalzell's review of "the special attributes of Internet communication" disclosed by the evidence convinced him that the First Amendment denies Congress the power to regulate the content of protected speech on the Internet. Id., at 867. His opinion explained at length why he believed the Act would abridge significant protected speech, particularly by noncommercial speakers, while "[p]erversely, commercial pornographers would remain relatively unaffected." Id., at 879. He construed our cases as requiring a "medium specific" approach to the analysis of the regulation of mass communication, id., at 873, and concluded that the Internet--as "the most participatory form of mass speech yet developed," id., at 883--is entitled to "the highest protection from governmental intrusion," ibid. [n.30]

The judgment of the District Court enjoins the Government from enforcing the prohibitions in §223(a)(1)(B) insofar as they relate to "indecent" communications, but expressly preserves the Government's right to investigate and prosecute the obscenity or child pornography activities prohibited therein. The injunction against enforcement of §§223(d)(1) and (2) is unqualified because those provisions contain no separate reference to obscenity or child pornography.

The Government appealed under the Act's special review provisions, §561, 110 Stat. 142-143, and we noted probable jurisdiction, see 519 U. S. ___ (1996). In its appeal, the Government argues that the District Court erred in holding that the CDA violated both the First Amendment because it is overbroad and the Fifth Amendment because it is vague. While we discuss the vagueness of the CDA because of its relevance to the First Amendment overbreadth inquiry, we conclude that the judgment should be affirmed without reaching the Fifth Amendment issue. We begin our analysis by reviewing the principal authorities on which the Government relies. Then, after describing the overbreadth of the CDA, we consider the Government's specific contentions, including its submission that we save portions of the statute either by severance or by fashioning judicial limitations on the scope of its coverage.

In arguing for reversal, the Government contends that the CDA is plainly constitutional under three of our prior decisions: (1) Ginsberg v. New York, 390 U.S. 629 (1968); (2) FCC v. Pacifica Foundation, 438 U.S. 726 (1978); and (3) Renton v. Playtime Theatres, Inc., 475 U.S. 41 (1986). A close look at these cases, however, raises--rather than relieves--doubts concerning the constitutionality of the CDA.

In Ginsberg, we upheld the constitutionality of a New York statute that prohibited selling to minors under 17 years of age material that was considered obscene as to them even if not obscene as to adults. We rejected the defendant's broad submission that "the scope of the constitutional freedom of expression secured to a citizen to read or see material concerned with sex cannot be made to depend on whether the citizen is an adult or a minor." 390 U. S., at 636. In rejecting that contention, we relied not only on the State's independent interest in the well being of its youth, but also on our consistent recognition of the principle that "the parents' claim to authority in their own household to direct the rearing of their children is basic in the structure of our society." [n.31] In four important respects, the statute upheld in Ginsberg was narrower than the CDA. First, we noted in Ginsberg that "the prohibition against sales to minors does not bar parents who so desire from purchasing the magazines for their children." Id., at 639. Under the CDA, by contrast, neither the parents' consent--nor even their participation--in the communication would avoid the application of the statute. [n.32] Second, the New York statute applied only to commercial transactions, id., at 647, whereas the CDA contains no such limitation. Third, the New York statute cabined its definition of material that is harmful to minors with the requirement that it be "utterly without redeeming social importance for minors." Id., at 646. The CDA fails to provide us with any definition of the term "indecent" as used in §223(a)(1) and, importantly, omits any requirement that the "patently offensive" material covered by §223(d) lack serious literary, artistic, political, or scientific value. Fourth, the New York statute defined a minor as a person under the age of 17, whereas the CDA, in applying to all those under 18 years, includes an additional year of those nearest majority.

In Pacifica, we upheld a declaratory order of the Federal Communications Commission, holding that the broadcast of a recording of a 12-minute monologue entitled "Filthy Words" that had previously been delivered to a live audience "could have been the subject of administrative sanctions." 438 U. S., at 730 (internal quotations omitted). The Commission had found that the repetitive use of certain words referring to excretory or sexual activities or organs "in an afternoon broadcast when children are in the audience was patently offensive" and concluded that the monologue was indecent "as broadcast." Id., at 735. The respondent did not quarrel with the finding that the afternoon broadcast was patently offensive, but contended that it was not "indecent" within the meaning of the relevant statutes because it contained no prurient appeal. After rejecting respondent's statutory arguments, we confronted its two constitutional arguments: (1) that the Commission's construction of its authority to ban indecent speech was so broad that its order had to be set aside even if the broadcast at issue was unprotected; and (2) that since the recording was not obscene, the First Amendment forbade any abridgement of the right to broadcast it on the radio.

In the portion of the lead opinion not joined by Justices Powell and Blackmun, the plurality stated that the First Amendment does not prohibit all governmental regulation that depends on the content of speech. Id., at 742-743. Accordingly, the availability of constitutional protection for a vulgar and offensive monologue that was not obscene depended on the context of the broadcast. Id., at 744-748. Relying on the premise that "of all forms of communication" broadcasting had received the most limited First Amendment protection, id., at 748-749, the Court concluded that the ease with which children may obtain access to broadcasts, "coupled with the concerns recognized in Ginsberg," justified special treatment of indecent broadcasting. Id., at 749-750.

As with the New York statute at issue in Ginsberg, there are significant differences between the order upheld in Pacifica and the CDA. First, the order in Pacifica, issued by an agency that had been regulating radio stations for decades, targeted a specific broadcast that represented a rather dramatic departure from traditional program content in order to designate when--rather than whether--it would be permissible to air such a program in that particular medium. The CDA's broad categorical prohibitions are not limited to particular times and are not dependent on any evaluation by an agency familiar with the unique characteristics of the Internet. Second, unlike the CDA, the Commission's declaratory order was not punitive; we expressly refused to decide whether the indecent broadcast "would justify a criminal prosecution." Id., at 750. Finally, the Commission's order applied to a medium which as a matter of history had "received the most limited First Amendment protection," id., at 748, in large part because warnings could not adequately protect the listener from unexpected program content. The Internet, however, has no comparable history. Moreover, the District Court found that the risk of encountering indecent material by accident is remote because a series of affirmative steps is required to access specific material.

In Renton, we upheld a zoning ordinance that kept adult movie theatres out of residential neighborhoods. The ordinance was aimed, not at the content of the films shown in the theaters, but rather at the "secondary effects"--such as crime and deteriorating property values--that these theaters fostered: " `It is th[e] secondary effect which these zoning ordinances attempt to avoid, not the dissemination of "offensive" speech.' " 475 U. S., at 49 (quoting Young v. American Mini Theatres, Inc., 427 U.S. 50, 71, n. 34 (1976)). According to the Government, the CDA is constitutional because it constitutes a sort of "cyberzoning" on the Internet. But the CDA applies broadly to the entire universe of cyberspace. And the purpose of the CDA is to protect children from the primary effects of "indecent" and "patently offensive" speech, rather than any "secondary" effect of such speech. Thus, the CDA is a content based blanket restriction on speech, and, as such, cannot be "properly analyzed as a form of time, place, and manner regulation." 475 U. S., at 46. See also Boos v. Barry, 485 U.S. 312, 321 (1988) ("Regulations that focus on the direct impact of speech on its audience" are not properly analyzed under Renton); Forsyth County v. Nationalist Movement, 505 U.S. 123, 134 (1992) ("Listeners' reaction to speech is not a content neutral basis for regulation").

These precedents, then, surely do not require us to uphold the CDA and are fully consistent with the application of the most stringent review of its provisions.

In Southeastern Promotions, Ltd. v. Conrad, 420 U.S. 546, 557 (1975), we observed that "[e]ach medium of expression . . . may present its own problems." Thus, some of our cases have recognized special justifications for regulation of the broadcast media that are not applicable to other speakers, see Red Lion Broadcasting Co. v. FCC, 395 U.S. 367 (1969); FCC v. Pacifica Foundation, 438 U.S. 726 (1978). In these cases, the Court relied on the history of extensive government regulation of the broadcast medium, see, e.g., Red Lion, 395 U. S., at 399-400; the scarcity of available frequencies at its inception, see, e.g., Turner Broadcasting System, Inc. v. FCC, 512 U.S. 622, 637-638 (1994); and its "invasive" nature, see Sable Communications of Cal., Inc. v. FCC, 492 U.S.

115, 128 (1989).

Those factors are not present in cyberspace. Neither before nor after the enactment of the CDA have the vast democratic fora of the Internet been subject to the type of government supervision and regulation that has attended the broadcast industry. [n.33] Moreover, the Internet is not as "invasive" as radio or television. The District Court specifically found that "[c]ommunications over the Internet do not `invade' an individual's home or appear on one's computer screen unbidden. Users seldom encounter content `by accident.' " 929 F. Supp., at 844 (finding 88). It also found that "[a]lmost all sexually explicit images are preceded by warnings as to the content," and cited testimony that " `odds are slim' that a user would come across a sexually explicit sight by accident." Ibid.

We distinguished Pacifica in Sable, 492 U. S., at 128, on just this basis. In Sable, a company engaged in the business of offering sexually oriented prerecorded telephone messages (popularly known as "dial a porn") challenged the constitutionality of an amendment to the Communications Act that imposed a blanket prohibition on indecent as well as obscene interstate commercial telephone messages. We held that the statute was constitutional insofar as it applied to obscene messages but invalid as applied to indecent messages. In attempting to justify the complete ban and criminalization of indecent commercial telephone messages, the Government relied on Pacifica, arguing that the ban was necessary to prevent children from gaining access to such messages. We agreed that "there is a compelling interest in protecting the physical and psychological well being of minors" which extended to shielding them from indecent messages that are not obscene by adult standards, 492 U. S., at 126, but distinguished our "emphatically narrow holding" in Pacifica because it did not involve a complete ban and because it involved a different medium of communication, id., at 127. We explained that "the dial it medium requires the listener to take affirmative steps to receive the communication." Id., at 127-128. "Placing a telephone call," we continued, "is not the same as turning on a radio and being taken by surprise by an indecent message." Id., at 128.

Finally, unlike the conditions that prevailed when Congress first authorized regulation of the broadcast spectrum, the Internet can hardly be considered a "scarce" expressive commodity. It provides relatively unlimited, low cost capacity for communication of all kinds. The Government estimates that "[a]s many as 40 million people use the Internet today, and that figure is expected to grow to 200 million by 1999." [n.34] This dynamic, multifaceted category of communication includes not only traditional print and news services, but also audio, video, and still images, as well as interactive, real time dialogue. Through the use of chat rooms, any person with a phone line can become a town crier with a voice that resonates farther than it could from any soapbox. Through the use of Web pages, mail exploders, and newsgroups, the same individual can become a pamphleteer. As the District Court found, "the content on the Internet is as diverse as human thought." 929 F. Supp., at 842 (finding 74). We agree with its conclusion that our cases provide no basis for qualifying the level of First Amendment scrutiny that should be applied to this medium.

Regardless of whether the CDA is so vague that it violates the Fifth Amendment, the many ambiguities concerning the scope of its coverage render it problematic for purposes of the First Amendment. For instance, each of the two parts of the CDA uses a different linguistic form. The first uses the word "indecent," 47 U. S. C. A. §223(a) (Supp. 1997), while the second speaks of material that "in context, depicts or describes, in terms patently offensive as measured by contemporary community standards, sexual or excretory activities or organs," §223(d). Given the absence of a definition of either term, [n.35] this difference in language will provoke uncertainty among speakers about how the two standards relate to each other [n.36] and just what they mean. [n.37] Could a speaker confidently assume that a serious discussion about birth control practices, homosexuality, the First Amendment issues raised by the Appendix to our Pacifica opinion, or the consequences of prison rape would not violate the CDA? This uncertainty undermines the likelihood that the CDA has been carefully tailored to the congressional goal of protecting minors from potentially harmful materials.

The vagueness of the CDA is a matter of special concern for two reasons. First, the CDA is a content based regulation of speech. The vagueness of such a regulation raises special First Amendment concerns because of its obvious chilling effect on free speech. See, e.g., Gentile v. State Bar of Nev., 501 U.S. 1030, 1048-1051 (1991). Second, the CDA is a criminal statute. In addition to the opprobrium and stigma of a criminal conviction, the CDA threatens violators with penalties including up to two years in prison for each act of violation. The severity of criminal sanctions may well cause speakers to remain silent rather than communicate even arguably unlawful words, ideas, and images. See, e.g., Dombrowski v. Pfister, 380 U.S. 479, 494 (1965). As a practical matter, this increased deterrent effect, coupled with the "risk of discriminatory enforcement" of vague regulations, poses greater First Amendment concerns than those implicated by the civil regulation reviewed in Denver Area Ed. Telecommunications Consortium, Inc. v. FCC, 518 U. S. ____ (1996).

The Government argues that the statute is no more vague than the obscenity standard this Court established in Miller v. California, 413 U.S. 15 (1973). But that is not so. In Miller, this Court reviewed a criminal conviction against a commercial vendor who mailed brochures containing pictures of sexually explicit activities to individuals who had not requested such materials. Id., at 18. Having struggled for some time to establish a definition of obscenity, we set forth in Miller the test for obscenity that controls to this day:

"(a) whether the average person, applying contemporary community standards would find that the work, taken as a whole, appeals to the prurient interest; (b) whether the work depicts or describes, in a patently offensive way, sexual conduct specifically defined by the applicable state law; and (c) whether the work, taken as a whole, lacks serious literary, artistic, political, or scientific value." Id., at 24 (internal quotation marks and citations omitted).

Because the CDA's "patently offensive" standard (and, we assume arguendo, its synonymous "indecent" standard) is one part of the three prong Miller test, the Government reasons, it cannot be unconstitutionally vague.

The Government's assertion is incorrect as a matter of fact. The second prong of the Miller test--the purportedly analogous standard--contains a critical requirement that is omitted from the CDA: that the proscribed material be "specifically defined by the applicable state law." This requirement reduces the vagueness inherent in the open ended term "patently offensive" as used in the CDA. Moreover, the Miller definition is limited to "sexual conduct," whereas the CDA extends also to include (1) "excretory activities" as well as (2) "organs" of both a sexual and excretory nature.

The Government's reasoning is also flawed. Just because a definition including three limitations is not vague, it does not follow that one of those limitations, standing by itself, is not vague. [n.38] Each of Miller's additional two prongs--(1) that, taken as a whole, the material appeal to the "prurient" interest, and (2) that it "lac[k] serious literary, artistic, political, or scientific value"--critically limits the uncertain sweep of the obscenity definition. The second requirement is particularly important because, unlike the "patently offensive" and "prurient interest" criteria, it is not judged by contemporary community standards. See Pope v. Illinois, 481 U.S. 497, 500 (1987). This "societal value" requirement, absent in the CDA, allows appellate courts to impose some limitations and regularity on the definition by setting, as a matter of law, a national floor for socially redeeming value. The Government's contention that courts will be able to give such legal limitations to the CDA's standards is belied by Miller's own rationale for having juries determine whether material is "patently offensive" according to community standards: that such questions are essentially ones of fact. [n.39]

In contrast to Miller and our other previous cases, the CDA thus presents a greater threat of censoring speech that, in fact, falls outside the statute's scope. Given the vague contours of the coverage of the statute, it unquestionably silences some speakers whose messages would be entitled to constitutional protection. That danger provides further reason for insisting that the statute not be overly broad. The CDA's burden on protected speech cannot be justified if it could be avoided by a more carefully drafted statute.

We are persuaded that the CDA lacks the precision that the First Amendment requires when a statute regulates the content of speech. In order to deny minors access to potentially harmful speech, the CDA effectively suppresses a large amount of speech that adults have a constitutional right to receive and to address to one another. That burden on adult speech is unacceptable if less restrictive alternatives would be at least as effective in achieving the legitimate purpose that the statute was enacted to serve.

In evaluating the free speech rights of adults, we have made it perfectly clear that "[s]exual expression which is indecent but not obscene is protected by the First Amendment." Sable, 492 U. S., at 126. See also Carey v. Population Services Int'l, 431 U.S. 678, 701 (1977) ("[W]here obscenity is not involved, we have consistently held that the fact that protected speech may be offensive to some does not justify its suppression"). Indeed, Pacifica itself

admonished that "the fact that society may find speech offensive is not a sufficient reason for suppressing it." 438 U. S., at 745.

It is true that we have repeatedly recognized the governmental interest in protecting children from harmful materials. See Ginsberg, 390 U. S., at 639; Pacifica, 438 U. S., at 749. But that interest does not justify an unnecessarily broad suppression of speech addressed to adults. As we have explained, the Government may not "reduc[e] the adult population . . . to . . . only what is fit for children." Denver, 518 U. S., at ___ (slip op., at 29) (internal quotation marks omitted) (quoting Sable, 492 U. S., at 128). [n.40] "[R]egardless of the strength of the government's interest" in protecting children, "[t]he level of discourse reaching a mailbox simply cannot be limited to that which would be suitable for a sandbox." Bolger v. Youngs Drug Products Corp., 463 U.S. 60, 74-75 (1983).

The District Court was correct to conclude that the CDA effectively resembles the ban on "dial a porn" invalidated in Sable. 929 F. Supp., at 854. In Sable, 492 U. S., at 129, this Court rejected the argument that we should defer to the congressional judgment that nothing less than a total ban would be effective in preventing enterprising youngsters from gaining access to indecent communications. Sable thus made clear that the mere fact that a statutory regulation of speech was enacted for the important purpose of protecting children from exposure to sexually explicit material does not foreclose inquiry into its validity. [n.41] As we pointed out last Term, that inquiry embodies an "over arching commitment" to make sure that Congress has designed its statute to accomplish its purpose "without imposing an unnecessarily great restriction on speech." Denver, 518 U. S., at ___ (slip op., at 11).

In arguing that the CDA does not so diminish adult communication, the Government relies on the incorrect factual premise that prohibiting a transmission whenever it is known that one of its recipients is a minor would not interfere with adult to adult communication. The findings of the District Court make clear that this premise is untenable.

Given the size of the potential audience for most messages, in the absence of a viable age verification process, the sender must be charged with knowing that one or more minors will likely view it. Knowledge that, for instance, one or more members of a 100 person chat group will be minor--and therefore that it would be a crime to send the group an indecent message--would surely burden communication among adults. [n.42]

The District Court found that at the time of trial existing technology did not include any effective method for a sender to prevent minors from obtaining access to its communications on the Internet without also denying access to adults. The Court found no effective way to determine the age of a user who is accessing material through e mail, mail exploders, newsgroups, or chat rooms. 929 F. Supp., at 845 (findings 90-94). As a practical matter, the Court also found that it would be prohibitively expensive for noncommercial--as well as some commercial--speakers who have Web sites to verify that their users are adults. Id., at 845-848 (findings 95-116). [n.43] These limitations must inevitably curtail a significant amount of adult communication on the Internet. By contrast, the District Court found that "[d]espite its limitations, currently available user based software suggests that a reasonably effective method by which parents can prevent their children from accessing sexually explicit and other material which parents may believe is inappropriate for their children will soon be widely available." Id., at 842 (finding 73) (emphases added).

The breadth of the CDA's coverage is wholly unprecedented. Unlike the regulations upheld in Ginsberg and Pacifica, the scope of the CDA is not limited to commercial speech or commercial entities. Its open ended prohibitions embrace all nonprofit entities and individuals posting indecent messages or displaying them on their own computers in the presence of minors. The general, undefined terms "indecent" and "patently offensive" cover large amounts of nonpornographic material with serious educational or other value. [n.44] Moreover, the "community standards" criterion as applied to the Internet means that any communication available to a nation wide audience will be judged by the standards of the community most likely to be offended by the message. [n.45] The regulated subject matter includes any of the seven "dirty words" used in the Pacifica monologue, the use of which the Government's expert acknowledged could constitute a felony. See Olsen Test., Tr. Vol. V, 53:16-54:10. It may also extend to discussions about prison rape or safe sexual practices, artistic images that include nude subjects, and arguably the card catalogue of the Carnegie Library.

For the purposes of our decision, we need neither accept nor reject the Government's submission that the First Amendment does not forbid a blanket prohibition on all "indecent" and "patently offensive" messages communicated to a 17 year old--no matter how much value the message may contain and regardless of parental approval. It is at least clear that the strength of the Government's interest in protecting minors is not equally strong throughout the coverage of this broad statute. Under the CDA, a parent allowing her 17 year old to use the family computer to obtain information on the Internet that she, in her parental judgment, deems appropriate could face a lengthy prison term. See 47 U. S. C. A. §223(a)(2) (Supp. 1997). Similarly, a parent who sent his 17 year old college freshman information on birth control via e mail could be incarcerated even though neither he, his child, nor anyone in their home community, found the material "indecent" or "patently offensive," if the college town's community thought otherwise.

The breadth of this content based restriction of speech imposes an especially heavy burden on the Government to explain why a less restrictive provision would not be as effective as the CDA. It has not done so. The arguments in this Court have referred to possible alternatives such as requiring that indecent material be "tagged" in a way that facilitates parental control of material coming into their homes, making exceptions for messages with artistic or educational value, providing some tolerance for parental choice, and regulating some portions of the Internet--such as commercial web sites--differently than others, such as chat rooms. Particularly in the light of the absence of any detailed findings by the Congress, or even hearings addressing the special problems of the CDA, we are persuaded that the CDA is not narrowly tailored if that requirement has any meaning at all.

In an attempt to curtail the CDA's facial overbreadth, the Government advances three additional arguments for sustaining the Act's affirmative prohibitions: (1) that the CDA is constitutional because it leaves open ample "alternative channels" of communication; (2) that the plain meaning of the Act's "knowledge" and "specific person" requirement significantly restricts its permissible applications; and (3) that the Act's prohibitions are "almost always" limited to material lacking redeeming social value.

The Government first contends that, even though the CDA effectively censors discourse on many of the Internet's modalities--such as chat groups, newsgroups, and mail exploders--it is nonetheless constitutional because it provides a "reasonable opportunity" for speakers to engage in the restricted speech on the World Wide Web. Brief for Appellants 39. This argument is unpersuasive because the CDA regulates speech on the basis of its content. A "time, place, and manner" analysis is therefore inapplicable. See Consolidated Edison Co. of N. Y. v. Public Serv. Comm'n of N. Y., 447 U.S. 530, 536 (1980). It is thus immaterial whether such speech would be feasible on the Web (which, as the Government's own expert acknowledged, would cost up to $10,000 if the speaker's interests were not accommodated by an existing Web site, not including costs for database management and age verification). The Government's position is equivalent to arguing that a statute could ban leaflets on certain subjects as long as individuals are free to publish books. In invalidating a number of laws that banned leafletting on the streets regardless of their content--we explained that "one is not to have the exercise of his liberty of expression in appropriate places abridged on the plea that it may be exercised in some other place." Schneider v. State (Town of Irvington), 308 U.S. 147, 163 (1939).

The Government also asserts that the "knowledge" requirement of both §§223(a) and (d), especially when coupled with the "specific child" element found in §223(d), saves the CDA from overbreadth. Because both sections prohibit the dissemination of indecent messages only to persons known to be under 18, the Government argues, it does not require transmitters to "refrain from communicating indecent material to adults; they need only refrain from disseminating such materials to persons they know to be under 18." Brief for Appellants 24. This argument ignores the fact that most Internet fora-- including chat rooms, newsgroups, mail exploders, and the Web--are open to all comers. The Government's assertion that the knowledge requirement somehow protects the communications of adults is therefore untenable. Even the strongest reading of the "specific person" requirement of §223(d) cannot save the statute. It would confer broad powers of censorship, in the form of a "heckler's veto," upon any opponent of indecent speech who might simply log on and inform the would be discoursers that his 17 year old child--a "specific person . . . under 18 years of age," 47 U. S. C. A. §223(d)(1)(A) (Supp. 1997)--would be present.

Finally, we find no textual support for the Government's submission that material having scientific, educational, or other redeeming social value will necessarily fall outside the CDA's "patently offensive" and "indecent" prohibitions. See also n. 37, supra.

The Government's three remaining arguments focus on the defenses provided in §223(e)(5). [n.46] First, relying on the "good faith, reasonable, effective, and appropriate actions" provision, the Government suggests that "tagging" provides a defense that saves the constitutionality of the Act. The suggestion assumes that transmitters may encode their indecent communications in a way that would indicate their contents, thus permitting recipients to block their reception with appropriate software. It is the requirement that the good faith action must be "effective" that makes this defense illusory. The Government recognizes that its proposed screening software does not currently exist. Even if it did, there is no way to know whether a potential recipient will actually block the encoded material. Without the impossible knowledge that every guardian in America is screening for the "tag," the transmitter could not reasonably rely on its action to be "effective."

For its second and third arguments concerning defenses--which we can consider together--the Government relies on the latter half of §223(e)(5), which applies when the transmitter has restricted access by requiring use of a verified credit card or adult identification. Such verification is not only technologically available but actually is used by commercial providers of sexually explicit material. These providers, therefore, would be protected by the defense. Under the findings of the District Court, however, it is not economically feasible for most noncommercial speakers to employ such verification. Accordingly, this defense would not significantly narrow the statute's burden on noncommercial speech. Even with respect to the commercial pornographers that would be protected by the defense, the Government failed to adduce any evidence that these verification techniques actually preclude minors from posing as adults. [n.47] Given that the risk of criminal sanctions "hovers over each content provider, like the proverbial sword of Damocles," [n.48] the District Court correctly refused to rely on unproven future technology to save the statute. The Government thus failed to prove that the proffered defense would significantly reduce the heavy burden on adult speech produced by the prohibition on offensive displays.

We agree with the District Court's conclusion that the CDA places an unacceptably heavy burden on protected speech, and that the defenses do not constitute the sort of "narrow tailoring" that will save an otherwise patently invalid unconstitutional provision. In Sable, 492 U. S., at 127, we remarked that the speech restriction at issue there amounted to " `burn[ing] the house to roast the pig.' " The CDA, casting a far darker shadow over free speech, threatens to torch a large segment of the Internet community.

At oral argument, the Government relied heavily on its ultimate fall back position: If this Court should conclude that the CDA is insufficiently tailored, it urged, we should save the statute's constitutionality by honoring the severability clause, see 47 U.S.C. § 608 and construing nonseverable terms narrowly. In only one respect is this argument acceptable.

A severability clause requires textual provisions that can be severed. We will follow §608's guidance by leaving constitutional textual elements of the statute intact in the one place where they are, in fact, severable. The "indecency" provision, 47 U. S. C. A. §223(a) (Supp. 1997), applies to "any comment, request, suggestion, proposal, image, or other communication which is obscene or indecent." (Emphasis added.) Appellees do not challenge the application of the statute to obscene speech, which, they acknowledge, can be banned totally because it enjoys no First Amendment protection. See Miller, 413 U. S., at 18. As set forth by the statute, the restriction of "obscene" material enjoys a textual manifestation separate from that for "indecent" material, which we have held unconstitutional. Therefore, we will sever the term "or indecent" from the statute, leaving the rest of §223(a) standing. In no other respect, however, can §223(a) or §223(d) be saved by such a textual surgery.

The Government also draws on an additional, less traditional aspect of the CDA's severability clause, 47 U. S. C., §608, which asks any reviewing court that holds the statute facially unconstitutional not to invalidate the CDA in application to "other persons or circumstances" that might be constitutionally permissible. It further invokes this Court's admonition that, absent "countervailing considerations," a statute should "be declared invalid to the extent it reaches too far, but otherwise left intact." Brockett v. Spokane Arcades, Inc., 472 U.S. 491, 503-504 (1985). There are two flaws in this argument.

First, the statute that grants our jurisdiction for this expedited review, 47 U. S. C. A. §561 (Supp. 1997), limits that jurisdictional grant to actions challenging the CDA "on its face." Consistent with §561, the plaintiffs who brought this suit and the three judge panel that decided it treated it as a facial challenge. We have no authority, in this particular posture, to convert this litigation into an "as applied" challenge. Nor, given the vast array of plaintiffs, the range of their expressive activities, and the vagueness of the statute, would it be practicable to limit our holding to a judicially defined set of specific applications.

Second, one of the "countervailing considerations" mentioned in Brockett is present here. In considering a facial challenge, this Court may impose a limiting construction on a statute only if it is "readily susceptible" to such a construction. Virginia v. American Bookseller's Assn., Inc., 484 U.S. 383, 397 (1988). See also Erznoznik, v. Jacksonville, 422 U.S. 205, 216 (1975) ("readily subject" to narrowing construction). The open ended character of the CDA provides no guidance whatever for limiting its coverage.

This case is therefore unlike those in which we have construed a statute narrowly because the text or other source of congressional intent identified a clear line that this Court could draw. Cf., e.g., Brockett, 472 U. S., at 504-505 (invalidating obscenity statute only to the extent that word "lust" was actually or effectively excised from statute); United States v. Grace, 461 U.S. 171, 180-183 (1983) (invalidating federal statute banning expressive displays only insofar as it extended to public sidewalks when clear line could be drawn between sidewalks and other grounds that comported with congressional purpose of protecting the building, grounds, and people therein). Rather, our decision in United States v. Treasury Employees, 513 U.S. 454, 479, n. 26 (1995), is applicable. In that case, we declined to "dra[w] one or more lines between categories of speech covered by an overly broad statute, when Congress has sent inconsistent signals as to where the new line or lines should be drawn" because doing so "involves a far more serious invasion of the legislative domain." [n.49] This Court "will not rewrite a . . . law to conform it to constitutional requirements." American Booksellers, 484 U. S., at 397. [n.50]

In this Court, though not in the District Court, the Government asserts that--in addition to its interest in protecting children--its "[e]qually significant" interest in fostering the growth of the Internet provides an independent basis for upholding the constitutionality of the CDA. Brief for Appellants 19. The Government apparently assumes that the unregulated availability of "indecent" and "patently offensive" material on the Internet is driving countless citizens away from the medium because of the risk of exposing themselves or their children to harmful material.

We find this argument singularly unpersuasive. The dramatic expansion of this new marketplace of ideas contradicts the factual basis of this contention. The record demonstrates that the growth of the Internet has been and continues to be phenomenal. As a matter of constitutional tradition, in the absence of evidence to the contrary, we presume that governmental regulation of the content of speech is more likely to interfere with the free exchange of ideas than to encourage it. The interest in encouraging freedom of expression in a democratic society outweighs any theoretical but unproven benefit of censorship.

For the foregoing reasons, the judgment of the district court is affirmed.

It is so ordered.

Notes

1 "Congress shall make no law . . . abridging the freedom of speech." U. S. Const., Amdt. 1.

2 The Court made 410 findings, including 356 paragraphs of the parties' stipulation and 54 findings based on evidence received in open court. See 929 F. Supp. at 830, n. 9, 842, n. 15.

3 An acronym for the network developed by the Advanced Research Project Agency.

4 Id., at 844 (finding 81).

5 Id., at 831 (finding 3).

6 Id., at 835 (finding 27).

7 Id., at 842 (finding 74).

8 Id., at 836 (finding 36).

9 "Web publishing is simple enough that thousands of individual users and small community organizations are using the Web to publish their own personal `home pages,'

the equivalent of individualized newsletters about the person or organization, which are available to everyone on the Web." Id., at 837 (finding 42).

10 Id., at 838 (finding 46).

11 Id., at 844 (finding 82).

12 Ibid. (finding 86).

13 Ibid. (finding 85).

14 Id., at 848 (finding 117).

15 Id., at 844-845 (finding 88).

16 Ibid.

17 Id., at 845 (finding 89).

18 Id., at 842 (finding 72).

19 Ibid. (finding 73).

20 Id., at 845 (finding 90): "An e mail address provides no authoritative information about the addressee, who may use an e mail `alias' or an anonymous remailer. There is also no universal or reliable listing of e mail addresses and corresponding names or telephone numbers, and any such listing would be or rapidly become incomplete. For these reasons, there is no reliable way in many instances for a sender to know if the e mail recipient is an adult or a minor. The difficulty of e mail age verification is compounded for mail exploders such as listservs, which automatically send information to all e mail addresses on a sender's list. Government expert Dr. Olsen agreed that no current technology could give a speaker assurance that only adults were listed in a particular mail exploder's mailing list."

21 Ibid. (finding 93).

22 Id., at 846 (finding 102).

23 Id., at 847 (findings 104-106):

"At least some, if not almost all, non commercial organizations, such as the ACLU, Stop Prisoner Rape or Critical Path AIDS Project, regard charging listeners to access their speech as contrary to their goals of making their materials available to a wide audience free of charge.

. . . . .

"There is evidence suggesting that adult users, particularly casual Web browsers, would be discouraged from retrieving information that required use of a credit card or password. Andrew Anker testified that Hot Wired has received many complaints from its members about HotWired's registration system, which requires only that a member supply a name, e mail address and self created password. There is concern by commercial content providers that age verification requirements would decrease advertising and revenue because advertisers depend on a demonstration that the sites are widely available and frequently visited."

24 See Exon Amendment No. 1268, 141 Cong. Rec. S8120 (June 9, 1995). See also id., at S8087. This amendment, as revised, became§502 of the Communications Act of 1996, 110 Stat. 133, 47 U. S. C. A. §§223(a)-%(e) (Supp. 1997). Some Members of the

House of Representatives opposed the Exon Amendment because they thought it "possible for our parents now to child proof the family computer with these products available in the private sector." They also thought the Senate's approach would "involve the Federal Government spending vast sums of money trying to define elusive terms that are going to lead to a flood of legal challenges while our kids are unprotected." These Members offered an amendment intended as a substitute for the Exon Amendment, but instead enacted as an additional section of the Act entitled "Online Family Empowerment." See 110 Stat. 137, 47 U. S. C. A. §230 (Supp. 1997); 141 Cong. Rec. H8468-H8472. No hearings were held on the provisions that became law. See S. Rep. No. 104-23 (1995), p. 9. After the Senate adopted the Exon amendment, however, its Judiciary Committee did conduct a one day hearing on "Cyberporn and Children." In his opening statement at that hearing, Senator Leahy observed:

"It really struck me in your opening statement when you mentioned, Mr. Chairman, that it is the first ever hearing, and you are absolutely right. And yet we had a major debate on the floor, passed legislation overwhelmingly on a subject involving the Internet, legislation that could dramatically change--some would say even wreak havoc-- on the Internet. The Senate went in willy nilly, passed legislation, and never once had a hearing, never once had a discussion other than an hour or so on the floor." Cyberporn and Children: The Scope of the Problem, The State of the Technology, and the Need for Congressional Action, Hearing on S. 892 before the Senate Committee on the Judiciary, 104th Cong., 1st Sess., 7-8 (1995).

25 Although the Government and the dissent break §223(d)(1) into two separate "patently offensive" and "display" provisions, we follow the convention of both parties below, as well the District Court's order and opinion, in describing §223(d)(1) as one provision.

26 In full, § 223(e)(5) provides:

"(5) It is a defense to a prosecution under subsection (a)(1)(B) or (d) of this section, or under subsection (a)(2) of this section with respect to the use of a facility for an activity under subsection (a)(1)(B) of this section that a person--

"(A) has taken, in good faith, reasonable, effective, and appropriate actions under the circumstances to restrict or prevent access by minors to a communication specified in such subsections, which may involve any appropriate measures to restrict minors from such communications, including any method which is feasible under available technology; or

"(B) has restricted access to such communication by requiring use of a verified credit card, debit account, adult access code, or adult personal identification number."

27 American Civil Liberties Union; Human Rights Watch; Electronic Privacy Information Center; Electronic Frontier Foundation; Journalism Education Association; Computer Professionals for Social Responsibility; National Writers Union; Clarinet Communications Corp.; Institute for Global Communications; Stop Prisoner Rape; AIDS Education Global Information System; Bibliobytes; Queer Resources Directory; Critical

Path AIDS Project, Inc.; Wildcat Press, Inc.; Declan McCullagh dba Justice on Campus; Brock Meeks dba Cyberwire Dispatch; John Troyer dba The Safer Sex Page; Jonathan Wallace dba The Ethical Spectacle; and Planned Parenthood Federation of America, Inc.

28 American Library Association; America Online, Inc.; American Booksellers Association, Inc.; American Booksellers Foundation for Free Expression; American Society of Newspaper Editors; Apple Computer, Inc.; Association of American Publishers, Inc.; Association of Publishers, Editors and Writers; Citizens Internet Empowerment Coalition; Commercial Internet Exchange Association; CompuServe Incorporated; Families Against Internet Censorship; Freedom to Read Foundation, Inc.; Health Sciences Libraries Consortium; Hotwired Ventures LLC; Interactive Digital Software Association; Interactive Services Association; Magazine Publishers of America; Microsoft Corporation; The Microsoft Network, L. L. C.; National Press Photographers Association; Netcom On Line Communication Services, Inc.; Newspaper Association of America; Opnet, Inc.; Prodigy Services Company; Society of Professional Journalists; Wired Ventures, Ltd.

29 110 Stat. 142-143, note following 47 U. S. C. A. §223 (Supp.1997).

30 See also 929 F. Supp., at 877: "Four related characteristics of Internet communication have a transcendent importance to our shared holding that the CDA is unconstitutional on its face. We explain these characteristics in our Findings of fact above, and I only rehearse them briefly here. First, the Internet presents very low barriers to entry. Second, these barriers to entry are identical for both speakers and listeners. Third, as a result of these low barriers, astoundingly diverse content is available on the Internet. Fourth, the Internet provides significant access to all who wish to speak in the medium, and even creates a relative parity among speakers." According to Judge Dalzell, these characteristics and the rest of the District Court's findings "lead to the conclusion that Congress may not regulate indecency on the Internet at all." Ibid. Because appellees do not press this argument before this Court, we do not consider it. Appellees also do not dispute that the Government generally has a compelling interest in protecting minors from "indecent" and "patently offensive" speech.

31 390 U. S., at 639. We quoted from Prince v. Massachusetts, 321 U.S. 158, 166 (1944): "It is cardinal with us that the custody, care and nurture of the child reside first in the parents, whose primary function and freedom include preparation for obligations the state can neither supply nor hinder."

32 Given the likelihood that many E mail transmissions from an adult to a minor are conversations between family members, it is therefore incorrect for the dissent to suggest that the provisions of the CDA, even in this narrow area, "are no different from the law we sustained in Ginsberg." Post, at 8.

33 Cf. Pacifica Foundation v. FCC, 556 F. 2d 9, 36 (CADC 1977) (Levanthal, J., dissenting), rev'd, FCC v. Pacifica Foundation, 438 U.S. 726 (1978). When Pacifica was decided, given that radio stations were allowed to operate only pursuant to federal license, and that Congress had enacted legislation prohibiting licensees from

broadcasting indecent speech, there was a risk that members of the radio audience might infer some sort of official or societal approval of whatever was heard over the radio, see 556 F. 2d, at 37, n. 18. No such risk attends messages received through the Internet, which is not supervised by any federal agency.

34 Juris. Statement 3 (citing 929 F. Supp., at 831 (finding 3)).

35 "Indecent" does not benefit from any textual embellishment at all. "Patently offensive" is qualified only to the extent that it involves "sexual or excretory activities or organs" taken "in context" and "measured by contemporary community standards."

36 See Gozlon Peretz v. United States, 498 U.S. 395, 404 (1991) ("Where Congress includes particular language in one section of a statute but omits it in another section of the same Act, it is generally presumed that Congress acts intentionally and purposely in the disparate inclusion and exclusion") (internal quotation marks omitted).

37 The statute does not indicate whether the "patently offensive" and "indecent" determinations should be made with respect to minors or the population as a whole. The Government asserts that the appropriate standard is "what is suitable material for minors." Reply Brief for Appellants 18, n. 13 (citing Ginsberg v. New York, 390 U.S. 629, 633 (1968)). But the Conferees expressly rejected amendments that would have imposed such a "harmful to minors" standard. See S. Conf. Rep. No. 104-230, p. 189 (1996) (S. Conf. Rep.), 142 Cong. Rec. H1145, H1165-1166 (Feb. 1, 1996). The Conferees also rejected amendments that would have limited the proscribed materials to those lacking redeeming value. See S. Conf. Rep., at 189, 142 Cong. Rec. H1165-1166 (Feb. 1, 1996).

38 Even though the word "trunk," standing alone, might refer to luggage, a swimming suit, the base of a tree, or the long nose of an animal, its meaning is clear when it is one prong of a three part description of a species of gray animals.

39 413 U. S., at 30 (Determinations of "what appeals to the `prurient interest' or is `patently offensive'. . . . are essentially questions of fact, and our Nation is simply too big and too diverse for this Court to reasonably expect that such standards could be articulated for all 50 States in a single formulation, even assuming the prerequisite consensus exists"). The CDA, which implements the "contemporary community standards" language of Miller, thus conflicts with the Conferees' own assertion that the CDA was intended "to establish a uniform national standard of content regulation." S. Conf. Rep., at 191.

40 Accord, Butler v. Michigan, 352 U.S. 380, 383 (1957) (ban on sale to adults of books deemed harmful to children unconstitutional); Sable Communications of Cal., Inc. v. FCC, 492 U.S. 115, 128 (1989) (ban on "dial a porn" messages unconstitutional); Bolger v. Youngs Drug Products Corp., 463 U.S. 60, 73 (1983) (ban on mailing of unsolicited advertisement for contraceptives unconstitutional).

41 The lack of legislative attention to the statute at issue in Sable suggests another parallel with this case. Compare 492 U. S., at 129-130 ("[A]side from conclusory statements during the debates by proponents of the bill, as well as similar assertions in hearings on a substantially identical bill the year before, . . . the congressional record

presented to us contains no evidence as to how effective or ineffective the FCC's most recent regulations were or might prove to be. . . . No Congressman or Senator purported to present a considered judgment with respect to how often or to what extent minors could or would circumvent the rules and have access to dial a porn messages") with n. 24, supra.

42 The Government agrees that these provisions are applicable whenever "a sender transmits a message to more than one recipient, knowing that at least one of the specific persons receiving the message is a minor." Opposition to Motion to Affirm and Reply to Juris. Statement 4-5, n. 1.

43 The Government asserts that "[t]here is nothing constitutionally suspect about requiring commercial Web site operators . . . to shoulder the modest burdens associated with their use." Brief for Appellants 35. As a matter of fact, however, there is no evidence that a "modest burden" would be effective.

44 Transmitting obscenity and child pornography, whether via the Internet or other means, is already illegal under federal law for both adults and juveniles. See 18 U.S.C. §§ 1464-1465 (criminalizing obscenity); §2251 (criminalizing child pornography). In fact, when Congress was considering the CDA, the Government expressed its view that the law was unnecessary because existing laws already authorized its ongoing efforts to prosecute obscenity, child pornography, and child solicitation. See 141 Cong. Rec. S8342 (June 14, 1995) (letter from Kent Markus, Acting Assistant Attorney General, U. S. Department of Justice, to Sen. Leahy).

45 Citing Church of Lukumi Babalu Aye, Inc. v. Hialeah, 508 U.S. 520 (1993), among other cases, appellees offer an additional reason why, in their view, the CDA fails strict scrutiny. Because so much sexually explicit content originates overseas, they argue, the CDA cannot be "effective." Brief for Appellees American Library Association et al. 33-34. This argument raises difficult issues regarding the intended, as well as the permissible scope of, extraterritorial application of the CDA. We find it unnecessary to address those issues to dispose of this case.

46 For the full text of §223(e)(5), see n. 26, supra.

47 Thus, ironically, this defense may significantly protect commercial purveyors of obscene postings while providing little (or no) benefit for transmitters of indecent messages that have significant social or artistic value.

48 929 F. Supp., at 855-856.

49 As this Court long ago explained, "It would certainly be dangerous if the Legislature could set a net large enough to catch all possible offenders and leave it to the courts to step inside and say who could be rightfully be detained and who should be set at large. This would, to some extent, substitute the judicial for the legislative department of the government." United States v. Reese, 92 U.S. 214, 221 (1876). In part because of these separation of powers concerns, we have held that a severability clause is "an aid merely; not an inexorable command." Dorchy v. Kansas, 264 U.S. 286, 290 (1924).

50 See also Osborne v. Ohio, 495 U.S. 103, 121 (1990) (judicial rewriting of

statutes would derogate Congress's "incentive to draft a narrowly tailored law in the first place").

## Burnham v. Ianni (Eighth Circuit) (July 11, 1997) [Notes omitted]

Before RICHARD S. ARNOLD, Chief Judge, McMILLIAN, JOHN R. GIBSON, FAGG, BOWMAN, WOLLMAN, BEAM, LOKEN, HANSEN, and MORRIS SHEPPARD ARNOLD, Circuit Judges, en banc.

BEAM, Circuit Judge.

In this section 1983 action, Chancellor Lawrence Ianni appeals from the district court's[1] denial of his motion for summary judgment based on qualified immunity. A panel of this court reversed. Our decision to grant en banc review vacated that decision. See Burnham v. Ianni, 98 F.3d 1007 (8th Cir.1996). We now affirm.

### I. BACKGROUND

Because discovery has not been conducted in this case, the facts are derived from the plaintiffs' pleadings and the affidavits submitted by the parties. Plaintiff Albert Burnham has been a part-time professor in the history department at the University of Minnesota-Duluth (UMD) since 1986. Plaintiff Ronald Marchese is a tenured professor in the University of Minnesota system. He is a professor of humanities, classics and history at UMD and a professor of ancient history and archaeology in the Center for Ancient Studies at the University of Minnesota-Minneapolis. The History Club, active for a number of years on campus, operates under the auspices of the UMD history department. At all relevant times, Professor Burnham was the faculty advisor to the Club.

During the fall quarter of 1991, two student members of the History Club, plaintiffs Michael and Louise Kohn,[2] conceived an idea for a project that was intended to publicize some of the areas of expertise and interest of the history department's faculty, while at the same time portraying the instructors in an informal, somewhat humorous way. The Kohns approached Professors Burnham and Marchese as well as other members of the department, all of whom agreed to participate. They agreed to pose for a picture with a "prop" that related to their areas of interest.

They also supplied information about their fields of expertise, academic background, and historical heroes, as well as a quotation to be used along with the above information and their photographs.

For his photograph, Professor Burnham posed with a .45 caliber military pistol, wearing a coonskin cap. His special interest in American history includes military history in particular. He listed John Adams and Davy Crockett among his historical heroes. Consistent with his professional interests, Professor Marchese elected to hold an ancient Roman short sword while wearing a cardboard laurel wreath. He listed his specialties as "Ancient Greece and Rome, Homeric Literature" and identified Homer and Alexander the Great as his historical heroes.

A total of eleven professors posed for or supplied pictures. The Kohns assembled an exhibit that incorporated these photographs along with the written comments submitted by each faculty member. The photographs and the accompanying written material were thought to communicate matters of public interest.[3] The exhibit was intended to be viewed by students and prospective students, as well as any members of the public who might be on the premises. It was designed to impart information about the professors and their attitudes toward history — as reflected, for example, in their choices of historical heroes.

The exhibit was put up in the history department's display case, located in the public corridor next to the classrooms used by the department, on March 27, 1992. The case and its contents are seen by students taking classes nearby, faculty members, and members of the general public. The display case is reserved for the use of the history department. It has contained, for a number of years, an exhibit on Roman siege warfare equipment that was assembled by Professor Marchese. The device has been used by members of the History Club as well as by the history department faculty. The case is used only to communicate matters that are considered to be of general interest. It is not used for private communications, like a mailbox or a message system.

The exhibit was, in fact, observed by hundreds, if not thousands, of people. Members of the department received many compliments on the presentation, as did the students who assembled it. For two weeks, no one expressed any criticism about the exhibit. To the contrary, the display appeared to contribute to morale and good relations within the department.

On April 10, 1992, Judith Karon, who was then UMD's affirmative action officer, and UMD Police Captain Harry Michalicek came to the history department and viewed the exhibit. This was in response to a complaint by Charlotte Macleod, an assistant professor who was the head of the UMD Commission on Women. Karon went to the departmental secretary, Elizabeth Kwapick, and demanded that the pictures of Professors Burnham and Marchese be removed. The department denied this demand.

Upon hearing of this attempt to remove the pictures, Professor Burnham called a lawyer in the University of Minnesota's Legal Department, who told him that she could find nothing wrong with the display as described. The history department agreed that the department should resist any attempt by the administration to censor the photographs, and the department declined to remove them.

On April 27, 1992, Karon sent a memorandum to the Dean of the College of Liberal Arts, John Red Horse, stating that she expected the pictures to be removed immediately because she found them to be "totally inappropriate." Dean Red Horse apparently refused to act on Karon's request. On April 30, 1992, Karon sent Professor Burnham a memorandum explaining her reasons for wanting to remove the photographs of Professors Burnham and Marchese. In her memorandum, Karon again stated that she ordered the exhibit taken down because she found the photographs "insensitive" and "inappropriate."

On the morning of April 29, 1992, Louise Kohn, Michael Kohn, Elizabeth

Kwapick and Professor Burnham met with Chancellor Ianni to explain the display and protest Karon's attempted censorship of the pictures and the students' work. During that meeting, Ianni said that he personally found nothing wrong with the photographs. On the afternoon of the same day, the history department held a meeting on this issue, which was also attended by Ianni, Karon, and Red Horse. During that meeting, Chancellor Ianni again stated that he personally saw nothing wrong with the photographs, but hinted that he might nevertheless support their removal.

When asked to explain why she wanted the photographs removed, Karon tried to connect them to a written threat against Professor Judith Trolander which had been found on March 16, 1992.[4] Members of the department told Karon that they thought her attempt to link the pictures to this deranged message was absurd. Karon also stated that she considered the photographs to constitute sexual harassment. She was unable to explain what she meant by this. She was also unable to state by what authority she could order the removal of a student departmental display.

On May 4, 1992, Chancellor Ianni ordered UMD Plant Services Director Kirk Johnson to remove the pictures of Professors Burnham and Marchese. Because Johnson was unable to obtain access to the pictures at that time, Ianni ordered the UMD police to remove the photos. The next day, UMD Police Captain Michalicek removed the photographs from the display. Only the two photographs with weapons were removed. The other nine photographs remained on display. Professors Burnham and Marchese then removed the balance of their contributions to the exhibit.

Following the removal of the photographs, Ianni explained that he removed them because Karon had claimed that she had received anonymous complaints about the display which objected to the depiction of faculty members with weapons. Karon also claimed that Professor Trolander had contacted her about the display's upsetting effect on her. Ianni expressed his belief that the campus was enshrouded in an atmosphere of anxiety due to the earlier threats against Trolander and others.[5] He further explained that his removal of the photographs was an attempt to stop the disruption caused by the display and to prevent aggravation of the atmosphere of fear. Plaintiffs dispute that any milieu of concern existed and contend that the campus atmosphere, whatever it may have been, was not aggravated or affected by the two photographs.

Copies of the photographs were later posted at the student center by a group of students protesting the administration's actions. The student center display advanced the subject of censorship and was entitled "The Administration Does Not Want You to See These." The students used the incidents surrounding the removal of the photographs as an example of impermissible actions under the First Amendment. Apparently, no complaints were lodged about the student center exhibit, nor was there any evidence of an institutional breakdown upon the showing of the photographs.

Plaintiffs, alleging First Amendment violations, filed this 42 U.S.C. § 1983 action against Chancellor Ianni and the University of Minnesota. Defendants moved for summary judgment, which the district court granted in part and denied in part. The court dismissed, with prejudice, all plaintiffs' claims against the University of Minnesota, all plaintiffs' claims for money damages against Ianni in his official capacity as Chancellor of UMD, and the Kohns' claims against Ianni for injunctive relief. The district court denied summary judgment on the remaining contentions, including the issue of qualified immunity for Chancellor Ianni.[6] The district court found that Chancellor Ianni's actions violated the plaintiffs' clearly established First Amendment rights, in a way that an objective university chancellor would have known. Burnham v. Ianni, 899 F.Supp. 395, 400 (D.Minn.1995). Ianni appeals the denial of summary judgment on this ground, contending that the plaintiffs' First Amendment rights were not clearly established, thereby rendering his actions protected by qualified immunity. We review the district court's conclusion on the qualified immunity issue de novo.[7] White v. Holmes, 21 F.3d 277, 279 (8th Cir.1994).

II. DISCUSSION

Since this matter is before the court on a motion for summary judgment based on qualified immunity, the court "ordinarily must look at the record in the light most favorable to the party [plaintiffs/appellees] opposing the motion, drawing all inferences most favorable to that party." Harlow v. Fitzgerald, 457 U.S. 800, 816 n. 26, 102 S.Ct. 2727, 2737, 73 L.Ed.2d 396 (1982). Qualified immunity shields government officials from suit unless their conduct violates a clearly established constitutional or statutory right of which a reasonable person would have known. Id. at 818, 102 S.Ct. at 2738; Yowell v. Combs, 89 F.3d 542, 544 (8th Cir.1996).

Chancellor Ianni's assertion that he is protected by qualified immunity triggers a three-pronged inquiry: (1) whether the plaintiffs have asserted a violation of a constitutional or statutory right; (2) if so, whether that right was clearly established at the time of the violation; and (3) whether, given the facts most favorable to the plaintiffs, there are no genuine issues of material fact as to whether a reasonable official would have known that the alleged action violated that right. Yowell, 89 F.3d at 544.[8] Ianni focuses on the second prong of this analysis. He argues that the plaintiffs' rights were not clearly established at the time of the removal of the photographs. Whether a legally protected interest is clearly established turns on the "objective legal reasonableness of an official's acts. Where an official could be expected to know that certain conduct would violate statutory or constitutional rights, he should be made to hesitate." Harlow, 457 U.S. at 819, 102 S.Ct. at 2739.

Ianni bears the burden of proving that the plaintiffs' First Amendment rights were not clearly established. See, e.g., Siegert v. Gilley, 500 U.S. 226, 231, 111 S.Ct. 1789, 1792-93, 114 L.Ed.2d 277 (1991); Watertown Equip. Co. v. Norwest Bank Watertown, 830 F.2d 1487, 1490 (8th Cir.1987). In an attempt to shoulder this burden, Ianni argues that: (1) some restrictions on speech in nonpublic forums are constitutionally acceptable and, thus, which restrictions are acceptable in a given situation is never "clearly established;" and (2) the professors were public employees[9] and their First Amendment rights were subject to the fact-intensive Pickering[10] balancing test, thus, precluding the rights from being "clearly established." These arguments will be addressed in turn.

First, however, we note that the expressive behavior at issue here, i.e., the posting of the photographs within the history department display, qualifies as constitutionally protected speech. See, e.g., Spence v. Washington, 418 U.S. 405, 410, 94 S.Ct. 2727, 2730, 41 L.Ed.2d 842 (1974); Tinker v. Des Moines Indep. Community Sch. Dist., 393 U.S. 503, 505-06, 89 S.Ct. 733, 735-36, 21 L.Ed.2d 731 (1969); Tindle v. Caudell, 56 F.3d 966, 969 (8th Cir.1995). Nonverbal conduct constitutes speech if it is intended to convey a particularized message and the likelihood is great that the message will be understood by those who view it, regardless of whether it is actually understood in a particular instance in such a way. Spence, 418 U.S. at 411, 94 S.Ct. at 2730-31. Burnham and Marchese, through their photographs, were attempting, at least in part, to convey and advocate their scholarly and professorial interests in military history and in military weaponry's part in their vocation. Michael and Louise Kohn, as well, were attempting to show their creativeness and interest in the scope of the teaching mission of the history department. The display was the Kohns' idea; they organized and exhibited it. Because these messages sufficiently satisfy the Spence test, the photographs and the display qualify as speech. Id. And, we do not understand that Ianni disputes this conclusion.

Although the right of free speech is not absolute, the First Amendment generally prevents the government from proscribing speech of any kind simply because of disapproval of the ideas expressed. R.A.V. v. City of St. Paul, 505 U.S. 377, 382, 112 S.Ct. 2538, 2542-43, 120 L.Ed.2d 305 (1992). Indeed, with a few exceptions, most speech receives First Amendment protection. Cohen v. California, 403 U.S. 15, 24, 91 S.Ct. 1780, 1787-88, 29 L.Ed.2d 284 (1971); see, e.g., New York v. Ferber, 458 U.S. 747, 756, 102 S.Ct. 3348, 3354, 73 L.Ed.2d 1113 (1982) (child pornography is unprotected speech); Miller v. California, 413 U.S. 15, 23, 93 S.Ct. 2607, 2614, 37 L.Ed.2d 419 (1973) (obscene speech is unprotected speech); Chaplinsky v. New Hampshire, 315 U.S. 568, 572, 62 S.Ct. 766, 769, 86 L.Ed. 1031 (1942) (fighting words are unprotected speech). The First Amendment's protection even extends to indecent speech. Sable Communications v. Federal Communications Comm'n, 492 U.S. 115, 126, 109 S.Ct. 2829, 2836-37, 106 L.Ed.2d 93 (1989). It also extends to speech unprotected on one basis (e.g., obscenity) but protected on another (e.g., content in opposition to governmental acts). R.A.V., 505 U.S. at 384-86, 112 S.Ct. at 2543-45. Clearly then, plaintiffs' speech is worthy of constitutional protection.

Because this case involves Ianni's suppression of plaintiffs' protected speech, plaintiffs have (at least for purposes of summary adjudication) sufficiently established a violation of a constitutional right — unless limitations indigenous to the forum lawfully permit restrictions on plaintiffs' First Amendment privileges. We turn to that inquiry.

A. The Forum

Access to and the character of speech on government-controlled areas may be limited depending upon the type of property at issue. Courts recognize three categories of property on which the government may, in greatly varying degrees, restrict speech: (1) public forums, places which by tradition have been devoted to assembly or debate; (2)

limited public forums,[11] properties which the state has opened for use by the public as places for expressive activity; and (3) nonpublic forums, places which are not by tradition or designation forums for public communication. Perry Educ. Ass'n v. Perry Local Educators' Ass'n, 460 U.S. 37, 45-46, 103 S.Ct. 948, 954-56, 74 L.Ed.2d 794 (1983). In public forums, the state's right to limit expression is "sharply circumscribed." Id. at 45, 103 S.Ct. at 954. In limited public and nonpublic forums, however, the state's right to regulate speech is more pervasive.

Ianni argues, and the district court found, that the history department display case is a nonpublic forum. Ianni further claims that because the expression occurred in a nonpublic forum, speech restrictions were permissible or, at least, the extent of any permissible restriction was unclear. Thus, Ianni states, plaintiffs' First Amendment rights were extinguished, limited or at a minimum, not clearly established. Therefore, Ianni says, the district court's denial of qualified immunity was error. We disagree.

In this case the nature of the forum makes little difference.[12] Even if the display case was a nonpublic forum, Ianni is not entitled to qualified immunity. The Supreme Court has declared that "the State may reserve [a nonpublic] forum for its intended purposes, communicative or otherwise, as long as the regulation on speech is reasonable and not an effort to suppress expression merely because public officials oppose the speaker's view." Perry, 460 U.S. at 46, 103 S.Ct. at 955; see also Lamb's Chapel v. Center Moriches Union Free Sch. Dist., 508 U.S. 384, 394, 113 S.Ct. 2141, 2147-48, 124 L.Ed.2d 352 (1993) (stating control over access to nonpublic forum can be based on subject matter and speaker identity so long as the distinctions drawn are reasonable in light of the purpose served by the forum and are viewpoint neutral); United States v. Kokinda, 497 U.S. 720, 732, 110 S.Ct. 3115, 3122-23, 111 L.Ed.2d 571 (1990) (stating constitutionality of regulation must be considered in light of the nature and function of the forum involved).

Here, we find that the suppression was unreasonable both in light of the purpose served by the forum and because of its view-point-based discrimination.

The display case was designated for precisely the type of activity for which the Kohns and Professors Burnham and Marchese were using it. It was intended to inform students, faculty and community members of events in and interests of the history department. The University was not obligated to create the display case, nor did it have to open the case for use by history department faculty and students. However, once it chose to open the case, it was prevented from unreasonably distinguishing among the types of speech it would allow within the forum. See, e.g., Lamb's Chapel, 508 U.S. at 392-93, 113 S.Ct. at 2146-47; Widmar v. Vincent, 454 U.S. 263, 267, 102 S.Ct. 269, 273, 70 L.Ed.2d 440 (1981). Since the purpose of the case was the dissemination of information about the history department, the suppression of exactly that type of information was simply not reasonable.

We recognize that UMD "may legally preserve the property under its control for the use to which it is dedicated." Lamb's Chapel, 508 U.S. at 390, 113 S.Ct. at 2146. However, as the Supreme Court has stated:

"[A]lthough a speaker may be excluded from a nonpublic forum if he wishes to address a topic not encompassed within the purpose of the forum ... or if he is not a member of the class of speakers for whose especial benefit the forum was created ..., the government violates the First Amendment when it denies access to a speaker solely to suppress the point of view he espouses on an otherwise includible subject."

Id. at 394, 113 S.Ct. at 2147 (quoting Cornelius v. NAACP Legal Defense & Educ. Fund, Inc., 473 U.S. 788, 806, 105 S.Ct. 3439, 3451, 87 L.Ed.2d 567 (1985)).

The suppression of this particular speech was also viewpoint-based discrimination. As the Supreme Court has noted, in determining whether the government may legitimately exclude a class of speech to preserve the limits of a forum,

we have observed a distinction between, on the one hand, content discrimination, which may be permissible if it preserves the purposes of that limited forum, and, on the other hand, viewpoint discrimination, which is presumed impermissible when directed against speech otherwise within the forum's limitations.

Rosenberger v. Rector and Visitors, 515 U.S. 819, 829, 115 S.Ct. 2510, 2517, 132 L.Ed.2d 700 (1995) (citing Perry, 460 U.S. at 46, 103 S.Ct. at 955-56). As Rosenberger illustrates, what occurred here was impermissible. The photographs of Professors Burnham and Marchese expressed the plaintiffs' view that the study of history necessarily involves a study of military history, including the use of military weapons. Because other persons on the UMD campus objected to this viewpoint, or, at least, to allowing this viewpoint to be expressed in this particular way, Ianni suppressed the speech to placate the complainants.[13] To put it simply, the photographs were removed because a handful of individuals apparently objected to the plaintiffs' views on the possession and the use of military-type weapons and especially to their exhibition on campus even in an historical context. Freedom of expression, even in a nonpublic forum, may be regulated only for a constitutionally valid reason; there was no such reason in this case.[14]

B. Reasonable Public Official

Ianni further claims that at the time the photographs were suppressed, a reasonably objective chancellor of a large public university would not have known that the conduct violated the plaintiffs' constitutional rights. We again disagree.[15]

As a basic matter, the Supreme Court stated in 1969 "[i]t can hardly be argued that either students or teachers shed their constitutional rights to freedom of speech or expression at the schoolhouse gate." Tinker, 393 U.S. at 506, 89 S.Ct. at 736. Indeed, a year earlier, the idea that a faculty member could be compelled to relinquish First Amendment rights in connection with employment at a public school was "unequivocally rejected" by the Supreme Court. Pickering v. Board of Educ., 391 U.S. 563, 568, 88 S.Ct. 1731, 1734-35, 20 L.Ed.2d 811 (1968).

Applying these long established tenets to this case, we note that our earlier quotation from Rosenberger, 515 U.S. at 829, 115 S.Ct. at 2517, links its observations on viewpoint discrimination within a nonpublic forum to Perry, 460 U.S. at 46, 103 S.Ct. at 955-56, a teacher speech case decided by the Supreme Court in 1983. Similarly, the language proscribing viewpoint discrimination found in Lamb's Chapel, 508 U.S. at 394, 113 S.Ct. at 2147-48, quotes directly from Cornelius, 473 U.S. at 806, 105 S.Ct. at 3451, a 1985 decision. In addition, Widmar's holding prohibiting unreasonable discrimination among "types of expression" within a specific forum, clearly made in the context of an analysis of the purpose of the particular forum, was available as early as 1981. Widmar, 454 U.S. at 265-67, 277, 102 S.Ct. at 272-73, 278.

Judge Heaney, writing for a panel of this court, recently noted that once a controlling opinion has been decided, a constitutional right has been clearly established.[16] See Waddell v. Forney, 108 F.3d 889, 893 (8th Cir.1997). And, admittedly, "[t]he contours of the right must be sufficiently clear that a reasonable official would understand that what he is doing violates that right." Anderson v. Creighton, 483 U.S. 635, 640, 107 S.Ct. 3034, 3039, 97 L.Ed.2d 523 (1987). But, as noted by Judge McMillian in his opinion for the court in Hayes v. Long, 72 F.3d 70, 73 (8th Cir.1995), "[t]his court has taken a broad view of what constitutes `clearly established law' for the purposes of a qualified immunity inquiry." More particularly, he stated, with regard to "clearly established" law, that:

"In order to determine whether a right is clearly established, it is not necessary that the Supreme Court has directly addressed the issue, nor does the precise action or omission in question need to have been held unlawful. In the absence of binding precedent, a court should look to all available decisional law including decisions of state courts, other circuits and district courts...."

Id. at 73-74 (quoting Norfleet v. Arkansas Dep't of Human Servs., 989 F.2d 289, 291 (8th Cir.1993)).

Here, of course, we have long established, binding precedent totally supportive of plaintiffs' claims. The Supreme Court and this court have both clearly and directly spoken on the subject on numerous occasions and in years long prior to the 1992 censorship by Ianni. Accordingly, Chancellor Ianni's "not clearly established" claim must be rejected.[17]

C. Pickering Balancing Argument

Finally, Chancellor Ianni seizes upon the two incidents involving threats to Ms. Featherman and Ms. Trolander in an attempt to interject First Amendment precedent not applicable to this dispute. We reject this endeavor.

Ianni contends that the plaintiffs' rights to express this particular speech must additionally be balanced against UMD's right to suppress it in the name of workplace efficiency and harmony. He urges this court to invoke a line of employee discipline and termination cases to summarily dispose of any violation of constitutional rights. See, e.g., Pickering, 391 U.S. 563, 88 S.Ct. 1731 (teacher discharged for writing letter to newspaper criticizing school board and school superintendent); Connick v. Myers, 461 U.S. 138, 103 S.Ct. 1684, 75 L.Ed.2d 708 (1983) (assistant district attorney discharged for distributing questionnaire concerning office morale, policy and confidence in supervisors). We decline to do so here.

The Supreme Court, in Pickering, held that in an employee discipline case, a court must determine whether the employee's speech was on matter of public concern, and if so, whether the employee's interest in that speech is outweighed by the governmental employer's interest in promoting the efficiency and effectiveness of the services it performs. Pickering, 391 U.S. at 568, 88 S.Ct. at 1734-35. In conjunction with his argument in favor of this balancing requirement, Ianni also advances the theory that government employers must always be granted qualified immunity under such circumstances. We not only find that the Pickering balancing test is inapposite under these facts, but we also disagree with Ianni's analysis of qualified immunity law.

The Pickering standard applies to determinations of whether a public employer has properly discharged or disciplined an employee for engaging in speech. Waters v. Churchill, 511 U.S. 661, 668, 114 S.Ct. 1878, 1884, 128 L.Ed.2d 686 (1994); Rankin v. McPherson, 483 U.S. 378, 384, 107 S.Ct. 2891, 2896-97, 97 L.Ed.2d 315 (1987); Kincade v. City of Blue Springs, 64 F.3d 389, 395 (8th Cir.1995), cert. denied, ____ U.S. ____, 116 S.Ct. 1565, 134 L.Ed.2d 665 (1996). In this case, it is argued that there is no adverse employment action (unless the censorship itself serves that purpose), against which the plaintiffs' free speech rights might be balanced.[18] Indeed, the district court found:

The gravamen of the complaint is not whether the photographs were the basis for adverse employment action; rather, the gravamen of the complaint is whether the ideas conveyed in the photographs fall within any of the exceptions to the general rule "that under our Constitution, the public expression of ideas may not be prohibited merely because the ideas are themselves offensive to some of the hearers."

Burnham, 899 F.Supp. at 400 (quoting Street v. New York, 394 U.S. 576, 592, 89 S.Ct. 1354, 1366, 22 L.Ed.2d 572 (1969)).

We need not decide whether an adverse employment action can be fashioned from the evidence, however, because Ianni has factually failed to put the Pickering balancing test in play. See, e.g., Kincade, 64 F.3d at 398. As this court recently observed, "it is critical to determine whether the defendants [employers] have put the Pickering balancing test at issue by producing evidence that the speech activity had an adverse effect on the efficiency of the ... employer's operations." Grantham v. Trickey, 21 F.3d 289, 294 (8th Cir.1994). As the district court found, "[t]his is not an employment case where there is a threatened disruption to the efficient delivery of services." Burnham, 899 F.Supp. at 400; see also Pickering, 391 U.S. at 570, 88 S.Ct. at 1736 (noting that "no evidence to support [professional damage to the school board and superintendent] was introduced at the hearing" and rejecting the workplace disruption argument of the board.)

As in our Kincade decision, we find that Ianni has failed to carry his burden on this prong of the Pickering rationale. Ianni has made no factual showing that the suppressed conduct "substantially" interfered with the efficiency of the workplace or UMD's educational mission. Kincade, 64 F.3d at 398. "In our system, undifferentiated fear or apprehension of disturbance is not enough to overcome the right to freedom of expression." Tinker, 393 U.S. at 508, 89 S.Ct. at 737. It is simply unreasonable, as a matter of law, to assert that a photograph of a cardboard laurel-wreath bedecked faculty member holding a Roman short sword, as part of an eleven-person faculty display, somehow exacerbated an unestablished ambiance of fear on the UMD campus.

And, even if the Pickering balancing test were somehow applicable, which it is not, Ianni's defense would fail. As stated earlier, the Pickering balancing test requires a court to determine whether the employee's speech involves a matter of public concern and, if so, how the employee's rights in the speech balance against the occurrence of workplace disruption. Both of these questions are issues of law for the court to decide. Kincade, 64 F.3d at 395.

To determine whether the speech at issue here involves a matter of public concern, we examine the "content, form and context" of the speech, given the record as a whole. Connick, 461 U.S. at 147-48, 103 S.Ct. at 1690. To be considered speech on a matter of public concern, the discourse must relate to a "matter of political, social, or other concern to the community." Id. at 146, 103 S.Ct. at 1690; see also Kincade, 64 F.3d at 396. That definition includes many types of speech, excluding mainly speech relating merely to internal office grievances. Connick, 461 U.S. at 148-49, 103 S.Ct. at 1690-91; see also Cox v. Dardanelle Pub. Sch. Dist., 790 F.2d 668, 672 (8th Cir.1986).

The history exhibit, displayed for public viewing, was intended, at least, to inform the University and surrounding community of the views and specialties of the history department and its faculty. As such, the speech involved more than a mere internal office grievance. See, e.g., Cox, 790 F.2d at 673 (stating "educational theories and practices employed by school administrators is clearly a question of public concern ... [h]ow we teach the young, what we teach them, and the environment in which we teach them are of the most central concern to every community in the nation"). See also Lewis v. Harrison Sch. Dist. No. 1, 805 F.2d 310, 314 (8th Cir.1986) (holding speech involving proposed transfer of teacher was on matter of public concern due to large turnout at meeting regarding transfer and teacher interest in the subject); Roberts v. Van Buren Pub. Schs., 773 F.2d 949, 955 (8th Cir.1985) (holding speech involving content of rules governing fifth grade field trip was on matter of public concern due to parental dissatisfaction with and interest in the subject).

Admittedly, the speech at issue here is not of the utmost public concern when compared with an assassination attempt against the President, as in Rankin. 483 U.S. at 381, 107 S.Ct. at 2895. However, when balancing an employee's interest against an employer's interest, the constitutional standard takes proportionality into account. "[T]he closer the employee's speech reflects on matters of public concern, the greater must be the employer's showing that the speech is likely to be disruptive before it may be punished." Jeffries v. Harleston, 52 F.3d 9, 13 (2d Cir.), cert. denied, ____ U.S. ____, 116 S.Ct. 173, 133 L.Ed.2d 114 (1995). The converse is also true. When weighed against the meager evidence of workplace disruption, the plaintiffs' speech clearly addresses matters of public concern within the meaning of the Pickering test. See supra n. 3.

Our next consideration is whether UMD's interest in suppressing the speech, to purportedly control workplace disruption, outweighs the plaintiffs' First Amendment rights in the display. See, e.g., Barnard v. Jackson County, Missouri, 43 F.3d 1218, 1224 (8th Cir.) (stating pertinent considerations for Pickering balancing test are "whether the employee's speech has a detrimental impact on working relationships where personal loyalty or confidence is necessary, and whether the speech impedes the efficient operation of the governmental entity's function"), cert. denied, ____ U.S. ____, 116 S.Ct. 53, 133 L.Ed.2d 17 (1995). The government employer must make a substantial showing that the speech is, in fact, disruptive before the speech may be punished. Waters, 511 U.S. at 673, 114 S.Ct. at 1886-87. We recognize that the government, as an employer, has broader powers in suppressing free speech than the government as a sovereign. Indeed, we have given some deference to an employer's predictions of workplace disruption. Id. However, we have never granted any deference to a government supervisor's bald assertions of harm based on conclusory hearsay and rank speculation. As stated above, the procedural posture of this case requires us to view the facts in the light most favorable to the nonmoving party, i.e., the plaintiffs. In so doing, we note that both Burnham and Marchese, by affidavit, expressly dispute that a "climate of fear and violence" existed on the campus, stating that campus life continued as normal, no classes were suspended or schedules altered and not a single act of violence occurred on UMD premises.

Even if we were to attempt to balance the plaintiffs' free speech rights against the purported disruption of the pedagogical tasks of UMD, it is clear that the impact of the speech on UMD's mission is totally unproven and unaddressed except in the most conclusory fashion. There is simply no evidence that establishes a nexus between the two photographs and an exacerbated climate of fear on the campus or, more importantly, that establishes a relationship between the photographs and a decrease in the efficiency and effectiveness of UMD's educational mission.

In sum, then, upholding Ianni's approach to the First Amendment would permit the suppression of too much speech on arbitrary and capricious grounds. Such a holding would presumably permit the suppression of Ms. Featherman's advocacy of gender and cultural diversity at UMD if Ianni felt that such speech contributed to an inefficient and negative working and learning environment on the campus because of unlawful or vehement opposition to Featherman's views.[19] "Vigilance is necessary to ensure that public employers do not use authority over employees to silence discourse, not because it hampers public functions but simply because superiors disagree with the content of employees' speech." Rankin, 483 U.S. at 384, 107 S.Ct. at 2897.

Finally, we hold that Ianni's failure to establish workplace disruption or, at least, to make a connection between the plaintiffs' speech and the workplace atmosphere, is fatal to his claim of qualified immunity under a Pickering analysis. Kincade is both directly on point and directly contradictory to Ianni's position. Kincade was discharged by Blue Springs for exercising his free speech rights. Because Kincade's speech, as here, touched on a matter of public concern, the Pickering balancing test was employed to review the district court's denial of a motion for summary judgment on qualified immunity grounds. After noting that the only evidence of workplace disruption was conclusory statements to that effect by the mayor and other city officials, Judge Hansen stated:

> the Appellants [city officials] have merely asserted that Kincade's speech adversely affected the efficiency of the City's operations and substantially disrupted the work environment without presenting any specific evidence to support this assertion. They therefore have not put the Pickering balancing test at issue, and accordingly, we reject their claim that they are entitled to qualified immunity because free speech questions for public employees, as a matter of law, cannot be "clearly established."

Kincade, 64 F.3d at 398-99. This is precisely the factual and legal situation we have in this case.

### III. CONCLUSION

The district court correctly found that Ianni is not entitled to qualified immunity from a suit seeking money damages for the violation of plaintiffs' First Amendment rights. Accordingly, we affirm.

## Rice v. Paladin Ent. (Fourth Circuit) (November 10, 1997) [Excerpt]

Before WILKINS, LUTTIG, and WILLIAMS, Circuit Judges.
LUTTIG, Circuit Judge:
[. . .]
I.

[. . .] Notwithstanding Paladin's extraordinary stipulations that it not only knew that its instructions might be used by murderers, but that it actually intended to provide assistance to murderers and would-be murderers which would be used by them "upon receipt," and that it in fact assisted Perry in particular in the commission of the murders of Mildred and Trevor Horn and Janice Saunders, the district court granted Paladin's motion for summary judgment and dismissed plaintiffs' claims that Paladin aided and abetted Perry, holding that these claims were barred by the First Amendment as a matter of law.

Because long-established caselaw provides that speech — even speech by the press — that constitutes criminal aiding and abetting does not enjoy the protection of the First Amendment, and because we are convinced that such caselaw is both correct and equally applicable to speech that constitutes civil aiding and abetting of criminal conduct (at least where, as here, the defendant has the specific purpose of assisting and encouraging commission of such conduct and the alleged assistance and encouragement takes a form other than abstract advocacy), we hold, as urged by the Attorney General and the Department of Justice, that the First Amendment does not pose a bar to a finding that Paladin is civilly liable as an aider and abetter of Perry's triple contract murder. We also hold that the plaintiffs have stated against Paladin a civil aiding and abetting claim under Maryland law sufficient to withstand Paladin's motion for summary judgment. For these reasons, which we fully explain below, the district court's grant of summary judgment in Paladin's favor is reversed and the case is remanded for trial.

II.

A.

In the seminal case of Brandenburg v. Ohio, 395 U.S. 444, 89 S.Ct. 1827, 23 L.Ed.2d 430 (1969), the Supreme Court held that abstract advocacy of lawlessness is protected speech under the First Amendment. Although the Court provided little explanation for this holding in its brief per curiam opinion, it is evident the Court recognized from our own history that such a right to advocate lawlessness is, almost paradoxically, one of the ultimate safeguards of liberty. Even in a society of laws, one of the most indispensable freedoms is that to express in the most impassioned terms the most passionate disagreement with the laws themselves, the institutions of, and created by, law, and the individual officials with whom the laws and institutions are entrusted. Without the freedom to criticize that which constrains, there is no freedom at all.

However, while even speech advocating lawlessness has long enjoyed protections under the First Amendment, it is equally well established that speech which, in its effect, is tantamount to legitimately proscribable nonexpressive conduct may itself be legitimately proscribed, punished, or regulated incidentally to the constitutional enforcement of generally applicable statutes. Cf. Cohen v. Cowles Media Co., 501 U.S. 663, 669, 111 S.Ct. 2513, 2518, 115 L.Ed.2d 586 (1991) (noting "well-established line of decisions holding that generally applicable laws do not offend the First Amendment simply because their enforcement against the press has incidental effects on its ability to gather and report the news"). As no less a First Amendment absolutist than Justice Black wrote for the Supreme Court almost fifty years ago in Giboney v. Empire Storage & Ice Co., in rejecting a First Amendment challenge to an injunction forbidding unionized distributors from picketing to force an illegal business arrangement:

It rarely has been suggested that the constitutional freedom for speech and press extends its immunity to speech or writing used as an integral part of conduct in violation of a valid criminal statute. We reject the contention now....

...

... It is true that the agreements and course of conduct here were as in most instances brought about through speaking or writing. But it has never been deemed an abridgment of freedom of speech or press to make a course of conduct illegal merely because the conduct was in part initiated, evidenced, or carried out by means of language, either spoken, written, or printed. Such an expansive interpretation of the constitutional guaranties of speech and press would make it practically impossible ever to enforce laws against agreements in restraint of trade as well as many other agreements and conspiracies deemed injurious to society.

336 U.S. 490, 498, 502, 69 S.Ct. 684, 688-89, 691, 93 L.Ed. 834 (1949) (citations omitted). And as the Court more recently reaffirmed:

566

Although agreements to engage in illegal conduct undoubtedly possess some element of association, the State may ban such illegal agreements without trenching on any right of association protected by the First Amendment. The fact that such an agreement necessarily takes the form of words does not confer upon it, or upon the underlying conduct, the constitutional immunities that the First Amendment extends to speech. [W]hile a solicitation to enter into an agreement arguably crosses the sometimes hazy line distinguishing conduct from pure speech, such a solicitation, even though it may have an impact in the political arena, remains in essence an invitation to engage in an illegal exchange for private profit, and may properly be prohibited.

[. . .]

Were the First Amendment to bar or to limit government regulation of such "speech brigaded with action," Brandenburg, 395 U.S. at 456, 89 S.Ct. at 1834 (Douglas, J., concurring), the government would be powerless to protect the public from countless of even the most pernicious criminal acts and civil wrongs. See, e.g., Model Penal Code § 223.4 (extortion or blackmail); id. § 240.2 (threats and other improper influences in official and political matters); id. § 241 (perjury and various cognate crimes); id. § 5.02 and § 2.06(3)(a)(i) (criminal solicitation); 18 U.S.C. § 871 (threatening the life of the President); Model Penal Code § 5.03 (conspiracy); id. § 250.4 (harassment); id. § 224.1 (forgery); id. § 210.5(2) (successfully soliciting another to commit suicide); id. § 250.3 (false public alarms); and the like. As Professor Greenawalt succinctly summarized:

The reasons of ordinary penal policy for covering communicative efforts to carry out ordinary crimes are obvious, and the criminal law sensibly draws no distinction between communicative and other acts. Although assertions of fact generally fall within a principle of freedom of speech, what these sorts of factual statements contribute to the general understanding of listeners is minimal, and the justifications for free speech that apply to speakers do not reach communications that are simply means to get a crime successfully committed.

Greenawalt, Speech, Crime, and the Uses of Language at 85 (1989).

In particular as it concerns the instant case, the speech-act doctrine has long been invoked to sustain convictions for aiding and abetting the commission of criminal offenses. Indeed, every court that has addressed the issue, including this court, has held that the First Amendment does not necessarily pose a bar to liability for aiding and abetting a crime, even when such aiding and abetting takes the form of the spoken or written word.

Thus, in a case indistinguishable in principle from that before us, the Ninth Circuit expressly held in United States v. Barnett, 667 F.2d 835 (9th Cir.1982), that the First Amendment does not provide publishers a defense as a matter of law to charges of aiding and abetting a crime through the publication and distribution of instructions on how to make illegal drugs. In rejecting the publisher's argument that there could be no probable cause to believe that a crime had been committed because its actions were shielded by the First Amendment, and thus a fortiori there was no probable cause to support the search pursuant to which the drug manufacturing instructions were found, the Court of Appeals explicitly foreclosed a First Amendment defense not only to the search itself, but also to a later prosecution:

> To the extent ... that Barnett appears to contend that he is immune from search or prosecution because he uses the printed word in encouraging and counseling others in the commission of a crime, we hold expressly that the first amendment does not provide a defense as a matter of law to such conduct.

Id. at 843 (emphasis in original); see also id. at 842 ("The first amendment does not provide a defense to a criminal charge simply because the actor uses words to carry out his illegal purpose. Crimes, including that of aiding and abetting, frequently involve the use of speech as part of the criminal transaction."). The Ninth Circuit derided as a "specious syllogism" with "no support in the law" the publisher's argument that the First Amendment protected his sale of the instruction manual simply because the First Amendment protects the written word. Id. at 842.

The principle of Barnett, that the provision of instructions that aid and abet another in the commission of a criminal offense is unprotected by the First Amendment, has been uniformly accepted, and the principle has been applied to the aiding and abetting of innumerable crimes.

Notably, then-Judge Kennedy, in express reliance upon Barnett, invoked the principle in United States v. Freeman to sustain convictions for the aiding and abetting of tax fraud. 761 F.2d 549, 552-53 (9th Cir.1985), cert. denied, 476 U.S. 1120, 106 S.Ct. 1982, 90 L.Ed.2d 664 (1986). In Freeman, the Ninth Circuit concluded that the defendant could be held criminally liable for counseling tax evasion at seminars held in protest of the tax laws, even though the speech that served as the predicate for the conviction "spr[ang] from the anterior motive to effect political or social change." 761 F.2d at 551. Said the court:

> [T]he First Amendment is quite irrelevant if the intent of the actor and the objective meaning of the words used are so close in time and purpose to a substantive evil as to become part of the ultimate crime itself. In those instances, where speech becomes an integral part of the crime, a First Amendment defense is foreclosed even if the prosecution rests on words alone.

Id. at 552 (citations omitted). Thus, the court held that a First Amendment instruction was required only for those counts as to which there was evidence that the speaker "directed his comments at the unfairness of the tax laws generally, without soliciting or counseling a violation of the law in an immediate sense [and] made statements that, at least arguably, were of abstract generality, remote from advice to commit a specific criminal act." Id. at 551-52. For those counts as to which the defendant, through his speech, directly assisted in the preparation and review of false tax returns, the court held that the defendant was not entitled to a First Amendment instruction at all. Id. at 552. See also United States v. Mendelsohn, 896 F.2d 1183, 1186 (9th Cir.1990) (holding Brandenburg inapplicable to a conviction for conspiring to transport and aiding and abetting the interstate transportation of wagering paraphernalia, where defendants disseminated a computer program that assisted others to record and analyze bets on sporting events; program was "too instrumental in and intertwined with the performance of criminal activity to retain first amendment protection").

[. . .]

Indeed, as the Department of Justice recently advised Congress, the law is now well established that the First Amendment, and Brandenburg's "imminence" requirement in particular, generally poses little obstacle to the punishment of speech that constitutes criminal aiding and abetting, because "culpability in such cases is premised, not on defendants' `advocacy' of criminal conduct, but on defendants' successful efforts to assist others by detailing to them the means of accomplishing the crimes." Department of Justice, "Report on the Availability of Bombmaking Information, the Extent to Which Its Dissemination is Controlled by Federal Law, and the Extent to Which Such Dissemination May Be Subject to Regulation Consistent with the First Amendment to the United States Constitution" 37 (April 1997) (footnote omitted) [hereinafter "DOJ Report"]; see also id. ("[T]he question of whether criminal conduct is `imminent' is relevant for constitutional purposes only where, as in Brandenburg itself, the government attempts to restrict advocacy, as such.").[3] And, while there is considerably less authority on the subject, we assume that those speech acts which the government may criminally prosecute with little or no concern for the First Amendment, the government may likewise subject to civil penalty or make subject to private causes of action. Compare Garrison v. Louisiana, 379 U.S. 64, 85 S.Ct. 209, 13 L.Ed.2d 125 (1964) (applying the same "actual malice" standard to both criminal libel prosecutions and private defamation actions) with New York Times Co. v. Sullivan, 376 U.S. 254, 84 S.Ct. 710, 11 L.Ed.2d 686 (1964). Cf. Cohen, 501 U.S. 663, 111 S.Ct. 2513, 115 L.Ed.2d 586 (finding in civil promissory estoppel case that First Amendment does not bar liability for newspaper's publication of confidential source's name); Zacchini v. Scripps-Howard Broadcasting Co., 433 U.S. 562, 97 S.Ct. 2849, 53 L.Ed.2d 965 (1977) (First Amendment does not bar liability for common law tort of unlawful appropriation of "right to publicity" where television station broadcast "human cannonball" act in its entirety without plaintiff's authorization); Harper & Row, Publishers, Inc. v. Nation Enterprises, 471 U.S. 539, 105 S.Ct. 2218, 85 L.Ed.2d 588 (1985) (rejecting First Amendment defense to copyright infringement action against magazine for printing unauthorized presidential memoir excerpts). Even if this is not universally so, we believe it must be true at least where the government's interest in preventing the particular conduct at issue is incontrovertibly compelling.

B.

We can envision only two possible qualifications to these general rules, neither of which, for reasons that we discuss more extensively below, is of special moment in the context of the particular aiding and abetting case before us.

1.

The first, which obviously would have practical import principally in the civil context, is that the First Amendment may, at least in certain circumstances, superimpose upon the speech-act doctrine a heightened intent requirement in order that preeminent values underlying that constitutional provision not be imperiled. See, e.g., New York Times, 376 U.S. 254, 84 S.Ct. 710, 11 L.Ed.2d 686; cf. United States v. Aguilar, 515 U.S. 593, 605, 115 S.Ct. 2357, 2365, 132 L.Ed.2d 520 (1995) (rejecting defendant's First Amendment construction in part because "the statute here in question does not impose such a restriction [on the disclosure of wiretap authorizations] generally, but only upon those who disclose wiretap information `in order to [ob]struct, impede, or prevent' a wiretap interception" (emphasis added)); Haig v. Agee, 453 U.S. 280, 308-09, 101 S.Ct. 2766, 2783, 69 L.Ed.2d 640 (1981) ("[The defendant's] disclosures, among other things, have the declared purpose of obstructing intelligence operations and the recruiting of intelligence personnel. They are clearly not protected by the Constitution." (emphasis added)); United States v. Featherston, 461 F.2d 1119, 1122 (5th Cir.1972) (rejecting First Amendment challenge to federal statute criminalizing the teaching or demonstration of the making of any explosive device after construing statute to require "intent or knowledge that the information disseminated would be used in the furtherance of a civil disorder"), cert. denied, 409 U.S. 991, 93 S.Ct. 339, 34 L.Ed.2d 258 (1972); National Mobilization Committee to End the War in Viet Nam v. Foran, 411 F.2d 934, 937 (7th Cir.1969). That is, in order to prevent the punishment or even the chilling of entirely innocent, lawfully useful speech, the First Amendment may in some contexts stand as a bar to the imposition of liability on the basis of mere foreseeability or knowledge that the information one imparts could be misused for an impermissible purpose. Where it is necessary, such a limitation would meet the quite legitimate, if not compelling, concern of those who publish, broadcast, or distribute to large, undifferentiated audiences, that the exposure to suit under lesser standards would be intolerable. See discussion infra, Part IV.

At the same time, it would not relieve from liability those who would, for profit or other motive, intentionally assist and encourage crime and then shamelessly seek refuge in the sanctuary of the First Amendment. Like our sister circuits, at the very least where a speaker — individual or media — acts with the purpose of assisting in the commission of crime, we do not believe that the First Amendment insulates that speaker from responsibility for his actions simply because he may have disseminated his message to a wide audience. See, e.g., Barnett, 667 F.2d 835 (holding that drug manufacturing instructions mailed to countless customers with whom the defendant had no personal contact could give rise to aiding and abetting conviction); Mendelsohn, 896 F.2d 1183 (holding that First Amendment did not forbid prosecution of aiding and abetting interstate transportation of wagering paraphernalia where computer programs for recording and analyzing illegal wagers were distributed generally and widely to the public); Buttorff, 572 F.2d at 622-23 (affirming, despite First Amendment challenges, convictions for providing tax-evasion information at "large public gatherings" to participants whom the defendants did not personally meet); Kelley, 769 F.2d 215 (similar); Moss, 604 F.2d 569 (similar); Freeman, 761 F.2d 549 (similar). This is certainly so, we are satisfied, where not only the speaker's dissemination or marketing strategy, but the nature of the speech itself, strongly suggest that the audience both targeted and actually reached is, in actuality, very narrowly confined, as in the case before us. See discussion infra at 253-256. Were the First Amendment to offer protection even in these circumstances, one could publish, by traditional means or even on the internet, the necessary plans and instructions for assassinating the President, for poisoning a city's water supply, for blowing up a skyscraper or public building, or for similar acts of terror and mass destruction, with the specific, indeed even the admitted, purpose of assisting such crimes — all with impunity.

We need not engage in an extended discussion of the existence or scope of an intent-based limitation today, however, because we are confident that the First Amendment poses no bar to the imposition of civil (or criminal) liability for speech acts which the plaintiff (or the prosecution) can establish were undertaken with specific, if not criminal, intent. See DOJ Report at 42-43 (advising that "the government may punish publication of dangerous instructional information where that publication is motivated by a desire to facilitate the unlawful [conduct as to which the instructions inform, or] [a]t the very least, publication with such an improper intent should not be constitutionally protected where it is foreseeable that the publication will be used for criminal purposes...."). In fact, this conclusion would seem to follow a fortiori from the Supreme Court's holding in New York Times, 376 U.S. 254, 84 S.Ct. 710, 11 L.Ed.2d 686, allowing the imposition of civil tort liability on a media defendant for reputational injury caused by mere reckless disregard of the truth of its published statements. And, here, as previously noted, see also discussion infra at 252-53, Paladin has stipulated that it provided its assistance to Perry with both the knowledge and the intent that the book would immediately be used by criminals and would-be criminals in the solicitation, planning, and commission of murder and murder for hire, and even absent the stipulations, a jury could reasonably find such specific intent, see discussion infra at 253-55. Thus, Paladin has stipulated to an intent, and a jury could otherwise reasonably find that Paladin acted with a kind and degree of intent, that would satisfy any heightened standard that might be required by the First Amendment prerequisite to the imposition of liability for aiding and abetting through speech conduct.[4]

2.

The second qualification is that the First Amendment might well (and presumably would) interpose the same or similar limitations upon the imposition of civil liability for abstract advocacy, without more, that it interposes upon the imposition of criminal punishment for such advocacy. In other words, the First Amendment might well circumscribe the power of the state to create and enforce a cause of action that would permit the imposition of civil liability, such as aiding and abetting civil liability, for speech that would constitute pure abstract advocacy, at least if that speech were not "directed to inciting or producing imminent lawless action, and ... likely to incite or produce such action." Brandenburg, 395 U.S. at 447, 89 S.Ct. at 1829. The instances in which such advocacy might give rise to civil liability under state statute would seem rare, but they are not inconceivable. Cf. Schenck v. United States, 249 U.S. 47, 39 S.Ct. 247, 63 L.Ed. 470 (1919) (criminal conspiracy prosecution predicated upon subversive advocacy); Frohwerk v. United States, 249 U.S. 204, 39 S.Ct. 249, 63 L.Ed. 561 (1919) (same); Debs v. United States, 249 U.S. 211, 39 S.Ct. 252, 63 L.Ed. 566 (1919) (criminal attempt prosecution predicated upon such advocacy). Again, however, an exhaustive analysis of this likely limitation is not required in this case.

Here, it is alleged, and a jury could reasonably find, see discussion infra Part III.A, that Paladin aided and abetted the murders at issue through the quintessential speech act of providing step-by-step instructions for murder (replete with photographs, diagrams, and narration) so comprehensive and detailed that it is as if the instructor were literally present with the would-be murderer not only in the preparation and planning, but in the actual commission of, and follow-up to, the murder; there is not even a hint that the aid was provided in the form of speech that might constitute abstract advocacy. As the district court itself concluded, Hit Man "merely teaches what must be done to implement a professional hit." J.A. at 218. Moreover, although we do not believe such would be necessary, we are satisfied a jury could readily find that the provided instructions not only have no, or virtually no, noninstructional communicative value, but also that their only instructional communicative "value" is the indisputably illegitimate one of training persons how to murder and to engage in the business of murder for hire. See id.; see also id. at 221 ("This Court, quite candidly, personally finds Hit Man to be reprehensible and devoid of any significant redeeming social value").

Aid and assistance in the form of this kind of speech bears no resemblance to the "theoretical advocacy," Scales v. United States, 367 U.S. 203, 235, 81 S.Ct. 1469, 1489, 6 L.Ed.2d 782 (1961), the advocacy of "principles divorced from action," Yates v. United States, 354 U.S. 298, 320, 77 S.Ct. 1064, 1077, 1 L.Ed.2d 1356 (1957), overruled on other grounds, Burks v. United States, 437 U.S. 1, 98 S.Ct. 2141, 57 L.Ed.2d 1 (1978), the "doctrinal justification," id. at 321, 77 S.Ct. at 1078, "the mere abstract teaching [of] the moral propriety or even moral necessity for a resort to force and violence," Brandenburg, 395 U.S. at 448, 89 S.Ct. at 1830 (quoting Noto v. United States, 367 U.S. 290, 297-98, 81 S.Ct. 1517, 1520-22, 6 L.Ed.2d 836 (1961)), or any of the other forms of discourse critical of government, its policies, and its leaders, which have always animated, and to this day continue to animate, the First Amendment. Indeed, this detailed, focused instructional assistance to those contemplating or in the throes of planning murder is the antithesis of speech protected under Brandenburg. It is the teaching of the "techniques" of violence, Scales, 367 U.S. at 233, 81 S.Ct. at 1488, the "advocacy and teaching of concrete action," Yates, 354 U.S. at 320, 77 S.Ct. at 1077, the "prepar[ation] ... for violent action and [the] steeling ... to such action," Brandenburg, 395 U.S. at 448, 89 S.Ct. at 1830 (quoting Noto, 367 U.S. at 297-98, 81 S.Ct. at 1520-21). It is the instruction in the methods of terror of which Justice Douglas spoke in Dennis v. United States, when he said, "If this were a case where those who claimed protection under the First Amendment were teaching the techniques of sabotage ... I would have no doubts. The freedom to speak is not absolute; the teaching of methods of terror ... should be beyond the pale...." 341 U.S. 494, 581, 71 S.Ct. 857, 903, 95 L.Ed. 1137 (1951) (Douglas, J., dissenting). As such, the murder instructions in Hit Man are, collectively, a textbook example of the type of speech that the Supreme Court has quite purposely left unprotected, and the prosecution of which, criminally or civilly, has historically been thought subject to few, if any, First Amendment constraints. Accordingly, we hold that the First Amendment does not pose a bar to the plaintiffs' civil aiding and abetting cause of action against Paladin Press. If, as precedent uniformly confirms, the states have the power to regulate speech that aids and abets crime, then certainly they have the power to regulate the speech at issue here.

III.

[. . .]

Finally, and significantly, Paladin also has stipulated to an intent that readily satisfies that required under Maryland law or the First Amendment. Even if the First Amendment imposes a heightened intent-based limitation on the state's ability to apply the tort of aiding and abetting to speech, see discussion supra at II.B.1, we are confident that, at the very least, the aiding and abetting of a malum in se crime such as murder with the specific purpose of assisting and encouraging another or others in that crime would satisfy such a limitation. Paladin has stipulated not only that it had knowledge that its publication would be used upon receipt by murderers and other criminals in the commission of murder, but that it even intended that the book be so used. Thus, the publisher stipulated, "defendants intended and had knowledge that their publications would be used, upon receipt, by criminals and would-be criminals to plan and execute the crime of murder for hire." J.A. at 59. Paladin has even stipulated that it "engaged in a marketing strategy intended to attract and assist criminals and would-be criminals who desire information and instructions on how to commit crimes." Id. These stipulations are more than sufficient to foreclose an absolute First Amendment defense to plaintiffs' suit. See DOJ Report at 43 & 44-45 n.71 ("[W]e believe that the district court in Rice v. Paladin erred insofar as it concluded that Brandenburg bars liability for dissemination of [instructions on murder] regardless of the publisher's intent.... [Defendant Paladin's] concession[s] would, for purposes of summary judgment, seem to foreclose a constitutional defense ...").

The district court was never required to consider the intent requirement under Maryland's law of aiding and abetting, much less whether the First Amendment imposes a heightened intent standard in the context of authorizing liability for speech acts, because of its mistaken conclusion that Maryland does not recognize a civil cause of action for aiding and abetting. In analogizing this case to the copycat cases (and seemingly in order to permit the analogy), however, the district court accepted Paladin's post hoc "clarification" that it meant by its stipulation only that it was reasonably foreseeable to the publisher that, once the book was published and publicly available, it would be used by murderers to plan and to commit murder. Thus, in accepting the defendants' belated clarification, the district court said:

Defendants conceded that they intended that their publications would be used by criminals to plan and execute murder as instructed in the manual.... However, Defendants clarify their concession by explaining that when they published, advertised and distributed both Hit Man and Silencers, they knew, and in that sense "intended," that the books would be purchased by all of the categories of readers previously described and used by them for the broad range of purposes previously described.

J.A. at 215-16 (citations omitted). Of course, the district court was without authority to allow Paladin to alter the parties' stipulation unilaterally, particularly given that Paladin was the party moving for summary judgment. If anything, the stipulation should have been, and in any event must now be, interpreted in the light most favorable to the plaintiffs.

Furthermore, even if the stipulation only established knowledge, summary judgment was yet inappropriate because a trier of fact could still conclude that Paladin acted with the requisite intent to support civil liability. Wholly apart from Paladin's stipulations, there are four bases upon which, collectively, if perhaps not individually, a reasonable jury could find that Paladin possessed the intent required under Maryland law, as well as the intent required under any heightened First Amendment standard. Compare DOJ Report, at 45 n.71 ("[E]ven assuming arguendo that the defendants' own construction of the `intent' stipulation were correct, that still would not justify the grant of summary judgment, since it would leave unanswered the question whether Paladin also had the specific purpose of facilitating murder.").

First, the declared purpose of Hit Man itself is to facilitate murder. Consistent with its declared purpose, the book is subtitled "A Technical Manual for Independent Contractors," and it unabashedly describes itself as "an instruction book on murder," Hit Man at ix. A jury need not, but plainly could, conclude from such prominent and unequivocal statements of criminal purpose that the publisher who disseminated the book intended to assist in the achievement of that purpose.

Second, the book's extensive, decided, and pointed promotion of murder is highly probative of the publisher's intent, and may be considered as such, whether or not that promotion, standing alone, could serve as the basis for liability consistent with the First Amendment. See Wisconsin v. Mitchell, 508 U.S. 476, 489, 113 S.Ct. 2194, 2201, 124 L.Ed.2d 436 (1993) ("The First Amendment ... does not prohibit the evidentiary use of speech to establish the elements of a crime or to prove motive or intent."); cf. Noto, 367 U.S. at 299, 81 S.Ct. at 1521-22.[7] After carefully and repeatedly reading Hit Man in its entirety, we are of the view that the book so overtly promotes murder in concrete, nonabstract terms that we regard as disturbingly disingenuous both Paladin's cavalier suggestion that the book is essentially a comic book whose "fantastical" promotion of murder no one could take seriously, and amici's reckless characterization of the book as "almost avuncular," see Br. of Amici at 8-9. The unique text of Hit Man alone, boldly proselytizing and glamorizing the crime of murder and the "profession" of murder as it dispassionately instructs on its commission, is more than sufficient to create a triable issue of fact as to Paladin's intent in publishing and selling the manual.

Third, Paladin's marketing strategy would more than support a finding of the requisite intent. Cf. Direct Sales v. United States, 319 U.S. 703, 712-13, 63 S.Ct. 1265, 1269-70, 87 L.Ed. 1674 (1943) (holding that jury may infer intent to assist a criminal operation based upon a drug distributor's marketing strategy). It is known through Paladin's stipulations that it "engaged in a marketing strategy intended to attract and assist criminals and would-be criminals who desire information and instructions on how to commit crimes." J.A. at 59. But an inference as to such a strategy would be permitted from Paladin's catalogue advertisement of Hit Man. The publisher markets the book as follows, invoking a disclaimer which, the district court's characterization notwithstanding, a jury could readily find to be transparent sarcasm designed to intrigue and entice:

Learn how a pro gets assignments, creates a false identity, makes a disposable silencer, leaves the scene without a trace, watches his mark unobserved and more. Feral reveals how to get in, do the job and get out without getting caught. For academic study only!

Paladin Press Catalog, Vol. 26, No. 2 at 41 (emphasis in original). See also infra note 10. From this statement by the publisher in its own promotional sales catalogue, a jury could conclude that Paladin marketed Hit Man directly and even primarily to murderers and would-be criminals, and, from this permissible conclusion, in turn conclude that Paladin possessed the requisite intent necessary to support liability.

Certainly, such a conclusion would be reasonable based upon this promotional description coupled with the singular character of Hit Man, which is so narrowly focused in its subject matter and presentation as to be effectively targeted exclusively to criminals. In other words, despite the fact that Paladin may technically offer the book for sale to all comers, we are satisfied that a jury could, based upon Hit Man's seemingly exclusive purpose to assist murderers in the commission of murder, reasonably conclude that Paladin essentially distributed Hit Man only to murderers and would-be murderers — that its conduct was not, at least in law, different from that of a publisher (or anyone else) who delivered Hit Man to a specific person or group of persons whom the publisher knew to be interested in murder. And even Paladin effectively concedes that it could be liable were such a finding permissibly made. Paladin's Memorandum in Support of Summary Judgment at 33 n.24.

A conclusion that Paladin directed Hit Man to a discrete group rather than to the public at large would be supported, even if not established, by the evidence that Hit Man is not generally available or sold to the public from the bookshelves of local bookstores, but, rather, is obtainable as a practical matter only by catalogue. Paladin Press is a mail order company, and for the most part does not sell books through retail outlets. In order to procure a copy of Hit Man, the prospective reader must first obtain a copy of Paladin's catalogue, typically by completing a request form reprinted in one of Paladin's advertisements in specialized magazines such as Soldier of Fortune. After obtaining that catalogue, the reader must scan the list of book titles and read the accompanying descriptions. Once the reader finds the book he desires, he must then complete and mail another form to order the book.

From the requirements of this process, together with the book's character, a jury need not, but could, permissibly find that Hit Man is not at all distributed to the general public and that, instead, it is available only to a limited, self-selected group of people interested in learning from and being trained by a self-described professional killer in various methods of killing for money, individuals who are then contemplating or highly susceptible to the commission of murder.

Finally, a jury could reasonably conclude that Paladin specifically intended to assist Perry and similar murderers by finding, contrary to Paladin's demurs, as would we, that Hit Man's only genuine use is the unlawful one of facilitating such murders.[8] Cf. J.A. at 221 (observation by district court that Hit Man is "devoid of any significant redeeming social value"). Although before us Paladin attempts to hypothesize lawful purposes for Hit Man, and it would doubtless advance the same hypotheses before a jury, at some point hypotheses are so implausible as to be deserving of little or no weight. The likelihood that Hit Man actually is, or would be, used in the legitimate manners hypothesized by Paladin is sufficiently remote that a jury could quite reasonably reject them altogether as alternative uses for the book. If there is a publication that could be found to have no other use than to facilitate unlawful conduct, then this would be it, so devoid is the book of any political, social, entertainment, or other legitimate discourse. Cf. Miller v. California, 413 U.S. 15, 93 S.Ct. 2607, 37 L.Ed.2d 419 (1973) (distinguishing obscene from nonobscene material in part on basis of "whether the work, taken as a whole, lacks serious literary, artistic, political, or scientific value"). Thus, for example, a jury would certainly not be unreasonable in dismissing (in fact, it arguably would be unreasonable in accepting) Paladin's contention that Hit Man has significant social value in that the book, in the course of instructing murderers how to murder, incidentally informs law enforcement on the techniques that the book's readers will likely employ in the commission of their murders. Likewise, a reasonable jury could simply refuse to accept Paladin's contention that this purely factual, instructional manual on murder has entertainment value to law-abiding citizens. And, just as a permissible inference as to Paladin's marketing strategy would be supportable by evidence as to the specialized process by which one acquires Hit Man, either of these conclusions as to the absence of lawful purpose could be reinforced by the same evidence.

In summary, a reasonable jury clearly could conclude from the stipulations of the parties, and, apart from the stipulations, from the text of Hit Man itself and the other facts of record, that Paladin aided and abetted in Perry's triple murder by providing detailed instructions on the techniques of murder and murder for hire with the specific intent of aiding and abetting the commission of these violent crimes.

[. . .]

Indeed, one finds in Hit Man little, if anything, even remotely characterizable as the abstract criticism that Brandenburg jealously protects. Hit Man's detailed, concrete instructions and adjurations to murder stand in stark contrast to the vague, rhetorical threats of politically or socially motivated violence that have historically been considered part and parcel of the impassioned criticism of laws, policies, and government indispensable in a free society and rightly protected under Brandenburg. The speech of Hit Man defies even comparison with the Klansman's chilling, but protected, statement in Brandenburg itself that, "[the Ku Klux Klan is] not a revengent organization, but if our President, our Congress, our Supreme Court, continues to suppress the white, Caucasian race, it's possible that there might have to be some revengeance taken," 395 U.S. at 446, 89 S.Ct. at 1829; the protestor's inciteful, but protected, chant in Hess v. Indiana, 414 U.S. 105, 108, 94 S.Ct. 326, 328-29, 38 L.Ed.2d 303 (1973) that "[w]e'll take the fucking street again"; the NAACP speaker's threat, rhetorical in its context, to boycott violators that "[i]f we catch any of you going in any of them racist stores, we're gonna break your damn neck," which was held to be protected in NAACP v. Claiborne Hardware Co., 458 U.S. 886, 902, 102 S.Ct. 3409, 3420, 73 L.Ed.2d 1215 (1982); or the draft protestor's crude, but protected, blustering in Watts that "[i]f they ever make me carry a rifle the first man I want to get in my sights is L.B.J," Watts v. United States, 394 U.S. 705, 706, 89 S.Ct. 1399, 1401, 22 L.Ed.2d 664 (1969).

Plaintiffs observed in their submissions before the district court that,

Hit Man is not political manifesto, not revolutionary diatribe, not propaganda, advocacy, or protest, not an outpouring of conscience or credo.

...

It contains no discussion of ideas, no argument, no information about politics, religion, science, art, or culture ... it offers no agenda for self-governance, no insight into the issues of the day....

Appellant's Br. at 32; Memorandum of Points and Authorities in Support of Plaintiffs' Opposition to Defendant's Motion for Summary Judgment at 31-32. And, this is apt observation. Hit Man is none of this. Ideas simply are neither the focus nor the burden of the book. To the extent that there are any passages within Hit Man's pages that arguably are in the nature of ideas or abstract advocacy, those sentences are so very few in number and isolated as to be legally of no significance whatsoever.[9] Cf. Kois v. Wisconsin, 408 U.S. 229, 231, 92 S.Ct. 2245, 2246, 33 L.Ed.2d 312 (1972) ("A quotation from Voltaire in the flyleaf of a book will not constitutionally redeem an otherwise obscene publication."); see also Miller, 413 U.S. at 24, 93 S.Ct. at 2614-15; Penthouse International, Ltd. v. McAuliffe, 610 F.2d 1353 (5th Cir.1980), cert. dismissed, 447 U.S. 931, 100 S.Ct. 3031, 65 L.Ed.2d 1131 (1980). Hit Man is, pure and simple, a step-by-step murder manual, a training book for assassins. There is nothing even arguably tentative or recondite in the book's promotion of, and instruction in, murder.[10] To the contrary, the book directly and unmistakably urges concrete violations of the laws against murder and murder for hire and coldly instructs on the commission of these crimes. The Supreme Court has never protected as abstract advocacy speech so explicit in its palpable entreaties to violent crime.

2.

In concluding that Hit Man is protected "advocacy," the district court appears to have misperceived the nature of the speech that the Supreme Court held in Brandenburg is protected under the First Amendment. In particular, the district court seems to have misunderstood the Court in Brandenburg as having distinguished between "advocating or teaching" lawlessness on the one hand, and "inciting or encouraging" lawlessness on the other, any and all of the former being entitled to First Amendment protection. The district court thus framed the issue before it as "whether Hit Man merely advocates or teaches murder or whether it incites or encourages murder." J.A. at 212. And, finding that Hit Man "merely teaches" in technical fashion the fundamentals of murder, it concluded that "[t]he book does not cross that line between permissible advocacy and impermissible incitation to crime or violence." Id. at 218.

The Court in Brandenburg, however, did not hold that "mere teaching" is protected; the Court never even used this phrase. And it certainly did not hold, as the district court apparently believed, that all teaching is protected. Rather, however inartfully it may have done so, the Court fairly clearly held only that the "mere abstract teaching" of principles, id. at 447-48, 89 S.Ct. at 1830 (quoting Noto, 367 U.S. at 297-98, 81 S.Ct. at 1520-21) (emphasis added), and "mere advocacy," 395 U.S. at 448-49, 89 S.Ct. at 1830-31 (emphasis added), are protected. In the final analysis, it appears the district court simply failed to fully appreciate the import of the qualification to the kind of "teaching" that the Supreme Court held to be protected in Brandenburg. See J.A. at 217 (defining "advocacy" as "mere teaching" rather than "mere abstract teaching" but citing to Brandenburg, 395 U.S. at 448, 89 S.Ct. at 1830 (quoting Noto, 367 U.S. at 297-98, 81 S.Ct. at 1520-21)). As the Supreme Court's approving quotation from its opinion in Noto confirms, it is not teaching simpliciter, but only "the mere abstract teaching ... of the moral propriety or even moral necessity" for resort to lawlessness, or its equivalent, that is protected under the commands of Brandenburg. 367 U.S. at 297-98, 81 S.Ct. at 1520-21 (emphasis added).[11]

Although we believe the district court's specific misreading of Brandenburg was plainly in error, we cannot fault the district court for its confusion over the opinion in that case. The short per curiam opinion in Brandenburg is, by any measure, elliptical.

In particular, the Court unmistakably draws the distinction discussed above, between "the mere abstract teaching ... of the moral propriety or even moral necessity for a resort to force and violence" on one hand, 395 U.S. at 448, 89 S.Ct. at 1830, and the "prepar[ation] [of] a group for violent action and steeling it to such action" on the other. Id. And it then recites in the very next sentence that "[a] statute which fails to draw this distinction," id. (emphasis added) — a seeming reference to the distinction between "mere abstract teaching" and "preparing and steeling" — is unconstitutional under the First Amendment. In the succeeding paragraph and a later footnote, however, the Court distinguishes between "mere advocacy" and "incitement to imminent lawless action," a distinction which, as a matter of common sense and common parlance, appears different from the first distinction drawn, because "preparation and steeling" can occur without "incitement," and vice-versa. See id. at 448, 89 S.Ct. at 1830 ("Neither the indictment nor the trial judge's instructions to the jury in any way refined the statute's bald definition of the crime in terms of mere advocacy not distinguished from incitement to imminent lawless action." (footnote omitted)); id. at 449 n. 4, 89 S.Ct. at 1831 n. 4 ("Statutes affecting the right of assembly, like those touching on freedom of speech, must observe the established distinctions between mere advocacy and incitement to imminent lawless action....").

It would have been natural, based upon its prior cases, for the Court actually to have contemplated and intended both distinctions, and to have developed the latter only, because the case before it turned exclusively on that distinction. It is more likely, however, that the Court did not focus at all on the seeming facial incongruity between the first and the latter two of these distinctions. The Court, therefore, may well have intended to equate the preparation and steeling of a group to violent action with speech that is directed to inciting imminent lawless action and likely to produce such action. In other words, the Court may well have meant to imply that one prepares and steels another or others for violent action only when he does so through speech that is "directed to inciting or producing imminent lawless action and ... [that is] likely to incite or produce such action," id. at 447, 89 S.Ct. at 1829, and thus that preparation and steeling is not per se unprotected. Compare id. at 447-48, 89 S.Ct. at 1829-30 ("As we said in Noto. ...") with Noto, 367 U.S. at 298, 81 S.Ct. at 1521 (describing preparation and steeling through "a call to violence"). Assuming that it did so mean to imply, however, we are confident it meant to do so only in the context of advocacy — speech that is part and parcel of political and social discourse — which was the only type of speech at issue in Brandenburg, Noto, and the other cases relied upon by the Court. See, e.g., 44 Liquormart v. Rhode Island, ____ U.S. ___, ___, 116 S.Ct. 1495, 1505, 134 L.Ed.2d 711 (1996) (Stevens, J., for plurality) (describing Brandenburg as setting forth "test for suppressing political speech"). The Court even so defined its own holding: "These later decisions have fashioned the principle that the constitutional guarantees of free speech and free press do not permit a State to forbid or proscribe advocacy of the use of force or of law violation except where such advocacy is directed to inciting or producing imminent lawless action and is likely to incite or produce such action." 395 U.S. at 447, 89 S.Ct. at 1829 (footnote omitted; emphases added). For, as this case reveals, and as the Court itself has always seemed to recognize, one obviously can prepare, and even steel, another to violent action not only through the dissident "call to violence," but also through speech, such as instruction in the methods of terror or other crime, that does not even remotely resemble advocacy, in either form or purpose. And, of course, to understand the Court as addressing itself to speech other than advocacy would be to ascribe to it an intent to revolutionize the criminal law, in a several paragraph per curiam opinion, by subjecting prosecutions to the demands of Brandenburg's "imminence" and "likelihood" requirements whenever the predicate conduct takes, in whole or in part, the form of speech — an intent that no lower court has discerned and that, this late in the day, we would hesitate to impute to the Supreme Court.

Accordingly, we hold that plaintiffs have stated, sufficient to withstand summary judgment, a civil cause of action against Paladin Enterprises for aiding and abetting the murders of Mildred and Trevor Horn and Janice Saunders on the night of March 3, 1993, and that this cause of action is not barred by the First Amendment to the United States Constitution.

IV.

Paladin, joined by a spate of media amici, including many of the major networks, newspapers, and publishers, contends that any decision recognizing even a potential cause of action against Paladin will have far-reaching chilling effects on the rights of free speech and press. See Br. of Amici at 3, 22 ("Allowing this lawsuit to survive will disturb decades of First Amendment jurisprudence and jeopardize free speech from the periphery to the core.... No expression — music, video, books, even newspaper articles — would be safe from civil liability."). That the national media organizations would feel obliged to vigorously defend Paladin's assertion of a constitutional right to intentionally and knowingly assist murderers with technical information which Paladin admits it intended and knew would be used immediately in the commission of murder and other crimes against society is, to say the least, breathtaking. But be that as it may, it should be apparent from the foregoing that the indisputably important First Amendment values that Paladin and amici argue would be imperiled by a decision recognizing potential liability under the peculiar facts of this case will not even arguably be adversely affected by allowing plaintiffs' action against Paladin to proceed. In fact, neither the extensive briefing by the parties and the numerous amici in this case, nor the exhaustive research which the court itself has undertaken, has revealed even a single case that we regard as factually analogous to this case.

Paladin and amici insist that recognizing the existence of a cause of action against Paladin predicated on aiding and abetting will subject broadcasters and publishers to liability whenever someone imitates or "copies" conduct that is either described or depicted in their broadcasts, publications, or movies. This is simply not true. In the "copycat" context, it will presumably never be the case that the broadcaster or publisher actually intends, through its description or depiction, to assist another or others in the commission of violent crime; rather, the information for the dissemination of which liability is sought to be imposed will actually have been misused vis-a-vis the use intended, not, as here, used precisely as intended. It would be difficult to overstate the significance of this difference insofar as the potential liability to which the media might be exposed by our decision herein is concerned.

And, perhaps most importantly, there will almost never be evidence proffered from which a jury even could reasonably conclude that the producer or publisher possessed the actual intent to assist criminal activity. In only the rarest case, as here where the publisher has stipulated in almost taunting defiance that it intended to assist murderers and other criminals, will there be evidence extraneous to the speech itself which would support a finding of the requisite intent; surely few will, as Paladin has, "stand up and proclaim to the world that because they are publishers they have a unique constitutional right to aid and abet murder." Appellant's Reply Br. at 20. Moreover, in contrast to the case before us, in virtually every "copycat" case, there will be lacking in the speech itself any basis for a permissible inference that the "speaker" intended to assist and facilitate the criminal conduct described or depicted. Of course, with few, if any, exceptions, the speech which gives rise to the copycat crime will not directly and affirmatively promote the criminal conduct, even if, in some circumstances, it incidentally glamorizes and thereby indirectly promotes such conduct.

Additionally, not only will a political, informational, educational, entertainment, or other wholly legitimate purpose for the description or depiction be demonstrably apparent; but the description or depiction of the criminality will be of such a character that an inference of impressible intent on the part of the producer or publisher would be unwarranted as a matter of law. So, for example, for almost any broadcast, book, movie, or song that one can imagine, an inference of unlawful motive from the description or depiction of particular criminal conduct therein would almost never be reasonable, for not only will there be (and demonstrably so) a legitimate and lawful purpose for these communications, but the contexts in which the descriptions or depictions appear will themselves negate a purpose on the part of the producer or publisher to assist others in their undertaking of the described or depicted conduct. Compare Miller, 413 U.S. 15, 93 S.Ct. 2607.

Paladin contends that exposing it to liability under the circumstances presented here will necessarily expose broadcasters and publishers of the news, in particular, to liability when persons mimic activity either reported on or captured on film footage and disseminated in the form of broadcast news. Appellee's Br. at 26 n.17. This contention, as well, is categorically wrong. News reporting, we can assume, no matter how explicit it is in its description or depiction of criminal activity, could never serve as a basis for aiding and abetting liability consistent with the First Amendment. It will be self-evident in the context of news reporting, if nowhere else, that neither the intent of the reporter nor the purpose of the report is to facilitate repetition of the crime or other conduct reported upon, but, rather, merely to report on the particular event, and thereby to inform the public.

A decision that Paladin may be liable under the circumstances of this case is not even tantamount to a holding that all publishers of instructional manuals may be liable for the misconduct that ensues when one follows the instructions which appear in those manuals. Admittedly, a holding that Paladin is not entitled to an absolute defense to the plaintiffs' claims here may not bode well for those publishers, if any, of factually detailed instructional books, similar to Hit Man, which are devoted exclusively to teaching the techniques of violent activities that are criminal per se. But, in holding that a defense to liability may not inure to publishers for their dissemination of such manuals of criminal conduct, we do not address ourselves to the potential liability of a publisher for the criminal use of published instructions on activity that is either entirely lawful, or lawful or not depending upon the circumstances of its occurrence. Assuming, as we do, that liability could not be imposed in these circumstances on a finding of mere foreseeability or knowledge that the instructions might be misused for a criminal purpose, the chances that claims arising from the publication of instructional manuals like these can withstand motions for summary judgment directed to the issue of intent seem to us remote indeed, at least absent some substantial confirmation of specific intent like that that exists in this case.

Thus, while the "horribles" paraded before us by Paladin and amici have quite properly prompted us to examine and reexamine the established authorities on which plaintiffs' case firmly rests, we regard them ultimately as but anticipatory of cases wholly unlike the one we must decide today.

Paladin Press in this case has stipulated that it specifically targeted the market of murderers, would-be murderers, and other criminals for sale of its murder manual. Paladin has stipulated both that it had knowledge and that it intended that Hit Man would immediately be used by criminals and would-be criminals in the solicitation, planning, and commission of murder and murder for hire. And Paladin has stipulated that, through publishing and selling Hit Man, it "assisted" Perry in particular in the perpetration of the brutal triple murders for which plaintiffs now seek to hold the publisher liable. Beyond these startling stipulations, it is alleged, and the record would support, that Paladin assisted Perry through the quintessential speech act of providing Perry with detailed factual instructions on how to prepare for, commit, and cover up his murders, instructions which themselves embody not so much as a hint of the theoretical advocacy of principles divorced from action that is the hallmark of protected speech. And it is alleged, and a jury could find, that Paladin's assistance assumed the form of speech with little, if any, purpose beyond the unlawful one of facilitating murder.

Paladin's astonishing stipulations, coupled with the extraordinary comprehensiveness, detail, and clarity of Hit Man's instructions for criminal activity and murder in particular, the boldness of its palpable exhortation to murder, the alarming power and effectiveness of its peculiar form of instruction, the notable absence from its text of the kind of ideas for the protection of which the First Amendment exists, and the book's evident lack of any even arguably legitimate purpose beyond the promotion and teaching of murder, render this case unique in the law. In at least these circumstances, we are confident that the First Amendment does not erect the absolute bar to the imposition of civil liability for which Paladin Press and amici contend. Indeed, to hold that the First Amendment forbids liability in such circumstances as a matter of law would fly in the face of all precedent of which we are aware, not only from the courts of appeals but from the Supreme Court of the United States itself. Hit Man is, we are convinced, the speech that even Justice Douglas, with his unrivaled devotion to the First Amendment, counseled without any equivocation "should be beyond the pale" under a Constitution that reserves to the people the ultimate and necessary authority to adjudge some conduct — and even some speech — fundamentally incompatible with the liberties they have secured unto themselves.

The judgment of the district court is hereby reversed, and the case remanded for trial.

It is so ordered.

## National Endowment for the Arts v. Finley (June 25, 1998)

Justice O'Connor delivered the opinion of the Court.

The National Foundation on the Arts and Humanities Act, as amended in 1990, requires the Chairperson of the National Endowment for the Arts (NEA) to ensure that "artistic excellence and artistic merit are the criteria by which [grant] applications are judged, taking into consideration general standards of decency and respect for the diverse beliefs and values of the American public." 20 U.S.C. § 954(d)(1). In this case, we review the Court of Appeals' determination that §954(d)(1), on its face, impermissibly discriminates on the basis of viewpoint and is void for vagueness under the First and Fifth Amendments. We conclude that §954(d)(1) is facially valid, as it neither inherently interferes with First Amendment rights nor violates constitutional vagueness principles.

I

A

With the establishment of the NEA in 1965, Congress embarked on a "broadly conceived national policy of support for the . . . arts in the United States," see §953(b), pledging federal funds to "help create and sustain not only a climate encouraging freedom of thought, imagination, and inquiry but also the material conditions facilitating the release of ... creative talent." §951(7). The enabling statute vests the NEA with substantial discretion to award grants; it identifies only the broadest funding priorities, including "artistic and cultural significance, giving emphasis to American creativity and cultural diversity," "professional excellence," and the encouragement of "public knowledge, education, understanding, and appreciation of the arts." See §§954(c)(1)—(10).

Applications for NEA funding are initially reviewed by advisory panels composed of experts in the relevant field of the arts. Under the 1990 Amendments to the enabling statute, those panels must reflect "diverse artistic and cultural points of view" and include "wide geographic, ethnic, and minority representation," as well as "lay individuals who are knowledgeable about the arts." §§959(c)(1)—(2). The panels report to the 26-member National Council on the Arts (Council), which, in turn, advises the NEA Chairperson. The Chairperson has the ultimate authority to award grants but may not approve an application as to which the Council has made a negative recommendation. §955(f).

Since 1965, the NEA has distributed over three billion dollars in grants to individuals and organizations, funding that has served as a catalyst for increased state, corporate, and foundation support for the arts. Congress has recently restricted the availability of federal funding for individual artists, confining grants primarily to qualifying organizations and state arts agencies, and constraining sub-granting. See Department of the Interior and Related Agencies Appropriations Act, 1998, Pub. L. 105—83, §329, 111 Stat. 1600. By far the largest portion of the grants distributed in fiscal year 1998 were awarded directly to state arts agencies. In the remaining categories, the most substantial grants were allocated to symphony orchestras, fine arts museums, dance theater foundations, and opera associations. See National Endowment for the Arts, FY 1998 Grants, Creation & Presentation 5—8, 21, 20, 27.

Throughout the NEA's history, only a handful of the agency's roughly 100,000 awards have generated formal complaints about misapplied funds or abuse of the public's trust. Two provocative works, however, prompted public controversy in 1989 and led to congressional revaluation of the NEA's funding priorities and efforts to increase oversight of its grant-making procedures. The Institute of Contemporary Art at the University of Pennsylvania had used $30,000 of a visual arts grant it received from the NEA to fund a 1989 retrospective of photographer Robert Mapplethorpe's work. The exhibit, entitled The Perfect Moment, included homoerotic photographs that several Members of Congress condemned as pornographic. See, e.g., 135 Cong. Rec. 22372 (1989). Members also denounced artist Andres Serrano's work Piss Christ, a photograph of a crucifix immersed in urine. See, e.g., id., at 9789. Serrano had been awarded a $15,000 grant from the Southeast Center for Contemporary Art, an organization that received NEA support.

When considering the NEA's appropriations for fiscal year 1990, Congress reacted to the controversy surrounding the Mapplethorpe and Serrano photographs by eliminating $45,000 from the agency's budget, the precise amount contributed to the two exhibits by NEA grant recipients. Congress also enacted an amendment providing that no NEA funds "may be used to promote, disseminate, or produce materials which in the judgment of [the NEA] may be considered obscene, including but not limited to, depictions of sadomasochism, homoeroticism, the sexual exploitation of children, or individuals engaged in sex acts and which, when taken as a whole, do not have serious literary, artistic, political, or scientific value." Department of the Interior and Related Agencies Appropriations Act, 1990, Pub. L. 101—121, 103 Stat. 738, 738—742. The NEA implemented Congress' mandate by instituting a requirement that all grantees certify in writing that they would not utilize federal funding to engage in projects inconsistent with the criteria in the 1990 appropriations bill. That certification requirement was subsequently invalidated as unconstitutionally vague by a Federal District Court, see Bella Lewitzky Dance Foundation v. Frohnmayer, 754 F. Supp. 774 (CD Cal. 1991), and the NEA did not appeal the decision.

In the 1990 appropriations bill, Congress also agreed to create an Independent Commission of constitutional law scholars to review the NEA's grant-making procedures and assess the possibility of more focused standards for public arts funding. The Commission's report, issued in September 1990, concluded that there is no constitutional obligation to provide arts funding, but also recommended that the NEA rescind the certification requirement and cautioned against legislation setting forth any content restrictions. Instead, the Commission suggested procedural changes to enhance the role of advisory panels and a statutory reaffirmation of "the high place the nation accords to the fostering of mutual respect for the disparate beliefs and values among us." See Independent Commission, Report to Congress on the National Endowment for the Arts 83—91 (Sept. 1990), 3 Record, Doc. No. 151, Exh. K (hereinafter Report to Congress).

Informed by the Commission's recommendations, and cognizant of pending judicial challenges to the funding limitations in the 1990 appropriations bill, Congress debated several proposals to reform the NEA's grant-making process when it considered the agency's reauthorization in the fall of 1990. The House rejected the Crane Amendment, which would have virtually eliminated the NEA, see 136 Cong. Rec. 28656— 28657 (1990), and the Rohrabacher Amendment, which would have introduced a prohibition on awarding any grants that could be used to "promote, distribute, disseminate, or produce matter that has the purpose or effect of denigrating the beliefs, tenets, or objects of a particular religion" or "of denigrating an individual, or group of individuals, on the basis of race, sex, handicap, or national origin," id., at 28657—28664. Ultimately, Congress adopted the Williams/Coleman Amendment, a bipartisan compromise between Members opposing any funding restrictions and those favoring some guidance to the agency. In relevant part, the Amendment became §954(d)(1), which directs the Chairperson, in establishing procedures to judge the artistic merit of grant applications, to "tak[e] into consideration general standards of decency and respect for the diverse beliefs and values of the American public."*

The NEA has not promulgated any official interpretation of the provision, but in December 1990, the Council unanimously adopted a resolution to implement §954(d)(1) merely by ensuring that the members of the advisory panels that conduct the initial review of grant applications represent geographic, ethnic, and aesthetic diversity. See Minutes of the Dec. 1990 Retreat of the National Council on the Arts, reprinted in App. 12—13; Transcript of the Dec. 1990 Retreat of the National Council on the Arts, reprinted in id., 32—33. John Frohnmayer, then Chairperson of the NEA, also declared that he would "count on [the] procedures" ensuring diverse membership on the peer review panels to fulfill Congress' mandate. See id., at 40.

B

The four individual respondents in this case, Karen Finley, John Fleck, Holly Hughes, and Tim Miller, are performance artists who applied for NEA grants before §954(d)(1) was enacted. An advisory panel recommended approval of respondents' projects, both initially and after receiving Frohnmayer's request to reconsider three of the applications. A majority of the Council subsequently recommended disapproval, and in June 1990, the NEA informed respondents that they had been denied funding. Respondents filed suit, alleging that the NEA had violated their First Amendment rights by rejecting the applications on political grounds, had failed to follow statutory procedures by basing the denial on criteria other than those set forth in the NEA's enabling statute, and had breached the confidentiality of their grant applications through the release of quotations to the press, in violation of the Privacy Act of 1974, 5 U.S.C. § 552(a). Respondents sought restoration of the recommended grants or reconsideration of their applications, as well as damages for the alleged Privacy Act violations. When Congress enacted §954(d)(1), respondents, now joined by the National Association of Artists' Organizations (NAAO), amended their complaint to challenge the provision as void for vagueness and impermissibly viewpoint based. First Amended Complaint, 1 Record, Doc. No. 16, p. 1 (Mar. 27, 1991).

The District Court denied the NEA's motion for judgment on the pleadings, 795 F. Supp. 1457, 1463—1468 (CD Cal. 1992), and, after discovery, the NEA agreed to settle the individual respondents' statutory and as-applied constitutional claims by paying the artists the amount of the vetoed grants, damages, and attorney's fees. See Stipulation and Settlement Agreement, 6 Record, Doc. No. 128, pp. 3—5 (June 11, 1993).

The District Court then granted summary judgment in favor of respondents on their facial constitutional challenge to §954(d)(1) and enjoined enforcement of the provision. See 795 F. Supp., at 1476. The court rejected the argument that the NEA could comply with §954(d)(1) by structuring the grant selection process to provide for diverse advisory panels. Id., at 1471. The provision, the court stated, "fails adequately to notify applicants of what is required of them or to circumscribe NEA discretion." Id., at 1472. Reasoning that "the very nature of our pluralistic society is that there are an infinite number of values and beliefs, and correlatively, there may be no national 'general standards of decency,' " the court concluded that §954(d)(1) "cannot be given effect consistent with the Fifth Amendment's due process requirement." Id., at 1471—1472 (citing Grayned v. City of Rockford, 408 U.S. 104, 108—109 (1972)). Drawing an analogy between arts funding and public universities, the court further ruled that the First Amendment constrains the NEA's grant-making process, and that because §954(d)(1) "clearly reaches a substantial amount of protected speech," it is impermissibly overbroad on its face. 795 F. Supp., at 1476. The Government did not seek a stay of the District Court's injunction, and consequently the NEA has not applied §954(d)(1) since June 1992.

A divided panel of the Court of Appeals affirmed the District Court's ruling. 100 F.3d 671 (CA9 1996). The majority agreed with the District Court that the NEA was compelled by the adoption of §954(d)(1) to alter its grant-making procedures to ensure that applications are judged according to the "decency and respect" criteria. The Chairperson, the court reasoned, "has no discretion to ignore this obligation, enforce only part of it, or give it a cramped construction." Id., at 680. Concluding that the "decency and respect" criteria are not "susceptible to objective definition," the court held that §954(d)(1) "gives rise to the danger of arbitrary and discriminatory application" and is void for vagueness under the First and Fifth Amendments. Id., at 680–681. In the alternative, the court ruled that §954(d)(1) violates the First Amendment's prohibition on viewpoint-based restrictions on protected speech. Government funding of the arts, the court explained, is both a "traditional sphere of free expression," Rust v. Sullivan, 500 U.S. 173, 200 (1991), and an area in which the Government has stated its intention to "encourage a diversity of views from private speakers," Rosenberger v. Rector and Visitors of Univ. of Va., 515 U.S. 819, 834 (1995). 100 F.3d, at 681–682. Accordingly, finding that §954(d)(1) "has a speech-based restriction as its sole rationale and operative principle," Rosenberger, supra, at 834, and noting the NEA's failure to articulate a compelling interest for the provision, the court declared it facially invalid. 100 F.3d, at 683.

The dissent asserted that the First Amendment protects artists' rights to express themselves as indecently and disrespectfully as they like, but does not compel the Government to fund that speech. Id., at 684 (Kleinfeld, J., dissenting). The challenged provision, the dissent contended, did not prohibit the NEA from funding indecent or offensive art, but merely required the agency to consider the "decency and respect" criteria in the grant selection process. Id., at 689–690. Moreover, according to the dissent's reasoning, the vagueness principles applicable to the direct regulation of speech have no bearing on the selective award of prizes, and the Government may draw distinctions based on content and viewpoint in making its funding decisions. Id., at 684–688. Three judges dissented from the denial of rehearing en banc, maintaining that the panel's decision gave the statute an "implausible construction," applied the " 'void for vagueness' doctrine where it does not belong," and extended "First Amendment principles to a situation that the First Amendment doesn't cover." 112 F.3d 1015, 1016–1017 (CA9 1997).

We granted certiorari, 522 U.S. __ (1997), and now reverse the judgment of the Court of Appeals.

II

A

Respondents raise a facial constitutional challenge to §954(d)(1), and consequently they confront "a heavy burden" in advancing their claim. Rust, supra, at 183. Facial invalidation "is, manifestly, strong medicine" that "has been employed by the Court sparingly and only as a last resort." Broadrick v. Oklahoma, 413 U.S. 601, 613 (1973); see also FW/PBS, Inc. v. Dallas, 493 U.S. 215, 223 (1990) (noting that "facial challenges to legislation are generally disfavored"). To prevail, respondents must demonstrate a substantial risk that application of the provision will lead to the suppression of speech. See Broadrick, supra, at 615.

Respondents argue that the provision is a paradigmatic example of viewpoint discrimination because it rejects any artistic speech that either fails to respect mainstream values or offends standards of decency. The premise of respondents' claim is that §954(d)(1) constrains the agency's ability to fund certain categories of artistic expression. The NEA, however, reads the provision as merely hortatory, and contends that it stops well short of an absolute restriction. Section 954(d)(1) adds "considerations" to the grant-making process; it does not preclude awards to projects that might be deemed "indecent" or "disrespectful," nor place conditions on grants, or even specify that those factors must be given any particular weight in reviewing an application. Indeed, the agency asserts that it has adequately implemented §954(d)(1) merely by ensuring the representation of various backgrounds and points of view on the advisory panels that analyze grant applications. See Declaration of Randolph McAusland, Deputy Chairman for Programs at the NEA, reprinted in App. 79 (stating that the NEA implements the provision "by ensuring that the peer review panels represent a variety of geographical areas, aesthetic views, professions, areas of expertise, races and ethnic groups, and gender, and include a lay person"). We do not decide whether the NEA's view—that the formulation of diverse advisory panels is sufficient to comply with Congress' command—is in fact a reasonable reading of the statute. It is clear, however, that the text of §954(d)(1) imposes no categorical requirement. The advisory language stands in sharp contrast to congressional efforts to prohibit the funding of certain classes of speech. When Congress has in fact intended to affirmatively constrain the NEA's grant-making authority, it has done so in no uncertain terms. See §954(d)(2) ("[O]bscenity is without artistic merit, is not protected speech, and shall not be funded").

Furthermore, like the plain language of §954(d), the political context surrounding the adoption of the "decency and respect" clause is inconsistent with respondents' assertion that the provision compels the NEA to deny funding on the basis of viewpoint discriminatory criteria. The legislation was a bipartisan proposal introduced as a counterweight to amendments aimed at eliminating the NEA's funding or substantially constraining its grant-making authority. See, e.g., 136 Cong. Rec. 28626, 28632, 28634 (1990). The Independent Commission had cautioned Congress against the adoption of distinct viewpoint-based standards for funding, and the Commission's report suggests that " additional criteria for selection, if any, should be incorporated as part of the selection process (perhaps as part of a definition of 'artistic excellence'), rather than isolated and treated as exogenous considerations." Report to Congress, at 89. In keeping with that recommendation, the criteria in §954(d)(1) inform the assessment of artistic merit, but Congress declined to disallow any particular viewpoints. As the sponsors of §954(d)(1) noted in urging rejection of the Rohrabacher Amendment, "if we start down that road of prohibiting categories of expression, categories which are indeed constitutionally protected speech, where do we end? Where one Member's aversions end, others with different sensibilities and with different values begin." 136 Cong. Rec. 28624 (statement of Rep. Coleman); see also id., at 28663 (statement of Rep. Williams) (arguing that the Rohrabacher Amendment would prevent the funding of Jasper Johns' flag series, "The Merchant of Venice," "Chorus Line," "Birth of a Nation," and the "Grapes of

Wrath"). In contrast, before the vote on §954(d)(1), one of its sponsors stated: "If we have done one important thing in this amendment, it is this. We have maintained the integrity of freedom of expression in the United States." Id., at 28674.

That §954(d)(1) admonishes the NEA merely to take "decency and respect" into consideration, and that the legislation was aimed at reforming procedures rather than precluding speech, undercut respondents' argument that the provision inevitably will be utilized as a tool for invidious viewpoint discrimination. In cases where we have struck down legislation as facially unconstitutional, the dangers were both more evident and more substantial. In R. A. V. v. St. Paul, 505 U.S. 377 (1992), for example, we invalidated on its face a municipal ordinance that defined as a criminal offense the placement of a symbol on public or private property " 'which one knows or has reasonable grounds to know arouses anger, alarm, or resentment in others on the basis of race, color, creed, religion, or gender.' " See id., at 380. That provision set forth a clear penalty, proscribed views on particular "disfavored subjects," id., at 391, and suppressed "distinctive idea[s], conveyed by a distinctive message," id., at 393.

In contrast, the "decency and respect" criteria do not silence speakers by expressly "threaten[ing] censorship of ideas." See ibid. Thus, we do not perceive a realistic danger that §954(d)(1) will compromise First Amendment values. As respondents' own arguments demonstrate, the considerations that the provision introduces, by their nature, do not engender the kind of directed viewpoint discrimination that would prompt this Court to invalidate a statute on its face. Respondents assert, for example, that "[o]ne would be hard-pressed to find two people in the United States who could agree on what the 'diverse beliefs and values of the American public' are, much less on whether a particular work of art 'respects' them"; and they claim that " '[d]ecency' is likely to mean something very different to a septegenarian in Tuscaloosa and a teenager in Las Vegas." Brief for Respondents 41. The NEA likewise views the considerations enumerated in §954(d)(1) as susceptible to multiple interpretations. See Department of the Interior and Related Agencies Appropriations for 1992, Hearing before the Subcommittee on Interior and Related Agencies of the House Committee on Appropriations, 102d Cong., 1st Sess., 234 (1991) (testimony of John Frohnmayer) ("[N]o one individual is wise enough to be able to consider general standards of decency and the diverse values and beliefs of the American people all by him or herself. These are group decisions"). Accordingly, the provision does not introduce considerations that, in practice, would effectively preclude or punish the expression of particular views. Indeed, one could hardly anticipate how "decency" or "respect" would bear on grant applications in categories such as funding for symphony orchestras.

Respondents' claim that the provision is facially unconstitutional may be reduced to the argument that the criteria in §954(d)(1) are sufficiently subjective that the agency could utilize them to engage in viewpoint discrimination. Given the varied interpretations of the criteria and the vague exhortation to "take them into consideration," it seems unlikely that this provision will introduce any greater element of selectivity than the determination of "artistic excellence" itself. And we are reluctant, in any event, to invalidate legislation "on the basis of its hypothetical application to situations not before the Court." FCC v. Pacifica Foundation, 438 U.S. 726, 743 (1978).

The NEA's enabling statute contemplates a number of indisputably constitutional applications for both the "decency" prong of §954(d)(1) and its reference to "respect for the diverse beliefs and values of the American public." Educational programs are central to the NEA's mission. See §951(9) ("Americans should receive in school, background and preparation in the arts and humanities"); §954(c)(5) (listing "projects and productions that will encourage public knowledge, education, understanding, and appreciation of the arts" among the NEA's funding priorities); National Endowment for the Arts, FY 1999 Application Guidelines 18—19 (describing "Education & Access" category); Brief for Twenty-six Arts, Broadcast, Library, Museum, and Publishing Amici Curiae 5, n. 2 (citing NEA Strategic Plan FY 1997—FY 2002, which identifies children's festivals and museums, art education, at-risk youth projects, and artists in schools as examples of the NEA's activities). And it is well established that "decency" is a permissible factor where "educational suitability" motivates its consideration. Board of Ed., Island Trees Union Free School Dist. No. 26 v. Pico, 457 U.S. 853, 871 (1982); see also Bethel School Dist. No. 403 v. Fraser, 478 U.S. 675, 683 (1986) ("Surely it is a highly appropriate function of public school education to prohibit the use of vulgar and offensive terms in public discourse").

Permissible applications of the mandate to consider "respect for the diverse beliefs and values of the American public" are also apparent. In setting forth the purposes of the NEA, Congress explained that "[i]t is vital to democracy to honor and preserve its multicultural artistic heritage." §951(10). The agency expressly takes diversity into account, giving special consideration to "projects and productions . . . that reach, or reflect the culture of, a minority, inner city, rural, or tribal community," §954(c)(4), as well as projects that generally emphasize "cultural diversity," §954(c)(1). Respondents do not contend that the criteria in §954(d)(1) are impermissibly applied when they may be justified, as the statute contemplates, with respect to a project's intended audience.

We recognize, of course, that reference to these permissible applications would not alone be sufficient to sustain the statute against respondents' First Amendment challenge. But neither are we persuaded that, in other applications, the language of §954(d)(1) itself will give rise to the suppression of protected expression. Any content-based considerations that may be taken into account in the grant-making process are a consequence of the nature of arts funding. The NEA has limited resources and it must deny the majority of the grant applications that it receives, including many that propose "artistically excellent" projects. The agency may decide to fund particular projects for a wide variety of reasons, "such as the technical proficiency of the artist, the creativity of the work, the anticipated public interest in or appreciation of the work, the work's contemporary relevance, its educational value, its suitability for or appeal to special audiences (such as children or the disabled), its service to a rural or isolated community, or even simply that the work could increase public knowledge of an art form." Brief for Petitioners 32. As the dissent below noted, it would be "impossible to have a highly selective grant program without denying money to a large amount of constitutionally protected expression." 100 F.3d, at 685 (Kleinfeld, J., dissenting). The "very assumption" of the NEA is that grants will be awarded according to the "artistic worth of competing applications," and absolute neutrality is simply "inconceivable." Advocates for the Arts v. Thomson, 532 F.2d 792, 795–796 (CA1), cert. denied, 429 U.S. 894 (1976).

Respondent's reliance on our decision in Rosenberger v. Rector and Visitors of Univ. of Va., 515 U.S. 819 (1995), is therefore misplaced. In Rosenberger, a public university declined to authorize disbursements from its Student Activities Fund to finance the printing of a Christian student newspaper. We held that by subsidizing the Student Activities Fund, the University had created a limited public forum, from which it impermissibly excluded all publications with religious editorial viewpoints. Id., at 837. Although the scarcity of NEA funding does not distinguish this case from Rosenberger, see id., at 835, the competitive process according to which the grants are allocated does. In the context of arts funding, in contrast to many other subsidies, the Government does not indiscriminately "encourage a diversity of views from private speakers," id., at 834. The NEA's mandate is to make aesthetic judgments, and the inherently content-based "excellence" threshold for NEA support sets it apart from the subsidy at issue in Rosenberger–which was available to all student organizations that were " 'related to the educational purpose of the University,' " id., at 824–and from comparably objective decisions on allocating public benefits, such as access to a school auditorium or a municipal theater, see Lamb's Chapel v. Center Moriches Union Free School Dist., 508 U.S. 384, 386 (1993); Southeastern Promotions, Ltd. v. Conrad, 420 U.S. 546, 555 (1975), or the second class mailing privileges available to " 'all newspapers and other periodical publications,' " see Hannegan v. Esquire, Inc., 327 U.S. 146, 148, n. 1 (1946).

Respondents do not allege discrimination in any particular funding decision. (In fact, after filing suit to challenge §954(d)(1), two of the individual respondents received NEA grants. See Exhibit 35 to Heins Declaration, 3 Record, Doc. Nos. 275 and 276 (Sept. 30, 1991 letters from the NEA informing respondents Hughes and Miller that they had been awarded Solo Performance Theater Artist Fellowships).) Thus, we have no occasion here to address an as-applied challenge in a situation where the denial of a grant may be shown to be the product of invidious viewpoint discrimination. If the NEA were to leverage its power to award subsidies on the basis of subjective criteria into a penalty on disfavored viewpoints, then we would confront a different case. We have stated that, even in the provision of subsidies, the Government may not "ai[m] at the suppression of dangerous ideas," Regan, supra, 461 U.S., at 550 (internal quotation marks omitted), and if a subsidy were "manipulated" to have a "coercive effect," then relief could be appropriate. See Arkansas Writers' Project, Inc. v. Ragland, 481 U.S. 221, 237 (1987) (Scalia, J., dissenting); see also Leathers v. Medlock, 499 U.S. 439, 447 (1991) ("[D]ifferential taxation of First Amendment speakers is constitutionally suspect when it threatens to suppress the expression of particular ideas or viewpoints"). In addition, as the NEA itself concedes, a more pressing constitutional question would arise if government funding resulted in the imposition of a disproportionate burden calculated to drive "certain ideas or viewpoints from the marketplace." Simon & Schuster, Inc. v. Members of N. Y. State Crime Victims Bd., 502 U.S. 105, 116 (1991); see Brief for Petitioners 38, n. 12. Unless and until §954(d)(1) is applied in a manner that raises concern about the suppression of disfavored viewpoints, however, we uphold the constitutionality of the provision. Cf. Red Lion Broadcasting Co. v. FCC, 395 U.S. 367, 396 (1969) ("[W]e will not now pass upon the constitutionality of these regulations by envisioning the most extreme applications conceivable, but will deal with those problems if and when they arise") (internal citation omitted).

B

Finally, although the First Amendment certainly has application in the subsidy context, we note that the Government may allocate competitive funding according to criteria that would be impermissible were direct regulation of speech or a criminal penalty at stake. So long as legislation does not infringe on other constitutionally protected rights, Congress has wide latitude to set spending priorities. See Regan v. Taxation with Representation of Wash., 461 U.S. 540, 549 (1983). In the 1990 Amendments that incorporated §954(d)(1), Congress modified the declaration of purpose in the NEA's enabling act to provide that arts funding should "contribute to public support and confidence in the use of taxpayer funds," and that "[p]ublic funds ... must ultimately serve public purposes the Congress defines." §951(5). And as we held in Rust, Congress may "selectively fund a program to encourage certain activities it believes to be in the public interest, without at the same time funding an alternative program which seeks to deal with the problem in another way." 500 U.S., at 193. In doing so, "the Government has not discriminated on the basis of viewpoint; it has merely chosen to fund one activity to the exclusion of the other." Ibid.; see also Maher v. Roe, 432 U.S. 464, 475 (1977) ("There is a basic difference between direct state interference with a protected activity and state encouragement of an alternative activity consonant with legislative policy").

III

The lower courts also erred in invalidating §954(d)(1) as unconstitutionally vague. Under the First and Fifth Amendments, speakers are protected from arbitrary and discriminatory enforcement of vague standards. See NAACP v. Button, 371 U.S. 415, 432−433 (1963). The terms of the provision are undeniably opaque, and if they appeared in a criminal statute or regulatory scheme, they could raise substantial vagueness concerns. It is unlikely, however, that speakers will be compelled to steer too far clear of any "forbidden area" in the context of grants of this nature. Compare Board of Airport Comm'rs of Los Angeles v. Jews for Jesus, Inc., 482 U.S. 569, 574 (1987) (facially invalidating a flat ban on any "First Amendment" activities in an airport); Hoffman Estates v. Flipside, Hoffman Estates, Inc., 455 U.S. 489, 499 (1982) ("prohibitory and stigmatizing effect" of a "quasi-criminal" ordinance relevant to the vagueness analysis); Grayned v. City of Rockford, 408 U.S., at 108 (requiring clear lines between "lawful and unlawful" conduct). We recognize, as a practical matter, that artists may conform their speech to what they believe to be the decision-making criteria in order to acquire funding. See Statement of Charlotte Murphy, Executive Director of NAAO, reprinted in App. 21– 22. But when the Government is acting as patron rather than as sovereign, the consequences of imprecision are not constitutionally severe.

In the context of selective subsidies, it is not always feasible for Congress to legislate with clarity. Indeed, if this statute is unconstitutionally vague, then so too are all government programs awarding scholarships and grants on the basis of subjective criteria such as "excellence." See, e.g., 2 U.S.C. § 802 (establishing the Congressional Award Program to "promote initiative, achievement, and excellence among youths in the areas of public service, personal development, and physical and expedition fitness"); 20 U.S.C. § 956(c)(1) (providing funding to the National Endowment for the Humanities to promote "progress and scholarship in the humanities"); §1134h(a) (authorizing the Secretary of Education to award fellowships to "students of superior ability selected on the basis of demonstrated achievement and exceptional promise"); 22 U.S.C. § 2452(a) (authorizing the award of Fulbright grants to "strengthen international cooperative relations"); 42 U.S.C. § 7382c (authorizing the Secretary of Energy to recognize teachers for "excellence in mathematics or science education"). To accept respondents' vagueness argument would be to call into question the constitutionality of these valuable government programs and countless others like them.

Section 954(d)(1) merely adds some imprecise considerations to an already subjective selection process. It does not, on its face, impermissibly infringe on First or Fifth Amendment rights. Accordingly, the judgment of the Court of Appeals is reversed and the case is remanded for further proceedings consistent with this opinion.

It is so ordered.

### Notes

1. * Title 20 U.S.C. § 954(d) provides in full that: "No payment shall be made under this section except upon application therefor which is submitted to the National Endowment for the Arts in accordance with regulations issued and procedures established by the Chairperson. In establishing such regulations and procedures, the Chairperson shall ensure that– "(1) artistic excellence and artistic merit are the criteria by which applications are judged, taking into consideration general standards of decency and respect for the diverse beliefs and values of the American public; and "(2) applications are consistent with the purposes of this section. Such regulations and procedures shall clearly indicate that obscenity is without artistic merit, is not protected speech, and shall not be funded."

## Aurelia Davis v. Monroe County Board of Education (May 24, 1999)

Justice O'Connor delivered the opinion of the Court.

Petitioner brought suit against the Monroe County Board of Education and other defendants, alleging that her fifth-grade daughter had been the victim of sexual harassment by another student in her class. Among petitioner's claims was a claim for monetary and injunctive relief under Title IX of the Education Amendments of 1972 (Title IX), 86 Stat. 373, as amended, 20 U.S.C. § 1681 et seq. The District Court dismissed petitioner's Title IX claim on the ground that "student-on-student," or peer, harassment provides no ground for a private cause of action under the statute. The Court of Appeals for the Eleventh Circuit, sitting en banc, affirmed. We consider here whether a private damages action may lie against the school board in cases of student-on-student harassment. We conclude that it may, but only where the funding recipient acts with deliberate indifference to known acts of harassment in its programs or activities. Moreover, we conclude that such an action will lie only for harassment that is so severe, pervasive, and objectively offensive that it effectively bars the victim's access to an educational opportunity or benefit.

I

Petitioner's Title IX claim was dismissed under Federal Rule of Civil Procedure 12(b)(6) for failure to state a claim upon which relief could be granted. Accordingly, in reviewing the legal sufficiency of petitioner's cause of action, "we must assume the truth of the material facts as alleged in the complaint." Summit Health, Ltd. v. Pinhas, 500 U.S. 322, 325 (1991).

A

Petitioner's minor daughter, LaShonda, was allegedly the victim of a prolonged pattern of sexual harassment by one of her fifth-grade classmates at Hubbard Elementary School, a public school in Monroe County, Georgia. According to petitioner's complaint, the harassment began in December 1992, when the classmate, G. F., attempted to touch LaShonda's breasts and genital area and made vulgar statements such as " 'I want to get in bed with you' " and " 'I want to feel your boobs.' " Complaint ¶7. Similar conduct allegedly occurred on or about January 4 and January 20, 1993. Ibid. LaShonda reported each of these incidents to her mother and to her classroom teacher, Diane Fort. Ibid. Petitioner, in turn, also contacted Fort, who allegedly assured petitioner that the school principal, Bill Querry, had been informed of the incidents. Ibid. Petitioner contends that, notwithstanding these reports, no disciplinary action was taken against G. F. Id., ¶16.

G. F.'s conduct allegedly continued for many months. In early February, G. F. purportedly placed a door stop in his pants and proceeded to act in a sexually suggestive manner toward LaShonda during physical education class. Id., ¶8. LaShonda reported G. F.'s behavior to her physical education teacher, Whit Maples. Ibid. Approximately one week later, G. F. again allegedly engaged in harassing behavior, this time while under the supervision of another classroom teacher, Joyce Pippin. Id., ¶9. Again, LaShonda allegedly reported the incident to the teacher, and again petitioner contacted the teacher to follow up. Ibid.

Petitioner alleges that G. F. once more directed sexually harassing conduct toward LaShonda in physical education class in early March, and that LaShonda reported the incident to both Maples and Pippen. Id., ¶10. In mid-April 1993, G. F. allegedly rubbed his body against LaShonda in the school hallway in what LaShonda considered a sexually suggestive manner, and LaShonda again reported the matter to Fort. Id., ¶11.

The string of incidents finally ended in mid-May, when G. F. was charged with, and pleaded guilty to, sexual battery for his misconduct. Id., ¶14. The complaint alleges that LaShonda had suffered during the months of harassment, however; specifically, her previously high grades allegedly dropped as she became unable to concentrate on her studies, id., ¶15, and, in April 1993, her father discovered that she had written a suicide note, ibid. The complaint further alleges that, at one point, LaShonda told petitioner that she " 'didn't know how much longer she could keep [G. F.] off her.' " Id., ¶12.

Nor was LaShonda G. F.'s only victim; it is alleged that other girls in the class fell prey to G. F.'s conduct. Id., ¶16. At one point, in fact, a group composed of LaShonda and other female students tried to speak with Principal Querry about G. F.'s behavior. Id., ¶10. According to the complaint, however, a teacher denied the students' request with the statement, " 'If [Querry] wants you, he'll call you.' " Ibid.

Petitioner alleges that no disciplinary action was taken in response to G. F.'s behavior toward LaShonda. Id., ¶16. In addition to her conversations with Fort and Pippen, petitioner alleges that she spoke with Principal Querry in mid-May 1993. When petitioner inquired as to what action the school intended to take against G. F., Querry simply stated, " 'I guess I'll have to threaten him a little bit harder.' " Id., ¶12. Yet, petitioner alleges, at no point during the many months of his reported misconduct was G. F. disciplined for harassment. Id., ¶16. Indeed, Querry allegedly asked petitioner why LaShonda " 'was the only one complaining.' " Id., ¶12.

Nor, according to the complaint, was any effort made to separate G. F. and LaShonda. Id., ¶16. On the contrary, notwithstanding LaShonda's frequent complaints, only after more than three months of reported harassment was she even permitted to change her classroom seat so that she was no longer seated next to G. F. Id., ¶13. Moreover, petitioner alleges that, at the time of the events in question, the Monroe County Board of Education (Board) had not instructed its personnel on how to respond to peer sexual harassment and had not established a policy on the issue. Id., ¶17.

B

On May 4, 1994, petitioner filed suit in the United States District Court for the Middle District of Georgia against the Board, Charles Dumas, the school district's superintendent, and Principal Querry. The complaint alleged that the Board is a recipient of federal funding for purposes of Title IX, that "[t]he persistent sexual advances and harassment by the student G. F. upon [LaShonda] interfered with her ability to attend school and perform her studies and activities," and that "[t]he deliberate indifference by Defendants to the unwelcome sexual advances of a student upon LaShonda created an intimidating, hostile, offensive and abus[ive] school environment in violation of Title IX." Id., ¶¶27, 28. The complaint sought compensatory and punitive damages, attorney's fees, and injunctive relief. Id., ¶32.

The defendants (all respondents here) moved to dismiss petitioner's complaint under Federal Rule of Civil Procedure 12(b)(6) for failure to state a claim upon which relief could be granted, and the District Court granted respondents' motion. See 862 F. Supp. 363, 368 (MD Ga. 1994). With regard to petitioner's claims under Title IX, the court dismissed the claims against individual defendants on the ground that only federally funded educational institutions are subject to liability in private causes of action under Title IX. Id., at 367. As for the Board, the court concluded that Title IX provided no basis for liability absent an allegation "that the Board or an employee of the Board had any role in the harassment." Ibid.

Petitioner appealed the District Court's decision dismissing her Title IX claim against the Board, and a panel of the Court of Appeals for the Eleventh Circuit reversed. 74 F.3d 1186, 1195 (1996). Borrowing from Title VII law, a majority of the panel determined that student-on-student harassment stated a cause of action against the Board under Title IX: "[W]e conclude that as Title VII encompasses a claim for damages due to a sexually hostile working environment created by co-workers and tolerated by the employer, Title IX encompasses a claim for damages due to a sexually hostile educational environment created by a fellow student or students when the supervising authorities knowingly fail to act to eliminate the harassment." Id., at 1193. The Eleventh Circuit panel recognized that petitioner sought to state a claim based on school "officials' failure to take action to stop the offensive acts of those over whom the officials exercised control," ibid., and the court concluded that petitioner had alleged facts sufficient to support a claim for hostile environment sexual harassment on this theory, id., at 1195.

The Eleventh Circuit granted the Board's motion for rehearing en banc, 91 F.3d 1418 (1996), and affirmed the District Court's decision to dismiss petitioner's Title IX claim against the Board, 120 F.3d 1390 (1998). The en banc court relied, primarily, on the theory that Title IX was passed pursuant to Congress' legislative authority under the Constitution's Spending Clause, U.S. Const., Art I, §8, cl. 1, and that the statute therefore must provide potential recipients of federal education funding with "unambiguous notice of the conditions they are assuming when they accept" it. 120 F.3d, at 1399. Title IX, the court reasoned, provides recipients with notice that they must stop their employees from engaging in discriminatory conduct, but the statute fails to provide a recipient with sufficient notice of a duty to prevent student-on-student harassment. Id., at 1401.

Writing in dissent, four judges urged that the statute, by declining to identify the perpetrator of discrimination, encompasses misconduct by third parties: "The identity of the perpetrator is simply irrelevant under the language" of the statute. Id., at 1412 (Barkett, J., dissenting). The plain language, the dissenters reasoned, also provides recipients with sufficient notice that a failure to respond to student-on-student harassment could trigger liability for the district. Id., at 1414.

We granted certiorari, 524 U.S. _____ (1998), in order to resolve a conflict in the Circuits over whether, and under what circumstances, a recipient of federal educational funds can be liable in a private damages action arising from student-on-student sexual harassment, compare 120 F.3d 1390 (CA11 1998) (case below), and Rowinsky v. Bryan Independent School Dist., 80 F.3d 1006, 1008 (CA5) (holding that private damages action for student-on-student harassment is available under Title IX only where funding recipient responds to these claims differently based on gender of victim), cert. denied, 519 U.S. 861 (1996), with Doe v. University of Illinois, 138 F.3d 653, 668 (CA7 1998) (upholding private damages action under Title IX for funding recipient's inadequate response to known student-on-student harassment), cert. pending, No. 98—126, Brzonkala v. Virginia Polytechnic Institute and State University, 132 F.3d 949, 960—961 (CA4 1997) (same), vacated and District Court decision affirmed en banc, 169 F.3d 820 (CA4 1999) (not addressing merits of Title IX hostile environment sexual harassment claim and directing District Court to hold this claim in abeyance pending this Court's decision in the instant case), and Oona, R. S. v. McCaffrey, 143 F.3d 473, 478 (CA9 1998) (rejecting qualified immunity claim and concluding that Title IX duty to respond to student-on-student harassment was clearly established by 1992—1993), cert. pending, No. 98—101. We now reverse.

II

Title IX provides, with certain exceptions not at issue here, that

"[n]o person in the United States shall, on the basis of sex, be excluded from participation in, be denied the benefits of, or be subjected to discrimination under any education program or activity receiving Federal financial assistance." 20 U.S.C. § 1681(a).

Congress authorized an administrative enforcement scheme for Title IX. Federal departments or agencies with the authority to provide financial assistance are entrusted to promulgate rules, regulations, and orders to enforce the objectives of §1681, see §1682, and these departments or agencies may rely on "any . . . means authorized by law," including the termination of funding, ibid., to give effect to the statute's restrictions.

There is no dispute here that the Board is a recipient of federal education funding for Title IX purposes. 74 F.3d, at 1189. Nor do respondents support an argument that student-on-student harassment cannot rise to the level of "discrimination" for purposes of Title IX. Rather, at issue here is the question whether a recipient of federal education funding may be liable for damages under Title IX under any circumstances for discrimination in the form of student-on-student sexual harassment.

A

Petitioner urges that Title IX's plain language compels the conclusion that the statute is intended to bar recipients of federal funding from permitting this form of discrimination in their programs or activities. She emphasizes that the statute prohibits a student from being "subjected to discrimination under any education program or activity receiving Federal financial assistance." 20 U.S.C. § 1681 (emphasis supplied). It is Title IX's "unmistakable focus on the benefited class," Cannon v. University of Chicago, 441

U.S. 677, 691 (1979), rather than the perpetrator, that, in petitioner's view, compels the conclusion that the statute works to protect students from the discriminatory misconduct of their peers.

Here, however, we are asked to do more than define the scope of the behavior that Title IX proscribes. We must determine whether a district's failure to respond to student-on-student harassment in its schools can support a private suit for money damages. See Gebser v. Lago Vista Independent School Dist., 524 U.S. 274, 283 (1998) ("In this case, . . . petitioners seek not just to establish a Title IX violation but to recover damages . . ."). This Court has indeed recognized an implied private right of action under Title IX, see Cannon v. University of Chicago, supra, and we have held that money damages are available in such suits, Franklin v. Gwinnett County Public Schools, 503 U.S. 60 (1992). Because we have repeatedly treated Title IX as legislation enacted pursuant to Congress' authority under the Spending Clause, however, see, e.g., Gebser v. Lago Vista Independent School Dist., supra, at 287 (Title IX); Franklin v. Gwinnett County Public Schools, supra, at 74–75, and n. 8 (Title IX); see also Guardians Assn. v. Civil Serv. Comm'n of New York City, 463 U.S. 582, 598–599 (1983) (opinion of White, J.) (Title VI), private damages actions are available only where recipients of federal funding had adequate notice that they could be liable for the conduct at issue. When Congress acts pursuant to its spending power, it generates legislation "much in the nature of a contract: in return for federal funds, the States agree to comply with federally imposed conditions." Pennhurst State School and Hospital v. Halderman, 451 U.S. 1, 17 (1981). In interpreting language in spending legislation, we thus "insis[t] that Congress speak with a clear voice," recognizing that "[t]here can, of course, be no knowing acceptance [of the terms of the putative contract] if a State is unaware of the conditions [imposed by the legislation] or is unable to ascertain what is expected of it." Ibid.; see also id., at 24–25.

Invoking Pennhurst, respondents urge that Title IX provides no notice that recipients of federal educational funds could be liable in damages for harm arising from student-on-student harassment. Respondents contend, specifically, that the statute only proscribes misconduct by grant recipients, not third parties. Respondents argue, moreover, that it would be contrary to the very purpose of Spending Clause legislation to impose liability on a funding recipient for the misconduct of third parties, over whom recipients exercise little control. See also Rowinsky v. Bryan Independent School Dist., 80 F.3d, at 1013.

We agree with respondents that a recipient of federal funds may be liable in damages under Title IX only for its own misconduct. The recipient itself must "exclud[e] [persons] from participation in, . . . den[y] [persons] the benefits of, or . . . subjec[t] [persons] to discrimination under" its "program[s] or activit[ies]" in order to be liable under Title IX. The Government's enforcement power may only be exercised against the funding recipient, see §1682, and we have not extended damages liability under Title IX to parties outside the scope of this power. See National Collegiate Athletic Assn. v. Smith, 525 U.S. ____, ____, n. 5 (1999) (slip op., at 7, n. 5) (rejecting suggestion "that the private right of action available under . . . §1681(a) is potentially broader than the Government's enforcement authority"); cf. Gebser v. Lago Vista Independent School Dist., supra, at 289 ("It would be unsound, we think, for a statute's express system of enforcement to require notice to the recipient and an opportunity to come into voluntary compliance while a judicially implied system of enforcement permits substantial liability without regard to the recipient's knowledge or its corrective actions upon receiving notice").

We disagree with respondents' assertion, however, that petitioner seeks to hold the Board liable for G. F.'s actions instead of its own. Here, petitioner attempts to hold the Board liable for its own decision to remain idle in the face of known student-on-student harassment in its schools. In Gebser, we concluded that a recipient of federal education funds may be liable in damages under Title IX where it is deliberately indifferent to known acts of sexual harassment by a teacher. In that case, a teacher had entered into a sexual relationship with an eighth grade student, and the student sought damages under Title IX for the teacher's misconduct. We recognized that the scope of liability in private damages actions under Title IX is circumscribed by Pennhurst's requirement that funding recipients have notice of their potential liability. 524 U.S., at 287–288. Invoking Pennhurst, Guardians Assn., and Franklin, in Gebser we once again required " that 'the receiving entity of federal funds [have] notice that it will be liable for a monetary award' " before subjecting it to damages liability. Id., at 287 (quoting Franklin v. Gwinnett County Public Schools, 503 U.S., at 74). We also recognized, however, that this limitation on private damages actions is not a bar to liability where a funding recipient intentionally violates the statute. Id., at 74–75; see also Guardians Assn. v. Civil Serv. Comm'n of New York City, supra, at 597–598 (opinion of White, J.) (same with respect to Title VI). In particular, we concluded that Pennhurst does not bar a private damages action under Title IX where the funding recipient engages in intentional conduct that violates the clear terms of the statute.

Accordingly, we rejected the use of agency principles to impute liability to the district for the misconduct of its teachers. 524 U.S., at 283. Likewise, we declined the invitation to impose liability under what amounted to a negligence standard–holding the district liable for its failure to react to teacher-student harassment of which it knew or should have known. Ibid. Rather, we concluded that the district could be liable for damages only where the district itself intentionally acted in clear violation of Title IX by remaining deliberately indifferent to acts of teacher-student harassment of which it had actual knowledge. Id., at 290. Contrary to the dissent's suggestion, the misconduct of the teacher in Gebser was not "treated as the grant recipient's actions." Post, at 8. Liability arose, rather, from "an official decision by the recipient not to remedy the violation." Gebser v. Lago Vista Independent School Dist., supra, at 290. By employing the "deliberate indifference" theory already used to establish municipal liability under Rev. Stat. §1979, 42 U.S.C. § 1983 see Gebser v. Lago Vista Independent School Dist., supra, at 290–291 (citing Board of Comm'rs of Bryan Cty. v. Brown, 520 U.S. 397 (1997), and Canton v. Harris, 489 U.S. 378 (1989)), we concluded in Gebser that recipients could be liable in damages only where their own deliberate indifference effectively "cause[d]" the discrimination, 524 U.S., at 291; see also Canton v. Harris, supra, at 385 (recognizing that a municipality will be liable under §1983 only if "the municipality itself causes the constitutional violation at issue" (emphasis in original)). The high standard imposed in Gebser sought to eliminate any "risk that the recipient would be liable in damages not for its own official decision but instead for its employees' independent actions." 524 U.S., at 290–291.

Gebser thus established that a recipient intentionally violates Title IX, and is subject to a private damages action, where the recipient is deliberately indifferent to known acts of teacher-student discrimination. Indeed, whether viewed as "discrimination" or "subject[ing]" students to discrimination, Title IX "[u]nquestionably . . . placed on [the Board] the duty not" to permit teacher-student harassment in its schools, Franklin v. Gwinnett County Public Schools, supra, at 75, and recipients violate Title IX's plain terms when they remain deliberately indifferent to this form of misconduct.

We consider here whether the misconduct identified in Gebser–deliberate indifference to known acts of harassment–amounts to an intentional violation of Title IX, capable of supporting a private damages action, when the harasser is a student rather than a teacher. We conclude that, in certain limited circumstances, it does. As an initial matter, in Gebser we expressly rejected the use of agency principles in the Title IX context, noting the textual differences between Title IX and Title VII. 524 U.S., at 283; cf. Faragher v. Boca Raton, 524 U.S. 775, 791–792 (1998) (invoking agency principles on ground that definition of "employer" in Title VII includes agents of employer); Meritor Savings Bank, FSB v. Vinson, 477 U.S. 57, 72 (1986) (same). Additionally, the regulatory scheme surrounding Title IX has long provided funding recipients with notice that they may be liable for their failure to respond to the discriminatory acts of certain non-agents. The Department of Education requires recipients to monitor third parties for discrimination in specified circumstances and to refrain from particular forms of interaction with outside entities that are known to discriminate. See, e.g., 34 CFR §§106.31(b)(6), 106.31(d), 106.37(a)(2), 106.38(a), 106.51(a)(3) (1998).

The common law, too, has put schools on notice that they may be held responsible under state law for their failure to protect students from the tortious acts of third parties. See Restatement (Second) of Torts §320, and Comment a (1965). In fact, state courts routinely uphold claims alleging that schools have been negligent in failing to protect their students from the torts of their peers. See, e.g., Rupp v. Bryant, 417 So. 2d 658, 666–667 (Fla. 1982); Brahatcek v. Millard School Dist., 202 Neb. 86, 99–100, 273 N. W. 2d 680, 688 (1979); McLeod v. Grant County School Dist. No. 128, 42 Wash. 2d 316, 320, 255 P.2d 360, 362–363 (1953).

This is not to say that the identity of the harasser is irrelevant. On the contrary, both the "deliberate indifference" standard and the language of Title IX narrowly circumscribe the set of parties whose known acts of sexual harassment can trigger some duty to respond on the part of funding recipients. Deliberate indifference makes sense as a theory of direct liability under Title IX only where the funding recipient has some control over the alleged harassment. A recipient cannot be directly liable for its indifference where it lacks the authority to take remedial action.

The language of Title IX itself–particularly when viewed in conjunction with the requirement that the recipient have notice of Title IX's prohibitions to be liable for damages–also cabins the range of misconduct that the statute proscribes. The statute's plain language confines the scope of prohibited conduct based on the recipient's degree of control over the harasser and the environment in which the harassment occurs. If a funding recipient does not engage in harassment directly, it may not be liable for damages unless its deliberate indifference "subject[s]" its students to harassment. That is, the deliberate indifference must, at a minimum, "cause [students] to undergo" harassment or "make them liable or vulnerable" to it. Random House Dictionary of the English Language 1415 (1966) (defining "subject" as "to cause to undergo the action of something specified; expose" or "to make liable or vulnerable; lay open; expose"); Webster's Third New International Dictionary of the English Language 2275 (1961) (defining "subject" as "to cause to undergo or submit to: make submit to a particular action or effect: EXPOSE"). Moreover, because the harassment must occur "under" "the operations of" a funding recipient, see 20 U.S.C. § 1681(a); §1687 (defining "program or activity"), the harassment must take place in a context subject to the school district's control, Webster's Third New International Dictionary of the English Language, supra, at 2487 (defining "under" as "in or into a condition of subjection, regulation, or subordination"; "subject to the guidance and instruction of"); Random House Dictionary of the English Language, supra, at 1543 (defining "under" as "subject to the authority, direction, or supervision of").

These factors combine to limit a recipient's damages liability to circumstances wherein the recipient exercises substantial control over both the harasser and the context in which the known harassment occurs. Only then can the recipient be said to "expose" its students to harassment or "cause" them to undergo it "under" the recipient's programs. We agree with the dissent that these conditions are satisfied most easily and most obviously when the offender is an agent of the recipient. Post, at 8. We rejected the use of agency analysis in Gebser, however, and we disagree that the term "under" somehow imports an agency requirement into Title IX. See ibid. As noted above, the theory in Gebser was that the recipient was directly liable for its deliberate indifference to discrimination. See supra, at 11. Liability in that case did not arise because the "teacher's actions [were] treated" as those of the funding recipient, post, at 8; the district was directly liable for its own failure to act. The terms "subjec[t]" and "under" impose limits, but nothing about these terms requires the use of agency principles.

Where, as here, the misconduct occurs during school hours and on school grounds–the bulk of G. F.'s misconduct, in fact, took place in the classroom–the misconduct is taking place "under" an "operation" of the funding recipient. See Doe v.

University of Illinois, 138 F.3d, at 661 (finding liability where school fails to respond properly to "student-on-student sexual harassment that takes place while the students are involved in school activities or otherwise under the supervision of school employees"). In these circumstances, the recipient retains substantial control over the context in which the harassment occurs. More importantly, however, in this setting the Board exercises significant control over the harasser. We have observed, for example, "that the nature of [the State's] power [over public schoolchildren] is custodial and tutelary, permitting a degree of supervision and control that could not be exercised over free adults." Vernonia School Dist. 47J v. Acton, 515 U.S. 646, 655 (1995). On more than one occasion, this Court has recognized the importance of school officials' "comprehensive authority . . ., consistent with fundamental constitutional safeguards, to prescribe and control conduct in the schools." Tinker v. Des Moines Independent Community School Dist., 393 U.S. 503, 507 (1969); see also New Jersey v. T. L. O., 469 U.S. 325, 342, n. 9 (1985) ("The maintenance of discipline in the schools requires not only that students be restrained from assaulting one another, abusing drugs and alcohol, and committing other crimes, but also that students conform themselves to the standards of conduct prescribed by school authorities"); 74 F.3d, at 1193 ("The ability to control and influence behavior exists to an even greater extent in the classroom than in the workplace . . ."). The common law, too, recognizes the school's disciplinary authority. See Restatement (Second) of Torts §152 (1965). We thus conclude that recipients of federal funding may be liable for "subject[ing]" their students to discrimination where the recipient is deliberately indifferent to known acts of student-on-student sexual harassment and the harasser is under the school's disciplinary authority.

At the time of the events in question here, in fact, school attorneys and administrators were being told that student-on-student harassment could trigger liability under Title IX. In March 1993, even as the events alleged in petitioner's complaint were unfolding, the National School Boards Association issued a publication, for use by "school attorneys and administrators in understanding the law regarding sexual harassment of employees and students," which observed that districts could be liable under Title IX for their failure to respond to student-on-student harassment. See National School Boards Association Council of School Attorneys, Sexual Harassment in the Schools: Preventing and Defending Against Claims v, 45 (rev. ed.). Drawing on Equal Employment Opportunity Commission guidelines interpreting Title VII, the publication informed districts that, "if [a] school district has constructive notice of severe and repeated acts of sexual harassment by fellow students, that may form the basis of a [T]itle IX claim." Id., at 45. The publication even correctly anticipated a form of Gebser's actual notice requirement: "It is unlikely that courts will hold a school district liable for sexual harassment by students against students in the absence of actual knowledge or notice to district employees." Sexual Harassment in the Schools, supra, at 45. Although we do not rely on this publication as an "indicium of congressional notice," see post, at 19, we do find support for our reading of Title IX in the fact that school attorneys have rendered an analogous interpretation.

 Likewise, although they were promulgated too late to contribute to the Board's notice of proscribed misconduct, the Department of Education's Office for Civil Rights (OCR) has recently adopted policy guidelines providing that student-on-student harassment falls within the scope of Title IX's proscriptions. See Department of Education, Office of Civil Rights, Sexual Harassment Guidance: Harassment of Students by School Employees, Other Students, or Third Parties, 62 Fed. Reg. 12034, 12039–12040 (1997) (OCR Title IX Guidelines); see also Department of Education, Racial Incidents and Harassment Against Students at Educational Institutions, 59 Fed. Reg. 11448, 11449 (1994).

 We stress that our conclusion here–that recipients may be liable for their deliberate indifference to known acts of peer sexual harassment–does not mean that recipients can avoid liability only by purging their schools of actionable peer harassment or that administrators must engage in particular disciplinary action. We thus disagree with respondents' contention that, if Title IX provides a cause of action for student-on-student harassment, "nothing short of expulsion of every student accused of misconduct involving sexual overtones would protect school systems from liability or damages." See Brief for Respondents 16; see also 120 F.3d, at 1402 (Tjoflat, J.) ("[A] school must immediately suspend or expel a student accused of sexual harassment"). Likewise, the dissent erroneously imagines that victims of peer harassment now have a Title IX right to make particular remedial demands. See post, at 34 (contemplating that victim could demand new desk assignment). In fact, as we have previously noted, courts should refrain from second guessing the disciplinary decisions made by school administrators. New Jersey v. T. L. O., supra, at 342–343, n. 9.

 School administrators will continue to enjoy the flexibility they require so long as funding recipients are deemed "deliberately indifferent" to acts of student-on-student harassment only where the recipient's response to the harassment or lack thereof is clearly unreasonable in light of the known circumstances. The dissent consistently mischaracterizes this standard to require funding recipients to "remedy" peer harassment, post at 5, 10, 16, 30, and to "ensur[e] that . . . students conform their conduct to" certain rules, post at 13. Title IX imposes no such requirements. On the contrary, the recipient must merely respond to known peer harassment in a manner that is not clearly unreasonable. This is not a mere "reasonableness" standard, as the dissent assumes. See post, at 26. In an appropriate case, there is no reason why courts, on a motion to dismiss, for summary judgment, or for a directed verdict, could not identify a response as not "clearly unreasonable" as a matter of law.

 Like the dissent, see post, at 11–15, we acknowledge that school administrators shoulder substantial burdens as a result of legal constraints on their disciplinary authority. To the extent that these restrictions arise from federal statutes, Congress can review these burdens with attention to the difficult position in which such legislation may place our Nation's schools. We believe, however, that the standard set out here is sufficiently flexible to account both for the level of disciplinary authority available to the school and for the potential liability arising from certain forms of disciplinary action. A university might not, for example, be expected to exercise the same degree of control over its students that a grade school would enjoy, see post, at 14, and it would be entirely reasonable for a school to refrain from a form of disciplinary action that would expose it to constitutional or statutory claims.

While it remains to be seen whether petitioner can show that the Board's response to reports of G. F.'s misconduct was clearly unreasonable in light of the known circumstances, petitioner may be able to show that the Board "subject[ed]" LaShonda to discrimination by failing to respond in any way over a period of five months to complaints of G. F.'s in-school misconduct from LaShonda and other female students.

B

The requirement that recipients receive adequate notice of Title IX's proscriptions also bears on the proper definition of "discrimination" in the context of a private damages action. We have elsewhere concluded that sexual harassment is a form of discrimination for Title IX purposes and that Title IX proscribes harassment with sufficient clarity to satisfy Pennhurst's notice requirement and serve as a basis for a damages action. See Gebser v. Lago Vista Independent School Dist., 524 U.S., at 281; Franklin v. Gwinnett County Public Schools, supra, at 74—75. Having previously determined that "sexual harassment" is "discrimination" in the school context under Title IX, we are constrained to conclude that student-on-student sexual harassment, if sufficiently severe, can likewise rise to the level of discrimination actionable under the statute. See Bennett v. Kentucky Dept. of Ed., 470 U.S. 656, 665—666 (1985) (rejecting claim of insufficient notice under Pennhurst where statute made clear that there were some conditions placed on receipt of federal funds, and noting that Congress need not "specifically identif[y] and proscrib[e]" each condition in the legislation). The statute's other prohibitions, moreover, help give content to the term "discrimination" in this context. Students are not only protected from discrimination, but also specifically shielded from being "excluded from participation in" or "denied the benefits of" any "education program or activity receiving Federal financial assistance." §1681(a). The statute makes clear that, whatever else it prohibits, students must not be denied access to educational benefits and opportunities on the basis of gender. We thus conclude that funding recipients are properly held liable in damages only where they are deliberately indifferent to sexual harassment, of which they have actual knowledge, that is so severe, pervasive, and objectively offensive that it can be said to deprive the victims of access to the educational opportunities or benefits provided by the school.

The most obvious example of student-on-student sexual harassment capable of triggering a damages claim would thus involve the overt, physical deprivation of access to school resources. Consider, for example, a case in which male students physically threaten their female peers every day, successfully preventing the female students from using a particular school resource—an athletic field or a computer lab, for instance.

District administrators are well aware of the daily ritual, yet they deliberately ignore requests for aid from the female students wishing to use the resource. The district's knowing refusal to take any action in response to such behavior would fly in the face of Title IX's core principles, and such deliberate indifference may appropriately be subject to claims for monetary damages. It is not necessary, however, to show physical exclusion to demonstrate that students have been deprived by the actions of another student or students of an educational opportunity on the basis of sex. Rather, a plaintiff must establish sexual harassment of students that is so severe, pervasive, and objectively offensive, and that so undermines and detracts from the victims' educational experience, that the victim-students are effectively denied equal access to an institution's resources and opportunities. Cf. Meritor Savings Bank, FSB v. Vinson, 477 U.S., at 67.

Whether gender-oriented conduct rises to the level of actionable "harassment" thus "depends on a constellation of surrounding circumstances, expectations, and relationships," Oncale v. Sundowner Offshore Services, Inc., 523 U.S. 75, 82 (1998), including, but not limited to, the ages of the harasser and the victim and the number of individuals involved, see OCR Title IX Guidelines 12041—12042. Courts, moreover, must bear in mind that schools are unlike the adult workplace and that children may regularly interact in a manner that would be unacceptable among adults. See, e.g., Brief for National School Boards Association et al. as Amici Curiae 11 (describing "dizzying array of immature . . . behaviors by students"). Indeed, at least early on, students are still learning how to interact appropriately with their peers. It is thus understandable that, in the school setting, students often engage in insults, banter, teasing, shoving, pushing, and gender-specific conduct that is upsetting to the students subjected to it. Damages are not available for simple acts of teasing and name-calling among school children, however, even where these comments target differences in gender. Rather, in the context of student-on-student harassment, damages are available only where the behavior is so severe, pervasive, and objectively offensive that it denies its victims the equal access to education that Title IX is designed to protect.

The dissent fails to appreciate these very real limitations on a funding recipient's liability under Title IX. It is not enough to show, as the dissent would read this opinion to provide, that a student has been "teased," post, at 25, or "called . . . offensive names," post, at 27—28. Comparisons to an "overweight child who skips gym class because the other children tease her about her size," the student "who refuses to wear glasses to avoid the taunts of 'four-eyes,'" and "the child who refuses to go to school because the school bully calls him a 'scardy-cat' at recess," post, at 25, are inapposite and misleading. Nor do we contemplate, much less hold, that a mere "decline in grades is enough to survive" a motion to dismiss. Ibid. The drop-off in LaShonda's grades provides necessary evidence of a potential link between her education and G.F.'s misconduct, but petitioner's ability to state a cognizable claim here depends equally on the alleged persistence and severity of G.F.'s actions, not to mention the Board's alleged knowledge and deliberate indifference. We trust that the dissent's characterization of our opinion will not mislead courts to impose more sweeping liability than we read Title IX to require.

Moreover, the provision that the discrimination occur "under any education program or activity" suggests that the behavior be serious enough to have the systemic effect of denying the victim equal access to an educational program or activity. Although, in theory, a single instance of sufficiently severe one-on-one peer harassment could be said to have such an effect, we think it unlikely that Congress would have thought such behavior sufficient to rise to this level in light of the inevitability of student misconduct and the amount of litigation that would be invited by entertaining claims of official indifference to a single instance of one-on-one peer harassment. By limiting private damages actions to cases having a systemic effect on educational programs or activities, we reconcile the general principle that Title IX prohibits official indifference to known peer sexual harassment with the practical realities of responding to student behavior, realities that Congress could not have meant to be ignored. Even the dissent suggests that Title IX liability may arise when a funding recipient remains indifferent to severe, gender-based mistreatment played out on a "widespread level" among students. Post, at 31.

The fact that it was a teacher who engaged in harassment in Franklin and Gebser is relevant. The relationship between the harasser and the victim necessarily affects the extent to which the misconduct can be said to breach Title IX's guarantee of equal access to educational benefits and to have a systemic effect on a program or activity. Peer harassment, in particular, is less likely to satisfy these requirements than is teacher-student harassment.

C

Applying this standard to the facts at issue here, we conclude that the Eleventh Circuit erred in dismissing petitioner's complaint. Petitioner alleges that her daughter was the victim of repeated acts of sexual harassment by G. F. over a 5-month period, and there are allegations in support of the conclusion that G. F.'s misconduct was severe, pervasive, and objectively offensive. The harassment was not only verbal; it included numerous acts of objectively offensive touching, and, indeed, G. F. ultimately pleaded guilty to criminal sexual misconduct. Moreover, the complaint alleges that there were multiple victims who were sufficiently disturbed by G. F.'s misconduct to seek an audience with the school principal. Further, petitioner contends that the harassment had a concrete, negative effect on her daughter's ability to receive an education. The complaint also suggests that petitioner may be able to show both actual knowledge and deliberate indifference on the part of the Board, which made no effort whatsoever either to investigate or to put an end to the harassment.

On this complaint, we cannot say "beyond doubt that [petitioner] can prove no set of facts in support of [her] claim which would entitle [her] to relief." Conley v. Gibson, 355 U.S. 41, 45—46 (1957). See also Scheuer v. Rhodes, 416 U.S. 232, 236 (1974) ("The issue is not whether a plaintiff will ultimately prevail but whether the claimant is entitled to offer evidence to support the claims"). Accordingly, the judgment of the United States Court of Appeals for the Eleventh Circuit is reversed, and the case is remanded for further proceedings consistent with this opinion.

It is so ordered.

### Erie v. Pap's AM (March 29, 2000) [Note omitted]

Justice O'Connor announced the judgment of the Court and delivered the opinion of the Court with respect to Parts I and II, and an opinion with respect to Parts III and IV, in which The Chief Justice, Justice Kennedy, and Justice Breyer join.

The city of Erie, Pennsylvania, enacted an ordinance banning public nudity. Respondent Pap's A. M. (hereinafter Pap's), which operated a nude dancing establishment in Erie, challenged the constitutionality of the ordinance and sought a permanent injunction against its enforcement. The Pennsylvania Supreme Court, although noting that this Court in Barnes v. Glen Theatre, Inc., 501 U. S. 560 (1991), had upheld an Indiana ordinance that was "strikingly similar" to Erie's, found that the public nudity sections of the ordinance violated respondent's right to freedom of expression under the United States Constitution. 553 Pa. 348, 356, 719 A. 2d 273, 277 (1998). This case raises the question whether the Pennsylvania Supreme Court properly evaluated the ordinance's constitutionality under the First Amendment. We hold that Erie's ordinance is a content-neutral regulation that satisfies the four-part test of United States v. O'Brien, 391 U. S. 367 (1968). Accordingly, we reverse the decision of the Pennsylvania Supreme Court and remand for the consideration of any remaining issues.

I

On September 28, 1994, the city council for the city of Erie, Pennsylvania, enacted Ordinance 75-1994, a public indecency ordinance that makes it a summary offense to knowingly or intentionally appear in public in a "state of nudity."[*]

Respondent Pap's, a Pennsylvania corporation, operated an establishment in Erie known as "Kandyland" that featured totally nude erotic dancing performed by women. To comply with the ordinance, these dancers must wear, at a minimum, "pasties" and a "G-string." On October 14, 1994, two days after the ordinance went into effect, Pap's filed a complaint against the city of Erie, the mayor of the city, and members of the city council, seeking declaratory relief and a permanent injunction against the enforcement of the ordinance.

The Court of Common Pleas of Erie County granted the permanent injunction and struck down the ordinance as unconstitutional. Civ. No. 60059-1994 (Jan. 18, 1995), Pet. for Cert. 40a. On cross appeals, the Commonwealth Court reversed the trial court's order. 674 A. 2d 338 (1996).

The Pennsylvania Supreme Court granted review and reversed, concluding that the public nudity provisions of the ordinance violated respondent's rights to freedom of expression as protected by the First and Fourteenth Amendments. 553 Pa. 348, 719 A. 2d 273 (1998). The Pennsylvania court first inquired whether nude dancing constitutes expressive conduct that is within the protection of the First Amendment. The court noted that the act of being nude, in and of itself, is not entitled to First Amendment protection because it conveys no message. Id., at 354, 719 A. 2d, at 276. Nude dancing, however, is expressive conduct that is entitled to some quantum of protection under the First Amendment, a view that the Pennsylvania Supreme Court noted was endorsed by eight Members of this Court in Barnes. 553 Pa., at 354, 719 A. 2d, at 276.

The Pennsylvania court next inquired whether the government interest in enacting the ordinance was content neutral, explaining that regulations that are unrelated to the suppression of expression are not subject to strict scrutiny but to the less stringent standard of United States v. O'Brien, supra, at 377. To answer the question whether the ordinance is content based, the court turned to our decision in Barnes. 553 Pa., at 355-356, 719 A. 2d, at 277. Although the Pennsylvania court noted that the Indiana statute at issue in Barnes "is strikingly similar to the Ordinance we are examining," it concluded that "[u]nfortunately for our purposes, the Barnes Court splintered and produced four separate, non-harmonious opinions." 553 Pa., at 356, 719 A. 2d, at 277. After canvassing these separate opinions, the Pennsylvania court concluded that, although it is permissible to find precedential effect in a fragmented decision, to do so a majority of the Court must have been in agreement on the concept that is deemed to be the holding. See Marks v. United States, 430 U. S. 188 (1977). The Pennsylvania court noted that "aside from the agreement by a majority of the Barnes Court that nude dancing is entitled to some First Amendment protection, we can find no point on which a majority of the Barnes Court agreed." 553 Pa., at 358, 719 A. 2d, at 278. Accordingly, the court concluded that "no clear precedent arises out of Barnes on the issue of whether the [Erie] ordinance . . . passes muster under the First Amendment." Ibid.

Having determined that there was no United States Supreme Court precedent on point, the Pennsylvania court conducted an independent examination of the ordinance to ascertain whether it was related to the suppression of expression. The court concluded that although one of the purposes of the ordinance was to combat negative secondary effects, "[i]nextricably bound up with this stated purpose is an unmentioned purpose . . . to impact negatively on the erotic message of the dance." Id., at 359, 719 A. 2d, at 279. As such, the court determined the ordinance was content based and subject to strict scrutiny. The ordinance failed the narrow tailoring requirement of strict scrutiny because the court found that imposing criminal and civil sanctions on those who commit sex crimes would be a far narrower means of combating secondary effects than the requirement that dancers wear pasties and G-strings. Id., at 361-362, 719 A. 2d, at 280.

Concluding that the ordinance unconstitutionally burdened respondent's expressive conduct, the Pennsylvania court then determined that, under Pennsylvania law, the public nudity provisions of the ordinance could be severed rather than striking the ordinance in its entirety. Accordingly, the court severed §§ 1(c) and 2 from the ordinance and reversed the order of the Commonwealth Court. Id., at 363-364, 719 A. 2d, at 281. Because the court determined that the public nudity provisions of the ordinance violated Pap's right to freedom of expression under the United States Constitution, it did not address the constitutionality of the ordinance under the Pennsylvania Constitution or the claim that the ordinance is unconstitutionally overbroad. Ibid.

In a separate concurrence, two justices of the Pennsylvania court noted that, because this Court upheld a virtually identical statute in Barnes, the ordinance should have been upheld under the United States Constitution. 553 Pa., at 364, 719 A. 2d, at 281. They reached the same result as the majority, however, because they would have held that the public nudity sections of the ordinance violate the Pennsylvania Constitution. Id., at 370, 719 A. 2d, at 284.

The city of Erie petitioned for a writ of certiorari, which we granted. 526 U. S. 1111 (1999). Shortly thereafter, Pap's filed a motion to dismiss the case as moot, noting that Kandyland was no longer operating as a nude dancing club, and Pap's was not operating a nude dancing club at any other location. Respondent's Motion to Dismiss as Moot 1. We denied the motion. 527 U. S. 1034 (1999).

II

As a preliminary matter, we must address the justiciability question. "`[A] case is moot when the issues presented are no longer "live" or the parties lack a legally cognizable interest in the outcome.' " County of Los Angeles v. Davis, 440 U. S. 625, 631 (1979) (quoting Powell v. McCormack, 395 U. S. 486, 496 (1969)). The underlying concern is that, when the challenged conduct ceases such that "`there is no reasonable expectation that the wrong will be repeated,' " United States v. W. T. Grant Co., 345 U. S. 629, 633 (1953), then it becomes impossible for the court to grant "`any effectual relief whatever' to [the] prevailing party," Church of Scientology of Cal. v. United States, 506 U. S. 9, 12 (1992) (quoting Mills v. Green, 159 U. S. 651, 653 (1895)). In that case, any opinion as to the legality of the challenged action would be advisory.

Here, Pap's submitted an affidavit stating that it had "ceased to operate a nude dancing establishment in Erie." Status Report Re Potential Issue of Mootness 1 (Sept. 8, 1999). Pap's asserts that the case is therefore moot because "[t]he outcome of this case will have no effect upon Respondent." Respondent's Motion to Dismiss as Moot 1. Simply closing Kandyland is not sufficient to render this case moot, however. Pap's is still incorporated under Pennsylvania law, and it could again decide to operate a nude dancing establishment in Erie. See Petitioner's Brief in Opposition to Motion to Dismiss 3. Justice Scalia differs with our assessment as to the likelihood that Pap's may resume its nude dancing operation. Several Members of this Court can attest, however, that the "advanced age" of Pap's owner (72) does not make it "absolutely clear" that a life of quiet retirement is his only reasonable expectation. Cf. Friends of Earth, Inc. v. Laidlaw Environmental Services (TOC), Inc., 528 U. S. 167 (2000). Moreover, our appraisal of Pap's affidavit is influenced by Pap's failure, despite its obligation to the Court, to mention a word about the potential mootness issue in its brief in opposition to the petition for writ of certiorari, which was filed in April 1999, even though, as Justice Scalia points out, Kandyland was closed and that property sold in 1998. See Board of License Comm'rs of Tiverton v. Pastore, 469 U. S. 238, 240 (1985) (per curiam). Pap's only raised the issue after this Court granted certiorari.

In any event, this is not a run of the mill voluntary cessation case. Here it is the plaintiff who, having prevailed below, now seeks to have the case declared moot. And it is the city of Erie that seeks to invoke the federal judicial power to obtain this Court's review of the Pennsylvania Supreme Court decision. Cf. ASARCO Inc. v. Kadish, 490 U. S. 605, 617-618 (1989). The city has an ongoing injury because it is barred from enforcing the public nudity provisions of its ordinance. If the challenged ordinance is found constitutional, then Erie can enforce it, and the availability of such relief is sufficient to prevent the case from being moot. See Church of Scientology of Cal. v. United States, supra, at 13. And Pap's still has a concrete stake in the outcome of this case because, to the extent Pap's has an interest in resuming operations, it has an interest in preserving the judgment of the Pennsylvania Supreme Court. Our interest in preventing litigants from attempting to manipulate the Court's jurisdiction to insulate a favorable decision from review further counsels against a finding of mootness here. See United States v. W. T. Grant Co., supra, at 632; cf. Arizonans for Official English v. Arizona, 520 U. S. 43, 74 (1997). Although the issue is close, we conclude that the case is not moot, and we turn to the merits.

III

Being "in a state of nudity" is not an inherently expressive condition. As we explained in Barnes, however, nude dancing of the type at issue here is expressive conduct, although we think that it falls only within the outer ambit of the First Amendment's protection. See Barnes v. Glen Theatre, Inc., 501 U. S., at 565-566 (plurality opinion); Schad v. Mount Ephraim, 452 U. S. 61, 66 (1981).

To determine what level of scrutiny applies to the ordinance at issue here, we must decide "whether the State's regulation is related to the suppression of expression." Texas v. Johnson, 491 U. S. 397, 403 (1989); see also United States v. O'Brien, 391 U. S., at 377. If the governmental purpose in enacting the regulation is unrelated to the suppression of expression, then the regulation need only satisfy the "less stringent" standard from O'Brien for evaluating restrictions on symbolic speech. Texas v. Johnson, supra, at 403; United States v. O'Brien, supra, at 377. If the government interest is related to the content of the expression, however, then the regulation falls outside the scope of the O'Brien test and must be justified under a more demanding standard. Texas v. Johnson, supra, at 403.

In Barnes, we analyzed an almost identical statute, holding that Indiana's public nudity ban did not violate the First Amendment, although no five Members of the Court agreed on a single rationale for that conclusion. We now clarify that government restrictions on public nudity such as the ordinance at issue here should be evaluated under the framework set forth in O'Brien for content-neutral restrictions on symbolic speech.

The city of Erie argues that the ordinance is a contentneutral restriction that is reviewable under O'Brien because the ordinance bans conduct, not speech; specifically, public nudity. Respondent counters that the ordinance targets nude dancing and, as such, is aimed specifically at suppressing expression, making the ordinance a content-based restriction that must be subjected to strict scrutiny.

The ordinance here, like the statute in Barnes, is on its face a general prohibition on public nudity. 553 Pa., at 354, 719 A. 2d, at 277. By its terms, the ordinance regulates conduct alone. It does not target nudity that contains an erotic message; rather, it bans all public nudity, regardless of whether that nudity is accompanied by expressive activity. And like the statute in Barnes, the Erie ordinance replaces and updates provisions of an "Indecency and Immorality" ordinance that has been on the books since 1866, predating the prevalence of nude dancing establishments such as Kandyland. Pet. for Cert. 7a; see Barnes v. Glen Theatre, Inc., supra, at 568.

Respondent and Justice Stevens contend nonetheless that the ordinance is related to the suppression of expression because language in the ordinance's preamble suggests that its actual purpose is to prohibit erotic dancing of the type performed at Kandyland. Post, at 318 (dissenting opinion). That is not how the Pennsylvania Supreme Court interpreted that language, however. In the preamble to the ordinance, the city council stated that it was adopting the regulation

"`for the purpose of limiting a recent increase in nude live entertainment within the City, which activity adversely impacts and threatens to impact on the public health, safety and welfare by providing an atmosphere conducive to violence, sexual harassment, public intoxication, prostitution, the spread of sexually transmitted diseases and other deleterious effects.'" 553 Pa., at 359, 719 A. 2d, at 279.

The Pennsylvania Supreme Court construed this language to mean that one purpose of the ordinance was "to combat negative secondary effects." Ibid.

As Justice Souter noted in Barnes, "on its face, the governmental interest in combating prostitution and other criminal activity is not at all inherently related to expression." 501 U. S., at 585 (opinion concurring in judgment). In that sense, this case is similar to O'Brien. O'Brien burned his draft registration card as a public statement of his antiwar views, and he was convicted under a statute making it a crime to knowingly mutilate or destroy such a card. This Court rejected his claim that the statute violated his First Amendment rights, reasoning that the law punished him for the "noncommunicative impact of his conduct, and for nothing else." 391 U. S., at 382. In other words, the Government regulation prohibiting the destruction of draft cards was aimed at maintaining the integrity of the Selective Service System and not at suppressing the message of draft resistance that O'Brien sought to convey by burning his draft card. So too here, the ordinance prohibiting public nudity is aimed at combating crime and other negative secondary effects caused by the presence of adult entertainment establishments like Kandyland and not at suppressing the erotic message conveyed by this type of nude dancing. Put another way, the ordinance does not attempt to regulate the primary effects of the expression, i. e., the effect on the audience of watching nude erotic dancing, but rather the secondary effects, such as the impacts on public health, safety, and welfare, which we have previously recognized are "caused by the presence of even one such" establishment. Renton v. Playtime Theatres, Inc., 475 U. S. 41, 47-48, 50 (1986); see also Boos v. Barry, 485 U. S. 312, 321 (1988).

Although the Pennsylvania Supreme Court acknowledged that one goal of the ordinance was to combat the negative secondary effects associated with nude dancing establishments, the court concluded that the ordinance was nevertheless content based, relying on Justice White's position in dissent in Barnes for the proposition that a ban of this type necessarily has the purpose of suppressing the erotic message of the dance. Because the Pennsylvania court agreed with Justice White's approach, it concluded that the ordinance must have another, "unmentioned" purpose related to the suppression of expression. 553 Pa., at 359, 719 A. 2d, at 279. That is, the Pennsylvania court adopted the dissent's view in Barnes that "`[s]ince the State permits the dancers to perform if they wear pasties and G-strings but forbids nude dancing, it is precisely because of the distinctive, expressive content of the nude dancing performances at issue in this case that the State seeks to apply the statutory prohibition." 553 Pa., at 359, 719 A. 2d, at 279 (quoting Barnes, supra, at 592 (White, J., dissenting)). A majority of the Court rejected that view in Barnes, and we do so again here.

Respondent's argument that the ordinance is "aimed" at suppressing expression through a ban on nude dancing—an argument that respondent supports by pointing to statements by the city attorney that the public nudity ban was not intended to apply to "legitimate" theater productions— is really an argument that the city council also had an illicit motive in enacting the ordinance. As we have said before, however, this Court will not strike down an otherwise constitutional statute on the basis of an alleged illicit motive. O'Brien, supra, at 382-383; Renton v. Playtime Theatres, Inc., supra, at 47-48 (that the "predominate" purpose of the statute was to control secondary effects was "more than adequate to establish" that the city's interest was unrelated to the suppression of expression). In light of the Pennsylvania court's determination that one purpose of the ordinance is to combat harmful secondary effects, the ban on public nudity here is no different from the ban on burning draft registration cards in O'Brien, where the Government sought to prevent the means of the expression and not the expression of antiwar sentiment itself.

Justice Stevens argues that the ordinance enacts a complete ban on expression. We respectfully disagree with that characterization. The public nudity ban certainly has the effect of limiting one particular means of expressing the kind of erotic message being disseminated at Kandyland. But simply to define what is being banned as the "message" is to assume the conclusion. We did not analyze the regulation in O'Brien as having enacted a total ban on expression. Instead, the Court recognized that the regulation against destroying one's draft card was justified by the Government's interest in preventing the harmful "secondary effects" of that conduct (disruption to the Selective Service System), even though that regulation may have some incidental effect on the expressive element of the conduct. Because this justification was unrelated to the suppression of O'Brien's antiwar message, the regulation was content neutral. Although there may be cases in which banning the means of expression so interferes with the message that it essentially bans the message, that is not the case here.

Even if we had not already rejected the view that a ban on public nudity is necessarily related to the suppression of the erotic message of nude dancing, we would do so now because the premise of such a view is flawed. The State's interest in preventing harmful secondary effects is not related to the suppression of expression. In trying to control the secondary effects of nude dancing, the ordinance seeks to deter crime and the other deleterious effects caused by the presence of such an establishment in the neighborhood. See Renton, supra, at 50-51. In Clark v. Community for Creative Non-Violence, 468 U. S. 288 (1984), we held that a National Park Service regulation prohibiting camping in certain parks did not violate the First Amendment when applied to prohibit demonstrators from sleeping in Lafayette Park and the Mall in Washington, D. C., in connection with a demonstration intended to call attention to the plight of the homeless. Assuming, arguendo, that sleeping can be expressive conduct, the Court concluded that the Government interest in conserving park property was unrelated to the demonstrators' message about homelessness. Id., at 299.

So, while the demonstrators were allowed to erect "symbolic tent cities," they were not allowed to sleep overnight in those tents. Even though the regulation may have directly limited the expressive element involved in actually sleeping in the park, the regulation was nonetheless content neutral.

Similarly, even if Erie's public nudity ban has some minimal effect on the erotic message by muting that portion of the expression that occurs when the last stitch is dropped, the dancers at Kandyland and other such establishments are free to perform wearing pasties and G-strings. Any effect on the overall expression is de minimis. And as Justice Stevens eloquently stated for the plurality in Young v. American Mini Theatres, Inc., 427 U. S. 50, 70 (1976), "even though we recognize that the First Amendment will not tolerate the total suppression of erotic materials that have some arguably artistic value, it is manifest that society's interest in protecting this type of expression is of a wholly different, and lesser, magnitude than the interest in untrammeled political debate," and "few of us would march our sons and daughters off to war to preserve the citizen's right to see" specified anatomical areas exhibited at establishments like Kandyland. If States are to be able to regulate secondary effects, then de minimis intrusions on expression such as those at issue here cannot be sufficient to render the ordinance content based. See Clark v. Community for Creative Non-Violence, supra, at 299; Ward v. Rock Against Racism, 491 U. S. 781, 791 (1989) (even if regulation has an incidental effect on some speakers or messages but not others, the regulation is content neutral if it can be justified without reference to the content of the expression).

This case is, in fact, similar to O'Brien, Community for Creative Non-Violence, and Ward. The justification for the government regulation in each case prevents harmful "secondary" effects that are unrelated to the suppression of expression. See, e. g., Ward v.

Rock Against Racism, supra, at 791-792 (noting that "[t]he principal justification for the sound-amplification guideline is the city's desire to control noise levels at bandshell events, in order to retain the character of the [adjacent] Sheep Meadow and its more sedate activities," and citing Renton for the proposition that "[a] regulation that serves purposes unrelated to the content of expression is deemed neutral, even if it has an incidental effect on some speakers or messages but not others"). While the doctrinal theories behind "incidental burdens" and "secondary effects" are, of course, not identical, there is nothing objectionable about a city passing a general ordinance to ban public nudity (even though such a ban may place incidental burdens on some protected speech) and at the same time recognizing that one specific occurrence of public nudity— nude erotic dancing—is particularly problematic because it produces harmful secondary effects.

Justice Stevens claims that today we "[f]or the first time" extend Renton `s secondary effects doctrine to justify restrictions other than the location of a commercial enterprise. Post, at 317 (dissenting opinion). Our reliance on Renton to justify other restrictions is not new, however. In Ward, the Court relied on Renton to evaluate restrictions on sound amplification at an outdoor bandshell, rejecting the dissent's contention that Renton was inapplicable. See Ward v. Rock Against Racism, supra, at 804, n. 1 (Marshall, J., dissenting) ("Today, for the first time, a majority of the Court applies Renton analysis to a category of speech far afield from that decision's original limited focus"). Moreover, Erie's ordinance does not effect a "total ban" on protected expression. Post, at 319.

In Renton, the regulation explicitly treated "adult" movie theaters differently from other theaters, and defined "adult" theaters solely by reference to the content of their movies. 475 U. S., at 44. We nonetheless treated the zoning regulation as content neutral because the ordinance was aimed at the secondary effects of adult theaters, a justification unrelated to the content of the adult movies themselves. Id., at 48. Here, Erie's ordinance is on its face a content-neutral restriction on conduct. Even if the city thought that nude dancing at clubs like Kandyland constituted a particularly problematic instance of public nudity, the regulation is still properly evaluated as a content-neutral restriction because the interest in combating the secondary effects associated with those clubs is unrelated to the suppression of the erotic message conveyed by nude dancing.

We conclude that Erie's asserted interest in combating the negative secondary effects associated with adult entertainment establishments like Kandyland is unrelated to the suppression of the erotic message conveyed by nude dancing. The ordinance prohibiting public nudity is therefore valid if it satisfies the four-factor test from O'Brien for evaluating restrictions on symbolic speech.

IV

Applying that standard here, we conclude that Erie's ordinance is justified under O'Brien. The first factor of the O'Brien test is whether the government regulation is within the constitutional power of the government to enact. Here, Erie's efforts to protect public health and safety are clearly within the city's police powers. The second factor is whether the regulation furthers an important or substantial government interest. The asserted interests of regulating conduct through a public nudity ban and of combating the harmful secondary effects associated with nude dancing are undeniably important. And in terms of demonstrating that such secondary effects pose a threat, the city need not "conduct new studies or produce evidence independent of that already generated by other cities" to demonstrate the problem of secondary effects, "so long as whatever evidence the city relies upon is reasonably believed to be relevant to the problem that the city addresses." Renton v. Playtime Theatres, Inc., supra, at 51-52. Because the nude dancing at Kandyland is of the same character as the adult entertainment at issue in Renton, Young v. American Mini Theatres, Inc., 427 U. S. 50 (1976), and California v. LaRue, 409 U. S. 109 (1972), it was reasonable for Erie to conclude that such nude dancing was likely to produce the same secondary effects. And Erie could reasonably rely on the evidentiary foundation set forth in Renton and American Mini Theatres to the effect that secondary effects are caused by the presence of even one adult entertainment establishment in a given neighborhood. See Renton v. Playtime Theatres, Inc., supra, at 51-52 (indicating that reliance on a judicial opinion that describes the evidentiary basis is sufficient). In fact, Erie expressly relied on Barnes and its discussion of secondary effects, including its reference to Renton and American Mini Theatres. Even in cases addressing regulations that strike closer to the core of First Amendment values, we have accepted a state or local government's reasonable belief that the experience of other jurisdictions is relevant to the problem it is addressing. See Nixon v. Shrink Missouri Government PAC, 528 U. S. 377, 393, n. 6 (2000). Regardless of whether Justice Souter now wishes to disavow his opinion in Barnes on this point, see post, at 316-317 (opinion concurring in part and dissenting in part), the evidentiary standard described in Renton controls here, and Erie meets that standard.

In any event, Erie also relied on its own findings. The preamble to the ordinance states that "the Council of the City of Erie has, at various times over more than a century, expressed its findings that certain lewd, immoral activities carried on in public places for profit are highly detrimental to the public health, safety and welfare, and lead to the debasement of both women and men, promote violence, public intoxication, prostitution and other serious criminal activity." Pet. for Cert. 6a (emphasis added). The city council members, familiar with commercial downtown Erie, are the individuals who would likely have had firsthand knowledge of what took place at and around nude dancing establishments in Erie, and can make particularized, expert judgments about the resulting harmful secondary effects. Analogizing to the administrative agency context, it is well established that, as long as a party has an opportunity to respond, an administrative agency may take official notice of such "legislative facts" within its special knowledge, and is not confined to the evidence in the record in reaching its expert judgment. See FCC v. National Citizens Comm. for Broadcasting, 436 U. S. 775 (1978); Republic Aviation Corp. v. NLRB, 324 U. S. 793 (1945); 2 K. Davis & R. Pierce, Administrative Law Treatise § 10.6 (3d ed. 1994). Here, Kandyland has had ample opportunity to contest the council's findings about secondary effects—before the council itself, throughout the state proceedings, and before this Court. Yet to this day, Kandyland has never challenged the city council's findings or cast any specific doubt on the validity of those findings. Instead, it has simply asserted that the council's evidentiary proof was lacking. In the absence of any reason to doubt it, the city's expert judgment should be credited. And the study relied on by amicus curiae does not cast any legitimate doubt on the Erie city council's judgment about Erie. See Brief for First Amendment Lawyers Association as Amicus Curiae 16-23.

Finally, it is worth repeating that Erie's ordinance is on its face a content-neutral restriction that regulates conduct, not First Amendment expression. And the government should have sufficient leeway to justify such a law based on secondary effects. On this point, O'Brien is especially instructive. The Court there did not require evidence that the integrity of the Selective Service System would be jeopardized by the knowing destruction or mutilation of draft cards. It simply reviewed the Government's various administrative interests in issuing the cards, and then concluded that "Congress has a legitimate and substantial interest in preventing their wanton and unrestrained destruction and assuring their continuing availability by punishing people who knowingly and willfully destroy or mutilate them." 391 U. S., at 378-380. There was no study documenting instances of draft card mutilation or the actual effect of such mutilation on the Government's asserted efficiency interests. But the Court permitted Congress to take official notice, as it were, that draft card destruction would jeopardize the system. The fact that this sort of leeway is appropriate in a case involving conduct says nothing whatsoever about its appropriateness in a case involving actual regulation of First Amendment expression. As we have said, so long as the regulation is unrelated to the suppression of expression, "[t]he government generally has a freer hand in restricting expressive conduct than it has in restricting the written or spoken word." Texas v. Johnson, 491 U. S., at 406. See, e. g., United States v. O'Brien, supra, at 377; United States v. Albertini, 472 U. S. 675, 689 (1985) (finding sufficient the Government's assertion that those who had previously been barred from entering the military installation pose a threat to the security of that installation); Clark v. Community for Creative Non-Violence, 468 U. S., at 299 (finding sufficient the Government's assertion that camping overnight in the park poses a threat to park property).

Justice Souter, however, would require Erie to develop a specific evidentiary record supporting its ordinance. Post, at 317 (opinion concurring in part and dissenting in part). Justice Souter agrees that Erie's interest in combating the negative secondary effects associated with nude dancing establishments is a legitimate government interest unrelated to the suppression of expression, and he agrees that the ordinance should therefore be evaluated under O'Brien. O'Brien, of course, required no evidentiary showing at all that the threatened harm was real. But that case is different, Justice Souter contends, because in O'Brien "there could be no doubt" that a regulation prohibiting the destruction of draft cards would alleviate the harmful secondary effects flowing from the destruction of those cards. Post, at 311, n. 1.

But whether the harm is evident to our "intuition," ibid., is not the proper inquiry. If it were, we would simply say there is no doubt that a regulation prohibiting public nudity would alleviate the harmful secondary effects associated with nude dancing. In any event, Justice Souter conflates two distinct concepts under O'Brien: whether there is a substantial government interest and whether the regulation furthers that interest. As to the government interest, i. e., whether the threatened harm is real, the city council relied on this Court's opinions detailing the harmful secondary effects caused by establishments like Kandyland, as well as on its own experiences in Erie. Justice Souter attempts to denigrate the city council's conclusion that the threatened harm was real, arguing that we cannot accept Erie's findings because the subject of nude dancing is "fraught with some emotionalism," post, at 314. Yet surely the subject of drafting our citizens into the military is "fraught" with more emotionalism than the subject of regulating nude dancing. Ibid. Justice Souter next hypothesizes that the reason we cannot accept Erie's conclusion is that, since the question whether these secondary effects occur is "amenable to empirical treatment," we should ignore Erie's actual experience and instead require such an empirical analysis. Post, at 314-315, n. 3 (referring to a "scientifically sound" study offered by an amicus curiae to show that nude dancing establishments do not cause secondary effects). In Nixon, however, we flatly rejected that idea. 528 U. S., at 394 (noting that the "invocation of academic studies said to indicate" that the threatened harms are not real is insufficient to cast doubt on the experience of the local government).

As to the second point—whether the regulation furthers the government interest—it is evident that, since crime and other public health and safety problems are caused by the presence of nude dancing establishments like Kandyland, a ban on such nude dancing would further Erie's interest in preventing such secondary effects. To be sure, requiring dancers to wear pasties and G-strings may not greatly reduce these secondary effects, but O'Brien requires only that the regulation further the interest in combating such effects. Even though the dissent questions the wisdom of Erie's chosen remedy, post, at 323 (opinion of Stevens, J.), the "'city must be allowed a reasonable opportunity to experiment with solutions to admittedly serious problems,'" Renton v. Playtime Theatres, Inc., 475 U. S., at 52 (quoting American Mini Theatres, 427 U. S., at 71 (plurality opinion)). It also may be true that a pasties and G-string requirement would not be as effective as, for example, a requirement that the dancers be fully clothed, but the city must balance its efforts to address the problem with the requirement that the restriction be no greater than necessary to further the city's interest.

The ordinance also satisfies O'Brien's third factor, that the government interest is unrelated to the suppression of free expression, as discussed supra, at 289-296. The fourth and final O'Brien factor—that the restriction is no greater than is essential to the furtherance of the government interest— is satisfied as well. The ordinance regulates conduct, and any incidental impact on the expressive element of nude dancing is de minimis. The requirement that dancers wear pasties and G-strings is a minimal restriction in furtherance of the asserted government interests, and the restriction leaves ample capacity to convey the dancer's erotic message. See Barnes v. Glen Theatre, Inc., 501 U. S., at 572 (plurality opinion of Rehnquist, C. J., joined by O'Connor and Kennedy, JJ.); id., at 587 (Souter, J., concurring in judgment). Justice Souter points out that zoning is an alternative means of addressing this problem. It is far from clear, however, that zoning imposes less of a burden on expression than the minimal requirement implemented here. In any event, since this is a content-neutral restriction, least restrictive means analysis is not required. See Ward, 491 U. S., at 798799, n. 6.

We hold, therefore, that Erie's ordinance is a content-neutral regulation that is valid under O'Brien. Accordingly, the judgment of the Pennsylvania Supreme Court is reversed, and the case is remanded for further proceedings.

It is so ordered.

## US v. Playboy Entertainment Group (May 22, 2000) [Appendix omitted]

Justice Kennedy delivered the opinion of the Court.

This case presents a challenge to §505 of the Telecommunications Act of 1996, Pub. L. 104—104, 110 Stat. 136, 47 U.S.C. § 561 (1994 ed., Supp. III). Section 505 requires cable television operators who provide channels "primarily dedicated to sexually-oriented programming" either to "fully scramble or otherwise fully block" those channels or to limit their transmission to hours when children are unlikely to be viewing, set by administrative regulation as the time between 10 p.m. and 6 a.m. 47 U.S.C. § 561(a) (1994 ed., Supp. III); 47 CFR § 76.227 (1999). Even before enactment of the statute, signal scrambling was already in use. Cable operators used scrambling in the regular course of business, so that only paying customers had access to certain programs. Scrambling could be imprecise, however; and either or both audio and visual portions of the scrambled programs might be heard or seen, a phenomenon known as "signal bleed." The purpose of §505 is to shield children from hearing or seeing images resulting from signal bleed.

To comply with the statute, the majority of cable operators adopted the second, or "time channeling," approach. The effect of the widespread adoption of time channeling was to eliminate altogether the transmission of the targeted programming outside the safe harbor period in affected cable service areas. In other words, for two-thirds of the day no household in those service areas could receive the programming, whether or not the household or the viewer wanted to do so.

Appellee Playboy Entertainment Group, Inc., challenged the statute as unnecessarily restrictive content-based legislation violative of the First Amendment. After a trial, a three-judge District Court concluded that a regime in which viewers could order signal blocking on a household-by-household basis presented an effective, less restrictive alternative to §505. 30 F. Supp. 2d 702, 719 (Del. 1998). Finding no error in this conclusion, we affirm.

I

Playboy Entertainment Group owns and prepares programs for adult television networks, including Playboy Television and Spice. Playboy transmits its programming to cable television operators, who retransmit it to their subscribers, either through monthly subscriptions to premium channels or on a so-called "pay-per-view" basis. Cable operators transmit Playboy's signal, like other premium channel signals, in scrambled form. The operators then provide paying subscribers with an "addressable converter," a box placed on the home television set. The converter permits the viewer to see and hear the descrambled signal. It is conceded that almost all of Playboy's programming consists of sexually explicit material as defined by the statute.

The statute was enacted because not all scrambling technology is perfect. Analog cable television systems may use either "RF" or "baseband" scrambling systems, which may not prevent signal bleed, so discernible pictures may appear from time to time on the scrambled screen. Furthermore, the listener might hear the audio portion of the program.

These imperfections are not inevitable. The problem is that at present it appears not to be economical to convert simpler RF or baseband scrambling systems to alternative scrambling technologies on a systemwide scale. Digital technology may one day provide another solution, as it presents no bleed problem at all. Indeed, digital systems are projected to become the technology of choice, which would eliminate the signal bleed problem. Digital technology is not yet in widespread use, however. With imperfect scrambling, viewers who have not paid to receive Playboy's channels may happen across discernible images of a sexually explicit nature. How many viewers, how discernible the scene or sound, and how often this may occur are at issue in this case.

Section 505 was enacted to address the signal bleed phenomenon. As noted, the statute and its implementing regulations require cable operators either to scramble a sexually explicit channel in full or to limit the channel's programming to the hours between 10 p.m. and 6 a.m. 47 U.S.C. § 561 (1994 ed., Supp. III); 47 CFR § 76.227 (1999). Section 505 was added by floor amendment, without significant debate, to the Telecommunications Act of 1996 (Act), a major legislative effort designed "to reduce regulation and encourage 'the rapid deployment of new telecommunications technologies.'" Reno v. American Civil Liberties Union, 521 U.S. 844, 857 (1997) (quoting 110 Stat. 56). "The Act includes seven Titles, six of which are the product of extensive committee hearings and the subject of discussion in Reports prepared by Committees of the Senate and the House of Representatives." Reno, supra, at 858. Section 505 is found in Title V of the Act, which is itself known as the Communications Decency Act of 1996 (CDA). 110 Stat. 133. Section 505 was to become effective on March 9, 1996, 30 days after the Act was signed by the President. Note following 47 U.S.C. § 561 (1994 ed., Supp. III).

On March 7, 1996, Playboy obtained a temporary restraining order (TRO) enjoining the enforcement of §505. 918 F. Supp. 813 (Del.), and brought this suit in a three-judge District Court pursuant to §561 of the Act, 110 Stat. 142, note following 47

U.S.C. § 223 (1994 ed., Supp. III). Playboy sought a declaration that §505 violates the Constitution and an injunction prohibiting the law's enforcement. The District Court denied Playboy a preliminary injunction, 945 F. Supp. 772 (Del. 1996), and we summarily affirmed, 520 U.S. 1141 (1997). The TRO was lifted, and the Federal Communications Commission announced it would begin enforcing §505 on May 18, 1997. In re Implementation of Section 505 of the Telecommunications Act of 1996, 12 FCC Rcd. 5212, 5214 (1997).

When the statute became operative, most cable operators had "no practical choice but to curtail [the targeted] programming during the [regulated] sixteen hours or risk the penalties imposed ... if any audio or video signal bleed occur[red] during [those] times." 30 F. Supp. 2d, at 711. The majority of operators—"in one survey, 69%"—complied with §505 by time channeling the targeted programmers. Ibid. Since "30 to 50% of all adult programming is viewed by households prior to 10 p.m.," the result was a significant restriction of communication, with a corresponding reduction in Playboy's revenues. Ibid.

In March 1998, the District Court held a full trial and concluded that §505 violates the First Amendment. 30 F. Supp. 2d, at 702. The District Court observed that §505 imposed a content-based restriction on speech. Id., at 714—715. It agreed that the interests the statute advanced were compelling but concluded the Government might further those interests in less restrictive ways. Id., at 717—720. One plausible, less restrictive alternative could be found in another section of the Act: §504, which requires a cable operator, "[u]pon request by a cable service subscriber . . . without charge, [to] fully scramble or otherwise fully block" any channel the subscriber does not wish to receive. 110 Stat. 136, 47 U.S.C. § 560 (1994 ed., Supp. III). As long as subscribers knew about this opportunity, the court reasoned, §504 would provide as much protection against unwanted programming as would §505. 30 F. Supp. 2d, at 718—720. At the same time, §504 was content neutral and would be less restrictive of Playboy's First Amendment rights. Ibid.

The court described what "adequate notice" would include, suggesting

"[operators] should communicate to their subscribers the information that certain channels broadcast sexually-oriented programming; that signal bleed ... may appear; that children may view signal bleed without their parents' knowledge or permission; that channel blocking devices ... are available free of charge ...; and that a request for a free device ... can be made by a telephone call to the [operator]." Id., at 719.

The means of providing this notice could include

"inserts in monthly billing statements, barker channels (preview channels of programming coming up on Pay-Per-View), and on-air advertisement on channels other than the one broadcasting the sexually explicit programming." Ibid.

The court added that this notice could be "conveyed on a regular basis, at reasonable intervals," and could include notice of changes in channel alignments. Ibid.

The District Court concluded that §504 so supplemented would be an effective, less restrictive alternative to §505, and consequently declared §505 unconstitutional and enjoined its enforcement. Id., at 719—720. The court also required Playboy to insist on these notice provisions in its contracts with cable operators. Ibid.

The United States filed a direct appeal in this Court pursuant to §561. The District Court thereafter dismissed for lack of jurisdiction two post-trial motions filed by the Government. App. to Juris. Statement 91a—92a. We noted probable jurisdiction, 527 U.S. 1021 (1999), and now affirm.

II

Two essential points should be understood concerning the speech at issue here. First, we shall assume that many adults themselves would find the material highly offensive; and when we consider the further circumstance that the material comes unwanted into homes where children might see or hear it against parental wishes or consent, there are legitimate reasons for regulating it. Second, all parties bring the case to us on the premise that Playboy's programming has First Amendment protection. As this case has been litigated, it is not alleged to be obscene; adults have a constitutional right to view it; the Government disclaims any interest in preventing children from seeing or hearing it with the consent of their parents; and Playboy has concomitant rights under the First Amendment to transmit it. These points are undisputed.

The speech in question is defined by its content; and the statute which seeks to restrict it is content based. Section 505 applies only to channels primarily dedicated to "sexually explicit adult programming or other programming that is indecent." The statute is unconcerned with signal bleed from any other channels. See 945 F. Supp., at 785 ("[Section 505] does not apply when signal bleed occurs on other premium channel networks, like HBO or the Disney Channel"). The overriding justification for the regulation is concern for the effect of the subject matter on young viewers. Section 505 is not "'justified without reference to the content of the regulated speech.'" Ward v. Rock Against Racism, 491 U.S. 781, 791 (1989) (quoting Clark v. Community for Creative Non&nbhyph;Violence, 468 U.S. 288, 293 (1984) (emphasis deleted)). It "focuses only on the content of the speech and the direct impact that speech has on its listeners." Boos v. Barry, 485 U.S. 312, 321 (1988) (opinion of O'Connor, J.). This is the essence of content-based regulation.

Not only does §505 single out particular programming content for regulation, it also singles out particular programmers. The speech in question was not thought by Congress to be so harmful that all channels were subject to restriction. Instead, the statutory disability applies only to channels "primarily dedicated to sexually-oriented programming." 47 U.S.C. § 561(a) (1994 ed., Supp. III). One sponsor of the measure even identified appellee by name. See 141 Cong. Rec. 15587 (1995) (statement of Sen. Feinstein) (noting the statute would apply to channels "such as the Playboy and Spice channels"). Laws designed or intended to suppress or restrict the expression of specific speakers contradict basic First Amendment principles. Section 505 limited Playboy's market as a penalty for its programming choice, though other channels capable of transmitting like material are altogether exempt.

The effect of the federal statute on the protected speech is now apparent. It is evident that the only reasonable way for a substantial number of cable operators to comply with the letter of §505 is to time channel, which silences the protected speech for two-thirds of the day in every home in a cable service area, regardless of the presence or likely presence of children or of the wishes of the viewers. According to the District Court, "30 to 50% of all adult programming is viewed by households prior to 10 p.m.," when the safe-harbor period begins. 30 F. Supp. 2d, at 711. To prohibit this much speech is a significant restriction of communication between speakers and willing adult listeners, communication which enjoys First Amendment protection. It is of no moment that the statute does not impose a complete prohibition. The distinction between laws burdening and laws banning speech is but a matter of degree. The Government's content-based burdens must satisfy the same rigorous scrutiny as its content-based bans.

Since §505 is a content-based speech restriction, it can stand only if it satisfies strict scrutiny. Sable Communications of Cal., Inc. v. FCC, 492 U.S. 115, 126 (1989). If a statute regulates speech based on its content, it must be narrowly tailored to promote a compelling Government interest. Ibid. If a less restrictive alternative would serve the Government's purpose, the legislature must use that alternative. Reno, 521 U.S., at 874 ("[The CDA's Internet indecency provisions'] burden on adult speech is unacceptable if less restrictive alternatives would be at least as effective in achieving the legitimate purpose that the statute was enacted to serve"); Sable Communications, supra, at 126 ("The Government may ... regulate the content of constitutionally protected speech in order to promote a compelling interest if it chooses the least restrictive means to further the articulated interest"). To do otherwise would be to restrict speech without an adequate justification, a course the First Amendment does not permit.

Our precedents teach these principles. Where the designed benefit of a content-based speech restriction is to shield the sensibilities of listeners, the general rule is that the right of expression prevails, even where no less restrictive alternative exists. We are expected to protect our own sensibilities "simply by averting [our] eyes." Cohen v. California, 403 U.S. 15, 21 (1971); accord, Erznoznik v. Jacksonville, 422 U.S. 205, 210–211 (1975). Here, of course, we consider images transmitted to some homes where they are not wanted and where parents often are not present to give immediate guidance. Cable television, like broadcast media, presents unique problems, which inform our assessment of the interests at stake, and which may justify restrictions that would be unacceptable in other contexts. See Denver Area Ed. Telecommunications Consortium, Inc. v. FCC, 518 U.S. 727, 744 (1996) (plurality opinion); id., at 804–805 (Kennedy, J., concurring in part, concurring in judgment in part, and dissenting in part); FCC v. Pacifica Foundation, 438 U.S. 726 (1978). No one suggests the Government must be indifferent to unwanted, indecent speech that comes into the home without parental consent. The speech here, all agree, is protected speech; and the question is what standard the Government must meet in order to restrict it. As we consider a content-based regulation, the answer should be clear: The standard is strict scrutiny. This case involves speech alone; and even where speech is indecent and enters the home, the objective of shielding children does not suffice to support a blanket ban if the protection can be accomplished by a less restrictive alternative.

In Sable Communications, for instance, the feasibility of a technological approach to controlling minors' access to "dial-a-porn" messages required invalidation of a complete statutory ban on the medium. 492 U.S., at 130—131. And, while mentioned only in passing, the mere possibility that user-based Internet screening software would "'soon be widely available'" was relevant to our rejection of an overbroad restriction of indecent cyberspeech. Reno, supra, at 876—877. Compare Rowan v. Post Office Dept., 397 U.S. 728, 729—730 (1970) (upholding statute "whereby any householder may insulate himself from advertisements that offer for sale 'matter which the addressee in his sole discretion believes to be erotically arousing or sexually provocative'" (quoting then 39 U.S.C. § 4009(a) (1964 ed., Supp. IV))), with Bolger v. Youngs Drug Products Corp., 463 U.S. 60, 75 (1983) (rejecting blanket ban on the mailing of unsolicited contraceptive advertisements). Compare also Ginsberg v. New York, 390 U.S. 629, 631 (1968) (upholding state statute barring the sale to minors of material defined as "obscene on the basis of its appeal to them"), with Butler v. Michigan, 352 U.S. 380, 381 (1957) (rejecting blanket ban of material "'tending to incite minors to violent or depraved or immoral acts, manifestly tending to the corruption of the morals of youth'" (quoting then Mich. Penal Code §343)). Each of these cases arose in a different context–Sable Communications and Reno, for instance, also note the affirmative steps necessary to obtain access to indecent material via the media at issue–but they provide necessary instruction for complying with accepted First Amendment principles.

Our zoning cases, on the other hand, are irrelevant to the question here. Post, at 4 (Breyer, J., dissenting) (citing Renton v. Playtime Theatres, Inc., 475 U.S. 41 (1986), and Young v. American Mini Theatres, Inc., 427 U.S. 50 (1976)). We have made clear that the lesser scrutiny afforded regulations targeting the secondary effects of crime or declining property values has no application to content-based regulations targeting the primary effects of protected speech. Reno, supra, at 867—868; Boos, 485 U.S., at 320—321. The statute now before us bur-dens speech because of its content; it must receive strict scrutiny.

There is, moreover, a key difference between cable television and the broadcasting media, which is the point on which this case turns: Cable systems have the capacity to block unwanted channels on a household-by-household basis. The option to block reduces the likelihood, so concerning to the Court in Pacifica, supra, at 744, that traditional First Amendment scrutiny would deprive the Government of all authority to address this sort of problem. The corollary, of course, is that targeted blocking enables the Government to support parental authority without affecting the First Amendment interests of speakers and willing listeners–listeners for whom, if the speech is unpopular or indecent, the privacy of their own homes may be the optimal place of receipt. Simply put, targeted blocking is less restrictive than banning, and the Government cannot ban speech if targeted blocking is a feasible and effective means of furthering its compelling interests. This is not to say that the absence of an effective blocking mechanism will in all cases suffice to support a law restricting the speech in question; but if a less restrictive means is available for the Government to achieve its goals, the Government must use it.

III

The District Court concluded that a less restrictive alternative is available: §504, with adequate publicity. 30 F. Supp. 2d, at 719–720. No one disputes that §504, which requires cable operators to block undesired channels at individual households upon request, is narrowly tailored to the Government's goal of supporting parents who want those channels blocked. The question is whether §504 can be effective.

When a plausible, less restrictive alternative is offered to a content-based speech restriction, it is the Government's obligation to prove that the alternative will be ineffective to achieve its goals. The Government has not met that burden here. In support of its position, the Government cites empirical evidence showing that §504, as promulgated and implemented before trial, generated few requests for household-by-household blocking. Between March 1996 and May 1997, while the Government was enjoined from enforcing §505, §504 remained in operation. A survey of cable operators determined that fewer than 0.5% of cable subscribers requested full blocking during that time. Id., at 712. The uncomfortable fact is that §504 was the sole blocking regulation in effect for over a year; and the public greeted it with a collective yawn.

The District Court was correct to direct its attention to the import of this tepid response. Placing the burden of proof upon the Government, the District Court examined whether §504 was capable of serving as an effective, less restrictive means of reaching the Government's goals. Id., at 715, 718–719. It concluded that §504, if publicized in an adequate manner, could be. Id., at 719–720.

The District Court employed the proper approach. When the Government restricts speech, the Government bears the burden of proving the constitutionality of its actions. Greater New Orleans Broadcasting Assn., Inc. v. United States, 527 U.S. 173, 183 (1999) ("[T]he Government bears the burden of identifying a substantial interest and justifying the challenged restriction"); Reno, 521 U.S., at 879 ("The breadth of this content-based restriction of speech imposes an especially heavy burden on the Government to explain why a less restrictive provision would not be as effective ..."); Edenfield v. Fane, 507 U.S. 761, 770–771 (1993) ("[A] governmental body seeking to sustain a restriction on commercial speech must demonstrate that the harms it recites are real and that its restriction will in fact alleviate them to a material degree"); Board of Trustees of State Univ. of N. Y. v. Fox, 492 U.S. 469, 480 (1989) ("[T]he State bears the burden of justifying its restrictions ..."); Tinker v. Des Moines Independent Community School Dist., 393 U.S. 503, 509 (1969) ("In order for the State ... to justify prohibition of a particular expression of opinion, it must be able to show that its action was caused by something more than a mere desire to avoid the discomfort and unpleasantness that always accompany an unpopular viewpoint"). When the Government seeks to restrict speech based on its content, the usual presumption of constitutionality afforded congressional enactments is reversed. "Content-based regulations are presumptively invalid," R. A. V. v. St. Paul, 505 U.S. 377, 382 (1992), and the Government bears the burden to rebut that presumption.

This is for good reason. "[T]he line between speech unconditionally guaranteed and speech which may legitimately be regulated, suppressed, or punished is finely drawn." Speiser v. Randall, 357 U.S. 513, 525 (1958). Error in marking that line exacts an extraordinary cost. It is through speech that our convictions and beliefs are influenced, expressed, and tested. It is through speech that we bring those beliefs to bear on Government and on society. It is through speech that our personalities are formed and expressed. The citizen is entitled to seek out or reject certain ideas or influences without Government interference or control.

When a student first encounters our free speech jurisprudence, he or she might think it is influenced by the philosophy that one idea is as good as any other, and that in art and literature objective standards of style, taste, decorum, beauty, and esthetics are deemed by the Constitution to be inappropriate, indeed unattainable. Quite the opposite is true. The Constitution no more enforces a relativistic philosophy or moral nihilism than it does any other point of view. The Constitution exists precisely so that opinions and judgments, including esthetic and moral judgments about art and literature, can be formed, tested, and expressed. What the Constitution says is that these judgments are for the individual to make, not for the Government to decree, even with the mandate or approval of a majority. Technology expands the capacity to choose; and it denies the potential of this revolution if we assume the Government is best positioned to make these choices for us.

It is rare that a regulation restricting speech because of its content will ever be permissible. Indeed, were we to give the Government the benefit of the doubt when it attempted to restrict speech, we would risk leaving regulations in place that sought to shape our unique personalities or to silence dissenting ideas. When First Amendment compliance is the point to be proved, the risk of non-persuasion–operative in all trials– must rest with the Government, not with the citizen. Id., at 526.

With this burden in mind, the District Court explored three explanations for the lack of individual blocking requests. 30 F. Supp. 2d, at 719. First, individual blocking might not be an effective alternative, due to technological or other limitations. Second, although an adequately advertised blocking provision might have been effective, §504 as written did not require sufficient notice to make it so. Third, the actual signal bleed problem might be far less of a concern than the Government at first had supposed. Ibid.

To sustain its statute, the Government was required to show that the first was the right answer. According to the District Court, however, the first and third possibilities were "equally consistent" with the record before it. Ibid. As for the second, the record was "not clear" as to whether enough notice had been issued to give §504 a fighting chance. Ibid. The case, then, was at best a draw. Unless the District Court's findings are clearly erroneous, the tie goes to free expression.

The District Court began with the problem of signal bleed itself, concluding "the Government has not convinced us that [signal bleed] is a pervasive problem." Id., at 708–709, 718. The District Court's thorough discussion exposes a central weakness in the Government's proof: There is little hard evidence of how widespread or how serious the problem of signal bleed is. Indeed, there is no proof as to how likely any child is to view a discernible explicit image, and no proof of the duration of the bleed or the quality of the pictures or sound. To say that millions of children are subject to a risk of viewing signal bleed is one thing; to avoid articulating the true nature and extent of the risk is quite another. Under §505, sanctionable signal bleed can include instances as fleeting as an image appearing on a screen for just a few seconds. The First Amendment requires a more careful assessment and characterization of an evil in order to justify a regulation as sweeping as this. Although the parties have taken the additional step of lodging with the Court an assortment of videotapes, some of which show quite explicit bleeding and some of which show television static or snow, there is no attempt at explanation or context; there is no discussion, for instance, of the extent to which any particular tape is representative of what appears on screens nationwide.

The Government relied at trial on anecdotal evidence to support its regulation, which the District Court summarized as follows:

"The Government presented evidence of two city councillors, eighteen individuals, one United States Senator, and the officials of one city who complained either to their [cable operator], to their local Congressman, or to the FCC about viewing signal bleed on television. In each instance, the local [cable operator] offered to, or did in fact, rectify the situation for free (with the exception of 1 individual), with varying degrees of rapidity. Included in the complaints was the additional concern that other parents might not be aware that their children are exposed to this problem. In addition, the Government presented evidence of a child exposed to signal bleed at a friend's house. Cindy Omlin set the lockout feature on her remote control to prevent her child from tuning to adult channels, but her eleven year old son was nevertheless exposed to signal bleed when he attended a slumber party at a friend's house.

"The Government has presented evidence of only a handful of isolated incidents over the 16 years since 1982 when Playboy started broadcasting. The Government has not presented any survey-type evidence on the magnitude of the 'problem.'" Id., at 709 (footnote and record citations omitted).

Spurred by the District Court's express request for more specific evidence of the problem, see 945 F. Supp., at 779, n. 16, the Government also presented an expert's spreadsheet estimate that 39 million homes with 29.5 million children had the potential to be exposed to signal bleed, 30 F. Supp. 2d, at 708–709. The Government made no attempt to confirm the accuracy of its estimate through surveys or other field tests, however. Accordingly, the District Court discounted the figures and made this finding:

"[T]he Government presented no evidence on the number of households actually exposed to signal bleed and thus has not quantified the actual extent of the problem of signal bleed." Id., at 709. The finding is not clearly erroneous; indeed it is all but required.

Once §505 went into effect, of course, a significant percentage of cable operators felt it necessary to time channel their sexually explicit programmers. Id., at 711, and n. 14. This is an indication that scrambling technology is not yet perfected. That is not to say, however, that scrambling is completely ineffective. Different cable systems use different scrambling systems, which vary in their dependability. "The severity of the problem varies from time to time and place to place, depending on the weather, the quality of the equipment, its installation, and maintenance." Id., at 708. At even the good end of the spectrum a system might bleed to an extent sufficient to trigger the time-channeling requirement for a cautious cable operator. (The statute requires the signal to be "fully block[ed]." 47 U.S.C. § 561(a) (1994 ed., Supp. III) (emphasis added).) A rational cable operator, faced with the possibility of sanctions for intermittent bleeding, could well choose to time channel even if the bleeding is too momentary to pose any concern to most households. To affirm that the Government failed to prove the existence of a problem, while at the same time observing that the statute imposes a severe burden on speech, is consistent with the analysis our cases require. Here, there is no probative evidence in the record which differentiates among the extent of bleed at individual households and no evidence which otherwise quantifies the signal bleed problem.

In addition, market-based solutions such as programmable televisions, VCR's, and mapping systems (which display a blue screen when tuned to a scrambled signal) may eliminate signal bleed at the consumer end of the cable. 30 F. Supp. 2d, at 708. Playboy made the point at trial that the Government's estimate failed to account for these factors. Id., at 708–709. Without some sort of field survey, it is impossible to know how widespread the problem in fact is, and the only indicator in the record is a handful of complaints. Cf. Turner Broadcasting System, Inc. v. FCC, 520 U.S. 180, 187 (1997) (reviewing "'a record of tens of thousands of pages' of evidence" developed through "three years of pre-enactment hearings, ... as well as additional expert submissions, sworn declarations and testimony, and industry documents" in support of complex must-carry provisions). If the number of children transfixed by even flickering pornographic television images in fact reached into the millions we, like the District Court, would have expected to be directed to more than a handful of complaints.

No support for the restriction can be found in the near barren legislative record relevant to this provision. Section 505 was added to the Act by floor amendment, accompanied by only brief statements, and without committee hearing or debate. See 141 Cong. Rec. 15586–15589 (1995). One of the measure's sponsors did indicate she considered time channeling to be superior to voluntary blocking, which "put[s] the burden of action on the subscriber, not the cable company." Id., at 15587 (statement of Sen. Feinstein). This sole conclusory statement, however, tells little about the relative efficacy of voluntary blocking versus time channeling, other than offering the unhelpful, self-evident generality that voluntary measures require voluntary action. The Court has declined to rely on similar evidence before. See Sable Communications, 492 U.S., at 129—130 ("[A]side from conclusory statements during the debates by proponents of the bill, ... the congressional record presented to us contains no evidence as to how effective or ineffective the ... regulations were or might prove to be" (footnote omitted)); Reno, 521 U.S., at 858, and n. 24, 875—876, n. 41 (same). This is not to suggest that a 10,000 page record must be compiled in every case or that the Government must delay in acting to address a real problem; but the Government must present more than anecdote and supposition. The question is whether an actual problem has been proven in this case. We agree that the Government has failed to establish a pervasive, nationwide problem justifying its nationwide daytime speech ban.

Nor did the District Court err in its second conclusion. The Government also failed to prove §504 with adequate notice would be an ineffective alternative to §505. Once again, the District Court invited the Government to produce its proof. See 945 F. Supp., at 781 ("If the §504 blocking option is not being promoted, it cannot become a meaningful alternative to the provisions of §505. At the time of the permanent injunction hearing, further evidence of the actual and predicted impact and efficacy of §504 would be helpful to us"). Once again, the Government fell short. See 30 F. Supp. 2d, at 719 ("[The Government's argument that §504 is ineffective] is premised on adequate notice to subscribers. It is not clear, however, from the record that notices of the provisions of §504 have been adequate"). There is no evidence that a well-promoted voluntary blocking provision would not be capable at least of informing parents about signal bleed (if they are not yet aware of it) and about their rights to have the bleed blocked (if they consider it a problem and have not yet controlled it themselves).

The Government finds at least two problems with the conclusion of the three-judge District Court. First, the Government takes issue with the District Court's reliance, without proof, on a "hypothetical, enhanced version of Section 504." Brief for United States et al. 32. It was not the District Court's obligation, however, to predict the extent to which an improved notice scheme would improve §504. It was for the Government, presented with a plausible, less restrictive alternative, to prove the alternative to be ineffective, and §505 to be the least restrictive available means. Indeed, to the extent the District Court erred, it was only in attempting to implement the less restrictive alternative through judicial decree by requiring Playboy to provide for expanded notice in its cable service contracts. The appropriate remedy was not to repair the statute, it was to enjoin the speech restriction. Given the existence of a less restrictive means, if the Legislature wished to improve its statute, perhaps in the process giving careful consideration to other alternatives, it then could do so.

The Government also contends a publicized §504 will be just as restrictive as §505, on the theory that the cost of installing blocking devices will outstrip the revenues from distributing Playboy's programming and lead to its cancellation. See 30 F. Supp. 2d, at 713. This conclusion rests on the assumption that a sufficient percentage of households, informed of the potential for signal bleed, would consider it enough of a problem to order blocking devices–an assumption for which there is no support in the record. Id., at 719. It should be noted, furthermore, that Playboy is willing to incur the costs of an effective §504. One might infer that Playboy believes an advertised §504 will be ineffective for its object, or one might infer the company believes the signal bleed problem is not widespread. In the absence of proof, it is not for the Court to assume the former.

It is no response that voluntary blocking requires a consumer to take action, or may be inconvenient, or may not go perfectly every time. A court should not assume a plausible, less restrictive alternative would be ineffective; and a court should not presume parents, given full information, will fail to act. If unresponsive operators are a concern, moreover, a notice statute could give cable operators ample incentive, through fines or other penalties for noncompliance, to respond to blocking requests in prompt and efficient fashion.

Having adduced no evidence in the District Court showing that an adequately advertised §504 would not be effective to aid desirous parents in keeping signal bleed out of their own households, the Government can now cite nothing in the record to support the point. The Government instead takes quite a different approach. After only an offhand suggestion that the success of a well-communicated §504 is "highly unlikely," the Government sets the point aside, arguing instead that society's independent interests will be unserved if parents fail to act on that information. Brief for United States et al. 32–33 ("[U]nder ... an enhanced version of Section 504, parents who had strong feelings about the matter could see to it that their children did not view signal bleed–at least in their own homes"); id., at 33 ("Even an enhanced version of Section 504 would succeed in blocking signal bleed only if, and after, parents affirmatively decided to avail themselves of the means offered them to do so. There would certainly be parents–perhaps a large number of parents–who out of inertia, indifference, or distraction, simply would take no action to block signal bleed, even if fully informed of the problem and even if offered a relatively easy solution"); Reply Brief for United States et al. 12 ([Society's] interest would of course be served in instances ... in which parents request blocking under an enhanced Section 504. But in cases in which parents fail to make use of an enhanced Section 504 procedure out of distraction, inertia, or indifference, Section 505 would be the only means to protect society's independent interest").

Even upon the assumption that the Government has an interest in substituting itself for informed and empowered parents, its interest is not sufficiently compelling to justify this widespread restriction on speech. The Government's argument stems from the idea that parents do not know their children are viewing the material on a scale or frequency to cause concern, or if so, that parents do not want to take affirmative steps to block it and their decisions are to be superseded. The assumptions have not been established; and in any event the assumptions apply only in a regime where the option of blocking has not been explained. The whole point of a publicized §504 would be to advise parents that indecent material may be shown and to afford them an opportunity to block it at all times, even when they are not at home and even after 10 p.m. Time channeling does not offer this assistance. The regulatory alternative of a publicized §504, which has the real possibility of promoting more open disclosure and the choice of an effective blocking system, would provide parents the information needed to engage in active supervision. The Government has not shown that this alternative, a regime of added communication and support, would be insufficient to secure its objective, or that any overriding harm justifies its intervention.

There can be little doubt, of course, that under a voluntary blocking regime, even with adequate notice, some children will be exposed to signal bleed; and we need not discount the possibility that a graphic image could have a negative impact on a young child. It must be remembered, however, that children will be exposed to signal bleed under time channeling as well. Time channeling, unlike blocking, does not eliminate signal bleed around the clock. Just as adolescents may be unsupervised outside of their own households, it is hardly unknown for them to be unsupervised in front of the television set after 10 p.m. The record is silent as to the comparative effectiveness of the two alternatives.

     \*   \*   \*

Basic speech principles are at stake in this case. When the purpose and design of a statute is to regulate speech by reason of its content, special consideration or latitude is not accorded to the Government merely because the law can somehow be described as a burden rather than outright suppression. We cannot be influenced, moreover, by the perception that the regulation in question is not a major one because the speech is not very important. The history of the law of free expression is one of vindication in cases involving speech that many citizens may find shabby, offensive, or even ugly. It follows that all content-based restrictions on speech must give us more than a moment's pause. If television broadcasts can expose children to the real risk of harmful exposure to indecent materials, even in their own home and without parental consent, there is a problem the Government can address. It must do so, however, in a way consistent with First Amendment principles. Here the Government has not met the burden the First Amendment imposes.

The Government has failed to show that §505 is the least restrictive means for addressing a real problem; and the District Court did not err in holding the statute violative of the First Amendment. In light of our ruling, it is unnecessary to address the second question presented: whether the District Court was divested of jurisdiction to consider the Government's postjudgment motions after the Government filed a notice of appeal in this Court. The judgment of the District Court is affirmed.

It is so ordered.

**Boy Scouts of America v. Dale (June 28, 2000) [Appendix omitted]**

Chief Justice Rehnquist delivered the opinion of the Court.

Petitioners are the Boy Scouts of America and the Monmouth Council, a division of the Boy Scouts of America (collectively, Boy Scouts). The Boy Scouts is a private, not-for-profit organization engaged in instilling its system of values in young people. The Boy Scouts asserts that homosexual conduct is inconsistent with the values it seeks to instill. Respondent is James Dale, a former Eagle Scout whose adult membership in the Boy Scouts was revoked when the Boy Scouts learned that he is an avowed homosexual and gay rights activist. The New Jersey Supreme Court held that New Jersey's public accommodations law requires that the Boy Scouts admit Dale. This case presents the question whether applying New Jersey's public accommodations law in this way violates the Boy Scouts' First Amendment right of expressive association. We hold that it does.

I

James Dale entered scouting in 1978 at the age of eight by joining Monmouth Council's Cub Scout Pack 142. Dale became a Boy Scout in 1981 and remained a Scout until he turned 18. By all accounts, Dale was an exemplary Scout. In 1988, he achieved the rank of Eagle Scout, one of Scouting's highest honors.

Dale applied for adult membership in the Boy Scouts in 1989. The Boy Scouts approved his application for the position of assistant scoutmaster of Troop 73. Around the same time, Dale left home to attend Rutgers University. After arriving at Rutgers, Dale first acknowledged to himself and others that he is gay. He quickly became involved with, and eventually became the copresident of, the Rutgers University Lesbian/Gay Alliance. In 1990, Dale attended a seminar addressing the psychological and health needs of lesbian and gay teenagers. A newspaper covering the event interviewed Dale about his advocacy of homosexual teenagers' need for gay role models. In early July 1990, the newspaper published the interview and Dale's photograph over a caption identifying him as the copresident of the Lesbian/Gay Alliance.

Later that month, Dale received a letter from Monmouth Council Executive James Kay revoking his adult membership. Dale wrote to Kay requesting the reason for Monmouth Council's decision. Kay responded by letter that the Boy Scouts "specifically forbid membership to homosexuals." App. 137.

In 1992, Dale filed a complaint against the Boy Scouts in the New Jersey Superior Court. The complaint alleged that the Boy Scouts had violated New Jersey's public accommodations statute and its common law by revoking Dale's membership based solely on his sexual orientation. New Jersey's public accommodations statute prohibits, among other things, discrimination on the basis of sexual orientation in places of public accommodation. N. J. Stat. Ann. §§10:5—4 and 10:5—5 (West Supp. 2000); see Appendix, infra, at 18—19.

The New Jersey Superior Court's Chancery Division granted summary judgment in favor of the Boy Scouts. The court held that New Jersey's public accommodations law was inapplicable because the Boy Scouts was not a place of public accommodation, and that, alternatively, the Boy Scouts is a distinctly private group exempted from coverage under New Jersey's law. The court rejected Dale's common-law claim holding that New Jersey's policy is embodied in the public accommodations law. The court also concluded that the Boy Scouts' position in respect of active homosexuality was clear and held that the First Amendment freedom of expressive association prevented the government from forcing the Boy Scouts to accept Dale as an adult leader.

The New Jersey Superior Court's Appellate Division affirmed the dismissal of Dale's common-law claim, but otherwise reversed and remanded for further proceedings. 308 N. J. Super. 516, 70 A. 2d 270 (1998). It held that New Jersey's public accommodations law applied to the Boy Scouts and that the Boy Scouts violated it. The Appellate Division rejected the Boy Scouts' federal constitutional claims.

The New Jersey Supreme Court affirmed the judgment of the Appellate Division. It held that the Boy Scouts was a place of public accommodation subject to the public accommodations law, that the organization was not exempt from the law under any of its express exceptions, and that the Boy Scouts violated the law by revoking Dale's membership based on his avowed homosexuality. After considering the state-law issues, the court addressed the Boy Scouts' claims that application of the public accommodations law in this case violated its federal constitutional rights " 'to enter into and maintain ... intimate or private relationships ... [and] to associate for the purpose of engaging in protected speech.' " 160 N. J. 562, 605, 734 A. 2d 1196, 1219 (1999) (quoting Board of Directors of Rotary Int'l v. Rotary Club of Duarte, 481 U.S. 537, 544 (1987)). With respect to the right to intimate association, the court concluded that the Boy Scouts' "large size, nonselectivity, inclusive rather than exclusive purpose, and practice of inviting or allowing nonmembers to attend meetings, establish that the organization is not 'sufficiently personal or private to warrant constitutional protection' under the freedom of intimate association.' " 160 N. J., at 608—609, 734 A. 2d, at 1221 (quoting Duarte, supra, at 546). With respect to the right of expressive association, the court "agree[d] that Boy Scouts expresses a belief in moral values and uses its activities to encourage the moral development of its members." Ibid., 734 A. 2d, at 1223. But the court concluded that it was "not persuaded ... that a shared goal of Boy Scout members is to associate in order to preserve the view that homosexuality is immoral." 160 N. J., at 613, 734 A. 2d, at 1223— 1224 (internal quotation marks omitted). Accordingly, the court held "that Dale's membership does not violate the Boy Scouts' right of expressive association because his inclusion would not 'affect in any significant way [the Boy Scouts'] existing members' ability to carry out their various purposes.' " Id., at 615, 734 A. 2d, at 1225 (quoting Duarte, supra, at 548). The court also determined that New Jersey has a compelling interest in eliminating "the destructive consequences of discrimination from our society," and that its public accommodations law abridges no more speech than is necessary to accomplish its purpose. 160 N. J., at 619—620, 734 A. 2d, at 1227—1228. Finally, the court addressed the Boy Scouts' reliance on Hurley v. Irish-American Gay, Lesbian and Bisexual Group of Boston, Inc., 515 U.S. 557 (1995), in support of its claimed First

Amendment right to exclude Dale. The court determined that Hurley did not require deciding the case in favor of the Boy Scouts because "the reinstatement of Dale does not compel Boy Scouts to express any message." 160 N. J., at 624, 734 A. 2d, at 1229.

We granted the Boy Scouts' petition for certiorari to determine whether the application of New Jersey's public accommodations law violated the First Amendment. 528 U.S. 1109 (2000).

II

In Roberts v. United States Jaycees, 468 U.S. 609, 622 (1984), we observed that "implicit in the right to engage in activities protected by the First Amendment" is "a corresponding right to associate with others in pursuit of a wide variety of political, social, economic, educational, religious, and cultural ends." This right is crucial in preventing the majority from imposing its views on groups that would rather express other, perhaps unpopular, ideas. See ibid. (stating that protection of the right to expressive association is "especially important in preserving political and cultural diversity and in shielding dissident expression from suppression by the majority"). Government actions that may unconstitutionally burden this freedom may take many forms, one of which is "intrusion into the internal structure or affairs of an association" like a "regulation that forces the group to accept members it does not desire." Id., at 623. Forcing a group to accept certain members may impair the ability of the group to express those views, and only those views, that it intends to express. Thus, "[f ]reedom of association ... plainly presupposes a freedom not to associate." Ibid.

The forced inclusion of an unwanted person in a group infringes the group's freedom of expressive association if the presence of that person affects in a significant way the group's ability to advocate public or private viewpoints. New York State Club Assn., Inc. v. City of New York, 487 U.S. 1, 13 (1988). But the freedom of expressive association, like many freedoms, is not absolute. We have held that the freedom could be overridden "by regulations adopted to serve compelling state interests, unrelated to the suppression of ideas, that cannot be achieved through means significantly less restrictive of associational freedoms." Roberts, supra, at 623.

To determine whether a group is protected by the First Amendment's expressive associational right, we must determine whether the group engages in "expressive association." The First Amendment's protection of expressive association is not reserved for advocacy groups. But to come within its ambit, a group must engage in some form of expression, whether it be public or private.

Because this is a First Amendment case where the ultimate conclusions of law are virtually inseparable from findings of fact, we are obligated to independently review the factual record to ensure that the state court's judgment does not unlawfully intrude on free expression. See Hurley, supra, at 567—568. The record reveals the following. The Boy Scouts is a private, nonprofit organization. According to its mission statement:

"It is the mission of the Boy Scouts of America to serve others by helping to instill values in young people and, in other ways, to prepare them to make ethical choices over their lifetime in achieving their full potential.

"The values we strive to instill are based on those found in the Scout Oath and Law:

"Scout Oath

"On my honor I will do my best

To do my duty to God and my country

and to obey the Scout Law;

To help other people at all times;

To keep myself physically strong,

mentally awake, and morally straight.

"Scout Law

"A Scout is:

"Trustworthy  Obedient

Loyal  Cheerful

Helpful  Thrifty

Friendly  Brave

Courteous  Clean

Kind  Reverent." App. 184.

Thus, the general mission of the Boy Scouts is clear: "[T]o instill values in young people." Ibid. The Boy Scouts seeks to instill these values by having its adult leaders spend time with the youth members, instructing and engaging them in activities like camping, archery, and fishing. During the time spent with the youth members, the scoutmasters and assistant scoutmasters inculcate them with the Boy Scouts' values–both expressly and by example. It seems indisputable that an association that seeks to transmit such a system of values engages in expressive activity. See Roberts, supra, at 636 (O'Connor, J., concurring) ("Even the training of outdoor survival skills or participation in community service might become expressive when the activity is intended to develop good morals, reverence, patriotism, and a desire for self-improvement").

Given that the Boy Scouts engages in expressive activity, we must determine whether the forced inclusion of Dale as an assistant scoutmaster would significantly affect the Boy Scouts' ability to advocate public or private viewpoints. This inquiry necessarily requires us first to explore, to a limited extent, the nature of the Boy Scouts' view of homosexuality.

The values the Boy Scouts seeks to instill are "based on" those listed in the Scout Oath and Law. App. 184. The Boy Scouts explains that the Scout Oath and Law provide "a positive moral code for living; they are a list of 'do's' rather than 'don'ts.' " Brief for Petitioners 3. The Boy Scouts asserts that homosexual conduct is inconsistent with the values embodied in the Scout Oath and Law, particularly with the values represented by the terms "morally straight" and "clean."

Obviously, the Scout Oath and Law do not expressly mention sexuality or sexual orientation. See supra, at 6—7. And the terms "morally straight" and "clean" are by no means self-defining. Different people would attribute to those terms very different meanings. For example, some people may believe that engaging in homosexual conduct is not at odds with being "morally straight" and "clean." And others may believe that engaging in homosexual conduct is contrary to being "morally straight" and "clean." The Boy Scouts says it falls within the latter category.

The New Jersey Supreme Court analyzed the Boy Scouts' beliefs and found that the "exclusion of members solely on the basis of their sexual orientation is inconsistent with Boy Scouts' commitment to a diverse and 'representative' membership ... [and] contradicts Boy Scouts' overarching objective to reach 'all eligible youth.' " 160 N. J., at 618, 734 A. 2d, at 1226. The court concluded that the exclusion of members like Dale "appears antithetical to the organization's goals and philosophy." Ibid. But our cases reject this sort of inquiry; it is not the role of the courts to reject a group's expressed values because they disagree with those values or find them internally inconsistent. See Democratic Party of United States v. Wisconsin ex rel. La Follette, 450 U.S. 107, 124 (1981) ("[A]s is true of all expressions of First Amendment freedoms, the courts may not interfere on the ground that they view a particular expression as unwise or irrational"); see also Thomas v. Review Bd. of Indiana Employment Security Div., 450 U.S. 707, 714 (1981) ("[R]eligious beliefs need not be acceptable, logical, consistent, or comprehensible to others to merit First Amendment protection").

The Boy Scouts asserts that it "teach[es] that homosexual conduct is not morally straight," Brief for Peti-
tioners 39, and that it does "not want to promote homosexual conduct as a legitimate form of behavior," Reply Brief for Petitioners 5. We accept the Boy Scouts' assertion. We need not inquire further to determine the nature of the Boy Scouts' expression with respect to homosexuality. But because the record before us contains written evidence of the Boy Scouts' viewpoint, we look
to it as instructive, if only on the question of the sincerity of the professed beliefs.

A 1978 position statement to the Boy Scouts' Executive Committee, signed by Downing B. Jenks, the President of the Boy Scouts, and Harvey L. Price, the Chief Scout Executive, expresses the Boy Scouts' "official position" with regard to "homosexuality and Scouting":

"Q. May an individual who openly declares himself to be a homosexual be a volunteer Scout leader?

"A. No. The Boy Scouts of America is a private, membership organization and leadership therein is a privilege and not a right. We do not believe that homosexuality and leadership in Scouting are appropriate. We will continue to select only those who in our judgment meet our standards and qualifications for leadership." App. 453–454.

Thus, at least as of 1978–the year James Dale entered Scouting–the official position of the Boy Scouts was that avowed homosexuals were not to be Scout leaders.

A position statement promulgated by the Boy Scouts in 1991 (after Dale's membership was revoked but before this litigation was filed) also supports its current view:

"We believe that homosexual conduct is inconsistent with the requirement in the Scout Oath that a Scout be morally straight and in the Scout Law that a Scout be clean in word and deed, and that homosexuals do not provide a desirable role model for Scouts." Id., at 457.

This position statement was redrafted numerous times but its core message remained consistent. For example, a 1993 position statement, the most recent in the record, reads, in part:

"The Boy Scouts of America has always reflected the expectations that Scouting families have had for the organization. We do not believe that homosexuals provide a role model consistent with these expectations. Accordingly, we do not allow for the registration of avowed homosexuals as members or as leaders of the BSA." Id., at 461.

The Boy Scouts publicly expressed its views with respect to homosexual conduct by its assertions in prior litigation. For example, throughout a California case with similar facts filed in the early 1980's, the Boy Scouts consistently asserted the same position with respect to homosexuality that it asserts today. See Curran v. Mount Diablo Council of Boy Scouts of America, No. C—365529 (Cal. Super. Ct., July 25, 1991); 48 Cal. App. 4th 670, 29 Cal. Rptr. 2d 580 (1994); 17 Cal. 4th 670, 952 P.2d 218 (1998). We cannot doubt that the Boy Scouts sincerely holds this view.

We must then determine whether Dale's presence as an assistant scoutmaster would significantly burden the Boy Scouts' desire to not "promote homosexual conduct as a legitimate form of behavior." Reply Brief for Petitioners 5. As we give deference to an association's assertions regarding the nature of its expression, we must also give deference to an association's view of what would impair its expression. See, e.g., La Follette, supra, at 123—124 (considering whether a Wisconsin law burdened the National Party's associational rights and stating that "a State, or a court, may not constitutionally substitute its own judgment for that of the Party"). That is not to say that an expressive association can erect a shield against antidiscrimination laws simply by asserting that mere acceptance of a member from a particular group would impair its message. But here Dale, by his own admission, is one of a group of gay Scouts who have "become leaders in their community and are open and honest about their sexual orientation." App. 11. Dale was the copresident of a gay and lesbian organization at college and remains a gay rights activist. Dale's presence in the Boy Scouts would, at the very least, force the organization to send a message, both to the youth members and the world, that the Boy Scouts accepts homosexual conduct as a legitimate form of behavior.

Hurley is illustrative on this point. There we considered whether the application of Massachusetts' public accommodations law to require the organizers of a private St. Patrick's Day parade to include among the marchers an Irish&nbhyph;American gay, lesbian, and bisexual group, GLIB, violated the parade organizers' First Amendment rights. We noted that the parade organizers did not wish to exclude the GLIB members because of their sexual orientations, but because they wanted to march behind a GLIB banner. We observed:

"[A] contingent marching behind the organization's banner would at least bear witness to the fact that some Irish are gay, lesbian, or bisexual, and the presence of the organized marchers would suggest their view that people of their sexual orientations have as much claim to unqualified social acceptance as heterosexuals ... . The parade's organizers may not believe these facts about Irish sexuality to be so, or they may object to unqualified social acceptance of gays and lesbians or have some other reason for wishing to keep GLIB's message out of the parade. But whatever the reason, it boils down to the choice of a speaker not to propound a particular point of view, and that choice is presumed to lie beyond the government's power to control." 515 U.S., at 574—575.

Here, we have found that the Boy Scouts believes that homosexual conduct is inconsistent with the values it seeks to instill in its youth members; it will not "promote homosexual conduct as a legitimate form of behavior." Reply Brief for Petitioners 5. As the presence of GLIB in Boston's St. Patrick's Day parade would have interfered with the parade organizers' choice not to propound a particular point of view, the presence of Dale as an assistant scoutmaster would just as surely interfere with the Boy Scout's choice not to propound a point of view contrary to its beliefs.

The New Jersey Supreme Court determined that the Boy Scouts' ability to disseminate its message was not significantly affected by the forced inclusion of Dale as an assistant scoutmaster because of the following findings:

"Boy Scout members do not associate for the purpose of disseminating the belief that homosexuality is immoral; Boy Scouts discourages its leaders from disseminating any views on sexual issues; and Boy Scouts includes sponsors and members who subscribe to different views in respect of homosexuality." 160 N. J., at 612, 734 A. 2d, at 1223.

We disagree with the New Jersey Supreme Court's conclusion drawn from these findings.

First, associations do not have to associate for the "purpose" of disseminating a certain message in order to be entitled to the protections of the First Amendment. An association must merely engage in expressive activity that could be impaired in order to be entitled to protection. For example, the purpose of the St. Patrick's Day parade in Hurley was not to espouse any views about sexual orientation, but we held that the parade organizers had a right to exclude certain participants nonetheless.

Second, even if the Boy Scouts discourages Scout leaders from disseminating views on sexual issues—a fact that the Boy Scouts disputes with contrary evidence—the First Amendment protects the Boy Scouts' method of expression. If the Boy Scouts wishes Scout leaders to avoid questions of sexuality and teach only by example, this fact does not negate the sincerity of its belief discussed above.

Third, the First Amendment simply does not require that every member of a group agree on every issue in order for the group's policy to be "expressive association." The Boy Scouts takes an official position with respect to homosexual conduct, and that is sufficient for First Amendment purposes. In this same vein, Dale makes much of the claim that the Boy Scouts does not revoke the membership of heterosexual Scout leaders that openly disagree with the Boy Scouts' policy on sexual orientation. But if this is true, it is irrelevant.1 The presence of an avowed homosexual and gay rights activist in an as-

sistant scoutmaster's uniform sends a distinctly different message from the presence of a heterosexual assistant scoutmaster who is on record as disagreeing with Boy Scouts policy. The Boy Scouts has a First Amendment right to choose to send one message but not the other. The fact that the organization does not trumpet its views

from the housetops, or that it tolerates dissent within

its ranks, does not mean that its views receive no First Amendment protection.

Having determined that the Boy Scouts is an expressive association and that the forced inclusion of Dale would significantly affect its expression, we inquire whether the application of New Jersey's public accommodations law to require that the Boy Scouts accept Dale as an assistant scoutmaster runs afoul of the Scouts' freedom of expressive association. We conclude that it does.

State public accommodations laws were originally enacted to prevent discrimination in traditional places of public accommodation–like inns and trains. See, e.g., Hurley, supra, at 571–572 (explaining the history of Massachusetts' public accommodations law); Romer v. Evans, 517 U.S. 620, 627–629 (1996) (describing the evolution of public accommodations laws). Over time, the public accommodations laws have expanded to cover more places.2 New Jersey's statutory definition of " '[a] place of public accommodation' " is extremely broad. The term is said to "include, but not be limited to," a list of over 50 types of places. N. J. Stat. Ann. §10:5–5(l) (West Supp. 2000); see Appendix, infra, at 18–19. Many on the list are what one would expect to be places where the public is invited. For example, the statute includes as places of public accommodation taverns, restaurants, retail shops, and public libraries. But the statute also includes places that often may not carry with them open invitations to the public, like summer camps and roof gardens. In this case, the New Jersey Supreme Court went a step further and applied its public accommodations law to a private entity without even attempting to tie the term "place" to a physical location.3 As the definition of "public accommodation" has expanded from clearly commercial entities, such as restaurants, bars, and hotels, to membership organizations such as the Boy Scouts, the potential for conflict between state public accommodations laws and the First Amendment rights of organizations has increased.

We recognized in cases such as Roberts and Duarte that States have a compelling interest in eliminating discrimination against women in public accommodations. But in each of these cases we went on to conclude that the enforcement of these statutes would not materially interfere with the ideas that the organization sought to express. In Roberts, we said "[i]ndeed, the Jaycees has failed to demonstrate ... any serious burden on the male members' freedom of expressive association." 468 U.S., at 626. In Duarte, we said:

"[I]mpediments to the exercise of one's right to choose one's associates can violate the right of association protected by the First Amendment. In this case, however, the evidence fails to demonstrate that admitting women to Rotary Clubs will affect in any significant way the existing members' ability to carry out their various purposes." 481 U.S., at 548 (internal quotation marks and citations omitted).

We thereupon concluded in each of these cases that the organizations' First Amendment rights were not violated by the application of the States' public accommodations laws.

In Hurley, we said that public accommodations laws "are well within the State's usual power to enact when a legislature has reason to believe that a given group is the target of discrimination, and they do not, as a general matter, violate the First or Fourteenth Amendments." 515 U.S., at 572. But we went on to note that in that case "the Massachusetts [public accommodations] law has been applied in a peculiar way" because "any contingent of protected individuals with a message would have the right to participate in petitioners' speech, so that the communication produced by the private organizers would be shaped by all those protected by the law who wish to join in with some expressive demonstration of their own." Id., at 572—573. And in the associational freedom cases such as Roberts, Duarte, and New York State Club Assn., after finding a compelling state interest, the Court went on to examine whether or not the application of the state law would impose any "serious burden" on the organization's rights of expressive association. So in these cases, the associational interest in freedom of expression has been set on one side of the scale, and the State's interest on the other.

Dale contends that we should apply the intermediate standard of review enunciated in United States v. O'Brien, 391 U.S. 367 (1968), to evaluate the competing interests. There the Court enunciated a four-part test for review of a governmental regulation that has only an incidental effect on protected speech—in that case the symbolic burning of a draft card. A law prohibiting the destruction of draft cards only incidentally affects the free speech rights of those who happen to use a violation of that law as a symbol of protest. But New Jersey's public accommodations law directly and immediately affects associational rights, in this case associational rights that enjoy First Amendment protection. Thus, O'Brien is inapplicable.

In Hurley, we applied traditional First Amendment analysis to hold that the application of the Massachusetts public accommodations law to a parade violated the First Amendment rights of the parade organizers. Although we did not explicitly deem the parade in Hurley an expressive association, the analysis we applied there is similar to the analysis we apply here. We have already concluded that a state requirement that the Boy Scouts retain Dale as an assistant scoutmaster would significantly burden the organization's right to oppose or disfavor homosexual conduct. The state interests embodied in New Jersey's public accommodations law do not justify such a severe intrusion on the Boy Scouts' rights to freedom of expressive association. That being the case, we hold that the First Amendment prohibits the State from imposing such a requirement through the application of its public accommodations law.4

Justice Stevens' dissent makes much of its observation that the public perception of homosexuality in this country has changed. See post, at 37—39. Indeed, it appears that homosexuality has gained greater societal acceptance. See ibid. But this is scarcely an argument for denying First Amendment protection to those who refuse to accept these views. The First Amendment protects expression, be it of the popular variety or not. See, e.g., Texas v. Johnson, 491 U.S. 397 (1989) (holding that Johnson's conviction for burning the American flag violates the First Amendment); Brandenburg v. Ohio, 395 U.S. 444 (1969) (holding that a Ku Klux Klan leaders' conviction for advocating unlawfulness as a means of political reform violates the First Amendment). And the fact that an idea may be embraced and advocated by increasing numbers of people is all the more reason to protect the First Amendment rights of those who wish to voice a different view.

Justice Stevens' extolling of Justice Brandeis' comments in New State Ice Co. v. Liebmann, 285 U.S. 262, 311 (1932) (dissenting opinion); see post, at 2, 40, confuses two entirely different principles. In New State Ice, the Court struck down an Oklahoma regulation prohibiting the manufacture, sale, and distribution of ice without a license. Justice Brandeis, a champion of state experimentation in the economic realm, dissented. But Justice Brandeis was never a champion of state experimentation in the suppression of free speech. To the contrary, his First Amendment commentary provides compelling support for the Court's opinion in this case. In speaking of the Founders of this Nation, Justice Brandeis emphasized that they "believed that the freedom to think as you will and to speak as you think are means indispensable

to the discovery and spread of political truth." Whitney v. California, 274 U.S. 357, 375 (concurring opinion). He continued:

"Believing in the power of reason as applied through public discussion, they eschewed silence coerced by law–the argument of force in its worst form. Recognizing the occasional tyrannies of governing majorities, they amended the Constitution so that free speech and assembly should be guaranteed." Id., at 375—376.

We are not, as we must not be, guided by our views of whether the Boy Scouts' teachings with respect to homosexual conduct are right or wrong; public or judicial disapproval of a tenet of an organization's expression does not justify the State's effort to compel the organization to accept members where such acceptance would derogate from the organization's expressive message. "While the law is free to promote all sorts of conduct in place of harmful behavior, it is not free to interfere with speech for no better reason than promoting an approved message or discouraging a disfavored one, however enlightened either purpose may strike the government." Hurley, 515 U.S., at 579.

The judgment of the New Jersey Supreme Court is reversed, and the cause remanded for further proceedings not inconsistent with this opinion.

It is so ordered.

Notes

1. The record evidence sheds doubt on Dale's assertion. For example, the National Director of the Boy Scouts certified that "any persons who advocate to Scouting youth that homosexual conduct is" consistent with Scouting values will not be registered as adult leaders. App. 746 (emphasis added). And the Monmouth Council Scout Executive testified that the advocacy of the morality of homosexuality to youth members by any adult member is grounds for revocation of the adult's membership. Id., at 761.

2. Public accommodations laws have also broadened in scope to cover more groups; they have expanded beyond those groups that have been given heightened equal protection scrutiny under our cases. See Romer, 517 U.S., at 629. Some municipal ordinances have even expanded to cover criteria such as prior criminal record, prior psychiatric treatment, military status, personal appearance, source of income, place of residence, and political ideology. See 1 Boston, Mass., Ordinance No. §12—9(7) (1999) (ex-offender, prior psychiatric treatment, and military status); D. C. Code Ann. §1—2519 (1999) (personal appearance, source of income, place of residence); Seattle, Wash., Municipal Code §14.08.090 (1999) (political ideology).

3. Four State Supreme Courts and one United States Court of Appeals have ruled that the Boy Scouts is not a place of public accommodation. Welsh v. Boy Scouts of America, 993 F.2d 1267 (CA7); cert. denied, 510 U.S. 1012 (1993); Curran v. Mount Diablo Council of the Boy Scouts of America, 17 Cal. 4th 670, 952 P.2d 218 (1998); Seabourn v. Coronado Area Council, Boy Scouts of America, 257 Kan. 178, 891 P.2d 385 (1995); Quinnipiac Council, Boy Scouts of America, Inc. v. Comm'n on Human Rights & Opportunities, 204 Conn. 287, 528 A. 2d 352 (1987); Schwenk v. Boy Scouts of America, 275 Ore. 327, 551 P.2d 465 (1976). No federal appellate court or state supreme court—except the New Jersey Supreme Court in this case—has reached a contrary result.

4. We anticipated this result in Hurley when we illustrated the reasons for our holding in that case by likening the parade to a private membership organization. 515 U.S., at 580. We stated: "Assuming the parade to be large enough and a source of benefits (apart from its expression) that would generally justify a mandated access provision, GLIB could nonetheless be refused admission as an expressive contingent with its own message just as readily as a private club could exclude an applicant whose manifest views were at odds with a position taken by the club's existing members." Id., at 580—581.

### Castorina v. Madison County School Bd. (Sixth Circuit) (March 8, 2001)

Before: MERRITT, KENNEDY, and GILMAN, Circuit Judges.
MERRITT, Circuit Judge.
Principal William Fultz of Madison County High School twice suspended students Timothy Castorina and Tiffany Dargavell for wearing T-shirts displaying the Confederate flag; the rationale for the suspensions was that the T-shirts violated the school dress code, which bans clothing containing any "illegal, immoral or racist

implications." Following their suspensions, the students brought suit challenging the constitutionality of the disciplinary actions and the district court granted summary judgment for the school board. After reviewing that decision, we find that we are unable to resolve the constitutionality of the school board's actions without knowing the manner in which the school board enforced its dress code and whether Madison County High School had actually experienced any racially based violence prior to the suspensions. As a result, material questions of fact remain which render this case inappropriate for summary judgment and we therefore remand this case to the district court for trial. Once the district court has made the necessary findings of fact, it should apply the legal framework set forth in this opinion.

I. Facts

In the fall of 1997, when all of the events in question took place, Timothy Castorina and Tiffany Dargavell were students at Madison Central High School, located in Madison County, Kentucky. Castorina was a junior and Dargavell a freshman. At the time, Castorina and Dargavell were dating. Neither had previously experienced any significant disciplinary problems.

On the morning of September 17, both plaintiffs arrived at school wearing matching Hank Williams, Jr. concert T-shirts given to them by Dargavell's father. Country music star Hank Williams, Jr. was pictured on the front of the T-shirts and two Confederate flags were displayed on the back, along with the phrase "Southern Thunder." The plaintiffs said that they were wearing the T-shirts in commemoration of Hank Williams, Sr.'s birthday and to express their southern heritage. When the two students went to the principal's office to change Dargavell's class schedule, the principal, William Fultz, informed them that the Confederate flag emblem violated the school's dress code. He gave the students the choice of either turning the shirts inside out for the rest of the day or returning home to change. Fultz based this instruction on his interpretation of the school's dress code, which prohibits students from wearing any clothing or emblem "that is obscene, sexually suggestive, disrespectful, or which contains slogans, words or in any way depicts alcohol, drugs, tobacco or any illegal, immoral, or racist implication." The dress code specified that if the violation could not be corrected at school, then the principal had the authority to send the offender home to change and to assign appropriate punishment. When Castorina and Dargavell refused to comply with his directives, Fultz called their parents. He explained to the parents that the clothing was a violation of the dress code, but that if the parents convinced the students to go home and change there would be no disciplinary action. If the students refused to change, they would be suspended for three days. The parents strongly supported their children's decision, and Fultz suspended each student. At the end of the three days, Castorina and Dargavell returned to school wearing the same shirts. Fultz again explained that the flag was offensive to other students and a violation of the dress code. When the parents reiterated their support for the students' desire to wear the T-shirts, Fultz suspended them for a second three-day period. Castorina and Dargavell never returned to Madison

Central and were subsequently given home-schooling by their parents.

In ruling on the students' suit challenging their suspensions, the district court found that wearing the T-shirts did not qualify as "speech" and that even if it were "speech," the plaintiffs failed to show a First Amendment violation. In addition, the court rejected the plaintiffs' contention that the school dress code was vague and overbroad. The Court then dismissed all supplemental state claims without prejudice.

II. Analysis

This case raises two main questions: (1) does wearing the Confederate flag T-shirts qualify as the type of speech covered by the First Amendment, and (2) if so, is that speech protected given the special rules governing schools' authority to regulate student speech? The district court's answer to the first question — that wearing the Hank Williams, Jr. T-shirts did not qualify as "speech" — was incorrect. The plaintiffs wore the shirts to express a certain viewpoint and that viewpoint was easily ascertainable by an observer. On the second question, viewing all of the facts in the light most favorable to the plaintiffs, it appears that the school board enforced the dress code in an uneven and viewpoint-specific manner, thereby violating core values of the First Amendment. In addition, the school has not shown that the plaintiffs' conduct creates a likelihood of violence or other disruption that warrants this kind of regulation.

1. The Plaintiffs' Conduct was Speech Governed by the First Amendment. — In Texas v. Johnson, 491 U.S. 397, 109 S.Ct. 2533, 105 L.Ed.2d 342 (1989) (the flag-burning case), the Supreme Court laid out the standard for what conduct constitutes expression protected by the First Amendment. This inquiry focused on "whether [a]n intent to convey a particularized message was present and [whether] the likelihood was great that the message would be understood by those who viewed it." Id. at 404, 109 S.Ct. 2533. In the instant case, the district court concluded that the plaintiffs intended to commemorate Hank Williams, Sr.'s birthday. The court found that this was a particularized message, but that this message was unascertainable based on the plaintiffs' decision to wear a Hank Williams, Jr. T-shirt. The court characterized the wearing of these T-shirts as a "mere display" of a confederate flag and ruled that this did not result in a finding of protected speech. Both plaintiffs, however, testified that they intended to convey pride in their southern heritage in addition to any message associated with Hank Williams, Sr. The school board does not dispute the plaintiffs' claim that they also intended to affirm their southern back-grounds.

The T-shirts prominently displayed two Confederate flags and the phrase "Southern Thunder." In addition, both Hank Williams, Sr. and Hank Williams, Jr. are singers whose songs have strong appeal in the South. We therefore conclude that the plaintiffs intended to express more than a mere appreciation for the life and music of either performer. Further, their decision to return to school at the end of the first suspension still wearing the T-shirts demonstrates that the students fully appreciated the message that school administrators understood the T-shirts to convey. Because the plaintiffs' intended expression was both a commemoration of Hank Williams, Sr.'s birthday as well as a statement affirming the plaintiffs' shared southern heritage, their decision to wear the Hank Williams T-shirts constitutes speech falling within the First Amendment.

2. The School Board's Authority To Regulate the Plaintiffs' Speech. — This case is governed by the Supreme Court's landmark decision concerning student speech, Tinker v. Des Moines Independent School District, 393 U.S. 503, 89 S.Ct. 733, 21 L.Ed.2d 731 (1969). While Tinker has been narrowed by two more recent cases, Bethel School District No. 403 v. Fraser, 478 U.S. 675, 106 S.Ct. 3159, 92 L.Ed.2d 549 (1986), and Hazelwood School District v. Kuhlmeier, 484 U.S. 260, 108 S.Ct. 562, 98 L.Ed.2d 592 (1988), neither of these decisions altered Tinker's core principles concerning the circumstances under which public schools may regulate student speech. In Tinker, the Supreme Court struck down the school district's ban on the wearing of black armbands to protest the Vietnam War. Central to the decision was the fact that the school district did not ban other clothing that expressed controversial views, including Iron Crosses, which were often understood as symbols of Hitler and the Nazis. Tinker, 393 U.S. at 506-511, 89 S.Ct. 733. This aspect of the decision is consistent with a number of later Supreme Court decisions signaling that viewpoint-specific speech restrictions are an egregious violation of the First Amendment. See, e.g., Rosenberger v. Rector and Visitors of the University of Virginia, 515 U.S. 819, 828-29, 115 S.Ct. 2510, 132 L.Ed.2d 700 (1995) ("Discrimination against speech because of its message is presumed to be unconstitutional"), R.A.V. v. St. Paul, 505 U.S. 377, 391-92, 112 S.Ct. 2538, 120 L.Ed.2d 305 (1992) (striking down a Minnesota hate-speech statute on the basis of impermissible viewpoint discrimination).

In contrast, Fraser concerned a school's decision to discipline a student after he used "offensively lewd and indecent speech" during a speech nominating a classmate for a position in the student assembly. The Court found that this was not protected speech and that the school had an interest in teaching students the boundaries of socially appropriate behavior that provided some room for a school to regulate speech which would otherwise be protected. Fraser, 478 U.S. at 682-685, 106 S.Ct. 3159. In Hazelwood, the Court upheld the school's decision to censor certain articles in the school newspaper. The Court found that the school newspaper was not a public forum and that school officials are entitled to exercise greater control over "school-sponsored" speech such as a school newspaper. Hazelwood, 484 U.S. at 268-273, 108 S.Ct. 562. Beyond the three "school-speech" Supreme Court cases and the well-developed line of Supreme Court decisions prohibiting viewpoint discrimination, two Court of Appeals decisions, Melton v. Young, 465 F.2d 1332 (6th Cir.1972), and West v. Derby Unified School District No. 260, 206 F.3d 1358 (10th Cir.2000), are relevant in that they uphold a public school's authority to ban Confederate flags in somewhat different factual circumstances.

The facts, when viewed in the light most favorable to the plaintiffs, distinguish the Madison County ban on Confederate flags from the bans upheld in all four of these cases. First, the plaintiffs testified that other members of the student body wore clothing venerating Malcolm X and were not disciplined. Second, the plaintiffs were wearing the disputed clothing in a manner that did not disrupt school activity or cause unrest during the school day. Third, Castorina and Dargavell were clearly making a personal statement in deciding to wear the Hank Williams, Jr. T-shirts; in other words, there is no way that their speech could be considered to be "school-sponsored," nor did the students use any school resources to express their views.

Taking these facts into consideration, the Madison County case is more analogous to Tinker than to either Fraser or Hazelwood. In Tinker, the Des Moines school board had adopted a policy specifically banning the wearing of black armbands. The policy stated that any students found in violation would be asked to remove the offending article; if the student refused, suspension would follow until the student returned without the armband. The plaintiffs intentionally violated the policy and were sent home. Following their legal challenge to the suspension, the Supreme Court struck down the school policy as unconstitutional. As a preliminary matter, the Court formally recognized the fact that students do not "shed their constitutional rights to freedom of speech or expression at the schoolhouse gate." Tinker, 393 U.S. at 506, 89 S.Ct. 733. Though schools have the authority to set regulations pertaining to the length of skirts or hair, the Court held that there was no basis for a policy that punished "silent, passive expression of opinion, unaccompanied by any disorder or disturbance on the part of petitioners." Id. at 508. The Court drew special attention to the fact that the plaintiffs' actions did not cause any interference "with schools' work or [] collision with the rights of other students to be secure and to be let alone." Id. In the lower court proceedings, the district court had based its decision upholding the school board's actions on the fear of disturbance, but the Supreme Court rejected this argument because "undifferentiated fear or apprehension of disturbance is not enough to overcome the right to freedom of expression." Id. In addition, the Supreme Court was clearly influenced by the fact that the school board adopted a policy that only banned black armbands, and not other potentially disruptive symbols. Id. at 510, 89 S.Ct. 733. For example, the Court specifically noted that the school board banned black armbands while allowing students to wear the Iron Cross, a symbol that obviously invoked images of Nazi Germany. Id. In the instant case, Dargavell and Castorina claim that students in Madison County wore clothing bearing the "X" symbol associated with Malcolm X and the Black Muslim movement. The school's refusal to bar the wearing of this apparel along with the Confederate flag gives the appearance of a targeted ban, something that the Supreme Court has routinely struck down as a violation of the First Amendment. See e.g., Police Department of Chicago v. Mosley, 408 U.S. 92, 92 S.Ct. 2286, 33 L.Ed.2d 212 (1972) (striking down a no-picketing law that contained an exception for only labor-related picketing), City of Madison, Joint School District No. 8 v. Wisconsin Employment Relations Commission, 429 U.S. 167, 97 S.Ct. 421, 50 L.Ed.2d 376 (1976) (holding that a school board cannot bar only non-union teachers from speaking at a public meeting concerning the board's labor relations). The Court has held that this type of ban is a "more blatant" violation of the First Amendment because "government regulation may not regulate speech based on its substantive content or the message it conveys." Rosenberger, 515 U.S. at 828-29, 115 S.Ct. 2510.

Viewing the facts in the light most favorable to the students, the school has banned only certain racial viewpoints without any showing of disruption. As a result, without any formal factual findings to guide us, we see no obvious differences between the Tinker and Madison County situations other than the fact that the Des Moines School Board adopted a formal policy banning black armbands before the students ever wore them, whereas the Madison County School Board banned Confederate flags in a more "ad hoc" manner. This means that in Tinker there was a formally targeted ban from the very beginning, whereas the Madison County dress code is a facially neutral policy that is enforced, according to the students, in a content-specific manner. If the students' claim is true, only certain ideological positions are barred from expression on school property. Based on the Supreme Court rulings in Tinker, Mosley and Rosenberger, the school board cannot single out Confederate flags for special treatment while allowing other controversial racial and political symbols to be displayed.

The more recent Supreme Court decisions discussing schools' authority to regulate student speech are not applicable to this situation. Both Fraser and Hazelwood — the two cases often cited for public schools' power to regulate their students' speech — contain important factual differences that distinguish them from the instant controversy. Fraser upheld the disciplining of the student's profane nominating speech based on the school's need to teach students about appropriate societal behavior; furthermore, the Court found that the school had wide latitude in determining the "manner of speech" that was permissible on school grounds. Fraser, 478 U.S. at 683, 106 S.Ct. 3159. In the instant case, however, the school is not attempting to regulate the "manner of speech." For example, a student would be permitted to attend class wearing a T-shirt with a flag on it if the flag was in support of the country's Olympic team. As a result, it is the content of speech, not the manner, that the Madison County School Board wishes to regulate. In addition, a clear underpinning of the Court's holding in Fraser was the disruptive nature of the plaintiff's nominating speech and the fact that the sanctions were not based on one particular political viewpoint. Id. at 685, 106 S.Ct. 3159. Assuming that there has not been any racially motivated violence or threat in the Madison County schools, the plaintiffs' display of the Confederate flag may not have had any significant disruptive effect. The defendants do claim that prior to the plaintiffs' suspension, there was a racially based altercation on school grounds, but plaintiffs contend that race was not the cause of the disturbance. This disagreement simply highlights the need for a trial to determine the precise facts of this situation.

Hazelwood concerned a public school's decision to censor two articles slated for appearance in the school newspaper: one concerned pregnant students at the school, the other discussed the impact of divorce on students. The pregnancy story was rejected because the principal feared that in spite of the pseudonyms used in the article, the subjects might still be identified by the school community. The divorce story was rejected because it contained negative information about school parents and there was insufficient time to permit them to respond to the facts set out in the article. The Supreme Court rejected the newspaper staff members' suit on a number of bases: the school paper was not a public forum, publishing the paper was a school-sponsored activity that was part of an advanced journalism class, and readers would perceive articles appearing in the school paper as being "school-approved" publications. Hazelwood, 484 U.S. at 268-73, 108 S.Ct. 562. In addition, the Court recognized the competing privacy interests of the pregnant students and the families going through a divorce. Id. All of these factors combined to create a set of circumstances where the Court allowed the school officials to regulate student speech. For the purposes of our current inquiry, the most important part of the Hazelwood holding is the Court's description of when a school has greater authority to regulate student speech (and the way Tinker differs from Hazelwood):

> [T]he standard articulated in Tinker for determining when a school may punish student expression need not also be the standard for determining when a school may refuse to lend its name and resources to the dissemination of student expression. Instead, we hold that educators do not offend the First Amendment by exercising editorial control over the style and content of student speech in school-sponsored expressive activities so long as their actions are reasonably related to legitimate pedagogical concerns. Id. at 272-73, 108 S.Ct. 562.

The Madison County School Board's actions cannot be judged using the more lenient Hazelwood standard because the special circumstances present in Hazelwood are so clearly absent in Madison County. Castorina and Dargavell's actions were not school sponsored, nor did the school supply any of the resources involved in their wearing the T-shirts. Most importantly, no reasonable observer could conclude that the school had somehow endorsed the students' display of the Confederate flag. As a result, Tinker is the most relevant of the three Supreme Court cases concerning school speech and sets forth the legal framework that the district court should apply to its factual findings. Using the Tinker standard that "silent, passive expression of opinion, unaccompanied by any disorder or disturbance on the part of petitioners" is not subject to regulation, Tinker, 393 U.S. at 508, 89 S.Ct. 733, it is clear that a formal factual finding with respect to the disturbance — if any — caused by the plaintiffs' actions is necessary before a final decision can be entered in this case.

In addition, the two Court of Appeals decisions upholding suspensions for Confederate flag displays, Melton v. Young, 465 F.2d 1332 (6th Cir.1972), and West v. Derby Unified School District No.260, 206 F.3d 1358 (10th Cir.2000), satisfy Tinker in ways that the Madison County suspension does not. In West, junior high school student T.W. drew a picture of a Confederate flag during his math class, thus violating the school's "Racial Harassment and Intimidation" policy. He was subsequently suspended and brought suit challenging the constitutionality of his punishment. The Tenth Circuit upheld the suspension as a legitimate exercise of the school's authority. Though this may appear facially similar to the Madison County controversy, in West there had been actual fights involving racial symbols (the Confederate flag in particular) in the school district and there was no evidence that the school district enforced the Racial Harassment and Intimidation policy in a manner that favored one type of potentially racially divisive symbols over another. As a result, the Tenth Circuit's decision in West merely demonstrates that a school board may ban racially divisive symbols when there has been actual racially motivated violence and when the policy is enforced without viewpoint discrimination. Since the Madison County action does not appear to satisfy either one of these criteria, the Tenth Circuit decision is of limited utility in the adjudication of the case before this court.

Similarly, this court's decision in Melton concerned a Chattanooga public school's 1970 suspension of a student for wearing a jacket with a Confederate flag patch. The school in question, which had previously been an all-white school, was integrated in 1966, only four years before the suspension. In that four year period, the high school in question experienced significant racial tension, much of which sprung from the school's symbol (the Confederate flag), the school's athletic nickname (the "Rebels") and the school's fight song ("Dixie"). Following these problems, a special committee convened to address these racial problems made a specific finding that the Confederate flag was a cause of unrest. Relying on that finding, the school board banned the display of the Confederate flag. Having been informed of the ban, plaintiff Melton then wore a jacket with a Confederate flag patch to school and was suspended. In reviewing his suspension, this court applied Tinker to the regulation, finding that the history of unrest amounted to a material disruption at the school and that the committee's specific findings showed that there was more than "an undifferentiated fear or apprehension of disturbance." Melton, 465 F.2d at 1334-35. As a result, the court recognized that though the case was a close one, the suspension was a valid exercise of the school board's constitutional authority under Tinker. Id.

The foregoing discussion of the three Supreme Court and two Court of Appeals cases demonstrates the importance of the factual circumstances in school speech cases and why a remand is necessary in this case so that the district court can resolve the plaintiffs' factual assertions. If the students' claims regarding the Malcolm X-inspired clothing (i.e. that other students wore this type of clothing and were not disciplined) and their claims that there were no prior disruptive altercations as a result of Confederate flags are found credible, the court below would be required to strike down the students' suspension as a violation of their rights of free speech as set forth in Tinker. In addition, even if there has been racial violence that necessitates a ban on racially divisive symbols, the school does not have the authority to enforce a viewpoint-specific ban on racially sensitive symbols and not others. Conversely, if the students cannot establish their factual claims, then the principal and school board may have acted within their constitutional authority to control student activity and behavior. In either circumstance, the facts are essential to the application of the legal framework discussed herein. Accordingly, the summary judgment is reversed and the case remanded to the district court for trial.

## Ashcroft v. Free Speech Coalition (April 16, 2002)

Justice Kennedy delivered the opinion of the Court.

We consider in this case whether the Child Pornography Prevention Act of 1996 (CPPA), 18 U.S.C. § 2251 et seq., abridges the freedom of speech. The CPPA extends the federal prohibition against child pornography to sexually explicit images that appear to depict minors but were produced without using any real children. The statute prohibits, in specific circumstances, possessing or distributing these images, which may be created by using adults who look like minors or by using computer imaging. The new technology, according to Congress, makes it possible to create realistic images of children who do not exist. See Congressional Findings, notes following 18 U.S.C. § 2251.

By prohibiting child pornography that does not depict an actual child, the statute goes beyond New York v. Ferber, 458 U.S. 747 (1982), which distinguished child pornography from other sexually explicit speech because of the State's interest in protecting the children exploited by the production process. See id., at 758. As a general rule, pornography can be banned only if obscene, but under Ferber, pornography showing minors can be proscribed whether or not the images are obscene under the definition set forth in Miller v. California, 413 U.S. 15 (1973). Ferber recognized that "[t]he Miller standard, like all general definitions of what may be banned as obscene, does not reflect the State's particular and more compelling interest in prosecuting those who promote the sexual exploitation of children." 458 U.S., at 761.

While we have not had occasion to consider the question, we may assume that the apparent age of persons engaged in sexual conduct is relevant to whether a depiction offends community standards. Pictures of young children engaged in certain acts might be obscene where similar depictions of adults, or perhaps even older adolescents, would not. The CPPA, however, is not directed at speech that is obscene; Congress has proscribed those materials through a separate statute. 18 U.S.C. § 1460—1466. Like the law in Ferber, the CPPA seeks to reach beyond obscenity, and it makes no attempt to conform to the Miller standard. For instance, the statute would reach visual depictions, such as movies, even if they have redeeming social value.

The principal question to be resolved, then, is whether the CPPA is constitutional where it proscribes a significant universe of speech that is neither obscene under Miller nor child pornography under Ferber.

I

Before 1996, Congress defined child pornography as the type of depictions at issue in Ferber, images made using actual minors. 18 U.S.C. § 2252 (1994 ed.). The CPPA retains that prohibition at 18 U.S.C. § 2256(8)(A) and adds three other prohibited categories of speech, of which the first, §2256(8)(B), and the third, §2256(8)(D), are at issue in this case. Section 2256(8)(B) prohibits "any visual depiction, including any photograph, film, video, picture, or computer or computer-generated image or picture" that "is, or appears to be, of a minor engaging in sexually explicit conduct." The prohibition on "any visual depiction" does not depend at all on how the image is produced. The section captures a range of depictions, sometimes called "virtual child pornography," which include computer-generated images, as well as images produced by more traditional means. For instance, the literal terms of the statute embrace a Renaissance painting depicting a scene from classical mythology, a "picture" that "appears to be, of a minor engaging in sexually explicit conduct." The statute also prohibits Hollywood movies, filmed without any child actors, if a jury believes an actor "appears to be" a minor engaging in "actual or simulated ... sexual intercourse." §2256(2).

These images do not involve, let alone harm, any children in the production process; but Congress decided the materials threaten children in other, less direct, ways. Pedophiles might use the materials to encourage children to participate in sexual activity. "[A] child who is reluctant to engage in sexual activity with an adult, or to pose for sexually explicit photographs, can sometimes be convinced by viewing depictions of other children 'having fun' participating in such activity." Congressional Findings, note (3) following §2251. Furthermore, pedophiles might "whet their own sexual appetites" with the pornographic images, "thereby increasing the creation and distribution of child pornography and the sexual abuse and exploitation of actual children." Id., notes (4), (10)(B). Under these rationales, harm flows from the content of the images, not from the means of their production. In addition, Congress identified another problem created by computer-generated images: Their existence can make it harder to prosecute pornographers who do use real minors. See id., note (6)(A). As imaging technology improves, Congress found, it becomes more difficult to prove that a particular picture was produced using actual children. To ensure that defendants possessing child pornography using real minors cannot evade prosecution, Congress extended the ban to virtual child pornography.

Section 2256(8)(C) prohibits a more common and lower tech means of creating virtual images, known as computer morphing. Rather than creating original images, pornographers can alter innocent pictures of real children so that the children appear to be engaged in sexual activity. Although morphed images may fall within the definition of virtual child pornography, they implicate the interests of real children and are in that sense closer to the images in Ferber. Respondents do not challenge this provision, and we do not consider it.

Respondents do challenge §2256(8)(D). Like the text of the "appears to be" provision, the sweep of this provision is quite broad. Section 2256(8)(D) defines child pornography to include any sexually explicit image that was "advertised, promoted, presented, described, or distributed in such a manner that conveys the impression" it depicts "a minor engaging in sexually explicit conduct." One Committee Report identified the provision as directed at sexually explicit images pandered as child pornography. See S. Rep. No. 104–358, p. 22 (1996) ("This provision prevents child pornographers and pedophiles from exploiting prurient interests in child sexuality and sexual activity through the production or distribution of pornographic material which is intentionally pandered as child pornography"). The statute is not so limited in its reach, however, as it punishes even those possessors who took no part in pandering. Once a work has been described as child pornography, the taint remains on the speech in the hands of subsequent possessors, making possession unlawful even though the content otherwise would not be objectionable.

Fearing that the CPPA threatened the activities of its members, respondent Free Speech Coalition and others challenged the statute in the United States District Court for the Northern District of California. The Coalition, a California trade association for the adult-entertainment industry, alleged that its members did not use minors in their sexually explicit works, but they believed some of these materials might fall within the CPPA's expanded definition of child pornography. The other respondents are Bold Type, Inc., the publisher of a book advocating the nudist lifestyle; Jim Gingerich, a painter of nudes; and Ron Raffaelli, a photographer specializing in erotic images. Respondents alleged that the "appears to be" and "conveys the impression" provisions are overbroad and vague, chilling them from producing works protected by the First Amendment. The District Court disagreed and granted summary judgment to the Government. The court dismissed the overbreadth claim because it was "highly unlikely" that any "adaptations of sexual works like 'Romeo and Juliet,' will be treated as 'criminal contraband.' " App. to Pet. for Cert. 62a–63a.

The Court of Appeals for the Ninth Circuit reversed. See 198 F.3d 1083 (1999). The court reasoned that the Government could not prohibit speech because of its tendency to persuade viewers to commit illegal acts. The court held the CPPA to be substantially overbroad because it bans materials that are neither obscene nor produced by the exploitation of real children as in New York v. Ferber, 458 U.S. 747 (1982). Judge Ferguson dissented on the ground that virtual images, like obscenity and real child pornography, should be treated as a category of speech unprotected by the First Amendment. 198 F.3d, at 1097. The Court of Appeals voted to deny the petition for rehearing en banc, over the dissent of three judges. See 220 F.3d 1113 (2000).

While the Ninth Circuit found the CPPA invalid on its face, four other Courts of Appeals have sustained it. See United States v. Fox, 248 F.3d 394 (CA5 2001); United States v. Mento, 231 F.3d 912 (CA4 2000); United States v. Acheson, 195 F.3d 645 (CA11 1999); United States v. Hilton, 167 F.3d 61 (CA1), cert. denied, 528 U.S. 844 (1999). We granted certiorari. 531 U.S. 1124 (2001).

II

The First Amendment commands, "Congress shall make no law ... abridging the freedom of speech." The government may violate this mandate in many ways, e.g., Rosenberger v. Rector and Visitors of Univ. of Va., 515 U.S. 819 (1995); Keller v. State Bar of Cal., 496 U.S. 1 (1990), but a law imposing criminal penalties on protected speech is a stark example of speech suppression. The CPPA's penalties are indeed severe. A first offender may be imprisoned for 15 years. §2252A(b)(1). A repeat offender faces a prison sentence of not less than 5 years and not more than 30 years in prison. Ibid. While even minor punishments can chill protected speech, see Wooley v. Maynard, 430 U.S. 705 (1977), this case provides a textbook example of why we permit facial challenges to statutes that burden expression. With these severe penalties in force, few legitimate movie producers or book publishers, or few other speakers in any capacity, would risk distributing images in or near the uncertain reach of this law. The Constitution gives significant protection from overbroad laws that chill speech within the First Amendment's vast and privileged sphere. Under this principle, the CPPA is unconstitutional on its face if it prohibits a substantial amount of protected expression. See Broadrick v. Oklahoma, 413 U.S. 601, 612 (1973).

The sexual abuse of a child is a most serious crime and an act repugnant to the moral instincts of a decent people. In its legislative findings, Congress recognized that there are subcultures of persons who harbor illicit desires for children and commit criminal acts to gratify the impulses. See Congressional Findings, notes following §2251; see also U.S. Dept. of Health and Human Services, Administration on Children, Youth and Families, Child Maltreatment 1999 (estimating that 93,000 children were victims of sexual abuse in 1999). Congress also found that surrounding the serious offenders are those who flirt with these impulses and trade pictures and written accounts of sexual activity with young children.

Congress may pass valid laws to protect children from abuse, and it has. E.g., 18 U.S.C. § 2241 2251. The prospect of crime, however, by itself does not justify laws suppressing protected speech. See Kingsley Int'l Pictures Corp. v. Regents of Univ. of N. Y., 360 U.S. 684, 689 (1959) ("Among free men, the deterrents ordinarily to be applied to prevent crime are education and punishment for violations of the law, not abridgment of the rights of free speech") (internal quotation marks and citation omitted)). It is also well established that speech may not be prohibited because it concerns subjects offending our sensibilities. See FCC v. Pacifica Foundation, 438 U.S. 726, 745 (1978) ("[T]he fact that society may find speech offensive is not a sufficient reason for suppressing it"); see also Reno v. American Civil Liberties Union, 521 U.S. 844, 874 (1997) ("In evaluating the free speech rights of adults, we have made it perfectly clear that '[s]exual expression which is indecent but not obscene is protected by the First Amendment' ") (quoting Sable Communications of Cal., Inc. v. FCC, 492 U.S. 115, 126 (1989); Carey v. Population Services Int'l, 431 U.S. 678, 701 (1977) ("[T]he fact that protected speech may be offensive to some does not justify its suppression").

As a general principle, the First Amendment bars the government from dictating what we see or read or speak or hear. The freedom of speech has its limits; it does not embrace certain categories of speech, including defamation, incitement, obscenity, and pornography produced with real children. See Simon & Schuster, Inc. v. Members of N. Y. State Crime Victims Bd., 502 U.S. 105, 127 (1991) (Kennedy, J., concurring). While these categories may be prohibited without violating the First Amendment, none of them includes the speech prohibited by the CPPA. In his dissent from the opinion of the Court of Appeals, Judge Ferguson recognized this to be the law and proposed that virtual child pornography should be regarded as an additional category of unprotected speech. See 198 F.3d, at 1101. It would be necessary for us to take this step to uphold the statute.

As we have noted, the CPPA is much more than a supplement to the existing federal prohibition on obscenity. Under Miller v. California, 413 U.S. 15 (1973), the Government must prove that the work, taken as a whole, appeals to the prurient interest, is patently offensive in light of community standards, and lacks serious literary, artistic, political, or scientific value. Id., at 24. The CPPA, however, extends to images that appear to depict a minor engaging in sexually explicit activity without regard to the Miller requirements. The materials need not appeal to the prurient interest. Any depiction of sexually explicit activity, no matter how it is presented, is proscribed. The CPPA applies to a picture in a psychology manual, as well as a movie depicting the horrors of sexual abuse. It is not necessary, moreover, that the image be patently offensive. Pictures of what appear to be 17-year-olds engaging in sexually explicit activity do not in every case contravene community standards.

The CPPA prohibits speech despite its serious literary, artistic, political, or scientific value. The statute proscribes the visual depiction of an idea–that of teenagers engaging in sexual activity–that is a fact of modern society and has been a theme in art and literature throughout the ages. Under the CPPA, images are prohibited so long as the persons appear to be under 18 years of age. 18 U.S.C. § 2256(1). This is higher than the legal age for marriage in many States, as well as the age at which persons may consent to sexual relations. See §2243(a) (age of consent in the federal maritime and territorial jurisdiction is 16); U.S. National Survey of State Laws 384—388 (R. Leiter ed., 3d ed. 1999) (48 States permit 16-year-olds to marry with parental consent); W. Eskridge & N. Hunter, Sexuality, Gender, and the Law 1021—1022 (1997) (in 39 States and the District of Columbia, the age of consent is 16 or younger). It is, of course, undeniable that some youths engage in sexual activity before the legal age, either on their own inclination or because they are victims of sexual abuse.

Both themes–teenage sexual activity and the sexual abuse of children–have inspired countless literary works. William Shakespeare created the most famous pair of teenage lovers, one of whom is just 13 years of age. See Romeo and Juliet, act I, sc. 2, l. 9 ("She hath not seen the change of fourteen years"). In the drama, Shakespeare portrays the relationship as something splendid and innocent, but not juvenile. The work has inspired no less than 40 motion pictures, some of which suggest that the teenagers consummated their relationship. E.g., Romeo and Juliet (B. Luhrmann director, 1996). Shakespeare may not have written sexually explicit scenes for the Elizabethan audience, but were modern directors to adopt a less conventional approach, that fact alone would not compel the conclusion that the work was obscene.

Contemporary movies pursue similar themes. Last year's Academy Awards featured the movie, Traffic, which was nominated for Best Picture. See Predictable and Less So, the Academy Award Contenders, N. Y. Times, Feb. 14, 2001, p. E11. The film portrays a teenager, identified as a 16-year-old, who becomes addicted to drugs. The viewer sees the degradation of her addiction, which in the end leads her to a filthy room to trade sex for drugs. The year before, American Beauty won the Academy Award for Best Picture. See "American Beauty" Tops the Oscars, N. Y. Times, Mar. 27, 2000, p. E1. In the course of the movie, a teenage girl engages in sexual relations with her teenage boyfriend, and another yields herself to the gratification of a middle-aged man. The film also contains a scene where, although the movie audience understands the act is not taking place, one character believes he is watching a teenage boy performing a sexual act on an older man.

Our society, like other cultures, has empathy and enduring fascination with the lives and destinies of the young. Art and literature express the vital interest we all have in the formative years we ourselves once knew, when wounds can be so grievous, disappointment so profound, and mistaken choices so tragic, but when moral acts and self-fulfillment are still in reach. Whether or not the films we mention violate the CPPA, they explore themes within the wide sweep of the statute's prohibitions. If these films, or hundreds of others of lesser note that explore those subjects, contain a single graphic depiction of sexual activity within the statutory definition, the possessor of the film would be subject to severe punishment without inquiry into the work's redeeming value. This is inconsistent with an essential First Amendment rule: The artistic merit of a work does not depend on the presence of a single explicit scene. See Book Named "John Cleland's Memoirs of a Woman of Pleasure" v. Attorney General of Mass., 383 U.S. 413, 419 (1966) (plurality opinion) ("[T]he social value of the book can neither be weighed against nor canceled by its prurient appeal or patent offensiveness"). Under Miller, the First Amendment requires that redeeming value be judged by considering the work as a whole. Where the scene is part of the narrative, the work itself does not for this reason become obscene, even though the scene in isolation might be offensive. See Kois v. Wisconsin, 408 U.S. 229, 231 (1972) (per curiam). For this reason, and the others we have noted, the CPPA cannot be read to prohibit obscenity, because it lacks the required link between its prohibitions and the affront to community standards prohibited by the definition of obscenity.

The Government seeks to address this deficiency by arguing that speech prohibited by the CPPA is virtually indistinguishable from child pornography, which may be banned without regard to whether it depicts works of value. See New York v. Ferber, 458 U.S., at 761. Where the images are themselves the product of child sexual abuse, Ferber recognized that the State had an interest in stamping it out without regard to any judgment about its content. Id., at 761, n. 12; see also id., at 775 (O'Connor, J., concurring) ("As drafted, New York's statute does not attempt to suppress the communication of particular ideas"). The production of the work, not its content, was the target of the statute. The fact that a work contained serious literary, artistic, or other value did not excuse the harm it caused to its child participants. It was simply "unrealistic to equate a community's toleration for sexually oriented materials with the permissible scope of legislation aimed at protecting children from sexual exploitation." Id., at 761, n. 12.

Ferber upheld a prohibition on the distribution and sale of child pornography, as well as its production, because these acts were "intrinsically related" to the sexual abuse of children in two ways. Id., at 759. First, as a permanent record of a child's abuse, the continued circulation itself would harm the child who had participated. Like a defamatory statement, each new publication of the speech would cause new injury to the child's reputation and emotional well-being. See id., at 759, and n. 10. Second, because the traffic in child pornography was an economic motive for its production, the State had an interest in closing the distribution network. "The most expeditious if not the only practical method of law enforcement may be to dry up the market for this material by imposing severe criminal penalties on persons selling, advertising, or otherwise promoting the product." Id., at 760. Under either rationale, the speech had what the Court in effect held was a proximate link to the crime from which it came.

Later, in Osborne v. Ohio, 495 U.S. 103 (1990), the Court ruled that these same interests justified a ban on the possession of pornography produced by using children. "Given the importance of the State's interest in protecting the victims of child pornography," the State was justified in "attempting to stamp out this vice at all levels in the distribution chain." Id., at 110. Osborne also noted the State's interest in preventing child pornography from being used as an aid in the solicitation of minors. Id., at 111. The Court, however, anchored its holding in the concern for the participants, those whom it called the "victims of child pornography." Id., at 110. It did not suggest that, absent this concern, other governmental interests would suffice. See infra, at 13—15.

In contrast to the speech in Ferber, speech that itself is the record of sexual abuse, the CPPA prohibits speech that records no crime and creates no victims by its production. Virtual child pornography is not "intrinsically related" to the sexual abuse of children, as were the materials in Ferber. 458 U.S., at 759. While the Government asserts that the images can lead to actual instances of child abuse, see infra, at 13—16, the causal link is contingent and indirect. The harm does not necessarily follow from the speech, but depends upon some unquantified potential for subsequent criminal acts.

The Government says these indirect harms are sufficient because, as Ferber acknowledged, child pornography rarely can be valuable speech. See 458 U.S., at 762 ("The value of permitting live performances and photographic reproductions of children engaged in lewd sexual conduct is exceedingly modest, if not *de minimis*"). This argument, however, suffers from two flaws. First, Ferber's judgment about child pornography was based upon how it was made, not on what it communicated. The case reaffirmed that where the speech is neither obscene nor the product of sexual abuse, it does not fall outside the protection of the First Amendment. See id., at 764—765 ("[T]he distribution of descriptions or other depictions of sexual conduct, not otherwise obscene, which do not involve live performance or photographic or other visual reproduction of live performances, retains First Amendment protection").

The second flaw in the Government's position is that Ferber did not hold that child pornography is by definition without value. On the contrary, the Court recognized some works in this category might have significant value, see id., at 761, but relied on virtual images–the very images prohibited by the CPPA–as an alternative and permissible means of expression: "[I]f it were necessary for literary or artistic value, a person over the statutory age who perhaps looked younger could be utilized. Simulation outside of the prohibition of the statute could provide another alternative." Id., at 763. Ferber, then, not only referred to the distinction between actual and virtual child pornography, it relied on it as a reason supporting its holding. Ferber provides no support for a statute that eliminates the distinction and makes the alternative mode criminal as well.

III

The CPPA, for reasons we have explored, is inconsistent with Miller and finds no support in Ferber. The Government seeks to justify its prohibitions in other ways. It argues that the CPPA is necessary because pedophiles may use virtual child pornography to seduce children. There are many things innocent in themselves, however, such as cartoons, video games, and candy, that might be used for immoral purposes, yet we would not expect those to be prohibited because they can be misused. The Government, of course, may punish adults who provide unsuitable materials to children, see Ginsberg v. New York, 390 U.S. 629 (1968), and it may enforce criminal penalties for unlawful solicitation. The precedents establish, however, that speech within the rights of adults to hear may not be silenced completely in an attempt to shield children from it. See Sable Communications of Cal., Inc. v. FCC, 492 U.S. 115 (1989). In Butler v. Michigan, 352 U.S. 380, 381 (1957), the Court invalidated a statute prohibiting distribution of an indecent publication because of its tendency to "incite minors to violent or depraved or immoral acts." A unanimous Court agreed upon the important First Amendment principle that the State could not "reduce the adult population ... to reading only what is fit for children." Id., at 383. We have reaffirmed this holding. See United States v. Playboy Entertainment Group, Inc., 529 U.S. 803, 814 (2000) ("[T]he objective of shielding children does not suffice to support a blanket ban if the protection can be accomplished by a less restrictive alternative"); Reno v. American Civil Liberties Union, 521 U.S., at 875 (The "governmental interest in protecting children from harmful materials ... does not justify an unnecessarily broad suppression of speech addressed to adults"); Sable Communications v. FCC, supra, at 130–131 (striking down a ban on "dial-a-porn" messages that had "the invalid effect of limiting the content of adult telephone conversations to that which is suitable for children to hear").

Here, the Government wants to keep speech from children not to protect them from its content but to protect them from those who would commit other crimes. The principle, however, remains the same: The Government cannot ban speech fit for adults simply because it may fall into the hands of children. The evil in question depends upon the actor's unlawful conduct, conduct defined as criminal quite apart from any link to the speech in question. This establishes that the speech ban is not narrowly drawn. The objective is to prohibit illegal conduct, but this restriction goes well beyond that interest by restricting the speech available to law-abiding adults.

The Government submits further that virtual child pornography whets the appetites of pedophiles and encourages them to engage in illegal conduct. This rationale cannot sustain the provision in question. The mere tendency of speech to encourage unlawful acts is not a sufficient reason for banning it. The government "cannot constitutionally premise legislation on the desirability of controlling a person's private thoughts." Stanley v. Georgia, 394 U.S. 557, 566 (1969). First Amendment freedoms are most in danger when the government seeks to control thought or to justify its laws for that impermissible end. The right to think is the beginning of freedom, and speech must be protected from the government because speech is the beginning of thought.

To preserve these freedoms, and to protect speech for its own sake, the Court's First Amendment cases draw vital distinctions between words and deeds, between ideas and conduct. See Kingsley Int'l Pictures Corp., 360 U.S., at 689; see also Bartnicki v. Vopper, 532 U.S. 514, 529 (2001) ("The normal method of deterring unlawful conduct is to impose an appropriate punishment on the person who engages in it"). The government may not prohibit speech because it increases the chance an unlawful act will be committed "at some indefinite future time." Hess v. Indiana, 414 U.S. 105, 108 (1973) (per curiam). The government may suppress speech for advocating the use of force or a violation of law only if "such advocacy is directed to inciting or producing imminent lawless action and is likely to incite or produce such action." Brandenburg v. Ohio, 395 U.S. 444, 447 (1969) (per curiam). There is here no attempt, incitement, solicitation, or conspiracy. The Government has shown no more than a remote connection between speech that might encourage thoughts or impulses and any resulting child abuse. Without a significantly stronger, more direct connection, the Government may not prohibit speech on the ground that it may encourage pedophiles to engage in illegal conduct.

The Government next argues that its objective of eliminating the market for pornography produced using real children necessitates a prohibition on virtual images as well. Virtual images, the Government contends, are indistinguishable from real ones; they are part of the same market and are often exchanged. In this way, it is said, virtual images promote the trafficking in works produced through the exploitation of real children. The hypothesis is somewhat implausible. If virtual images were identical to illegal child pornography, the illegal images would be driven from the market by the indistinguishable substitutes. Few pornographers would risk prosecution by abusing real children if fictional, computerized images would suffice.

In the case of the material covered by Ferber, the creation of the speech is itself the crime of child abuse; the prohibition deters the crime by removing the profit motive. See Osborne, 495 U.S., at 109—110. Even where there is an underlying crime, however, the Court has not allowed the suppression of speech in all cases. E.g., Bartnicki, supra, at 529 (market deterrence would not justify law prohibiting a radio commentator from distributing speech that had been unlawfully intercepted). We need not consider where to strike the balance in this case, because here, there is no underlying crime at all. Even if the Government's market deterrence theory were persuasive in some contexts, it would not justify this statute.

Finally, the Government says that the possibility of producing images by using computer imaging makes it very difficult for it to prosecute those who produce pornography by using real children. Experts, we are told, may have difficulty in saying whether the pictures were made by using real children or by using computer imaging. The necessary solution, the argument runs, is to prohibit both kinds of images. The argument, in essence, is that protected speech may be banned as a means to ban unprotected speech. This analysis turns the First Amendment upside down.

The Government may not suppress lawful speech as the means to suppress unlawful speech. Protected speech does not become unprotected merely because it resembles the latter. The Constitution requires the reverse. "[T]he possible harm to society in permitting some unprotected speech to go unpunished is outweighed by the possibility that protected speech of others may be muted ... ." Broadrick v. Oklahoma, 413 U.S., at 612. The overbreadth doctrine prohibits the Government from banning unprotected speech if a substantial amount of protected speech is prohibited or chilled in the process.

To avoid the force of this objection, the Government would have us read the CPPA not as a measure suppressing speech but as a law shifting the burden to the accused to prove the speech is lawful. In this connection, the Government relies on an affirmative defense under the statute, which allows a defendant to avoid conviction for nonpossession offenses by showing that the materials were produced using only adults and were not otherwise distributed in a manner conveying the impression that they depicted real children. See 18 U.S.C. § 2252A(c).

The Government raises serious constitutional difficulties by seeking to impose on the defendant the burden of proving his speech is not unlawful. An affirmative defense applies only after prosecution has begun, and the speaker must himself prove, on pain of a felony conviction, that his conduct falls within the affirmative defense. In cases under the CPPA, the evidentiary burden is not trivial. Where the defendant is not the producer of the work, he may have no way of establishing the identity, or even the existence, of the actors. If the evidentiary issue is a serious problem for the Government, as it asserts, it will be at least as difficult for the innocent possessor. The statute, moreover, applies to work created before 1996, and the producers themselves may not have preserved the records necessary to meet the burden of proof. Failure to establish the defense can lead to a felony conviction.

We need not decide, however, whether the Government could impose this burden on a speaker. Even if an affirmative defense can save a statute from First Amendment challenge, here the defense is incomplete and insufficient, even on its own terms. It allows persons to be convicted in some instances where they can prove children were not exploited in the production. A defendant charged with possessing, as opposed to distributing, proscribed works may not defend on the ground that the film depicts only adult actors. See ibid. So while the affirmative defense may protect a movie producer from prosecution for the act of distribution, that same producer, and all other persons in the subsequent distribution chain, could be liable for possessing the prohibited work. Furthermore, the affirmative defense provides no protection to persons who produce speech by using computer imaging, or through other means that do not involve the use of adult actors who appear to be minors. See ibid. In these cases, the defendant can demonstrate no children were harmed in producing the images, yet the affirmative defense would not bar the prosecution. For this reason, the affirmative defense cannot save the statute, for it leaves unprotected a substantial amount of speech not tied to the Government's interest in distinguishing images produced using real children from virtual ones.

In sum, §2256(8)(B) covers materials beyond the categories recognized in Ferber and Miller, and the reasons the Government offers in support of limiting the freedom of speech have no justification in our precedents or in the law of the First Amendment. The provision abridges the freedom to engage in a substantial amount of lawful speech. For this reason, it is overbroad and unconstitutional.

IV

Respondents challenge §2256(8)(D) as well. This provision bans depictions of sexually explicit conduct that are "advertised, promoted, presented, described, or distributed in such a manner that conveys the impression that the material is or contains a visual depiction of a minor engaging in sexually explicit conduct." The parties treat the section as nearly identical to the provision prohibiting materials that appear to be child pornography. In the Government's view, the difference between the two is that "the 'conveys the impression' provision requires the jury to assess the material at issue in light of the manner in which it is promoted." Brief for Petitioners 18, n. 3. The Government's assumption, however, is that the determination would still depend principally upon the content of the prohibited work.

We disagree with this view. The CPPA prohibits sexually explicit materials that "conve[y] the impression" they depict minors. While that phrase may sound like the "appears to be" prohibition in §2256(8)(B), it requires little judgment about the content of the image. Under §2256(8)(D), the work must be sexually explicit, but otherwise the content is irrelevant. Even if a film contains no sexually explicit scenes involving minors, it could be treated as child pornography if the title and trailers convey the impression that the scenes would be found in the movie. The determination turns on how the speech is presented, not on what is depicted. While the legislative findings address at length the problems posed by materials that look like child pornography, they are silent on the evils posed by images simply pandered that way.

The Government does not offer a serious defense of this provision, and the other arguments it makes in support of the CPPA do not bear on §2256(8)(D). The materials, for instance, are not likely to be confused for child pornography in a criminal trial. The Court has recognized that pandering may be relevant, as an evidentiary matter, to the question whether particular materials are obscene. See Ginzburg v. United States, 383 U.S. 463, 474 (1966) ("[I]n close cases evidence of pandering may be probative with respect to the nature of the material in question and thus satisfy the [obscenity] test"). Where a defendant engages in the "commercial exploitation of erotica solely for the sake of their prurient appeal," id., at 466, the context he or she creates may itself be relevant to the evaluation of the materials.

Section 2256(8)(D), however, prohibits a substantial amount of speech that falls outside Ginzburg's rationale. Materials falling within the proscription are tainted and unlawful in the hands of all who receive it, though they bear no responsibility for how it was marketed, sold, or described. The statute, furthermore, does not require that the context be part of an effort at "commercial exploitation." Ibid. As a consequence, the CPPA does more than prohibit pandering. It prohibits possession of material described, or pandered, as child pornography by someone earlier in the distribution chain. The provision prohibits a sexually explicit film containing no youthful actors, just because it is placed in a box suggesting a prohibited movie. Possession is a crime even when the possessor knows the movie was mislabeled. The First Amendment requires a more precise restriction. For this reason, §2256(8)(D) is substantially overbroad and in violation of the First Amendment.

V

For the reasons we have set forth, the prohibitions of §§2256(8)(B) and 2256(8)(D) are overbroad and unconstitutional. Having reached this conclusion, we need not address respondents' further contention that the provisions are unconstitutional because of vague statutory language.

The judgment of the Court of Appeals is affirmed.

It is so ordered.

## Los Angeles v. Alameda Books, Inc. (May 13, 2002)

Justice O'Connor announced the judgment of the Court and delivered an opinion, in which The Chief Justice, Justice Scalia, and Justice Thomas join.

Los Angeles Municipal Code §12.70(C) (1983), as amended, prohibits "the establishment or maintenance of more than one adult entertainment business in the same building, structure or portion thereof." Respondents, two adult establishments that each operated an adult bookstore and an adult video arcade in the same building, filed a suit under Rev. Stat. §1979, 42 U.S.C. § 1983 (1994 ed., Supp. V), alleging that §12.70(C) violates the First Amendment and seeking declaratory and injunctive relief. The District Court granted summary judgment to respondents, finding that the city of Los Angeles' prohibition was a content-based regulation of speech that failed strict scrutiny. The Court of Appeals for the Ninth Circuit affirmed, but on different grounds. It held that, even if §12.70(C) were a content-neutral regulation, the city failed to demonstrate that the prohibition was designed to serve a substantial government interest. Specifically, the Court of Appeals found that the city failed to present evidence upon which it could reasonably rely to demonstrate a link between multiple-use adult establishments and negative secondary effects. Therefore, the Court of Appeals held the Los Angeles prohibition on such establishments invalid under Renton v. Playtime Theatres, Inc., 475 U.S. 41 (1986), and its precedents interpreting that case. 222 F.3d 719, 723—728 (2000). We reverse and remand. The city of Los Angeles may reasonably rely on a study it conducted some years before enacting the present version of §12.70(C) to demonstrate that its ban on multiple-use adult establishments serves its interest in reducing crime.

   I

   In 1977, the city of Los Angeles conducted a comprehensive study of adult establishments and concluded that concentrations of adult businesses are associated with higher rates of prostitution, robbery, assaults, and thefts in surrounding communities. See App. 35—162 (Los Angeles Dept. of City Planning, Study of the Effects of the Concentration of Adult Entertainment Establishments in the City of Los Angeles (City Plan Case No. 26475, City Council File No. 74—4521—S.3, June 1977)). Accordingly, the city enacted an ordinance prohibiting the establishment, substantial enlargement, or transfer of ownership of an adult arcade, bookstore, cabaret, motel, theater, or massage parlor or a place for sexual encounters within 1,000 feet of another such enterprise or within 500 feet of any religious institution, school, or public park. See Los Angeles Municipal Code §12.70(C) (1978).

   There is evidence that the intent of the city council when enacting this prohibition was not only to disperse distinct adult establishments housed in separate buildings, but also to disperse distinct adult businesses operated under common ownership and housed in a single structure. See App. 29 (Los Angeles Dept. of City Planning, Amendment—Proposed Ordinance to Prohibit the Establishment of More than One Adult Entertainment Business at a Single Location (City Plan Case No. 26475, City Council File No. 82—0155, Jan. 13, 1983)). The ordinance the city enacted, however, directed that "[t]he distance between any two adult entertainment businesses shall be measured in a straight line ... from the closest exterior structural wall of each business." Los Angeles Municipal Code §12.70(D) (1978). Subsequent to enactment, the city realized that this method of calculating distances created a loophole permitting the concentration of multiple adult enterprises in a single structure.

   Concerned that allowing an adult-oriented department store to replace a strip of adult establishments could defeat the goal of the original ordinance, the city council amended §12.70(C) by adding a prohibition on "the establishment or maintenance of more than one adult entertainment business in the same building, structure or portion thereof." Los Angeles Municipal Code §12.70(C) (1983). The amended ordinance defines an "Adult Entertainment Business" as an adult arcade, bookstore, cabaret, motel, theater, or massage parlor or a place for sexual encounters, and notes that each of these enterprises "shall constitute a separate adult entertainment business even if operated in conjunction with another adult entertainment business at the same establishment." §12.70(B)(17). The ordinance uses the term "business" to refer to certain types of goods or services sold in adult establishments, rather than the establishment itself. Relevant for purposes of this case are also the ordinance's definitions of adult bookstores and arcades. An "Adult Bookstore" is an operation that "has as a substantial portion of its stock-in-trade and offers for sale" printed matter and videocassettes that emphasize the depiction of specified sexual activities. §12.70(B)(2)(a). An adult arcade is an operation where, "for any form of consideration," five or fewer patrons together may view films or videocassettes that emphasize the depiction of specified sexual activities. §12.70(B)(1).

Respondents, Alameda Books, Inc., and Highland Books, Inc., are two adult establishments operating in Los Angeles. Neither is located within 1,000 feet of another adult establishment or 500 feet of any religious institution, public park, or school. Each establishment occupies less than 3,000 square feet. Both respondents rent and sell sexually oriented products, including videocassettes. Additionally, both provide booths where patrons can view videocassettes for a fee. Although respondents are located in different buildings, each operates its retail sales and rental operations in the same commercial space in which its video booths are located. There are no physical distinctions between the different operations within each establishment and each establishment has only one entrance. 222 F.3d, at 721. Respondents concede they are openly operating in violation of §12.70(C) of the city's Code, as amended. Brief for Respondents 7; Brief for Petitioner 9.

After a city building inspector found in 1995 that Alameda Books, Inc., was operating both as an adult bookstore and an adult arcade in violation of the city's adult zoning regulations, respondents joined as plaintiffs and sued under 42 U.S.C. § 1983 for declaratory and injunctive relief to prevent enforcement of the ordinance. 222 F.3d, at 721. At issue in this case is count I of the complaint, which alleges a facial violation of the First Amendment. Both the city and respondents filed cross-motions for summary judgment.

The District Court for the Central District of California initially denied both motions on the First Amendment issues in count I, concluding that there was "a genuine issue of fact whether the operation of a combination video rental and video viewing business leads to the harmful secondary effects associated with a concentration of separate businesses in a single urban area." App. 255. After respondents filed a motion for reconsideration, however, the District Court found that Los Angeles' prohibition on multiple-use adult establishments was not a content-neutral regulation of speech. App. to Pet. for Cert. 51. It reasoned that the neither the city's 1977 study nor a report cited in Hart Book Stores v. Edmisten, 612 F.2d 821 (CA4 1979) (upholding a North Carolina statute that also banned multiple-use adult establishments), supported a reasonable belief that multiple-use adult establishments produced the secondary effects the city asserted as content-neutral justifications for its prohibition. App. to Pet. for Cert. 34—47. Therefore, the District Court proceeded to subject the Los Angeles ordinance to strict scrutiny. Because it felt that the city did not offer evidence to demonstrate that its prohibition is necessary to serve a compelling government interest, the District Court granted summary judgment for respondents and issued a permanent injunction enjoining the enforcement of the ordinance against respondents. Id., at 51.

The Court of Appeals for the Ninth Circuit affirmed, although on different grounds. The Court of Appeals determined that it did not have to reach the District Court's decision that the Los Angeles ordinance was content based because, even if the ordinance were content neutral, the city failed to present evidence upon which it could reasonably rely to demonstrate that its regulation of multiple-use establishments is "designed to serve" the city's substantial interest in reducing crime. The challenged ordinance was therefore invalid under Renton, 475 U.S. 41. 222 F.3d, at 723—724. We granted certiorari, 532 U.S. 902 (2001), to clarify the standard for determining whether an ordinance serves a substantial government interest under Renton, supra.

II

In Renton v. Playtime Theatres, Inc., supra, this Court considered the validity of a municipal ordinance that prohibited any adult movie theater from locating within 1,000 feet of any residential zone, family dwelling, church, park, or school. Our analysis of the ordinance proceeded in three steps. First, we found that the ordinance did not ban adult theaters altogether, but merely required that they be distanced from certain sensitive locations. The ordinance was properly analyzed, therefore, as a time, place, and manner regulation. Id., at 46. We next considered whether the ordinance was content neutral or content based. If the regulation were content based, it would be considered presumptively invalid and subject to strict scrutiny. Simon & Schuster, Inc. v. Members of N. Y. State Crime Victims Bd., 502 U.S. 105, 115, 118 (1991); Arkansas Writers' Project, Inc. v. Ragland, 481 U.S. 221, 230—231 (1987). We held, however, that the Renton ordinance was aimed not at the content of the films shown at adult theaters, but rather at the secondary effects of such theaters on the surrounding community, namely at crime rates, property values, and the quality of the city's neighborhoods. Therefore, the ordinance was deemed content neutral. Renton, supra, at 47—49. Finally, given this finding, we stated that the ordinance would be upheld so long as the city of Renton showed that its ordinance was designed to serve a substantial government interest and that reasonable alternative avenues of communication remained available. 475 U.S., at 50. We concluded that Renton had met this burden, and we upheld its ordinance. Id., at 51—54.

The Court of Appeals applied the same analysis to evaluate the Los Angeles ordinance challenged in this case. First, the Court of Appeals found that the Los Angeles ordinance was not a complete ban on adult entertainment establishments, but rather a sort of adult zoning regulation, which Renton considered a time, place, and manner regulation. 222 F.3d, at 723. The Court of Appeals turned to the second step of the Renton analysis, but did not draw any conclusions about whether the Los Angeles ordinance was content based. It explained that, even if the Los Angeles ordinance were content neutral, the city had failed to demonstrate, as required by the third step of the Renton analysis, that its prohibition on multiple-use adult establishments was designed to serve its substantial interest in reducing crime. The Court of Appeals noted that the primary evidence relied upon by Los Angeles to demonstrate a link between combination adult businesses and harmful secondary effects was the 1977 study conducted by the city's planning department. The Court of Appeals found, however, that the city could not rely on that study because it did not " 'suppor[t] a reasonable belief that [the] combination [of] businesses ... produced harmful secondary effects of the type asserted." 222 F.3d, at 724. For similar reasons, the Court of Appeals also rejected the city's attempt to rely on a report on health conditions inside adult video arcades described in Hart Book Stores, a case that upheld a North Carolina statute similar to the Los Angeles ordinance challenged in this case. 612 F.2d 821.

The central component of the 1977 study is a report on city crime patterns provided by the Los Angeles Police Department. That report indicated that, during the period from 1965 to 1975, certain crime rates grew much faster in Hollywood, which had the largest concentration of adult establishments in the city, than in the city of Los Angeles as a whole. For example, robberies increased 3 times faster and prostitution 15 times faster in Hollywood than citywide. App. 124–125.

The 1977 study also contains reports conducted directly by the staff of the Los Angeles Planning Department that examine the relationship between adult establishments and property values. These staff reports, however, are inconclusive. Not surprisingly, the parties focus their dispute before this Court on the report by the Los Angeles Police Department. Because we find that reducing crime is a substantial government interest and that the police department report's conclusions regarding crime patterns may reasonably be relied upon to overcome summary judgment against the city, we also focus on the portion of the 1977 study drawn from the police department report.

The Court of Appeals found that the 1977 study did not reasonably support the inference that a concentration of adult operations within a single adult establishment produced greater levels of criminal activity because the study focused on the effect that a concentration of establishments–not a concentration of operations within a single establishment–had on crime rates. The Court of Appeals pointed out that the study treated combination adult bookstore/arcades as single establishments and did not study the effect of any separate-standing adult bookstore or arcade. 222 F.3d, at 724.

The Court of Appeals misunderstood the implications of the 1977 study. While the study reveals that areas with high concentrations of adult establishments are associated with high crime rates, areas with high concentrations of adult establishments are also areas with high concentrations of adult operations, albeit each in separate establishments. It was therefore consistent with the findings of the 1977 study, and thus reasonable, for Los Angeles to suppose that a concentration of adult establishments is correlated with high crime rates because a concentration of operations in one locale draws, for example, a greater concentration of adult consumers to the neighborhood, and a high density of such consumers either attracts or generates criminal activity. The assumption behind this theory is that having a number of adult operations in one single adult establishment draws the same dense foot traffic as having a number of distinct adult establishments in close proximity, much as minimalls and department stores similarly attract the crowds of consumers. Brief for Petitioner 28. Under this view, it is rational for the city to infer that reducing the concentration of adult operations in a neighborhood, whether within separate establishments or in one large establishment, will reduce crime rates.

Neither the Court of Appeals, nor respondents, nor the dissent provides any reason to question the city's theory. In particular, they do not offer a competing theory, let alone data, that explains why the elevated crime rates in neighborhoods with a concentration of adult establishments can be attributed entirely to the presence of permanent walls between, and separate entrances to, each individual adult operation. While the city certainly bears the burden of providing evidence that supports a link between concentrations of adult operations and asserted secondary effects, it does not bear the burden of providing evidence that rules out every theory for the link between concentrations of adult establishments that is inconsistent with its own.

The error that the Court of Appeals made is that it required the city to prove that its theory about a concentration of adult operations attracting crowds of customers, much like a minimall or department store does, is a necessary consequence of the 1977 study. For example, the Court of Appeals refused to allow the city to draw the inference that "the expansion of an adult bookstore to include an adult arcade would increase" business activity and "produce the harmful secondary effects identified in the Study." 222 F.3d, at 726. It reasoned that such an inference would justify limits on the inventory of an adult bookstore, not a ban on the combination of an adult bookstore and an adult arcade. The Court of Appeals simply replaced the city's theory–that having many different operations in close proximity attracts crowds–with its own–that the size of an operation attracts crowds. If the Court of Appeals' theory is correct, then inventory limits make more sense. If the city's theory is correct, then a prohibition on the combination of businesses makes more sense. Both theories are consistent with the data in the 1977 study. The Court of Appeals' analysis, however, implicitly requires the city to prove that its theory is the only one that can plausibly explain the data because only in this manner can the city refute the Court of Appeals' logic.

Respondents make the same logical error as the Court of Appeals when they suggest that the city's prohibition on multiuse establishments will raise crime rates in certain neighborhoods because it will force certain adult businesses to relocate to areas without any other adult businesses. Respondents' claim assumes that the 1977 study proves that all adult businesses, whether or not they are located near other adult businesses, generate crime. This is a plausible reading of the results from the 1977 study, but respondents do not demonstrate that it is a compelled reading. Nor do they provide evidence that refutes the city's interpretation of the study, under which the city's prohibition should on balance reduce crime. If this Court were nevertheless to accept respondents' speculation, it would effectively require that the city provide evidence that not only supports the claim that its ordinance serves an important government interest, but also does not provide support for any other approach to serve that interest.

In Renton, we specifically refused to set such a high bar for municipalities that want to address merely the secondary effects of protected speech. We held that a municipality may rely on any evidence that is "reasonably believed to be relevant" for demonstrating a connection between speech and a substantial, independent government interest. 475 U.S., at 51—52; see also, e.g., Barnes v. Glen Theatre, Inc., 501 U.S. 560, 584 (1991) (Souter, J., concurring in judgment) (permitting municipality to use evidence that adult theaters are correlated with harmful secondary effects to support its claim that nude dancing is likely to produce the same effects). This is not to say that a municipality can get away with shoddy data or reasoning. The municipality's evidence must fairly support the municipality's rationale for its ordinance. If plaintiffs fail to cast direct doubt on this rationale, either by demonstrating that the municipality's evidence does not support its rationale or by furnishing evidence that disputes the municipality's factual findings, the municipality meets the standard set forth in Renton. If plaintiffs succeed in casting doubt on a municipality's rationale in either manner, the burden shifts back to the municipality to supplement the record with evidence renewing support for a theory that justifies its ordinance. See, e.g., Erie v. Pap's A. M., 529 U.S. 277, 298 (2000) (plurality opinion). This case is at a very early stage in this process. It arrives on a summary judgment motion by respondents defended only by complaints that the 1977 study fails to prove that the city's justification for its ordinance is necessarily correct. Therefore, we conclude that the city, at this stage of the litigation, has complied with the evidentiary requirement in Renton.

Justice Souter faults the city for relying on the 1977 study not because the study fails to support the city's theory that adult department stores, like adult minimalls, attract customers and thus crime, but because the city does not demonstrate that free-standing single-use adult establishments reduce crime. See post, at 8—9 (dissenting opinion). In effect, Justice Souter asks the city to demonstrate, not merely by appeal to common sense, but also with empirical data, that its ordinance will successfully lower crime. Our cases have never required that municipalities make such a showing, certainly not without actual and convincing evidence from plaintiffs to the contrary. See, e.g., Barnes, supra, at 583—584 (Souter, J., concurring in judgment). Such a requirement would go too far in undermining our settled position that municipalities must be given a " 'reasonable opportunity to experiment with solutions' " to address the secondary effects of protected speech. Renton, supra, at 52 (quoting Young v. American Mini Theatres, Inc., 427 U.S. 50, 71 (1976) (plurality opinion)). A municipality considering an innovative solution may not have data that could demonstrate the efficacy of its proposal because the solution would, by definition, not have been implemented previously. The city's ordinance banning multiple-use adult establishments is such a solution. Respondents contend that there are no adult video arcades in Los Angeles County that operate independently of adult bookstores. See Brief for Respondents 41. But without such arcades, the city does not have a treatment group to compare with the control group of multiple-use adult establishments, and without such a comparison Justice Souter would strike down the city's ordinance. This leaves the city with no means to address the secondary effects with which it is concerned.

Our deference to the evidence presented by the city of Los Angeles is the product of a careful balance between competing interests. One the one hand, we have an "obligation to exercise independent judgment when First Amendment rights are implicated." Turner Broadcasting System, Inc. v. FCC, 512 U.S. 622, 666 (1994) (plurality opinion); see also Landmark Communications, Inc. v. Virginia, 435 U.S. 829, 843—844 (1978). On the other hand, we must acknowledge that the Los Angeles City Council is in a better position than the Judiciary to gather and evaluate data on local problems. See Turner, supra, at 665—666; Erie v. Pap's A. M., supra, at 297—298 (plurality opinion). We are also guided by the fact that Renton requires that municipal ordinances receive only intermediate scrutiny if they are content neutral. Renton, supra, at 48—50. There is less reason to be concerned that municipalities will use these ordinances to discriminate against unpopular speech. See Erie, supra, at 298—299.

Justice Souter would have us rethink this balance, and indeed the entire Renton framework. In Renton, the Court distinguished the inquiry into whether a municipal ordinance is content neutral from the inquiry into whether it is "designed to serve a substantial government interest and do not unreasonably limit alternative avenues of communication." 475 U.S., at 47—54. The former requires courts to verify that the "predominate concerns" motivating the ordinance "were with the secondary effects of adult [speech], and not with the content of adult [speech]." Id., at 47. The latter inquiry goes one step further and asks whether the municipality can demonstrate a connection between the speech regulated by the ordinance and the secondary effects that motivated the adoption of the ordinance. Only at this stage did Renton contemplate that courts would examine evidence concerning regulated speech and secondary effects. Id., at 50—52. Justice Souter would either merge these two inquiries or move the evidentiary analysis into the inquiry on content neutrality, and raise the evidentiary bar that a municipality must pass. His logic is that verifying that the ordinance actually reduces the secondary effects asserted would ensure that zoning regulations are not merely content-based regulations in disguise. See post, at 5—6.

We think this proposal unwise. First, none of the parties request the Court to depart from the Renton framework. Nor is the proposal fairly encompassed in the question presented, which focuses on the sorts of evidence upon which the city may rely to demonstrate that its ordinance is designed to serve a substantial governmental interest. Pet. for Cert. i. Second, there is no evidence suggesting that courts have difficulty determining whether municipal ordinances are motivated primarily by the content of adult speech or by its secondary effects without looking to evidence connecting such speech to the asserted secondary effects. In this case, the Court of Appeals has not yet had an opportunity to address the issue, having assumed for the sake of argument that the city's ordinance is content neutral. 222 F.3d, at 723. It would be inappropriate for this Court to reach the question of content neutrality before permitting the lower court to pass upon it. Finally, Justice Souter does not clarify the sort of evidence upon which municipalities may rely to meet the evidentiary burden he would require. It is easy to say that courts must demand evidence when "common experiences" or "common assumptions" are incorrect, see post, at 6–7, but it is difficult for courts to know ahead of time whether that condition is met. Municipalities will, in general, have greater experience with and understanding of the secondary effects that follow certain protected speech than will the courts. See Pap's A. M., 529 U.S., at 297–298 (plurality opinion). For this reason our cases require only that municipalities rely upon evidence that is "reasonably believed to be relevant" to the secondary effects that they seek to address.

### III

The city of Los Angeles argues that its prohibition on multiuse establishments draws further support from a study of the poor health conditions in adult video arcades described in Hart Book Stores, a case that upheld a North Carolina ordinance similar to that challenged here. See 612 F.2d, at 828, n. 9. Respondents argue that the city cannot rely on evidence from Hart Book Stores because the city cannot prove it examined that evidence before it enacted the current version of §12.70(C). Brief for Respondents 21. Respondents note, moreover, that unsanitary conditions in adult video arcades would persist regardless of whether arcades were operated in the same buildings as, say, adult bookstores. Ibid.

We do not, however, need to resolve the parties' dispute over evidence cited in Hart Book Stores. Unlike the city of Renton, the city of Los Angeles conducted its own study of adult businesses. We have concluded that the Los Angeles study provides evidence to support the city's theory that a concentration of adult operations in one locale attracts crime, and can be reasonably relied upon to demonstrate that Los Angeles Municipal Code §12.70(C) (1983) is designed to promote the city's interest in reducing crime. Therefore, the city need not present foreign studies to overcome the summary judgment against it.

Before concluding, it should be noted that respondents argue, as an alternative basis to sustain the Court of Appeals' judgment, that the Los Angeles ordinance is not a typical zoning regulation. Rather, respondents explain, the prohibition on multiuse adult establishments is effectively a ban on adult video arcades because no such business exists independently of an adult bookstore. Brief for Respondents 12–13. Respondents request that the Court hold that the Los Angeles ordinance is not a time, place, and manner regulation, and that the Court subject the ordinance to strict scrutiny. This also appears to be the theme of Justice Kennedy's concurrence. He contends that "[a] city may not assert that it will reduce secondary effects by reducing speech in the same proportion." Post, at 7 (opinion concurring in judgment). We consider that unobjectionable proposition as simply a reformulation of the requirement that an ordinance warrants intermediate scrutiny only if it is a time, place, and manner regulation and not a ban. The Court of Appeals held, however, that the city's prohibition on the combination of adult bookstores and arcades is not a ban and respondents did not petition for review of that determination.

Accordingly, we reverse the Court of Appeals' judgment granting summary judgment to respondents and remand the case for further proceedings.

It is so ordered.

## Virginia v. Black (April 7, 2003)

Justice O'Connor announced the judgment of the Court and delivered the opinion of the Court with respect to Parts I, II, and III, and an opinion with respect to Parts IV and V, in which The Chief Justice, Justice Stevens, and Justice Breyer join.

In this case we consider whether the Commonwealth of Virginia's statute banning cross burning with "an intent to intimidate a person or group of persons" violates the First Amendment. Va. Code Ann. §18.2—423 (1996). We conclude that while a State, consistent with the First Amendment, may ban cross burning carried out with the intent to intimidate, the provision in the Virginia statute treating any cross burning as prima facie evidence of intent to intimidate renders the statute unconstitutional in its current form.

I

Respondents Barry Black, Richard Elliott, and Jonathan O'Mara were convicted separately of violating Virginia's cross-burning statute, §18.2—423. That statute provides:

"It shall be unlawful for any person or persons, with the intent of intimidating any person or group of persons, to burn, or cause to be burned, a cross on the property of another, a highway or other public place. Any person who shall violate any provision of this section shall be guilty of a Class 6 felony.

"Any such burning of a cross shall be prima facie evidence of an intent to intimidate a person or group of persons."

On August 22, 1998, Barry Black led a Ku Klux Klan rally in Carroll County, Virginia. Twenty-five to thirty people attended this gathering, which occurred on private property with the permission of the owner, who was in attendance. The property was located on an open field just off Brushy Fork Road (State Highway 690) in Cana, Virginia.

When the sheriff of Carroll County learned that a Klan rally was occurring in his county, he went to observe it from the side of the road. During the approximately one hour that the sheriff was present, about 40 to 50 cars passed the site, a "few" of which stopped to ask the sheriff what was happening on the property. App. 71. Eight to ten houses were located in the vicinity of the rally. Rebecca Sechrist, who was related to the owner of the property where the rally took place, "sat and watched to see wha[t] [was] going on" from the lawn of her in-laws' house. She looked on as the Klan prepared for the gathering and subsequently conducted the rally itself. Id., at 103.

During the rally, Sechrist heard Klan members speak about "what they were" and "what they believed in." Id., at 106. The speakers "talked real bad about the blacks and the Mexicans." Id., at 109. One speaker told the assembled gathering that "he would love to take a .30/.30 and just random[ly] shoot the blacks." Ibid. The speakers also talked about "President Clinton and Hillary Clinton," and about how their tax money "goes to ... the black people." Ibid. Sechrist testified that this language made her "very ... scared." Id., at 110.

At the conclusion of the rally, the crowd circled around a 25- to 30-foot cross. The cross was between 300 and 350 yards away from the road. According to the sheriff, the cross "then all of a sudden ... went up in a flame." Id., at 71. As the cross burned, the Klan played Amazing Grace over the loudspeakers. Sechrist stated that the cross burning made her feel "awful" and "terrible." Id., at 110.

When the sheriff observed the cross burning, he informed his deputy that they needed to "find out who's responsible and explain to them that they cannot do this in the State of Virginia." Id., at 72. The sheriff then went down the driveway, entered the rally, and asked "who was responsible for burning the cross." Id., at 74. Black responded, "I guess I am because I'm the head of the rally." Ibid. The sheriff then told Black, "[T]here's a law in the State of Virginia that you cannot burn a cross and I'll have to place you under arrest for this." Ibid.

Black was charged with burning a cross with the intent of intimidating a person or group of persons, in violation of §18.2—423. At his trial, the jury was instructed that "intent to intimidate means the motivation to intentionally put a person or a group of persons in fear of bodily harm. Such fear must arise from the willful conduct of the accused rather than from some mere temperamental timidity of the victim." Id., at 146. The trial court also instructed the jury that "the burning of a cross by itself is sufficient evidence from which you may infer the required intent." Ibid. When Black objected to this last instruction on First Amendment grounds, the prosecutor responded that the instruction was "taken straight out of the [Virginia] Model Instructions." Id., at 134. The jury found Black guilty, and fined him $2,500. The Court of Appeals of Virginia affirmed Black's conviction. Rec. No. 1581—99—3 (Va. App., Dec. 19, 2000), App. 201.

On May 2, 1998, respondents Richard Elliott and Jonathan O'Mara, as well as a third individual, attempted to burn a cross on the yard of James Jubilee. Jubilee, an African-American, was Elliott's next-door neighbor in Virginia Beach, Virginia. Four months prior to the incident, Jubilee and his family had moved from California to Virginia Beach. Before the cross burning, Jubilee spoke to Elliott's mother to inquire about shots being fired from behind the Elliott home. Elliott's mother explained to Jubilee that her son shot firearms as a hobby, and that he used the backyard as a firing range.

On the night of May 2, respondents drove a truck onto Jubilee's property, planted a cross, and set it on fire. Their apparent motive was to "get back" at Jubilee for complaining about the shooting in the backyard. Id., at 241. Respondents were not affiliated with the Klan. The next morning, as Jubilee was pulling his car out of the driveway, he noticed the partially burned cross approximately 20 feet from his house. After seeing the cross, Jubilee was "very nervous" because he "didn't know what would be the next phase," and because "a cross burned in your yard ... tells you that it's just the first round." Id., at 231.

Elliott and O'Mara were charged with attempted cross burning and conspiracy to commit cross burning. O'Mara pleaded guilty to both counts, reserving the right to challenge the constitutionality of the cross-burning statute. The judge sentenced O'Mara to 90 days in jail and fined him $2,500. The judge also suspended 45 days of the sentence and $1,000 of the fine.

At Elliott's trial, the judge originally ruled that the jury would be instructed "that the burning of a cross by itself is sufficient evidence from which you may infer the required intent." Id., at 221—222. At trial, however, the court instructed the jury that the Commonwealth must prove that "the defendant intended to commit cross burning," that "the defendant did a direct act toward the commission of the cross burning," and that "the defendant had the intent of intimidating any person or group of persons." Id., at 250. The court did not instruct the jury on the meaning of the word "intimidate," nor on the prima facie evidence provision of §18.2—423. The jury found Elliott guilty of attempted cross burning and acquitted him of conspiracy to commit cross burning. It sentenced Elliott to 90 days in jail and a $2,500 fine. The Court of Appeals of Virginia affirmed the convictions of both Elliott and O'Mara. O'Mara v. Commonwealth, 33 Va. App. 525, 535 S. E. 2d 175 (2000).

Each respondent appealed to the Supreme Court of Virginia, arguing that §18.2—423 is facially unconstitutional. The Supreme Court of Virginia consolidated all three cases, and held that the statute is unconstitutional on its face. 262 Va. 764, 553 S. E. 2d 738 (2001). It held that the Virginia cross-burning statute "is analytically indistinguishable from the ordinance found unconstitutional in R. A. V. [v. St. Paul, 505 U.S. 377 (1992)]." Id., at 772, 553 S. E. 2d, at 742. The Virginia statute, the court held, discriminates on the basis of content since it "selectively chooses only cross burning because of its distinctive message." Id., at 774, 553 S. E. 2d, at 744. The court also held that the prima facie evidence provision renders the statute overbroad because "[t]he enhanced probability of prosecution under the statute chills the expression of protected speech." Id., at 777, 553 S. E. 2d, at 746.

Three justices dissented, concluding that the Virginia cross-burning statute passes constitutional muster because it proscribes only conduct that constitutes a true threat. The justices noted that unlike the ordinance found unconstitutional in R. A. V. v. St. Paul, 505 U.S. 377 (1992), the Virginia statute does not just target cross burning "on the basis of race, color, creed, religion or gender." 262 Va., at 791, 553 S. E. 2d, at 791. Rather, "the Virginia statute applies to any individual who burns a cross for any reason provided the cross is burned with the intent to intimidate." Ibid. The dissenters also disagreed with the majority's analysis of the prima facie provision because the inference alone "is clearly insufficient to establish beyond a reasonable doubt that a defendant burned a cross with the intent to intimidate." Id., at 795, 553 S. E. 2d, at 756. The dissent noted that the burden of proof still remains on the Commonwealth to prove intent to intimidate. We granted certiorari. 535 U.S. 1094 (2002).1

II

Cross burning originated in the 14th century as a means for Scottish tribes to signal each other. See M. Newton & J. Newton, The Ku Klux Klan: An Encyclopedia 145 (1991). Sir Walter Scott used cross burnings for dramatic effect in The Lady of the Lake, where the burning cross signified both a summons and a call to arms. See W. Scott, The Lady of The Lake, canto third. Cross burning in this country, however, long ago became unmoored from its Scottish ancestry. Burning a cross in the United States is inextricably intertwined with the history of the Ku Klux Klan.

The first Ku Klux Klan began in Pulaski, Tennessee, in the spring of 1866. Although the Ku Klux Klan started as a social club, it soon changed into something far different. The Klan fought Reconstruction and the corresponding drive to allow freed blacks to participate in the political process. Soon the Klan imposed "a veritable reign of terror" throughout the South. S. Kennedy, Southern Exposure 31 (1991) (hereinafter Kennedy). The Klan employed tactics such as whipping, threatening to burn people at the stake, and murder. W. Wade, The Fiery Cross: The Ku Klux Klan in America 48—49 (1987) (hereinafter Wade). The Klan's victims included blacks, southern whites who disagreed with the Klan, and "carpetbagger" northern whites.

The activities of the Ku Klux Klan prompted legislative action at the national level. In 1871, "President Grant sent a message to Congress indicating that the Klan's reign of terror in the Southern States had rendered life and property insecure." Jett v. Dallas Independent School Dist., 491 U.S. 701, 722 (1989) (internal quotation marks and alterations omitted). In response, Congress passed what is now known as the Ku Klux Klan Act. See "An Act to enforce the Provisions of the Fourteenth Amendment to the Constitution of the United States, and for other Purposes," 17 Stat. 13 (now codified at 42 U.S.C. § 1983 1985, and 1986). President Grant used these new powers to suppress the Klan in South Carolina, the effect of which severely curtailed the Klan in other States as well. By the end of Reconstruction in 1877, the first Klan no longer existed.

The genesis of the second Klan began in 1905, with the publication of Thomas Dixon's The Clansmen: An Historical Romance of the Ku Klux Klan. Dixon's book was a sympathetic portrait of the first Klan, depicting the Klan as a group of heroes "saving" the South from blacks and the "horrors" of Reconstruction. Although the first Klan never actually practiced cross burning, Dixon's book depicted the Klan burning crosses to celebrate the execution of former slaves. Id., at 324—326; see also Capitol Square Review and Advisory Bd. v. Pinette, 515 U.S. 753, 770—771 (1995) (Thomas, J., concurring). Cross burning thereby became associated with the first Ku Klux Klan. When D. W. Griffith turned Dixon's book into the movie The Birth of a Nation in 1915, the association between cross burning and the Klan became indelible. In addition to the cross burnings in the movie, a poster advertising the film displayed a hooded Klansman riding a hooded horse, with his left hand holding the reins of the horse and his right hand holding a burning cross above his head. Wade 127. Soon thereafter, in November 1915, the second Klan began.

From the inception of the second Klan, cross burnings have been used to communicate both threats of violence and messages of shared ideology. The first initiation ceremony occurred on Stone Mountain near Atlanta, Georgia. While a 40-foot cross burned on the mountain, the Klan members took their oaths of loyalty. See Kennedy 163. This cross burning was the second recorded instance in the United States. The first known cross burning in the country had occurred a little over one month before the Klan initiation, when a Georgia mob celebrated the lynching of Leo Frank by burning a "gigantic cross" on Stone Mountain that was "visible throughout" Atlanta. Wade 144 (internal quotation marks omitted).

The new Klan's ideology did not differ much from that of the first Klan. As one Klan publication emphasized, "We avow the distinction between [the] races, ... and we shall ever be true to the faithful maintenance of White Supremacy and will strenuously oppose any compromise thereof in any and all things." Id., at 147—148 (internal quotation marks omitted). Violence was also an elemental part of this new Klan. By September 1921, the New York World newspaper documented 152 acts of Klan violence, including 4 murders, 41 floggings, and 27 tar-and-featherings. Wade 160.

Often, the Klan used cross burnings as a tool of intimidation and a threat of impending violence. For example, in 1939 and 1940, the Klan burned crosses in front of synagogues and churches. See Kennedy 175. After one cross burning at a synagogue, a Klan member noted that if the cross burning did not "shut the Jews up, we'll cut a few throats and see what happens." Ibid. (internal quotation marks omitted). In Miami in 1941, the Klan burned four crosses in front of a proposed housing project, declaring, "We are here to keep niggers out of your town ... . When the law fails you, call on us." Id., at 176 (internal quotation marks omitted). And in Alabama in 1942, in "a whirlwind climax to weeks of flogging and terror," the Klan burned crosses in front of a union hall and in front of a union leader's home on the eve of a labor election. Id., at 180. These cross burnings embodied threats to people whom the Klan deemed antithetical to its goals. And these threats had special force given the long history of Klan violence.

The Klan continued to use cross burnings to intimidate after World War II. In one incident, an African-American "school teacher who recently moved his family into a block formerly occupied only by whites asked the protection of city police ... after the burning of a cross in his front yard." Richmond News Leader, Jan. 21, 1949, p. 19, App. 312. And after a cross burning in Suffolk, Virginia during the late 1940's, the Virginia Governor stated that he would "not allow any of our people of any race to be subjected to terrorism or intimidation in any form by the Klan or any other organization." D.

Chalmers, Hooded Americanism: The History of the Ku Klux Klan 333 (1980) (hereinafter Chalmers). These incidents of cross burning, among others, helped prompt Virginia to enact its first version of the cross-burning statute in 1950.

The decision of this Court in Brown v. Board of Education, 347 U.S. 483 (1954), along with the civil rights movement of the 1950's and 1960's, sparked another outbreak of Klan violence. These acts of violence included bombings, beatings, shootings, stabbings, and mutilations. See, e.g., Chalmers 349–350; Wade 302–303. Members of the Klan burned crosses on the lawns of those associated with the civil rights movement, assaulted the Freedom Riders, bombed churches, and murdered blacks as well as whites whom the Klan viewed as sympathetic toward the civil rights movement.

Throughout the history of the Klan, cross burnings have also remained potent symbols of shared group identity and ideology. The burning cross became a symbol of the Klan itself and a central feature of Klan gatherings. According to the Klan constitution (called the kloran), the "fiery cross" was the "emblem of that sincere, unselfish devotedness of all klansmen to the sacred purpose and principles we have espoused." The Ku Klux Klan Hearings before the House Committee on Rules, 67th Cong., 1st Sess., 114, Exh. G (1921); see also Wade 419. And the Klan has often published its newsletters and magazines under the name The Fiery Cross. See Wade 226, 489.

At Klan gatherings across the country, cross burning became the climax of the rally or the initiation. Posters advertising an upcoming Klan rally often featured a Klan member holding a cross. See N. MacLean, Behind the Mask of Chivalry: The Making of the Second Ku Klux Klan 142–143 (1994). Typically, a cross burning would start with a prayer by the "Klavern" minister, followed by the singing of Onward Christian Soldiers. The Klan would then light the cross on fire, as the members raised their left arm toward the burning cross and sang The Old Rugged Cross. Wade 185. Throughout the Klan's history, the Klan continued to use the burning cross in their ritual ceremonies.

For its own members, the cross was a sign of celebration and ceremony. During a joint Nazi-Klan rally in 1940, the proceeding concluded with the wedding of two Klan members who "were married in full Klan regalia beneath a blazing cross." Id., at 271. In response to antimasking bills introduced in state legislatures after World War II, the Klan burned crosses in protest. See Chalmers 340. On March 26, 1960, the Klan engaged in rallies and cross burnings throughout the South in an attempt to recruit 10 million members. See Wade 305. Later in 1960, the Klan became an issue in the third debate between Richard Nixon and John Kennedy, with both candidates renouncing the Klan. After this debate, the Klan reiterated its support for Nixon by burning crosses. See id., at 309. And cross burnings featured prominently in Klan rallies when the Klan attempted to move toward more nonviolent tactics to stop integration. See id., at 323; cf. Chalmers 368–369, 371–372, 380, 384. In short, a burning cross has remained a symbol of Klan ideology and of Klan unity.

To this day, regardless of whether the message is a political one or whether the message is also meant to intimidate, the burning of a cross is a "symbol of hate." Capitol

Square Review and Advisory Bd. v. Pinette, 515 U.S., at 771 (Thomas, J., concurring). And while cross burning sometimes carries no intimidating message, at other times the intimidating message is the only message conveyed. For example, when a cross burning is directed at a particular person not affiliated with the Klan, the burning cross often serves as a message of intimidation, designed to inspire in the victim a fear of bodily harm. Moreover, the history of violence associated with the Klan shows that the possibility of injury or death is not just hypothetical. The person who burns a cross directed at a particular person often is making a serious threat, meant to coerce the victim to comply with the Klan's wishes unless the victim is willing to risk the wrath of the Klan. Indeed, as the cases of respondents Elliott and O'Mara indicate, individuals without Klan affiliation who wish to threaten or menace another person sometimes use cross burning because of this association between a burning cross and violence.

In sum, while a burning cross does not inevitably convey a message of intimidation, often the cross burner intends that the recipients of the message fear for their lives. And when a cross burning is used to intimidate, few if any messages are more powerful.

III

A

The First Amendment, applicable to the States through the Fourteenth Amendment, provides that "Congress shall make no law ... abridging the freedom of speech." The hallmark of the protection of free speech is to allow "free trade in ideas"– even ideas that the overwhelming majority of people might find distasteful or discomforting. Abrams v. United States, 250 U.S. 616, 630 (1919) (Holmes, J., dissenting); see also Texas v. Johnson, 491 U.S. 397, 414 (1989) ("If there is a bedrock principle underlying the First Amendment, it is that the government may not prohibit the expression of an idea simply because society finds the idea itself offensive or disagreeable"). Thus, the First Amendment "ordinarily" denies a State "the power to prohibit dissemination of social, economic and political doctrine which a vast majority of its citizens believes to be false and fraught with evil consequence." Whitney v. California, 274 U.S. 357, 374 (1927) (Brandeis, J., dissenting). The First Amendment affords protection to symbolic or expressive conduct as well as to actual speech. See, e.g., R. A. V. v. City of St. Paul, 505 U.S., at 382; Texas v. Johnson, supra, at 405–406; United States v. O'Brien, 391 U.S. 367, 376–377 (1968); Tinker v. Des Moines Independent Community School Dist., 393 U.S. 503, 505 (1969).

The protections afforded by the First Amendment, however, are not absolute, and we have long recognized that the government may regulate certain categories of expression consistent with the Constitution. See, e.g., Chaplinsky v. New Hampshire, 315 U.S. 568, 571–572 (1942) ("There are certain well-defined and narrowly limited classes of speech, the prevention and punishment of which has never been thought to raise any Constitutional problem"). The First Amendment permits "restrictions upon the content of speech in a few limited areas, which are 'of such slight social value as a step to truth that any benefit that may be derived from them is clearly outweighed by the social interest in order and morality.' " R. A. V. v. City of St. Paul, supra, at 382–383 (quoting Chaplinsky v. New Hampshire, supra, at 572).

Thus, for example, a State may punish those words "which by their very utterance inflict injury or tend to incite an immediate breach of the peace." Chaplinsky v. New Hampshire, supra, at 572; see also R. A. V. v. City of St. Paul, supra, at 383 (listing limited areas where the First Amendment permits restrictions on the content of speech). We have consequently held that fighting words–"those personally abusive epithets which, when addressed to the ordinary citizen, are, as a matter of common knowledge, inherently likely to provoke violent reaction"–are generally proscribable under the First Amendment. Cohen v. California, 403 U.S. 15, 20 (1971); see also Chaplinsky v. New Hampshire, supra, at 572. Furthermore, "the constitutional guarantees of free speech and free press do not permit a State to forbid or proscribe advocacy of the use of force or of law violation except where such advocacy is directed to inciting or producing imminent lawless action and is likely to incite or produce such action." Brandenburg v. Ohio, 395 U.S. 444, 447 (1969) (per curiam). And the First Amendment also permits a State to ban a "true threat." Watts v. United States, 394 U.S. 705, 708 (1969) (per curiam) (internal quotation marks omitted); accord, R. A. V. v. City of St. Paul, supra, at 388 ("[T]hreats of violence are outside the First Amendment"); Madsen v. Women's Health Center, Inc., 512 U.S. 753, 774 (1994); Schenck v. Pro-Choice Network of Western N. Y., 519 U.S. 357, 373 (1997).

"True threats" encompass those statements where the speaker means to communicate a serious expression of an intent to commit an act of unlawful violence to a particular individual or group of individuals. See Watts v. United States, supra, at 708 ("political hyberbole" is not a true threat); R. A. V. v. City of St. Paul, 505 U.S., at 388. The speaker need not actually intend to carry out the threat. Rather, a prohibition on true threats "protect[s] individuals from the fear of violence" and "from the disruption that fear engenders," in addition to protecting people "from the possibility that the threatened violence will occur." Ibid. Intimidation in the constitutionally proscribable sense of the word is a type of true threat, where a speaker directs a threat to a person or group of persons with the intent of placing the victim in fear of bodily harm or death. Respondents do not contest that some cross burnings fit within this meaning of intimidating speech, and rightly so. As noted in Part II, supra, the history of cross burning in this country shows that cross burning is often intimidating, intended to create a pervasive fear in victims that they are a target of violence.

B

The Supreme Court of Virginia ruled that in light of R. A. V. v. City of St. Paul, supra, even if it is constitutional to ban cross burning in a content-neutral manner, the Virginia cross-burning statute is unconstitutional because it discriminates on the basis of content and viewpoint. 262 Va., at 771–776, 553 S. E. 2d, at 742–745. It is true, as the Supreme Court of Virginia held, that the burning of a cross is symbolic expression. The reason why the Klan burns a cross at its rallies, or individuals place a burning cross on someone else's lawn, is that the burning cross represents the message that the speaker wishes to communicate. Individuals burn crosses as opposed to other means of communication because cross burning carries a message in an effective and dramatic manner.2

The fact that cross burning is symbolic expression, however, does not resolve the constitutional question. The Supreme Court of Virginia relied upon R. A. V. v. City of St. Paul, supra, to conclude that once a statute discriminates on the basis of this type of content, the law is unconstitutional. We disagree.

In R. A. V., we held that a local ordinance that banned certain symbolic conduct, including cross burning, when done with the knowledge that such conduct would " 'arouse anger, alarm or resentment in others on the basis of race, color, creed, religion or gender' " was unconstitutional. Id., at 380 (quoting the St. Paul Bias-Motivated Crime Ordinance, St. Paul, Minn., Legis. Code §292.02 (1990)). We held that the ordinance did not pass constitutional muster because it discriminated on the basis of content by targeting only those individuals who "provoke violence" on a basis specified in the law. 505 U.S., at 391. The ordinance did not cover "[t]hose who wish to use 'fighting words' in connection with other ideas–to express hostility, for example, on the basis of political affiliation, union membership, or homosexuality." Ibid. This content-based discrimination was unconstitutional because it allowed the city "to impose special prohibitions on those speakers who express views on disfavored subjects." Ibid.

We did not hold in R. A. V. that the First Amendment prohibits all forms of content-based discrimination within a proscribable area of speech. Rather, we specifically stated that some types of content discrimination did not violate the First Amendment:

"When the basis for the content discrimination consists entirely of the very reason the entire class of speech at issue is proscribable, no significant danger of idea or viewpoint discrimination exists. Such a reason, having been adjudged neutral enough to support exclusion of the entire class of speech from First Amendment protection, is also neutral enough to form the basis of distinction within the class." Id., at 388.

Indeed, we noted that it would be constitutional to ban only a particular type of threat: "[T]he Federal Government can criminalize only those threats of violence that are directed against the President ... since the reasons why threats of violence are outside the First Amendment ... have special force when applied to the person of the President." Ibid. And a State may "choose to prohibit only that obscenity which is the most patently offensive in its prurience–i.e., that which involves the most lascivious displays of sexual activity." Ibid. (emphasis in original). Consequently, while the holding of R. A. V. does not permit a State to ban only obscenity based on "offensive political messages," ibid., or "only those threats against the President that mention his policy on aid to inner cities," ibid., the First Amendment permits content discrimination "based on the very reasons why the particular class of speech at issue ... is proscribable," id., at 393.

Similarly, Virginia's statute does not run afoul of the First Amendment insofar as it bans cross burning with intent to intimidate. Unlike the statute at issue in R. A. V., the Virginia statute does not single out for opprobrium only that speech directed toward "one of the specified disfavored topics." Id., at 391. It does not matter whether an individual burns a cross with intent to intimidate because of the victim's race, gender, or religion, or because of the victim's "political affiliation, union membership, or homosexuality." Ibid. Moreover, as a factual matter it is not true that cross burners direct their intimidating conduct solely to racial or religious minorities. See, e.g., supra, at 8 (noting the instances of cross burnings directed at union members); State v. Miller, 6 Kan. App. 2d 432, 629 P.2d 748 (1981) (describing the case of a defendant who burned a cross in the yard of the lawyer who had previously represented him and who was currently prosecuting him). Indeed, in the case of Elliott and O'Mara, it is at least unclear whether the respondents burned a cross due to racial animus. See 262 Va., at 791, 553 S. E. 2d, at 753 (Hassell, J., dissenting) (noting that "these defendants burned a cross because they were angry that their neighbor had complained about the presence of a firearm shooting range in the Elliott's yard, not because of any racial animus").

The First Amendment permits Virginia to outlaw cross burnings done with the intent to intimidate because burning a cross is a particularly virulent form of intimidation. Instead of prohibiting all intimidating messages, Virginia may choose to regulate this subset of intimidating messages in light of cross burning's long and pernicious history as a signal of impending violence. Thus, just as a State may regulate only that obscenity which is the most obscene due to its prurient content, so too may a State choose to prohibit only those forms of intimidation that are most likely to inspire fear of bodily harm. A ban on cross burning carried out with the intent to intimidate is fully consistent with our holding in R. A. V. and is proscribable under the First Amendment.

IV

The Supreme Court of Virginia ruled in the alternative that Virginia's cross-burning statute was unconstitutionally overbroad due to its provision stating that "[a]ny such burning of a cross shall be prima facie evidence of an intent to intimidate a person or group of persons." Va. Code Ann. §18.2—423 (1996). The Commonwealth added the prima facie provision to the statute in 1968. The court below did not reach whether this provision is severable from the rest of the cross-burning statute under Virginia law. See §1—17.1 ("The provisions of all statutes are severable unless ... it is apparent that two or more statutes or provisions must operate in accord with one another"). In this Court, as in the Supreme Court of Virginia, respondents do not argue that the prima facie evidence provision is unconstitutional as applied to any one of them. Rather, they contend that the provision is unconstitutional on its face.

The Supreme Court of Virginia has not ruled on the meaning of the prima facie evidence provision. It has, however, stated that "the act of burning a cross alone, with no evidence of intent to intimidate, will nonetheless suffice for arrest and prosecution and will insulate the Commonwealth from a motion to strike the evidence at the end of its case-in-chief." 262 Va., at 778, 553 S. E. 2d, at 746. The jury in the case of Richard Elliott did not receive any instruction on the prima facie evidence provision, and the provision was not an issue in the case of Jonathan O'Mara because he pleaded guilty. The court in Barry Black's case, however, instructed the jury that the provision means: "The burning of a cross, by itself, is sufficient evidence from which you may infer the required intent." App. 196. This jury instruction is the same as the Model Jury Instruction in the Commonwealth of Virginia. See Virginia Model Jury Instructions, Criminal, Instruction No. 10.250 (1998 and Supp. 2001).

The prima facie evidence provision, as interpreted by the jury instruction, renders the statute unconstitutional. Because this jury instruction is the Model Jury Instruction, and because the Supreme Court of Virginia had the opportunity to expressly disavow the jury instruction, the jury instruction's construction of the prima facie provision "is a ruling on a question of state law that is as binding on us as though the precise words had been written into" the statute. E.g., Terminiello v. Chicago, 337 U.S. 1, 4 (1949) (striking down an ambiguous statute on facial grounds based upon the instruction given to the jury); see also New York v. Ferber, 458 U.S. 747, 768 n. 21 (1982) (noting that Terminiello involved a facial challenge to the statute); Secretary of State of Md. v. Joseph H. Munson Co., 467 U.S. 947, 965, n. 13 (1984); Note, The First Amendment Overbreadth Doctrine, 83 Harv. L. Rev. 844, 845–846, n. 8 (1970); Monaghan, Overbreadth, 1981 S. Ct. Rev. 1, 10–12; Blakey & Murray, Threats, Free Speech, and the Jurisprudence of the Federal Criminal Law, 2002 B. Y. U. L. Rev. 829, 883, n. 133. As construed by the jury instruction, the prima facie provision strips away the very reason why a State may ban cross burning with the intent to intimidate. The prima facie evidence provision permits a jury to convict in every cross-burning case in which defendants exercise their constitutional right not to put on a defense. And even where a defendant like Black presents a defense, the prima facie evidence provision makes it more likely that the jury will find an intent to intimidate regardless of the particular facts of the case. The provision permits the Commonwealth to arrest, prosecute, and convict a person based solely on the fact of cross burning itself.

It is apparent that the provision as so interpreted " 'would create an unacceptable risk of the suppression of ideas.' " Secretary of State of Md. v. Joseph H. Munson Co., supra, at 965, n. 13 (quoting Members of City Council of Los Angeles v. Taxpayers for Vincent, 466 U.S. 789, 797 (1984)). The act of burning a cross may mean that a person is engaging in constitutionally proscribable intimidation. But that same act may mean only that the person is engaged in core political speech. The prima facie evidence provision in this statute blurs the line between these two meanings of a burning cross. As interpreted by the jury instruction, the provision chills constitutionally protected political speech because of the possibility that a State will prosecute—and potentially convict—somebody engaging only in lawful political speech at the core of what the First Amendment is designed to protect.

As the history of cross burning indicates, a burning cross is not always intended to intimidate. Rather, sometimes the cross burning is a statement of ideology, a symbol of group solidarity. It is a ritual used at Klan gatherings, and it is used to represent the Klan itself. Thus, "[b]urning a cross at a political rally would almost certainly be protected expression." R. A. V. v. St. Paul, 505 U.S., at 402, n. 4 (White, J., concurring in judgment) (citing Brandenburg v. Ohio, 395 U.S., at 445). Cf. National Socialist Party of America v. Skokie, 432 U.S. 43 (1977) (per curiam). Indeed, occasionally a person who burns a cross does not intend to express either a statement of ideology or intimidation. Cross burnings have appeared in movies such as Mississippi Burning, and in plays such as the stage adaptation of Sir Walter Scott's The Lady of the Lake.

The prima facie provision makes no effort to distinguish among these different types of cross burnings. It does not distinguish between a cross burning done with the purpose of creating anger or resentment and a cross burning done with the purpose of threatening or intimidating a victim. It does not distinguish between a cross burning at a public rally or a cross burning on a neighbor's lawn. It does not treat the cross burning directed at an individual differently from the cross burning directed at a group of like-minded believers. It allows a jury to treat a cross burning on the property of another with the owner's acquiescence in the same manner as a cross burning on the property of another without the owner's permission. To this extent I agree with Justice Souter that the prima facie evidence provision can "skew jury deliberations toward conviction in cases where the evidence of intent to intimidate is relatively weak and arguably consistent with a solely ideological reason for burning." Post, at 6 (opinion concurring in judgment and dissenting in part).

It may be true that a cross burning, even at a political rally, arouses a sense of anger or hatred among the vast majority of citizens who see a burning cross. But this sense of anger or hatred is not sufficient to ban all cross burnings. As Gerald Gunther has stated, "The lesson I have drawn from my childhood in Nazi Germany and my happier adult life in this country is the need to walk the sometimes difficult path of denouncing the bigot's hateful ideas with all my power, yet at the same time challenging any community's attempt to suppress hateful ideas by force of law." Casper, Gerry, 55 Stan. L. Rev. 647, 649 (2002) (internal quotation marks omitted). The prima facie evidence provision in this case ignores all of the contextual factors that are necessary to decide whether a particular cross burning is intended to intimidate. The First Amendment does not permit such a shortcut.

For these reasons, the prima facie evidence provision, as interpreted through the jury instruction and as applied in Barry Black's case, is unconstitutional on its face. We recognize that the Supreme Court of Virginia has not authoritatively interpreted the meaning of the prima facie evidence provision. Unlike Justice Scalia, we refuse to speculate on whether any interpretation of the prima facie evidence provision would satisfy the First Amendment. Rather, all we hold is that because of the interpretation of the prima facie evidence provision given by the jury instruction, the provision makes the statute facially invalid at this point. We also recognize the theoretical possibility that the court, on remand, could interpret the provision in a manner different from that so far set forth in order to avoid the constitutional objections we have described. We leave open that possibility. We also leave open the possibility that the provision is severable, and if so, whether Elliott and O'Mara could be retried under §18.2—423.

V

With respect to Barry Black, we agree with the Supreme Court of Virginia that his conviction cannot stand, and we affirm the judgment of the Supreme Court of Virginia. With respect to Elliott and O'Mara, we vacate the judgment of the Supreme Court of Virginia, and remand the case for further proceedings.

It is so ordered.

Notes

1. After we granted certiorari, the Commonwealth enacted another statute designed to remedy the constitutional problems identified by the state court. See Va. Code Ann. §18.2—423.01 (2002). Section 18.2—

423.01 bans the burning of "an object" when done "with the intent of intimidating any person or group of persons." The statute does not contain any prima facie evidence provision. Section 18.2—423.01, however, did not repeal §18.2—423, the cross-burning statute at issue in this case.

2. Justice Thomas argues in dissent that cross burning is "conduct, not expression." Post, at 8. While it is of course true that burning a cross is conduct, it is equally true that the First Amendment protects symbolic conduct as well as pure speech. See supra at 12. As Justice Thomas has previously recognized, a burning cross is a "symbol of hate," and a "a symbol of white supremacy." Capitol Square Review and Advisory Bd. v. Pinette, 515 U.S. 753, 770—771 (1995) (Thomas, J., concurring).

## Lawrence v. Texas (June 26, 2003)

Justice Kennedy delivered the opinion of the Court.

Liberty protects the person from unwarranted government intrusions into a dwelling or other private places. In our tradition the State is not omnipresent in the home. And there are other spheres of our lives and existence, outside the home, where the State should not be a dominant presence. Freedom extends beyond spatial bounds. Liberty presumes an autonomy of self that includes freedom of thought, belief, expression, and certain intimate conduct. The instant case involves liberty of the person both in its spatial and more transcendent dimensions.

I

The question before the Court is the validity of a Texas statute making it a crime for two persons of the same sex to engage in certain intimate sexual conduct.

In Houston, Texas, officers of the Harris County Police Department were dispatched to a private residence in response to a reported weapons disturbance. They entered an apartment where one of the petitioners, John Geddes Lawrence, resided. The right of the police to enter does not seem to have been questioned. The officers observed Lawrence and another man, Tyron Garner, engaging in a sexual act. The two petitioners were arrested, held in custody over night, and charged and convicted before a Justice of the Peace.

The complaints described their crime as "deviate sexual intercourse, namely anal sex, with a member of the same sex (man)." App. to Pet. for Cert. 127a, 139a. The applicable state law is Tex. Penal Code Ann. §21.06(a) (2003). It provides: "A person commits an offense if he engages in deviate sexual intercourse with another individual of the same sex." The statute defines "[d]eviate sexual intercourse" as follows:

"(A) any contact between any part of the genitals of one person and the mouth or anus of another person; or

"(B) the penetration of the genitals or the anus of another person with an object." §21.01(1).

The petitioners exercised their right to a trial de novo in Harris County Criminal Court. They challenged the statute as a violation of the Equal Protection Clause of the Fourteenth Amendment and of a like provision of the Texas Constitution. Tex. Const., Art. 1, §3a. Those contentions were rejected. The petitioners, having entered a plea of nolo contendere, were each fined $200 and assessed court costs of $141.25. App. to Pet. for Cert. 107a–110a.

The Court of Appeals for the Texas Fourteenth District considered the petitioners' federal constitutional arguments under both the Equal Protection and Due Process Clauses of the Fourteenth Amendment. After hearing the case en banc the court, in a divided opinion, rejected the constitutional arguments and affirmed the convictions. 41 S. W. 3d 349 (Tex. App. 2001). The majority opinion indicates that the Court of Appeals considered our decision in Bowers v. Hardwick, 478 U.S. 186 (1986), to be controlling on the federal due process aspect of the case. Bowers then being authoritative, this was proper.

We granted certiorari, 537 U.S. 1044 (2002), to consider three questions:

"1. Whether Petitioners' criminal convictions under the Texas "Homosexual Conduct" law–which criminalizes sexual intimacy by same-sex couples, but not identical behavior by different-sex couples–violate the Fourteenth Amendment guarantee of equal protection of laws?

"2. Whether Petitioners' criminal convictions for adult consensual sexual intimacy in the home violate their vital interests in liberty and privacy protected by the Due Process Clause of the Fourteenth Amendment?

"3. Whether Bowers v. Hardwick, 478 U.S. 186 (1986), should be overruled?" Pet. for Cert. i.

The petitioners were adults at the time of the alleged offense. Their conduct was in private and consensual.

II

We conclude the case should be resolved by determining whether the petitioners were free as adults to engage in the private conduct in the exercise of their liberty under the Due Process Clause of the Fourteenth Amendment to the Constitution. For this inquiry we deem it necessary to reconsider the Court's holding in Bowers.

There are broad statements of the substantive reach of liberty under the Due Process Clause in earlier cases, including Pierce v. Society of Sisters, 268 U.S. 510 (1925), and Meyer v. Nebraska, 262 U.S. 390 (1923); but the most pertinent beginning point is our decision in Griswold v. Connecticut, 381 U.S. 479 (1965).

In Griswold the Court invalidated a state law prohibiting the use of drugs or devices of contraception and counseling or aiding and abetting the use of contraceptives. The Court described the protected interest as a right to privacy and placed emphasis on the marriage relation and the protected space of the marital bedroom. Id., at 485.

After Griswold it was established that the right to make certain decisions regarding sexual conduct extends beyond the marital relationship. In Eisenstadt v. Baird, 405 U.S. 438 (1972), the Court invalidated a law prohibiting the distribution of contraceptives to unmarried persons. The case was decided under the Equal Protection Clause, id., at 454; but with respect to unmarried persons, the Court went on to state the fundamental proposition that the law impaired the exercise of their personal rights, ibid. It quoted from the statement of the Court of Appeals finding the law to be in conflict with fundamental human rights, and it followed with this statement of its own:

"It is true that in Griswold the right of privacy in question inhered in the marital relationship.... If the right of privacy means anything, it is the right of the individual, married or single, to be free from unwarranted governmental intrusion into matters so fundamentally affecting a person as the decision whether to bear or beget a child." Id., at 453.

The opinions in Griswold and Eisenstadt were part of the background for the decision in Roe v. Wade, 410 U.S. 113 (1973). As is well known, the case involved a challenge to the Texas law prohibiting abortions, but the laws of other States were affected as well. Although the Court held the woman's rights were not absolute, her right to elect an abortion did have real and substantial protection as an exercise of her liberty under the Due Process Clause. The Court cited cases that protect spatial freedom and cases that go well beyond it. Roe recognized the right of a woman to make certain fundamental decisions affecting her destiny and confirmed once more that the protection of liberty under the Due Process Clause has a substantive dimension of fundamental significance in defining the rights of the person.

In Carey v. Population Services Int'l, 431 U.S. 678 (1977), the Court confronted a New York law forbidding sale or distribution of contraceptive devices to persons under 16 years of age. Although there was no single opinion for the Court, the law was invalidated. Both Eisenstadt and Carey, as well as the holding and rationale in Roe, confirmed that the reasoning of Griswold could not be confined to the protection of rights of married adults. This was the state of the law with respect to some of the most relevant cases when the Court considered Bowers v. Hardwick.

The facts in Bowers had some similarities to the instant case. A police officer, whose right to enter seems not to have been in question, observed Hardwick, in his own bedroom, engaging in intimate sexual conduct with another adult male. The conduct was in violation of a Georgia statute making it a criminal offense to engage in sodomy. One difference between the two cases is that the Georgia statute prohibited the conduct whether or not the participants were of the same sex, while the Texas statute, as we have seen, applies only to participants of the same sex. Hardwick was not prosecuted, but he brought an action in federal court to declare the state statute invalid. He alleged he was a practicing homosexual and that the criminal prohibition violated rights guaranteed to him by the Constitution. The Court, in an opinion by Justice White, sustained the Georgia law. Chief Justice Burger and Justice Powell joined the opinion of the Court and filed separate, concurring opinions. Four Justices dissented. 478 U.S., at 199 (opinion of Blackmun, J., joined by Brennan, Marshall, and Stevens, JJ.); id., at 214 (opinion of Stevens, J., joined by Brennan and Marshall, JJ.).

The Court began its substantive discussion in Bowers as follows: "The issue presented is whether the Federal Constitution confers a fundamental right upon homosexuals to engage in sodomy and hence invalidates the laws of the many States that still make such conduct illegal and have done so for a very long time." Id., at 190. That statement, we now conclude, discloses the Court's own failure to appreciate the extent of the liberty at stake. To say that the issue in Bowers was simply the right to engage in certain sexual conduct demeans the claim the individual put forward, just as it would demean a married couple were it to be said marriage is simply about the right to have sexual intercourse. The laws involved in Bowers and here are, to be sure, statutes that purport to do no more than prohibit a particular sexual act. Their penalties and purposes, though, have more far-reaching consequences, touching upon the most private human conduct, sexual behavior, and in the most private of places, the home. The statutes do seek to control a personal relationship that, whether or not entitled to formal recognition in the law, is within the liberty of persons to choose without being punished as criminals.

This, as a general rule, should counsel against attempts by the State, or a court, to define the meaning of the relationship or to set its boundaries absent injury to a person or abuse of an institution the law protects. It suffices for us to acknowledge that adults may choose to enter upon this relationship in the confines of their homes and their own private lives and still retain their dignity as free persons. When sexuality finds overt expression in intimate conduct with another person, the conduct can be but one element in a personal bond that is more enduring. The liberty protected by the Constitution allows homosexual persons the right to make this choice.

Having misapprehended the claim of liberty there presented to it, and thus stating the claim to be whether there is a fundamental right to engage in consensual sodomy, the Bowers Court said: "Proscriptions against that conduct have ancient roots." Id., at 192. In academic writings, and in many of the scholarly amicus briefs filed to assist the Court in this case, there are fundamental criticisms of the historical premises relied upon by the majority and concurring opinions in Bowers. Brief for Cato Institute as Amicus Curiae 16—17; Brief for American Civil Liberties Union et al. as Amici Curiae 15—21; Brief for Professors of History et al. as Amici Curiae 3—10. We need not enter this debate in the attempt to reach a definitive historical judgment, but the following considerations counsel against adopting the definitive conclusions upon which Bowers placed such reliance.

At the outset it should be noted that there is no longstanding history in this country of laws directed at homosexual conduct as a distinct matter. Beginning in colonial times there were prohibitions of sodomy derived from the English criminal laws passed in the first instance by the Reformation Parliament of 1533. The English prohibition was understood to include relations between men and women as well as relations between men and men. See, e.g., King v. Wiseman, 92 Eng. Rep. 774, 775 (K. B. 1718) (interpreting "mankind" in Act of 1533 as including women and girls). Nineteenth-century commentators similarly read American sodomy, buggery, and crime-against-nature statutes as criminalizing certain relations between men and women and between men and men. See, e.g., 2 J. Bishop, Criminal Law §1028 (1858); 2 J. Chitty, Criminal Law 47—50 (5th Am. ed. 1847); R. Desty, A Compendium of American Criminal Law 143 (1882); J. May, The Law of Crimes §203 (2d ed. 1893). The absence of legal prohibitions focusing on homosexual conduct may be explained in part by noting that according to some scholars the concept of the homosexual as a distinct category of person did not emerge until the late 19th century. See, e.g., J. Katz, The Invention of Heterosexuality 10 (1995); J. D'Emilio & E. Freedman, Intimate Matters: A History of Sexuality in America 121 (2d ed. 1997) (" The modern terms homosexuality and heterosexuality do not apply to an era that had not yet articulated these distinctions"). Thus early American sodomy laws were not directed at homosexuals as such but instead sought to prohibit nonprocreative sexual activity more generally. This does not suggest approval of homosexual conduct. It does tend to show that this particular form of conduct was not thought of as a separate category from like conduct between heterosexual persons.

Laws prohibiting sodomy do not seem to have been enforced against consenting adults acting in private. A substantial number of sodomy prosecutions and convictions for which there are surviving records were for predatory acts against those who could not or did not consent, as in the case of a minor or the victim of an assault. As to these, one purpose for the prohibitions was to ensure there would be no lack of coverage if a predator committed a sexual assault that did not constitute rape as defined by the criminal law. Thus the model sodomy indictments presented in a 19th-century treatise, see 2 Chitty, supra, at 49, addressed the predatory acts of an adult man against a minor girl or minor boy. Instead of targeting relations between consenting adults in private, 19th-century sodomy prosecutions typically involved relations between men and minor girls or minor boys, relations between adults involving force, relations between adults implicating disparity in status, or relations between men and animals.

To the extent that there were any prosecutions for the acts in question, 19th-century evidence rules imposed a burden that would make a conviction more difficult to obtain even taking into account the problems always inherent in prosecuting consensual acts committed in private. Under then-prevailing standards, a man could not be convicted of sodomy based upon testimony of a consenting partner, because the partner was considered an accomplice. A partner's testimony, however, was admissible if he or she had not consented to the act or was a minor, and therefore incapable of consent. See, e.g., F. Wharton, Criminal Law 443 (2d ed. 1852); 1 F. Wharton, Criminal Law 512 (8th ed. 1880). The rule may explain in part the infrequency of these prosecutions. In all events that infrequency makes it difficult to say that society approved of a rigorous and systematic punishment of the consensual acts committed in private and by adults. The longstanding criminal prohibition of homosexual sodomy upon which the Bowers decision placed such reliance is as consistent with a general condemnation of nonprocreative sex as it is with an established tradition of prosecuting acts because of their homosexual character.

The policy of punishing consenting adults for private acts was not much discussed in the early legal literature. We can infer that one reason for this was the very private nature of the conduct. Despite the absence of prosecutions, there may have been periods in which there was public criticism of homosexuals as such and an insistence that the criminal laws be enforced to discourage their practices. But far from possessing "ancient roots," Bowers, 478 U.S., at 192, American laws targeting same-sex couples did not develop until the last third of the 20th century. The reported decisions concerning the prosecution of consensual, homosexual sodomy between adults for the years 1880—1995 are not always clear in the details, but a significant number involved conduct in a public place. See Brief for American Civil Liberties Union et al. as Amici Curiae 14—15, and n. 18.

It was not until the 1970's that any State singled out same-sex relations for criminal prosecution, and only nine States have done so. See 1977 Ark. Gen. Acts no. 828; 1983 Kan. Sess. Laws p. 652; 1974 Ky. Acts p. 847; 1977 Mo. Laws p. 687; 1973 Mont. Laws p. 1339; 1977 Nev. Stats. p. 1632; 1989 Tenn. Pub. Acts ch. 591; 1973 Tex. Gen. Laws ch. 399; see also Post v. State, 715 P.2d 1105 (Okla. Crim. App. 1986) (sodomy law invalidated as applied to different-sex couples). Post-Bowers even some of these States did not adhere to the policy of suppressing homosexual conduct. Over the course of the last decades, States with same-sex prohibitions have moved toward abolishing them. See, e.g., Jegley v. Picado, 349 Ark. 600, 80 S. W. 3d 332 (2002); Gryczan v. State, 283 Mont. 433, 942 P.2d 112 (1997); Campbell v. Sundquist, 926 S. W. 2d 250 (Tenn. App. 1996); Commonwealth v. Wasson, 842 S. W. 2d 487 (Ky. 1992); see also 1993 Nev. Stats. p. 518 (repealing Nev. Rev. Stat. §201.193).

In summary, the historical grounds relied upon in Bowers are more complex than the majority opinion and the concurring opinion by Chief Justice Burger indicate. Their historical premises are not without doubt and, at the very least, are overstated.

It must be acknowledged, of course, that the Court in Bowers was making the broader point that for centuries there have been powerful voices to condemn homosexual conduct as immoral. The condemnation has been shaped by religious beliefs, conceptions of right and acceptable behavior, and respect for the traditional family. For many persons these are not trivial concerns but profound and deep convictions accepted as ethical and moral principles to which they aspire and which thus determine the course of their lives. These considerations do not answer the question before us, however. The issue is whether the majority may use the power of the State to enforce these views on the whole society through operation of the criminal law. "Our obligation is to define the liberty of all, not to mandate our own moral code." Planned Parenthood of Southeastern Pa. v. Casey, 505 U.S. 833, 850 (1992).

Chief Justice Burger joined the opinion for the Court in Bowers and further explained his views as follows: "Decisions of individuals relating to homosexual conduct have been subject to state intervention throughout the history of Western civilization. Condemnation of those practices is firmly rooted in Judeao-Christian moral and ethical standards." 478 U.S., at 196. As with Justice White's assumptions about history, scholarship casts some doubt on the sweeping nature of the statement by Chief Justice Burger as it pertains to private homosexual conduct between consenting adults. See, e.g., Eskridge, Hardwick and Historiography, 1999 U. Ill. L. Rev. 631, 656. In all events we think that our laws and traditions in the past half century are of most relevance here. These references show an emerging awareness that liberty gives substantial protection to adult persons in deciding how to conduct their private lives in matters pertaining to sex. "[H]istory and tradition are the starting point but not in all cases the ending point of the substantive due process inquiry." County of Sacramento v. Lewis, 523 U.S. 833, 857 (1998) (Kennedy, J., concurring).

This emerging recognition should have been apparent when Bowers was decided. In 1955 the American Law Institute promulgated the Model Penal Code and made clear that it did not recommend or provide for "criminal penalties for consensual sexual relations conducted in private." ALI, Model Penal Code §213.2, Comment 2, p. 372 (1980). It justified its decision on three grounds: (1) The prohibitions undermined respect for the law by penalizing conduct many people engaged in; (2) the statutes regulated private conduct not harmful to others; and (3) the laws were arbitrarily enforced and thus invited the danger of blackmail. ALI, Model Penal Code, Commentary 277—280 (Tent. Draft No. 4, 1955). In 1961 Illinois changed its laws to conform to the Model Penal Code. Other States soon followed. Brief for Cato Institute as Amicus Curiae 15—16.

In Bowers the Court referred to the fact that before 1961 all 50 States had outlawed sodomy, and that at the time of the Court's decision 24 States and the District of Columbia had sodomy laws. 478 U.S., at 192—193. Justice Powell pointed out that these prohibitions often were being ignored, however. Georgia, for instance, had not sought to enforce its law for decades. Id., at 197—198, n. 2 ("The history of nonenforcement suggests the moribund character today of laws criminalizing this type of private, consensual conduct").

The sweeping references by Chief Justice Burger to the history of Western civilization and to Judeo-Christian moral and ethical standards did not take account of other authorities pointing in an opposite direction. A committee advising the British Parliament recommended in 1957 repeal of laws punishing homosexual conduct. The Wolfenden Report: Report of the Committee on Homosexual Offenses and Prostitution (1963). Parliament enacted the substance of those recommendations 10 years later. Sexual Offences Act 1967, §1.

Of even more importance, almost five years before Bowers was decided the European Court of Human Rights considered a case with parallels to Bowers and to today's case. An adult male resident in Northern Ireland alleged he was a practicing homosexual who desired to engage in consensual homosexual conduct. The laws of Northern Ireland forbade him that right. He alleged that he had been questioned, his home had been searched, and he feared criminal prosecution. The court held that the laws proscribing the conduct were invalid under the European Convention on Human Rights. Dudgeon v. United Kingdom, 45 Eur. Ct. H. R. (1981) ¶52. Authoritative in all countries that are members of the Council of Europe (21 nations then, 45 nations now), the decision is at odds with the premise in Bowers that the claim put forward was insubstantial in our Western civilization.

In our own constitutional system the deficiencies in Bowers became even more apparent in the years following its announcement. The 25 States with laws prohibiting the relevant conduct referenced in the Bowers decision are reduced now to 13, of which 4 enforce their laws only against homosexual conduct. In those States where sodomy is still proscribed, whether for same-sex or heterosexual conduct, there is a pattern of nonenforcement with respect to consenting adults acting in private. The State of Texas admitted in 1994 that as of that date it had not prosecuted anyone under those circumstances. State v. Morales, 869 S. W. 2d 941, 943.

Two principal cases decided after Bowers cast its holding into even more doubt. In Planned Parenthood of Southeastern Pa. v. Casey, 505 U.S. 833 (1992), the Court reaffirmed the substantive force of the liberty protected by the Due Process Clause. The Casey decision again confirmed that our laws and tradition afford constitutional protection to personal decisions relating to marriage, procreation, contraception, family relationships, child rearing, and education. Id., at 851. In explaining the respect the Constitution demands for the autonomy of the person in making these choices, we stated as follows:

" These matters, involving the most intimate and personal choices a person may make in a lifetime, choices central to personal dignity and autonomy, are central to the liberty protected by the Fourteenth Amendment. At the heart of liberty is the right to define one's own concept of existence, of meaning, of the universe, and of the mystery of human life. Beliefs about these matters could not define the attributes of personhood were they formed under compulsion of the State." Ibid.

Persons in a homosexual relationship may seek autonomy for these purposes, just as heterosexual persons do. The decision in Bowers would deny them this right.

The second post-Bowers case of principal relevance is Romer v. Evans, 517 U.S. 620 (1996). There the Court struck down class-based legislation directed at homosexuals as a violation of the Equal Protection Clause. Romer invalidated an amendment to Colorado's constitution which named as a solitary class persons who were homosexuals, lesbians, or bisexual either by "orientation, conduct, practices or relationships," id., at 624 (internal quotation marks omitted), and deprived them of protection under state antidiscrimination laws. We concluded that the provision was "born of animosity toward the class of persons affected" and further that it had no rational relation to a legitimate governmental purpose. Id., at 634.

As an alternative argument in this case, counsel for the petitioners and some amici contend that Romer provides the basis for declaring the Texas statute invalid under the Equal Protection Clause. That is a tenable argument, but we conclude the instant case requires us to address whether Bowers itself has continuing validity. Were we to hold the statute invalid under the Equal Protection Clause some might question whether a prohibition would be valid if drawn differently, say, to prohibit the conduct both between same-sex and different-sex participants.

Equality of treatment and the due process right to demand respect for conduct protected by the substantive guarantee of liberty are linked in important respects, and a decision on the latter point advances both interests. If protected conduct is made criminal and the law which does so remains unexamined for its substantive validity, its stigma might remain even if it were not enforceable as drawn for equal protection reasons. When homosexual conduct is made criminal by the law of the State, that declaration in and of itself is an invitation to subject homosexual persons to discrimination both in the public and in the private spheres. The central holding of Bowers has been brought in question by this case, and it should be addressed. Its continuance as precedent demeans the lives of homosexual persons.

The stigma this criminal statute imposes, moreover, is not trivial. The offense, to be sure, is but a class C misdemeanor, a minor offense in the Texas legal system. Still, it remains a criminal offense with all that imports for the dignity of the persons charged. The petitioners will bear on their record the history of their criminal convictions. Just this Term we rejected various challenges to state laws requiring the registration of sex offenders. Smith v. Doe, 538 U.S. __ (2003); Connecticut Dept. of Public Safety v. Doe, 538 U.S. 1 (2003). We are advised that if Texas convicted an adult for private, consensual homosexual conduct under the statute here in question the convicted person would come within the registration laws of a least four States were he or she to be subject to their jurisdiction. Pet. for Cert. 13, and n. 12 (citing Idaho Code §§18—8301 to 18—8326 (Cum. Supp. 2002); La. Code Crim. Proc. Ann., §§15:540—15:549 (West 2003); Miss. Code Ann. §§45—33—21 to 45—33—57 (Lexis 2003); S. C. Code Ann. §§23—3—400 to 23—3—490 (West 2002)). This underscores the consequential nature of the punishment and the state-sponsored condemnation attendant to the criminal prohibition. Furthermore, the

Texas criminal conviction carries with it the other collateral consequences always following a conviction, such as notations on job application forms, to mention but one example.

The foundations of Bowers have sustained serious erosion from our recent decisions in Casey and Romer. When our precedent has been thus weakened, criticism from other sources is of greater significance. In the United States criticism of Bowers has been substantial and continuing, disapproving of its reasoning in all respects, not just as to its historical assumptions. See, e.g., C. Fried, Order and Law: Arguing the Reagan Revolution–A Firsthand Account 81–84 (1991); R. Posner, Sex and Reason 341–350 (1992). The courts of five different States have declined to follow it in interpreting provisions in their own state constitutions parallel to the Due Process Clause of the Fourteenth Amendment, see Jegley v. Picado, 349 Ark. 600, 80 S. W. 3d 332 (2002); Powell v. State, 270 Ga. 327, 510 S. E. 2d 18, 24 (1998); Gryczan v. State, 283 Mont. 433, 942 P.2d 112 (1997); Campbell v. Sundquist, 926 S. W. 2d 250 (Tenn. App. 1996); Commonwealth v. Wasson, 842 S. W. 2d 487 (Ky. 1992).

To the extent Bowers relied on values we share with a wider civilization, it should be noted that the reasoning and holding in Bowers have been rejected elsewhere. The European Court of Human Rights has followed not Bowers but its own decision in Dudgeon v. United Kingdom. See P. G. & J. H. v. United Kingdom, App. No. 00044787/98, ¶56 (Eur. Ct. H. R., Sept. 25, 2001); Modinos v. Cyprus, 259 Eur. Ct. H. R. (1993); Norris v. Ireland, 142 Eur. Ct. H. R. (1988). Other nations, too, have taken action consistent with an affirmation of the protected right of homosexual adults to engage in intimate, consensual conduct. See Brief for Mary Robinson et al. as Amici Curiae 11–12. The right the petitioners seek in this case has been accepted as an integral part of human freedom in many other countries. There has been no showing that in this country the governmental interest in circumscribing personal choice is somehow more legitimate or urgent.

The doctrine of stare decisis is essential to the respect accorded to the judgments of the Court and to the stability of the law. It is not, however, an inexorable command. Payne v. Tennessee, 501 U.S. 808, 828 (1991) ("Stare decisis is not an inexorable command; rather, it 'is a principle of policy and not a mechanical formula of adherence to the latest decision' ") (quoting Helvering v. Hallock, 309 U.S. 106, 119 (1940))). In Casey we noted that when a Court is asked to overrule a precedent recognizing a constitutional liberty interest, individual or societal reliance on the existence of that liberty cautions with particular strength against reversing course. 505 U.S., at 855–856; see also id., at 844 ("Liberty finds no refuge in a jurisprudence of doubt"). The holding in Bowers, however, has not induced detrimental reliance comparable to some instances where recognized individual rights are involved. Indeed, there has been no individual or societal reliance on Bowers of the sort that could counsel against overturning its holding once there are compelling reasons to do so. Bowers itself causes uncertainty, for the precedents before and after its issuance contradict its central holding.

The rationale of Bowers does not withstand careful analysis. In his dissenting opinion in Bowers Justice Stevens came to these conclusions:

"Our prior cases make two propositions abundantly clear. First, the fact that the governing majority in a State has traditionally viewed a particular practice as immoral is not a sufficient reason for upholding a law prohibiting the practice; neither history nor tradition could save a law prohibiting miscegenation from constitutional attack. Second, individual decisions by married persons, concerning the intimacies of their physical relationship, even when not intended to produce offspring, are a form of "liberty" protected by the Due Process Clause of the Fourteenth Amendment. Moreover, this protection extends to intimate choices by unmarried as well as married persons." 478 U.S., at 216 (footnotes and citations omitted).

Justice Stevens' analysis, in our view, should have been controlling in Bowers and should control here.

Bowers was not correct when it was decided, and it is not correct today. It ought not to remain binding precedent. Bowers v. Hardwick should be and now is overruled.

The present case does not involve minors. It does not involve persons who might be injured or coerced or who are situated in relationships where consent might not easily be refused. It does not involve public conduct or prostitution. It does not involve whether the government must give formal recognition to any relationship that homosexual persons seek to enter. The case does involve two adults who, with full and mutual consent from each other, engaged in sexual practices common to a homosexual lifestyle. The petitioners are entitled to respect for their private lives. The State cannot demean their existence or control their destiny by making their private sexual conduct a crime. Their right to liberty under the Due Process Clause gives them the full right to engage in their conduct without intervention of the government. "It is a promise of the Constitution that there is a realm of personal liberty which the government may not enter." Casey, supra, at 847. The Texas statute furthers no legitimate state interest which can justify its intrusion into the personal and private life of the individual.

Had those who drew and ratified the Due Process Clauses of the Fifth Amendment or the Fourteenth Amendment known the components of liberty in its manifold possibilities, they might have been more specific. They did not presume to have this insight. They knew times can blind us to certain truths and later generations can see that laws once thought necessary and proper in fact serve only to oppress. As the Constitution endures, persons in every generation can invoke its principles in their own search for greater freedom.

The judgment of the Court of Appeals for the Texas Fourteenth District is reversed, and the case is remanded for further proceedings not inconsistent with this opinion.

It is so ordered.

## Ashcroft v. American Civil Liberties Union II (June 29, 2004)

Justice Kennedy delivered the opinion of the Court.

This case presents a challenge to a statute enacted by Congress to protect minors from exposure to sexually explicit materials on the Internet, the Child Online Protection Act (COPA). 112 Stat. 2681—736, codified at 47 U.S.C. § 231. We must decide whether the Court of Appeals was correct to affirm a ruling by the District Court that enforcement of COPA should be enjoined because the statute likely violates the First Amendment.

In enacting COPA, Congress gave consideration to our earlier decisions on this subject, in particular the decision in Reno v. American Civil Liberties Union, 521 U.S. 844 (1997). For that reason, "the Judiciary must proceed with caution and . . . with care before invalidating the Act." Ashcroft v. American Civil Liberties Union, 535 U.S. 564, 592 (Ashcroft I) (Kennedy, J., concurring in judgment). The imperative of according respect to the Congress, however, does not permit us to depart from well-established First Amendment principles. Instead, we must hold the Government to its constitutional burden of proof.

Content-based prohibitions, enforced by severe criminal penalties, have the constant potential to be a repressive force in the lives and thoughts of a free people. To guard against that threat the Constitution demands that content-based restrictions on speech be presumed invalid, R. A. V. v. St. Paul, 505 U.S. 377, 382 (1992), and that the Government bear the burden of showing their constitutionality. United States v. Playboy Entertainment Group, Inc., 529 U.S. 803, 817 (2000). This is true even when Congress twice has attempted to find a constitutional means to restrict, and punish, the speech in question.

This case comes to the Court on certiorari review of an appeal from the decision of the District Court granting a preliminary injunction. The Court of Appeals reviewed the decision of the District Court for abuse of discretion. Under that standard, the Court of Appeals was correct to conclude that the District Court did not abuse its discretion in granting the preliminary injunction. The Government has failed, at this point, to rebut the plaintiffs' contention that there are plausible less restrictive alternatives to the statute. Substantial practical considerations, furthermore, argue in favor of upholding the injunction and allowing the case to proceed to trial. For those reasons, we affirm the decision of the Court of Appeals upholding the preliminary injunction, and we remand the case so that it may be returned to the District Court for trial on the issues presented.

I

A

COPA is the second attempt by Congress to make the Internet safe for minors by criminalizing certain Internet speech.    The first attempt was the Communications

Decency Act of 1996, Pub. L. 104–104, §502, 110 Stat. 133, 47 U.S.C. § 223 (1994 ed., Supp. II). The Court held the CDA unconstitutional because it was not narrowly tailored to serve a compelling governmental interest and because less restrictive alternatives were available. Reno, supra.

In response to the Court's decision in Reno, Congress passed COPA. COPA imposes criminal penalties of a $50,000 fine and six months in prison for the knowing posting, for "commercial purposes," of World Wide Web content that is "harmful to minors." §231(a)(1). Material that is "harmful to minors" is defined as:

"any communication, picture, image, graphic image file, article, recording, writing, or other matter of any kind that is obscene or that–

"(A) the average person, applying contemporary community standards, would find, taking the material as a whole and with respect to minors, is designed to
appeal to, or is designed to pander to, the prurient
interest;

"(B) depicts, describes, or represents, in a manner patently offensive with respect to minors, an actual or simulated sexual act or sexual contact, an actual or simulated normal or perverted sexual act, or a lewd exhibition of the genitals or post-pubescent female breast; and

"(C) taken as a whole, lacks serious literary, artistic, political, or scientific value for minors." §231(e)(6).

"Minors" are defined as "any person under 17 years of age." §231(e)(7). A person acts for "commercial purposes only if such person is engaged in the business of making such communications." "Engaged in the business," in turn,

"means that the person who makes a communication, or offers to make a communication, by means of the World Wide Web, that includes any material that is harmful to minors, devotes time, attention, or labor to such activities, as a regular course of such person's trade or business, with the objective of earning a profit as a result of such activities (although it is not necessary that the person make a profit or that the making or offering to make such communications be the person's sole or principal business or source of income)." §231(e)(2).

While the statute labels all speech that falls within these definitions as criminal speech, it also provides an affirmative defense to those who employ specified means to prevent minors from gaining access to the prohibited materials on their Web site. A person may escape conviction under the statute by demonstrating that he

"has restricted access by minors to material that is harmful to minors–

"(A) by requiring use of a credit card, debit account, adult access code, or adult personal identification number;

"(B) by accepting a digital certificate that verifies age, or

"(C) by any other reasonable measures that are feasible under available technology." §231(c)(1).

Since the passage of COPA, Congress has enacted additional laws regulating the Internet in an attempt to protect minors. For example, it has enacted a prohibition on misleading Internet domain names, 18 U.S.C. A. §2252B (Supp. 2004), in order to prevent Web site owners from disguising pornographic Web sites in a way likely to cause uninterested persons to visit them. See Brief for Petitioner 7 (giving, as an example, the Web site "whitehouse.com"). It has also passed a statute creating a "Dot Kids" second-level Internet domain, the content of which is restricted to that which is fit for minors under the age of 13. 47 U.S.C. A. §941 (Supp. 2004).

B

Respondents, Internet content providers and others concerned with protecting the freedom of speech, filed suit in the United States District Court for the Eastern District of Pennsylvania. They sought a preliminary injunction against enforcement of the statute. After considering testimony from witnesses presented by both respondents and the Government, the District Court issued an order granting the preliminary injunction. The court first noted that the statute would place a burden on some protected speech. American Civil Liberties Union v. Reno, 31 F. Supp. 2d 473, 495 (1999). The court then concluded that respondents were likely to prevail on their argument that there were less restrictive alternatives to the statute: "On the record to date, it is not apparent ... that [petitioner] can meet its burden to prove that COPA is the least restrictive means available to achieve the goal of restricting the access of minors" to harmful material. Id., at 497. In particular, it noted that "[t]he record before the Court reveals that blocking or filtering technology may be at least as successful as COPA would be in restricting minors' access to harmful material online without imposing the burden on constitutionally protected speech that COPA imposes on adult users or Web site operators." Ibid.

The Government appealed the District Court's decision to the United States Court of Appeals for the Third Circuit. The Court of Appeals affirmed the preliminary injunction, but on a different ground. 217 F.3d 162, 166 (2000). The court concluded that the "community standards" language in COPA by itself rendered the statute unconstitutionally overbroad. Id., at 166. We granted certiorari and reversed, holding that the community-standards language did not, standing alone, make the statute unconstitutionally overbroad. Ashcroft I, 535 U.S., at 585. We emphasized, however, that our decision was limited to that narrow issue. Ibid. We remanded the case to the Court of Appeals to reconsider whether the District Court had been correct to grant the preliminary injunction. On remand, the Court of Appeals again affirmed the District Court. 322 F.3d 240 (2003). The Court of Appeals concluded that the statute was not narrowly tailored to serve a compelling Government interest, was overbroad, and was not the least restrictive means available for the Government to serve the interest of preventing minors from using the Internet to gain access to materials that are harmful to them. Id., at 266–271. The Government once again sought review from this Court, and we again granted certiorari. 540 U.S. 944 (2003).

II

A

"This Court, like other appellate courts, has always applied the abuse of discretion standard on the review of a preliminary injunction." Walters v. National Assn. of Radiation Survivors, 473 U.S. 305, 336 (1985) (O'Connor, J., concurring) (internal quotation marks omitted). "The grant of appellate jurisdiction under [28 U.S.C.] §1252 does not give the Court license to depart from established standards of appellate review." Ibid. If the underlying constitutional question is close, therefore, we should uphold the injunction and remand for trial on the merits. Applying this mode of inquiry, we agree with the Court of Appeals that the District Court did not abuse its discretion in entering the preliminary injunction. Our reasoning in support of this conclusion, however, is based on a narrower, more specific grounds than the rationale the Court of Appeals adopted. The Court of Appeals, in its opinion affirming the decision of the District Court, construed a number of terms in the statute, and held that COPA, so construed, was unconstitutional. None of those constructions of statutory terminology, however, were relied on by or necessary to the conclusions of the District Court. Instead, the District Court concluded only that the statute was likely to burden some speech that is protected for adults, 31 F. Supp.2d, at 495, which petitioner does not dispute. As to the definitional disputes, the District Court concluded only that respondents' interpretation was "not unreasonable," and relied on their interpretation only to conclude that respondents had standing to challenge the statute, id., at 481, which, again, petitioner does not dispute. Because we affirm the District Court's decision to grant the preliminary injunction for the reasons relied on by the District Court, we decline to consider the correctness of the other arguments relied on by the Court of Appeals.

The District Court, in deciding to grant the preliminary injunction, concentrated primarily on the argument that there are plausible, less restrictive alternatives to COPA. A statute that "effectively suppresses a large amount of speech that adults have a constitutional right to receive and to address to one another ... is unacceptable if less restrictive alternatives would be at least as effective in achieving the legitimate purpose that the statute was enacted to serve." Reno, 521 U.S., at 874. When plaintiffs challenge a content-based speech restriction, the burden is on the Government to prove that the proposed alternatives will not be as effective as the challenged statute. Id., at 874.

In considering this question, a court assumes that certain protected speech may be regulated, and then asks what is the least restrictive alternative that can be used to achieve that goal. The purpose of the test is not to consider whether the challenged restriction has some effect in achieving Congress' goal, regardless of the restriction it imposes. The purpose of the test is to ensure that speech is restricted no further than necessary to achieve the goal, for it is important to assure that legitimate speech is not chilled or punished. For that reason, the test does not begin with the status quo of existing regulations, then ask whether the challenged restriction has some additional ability to achieve Congress' legitimate interest. Any restriction on speech could be justified under that analysis. Instead, the court should ask whether the challenged regulation is the least restrictive means among available, effective alternatives.

In deciding whether to grant a preliminary injunction stage, a district court must consider whether the plaintiffs have demonstrated that they are likely to prevail on the merits. See, e.g., Doran v. Salem Inn, Inc., 422 U.S. 922, 931 (1975). (The court also considers whether the plaintiff has shown irreparable injury, see id., at 931, but the parties in this case do not contest the correctness of the District Court's conclusion that a likelihood of irreparable injury had been established. See 31 F. Supp. 2d, at 497–498). As the Government bears the burden of proof on the ultimate question of COPA's constitutionality, respondents must be deemed likely to prevail unless the Government has shown that respondents' proposed less restrictive alternatives are less effective than COPA. Applying that analysis, the District Court concluded that respondents were likely to prevail. Id., at 496–497. That conclusion was not an abuse of discretion, because on this record there are a number of plausible, less restrictive alternatives to the statute.

The primary alternative considered by the District Court was blocking and filtering software. Blocking and filtering software is an alternative that is less restrictive than COPA, and, in addition, likely more effective as a means of restricting children's access to materials harmful to them. The District Court, in granting the preliminary injunction, did so primarily because the plaintiffs had proposed that filters are a less restrictive alternative to COPA and the Government had not shown it would be likely to disprove the plaintiffs' contention at trial. Ibid.

Filters are less restrictive than COPA. They impose selective restrictions on speech at the receiving end, not universal restrictions at the source. Under a filtering regime, adults without children may gain access to speech they have a right to see without having to identify themselves or provide their credit card information. Even adults with children may obtain access to the same speech on the same terms simply by turning off the filter on their home computers. Above all, promoting the use of filters does not condemn as criminal any category of speech, and so the potential chilling effect is eliminated, or at least much diminished. All of these things are true, moreover, regardless of how broadly or narrowly the definitions in COPA are construed.

Filters also may well be more effective than COPA. First, a filter can prevent minors from seeing all pornography, not just pornography posted to the Web from America. The District Court noted in its factfindings that one witness estimated that 40% of harmful-to-minors content comes from overseas. Id., at 484. COPA does not prevent minors from having access to those foreign harmful materials. That alone makes it possible that filtering software might be more effective in serving Congress' goals. Effectiveness is likely to diminish even further if COPA is upheld, because the providers of the materials that would be covered by the statute simply can move their operations overseas. It is not an answer to say that COPA reaches some amount of materials that are harmful to minors; the question is whether it would reach more of them than less restrictive alternatives. In addition, the District Court found that verification systems may be subject to evasion and circumvention, for example by minors who have their own credit cards. See id., at 484, 496–497. Finally, filters also may be more effective because they can be applied to all forms of Internet communication, including e-mail, not just communications available via the World Wide Web.

That filtering software may well be more effective than COPA is confirmed by the findings of the Commission on Child Online Protection, a blue-ribbon commission created by Congress in COPA itself. Congress directed the Commission to evaluate the relative merits of different means of restricting minors' ability to gain access to harmful materials on the Internet. Note following 47 U.S.C. § 231. It unambiguously found that filters are more effective than age-verification requirements. See Commission on Child Online Protection (COPA), Report to Congress, at 19–21, 23–25, 27 (Oct. 20, 2000) (assigning a score for "Effectiveness" of 7.4 for server-based filters and 6.5 for client-based filters, as compared to 5.9 for independent adult-id verification, and 5.5 for credit card verification). Thus, not only has the Government failed to carry its burden of showing the District Court that the proposed alternative is less effective, but also a Government Commission appointed to consider the question has concluded just the opposite. That finding supports our conclusion that the District Court did not abuse its discretion in enjoining the statute.

Filtering software, of course, is not a perfect solution to the problem of children gaining access to harmful-to-minors materials. It may block some materials that are not harmful to minors and fail to catch some that are. See 31 F. Supp. 2d, at 492. Whatever the deficiencies of filters, however, the Government failed to introduce specific evidence proving that existing technologies are less effective than the restrictions in COPA. The District Court made a specific factfinding that "[n]o evidence was presented to the Court as to the percentage of time that blocking and filtering technology is over- or underinclusive." Ibid. In the absence of a showing as to the relative effectiveness of COPA and the alternatives proposed by respondents, it was not an abuse of discretion for the District Court to grant the preliminary injunction. The Government's burden is not merely to show that a proposed less restrictive alternative has some flaws; its burden is to show that it is less effective. Reno, 521 U.S., at 874. It is not enough for the Government to show that COPA has some effect. Nor do respondents bear a burden to introduce, or offer to introduce, evidence that their proposed alternatives are more effective. The Government has the burden to show they are less so. The Government having failed to carry its burden, it was not an abuse of discretion for the District Court to grant the preliminary injunction.

One argument to the contrary is worth mentioning–the argument that filtering software is not an available alternative because Congress may not require it to be used. That argument carries little weight, because Congress undoubtedly may act to encourage the use of filters. We have held that Congress can give strong incentives to schools and libraries to use them. United States v. American Library Assn., Inc, 539 U. S 194 (2003). It could also take steps to promote their development by industry, and their use by parents. It is incorrect, for that reason, to say that filters are part of the current regulatory status quo. The need for parental cooperation does not automatically disqualify a proposed less restrictive alternative. Playboy Entertainment Group, 529 U.S., at 824. ("A court should not assume a plausible, less restrictive alternative would be ineffective; and a court should not presume parents, given full information, will fail to act"). In enacting COPA, Congress said its goal was to prevent the "widespread availability of the Internet" from providing "opportunities for minors to access materials through the World Wide Web in a manner that can frustrate parental supervision or control." Congressional Findings, note following 47 U.S.C. § 231 (quoting Pub. L. 105–277, Tit. XIV, §1402(1), 112 Stat. 2681–736). COPA presumes that parents lack the ability, not the will, to monitor what their children see. By enacting programs to promote use of filtering software, Congress could give parents that ability without subjecting protected speech to severe penalties.

The closest precedent on the general point is our decision in Playboy Entertainment Group. Playboy Entertainment Group, like this case, involved a content-based restriction designed to protect minors from viewing harmful materials. The choice was between a blanket speech restriction and a more specific technological solution that was available to parents who chose to implement it. 529 U.S., at 825. Absent a showing that the proposed less restrictive alternative would not be as effective, we concluded, the more restrictive option preferred by Congress could not survive strict scrutiny. Id., at 826 (reversing because "[t]he record is silent as to the comparative effectiveness of the two alternatives"). In the instant case, too, the Government has failed to show, at this point, that the proposed less restrictive alternative will be less effective. The reasoning of Playboy Entertainment Group, and the holdings and force of our precedents require us to affirm the preliminary injunction. To do otherwise would be to do less than the First Amendment commands. "The starch in our constitutional standards cannot be sacrificed to accommodate the enforcement choices of the Government." Id., at 830 (Thomas, J., concurring).

B

There are also important practical reasons to let the injunction stand pending a full trial on the merits. First, the potential harms from reversing the injunction outweigh those of leaving it in place by mistake. Where a prosecution is a likely possibility, yet only an affirmative defense is available, speakers may self-censor rather than risk the perils of trial. There is a potential for extraordinary harm and a serious chill upon protected speech. Cf. id., at 817 ("Error in marking that line exacts an extraordinary cost"). The harm done from letting the injunction stand pending a trial on the merits, in contrast, will not be extensive. No prosecutions have yet been undertaken under the law, so none will be disrupted if the injunction stands. Further, if the injunction is upheld, the Government in the interim can enforce obscenity laws already on the books.

Second, there are substantial factual disputes remaining in the case. As mentioned above, there is a serious gap in the evidence as to the effectiveness of filtering software. See supra, at 9. For us to assume, without proof, that filters are less effective than COPA would usurp the District Court's factfinding role. By allowing the preliminary injunction to stand and remanding for trial, we require the Government to shoulder its full constitutional burden of proof respecting the less restrictive alternative argument, rather than excuse it from doing so.

Third, and on a related point, the factual record does not reflect current technological reality–a serious flaw in any case involving the Internet. The technology of the Internet evolves at a rapid pace. Yet the factfindings of the District Court were entered in February 1999, over five years ago. Since then, certain facts about the Internet are known to have changed. Compare, e.g., 31 F. Supp. 2d, at 481 (36.7 million Internet hosts as of July 1998) with Internet Systems Consortium, Internet Domain Survey, Jan. 2004, http://www.isc.org/index.pl?/ops/ds (as visited June 22, 2004, and available in the Clerk of Court's case file) (233.1 million hosts as of Jan. 2004). It is reasonable to assume that other technological developments important to the First Amendment analysis have also occurred during that time. More and better filtering alternatives may exist than when the District Court entered its findings. Indeed, we know that after the District Court entered its factfindings, a congressionally appointed commission issued a report that found that filters are more effective than verification screens. See supra, at 8.

Delay between the time that a district court makes factfindings and the time that a case reaches this Court is inevitable, with the necessary consequence that there will be some discrepancy between the facts as found and the facts at the time the appellate court takes up the question. See, e.g., Benjamin, Stepping into the Same River Twice: Rapidly Changing Facts and the Appellate Process, 78 Texas L. Rev. 269, 290–296 (1999) (noting the problems presented for appellate courts by changing facts in the context of cases involving the Internet, and giving as a specific example the Court's decision in Reno, 521 U.S. 844). We do not mean, therefore, to set up an insuperable obstacle to fair review. Here, however, the usual gap has doubled because the case has been through the Court of Appeals twice. The additional two years might make a difference. By affirming the preliminary injunction and remanding for trial, we allow the parties to update and supplement the factual record to reflect current technological realities.

Remand will also permit the District Court to take account of a changed legal landscape. Since the District Court made its factfindings, Congress has passed at least two further statutes that might qualify as less restrictive alternatives to COPA–a prohibition on misleading domain names, and a statute creating a minors-safe "Dot Kids" domain. See supra, at 4. Remanding for trial will allow the District Court to take into account those additional potential alternatives.

On a final point, it is important to note that this opinion does not hold that Congress is incapable of enacting any regulation of the Internet designed to prevent minors from gaining access to harmful materials. The parties, because of the conclusion of the Court of Appeals that the statute's definitions rendered it unconstitutional, did not devote their attention to the question whether further evidence might be introduced on the relative restrictiveness and effectiveness of alternatives to the statute. On remand, however, the parties will be able to introduce further evidence on this point. This opinion does not foreclose the District Court from concluding, upon a proper showing by the Government that meets the Government's constitutional burden as defined in this opinion, that COPA is the least restrictive alternative available to accomplish Congress' goal.

\* \* \*

On this record, the Government has not shown that the less restrictive alternatives proposed by respondents should be disregarded. Those alternatives, indeed, may be more effective than the provisions of COPA. The District Court did not abuse its discretion when it entered the preliminary injunction. The judgment of the Court of Appeals is affirmed, and the case is remanded for proceedings consistent with this opinion.

It is so ordered.

## Christian Legal Society v. Martinez (June 28, 2010) [Notes omitted]

Justice Ginsburg delivered the opinion of the Court.

In a series of decisions, this Court has emphasized that the First Amendment generally precludes public universities from denying student organizations access to school-sponsored forums because of the groups' viewpoints. See Rosenberger v. Rector and Visitors of Univ. of Va., 515 U. S. 819 (1995); Widmar v. Vincent, 454 U. S. 263 (1981); Healy v. James, 408 U. S. 169 (1972). This case concerns a novel question regarding student activities at public universities: May a public law school condition its official recognition of a student group—and the attendant use of school funds and facilities—on the organization's agreement to open eligibility for membership and leadership to all students?

In the view of petitioner Christian Legal Society (CLS), an accept-all-comers policy impairs its First Amendment rights to free speech, expressive association, and free exercise of religion by prompting it, on pain of relinquishing the advantages of recognition, to accept members who do not share the organization's core beliefs about religion and sexual orientation. From the perspective of respondent Hastings College of the Law (Hastings or the Law School), CLS seeks special dispensation from an across-the-board open-access requirement designed to further the reasonable educational purposes underpinning the school's student-organization program.

In accord with the District Court and the Court of Appeals, we reject CLS's First Amendment challenge. Compliance with Hastings' all-comers policy, we conclude, is a reasonable, viewpoint-neutral condition on access to the student-organization forum. In requiring CLS—in common with all other student organizations—to choose between welcoming all students and forgoing the benefits of official recognition, we hold, Hastings did not transgress constitutional limitations. CLS, it bears emphasis, seeks not parity with other organizations, but a preferential exemption from Hastings' policy. The First Amendment shields CLS against state prohibition of the organization's expressive activity, however exclusionary that activity may be. But CLS enjoys no constitutional right to state subvention of its selectivity.

I

Founded in 1878, Hastings was the first law school in the University of California public-school system. Like many institutions of higher education, Hastings encourages students to form extracurricular associations that "contribute to the Hastings community and experience." App. 349. These groups offer students "opportunities to pursue academic and social interests outside of the classroom [to] further their education" and to help them "develo[p] leadership skills." Ibid.

Through its "Registered Student Organization" (RSO) program, Hastings extends official recognition to student groups. Several benefits attend this school-approved status. RSOs are eligible to seek financial assistance from the Law School, which subsidizes their events using funds from a mandatory student-activity fee imposed on all students. Id., at 217. RSOs may also use Law-School channels to communicate with students: They may place announcements in a weekly Office-of-Student-Services newsletter, advertise events on designated bulletin boards, send e-mails using a Hastings-organization address, and participate in an annual Student Organizations Fair designed to advance recruitment efforts. Id., at 216–219. In addition, RSOs may apply for permission to use the Law School's facilities for meetings and office space. Id., at 218–219. Finally, Hastings allows officially recognized groups to use its name and logo. Id., at 216.

In exchange for these benefits, RSOs must abide by certain conditions. Only a "non-commercial organization whose membership is limited to Hastings students may become [an RSO]." App. to Pet. for Cert. 83a. A prospective RSO must submit its bylaws to Hastings for approval, id., at 83a–84a; and if it intends to use the Law School's name or logo, it must sign a license agreement, App. 219. Critical here, all RSOs must undertake to comply with Hastings' "Policies and Regulations Applying to College Activities, Organizations and Students." Ibid. 1

The Law School's Policy on Nondiscrimination (Nondiscrimination Policy), which binds RSOs, states:

"[Hastings] is committed to a policy against legally impermissible, arbitrary or unreasonable discriminatory practices. All groups, including administration, faculty, student governments, [Hastings]-owned student residence facilities and programs sponsored by [Hastings], are governed by this policy of nondiscrimination. [Hasting's] policy on nondiscrimination is to comply fully with applicable law.

"[Hastings] shall not discriminate unlawfully on the basis of race, color, religion, national origin, ancestry, disability, age, sex or sexual orientation. This nondiscrimination policy covers admission, access and treatment in Hastings-sponsored programs and activities." Id., at 220.

Hastings interprets the Nondiscrimination Policy, as it relates to the RSO program, to mandate acceptance of all comers: School-approved groups must "allow any student to participate, become a member, or seek leadership positions in the organization, regardless of [her] status or beliefs." Id., at 221. 2 Other law schools have adopted similar all-comers policies. See, e.g., Georgetown University Law Center, Office of Student Life: Student Organi zations, available at http://www.law.georgetown.edu/ StudentLife/StudentOrgs/NewGroup.htm (All Internet materials as visited June 24, 2010, and included in Clerk of Court's case file) (Membership in registered groups must be "open to all students."); Hofstra Law School Student Handbook 2009–2010, p. 49, available at http:// law.hofstra.edu/pdf/StudentLife/StudentAffairs/Handbook/ stuhb_handbook.pdf ("[Student] organizations are open to all students."). From Hastings' adoption of its Nondiscrimination Policy in 1990 until the events stirring this litigation, "no student organization at Hastings ... ever sought an exemption from the Policy." App. 221.

In 2004, CLS became the first student group to do so. At the beginning of the academic year, the leaders of a predecessor Christian organization—which had been an RSO at Hastings for a decade—formed CLS by affiliating with the national Christian Legal Society (CLS-National). Id., at 222–223, 225. CLS-National, an association of Christian lawyers and law students, charters student chapters at law schools throughout the country. Id., at 225. CLS chapters must adopt bylaws that, inter alia, require members and officers to sign a "Statement of Faith" and to conduct their lives in accord with prescribed principles. Id., at 225–226; App. to Pet. for Cert. 101a. 3 Among those tenets is the belief that sexual activity should not occur outside of marriage between a man and a woman; CLS thus interprets its bylaws to exclude from affiliation anyone who engages in "unrepentant homosexual conduct." App. 226. CLS also excludes students who hold religious convictions different from those in the Statement of Faith. Id., at 227.

On September 17, 2004, CLS submitted to Hastings an application for RSO status, accompanied by all required documents, including the set of bylaws mandated by CLS-National. Id., at 227–228. Several days later, the Law School rejected the application; CLS's bylaws, Hastings explained, did not comply with the Nondiscrimination Policy because CLS barred students based on religion and sexual orientation. Id., at 228.

CLS formally requested an exemption from the Nondiscrimination Policy, id., at 281, but Hastings declined to grant one. "[T]o be one of our student-recognized organizations," Hastings reiterated, "CLS must open its membership to all students irrespective of their religious beliefs or sexual orientation." Id., at 294. If CLS instead chose to operate outside the RSO program, Hastings stated, the school "would be pleased to provide [CLS] the use of Hastings facilities for its meetings and activities." Ibid. CLS would also have access to chalkboards and generally available campus bulletin boards to announce its events. Id., at 219, 233. In other words, Hastings would do nothing to suppress CLS's endeavors, but neither would it lend RSO-level support for them.

Refusing to alter its bylaws, CLS did not obtain RSO status. It did, however, operate independently during the 2004–2005 academic year. CLS held weekly Bible-study meetings and invited Hastings students to Good Friday and Easter Sunday church services. Id., at 229. It also hosted a beach barbeque, Thanksgiving dinner, campus lecture on the Christian faith and the legal practice, several fellowship dinners, an end-of-year banquet, and other informal social activities. Ibid.

On October 22, 2004, CLS filed suit against various Hastings officers and administrators under 42 U. S. C. §1983. Its complaint alleged that Hastings' refusal to grant the organization RSO status violated CLS's First and Fourteenth Amendment rights to free speech, expressive association, and free exercise of religion. The suit sought injunctive and declaratory relief. 4

On cross-motions for summary judgment, the U. S. District Court for the Northern District of California ruled in favor of Hastings. The Law School's all-comers condition on access to a limited public forum, the court held, was both reasonable and viewpoint neutral, and therefore did not violate CLS's right to free speech. App. to Pet. for Cert. 27a–38a.

Nor, in the District Court's view, did the Law School impermissibly impair CLS's right to expressive association. "Hastings is not directly ordering CLS to admit [any] studen[t]," the court observed, id., at 42a; "[r]ather, Hastings has merely placed conditions on" the use of its facilities and funds, ibid. "Hastings' denial of official recognition," the court added, "was not a substantial impediment to CLS's ability to meet and communicate as a group." Id., at 49a.

The court also rejected CLS's Free Exercise Clause argument. "[T]he Nondiscrimination Policy does not target or single out religious beliefs," the court noted; rather, the policy "is neutral and of general applicability." Id., at 63a. "CLS may be motivated by its religious beliefs to exclude students based on their religion or sexual orientation," the court explained, "but that does not convert the reason for Hastings' [Nondiscrimination Policy] to be one that is religiously-based." Id., at 63a–64a.

On appeal, the Ninth Circuit affirmed in an opinion that stated, in full:

"The parties stipulate that Hastings imposes an open membership rule on all student groups—all groups must accept all comers as voting members even if those individuals disagree with the mission of the group. The conditions on recognition are therefore viewpoint neutral and reasonable. Truth v. Kent Sch. Dist., 542 F. 3d 634, 649–50 (9th Cir. 2008)." Christian Legal Soc. Chapter of Univ. of Cal. v. Kane, 319 Fed. Appx. 645, 645–646 (CA9 2009).

We granted certiorari, 558 U. S. _____ (2009), and now affirm the Ninth Circuit's judgment.

II

Before considering the merits of CLS's constitutional arguments, we must resolve a preliminary issue: CLS urges us to review the Nondiscrimination Policy as written— prohibiting discrimination on several enumerated bases, including religion and sexual orientation—and not as a requirement that all RSOs accept all comers. The written terms of the Nondiscrimination Policy, CLS contends, "targe[t] solely those groups whose beliefs are based on religion or that disapprove of a particular kind of sexual behavior," and leave other associations free to limit membership and leadership to individuals committed to the group's ideology. Brief for Petitioner 19 (internal quotation marks omitted). For example, "[a] political ... group can insist that its leaders support its purposes and beliefs," CLS alleges, but "a religious group cannot." Id., at 20.

CLS's assertion runs headlong into the stipulation of facts it jointly submitted with Hastings at the summary-judgment stage. In that filing, the parties specified:

"Hastings requires that registered student organizations allow any student to participate, become a member, or seek leadership positions in the organization, regardless of [her] status or beliefs. Thus, for example, the Hastings Democratic Caucus cannot bar students holding Republican political beliefs from becoming members or seeking leadership positions in the organization." App. 221 (Joint Stipulation ¶18) (emphasis added; citations omitted). 5

Under the District Court's local rules, stipulated facts are deemed "undisputed." Civil Local Rule 56–2 (ND Cal. 2010). See also Pet. for Cert. 2 ("The material facts of this case are undisputed."). 6

Litigants, we have long recognized, "[a]re entitled to have [their] case tried upon the assumption that ... facts, stipulated into the record, were established." H. Hackfeld & Co. v. United States, 197 U. S. 442, 447 (1905) . 7 This entitlement is the bookend to a party's undertaking to be bound by the factual stipulations it submits. See post, at 10 ( Alito, J ., dissenting) (agreeing that "the parties must be held to their Joint Stipulation"). As a leading legal reference summarizes:

"[Factual stipulations are] binding and conclusive ..., and the facts stated are not subject to subsequent variation. So, the parties will not be permitted to deny the truth of the facts stated, ... or to maintain a contention contrary to the agreed statement, ... or to suggest, on appeal, that the facts were other than as stipulated or that any material fact was omitted. The burden is on the party seeking to recover to show his or her right from the facts actually stated." 83 C. J. S., Stipulations §93 (2000) (footnotes omitted).

This Court has accordingly refused to consider a party's argument that contradicted a joint "stipulation [entered] at the outset of th[e] litigation." Board of Regents of Univ. of Wis. System v. Southworth, 529 U. S. 217, 226 (2000) . Time and again, the dissent races away from the facts to which CLS stipulated. See, e.g., post, at 2, 3, 5, 6, 7, 8, 11, 24. 8 But factual stipulations are "formal concessions ... that have the effect of withdrawing a fact from issue and dispensing wholly with the need for proof of the fact. Thus, a judicial admission ... is conclusive in the case." 2 K. Broun, McCormick on Evidence §254, p. 181 (6th ed. 2006) (footnote omitted). See also, e.g., Oscanyan v. Arms Co., 103 U. S. 261, 263 (1881) ("The power of the court to act in the disposition of a trial upon facts conceded by counsel is as plain as its power to act upon the evidence produced."). 9

In light of the joint stipulation, both the District Court and the Ninth Circuit trained their attention on the constitutionality of the all-comers requirement, as described in the parties' accord. See 319 Fed. Appx., at 645–646; App. to Pet. for Cert. 32a; id., at 36a. We reject CLS's unseemly attempt to escape from the stipulation and shift its target to Hastings' policy as written. This opinion, therefore, considers only whether conditioning access to a student-organization forum on compliance with an all-comers policy violates the Constitution. 10

III

A

In support of the argument that Hastings' all-comers policy treads on its First Amendment rights to free speech and expressive association, CLS draws on two lines of decisions. First, in a progression of cases, this Court has employed forum analysis to determine when a governmental entity, in regulating property in its charge, may place limitations on speech. 11 Recognizing a State's right "to preserve the property under its control for the use to which it is lawfully dedicated," Cornelius v. NAACP Legal Defense & Ed. Fund, Inc., 473 U. S. 788, 800 (1985) (internal quotation marks omitted), the Court has permitted restrictions on access to a limited public forum, like the RSO program here, with this key caveat: Any access barrier must be reasonable and viewpoint neutral, e.g., Rosenberger, 515 U. S., at 829. See also, e.g., Good News Club v. Milford Central School, 533 U. S. 98, 106–107 (2001); Lamb's Chapel v. Center Moriches Union Free School Dist., 508 U. S. 384, 392–393 (1993); Perry Ed. Assn. v. Perry Local Educators' Assn., 460 U. S. 37, 46 (1983) . 12

Second, as evidenced by another set of decisions, this Court has rigorously reviewed laws and regulations that constrain associational freedom. In the context of public accommodations, we have subjected restrictions on that freedom to close scrutiny; such restrictions are permitted only if they serve "compelling state interests" that are "unrelated to the suppression of ideas"—interests that cannot be advanced "through ... significantly less restrictive [means]." Roberts v. United States Jaycees, 468 U. S. 609, 623 (1984) . See also, e.g., Boy Scouts of America v. Dale, 530 U. S. 640, 648 (2000) . "Freedom of association," we have recognized, "plainly presupposes a freedom not to associate." Roberts, 468 U. S., at 623. Insisting that an organization embrace unwelcome members, we have therefore concluded, "directly and immediately affects associational rights." Dale, 530 U. S., at 659.

CLS would have us engage each line of cases independently, but its expressive-association and free-speech arguments merge: Who speaks on its behalf, CLS reasons, colors what concept is conveyed. See Brief for Petitioner 35 (expressive association in this case is "the functional equivalent of speech itself"). It therefore makes little sense to treat CLS's speech and association claims as discrete. See Citizens Against Rent Control/Coalition for Fair Housing v. Berkeley, 454 U. S. 290, 300 (1981) . Instead, three observations lead us to conclude that our limited-public-forum precedents supply the appropriate framework for assessing both CLS's speech and association rights.

First, the same considerations that have led us to apply a less restrictive level of scrutiny to speech in limited public forums as compared to other environments, see supra, at 12–13, and n. 11, apply with equal force to expressive association occurring in limited public forums. As just noted, speech and expressive-association rights are closely linked. See Roberts, 468 U. S., at 622 (Associational freedom is "implicit in the right to engage in activities protected by the First Amendment ."). When these intertwined rights arise in exactly the same context, it would be anomalous for a restriction on speech to survive constitutional review under our limited-public-forum test only to be invalidated as an impermissible infringement of expressive association. Accord Brief for State Universities and State University Systems as Amici Curiae 37–38. That result would be all the more anomalous in this case, for CLS suggests that its expressive-association claim plays a part auxiliary to speech's starring role. See Brief for Petitioner 18.

Second, and closely related, the strict scrutiny we have applied in some settings to laws that burden expressive association would, in practical effect, invalidate a defining characteristic of limited public forums—the State may "reserv[e] [them] for certain groups." Rosenberger, 515 U. S., at 829. See also Perry Ed. Assn., 460 U. S., at 49 ("Implicit in the concept" of a limited public forum is the State's "right to make distinctions in access on the basis of ... speaker identity."); Cornelius, 473 U. S., at 806 ("[A] speaker may be excluded from" a limited public forum "if he is not a member of the class of speakers for whose especial benefit the forum was created.").

An example sharpens the tip of this point: Schools, including Hastings, see App. to Pet. for Cert. 83a, ordinarily, and without controversy, limit official student-group recognition to organizations comprising only students—even if those groups wish to associate with nonstudents. See, e.g., Volokh, Freedom of Expressive Association and Government Subsidies, 58 Stan. L. Rev. 1919, 1940 (2006). The same ground rules must govern both speech and association challenges in the limited-public-forum context, lest strict scrutiny trump a public university's ability to "confin[e] a [speech] forum to the limited and legitimate purposes for which it was created." Rosenberger, 515 U. S., at 829. See also Healy, 408 U. S., at 189 ("Associational activities need not be tolerated where they infringe reasonable campus rules.").

Third, this case fits comfortably within the limited-public-forum category, for CLS, in seeking what is effectively a state subsidy, faces only indirect pressure to modify its membership policies; CLS may exclude any person for any reason if it forgoes the benefits of official recognition. 13 The expressive-association precedents on which CLS relies, in contrast, involved regulations that compelled a group to include unwanted members, with no choice to opt out. See, e.g., Dale, 530 U. S., at 648 (regulation "forc[ed] [the Boy Scouts] to accept members it [did] not desire" (internal quotation marks omitted)); Roberts, 468 U. S., at 623 ("There can be no clearer example of an intrusion into the internal structure or affairs of an association than" forced inclusion of unwelcome participants.). 14

In diverse contexts, our decisions have distinguished between policies that require action and those that withhold benefits. See, e.g., Grove City College v. Bell, 465 U. S. 555, 575–576 (1984); Bob Jones Univ. v. United States, 461 U. S. 574, 602–604 (1983) . Application of the less-restrictive limited-public-forum analysis better accounts for the fact that Hastings, through its RSO program, is dangling the carrot of subsidy, not wielding the stick of prohibition. Cf. Norwood v. Harrison, 413 U. S. 455, 463 (1973) ("That the Constitution may compel toleration of private discrimination in some circumstances does not mean that it requires state support for such discrimination.").

In sum, we are persuaded that our limited-public-forum precedents adequately respect both CLS's speech and expressive-association rights, and fairly balance those rights against Hastings' interests as property owner and educational institution. We turn to the merits of the instant dispute, therefore, with the limited-public-forum decisions as our guide.

B

As earlier pointed out, supra, at 1, 12–13, we do not write on a blank slate; we have three times before considered clashes between public universities and student groups seeking official recognition or its attendant benefits. First, in Healy, a state college denied school affiliation to a student group that wished to form a local chapter of Students for a Democratic Society (SDS). 408 U. S., at 170. Characterizing SDS's mission as violent and disruptive, and finding the organization's philosophy repugnant, the college completely banned the SDS chapter from campus; in its effort to sever all channels of communication between students and the group, university officials went so far as to disband a meeting of SDS members in a campus coffee shop. Id., at 174–176. The college, we noted, could require "that a group seeking official recognition affirm in advance its willingness to adhere to reasonable campus law," including "reasonable standards respecting conduct." Id., at 193. But a public educational institution exceeds constitutional bounds, we held, when it "restrict[s] speech or association simply because it finds the views expressed by [a] group to be abhorrent." Id., at 187–188. 15

We later relied on Healy in Widmar . In that case, a public university, in an effort to avoid state support for religion, had closed its facilities to a registered student group that sought to use university space for religious worship and discussion. 454 U. S., at 264–265. "A university's mission is education," we observed, "and decisions of this Court have never denied a university's authority to impose reasonable regulations compatible with that mission upon the use of its campus and facilities." Id., at 268, n. 5. But because the university singled out religious organizations for disadvantageous treatment, we subjected the university's regulation to strict scrutiny. Id., at 269–270. The school's interest "in maintaining strict separation of church and State," we held, was not "sufficiently compelling to justify ... [viewpoint] discrimination against ... religious speech." Id., at 270, 276 (internal quotation marks omitted).

Most recently and comprehensively, in Rosenberger, we reiterated that a university generally may not withhold benefits from student groups because of their religious outlook. The officially recognized student group in Rosenberger was denied student-activity-fee funding to distribute a newspaper because the publication discussed issues from a Christian perspective. 515 U. S., at 825–827. By "select[ing] for disfavored treatment those student journalistic efforts with religious editorial viewpoints," we held, the university had engaged in "viewpoint discrimination, which is presumed impermissible when directed against speech otherwise within the forum's limitations." Id., at 831, 830.

In all three cases, we ruled that student groups had been unconstitutionally singled out because of their points of view. "Once it has opened a limited [public] forum," we emphasized, "the State must respect the lawful boundaries it has itself set." Id., at 829. The constitutional constraints on the boundaries the State may set bear repetition here: "The State may not exclude speech where its distinction is not reasonable in light of the purpose served by the forum, ... nor may it discriminate against speech on the basis of ... viewpoint." Ibid . (internal quotation marks omitted).

C

We first consider whether Hastings' policy is reasonable taking into account the RSO forum's function and "all the surrounding circumstances." Cornelius, 473 U. S., at 809.

1

Our inquiry is shaped by the educational context in which it arises: " First Amendment rights," we have observed, "must be analyzed in light of the special characteristics of the school environment." Widmar, 454 U. S., at 268, n. 5 (internal quotation marks omitted). This Court is the final arbiter of the question whether a public university has exceeded constitutional constraints, and we owe no deference to universities when we consider that question. Cf. Pell v. Procunier, 417 U. S. 817, 827 (1974) ("Courts cannot, of course, abdicate their constitutional responsibility to delineate and protect fundamental liberties."). Cognizant that judges lack the on-the-ground expertise and experience of school administrators, however, we have cautioned courts in various contexts to resist "substitut[ing] their own notions of sound educational policy for those of the school authorities which they review." Board of Ed. of Hendrick Hudson Central School Dist., Westchester Cty. v. Rowley, 458 U. S. 176, 206 (1982) . See also, e.g., Hazelwood School Dist. v. Kuhlmeier, 484 U. S. 260, 273 (1988) (noting our "oft-expressed view that the education of the Nation's youth is primarily the responsibility of parents, teachers, and state and local school officials, and not of federal judges"); Healy, 408 U. S., at 180 ("[T]his Court has long recognized 'the need for affirming the comprehensive authority of the States and of school officials, consistent with fundamental constitutional safeguards, to prescribe and control conduct in the schools.' " (quoting Tinker v. Des Moines Independent Community School Dist., 393 U. S. 503, 507 (1969) )).

A college's commission—and its concomitant license to choose among pedagogical approaches—is not confined to the classroom, for extracurricular programs are, today, essential parts of the educational process. See Board of Ed. of Independent School Dist. No. 92 of Pottawatomie Cty. v. Earls, 536 U. S. 822, 831, n. 4 (2002) (involvement in student groups is "a significant contributor to the breadth and quality of the educational experience" (internal quotation marks omitted)). Schools, we have emphasized, enjoy "a significant measure of authority over the type of officially recognized activities in which their students participate." Board of Ed. of Westside Community Schools (Dist. 66) v. Mergens, 496 U. S. 226, 240 (1990) . We therefore "approach our task with special caution," Healy, 408 U. S., at 171, mindful that Hastings' decisions about the character of its student-group program are due decent respect. 16

2

  With appropriate regard for school administrators' judgment, we review the justifications Hastings offers in defense of its all-comers requirement. 17 First, the open-access policy "ensures that the leadership, educational, and social opportunities afforded by [RSOs] are available to all students." Brief for Hastings 32; see Brief for American Civil Liberties Union et al. as Amici Curiae 11. Just as "Hastings does not allow its professors to host classes open only to those students with a certain status or belief," so the Law School may decide, reasonably in our view, "that the ... educational experience is best promoted when all participants in the forum must provide equal access to all students." Brief for Hastings 32. RSOs, we count it significant, are eligible for financial assist- ance drawn from mandatory student-activity fees, see supra, at 3; the all-comers policy ensures that no Hastings student is forced to fund a group that would reject her as a member. 18

  Second, the all-comers requirement helps Hastings police the written terms of its Nondiscrimination Policy without inquiring into an RSO's motivation for membership restrictions. To bring the RSO program within CLS's view of the Constitution's limits, CLS proposes that Hastings permit exclusion because of belief but forbid discrimination due to status . See Tr. of Oral Arg. 18. But that proposal would impose on Hastings a daunting labor. How should the Law School go about determining whether a student organization cloaked prohibited status exclusion in belief-based garb? If a hypothetical Male-Superiority Club barred a female student from running for its presidency, for example, how could the Law School tell whether the group rejected her bid because of her sex or because, by seeking to lead the club, she manifested a lack of belief in its fundamental philosophy?

  This case itself is instructive in this regard. CLS contends that it does not exclude individuals because of sexual orientation, but rather "on the basis of a conjunction of conduct and the belief that the conduct is not wrong." Brief for Petitioner 35–36 (emphasis deleted). Our decisions have declined to distinguish between status and conduct in this context. See Lawrence v. Texas, 539 U. S. 558, 575 (2003) ("When homosexual conduct is made criminal by the law of the State, that declaration in and of itself is an invitation to subject homosexual persons to discrimination." (emphasis added)); id., at 583 (O'Connor, J., concurring in judgment) ("While it is true that the law applies only to conduct, the conduct targeted by this law is conduct that is closely correlated with being homosexual. Under such circumstances, [the] law is targeted at more than conduct. It is instead directed toward gay persons as a class."); cf. Bray v.

Alexandria Women's Health Clinic, 506 U. S. 263, 270 (1993) ("A tax on wearing yarmulkes is a tax on Jews."). See also Brief for Lambda Legal Defense and Education Fund, Inc., et al. as Amici Curiae 7–20.

Third, the Law School reasonably adheres to the view that an all-comers policy, to the extent it brings together individuals with diverse backgrounds and beliefs, "encourages tolerance, cooperation, and learning among students." App. 349. 19 And if the policy sometimes produces discord, Hastings can rationally rank among RSO-program goals development of conflict-resolution skills, toleration, and readiness to find common ground.

Fourth, Hastings' policy, which incorporates—in fact, subsumes—state-law proscriptions on discrimination, conveys the Law School's decision "to decline to subsidize with public monies and benefits conduct of which the people of California disapprove." Brief for Hastings 35; id., at 33–34 (citing Cal. Educ. Code §66270 (prohibiting discrimination on various bases)). State law, of course, may not command that public universities take action impermissible under the First Amendment . But so long as a public university does not contravene constitutional limits, its choice to advance state-law goals through the school's educational endeavors stands on firm footing.

In sum, the several justifications Hastings asserts in support of its all-comers requirement are surely reasonable in light of the RSO forum's purposes. 20

3

The Law School's policy is all the more credit-worthy in view of the "substantial alternative channels that remain open for [CLS-student] communication to take place." Perry Ed. Assn., 460 U. S., at 53. If restrictions on access to a limited public forum are viewpoint discriminatory, the ability of a group to exist outside the forum would not cure the constitutional shortcoming. But when access barriers are viewpoint neutral, our decisions have counted it significant that other available avenues for the group to exercise its First Amendment rights lessen the burden created by those barriers. See ibid.; Cornelius, 473 U. S., at 809; Greer v. Spock, 424 U. S. 828, 839 (1976); Pell, 417 U. S., at 827–828.

In this case, Hastings offered CLS access to school facilities to conduct meetings and the use of chalkboards and generally available bulletin boards to advertise events. App. 232–233. Although CLS could not take advantage of RSO-specific methods of communication, see supra, at 3, the advent of electronic media and social-networking sites reduces the importance of those channels. See App. 114–115 (CLS maintained a Yahoo! message group to disseminate information to students.); Christian Legal Society v. Walker, 453 F. 3d 853, 874 (CA7 2006) (Wood, J., dissenting) ("Most universities and colleges, and most college-aged students, communicate through email, websites, and hosts like MySpace ... . If CLS had its own website, any student at the school with access to Google—that is, all of them—could easily have found it."). See also Brief for Associated Students of the University of California, Hastings College of Law as Amicus Curiae 14–18 (describing host of ways CLS could communicate with Hastings' students outside official channels).

Private groups, from fraternities and sororities to social clubs and secret societies, commonly maintain a presence at universities without official school affiliation. 21 Based on the record before us, CLS was similarly situated: It hosted a variety of activities the year after Hastings denied it recognition, and the number of students attending those meetings and events doubled. App. 224, 229–230. "The variety and type of alternative modes of access present here," in short, "compare favorably with those in other [limited public] forum cases where we have upheld restrictions on access." Perry Ed. Assn., 460 U. S., at 53–54. It is beyond dissenter's license, we note again, see supra, at 21, n. 17, constantly to maintain that nonrecognition of a student organization is equivalent to prohibiting its members from speaking.

4

CLS nevertheless deems Hastings' all-comers policy "frankly absurd." Brief for Petitioner 49. "There can be no diversity of viewpoints in a forum," it asserts, "if groups are not permitted to form around viewpoints." Id., at 50; accord post, at 25 ( Alito, J ., dissenting). This catchphrase confuses CLS's preferred policy with constitutional limitation—the advisability of Hastings' policy does not control its permissibility . See Wood v. Strickland, 420 U. S. 308, 326 (1975) . Instead, we have repeatedly stressed that a State's restriction on access to a limited public forum "need not be the most reasonable or the only reasonable limitation." Cornelius, 473 U. S., at 808. 22

CLS also assails the reasonableness of the all-comers policy in light of the RSO forum's function by forecasting that the policy will facilitate hostile takeovers; if organizations must open their arms to all, CLS contends, saboteurs will infiltrate groups to subvert their mission and message. This supposition strikes us as more hypothetical than real. CLS points to no history or prospect of RSO-hijackings at Hastings. Cf. National Endowment for Arts v. Finley, 524 U. S. 569, 584 (1998) ("[W]e are reluctant ... to invalidate legislation on the basis of its hypothetical application to situations not before the Court." (internal quotation marks omitted)). Students tend to self-sort and presumably will not endeavor en masse to join—let alone seek leadership positions in—groups pursuing missions wholly at odds with their personal beliefs. And if a rogue student intent on sabotaging an organization's objectives nevertheless attempted a takeover, the members of that group would not likely elect her as an officer.

RSOs, moreover, in harmony with the all-comers policy, may condition eligibility for membership and leadership on attendance, the payment of dues, or other neutral requirements designed to ensure that students join because of their commitment to a group's vitality, not its demise. See supra, at 4, n. 2. Several RSOs at Hastings limit their membership rolls and officer slates in just this way. See, e.g., App. 192 (members must "[p]ay their dues on a timely basis" and "attend meetings regularly"); id., at 173 (members must complete an application and pay dues; "[a]ny active member who misses a semester of regularly scheduled meetings shall be dropped from rolls"); App. to Pet. for Cert. 129a ("Only Hastings students who have held membership in this organization for a minimum of one semester shall be eligible to be an officer."). 23

Hastings, furthermore, could reasonably expect more from its law students than the disruptive behavior CLS hypothesizes—and to build this expectation into its educational approach. A reasonable policy need not anticipate and preemptively close off every opportunity for avoidance or manipulation. If students begin to exploit an all-comers policy by hijacking organizations to distort or destroy their missions, Hastings presumably would revisit and revise its policy. See Tr. of Oral Arg. 41 (counsel for Hastings); Brief for Hastings 38.

Finally, CLS asserts (and the dissent repeats, post, at 29) that the Law School lacks any legitimate interest—let alone one reasonably related to the RSO forum's purposes—in urging "religious groups not to favor co-religionists for purposes of their religious activities." Brief for Petitioner 43; id., at 50. CLS's analytical error lies in focusing on the benefits it must forgo while ignoring the interests of those it seeks to fence out: Exclusion, after all, has two sides. Hastings, caught in the crossfire between a group's desire to exclude and students' demand for equal access, may reasonably draw a line in the sand permitting all organizations to express what they wish but no group to discriminate in membership. 24

D

We next consider whether Hastings' all-comers policy is viewpoint neutral.

1

Although this aspect of limited-public-forum analysis has been the constitutional sticking point in our prior decisions, as earlier recounted, supra, at 17–19, we need not dwell on it here. It is, after all, hard to imagine a more viewpoint-neutral policy than one requiring all student groups to accept all comers. In contrast to Healy, Widmar, and Rosenberger, in which universities singled out organizations for disfavored treatment because of their points of view, Hastings' all-comers requirement draws no distinction between groups based on their message or perspective. An all-comers condition on access to RSO status, in short, is textbook viewpoint neutral. 25

2

Conceding that Hastings' all-comers policy is "nominally neutral," CLS attacks the regulation by pointing to its effect: The policy is vulnerable to constitutional assault, CLS contends, because "it systematically and predictably burdens most heavily those groups whose viewpoints are out of favor with the campus mainstream." Brief for Petitioner 51; cf. post, at 1 ( Alito, J ., dissenting) (charging that Hastings' policy favors "political[ly] correc[t]" student expression). This argument stumbles from its first step because "[a] regulation that serves purposes unrelated to the content of expression is deemed neutral, even if it has an incidental effect on some speakers or messages but not others." Ward v. Rock Against Racism, 491 U. S. 781, 791 (1989) . See also Madsen v. Women's Health Center, Inc., 512 U. S. 753, 763 (1994) ("[T]he fact that the injunction covered people with a particular viewpoint does not itself render the injunction content or viewpoint based.").

Even if a regulation has a differential impact on groups wishing to enforce exclusionary membership policies, "[w]here the [State] does not target conduct on the basis of its expressive content, acts are not shielded from regulation merely because they express a discriminatory idea or philosophy." R. A. V. v. St. Paul, 505 U. S. 377, 390 (1992) . See also Roberts, 468 U. S., at 623 (State's nondiscrimination law did not "distinguish between prohibited and permitted activity on the basis of viewpoint."); Board of Directors of Rotary Int'l v. Rotary Club of Duarte, 481 U. S. 537, 549 (1987) (same).

Hastings' requirement that student groups accept all comers, we are satisfied, "is justified without reference to the content [or viewpoint] of the regulated speech." Ward, 491 U. S., at 791 (internal quotation marks and emphasis omitted). The Law School's policy aims at the act of rejecting would-be group members without reference to the reasons motivating that behavior: Hastings' "desire to redress th[e] perceived harms" of exclusionary membership policies "provides an adequate explanation for its [all-comers condition] over and above mere disagreement with [any student group's] beliefs or biases." Wisconsin v. Mitchell, 508 U. S. 476, 488 (1993) . CLS's conduct—not its Christian perspective—is, from Hastings' vantage point, what stands between the group and RSO status. "In the end," as Hastings observes, "CLS is simply confusing its own viewpoint-based objections to ... nondiscrimination laws (which it is entitled to have and [to] voice) with viewpoint discrimination ." Brief for Hastings 31. 26

Finding Hastings' open-access condition on RSO status reasonable and viewpoint neutral, we reject CLS' free-speech and expressive-association claims. 27

IV

In its reply brief, CLS contends that "[t]he peculiarity, incoherence, and suspect history of the all-comers policy all point to pretext." Reply Brief 23. Neither the District Court nor the Ninth Circuit addressed an argument that Hastings selectively enforces its all-comers policy, and this Court is not the proper forum to air the issue in the first instance. 28 On remand, the Ninth Circuit may consider CLS's pretext argument if, and to the extent, it is preserved. 29

*   *   *

For the foregoing reasons, we affirm the Court of Appeals' ruling that the all-comers policy is constitutional and remand the case for further proceedings consistent with this opinion.

It is so ordered.

## US v. Stevens (April 20, 2010)

Chief Justice Roberts delivered the opinion of the Court.

Congress enacted 18 U. S. C. §48 to criminalize the commercial creation, sale, or possession of certain depictions of animal cruelty. The statute does not address underlying acts harmful to animals, but only portrayals of such conduct. The question presented is whether the prohibition in the statute is consistent with the freedom of speech guaranteed by the First Amendment.

I

Section 48 establishes a criminal penalty of up to five years in prison for anyone who knowingly "creates, sells, or possesses a depiction of animal cruelty," if done "for commercial gain" in interstate or foreign commerce. §48(a). 1 A depiction of "animal cruelty" is defined as one "in which a living animal is intentionally maimed, mutilated, tortured, wounded, or killed," if that conduct violates federal or state law where "the creation, sale, or possession takes place." §48(c)(1). In what is referred to as the "exceptions clause," the law exempts from prohibition any depiction "that has serious religious, political, scientific, educational, journalistic, historical, or artistic value." §48(b).

The legislative background of §48 focused primarily on the interstate market for "crush videos." According to the House Committee Report on the bill, such videos feature the intentional torture and killing of helpless animals, including cats, dogs, monkeys, mice, and hamsters. H. R. Rep. No. 106–397, p. 2 (1999) (hereinafter H. R. Rep.). Crush videos often depict women slowly crushing animals to death "with their bare feet or while wearing high heeled shoes," sometimes while "talking to the animals in a kind of dominatrix patter" over "[t]he cries and squeals of the animals, obviously in great pain." Ibid. Apparently these depictions "appeal to persons with a very specific sexual fetish who find them sexually arousing or otherwise exciting." Id., at 2–3. The acts depicted in crush videos are typically prohibited by the animal cruelty laws enacted by all 50 States and the District of Columbia. See Brief for United States 25, n. 7 (listing statutes). But crush videos rarely disclose the participants' identities, inhibiting prosecution of the underlying conduct. See H. R. Rep., at 3; accord, Brief for State of Florida et al. as Amici Curiae 11.

This case, however, involves an application of §48 to depictions of animal fighting. Dogfighting, for example, is unlawful in all 50 States and the District of Columbia, see Brief for United States 26, n. 8 (listing statutes), and has been restricted by federal law since 1976. Animal Welfare Act Amendments of 1976, §17, 90 Stat. 421, 7 U. S. C. §2156. Respondent Robert J. Stevens ran a business, "Dogs of Velvet and Steel," and an associated Web site, through which he sold videos of pit bulls engaging in dogfights and attacking other animals. Among these videos were Japan Pit Fights and Pick-A-Winna: A Pit Bull Documentary, which include contemporary footage of dogfights in Japan (where such conduct is allegedly legal) as well as footage of American dogfights from the 1960's and 1970's. 2 A third video, Catch Dogs and Country Living, depicts the use of pit bulls to hunt wild boar, as well as a "gruesome" scene of a pit bull attacking a domestic farm pig. 533 F. 3d 218, 221 (CA3 2008) (en banc). On the basis of these videos, Stevens was indicted on three counts of violating §48.

Stevens moved to dismiss the indictment, arguing that §48 is facially invalid under the First Amendment . The District Court denied the motion. It held that the depictions subject to §48, like obscenity or child pornography, are categorically unprotected by the First Amendment . 2:04–cr–00051–ANB (WD Pa., Nov. 10, 2004), App. to Pet. for Cert. 65a–71a. It went on to hold that §48 is not substantially overbroad, because the exceptions clause sufficiently narrows the statute to constitutional applications. Id., at 71a–75a. The jury convicted Stevens on all counts, and the District Court sentenced him to three concurrent sentences of 37 months' imprisonment, followed by three years of supervised release. App. 37.

The en banc Third Circuit, over a three-judge dissent, declared §48 facially unconstitutional and vacated Stevens's conviction. 533 F. 3d 218. The Court of Appeals first held that §48 regulates speech that is protected by the First Amendment . The Court declined to recognize a new category of unprotected speech for depictions of animal cruelty, id., at 224, and n. 6, and rejected the Government's analogy between animal cruelty depictions and child pornography, id., at 224–232.

The Court of Appeals then held that §48 could not survive strict scrutiny as a content-based regulation of protected speech. Id., at 232. It found that the statute lacked a compelling government interest and was neither narrowly tailored to preventing animal cruelty nor the least restrictive means of doing so. Id., at 232–235. It therefore held §48 facially invalid.

In an extended footnote, the Third Circuit noted that §48 "might also be unconstitutionally overbroad," because it "potentially covers a great deal of constitutionally protected speech" and "sweeps [too] widely" to be limited only by prosecutorial discretion. Id., at 235, n. 16. But the Court of Appeals declined to rest its analysis on this ground.

We granted certiorari. 556 U. S. ___ (2009).

II

The Government's primary submission is that §48 necessarily complies with the Constitution because the banned depictions of animal cruelty, as a class, are categorically unprotected by the First Amendment. We disagree.

The First Amendment provides that "Congress shall make no law ... abridging the freedom of speech." "[A]s a general matter, the First Amendment means that government has no power to restrict expression because of its message, its ideas, its subject matter, or its content." Ashcroft v. American Civil Liberties Union , 535 U. S. 564, 573 (2002) (internal quotation marks omitted). Section 48 explicitly regulates expression based on content: The statute restricts "visual [and] auditory depiction[s]," such as photographs, videos, or sound recordings, depending on whether they depict conduct in which a living animal is intentionally harmed. As such, §48 is " 'presumptively invalid,' and the Government bears the burden to rebut that presumption." United States v. Playboy Entertainment Group, Inc. , 529 U. S. 803, 817 (2000) (quoting R. A. V. v. St. Paul , 505 U. S. 377, 382 (1992) ; citation omitted).

"From 1791 to the present," however, the First Amendment has "permitted restrictions upon the content of speech in a few limited areas," and has never "include[d] a freedom to disregard these traditional limitations." Id., at 382–383. These "historic and traditional categories long familiar to the bar," Simon & Schuster, Inc. v. Members of N. Y. State Crime Victims Bd. , 502 U. S. 105, 127 (1991) ( Kennedy, J. , concurring in judgment)—including obscenity, Roth v. United States , 354 U. S. 476, 483 (1957) , defamation, Beauharnais v. Illinois , 343 U. S. 250, 254–255 (1952) , fraud, Virginia Bd. of Pharmacy v. Virginia Citizens Consumer Council, Inc. , 425 U. S. 748, 771 (1976) , incitement, Brandenburg v. Ohio , 395 U. S. 444, 447–449 (1969) ( per curiam ), and speech integral to criminal conduct, Giboney v. Empire Storage & Ice Co. , 336 U. S. 490, 498 (1949) —are "well-defined and narrowly limited classes of speech, the prevention and punishment of which have never been thought to raise any Constitutional problem." Chaplinsky v. New Hampshire , 315 U. S. 568, 571–572 (1942) .

The Government argues that "depictions of animal cruelty" should be added to the list. It contends that depictions of "illegal acts of animal cruelty" that are "made, sold, or possessed for commercial gain" necessarily "lack expressive value," and may accordingly "be regulated as unprotected speech." Brief for United States 10 (emphasis added). The claim is not just that Congress may regulate depictions of animal cruelty subject to the First Amendment , but that these depictions are outside the reach of that Amendment altogether—that they fall into a " ' First Amendment Free Zone.' " Board of Airport Comm'rs of Los Angeles v. Jews for Jesus, Inc. , 482 U. S. 569, 574 (1987) .

As the Government notes, the prohibition of animal cruelty itself has a long history in American law, starting with the early settlement of the Colonies. Reply Brief 12, n. 8; see, e.g., The Body of Liberties §92 (Mass. Bay Colony 1641), reprinted in American Historical Documents 1000–1904, 43 Harvard Classics 66, 79 (C. Eliot ed. 1910) ("No man shall exercise any Tirranny or Crueltie towards any bruite Creature which are usuallie kept for man's use"). But we are unaware of any similar tradition excluding depictions of animal cruelty from "the freedom of speech" codified in the First Amendment , and the Government points us to none.

The Government contends that "historical evidence" about the reach of the First Amendment is not "a necessary prerequisite for regulation today," Reply Brief 12, n. 8, and that categories of speech may be exempted from the First Amendment 's protection without any long-settled tradition of subjecting that speech to regulation. Instead, the Government points to Congress's " 'legislative judgment that ... depictions of animals being intentionally tortured and killed [are] of such minimal redeeming value as to render [them] unworthy of First Amendment protection,' " Brief for United States 23 (quoting 533 F. 3d, at 243 (Cowen, J., dissenting)), and asks the Court to uphold the ban on the same basis. The Government thus proposes that a claim of categorical exclusion should be considered under a simple balancing test: "Whether a given category of speech enjoys First Amendment protection depends upon a categorical balancing of the value of the speech against its societal costs." Brief for United States 8; see also id., at 12.

As a free-floating test for First Amendment coverage, that sentence is startling and dangerous. The First Amendment 's guarantee of free speech does not extend only to categories of speech that survive an ad hoc balancing of relative social costs and benefits. The First Amendment itself reflects a judgment by the American people that the benefits of its restrictions on the Government outweigh the costs. Our Constitution forecloses any attempt to revise that judgment simply on the basis that some speech is not worth it. The Constitution is not a document "prescribing limits, and declaring that those limits may be passed at pleasure." Marbury v. Madison , 1 Cranch 137, 178 (1803).

To be fair to the Government, its view did not emerge from a vacuum. As the Government correctly notes, this Court has often described historically unprotected categories of speech as being " 'of such slight social value as a step to truth that any benefit that may be derived from them is clearly outweighed by the social interest in order and morality.' " R. A. V. , supra , at 383 (quoting Chaplinsky , supra , at 572). In New York v. Ferber , 458 U. S. 747 (1982) , we noted that within these categories of unprotected speech, "the evil to be restricted so overwhelmingly outweighs the expressive interests, if any, at stake, that no process of case-by-case adjudication is required," because "the balance of competing interests is clearly struck," id., at 763–764. The Government derives its proposed test from these descriptions in our precedents. See Brief for United States 12–13.

But such descriptions are just that—descriptive. They do not set forth a test that may be applied as a general matter to permit the Government to imprison any speaker so long as his speech is deemed valueless or unnecessary, or so long as an ad hoc calculus of costs and benefits tilts in a statute's favor.

When we have identified categories of speech as fully outside the protection of the First Amendment , it has not been on the basis of a simple cost-benefit analysis. In Ferber , for example, we classified child pornography as such a category, 458 U. S., at 763. We noted that the State of New York had a compelling interest in protecting children from abuse, and that the value of using children in these works (as opposed to simulated conduct or adult actors) was de minimis . Id., at 756–757, 762. But our decision did not rest on this "balance of competing interests" alone. Id. , at 764. We made clear that Ferber presented a special case: The market for child pornography was "intrinsically related" to the underlying abuse, and was therefore "an integral part of the production of such materials, an activity illegal throughout the Nation." Id., at 759, 761. As we noted, " '[i]t rarely has been suggested that the constitutional freedom for speech and press extends its immunity to speech or writing used as an integral part of conduct in violation of a valid criminal statute.' " Id., at 761–762 (quoting Giboney , supra , at 498). Ferber thus grounded its analysis in a previously recognized, long-established category of unprotected speech, and our subsequent decisions have shared this understanding. See Osborne v. Ohio , 495 U. S. 103, 110 (1990) (describing Ferber as finding "persuasive" the argument that the advertising and sale of child pornography was "an integral part" of its unlawful production (internal quotation marks omitted)); Ashcroft v. Free Speech Coalition , 535 U. S. 234, 249–250 (2002) (noting that distribution and sale "were intrinsically related to the sexual abuse of children," giving the speech at issue "a proximate link to the crime from which it came" (internal quotation marks omitted)).

Our decisions in Ferber and other cases cannot be taken as establishing a freewheeling authority to declare new categories of speech outside the scope of the First Amendment . Maybe there are some categories of speech that have been historically unprotected, but have not yet been specifically identified or discussed as such in our case law. But if so, there is no evidence that "depictions of animal cruelty" is among them. We need not foreclose the future recognition of such additional categories to reject the Government's highly manipulable balancing test as a means of identifying them.

III

Because we decline to carve out from the First Amendment any novel exception for §48, we review Stevens's First Amendment challenge under our existing doctrine.

A

Stevens challenged §48 on its face, arguing that any conviction secured under the statute would be unconstitutional. The court below decided the case on that basis, 533 F. 3d, at 231, n. 13, and we granted the Solicitor General's petition for certiorari to determine "whether 18 U. S. C. 48 is facially invalid under the Free Speech Clause of the First Amendment ," Pet. for Cert. i.

To succeed in a typical facial attack, Stevens would have to establish "that no set of circumstances exists under which [§48] would be valid," United States v. Salerno , 481 U. S. 739, 745 (1987) , or that the statute lacks any "plainly legitimate sweep," Washington v. Glucksberg , 521 U. S. 702 , n. 7 (1997) ( Stevens, J. , concurring in judgments) (internal quotation marks omitted). Which standard applies in a typical case is a matter of dispute that we need not and do not address, and neither Salerno nor Glucksberg is a speech case. Here the Government asserts that Stevens cannot prevail because §48 is plainly legitimate as applied to crush videos and animal fighting depictions. Deciding this case through a traditional facial analysis would require us to resolve whether these applications of §48 are in fact consistent with the Constitution.

In the First Amendment context, however, this Court recognizes "a second type of facial challenge," whereby a law may be invalidated as overbroad if "a substantial number of its applications are unconstitutional, judged in relation to the statute's plainly legitimate sweep." Washington State Grange v. Washington State Republican Party , 552 U. S. 442 , n. 6 (2008) (internal quotation marks omitted). Stevens argues that §48 applies to common depictions of ordinary and lawful activities, and that these depictions constitute the vast majority of materials subject to the statute. Brief for Respondent 22–25. The Government makes no effort to defend such a broad ban as constitutional. Instead, the Government's entire defense of §48 rests on interpreting the statute as narrowly limited to specific types of "extreme" material. Brief for United States 8. As the parties have presented the issue, therefore, the constitutionality of §48 hinges on how broadly it is construed. It is to that question that we now turn. 3

B

As we explained two Terms ago, "[t]he first step in overbreadth analysis is to construe the challenged statute; it is impossible to determine whether a statute reaches too far without first knowing what the statute covers." United States v. Williams , 553 U. S. 285, 293 (2008) . Because §48 is a federal statute, there is no need to defer to a state court's authority to interpret its own law.

We read §48 to create a criminal prohibition of alarming breadth. To begin with, the text of the statute's ban on a "depiction of animal cruelty" nowhere requires that the depicted conduct be cruel. That text applies to "any ... depiction" in which "a living animal is intentionally maimed, mutilated, tortured, wounded, or killed." §48(c)(1). "[M]aimed, mutilated, [and] tortured" convey cruelty, but "wounded" or "killed" do not suggest any such limitation.

The Government contends that the terms in the definition should be read to require the additional element of "accompanying acts of cruelty." Reply Brief 6; see also Tr. of Oral Arg. 17–19. (The dissent hinges on the same assumption. See post, at 6, 9.) The Government bases this argument on the definiendum, "depiction of animal cruelty," cf. Leocal v. Ashcroft , 543 U. S. 1, 11 (2004) , and on " 'the commonsense canon of noscitur a sociis .' " Reply Brief 7 (quoting Williams , 553 U. S., at 294). As that canon recognizes, an ambiguous term may be "given more precise content by the neighboring words with which it is associated." Ibid . Likewise, an unclear definitional phrase may take meaning from the term to be defined, see Leocal , supra, at 11 (interpreting a " 'substantial risk' " of the "us[e]" of "physical force" as part of the definition of " 'crime of violence' ").

But the phrase "wounded ... or killed" at issue here contains little ambiguity. The Government's opening brief properly applies the ordinary meaning of these words, stating for example that to " 'kill' is 'to deprive of life.' " Brief for United States 14 (quoting Webster's Third New International Dictionary 1242 (1993)). We agree that "wounded" and "killed" should be read according to their ordinary meaning. Cf. Engine Mfrs. Assn. v. South Coast Air Quality Management Dist. , 541 U. S. 246, 252 (2004) . Nothing about that meaning requires cruelty.

While not requiring cruelty, §48 does require that the depicted conduct be "illegal." But this requirement does not limit §48 along the lines the Government suggests. There are myriad federal and state laws concerning the proper treatment of animals, but many of them are not designed to guard against animal cruelty. Protections of endangered species, for example, restrict even the humane "wound[ing] or kill[ing]" of "living animal[s]." §48(c)(1). Livestock regulations are often designed to protect the health of human beings, and hunting and fishing rules (seasons, licensure, bag limits, weight requirements) can be designed to raise revenue, preserve animal populations, or prevent accidents. The text of §48(c) draws no distinction based on the reason the intentional killing of an animal is made illegal, and includes, for example, the humane slaughter of a stolen cow. 4

What is more, the application of §48 to depictions of illegal conduct extends to conduct that is illegal in only a single jurisdiction. Under subsection (c)(1), the depicted conduct need only be illegal in "the State in which the creation, sale, or possession takes place, regardless of whether the ... wounding ... or killing took place in [that] State." A depiction of entirely lawful conduct runs afoul of the ban if that depiction later finds its way into another State where the same conduct is unlawful. This provision greatly expands the scope of §48, because although there may be "a broad societal consensus" against cruelty to animals, Brief for United States 2, there is substantial disagreement on what types of conduct are properly regarded as cruel. Both views about cruelty to animals and regulations having no connection to cruelty vary widely from place to place.

In the District of Columbia, for example, all hunting is unlawful. D. C. Munic. Regs., tit. 19, §1560 (2009). Other jurisdictions permit or encourage hunting, and there is an enormous national market for hunting-related depictions in which a living animal is intentionally killed. Hunting periodicals have circulations in the hundreds of thousands or millions, see Mediaweek, Sept. 29, 2008, p. 28, and hunting television programs, videos, and Web sites are equally popular, see Brief for Professional Outdoor Media Association et al. as Amici Curiae 9–10. The demand for hunting depictions exceeds the estimated demand for crush videos or animal fighting depictions by several orders of magnitude. Compare ibid. and Brief for National Rifle Association of America, Inc., as Amicus Curiae 12 (hereinafter NRA Brief) (estimating that hunting magazines alone account for $135 million in annual retail sales) with Brief for United States 43–44, 46 (suggesting $1 million in crush video sales per year, and noting that Stevens earned $57,000 from his videos). Nonetheless, because the statute allows each jurisdiction to export its laws to the rest of the country, §48(a) extends to any magazine or video depicting lawful hunting, so long as that depiction is sold within the Nation's Capital.

Those seeking to comply with the law thus face a bewildering maze of regulations from at least 56 separate jurisdictions. Some States permit hunting with crossbows, Ga. Code Ann. §27–3–4(1) (2007); Va. Code Ann. §29.1–519(A)(6) (Lexis 2008 Cum. Supp.), while others forbid it, Ore. Admin. Reg. 635–065–0725 (2009), or restrict it only to the disabled, N. Y. Envir. Conserv. Law Ann. §11–0901(16) (West 2005). Missouri allows the "canned" hunting of ungulates held in captivity, Mo. Code Regs. Ann., tit. 3, 10–9.560(1), but Montana restricts such hunting to certain bird species, Mont. Admin. Rule 12.6.1202(1) (2007). The sharp-tailed grouse may be hunted in Idaho, but not in Washington. Compare Idaho Admin. Code §13.01.09.606 (2009) with Wash. Admin. Code §232–28–342 (2009).

The disagreements among the States—and the "commonwealth[s], territor[ies], or possession[s] of the United States," 18 U. S. C. §48(c)(2)—extend well beyond hunting. State agricultural regulations permit different methods of livestock slaughter in different places or as applied to different animals. Compare, e.g., Fla. Stat. §828.23(5) (2007) (excluding poultry from humane slaughter requirements) with Cal. Food & Agric. Code Ann. §19501(b) (West 2001) (including some poultry). California has recently banned cutting or "docking" the tails of dairy cattle, which other States permit. 2009 Cal. Legis. Serv. Ch. 344 (S. B. 135) (West). Even cockfighting, long considered immoral in much of America, see Barnes v. Glen Theatre, Inc. , 501 U. S. 560, 575 (1991) ( Scalia, J. , concurring in judgment), is legal in Puerto Rico, see 15 Laws P. R. Ann. §301 (Supp. 2008); Posadas de Puerto Rico Associates v. Tourism Co. of P. R. , 478 U. S. 328, 342 (1986) , and was legal in Louisiana until 2008, see La. Stat. Ann. §14:102.23 (West) (effective Aug. 15, 2008). An otherwise-lawful image of any of these practices, if sold or possessed for commercial gain within a State that happens to forbid the practice, falls within the prohibition of §48(a).

### C

The only thing standing between defendants who sell such depictions and five years in federal prison—other than the mercy of a prosecutor—is the statute's exceptions clause. Subsection (b) exempts from prohibition "any depiction that has serious religious, political, scientific, educational, journalistic, historical, or artistic value." The Government argues that this clause substantially narrows the statute's reach: News reports about animal cruelty have "journalistic" value; pictures of bullfights in Spain have "historical" value; and instructional hunting videos have "educational" value. Reply Brief 6. Thus, the Government argues, §48 reaches only crush videos, depictions of animal fighting (other than Spanish bullfighting, see Brief for United States 47–48), and perhaps other depictions of "extreme acts of animal cruelty." Id., at 41.

The Government's attempt to narrow the statutory ban, however, requires an unrealistically broad reading of the exceptions clause. As the Government reads the clause, any material with "redeeming societal value," id. , at 9, 16, 23, " 'at least some minimal value,' " Reply Brief 6 (quoting H. R. Rep., at 4), or anything more than "scant social value," Reply Brief 11, is excluded under §48(b). But the text says "serious" value, and "serious" should be taken seriously. We decline the Government's invitation— advanced for the first time in this Court—to regard as "serious" anything that is not "scant." (Or, as the dissent puts it, " 'trifling.' " Post , at 6.) As the Government recognized below, "serious" ordinarily means a good bit more. The District Court's jury instructions required value that is "significant and of great import," App. 132, and the Government defended these instructions as properly relying on "a commonly accepted meaning of the word 'serious,' " Brief for United States in No. 05–2497 (CA3), p. 50.

Quite apart from the requirement of "serious" value in §48(b), the excepted speech must also fall within one of the enumerated categories. Much speech does not. Most hunting videos, for example, are not obviously instructional in nature, except in the sense that all life is a lesson. According to Safari Club International and the Congressional Sportsmen's Foundation, many popular videos "have primarily entertainment value" and are designed to "entertai[n] the viewer, marke[t] hunting equipment, or increas[e] the hunting community." Brief for Safari Club International et al. as Amici Curiae 12. The National Rifle Association agrees that "much of the content of hunting media ... is merely recreational in nature." NRA Brief 28. The Government offers no principled explanation why these depictions of hunting or depictions of Spanish bullfights would be inherently valuable while those of Japanese dogfights are not. The dissent contends that hunting depictions must have serious value because hunting has serious value, in a way that dogfights presumably do not. Post, at 6–8. But §48(b) addresses the value of the depictions , not of the underlying activity. There is simply no adequate reading of the exceptions clause that results in the statute's banning only the depictions the Government would like to ban.

The Government explains that the language of §48(b) was largely drawn from our opinion in Miller v. California , 413 U. S. 15 (1973) , which excepted from its definition of obscenity any material with "serious literary, artistic, political, or scientific value," id., at 24. See Reply Brief 8, 9, and n. 5. According to the Government, this incorporation of the Miller standard into §48 is therefore surely enough to answer any First Amendment objection. Reply Brief 8–9.

In Miller we held that "serious" value shields depictions of sex from regulation as obscenity. 413 U. S., at 24–25. Limiting Miller 's exception to "serious" value ensured that " '[a] quotation from Voltaire in the flyleaf of a book [would] not constitutionally redeem an otherwise obscene publication.' " Id., at 25, n. 7 (quoting Kois v. Wisconsin , 408 U. S. 229, 231 (1972) ( per curiam )). We did not, however, determine that serious value could be used as a general precondition to protecting other types of speech in the first place. Most of what we say to one another lacks "religious, political, scientific, educational, journalistic, historical, or artistic value" (let alone serious value), but it is still sheltered from government regulation. Even " '[w]holly neutral futilities ... come under the protection of free speech as fully as do Keats' poems or Donne's sermons.' " Cohen v. California , 403 U. S. 15, 25 (1971) (quoting Winters v. New York , 333 U. S. 507, 528 (1948) (Frankfurter, J., dissenting); alteration in original).

Thus, the protection of the First Amendment presumptively extends to many forms of speech that do not qualify for the serious-value exception of §48(b), but nonetheless fall within the broad reach of §48(c).

D

Not to worry, the Government says: The Executive Branch construes §48 to reach only "extreme" cruelty, Brief for United States 8, and it "neither has brought nor will bring a prosecution for anything less," Reply Brief 6–7. The Government hits this theme hard, invoking its prosecutorial discretion several times. See id., at 6–7, 10, and n. 6, 19, 22. But the First Amendment protects against the Government; it does not leave us at the mercy of noblesse oblige . We would not uphold an unconstitutional statute merely because the Government promised to use it responsibly. Cf. Whitman v. American Trucking Assns., Inc. , 531 U. S. 457, 473 (2001) .

This prosecution is itself evidence of the danger in putting faith in government representations of prosecutorial restraint. When this legislation was enacted, the Executive Branch announced that it would interpret §48 as covering only depictions "of wanton cruelty to animals designed to appeal to a prurient interest in sex." See Statement by President William J. Clinton upon Signing H. R. 1887, 34 Weekly Comp. Pres. Doc. 2557 (Dec. 9, 1999). No one suggests that the videos in this case fit that description. The

Government's assurance that it will apply §48 far more restrictively than its language provides is pertinent only as an implicit acknowledgment of the potential constitutional problems with a more natural reading.

Nor can we rely upon the canon of construction that "ambiguous statutory language [should] be construed to avoid serious constitutional doubts." FCC v. Fox Television Stations, Inc. , 556 U. S. ___, ___ (2009) (slip op., at 12). "[T]his Court may impose a limiting construction on a statute only if it is 'readily susceptible' to such a construction." Reno v. American Civil Liberties Union , 521 U. S. 844, 884 (1997) . We " 'will not rewrite a ... law to conform it to constitutional requirements,' " id., at 884–885 (quoting Virginia v. American Booksellers Assn., Inc. , 484 U. S. 383, 397 (1988) ; omission in original), for doing so would constitute a "serious invasion of the legislative domain," United States v. Treasury Employees , 513 U. S. 454, 479, n. 26 (1995) , and sharply diminish Congress's "incentive to draft a narrowly tailored law in the first place," Osborne, 495 U. S., at 121. To read §48 as the Government desires requires rewriting, not just reinterpretation.

\*    \*    \*

Our construction of §48 decides the constitutional question; the Government makes no effort to defend the constitutionality of §48 as applied beyond crush videos and depictions of animal fighting. It argues that those particular depictions are intrinsically related to criminal conduct or are analogous to obscenity (if not themselves obscene), and that the ban on such speech is narrowly tailored to reinforce restrictions on the underlying conduct, prevent additional crime arising from the depictions, or safeguard public mores. But the Government nowhere attempts to extend these arguments to depictions of any other activities—depictions that are presumptively protected by the First Amendment but that remain subject to the criminal sanctions of §48.

Nor does the Government seriously contest that the presumptively impermissible applications of §48 (properly construed) far outnumber any permissible ones. However "growing" and "lucrative" the markets for crush videos and dogfighting depictions might be, see Brief for United States 43, 46 (internal quotation marks omitted), they are dwarfed by the market for other depictions, such as hunting magazines and videos, that we have determined to be within the scope of §48. See supra , at 13–14. We therefore need not and do not decide whether a statute limited to crush videos or other depictions of extreme animal cruelty would be constitutional. We hold only that §48 is not so limited but is instead substantially overbroad, and therefore invalid under the First Amendment.

The judgment of the United States Court of Appeals for the Third Circuit is affirmed.

It is so ordered.

Notes

1 The statute reads in full: "§48. Depiction of animal cruelty "(a) Creation, Sale,

or Possession.—Whoever knowingly creates, sells, or possesses a depiction of animal cruelty with the intention of placing that depiction in interstate or foreign commerce for commercial gain, shall be fined under this title or imprisoned not more than 5 years, or both. "(b) Exception.—Subsection (a) does not apply to any depiction that has serious religious, political, scientific, educational, journalistic, historical, or artistic value. "(c) Definitions.—In this section— "(1) the term 'depiction of animal cruelty' means any visual or auditory depiction, including any photograph, motion-picture film, video recording, electronic image, or sound recording of conduct in which a living animal is intentionally maimed, mutilated, tortured, wounded, or killed, if such conduct is illegal under Federal law or the law of the State in which the creation, sale, or possession takes place, regardless of whether the maiming, mutilation, torture, wounding, or killing took place in the State; and "(2) the term 'State' means each of the several States, the District of Columbia, the Commonwealth of Puerto Rico, the Virgin Islands, Guam, American Samoa, the Commonwealth of the Northern Mariana Islands, and any other commonwealth, territory, or possession of the United States."

2 The Government contends that these dogfights were unlawful at the time they occurred, while Stevens disputes the assertion. Reply Brief for United States 25, n. 14 (hereinafter Reply Brief); Brief for Respondent 44, n. 18.

3 The dissent contends that because there has not been a ruling on the validity of the statute as applied to Stevens, our consideration of his facial overbreadth claim is premature. Post, at 1, and n. 1, 2–3 (opinion of Alito, J.). Whether or not that conclusion follows, here no as-applied claim has been preserved. Neither court below construed Stevens's briefs as adequately developing a separate attack on a defined subset of the statute's applications (say, dogfighting videos). See 533 F. 3d 218, 231, n. 13 (CA3 2008) (en banc) ("Stevens brings a facial challenge to the statute"); App. to Pet. for Cert. 65a, 74a. Neither did the Government, see Brief for United States in No. 05–2497 (CA3), p. 28 (opposing "the appellant's facial challenge"); accord, Brief for United States 4. The sentence in Stevens's appellate brief mentioning his unrelated sufficiency-of-the-evidence challenge hardly developed a First Amendment as-applied claim. See post, at 1, n. 1. Stevens's constitutional argument is a general one. And unlike the challengers in Washington State Grange, Stevens does not "rest on factual assumptions ... that can be evaluated only in the context of an as-applied challenge." 552 U. S., at 444.

4 The citations in the dissent's appendix are beside the point. The cited statutes stand for the proposition that hunting is not covered by animal cruelty laws. But the reach of §48 is, as we have explained, not restricted to depictions of conduct that violates a law specifically directed at animal cruelty. It simply requires that the depicted conduct be "illegal." §48(c)(1). The Government implicitly admits as much, arguing that "instructional videos for hunting" are saved by the statute's exceptions clause, not that they fall outside the prohibition in the first place. Reply Brief 6.

**Snyder v. Phelps (March 2, 2011)**

Chief Justice Roberts delivered the opinion of the Court.

A jury held members of the Westboro Baptist Church liable for millions of dollars in damages for picketing near a soldier's funeral service. The picket signs reflected the church's view that the United States is overly tolerant of sin and that God kills American soldiers as punishment. The question presented is whether the First Amendment shields the church members from tort liability for their speech in this case.

I

A

Fred Phelps founded the Westboro Baptist Church in Topeka, Kansas, in 1955. The church's congregation believes that God hates and punishes the United States for its tolerance of homosexuality, particularly in America's military. The church frequently communicates its views by picketing, often at military funerals. In the more than 20 years that the members of Westboro Baptist have publicized their message, they have picketed nearly 600 funerals. Brief for Rutherford Institute as Amicus Curiae 7, n. 14.

Marine Lance Corporal Matthew Snyder was killed in Iraq in the line of duty. Lance Corporal Snyder's father selected the Catholic church in the Snyders' hometown of Westminster, Maryland, as the site for his son's funeral. Local newspapers provided notice of the time and location of the service.

Phelps became aware of Matthew Snyder's funeral and decided to travel to Maryland with six other Westboro Baptist parishioners (two of his daughters and four of his grandchildren) to picket. On the day of the memorial service, the Westboro congregation members picketed on public land adjacent to public streets near the Maryland State House, the United States Naval Academy, and Matthew Snyder's funeral. The Westboro picketers carried signs that were largely the same at all three locations. They stated, for instance: "God Hates the USA/Thank God for 9/11," "America is Doomed," "Don't Pray for the USA," "Thank God for IEDs," "Thank God for Dead Soldiers," "Pope in Hell," "Priests Rape Boys," "God Hates Fags," "You're Going to Hell," and "God Hates You."

The church had notified the authorities in advance of its intent to picket at the time of the funeral, and the picketers complied with police instructions in staging their demonstration. The picketing took place within a 10- by 25-foot plot of public land adjacent to a public street, behind a temporary fence. App. to Brief for Appellants in No. 08–1026 (CA4), pp. 2282–2285 (hereinafter App.). That plot was approximately 1,000 feet from the church where the funeral was held. Several buildings separated the picket site from the church. Id ., at 3758. The Westboro picketers displayed their signs for about 30 minutes before the funeral began and sang hymns and recited Bible verses. None of the picketers entered church property or went to the cemetery. They did not yell or use profanity, and there was no violence associated with the picketing. Id ., at 2168, 2371, 2286, 2293.

The funeral procession passed within 200 to 300 feet of the picket site.

Although Snyder testified that he could see the tops of the picket signs as he drove to the funeral, he did not see what was written on the signs until later that night, while watching a news broadcast covering the event. Id., at 2084–2086. 1

B

Snyder filed suit against Phelps, Phelps's daughters, and the Westboro Baptist Church (collectively Westboro or the church) in the United States District Court for the District of Maryland under that court's diversity jurisdiction. Snyder alleged five state tort law claims: defamation, publicity given to private life, intentional infliction of emotional distress, intrusion upon seclusion, and civil conspiracy. Westboro moved for summary judgment contending, in part, that the church's speech was insulated from liability by the First Amendment . See 533 F. Supp. 2d 567, 570 (Md. 2008).

The District Court awarded Westboro summary judgment on Snyder's claims for defamation and publicity given to private life, concluding that Snyder could not prove the necessary elements of those torts. Id., at 572–573. A trial was held on the remaining claims. At trial, Snyder described the severity of his emotional injuries. He testified that he is unable to separate the thought of his dead son from his thoughts of Westboro's picketing, and that he often becomes tearful, angry, and physically ill when he thinks about it. Id., at 588–589. Expert witnesses testified that Snyder's emotional anguish had resulted in severe depression and had exacerbated pre-existing health conditions.

A jury found for Snyder on the intentional infliction of emotional distress, intrusion upon seclusion, and civil conspiracy claims, and held Westboro liable for $2.9 million in compensatory damages and $8 million in punitive damages. Westboro filed several post-trial motions, including a motion contending that the jury verdict was grossly excessive and a motion seeking judgment as a matter of law on all claims on First Amendment grounds. The District Court remitted the punitive damages award to $2.1 million, but left the jury verdict otherwise intact. Id., at 597.

In the Court of Appeals, Westboro's primary argument was that the church was entitled to judgment as a matter of law because the First Amendment fully protected Westboro's speech. The Court of Appeals agreed. 580 F. 3d 206, 221 (CA4 2009). The court reviewed the picket signs and concluded that Westboro's statements were entitled to First Amendment protection because those statements were on matters of public concern, were not provably false, and were expressed solely through hyperbolic rhetoric. Id., at 222–224. 2

We granted certiorari. 559 U. S. ___ (2010).

II

To succeed on a claim for intentional infliction of emotional distress in Maryland, a plaintiff must demonstrate that the defendant intentionally or recklessly engaged in extreme and outrageous conduct that caused the plaintiff to suffer severe emotional distress. See Harris v. Jones, 281 Md. 560, 565–566, 380 A. 2d 611, 614 (1977). The Free Speech Clause of the First Amendment —"Congress shall make no law ... abridging the freedom of speech"—can serve as a defense in state tort suits, including suits for intentional infliction of emotional distress. See, e.g., Hustler Magazine, Inc. v. Falwell, 485 U. S. 46, 50–51 (1988). 3

Whether the First Amendment prohibits holding Westboro liable for its speech in this case turns largely on whether that speech is of public or private concern, as determined by all the circumstances of the case. "[S]peech on 'matters of public concern' ... is 'at the heart of the First Amendment 's protection.' " Dun & Bradstreet, Inc. v. Greenmoss Builders, Inc., 472 U. S. 749, 758–759 (1985) (opinion of Powell, J.) (quoting First Nat. Bank of Boston v. Bellotti, 435 U. S. 765, 776 (1978)). The First Amendment reflects "a profound national commitment to the principle that debate on public issues should be uninhibited, robust, and wide-open." New York Times Co. v. Sullivan, 376 U. S. 254, 270 (1964). That is because "speech concerning public affairs is more than self-expression; it is the essence of self-government." Garrison v. Louisiana, 379 U. S. 64, 74–75 (1964). Accordingly, "speech on public issues occupies the highest rung of the hierarchy of First Amendment values, and is entitled to special protection." Connick v. Myers, 461 U. S. 138, 145 (1983) (internal quotation marks omitted).

" '[N]ot all speech is of equal First Amendment importance,' " however, and where matters of purely private significance are at issue, First Amendment protections are often less rigorous. Hustler, supra, at 56 (quoting Dun & Bradstreet, supra, at 758); see Connick, supra, at 145–147. That is because restricting speech on purely private matters does not implicate the same constitutional concerns as limiting speech on matters of public interest: "[T]here is no threat to the free and robust debate of public issues; there is no potential interference with a meaningful dialogue of ideas"; and the "threat of liability" does not pose the risk of "a reaction of self-censorship" on matters of public import. Dun & Bradstreet, supra, at 760 (internal quotation marks omitted).

We noted a short time ago, in considering whether public employee speech addressed a matter of public concern, that "the boundaries of the public concern test are not well defined." San Diego v. Roe, 543 U. S. 77, 83 (2004) (per curiam). Although that remains true today, we have articulated some guiding principles, principles that accord broad protection to speech to ensure that courts themselves do not become inadvertent censors.

Speech deals with matters of public concern when it can "be fairly considered as relating to any matter of political, social, or other concern to the community," Connick, supra, at 146, or when it "is a subject of legitimate news interest; that is, a subject of general interest and of value and concern to the public," San Diego, supra, at 83–84. See Cox Broadcasting Corp. v. Cohn, 420 U. S. 469, 492–494 (1975); Time, Inc. v. Hill, 385 U. S. 374 – 388 (1967). The arguably "inappropriate or controversial character of a statement is irrelevant to the question whether it deals with a matter of public concern." Rankin v. McPherson, 483 U. S. 378, 387 (1987).

Our opinion in Dun & Bradstreet, on the other hand, provides an example of speech of only private concern. In that case we held, as a general matter, that information about a particular individual's credit report "concerns no public issue." 472 U. S., at 762.

The content of the report, we explained, "was speech solely in the individual interest of the speaker and its specific business audience." Ibid. That was confirmed by the fact that the particular report was sent to only five subscribers to the reporting service, who were bound not to disseminate it further. Ibid. To cite another example, we concluded in San Diego v. Roe that, in the context of a government employer regulating the speech of its employees, videos of an employee engaging in sexually explicit acts did not address a public concern; the videos "did nothing to inform the public about any aspect of the [employing agency's] functioning or operation." 543 U. S., at 84.

Deciding whether speech is of public or private concern requires us to examine the " 'content, form, and context' " of that speech, " 'as revealed by the whole record.' " Dun & Bradstreet, supra, at 761 (quoting Connick, supra, at 147–148). As in other First Amendment cases, the court is obligated "to 'make an independent examination of the whole record' in order to make sure that 'the judgment does not constitute a forbidden intrusion on the field of free expression.' " Bose Corp. v. Consumers Union of United States, Inc., 466 U. S. 485, 499 (1984) (quoting New York Times, supra, at 284–286). In considering content, form, and context, no factor is dispositive, and it is necessary to evaluate all the circumstances of the speech, including what was said, where it was said, and how it was said.

The "content" of Westboro's signs plainly relates to broad issues of interest to society at large, rather than matters of "purely private concern." Dun & Bradstreet, supra, at 759. The placards read "God Hates the USA/Thank God for 9/11," "America is Doomed," "Don't Pray for the USA," "Thank God for IEDs," "Fag Troops," "Semper Fi Fags," "God Hates Fags," "Maryland Taliban," "Fags Doom Nations," "Not Blessed Just Cursed," "Thank God for Dead Soldiers," "Pope in Hell," "Priests Rape Boys," "You're Going to Hell," and "God Hates You." App. 3781–3787. While these messages may fall short of refined social or political commentary, the issues they highlight—the political and moral conduct of the United States and its citizens, the fate of our Nation, homosexuality in the military, and scandals involving the Catholic clergy—are matters of public import. The signs certainly convey Westboro's position on those issues, in a manner designed, unlike the private speech in Dun & Bradstreet, to reach as broad a public audience as possible. And even if a few of the signs—such as "You're Going to Hell" and "God Hates You"—were viewed as containing messages related to Matthew Snyder or the Snyders specifically, that would not change the fact that the overall thrust and dominant theme of Westboro's demonstration spoke to broader public issues.

Apart from the content of Westboro's signs, Snyder contends that the "context" of the speech—its connection with his son's funeral—makes the speech a matter of private rather than public concern. The fact that Westboro spoke in connection with a funeral, however, cannot by itself transform the nature of Westboro's speech. Westboro's signs, displayed on public land next to a public street, reflect the fact that the church finds much to condemn in modern society. Its speech is "fairly characterized as constituting speech on a matter of public concern," Connick, 461 U. S., at 146, and the funeral setting does not alter that conclusion.

Snyder argues that the church members in fact mounted a personal attack on Snyder and his family, and then attempted to "immunize their conduct by claiming that they were actually protesting the United States' tolerance of homosexuality or the supposed evils of the Catholic Church." Reply Brief for Petitioner 10. We are not concerned in this case that Westboro's speech on public matters was in any way contrived to insulate speech on a private matter from liability. Westboro had been actively engaged in speaking on the subjects addressed in its picketing long before it became aware of Matthew Snyder, and there can be no serious claim that Westboro's picketing did not represent its "honestly believed" views on public issues. Garrison, 379 U. S., at 73. There was no pre-existing relationship or conflict between Westboro and Snyder that might suggest Westboro's speech on public matters was intended to mask an attack on Snyder over a private matter. Contrast Connick, supra, at 153 (finding public employee speech a matter of private concern when it was "no coincidence that [the speech] followed upon the heels of [a] transfer notice" affecting the employee).

Snyder goes on to argue that Westboro's speech should be afforded less than full First Amendment protection "not only because of the words" but also because the church members exploited the funeral "as a platform to bring their message to a broader audience." Brief for Petitioner 44, 40. There is no doubt that Westboro chose to stage its picketing at the Naval Academy, the Maryland State House, and Matthew Snyder's funeral to increase publicity for its views and because of the relation between those sites and its views—in the case of the military funeral, because Westboro believes that God is killing American soldiers as punishment for the Nation's sinful policies.

Westboro's choice to convey its views in conjunction with Matthew Snyder's funeral made the expression of those views particularly hurtful to many, especially to Matthew's father. The record makes clear that the applicable legal term—"emotional distress"—fails to capture fully the anguish Westboro's choice added to Mr. Snyder's already incalculable grief. But Westboro conducted its picketing peacefully on matters of public concern at a public place adjacent to a public street. Such space occupies a "special position in terms of First Amendment protection." United States v. Grace, 461 U. S. 171, 180 (1983). "[W]e have repeatedly referred to public streets as the archetype of a traditional public forum," noting that " '[t]ime out of mind' public streets and sidewalks have been used for public assembly and debate." Frisby v. Schultz, 487 U. S. 474, 480 (1988). 4

That said, "[e]ven protected speech is not equally permissible in all places and at all times." Id., at 479 (quoting Cornelius v. NAACP Legal Defense & Ed. Fund, Inc., 473 U. S. 788, 799 (1985)). Westboro's choice of where and when to conduct its picketing is not beyond the Government's regulatory reach—it is "subject to reasonable time, place, or manner restrictions" that are consistent with the standards announced in this Court's precedents. Clark v. Community for Creative Non-Violence, 468 U. S. 288, 293 (1984). Maryland now has a law imposing restrictions on funeral picketing, Md. Crim. Law Code

Ann. §10–205 (Lexis Supp. 2010), as do 43 other States and the Federal Government. See Brief for American Legion as Amicus Curiae 18–19, n. 2 (listing statutes). To the extent these laws are content neutral, they raise very different questions from the tort verdict at issue in this case. Maryland's law, however, was not in effect at the time of the events at issue here, so we have no occasion to consider how it might apply to facts such as those before us, or whether it or other similar regulations are constitutional. 5

We have identified a few limited situations where the location of targeted picketing can be regulated under provisions that the Court has determined to be content neutral. In Frisby, for example, we upheld a ban on such picketing "before or about" a particular residence, 487 U. S., at 477. In Madsen v. Women's Health Center, Inc., we approved an injunction requiring a buffer zone between protesters and an abortion clinic entrance. 512 U. S. 753, 768 (1994). The facts here are obviously quite different, both with respect to the activity being regulated and the means of restricting those activities.

Simply put, the church members had the right to be where they were. Westboro alerted local authorities to its funeral protest and fully complied with police guidance on where the picketing could be staged. The picketing was conducted under police supervision some 1,000 feet from the church, out of the sight of those at the church. The protest was not unruly; there was no shouting, profanity, or violence.

The record confirms that any distress occasioned by Westboro's picketing turned on the content and viewpoint of the message conveyed, rather than any interference with the funeral itself. A group of parishioners standing at the very spot where Westboro stood, holding signs that said "God Bless America" and "God Loves You," would not have been subjected to liability. It was what Westboro said that exposed it to tort damages.

Given that Westboro's speech was at a public place on a matter of public concern, that speech is entitled to "special protection" under the First Amendment . Such speech cannot be restricted simply because it is upsetting or arouses contempt. "If there is a bedrock principle underlying the First Amendment, it is that the government may not prohibit the expression of an idea simply because society finds the idea itself offensive or disagreeable." Texas v. Johnson, 491 U. S. 397, 414 (1989). Indeed, "the point of all speech protection ... is to shield just those choices of content that in someone's eyes are misguided, or even hurtful." Hurley v. Irish-American Gay, Lesbian and Bisexual Group of Boston, Inc., 515 U. S. 557, 574 (1995).

The jury here was instructed that it could hold Westboro liable for intentional infliction of emotional distress based on a finding that Westboro's picketing was "outrageous." "Outrageousness," however, is a highly malleable standard with "an inherent subjectiveness about it which would allow a jury to impose liability on the basis of the jurors' tastes or views, or perhaps on the basis of their dislike of a particular expression." Hustler, 485 U. S., at 55 (internal quotation marks omitted). In a case such as this, a jury is "unlikely to be neutral with respect to the content of [the] speech," posing "a real danger of becoming an instrument for the suppression of ... 'vehement, caustic, and sometimes unpleasan[t]' " expression. Bose Corp., 466 U. S., at 510 (quoting New York Times, 376 U. S., at 270). Such a risk is unacceptable; "in public debate [we] must tolerate insulting, and even outrageous, speech in order to provide adequate 'breathing space' to the freedoms protected by the First Amendment ." Boos v. Barry, 485 U. S. 312, 322 (1988) (some internal quotation marks omitted). What Westboro said, in the whole context of how and where it chose to say it, is entitled to "special protection" under the First Amendment, and that protection cannot be overcome by a jury finding that the picketing was outrageous.

For all these reasons, the jury verdict imposing tort liability on Westboro for intentional infliction of emotional distress must be set aside.

III

The jury also found Westboro liable for the state law torts of intrusion upon seclusion and civil conspiracy. The Court of Appeals did not examine these torts independently of the intentional infliction of emotional distress tort. Instead, the Court of Appeals reversed the District Court wholesale, holding that the judgment wrongly "attache[d] tort liability to constitutionally protected speech." 580 F. 3d, at 226.

Snyder argues that even assuming Westboro's speech is entitled to First Amendment protection generally, the church is not immunized from liability for intrusion upon seclusion because Snyder was a member of a captive audience at his son's funeral. Brief for Petitioner 45–46. We do not agree. In most circumstances, "the Constitution does not permit the government to decide which types of otherwise protected speech are sufficiently offensive to require protection for the unwilling listener or viewer. Rather, ... the burden normally falls upon the viewer to avoid further bombardment of [his] sensibilities simply by averting [his] eyes." Erznoznik v. Jacksonville, 422 U. S. 205, 210–211 (1975) (internal quotation marks omitted). As a result, "[t]he ability of government, consonant with the Constitution, to shut off discourse solely to protect others from hearing it is ... dependent upon a showing that substantial privacy interests are being invaded in an essentially intolerable manner." Cohen v. California, 403 U. S. 15, 21 (1971).

As a general matter, we have applied the captive audience doctrine only sparingly to protect unwilling listeners from protected speech. For example, we have upheld a statute allowing a homeowner to restrict the delivery of offensive mail to his home, see Rowan v. Post Office Dept., 397 U. S. 728, 736–738 (1970), and an ordinance prohibiting picketing "before or about" any individual's residence, Frisby, 487 U. S., at 484–485.

Here, Westboro stayed well away from the memorial service. Snyder could see no more than the tops of the signs when driving to the funeral. And there is no indication that the picketing in any way interfered with the funeral service itself. We decline to expand the captive audience doctrine to the circumstances presented here.

Because we find that the First Amendment bars Snyder from recovery for intentional infliction of emotional distress or intrusion upon seclusion—the alleged unlawful activity Westboro conspired to accomplish—we must likewise hold that Snyder cannot recover for civil conspiracy based on those torts.

IV

Our holding today is narrow. We are required in First Amendment cases to carefully review the record, and the reach of our opinion here is limited by the particular facts before us. As we have noted, "the sensitivity and significance of the interests presented in clashes between First Amendment and [state law] rights counsel relying on limited principles that sweep no more broadly than the appropriate context of the instant case." Florida Star v. B. J. F., 491 U. S. 524, 533 (1989).

Westboro believes that America is morally flawed; many Americans might feel the same about Westboro. Westboro's funeral picketing is certainly hurtful and its con-tribution to public discourse may be negligible. But Westboro addressed matters of public import on public property, in a peaceful manner, in full compliance with the guidance of local officials. The speech was indeed planned to coincide with Matthew Snyder's funeral, but did not itself disrupt that funeral, and Westboro's choice to conduct its picketing at that time and place did not alter the nature of its speech.

Speech is powerful. It can stir people to action, move them to tears of both joy and sorrow, and—as it did here—inflict great pain. On the facts before us, we cannot react to that pain by punishing the speaker. As a Nation we have chosen a different course—to protect even hurtful speech on public issues to ensure that we do not stifle public debate. That choice requires that we shield Westboro from tort liability for its picketing in this case.

The judgment of the United States Court of Appeals for the Fourth Circuit is affirmed.

It is so ordered.


Notes

1 A few weeks after the funeral, one of the picketers posted a message on Westboro's Web site discussing the picketing and containing religiously oriented denunciations of the Snyders, interspersed among lengthy Bible quotations. Snyder discovered the posting, referred to by the parties as the "epic," during an Internet search for his son's name. The epic is not properly before us and does not factor in our analysis. Although the epic was submitted to the jury and discussed in the courts below, Snyder never mentioned it in his petition for certiorari. See Pet. for Cert. i ("Snyder's claim arose out of Phelps' intentional acts at Snyder's son's funeral" (emphasis added)); this Court's Rule 14.1(g) (petition must contain statement "setting out the facts material to consideration of the question presented"). Nor did Snyder respond to the statement in the opposition to certiorari that "[t]hough the epic was asserted as a basis for the claims at trial, the petition ... appears to be addressing only claims based on the picketing." Brief in Opposition 9. Snyder devoted only one paragraph in the argument section of his opening merits brief to the epic. Given the foregoing and the fact that an Internet posting may raise distinct issues in this context, we decline to consider the epic in deciding this case.

See Ontario v. Quon, 560 U. S. ___, ___ – ___ (2010) (slip op., at 10–12).

2 One judge concurred in the judgment on the ground that Snyder had failed to introduce sufficient evidence at trial to support a jury verdict on any of his tort claims. 580 F. 3d, at 227 (opinion of Shedd, J.). The Court of Appeals majority determined that the picketers had "voluntarily waived" any such contention on appeal. Id., at 216. Like the court below, we proceed on the unexamined premise that respondents' speech was tortious.

3 The dissent attempts to draw parallels between this case and hypothetical cases involving defamation or fighting words. Post, at 10–11 (opinion of Alito, J.). But, as the court below noted, there is "no suggestion that the speech at issue falls within one of the categorical exclusions from First Amendment protection, such as those for obscenity or 'fighting words.'" 580 F. 3d, at 218, n. 12; see United States v. Stevens, 559 U. S. ___, ___ (2010) (slip op., at 5).

4 The dissent is wrong to suggest that the Court considers a public street "a free-fire zone in which otherwise actionable verbal attacks are shielded from liability." Post, at 10–11. The fact that Westboro conducted its picketing adjacent to a public street does not insulate the speech from liability, but instead heightens concerns that what is at issue is an effort to communicate to the public the church's views on matters of public concern. That is why our precedents so clearly recognize the special significance of this traditional public forum.

5 The Maryland law prohibits picketing within 100 feet of a funeral service or funeral procession; Westboro's picketing would have complied with that restriction.

## Brown v. Entertainment Merchants Association (June 27, 2011)

Justice Scalia delivered the opinion of the Court.

We consider whether a California law imposing restrictions on violent video games comports with the First Amendment.

I

California Assembly Bill 1179 (2005), Cal. Civ. Code Ann. §§1746–1746.5 (West 2009) (Act), prohibits the sale or rental of "violent video games" to minors, and requires their packaging to be labeled "18." The Act covers games "in which the range of options available to a player includes killing, maiming, dismembering, or sexually assaulting an image of a human being, if those acts are depicted" in a manner that "[a] reasonable person, considering the game as a whole, would find appeals to a deviant or morbid interest of minors," that is "patently offensive to prevailing standards in the community as to what is suitable for minors," and that "causes the game, as a whole, to lack serious literary, artistic, political, or scientific value for minors." §1746(d)(1)(A). Violation of the Act is punishable by a civil fine of up to $1,000. §1746.3.

Respondents, representing the video-game and software industries, brought a preenforcement challenge to the Act in the United States District Court for the Northern

District of California. That court concluded that the Act violated the First Amendment and permanently enjoined its enforcement. Video Software Dealers Assn. v. Schwarzenegger, No. C–05–04188 RMW (2007), App. to Pet. for Cert. 39a. The Court of Appeals affirmed, Video Software Dealers Assn. v. Schwarzenegger, 556 F. 3d 950 (CA9 2009), and we granted certiorari, 559 U. S. _____ (2010).

> II

California correctly acknowledges that video games qualify for First Amendment protection. The Free Speech Clause exists principally to protect discourse on public matters, but we have long recognized that it is difficult to distinguish politics from entertainment, and dangerous to try. "Everyone is familiar with instances of propaganda through fiction. What is one man's amusement, teaches another's doctrine." Winters v. New York, 333 U. S. 507, 510 (1948). Like the protected books, plays, and movies that preceded them, video games communicate ideas—and even social messages—through many familiar literary devices (such as characters, dialogue, plot, and music) and through features distinctive to the medium (such as the player's interaction with the virtual world). That suffices to confer First Amendment protection. Under our Constitution, "esthetic and moral judgments about art and literature ... are for the individual to make, not for the Government to decree, even with the mandate or approval of a majority." United States v. Playboy Entertainment Group, Inc., 529 U. S. 803, 818 (2000). And whatever the challenges of applying the Constitution to ever-advancing technology, "the basic principles of freedom of speech and the press, like the First Amendment 's command, do not vary" when a new and different medium for communication appears. Joseph Burstyn, Inc. v. Wilson, 343 U. S. 495, 503 (1952).

The most basic of those principles is this: "[A]s a general matter, ... government has no power to restrict expression because of its message, its ideas, its subject matter, or its content." Ashcroft v. American Civil Liberties Union, 535 U. S. 564, 573 (2002) (internal quotation marks omitted). There are of course exceptions. " 'From 1791 to the present,' ... the First Amendment has 'permitted restrictions upon the content of speech in a few limited areas,' and has never 'include[d] a freedom to disregard these traditional limitations.' " United States v. Stevens, 559 U. S. ___, ___ (2010) (slip op., at 5) (quoting R. A. V. v. St. Paul, 505 U. S. 377, 382–383 (1992)). These limited areas—such as obscenity, Roth v. United States, 354 U. S. 476, 483 (1957), incitement, Brandenburg v. Ohio, 395 U. S. 444, 447–449 (1969) (per curiam), and fighting words, Chaplinsky v. New Hampshire, 315 U. S. 568, 572 (1942)—represent "well-defined and narrowly limited classes of speech, the prevention and punishment of which have never been thought to raise any Constitutional problem," id., at 571–572.

Last Term, in Stevens, we held that new categories of unprotected speech may not be added to the list by a legislature that concludes certain speech is too harmful to be tolerated. Stevens concerned a federal statute purporting to criminalize the creation, sale, or possession of certain depictions of animal cruelty. See 18 U. S. C. §48 (amended 2010). The statute covered depictions "in which a living animal is intentionally maimed, mutilated, tortured, wounded, or killed" if that harm to the animal was illegal where the "the creation, sale, or possession t[ook] place," §48(c)(1). A saving clause largely borrowed from our obscenity jurisprudence, see Miller v. California, 413 U. S. 15, 24 (1973), exempted depictions with "serious religious, political, scientific, educational, journalistic, historical, or artistic value," §48(b). We held that statute to be an impermissible content-based restriction on speech. There was no American tradition of forbidding the depiction of animal cruelty—though States have long had laws against committing it.

The Government argued in Stevens that lack of a historical warrant did not matter; that it could create new categories of unprotected speech by applying a "simple balancing test" that weighs the value of a particular category of speech against its social costs and then punishes that category of speech if it fails the test. Stevens, 559 U. S., at ____ (slip op., at 7). We emphatically rejected that "startling and dangerous" proposition. Ibid. "Maybe there are some categories of speech that have been historically unprotected, but have not yet been specifically identified or discussed as such in our case law." Id., at ____ (slip op., at 9). But without persuasive evidence that a novel restriction on content is part of a long (if heretofore unrecognized) tradition of proscription, a legislature may not revise the "judgment [of] the American people," embodied in the First Amendment, "that the benefits of its restrictions on the Government outweigh the costs." Id., at ____ (slip op., at 7).

That holding controls this case. 1 As in Stevens, California has tried to make violent-speech regulation look like obscenity regulation by appending a saving clause required for the latter. That does not suffice. Our cases have been clear that the obscenity exception to the First Amendment does not cover whatever a legislature finds shocking, but only depictions of "sexual conduct," Miller, supra, at 24. See also Cohen v. California, 403 U. S. 15, 20 (1971); Roth, supra, at 487, and n. 20.

Stevens was not the first time we have encountered and rejected a State's attempt to shoehorn speech about violence into obscenity. In Winters, we considered a New York criminal statute "forbid[ding] the massing of stories of bloodshed and lust in such a way as to incite to crime against the person," 333 U. S., at 514. The New York Court of Appeals upheld the provision as a law against obscenity. "[T]here can be no more precise test of written indecency or obscenity," it said, "than the continuing and changeable experience of the community as to what types of books are likely to bring about the corruption of public morals or other analogous injury to the public order. " Id., at 514 (internal quotation marks omitted). That is of course the same expansive view of governmental power to abridge the freedom of speech based on interest-balancing that we rejected in Stevens . Our opinion in Winters, which concluded that the New York statute failed a heightened vagueness standard applicable to restrictions upon speech entitled to First Amendment protection, 333 U. S., at 517–519, made clear that violence is not part of the obscenity that the Constitution permits to be regulated. The speech reached by the statute contained "no indecency or obscenity in any sense heretofore known to the law." Id., at 519.

Because speech about violence is not obscene, it is of no consequence that California's statute mimics the New York statute regulating obscenity-for-minors that we upheld in Ginsberg v. New York, 390 U. S. 629 (1968). That case approved a prohibition on the sale to minors of sexual material that would be obscene from the perspective of a child. 2 We held that the legislature could "adjus[t] the definition of obscenity 'to social realities by permitting the appeal of this type of material to be assessed in terms of the sexual interests ...' of ... minors. " Id., at 638 (quoting Mishkin v. New York, 383 U. S. 502, 509 (1966)). And because "obscenity is not protected expression," the New York statute could be sustained so long as the legislature's judgment that the proscribed materials were harmful to children "was not irrational." 390 U. S., at 641.

The California Act is something else entirely. It does not adjust the boundaries of an existing category of unprotected speech to ensure that a definition designed for adults is not uncritically applied to children. California does not argue that it is empowered to prohibit selling offensively violent works to adults —and it is wise not to, since that is but a hair's breadth from the argument rejected in Stevens . Instead, it wishes to create a wholly new category of content-based regulation that is permissible only for speech directed at children.

That is unprecedented and mistaken. "[M]inors are entitled to a significant measure of First Amendment protection, and only in relatively narrow and well-defined circumstances may government bar public dissemination of protected materials to them." Erznoznik v. Jacksonville, 422 U. S. 205, 212–213 (1975) (citation omitted). No doubt a State possesses legitimate power to protect children from harm, Ginsberg, supra, at 640–641; Prince v. Massachusetts, 321 U. S. 158, 165 (1944), but that does not include a free-floating power to restrict the ideas to which children may be exposed. "Speech that is neither obscene as to youths nor subject to some other legitimate proscription cannot be suppressed solely to protect the young from ideas or images that a legislative body thinks unsuitable for them." Erznoznik, supra, at 213–214. 3

California's argument would fare better if there were a longstanding tradition in this country of specially restricting children's access to depictions of violence, but there is none. Certainly the books we give children to read—or read to them when they are younger—contain no shortage of gore. Grimm's Fairy Tales, for example, are grim indeed. As her just deserts for trying to poison Snow White, the wicked queen is made to dance in red hot slippers "till she fell dead on the floor, a sad example of envy and jealousy." The Complete Brothers Grimm Fairy Tales 198 (2006 ed.). Cinderella's evil stepsisters have their eyes pecked out by doves. Id., at 95. And Hansel and Gretel (children!) kill their captor by baking her in an oven. Id., at 54.

High-school reading lists are full of similar fare. Homer's Odysseus blinds Polyphemus the Cyclops by grinding out his eye with a heated stake. The Odyssey of Homer, Book IX, p. 125 (S. Butcher & A. Lang transls. 1909) ("Even so did we seize the fiery-pointed brand and whirled it round in his eye, and the blood flowed about the heated bar. And the breath of the flame singed his eyelids and brows all about, as the ball of the eye burnt away, and the roots thereof crackled in the flame"). In the Inferno, Dante and Virgil watch corrupt politicians struggle to stay submerged beneath a lake of boiling pitch, lest they be skewered by devils above the surface. Canto XXI, pp. 187–189 (A. Mandelbaum transl. Bantam Classic ed. 1982). And Golding's Lord of the Flies recounts how a schoolboy called Piggy is savagely murdered by other children while marooned on an island. W. Golding, Lord of the Flies 208–209 (1997 ed.). 4

      This is not to say that minors' consumption of violent entertainment has never encountered resistance. In the 1800's, dime novels depicting crime and "penny dreadfuls" (named for their price and content) were blamed in some quarters for juvenile delinquency. See Brief for Cato Institute as Amicus Curiae 6–7. When motion pictures came along, they became the villains instead. "The days when the police looked upon dime novels as the most dangerous of textbooks in the school for crime are drawing to a close... . They say that the moving picture machine ... tends even more than did the dime novel to turn the thoughts of the easily influenced to paths which sometimes lead to prison." Moving Pictures as Helps to Crime, N. Y. Times, Feb. 21, 1909, quoted in Brief for Cato Institute, at 8. For a time, our Court did permit broad censorship of movies because of their capacity to be "used for evil," see Mutual Film Corp. v. Industrial Comm'n of Ohio, 236 U. S. 230, 242 (1915), but we eventually reversed course, Joseph Burstyn, Inc., 343 U. S., at 502; see also Erznoznik, supra, at 212–214 (invalidating a drive-in movies restriction designed to protect children). Radio dramas were next, and then came comic books. Brief for Cato Institute, at 10–11. Many in the late 1940's and early 1950's blamed comic books for fostering a "preoccupation with violence and horror" among the young, leading to a rising juvenile crime rate. See Note, Regulation of Comic Books, 68 Harv.L.Rev. 489, 490 (1955). But efforts to convince Congress to restrict comic books failed. Brief for Comic Book Legal Defense Fund as Amicus Curiae 11–15. 5 And, of course, after comic books came television and music lyrics.

      California claims that video games present special problems because they are "interactive," in that the player participates in the violent action on screen and determines its outcome. The latter feature is nothing new: Since at least the publication of The Adventures of You: Sugarcane Island in 1969, young readers of choose-your-own-adventure stories have been able to make decisions that determine the plot by following instructions about which page to turn to. Cf. Interactive Digital Software Assn. v. St. Louis County, 329 F. 3d 954, 957–958 (CA8 2003). As for the argument that video games enable participation in the violent action, that seems to us more a matter of degree than of kind. As Judge Posner has observed, all literature is interactive. "[T]he better it is, the more interactive. Literature when it is successful draws the reader into the story, makes him identify with the characters, invites him to judge them and quarrel with them, to experience their joys and sufferings as the reader's own." American Amusement Machine Assn. v. Kendrick, 244 F. 3d 572, 577 (CA7 2001) (striking down a similar restriction on violent video games).

Justice Alito has done considerable independent re-search to identify, see post, at 14–15, nn. 13–18, video games in which "the violence is astounding," post, at 14. "Victims are dismembered, decapitated, disemboweled, set on fire, and chopped into little pieces. . . . Blood gushes, splatters, and pools." Ibid. Justice Alito recounts all these disgusting video games in order to disgust us—but disgust is not a valid basis for restricting expression. And the same is true of Justice Alito 's description, post, at 14–15, of those video games he has discovered that have a racial or ethnic motive for their violence—" 'ethnic cleansing' [of] . . . African Americans, Latinos, or Jews." To what end does he relate this? Does it somehow increase the "aggressiveness" that California wishes to suppress? Who knows? But it does arouse the reader's ire, and the reader's desire to put an end to this horrible message. Thus, ironically, Justice Alito 's argument highlights the precise danger posed by the California Act: that the ideas expressed by speech—whether it be violence, or gore, or racism—and not its objective effects, may be the real reason for governmental proscription.

III

Because the Act imposes a restriction on the content of protected speech, it is invalid unless California can demonstrate that it passes strict scrutiny—that is, unless it is justified by a compelling government interest and is narrowly drawn to serve that interest. R. A. V., 505 U. S., at 395. The State must specifically identify an "actual problem" in need of solving, Playboy, 529 U. S., at 822–823, and the curtailment of free speech must be actually necessary to the solution, see R. A. V., supra, at 395. That is a demanding standard. "It is rare that a regulation restricting speech because of its content will ever be permissible." Playboy, supra, at 818.

California cannot meet that standard. At the outset, it acknowledges that it cannot show a direct causal link between violent video games and harm to minors. Rather, relying upon our decision in Turner Broadcasting System, Inc. v. FCC, 512 U. S. 622 (1994), the State claims that it need not produce such proof because the legislature can make a predictive judgment that such a link exists, based on competing psychological studies. But reliance on Turner Broadcasting is misplaced. That decision applied intermediate scrutiny to a content-neutral regulation. Id., at 661–662. California's burden is much higher, and because it bears the risk of uncertainty, see Playboy, supra, at 816–817, ambiguous proof will not suffice.

The State's evidence is not compelling. California relies primarily on the research of Dr. Craig Anderson and a few other research psychologists whose studies purport to show a connection between exposure to violent video games and harmful effects on children. These studies have been rejected by every court to consider them, 6 and with good reason: They do not prove that violent video games cause minors to act aggressively (which would at least be a beginning). Instead, "[n]early all of the research is based on correlation, not evidence of causation, and most of the studies suffer from significant, admitted flaws in methodology." Video Software Dealers Assn. 556 F. 3d, at 964. They show at best some correlation between exposure to violent entertainment and minuscule real-world effects, such as children's feeling more aggressive or making louder noises in the few minutes after playing a violent game than after playing a nonviolent game. 7

Even taking for granted Dr. Anderson's conclusions that violent video games produce some effect on children's feelings of aggression, those effects are both small and indistinguishable from effects produced by other media. In his testimony in a similar lawsuit, Dr. Anderson admitted that the "effect sizes" of children's exposure to violent video games are "about the same" as that produced by their exposure to violence on television. App. 1263. And he admits that the same effects have been found when children watch cartoons starring Bugs Bunny or the Road Runner, id., at 1304, or when they play video games like Sonic the Hedgehog that are rated "E" (appropriate for all ages), id., at 1270, or even when they "vie[w] a picture of a gun," id., at 1315–1316. 8

Of course, California has (wisely) declined to restrict Saturday morning cartoons, the sale of games rated for young children, or the distribution of pictures of guns. The consequence is that its regulation is wildly underinclusive when judged against its asserted justification, which in our view is alone enough to defeat it. Underinclusiveness raises serious doubts about whether the government is in fact pursuing the interest it invokes, rather than disfavoring a particular speaker or viewpoint. See City of Ladue v. Gilleo, 512 U. S. 43, 51 (1994); Florida Star v. B. J. F., 491 U. S. 524, 540 (1989). Here, California has singled out the purveyors of video games for disfavored treatment—at least when compared to booksellers, cartoonists, and movie producers— and has given no persuasive reason why.

The Act is also seriously underinclusive in another respect—and a respect that renders irrelevant the contentions of the concurrence and the dissents that video games are qualitatively different from other portrayals of violence. The California Legislature is perfectly willing to leave this dangerous, mind-altering material in the hands of children so long as one parent (or even an aunt or uncle) says it's OK. And there are not even any requirements as to how this parental or avuncular relationship is to be verified; apparently the child's or putative parent's, aunt's, or uncle's say-so suffices. That is not how one addresses a serious social problem.

California claims that the Act is justified in aid of parental authority: By requiring that the purchase of violent video games can be made only by adults, the Act ensures that parents can decide what games are appropriate. At the outset, we note our doubts that punishing third parties for conveying protected speech to children just in case their parents disapprove of that speech is a proper governmental means of aiding parental authority. Accepting that position would largely vitiate the rule that "only in relatively narrow and well-defined circumstances may government bar public dissemination of protected materials to [minors]." Erznoznik, 422 U. S., at 212–213.

But leaving that aside, California cannot show that the Act's restrictions meet a substantial need of parents who wish to restrict their children's access to violent video games but cannot do so. The video-game industry has in place a voluntary rating system designed to inform consumers about the content of games. The system, implemented by the Entertainment Software Rating Board (ESRB), assigns age-specific ratings to each video game submitted: EC (Early Childhood); E (Everyone); E10+ (Everyone 10 and older); T (Teens); M (17 and older); and AO (Adults Only—18 and older). App. 86. The Video Software Dealers Association encourages retailers to prominently display information about the ESRB system in their stores; to refrain from renting or selling adults-only games to minors; and to rent or sell "M" rated games to minors only with parental consent. Id., at 47. In 2009, the Federal Trade Commission (FTC) found that, as a result of this system, "the video game industry outpaces the movie and music industries" in "(1) restricting target-marketing of mature-rated products to children; (2) clearly and prominently disclosing rating information; and (3) re-stricting children's access to mature-rated products at retail." FTC, Report to Congress, Marketing Violent Entertainment to Children 30 (Dec. 2009), online at http:// www.ftc.gov / os/ 2009 / 12/ P994511violententertainment.pdf (as visited June 24, 2011, and available in Clerk of Court's case file) (FTC Report). This system does much to ensure that minors cannot purchase seriously violent games on their own, and that parents who care about the matter can readily evaluate the games their children bring home. Filling the remaining modest gap in concerned-parents' control can hardly be a compelling state interest. 9

And finally, the Act's purported aid to parental authority is vastly overinclusive. Not all of the children who are forbidden to purchase violent video games on their own have parents who care whether they purchase violent video games. While some of the legislation's effect may indeed be in support of what some parents of the restricted children actually want, its entire effect is only in support of what the State thinks parents ought to want. This is not the narrow tailoring to "assisting parents" that restriction of First Amendment rights requires.

     \*     \*     \*

California's effort to regulate violent video games is the latest episode in a long series of failed attempts to censor violent entertainment for minors. While we have pointed out above that some of the evidence brought forward to support the harmfulness of video games is unpersuasive, we do not mean to demean or disparage the concerns that underlie the attempt to regulate them—concerns that may and doubtless do prompt a good deal of parental oversight. We have no business passing judgment on the view of the California Legislature that violent video games (or, for that matter, any other forms of speech) corrupt the young or harm their moral development. Our task is only to say whether or not such works constitute a "well-defined and narrowly limited clas[s] of speech, the prevention and punishment of which have never been thought to raise any Constitutional problem," Chaplinsky, 315 U. S., at 571–572 (the answer plainly is no); and if not, whether the regulation of such works is justified by that high degree of necessity we have described as a compelling state interest (it is not). Even where the protection of children is the object, the constitutional limits on governmental action apply.

California's legislation straddles the fence between (1) addressing a serious social problem and (2) helping concerned parents control their children. Both ends are legitimate, but when they affect First Amendment rights they must be pursued by means that are neither seriously underinclusive nor seriously overinclusive. See Church of Lukumi Babalu Aye, Inc. v. Hialeah, 508 U. S. 520, 546 (1993). As a means of protecting children from portrayals of violence, the legislation is seriously underinclusive, not only because it excludes portrayals other than video games, but also because it permits a parental or avuncular veto. And as a means of assisting concerned parents it is seriously overinclusive because it abridges the First Amendment rights of young people whose parents (and aunts and uncles) think violent video games are a harmless pastime. And the overbreadth in achieving one goal is not cured by the underbreadth in achieving the other. Legislation such as this, which is neither fish nor fowl, cannot survive strict scrutiny.

We affirm the judgment below.

It is so ordered.

Notes

1 Justice Alito distinguishes Stevens on several grounds that seem to us ill founded. He suggests, post, at 10 (opinion concurring in judgment), that Stevens did not apply strict scrutiny. If that is so (and we doubt it), it would make this an a fortiori case. He says, post, at 9, 10, that the California Act punishes the sale or rental rather than the "creation" or "possession" of violent depictions. That distinction appears nowhere in Stevens itself, and for good reason: It would make permissible the prohibition of printing or selling books—though not the writing of them. Whether government regulation applies to creating, distributing, or consuming speech makes no difference. And finally, Justice Alito points out, post, at 10, that Stevens "left open the possibility that a more narrowly drawn statute" would be constitutional. True, but entirely irrelevant. Stevens said, 559 U. S., at ___ (slip op., at 19), that the "crush-video" statute at issue there might pass muster if it were limited to videos of acts of animal cruelty that violated the law where the acts were performed. There is no contention that any of the virtual characters depicted in the imaginative videos at issue here are criminally liable.

2 The statute in Ginsberg restricted the sale of certain depictions of "nudity, sexual conduct, sexual excitement, or sado-masochistic abuse," that were " '[h]armful to minors.' " A depiction was harmful to minors if it: "(i) predominantly appeals to the prurient, shameful or morbid interests of minors, and "(ii) is patently offensive to prevailing standards in the adult community as a whole with respect to what is suitable material for minors, and "(iii) is utterly without redeeming social importance for minors." 390 U. S., at 646 (Appendix A to opinion of the Court) (quoting N. Y. Penal Law §484–h(1)(f)).

3 Justice Thomas ignores the holding of Erznoznik, and denies that persons under 18 have any constitutional right to speak or be spoken to without their parents' consent. He cites no case, state or federal, supporting this view, and to our knowledge

there is none. Most of his dissent is devoted to the proposition that parents have traditionally had the power to control what their children hear and say. This is true enough. And it perhaps follows from this that the state has the power to enforce parental prohibitions—to require, for example, that the promoters of a rock concert exclude those minors whose parents have advised the promoters that their children are forbidden to attend. But it does not follow that the state has the power to prevent children from hearing or saying anything without their parents' prior consent. The latter would mean, for example, that it could be made criminal to admit persons under 18 to a political rally without their parents' prior written consent—even a political rally in support of laws against corporal punishment of children, or laws in favor of greater rights for minors. And what is good for First Amendment rights of speech must be good for First Amendment rights of religion as well: It could be made criminal to admit a person under 18 to church, or to give a person under 18 a religious tract, without his parents' prior consent. Our point is not, as Justice Thomas believes, post, at 16, n. 2, merely that such laws are "undesirable." They are obviously an infringement upon the religious freedom of young people and those who wish to proselytize young people. Such laws do not enforce parental authority over children's speech and religion; they impose governmental authority, subject only to a parental veto. In the absence of any precedent for state control, uninvited by the parents, over a child's speech and religion (Justice Thomas cites none), and in the absence of any justification for such control that would satisfy strict scrutiny, those laws must be unconstitutional. This argument is not, as Justice Thomas asserts, "circular," ibid. It is the absence of any historical warrant or compelling justification for such restrictions, not our ipse dixit, that renders them invalid.

4 Justice Alito accuses us of pronouncing that playing violent video games "is not different in 'kind' " from reading violent literature. Post, at 2. Well of course it is different in kind, but not in a way that causes the provision and viewing of violent video games, unlike the provision and reading of books, not to be expressive activity and hence not to enjoy First Amendment protection. Reading Dante is unquestionably more cultured and intellectually edifying than playing Mortal Kombat. But these cultural and intellectual differences are not constitutional ones. Crudely violent video games, tawdry TV shows, and cheap novels and magazines are no less forms of speech than The Divine Comedy, and restrictions upon them must survive strict scrutiny—a question to which we devote our attention in Part III, infra. Even if we can see in them "nothing of any possible value to society . . ., they are as much entitled to the protection of free speech as the best of literature." Winters v. New York, 333 U. S. 507, 510 (1948).

5 The crusade against comic books was led by a psychiatrist, Frederic Wertham, who told the Senate Judiciary Committee that "as long as the crime comic books industry exists in its present forms there are no secure homes." Juvenile Delinquency (Comic Books): Hearings before the Subcommittee to Investigate Juvenile Delinquency, 83d Cong., 2d Sess., 84 (1954). Wertham's objections extended even to Superman comics, which he described as "particularly injurious to the ethical development of children." Id.,

at 86. Wertham's crusade did convince the New York Legislature to pass a ban on the sale of certain comic books to minors, but it was vetoed by Governor Thomas Dewey on the ground that it was unconstitutional given our opinion in Winters, supra. See People v. Bookcase, Inc., 14 N. Y. 2d 409, 412–413, 201 N. E. 2d 14, 15–16 (1964).

6 See Video Software Dealers Assn. v. Schwarzenegger, 556 F. 3d 950, 963–964 (CA9 2009); Interactive Digital Software Assn. v. St. Louis County, 329 F. 3d 954 (CA8 2003); American Amusement Machine Assn. v. Kendrick, 244 F. 3d 572, 578–579 (CA7 2001); Entertainment Software Assn. v. Foti, 451 F. Supp. 2d 823, 832–833 (MD La. 2006); Entertainment Software Assn. v. Hatch, 443 F. Supp. 2d 1065, 1070 (Minn. 2006), aff'd, 519 F. 3d 768 (CA8 2008); Entertainment Software Assn. v. Granholm, 426 F. Supp. 2d 646, 653 (ED Mich. 2006); Entertainment Software Assn. v. Blagojevich, 404 F. Supp. 2d 1051, 1063 (ND Ill. 2005), aff'd, 469 F. 3d 641 (CA7 2006).

7 One study, for example, found that children who had just finished playing violent video games were more likely to fill in the blank letter in "explo_e" with a "d" (so that it reads "explode") than with an "r" ("explore"). App. 496, 506 (internal quotation marks omitted). The prevention of this phenomenon, which might have been anticipated with common sense, is not a compelling state interest.

8 Justice Alito is mistaken in thinking that we fail to take account of "new and rapidly evolving technology," post, at 1. The studies in question pertain to that new and rapidly evolving technology, and fail to show, with the degree of certitude that strict scrutiny requires, that this subject-matter restriction on speech is justified. Nor is Justice Alito correct in attributing to us the view that "violent video games really present no serious problem." Post, at 2. Perhaps they do present a problem, and perhaps none of us would allow our own children to play them. But there are all sorts of "problems"—some of them surely more serious than this one—that cannot be addressed by governmental restriction of free expression: for example, the problem of encouraging anti-Semitism (National Socialist Party of America v. Skokie, 432 U. S. 43 (1977) (per curiam)), the problem of spreading a political philosophy hostile to the Constitution (Noto v. United States, 367 U. S. 290 (1961)), or the problem of encouraging disrespect for the Nation's flag (Texas v. Johnson, 491 U. S. 397 (1989)). Justice Breyer would hold that California has satisfied strict scrutiny based upon his own research into the issue of the harmfulness of violent video games. See post, at 20–35 (Appendixes to dissenting opinion) (listing competing academic articles discussing the harmfulness vel non of violent video games). The vast preponderance of this research is outside the record—and in any event we do not see how it could lead to Justice Breyer's conclusion, since he admits he cannot say whether the studies on his side are right or wrong. Post, at 15. Similarly, Justice Alito says he is not "sure" whether there are any constitutionally dispositive differences between video games and other media. Post, at 2. If that is so, then strict scrutiny plainly has not been satisfied.

9 Justice Breyer concludes that the remaining gap is compelling because, according to the FTC's report, some "20% of those under 17 are still able to buy M-rated

games." Post, at 18 (citing FTC Report 28). But some gap in compliance is unavoidable. The sale of alcohol to minors, for example, has long been illegal, but a 2005 study suggests that about 18% of retailers still sell alcohol to those under the drinking age. Brief for State of Rhode Island et al. as Amici Curiae 18. Even if the sale of violent video games to minors could be deterred further by increasing regulation, the government does not have a compelling interest in each marginal percentage point by which its goals are advanced.

## United States v. Alvarez (June 28, 2012)

Justice Kennedy announced the judgment of the Court and delivered an opinion, in which The Chief Justice, Justice Ginsburg, and Justice Sotomayor join.

Lying was his habit. Xavier Alvarez, the respondent here, lied when he said that he played hockey for the Detroit Red Wings and that he once married a starlet from Mexico. But when he lied in announcing he held the Congressional Medal of Honor, respondent ventured onto new ground; for that lie violates a federal criminal statute, the Stolen Valor Act of 2005. 18 U. S. C. §704.

In 2007, respondent attended his first public meeting as a board member of the Three Valley Water District Board. The board is a governmental entity with headquarters in Claremont, California. He introduced himself as follows: "I'm a retired marine of 25 years. I retired in the year 2001. Back in 1987, I was awarded the Congressional Medal of Honor. I got wounded many times by the same guy." 617 F. 3d 1198, 1201–1202 (CA9 2010). None of this was true. For all the record shows, respondent's statements were but a pathetic attempt to gain respect that eluded him. The statements do not seem to have been made to secure employment or financial benefits or admission to privileges reserved for those who had earned the Medal.

Respondent was indicted under the Stolen Valor Act for lying about the Congressional Medal of Honor at the meeting. The United States District Court for the Central District of California rejected his claim that the statute is invalid under the First Amendment. Respondent pleaded guilty to one count, reserving the right to appeal on his First Amendment claim. The United States Court of Appeals for the Ninth Circuit, in a decision by a divided panel, found the Act invalid under the First Amendment and reversed the conviction. Id., at 1218. With further opinions on the issue, and over a dissent by seven judges, rehearing en banc was denied. 638 F. 3d 666 (2011). This Court granted certiorari. 565 U. S. ____ (2011).

After certiorari was granted, and in an unrelated case, the United States Court of Appeals for the Tenth Circuit, also in a decision by a divided panel, found the Act constitutional. United States v. Strandlof, 667 F. 3d 1146 (2012). So there is now a conflict in the Courts of Appeals on the question of the Act's validity.

This is the second case in two Terms requiring the Court to consider speech that can disparage, or attempt to steal, honor that belongs to those who fought for this Nation in battle. See Snyder v. Phelps, 562 U. S. ___ (2011) (hateful protests directed at the funeral of a serviceman who died in Iraq). Here the statement that the speaker held the Medal was an intended, undoubted lie.

It is right and proper that Congress, over a century ago, established an award so the Nation can hold in its highest respect and esteem those who, in the course of carrying out the "supreme and noble duty of contributing to the defense of the rights and honor of the nation," Selective Draft Law Cases, 245 U. S. 366, 390 (1918), have acted with extraordinary honor. And it should be uncontested that this is a legitimate Government objective, indeed a most valued national aspiration and purpose. This does not end the inquiry, however. Fundamental constitutional principles require that laws enacted to honor the brave must be consistent with the precepts of the Constitution for which they fought.

The Government contends the criminal prohibition isa proper means to further its purpose in creating and awarding the Medal. When content-based speech regulation is in question, however, exacting scrutiny is required. Statutes suppressing or restricting speech must be judged by the sometimes inconvenient principles of the First Amendment. By this measure, the statutory provisions under which respondent was convicted must be held invalid, and his conviction must be set aside.

I

Respondent's claim to hold the Congressional Medal of Honor was false. There is no room to argue about interpretation or shades of meaning. On this premise, respondent violated §704(b); and, because the lie concerned the Congressional Medal of Honor, he was subject to an enhanced penalty under subsection (c). Those statutory provisions are as follows:

"(b) False Claims About Receipt of Military Decorations or Medals.––Whoever falsely represents himself or herself, verbally or in writing, to have been awarded any decoration or medal authorized by Congress for the Armed Forces of the United States . . . shall be fined under this title, imprisoned not more than six months, or both.

"(c) Enhanced Penalty for Offenses Involving Congressional Medal of Honor.––

"(1) In General.––If a decoration or medal involved in an offense under subsection (a) or (b) is a Congressional Medal of Honor, in lieu of the punishment provided in that subsection, the offender shall be fined under this title, imprisoned not more than 1 year, or both."

Respondent challenges the statute as a content-based suppression of pure speech, speech not falling within any of the few categories of expression where content-based regulation is permissible. The Government defends the statute as necessary to preserve the integrity and purpose of the Medal, an integrity and purpose it contends are compromised and frustrated by the false statements the statute prohibits. It argues that false statements "have no First Amendment value in themselves," and thus "are protected only to the extent needed to avoid chilling fully protected speech." Brief for United States 18, 20. Al-though the statute covers respondent's speech, the Government argues that it leaves breathing room for protected speech, for example speech which might criticize the idea of the Medal or the importance of the military. The Government's arguments cannot suffice to save the statute.

II

"[A]s a general matter, the First Amendment means that government has no power to restrict expression because of its message, its ideas, its subject matter, or its content." Ashcroft v. American Civil Liberties Union, 535 U. S. 564, 573 (2002) (internal quotation marks omitted). As a result, the Constitution "demands that content-based restrictions on speech be presumed invalid . . . and that the Government bear the burden of showing their constitutionality." Ashcroft v. American Civil Liberties Union, 542 U. S. 656, 660 (2004).

In light of the substantial and expansive threats to free expression posed by content-based restrictions, this Court has rejected as "startling and dangerous" a "free-floating test for First Amendment coverage . . . [based on] an ad hoc balancing of relative social costs and benefits." United States v. Stevens, 559 U. S. ___, ___ (2010) (slip op., at 7). Instead, content-based restrictions on speech have been permitted, as a general matter, only when confined to the few " 'historic and traditional categories [of expression] long familiar to the bar,' " Id., at ___ (slip op., at 5) (quoting Simon & Schuster, Inc. v. Members of N. Y. State Crime Victims Bd., 502 U. S. 105, 127 (1991) (Kennedy, J., concurring in judgment)). Among these categories are advocacy intended, and likely, to incite imminent lawless action, see Brandenburg v. Ohio, 395 U. S. 444 (1969) (per curiam); obscenity, see, e.g., Miller v. California, 413 U. S. 15 (1973); defamation, see, e.g., New York Times Co. v. Sullivan, 376 U. S. 254 (1964) (providing substantial protection for speech about public figures); Gertz v. Robert Welch, Inc., 418 U. S. 323 (1974) (imposing some limits on liability for defaming a private figure); speech integral to criminal conduct, see, e.g., Giboney v. Empire Storage & Ice Co., 336 U. S. 490 (1949); so-called "fighting words," see Chaplinsky v. New Hampshire, 315 U. S. 568 (1942); child pornography, see New York v. Ferber, 458 U. S. 747 (1982); fraud, see Virginia Bd. of Pharmacy v. Virginia Citizens Consumer Council, Inc., 425 U. S. 748, 771 (1976); true threats, see Watts v. United States, 394 U. S. 705 (1969) (per curiam); and speech presenting some grave and imminent threat the government has the power to prevent, see Near v. Minnesota ex rel. Olson, 283 U. S. 697, 716 (1931), although a restriction under the last category is most difficult to sustain, see New York Times Co. v. United States, 403 U. S. 713 (1971) (per curiam). These categories have a historical foundation in the Court's free speech tradition. The vast realm of free speech and thought always protected in our tradition can still thrive, and even be furthered, by adherence to those categories and rules.

Absent from those few categories where the law allows content-based regulation of speech is any general exception to the First Amendment for false statements. This comports with the common understanding that some false statements are inevitable if there is to be an open and vigorous expression of views in public and private conversation, expression the First Amendment seeks to guarantee. See Sullivan, supra, at 271 ("Th[e] erroneous statement is inevitable in free debate").

The Government disagrees with this proposition. It cites language from some of this Court's precedents to support its contention that false statements have no value and hence no First Amendment protection. See also Brief for Eugene Volokh et al. as Amici Curiae 2–11. These isolated statements in some earlier decisions do not support the Government's submission that false statements, as a general rule, are beyond constitutional protection. That conclusion would take the quoted language far from its proper context. For instance, the Court has stated "[f]alse statements of fact are particularly valueless [because] they interfere with the truth-seeking function of the marketplace of ideas," Hustler Magazine, Inc. v. Falwell, 485 U. S. 46, 52 (1988), and that false statements "are not protected by the First Amendment in the same manner as truthful statements," Brown v. Hartlage, 456 U. S. 45–61 (1982). See also, e.g., Virginia Bd. of Pharmacy, supra, at 771 ("Untruthful speech, commercial or otherwise, has never been protected for its own sake"); Herbert v. Lando, 441 U. S. 153, 171 (1979) ("Spreading false information in and of itself carries no First Amendment credentials"); Gertz, supra, at 340 ("[T]here is no constitutional value in false statements of fact"); Garrison v. Louisiana, 379 U. S. 64, 75 (1964) ("[T]he knowingly false statement and the false statement made with reckless disregard of the truth, do not enjoy constitutional protection").

These quotations all derive from cases discussing defamation, fraud, or some other legally cognizable harm associated with a false statement, such as an invasion of privacy or the costs of vexatious litigation. See Brief for United States 18–19. In those decisions the falsity of the speech at issue was not irrelevant to our analysis, but neither was it determinative. The Court has never endorsed the categorical rule the Government advances: that false statements receive no First Amendment protection. Our prior decisions have not confronted a measure, like the Stolen Valor Act, that targets falsity and nothing more.

Even when considering some instances of defamation and fraud, moreover, the Court has been careful to instruct that falsity alone may not suffice to bring the speech outside the First Amendment. The statement must be a knowing or reckless falsehood. See Sullivan, supra, at 280 (prohibiting recovery of damages for a defamatory falsehood made about a public official unless the statement was made "with knowledge that it was false or with reckless disregard of whether it was false or not"); see also Garrison, supra, at 73 ("[E]ven when the utterance is false, the great principles of the Constitution which secure freedom of expression . . . preclude attaching adverse consequences to any except the knowing or reckless falsehood"); Illinois ex rel. Madigan v. Telemarketing Associates, Inc., 538 U. S. 600, 620 (2003) ("False statement alone does not subject a fundraiser to fraud liability").

The Government thus seeks to use this principle for a new purpose. It seeks to convert a rule that limits liability even in defamation cases where the law permits recovery for tortious wrongs into a rule that expands liability in a different, far greater realm of discourse and expression. That inverts the rationale for the exception. The requirements of a knowing falsehood or reckless disregard for the truth as the condition for recovery in certain defamation cases exists to allow more speech, not less. A rule designed to tolerate certain speech ought not blossom to become a rationale for a rule restricting it.

The Government then gives three examples of regulations on false speech that courts generally have found permissible: first, the criminal prohibition of a false statement made to a Government official, 18 U. S. C. §1001; second, laws punishing perjury; and third, prohibitions on the false representation that one is speaking as a Government official or on behalf of the Government, see, e.g., §912; §709. These restrictions, however, do not establish a principle that all proscriptions of false statements are exempt from exacting First Amendment scrutiny.

The federal statute prohibiting false statements to Government officials punishes "whoever, in any matter within the jurisdiction of the executive, legislative, or judicial branch of the Government . . . makes any materially false, fictitious, or fraudulent statement or representation." §1001. Section 1001's prohibition on false statements made to Government officials, in communications concerning official matters, does not lead to the broader proposition that false statements are unprotected when made to any person, at any time, in any context.

The same point can be made about what the Court has confirmed is the "unquestioned constitutionality of perjury statutes," both the federal statute, §1623, and its state-law equivalents. United States v. Grayson, 438 U. S. 41, 54 (1978). See also Konigsberg v. State Bar of Cal., 366 U. S. 36, n. 10 (1961). It is not simply because perjured statements are false that they lack First Amendment protection. Perjured testimony "is at war with justice" because it can cause a court to render a "judgment not resting on truth." In re Michael, 326 U. S. 224, 227 (1945). Perjury undermines the function and province of the law and threatens the integrity of judgments that are the basis of the legal system. See United States v. Dunnigan, 507 U. S. 87, 97 (1993) ("To uphold the integrity of our trial system . . . the constitutionality of perjury statutes is unquestioned"). Unlike speech in other contexts, testimony under oath has the formality and gravity necessary to remind the witness that his or her statements will be the basis for official governmental action, action that often affects the rights and liberties of others. Sworn testimony is quite distinct from lies not spoken under oath and sim-ply intended to puff up oneself.

Statutes that prohibit falsely representing that one is speaking on behalf of the Government, or that prohibit impersonating a Government officer, also protect the integrity of Government processes, quite apart from merely restricting false speech. Title 18 U. S. C. §912, for ex-ample, prohibits impersonating an officer or employee of the United States. Even if that statute may not require proving an "actual financial or property loss" resulting from the deception, the statute is itself confined to "maintain[ing] the general good repute and dignity of . . . government . . . service itself." United States v. Lepowitch, 318 U. S. 702, 704 (1943) (internal quotation marks omitted). The same can be said for prohibitions on the unauthorized use of the names of federal agencies such as the Federal Bureau of Investigation in a manner calculated to convey that the communication is approved, see §709, or using words such as "Federal" or "United States" in the collection of private debts in order to convey that the communication has official authorization, see §712. These examples, to the extent that they implicate fraud or speech integral to criminal conduct, are inapplicable here.

As our law and tradition show, then, there are instances in which the falsity of speech bears upon whether it is protected. Some false speech may be prohibited even if analogous true speech could not be. This opinion does not imply that any of these targeted prohibitions are somehow vulnerable. But it also rejects the notion that false speech should be in a general category that is presumptively unprotected.

Although the First Amendment stands against any "freewheeling authority to declare new categories of speech outside the scope of the First Amendment," Stevens, 559 U. S., at ____ (slip op., at 9), the Court has acknowledged that perhaps there exist "some categories of speech that have been historically unprotected . . . but have not yet been specifically identified or discussed . . . in our case law." Ibid. Before exempting a category of speech from the normal prohibition on content-based restrictions, however, the Court must be presented with "persuasive evidence that a novel restriction on content is part of a long (if heretofore unrecognized) tradition of proscription," Brown v. Entertainment Merchants Assn., 564 U. S. ____, ____ (2011) (slip op., at 4). The Government has not demonstrated that false statements generally should constitute a new category of unprotected speech on this basis.

III

The probable, and adverse, effect of the Act on freedom of expression illustrates, in a fundamental way, the reasons for the Law's distrust of content-based speech prohibitions.

The Act by its plain terms applies to a false statement made at any time, in any place, to any person. It can be assumed that it would not apply to, say, a theatrical performance. See Milkovich v. Lorain Journal Co., 497 U. S. 1, 20 (1990) (recognizing that some statements nominally purporting to contain false facts in reality "cannot reasonably be interpreted as stating actual facts about an individual" (internal quotation marks and brackets omitted)). Still, the sweeping, quite unprecedented reach of the statute puts it in conflict with the First Amendment. Here the lie was made in a public meeting, but the statute would apply with equal force to personal, whispered conversations within a home. The statute seeks to control and suppress all false statements on this one subject in almost limitless times and settings. And it does so entirely without regard to whether the lie was made for the purpose of material gain. See San Francisco Arts & Athletics, Inc. v. United States Olympic Comm., 483 U. S. 522–540 (1987) (prohibiting a nonprofit corporation from exploiting the "commercial magnetism" of the word "Olympic" when organizing an athletic competition (internal quotation marks omitted)).

Permitting the government to decree this speech to bea criminal offense, whether shouted from the rooftops or made in a barely audible whisper, would endorse government authority to compile a list of subjects about which false statements are punishable. That governmental power has no clear limiting principle. Our constitutional tradition stands against the idea that we need Oceania's Ministry of Truth. See G. Orwell, Nineteen Eighty-Four (1949) (Centennial ed. 2003). Were this law to be sustained, there could be an endless list of subjects the National Government or the States could single out. Where false claims are made to effect a fraud or secure moneys or other valuable considerations, say offers of employment, it is well established that the Government may restrict speech without affronting the First Amendment. See, e.g., Virginia Bd. of Pharmacy, 425 U. S., at 771 (noting that fraudulent speech generally falls outside the protections of the First Amendment). But the Stolen Valor Act is not so limited in its reach. Were the Court to hold that the interest in truthful discourse alone is sufficient to sustain a ban on speech, absent any evidence that the speech was used to gain a material advantage, it would give government a broad censorial power unprecedented in this Court's cases or in our constitutional tradition. The mere potential for the exercise of that power casts a chill, a chill the First Amendment cannot permit if free speech, thought, and discourse are to remain a foundation of our freedom.

IV

The previous discussion suffices to show that the Act conflicts with free speech principles. But even when examined within its own narrow sphere of operation, the Act cannot survive. In assessing content-based restrictionson protected speech, the Court has not adopted a free-wheeling approach, see Stevens, 559 U. S., at ____ (slip op., at 7) ("The First Amendment's guarantee of free speech does not extend only to categories of speech that survive an ad hoc balancing of relative social costs and benefits"), but rather has applied the "most exacting scrutiny." Turner Broadcasting System, Inc. v. FCC, 512 U. S. 622, 642 (1994). Although the objectives the Government seeks to further by the statute are not without significance, the Court must, and now does, find the Act does not satisfy exacting scrutiny.

The Government is correct when it states military medals "serve the important public function of recognizing and expressing gratitude for acts of heroism and sacrifice in military service," and also " 'foste[r] morale, mission accomplishment and esprit de corps' among service members." Brief for United States 37, 38. General George Washington observed that an award for valor would "cherish a virtuous ambition in . . . soldiers, as well as foster and encourage every species of military merit." General Orders of George Washington Issued at Newburgh on the Hudson, 1782–1783 (Aug. 7, 1782), p. 30 (E. Boynton ed. 1883). Time has not diminished this idea. In periods of war and peace alike public recognition of valor and noble sacrifice by men and women in uniform reinforces the pride and national resolve that the military relies upon to fulfill its mission.

These interests are related to the integrity of the military honors system in general, and the Congressional Medal of Honor in particular. Although millions have served with brave resolve, the Medal, which is the highest military award for valor against an enemy force, has been given just 3, 476 times. Established in 1861, the Medal is reserved for those who have distinguished themselves "conspicuously by gallantry and intrepidity at the risk of his life above and beyond the call of duty." 10 U. S. C. §§3741 (Army), 6241 (Navy and Marine Corps), 8741 (Air Force), 14 U. S. C. §491 (Coast Guard). The stories of those who earned the Medal inspire and fascinate, from Dakota Meyer who in 2009 drove five times into the midst of a Taliban ambush to save 36 lives, see Curtis, President Obama Awards Medal of Honor to Dakota Meyer, The White House Blog (Sept. 15, 2011) (all Internet materials as visited June 25, 2012, and available in Clerk of Court's case file); to Desmond Doss who served as an army medic on Okinawa and on June 5, 1945, rescued 75 fellow soldiers, and who, after being wounded, gave up his own place on a stretcher so others could be taken to safety, see America's Heroes 88–90 (J. Willbanks ed. 2011); to William Carney who sustained multiple gunshot wounds to the head, chest, legs, and arm, and yet carried the flagto ensure it did not touch the ground during the Union army's assault on Fort Wagner in July 1863, id., at 44–45. The rare acts of courage the Medal celebrates led President Truman to say he would "rather have that medal round my neck than . . . be president of the United States." Truman Gives No. 1 Army Medal to 15 Heroes, Washington Post, Oct. 13, 1945, p. 5. The Government's interest in protecting the integrity of the Medal of Honor is beyond question.

But to recite the Government's compelling interests is not to end the matter. The First Amendment requires that the Government's chosen restriction on the speech at issue be "actually necessary" to achieve its interest. Entertainment Merchants Assn., 564 U. S., at ___ (slip op., at 12). There must be a direct causal link between the restriction imposed and the injury to be prevented. See ibid. The link between the Government's interest in protecting the integrity of the military honors system and the Act's restriction on the false claims of liars like respondent has not been shown. Although appearing to concede that "an isolated misrepresentation by itself would not tarnish the meaning of military honors," the Government asserts it is "common sense that false representations have the tendency to dilute the value and meaning of military awards," Brief for United States 49, 54. It must be acknowledged that when a pretender claims the Medal to be his own, the lie might harm the Government by demeaning the high purpose of the award, diminishing the honor it confirms, and creating the appearance that the Medal is awarded more often than is true. Furthermore, the lie may offend the true holders of the Medal. From one perspective it in-sults their bravery and high principles when falsehood puts them in the unworthy company of a pretender.

Yet these interests do not satisfy the Government's heavy burden when it seeks to regulate protected speech. See United States v. Playboy Entertainment Group, Inc., 529 U. S. 803, 818 (2000). The Government points to no evidence to support its claim that the public's general perception of military awards is diluted by false claims such as those made by Alvarez. Cf. Entertainment Merchants Assn., supra, at \_\_\_\_–\_\_\_\_ (slip op., at 12–13) (analyzing and rejecting the findings of research psychologists demonstrating the causal link between violent video games and harmful effects on children). As one of the Government's amici notes "there is nothing that charlatans such as Xavier Alvarez can do to stain [the Medal winners'] honor." Brief for Veterans of Foreign Wars of the United States et al. as Amici Curiae 1. This general proposition is sound, even if true holders of the Medal might experience anger and frustration.

The lack of a causal link between the Government's stated interest and the Act is not the only way in which the Act is not actually necessary to achieve the Government's stated interest. The Government has not shown, and cannot show, why counterspeech would not suffice to achieve its interest. The facts of this case indicate that the dynamics of free speech, of counterspeech, of refutation, can overcome the lie. Respondent lied at a public meeting. Even before the FBI began investigating him for his false statements "Alvarez was perceived as a phony," 617 F. 3d, at 1211. Once the lie was made public, he was ridiculed online, see Brief for Respondent 3, his actions were reported in the press, see Ortega, Alvarez Again Denies Claim, Ontario, CA, Inland Valley Daily Bulletin (Sept. 27, 2007), and a fellow board member called for his resignation, see, e.g., Bigham, Water District Rep Requests Alvarez Resign in Wake of False Medal Claim, San Bernardino Cty., CA, The Sun (May 21, 2008). There is good reason to believe that a similar fate would befall other false claimants. See Brief for Reporters Committee for Freedom of the Press et al. as Amici Curiae 30–33 (listing numerous examples of public exposure of false claimants). Indeed, the outrage and contempt expressed for respondent's lies can serve to reawaken and reinforce the public's respect for the Medal, its recipients, and its high purpose. The acclaim that recipients of the Congressional Medal of Honor receive also casts doubt on the proposition that the public will be misled by the claims of charlatans or become cynical of those whose heroic deeds earned them the Medal by right. See, e.g., Well Done, Washington Post, Feb. 5, 1943, p. 8 (reporting on President Roosevelt's awarding the Congressional Medal of Honor to Maj. Gen. Alexander Vandegrift); Devroy, Medal of Honor Given to 2 Killed in Somalia, Washington Post, May 24, 1994, p. A6 (reporting on President Clinton's awarding the Congressional Medal of Honor to two special forces soldiers killed during operations in Somalia).

The remedy for speech that is false is speech that is true. This is the ordinary course in a free society. The response to the unreasoned is the rational; to the uninformed, the enlightened; to the straight-out lie, the simple truth. See Whitney v. California, 274 U. S. 357, 377 (1927) (Brandeis, J., concurring) ("If there be time to expose through discussion the falsehood and fallacies, to avert the evil by the processes of education, the remedy to be ap-plied is more speech, not enforced silence"). The theory of our Constitution is "that the best test of truth is the power of the thought to get itself accepted in the competition of the market," Abrams v. United States, 250 U. S. 616, 630 (1919) (Holmes, J., dissenting). The First Amendment itself ensures the right to respond to speech we do not like, and for good reason. Freedom of speech and thought flows not from the beneficence of the state but from the inalienable rights of the person. And suppression of speech by the government can make exposure of falsity more difficult, not less so. Society has the right and civic duty to engage in open, dynamic, rational discourse. These ends are not well served when the government seeks to orchestrate public discussion through content-based mandates.

Expressing its concern that counterspeech is insuf-ficient, the Government responds that because "some military records have been lost . . . some claims [are] un-verifiable," Brief for United States 50. This proves little, however; for without verifiable records, successful criminal prosecution under the Act would be more difficult in any event. So, in cases where public refutation will not serve the Government's interest, the Act will not either. In addition, the Government claims that "many [false claims] will remain unchallenged." Id., at 55. The Government provides no support for the contention. And in any event, in order to show that public refutation is not an adequate alternative, the Government must demonstrate that unchallenged claims undermine the public's perception of the military and the integrity of its awards system. This showing has not been made.

It is a fair assumption that any true holders of the Medal who had heard of Alvarez's false claims would have been fully vindicated by the community's expression of outrage, showing as it did the Nation's high regard for the Medal. The same can be said for the Government's interest. The American people do not need the assistance of a government prosecution to express their high regard for the special place that military heroes hold in our tradi-tion. Only a weak society needs government protection or intervention before it pursues its resolve to preserve the truth. Truth needs neither handcuffs nor a badge for its vindication.

In addition, when the Government seeks to regulate protected speech, the restriction must be the "least restrictive means among available, effective alternatives." Ashcroft, 542 U. S., at 666. There is, however, at least one less speech-restrictive means by which the Government could likely protect the integrity of the military awards system. A Government-created database could list Congressional Medal of Honor winners. Were a database accessible through the Internet, it would be easy to verify and expose false claims. It appears some private individuals have already created databases similar to this, see Brief for Respondent 25, and at least one data-base of past winners is online and fully searchable, see Congressional Medal of Honor Society, Full Archive, http://www.cmohs.org/recipient-archive.php. The Solicitor General responds that although Congress and the Department of Defense investigated the feasibility of establishing a database in 2008, the Government "concluded that such a database would be impracticable and insuf-ficiently comprehensive." Brief for United States 55. Without more explanation, it is difficult to assess the Gov-ernment's claim, especially when at least one database of Congressional Medal of Honor winners already exists.

The Government may have responses to some of these criticisms, but there has been no clear showing of the necessity of the statute, the necessity required by exacting scrutiny.

\*     \*     \*

The Nation well knows that one of the costs of the First Amendment is that it protects the speech we detest as well as the speech we embrace. Though few might find respondent's statements anything but contemptible, his right to make those statements is protected by the Constitution's guarantee of freedom of speech and expression. The Stolen Valor Act infringes upon speech protected by the First Amendment.

The judgment of the Court of Appeals is affirmed.

It is so ordered.

## US v. Kebodeaux (June 24, 2013)

Justice BREYER delivered the opinion of the Court.

In 1999 a special court-martial convicted Anthony Kebodeaux, a member of the United States Air Force, of a sex offense. It imposed a sentence of three months' imprisonment and a bad conduct discharge. In 2006, several years after Kebodeaux had served his sentence and been discharged, Congress enacted the Sex Offender Registration and Notification Act (SORNA), 120 Stat. 590, 42 U.S.C. § 16901 et seq., a federal statute that requires those convicted of federal sex offenses to register in the States where they live, study, and work. § 16913(a); 18 U.S.C. § 2250(a). And, by regulation, the Federal Government made clear that SORNA's registration requirements apply to federal sex offenders who, when SORNA became law, had already completed their sentences. 42 U.S.C. § 16913(d) (Attorney General's authority to issue regulations); 28 CFR § 72.3 (2012) (regulation specifying application to pre-SORNA offenders).

We here must decide whether the Constitution's Necessary and Proper Clause grants Congress the power to enact SORNA's registration requirements and apply them to a federal offender who had completed his sentence prior to the time of SORNA's enactment. For purposes of answering this question, we assume that Congress has complied with the Constitution's Ex Post Facto and Due Process Clauses. See Smith v. Doe, 538 U.S. 84, 105-106, 123 S.Ct. 1140, 155 L.Ed.2d 164 (2003) (upholding a similar Alaska statute against ex post facto challenge); Supp. Brief for Kebodeaux on Rehearing En Banc in No. 08-51185 (CA5) (not raising any Due Process challenge); Brief for Respondent (same). We conclude that the Necessary and Proper Clause grants Congress adequate power to enact SORNA and to apply it here.

I

As we have just said, in 1999 a special court-martial convicted Kebodeaux, then a member of the Air Force, of a federal sex offense. He served his 3-month sentence; the Air Force released him with a bad conduct discharge. And then he moved to Texas. In 2004 Kebodeaux registered as a sex offender with Texas state authorities. Brief for Respondent 6-7. In 2006 Congress enacted SORNA. In 2007 Kebodeaux moved within Texas from San Antonio to El Paso, updating his sex offender registration. App. to Pet. for Cert. 167a-

168a. But later that year he returned to San Antonio without making the legally required sex-offender registration changes. Id., at 169a. And the Federal Government, acting under SORNA, prosecuted Kebodeaux for this last-mentioned SORNA registration failure.

A Federal District Court convicted Kebodeaux of having violated SORNA. See 687 F.3d 232, 234 (C.A.5 2012) (en banc). On appeal a panel of the United States Court of Appeals for the Fifth Circuit initially upheld the conviction. 647 F.3d 137 (2011) (per curiam). But the Circuit then heard the appeal en banc and, by a vote of 10 to 6, reversed. 687 F.3d, at 234. The court stated that, by the time Congress enacted SORNA, Kebodeaux had "fully served" his sex-offense sentence; he was "no longer in federal custody, in the military, under any sort of supervised release or parole, or in any other special relationship with the federal government." Ibid.

The court recognized that, even before SORNA, federal law required certain federal sex offenders to register. Id., at 235, n. 4. See Jacob Wetterling Crimes Against Children and Sexually Violent Offender Registration Act, § 170101, 108 Stat. 2038-2042. But it believed that the pre-SORNA federal registration requirements did not apply to Kebodeaux. 687 F.3d, at 235, n. 4. Hence, in the Circuit's view, Kebodeaux had been "unconditionally let ... free." Id., at 234. And, that being so, the Federal Government lacked the power under Article I's Necessary and Proper Clause to regulate through registration Kebodeaux's intrastate movements. Id., at 234-235. In particular, the court said that after "the federal government has unconditionally let a person free ... the fact that he once committed a crime is not a jurisdictional basis for subsequent regulation and possible criminal prosecution." Ibid.

The Solicitor General sought certiorari. And, in light of the fact that a Federal Court of Appeals has held a federal statute unconstitutional, we granted the petition. See, e.g., United States v. Morrison, 529 U.S. 598, 605, 120 S.Ct. 1740, 146 L.Ed.2d 658 (2000); United States v. Edge Broadcasting Co., 509 U.S. 418, 425, 113 S.Ct. 2696, 125 L.Ed.2d 345 (1993).

II

We do not agree with the Circuit's conclusion. And, in explaining our reasons, we need not go much further than the Circuit's critical assumption that Kebodeaux's release was "unconditional," i.e., that after Kebodeaux's release, he was not in "any ... special relationship with the federal government." 687 F.3d, at 234. To the contrary, the Solicitor General, tracing through a complex set of statutory cross-references, has pointed out that at the time of his offense and conviction Kebodeaux was subject to the federal Wetterling Act, an Act that imposed upon him registration requirements very similar to those that SORNA later mandated. Brief for United States 18-29.

Congress enacted the Wetterling Act in 1994 and updated it several times prior to Kebodeaux's offense. Like SORNA, it used the federal spending power to encourage States to adopt sex offender registration laws. 42 U.S.C. § 14071(i) (2000 ed.); Smith, supra, at 89-90, 123 S.Ct. 1140. Like SORNA, it applied to those who committed federal sex crimes. § 14071(b)(7)(A). And like SORNA, it imposed federal penalties upon federal sex offenders who failed to register in the States in which they lived, worked, and studied. §§ 14072(i)(3)-(4).

In particular, § 14072(i)(3) imposed federal criminal penalties upon any "person who is ... described in section 4042(c)(4) of title 18, and knowingly fails to register in any State in which the person resides." The cross-referenced § 4042(c)(4) said that a "person is described in this paragraph if the person was convicted of" certain enumerated offenses or "[a]ny other offense designated by the Attorney General as a sexual offense for purposes of this subsection." 18 U.S.C. § 4042(c)(4). In 1998 the Attorney General "delegated this authority [to designate sex offenses] to the Director of the Bureau of Prisons." Dept. of Justice, Bureau of Prisons, Designation of Offenses Subject to Sex Offender Release Notification, 63 Fed.Reg. 69386. And that same year the Director of the Bureau of Prisons "designate[d]" the offense of which Kebodeaux was convicted, namely the military offense of "carnal knowledge" as set forth in Article 120(B) of the Code of Military Justice. Id., at 69387 See 28 CFR § 571.72(b)(2) (1999). A full reading of these documents makes clear that, contrary to Kebodeaux's contention, the relevant penalty applied to crimes committed by military personnel.

Moreover, a different Wetterling Act section imposed federal criminal penalties upon any "person who is ... sentenced by a court martial for conduct in a category specified by the Secretary of Defense under section 115(a)(8)(C) of title I of Public Law 105-119, and knowingly fails to register in any State in which the person resides." 42 U.S.C. § 14072(i)(4) (2000 ed.). The cross-referenced section, § 115(a)(8)(C), said that the "Secretary of Defense shall specify categories of conduct punishable under the Uniform Code of Military Justice which encompass a range of conduct comparable to that described in [certain provisions of the Violent Crime Control and Law Enforcement Act of 1994], and such other conduct as the Secretary deems appropriate." 1998 Appropriations Act, § 115(a)(8)(C)(i), 111 Stat. 2466. See note following 10 U.S.C. § 951 (2000 ed.). The Secretary had delegated certain types of authority, such as this last mentioned "deem[ing]" authority, to an Assistant Secretary of Defense. DoD Directive 5124.5, p. 4 (Oct. 31, 1994). And in December 1998 an Assistant Secretary, acting pursuant to this authority, published a list of military crimes that included the crime of which Kebodeaux was convicted, namely Article 120(B) of the Uniform Code of Military Justice. App. to Pet. for Cert. 171a-175a. The provision added that "[c]onvictions ... shall trigger requirements to notify state and local law enforcement agencies and to provide information to inmates concerning sex offender registration requirements." Id., at 175a. And, the provision says (contrary to Kebodeaux's reading, Brief for Respondent 57), that it shall "take effect immediately." It contains no expiration date. App. to Pet. for Cert. 175a.

We are not aware of any plausible counterargument to the obvious conclusion, namely that as of the time of Kebodeaux's offense, conviction and release from federal custody, these Wetterling Act provisions applied to Kebodeaux and imposed upon him registration requirements very similar to those that SORNA later imposed. Contrary to what the Court of Appeals may have believed, the fact that the federal law's requirements in part involved compliance with state-law requirements made them no less requirements of federal law. See generally United States v. Sharpnack, 355 U.S. 286, 293-294, 78 S.Ct. 291, 2 L.Ed.2d 282 (1958) (Congress has the power to adopt as federal law the laws of a State and to apply them in federal enclaves); Gibbons v. Ogden, 9 Wheat. 1, 207-208, 6 L.Ed. 23 (1824) ("Although Congress cannot enable a State to legislate, Congress may adopt the provisions of a State on any subject.... The act [adopts state systems for regulation of pilots] and gives [them] the same validity as if its provisions had been specially made by Congress").

III

Both the Court of Appeals and Kebodeaux come close to conceding that if, as of the time of Kebodeaux's offense, he was subject to a federal registration requirement, then the Necessary and Proper Clause authorized Congress to modify the requirement as in SORNA and to apply the modified requirement to Kebodeaux. See 687 F.3d, at 234-235, and n. 4; Tr. of Oral Arg. 38-39. And we believe they would be right to make this concession.

No one here claims that the Wetterling Act, as applied to military sex offenders like Kebodeaux, falls outside the scope of the Necessary and Proper Clause. And it is difficult to see how anyone could persuasively do so. The Constitution explicitly grants Congress the power to "make Rules for the ... Regulation of the land and naval Forces." Art. I, § 8, cl. 14. And, in the Necessary and Proper Clause itself, it grants Congress the power to "make all Laws which shall be necessary and proper for carrying into Execution the foregoing Powers" and "all other Powers" that the Constitution vests "in the Government of the United States, or in any Department or Officer thereof." Id., cl. 18.

The scope of the Necessary and Proper Clause is broad. In words that have come to define that scope Chief Justice Marshall long ago wrote:

"Let the end be legitimate, let it be within the scope of the constitution, and all means which are appropriate, which are plainly adapted to that end, which are not prohibited, but consist with the letter and spirit of the constitution, are constitutional." McCulloch v. Maryland, 4 Wheat. 316, 421, 4 L.Ed. 579 (1819).

As we have come to understand these words and the provision they explain, they "leav[e] to Congress a large discretion as to the means that may be employed in executing a given power." Lottery Case, 188 U.S. 321, 355, 23 S.Ct. 321, 47 L.Ed. 492 (1903). See Morrison, 529 U.S., at 607, 120 S.Ct. 1740. The Clause allows Congress to "adopt any means, appearing to it most eligible and appropriate, which are adapted to the end to be accomplished and consistent with the letter and spirit of the Constitution." James Everard's Breweries v. Day, 265 U.S. 545, 559, 44 S.Ct. 628, 68 L.Ed. 1174 (1924).

The Constitution, for example, makes few explicit references to federal criminal law, but the Necessary and Proper Clause nonetheless authorizes Congress, in the implementation of other explicit powers, to create federal crimes, to confine offenders to prison, to hire guards and other prison personnel, to provide prisoners with medical care and educational training, to ensure the safety of those who may come into contact with prisoners, to ensure the public's safety through systems of parole and supervised release, and, where a federal prisoner's mental condition so requires, to confine that prisoner civilly after the expiration of his or her term of imprisonment. See United States v. Comstock, 560 U.S. 126, 136-137, 130 S.Ct. 1949, 176 L.Ed.2d 878 (2010).

Here, under the authority granted to it by the Military Regulation and Necessary and Proper Clauses, Congress could promulgate the Uniform Code of Military Justice. It could specify that the sex offense of which Kebodeaux was convicted was a military crime under that Code. It could punish that crime through imprisonment and by placing conditions upon Kebodeaux's release. And it could make the civil registration requirement at issue here a consequence of Kebodeaux's offense and conviction. This civil requirement, while not a specific condition of Kebodeaux's release, was in place at the time Kebodeaux committed his offense, and was a consequence of his violation of federal law.

And Congress' decision to impose such a civil requirement that would apply upon the release of an offender like Kebodeaux is eminently reasonable. Congress could reasonably conclude that registration requirements applied to federal sex offenders after their release can help protect the public from those federal sex offenders and alleviate public safety concerns. See Smith, 538 U.S., at 102-103, 123 S.Ct. 1140 (sex offender registration has "a legitimate nonpunitive purpose of `public safety, which is advanced by alerting the public to the risk of sex offenders in their community'"). There is evidence that recidivism rates among sex offenders are higher than the average for other types of criminals. See Dept. of Justice, Bureau of Justice Statistics, P. Langan, E. Schmitt, & M. Durose, Recidivism of Sex Offenders Released in 1994, p. 1 (Nov. 2003) (reporting that compared to non-sex offenders, released sex offenders were four times more likely to be rearrested for a sex crime, and that within the first three years following release 5.3% of released sex offenders were rearrested for a sex crime). There is also conflicting evidence on the point. Cf. R. Tewsbury, W. Jennings, & K. Zgoba, Final Report on Sex Offenders: Recidivism and Collateral Consequences (Sept. 2011) (concluding that sex offenders have relatively low rates of recidivism, and that registration requirements have limited observable benefits regarding recidivism). But the Clause gives Congress the power to weigh the evidence and to reach a rational conclusion, for example, that safety needs justify postrelease registration rules. See Lambert v. Yellowley, 272 U.S. 581, 594-595, 47 S.Ct. 210, 71 L.Ed. 422 (1926) (upholding congressional statute limiting the amount of spirituous liquor that may be prescribed by a physician, and noting that Congress' "finding [regarding the appropriate amount], in the presence of the well-known diverging opinions of physicians, cannot be regarded as arbitrary or without a reasonable basis"). See also Gonzales v. Raich, 545 U.S. 1, 22, 125 S.Ct. 2195, 162 L.Ed.2d 1 (2005) ("In assessing the scope of Congress' authority under the Commerce Clause, we stress that the task before us is a modest one. We need not determine whether respondents' activities, taken in the aggregate, substantially affect interstate commerce in fact, but only whether a `rational basis' exists for so concluding"). See also H.R.Rep. No. 109-218, pt. 1, pp. 22,

23 (2005) (House Report) (citing statistics compiled by the Justice Department as support for SORNA's sex offender registration regime).

At the same time, "it is entirely reasonable for Congress to have assigned the Federal Government a special role in ensuring compliance with SORNA's registration requirements by federal sex offenders — persons who typically would have spent time under federal criminal supervision." Carr v. United States, 560 U.S. 438, ___, 130 S.Ct. 2229, 176 L.Ed.2d 1152 (2010). The Federal Government has long kept track of former federal prisoners through probation, parole, and supervised release in part to prevent further crimes thereby protecting the public against the risk of recidivism. See Parole Act, 36 Stat. 819; Probation Act, ch. 521, 43 Stat. 1259; Sentencing Reform Act of 1984, ch. II, 98 Stat. 1987. See also 1 N. Cohen, The Law of Probation and Parole §§ 7:3, 7:4 (2d ed. 1999) (principal purposes of postrelease conditions are to rehabilitate the convict, thus preventing him from recidivating, and to protect the public). Neither, as of 1994, was registration particularly novel, for by then States had implemented similar requirements for close to half a century. See W. Logan, Knowledge as Power: Criminal Registration and Community Notification Laws in America 30-31 (2009). Moreover, the Wetterling Act took state interests into account by, for the most part, requiring released federal offenders to register in accordance with state law. At the same time, the Wetterling Act's requirements were reasonably narrow and precise, tying time limits to the type of sex offense, incorporating state-law details, and relating penalties for violations to the sex crime initially at issue. See 42 U.S.C. § 14071(b) (2000 ed.).

The upshot is that here Congress did not apply SORNA to an individual who had, prior to SORNA's enactment, been "unconditionally released," i.e., a person who was not in "any ... special relationship with the federal government," but rather to an individual already subject to federal registration requirements that were themselves a valid exercise of federal power under the Military Regulation and Necessary and Proper Clauses. But cf. post, at 2509-2510 (SCALIA, J., dissenting).

SORNA, enacted after Kebodeaux's release, somewhat modified the applicable registration requirements. In general, SORNA provided more detailed definitions of sex offenses, described in greater detail the nature of the information registrants must provide, and imposed somewhat different limits upon the length of time that registration must continue and the frequency with which offenders must update their registration. 42 U.S.C. §§ 16911, 16913-16916 (2006 ed. and Supp. V). But the statute, like the Wetterling Act, used Spending Clause grants to encourage States to adopt its uniform definitions and requirements. It did not insist that the States do so. See §§ 16925(a), (d) (2006 ed.) ("The provisions of this subchapter that are cast as directions to jurisdictions or their officials constitute, in relation to States, only conditions required to avoid the reduction of Federal funding under this section").

As applied to an individual already subject to the Wetterling Act like Kebodeaux, SORNA makes few changes. In particular, SORNA modified the time limitations for a sex offender who moves to update his registration to within three business days of the move from both seven days before and seven days after the move, as required by the Texas law enforced under the Wetterling Act. Compare 42 U.S.C. § 16913(c) with App. to Pet. for Cert. 167a-168a. SORNA also increased the federal penalty for a federal offender's registration violation to a maximum of 10 years from a maximum of 1 year for a first offense. Compare 18 U.S.C. § 2250(a) with 42 U.S.C. § 14072(i) (2000 ed.). Kebodeaux was sentenced to one year and one day of imprisonment. For purposes of federal law, SORNA reduced the duration of Kebodeaux's registration requirement to 25 years from the lifetime requirement imposed by Texas law, compare 42 U.S.C. § 16915(a) (2006 ed.) with App. to Pet. for Cert. 167a, and reduced the frequency with which Kebodeaux must update his registration to every six months from every 90 days as imposed by Texas law, compare 42 U.S.C. § 16916(2) with App. to Pet. for Cert. 167a. And as far as we can tell, while SORNA punishes violations of its requirements (instead of violations of state law), the Federal Government has prosecuted a sex offender for violating SORNA only when that offender also violated state-registration requirements.

SORNA's general changes were designed to make more uniform what had remained "a patchwork of federal and 50 individual state registration systems," Reynolds v. United States, 565 U.S. ___, ___, 132 S.Ct. 975, 978, 181 L.Ed.2d 935 (2012), with "loopholes and deficiencies" that had resulted in an estimated 100,000 sex offenders becoming "missing" or "lost," House Report 20, 26. See S.Rep. No. 109-369, pp. 16-17 (2006). See also Jinks v. Richland County, 538 U.S. 456, 462-463, 123 S.Ct. 1667, 155 L.Ed.2d 631 (2003) (holding that a statute is authorized by the Necessary and Proper Clause when it "provides an alternative to [otherwise] unsatisfactory options" that are "obviously inefficient"). SORNA's more specific changes reflect Congress' determination that the statute, changed in respect to frequency, penalties, and other details, will keep track of more offenders and will encourage States themselves to adopt its uniform standards. No one here claims that these changes are unreasonable or that Congress could not reasonably have found them "necessary and proper" means for furthering its pre-existing registration ends.

We conclude that the SORNA changes as applied to Kebodeaux fall within the scope Congress' authority under the Military Regulation and Necessary and Proper Clauses. The Fifth Circuit's judgment to the contrary is reversed, and the case is remanded for further proceedings consistent with this opinion.

It is so ordered.

## Shoemaker v. Taylor (Ninth Circuit) (August 6, 2013, amended September 13, 2013)

Before: HARRY PREGERSON, RICHARD A. PAEZ, and ANDREW D. HURWITZ, Circuit Judges.

ORDER

The Opinion filed on August 6, 2013 is amended as follows:

On slip opinion page 5, line 4, remove the following text:

On page 5, line 4, insert the following text:

An amended opinion is filed concurrently with this order.

No further petitions for rehearing or rehearing en banc will be entertained.

OPINION

PREGERSON, Circuit Judge:

A California jury convicted Stephen Shoemaker of eight misdemeanor counts of possession of child pornography in violation of California Penal Code § 311.11(a) and one misdemeanor count of duplicating child pornography in violation of California Penal Code § 311.3(a). Shoemaker was sentenced to 90 days in custody, 36 months probation, a $17,000 fine, and a one-year sexual compulsiveness program. He was also required to register as a sex offender for life. Shoemaker exhausted his state remedies through the filing of a direct appeal and a petition for writ of habeas corpus. Both the California Court of Appeal and the California Supreme Court issued summary denials of Shoemaker's state habeas petitions. Shoemaker then filed his federal habeas petition under 28 U.S.C. § 2254, which the district court denied.

On appeal from the district court's denial, Shoemaker argues that: (1) because six of the images at issue were not lewd, the jury erred in finding those six images to be child pornography; (2) because the remaining two images were digitally "morphed" so that the children only appeared to be engaging in sexual activity, the jury erred in finding those images to be child pornography; (3) the court erred when it instructed the jury, and permitted the prosecutor to argue, that the jury could consider the context in which the images were displayed to determine whether those images were child pornography; and (4) Shoemaker's convictions were not supported by substantial evidence. We have jurisdiction under 28 U.S.C. § 2253. Constrained by the stringent standards of the Antiterrorism and Effective Death Penalty Act ("AEDPA"), we affirm.

BACKGROUND

A. Seizure of the Images

While executing a warrant to search Stephen Shoemaker's business, Redondo Beach police found eight images they suspected to be child pornography. The images were located on two computer servers. One server hosted the adult website Blowout.com ("Blowout"); the other hosted the adult website Beachbaby.com ("Beachbaby"). Shoemaker owned both websites. Additionally, as the systems operator for Blowout, Shoemaker managed content for the site and approved images for posting on the site. Shoemaker had one employee, the systems operator for Beachbaby.

In addition to Blowout and Beachbaby, Shoemaker's business hosted five other websites that also contained adult pornography. Police seized more than 3,700 photos from the hard drives at the business. Eight of those images formed the basis for Shoemaker's child pornography convictions.

Six of the eight images (Exhibits 3, 5, 7, 8, 9, and 12) were found on the Beachbaby website. The remaining two images (Exhibits 13 and 14) were not posted on any website but instead were found in a subdirectory of the Beachbaby server named "shoe." Copies of these two images were also found on the Blowout server in a subdirectory named "shoe."

B. The Images

Shoemaker contends that two of the images, Exhibits 8 and 14, were innocent images of children digitally altered, or "morphed," so that the children appear to be engaging in sexual activity. Morphed images are often created by superimposing images of real children's heads on images of bodies of adults or bodies of other children. The following description of the images (Exhibits 3, 5, 7, 8, 9, 12, 13, and 14) are taken from the Appellate Division of the Superior Court of Los Angeles County's Memorandum Judgment.

• Exhibit 3 "portrays a nude girl, from the knees up, sitting on the edge of a sailboat. Her breasts and pubic hair are visible."

• Exhibit 5 "is a full-length portrayal of a nude girl sitting astride a seesaw. Her breasts and pubic hair are visible."

• Exhibit 7 "portrays a nude girl, from the knees up, sitting on the edge of the bathtub, slightly wet with soap suds. She is facing the viewer and her breasts and pubic area are visible."

• Exhibit 8 "portrays a nude girl and a nude boy, from the knees up. The girl's breasts and pubic area are visible, and the boy's penis and testes are visible. The boy is leaning back and the girl is leaning towards the boy, with one arm behind his head." Shoemaker contends that this image was morphed.

• Exhibit 9 "is a full-length portrayal of six nude girls standing before a crowd. All of the girls' breasts and pubic areas are visible, with varying amounts of pubic hair."

• Exhibit 12 "portrays a nude girl, from the mid-thigh up, standing in front of a shower attachment, with a detachable shower head aiming running water at her body. Her breasts and pubic area are visible."

• Exhibit 13 "is a full-length portrayal of a nude girl, holding a large piece of fabric behind her back, with a flower in her hair. Her breasts and pubic area are visible."

• Exhibit 14 "portrays two nude boys and one nude girl on what appears to be a bed. The girl is lying on her back, spread-eagled, and her breasts and genitals are exposed. One boy is kneeling over her and his erect penis is in the girl's mouth. The other boy is on his knees, holding the girl's feet, and his erect penis is penetrating the girl." Shoemaker contends that this image was also morphed.

C. State Court Criminal Proceedings

Shoemaker was charged with possession of child pornography under California Penal Code § 311.11 and duplication of child pornography under California Penal Code § 311.3.[1] At trial, Shoemaker sought a directed verdict, which the trial court denied. Shoemaker argued that the images in question were innocuous photographs at the time they were created (at nudist camps and the like), and that the display of such images on a pornographic website could not convert them into child pornography. The trial judge rejected this argument and stated: "The prosecution will be able to argue that [a] photograph [that is alleged to be child pornography] included in the other photographs on the same [pornographic] website ... imbues it with the essence of the violation.... To this court's mind, it is the use of the photograph.... You can take an innocuous photograph and make it illegal. I can take a questionable photograph and make it legal. It's all in the use of the photograph."

The trial court then instructed the jury that in determining whether an image met the statutory definition of child pornography, it could consider five factors:

(1) "whether the focal point is on the child's genitalia or pubic or rectal area"; (2) "whether the setting is sexually suggestive; that is, in a place or pose generally associated with sexual activity"; (3) "whether the child is in an unnatural pose, or inappropriate attire considering the age of the child"; (4) "whether the child is fully or partially clothed or nude"; and (5) "whether the child's conduct suggests sexual coyness or a willingness to engage in sexual activity."

In determining whether there has been a prohibited exhibition of a minor child's genitals, pubic, or rectal area based upon the above factors, it is not necessary to conclude that all factors 1 through 5 are present.[2]

At closing, the trial court allowed the prosecutor to argue that the placement of six of the images on Shoemaker's adult pornography website, Beachbaby, was evidence that those images were child pornography. After addressing the allegedly morphed images that more obviously showed sexual activity (Exhibits 8 and 14), the prosecutor turned to the other six images. He began by stating:

So when my family and I visit the nudist camp, and my kids are getting out of the pool, and we are having a great time, and I click, click, click, and I take some pictures of them and I send them to Photomat. And I get them developed, and they come back and someone gets a hold of them like Mr. Shoemaker or [his co-defendant] and they put them on their website among other pictures, other pornographic pictures of adults, children, animals, people drinking urine, it is that context, ladies and gentlemen, of my child, anyone's child on the bear skin rug in the bathtub with the soapy hair, with the little brother, the little sister laughing in the bathtub naked. It is when you see that image in the context of how it appears when a person looks at that photo placed amongst others by [codefendant] and Mr. Shoemaker that make that image the exhibition of the genitals for the purpose of stimulation of the viewer. (emphasis added)

The prosecutor then repeated to the jury all five factors from the instructions, stating: "Those are the factors that you should be looking at, ladies and gentlemen, when deciding these images in the context in which we find them ... meet the requirement of an exhibition of the genitals for the purposes of sexual stimulation of the viewer." The prosecutor also repeatedly emphasized, however, that six of the images were found in the context of Beachbaby, an adult pornographic website. The prosecutor explained that, even assuming the nude photographs were not child pornography when viewed in isolation, their placement on the Beachbaby website was "for the purpose of stimulation of the viewer," and thus evidence of child pornography under California law. Regarding one of the images, the prosecutor argued:

Maybe there is nothing particular[ly] odd about this photograph. It is in a nudist camp and everybody is walking around naked. The child is just posing for the camera as many kids may do. Again, it is the placing in the context of the website. And interestingly enough this one is, again, on the Teens section of Beachbaby.com.

Shoemaker was convicted of eight counts of misdemeanor possession of child pornography based on all eight images, and one count of duplication based on Exhibits 13 and 14, which were copied from the Beachbaby server to the Blowout server. Shoemaker was sentenced to 90 days in custody, 36 months probation, a $17,000 fine, and a one-year sexual compulsiveness counseling program. Shoemaker was also required to register as a sex offender for life.

D. Shoemaker's Appeal & Habeas Petition

Shoemaker appealed to the Appellate Division of the Superior Court of Los Angeles County, which affirmed the judgment. Shoemaker filed a petition for writ of habeas corpus with the California Court of Appeal, which issued a summary denial. Shoemaker then filed a habeas petition with the California Supreme Court, which also issued a summary denial.

In September 2007, Shoemaker filed his federal habeas petition. The district court rejected the same arguments that Shoemaker raises here and denied his petition.

STANDARD OF REVIEW

We review a district court's denial of a petition for writ of habeas corpus de novo. Lopez v. Thompson, 202 F.3d 1110, 1116 (9th Cir.2000) (en banc).

In the case of a habeas petition implicating the First Amendment, we first "must, as a reviewing court, conduct our own independent review of the record. In so doing, we must exercise independent judgment as to the legal issue of whether [the habeas petitioner]'s speech and association were protected." McCoy v. Stewart, 282 F.3d 626, 629 (9th Cir.2002) (conducting an independent review prior to conducting a habeas analysis in a habeas claim implicating the First Amendment).

Under AEDPA, we may grant habeas relief on a claim that was adjudicated on the merits in state court proceedings only where the state court's decision was: (1) "contrary to, or involved an unreasonable application of clearly established Federal law, as determined by the Supreme Court," or (2) "based on an unreasonable determination of the facts in light of the evidence presented in the State court proceeding." 28 U.S.C. § 2254(d). Under § 2254(d)(1), clearly established Federal law consists of "the holdings, as opposed to the dicta, of [the] Court's decisions as of the time of the relevant state-court decision." Williams v. Taylor, 529 U.S. 362, 412, 120 S.Ct. 1495, 146 L.Ed.2d 389 (2000). Section 2254(d)(1)'s "unreasonable application" applies where, as here, there have only been summary denials of habeas relief by the state courts. Harrington v. Richter, ____ U.S. ____, 131 S.Ct. 770, 784, 178 L.Ed.2d 624 (2011). "Where a state court's decision is unaccompanied by an explanation, the habeas petitioner's burden still must be met by showing there was no reasonable basis for the state court to deny relief." Id.

DISCUSSION

Shoemaker argues that it was contrary to, or an unreasonable application of, clearly established federal law for the state court to uphold: (1) the jury's determination that Exhibits 3, 5, 7, 9, 12, and 13 were child pornography, where those images were innocuous portrayals of nude children; (2) the jury's determination that Exhibits 8 and 14 were child pornography, where those images were morphed; (3) the jury instructions and the prosecutor's argument that allowed the jury to consider the context in which the images were displayed in determining whether the images were child pornography; and (4) the sufficiency of the evidence supporting his convictions. Although we agree that the prosecutor's argument was error, constrained by AEDPA, we conclude that the error was harmless, and we otherwise reject Shoemaker's remaining arguments.

A. Nude Images—Exhibits 3, 5, 7, 9, 12, and 13

First, Shoemaker argues that Exhibits 3, 5, 7, 9, 12, and 13 were simply innocent pictures of nude children, and thus protected speech. Upon independent review of the images, McCoy, 282 F.3d at 629, we cannot conclude that these images are protected by the First Amendment. Therefore, we hold that the state court was not unreasonable to determine that Exhibits 3, 5, 7, 9, 12, and 13 were not protected speech.

The Supreme Court has clearly established that not all images of nude children amount to child pornography because "nudity, without more[,] is protected expression." New York v. Ferber, 458 U.S. 747, 765 n. 18, 102 S.Ct. 3348, 73 L.Ed.2d 1113 (1982); see also Osborne v. Ohio, 495 U.S. 103, 112, 110 S.Ct. 1691, 109 L.Ed.2d 98 (1990). "For example, a family snapshot of a nude child bathing presumably would not be criminal." United States v. Hill, 459 F.3d 966, 970 (9th Cir.2006) (internal quotation omitted). The Supreme Court has, however, upheld statutes criminalizing the possession of "lewd" or "lascivious" depictions of nude children. United States v. X-Citement Video, Inc., 513 U.S. 64, 115 S.Ct. 464, 130 L.Ed.2d 372 (1994) (holding that "lascivious" and "lewd" are indistinguishable and that federal child pornography statute 18 U.S.C. § 2252 criminalizing the possession of images depicting "lascivious exhibition of the genitals" was not vague or overbroad); Osborne, 495 U.S. at 112-13, 110 S.Ct. 1691; Ferber, 458 U.S. at 765, 102 S.Ct. 3348 (upholding New York law prohibiting images amounting to a "lewd exhibition of the genitals").

We have held that "'lascivious' is a 'commonsensical term' and that whether a given photo is lascivious is a question of fact.... [W]hether the item to be judged is lewd, lascivious, or obscene is a determination that lay persons can and should make." United States v. Arvin, 900 F.2d 1385, 1390 (9th Cir.1990) (citations omitted). To determine whether depictions of nude children are "lascivious," "lewd," or "for the purpose of sexual stimulation of the viewer," and thus child pornography, our court and other circuits have relied on the Dost factors, set forth in United States v. Dost, 636 F.Supp. 828 (S.D.Cal.1986), aff'd sub nom. United States v. Wiegand, 812 F.2d 1239 (9th Cir.1987). See, e.g., Hill, 459 F.3d at 972; Doe v. Chamberlin, 299 F.3d 192, 196 (3d Cir.2002);

United States v. Brunette, 256 F.3d 14, 17-18 (1st Cir.2001); United States v. Boudreau, 250 F.3d 279, 282-83 (5th Cir.2001); United States v. Moore, 215 F.3d 681, 686-87 (7th Cir.2000). The Dost test sets forth six factors for determining lewdness or lasciviousness:

(1) whether the focal point of the visual depiction is on the child's genitalia or pubic area;

(2) whether the setting of the visual depiction is sexually suggestive, i.e. in a place or pose generally associated with sexual activity;

(3) whether the child is depicted in an unnatural pose, or in inappropriate attire, considering the age of the child;

(4) whether the child is fully or partially clothed, or nude;

(5) whether the visual depiction suggests sexual coyness or a willingness to engage in sexual activity; and

(6) whether the visual depiction is intended or designed to elicit a sexual response in the viewer.

636 F.Supp. at 832. We have stated that "the [Dost] factors are neither exclusive nor conclusive" but rather "general principles as guides for analysis" and "a starting point" in determining whether an image constitutes child pornography. Hill, 459 F.3d at 972.

Considering these factors on de novo review of the images, we conclude that the six images that Shoemaker claims are innocuous nude photographs are in fact child pornography. We find, just as the district court found after independently reviewing the photographs, that several of the Dost factors are present in Exhibits 3, 5, 7, 9, 12, and 13, including: nudity, expressions of sexual coyness, focus on genitals and pubic areas, and girls "arrayed for the sexual stimulation of the viewers."

Therefore, the state court's determination was not unreasonable.

Indeed, the jury in Shoemaker's case was instructed to consider five of the six Dost factors to determine whether the images were "exhibition of the genitals or pubic or rectal area for the purpose of sexual stimulation of the viewer" under California Penal Code § 311.11. Given the presence of several Dost factors in Exhibits 3, 5, 7, 9, 12, and 13, the state court did not unreasonably apply Ferber or Osborne when it rejected Shoemaker's argument that the images were innocuous nude photographs.

B. Morphed Images—Exhibits 8 and 14

Shoemaker argues that the jury wrongly found Exhibits 8 and 14 to be child pornography because those images were morphed, and the state court unreasonably applied clearly established federal law by failing to afford him habeas relief on this ground.

Upon an independent review of the record, it is clear that the images depict children engaging in sexually explicit behavior and would thus not be protected by the First Amendment if not "morphed." Irrespective of whether the images are in fact morphed, Shoemaker's claim fails because there is no clearly established Supreme Court law holding that images of real children morphed to look like child pornography constitute protected speech.

Morphed images of children engaged in sexual activity directly implicate the interest of protecting children from harm, an interest the Supreme Court deemed compelling in Ferber. There, the Court explained that states have a compelling interest in "safeguarding the physical and psychological well-being of a minor" and the "prevention of sexual exploitation and abuse of children." 458 U.S. at 756-57, 102 S.Ct. 3348 (internal quotation omitted). The Court further noted that actual child pornography is "intrinsically related to the sexual abuse of children" because it is "a permanent record of the children's participation and the harm to the child is exacerbated by [its] circulation." Id. at 759, 102 S.Ct. 3348 (emphasis added).

Morphed images are different from traditional child pornography because the children depicted may not have been sexually abused or physically harmed during the images' production. But, morphed images are like traditional child pornography in that they are records of the harmful sexual exploitation of children. The children, who are identifiable in the images, are violated by being falsely portrayed as engaging in sexual activity. As with traditional child pornography, the children are sexually exploited and psychologically harmed by the existence of the images, and subject to additional reputational harm as the images are circulated.

For this reason, at least three other circuits have held that morphed images of children engaging in sexual activity constitute unprotected speech. See Doe v. Boland, 698 F.3d 877 (6th Cir.2012); United States v. Hotaling, 634 F.3d 725 (2d Cir.2011), cert. denied, ____ U.S. ____, 132 S.Ct. 843, 181 L.Ed.2d 548 (2011); United States v. Bach, 400 F.3d 622 (8th Cir.2005). In Hotaling, the Second Circuit explained that the "underlying inquiry is whether an image of child pornography implicates the interests of an actual minor." 634 F.3d at 729. The court held that "[s]exually explicit images that use the faces of actual minors are not protected expressive speech under the First Amendment" because, when a minor's face is used, her interests are implicated and she is placed "at risk of reputational harm and ... psychological harm." Id. at 730. In Bach, the Eighth Circuit similarly reasoned,

Although there is no contention that the nude body actually is that of AC or that he was involved in the production of the image, a lasting record has been created of AC, an identifiable minor child, seemingly engaged in sexually explicit activity. He is thus victimized every time the picture is displayed.

400 F.3d at 632.

As the foregoing underscores, the Supreme Court has not clearly established that images morphed to depict children engaged in sexual activity are protected by the First Amendment. Indeed, the Court has expressly left open the question whether morphed images can constitute child pornography. Ashcroft v. Free Speech Coalition, 535 U.S. 234, 242, 122 S.Ct. 1389, 152 L.Ed.2d 403 (2002). In Free Speech Coalition, the Court held that virtual child pornography—images of naked children created entirely digitally without the use of any real children—was protected speech. Id. at 239, 122 S.Ct. 1389. The

Court thus declared unconstitutional those portions of the federal Child Pornography Protection Act prohibiting such pornography. Id. The Court, however, expressly declined to rule on the section of the Act that covered morphed images: "Although morphed images may fall within the definition of virtual child pornography, they implicate the interests of real children and are in that sense closer to the images in Ferber. Respondents do not challenge this provision, and we do not consider it." Id. at 242, 122 S.Ct. 1389. In fact, by stating that morphed images are "closer to the images in Ferber," the Court noted that morphed images were more likely to be considered unprotected speech like the actual child pornography at issue in Ferber, rather than protected speech.

Second, we are unpersuaded by Shoemaker's argument that it is clearly established that all speech is protected by the First Amendment unless the Supreme Court has expressly carved out an exception from First Amendment protection. Specifically, Shoemaker contends that unless and until the Court determines that morphed images of children engaging in sexual activity are unprotected, the law is clearly established that such images are protected. This argument rests on an overly narrow and static conception of categories of speech.

Contrary to Shoemaker's argument, if speech does not squarely fall within a category of unprotected speech, that speech's protection under the First Amendment is not clearly established. Rather, the "appellate court has an obligation to make an independent examination of the whole record" to evaluate whether the speech is protected or whether it actually falls into a category of unprotected speech and thus may be lawfully restricted under the First Amendment. Bose Corp. v. Consumers Union of U.S., Inc., 466 U.S. 485, 499, 104 S.Ct. 1949, 80 L.Ed.2d 502 (1984) (internal quotation omitted); Ferber, 458 U.S. at 774 n. 28, 102 S.Ct. 3348. During this independent examination, the court checks whether the speech falls within any unprotected category and, if so, "confine[s] the perimeters of [the] unprotected category within acceptably narrow limits in an effort to ensure that protected expression will not be inhibited." Bose, 466 U.S. at 505, 104 S.Ct. 1949. Through the independent examination process, the parameters of unprotected speech categories are continually being defined. For this reason, there is no need for the Court to carve out a separate exception for morphed images of children engaging in sexual activity in order to hold that such speech is unprotected. Instead, on independent review, the Court may decide that such speech is unprotected as a part of an existing category of unprotected speech like child pornography.

Therefore, we reject Shoemaker's invitation to invert AEDPA's standard of review in the First Amendment context. In sum, we conclude that the Supreme Court has not clearly established that morphed images are protected by the First Amendment. Accordingly, we hold that under § 2254(d), the state court reasonably rejected Shoemaker's claim that Exhibits 8 and 14 cannot be considered pornographic.

C. Context in Which the Images Were Shown

Shoemaker contends that the court erred when it allowed the jury to consider the context in which the images were displayed in determining whether the images were child pornography. Specifically, Shoemaker alleges error in the jury instructions, which allowed the jury to consider the "setting" of the images, and the prosecutor's arguments regarding the adult website on which six of the images were displayed. Shoemaker argues that Free Speech Coalition established that context is irrelevant in determining whether an image is child pornography. Shoemaker misreads Free Speech Coalition.

In Free Speech Coalition, the Supreme Court struck down a federal law that banned materials marketed in such a way that "conveys the impression" that such materials depict minors engaged in sexually explicit conduct. Id. at 257, 122 S.Ct. 1389. The Court was concerned that "[e]ven if a film contains no sexually explicit scenes involving minors, it could be treated as child pornography if the title and trailers convey the impression that [such] scenes would be found in the movie." Id. The Court found the law overbroad because its analysis would not "depend principally upon the content of the prohibited work" but would instead "turn[ ] on how the speech is presented, not on what is depicted." Id. The Court did not state, however, that the context in which an image is displayed may never be considered in determining whether an image is child pornography. In fact, the Court noted that how an image is pandered may be relevant in determining whether particular materials are obscene, citing Ginzburg v. United States, 383 U.S. 463, 474, 86 S.Ct. 942, 16 L.Ed.2d 31 (1966). 535 U.S. at 257-58, 122 S.Ct. 1389. Thus, the Court left open the question whether the context in which an image is displayed may be considered as a factor in a child pornography determination.

However, Free Speech Coalition does tell us that a child pornography determination may not "turn on" the context in which an image is presented. We read "turn on" to mean to "depend principally on." In Free Speech Coalition, the Court rejected the government's argument that "the determination [of child pornography] would still depend principally upon the content of the prohibited work." Id. at 257, 122 S.Ct. 1389 (emphasis added). The Court instead found that "[t]he determination turns on how the speech is presented, not what is depicted" and therefore held that the challenged law was unconstitutional. Id. (emphasis added). The juxtaposition in the opinion between "depend principally upon" and "turns on" supports our view that the two phrases are treated as synonymous. Thus, we read Free Speech Coalition as clearly establishing that the context of how an image is presented may not be the principal consideration in determining whether that image is child pornography.

We now turn to whether the state court unreasonably applied Free Speech Coalition in rejecting Shoemaker's habeas claim regarding the jury instructions. The instructions allowed the jury to consider "[w]hether the `setting' was sexually suggestive."

The jury may have understood "setting" to mean the backdrop depicted within the four corners of the photograph—for example, the sailboat in Exhibit 1 or the bathtub in Exhibit 7. This would make "setting" a factor relating to the content of the images rather than to the context in which they were displayed. Therefore, we cannot say that the state court was unreasonable in finding that the jury instructions, which tracked the widely-used Dost factors, were proper.

The state court's decision upholding the prosecutor's closing argument presents a different question. The prosecutor repeatedly emphasized the context of the adult Beachbaby website on which six of the pictures were displayed. At the outset of his closing, the prosecutor argued that when someone like Shoemaker gets his hands on hypothetical innocent photos of someone's children at a nudist camp and:

put[s] them on [his] website among other pictures, other pornographic pictures... it is that context, ladies and gentlemen, of my child, anyone's child on the bear skin rug in the bathtub with the soapy hair, with the little brother, the little sister laughing in the bathtub naked. It is when you see that image in the context of how it appears when a person looks at that photo placed amongst others by [co-defendant] and Mr. Shoemaker that make that image the exhibition of the genitals for the purpose of stimulation of the viewer. (emphasis added).

He said of each image in various formulations:

Let's assume for a minute that this image was taken at a nudist camp. Perfectly natural behavior for a nudist camp. Naturalist. When you take an image of a child out of their setting and put that into the setting of Beachbaby.com, of Blowout.com, this image is designed to stimulate the sexual desires of the viewer.

And referring to another image, he said:

Maybe there is nothing particular[ly] odd about the photograph. It is in a nudist camp and everybody is walking around naked. The child is just posing for the camera as many kids may do. Again, it is the placing in the context of the website. And interestingly enough this one is, again, on the teens section of Beachbaby.com.

In effect, the prosecutor argued that even if the nude images of children at issue here were not child pornography before they were on the website, they became child pornography in the context in which they were placed. In making this argument, the prosecutor did exactly what Free Speech Coalition forbid—he argued to the jury that its determination could "turn on" the fact that otherwise innocuous images were displayed in a pornographic context. Under clearly established Supreme Court precedent, the prosecutor erred.

Nonetheless, we hold that the prosecutor's error did not have a "substantial and injurious effect or influence in determining the jury's verdict." Brecht v. Abrahamson, 507 U.S. 619, 631, 113 S.Ct. 1710, 123 L.Ed.2d 353 (1993); Fry v. Pliler, 551 U.S. 112, 121-22, 127 S.Ct. 2321, 168 L.Ed.2d 16 (2007) (holding that "in § 2254 proceedings a court must assess the prejudicial impact of constitutional error in a state-court criminal trial under the `substantial and injurious effect' standard set forth in Brecht, whether or not the state appellate court recognized the error"). Here, as we have already independently determined, the images in question were child pornography and several of the Dost factors were present in each. Each image presented a nude girl, a factor that the prosecutor also emphasized throughout his closing argument. Although we hold that portions of the prosecutor's argument were erroneous, the prosecutor also repeated the instructions regarding the five factors that the jury should consider in determining whether the images were child pornography. In so doing, the whole of the prosecutor's argument made the jury aware that its decision should rest on multiple factors.

Thus, although the state court unreasonably applied Free Speech Coalition when it rejected Shoemaker's prosecutorial error argument, we reject Shoemaker's claim because the error was harmless.

D. Sufficiency of the Evidence

Lastly, Shoemaker requests that we expand the certificate of appealability to consider the issue whether his convictions were based on insufficient evidence and thus a violation of the Due Process Clause. A conviction based on insufficient evidence violates a defendant's due process rights. In re Winship, 397 U.S. 358, 90 S.Ct. 1068, 25 L.Ed.2d 368 (1970). Evidence is insufficient if, viewed in the light most favorable to the prosecution, no reasonable trier of fact could have found the defendant guilty beyond a reasonable doubt. Jackson v. Virginia, 443 U.S. 307, 319, 99 S.Ct. 2781, 61 L.Ed.2d 560 (1979).

The standard for expanding a certificate of appealability is low. A certificate of appealability should issue if "reasonable jurists could debate whether" (1) the district court's assessment of the claim was debatable or wrong; or (2) the issue presented is "adequate to deserve encouragement to proceed further." Slack v. McDaniel, 529 U.S. 473, 484, 120 S.Ct. 1595, 146 L.Ed.2d 542 (2000) (citation and internal quotation marks omitted); see also Miller-El v. Cockrell, 537 U.S. 322, 338, 123 S.Ct. 1029, 154 L.Ed.2d 931 (2003).

Even if the standard to expand the certificate of appealability is met, Shoemaker cannot meet his burden to show that the state court was unreasonable to decide that sufficient evidence existed to support his convictions. First, the state court was not unreasonable when it rejected Shoemaker's claim that insufficient evidence existed to support his conviction for knowingly possessing or controlling child pornography. Shoemaker owned the Beachbaby and Blowout websites; the servers for these websites were located in his business office; two of the images were in a folder titled "shoe," which are the first four letters of Shoemaker's last name; the "shoe" folder also contained images of Shoemaker, his friends, and his residence; and the systems operator for Beachbaby was Shoemaker's sole employee. In light of this evidence, the state court did not unreasonably apply Jackson v. Virginia in rejecting Shoemaker's habeas claim that insufficient evidence existed to support his convictions for possession of child pornography.

Nor was the state court objectively unreasonable to reject Shoemaker's claim that insufficient evidence existed to support his conviction for duplicating child pornography (based on Exhibits 13 and 14). The copies of these images were located in a folder on the Blowout server titled "shoe"; the "shoe" folder also contained images of Shoemaker, his friends, and his residence; the user "Staff" was moving Shoemaker's personal images around on the same day the copy of the "shoe" folder appeared on the Blowout server; and Shoemaker was the systems operator for the Blowout server. Given this evidence, the state court did not unreasonably apply Jackson v. Virginia in rejecting Shoemaker's claim that insufficient evidence existed to support his conviction for duplicating child pornography.

CONCLUSION

For the reasons set forth in this opinion, Shoemaker is not entitled to relief. Although the state court unreasonably applied Free Speech Coalition, the error was harmless. The district court's denial of Shoemaker's petition for writ of habeas corpus is therefore AFFIRMED.

Notes

[1] California Penal Code § 311.11 makes it a crime for a person to "knowingly possess[ ] or control[ ] any matter, representation of information, data, or image ... the production of which involves the use of a person under the age of 18 years, knowing that the matter depicts a person under the age of 18 years personally engaging in or simulating sexual conduct, as defined in subdivision (d) of Section 311.4."

California Penal Code § 311.4(d) defines "sexual conduct" as including actual or simulated "sexual intercourse" and "exhibition of the genitals or pubic or rectal area for the purpose of sexual stimulation of the viewer." (emphasis added).

California Penal Code § 311.3 makes it a crime to "knowingly develop[ ], duplicate[ ], print[ ], or exchange[ ] any representation of information, data or image ... that depicts a person under the age of 18 years engaged in an act of sexual conduct." This section defines "sexual conduct" in substantively the same way as § 311.4.

[2] These five factors were established in United States v. Dost, 636 F.Supp. 828, 832 (S.D.Cal. 1986).

## Vivid Entm't v. Fielding (Ninth Circuit) (Dec 15, 2014) [Appendices omitted]

GRABER, Circuit Judge:

Plaintiffs Vivid Entertainment, LLC; Califa Productions, Inc.; Kayden Kross; and Logan Pierce are organizations and individuals who make adult films in Los Angeles County. The Los Angeles County Department of Public Health, whose director is a defendant here, sent Plaintiffs a letter stating its intention to enforce the voter-initiated County of Los Angeles Safer Sex in the Adult Film Industry Act (2012) (commonly known as Measure B) (codified at Los Angeles County, Cal., Code tit. 11, div. 1, ch. 11.39, and amending tit. 22, div. 1, ch. 22.56.1925). Measure B imposes a permitting system and additional production obligations on the makers of adult films, including a requirement that performers wear condoms in certain contexts. Plaintiffs sued for declaratory and injunctive relief, arguing that Measure B burdens their freedom of expression in violation of the First Amendment. Defendant Los Angeles County answered that, although it would enforce the ordinance unless ordered by a court not to, it did not intend to defend Measure B because it took a "position of neutrality" with respect to the ordinance's constitutionality. The official proponents of Measure B intervened to defend it.

The district court issued a preliminary injunction forbidding Defendants from enforcing Measure B's fee- setting provision, which gave Defendants discretion to set fees for permits; a provision that allowed warrantless searches by county health officers of any location suspected of producing adult films; and the broad permit modification, suspension, and revocation process. The court denied preliminary injunctive relief, though, for much of the ordinance, including its condom and permitting requirements. Plaintiffs appeal the district court's decision not to enjoin Measure B in full.1 We affirm.

FACTUAL AND PROCEDURAL HISTORY

The citizens of Los Angeles County enacted Measure B in November 2012 by means of the initiative process; it became law on December 14, 2012. The text of the ordinance declared that it was passed in response to documentation by the Los Angeles County Department of Public Health of the widespread transmission of sexually transmitted infections among workers in the adult film industry. Under Measure B, producers of adult films2 must obtain a newly designated "public health permit" before shooting an adult film in Los Angeles County.

Under Measure B as enacted, to obtain such a permit, producers of adult films must pay a fee, provide the Department with proof that certain employees have completed a county-approved training program concerning blood-borne pathogens, display the permit while filming, post a notice at the film site that the use of condoms is required, report to the Department any changes in the permitted business, and comply with all applicable laws, including title 8, section 5193 of the California Code of Regulations. Measure B 11.39.080, .090, .100, .110. Section 5193 mandates barrier protection for all employees who are exposed to blood-borne pathogens, which Measure B interprets to require condoms for performers who engage in vaginal or anal intercourse. Id. 11.39.090. Measure B also provides that a public health permit may be suspended or revoked, and fines or criminal penalties imposed, for failure to comply with all permitting requirements. Id. 11.39.110. A producer who faces modification, suspension, or revocation of a permit may apply for an undefined form of "administrative review." Id. 11.39.110(C).

In addition to providing for monetary and criminal penalties, Measure B allows enforcement of the permitting requirements through a surprise inspection by a Los Angeles County health officer at "any location suspected of conducting any activity regulated by this chapter." Id.

11.39.130. "[F]or purposes of enforcing this chapter," the health officer "may issue notices and impose fines therein and take possession of any sample, photograph, record or other evidence, including any documents bearing upon adult film producer's compliance with the provision of the chapter." Id.

Measure B authorizes the district attorney to bring a civil enforcement action for injunctive relief against any producer who fails to cooperate with the health officer. Id. 11.39.140.

On the day that Measure B took effect, Defendant Department of Public Health mailed Plaintiffs a letter notifying them of the new ordinance and stating that it had established provisional permitting fees of $2,000 to $2,500 per year. Plaintiffs then filed this action challenging Measure B as facially unconstitutional under the First Amendment.3

Plaintiffs allege that Measure B's permitting scheme and its condom requirement operate as prior restraints on Plaintiffs' ability to create expression, in the form of adult films, which is protected by the First Amendment.

Over Plaintiffs' objection, the district court allowed supporters of Measure B to intervene. Following the Supreme Court's decision in Hollingsworth v. Perry, 133 S. Ct. 2652 (2013), Plaintiffs asked the court to reconsider because, they argued, Intervenors lacked Article III standing. The district court denied the motion to reconsider.

The district court granted in part and denied in part Intervenors' motion to dismiss, and granted in part and denied in part Plaintiffs' request for a preliminary injunction. In granting preliminary injunctive relief, the district court severed one chapter of Measure B in its entirety and severed portions of three other chapters. Appendix A contains Measure B and shows the parts that the district court enjoined and severed.

Plaintiffs timely appeal the denial of complete preliminary injunctive relief.4 They argue that the enjoined provisions are not properly severable, so the likely invalidity of some parts of the ordinance requires enjoining the entire ordinance. In the alternative, Plaintiffs argue that the district court erred in denying preliminary injunctive relief with respect to Measure B's requirements that producers:

(1) acquire a permit before beginning production on an adult film; (2) demonstrate that employees have completed a county-approved training program concerning blood-borne pathogens as a condition precedent to issuance of the permit; and (3) require performers to use condoms "during any acts of vaginal or anal sexual intercourse."

STANDARD OF REVIEW

We review for abuse of discretion denial of a preliminary injunction. Alliance for the Wild Rockies v. Cottrell, 632 F.3d 1127, 1131 (9th Cir. 2011). "As long as the district court got the law right, it will not be reversed simply because we would have arrived at a different result if we had applied the law to the facts of the case." A&M Records, Inc. v. Napster, Inc., 284 F.3d 1091, 1096 (9th Cir. 2002) (internal quotation marks and brackets omitted). A district court abuses its discretion, however, if it applies an incorrect legal standard. Does 1–5 v. Chandler, 83 F.3d 1150, 1152 (9th Cir. 1996). Accordingly, we review de novo the "legal premises underlying a preliminary injunction." A&M Records, 284 F.3d at 1096.

DISCUSSION

A. Jurisdiction

Citing Perry, Plaintiffs argue that we lack jurisdiction over this appeal, because Intervenors lack Article III standing. We disagree with their reading of Perry and with their contention that Intervenors must have standing for this appeal to proceed.

The Supreme Court has held that a party must have Article III standing both to initiate an action and to seek review on appeal. Arizonans for Official English v. Arizona, 520 U.S. 43, 64 (1997). But an intervenor who performs neither of those functions and no other function that invokes the power of the federal courts need not meet Article III standing requirements. Yniguez v. Arizona, 939 F.2d 727, 731 (9th Cir. 1991), vacated by Arizonans for Official English, 520 U.S. at 80, as recognized in League of United Latin Am. Citizens v. Wilson, 131 F.3d 1297, 1305 n.5 (9th Cir. 1997); see also Perry, 133 S. Ct. at 2661 (citing Art. III, § 2) (holding that "any person invoking the power of a federal court must demonstrate standing to do so" (emphasis added)). Nothing in Perry, which concerned the question whether an intervenor who sought to appeal had Article III standing, affects that conclusion. Plaintiffs have standing, and it is they alone who have invoked the federal courts' jurisdiction. For that reason, we need not and do not decide whether Intervenors satisfy the requirements of Article III standing.

To the extent that Plaintiffs contend that the district court erred in granting intervention, we cannot consider their challenge. An order allowing intervention under Federal Rule of Civil Procedure 24(a) is not a final order and is not an interlocutory order appealable by statute, so an appeal on that issue is premature until entry of final judgment. Alsea Valley Alliance v. Dep't of Commerce, 358 F.3d 1181, 1187 (9th Cir. 2004).

B. Severability

Plaintiffs next urge that, having held that they are likely to succeed on the merits with respect to some provisions of Measure B, the district court had to enjoin operation of the entire ordinance whether or not the remainder independently satisfies the standards for injunctive relief. For the reasons that follow, we disagree.

Federal courts should avoid "judicial legislation"—that is, amending, rather than construing, statutory text—out of respect for the separation-of-powers principle that only legislatures ought to make positive law. United States v. Nat'l Treasury Emps. Union, 513 U.S. 454, 479 (1995). But, because of countervailing separation-of-powers principles, courts must respect the laws made by legislatures and, therefore, should avoid nullifying an entire statute when only a portion is invalid. Brockett v. Spokane Arcades, Inc., 472 U.S. 491, 502 (1985). These concerns have led to the judicial doctrine of severability, that is, the "elementary principle that the same statute may be in part constitutional and in part unconstitutional, and that if the parts are wholly independent of each other, that which is constitutional may stand while that which is unconstitutional will be rejected."

Id. (internal quotation marks omitted). The need for deference and restraint in severing a state or local enactment is all the more acute because of our respect for federalism and local control. See City of Lakewood v. Plain Dealer Publ'g Co., 486 U.S. 750, 772 (1988).

Because a court may not use severability as a fig leaf for judicial legislation, courts have fashioned limits on when a statute may be severed. See Yu Cong Eng v.

Trinidad, 271 U.S. 500, 518 (1926) ("[I]t is very clear that amendment may not be substituted for construction, and that a court may not exercise legislative functions to save the law from conflict with constitutional limitation."). In keeping with federalism principles, the "[s]everability of a local ordinance is a question of state law." City of Lakewood, 486 U.S. at 772.

California law directs courts to consider first the inclusion of a severability clause in the legislation. Cal. Redev. Ass'n v. Matosantos, 267 P.3d 580, 607 (Cal. 2011). "The presence of such a clause establishes a presumption in favor of severance." Id. "Although not conclusive, a severability clause normally calls for sustaining the valid part of the enactment . . . ." Santa Barbara Sch. Dist. v. Superior Court, 530 P.2d 605, 618 (Cal. 1975) (internal quotation marks omitted).

Measure B contains this severability clause:

If any provision of this Act, or part thereof, is for any reason held to be invalid or unconstitutional, the remaining provisions shall not be affected, but shall remain in full force and effect, and to this end the provisions of the Act are severable.

Measure B § 8. Section 8 states clearly that the people, acting in their legislative capacity, intended any provision and any part of a provision, if invalid or unconstitutional, to be severed from the ordinance. The district court thus properly held that Measure B's severability clause establishes a presumption of severability.

Next, California law directs courts to "consider three additional criteria: The invalid provision must be grammatically, functionally, and volitionally separable." Cal. Redev. Ass'n, 267 P.3d at 607 (internal quotation marks and brackets omitted). We will consider each criterion in turn.

"Grammatical separability, also known as mechanical separability, depends on whether the invalid parts can be removed as a whole without affecting the wording or coherence of what remains." Id. (internal quotation marks omitted). "[T]he 'grammatical' component of the test for severance is met by the severability clause considered in conjunction with the separate and discrete provisions of [the statute]." Barlow v. Davis, 85 Cal. Rptr. 2d 752, 757 (Ct. App. 1999). "To be grammatically separable, the valid and invalid parts of the statute can be separated by paragraph, sentence, clause, phrase, or even single words." People v. Nguyen, 166 Cal. Rptr. 3d 590, 609 (Ct. App. 2014) (internal quotation marks omitted). "[Where] the defect cannot be cured by excising any word or group of words, the problem is quite different and more difficult of solution." Ex parte Blaney, 184 P.2d 892, 900 (Cal. 1947); Santa Barbara Sch. Dist., 530 P.2d at 617.

Here, Plaintiffs contend that the district court abused its discretion by striking individual words and groups of words from the definition of an adult film. Specifically, the district court struck part of 11.39.010 of Measure B as follows:

An "adult film" is defined as any film, video, multimedia or other representation of sexual intercourse in which performers actually engage in oral, vaginal, or anal penetration, including, but not limited to, penetration by a penis, finger, or inanimate object; oral contact with the anus or genitals of another performer; and/or any other sexual activity that may result in the transmission of blood and/or any other potentially infectious materials.

In large part, as can be seen, the district court severed distinct clauses. The district court also severed some individual words but, grammatically, they are understood by the reader to include complete clauses. For example, the compound clause "engage in oral, vaginal, or anal penetration" means—and easily could have been drafted to say—"engage in oral penetration, engage in vaginal penetration, or engage in anal penetration." For that reason, the district court did, in fact, sever only distinct provisions from Measure B, and that severance did not alter the meaning of the remaining text in any way. California courts have long held that parts of a compound clause are grammatically severable from a statute if their omission would not affect the meaning of the remaining text. Ex parte Blaney, 184 P.2d at 900; Santa Barbara Sch. Dist., 530 P.2d at 617; see also Legislature v. Eu, 816 P.2d 1309, 1335–36 (Cal. 1991) (holding as grammatically severable "or serving in" from "elected to or serving in the Legislature on or after November 1, 1990"); Borikas v. Alameda Unified Sch. Dist., 154 Cal. Rptr. 3d 186, 212 (Ct. App. 2013) (holding as grammatically severable "residential" from "[o]n each taxable, residential parcel at the rate of $120 per year"); City of Dublin v. County of Alameda, 17 Cal. Rptr. 2d 845, 850–51 (Ct. App. 1993) (holding as grammatically severable "incorporated and" from "the geographic entity, including both the incorporated and unincorporated areas"). In short, the district court permissibly held that the disputed portions of Measure B are grammatically severable.5

Our next consideration, functional severability, "depends on whether the remainder [of the statute] is complete in itself." Santa Barbara Sch. Dist., 530 P.2d at 618 (internal quotation marks omitted). To be functionally severable, "[t]he remaining provisions must stand on their own, unaided by the invalid provisions nor rendered vague by their absence nor inextricably connected to them by policy considerations. They must be capable of separate enforcement." People's Advocate, Inc. v. Superior Court, 226 Cal. Rptr. 640, 649 (Ct. App. 1986). Here, the district court enjoined the provisions of Measure B that allowed for modification, suspension, and revocation of permits; that authorized administrative searches; and that allowed discretion in setting fees. The rest of the ordinance remains intact: the permitting scheme, with its condom and educational requirements; and enforcement through fines and criminal charges. In addition, as the district court noted, even in the absence of the administrative search provision, Defendants can obtain a warrant to enforce Measure B. Because the remaining parts of Measure B operate independently, are not rendered vague in the absence of the invalid provisions, and are capable of separate enforcement, the district court permissibly ruled that the provisions are functionally severable.

Our final consideration, volitional severability, "depends on whether the remainder [of the statute] is complete in itself and would have been adopted by the legislative body had [it] foreseen the partial invalidation of the statute." Santa Barbara Sch. Dist., 530 P.2d at 618 (internal quotation marks omitted). With respect to ballot initiatives, the test for volitional severability "is whether it can be said with confidence that the electorate's attention was sufficiently focused upon the parts to be severed so that it would have separately considered and adopted them in the absence of the invalid portions." Gerken v. Fair Political Practices Comm'n, 863 P.2d 694, 699 (Cal. 1993) (internal quotation marks and emphasis omitted).

The district court preserved the requirements that producers of adult films in Los Angeles County obtain permits, train employees about the sexual transmission of disease, and require performers to wear condoms when engaged in vaginal or anal intercourse. The district court also preserved the enforcement mechanisms of fines and criminal penalties. As the court correctly noted, the "Findings and Declaration" section of the initiative emphasizes (1) a growing public concern over the spread of HIV/AIDS and other sexually transmitted infections in the adult film industry; (2) the importance of safe sex practices, and the use of condoms in particular, in limiting the spread of HIV/AIDS and other sexually transmitted infections; and (3) a failure to enforce current state laws mandating the use of condoms by performers in adult films. Measure B § 2. Thus, the Declaration demonstrates that the public's attention was focused primarily on heightening enforcement of the condom requirement. That is, even in the absence of the severed segments, the remaining provisions centrally address the voters' stated concerns. The district court permissibly concluded that the condom and permitting requirements are volitionally severable from the fee-setting, inspections, and administrative procedures.

Plaintiffs counter that the fee provisions are not volitionally severable, because the voters would not have passed Measure B as an "unfunded mandate." But the Declaration contained in Measure B says nothing about money or revenue neutrality. Rather, the text demonstrates that the core purpose of the initiative "was presented to the electorate as a distinct aim, separate and apart from the measure's funding mandate." McMahan v. City of San Francisco, 26 Cal. Rptr. 3d 509, 513 (Ct. App. 2005) (holding that a funding provision was volitionally severable from the primary regulatory scheme).

In sum, the district court did not abuse its discretion in granting preliminary injunctive relief with respect to only certain parts of Measure B, while allowing enforcement of other provisions as severable. We now turn to Plaintiffs' assertion that, even if severance is permissible, the district court erred in denying preliminary injunctive relief with respect to additional parts of the ordinance: the condom mandate and the permitting requirement.

C. Denial of Preliminary Injunctive Relief

In deciding whether a preliminary injunction should issue, a district court must consider four factors: (1) whether the plaintiff has shown a likelihood of success on the merits; (2) whether the plaintiff has shown a likelihood of irreparable harm in the absence of preliminary relief; (3) whether the balance of equities tips in the plaintiff's favor; and

(4) whether preliminary relief is in the public interest. Winter v. Natural Res. Def.

Council, Inc., 555 U.S. 7, 20 (2008).

Courts asked to issue preliminary injunctions based on First Amendment grounds face an inherent tension: the moving party bears the burden of showing likely success on the merits . . . and yet within that merits determination the government bears the burden of justifying its speech-restrictive law. . . .

. . . .

Therefore, in the First Amendment context, the moving party bears the initial burden of making a colorable claim that its First Amendment rights have been infringed,
. . . at which point the burden shifts to the government to justify the restriction.

Thalheimer v. City of San Diego, 645 F.3d 1109, 1115–16 (9th Cir. 2011). But even if the plaintiff demonstrates likely success on the merits, the plaintiff still must demonstrate irreparable injury, a favorable balance of equities, and the tipping of the public interest in favor of an injunction. Id. at 1128. That is, although

a First Amendment claim "certainly raises the specter" of irreparable harm and public interest considerations, proving the likelihood of such a claim is not enough to satisfy

Winter. Stormans, [Inc. v. Selecky, 586 F.3d 1109,] 1138 [(9th Cir. 2009)]; see also Klein v. City of San Clemente, 584 F.3d 1196, 1207 (9th Cir. 2009) (even where the plaintiff was likely to succeed on the merits of his First Amendment claim, he "must also demonstrate that he is likely to suffer irreparable injury in the absence of a preliminary injunction, and that the balance of equities and the public interest tip in his favor") (citing Winter, 555 U.S. at 20).

DISH Network Corp. v. FCC, 653 F.3d 771, 776 (9th Cir. 2011).

1. Condom Mandate

The district court held that Plaintiffs are unlikely to succeed on the merits of their First Amendment challenge to the condom requirement. The court did not abuse its discretion in declining to enjoin the enforcement of the condom mandate. The condom mandate survives intermediate scrutiny because it has only a de minimis effect on expression, is narrowly tailored to achieve the substantial governmental interest of reducing the rate of sexually transmitted infections, and leaves open adequate alternative means of expression.

As a threshold matter, Plaintiffs argue that the district court applied the wrong standard—intermediate scrutiny— and that the condom mandate should be subject to strict scrutiny. We disagree.

The Supreme Court has recognized that nearly all regulation of the adult entertainment industry is content based. See City of Los Angeles v. Alameda Books, Inc., 535 U.S. 425, 448 (2002) (Kennedy, J., concurring in the judgment). Content-based regulation of speech generally receives strict scrutiny, but we have fashioned an exception, grounded in Alameda Books, that applies intermediate scrutiny if two conditions are met. Ctr. for Fair Pub. Policy v. Maricopa County, 336 F.3d 1153, 1161, 1164–65 (9th Cir. 2003) (citing Alameda Books, 535 U.S. at 434) (recognizing Justice

Kennedy's concurrence as controlling). First, the ordinance must regulate "speech that is sexual or pornographic in nature." Gammoh v. City of La Habra, 395 F.3d 1114, 1123, amended on denial of reh'g, 402 F.3d 875 (9th Cir. 2005). Second, "the primary motivation behind the regulation [must be] to prevent secondary effects." Id.

But even if those two conditions are met, strict scrutiny may still apply if the regulation amounts to a complete ban on expression. Dream Palace v. County of Maricopa, 384 F.3d 990, 1021 (9th Cir. 2004).

We assume, but need not and do not decide, that Measure B's condom mandate is a content-based regulation of speech. Nonetheless, Measure B regulates sexual speech in order to prevent the secondary effects of sexually transmitted infections, thus falling within the Alameda Books exception. Plaintiffs argue that, despite that exception, the district court should have applied strict scrutiny because the condom mandate amounts to a complete ban on their protected expression.

As an initial matter, Plaintiffs' argument presupposes that their relevant expression for First Amendment purposes is the depiction of condomless sex. But "simply to define what is being banned as the 'message' is to assume the conclusion." City of Erie v. Pap's A.M., 529 U.S. 277, 293 (2000). In Pap's A.M., a plurality of the Supreme Court concluded that a general ban on public nudity, which required erotic dancers to wear at least pasties and a G-string while dancing, did not violate the First Amendment. Id. at 302. In reaching that conclusion, the opinion rejected the argument that the pasties- and-G-string requirement functioned as a complete ban on the dancers' expression of "nude dancing." Id. at 292–93. Instead, the opinion defined the relevant expression more broadly as "the dancer's erotic message." Id. at 301. We undertook a similar analysis, albeit without reference to Pap's A.M., in Gammoh, in which we upheld an ordinance that required dancers to stay at least two feet away from patrons during their performances. 395 F.3d at 1123. The plaintiffs there argued that the ordinance completely banned their expression, which they defined as "proximate dancing." Id.

In response, we stressed that "the 'expression' at issue could always be defined to include the contested restriction," but "virtually no ordinance would survive this analysis." Id. We instead defined the relevant expression as "the dancer's erotic message" and upheld the ordinance. Id. at 1128.

In light of those cases, we must examine more carefully whether Plaintiffs' relevant expression is the depiction of condomless sex. Plaintiffs submitted declarations stating that condomless sex differs from sex generally because condoms remind the audience about real-world concerns such as pregnancy and disease. Under this view, films depicting condomless sex convey a particular message about sex in a world without those risks. The Supreme Court has cautioned, however, that "'[i]t is possible to find some kernel of expression in almost every activity a person undertakes—for example, walking down the street or meeting one's friends at a shopping mall—but such a kernel is not sufficient to bring the activity within the protection of the First Amendment.'"

Barnes v. Glen Theatre, Inc., 501 U.S. 560, 570 (1991) (quoting City of Dallas v. Stanglin, 490 U.S. 19, 25 (1989)).

To determine whether conduct is protected by the First Amendment, we ask not only whether someone intended to convey a particular message through that conduct, but also whether there is a "great" likelihood "that the message would be understood by those who viewed it." Spence v. Washington, 418 U.S. 405, 410–11 (1974) (per curiam). Here, we agree with the district court that, whatever unique message Plaintiffs might intend to convey by depicting condomless sex, it is unlikely that viewers of adult films will understand that message. So condomless sex is not the relevant expression for First Amendment purposes;6 instead, the relevant expression is more generally the adult films' erotic message. See Pap's A.M., 529 U.S. at 293; Gammoh, 395 F.3d at 1123.

With Plaintiffs' expression so defined, we conclude that strict scrutiny is inappropriate because the condom mandate does not ban the relevant expression completely. Rather, it imposes a de minimis restriction. In Pap's A.M., the Supreme Court held that the pasties-and-G-string requirement did not violate the First Amendment because, even if the ban "has some minimal effect on the erotic message by muting that portion of the expression that occurs when the last stitch is dropped," that effect was de minimis. 529 U.S. at 294 (emphasis added). That was so even though the ban "certainly ha[d] the effect of limiting one particular means of expressing the kind of erotic message being disseminated."

Id. at 292–93; see also Barnes, 501 U.S. at 571 (noting that a requirement that erotic dancers wear pasties and G-strings "does not deprive the dance of whatever erotic message it conveys; it simply makes the message slightly less graphic").

Many of our sister circuits have relied on Pap's A.M. in upholding de minimis restrictions on speech using intermediate scrutiny. See, e.g., Sensations, Inc. v. City of Grand Rapids, 526 F.3d 291, 299 (6th Cir. 2008) (upholding a nudity ban under intermediate scrutiny because Pap's A.M. and Barnes had characterized a similar regulation as de minimis); Fantasy Ranch Inc. v. City of Arlington, 459 F.3d 546, 562 (5th Cir. 2006) (rejecting an argument that an ordinance requiring a certain distance between dancers and the audience enacted a "complete ban on proximate nude dancing"); Heideman v. S. Salt Lake City, 348 F.3d 1182, 1195–96 (10th Cir. 2003) (applying Pap's A.M. to conclude that a ban on nude erotic dancing was not a "total ban" on speech). And, as noted, we followed this same analytical approach in Gammoh, 395 F.3d at 1122–23.

A similar analysis applies to the condom mandate. The requirement that actors in adult films wear condoms while engaging in sexual intercourse might have "some minimal effect" on a film's erotic message, but that effect is certainly no greater than the effect of pasties and G-strings on the erotic message of nude dancing. In light of Pap's A.M. and the other precedent cited above, we conclude that the restriction on expression in this case is de minimis. And a de minimis restriction on expression is, by definition, not a complete ban on expression, and so does not trigger strict scrutiny. Accordingly, the mandate is subject to intermediate scrutiny.

The district court properly exercised its discretion in concluding that the condom requirement likely would survive intermediate scrutiny. "A statute will survive intermediate scrutiny if it: (1) is designed to serve a substantial government interest; (2) is narrowly tailored to serve that interest; and (3) does not unreasonably limit alternative avenues of communication." Gammoh, 395 F.3d at 1125–26, as amended on denial of reh'g, 402 F.3d at 876.

The purpose of Measure B is twofold: (1) to decrease the spread of sexually transmitted infections among performers within the adult film industry, (2) thereby stemming the transmission of sexually transmitted infections to the general population among whom the performers dwell. Plaintiffs do not contest that the government has a substantial interest in preventing certain secondary effects of the adult film industry, including the spread of sexually transmitted infections. See Rubin v. Coors Brewing Co., 514 U.S. 476, 485 (1995) (stating that "the Government . . . has a significant interest in protecting the health, safety, and welfare of its citizens"); Ctr. for Fair Pub. Policy, 336 F.3d at 1166 ("It is beyond peradventure at this point in the development of the doctrine that a state's interest in curbing the secondary effects associated with adult entertainment establishments is substantial."). Rather, Plaintiffs contend that Measure B's condom mandate is not narrowly tailored to serve the government's interest.

In order to be narrowly tailored for purposes of intermediate scrutiny, the regulation "'need not be the least restrictive or the least intrusive means' available to achieve the government's legitimate interests." Berger v. City of Seattle, 569 F.3d 1029, 1041 (9th Cir. 2009) (en banc) (quoting Ward v. Rock Against Racism, 491 U.S. 781, 798 (1989)). "Rather, the requirement of narrow tailoring is satisfied so long as the regulation promotes a substantial government interest that would be achieved less effectively absent the regulation." Colacurcio v. City of Kent, 163 F.3d 545, 553 (9th Cir. 1998) (internal quotation marks and ellipsis omitted). This is not to say that narrow tailoring allows a regulation to burden more speech than is necessary to satisfy the interest, but we may not invalidate such a regulation "simply because there is some imaginable alternative that might be less burdensome on speech." United States v. Albertini, 472 U.S. 675, 689 (1985).

Plaintiffs' narrow-tailoring argument rests largely on the proposition that Measure B duplicates a voluntary testing and monitoring scheme that already is in place in the industry. The adult film industry and its trade associations have established the Adult Protection Health & Safety Service, which has implemented a program whereby performers are tested, either monthly or more frequently, and the test results are made available in a database. In addition, if the Safety Service receives notification of a positive test result, it must inform the Department of Public Health. Adult film producers and performers have access to the database in order to verify that performers have been tested and that those tests have been negative. Certain employers require their performers, by contract, to submit to testing at various intervals. For example, Plaintiff Kross' contract requires testing every 15 days, Plaintiff Pierce is tested every 14 days, and all of Plaintiff Vivid Entertainment's performers are tested at least once every 28 days.

On the day of production, Plaintiff Vivid Entertainment requires each performer to provide identification, and each performer's test history is drawn from the Safety Service database. Plaintiff Vivid Entertainment allows participation in the production only by performers with a current test status and a negative result. Plaintiffs Kross and Pierce declare that they undertake this screening process before every explicit scene in which they perform, and both Plaintiffs Kross and Pierce declare that they would not take part in an explicit scene if the screening measures were not in place. Plaintiffs also provided testimony from industry officials that this testing system is effective.

The district court considered Plaintiffs' evidence and weighed it against contradictory evidence that the industry's testing scheme is ineffective. In particular, the district court considered a 2009 letter from the County of Los Angeles Department of Public Health to support the conclusion that Measure B, passed in 2012, was designed to address the spread of disease and is narrowly tailored to that end.7 The Findings and Declaration section of Measure B refers specifically to documentation by the Los Angeles County Department of Public Health of the spread of HIV/AIDS and other sexually transmitted infections in the adult film industry. Measure B § 2.

In the 2009 letter, the Department of Public Health reported that its analysis of 2008 data showed a markedly higher rate of sexually transmitted infections for performers within the adult film industry, 20%, than for the general public, 2.4%, and even for the county area with the highest rate of infection, 4.5%. The Department of Public Health also found that 20.2% of performers in adult films diagnosed with an infection were reinfected within one year. Further, the Department of Public Health opined that the data with respect to infection rates were likely underestimated, because rectal and oral screenings were not completed with regularity among workers in the industry.

The district court weighed all the evidence before it and, finding the 2009 letter especially compelling, held that Plaintiffs were unlikely to succeed on the merits in their First Amendment challenge to the condom mandate. In so doing, the district court did not abuse its discretion.8

On appeal, Plaintiffs also argue that Measure B's condom mandate is not narrowly tailored, and is largely ineffective, because makers of adult films can produce films across county lines without having performers wear condoms. As an initial matter, it bears noting that Plaintiffs offered evidence before the district court that Measure B has drastically reduced the number of adult films produced by the industry because the productions, which depend heavily on the "regular" film industry's infrastructure in Los Angeles County, cannot be moved elsewhere. That evidence undermines Plaintiffs' new contention that Measure B is ineffective because of the adult film industry's ready mobility.

But, more importantly, Plaintiffs' argument overstates the standard for narrow tailoring, which simply requires that the regulation "promote[] a substantial government interest that would be achieved less effectively absent the regulation."

Colacurcio, 163 F.3d at 553. The regulation need not be the most effective way to achieve the government's substantial interest, nor must it be shown that the regulation cannot be circumvented. Rather, it suffices if the regulation helps to achieve the substantial government interest effectively. Id.

Finally, Plaintiffs contend that Measure B's condom mandate unconstitutionally forecloses alternative channels of communication. As we noted in Gammoh, "[t]his inquiry is analogous" to our analysis of whether the condom mandate is a complete ban on expression. 395 F.3d at 1128. In

Gammoh, we held that the required two-foot separation between dancers and patrons left open alternative channels of communication because the requirement "slightly impaired [the message]," but "the dancer's erotic message [could] still be communicated from a slight distance." Id. The same is true here. Measure B is a minimal restriction on Plaintiffs' expression that "leaves ample capacity to convey [Plaintiffs'] erotic message." Pap's A.M., 529 U.S. at 301. Accordingly, the district court did not abuse its discretion in holding that the condom requirement leaves alternative channels of expression available.

2. Permitting System

The portions of Measure B's permitting system left in place by the district court also survive constitutional scrutiny.9 Plaintiffs first argue that the remaining permitting requirements are impermissibly content based and therefore unconstitutional. But a licensing scheme that regulates adult entertainment is not unconstitutional simply because it is content based. See Dream Palace, 384 F.3d at 1001. Plaintiffs also argue "that the remnants of Measure B's permitting regime left intact are [not] narrowly tailored." See Forsyth County v. Nationalist Movement, 505 U.S. 123, 130 (1992) (holding that "any permit scheme . . . must be narrowly tailored"). As discussed above, narrow tailoring requires only that the remaining portions of the permitting scheme "promote[] a substantial government interest that would be achieved less effectively absent the regulation."

Colacurcio, 163 F.3d at 553 (internal quotation marks omitted). The permitting system's requirements that adult film producers complete training about blood-borne pathogens and post a permit during shooting still serve the County's interest in preventing sexually transmitted infections. That remains so even in light of the other portions of the permitting system that the district court enjoined. Finally, Plaintiffs argue that the permitting scheme grants county officials too much discretion, but the district court correctly concluded that the remaining permitting provisions leave little, if any, discretion to government officials. Accordingly, the district court did not abuse its discretion in denying preliminary injunctive relief with respect to Measure B's remaining permitting requirements.

CONCLUSION

We have jurisdiction over this appeal whether or not Intervenors have demonstrated Article III standing. The district court did not abuse its discretion in holding that the invalid portions of Measure B are severable. Nor did the district court abuse its discretion in denying a preliminary injunction with respect to the condom and permitting provisions of Measure B.

AFFIRMED.

Notes

1 No one challenges the partial grant of preliminary injunctive relief.

2 Measure B defines "producer of adult film" as "any person or entity that produces, finances, or directs, adult films for commercial purposes." Measure B, § 4, pt. 11.39.075 (all citations herein are to parts of section 4 unless otherwise noted).

3 Plaintiffs raised other theories as well, but they are not at issue in this appeal.

4 We have jurisdiction under 28 U.S.C. § 1292(a)(1).

5 Plaintiffs rely on Acosta v. City of Costa Mesa, 718 F.3d 800, 820–21 (9th Cir. 2013) (per curiam), for the broad principle that a court necessarily abuses its discretion if it holds that a single word or group of words is grammatically severable under California law. Acosta is distinguishable, and we decline to extend it in a way that would contradict governing California law.

In Acosta, the severability clause itself was narrow, providing that only "sections, paragraphs, clauses and phrases" were severable from the ordinance in question. Id. at 820. We interpreted that particularized list to prohibit, by inference, the severance of "individual words." Id. As directed by California law, we read that narrow severability clause "'in conjunction with the separate and discrete provisions of' the text to determine whether the 'grammatical component of the test for severance is met.'" Id. (quoting Barlow, 85 Cal. Rptr. 2d at 757). Reading the text and severance clause together, we held that the single adjective "insolent" and the list of adjectives "personal, impertinent, profane, insolent" were not grammatically severable from the ordinance because, in context, the words did not express a single "legislative thought." Id. at 820–21.

Here, by contrast, Measure B contains a broad severability clause that does not prohibit the severance of individual words. Under Measure B, any provision or part of any provision shall be severed. Moreover, as noted, the challenged severance in this case involves discrete legislative thoughts.

6 We also note that even if the relevant expression were the depiction of condomless sex, Measure B still might warrant intermediate scrutiny. On its face, Measure B does not ban expression; it does not prohibit the depiction of condomless sex, but rather limits only the way the film is produced. In that way, Measure B's condom mandate is akin to the two- foot required distance between exotic dancers and patrons that we upheld in Gammoh, which did not "ban any form of dance" or address the content of the dance. 395 F.3d at 1123. When the district court adjudicates the First Amendment claim on the merits, if the court were to find that special effects could be used to edit

condoms out of adult films, that would provide yet another reason to apply intermediate scrutiny.

7 The district court properly relied on the letter because it is referred to in Measure B itself. Moreover, the letter is "not subject to reasonable dispute" because it "can be accurately and readily determined from sources whose accuracy cannot reasonably be questioned." Fed. R. Evid. 201(b); see Sachs v. Republic of Austria, 737 F.3d 584, 596 n.10 (9th Cir. 2013) (en banc) (taking notice of legislative facts necessary to discern legislative intent as directed by Rule 201(a), advisory note to 1972 amendments, but noting also that the court could properly notice such facts as adjudicative facts under Rule 201(b)), petition for cert. filed, 82 U.S.L.W. 3573 (U.S. Mar. 5, 2014) (No. 13-1067).

8 That the condom mandate has a de minimis effect on expression also supports the conclusion that the ordinance is narrowly tailored. Cf. Sensations, Inc., 526 F.3d at 299 (citing Pap's A.M. and Barnes in holding that a ban on public nudity was narrowly tailored to suppress negative secondary effects).

9 Plaintiffs also argue that the district court failed to conduct a narrow- tailoring analysis with respect to the permitting provisions. We reject their procedural objection for two reasons. First, the district court analyzed the merits of this issue, albeit in the context of considering the motion to dismiss. Second, because Measure B's condom mandate, which the district court analyzed at length with specific reference to narrow tailoring, is part of the permitting process, the court necessarily conducted a narrow-tailoring analysis of the permitting scheme as part of its consideration of the condom mandate.

## Esquivel-Quintana v. Sessions (May 30, 2017) [Appendix omitted]

Justice Thomas delivered the opinion of the Court.

The Immigration and Nationality Act (INA), 66Stat. 163, as amended, provides that "[a]ny alien who is convicted of an aggravated felony after admission" to the United States may be removed from the country by the Attorney General. 8 U. S. C. §1227(a)(2)(A)(iii). One of the many crimes that constitutes an aggravated felony under the INA is "sexual abuse of a minor." §1101(a)(43)(A). A conviction for sexual abuse of a minor is an aggravated felony regardless of whether it is for a "violation of Federal or State law." §1101(a)(43). The INA does not expressly define sexual abuse of a minor.

We must decide whether a conviction under a state statute criminalizing consensual sexual intercourse between a 21-year-old and a 17-year-old qualifies as sexual abuse of a minor under the INA. We hold that it does not.

I

Petitioner Juan Esquivel-Quintana is a native and citizen of Mexico. He was admitted to the United States as a lawful permanent resident in 2000. In 2009, he pleaded no contest in the Superior Court of California to a statutory rape offense: "unlawful sexual intercourse with a minor who is more than three years younger than the perpetrator," Cal. Penal Code Ann. §261.5(c) (West 2014); see also §261.5(a) ("Unlawful sexual intercourse is an act of sexual intercourse accomplished with a person who is not the spouse of the perpetrator, if the person is a minor"). For purposes of that offense, California defines "minor" as "a person under the age of 18 years." Ibid.

The Department of Homeland Security initiated removal proceedings against petitioner based on that conviction. An Immigration Judge concluded that the conviction qualified as "sexual abuse of a minor," 8 U. S. C. §1101(a)(43)(A), and ordered petitioner removed to Mexico. The Board of Immigration Appeals (Board) dismissed his appeal. 26 I. & N. Dec. 469 (2015). "[F]or a statutory rape offense involving a 16- or 17-year-old victim" to qualify as " 'sexual abuse of a minor,' " it reasoned, "the statute must require a meaningful age difference between the victim and the perpetrator." Id., at 477. In its view, the 3-year age difference required by Cal. Penal Code §261.5(c) was meaningful. Id., at 477. Accordingly, the Board concluded that petitioner's crime of conviction was an aggravated felony, making him removable under the INA. Ibid. A divided Court of Appeals denied Esquivel-Quintana's petition for review, deferring to the Board's interpretation of sexual abuse of a minor under Chevron U. S. A. Inc. v. Natural Resources Defense Council, Inc., 467 U. S. 837 (1984) . 810 F. 3d 1019 (CA6 2016); see also id., at 1027 (Sutton, J., concurring in part and dissenting in part). We granted certiorari, 580 U. S. ___ (2016), and now reverse.

II

Section 1227(a)(2)(A)(iii) makes aliens removable based on the nature of their convictions, not based on their actual conduct. See Mellouli v. Lynch, 575 U. S. ___, ___ (2015) (slip op., at 7). Accordingly, to determine whether an alien's conviction qualifies as an aggravated felony under that section, we "employ a categorical approach by looking to the statute . . . of conviction, rather than to the specific facts underlying the crime." Kawashima v. Holder, 565 U. S. 478, 483 (2012) ; see, e.g., Gonzales v. Duenas-Alvarez, 549 U. S. 183, 186 (2007) (applying the categorical approach set forth in Taylor v. United States, 495 U. S. 575 (1990) , to the INA). Under that approach, we ask whether " 'the state statute defining the crime of conviction' categorically fits within the 'generic' federal definition of a corresponding aggravated felony." Moncrieffe v. Holder, 569 U. S. 184, 190 (2013) (quoting Duenas-Alvarez, supra, at 186). In other words, we presume that the state conviction "rested upon . . . the least of th[e] acts" criminalized by the statute, and then we determine whether that conduct would fall within the federal definition of the crime. Johnson v. United States, 559 U. S. 133, 137 (2010) ; see also Moncrieffe, supra, at 191 (focusing "on the minimum conduct criminalized by the state statute"). 1 Petitioner's state conviction is thus an "aggravated felony" under the INA only if the least of the acts criminalized by the state statute falls within the generic federal definition of sexual abuse of a minor.

A

Because Cal. Penal Code §261.5(c) criminalizes "unlawful sexual intercourse with a minor who is more than three years younger than the perpetrator" and defines a minor as someone under age 18, the conduct criminalized under this provision would be, at a minimum, consensual sexual intercourse between a victim who is almost 18 and a perpetrator who just turned 21. Regardless of the actual facts of petitioner's crime, we must presume that his conviction was based on acts that were no more criminal than that. If those acts do not constitute sexual abuse of a minor under the INA, then petitioner was not convicted of an aggravated felony and is not, on that basis, removable.

Petitioner concedes that sexual abuse of a minor under the INA includes some statutory rape offenses. But he argues that a statutory rape offense based solely on the partners' ages (like the one here) is " 'abuse' " "only when the younger partner is under 16." Reply Brief 2. Because the California statute criminalizes sexual intercourse when the victim is up to 17 years old, petitioner contends that it does not categorically qualify as sexual abuse of a minor.

B

We agree with petitioner that, in the context of statutory rape offenses that criminalize sexual intercourse based solely on the age of the participants, the generic federal definition of sexual abuse of a minor requires that the victim be younger than 16. Because the California statute at issue in this case does not categorically fall within that definition, a conviction pursuant to it is not an aggravated felony under §1101(a)(43)(A). We begin, as always, with the text.

1

Section 1101(a)(43)(A) does not expressly define sexual abuse of a minor, so we interpret that phrase using the normal tools of statutory interpretation. "Our analysis begins with the language of the statute." Leocal v. Ashcroft, 543 U. S. 1, 8 (2004) ; see also Lopez v. Gonzales, 549 U. S. 47, 53 (2006) ("The everyday understanding of" the term used in §1101 "should count for a lot here, for the statutes in play do not define the term, and so remit us to regular usage to see what Congress probably meant").

Congress added sexual abuse of a minor to the INA in 1996, as part of a comprehensive immigration reform act. See Illegal Immigration Reform and Immigrant Responsibility Act of 1996, §321(a)(i), 110Stat. 3009–627. At that time, the ordinary meaning of "sexual abuse" included "the engaging in sexual contact with a person who is below a specified age or who is incapable of giving consent because of age or mental or physical incapacity." Merriam-Webster's Dictionary of Law 454 (1996). By providing that the abuse must be "of a minor," the INA focuses on age, rather than mental or physical incapacity. Accordingly, to qualify as sexual abuse of a minor, the statute of conviction must prohibit certain sexual acts based at least in part on the age of the victim.

Statutory rape laws are one example of this category of crimes. Those laws generally provide that an older person may not engage in sexual intercourse with a younger person under a specified age, known as the "age of consent." See id., at 20 (defining "age of consent" as "the age at which a person is deemed competent by law to give consent esp. to sexual intercourse" and cross-referencing "statutory rape"). Many laws also require an age differential between the two partners.

Although the age of consent for statutory rape purposes varies by jurisdiction, see infra, at 9, reliable dictionaries provide evidence that the "generic" age—in 1996 and today—is 16. See B. Garner, A Dictionary of Modern Legal Usage 38 (2d ed. 1995) ("Age of consent, usu[ally] 16, denotes the age when one is legally capable of agreeing . . . to sexual intercourse" and cross-referencing "statutory rape"); Black's Law Dictionary 73 (10th ed. 2014) (noting that the age of consent is "usu[ally] defined by statute as 16 years").

2

Relying on a different dictionary (and "sparse" legislative history), the Government suggests an alternative " 'everyday understanding' " of "sexual abuse of a minor." Brief for Respondent 16–17 (citing Black's Law Dictionary 1375 (6th ed. 1990)). Around the time sexual abuse of a minor was added to the INA's list of aggravated felonies, that dictionary defined "[s]exual abuse" as "[i]llegal sex acts performed against a minor by a parent, guardian, relative, or acquaintance," and defined "[m]inor" as "[a]n infant or person who is under the age of legal competence," which in "most states" was "18." Id., at 997, 1375. " 'Sexual abuse of a minor,' " the Government accordingly contends, "most naturally connotes conduct that (1) is illegal, (2) involves sexual activity, and (3) is directed at a person younger than 18 years old." Brief for Respondent 17.

We are not persuaded that the generic federal offense corresponds to the Government's definition. First, the Government's proposed definition is flatly inconsistent with the definition of sexual abuse contained in the very dictionary on which it relies; the Government's proposed definition does not require that the act be performed "by a parent, guardian, relative, or acquaintance." Black's Law Dictionary 1375 (6th ed. 1990) (emphasis added). In any event, as we explain below, offenses predicated on a special relationship of trust between the victim and offender are not at issue here and frequently have a different age requirement than the general age of consent. Second, in the context of statutory rape, the prepositional phrase "of a minor" naturally refers not to the age of legal competence (when a person is legally capable of agreeing to a contract, for example), but to the age of consent (when a person is legally capable of agreeing to sexual intercourse). Third, the Government's definition turns the categorical approach on its head by defining the generic federal offense of sexual abuse of a minor as whatever is illegal under the particular law of the State where the defendant was convicted. Under the Government's preferred approach, there is no "generic" definition at all. See Taylor, 495 U. S., at 591 (requiring "a clear indication that . . . Congress intended to abandon its general approach of using uniform categorical definitions to identify predicate offenses"); id., at 592 ("We think that 'burglary' in §924(e) must have some uniform definition independent of the labels employed by the various States' criminal codes").

C

The structure of the INA, a related federal statute, and evidence from state criminal codes confirm that, for a statutory rape offense to qualify as sexual abuse of a minor under the INA based solely on the age of the participants, the victim must be younger than 16.

789

1

Surrounding provisions of the INA guide our interpretation of sexual abuse of a minor. See A. Scalia & B. Garner, Reading Law: The Interpretation of Legal Texts 167 (2012). This offense is listed in the INA as an "aggravated felony." 8 U. S. C. §1227(a)(2)(A)(iii) (emphasis added). "An 'aggravated' offense is one 'made worse or more serious by circumstances such as violence, the presence of a deadly weapon, or the intent to commit another crime.' " Carachuri-Rosendo v. Holder, 560 U. S. 563, 574 (2010) (quoting Black's Law Dictionary 75 (9th ed. 2009)). Moreover, the INA lists sexual abuse of a minor in the samesubparagraph as "murder" and "rape," §1101(a)(43)(A)— among the most heinous crimes it defines as aggravated felonies. §1227(a)(2)(A)(iii). The structure of the INA therefore suggests that sexual abuse of a minor encompasses only especially egregious felonies.

A closely related federal statute, 18 U. S. C. §2243, provides further evidence that the generic federal definition of sexual abuse of a minor incorporates an age of consent of 16, at least in the context of statutory rape offenses predicated solely on the age of the participants. Cf. Leocal, 543 U. S., at 12–13, n. 9 (concluding that Congress' treatment of 18 U. S. C. §16 in an Act passed "just nine months earlier" provided "stron[g] suppor[t]" for our interpretation of §16 as incorporated into the INA); Powerex Corp. v. Reliant Energy Services, Inc., 551 U. S. 224, 232 (2007) . Section 2243, which criminalizes "[s]exual abuse of a minor or ward," contains the only definition of that phrase in the United States Code. As originally enacted in 1986, §2243 proscribed engaging in a "sexual act" with a person between the ages of 12 and 16 if the perpetrator was at least four years older than the victim. In 1996, Congress expanded §2243 to include victims who were younger than 12, thereby protecting anyone under the age of 16. §2243(a); see also §2241(c). Congress did this in the same omnibus law that added sexual abuse of a minor to the INA, which suggests that Congress understood that phrase to cover victims under age 16. 2 See Omnibus Consolidated Appropriations Act, 1997, §§121(7), 321, 110Stat. 3009–31, 3009–627.

Petitioner does not contend that the definition in §2243(a) must be imported wholesale into the INA, Brief for Petitioner 17, and we do not do so. One reason is that the INA does not cross-reference §2243(a), whereas many other aggravated felonies in the INA are defined by cross-reference to other provisions of the United States Code, see, e.g., §1101(a)(43)(H) ("an offense described in section 875, 876, 877, or 1202 of Title 18 (relating to the demand for or receipt of ransom)"). Another is that §2243(a) requires a 4-year age difference between the perpetrator and the victim. Combining that element with a 16-year age of consent would categorically exclude the statutory rape laws of most States. See Brief for Respondent 34–35; cf. Taylor, 495 U. S., at 594 (declining to "constru[e] 'burglary' to mean common-law burglary," because that "would come close to nullifying that term's effect in the statute," since "few of the crimes now generally recognized as burglaries would fall within the common-law definition"). Accordingly, we rely on §2243(a) for evidence of the meaning of sexual abuse of a minor, but not as providing the complete or exclusive definition.

2

As in other cases where we have applied the categorical approach, we look to state criminal codes for additional evidence about the generic meaning of sexual abuse of a minor. See Taylor, 495 U. S., at 598 (interpreting " 'bur-glary' " under the Armed Career Criminal Act of 1984 according to "the generic sense in which the term is now used in the criminal codes of most States"); Duenas-Alvarez, 549 U. S., at 190 (interpreting "theft" in the INA in the same manner). When "sexual abuse of a minor" was added to the INA in 1996, thirty-one States and the District of Columbia set the age of consent at 16 for statutory rape offenses that hinged solely on the age of the participants. As for the other States, one set the age of consent at 14; two set the age of consent at 15; six set the age of consent at 17; and the remaining ten, including California, set the age of consent at 18. See Appendix, infra; cf. ALI, Model Penal Code §213.3(1)(a) (1980) (in the absence of a special relationship, setting the default age of consent at 16 for the crime of "[c]orruption of [m]inors"). 3 A significant majority of jurisdictions thus set the age of consent at 16 for statutory rape offenses predicated exclusively on the age of the participants.

Many jurisdictions set a different age of consent for offenses that include an element apart from the age of the participants, such as offenses that focus on whether the perpetrator is in some special relationship of trust with the victim. That was true in the two States that had offenses labeled "sexual abuse of a minor" in 1996. See Alaska Stat. §11.41.438 (1996) (age of consent for third-degree "sexual abuse of a minor" was 16 generally but 18 where "the offender occupie[d] a position of authority in relation to the victim"); Me. Rev. Stat. Ann., Tit. 17–A, §254(1) (1983), as amended by 1995 Me. Laws p. 123 (age of consent for "[s]exual abuse of minors" was 16 generally but 18 where the victim was "a student" and the offender was "a teacher, employee or other official in the . . . school . . . in which the student [was] enrolled"). And that is true in four of the five jurisdictions that have offenses titled "sexual abuse of a minor" today. Compare, e.g., D. C. Code §§22–3001 (2012), 22–3008 (2016 Cum. Supp.) (age of consent is 16 in the absence of a significant relationship) with §22–3009.01 (age of consent is 18 where the offender "is in a significant relationship" with the victim); see also Brief for Respondent 31 (listing statutes with that title). Accordingly, the generic crime of sexual abuse of a minor may include a different age of consent where the perpetrator and victim are in a significant relationship of trust. As relevant to this case, however, the general consensus from state criminal codes points to the same generic definition as dictionaries and federal law: Where sexual intercourse is abusive solely because of the ages of the participants, the victim must be younger than 16.

D

The laws of many States and of the Federal Government include a minimum age differential (in addition to an age of consent) in defining statutory rape. We need not and do not decide whether the generic crime of sexual abuse of a minor under 8 U. S. C. §1101(a)(43)(A) includes an additional element of that kind. Petitioner has "show[n] something special about California's version of the doctrine"—that the age of consent is 18, rather than 16—and needs no more to prevail. Duenas-Alvarez, supra, at 191. Absent some special relationship of trust, consensual sexual conduct involving a younger partner who is at least 16 years of age does not qualify as sexual abuse of a minor under the INA, regardless of the age differential between the two participants. We leave for another day whether the generic offense requires a particular age differential between the victim and the perpetrator, and whether the generic offense encompasses sexual intercourse involving victims over the age of 16 that is abusive because of the nature of the relationship between the participants.

III

Finally, petitioner and the Government debate whether the Board's interpretation of sexual abuse of a minor is entitled to deference under Chevron, 467 U. S. 837. Petitioner argues that any ambiguity in the meaning of this phrase must be resolved in favor of the alien under the rule of lenity. See Brief for Petitioner 41–45. The Government responds that ambiguities should be resolved by deferring to the Board's interpretation. See Brief for Respondent 45–53. We have no need to resolve whether the rule of lenity or Chevron receives priority in this case because the statute, read in context, unambiguously forecloses the Board's interpretation. Therefore, neither the rule of lenity nor Chevron applies.

\*    \*    \*

We hold that in the context of statutory rape offenses focused solely on the age of the participants, the generic federal definition of "sexual abuse of a minor" under §1101(a)(43)(A) requires the age of the victim to be less than 16. The judgment of the Court of Appeals, accordingly, is reversed.

It is so ordered.


Notes

1 Where a state statute contains several different crimes that are described separately, we employ what is known as the "modified categorical approach." See Gonzales v. Duenas-Alvarez, 549 U. S. 183, 187 (2007) (internal quotation marks omitted). Under that approach, which is not at issue here, the court may review the charging documents, jury instructions, plea agreement, plea colloquy, and similar sources to determine the actual crime of which the alien was convicted. See ibid.

2 To eliminate a redundancy, Congress later amended §2243(a) to revert to the pre-1996 language. See Protection of Children From Sexual Predators Act of 1998, §301(b), 112Stat. 2979. That amendment does not change Congress' understanding in 1996, when it added sexual abuse of a minor to the INA.

3 The Government notes that this sort of multijurisdictional analysis can "be useful insofar as it helps shed light on the 'common understanding and meaning' of the federal provision being interpreted," but that it is not required by the categorical approach. Brief for Respondent 23–25 (quoting Perrin v. United States, 444 U. S. 37, 45

(1979) ). We agree. In this case, state criminal codes aid our interpretation of "sexual abuse of a minor" by offering useful context.

## Doe v. Boyertown Area School District (Third Circuit) (June 18, 2018) [Notes omitted]

Before: McKEE, SHWARTZ and NYGAARD, Circuit Judges.

McKEE, Circuit Judge.

This appeal requires us to decide whether the District Court correctly refused to enjoin the defendant School District from allowing transgender students to use bathrooms and locker rooms that are consistent with the students' gender identities as opposed to the sex they were determined to have at birth. The plaintiffs—a group of high school students who identify as being the same sex they were determined to have at birth (cisgender) —believe the policy violated their constitutional rights of bodily privacy, as well as Title IX, and Pennsylvania tort law. As we shall explain, we conclude that, under the circumstances here, the presence of transgender students in the locker and restrooms is no more offensive to constitutional or Pennsylvania-law privacy interests than the presence of the other students who are not transgender. Nor does their presence infringe on the plaintiffs' rights under Title IX.

In an exceedingly thorough, thoughtful, and well-reasoned opinion, the District Court denied the requested injunction based upon its conclusion that the plaintiffs had not shown that they are likely to succeed on the merits and because they had not shown that they will be irreparably harmed absent the injunction. Although we amplify the District Court's reasoning because of the interest in this issue, we affirm substantially for the reasons set forth in the District Court's opinion.

I. BACKGROUND

A. The Setting.

Because such seemingly familiar terms as "sex" and "gender" can be misleading in the context of the issues raised by this litigation, we will begin by explaining and defining relevant terms. Our explanation is based on the District Court testimony of Dr. Scott Leibowitz, an expert in gender dysphoria and gender-identity issues in children and adolescents, and the findings that the District Court made based upon that expert's testimony.

"Sex" is defined as the "anatomical and physiological processes that lead to or denote male or female."[1] Typically, sex is determined at birth based on the appearance of external genitalia.[2]

"Gender" is a "broader societal construct" that encompasses how a "society defines what male or female is within a certain cultural context."[3] A person's gender identity is their subjective, deep-core sense of self as being a particular gender.[4] As suggested by the parenthetical in our opening paragraph, "cisgender" refers to a person who identifies with the sex that person was determined to have at birth.[5] The term "transgender" refers to a person whose gender identity does not align with the sex that person was determined to have at birth.[6] A transgender boy is therefore a person who has a lasting, persistent male gender identity, though that person's sex was determined to be female at birth.[7] A transgender girl is a person who has a lasting, persistent female gender identity though that person's sex was determined to be male at birth.[8]

Approximately 1.4 million adults—or 0.6 percent of the adult population of the United States—identify as transgender.[9] Transgender individuals may experience "gender dysphoria," which is characterized by significant and substantial distress as a result of their birth-determined sex being different from their gender identity.[10] Treatment for children and adolescents who experience gender dysphoria includes social gender transition and physical interventions such as puberty blockers, hormone therapy, and sometimes surgery.[11]

"Social gender transition" refers to steps that transgender individuals take to present themselves as being the gender they most strongly identify with.[12] This typically includes adopting a different name that is consistent with that gender and using the corresponding pronoun set, wearing clothing and hairstyles typically associated with their gender identity rather than the sex they were determined to have at birth, and using sex-segregated spaces and engaging in sex-segregated activities that correspond to their gender identity rather than their birth-determined sex.[13] For transgender individuals, an important part of social gender transition is having others perceive them as being the gender the transgender individual most strongly identifies with.[14] Social gender transition can help alleviate gender dysphoria and is a useful and important tool for clinicians to ascertain whether living in the affirmed gender improves the psychological and emotional function of the individual.[15]

Policies that exclude transgender individuals from privacy facilities that are consistent with their gender identities "have detrimental effects on the physical and mental health, safety, and well-being of transgender individuals."[16] These exclusionary policies exacerbate the risk of "anxiety and depression, low self-esteem, engaging in self-injurious behaviors, suicide, substance use, homelessness, and eating disorders among other adverse outcomes."[17] The risk of succumbing to these conditions is already very high in individuals who are transgender. In a survey of 27,000 transgender individuals, 40% reported a suicide attempt (a rate nine times higher than the general population).[18] Yet, when transgender students are addressed with gender appropriate pronouns and permitted to use facilities that conform to their gender identity, those students "reflect the same, healthy psychological profile as their peers."[19]

Forcing transgender students to use bathrooms or locker rooms that do not match their gender identity is particularly harmful. It causes "severe psychological distress often leading to attempted suicide."[20] The result is that those students "avoid going to the bathroom by fasting, dehydrating, or otherwise forcing themselves not to use the restroom throughout the day."[21] This behavior can lead to medical problems and decreases in academic learning.[22]

We appreciate that there is testimony on this record that the cisgender plaintiffs have also reduced water intake, fasted, etc. in order to reduce the number of times they need to visit the bathroom so they can minimize or avoid encountering transgender students there. For reasons we discuss below, we do not view the level of stress that cisgender students may experience because of appellees' bathroom and locker room policy as comparable to the plight of transgender students who are not allowed to use facilities consistent with their gender identity. Given the majority of the testimony here and the District Court's well-supported findings, those situations are simply not analogous.

Dr. Leibowitz testified that forcing transgender students to use facilities that are not aligned with their gender identities "chips away and erodes at [the individual's] psychological wellbeing and wholeness."[23] It can exacerbate gender dysphoria symptoms by reinforcing that the "world does not appreciate or understand" transgender students.[24] In short, it is "society reducing them to their genitals."[25] Dr. Leibowitz also noted that "hundreds of thousands of physicians in the United States . . . take the position that individuals with gender dysphoria should not be forced to use a restroom that is not in accordance with their gender identity."[26] We have already noted the disparate suicide rates between transgender and cisgender students.

Prior to the 2016-17 school year, Boyertown Area School District required students at Boyertown Area Senior High School ("BASH") to use locker rooms and bathrooms that aligned with their birth-determined sex.[27] BASH changed this policy in 2016 and for the first time permitted transgender students to use restrooms and locker rooms consistent with their gender identity. In initiating this policy, BASH adopted a very careful process that included student-specific analysis. Permission was granted on a case-by-case basis.[28]

The District required the student claiming to be transgender to meet with counselors who were trained and licensed to address these issues and the counselors often consulted with additional counselors, principals, and school administrators.[29] Once a transgender student was approved to use the bathroom or locker room that aligned with his or her gender identity, the student was required to use only those facilities. The student could no longer use the facilities corresponding to that student's sex at birth.[30]

BASH has several multi-user bathrooms.[31] Each has individual toilet stalls.[32] Additionally, BASH has between four and eight single-user restrooms that are available to all students, depending on the time of day.[33] Four of these restrooms are always available for student use.[34]

The locker rooms at BASH consist of common areas, private "team rooms," and shower facilities.[35] Over the past (approximately) two years, BASH has renovated its locker rooms. The "gang showers" were replaced with single-user showers which have privacy curtains.[36] BASH does not require a student to change in the locker room prior to gym class, although the student must change into gym clothes.[37] A student who is uncomfortable changing in the locker room can change privately in one of the single-user facilities, the private shower stalls, or team rooms.[38]

B. The Litigation.

Four plaintiffs—proceeding pseudonymously under the names Joel Doe, Jack Jones, Mary Smith, and Macy Roe— sued the District after it changed its bathroom and locker room policy to the policy we have described above.[39] Their claims were based on encounters between some of the plaintiffs and transgender students in locker rooms or multi-user bathrooms. The plaintiffs sought to enjoin BASH's policy of permitting transgender students to use the bathrooms and locker rooms that aligned with their gender identities. They sought a preliminary injunction on three grounds. First, the plaintiffs alleged that the School District's policy violated their constitutional right to bodily privacy. Next, they claimed that the School District's policy violated Title IX of the Education Amendments of 1972 (Title IX).[40] Finally, they alleged that the policy was contrary to Pennsylvania tort law. After discovery and evidentiary hearings, the District Court filed the extensive and well-reasoned opinion we have already referred to, in which it explained that the plaintiffs had not demonstrated that they were likely to succeed on the merits of any of their claims and that plaintiffs had not shown that they would be irreparably harmed absent an injunction.

For reasons the court identified, it concluded that even if the School District's policy implicated the plaintiffs' constitutional right to privacy, the state had a compelling interest in not discriminating against transgender students. The court also determined that the School District's policy was narrowly tailored to serve that interest. Accordingly, the District Court ruled that even if a cisgender plaintiff had been viewed by a transgender student, it would not have violated the cisgender student's constitutional right to privacy. We agree.

The District Court rejected the plaintiffs' Title IX claim for two reasons. First, it found that the School District's policy did not discriminate on the basis of sex, because it applied equally to all students—cisgender male and cisgender female, as well as transgender male and transgender female students— alike. The court also concluded that the plaintiffs had not identified any conduct that was sufficiently serious to constitute Title IX harassment. The mere presence of a transgender student in a locker room should not be objectively offensive to a reasonable person given the safeguards of the school's policy.

For essentially the reasons described above, the District Court also declined to issue an injunction based on the Pennsylvania tort of intrusion upon seclusion. It found that there was insufficient evidence in the record to demonstrate that a transgender student ever viewed a partially clothed plaintiff, and that the presence of a transgender student would not be highly offensive to a reasonable person.

The District Court rejected the plaintiffs' theory of irreparable harm that posited that the plaintiffs were being forced to give up a constitutional right to use segregated locker rooms and bathrooms. It noted that the School District permitted the students to use the locker room facilities "without limitation."[41] Any student who was uncomfortable being in a state of undress or going to the bathroom with transgender students could use the single-user bathrooms or team rooms that BASH has made available.

Having found that the plaintiffs had no likelihood of success on the merits and did not face irreparable harm, the District Court entered an order on August 25, 2017 denying the injunction. This appeal followed.[42]

II. DISCUSSION[43]

Preliminary injunctive relief is an "extraordinary remedy."[44] It may be granted only when the moving party shows "(1) a likelihood of success on the merits; (2) that [the movant] will suffer irreparable harm if the injunction is denied; (3) that granting preliminary relief will not result in even greater harm to the nonmoving party; and (4) that the public interest favors such relief."[45] The movants must establish entitlement to relief by clear evidence.[46] We review the denial of a preliminary injunction for "an abuse of discretion, an error of law, or a clear mistake in the consideration of proof."[47] We exercise plenary review of the lower court's conclusions of law but review its findings of fact for clear error.[48]

A. Likelihood of Success on the Merits

The District Court correctly concluded that the appellants were not entitled to an injunction because none of their claims are likely to succeed on the merits.

The District Court correctly concluded that the appellants' constitutional right to privacy claim was unlikely to succeed on the merits.

The appellants contend that the District Court erroneously concluded they were unlikely to succeed on their claim that the School District's policy violated their constitutional right to privacy. They assert that the District Court (1) failed to recognize the "contours" of the right to privacy; (2) failed to recognize that a policy opening up facilities to persons of the opposite sex necessarily violates that right; (3) erroneously concluded that the School District's policy advanced a compelling interest; and (4) incorrectly found that the policy was narrowly tailored to serve that interest. We reject each of these arguments in turn.

The appellants' challenge to the School District's policy was brought as a civil rights claim pursuant to 42 U.S.C. § 1983. Section 1983 claims can succeed only if the underlying act—here, the alleged exposure of the appellants' partially clothed bodies to transgender students whose birth-determined sex differed from the appellants—violated a constitutional right.[49] When a plaintiff's § 1983 claim is premised on a violation of the constitutional right to privacy, it will succeed only if it is "limited to those rights of privacy which are fundamental or implicit in the concept of ordered liberty."[50]

The touchstone of constitutional privacy protection is whether the information at issue is "within an individual's reasonable expectations of confidentiality."[51] The Supreme Court has acknowledged two types of constitutional privacy interests rooted in the Fourteenth Amendment—"the individual interest in avoiding disclosure of personal matters" and the "interest in independence in making certain kinds of important decisions."[52] Based on the first principal described above, we have held that a person has a constitutionally protected privacy interest in his or her partially clothed body.[53]

The appellants advance two main arguments in support of their contention that their right to privacy was violated by the School District's policy of permitting transgender students to use bathrooms and locker rooms that aligned with their gender identities. Neither is persuasive.

First, the appellants claim that their right to privacy was violated because the policy permitted them to be viewed by members of the opposite sex while partially clothed.[54] Regardless of the degree of the appellants' undress at the time of the encounters, the District Court correctly found that this would not give rise to a constitutional violation because the School District's policy served a compelling interest—preventing discrimination against transgender students—and was narrowly tailored to that interest.

The constitutional right to privacy is not absolute.[55] It must be weighed against important competing governmental interests.[56] Only unjustified invasions of privacy by the government are actionable in a § 1983 claim.[57] That is, the constitution forbids governmental infringement on certain fundamental interests unless that infringement is sufficiently tailored to serve a compelling state interest.[58] The District Court found that the School District's policy served "a compelling state interest in not discriminating against transgender students" and was narrowly tailored to that interest.[59] We agree.

As set forth in detail above, transgender students face extraordinary social, psychological, and medical risks and the School District clearly had a compelling state interest in shielding them from discrimination. There can be "no denying that transgender individuals face discrimination, harassment, and violence because of their gender identity."[60] The risk of experiencing substantial clinical distress as a result of gender dysphoria is particularly high among children and may intensify during puberty.[61] The Supreme Court has regularly held that the state has a compelling interest in protecting the physical and psychological well-being of minors.[62] We have similarly found that the government has a compelling interest in protecting and caring for children in various contexts.[63] Mistreatment of transgender students can exacerbate gender dysphoria, lead to negative educational outcomes, and precipitate self-injurious behavior. When transgender students face discrimination in schools, the risk to their wellbeing cannot be overstated—indeed, it can be life threatening. This record clearly supports the District Court's conclusion that the School District had a compelling state interest in protecting transgender students from discrimination.

Moreover, the School District's policy fosters an environment of inclusivity, acceptance, and tolerance. As the appellees' amicus brief from the National Education Association convincingly explains, these values serve an important educational function for both transgender and cisgender students.[64] When a school promotes diversity and inclusion, "classroom discussion is livelier, more spirited, and simply more enlightening and interesting [because] the students have the greatest possible variety of backgrounds."[65] Students in diverse learning environments have higher academic achievement leading to better outcomes for all students.[66] Public education "must prepare pupils for citizenship in the Republic,"[67] and inclusive classrooms reduce prejudices and promote diverse relationships which later benefit students in the workplace and in their communities.[68] Accordingly, the School District's policy not only serves the compelling interest of protecting transgender students, but it benefits all students by promoting acceptance.

As we have already noted, we do not intend to minimize or ignore testimony suggesting that some of the appellants now avoid using the restrooms and reduce their water intake in order to reduce the number of times they need to use restrooms under the new policy. Nor do we discount the surprise the appellants reported feeling when in an intimate space with a student they understood was of the opposite biological sex.[69] We cannot, however, equate the situation the appellants now face with the very drastic consequences that the transgender students must endure if the school were to ignore the latter's needs and concerns. Moreover, as we have mentioned, those cisgender students who feel that they must try to limit trips to the restroom to avoid contact with transgender students can use the single-user bathrooms in the school.

Assuming the policy is subject to strict scrutiny, it must advance a compelling state interest and the means of achieving that interest must be "specifically and narrowly framed to accomplish that purpose."[70] Having correctly identified a compelling state interest, the District Court correctly held that the School District's policy was narrowly tailored. The appellants contend that "a much more tailored solution is to provide single-user accommodations."[71] They reason that "all students would be allowed to access the individual facilities, [so] no stigma would attach to the professed transgender students' using them, and preserving the sex-specific communal facilities to single-sex use would resolve all privacy concerns."[72]

This argument is not only unpersuasive, it fails to comprehend the depths of the problems the School District's policy was trying to remedy or the steps taken to address them. The School District already provides single-user accommodations for all students. Any student who is uncomfortable changing around their peers in private spaces, whether transgender or cisgender, may change in a bathroom stall, single-user bathroom, or the private team rooms.[73] The appellants seemingly admit that these accommodations "resolve all privacy concerns."[74] Yet they insist that the policy should be changed to require that transgender students use individual bathrooms if they do not wish to use the communal facilities that align with their birth-determined sex. Not only would forcing transgender students to use single-user facilities or those that correspond to their birth sex not serve the compelling interest that the School District has identified here, it would significantly undermine it.[75] As the Court of Appeals for the Seventh Circuit has recognized, a school district's policy that required a transgender student to use single-user facilities "actually invited more scrutiny and attention from his peers."[76] Adopting the appellants' position would very publicly brand all transgender students with a scarlet "T," and they should not have to endure that as the price of attending their public school.

Nothing in the record suggests that cisgender students who voluntarily elect to use single-user facilities to avoid transgender students face the same extraordinary consequences as transgender students would if they were forced to use them. As we explain more fully below, requiring transgender students to use single user or birth-sex-aligned facilities is its own form of discrimination.

It is therefore clear that the District Court was correct in concluding that the appellants are unlikely to succeed in establishing a violation of their right to privacy based on a transgender student potentially viewing them in a state of undress in a locker room or restroom. The challenged policy is narrowly tailored to serve a compelling governmental interest. There is no constitutional violation.

The appellants also urge us to recognize constitutional privacy protections for alleged violations that resulted from conduct other than being viewed by transgender students in a locker room or bathroom. They assert that "government actors cannot force minors to endure the risk of unconsented intimate exposure to the opposite sex as a condition for using the very facilities set aside to protect their privacy."[77] They claim that their constitutional privacy rights were violated "when the sexes intermingle[d]" in the bathrooms and locker rooms.[78] They also argue that the female appellants' privacy rights are violated if they are forced to attend to their menstrual hygiene in a facility where members of the opposite sex may potentially be present.[79] In other words, they contend that their constitutional right to privacy is necessarily violated because they are forced to share bathrooms and locker rooms with transgender students whose gender identities correspond with the sex-segregated space, but do not do not align with their birth sex.

We reject the premise of this argument because BASH's policy does not force any cisgender student to disrobe in the presence of any student—cisgender or transgender. BASH has provided facilities for any student who does not feel comfortable being in the confines of a communal restroom or locker room. BASH has installed privacy stalls and set some bathrooms aside as single-user facilities so that any student who is uneasy undressing or using a restroom in the presence of others can take steps to avoid contact. BASH's policy does not compel a privacy violation for any student.

In any event, we decline to recognize such an expansive constitutional right to privacy—a right that would be violated by the presence of students who do not share the same birth sex. Moreover, no court has ever done so. As counsel for the School District noted during oral argument, the appellants are claiming a very broad right of personal privacy in a space that is, by definition and common usage, just not that private. School locker rooms and restrooms are spaces where it is not only common to encounter others in various stages of undress, it is expected. The facilities exist so that students can attend to their personal biological and hygienic needs and change their clothing. As the Supreme Court has stated, "[p]ublic school locker rooms . . . are not notable for the privacy they afford."[80]

Thus, we are unpersuaded to the extent that the appellants' asserted privacy interest requires protection from the risk of encountering students in a bathroom or locker room whom appellants identify as being members of the opposite sex. As the Seventh Circuit noted in Whitaker "[a] transgender student's presence in the restroom provides no more of a risk to other students' privacy rights than the presence of an overly curious student of the same biological sex who decides to sneak glances at his or her classmates performing their bodily functions."[81]

None of the cases cited by the appellants is to the contrary.[82] For example, in their brief and at argument, they placed substantial reliance on Faulkner v. Jones[83] for the proposition that "society [has] undisputed[ly] approv[ed] separate public restrooms for men and women based on privacy concerns. The need for privacy justifies separation. . . ."[84] But that case did not recognize a constitutional mandate that bathrooms and locker rooms must be segregated by birth-determined sex. Although it acknowledged that privacy concerns may justify separate facilities for men and women in certain circumstances,[85] it did not hold that the Constitution compels separate bathroom facilities. Moreover, as we have explained and as the District Court more thoroughly described, BASH has carefully crafted a policy that attempts to address the concerns that some cisgender students may have. To its credit, it has done so in a way that recognizes those concerns as well as the needs, humanity, and decency of transgender students.

The appellants' reliance on Chaney v. Plainfield Healthcare Center[86] is similarly unconvincing. That was an appeal from a Title VII suit brought against a nursing home after a Black nursing assistant was fired for protesting a patient's demand that he receive care only from White nursing aids.[87] The court distinguished medical care based on race from medical care based on sex, noting that just as "the law tolerates same-sex restrooms or same-sex dressing rooms . . . to accommodate privacy needs, Title VII allows an employer to respect a preference for same-sex health providers, but not same-race providers."[88] Like Faulkner, Chaney held that the Constitution tolerates single-sex accommodations. It did not hold that the constitution demands it.

Equally unpersuasive is the appellants' reliance on cases discussing far more intrusive invasions of privacy than allowed by BASH's policy. Cases about strip searches[89] and a criminal conviction for voyeurism after a person repeatedly looked at women in the stalls of public restrooms[90] are wholly unhelpful to our analysis. Those cases involve inappropriate conduct as well as conduct that intruded into far more "intimate aspects of human affairs" than here.[91] There is simply nothing inappropriate about transgender students using the restrooms or locker rooms that correspond to their gender identity under the policy BASH has initiated, and we reject appellants' attempt to argue that there is. Appellants do not contend that transgender Students A or B did anything remotely out of the ordinary while using BASH's facilities. Indeed, the appellants' privacy complaint is not with transgender students' conduct, but with their mere presence. We have already explained that the presence of transgender students in these spaces does not offend the constitutional right of privacy any more than the presence of cisgender students in those spaces.

In an argument that completely misses (or deliberately ignores) the reason for the disputed policy or the circumstances it addresses, the appellants insist that it is improper to consider a student's transgender status when conducting this privacy analysis and that we must only look at the student's anatomy.[92] We disagree. Constitutional right to privacy cases "necessarily require fact-intensive and context-specific analyses."[93] Bright line rules cannot be drawn.[94] Put simply—the facts of a given case are critically important when assessing whether a constitutional right to privacy has been violated. A case involving transgender students using facilities aligned with their gender identities after seeking and receiving approval from trained school counselors and administrators implicates different privacy concerns than, for example, a case involving an adult stranger sneaking into a locker room to watch a fourteen year-old girl shower. The latter scenario—taken from a case the appellants rely upon[95] — is simply not analogous to the circumstances here.

1. The District Court correctly concluded that the appellants' Title IX claim was unlikely to succeed on the merits.

The District Court rejected the appellants' Title IX claim because the School District's policy treated all students equally and therefore did not discriminate on the basis of sex, and because the appellants had failed to meet the elements of a "hostile environment harassment" claim. We again agree. We also agree with the School District's position that barring transgender students from restrooms that align with their gender identity would itself pose a potential Title IX violation.

Title IX prohibits discrimination based on sex in all educational programs that receive funds from the federal government.[96] However, discrimination with regard to privacy facilities is exempt from that blanket prohibition. An institution "may provide separate toilet, locker room, and shower facilities on the basis of sex, but such facilities provided for students of one sex shall be comparable to such facilities provided for students of the other sex."[97] This exception is permissive—Title IX does not require that an institution provide separate privacy facilities for the sexes.

Title IX also supports a cause of action for "hostile environment harassment."[98] To recover on such a claim, a plaintiff must establish sexual harassment that is so severe, pervasive, or objectively offensive and that "so undermines and detracts from the victims' educational experience that [he or she] is effectively denied equal access to an institution's resources and opportunities."[99] To support a claim of hostile environment harassment, a plaintiff must demonstrate that the offensive conduct occurred because of his or her sex.[100]

Title IX's "hostile environment harassment" cause of action originated in a series of cases decided under Title VII of the Civil Rights Act of 1964 ("Title VII").[101] The Supreme Court has "extended an analogous cause of action to students under Title IX."[102] Title VII cases are therefore instructive.[103]

Title VII prohibits employers from discriminating based on sex.[104] In Oncale, the Supreme Court considered whether Title VII prohibited "discrimination because of sex" when the harasser and the harassed employee were the same sex.[105] In concluding that Title VII could support such a claim, the Court held that Title VII is concerned only with "discrimination because of sex."[106] It noted that the Court had never held that "workplace harassment, even harassment between men and women, is automatically discrimination because of sex merely because the words used have sexual content or connotations."[107] Rather, "the critical issue . . . is whether members of one sex are exposed to disadvantageous terms or conditions of employment to which members of the other sex are not exposed."[108] The plaintiffs in a Title VII action must therefore always "prove that the conduct at issue was not merely tinged with offensive sexual connotations, but actually constituted discrimination because of sex."[109] The same requirement holds true for Title IX claims.

The appellants have not provided any authority—either in the District Court or on appeal—to suggest that a sex-neutral policy can give rise to a Title IX claim. Instead, they simply hypothesize that "harassment" that targets both sexes equally would violate Title IX; that is simply not the law.[110] The touchstone of both Title VII and Title IX claims is disparate treatment based on sex.[111] The School District's policy allows all students to use bathrooms and locker rooms that align with their gender identity. It does not discriminate based on sex, and therefore does not offend Title IX.

The District Court also correctly found that the appellants had not met their burden of establishing that the mere presence of transgender students in bathrooms and locker rooms constitutes sexual harassment so severe, pervasive, or objectively offensive and "that so undermines and detracts from the victims' educational experience that [the plaintiff] is effectively denied equal access to an institution's resources and opportunities."[112] That is particularly true given the many safeguards the School District put in place as part of the challenged policy.

Rather than relying on relevant legal authority to establish that the mere presence of a transgender student in a locker room or bathroom rises to the level of harassment, the appellants again cite inapposite cases that involve egregious harassment. That is not surprising since we have found no authority that supports the appellants' claims. Two cases that the appellants attempt to analogize to their situation are particularly illustrative of the weakness of their position— Lewis v. Triborough Bridge and Tunnel Authority[113] and Schonauer v. DCR Entertainment Inc.[114] Lewis involved harassment that is worlds apart from anything in the present record. There, cisgender men not only entered a locker room while cisgender female employees were changing, they "leer[ed]" at them, "crowd[ed] the entrance to the locker room, forcing [them] to `run the gauntlet[,]' and brush[ed] up against them."[115] When a supervisor was informed, he referred to the female employees as "cunts" and "the biggest bunch of fucking crybabies."[116] Any comparison to the circumstances the appellants face here is patently frivolous.

Schonauer is also distinguishable. There, the plaintiff was employed as a beverage server at a topless nightclub and alleged that she had been harassed by a manager.[117] In addition to entering the women's changing facility, the manager repeatedly encouraged the plaintiff to enter nude dance contests, asked questions about her sexual fantasies, and probed her sexual history.[118] When the plaintiff resisted these advances, she was fired.[119] The Washington Court of Appeals found that this behavior could constitute harassment not simply because the manager entered the changing facility, but because he pressed the plaintiff to "provide sexually explicit information and to dance on stage in a sexually provocative way."[120]

The District Court no doubt realized that the appellants' attempt to seize upon Lewis and Schonauer demonstrated the weakness of their arguments. Here, there are no allegations of harassment, let alone any that are even remotely as "severe, pervasive, [or] objectively offensive."[121] Still, the appellants unconvincingly try to equate mere presence in a space with harassing activity.

This case is far more analogous to Cruzan v. Special School Dist., No. 1,[122] a Title VII case from the Court of Appeals for the Eighth Circuit. Cruzan held that a transgender individual in a bathroom did not create a hostile environment because there was no evidence that the individual "engaged in any inappropriate conduct other than merely being present in the women's faculty restroom."[123] That is, a transgender person in a restroom did not create an environment that was "permeated with discriminatory intimidation, ridicule, and insult" as required to sustain a harassment claim under Title VII.[124] We agree with the Eight Circuit's conclusion. As we have emphasized, the appellants' real objection is to the presence of transgender students, not to any "environment" their presence creates. Indeed, the allegations here include an assertion that a cisgender student was harassed merely by a transgender student washing that student's own hands in a bathroom or changing in a locker room. That is not the type of conduct that supports a Title IX hostile environment claim.[125] The District Court recognized this and correctly ruled that this claim was unlikely to succeed.

The School District, on the other hand, contends that barring transgender students from using privacy facilities that align with their gender identity would, itself, constitute discrimination under a sex-stereotyping theory in violation of Title IX.[126] We need not decide that very different issue here. We note only that the School District's argument finds support in the very persuasive opinion from the Seventh Circuit in Whitaker, and the analysis there supports the District Court's conclusion that appellants were not likely to succeed on the merits of their Title IX claim.

In Whitaker, a transgender boy sued the Kenosha Unified School District for prohibiting him from using the boys' bathrooms and locker room.[127] He alleged that Kenosha's policy violated Title IX and denied him equal protection.[128] The District Court agreed and the school district appealed.[129] The Court of Appeals for the Seventh Circuit affirmed, finding that Kenosha's policy constituted sex-based discrimination.

Specifically, Whitaker held that Kenosha's policy violated Title IX because it discriminated against transgender people based on their failure to conform to sex stereotypes.[130] "By definition, a transgender individual does not conform to the sex-based stereotypes of the sex that he or she was assigned at birth."[131] Accordingly, Kenosha's policy subjected Whitaker, "as a transgender student, to different rules, sanctions, and treatment than non-transgender students, in violation of Title IX."[132] The court also dismissed Kenosha's argument that gender-neutral bathroom alternatives were sufficient because such a policy would itself violate the Act.[133]

Whitaker explained that the Supreme Court has adopted an expansive view of "sex" under Title VII.[134] Rather than limit the definition of sex to one's anatomy, a plurality of the Supreme Court held in Price Waterhouse that Title VII "intended to strike at the entire spectrum of disparate treatment of men and women resulting from sex stereotypes."[135] The Supreme Court reiterated Title VII's broad view of "sex" in Oncale, wherein Justice Scalia wrote that "statutory provisions often go beyond the principal evil to cover reasonably comparable evils, and it is ultimately the provisions of our laws rather than the principal concern of our legislators by which we are governed."[136] Whitaker noted that, following Price Waterhouse, many courts (including the Third Circuit) have recognized a cause of action under Title VII when an employee faces discrimination for failing to conform to sex stereotypes.[137]

The injunction that the appellants have requested here would essentially have replicated the Kenosha policy. The Boyertown Area School District can hardly be faulted for being proactive in adopting a policy that avoids the issues that would have otherwise arisen under Title IX. Contrary to the appellants' assertions, "sex" has not been narrowly limited to a person's anatomy under Title VII—nor by analogy is it so limited under Title IX.

This conclusion is a natural extension of our decision in Prowel v. Wise Business Forms, Inc, where we recognized that a plaintiff can state a claim under Title VII for sexual discrimination based on gender stereotyping.[138] While Prowel did not involve a transgender person, we did consider whether a man who did not adhere to male gender stereotypes could state a claim for sex discrimination under Title VII.[139] Relying on Price Waterhouse, we held that Title VII's prohibition on discrimination "because of sex" also prohibited discriminating against someone who did not conform to gender stereotypes.[140]

Title IX prohibits discrimination against transgender students in school facilities just as Title VII prohibited discrimination against Prowel in the workplace. Therefore a court may not issue an injunction that would subject the transgender students to different conditions than their cisgender peers are subjected to.

We are not alone in reaching this conclusion. In addition to the Seventh Circuit's decision in Whitaker, the Courts of Appeals for the Eleventh and Sixth Circuits have concluded that discriminating against transgender individuals constitutes sex discrimination.[141] Similarly, the First Circuit has relied on Title VII in holding that a person may state a claim under the Equal Credit Opportunity Act, which prohibits discrimination "with respect to . . . sex[,]" if that person does not conform to sex stereotypes.[142] The Ninth Circuit has also looked to Title VII and held that a transgender female inmate who did not conform to sex stereotypes could state a claim under the Gender Motivated Violence Act.[143]

We therefore hold that the District Court correctly declined to issue an injunction based on the appellants' Title IX claim.

2. The District Court correctly concluded that the appellants' state law tort claim was unlikely to succeed on the merits.

Finally, the appellants contend that the District Court erred in denying the injunction as to their Pennsylvania-law tort claim for intrusion upon seclusion. Pennsylvania has adopted the Second Restatement of Torts' definition of intrusion upon seclusion:

One who intentionally intrudes, physically or otherwise, upon the solitude or seclusion of another or his private affairs or concerns, is subject to the other for invasion of his privacy, if the intrusion would be highly offensive to a reasonable person.[144]

In denying this claim, the District Court concluded that the mere presence of a transgender individual in a bathroom or locker room is not the type of conduct that would be highly offensive to a reasonable person. As we have noted, students in a locker room expect to see other students in varying stages of undress, and they expect that other students will see them in varying stages of undress. We will affirm the District Court's rejection of the appellants' tort claim.

B. Irreparable Harm

In addition to finding that the appellants were unlikely to succeed on the merits of their claims, the District Court denied injunctive relief because they had not demonstrated that the failure to issue an injunction would result in irreparable harm. The District Court found that:

On a practical level . . . the privacy protections that are in place at BASH, which include the bathroom stalls and shower stalls in the locker rooms, the bathroom stalls in the multi-user bathrooms, the availability of a number of single-user bathrooms (a few of which will have lockers for storing items), the [ability] of students to store personal items in their locker or leave those items with the gym teacher, and the availability of the team rooms in the locker rooms (which would not involve students passing through the common area of the locker room), and the overall willingness of the [appellees] to work with the students and their families to assure that the students are comfortable at BASH, mitigates against a finding of irreparable harm. . . . The privacy protections available to students in 2017-18 are more than suitable to address any privacy concerns relating to the presence of transgender students in the locker rooms and bathrooms at BASH.[145]

We agree that the appellants did not demonstrate irreparable harm would result from denying an injunction. The School District has provided adequate privacy facilities for the appellants to use during this litigation. Even if the appellants could otherwise succeed on one or more of their claims (and, as explained above, we do not suggest that they can), the single-user facilities ensure that no appellant faces irreparable harm in the meantime.

### III. CONCLUSION

The Boyertown Area School District has adopted a very thoughtful and carefully tailored policy in an attempt to address some very real issues while faithfully discharging its obligation to maintain a safe and respectful environment in which everyone can both learn and thrive.

The District Court correctly concluded that the appellants' attempt to enjoin that policy based on an alleged violation of their privacy rights and their rights under Title IX and Pennsylvania tort law is not likely to succeed on the merits. The District Court was also correct in deciding that denying the injunction would not irreparably harm the appellants. For the reasons set forth above and in the well-reasoned District Court opinion, we will affirm the District Court's denial of the requested preliminary injunction.

## Free the Nipple v. City of Fort Collins, Colo. (Tenth Circuit) (Feb 15, 2019) [Notes omitted]

Before BRISCOE, HARTZ, and PHILLIPS, Circuit Judges.

PHILLIPS, Circuit Judge.

The city of Fort Collins, Colorado, enacted a public-nudity ordinance that imposes no restrictions on male toplessness but prohibits women from baring their breasts below the areola. See Fort Collins, Colo., Mun. Code § 17-142 (2015). In response, Free the Nipple, an unincorporated association, and two individuals, Brittiany Hoagland and Samantha Six (collectively, "the Plaintiffs"), sued the City in federal district court. They alleged (among other things) that the ordinance violated the Equal Protection Clause, U.S. Const. amend. XIV, § 1, and they asked for a preliminary injunction to halt enforcement of the ordinance. The district court agreed. It enjoined the City, pending the resolution of the case's merits, from implementing the ordinance "to the extent that it prohibits women, but not men, from knowingly exposing their breasts in public." Free the Nipple-Fort Collins v. City of Fort Collins, 237 F.Supp.3d 1126, 1135 (D. Colo. 2017). The City then brought this interlocutory appeal to challenge the injunction.

The appeal presents a narrow question: Did the district court reversibly err in issuing the preliminary injunction? We answer no. Exercising interlocutory jurisdiction under 28 U.S.C. § 1292(a)(1), we affirm the district court's judgment and remand the case to that court for further proceedings consistent with this opinion.

### BACKGROUND

In 2015, after substantial public debate, the Fort Collins city council enacted this public-nudity ordinance:

No female who is ten (10) years of age or older shall knowingly appear in any public place with her breast exposed below the top of the areola and nipple while located: (1) In a public right-of-way, in a natural area, recreation area or trail, or recreation center, in a public building, in a public square, or while located in any other public place; or (2) On private property if the person is in a place that can be viewed from the ground level by another who is located on public property and who does not take extraordinary steps, such as climbing a ladder or peering over a screening fence, in order to achieve a point of vantage. .... The prohibition [on female toplessness] does not extend to women breastfeeding in places they are legally entitled to be.

Fort Collins, Colo., Mun. Code § 17-142(b), (d). Any person who violates this ordinance "shall be guilty of a misdemeanor" and "shall be punished" by a fine of up to $2,650, or up to 180 days in jail, or both. Id. § 1-15(a).

The Plaintiffs immediately sued the City in federal district court, alleging that the public-nudity ordinance violates the Free Speech Clause of the First Amendment and the Equal Protection Clause of the Fourteenth Amendment to the U.S. Constitution, as well as the Equal Rights Amendment to the Colorado Constitution. Their complaint includes a jury-trial demand and a prayer for relief asking the court (1) to declare the ordinance "unconstitutional on its face and as applied to [the] Plaintiffs" and (2) to prevent the ordinance's enforcement. Appellant's App. vol. 1 at 20. Separately, the Plaintiffs moved for a preliminary injunction blocking enforcement of the ordinance and "prohibit[ing] [the City] from discriminatorily arresting [the] Plaintiffs, and all others similarly situated, when they engage in the protected activity of standing topless in public places in Fort Collins, Colorado." Id. at 22.

The City countered with a motion to dismiss arguing that the Plaintiffs had failed to state any claim on which relief could be granted, see Fed. R. Civ. P. 12(b)(6), and a response to the Plaintiffs' preliminary-injunction motion. In the latter, the City asserted that a preliminary injunction would unfairly burden the public "by exposure to public nudity" and urged the court to deny the motion. Appellant's App. vol. 2 at 33.

The district court first addressed the City's motion to dismiss. It granted the motion on the Plaintiffs' free-speech claim, agreeing with the City that "topless protests" aren't protected speech, but allowed the Plaintiffs' (federal) Equal Protection Clause and (state) Equal Rights Amendment claims to proceed. Free the Nipple-Fort Collins v. City of Fort Collins, 216 F.Supp.3d 1258, 1262 (D. Colo. 2016). Next, the court turned to the Plaintiffs' preliminary-injunction motion. After holding a hearing on the matter, it granted the motion, ruling that the ordinance likely violated the Equal Protection Clause,[1] and issued the requested injunction. Free the Nipple, 237 F.Supp.3d at 1128. Pending trial (or other resolution of the case), the preliminary injunction blocks the City from enforcing its public-nudity ordinance "to the extent that it prohibits women, but not men, from knowingly exposing their breasts in public." Id. at 1135.

The City then brought this interlocutory appeal defending the constitutionality of its public-nudity ordinance and challenging the preliminary injunction.

DISCUSSION

In its appeal, the City asks us to vacate the district court's preliminary injunction so that it can fully enforce its public-nudity ordinance.[2] The City argues that the ordinance's unequal treatment of male and female toplessness survives constitutional scrutiny, making it likely that the Plaintiffs will lose a merits trial and, in the meantime, precluding them from getting injunctive relief. Before we address the City's argument, we define our standard of review and explain the rules governing the grant (or denial) of a preliminary injunction. We'll then apply that framework to determine whether the district court reversibly erred when it issued the preliminary injunction.

I. Standard of Review

District courts have discretion over whether to grant preliminary injunctions, United States ex rel. Citizen Band Potawatomi Indian Tribe v. Enter. Mgmt. Consultants, Inc., 883 F.2d 886, 889 (10th Cir. 1989), and we will disturb their decisions only if they abuse that discretion, Fish v. Kobach, 840 F.3d 710, 723 (10th Cir. 2016). A district court's decision crosses the abuse-of-discretion line if it rests on an erroneous legal conclusion or lacks a rational basis in the record. Id. (quoting Awad v. Ziriax, 670 F.3d 1111, 1125 (10th Cir. 2012)). As we review a district court's decision to grant or deny a preliminary injunction, we thus examine the court's factual findings for clear error and its legal conclusions de novo. Id.

II. The Legal Standards Governing Preliminary Injunctions

"A preliminary injunction is an extraordinary remedy, the exception rather than the rule." Enter. Mgmt. Consultants, Inc., 883 F.2d at 888. To succeed on a typical preliminary-injunction motion, the moving party needs to prove four things: (1) that she's "substantially likely to succeed on the merits," (2) that she'll "suffer irreparable injury" if the court denies the injunction, (3) that her "threatened injury" (without the injunction) outweighs the opposing party's under the injunction, and (4) that the injunction isn't "adverse to the public interest." Beltronics USA, Inc. v. Midwest Inventory Distrib., LLC, 562 F.3d 1067, 1070 (10th Cir. 2009).

But courts "disfavor" some preliminary injunctions and so require more of the parties who request them. See Schrier v. Univ. of Colo., 427 F.3d 1253, 1258-59 (10th Cir. 2005). Disfavored preliminary injunctions don't merely preserve the parties' relative positions pending trial. Id. Instead, a disfavored injunction may exhibit any of three characteristics: (1) it mandates action (rather than prohibiting it), (2) it changes the status quo, or (3) it grants all the relief that the moving party could expect from a trial win. Awad, 670 F.3d at 1125 (citing Summum v. Pleasant Grove City, 483 F.3d 1044, 1048-49 (10th Cir. 2007)); see also Phillip v. Fairfield Univ., 118 F.3d 131, 133 (2d Cir. 1997) (explaining that an injunction is "mandatory" if "its terms would alter, rather than preserve, the status quo by commanding some positive act"). To get a disfavored injunction, the moving party faces a heavier burden on the likelihood-of-success-on-the-merits and the balance-of-harms factors: She must make a "strong showing" that these tilt in her favor. Fish, 840 F.3d at 724 (quoting Beltronics, 562 F.3d at 1071).

On appeal, the City invokes an even higher standard that requires movants who, like the Plaintiffs, seek to disturb the status quo to "demonstrate not only that the four requirements for a preliminary injunction are met but also that they weigh heavily and compellingly in [the movants'] favor." Appellant's Opening Br. at 8 (quoting Kikumura v. Hurley, 242 F.3d 950, 955 (10th Cir. 2001)). But we "jettison[ed]" the heavily-and-compellingly requirement over a decade ago. O Centro Espirita Beneficiente Uniao do Vegetal v. Ashcroft, 389 F.3d 973, 975 (10th Cir. 2004) (per curiam), aff'd sub nom Gonzales v. O Centro Espirita Beneficiente Uniao do Vegetal, 546 U.S. 418, 126 S.Ct. 1211, 163 L.Ed.2d 1017 (2006). Today, "the requirement that a movant requesting a disfavored injunction must make a showing that the traditional four factors weigh heavily and compellingly in [the movant's] favor is no longer the law of the circuit." Schrier, 427 F.3d at 1261.

The preliminary injunction at issue here prevents the City from fully enforcing its public-nudity ordinance. In so doing, the district court concluded that the injunction both "alters the status quo and affords the movants all the relief they could recover at the conclusion of a full trial on the merits." Free the Nipple, 237 F.Supp.3d at 1130. This conclusion led the district court to apply the heightened disfavored-injunction standard and to require strong showings from the Plaintiffs on the first and third factors. Id. And though we have doubts that the heightened standard applies here, we need not decide which standard to apply— the plaintiffs prevail under the heightened standard and, therefore, under both.[3]

III. Application

On appeal, the City disputes that the Plaintiffs can prevail on any of the four preliminary-injunction factors, but its argument hinges on the first factor: the likelihood that the Plaintiffs will succeed on the merits. According to the City, all four preliminary-injunction factors favor the City because the Plaintiffs lack a viable equal-protection claim and will likely lose on the merits. The fate of this preliminary injunction thus turns largely, if not entirely, on the strength of the Plaintiffs' equal-protection claim. But the City challenges each preliminary-injunction factor, so we address each (though we focus on the first).

A. The First Factor: Likelihood of Success on the Merits

The heightened standard applicable to disfavored preliminary injunctions requires the Plaintiffs to make a strong showing that their equal-protection claim is substantially likely to succeed on its merits. Fish, 840 F.3d at 723-24. The City contests the district court's conclusion that the Plaintiffs made this showing. That conclusion, according to the City, reflects "a fundamental misunderstanding" of Supreme Court precedent and "a misapprehension of the purpose and effect" of the public-nudity ordinance. Appellant's Opening Br. at 9.

We begin our analysis with an outline of the relevant equal-protection principles. Applying those principles, we then assess the merits of the Plaintiffs' equal-protection claim to determine whether the district court abused its discretion when it concluded that the likelihood-of-success factor tilts toward the Plaintiffs.

1. The Equal Protection Clause and Gender-Based Classifications

"No State shall ... deny to any person within its jurisdiction the equal protection of the laws." U.S. Const. amend. XIV, § 1. The Equal Protection Clause, as the U.S. Supreme Court has interpreted it, directs "that all persons similarly situated should be treated alike." City of Cleburne v. Cleburne Living Ctr., 473 U.S. 432, 439, 105 S.Ct. 3249, 87 L.Ed.2d 313 (1985). "At a minimum," it requires that any statutory classification be "rationally related to a legitimate governmental purpose." Clark v. Jeter, 486 U.S. 456, 461, 108 S.Ct. 1910, 100 L.Ed.2d 465 (1988). But more stringent judicial scrutiny attaches to classifications based on certain "suspect" characteristics. See City of Cleburne, 473 U.S. at 440, 105 S.Ct. 3249. These (often immutable) characteristics seldom provide a "sensible ground for differential treatment." Id.

Gender, for instance, "frequently bears no relation to ability to perform or contribute to society," and statutes that differentiate between men and women "very likely reflect outmoded notions" about their "relative capabilities." Id. at 440-41, 105 S.Ct. 3249 (quoting Frontiero v. Richardson, 411 U.S. 677, 686, 93 S.Ct. 1764, 36 L.Ed.2d 583 (1973)). As a result, gender-based classifications "call for a heightened standard of review," id. at 440, 105 S.Ct. 3249, a standard dubbed "intermediate scrutiny" because it lies "[b]etween the[ ] extremes of rational basis review and strict scrutiny." Clark, 486 U.S. at 461, 108 S.Ct. 1910. To survive intermediate scrutiny, a gender-based classification needs "an exceedingly persuasive justification." J.E.B. v. Alabama ex rel. T.B., 511 U.S. 127, 136, 114 S.Ct. 1419, 128 L.Ed.2d 89 (1994). The classification must serve "important governmental objectives" through means "substantially related to" achieving those objectives. United States v. Virginia, 518 U.S. 515, 533, 116 S.Ct. 2264, 135 L.Ed.2d 735 (1996) (quoting Miss. Univ. for Women v. Hogan, 458 U.S. 718, 724, 102 S.Ct. 3331, 73 L.Ed.2d 1090 (1982)); see also Craig v. Boren, 429 U.S. 190, 197-99, 97 S.Ct. 451, 50 L.Ed.2d 397 (1976) (defining, for the first time, this level of means-ends scrutiny).

The City acknowledges that a female-only topless ban is a gender-based classification and that, to pass muster under the Equal Protection Clause, gender-based classifications must satisfy intermediate scrutiny. But instead of drawing the logical conclusion—that female-only topless bans warrant intermediate scrutiny—the City interrupts the syllogism. It asserts that "[t]he fundamental requirement of any cognizable gender discrimination claim is invidious discrimination, not simply classification on the basis of gender." Appellant's Opening Br. at 10 (bolding removed).

Some of the Court's early equal-protection cases, such as 1979's Parham v. Hughes, did treat invidiousness as a "threshold" inquiry. 441 U.S. 347, 351, 99 S.Ct. 1742, 60 L.Ed.2d 269 (1979). Yet Parham, if never overruled, is outdated in light of the Court's more modern equal-protection jurisprudence.[4] Since then, the Court has "consistently" recognized that statutes supposedly based on "reasonable considerations" may in fact reflect "archaic and overbroad generalizations about gender" or "outdated misconceptions concerning the role of females in the home rather than in the marketplace and world of ideas." J.E.B., 511 U.S. at 135, 114 S.Ct. 1419 (quoting Schlesinger v. Ballard, 419 U.S. 498, 506-07, 95 S.Ct. 572, 42 L.Ed.2d 610 (1975), and Craig, 429 U.S. at 198-99, 97 S.Ct. 451). Today, heightened scrutiny "attends `all gender-based classifications.'" Morales-Santana, 137 S.Ct. at 1689 (quoting J.E.B., 511 U.S. at 136, 114 S.Ct. 1419).

Invidiousness still matters, but only in challenges to facially gender-neutral statutes that disproportionately and adversely impact one gender. See Personnel Adm'r v. Feeney, 442 U.S. 256, 259, 273-74, 99 S.Ct. 2282, 60 L.Ed.2d 870 (1979) (challenging Massachusetts's hiring preference for veterans, which worked "overwhelmingly to the advantage of males"). Here, however, the City has enacted, and the Plaintiffs have challenged, a public-nudity ordinance that prescribes one rule for women, requiring them to cover their breasts below the areola, and a different rule for men, allowing them to go topless as they please. Fort Collins, Colo., Mun. Code § 17-142(b). The ordinance creates a gender classification on its face, taking invidiousness out of the equation. The success of the Plaintiffs' equal-protection claim depends only on whether the ordinance survives intermediate scrutiny.

We turn to that question next, as we address the City's attack on the merits of the Plaintiffs' equal-protection claim and defense of its public-nudity ordinance.

2. The Merits of the Plaintiffs' Equal-Protection Claim

The district court characterized as "little more than speculation" the City's claim that banning only female toplessness furthered important governmental objectives. Free the Nipple, 237 F.Supp.3d at 1131. Instead, the court found:

The ordinance discriminates against women based on the generalized notion that, regardless of a woman's intent, the exposure of her breasts in public (or even in her private home if viewable by the public) is necessarily a sexualized act. Thus, it perpetuates a stereotype engrained in our society that female breasts are primarily objects of sexual desire whereas male breasts are not.

Id. at 1132. As a result, the court concluded, the Plaintiffs demonstrated "a strong likelihood that they will succeed at the permanent injunction trial in establishing that [the City's public-nudity ordinance] violates the Equal Protection Clause." Id. at 1133.

The City challenges this conclusion on appeal. It argues that, "in light of the differences between male and female breasts," prohibiting only female toplessness is substantially related to an important governmental objective, as a sizeable majority of other courts have found. Appellant's Opening Br. at 19. We address the City's argument in two parts. First, we discuss the focus of the City's defense— the physical differences between male and female breasts—and explain how such differences affect the constitutional analysis. Second, we determine whether the City's female-only toplessness ban survives constitutional scrutiny.

a. Physical Differences

In defending the constitutionality of its public-nudity ordinance, the City emphasizes the physical, social, and sexual characteristics particular to the female breast. Citing a Wikipedia article (which is titled "Breast" but discusses only the female version) the City argues that women's breasts "have social and sexual characteristics," although their "primary function" is breastfeeding infants. Appellant's Opening Br. at 12; see

Breast, Wikipedia: The Free Encyclopedia, https://en.wikipedia.org/wiki/ Breast (last visited Apr. 18, 2018). The article, as quoted by the City, describes female breasts ("and especially the nipples") as "among the various human erogenous zones" and claims that "it is common to press or massage them with hands or orally before or during sexual activity." Appellant's Opening Br. at 12. Breasts, the City claims, "can figure prominently in a woman's perception of her body image and sexual attractiveness" and "have a hallowed sexual status" in Western culture, "arguably more fetishized than either sex's genitalia." Id. But "the sexualization of women's breasts," according to the City, "is not solely a product of societal norms, but of biology." Id. at 13. Research suggests that women's breasts have greater "tactile sensitivity" than men's. Id. at 13-14 (citing J.E. Robinson & R.V. Short, Changes in Breast Sensitivity at Puberty, During the Menstrual Cycle, and at Parturition, British Medical Journal 1, 1188-91 (1977)).[5]

Though we're wary of Wikipedia's user-generated content, we agree with the district court that "[o]f course" inherent physical differences exist between women's and men's breasts—most obviously, the unique potential to nourish children. Free the Nipple, 237 F.Supp.3d at 1132; see also Crispin v. Christian Audigier, Inc., 717 F.Supp.2d 965, 976 n.19 (C.D. Cal. 2010) (discussing the dangers of relying on Wikipedia); R. Jason Richards, Courting Wikipedia, 44 Trial 62 (Apr. 2008) ("Since when did a Web site that any Internet surfer can edit become an authoritative source by which ... lawyers could craft legal arguments[] and judges could issue precedents?"). But that doesn't resolve the constitutional question.

"Physical differences between men and women," the Court has recognized, "are enduring." Virginia, 518 U.S. at 533, 116 S.Ct. 2264. And in some cases, the Court has found, such differences justify differential treatment. See, e.g., Nguyen v. INS, 533 U.S. 53, 58-59, 68, 121 S.Ct. 2053, 150 L.Ed.2d 115 (2001) (upholding a paternal-acknowledgment requirement in a citizenship statute that treated unwed mothers differently than unwed fathers, in part because the statute addressed "an undeniable difference" between women and men: "at the moment of birth ... the mother's knowledge of the child and the fact of parenthood have been established in a way not guaranteed in the case of the unwed father"). But not always.

Any law premised on "generalizations about `the way women are'"—or the way men are—will fail constitutional scrutiny because it serves no important governmental objective. Virginia, 518 U.S. at 550, 116 S.Ct. 2264; see also Morales-Santana, 137 S.Ct. at 1692 (rejecting, as one such generalization, "the obsolescing view that `unwed fathers [are] invariably less qualified and entitled than mothers' to take responsibility for nonmarital children"). Generalizations, the Court has explained, "have a constraining impact, descriptive though they may be of the way many people still order their lives." Morales-Santana, 137 S.Ct. at 1692-93. They "may `creat[e] a self-fulfilling cycle of discrimination that force[s] women to continue to assume the role of primary family caregiver.'" Id. at 1693 (alteration in original) (quoting Nev. Dep't of Human Res. v. Hibbs, 538 U.S. 721, 736, 123 S.Ct. 1972, 155 L.Ed.2d 953 (2003)).

So, as we inquire into a gender-based classification's objectives, we must beware of stereotypes and their potential to perpetuate inequality. "Even if stereotypes frozen into legislation have `statistical support,'" we must "reject measures that classify unnecessarily and overbroadly by gender when more accurate and impartial lines can be drawn." Morales-Santana, 137 S.Ct. at 1693 n.13 (citing J.E.B., 511 U.S. at 139 n.11, 114 S.Ct. 1419); see also Cary Franklin, The Anti-Stereotyping Principle in Constitutional Sex Discrimination Law, 85 N.Y.U. L. Rev. 83, 138 n.296 (2010) ("The anti-stereotyping principle pervades both stages of [intermediate scrutiny], shaping what constitutes an important interest and what means qualify as sufficiently narrowly tailored to serve this interest.").

With those principles in mind, we now apply the intermediate-scrutiny doctrine to the City's female-only toplessness ban.

b. Intermediate Scrutiny

To determine whether the City's public-nudity ordinance survives intermediate scrutiny, we first identify the City's proffered reasons for enacting a gender-based classification. Then, we ask whether the City's reasons qualify as important governmental objectives and, if so, whether the gender-based means employed substantially serve those objectives. See Morales-Santana, 137 S.Ct. at 1690 (citing Virginia, 518 U.S. at 533, 116 S.Ct. 2264).

The City argues that the inherently sexual nature of the female breast, as opposed to the male breast, raises "myriad concerns" with "permitting adult females to go topless in public without restriction." Appellant's Opening Br. at 18. The City refers us to the preliminary-injunction hearing, where three city officials—the deputy city manager, the assistant chief of police, and the city aquatics supervisor— described some of these concerns. The officials testified that female toplessness could disrupt public order, lead to distracted driving, and endanger children. Citing these concerns, the City claims that prohibiting only female toplessness serves to protect children from public nudity, to maintain public order, and to promote traffic safety.[6] We address each rationale in turn.

i. Protecting Children from Public Nudity[7]

The capacity to breastfeed is the first attribute that, the City claims, sets the female breast apart. Yet the City's public-nudity ordinance expressly exempts breastfeeding women from the female-toplessness ban, so even children who weren't exposed to their mothers' breasts as breastfeeding infants may still see a naked female breast if they pass a woman breastfeeding in public—her right under state law. Fort Collins, Colo., Mun. Code § 17-142(d); see also Colo. Rev. Stat. § 25-6-302 (2017) ("A mother may breast-feed in any place she has a right to be."). In that context, few would consider the sight of the woman's breast dangerous.

The need to protect children arises, instead, from the City's fear of topless women "parading in front of elementary schools, or swimming topless in the public pool"— scenarios that it described to the court at the preliminary-injunction hearing. Free the

Nipple, 237 F.Supp.3d at 1131. But laws in the neighboring cities of Boulder and Denver, and in many other jurisdictions, allow female toplessness, and the City presented no evidence of any harmful fallout. Id.; see also Boulder, Colo. Mun. Code § 5-6-13 (2017); Denver, Colo. Mun. Code § 38-157.1 (2017). In fact, the district court found, the City presented no evidence "that a law permitting public exposure of female breasts would have a significantly negative impact on the public." Free the Nipple, 237 F.Supp.3d at 1131. And absent contrary proof we, like the district court, doubt that without a female-toplessness ban on the books, topless women would "regularly walk[] through downtown Fort Collins," "parad[e]" past elementary schools, or swim in public pools. Id.

We're left, as the district court was, to suspect that the City's professed interest in protecting children derives not from any morphological differences between men's and women's breasts but from negative stereotypes depicting women's breasts, but not men's breasts, as sex objects. Id. ("[C]hildren do not need to be protected from the naked female breast itself but from the negative societal norms, expectations, and stereotypes associated with it."); cf. Tagami v. City of Chicago, 875 F.3d 375, 382 (7th Cir. 2017) (Rovner, J., dissenting) ("The City's claim therefore boils down to a desire to perpetuate a stereotype that female breasts are primarily the objects of desire, and male breasts are not."), cert. denied, ___ U.S. ___, 138 S.Ct. 1577, 200 L.Ed.2d 747 (2018).

In support of this view, the district court relied on the testimony of Dr. Tomi-Ann Roberts, a psychology professor and witness for the Plaintiffs. At the preliminary-injunction hearing, Dr. Roberts testified that our society's sexualization of women's breasts—rather than any unique physical characteristic—has engrained in us the stereotype that the primary purpose of women's breasts is sex, not feeding babies. The district court found Dr. Roberts credible and concluded, based on her testimony, that "the naked female breast is seen as disorderly or dangerous because society, from Renaissance paintings to Victoria's Secret commercials, has conflated female breasts with genitalia and stereotyped them as such." Free the Nipple, 237 F.Supp.3d at 1133.

But laws grounded in stereotypes about the way women are serve no important governmental interest. Morales-Santana, 137 S.Ct. at 1692-93; Virginia, 518 U.S. at 550, 116 S.Ct. 2264. To the contrary, legislatively reinforced stereotypes tend to "create[] a self-fulfilling cycle of discrimination." Hibbs, 538 U.S. at 736, 123 S.Ct. 1972. Thus, the sex-object stereotype, according to Dr. Roberts, "serves the function of keeping women in their place." Appellant's App. vol. 3 at 192:11. And as the district court found, perpetuating the sex-object stereotype "leads to negative cognitive, behavioral, and emotional outcomes for both women and men." Free the Nipple, 237 F.Supp.3d at 1132. The court noted, for instance, that Dr. Roberts had testified about research linking the sexual objectification of women to the view that, at younger and younger ages, women are "appropriate targets of [sexual] assault." Appellant's App. vol. 3 at 194:22-23.

Accordingly, we reject the City's claim that protecting children from public nudity qualifies as an important governmental objective substantially served by the City's female-only toplessness ban.

ii. Maintaining Public Order and Promoting Traffic Safety

In the abstract, we agree that public order and traffic safety are important governmental objectives. The absence of either could be fatal. But the justification for a gender-based classification "must be genuine, not hypothesized," and "it must not rely on overbroad generalizations." Virginia, 518 U.S. at 533, 116 S.Ct. 2264. Here, we suspect that enacting the public-nudity ordinance had less to do with the City's professed objectives and more to do with the sex-object stereotype that the district court described. See Free the Nipple, 237 F.Supp.3d at 1132.

For one thing, in asserting that its female-only toplessness ban substantially furthers important governmental objectives, the City mostly relies on cases holding that nebulous concepts of public morality—not traffic safety or public order— justified similar bans. In one of those cases, for example, the Fourth Circuit tied a public-nudity ordinance like the City's to the "widely recognized" governmental interest in "protecting the moral sensibilities of that substantial segment of society that still does not want to be exposed willy-nilly to public displays of various portions of their fellow citizens' anatomies that traditionally in this society have been regarded as erogenous zones," portions that "still include (whether justifiably or not in the eyes of all) the female, but not the male, breast." United States v. Biocic, 928 F.2d 112, 115-16 (4th Cir. 1991); accord Tagami, 875 F.3d at 379; Ways v. City of Lincoln, 331 F.3d 596, 600 (8th Cir. 2003).

For another thing, although the City itself never asserted public morality as a justification for banning female toplessness, notions of morality may well underlie its assertions that conflicts will break out, and distracted drivers will crash, if it allows women to be topless in public. But such notions, like the fear that topless women will endanger children, originate from the sex-object stereotype of women's breasts. And as we've explained, that stereotype doesn't stand up to scrutiny. Cf. People v. Santorelli, 80 N.Y.2d 875, 587 N.Y.S.2d 601, 600 N.E.2d 232, 236 (1992) (Titone, J., concurring) ("One of the most important purposes to be served by the Equal Protection Clause is to ensure that `public sensibilities' grounded in prejudice and unexamined stereotypes do not become enshrined as part of the official policy of government."); accord Obergefell v. Hodges, ____ U.S. ____, 135 S.Ct. 2584, 2603, 192 L.Ed.2d 609 (2015); see also Planned Parenthood of Se. Penn. v. Casey, 505 U.S. 833, 850, 112 S.Ct. 2791, 120 L.Ed.2d 674 (1992) ("Our obligation is to define the liberty of all, not to mandate our own moral code.").

So what's left? A female-only toplessness ban strikes us as an unnecessary and overbroad means to maintain public order and promote traffic safety "when more accurate and impartial lines can be drawn." Morales-Santana, 137 S.Ct. at 1693 n.13; see also Craig, 429 U.S. at 208-09 & n.22, 97 S.Ct. 451 (striking down a gender-based differential in the age at which men and women could legally buy 3.2% beer because "the principles embodied in the Equal Protection Clause are not to be rendered inapplicable by statistically measured but loose-fitting generalities concerning the drinking tendencies of aggregate groups"). For instance, the City could abate sidewalk confrontations by increasing the penalties for engaging in offensive conduct. And to reduce distracted driving, the City could target billboards designed to draw drivers' eyes from the road. But the City can't impede women's (and not men's) ability to go topless unless it establishes the tight means-ends fit that intermediate scrutiny demands.

We recognize that ours is the minority viewpoint. Most other courts, including a recent (split) Seventh Circuit panel, have rejected equal-protection challenges to female-only toplessness bans. E.g., Tagami, 875 F.3d at 380.[8] But see id. at 383 (Rovner, J., dissenting) ("Whether out of reverence or fear of female breasts, Chicago's ordinance calls attention to and sexualizes the female form and imposes a burden of public modesty on women alone, with ramifications that likely extend beyond the public way." (citing Free the Nipple, 237 F.Supp.3d at 1133)); Santorelli, 587 N.Y.S.2d 601, 600 N.E.2d at 237 (Titone, J., concurring) ("[T]he People have offered nothing to justify a law that discriminates against women by prohibiting them from removing their tops and exposing their bare chests in public as men are routinely permitted to do."). None of these decisions binds us, though; nor does their sheer volume sway our analysis.

As we interpret the arc of the Court's equal-protection jurisprudence, ours is the constitutionally sound result. At least since Virginia, that arc bends toward requiring more—not less—judicial scrutiny when asserted physical differences are raised to justify gender-based discrimination, while casting doubt on public morality as a constitutional reason for gender-based classifications. See, e.g., Morales-Santana, 137 S.Ct. at 1689 (clarifying that "all gender-based classifications" are subject to "heightened scrutiny" (quoting J.E.B., 511 U.S. at 136, 114 S.Ct. 1419)); Virginia, 518 U.S. at 533, 116 S.Ct. 2264 ("`Inherent differences' between men and women, we have come to appreciate, remain cause for celebration, but not for denigration of the members of either sex or for artificial constraints on an individual's opportunity."); Franklin, supra, at 145-46 ("[T]he Court's opinion [in Virginia] suggests that equal protection law should be particularly alert to the possibility of sex stereotyping in contexts where `real' differences are involved, because these are the contexts in which sex classifications have most often been used to perpetuate sex-based inequality.").

For these reasons, we believe that the district court correctly analyzed the Plaintiffs' equal-protection claim. The court didn't abuse its discretion in concluding that because the Plaintiffs made a strong showing of their likelihood of success on the merits, the first preliminary-injunction factor weighed in their favor.

B. The Second Factor: Irreparable Injury

The second preliminary-injunction factor asks whether irreparable injury will befall the movants without an injunction. Awad, 670 F.3d at 1131. Most courts consider the infringement of a constitutional right enough and require no further showing of irreparable injury. Id.; accord Wright & Miller, supra, § 2948.1. The district court applied that principle here, concluding that the City's public-nudity ordinance inflicts irreparable harm by violating the Plaintiffs' right to equal protection under the law. See Free the Nipple, 237 F.Supp.3d at 1134.

On appeal, the City acknowledges that well-settled law supports the constitutional-violation-as-irreparable-injury principle. See, e.g., Elrod v. Burns, 427 U.S. 347, 373-74, 96 S.Ct. 2673, 49 L.Ed.2d 547 (1976); Awad, 670 F.3d at 1131; accord Wright et al., supra, § 2948.1. And the City seems to concede that in the context of constitutional claims, the principle collapses the first and second preliminary-injunction factors, equating likelihood of success on the merits with a demonstration of irreparable injury. The City nevertheless contests its application here on the ground that neither the district court nor the Plaintiffs cited a decision analyzing the specific injury asserted here: an equal-protection violation from a prohibition on public nudity.

We're not persuaded. What makes an injury "irreparable" is the inadequacy of, and the difficulty of calculating, a monetary remedy after a full trial. Awad, 670 F.3d at 1131. Any deprivation of any constitutional right fits that bill. See Adams ex rel. Adams v. Baker, 919 F.Supp. 1496, 1504-05 (D. Kan. 1996) (concluding that excluding the plaintiff from the wrestling team because of her gender deprived her of her right to equal protection and that this deprivation "itself" constituted irreparable harm). Here, absent the preliminary injunction, the Plaintiffs, and all women in Fort Collins, risk criminal sanctions for making a choice—to appear topless in public—that men may make scot-free. See Fort Collins, Colo. Mun. Code § 17-142. We've already concluded that this gender disparity violates the Equal Protection Clause, so we agree with the district court that the Plaintiffs need to show no further irreparable harm.

Accordingly, we conclude that the district court didn't abuse its discretion in concluding that the Plaintiffs met the irreparable-injury requirement.

C. The Third Factor: The Balance of Harms

The third preliminary-injunction factor involves balancing the irreparable harms identified above against the harm that the preliminary injunction causes the City. Fish, 840 F.3d at 754. Under the heightened disfavored-injunction standard, the Plaintiffs need to make a strong showing that the balance of harms tips in their favor. Awad, 670 F.3d at 1131. When a constitutional right hangs in the balance, though, "even a temporary loss" usually trumps any harm to the defendant. Wright et al., supra, § 2948.2 & n.10. In this case, according to the district court, the Plaintiffs met their third-factor burden because the deprivation of their right to equal protection outweighed the stakes for the City, which the court defined as the public's interest in morality. Free the Nipple, 237 F.Supp.3d at 1134.

The City contests that conclusion on appeal, asking "how any injury [the Plaintiffs] might sustain from being required to wait to bare their breasts in public until after this matter is concluded outweighs the City's interest in maintaining a law that was supported by the majority of its citizens and unanimously adopted by its City Council." Appellant's Opening Br. at 35. But "being required to wait to bare their breasts in public" deprives the Plaintiffs of a constitutional right, while the City has no interest in keeping an unconstitutional law on the books. Cf. Awad, 670 F.3d at 1131 ("[W]hen the law that voters wish to enact is likely unconstitutional, their interests do not outweigh [a plaintiff's interest] in having his constitutional rights protected.").

For these reasons, we conclude that the district court didn't abuse its discretion in determining that the balance of harms tips in the Plaintiffs' favor, even under the "strong showing" standard applicable to disfavored injunctions.

D. The Fourth Factor: The Public Interest

The last preliminary-injunction factor requires that the injunction not be against the public interest. Awad, 670 F.3d at 1132. But as the district court wrote, it's "always in the public interest to prevent the violation of a party's constitutional rights." Free the Nipple, 237 F.Supp.3d at 1134 (quoting Connection Distrib. Co. v. Reno, 154 F.3d 281, 288 (6th Cir. 1998)). On appeal, the City disputes that the public-nudity ordinance is unconstitutional, but it cites no law casting doubt on the public's interest in preserving constitutional rights. See Awad, 670 F.3d at 1132; see also Baker, 919 F.Supp. at 1505 ("The public interest would best be served by enjoining the defendants from infringing on the plaintiff's right to equal protection.").

As we explained above, the ordinance likely is unconstitutional, so we find the City's argument unconvincing. We conclude that the district court didn't abuse its discretion in ruling that the public-interest factor weighs in the Plaintiffs' favor.

\* \* \*

In sum, because we agree with the district court that each preliminary-injunction factor favored the Plaintiffs, we also agree that the Plaintiffs should prevail on their preliminary-injunction motion. Thus, the district court didn't abuse its discretion in issuing the injunction.

CONCLUSION

For these reasons, we affirm the district court's order granting the Plaintiffs' motion for a preliminary injunction, and we remand the case to the district court for further proceedings consistent with this opinion.

## Edge v. Everett, WA (Ninth Circuit) (July 3, 2019) [Notes omitted]

Before: Sandra S. Ikuta and Morgan Christen, Circuit Judges, and Jennifer Choe-Groves,[*] Judge.

CHRISTEN, Circuit Judge:

"Bikini barista" stands are drive-through businesses where scantily clad employees sell coffee and other non-alcoholic beverages. In Everett, Washington, a police investigation confirmed complaints that some baristas were engaging in lewd conduct at these establishments, that some baristas had been victimized by patrons, and that other crimes were associated with the stands. The City responded by adopting Everett Municipal Code (EMC) § 5.132.010-060 (the Dress Code Ordinance) requiring that the dress of employees, owners, and operators of Quick-Service Facilities cover "minimum body areas." Separately, the City also broadened its lewd conduct misdemeanor by expanding the Everett Municipal Code's definition of "lewd act" to include the public display of specific parts of the body. EMC § 10.24.010. The City also created a new misdemeanor called Facilitating Lewd Conduct for those who permit, cause or encourage lewd conduct. EMC § 10.24.020.

A stand owner and several baristas sued the City pursuant to 42 U.S.C. § 1983, contending that the Dress Code Ordinance and the amendments to the Lewd Conduct Ordinances violate their First and Fourteenth Amendment rights. The district court granted plaintiffs' motion for a preliminary injunction and enjoined enforcement of these provisions. The City appeals. We have jurisdiction over the City's interlocutory appeal pursuant to 28 U.S.C. § 1292. Because we conclude that plaintiffs did not show a likelihood of success on the merits of their two Fourteenth Amendment void-for-vagueness challenges, nor on their First Amendment free expression claim, we vacate the district court's preliminary injunction and remand this case for further proceedings.

I. Factual Background

Bikini barista stands have operated in and around Everett since at least 2009. The baristas working at these stands wear what they call "bikinis," but the City describes them as "nearly nude employees," and the district court made clear that their attire is significantly more revealing than a typical bikini. The district court's finding that at least some of the baristas wear little more than pasties and g-strings is well-supported by the record.

Beginning in summer 2009, the Everett Police Department (EPD) began fielding numerous citizen complaints related to bikini barista stands. One complainant asserted that she observed a female barista wearing "pasties" and "a thong and what appeared to be garter belts sitting perched in the window with her feet on the ledge[.]" The complainant went on to describe how a customer in a truck approached the window and began "groping" the barista in intimate areas. According to the complainant, "the next customer in line... was clearly touching his genitals through his clothes as he was waiting his turn." Stuck in traffic, the complainant wrote that she "had to sit there w/ my 2 young daughters and was so disgusted[.]"

After receiving upwards of forty complaints, EPD launched an undercover investigation and documented that some baristas at this type of stand were openly violating the existing criminal code prohibiting various forms of lewd conduct. At the time, EMC § 10.24.010 defined lewd conduct to include exposure or display of one's genitals, anus or any portion of the areola or nipple of the female breast, but EPD's investigation revealed that some of the bikini baristas removed their costumes entirely. EPD also discovered that some baristas were not paid hourly wages and worked for tips only, resulting in pressure to engage in lewd acts, and that other baristas were paid wages but still performed lewd acts in exchange for large tips. Everett undercover police officers took a series of graphic photos documenting the extremely revealing nature of the baristas' garb and instances in which baristas removed their tops and bottoms altogether. Officers also documented a wide variety of customer-barista physical contact. At least one bikini stand owner was convicted of sexually exploiting a minor after he was caught employing a sixteen-year old at one of the bikini stands. See State v. Wheeler, No. 72660-9-I, 2016 WL 1306132, at *1-3 (Wash. Ct. App. 2016). Another stand turned out to be a front for a prostitution ring, and some of the baristas, who worked in isolated locations late at night, reported being victims of sexual violence. A Snohomish County Sheriff's Deputy was convicted of a criminal offense after helping an owner evade the City's undercover officers in exchange for sexual favors.

Enforcing the City's existing lewd conduct ordinance required extensive use of undercover officers and proved to be both expensive and time consuming. The City also complained that policing the stands detracted from EPD's efforts to address the City's other priorities.

After five years of using undercover operations to prosecute individual offenders, EPD decided its "investigative approach was an ineffective and resource-intensive method of motivating stand owners to stop the illegal conduct" and it began collaborating with the City on a legislative fix. The City complied by enacting EMC §§ 5.132.010-060, a Dress Code Ordinance applicable only to "Quick-Service Facilities" like drive-throughs and coffee stands. The City also amended its criminal code to broaden the definition of "lewd act" and created the crime of Facilitating Lewd Conduct. See EMC §§ 10.24.010; 10.24.025. Because the constitutional challenges in this case focus on the text and effect of these enactments, we describe each in some detail.

A. The Lewd Conduct Amendments

The Lewd Conduct Amendments expanded the definition of "lewd act" to include:

An exposure or display of one's genitals, anus, bottom one-half of the anal cleft, or any portion of the areola or nipple of the female breast[] or [a]n exposure of more than one-half of the part of the female breast located below the top of the areola; provided that the covered area shall be covered by opaque material and coverage shall be contiguous to the areola.

EMC § 10.24.010(A)(1)-(2). An "owner, lessee, lessor, manager, operator, or other person in charge of a public place" commits the offense of Facilitating Lewd Conduct if that person "knowingly permits, encourages, or causes to be committed lewd conduct" as defined in the ordinance. Id. § 10.24.025(A). Findings supporting the City's Lewd Conduct Amendments state that the City "seeks to protect its citizens from those who profit from facilitating others to engage in the crime of Lewd Conduct, and so deems it necessary ... to create the new crime Facilitating Lewd Conduct, a gross misdemeanor punishable by a maximum penalty of 364 days in jail and a $ 5,000.00 fine[.]"

B. The Dress Code Ordinance

The City did not hide its effort to specifically address the problems associated with the bikini barista stands when it adopted the Dress Code Ordinance. The very first factual finding in the enactment establishing the Dress Code stated that "[t]he City has seen a proliferation of crimes of a sexual nature occurring at bikini barista stands throughout the City[.]" The next paragraph memorialized the City's conclusion "that the minimalistic nature of the clothing worn by baristas at these `bikini' stands lends itself to criminal conduct[.]"

The Dress Code Ordinance requires all employees, owners, and operators of "Quick-Service Facilities" to comply with a "dress requirement" mandating coverage of "minimum body areas." EMC § 5.132.020(A). Minimum body areas are further defined as "the upper and lower body (breast/pectorals, stomach, back below the shoulder blades, buttocks, top three inches of legs below the buttocks, pubic area and genitals)." Id. § 5.132.020(B). The Dress Code Ordinance defines Quick-Service Facilities as "coffee stands, fast food restaurants, delis, food trucks, and coffee shops" in addition to all other drive-through restaurants. Id. § 5.132.020(C). This ordinance prohibits owners of Quick-Service Facilities from operating their businesses if any employee is not in full compliance with the dress requirement. EMC § 5.132.040(A)(1). Violations are deemed civil infractions. Id. To ensure that stand owners are motivated to enforce the dress code, the City instituted a $ 250 fine for first time offenders. EMC § 5.132.040(B)(1). Repeat offenders face stiffer fines and risk losing their business licenses. EMC § 5.132.040(B)(1)-(2). In enacting these provisions, the City expressed its intent to "provide powerful tools for reducing the illegal conduct that has occurred at bikini barista stands in a cost-effective manner."

II. Procedural Background

Plaintiff Jovanna Edge owns Hillbilly Hotties, a bikini barista stand in Everett. Plaintiffs Leah Humphrey, Liberty Ziska, Amelia Powell, Natalie Bjerke, and Matteson Hernandez are, or at one time were, baristas employed at Hillbilly Hotties. Approximately one week after the Lewd Conduct Amendments and Dress Code Ordinance went into effect, plaintiffs filed this lawsuit alleging multiple constitutional violations, two of which are relevant to this appeal. Plaintiffs' complaint alleges: (1) that the Dress Code Ordinance and the Lewd Conduct Amendments violate their First Amendment rights to free expression, and (2) that the new provisions violate the Due Process Clause because they are unconstitutionally vague.

Plaintiffs' First Amendment free expression claim asserts that the baristas convey messages such as "female empowerment," "confiden[ce]," and "fearless body acceptance" by wearing bikinis while working. In support of their motion for a preliminary injunction, plaintiffs submitted declarations from several baristas explaining their views that "a bikini is not a sexual message, [it's] more a message of empowerment," "we are empowered to be comfortable in our bodies," "[t]he bikini sends the message that I am approachable," "the message I send is freedom[,]" and "my employees expose messages through tattoos and scars."[1] The baristas assert that their choice of clothing demonstrates that they are "fun and more open," and that wearing bikinis at work shows they are "empowered, confident, and free." Plaintiff Edge, owner of Hillbilly Hotties, explained that her employees' dress allows them to "tell stories of who they are[.]"

Notably, in the district court and on appeal, plaintiffs persistently disavow that they are nude dancers or that they engage in erotic performances, conduct that is expressly protected under the First Amendment. See Barnes v. Glen Theatre, Inc., 501

U.S. 560, 566, 111 S.Ct. 2456, 115 L.Ed.2d 504 (1991).[2] Plaintiffs' argument is that simply wearing what they refer to as bikinis is itself sufficiently expressive to warrant First Amendment protection, and that the City's new ordinance and amendments therefore impermissibly burden their speech.

The City disputes the baristas' premise that the act of wearing pasties and g-strings at work constitutes speech. The City also offers extensive evidence of adverse secondary effects associated with the stands, including prostitution and sexual violence, and argues that the new ordinance and Lewd Conduct Amendments are aimed at those effects.

Plaintiffs' motion for a preliminary injunction alleged that the new measures are impermissibly vague because they use ambiguous language to define parts of the body that must be covered by employees, owners, and operators of barista stands, and that a person of ordinary intelligence is denied a reasonable opportunity to know what conduct the City now prohibits. The City's opposition denied that the text of the Dress Code Ordinance and Lewd Conduct Amendments is vague or ambiguous, but the City voluntarily agreed to suspend enforcement of the new measures pending resolution of plaintiffs' motion for a preliminary injunction.

III. The Preliminary Injunction

In Winter v. Natural Resources Defense Council, the Supreme Court held that a plaintiff seeking a preliminary injunction must establish "[(1)] that he is likely to succeed on the merits, [(2)] that he is likely to suffer irreparable harm in the absence of preliminary relief, [(3)] that the balance of equities tips in his favor, and [(4)] that an injunction is in the public interest." Coffman v. Queen of Valley Med. Ctr., 895 F.3d 717, 725 (9th Cir. 2018) (quoting Winter v. Nat. Res. Def. Council, Inc., 555 U.S. 7, 20, 129 S.Ct. 365, 172 L.Ed.2d 249 (2008)) (alterations in original). "Likelihood of success on the merits is the most important factor; if a movant fails to meet this threshold inquiry, we need not consider the other factors." California v. Azar, 911 F.3d 558, 575 (9th Cir. 2018) (internal quotation marks omitted).

The district court applied the Winter factors and concluded that plaintiffs had demonstrated a likelihood of success on the merits of their vagueness challenges. The court expressed concern that the compound term "anal cleft" in the definition of "lewd act" is vague, and also ruled that both ordinances are susceptible to "arbitrary enforcement." Separately, the court concluded that plaintiffs had established a likelihood of success on the merits of their First Amendment free expression challenge to the Dress Code Ordinance, a ruling based on the court's conclusion that the act of wearing pasties and g-strings at Quick-Service Facilities was sufficiently expressive to merit constitutional protection.

The district court decided that plaintiffs had satisfied the remaining Winter factors, see 555 U.S. at 7, 129 S.Ct. 365, and enjoined enforcement of the new ordinances and amendments.

IV. Standard of Review

We review the district court's order granting a preliminary injunction "for an abuse of discretion," Gorbach v. Reno, 219 F.3d 1087, 1091 (9th Cir. 2000) (en banc), but "legal issues underlying the injunction are reviewed de novo because a district court would necessarily abuse its discretion if it based its ruling on an erroneous view of law." adidas Am., Inc. v. Skechers USA, Inc., 890 F.3d 747, 753 (9th Cir. 2018) (quoting GoTo.com, Inc. v. Walt Disney Co., 202 F.3d 1199, 1204 (9th Cir. 2000)). When an injunction involves a First Amendment challenge, constitutional questions of fact (such as whether certain restrictions create a severe burden on an individual's First Amendment rights) are reviewed de novo. See Prete v. Bradbury, 438 F.3d 949, 960 (9th Cir. 2006) (citing Planned Parenthood of the Columbia/Willamette, Inc. v. Am. Coal. of Life Activists, 290 F.3d 1058, 1070 (9th Cir. 2002)).

V. The Lewd Conduct Amendments

We first analyze the Lewd Conduct Amendments, which expanded the definition of "lewd act" and also created the misdemeanor offense of Facilitating Lewd Conduct.

"It is a basic principle of due process that an enactment is void for vagueness if its prohibitions are not clearly defined." Grayned v. City of Rockford, 408 U.S. 104, 108, 92 S.Ct. 2294, 33 L.Ed.2d 222 (1972). That said, we recognize that "[c]ondemned to the use of words, we can never expect mathematical certainty from our language." Id. at 110, 92 S.Ct. 2294. To put a finer point on it: "perfect clarity and precise guidance have never been required even of regulations that restrict expressive activity." United States v. Williams, 553 U.S. 285, 304, 128 S.Ct. 1830, 170 L.Ed.2d 650 (2008) (quoting Ward v. Rock Against Racism, 491 U.S. 781, 794, 109 S.Ct. 2746, 105 L.Ed.2d 661 (1989)).

The vagueness doctrine incorporates two related requirements. First, "laws [must] give the person of ordinary intelligence a reasonable opportunity to know what is prohibited, so that he may act accordingly." Grayned, 408 U.S. at 108, 92 S.Ct. 2294. Typically, all that is required to satisfy this due process concern is "`fair notice' of the conduct a statute proscribes." Sessions v. Dimaya, ___ U.S. ___, 138 S. Ct. 1204, 1212, 200 L.Ed.2d 549 (2018). But "where [F]irst [A]mendment freedoms are at stake, an even greater degree of specificity and clarity of laws is required," Kev, Inc. v. Kitsap Cty., 793 F.2d 1053, 1057 (9th Cir. 1986) (citing Grayned, 408 U.S. at 108-09, 92 S.Ct. 2294), and courts ask whether language is sufficiently murky that "speakers will be compelled to steer too far clear of any forbidden area[s.]" Nat'l Endowment for the Arts v. Finley, 524 U.S. 569, 588, 118 S.Ct. 2168, 141 L.Ed.2d 500 (1998) (internal quotation marks omitted). This enhanced standard protects against laws and regulations that might have the effect of chilling protected speech or expression by discouraging participation.

The vagueness doctrine's second requirement aims to avoid "arbitrary and discriminatory enforcement," and demands that laws "provide explicit standards for those who apply them." Grayned, 408 U.S. at 108, 92 S.Ct. 2294. A law that relies on a subjective standard—such as whether conduct amounts to an "annoyance"—is constitutionally suspect. See id. at 113, 92 S.Ct. 2294. In Coates v. Cincinnati, 402 U.S. 611, 614, 91 S.Ct. 1686, 29 L.Ed.2d 214 (1971), for example, an ordinance was deemed unconstitutionally vague because it criminalized the assembly of three or more persons on city sidewalks if they conducted themselves in a manner annoying to passers by. The Supreme Court observed that "[c]onduct that annoys some people does not annoy others," id., and it struck down the ordinance because "men of common intelligence must necessarily guess at its meaning." Id. (quoting Connally v. Gen. Constr. Co., 269 U.S. 385, 391, 46 S.Ct. 126, 70 L.Ed. 322 (1926)).

Here, the district court concluded that the amended definition of "lewd act" similarly fails to give a person of ordinary intelligence a reasonable opportunity to conform his or her conduct to the City's law. The court explained that it was "uncertain as to the meaning of the compound term `anal cleft' as used" in the amended definition, because "[t]he term `bottom one-half of the anal cleft' is not well-defined or reasonably understandable[.]" We reach the opposite conclusion. Having examined the text adopted by the City, we are not persuaded that the public will be left to guess at the meaning of the term "anal cleft," particularly because the meanings of both "anal" and "cleft" are easily discerned through recourse to a common dictionary. See, e.g., United States v. Wyatt, 408 F.3d 1257, 1261 (9th Cir. 2005) (relying in part on the dictionary definition of an allegedly ambiguous term); Kev, Inc., 793 F.2d at 1057 (same).[3] Moreover, "[t]his circuit has previously recognized that otherwise imprecise terms may avoid vagueness problems when used in combination with terms that provide sufficient clarity." Gammoh v. City of La Habra, 395 F.3d 1114, 1120 (9th Cir. 2005) (citing Kev, Inc., 793 F.2d at 1057). The Lewd Conduct Ordinance uses the term "anal cleft" in near proximity to a list of other intimate body parts. Viewing these facts together, we conclude that a person of ordinary intelligence reading the ordinance in its entirety will be adequately informed about what body areas cannot be exposed or displayed "in a public place or under circumstances where such act is likely to be observed by any member of the public." EMC § 10.24.020. Likewise, we conclude that the modifier "bottom one-half" does no more than specify an easily ascertained fractional part of an otherwise well-understood area of the body. Plaintiffs do not expressly challenge the new misdemeanor Facilitating Lewd Conduct on vagueness grounds, but we note that this provision does no more than prohibit owners, operators, lessors, lessees or any person "in charge of a public place" from knowingly permitting, or causing another person to commit lewd conduct as defined in EMC § 10.24.010. This prohibition is clear, as is the definition of lewd conduct. We therefore hold that the activity the Lewd Conduct Amendments prohibit is reasonably ascertainable to a person of ordinary intelligence.[4]

The second part of the vagueness test concerns whether the Lewd Conduct Amendments are amenable to unchecked law enforcement discretion. See, e.g., Papachristou v. City of Jacksonville, 405 U.S. 156, 169-70, 92 S.Ct. 839, 31 L.Ed.2d 110 (1972).[5] Definitions of proscribed conduct that rest wholly or principally on the subjective viewpoint of a law enforcement officer run the risk of unconstitutional murkiness. See, e.g., Gammoh, 395 F.3d at 1119-20 (collecting cases); Tucson Woman's Clinic v. Eden, 379 F.3d 531, 554-55 (9th Cir. 2004). Everett's definition of lewd conduct requires that certain areas of the body be covered in public and as we have explained, the definition is not ambiguous. Nor does the definition rely on the subjective assessment of an enforcing officer. The term "anal cleft" is clear and ascertainable and what constitutes the "bottom half" of this unambiguously described part of the human body is also an objective standard. In short, EMC § 10.24.010's description of the body parts that must be covered in public does not create a constitutional problem by inviting discretionary enforcement because there are "standards governing the exercise of the discretion granted by the ordinance[.]" Papachristou, 405 U.S. at 170, 92 S.Ct. 839.

Plaintiffs argue that there will be close cases requiring some degree of law enforcement subjectivity when the Lewd Conduct Amendments are enforced, and the district court shared this concern. But "the mere fact that close cases can be envisioned" does not render an otherwise permissible statute unconstitutionally vague. Williams, 553 U.S. at 305, 128 S.Ct. 1830. The Supreme Court has observed in other criminal contexts that close cases are addressed "not by the doctrine of vagueness, but by the requirement of proof beyond a reasonable doubt." Id. at 306, 128 S.Ct. 1830. Put another way, in close cases, a fact finder will decide whether the City has met its burden by the required standard of proof. That determination does not raise constitutional vagueness concerns so long as the legal standard against which it is measured is sufficiently clear. All a statute must define with specificity is what the fact finder is required to decide in any given case. See id. ("What renders a statute vague is not the possibility that it will sometimes be difficult to determine whether the incriminating fact it establishes has been proved; but rather the indeterminacy of precisely what that fact is." (emphasis added)).

The district court abused its discretion by ruling that plaintiffs are likely to succeed on the merits of their void-for-vagueness challenge to the Lewd Conduct Amendments. We therefore vacate the district court's preliminary injunction with respect to the Lewd Conduct Amendments.

VI. The Dress Code Ordinance

We next consider the district court's order enjoining enforcement of the Dress Code Ordinance. EMC § 5.132.030 mandates that employees, operators, and owners of "Quick-Service Facilities" comply with the City's dress requirement. The Dress Code Ordinance makes it unlawful to serve customers or operate a Quick-Service Facility if "minimum body areas" of the owner or any employee are not covered. EMC § 5.132.030. "Minimum body areas" are defined as: "breast/pectorals, stomach, back below the shoulder blades, buttocks, top three inches of legs below the buttocks, pubic area and genitals." EMC § 5.132.020(B). The district court enjoined the Dress Code Ordinance for two distinct reasons: (1) the court concluded that the Dress Code Ordinance's susceptibility to arbitrary enforcement renders it unconstitutionally vague; and (2) the district court concluded that the Dress Code Ordinance likely fails First Amendment review because it impermissibly burdens plaintiffs' rights to free expression. We address each rationale in turn.

A. Vagueness

The vagueness principles governing our analysis of the Lewd Conduct Amendments apply with equal force to the Dress Code Ordinance. The fact that law enforcement may have to make some close judgment calls regarding compliance with these provisions does not, perforce, mean that police are vested with impermissibly broad discretion. See Williams, 553 U.S. at 306, 128 S.Ct. 1830. The terms of the Dress Code Ordinance are sufficiently clear to preclude enforcement on "an ad hoc and subjective basis" because the dress requirement clearly defines areas of the body that owners and employees must cover while operating Quick-Service Facilities, using commonly understood names for those body areas. Hunt v. City of L.A., 638 F.3d 703, 712 (9th Cir. 2011). Enforcement does not require subjective judgments. Id. All an officer must determine is whether the upper body (specifically, the breast/pectorals, stomach, back below the shoulder blades) and lower body (the buttocks, top three inches of legs below the buttocks, pubic area and genitals) are covered. The meaning of these parts of the body is not beyond the common experience of an ordinary layperson, and the ordinance does not require that officers assessing potential violations delve into subjective questions. Cf. id. (observing that what constitutes a "religious, political, philosophical, or ideological" message is subjective). Because the Dress Code Ordinance is not open to the kind of arbitrary enforcement that triggers due process concerns, the vagueness doctrine does not warrant an injunction prohibiting enforcement of the Dress Code Ordinance.

B. Free Expression

The district court also concluded that plaintiffs demonstrated a likelihood of success on the merits of their First Amendment challenge to the Dress Code Ordinance. This part of the court's order relied on its determination that the baristas' choice to wear provocative attire (pasties and g-strings) constituted sufficiently expressive conduct to warrant First Amendment protection, that the Dress Code Ordinance amounted to a content-neutral restriction on the baristas' speech, and that the Dress Code Ordinance failed intermediate scrutiny under the "secondary effects" line of cases. See City of Renton v. Playtime Theatres, Inc., 475 U.S. 41, 48, 106 S.Ct. 925, 89 L.Ed.2d 29 (1986) (applying intermediate scrutiny to ordinances aimed at combating the side-effects of adult and sexually oriented businesses).

"The First Amendment literally forbids the abridgment only of `speech,'" but the United States Supreme Court has "long recognized that its protection does not end at the spoken or written word." Texas v. Johnson, 491 U.S. 397, 404, 109 S.Ct. 2533, 105 L.Ed.2d 342 (1989). The Supreme Court refers to non-speech activity that is within the ambit of the First Amendment's protections as "expressive conduct." See, e.g., Clark v. Cmty. for Creative Non-Violence, 468 U.S. 288, 293, 104 S.Ct. 3065, 82 L.Ed.2d 221 (1984). Conduct that is "sufficiently imbued with elements of communication" is protected by the First Amendment, Johnson, 491 U.S. at 404, 109 S.Ct. 2533 (quoting Spence v. Washington, 418 U.S. 405, 409, 94 S.Ct. 2727, 41 L.Ed.2d 842 (1974) (per curiam)), but the Court "has consistently rejected `the view that an apparently limitless variety of conduct can be labeled `speech' whenever the person engaging in the conduct intends thereby to express an idea.'" Anderson v. City of Hermosa Beach, 621 F.3d 1051, 1058 (9th Cir. 2010) (quoting United States v. O'Brien, 391 U.S. 367, 376, 88 S.Ct. 1673, 20 L.Ed.2d 672 (1968)). The Court has never "invalidated the application of a general law simply because the conduct that it reached was being engaged in for expressive purposes and the government could not demonstrate a sufficiently important state interest." Barnes, 501 U.S. at 577, 111 S.Ct. 2456 (Scalia, J., concurring). "Because the Court has eschewed a rule that `all conduct is presumptively expressive,' individuals claiming the protection of the First Amendment must carry the burden of demonstrating that their nonverbal conduct meets the applicable standard." Knox v. Brnovich, 907 F.3d 1167, 1181 (9th Cir. 2018) (quoting Clark, 468 U.S. at 293 n.5, 104 S.Ct. 3065).

Expressive conduct is characterized by two requirements: (1) "an intent to convey a particularized message" and (2) a "great" "likelihood ... that the message would be understood by those who viewed it." Johnson, 491 U.S. at 404, 109 S.Ct. 2533 (quoting Spence, 418 U.S. at 410-11, 94 S.Ct. 2727); see also Vivid Entm't, LLC v. Fielding, 774 F.3d 566, 579 (9th Cir. 2014). With respect to the first requirement—an intent to convey a particularized message—First Amendment protection is only granted to the act of wearing particular clothing or insignias where circumstances establish that an unmistakable communication is being made. See, e.g., Nat'l Socialist Party of Am. v. Village of Skokie, 432 U.S. 43, 97 S.Ct. 2205, 53 L.Ed.2d 96 (1977) (per curiam) (declining to enjoin Nazi marchers from wearing symbols of ideology in parade); Cohen v. California, 403 U.S. 15, 18, 91 S.Ct. 1780, 29 L.Ed.2d 284 (1971) (concluding that a person wearing a jacket bearing the inscription "F— the Draft" was entitled to First Amendment protections); Tinker v. Des Moines Indep. Cmty. Sch. Dist., 393 U.S. 503, 505-06, 89 S.Ct. 733, 21 L.Ed.2d 731 (1969) (holding that students who wore black armbands to protest Vietnam War engaged in expressive conduct "`closely akin to pure speech[.]'").

Even if plaintiffs could show that their intent is to convey a particularized message, and thereby satisfy the first requirement for classification as expressive conduct, Johnson, 491 U.S. at 404, 109 S.Ct. 2533, plaintiffs' First Amendment claim falters for failure to show a great likelihood that their intended message will be understood by those who receive it. See id.

Context is everything when deciding whether others will likely understand an intended message conveyed through expressive conduct. To decide whether the public is likely to understand the baristas' intended messages related to empowerment and confidence, we consider "the surrounding circumstances[.]" Spence, 418 U.S. at 411, 94 S.Ct. 2727. The Supreme Court made this clear in Spence, where a college student displayed a flag with an attached peace symbol from his university dorm room "roughly simultaneous with" the United States' invasion of Cambodia and the Kent State shootings. Id. at 410, 94 S.Ct. 2727. Under these circumstances, the Supreme Court observed that "it would have been difficult for the great majority of citizens to miss the drift of [the student's] point at the time that he made it." Id. Likewise, the choice to wear military medals—even medals one has not earned—"communicates that the wearer was awarded that medal and is entitled to the nation's recognition and gratitude `for acts of heroism and sacrifice in military service.'" United States v. Swisher, 811 F.3d 299, 314 (9th Cir. 2016) (en banc) (quoting United States v. Alvarez, 567 U.S. 709, 724, 132 S.Ct. 2537, 183 L.Ed.2d 574 (2012) (Kennedy, J., plurality opinion)). In the same way, a student group's choice to wear black arm bands to school during the 1965 holiday season was protected by the First Amendment because the group's intended anti-Vietnam War message "was closely akin to `pure speech[.]'" Tinker, 393 U.S. at 505, 89 S.Ct. 733.

The context here is starkly different from cases where First Amendment protection has been extended to expressive clothing or symbols. The Dress Code Ordinance applies at Quick-Service Facilities—coffee stands, fast food restaurants, delis, food trucks, coffee shops and drive-throughs. See EMC § 5.132.020(C). In other words, it applies at retail establishments that invite commercial transactions, and in these transactions, the baristas undisputedly solicit tips. The baristas' act of wearing pasties and g-strings in close proximity to paying customers creates a high likelihood that the message sent by the baristas' nearly nonexistent outfits vastly diverges from those described in plaintiffs' declarations. The commercial setting and close proximity to the baristas' customers makes the difference.

Because plaintiffs have not demonstrated a "great likelihood" that their intended messages related to empowerment and confidence will be understood by those who view them, we conclude that the mode of dress at issue in this case is not sufficiently communicative to merit First Amendment protection.

We stress that plaintiffs deny that they engage in nude dancing and erotic performances, thereby disavowing the First Amendment protections available for that conduct. See Barnes, 501 U.S. at 566, 111 S.Ct. 2456. The outcome of this case turns on the plaintiffs' contention that the act of wearing almost no clothing while serving coffee in a retail establishment constitutes speech. Because wearing pasties and g-strings while working at Quick-Service Facilities is not "expressive conduct" within the meaning of the First Amendment, the Dress Code Ordinance does not burden protected expression.

The district court's application of intermediate scrutiny under the "secondary effects" line of authority was inapposite because that doctrine applies to regulations that burden speech within the ambit of the First Amendment's sphere of protection. See World Wide Video of Wash., Inc. v. City of Spokane, 368 F.3d 1186, 1192 (9th Cir. 2004). Here, because the Dress Code Ordinance does not burden expressive conduct protected by the First Amendment, the City need only demonstrate that it "promotes a substantial government interest that would be achieved less effectively absent the regulation." Rumsfeld v. Forum for Acad. & Institutional Rights, Inc., 547 U.S. 47, 67, 126 S.Ct. 1297, 164 L.Ed.2d 156 (2006) (quoting United States v. Albertini, 472 U.S. 675, 689, 105 S.Ct. 2897, 86 L.Ed.2d 536 (1985)). The district court did not analyze the ordinance under this framework, so we vacate its preliminary injunction and remand for further proceedings.

VACATED AND REMANDED.

Printed in the USA
CPSIA information can be obtained
at www.ICGtesting.com
LVHW080826141223
766408LV00005B/404